Gallaudet
Encyclopedia of
DEAF PEOPLE
AND DEAFNESS

2

H–R

John V. Van Cleve, Editor in Chief
Gallaudet College

McGraw-Hill Book Company, Inc.

New York • St. Louis • San Francisco • Auckland • Bogotá • Hamburg
Johannesburg • London • Madrid • Mexico • Milan • Montreal • New Delhi
Panama • Paris • São Paulo • Singapore • Sydney • Tokyo • Toronto

GALLAUDET ENCYCLOPEDIA OF DEAF PEOPLE AND DEAFNESS

1 2 3 4 5 6 7 8 9 0 HAHA 8 9 4 3 2 1 0 9 8 7

ISBN 0-07-079229-1

Library of Congress Cataloging in Publication Data

Gallaudet encyclopedia of deaf people and deafness.

   Includes bibliographies and index.
   1. Deaf—Dictionaries.   2. Deafness—Dictionaries.
I. Van Cleve, John V.   II. Gallaudet College.
HV2365.G35   1987   362.4′2′0321   86-15396
ISBN 0-07-079229-1 (set)

Gallaudet Encyclopedia of DEAF PEOPLE AND DEAFNESS

2

H–R

Gallaudet Encyclopedia of DEAF PEOPLE AND DEAFNESS

2

H–R

H

HANSON, OLOF
(1862–1933)

Born on September 10, 1862, in Fjelkinge, Sweden, Olof Hanson became an American architect, ordained minister, and advocate for deaf people. He became deaf at age 10, after exposure to severe cold in a snowstorm. He is best known for his design of the North Dakota School for the Deaf (Devil's Lake, about 1895), a boys' dormitory at Gallaudet College (Washington, D.C., 1895) now known as Dawes House, and the Washington State School for the Deaf (Vancouver, Washington, 1911–1912). Hanson became interested in architecture while an undergraduate student at Gallaudet College (1881–1886). With the help of Senator William Drew Washburn, the father of his roommate Cadwallader Washburn, he began his architectural career with the firm of Hodgson and Son in Minneapolis, Minnesota. *See* GALLAUDET COLLEGE; WASHBURN, CADWALLADER.

Hanson left the firm in 1889 to spend a year of study and travel in Europe. For five months he was a special student at the Ecole des Beaux Arts in Paris. In addition to studying architectural monuments in England, Scotland, Italy, Switzerland, and Germany, Hanson visited schools for deaf students in each of the countries on his tour, indicating his early interest and commitment to the education of deaf people.

Upon his return to the United States, Hanson was employed by Wilson Brothers and Company in Philadelphia, and worked on plans for the Pennsylvania School for the Deaf. He then returned to Minnesota, where he had spent his childhood, but the economic depression of 1893 forced him to suspend his architectural career and to accept a teaching position for two years at his alma mater, the Minnesota School for the Deaf.

When the economy improved, Hanson established his own architectural office in Faribault, Minnesota. Although he was able to develop a satisfactory practice on his own, he decided in 1901

Olof Hanson. (Gallaudet College Archives)

to become a partner of Frank Thayer, who was located in the larger town of Mankato. They moved to Seattle, Washington, in the following year. While there, Hanson did the plans for the Greek Revival-style federal court house in Juneau, Alaska. During World War I, Hanson worked in St. Paul, Minnesota, and Omaha, Nebraska. He ultimately made Seattle his permanent home, where he secured a position as an architect and drafter for the University of Washington. He was employed by the university until his death in 1933.

While practicing architecture in the private sector in Minnesota, Nebraska, and Washington, Hanson designed more than 50 buildings, which included residences, schools, churches, small commercial buildings, and hotels. He was characteristic of the new breed of American architects who had not studied in the Beaux Arts tradition but had received their principal training in American-based architecture schools or, as in Hanson's case, by working in architects' offices. Projects such as the North Dakota School for the Deaf and the Faribault Public School indicated Hanson's familiarity with the restraint and simplicity of H. H. Richardson's mature style (as evidenced in Sever Hall in Cambridge, England, 1878–1880). Hanson's use of hipped roofs with dormers, high chimneys, turrets, arched doorways and windows, and the combination of bricks and shingles drew heavily from the Queen Anne style, popular in the late nineteenth century.

In addition to his professional career, Hanson was an important advocate for deaf people. He served as president of the National Association of the Deaf (NAD) from 1910 to 1913. He was a member of the Puget Sound Association of the Deaf, the Washington State Association of the Deaf, and the National Fraternal Society of the Deaf. His involve-

ment with deaf organizations on local and national levels made him a recognized and respected spokesperson for the deaf community. For example, in 1912 Hanson was called upon by the Seattle police department to assist in interrogating a "deaf" panhandler, Roy Thompson. After a lengthy written interview with the accused man, Hanson was convinced that Thompson was not deaf, but an imposter. He strongly expressed in a letter to the police judge the great harm that such persons did to the cause of honest, hardworking deaf people, and urged the judge to impose stiff fines and penalties in such cases. Hanson's insistence that Thompson was not deaf led to exposition and conviction. *See* NATIONAL ASSOCIATION OF THE DEAF; NATIONAL FRATERNAL SOCIETY OF THE DEAF.

Hanson was vitally concerned that deaf people be able to use a combined system of communication in order to derive full benefit from their educational opportunities. He argued in a 1910 paper delivered to the ninth Convention of the NAD and the World Federation of the Deaf that the prohibition of sign language was reprehensible. In his presentation, "The Combined System vs. Oral," he said: "Let the deaf learn to speak and read lips as far as they can, and those who find it serviceable will keep it up. But let them learn the sign language while in school in order to give them the broader and often more satisfactory means of communication." Only through a combined system of signs, speech, and lipreading, Hanson argued, would the deaf child be able to reach full intellectual potential. Despite the efforts of Hanson and the NAD, the Nebraska legislature passed a bill in 1911 which forbade the use of fingerspelling and sign language in the state school. *See* HISTORY: Sign Language Controversy; WORLD FEDERATION OF THE DEAF.

Employment was the other critical area in which Hanson felt the general public needed more accurate information about deaf people. He was the key spokesperson for the deaf community's opposition to the 1906 executive order which barred deaf people from taking the United States civil service examination and therefore excluded them from many areas of federal employment. Hanson wrote to President Theodore Roosevelt in 1908 asking him to personally intervene on behalf of deaf people. He pointed out that there were 28 deaf people in government service in the state of Washington alone, of whom 8 had been appointed after successfully passing the required examination. He went on to say, "The deaf do not ask for appointments to duties which they cannot perform [but only for fair consideration]." On April 4, 1908, the executive order was amended to permit deaf persons to be admitted to civil service examinations for all positions they may be considered capable of performing.

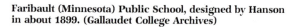

Faribault (Minnesota) Public School, designed by Hanson in about 1899. (Gallaudet College Archives)

Hanson was an important figure in the Episcopal church and became involved in missionary work in 1908. He was ordained a deacon in 1924, and in 1929 became one of 24 deaf men ordained as priests. Although he could not devote full time to the ministry because of financial reasons, Hanson traveled throughout Washington and Oregon, conducting services for deaf parishioners several times a month. He served as chairperson of the Survey Committee of the Church Mission to the Deaf, which assessed through questionnaires the extent of service being rendered to deaf people by the Episcopal church throughout the nation. *See* RELIGION, PROTESTANT.

Hanson married Agatha Tiegel, the first woman graduate of Gallaudet College, in 1893; they had three daughters. His contributions to his profession and the deaf community were recognized by the granting of an honorary doctor of science degree from Gallaudet College in 1899. Hanson died in Seattle on August 8, 1933.

Bibliography

Gallaudet College Archives.

Hanson, Olof: "An Autobiography," *The Companion*, vol. 16, May 5, 1932.

Judy Mannes

HEARING

An integral part of the human sensory input, the auditory system serves an important function for orientation to the outside world. Hearing is not as passive a process as the usual description of listening makes it seem. From the many acoustic signals that are received, an organized world of useful sound is actively created. Thus, a useful auditory system must be more than a positive receiver of sound signals; it must recognize sound sources and what those sources are doing that may affect the listener. It brings awareness of events that are not visible either because of intervening walls or other obstacles or because the sound source is not in the visible quadrant. This awareness can be especially valuable because there is also an immediate perception of the location of sounds not necessarily in the field of vision, and this may sometimes mean an appropriate action is taken to avoid danger. According to biologists, organisms without the capability of receiving vibratory signals have not survived the course of evolution. The advantage of a sensory input that provides information about events not in the field of vision is apparent to those people who do not have normal hearing sensitivity.

Immediate categorization of many familiar sounds (automobile horns, telephones, sirens), the capacity to recognize an impressive number of voices from a mere single spoken phrase (such as "hello" on the telephone), and the ability to interpret small changes in everyday sounds are auditory advantages that tend to be taken as a matter of course.

Listening to music, though it could scarcely be claimed an indispensable necessity, is for many people an enjoyable auditory activity and demonstrates the complexity of the listening process. The skilled listener can "hear out" one instrument in the presence of others, and it is usually not difficult to hear the solo voice or instrument in the presence of strong accompanying background. Such processing of mixed acoustic signals is physically much more difficult than effortless listening would indicate; the compelling subjective impression is that the signals from different sources are already cleanly separated.

SPATIAL HEARING

The localization of sound is not as highly developed in the human as in those species that depend on this function for survival, but humans do experience a useful auditory space and do register effortlessly the relative location of most sound sources of interest. The importance attached to this auditory space is attested in a number of ways, one of them being the premium many listeners place on stereophonic sound reproduction. Other evidence of the advantage of spatial hearing comes from the listening discomfort of the individual with a monaural hearing loss, and the person's comparative inability to separate out the desired signal in the presence of competing speech or noise. That the auditory system can develop even greater spatial capability is shown by the performance of some blind listeners whose skill at sensing acoustic obstacles and discerning the location and nature of acoustic boundaries can be truly impressive.

SPEECH PERCEPTION AND NOISE

For most listeners, the auditory system is pushed to its highest level of accomplishment in processing the sounds of ongoing speech. Perhaps the most impressive evidence that the perception of speech is a prodigious feat is the inability of even the most versatile computers and the most expert computer engineers to duplicate the speech-reception accomplishments of the normal auditory system. Also impressive is the ability to process speech even in the presence of other sounds. People tend to take advantage of this capability by creating communication situations that permit "tuning in" to any one of several simultaneous messages or, frequently, by creating or permitting overlapping messages during group communication efforts. Beyond that, music or other background may be added, either for pleasure or for purposes of privacy, at levels that make it difficult for computers or other electronic devices to process, or even select, the speech signal. *See* SPEECH PERCEPTION.

This ability to attend at least partially to other incoming messages is fortunate for the sense of awareness of warnings, even when attending to other auditory messages. However, it may not be advantageous to be able to work and communicate in background noise. It has been suspected for some time that the gradual high-frequency loss that comes with advancing age is at least partly attributable to constant exposure to noise. A study of schoolchildren, measuring the average level of background noise exposure for 24-hour periods (a noise dosimeter study) indicated that even for this population the level of background noise is sufficiently high to increase the risk of some loss of hearing sensitivity. If the auditory system were not so adept at selecting speech signals from background noise, quieter backgrounds might be the rule. *See* HEARING LOSS: Noise-Induced.

An additional circumstance that further complicates the listening process is the fact that much activity requires communication and takes place in environments that reflect sound, so that people usually communicate in the presence of reverberation. The normal auditory system, particularly the binaural system, appears well equipped to perform in this situation, or at least there seems to have been a good adaptation to listening in partially reverberant spaces as evidenced by the ability of the system to squelch echoes. Only under extreme echoic (reverberant) conditions does the system appear to exhibit any signal-processing impairment. Were this not the case, considering the high sensitivity and tremendous range of the system, echolike phenomena would frequently be heard in rooms the size of classrooms or when the listener is more than 5 to 10 feet (1.5 to 3 meters) from a reflecting surface. However, when normal binaural listening is not possible, even average amounts of sound reflection and echoes can lead to difficulty in speech perception.

People frequently do communicate in the presence of a high level of sound background or in very poor signal-to-noise ratio. As a result, auditory systems that do not operate normally have inordinate difficulty. Hearing-aid wearers, or persons who by audiological test measures have poorer hearing than average but should not need amplification in the simple listening situation, find that too many communication situations are of the noisy or competing-message variety. Frequently they give up trying to communicate in such circumstances.

EFFECT ON SPEECH

For the human species, hearing takes on additional importance with the recognition of the dependence of normal speech development on hearing. This is convincingly evident during a child's early years. The foundation for vocal communication appears to be laid very early—perhaps as soon as a few months of age when the child's babbling begins to show some variety. Although to the inexpert eye the child does not seem to be accomplishing anything systematic during this prelanguage period, expert observation and measures of linguistic progress indicate quite the opposite; namely, that lack of auditory stimulation during this very critical period may create an irremediable lag.

The accomplishments of the normally developing child in the realm of speech and language are truly phenomenal during this early period, but this impressive development requires the reception of acoustic signals from others as well as the capability of the child to monitor his or her own vocal efforts. Thus, with the growing realization of the dependence of early communication development on hearing has come an increased emphasis on early measurement. Furthermore, although a number of poorly controlled variables make it difficult to gather hard evidence, there appears to be at least a rough correlation between the degree of hearing loss and the amount of oral communication handicap, making accurate assessment at an early age more imperative. Fortunately, both behavioral response measurement and measurement of electric activity of the brain have become increasingly accurate and reliable. *See* SPEECH DEVELOPMENT.

SOCIAL OR EMOTIONAL SIGNIFICANCE

It is not surprising that an individual who cannot participate fully in the normal activities of communication may experience more difficulty than the average person in personal adjustment. Numerous studies have been made of the personal and social adjustment of deaf and hearing-impaired individuals. Though the pattern differs from one individual to another and though the differences found are small, on the average there is evidence of some increased degree of anxiety or depression, of introversion, and occasionally of aggression. Also, the behavioral impact of a loss of hearing appears to be greater in the case of a loss of hearing later in life than in those who experience it at birth. *See* PSYCHOLOGY: Mental Health.

Auditory rehabilitation programs actively address themselves to these problems, reportedly with some degree of success. Unfortunately, the proportion of persons with hearing loss who participate in rehabilitation programs is not high.

Earl D. Schubert

NEWBORNS

Babies are capable of hearing at birth. In fact, physiologically, the human cochlea is capable of many normal adult functions after the twentieth week of gestation. However, it is necessary to distinguish between "ears" and "hearing" as well as between "hearing" and "responding to sound." The embryologic development of the ear can be studied, but development of the structures of the ear is not sufficient evidence to tell whether a baby can hear. Absence of the development of auditory structures in the fetus may correlate with lack of hearing or deafness, but presence of these structures does not guarantee hearing. In addition, it is possible to stimulate a baby at birth and watch for a response to sound, but this reflexive reaction does not give direct evidence of hearing.

Prenatal Development   The auditory system develops structurally and functionally quite early. In fact, it has been argued that a premature infant hears at birth. Therefore, had that infant not been born prematurely, it would have been able to hear at that same gestational age (that is, after the twentieth week), although development of the middle and external ear would continue. Detailed studies of the development of the temporal bone, which contains the organs of hearing, has aided in understanding the development of auditory behavior. In addition, fetal response to loud sounds have been reported for over 60 years, and more recently by using sophisticated measurement techinques such as changes in fetal heart rate and monitoring of fetal movement.

The normal infant has thus been responding physiologically to fluid-borne sounds for at least four months before birth. Of course, during prenatal development, the middle ear of the fetus is filled with fluid from the surrounding uterine environment. At the time of birth, with the first few breaths, the middle ear drains and becomes air-filled, as it is designed to remain normally during the course of a lifetime. *See* EAR: Anatomy.

Hearing-Behavioral Measures   In the newborn, the earliest behavioral manifestations of response to sound are reflex actions. Included in this type of unlearned response is the most obvious auditory reflex observed early in life, the auropalpebral or eyeblink reflex, as well as the Moro or whole-body startle reflex, facial grimacing, increase or reduction in depth or rate of breathing, expression of pleasure, general limb movement, crying, waking from sleep, sucking, and interruption of nursing. With increasing age, reflexes tend to drop out of the infant's behavioral repertory. In the first few weeks of life, learned responses such as eye orientation motion, head turning, and turning of the entire body toward the source of sound begin to develop.

Many difficult sounds have been used to elicit behavioral responses in newborns. Early studies used such direct, live signals as bells, whistles, rattles, and clackers. However, these sounds usually are uncalibrated, which means they cannot always be faithfully reproduced at the same levels or with the same spectrum. Therefore, various measurable and calibrated signals such as white noise (a hissing noise), wide- or narrow-band noise, and frequency-modulated tones have been used to elicit responses from newborns. These calibrated signals are no more efficient at eliciting a response from a newborn than uncalibrated signals; they are just more controllable and repeatable. One signal recommended for eliciting responses in newborns is a high-pass filtered broad-band noise. It has been shown that newborns can discriminate sound on the basis of frequency, intensity, and stimulus-dimensionality. There is ample evidence to demonstrate that at birth the infant can differentiate speech signals and, for example, distinguish its mother's voice from others. It was demonstrated that newborns would suck differentially on a nonnutritive nipple in order to hear their mother's tape-recorded voice in preference to the voice of another infant's mother.

The degree of behavioral responsibility shown by a newborn to any given signal will be influenced by the prestimulus state; that is, the lower the initial state, the greater is the increase in the level of activity upon stimulation. This means that any newborn may show an increase or decrease in activity, or not change at all, depending on the prestimulus state. Light sleep is reported to be the optimal state for observing a response to sound. *See* AUDIOMETRY: Auditory Evoked Potentials.

Hearing-Electrophysiological Measures   In addition to behavioral measures in response to sound, the newborn infant demonstrates an array of electrophysiologic (changes in the electric activity of various aspects of the body) responses to sound. Investigators have studied changes in heart rate activity, respiration, middle-ear impedance, and the electric activity of the cochlea, brainstem, and brain as measures of hearing in newborns. A great deal of information also has been derived from studies of sucking, such as that described above, in which a nonnutritive nipple is connected to a pressure sensor and recording device. By way of these various techniques, it is possible to record subtle changes in electric activity of, or generated by, the newborn in response to sound, which may not be observable to the naked eye. By using electrophysiologic techniques such as those just described, it is possible to test the hearing of a newborn within hours of birth in order to detect the presence of a hearing loss. *See* AUDIOMETRY: Electrophysiologic.

Bibliography

Anson, B. J.: "Developmental Anatomy of the Ear," in M. M. Paparella and D. A. Shumrick (eds.), *Otolaryngology*, Saunders, Philadelphia, 1973.

DeCasper, A. J., and W. P. Fifer: "Of Human Bonding: Newborns Prefer Their Mothers' Voices," *Science*, 208: 1174–1176, 1980.

Eisenberg, R. B.: "The Development of Hearing in Man: An Assessment of Current Status," *Asha*, 12:119–123, 1970.

Gerber, S. E. (ed.): "Audiometry in Infancy," Grune and Stratton, New York, 1977.

Hunter-Duvar, I.: "Anatomy of the Inner Ear," in S. E. Gerber and G. T. Mencher (eds.), *The Development of Auditory Behavior*, Grune and Stratton, New York, 1983.

Mencher, G. T. (ed.): *Early Identification of Hearing Loss*, S. Karger, Basel, 1976.

Mendel, M. I.: "Infant Responses to Recorded Sounds," *Journal of Speech and Hearing Research*, 11:811–816, 1968.

Northern, J. L., and M. P. Downs (eds.): *Hearing in Children*, Williams and Wilkins, Baltimore, 1984.

Taylor, D. J., and G. T. Mencher: "Neonate Response: The Effect of Infant State and Auditory Stimuli," *Archives of Otolaryngology*, 95:120–124, 1972.

Maurice I. Mendel

HEARING AIDS

A hearing aid may be defined as any device designed to bring sound more effectively to the ear. Modern hearing aids are wearable electronic instruments that amplify sound for persons with impaired hearing.

Contemporary hearing aids may deliver amplified sound to the wearer either by bone-conduction or air-conduction reception. In bone conduction the amplified sound is applied to the skull, most commonly at the mastoid bone area, by means of a vibrator held behind the ear by eyeglass temples or by a headband. In air conduction the amplified sound exits the hearing aid through a miniature earphone or receiver to which is attached an earmold through which the sound is delivered into the ear canal. The majority of contemporary hearing aids are the air-conduction type. *See* HEARING.

Hearing instruments designed for use in classrooms for hearing-impaired students are usually not wearable; if wearable, they require an external input separate from the main device. These are usually referred to as auditory trainers. Cochlear implants are usually not categorized as hearing aids. *See* COCHLEAR IMPLANTS; SENSORY AIDS.

Electronic hearing aids consist of three major parts: a microphone that picks up speech and other sounds, the amplifier, and an earphone or receiver that delivers the amplified sound to the ear. An integral part of the amplifier is a power supply, which is a small battery. For most hearing aids, there also is an earmold, attached to the output of the receiver, and a volume control to adjust the loudness of the amplified sound. With some hearing aids there may be additional circuitry or controls, such as a tone control or other provisions to alter the frequency response of the aid or the microphone directionality; and a telephone call to allow direct electromagnetic pickup from a telephone.

Sound pressure changes, such as are created by speech or music, arrive at the microphone and are transduced or changed from acoustic to electric energy—a function which the microphone should perform as faithfully as possible. From the microphone the electric signal is fed into the amplifier, which increases the size of the signal, and usually alters the frequency response. The amplified signal is then fed to the output transducer, the receiver or earphone, where it is changed from an electric signal back to acoustic energy. From the receiver, the amplified sound is directed to the external ear canal of the wearer. For many hearing aids there is a plastic earhook and a short length of clear tubing between the receiver and the earmold. The physical cost of the amplification is the gradual reduction in the strength of the battery.

Kenneth W. Berger

DISTRIBUTION AND SALES

Hearing aid dispensing dates back to the turn of the century. During the period 1930–1960, when hearing aid dealerships were increasing rapidly, hearing aid dispensers traditionally affiliated with a single hearing aid manufacturer. In time, the trend toward independent operation and legal challenges to the single-company dealership combined to create more varied hearing aid dispensing operations.

Federal Regulations Two federal regulations stimulated the entry of otolaryngologists and audiologists into the hearing aid field, adding to the diversity of the hearing aid dispensing community. In 1977 the Food and Drug Administration (FDA) placed certain restrictions on the sale of hearing aids. These regulations provided a uniform standard relating primarily to labeling and warning and instructional statements. Medical examination within the six months preceding the purchase of a hearing aid was recommended, although consumers were given the option of waiving this examination. Otolaryngologists became the preferred physicians for medical referral.

In 1978 the United States Supreme Court ruled that professional and scientific associations could not establish ethical restrictions to limit competition among their members. Partially as a result of that ruling, the American Speech-Language-Hearing Association (ASHA) adopted its "Principles Governing Hearing Aid Dispensing." Thus, ASHA's audiologist members were free to engage in hearing aid dispensing without restrictions from the association. *See* AMERICAN SPEECH-LANGUAGE-HEARING ASSOCIATION.

Prevailing Conditions and Trends Federal regulations have been supplemented by state licensing laws. Individuals involved in hearing aid dispensing must be licensed or registered in 45 states

(Alaska, Massachusetts, Minnesota, New York, and Vermont are excluded) and the District of Columbia. Thirty-one states have enacted legislation to license audiologists. Persons licensed as audiologists under state laws may dispense hearing aids, or persons must be licensed as hearing aid dealers.

The traditional hearing aid dispensers (hearing aid specialists) are mainly represented by the National Hearing Aid Society (NHAS), which sets and maintains certification standards for its membership. NHAS was also instrumental in the development of the National Board of Certification in Hearing Instrument Sciences (NBC).

Total hearing aid sales in the United States increased an average of 100,000 aids per year from 1977 to 1983; 1984 sales reached the 1 million mark for the first time. A large share of this increase was credited to the announcement that President Ronald Reagan was fitted with an all-in-the-ear canal hearing aid.

Hearing aid sales in the United States are distributed as follows: behind-the-ear, 50.92 percent; in-the-ear, 43.3 percent; eyeglass type, 2.96 percent; and body type, 2.74 percent.

The sales of in-the-ear hearing aids have increased significantly since 1977, while body-type and eyeglass hearing aid sales have decreased. All-in-the-ear canal hearing aid sales are expected to rise dramatically. Most hearing aid sales are of the air-conduction type, with relatively few bone-conduction-type sales.

Binaural hearing aids amount to 28 percent of sales; monaural hearing aids, 72 percent. Trial or rental periods are offered almost universally, generally for durations of 30 days.

More than half of all hearing aids in the United States are sold to persons over 65 years of age. Another 25 to 30 percent are sold to individuals between ages 40 and 60, with the remainder being sold to younger persons.

Third-party payment of hearing aids occurs in about 15 percent of the cases. Free hearing aids are distributed by federal and state vocational rehabilitation agencies, the Veterans Administration, and various governmental child care agencies (such as Crippled Children, and Maternal and Child Care).

Increases are expected to continue in the senior citizen market in third-party sales, in medical- and audiological-type dispensing practices, and in multiple hearing aid sales office corporations with computer and market analysis capability. New fitting methods, advanced technology, and a large influx of well-educated people contribute to a bright outlook for the hearing aid industry.

Bibliography
Food and Drug Regulations: *Federal Register*, pp. 9286–9296, February 15, 1977.

Radcliff, D., and W. J. Mahon: "Who Is Today's Dispenser," *Hearing Aid Journal*, vol. 36, no. 5, May 1983.

Skadegard, H. J.: "International Trends in Supply and Consumption of Hearing Aids," *Hearing Instruments*, vol. 32, no. 10, 1981.

Skafte, M., and K. Cranmer: *"Hearing Instruments" Survey 1983*, Duluth, Minnesota.

E. Robert Libby

HISTORY

The history of hearing aids may be conveniently divided into three eras: preelectric instruments, electric (carbon microphone) instruments, and electronic instruments. Electronic instrument history may be further divided chronologically into two-piece vacuum-tube hearing aids; one-piece vacuum-tube wearable aids; transistor aids; and hearing aids with integrated circuits.

Nonelectric Aids The first nonelectric hearing aid is lost in prehistory. It might be assumed that someone found that cupping the hand behind the ear permitted better reception of sound than unassisted hearing. At some later date it is probable that hollowed-out animal horns provided for wider collection of sound and deliver of that additional sound to the ear. The earliest ear trumpets are reminiscent of animal horns. Bone-conduction devices also appear early in historical references to hearing aids.

The first known printed mention of an instrument specifically designed for assisting impaired hearing is in a book published by Sir Francis Bacon in 1627. In a single short paragraph Bacon describes a simple funnel-type ear trumpet and mentions that in Spain there is an instrument "in use to be set to the ear, that helpeth somewhat those that are thick of hearing." In the latter part of the 1600s and through the 1700s more frequent published references to ear trumpets and some illustrations of them may be found.

Ear trumpets were most typically of conical shape, and perhaps originally were merely an imitation of an animal horn. The opening of the ear trumpet, other things being equal, was a major determinant of how much amplification the device afforded. If

Conical ear trumpet with large collector. (From K. W. Berger, *The Hearing Aid: Its Operation and Development*, 3d ed., National Hearing Aid Society, 1983)

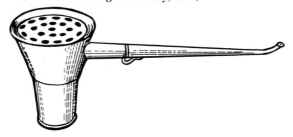

Simple dome trumpet. (From K. W. Berger, *The Hearing Aid: Its Operation and Development*, 3d ed., National Hearing Aid Society, 1983)

there was a large opening, this collected and then directed more sound to the ear canal than if there was a small opening. But, the larger the trumpet, the more obvious it was and the more cumbersome it was to use.

One of the popular later trumpet types was in the shape of a dome. It had part of the tubing bent inside the dome, thereby making the device more compact. For mild hearing losses, a trumpet could be flattened at the side and held at the ear by a headband. This type of instrument often is referred to as an ear cornet. The ear cornet provided about as much increase in signal as holding one's hand behind the ear.

As the ear trumpet and ear cornet developed, a host of ingenious schemes hid the devices in men's hats or in women's bonnets; trumpets were mounted on cane heads, built into chairs and thrones, or disguised as vases or other objects.

Materials used in ear trumpets include metal,

Curriers duplex earpiece, a speaking tube for training the hearing-impaired. (From K. W. Berger, *The Hearing Aid: Its Operation and Development*, 3d ed., National Hearing Aid Society, 1983)

tortoise shell, vulcanite (hard rubber), mother of pearl, and plastics. The eartip was usually of vulcanite, but a few of the more expensive ones were of ivory. Some trumpets included engraving or other forms of decoration.

Another nonelectric device that was popular and is still made in limited quantities in Europe is the speaking tube. The speaking tube consists of a small bell-shaped speaking end made of vulcanite or plastic, a length (perhaps two to three feet) of flexible tubing, and a small eartip made of the same material as the speaking end. The tubing usually is a spring wire covered by cloth. The speaking tube is efficient in one-to-one communication because the speech goes directly from the speaker to the listener, thereby providing a good signal-to-noise ratio.

Bone-conduction hearing aids in the preelectric era were not as popular as ear trumpets, but these, too, often were made to look like something other than a hearing aid. One interesting bone conduction instrument, popular around the early 1900s, was the hearing fan. The person with a conductive-type hearing loss could clasp the top edge of the fan blade between the teeth and pull a series of strings to hold the body of the thin vulcanite fan tense. Sound was picked up by the fan blade and delivered to the teeth. The acoustic fan made use of the phenomenon that sound travels efficiently from the teeth through bone to the inner ear.

Electric Hearing Aids   The carbon hearing aid made its appearance about 1899, at first in a table-sized instrument. By 1902 the first wearable carbon hearing aids were placed on the market in the United States and several years later in Germany. Typically, these consisted of a carbon microphone (or transmitter), an earphone, and a battery. The microphone was about the diameter of a coffee cup; if the hearing loss was greater than mild, two or more microphones were connected. In addition to wearable carbon models with one or two microphones, there were models with three or more microphones in resonant boxes, microphones along with the battery carried in specially designed purses, and multiple microphones for use in churches and auditoriums.

The earphone was later reduced in size, at which time an eartip and then an earmold was attached to it. The small earphone is usually referred to as a receiver. The receiver with earmold was more comfortable to the hearing-aid wearer than the earphone, was less bulky, and permitted more efficient delivery of the amplified sound to the ear canal. Another improvement was the addition of a combination on-off and volume control. Carbon hearing aids had limited amplification and were of some value to the hard-of-hearing individual but of little use to persons with severe hearing loss.

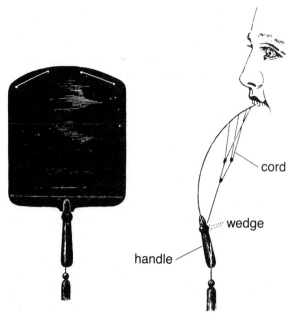

Acoustic fan. (From K. W. Berger, *The Hearing Aid: Its Operation and Development*, 3d ed., National Hearing Aid Society, 1983)

Electronic Hearing Aids The first vacuum-tube hearing aid appeared in 1921. However, it had little more power than the previous carbon models, and it was portable but not wearable. It was not until the late 1930s that wearable vacuum-tube hearing aids appeared and gradually replaced the carbon types. The vacuum-tube aids permitted virtually unlimited gain (increase in the signal) and, therefore, were useful to those with many degrees of hearing loss. The first vacuum-tube hearing aids were bulky, composed of a two-battery pack of large dimensions, the amplifier itself, and a cord leading to a receiver that connected to an earmold. With vacuum-tube hearing aids, a crystal microphone replaced the older carbon microphone.

In the 1940s the vacuum-tube hearing aid became a monopack, that is, the amplifier and batteries were housed in a single metal or plastic enclosure. The reduction in size resulted from smaller vacuum tubes which, in turn, required batteries of lesser voltage and smaller size.

In the 1950s the transistor era ushered in smaller units (now called body aids, or pocket aids) as well as several new types: eyeglass, barrette, behind-the-ear, and, somewhat later, models built entirely in the shell of an earmold, the in-the-ear aid. Barrettes were popular for only a short time in the late 1950s. The new types were made possible not only by the transistor and its smaller battery voltage requirement, but also by new battery types and other technologic developments. For transistor hearing aids, a magnetic microphone replaced the crystal microphone which had been used in vac-uum-tube models. Later, a ceramic microphone was employed in many models, and ultimately an electret microphone became standard. Transistor models also readily allowed an aid to be worn at each ear, thereby permitting binaural-aided hearing.

Within a relatively short time, major technologic changes appeared which permitted the hearing aid to become smaller and smaller, but at the same time more flexible electroacoustically and less costly to operate per hour of use. The latest hearing aid type is the canal aid. This consists of a small in-the-ear unit which fits into the external auditory canal, with only a portion extending out into the bowl (the concha) of the external ear flap.

Sales statistics for the period 1950–1985 showed a definite decline in the popularity of body- and eyeglass-type hearing aids. At the same time, the behind-the-ear and in-the-ear types have increased in popularity. These changes represent the greater cosmetic acceptability of the latter types resulting largely from technologic developments that have permitted more amplification power to be placed in smaller enclosures. Much of the reduction in size has been made possible by integrated circuits, which replace transistors and other circuit components. At the same time there has been a dramatic improvement of microphones (such as the electret microphone), some of which have directional capabilities.

Batteries The first electric hearing aids employed a battery about twice the size of today's large flashlight battery. Vacuum-tube hearing aids required two large batteries, one to heat the filament of the vacuum tubes and the other to accomplish amplification. Gradually, the batteries in vacuum-tube hearing aids were reduced in size as a result of vacuum-tube miniaturization and their smaller voltage need, but battery costs to the user remained relatively high. Batteries at that time needed to be rested periodically and stored in a cool place.

The transistor and the integrated circuit require only one battery, and in some instruments it may be as small as an aspirin tablet. Contemporary batteries are of the mercury, silver oxide, or zinc-carbon type. These do not need to be rested or stored in a cool place. They all have a long shelf-life (especially the zinc-air cell), that is, they do not deteriorate quickly when they are not being used.

Earmolds The earmold developed from a simple eartip which was attached to the earliest receivers. In the 1920s custom-made earmolds of vulcanite were introduced. Because these earmolds followed the contours of the wearer's external ear, they were more comfortable to wear than the earphone or the receiver with eartip. A few years later Lucite plastic was employed for earmolds, and this remains a common material for earmolds today. Other materials for earmolds include several softer or rubbery materials, as well as nonallergenic materials. Although the earmold is not usually considered an inherent part of a hearing aid, it has considerable effect on the acoustic output of the instrument. The marking of earmolds and their modification for specific hearing loss patterns has become a specialized technical craft.

Bibliography

Berger, K. W.: *The Hearing Aid: Its Operation and Development*, 3d ed., National Hearing Aid Society, Livonia, Michigan, 1983.

Kenneth W. Berger

Principles of Function

A contemporary hearing aid comprises five basic parts: microphone, amplifier, battery, receiver, and earmold.

The microphone picks up sound and converts it to electrical signals. The electret microphone is widely used and has good sensitivity and frequency response, along with tiny size and high reliability. Microphones may be omnidirectional, that is, capable of picking up sounds almost equally from any direction, or directional, usually emphasizing sounds from the front.

The amplifier greatly increases the strength of the electrical signal from the microphone. An amplifier may consist of individual transistors plus other needed components. The integrated circuit amplifier is widely used, with transistors, resistors, diodes, and electrical interconnections formed on a tiny silicon chip. A user-operated gain (volume) control on the amplifier allows amplification to be adjusted as needed. Other controls may be a tone control to change frequency response or a limiting control to adjust the output so that it is below the user's discomfort level. Some amplifiers incorporate automatic gain control (AGC), or compression, to reduce the gain of the amplifier as the incoming sound level increases. A major purpose of AGC is to prevent excessively loud sounds from being delivered suddenly to the ear. A wide variety of AGC types is available. Other amplifier functions that have been explored are multichannel compression, acoustic feedback reduction, and unwanted noise cancellation. Digital techniques have been employed increasingly for these purposes.

The battery provides electric power for the amplifier and microphone. Mercury (1.3 volts), zinc-air (1.3 V), and silver (1.5 V) types of cells are used. The batteries or cells range from aspirin size to cylindrical cells about 1⅛ inch long. In high-output body aids, two cells may be used instead of the usual one. Battery life depends on battery size and amplifier current requirements.

The receiver or earphone converts amplified electrical signals back to amplified sound. The balanced-armature magnetic type, which has high sensitivity, good frequency response, small size, and good reliability, is widely used. For body aids and auditory trainers, larger receivers may be used. Bone conduction receivers are infrequently used on hearing aids. They produce mechanical vibrations that reach the cochlea through the bony structure of the head.

The earmold couples the receiver to the ear canal. In behind-the-ear and eyeglass aids, flexible plastic tubing carries amplified sound from the aid to a custom-molded plastic plug that fits into the concha and ear canal. For in-the-ear and in-the-canal aids, the custom-molded case serves as the external portion of the earmold. The inside diameter of the earmold tubing or the earmold hole can significantly affect response and output. Special tubing systems can enhance high-frequency response. On low- and medium-gain aids, a vent (a hole from the tip of the earmold to the outside air) can be used to modify low-frequency response. Open molds that allow low-frequency sounds to enter the ear canal directly are useful when low-frequency hearing loss is small. An earmold must fit comfortably. In high-gain aids, the fit must be snug to prevent the escape of sound that would cause acoustic feedback (whistling).

Construction of a small behind-the-ear hearing aid. (Radioear Marketing Corporation)

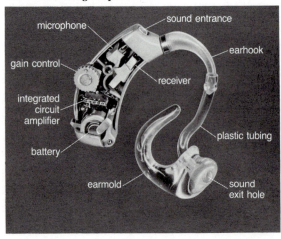

Bibliography

American National Standard Specification of Hearing Aid Characteristics, S3.22-1982, Acoustical Society of America, New York.

Berger, K. W.: *The Hearing Aid: Its Operation and Development*, National Hearing Aid Society, Detroit, 1984.

———, E. N. Hagberg, and R. L. Rane: *Prescription of Hearing Aids: Rationale, Procedure and Results*, Herald Publishing House, Kent, Ohio, 1979.

Burkhard, M. D., and R. M. Sachs: "Anthropometric Manikin for Acoustic Research," *Journal of the Acoustical Society of America*, 58:214–222, 1975.

Burnett, E. D., in *Veterans Administration Handbook of Hearing Aid Measurement*, 1982.

Harford, E. R.: "The Use of a Miniature Microphone in the Ear Canal for the Verification of Hearing Aid Performance," *Ear and Hearing*, 11(6):329–337, 1980.

Katz, J.: *Handbook of Clinical Audiology*, 3d ed., Williams and Wilkins, Baltimore, 1985.

McCandless, G. A., and P. E. Lyregaard: "Prescription of Gain/Output (POGO) for Hearing Aids," *Hearing Instruments*, 34(1):16–21, January 1983.

Mahon, W. J.: "The Million-Unit Year: 1983 Hearing Aid Sales and Statistical Summary, *Hearing Journal*, vol. 36, no. 12, December 1983.

Pascoe, D. P.: "Frequency Responses of Hearing Aids and Their Effects on the Speech Reception of Hearing Impaired Subjects," *Annals of Otology, Rhinology and Laryngology*, supp. 23, vol. 84, no. 5, part 2, 1975.

Zwislocki, J. J.: *An Earlike Coupler for Earphone Calibration*, Report LSC-S-9, Laboratory Sensory Communication, Syracuse University, 1971.

Samuel F. Lybarger

SELECTION PROCEDURES

There are many different hearing aid selection procedures, but all have a common purpose: to identify an amplification system that will promote the intelligibility of the speech signal for the hearing-impaired individual without making the sound uncomfortably loud. A selection procedure must take into account the communication needs of a particular hearing-impaired listener and the characteristics of his or her hearing loss.

Determining Candidacy The first step in any selection procedure is to decide whether a person is a candidate for amplification. Anyone who experiences difficulty hearing speech in the daily environment should consider wearing a hearing aid. However, each person has different communicative needs which should always be considered. An audiologic evaluation should be carried out prior to any hearing aid selection procedure. Hearing poorer than 40 dB HL often is used as an indication that a hearing aid may be warranted, but persons with even a smaller hearing loss may benefit from a hearing aid in specific situations. The clinician will interview the hearing-impaired person to obtain information about specific situations that cause particular difficulty and a decision regarding the advisability of amplification will be reached jointly by the clinician and the hearing-impaired person.

A medical examination is also advisable before actually trying any hearing aids. Preferably, evaluation should be done by an otolaryngologist, a medical doctor who specializes in the diagnosis and treatment of diseases of the ears, nose, and throat. Certain types of hearing problems, particularly those involving the middle-ear system, may be improved through medical intervention. In these cases, treatment may make use of a hearing aid unnecessary. In other cases, a hearing loss may be a sign of a particular medical problem requiring attention before a hearing aid can be considered. *See* AUDITORY DISORDERS, REMEDIATION OF.

Selecting the Type An initial consideration in the selection procedure is the type of hearing aid, that is, body, postauricular, on in-the-ear. In the past, the size of the hearing aid was directly related to available power. Therefore, those individuals requiring powerful hearing aids were limited to using body aids. This is no longer the case. Because of technical advances, a person with a severe or profound degree of hearing loss may satisfactorily use a postauricular hearing aid, and those with up to a severe degree of hearing loss may use an in-the-ear aid. Thus, other factors such as user preference, manual dexterity, and ease of use may be taken into consideration in this aspect of the hearing aid selection procedure. The decision about the type of hearing aid to be selected should also be made jointly with the prospective hearing aid user.

One or Two Aids When a person has a hearing loss in both ears, the question of whether to recommend one or two hearing aids arises. When the hearing loss is identical in the two ears, it is appropriate to recommend two hearing aids because of the possibility of providing the advantages of listening with both ears. These advantages include increases in the loudness of sound, in the ability to localize the source of sound, and in the ability to understand speech in noisy situations. When the amount of hearing loss in the two ears is different, the question of whether to recommend two hearing aids is more difficult to answer. Evidence suggests that even with a difference in sensitivity between ears, two hearing aids are better than one. Often the decision as to whether one or two hearing aids should be recommended is made in conjunction with the hearing-impaired person, after assessing performance with a single hearing aid and then with two hearing aids.

Specifying Electroacoustic Characteristics The determination of the exact specifications or electroacoustic characteristics of the hearing aid is the final and most crucial stage of the hearing aid selection procedure. This involves specifying the gain or amount of amplification that should be given, the frequency response or appropriate filter characteristic of the hearing aid, the maximum power output or the strongest sound that should be allowed to reach the ear through the hearing aid, and the type of earmold that should be used with the hearing aid.

The method of obtaining all necessary information varies. Two commonly used methods are a comparative evaluation approach and a prescriptive approach.

Comparative Evaluation The comparative approach involves comparing performance on speech tests obtained on several hearing aids under controlled test conditions and selecting the hearing aid that yields the best performance. The prototype for this comparative procedure was developed by R. Carhart and his coworkers in the late 1940s. In this procedure, four measures are taken, first without a hearing aid and then with several hearing aids. These measures are threshold for speech, loudness discomfort levels, and speech discrimination in quiet and in noise. Threshold for speech is the lowest level at which the listener can correctly repeat the words that were heard. Loudness discomfort level is the level at which sound becomes uncomfortably loud. Speech discrimination testing measures the listener's ability to repeat single-syllable words presented either in quiet or in noise. The hearing aid that brings the speech threshold closest to normal and that provides the best speech discrimination without causing discomfort would be recommended as the appropriate hearing aid. In practice, many people perform similarly with different hearing aids, and factors such as appearance, size, and ease of operation are used to make the final selection.

The procedure described by Carhart did not specify how to choose the hearing aids that would be evaluated. Modifications of the Carhart evaluation often use some of the guidelines provided by prescriptive procedures to choose hearing aids for evaluation. These modifications may also include slightly different test conditions. However, the hallmark of the comparative procedure is the use of speech measurements on several hearing aids and selection based on differences in performance on these speech tasks.

Prescriptive Evaluation: Prescriptive procedures use information about the person's hearing loss obtained with tones or with narrow bands of noise to predict the characteristics of the hearing aid that is best for an individual. Although the goal of the procedure is to maximize the understanding of speech, speech discrimination measurements are not necessarily used as part of the selection procedure. Instead, information about the nature of speech is used in conjunction with the information about the hearing loss at each frequency to determine the amount of amplification necessary.

Several prescriptive methods base the determination of gain and frequency response on threshold measurements. In these procedures, the amount of gain recommended at each frequency is equal to approximately half of the loss at that frequency. A correction is applied at various frequencies to reflect the amount of energy contained in an average speech at those frequencies. For example, because there is more low-frequency energy in speech than high-frequency, slightly more gain is necessary in the higher frequencies in order to make the speech audible.

Other prescriptive methods base the determination of gain and frequency response on measurements of the most comfortable loudness level at different frequenices. Frequency response and gain are calculated so as to place an average speech signal at comfort level across the frequency range.

After calculating the characteristics of the appropriate hearing aid and finding an instrument that matches these specifications, threshold measurements are made with the recommended hearing aid to determine whether the hearing aid is providing the amount of amplification predicted. If the expected amount of amplification is not achieved, modification in the frequency response and gain characteristics is made and the person is retested to verify that amplification goals have been met.

The maximum power output of the hearing aid typically is determined by obtaining measurements of the loudness discomfort level. The maximum power output is chosen so as not to exceed that level.

Earmold: Specification of the earmold is an important part of the selection procedure. The type of earmold can dramatically affect the amount of low-frequency and high-frequency energy that will reach the ear. The actual earmold that the person will use is a part of the amplification system and should be used in the hearing aid selection procedure. In the comparative procedure, this involves using the earmold while the comparative speech measures are being obtained. For the prescriptive procedures, this involves using the earmold while the measurements with the prescribed hearing aid are made.

Follow-Up   The selection procedure does not end with the recommendation that a hearing aid be purchased. After the hearing aid is obtained, each hearing-impaired individual should be checked with the hearing aid to assure that the instrument is functioning properly. If the indivdiual has not previously worn a hearing aid, instruction about its use should be provided.

Bibliography

Carhart, R.: "Tests for Selection of Hearing Aids," *Laryngoscope*, 56:780–794, 1946.

Pollack, M. C. (ed.): *Amplification for the Hearing Impaired*, Grune and Stratton, New York, 1980.

Ross, M.: "Hearing Aid Evaluation," in J. Katz (ed.), *Handbook of Clinical Audiology*, 2d ed., Williams and Wilkins, Maryland, 1978.

Arlene Neuman

TYPES

Five types of hearing aids are available. These are body aids, eyeglass aids, behind-the-ear aids, in-the-ear aids, and canal aids. Different types of hearing aids should not be confused with different makes. Most manufacturers make all types of aids.

The most common types worn today are those that fit behind the ear or into it. These place sound where it should be picked up, are convenient to wear, and are not plagued by clothing noise. However, the miniature units may be difficult to operate by persons who lack finger dexterity or fine motor control due, for example, to arthirtis or cerebral palsy. In these cases, the larger body aid will be appropriate. Each type of aid has advantages and disadvantages; no one type is the best. The goal is to select the type of aid that best meets an individual's special needs.

Body Aid A body unit, half the size of a cigarette pack, houses the microphone, batteries, amplifier, and controls. There is always a volume control and means of turning the aid on and off. A tone control and a microphone/telephone selection switch may be included. All types of aids that offer the microphone/telephone option permit the electromagnetic pickup of telephone conversations without picking up environmental sound. A thin wire connects the body aid to a receiver (earphone) which turns the electric signal into sound. A personal earmold couples the receiver to the ear. The body aid is the least frequently fitted aid because of its size, body placement, and the problem of noise from clothing rub. However, body aids are useful for persons who need larger controls, and they are commonly fitted to infants until they can wear ear-level units.

Eyeglass Aid In an eyeglass aid all components are enclosed in a thickened temple bar of the glasses. A small plastic tube connects the earmold to the temple. Few such aids are now fitted. Combining the aid with the glasses means that a problem with one means loss of use of the other during repairs. Maintaining a snug fit of the frame also is difficult because of the weight of the hearing-aid components.

Behind-the-Ear Aids These aids sit snugly behind the ear. They are effective for all but the most severe hearing problems. The components are housed in a curved plastic case which terminates in a plastic horn. This serves to hold the aid on the pinna or auricle and to convey sound to the ear through a clear plastic tube inserted in the earmold. A miniature battery is housed in the base of the aid. The on/off control may be combined with the volume control or may be separate. A telephone switch is an option, though all types of aids will amplify speech acoustically from the phone if the phone receiver is brought close to the hearing aid microphone. Tone controls on the aid allow tailoring of amplification characteristics to the wearer's needs.

In-the-Ear Aids In-the-ear aids are increasingly popular because they fit completely into the ear, the whole unit being housed in a custom earmold shell. The bulk of the unit sits in the concha, the space in the external ear that leads to the ear canal, while the remainder projects into the canal. The microphone, on/off volume control, and miniaturized battery compartment are on the flat outer surface. This part of the aid is visible unless covered by the hair. Disadvantages of this type of aid are the inability to accommodate severe hearing impairment or unusual patterns of loss, the extremely small controls, and the fact that modifications in its amplification specifications can only be made at the factory.

Canal Aids Even smaller than the in-the-ear aid, canal aids fit almost completely into the ear canal. The aid is, therefore, cosmetically most appealing. To use a canal aid, the wearer must have the necessary skill to insert and remove the very small unit, be able to adjust the tiny volume control, and be able to change the miniature battery. This type of aid can only be fit for hearing losses no greater than moderate.

Special Fittings The many types of hearing loss and the special requirements of individual hearing aid users often necessitate amplification systems more complex than those described above.

Binaural Aids. Any type of aid may be fitted to one or both ears. The choice is influenced by the client's needs, willingness to wear two aids, demonstrable benefits, usefulness of residual hearing in both ears, and cost. In many instances, binaural amplification provides superior hearing to monaural. It affords more natural stereophonic sound reception, ability to hear speakers on both sides, better listening in noise, and better sound localization.

Contralateral Routing of Signal (CROS) Aids. This type of fitting is for persons with normal hearing in one ear and unaidable hearing in the other. The fitting allows the good ear to hear sound picked up on the unaidable side. It also is used to prevent the whistle known as feedback, which occurs when powerful amplification causes leakage of sound back into the microphone because of its proximity to the receiver.

Two hearing aid cases are worn in a CROS fitting, one behind each ear. The case on the unamplified side contains a microphone, an amplifier, and the controls. A partial mold helps retain this unit on the ear. The unit on the normal ear contains the earphone or receiver. This converts the amplified electric signal back into sound, feeding it to the good ear through a special mold which does not block the canal. The amplified sound from the hearing aid on one side mixes with unamplified sound entering the normal ear on the other side. The two units may be linked by a thin wire or, preferably, may be cordless, linked by a built-in FM radio signal system. One of the advantages of the CROS type of aid is the improvement in the ability of the listener to know from which direction speech and other sounds are coming.

Bilateral Contralateral Routing of Signal (BI-CROS). This fitting is used when both ears are impaired but only one is aidable. It differs from a CROS aid only because the unit on the aidable ear also contains a microphone and amplifier. Thus, the sound is picked up by a microphone on each ear, mixed, amplified, and fed into the ear with usable hearing.

CRIS-CROS. A person with several bilateral hearing impairment may be unable to wear ear-level aids because of feedback problems. A CRIS-CROS fitting overcomes this problem by fitting two CROS-type aids. Each unit houses the microphone for the other side.

Surprisingly, in most instances the brain adapts to the unusual system of sound presentation in special fittings. Thus, persons are able to obtain amplification who otherwise would not be able to.

Bibliography

Armbruster, Joan M., and Maurice H. Miller: *Getting the Most Out of Your Hearing Aid*, Alexander Graham Bell Association for the Deaf, Spring/Summer 1984.

Harford, Earl, and Elizabeth Dodds: *Helpful Hearing and Hints.* Alexander Graham Bell Association for the Deaf, Spring/Summer 1984.

Montgomery County, Maryland, Public Schools: *All About Hearing Aids: Auditory Services Program*, Alexander Graham Bell Association for the Deaf, Spring/Summer 1984.

Pollack, M. C. (ed.): *Amplification for the Hearing Impaired*, 2d ed., Grune and Stratton, New York, 1980.

Ronnei, Eleavor, and Joan Porter: *Tim and His Hearing Aid*, Alexander Graham Bell Association for the Deaf, Spring/Summer 1984.

Sanders, D. A.: "Amplification for the Hearing Impaired Person," in D. A. Sanders, *Aural Rehabilitation: A Management Approach*, Prentice-Hall, Englewood Cliffs, New Jersey, 1982.

Derek A. Sanders

HEARING LOSS

Hearing loss has been defined in many ways; one authoritative definition is diminished hearing sensitivity measured in decibels (dB), which are units indicating the magnitude of a sound. For clinical purposes, the zero or reference decibel measure is calibrated to the threshold level of responses of the average, young normal adult to tones of different frequencies used in hearing evaluation. Threshold hearing levels for a patient are plotted on a graph called an audiogram. When an adult's hearing mechanism is sensitive to these tones at levels no stronger than approximately 25 decibels, the person is said to have hearing within normal limits for communication purposes. If sounds must be made stronger than that level in order to be heard, the person is said to have a hearing loss. Some professionals prefer to use the term hearing threshold level, however, because it is difficult to use the term loss with a child, for example, who is born with less than normal hearing sensitivity. The child has not suffered a loss as he or she never had normal hearing. Hearing loss also is used by some to cover a loss of understanding for speech or an inability to derive meaning from auditory signals because of faulty processing of sounds by the hearing mechanism. However, most professionals imply hearing loss to mean less than normal auditory sensitivity as depicted on an audiogram.

A person processes sound through the ear or peripheral auditory mechanism but actually perceives the meaning of sound with the brain or central auditory mechanism. Nevertheless, hearing sensitivity can be impaired only by some damage to the structures or by some impairment of the function of the peripheral auditory mechanism. Thus, loss of hearing sensitivity is incurred as a result of an inborn or an acquired dysfunction of some portion of the peripheral auditory system.

TYPES

The peripheral auditory system includes all of the anatomic structures from the pinna or auricle to the termination of the auditory nerve in the brain. The periphery usually is divided arbitrarily into the outer, middle, and inner ear mechanisms. Pathologic conditions affecting each of these systems individually or in combination can adversely affect the hearing ability of a person. If a condition such as impacted earwax in the outer ear or fluid in the middle ear blocks sound from reaching the inner ear, one's hearing sensitivity is reduced and a conductive hearing loss is said to exist. If, on the other hand, a condition affects the sensory cells of the cochlea in the inner ear, both hearing sensitivity and understanding of a message may be affected, and a sensory hearing loss is viewed as present. If the auditory nerve to the brain is compressed by a tumor, for example, the ensuing sensitivity impairment is termed a neural loss; in addition, the same pathologic condition often seriously affects the clarity of the sound that is heard. Because both sensory and neural losses often occur together and may be indistinguishable from each other, the descriptive term sensory-neural hearing loss often is used. A mixed hearing loss is said to exist when a loss results from conditions affecting both the conductive and sensory-neural auditory mechanisms.

DEGREE

A hearing loss can vary from a mild loss, minimally affecting one's ability to communicate, to a profound loss, making any understanding of speech impossible. Losses can begin before birth from inherited or genetic effects or from congenital (unfavorable uterine environmental) causes. They can exist from conditions incurred during birth or be acquired at any time after birth from a variety of factors. When a child suffers from a hearing impairment at birth, or early thereafter, so severe that language cannot be learned through hearing alone, the child is considered deaf. Deafness can also occur at any time in life when hearing impairment becomes so severe that understanding of speech through hearing alone is not possible.

A hearing impairment that exists prior to the learning of spoken language is termed a prelingual loss. A loss that occurs after spoken language is acquired is called a postlingual loss.

ORIENTATION OF EVALUATION

Hearing loss can be evaluated for the purpose of diagnosing a faulty auditory mechanism and used as part of the information needed in determining medical or surgical treatment of the ear. Hearing loss also can be evaluated for the purpose of assessing an aberrant avenue of communication and used as part of the information needed in determining habilitative and rehabilitative measures. In the first approach, hearing is viewed mainly from the aspect of how much hearing is lost, that is, the determination of the type and extent of a hearing disorder. In the second approach, however, there is more interest in how much hearing remains after the loss is assessed and in how to best use that residual hearing for improved everyday communication.

Bibliography

Davis, Hallowell, and S. Richard Silverman: *Hearing and Deafness*, Holt, Rinehart and Winston, New York, 1978.

Goldstein, Robert: "Neurophysiology of Hearing," in Norman J. Lass et al. (eds.), *Speech, Language and Hearing*, vol. 1: *Normal Processes*, W. B. Saunders, Philadelphia, 1982.

Martin, Frederick N.: *Introduction to Audiology*, Prentice-Hall, Englewood Cliffs, New Jersey, 1981.

Sanders, Derek A.: *Aural Rehabilitation*, Prentice-Hall, Englewood Cliffs, New Jersey, 1982.

Carol C. McRandle

Incidence and Prevalence

Hearing loss refers to all degrees of reduced sensitivity to sound. Because the range of human hearing theoretically extends from 20 to 20,000 hertz (Hz), decrements at any of these frequencies might be considered. Most studies, however, focus on reduced ability to hear in the range 500 to 2000 Hz, the so-called speech frequencies, because losses in this range interfere with aural communication.

Two other factors must be specified to make meaningful the data that follow: degree of loss and age at onset of the loss. Typically, increases in thresholds beyond 25 decibels (dB) are deemed medically significant. However, some research suggests that individuals do not label themselves hearing-impaired until their hearing levels for speech reach 30 dB. When prevalence estimates are based on self-reports, this respondent characteristic should be borne in mind. Many large-scale surveys differentiate degrees of loss with broad adjectives such as mild, moderate, severe, and profound. These adjectives often are presented without audiometric and functional correlates and, therefore, are difficult to interpret. The intended qualifications of the data do not satisfy the demands of scientific rigor, but the qualitative distinctions are noted nonetheless. A person is considered deaf when hearing losses become so severe that aural communication is impossible, even with best amplification. *See* DEAF POPULATION: Demography.

Much confusion about hearing loss was engendered in earlier statistical reports by incorporating, directly or indirectly, the age at onset into the definition. Thus, the U.S. Bureau of the Census in its surveys from 1830 to 1930 only counted persons whose losses were associated with muteness, thereby assuming prelingual onset of deafness. The Conference of Executives of American Schools for the Deaf formerly called students deaf if their speech was unintelligible, and hard-of-hearing if they had intelligible speech. Present practice differs in that the age at onset is specified separately by adding an adjective; for example, prelingual deafness means deafness that occurs before three years of age or before substantial development of language, while deafness unmodified means without regard to when it occurred in the individual's development. This practice avoids the confounding nature of defining hearing loss in terms of another difficult-to-measure ability, speech.

INCIDENCE DATA

The occurrence of hearing impairment has been poorly studied in the United States. Authorities relying on partial data and intuition have estimated the incidence of hearing impairments among live births to be of the order of 100 per 100,000. However, there is little empirical evidence on which to base that guess. Countries that have socialized medicine do occasionally obtain reliable incidence data. Sweden estimated for recent years that 70 per 100,000 children were born with a severe hearing loss. Studies in Northumberland and Durham, England, also yielded a 70 per 100,000 rate for severe hearing loss at birth. Several authorities now use this latter estimate for all European countries, a practice that will be discussed below. *See* ENGLAND, EDUCATION IN; SWEDEN.

Epidemics markedly affect the incidence of hearing impairments. During the 1951 rubella epidemic in that country, Sweden found that 8 percent of mothers infected during the first trimester delivered severely hearing-impaired infants. English investigators followed children whose mothers had had rubella while carrying them and determined an incidence for hearing loss of 19 percent, compared to 0.04 percent for a control group of children whose mothers were unaffected. The latter rate (40 per 100,000), it should be noted, is lower than the Swedish, Durham, and Northumberland rates cited above.

No substantial body of data exists about the incidence of hearing loss in adults. Yet, the correlation between age and the prevalence of hearing loss is very high. Studies of adult cohorts are needed to determine age-sex specific incidence rates for various geographical regions. Inferences from prevalences noted among elderly persons suggest that very high incidences must occur in the age decades beyond 50 years, but precise estimates of incidence have not been gathered.

PREVALENCE DATA

While much simpler to obtain, prevalence data are no less useful than incidence data; they merely serve other purposes. The United States has considerable prevalence data. The most extensive comes from the National Center for Health Statistics which periodically studies hearing impairment by household interviews (Health Interview Survey, HIS) and by physical examinations of samples of the population (Health Examination Survey, HES). As noted above, audiometric surveys are likely to differ from self-report studies in their estimates of hearing loss in a population. However, the National Health Survey found that rates for adult hearing loss derived from the Health Examination Survey and the Health Interview Survey matched exactly, when the rates for those with hearing levels for speech at and above 30 dB were compared to those who reported having varying degrees of difficulty understanding conversation. In both cases, the rates were 2.7 percent in 1963.

A more incisive survey of the United States population conducted by the Health Interview Survey in 1971 found that 7.1 percent of the United States population reported some difficulty hearing (including tinnitus), with almost half (3.2 percent) reporting a significant, bilateral loss. The rate for deafness in the population emerged at 0.87 percent. When age at onset was taken into account, 0.2 percent of the population became deaf before 19 years of age. The rate for prelingual deafness was estimated at 0.1 percent. Results of follow-up Health Interview Surveys from 1977 through 1981 are shown in Table 1. These figures include all hearing impairments and do not differentiate as to age at onset. They portray a tendency, even over the short span of five years, for the prevalence rates to increase. Future studies will be needed to determine the etiological contributions to these increases in prevalences. Note that subtracting successive prevalence rates will not permit calculation of the intervening incidence rates.

Age Table 1 displays the rates for reports of hearing impairments by age. It is clear that as age increases the proportion of the population having a hearing impairment dramatically increases. Under 17 years of age, less than 2 percent of the population complains of a hearing impairment. This rate increases gradually until, after 64 years of age, nearly 30 percent of the population indicates a hearing impairment. Projections of these data predict that by the year 2050 at least 40 percent of the population over 64 years of age will be hearing-impaired. The seriousness of that prediction should be considered with the realization that by that time one of every five members of the United States population will be over 64 years of age.

Sex Up to 65 years of age, males have a higher proportion of hearing loss than females. From 65 years of age, both have about the same rates. Because females tend to live longer, combining the rates for all ages over 64 years gives females a slightly higher rate, but more specific age breakdowns correct for this error and show that members of both groups have about the same proportion of hearing loss. Why the two rates differ in the earlier years has not been satisfactorily explained. It has been suggested that otitis media, a leading cause of

Table 1. Prevalence Rates per 100,000 Persons with Hearing Impairments (Including Tinnitus), Reported in Health Interviews, by Age and Year of Interview: United States

Age, Years	Year of Interview					
	1981	1980	1979	1978	1977	1971
All ages	8,290	7,970	7,720	7,740	7,640	7,160
Under 17	1,770	1,810	1,440	1,620	1,430	1,300
17 to 44	4,380	4,380	4,490	4,290	4,020	4,240
45 to 64	14,290	12,660	11,920	12,230	12,370	11,410
65 and over	28,380	28,250	28,160	28,420	29,270	29,430

Source: National Center for Health Statistics.

hearing impairment, may be more frequent in males because they have greater unprotected exposure to inclement weather than females. Males also tend to be employed more frequently in noisy environments. Incidence studies would shed light on the underlying reasons for the preponderance of hearing impairment in males.

Race Whites appear to have more hearing losses than blacks. While this finding remains true for overall prevalence, it should not be interpreted to mean that this results from a genetic factor influencing susceptibility to hearing impairment. That may be true, but it cannot be discovered alone from prevalence data. For example, because of poorer medical care, black children are more apt to die from bouts of spinal meningitis that white children survive, with an accompanying loss of hearing. Because such explanation cannot be ruled out, the reasons for the reduced prevalence rates for hearing loss among nonwhites remain an enigma.

Place and Time The data in Table 1 support what other studies show—that prevalence rates for hearing loss differ over time. In the United States prevalence rates generally have grown larger since 1930. That need not be true for the future, though such trends are expected to continue. Switzerland offers an example of lowered rates. From 1915 to 1922 the incidence of hearing loss ranged from 1.2 to 1.7 per 1000 births. By 1925 the rate dropped to 0.4 per 1000 births, the generally expected rate for Europe. The introduction of preventive measures resulted in a sharp reduction in the number of cases, just as an increase in the incidence rate could result because of an epidemic of rubella. *See* SWITZERLAND.

Geographically rates for hearing loss, as for deafness, vary widely. Table 2 shows the rates for hearing impairments in the United States by four census regions. As the data show, the prevalence rates for hearing impairments differ for the various portions of the country. Similar data on a worldwide basis make the same case for deafness.

RECONCILIATION

Based on the data, for any particular area at any particular time rates should be specifically determined. Using a national rate for hearing impairment, such as that in Table 2, to determine the amount of hearing loss, say, in California would result in a substantial underestimate (6603 vs. 7170 per 100,000). The same holds true for using rates from one period to estimate incidence or prevalence at a later period. Consider only the differences between the 1971 and 1981 national estimates for the prevalence of hearing impairment nationally. It has increased by 15 percent, from 7160 to 8290 per 100,000.

These statistics show that the incidence and prevalence of hearing loss are not static; they differ

Table 2. Prevalence Rates per 100,000 Persons with Hearing Impairments, by Census Regions: United States, 1971

Census Region	Prevalence Rate
United States	6603
Northeast	5977
North Central	6563
South	6807
West	7107

Source: Jerome D. Schein and Marcus T. Delk: *The Deaf Population of the United States*, National Association of the Deaf, Silver Spring, Maryland, 1974.

from place to place and over time. The astute consumers of statistics will not accept obsolete data; nor will they apply data from one area to another. Fresh, tailormade statistics are needed for research and planning.

Bibliography

Gentile, Augustine, Jerome D. Schein, and Kenneth Haase: "Characteristics of Persons with Impaired Hearing: United States, July 1962–June 1963," *Vital and Health Statistics*, ser. 10, no. 35, 1967.

Schein, Jerome D.: "Hearing Disorders," in L. T. Kurland, J. F. Kurtzke, and I. D. Goldberg (eds.), *Epidemiology of Neurologic and Sense Organ Disorders*, Harvard University Press, Cambridge, Massachusetts, 1973.

——— and Marcus T. Delk: *The Deaf Population of the United States*, National Association of the Deaf, Silver Spring, Maryland, 1974.

Jerome D. Schein

Noise-Induced

That sustained exposure to intense sound can cause damage to hearing has been known for millennia. Pliny the Elder, for example, commented on deafness among persons who lived near the Cataracts of the Nile. With the development of gunpowder, hearing loss following gunfire, even after a single explosion, became commonplace. Somewhat slower to be recognized, however, was the gradual progressive loss of hearing associated with repeated daily exposure to noises that, although loud, were far from painful. Indeed, only since 1948, when workers' compensation for partial loss of hearing was first awarded to a retired drop forge worker, have serious attempts been made to determine quantitative relations between hearing damage and noise exposure.

Progress in this direction has been slow, not only because damage is manifested in many ways, but also because noise exposures exist in great variety. Damage may refer either to morphologic and biochemical changes in the auditory system or to a loss of ability to detect or to discriminate among acoustic events such as pure tones or speech sounds. Similarly, noise exposures differ in intensity, spectrum (frequency composition), duration, and temporal pattern, all of which are relevant to the production of damage. Finally, even when the exposure is held constant, individual differences in susceptibility to damage are large. It is not surprising, therefore, that the field of noise-induced hearing damage remains controversial.

PHYSIOLOGIC DAMAGE

Damage to the auditory mechanism by noise occurs primarily in the cochlea, so that the resultant hearing loss is classified as sensory. Animal experiments have demonstrated that after exposures of moderate severity, subtle effects may be measured such as swelling and twisting of the hair cells that are the primary sensory receptors, disarray of the tiny hairs (stereocilia) on the top of the hair cells, reduction of enzymes and energy sources in the cochlear fluids, and changes in the structure of the stria vascularis, the cochlear structure thought to provide most of the nourishment to the hair cells. These changes are accompanied by a loss of auditory sensitivity. As the severity of the exposure increases, these alterations are accentuated and eventually become irreversible: stereocilia become fused together or disappear, hair cells and supporting structures disintegrate, and a few weeks later the nerve fibers that had innervated the hair cells disappear. The damage is then permanent, as hair cells do not regenerate. *See* EAR: Anatomy.

These effects are accentuated in acoustic trauma; the result of a single exposure of relatively short duration but very high intensity. When the severity of a sound exceeds some critical value, the mechanical system, the inner ear, is vibrated so violently that its elastic limit is exceeded. Attachments of the several elements of the inner ear are disrupted, hair cells are torn completely from the basilar membrane on which they normally rest, and that or one of the other membranes in the cochlea may be ruptured, leading to an intermixture of fluids of different composition that may result in poisoning of those hair cells that have survived the mechanical stress.

HEARING LOSS

Because physiologic destruction cannot be evaluated in the living organism, the aspect of damage most commonly measured in humans is the loss of sensitivity to pure tones, a change for the worse in hearing threshold levels at specific audiometric frequencies. Although from a practical viewpoint an index of damage based on auditory handicap, that is, the loss of ability to understand ordinary speech, would be preferable, little agreement exists as to how handicap is to be determined. Elevated pure-tone thresholds at the frequencies important for speech perception, 500 to 6000 Hz, have tra-ditionally been used as the measure of auditory damage. *See* AUDIOMETRY: Pure-Tone Audiogram.

Noise-induced hearing loss usually appears first at 4000 Hz, corresponding to damage in the cochlea at a point about one-third of the distance toward the apex from the oval window. This occurs because sound energy in that frequency region is most efficiently conducted to the inner ear due to the particular shape of the outer and middle ears. Even though most real-life noises are actually broadband (contain many frequencies), the 3000–4000 Hz components will almost always be the most intense ones reaching the cochlea; hence the corresponding receptors will be the first to be damaged.

With increasing exposure, the 4000-Hz tonal gap grows deeper and broader, higher frequencies generally being affected more rapidly than the lower frequencies, until in extreme cases high-frequency perception may be lost completely, although some low-frequency hearing capability remains.

Noise-induced hearing loss is not progressive; that is, if noise exposure ceases, thresholds of laboratory animals do not show further deterioration beyond that attributable to the aging process (presbycusis). The same would presumably be true for humans. However, most individuals in the modern world often are exposed to potentially hazardous noises in everyday life, and so even people who have never worked in a noisy industry will show increasing hearing loss with time over and above that caused by presbycusis and by nosoacusis (losses produced by genetic factors, drugs and chemicals, diseases, barotrauma, head blows, and other non-acoustic causes of damage). This loss of hearing due to noises not associated with employment is termed sociacusis. *See* PRESBYCUSIS.

NOISE EXPOSURE MEASUREMENT

The fact that an individual's hearing threshold levels will reflect not only the effects of industrial noise exposure but also sociacusis, nosoacusis, and presbycusis has made it difficult to infer relations between noise exposure and hearing loss from data on humans. An additional problem is posed by the lack of a valid yet simple measure of noise exposure. Although the total-energy theory of damage proposes that hearing loss is dependent only on the acoustic energy (the product of the intensity and duration of the sound) that has entered the ear, this theory is correct only for single uninterrupted exposures to a specific noise. Damage drops significantly if an exposure is broken by periods of relative quiet during which recovery processes can act. Furthermore, less damage is produced by low-frequency components of a noise than by high frequencies. The latter problem has been addressed by expressing sound intensity in terms of A-weighted sound level, a procedure that automatically deemphasizes low frequencies. However, how to take into account the effect of intermittence in exposure remains an unsolved problem.

SAFE DAILY NOISE DOSE

Hearing loss data from industry indicate that habitual exposure to steady workplace noise, 8 hours per day, 5 days per week, 50 weeks per year, will produce no effect if the noise level does not exceed 80 dB. As 80 dB is exceeded, damage increases: daily exposure at 85 dB produces a slight effect after many years of exposure. However, not until the noise level reaches 90 dB is there a significant effect, a loss of about 15 dB at the most sensitive frequencies of 3000, 4000, and 6000 Hz. For this reason, an 8-hour exposure to 90 dB has been widely adopted as a just-tolerable noise dose.

The daily permissible dose of 8 hours at 90 dB has been generalized to shorter or intermittent daily exposures in two different ways. The International Standards Organization has accepted the equal-energy variant of the total-energy theory by postulating that the daily dose be 90 dB for 8 hours (480 minutes) or its energy equivalent, for example, 93 dB for 4 hours, or 100 dB for 48 minutes, or 110 dB for 4.8 minutes. In the United States, however, an attempt has been made to approximate the effect of intermittence by allowing a 5-dB increase in level if the duration is cut in half: 95 dB for 4 hours, 100 dB for 2 hours, and so on, up to 115 dB for 15 minutes. Both of these systems are only approximations whose validity is still unknown, although the equal-energy theory appears to be more accurate in predicting the effect of very short exposures at high intensities, as in the case of gunfire.

INDIVIDUAL DIFFERENCES IN SUSCEPTIBILITY TO DAMAGE

The fact that habitual exposure to 90 dB will produce an average hearing loss of 15 dB at 3000, 4000, and 6000 Hz does not imply that everyone who works in a 90-dB noise will have precisely these values. Some ears will remain unaffected, while others will show losses of 30 dB or more. Part of this variability can be ascribed to undetected differences in exposure, either in or out of the workplace. For example, in the general population better hearing is found in women than in men, in blacks than in whites, and in right ears than in left ears; it is highly likely that these reflect differences in sociacusis and nosoacusis between the groups concerned.

On the other hand, it is conceivable that these differences could represent the effects of real morphologic differences that determine the amount of sound reaching the cochlea and hence the degree of damage. Thus, workers with conductive hearing losses will show better hearing by bone conduction than those with normal conductive mechanisms because the conductive loss reduces the sound reaching the cochlea just as an earplug does. By the same token, the size and shape of the pinna and the length of the auditory canal, the area of the eardrum, the mass of the ossicular chain, and the strength of the middle-ear muscles would be expected to be important, as would structural differences in the inner ear such as stiffness of the cochlear partition, the thickness of the various membranes, the blood supply to the cochlea, and the rate of oxygen metabolism.

Under some conditions, noise-induced hearing loss can be exacerbated. The best-established of these synergistic agents are ototoxic drugs such as kanamycin and neomycin; a noise dose that would ordinarily leave the ear unaffected may produce significant damage when combined with a drug dose that is also innocuous by itself. Fortunately, such synergism is rare. Although attempts have been made to link susceptibility to noise damage with general health, smoking habits, use of artificial food additives, poor posture, use of so-called social drugs or stimulants, and the like, no reliable causal relation has yet emerged.

Unfortunately, it is also true that no medications have yet proven to be of value in ameliorating the effects of noise. While claims have been made that substances such as vitamin A, nicotinic acid, procaine, nylidrin, adenosine triphosphate, brain cortex gangliosides, dextran, and carbogen will reduce damage from noise exposure, well-controlled studies have subsequently failed to confirm such assertions. Experience also is irrelevant: those who work in noise do not gradually become less susceptible to damage (nor more susceptible).

Attempts to predict suceptibility in order to identify persons most at risk in a given industrial noise have been equally unsuccessful. Although it is reasonable to expect that the best predictor of permanent damage from long or intense exposure would be the reversible temporary hearing loss following a more moderate exposure, little evidence of the validity of such an index exists. While individual differences in the amount of auditory fatigue produced by exposure to a particular spectrum of sound and in the rate of recovery from this fatigue have been studied extensively, only a few studies have been able to demonstrate a correlation between these temporary losses and subsequent permanent hearing losses that is statistically significant. Even in these cases the correlation is so low that it is not of practical importance.

The only way to prevent hearing loss from noise, therefore, is to reduce the noise reaching the inner ear to daily doses of 80 dB for 8 hours or its equivalent, either by lowering noise levels or through the use of ear protectors. Where this is not possible, only regular audiometry will permit the identification and the removal from noise of those individuals most susceptible to noise damage, at a point at which their hearing losses are not yet severe enough to cause problems in understanding speech.

Bibliography
Cantrell, R. W. (ed.): *Noise: Its Effects and Control*, Otolaryngologic Clinics of North America, vol. 12, no. 3, Saunders, Philadelphia, 1979.

Jones, D. M., and A. J. Chapman (eds.): *Noise and Society*, Wiley, London, 1984.

Sulkowski, W. J.: *Industrial Noise Pollution and Hearing Impairment*, National Technical Information Service, Springfield, Virginia, 1980.

Tobias, J. V., G. Jansen, and W. D. Ward (eds.): *Noise as a Public Health Problem*, ASHA Reports, no. 10, American Speech-Language-Hearing Association, Rockville, Maryland, 1980.

W. Dixon Ward

Genetic Causes

Hearing loss from genetic causes may occur at any stage in an individual's life. Genetically caused hearing loss in adult life is frequent and often only moderate, while in childhood it is less frequent but often severe.

ADULTHOOD

Hearing loss in adult life is a common disability. Indeed, some sensorineural loss of hearing, especially in the high frequencies, is a normal accompaniment of the aging process. The degree and type of hearing loss is at least in part under genetic influence. In most cases, this influence is complex, involving the interactions of many genes, but in some families hearing loss in adult life is under simple control by one specific gene. In such cases, Mendelian inheritance operates through well-known laws and patterns.

Thus, otosclerosis, a common cause of hearing loss in adult life, may be inherited in a proportion of cases in a Mendelian autosomal dominant manner. This means that one of the two genes is abnormal at a specific place, or locus, on the paired autosomes. (These are all the chromosomes except the sex chromosomes, X and Y. A female is of XX sex chromosomal constitution, a male of XY. There are 22 pairs of autosomes, making 46 chromosomes in all.) This abnormal form (allele or allelomorph) of the gene at that particular chromosomal locus causes a tendency to develop otosclerosis, but individuals who possess this abnormal allele will not all manifest the condition (reduced penetrance) and, if they do, it may be of very variable degree (variable expressivity). Thus, when considering whether the members of such a family actually complain of the symptoms of otosclerosis, or

whether they show signs, an irregular pattern of inheritance may be seen. In some families, on the other hand, all persons who possess the abnormal allele may complain of symptoms of, or show signs of, otosclerosis. In such families, the typical pattern of Mendelian autosomal dominant inheritance is seen, namely, that a person who possesses the abnormal allele will, on the average, pass it on to half of his or her offspring.

The situation is similar for sensorineural hearing losses of adult life. In most cases, these are under the control of complex systems of interacting genes and, although some familial aggregation may be seen, there is no regular pattern of inheritance. In other cases, this familial aggregation is more noticeable, and one may suspect the operation of a single abnormal allele with failure of penetrance and variable expressivity affecting the pattern of transmission. The situation is further complicated by the fact that abnormal alleles not only can give rise to variable hearing losses but may also be unilateral in their effect; unilateral hearing loss normally does not give rise to serious symptoms and may not even be noticed.

In many large families, however, mild to moderate sensorineural hearing loss in adolescents and adults is inherited in a regular autosomal dominant manner. Even the type of hearing loss may be characteristic of the family, and there may be predominantly high-, middle-, or low-tone loss patterns in the audiogram. A particularly well-known type of autosomal dominant sensorineural hearing loss of moderately severe degree with onset typically in adolescence occurs in the Alport syndrome (impaired hearing with kidney involvement or nephritis). The pattern of inheritance is complicated by the fact that male family members tend to be more severely affected than female family members, with respect to both the deafness and the nephritis. Eye involvement also may occur.

CHILDHOOD

Some of the genetic conditions mentioned above may show onset in childhood rather than later, but mild or moderate hearing loss in childhood often is due primarily to illness rather than to genetic causes. Such genetic causes, however, play an important part in the causation of profound hearing losses in childhood and are responsible for a half or more of all such cases.

Autosomal Recessive In contrast to the autosomal dominant pattern of Mendelian transmission, characteristic of less severe hearing losses, genetically determined profound hearing impairment of childhood is mainly autosomal recessive. In this type of inheritance, both parents carry an abnormal allele at the same chromosomal locus, but in contrast to autosomal dominant inheritance, these abnormal alleles do not cause any hearing impairment in the carrier parents, each of whom has a normal allele on the paired chromosome which counteracts the effects of the abnormal allele. Thus, in autosomal dominant inheritance, the effect of the abnormal allele is dominant to that of the normal, whereas in autosomal recessive inheritance it is recessive. This effect becomes uncovered, however, in one-quarter of the children of such a couple who inherit an abnormal allele from each parent and who have no normal allele at the locus in question to counteract the two abnormal alleles. These children with the paired abnormal alleles are profoundly deaf.

Autosomal recessive profound childhood deafness can be determined at any one of a large number of chromsomal loci. The exact number is unknown but it is substantial, perhaps 100 or more. Most of these genetically determined forms are rare; a few are relatively common. There is no way of identifying the particular locus concerned by any current laboratory test, and thus most of them are indistinguishable. In a few types, however, recognition is possible because of associated clinical features which are additional effects of the allele that causes the deafness. Thus, in the Pendred syndrome, which is an autosomal recessive condition of this type, deafness is associated with enlargement (goiter) of the thyroid gland. This enlargement occurs because of attempts by the body's regulating mechanisms to compensate for a partial defect in the synthesis of thyroid hormones. The biochemical nature of this defect has been defined to some extent, and it lies at the stage when inorganic iodide trapped by the thyroid gland is incorporated into organic form within the proteins of the gland. This is normally the first phase of the conversion of inorganic iodide to thyroid hormone. In general, the compensatory overgrowth is sufficient, and these individuals do not suffer from lack of thyroid hormone. They do have problems with goiter, which may have to be removed surgically. However, medical treatment is preferred, because if thyroid hormone is supplied as a drug on a permanent basis, the compensatory mechanism is not called into play and no overgrowth of the gland occurs. Such treatment can even lead to a reduction in the size of an already established goiter. It does not, however, have any effect on hearing loss that remains profound.

The Pendred syndrome is among the more common forms of autosomal recessive profound childhood deafness, as is the association of such deafness with retinitis pigmentosa, known as the Usher syndrome. A third clinically distinguishable cause of profound childhood deafness is the syndrome of Jervell and Lange-Nielson. In this condition, the accompanying clinical feature is the periodic occurrence of fainting attacks. Unfortunately, these attacks are far from being benign and are due to an unusual disturbance in cardiac conduction characterized by a bizarre electrocardiogram. Indeed, many of these children die of cardiac syncope in one of these attacks. This condition is not as common as the Pendred or Usher syndromes, and there is a large number of even rarer autosomal recessive conditions in which deafness is accompanied by distinctive clinical features. These other conditions often have been described in one or two families only and are too numerous to list individually. In most of these syndromes the hearing loss is sensorineural in nature and tends to be greater for the high frequencies. In a minority of these syndromes, the deafness includes a conductive component and is associated with malformations of the outer, middle, or inner ears.

The majority of cases of autosomal recessive deafness are not distinguishable by such clinical accompaniments. There are various lines of evidence that even such clinically undifferentiated autosomal recessive deafness may be determined at a large number, probably several dozen, of chromosomal loci. One line of evidence comes from marriages between deaf persons where there is clear evidence that both partners have autosomal recessive deafness. If this were determined at the same locus, all their children would be expected to be deaf because they cannot inherit any normal allele at this locus. However, the children of a large majority of such unions all are hearing, suggesting that the autosomal recessive deafness in the two parents is determined at two distinct loci.

In various populations studied in economically developed countries, the incidence of autosomal recessive profound childhood deafness is about 1 in 3000. Thus, it is not a very rare entity but, because it may be caused at any one of several dozen chromosomal loci, each one of these genetic subtypes is much rarer. Because of this rarity of the abnormal alleles concerned, it is not uncommon to find that the parents of such a deaf child are related, often as first cousins and sometimes more distantly. If an individual carries such a rare allele, it is much more likely that a related spouse should carry it also than that a spouse from the general population should do so.

Autosomal Dominant Autosomal dominant profound childhood deafness is much less frequent than the autosomal recessive variety, the incidence of the two being approximately in the proportion of 1 to 3. The same degree of biological heterogeneity is seen among forms of autosomal dominant as among forms of autosomal recessive deafness. Once again, forms exist where the deafness seems to be an isolated phenomenon, while in others it is associated with concomitant clinical features in other systems. A particularly well-delineated group of such syndromes is that in which impaired hearing occurs together with pigmentary anomalies. In the classical form of this condition, known as the Waardenburg syndrome, a hearing loss coexists with hypopigmentation which may affect large patches of skin, the hair, eye lashes, the irises, and ocular fundi. Because the hypopigmentation is segmental, the very striking phenomenon of heterochromia or color mixture of the irises may occur, with different colors appearing in the two irises. This heterochromia may be total, so that each iris is a different color (usually blue and brown), or segmental, indicating that segments of different coloration occur in one or both irises. This is a striking phenomenon and, together with the leucism or partial depigmentation of skin and hair, serves to identify such children. In addition, the children show an unusual morphologic anomaly of the facial structure known as telecanthus, involving a lateral displacement of the medial canthi (that is, inner corners) of the eyelid. While the Waardenburg syndrome is inherited in a dominant manner, the concepts of variable expressivity and penetrance alluded to above are of utmost importance in this condition. Thus, only a few persons who possess the abnormal allele show all the features of the syndrome, and only a small minority are affected with profound bilateral deafness, which is the sole detrimental feature of the condition. Many may, in fact, escape hearing loss.

There seems to be some basic connection between the development of pigmentation and of hearing during embryogenesis because the Waardenburg syndrome is by no means the only condition in which disorders of the two are associated. Two or even possibly three such distinct autosomal dominant conditions exist. It is not clear whether these autosomal dominant associations of hearing loss with pigmentary anomalies are determined at the same or at different gene loci, but an important discriminating feature is that the morphologic anomaly of the eyelid occurs in most members of some families but not in affected members of other families. This suggests that at least two distinct genetic entities may be involved.

The hearing disorder in these conditions in which pigmentary anomalies are associated is of the sensorineural type, but other autosomal dominant types of hearing loss exist in which the bony or osseous part of the auditory apparatus is involved in a malformation affecting a wider area of the facial skeleton, thus giving rise to a primarily conductive form of hearing loss. The best known of these is the Treacher Collins syndrome (mandibulofacial dysostosis). This consists of abnormalities of the outer, middle, and, occasionally, the internal ear, associated with antimongoloid palpebral (eyelid) fissures, coloboma or notch of the lower eyelids, hypoplasia or incomplete development of the malar (cheek) bone and mandible or lower jaw, macrostomia (abnormally large mouth size), high palate and malformed teeth, blind fistulae (abnormal sinuses or passages) between the angles of the mouth and the ears, and abnormal implantation of the facial hair. These deformities may occur in any combination and with varying degrees of severity. They may often be unilateral. Because of this marked variability, mandibulofacial dysostosis does not often lead to profound childhood deafness.

Apart from these syndromes, as in the case of autosomal recessive hearing loss, forms of autosomal dominant hearing loss exist that represent an isolated lesion without evidence of involvement of other body systems. Again, variable expressivity and lack of penetrance are rather common, though the extent seems to vary from family to family, probably because, as in the case of autosomal recessive inheritance, different gene loci are involved. Thus, in some families expressivity and penetrance are complete and profound bilateral childhood deafness is transmitted in a regular Mendelian manner to half the offspring of affected persons, while in others the pattern is far more irregular and some persons carrying the abnormal allele may be unilaterally affected, mildly affected, or both.

Sex-Linked A small minority of cases of profound childhood deafness in males (2–3 percent) is due to sex-linked or X-linked recessive inheritance. This means that the abnormal allele determining deafness lies on the X chromosome. The male has only one X chromosome, paired with a Y chromosome which contains very little genetic material. Thus, there can be no normal allele to counteract the effects of the abnormal one, and deafness results. These alleles are rare and it would be extremely unusual to find an affected woman, because she would need to have abnormal alleles on both her X chromosomes. Even in the case of this very rare entity of sex-linked recessive deafness, there is evidence of genetic heterogeneity; that is, the existence of different genetic subtypes determined by distinct loci on the X chromosome. One such subtype has been described where the deafness is not purely sensorineural but includes a conductive component due to fixation of the footplate of the stapes.

CONGENITAL MALFORMATIONS

Sometimes deafness may occur as part of a congenital malformation syndrome. One inherited example discussed above is the mandibulofacial dysostosis or Treacher Collins syndrome. A substantial proportion of such congenital malformation syndromes are not, however, determined in a simple genetic manner but are presumably due to the synergistic effects of multiple genes, possibly interacting with environmental factors. An example of this group of conditions may well be the Wildervanck syndrome, which combines hearing loss associated with malformations of the outer, middle, or internal ear, with the Klippel-Feil anomaly of the spine. Although the Klippel-Feil malformation itself seems to occur with equal frequency in females and males, its association with impaired hearing occurs much more often in the former, in the ratio of 10 or more to 1. The reason is not clear, but a predilection for one or the other sex is a characteristic feature of congenital malformations as a whole, though it is usually less pronounced. Presumably this phenomenon occurs because one sex has a lower threshold of resistance to the combination of genetic and environmental factors determining a particular defect of embryogenesis. Because embryogenesis takes a substantially different course in the two sexes, such variations in resistance would not be surprising.

Bibliography

Fraser, G. R.: *The Causes of Profound Deafness in Childhood: A Study of 3,535 Individuals with Severe Hearing Loss Present at Birth or of Childhood Onset*, Johns Hopkins University Press, Baltimore, 1976.

Konigsmark, B. W., and R. J. Gorlin: *Genetic and Metabolic Deafness*, Saunders, Philadelphia, 1976.

G. R. Fraser

Prenatal Causes

Hearing loss from prenatal causes has been reported in 7 to 20 percent of the total deaf and hard-of-hearing population. Prenatal deafness and hearing loss result from a variety of intrauterine conditions that fall into three categories: viral diseases, drugs, and miscellaneous intrauterine conditions. However, the effect of these conditions on the fetus is subject to the influence of genetic factors that can vary the response of the fetus to the condition. For example, the extent and nature of the harmful effects of maternal viral infections such as rubella (German measles) depend to a substantial degree on both maternal and fetal genes that determine susceptibility and resistance. Thus, possibly there is no pure cause of deafness. All of the prenatal causes of deafness are preventable; it is thus imperative to be aware of their effects.

VIRAL DISEASES

A number of viral infections contracted by the mother during or before pregnancy comprise the largest number of causes of prenatal deafness. They have been termed the TORCH complex of diseases, an acronym derived from toxoplasmosis, other (specifically syphilis), rubella, cytomegalovirus inclusion disease, and herpes simplex.

Toxoplasmosis This infection is caused by a parasite transmitted through uncooked meat or by contact with feces of infected cats. It is acquired by 2 in 1000 pregnant women; 30 percent of these will have infected infants, of which 17 percent will have hearing loss. Thus, the hearing loss from toxoplasmosis is fairly rare but remains a constant threat.

Other This miscellaneous category is concerned mainly with syphilis, which can eventually cause hearing loss in a child when transmitted in utero from an infected mother. Transmission to the child occurs in a large number of cases, and 35 percent of these children will eventually become deaf. The losses from this cause are not numerous, but the exact incidence is hard to identify because the loss becomes evident usually suddenly, later in childhood or even in adulthood. If the hearing loss appears before the age of 10, it is usually profound. The hearing loss from syphilis is particularly handicapping because it affects the neural part of the auditory system, a pathologic condition that results in poor understanding of speech even with amplification.

Rubella Often called German measles, this viral disease can cause hearing loss 50 percent of the time when the mother contracts it during pregnancy. Even exposure of the mother to the disease without her development of overt symptoms can result in deafness in the child, and the effects can be present regardless of the period of gestation during which exposure occurs. The hearing loss may progress further in the early years of life. The hearing loss of rubella affects the sensory part of the ear (the cochlea). Fortunately, there is usually good understanding of speech with amplification if there is residual hearing. A 1963–1965 epidemic deafened 8000 children in the United States, and during that decade rubella was responsible for over 20 percent of all deafness. Since then the introduction of a successful rubella vaccine has reduced the number to less than 5 percent of all deafness.

Cytomegalovirus (CMV) Inclusion Disease The cytomegalovirus that causes this disease is a common virus and is acquired by close personal contact, particularly with body secretions. It is harmless to most people but can be devastating to the developing fetus if the mother becomes infected for the first time during pregnancy. A study of newborn infants found that 0.5 percent had congenital CMV infection, of which 10 percent had some degree of hearing impairment. The losses most often are profound, but milder losses are occasionally found. When residual hearing is present, the child will benefit greatly from hearing aid use. It is possible that CMV is replacing rubella as the most common viral cause of prenatal hearing loss, with different reports placing it at 2 to 40 percent of all congenital deafness.

Herpes Simplex Virus Herpes is a sexually transmitted disease; the virus (type II) is acquired by the fetus during birth if the mother is infected. It causes death in a majority of infants affected, but the survivors may have hearing loss.

DRUGS

Some drugs are known to be ototoxic, that is, they are damaging to the sensorineural structures of the ear. These include thalidomide, the aminoglycosides, alcohol, and hard drugs.

Thalidomide This drug, taken during pregnancy, caused a large number of ear malformations and hearing loss in Europe during the 1960s. Fortunately the drug was never released in the United States by the Federal Food and Drug Administration, so it did not cause a significant number of losses other than in a few babies of women who had brought the drug to the United States from Europe.

Aminoglycosides Kanamycin, neomycin, gentamicin, tobramycin, and amikacin cause hearing loss in adults or children who receive them over a long period of time or who have kidney problems while taking the drug. However, the only reports of hearing loss resulting from use of these drugs during pregnancy are of infants whose mothers had kidney problems and received ethacrynic acid and furosimide, which are diuretics, in addition to an aminoglycoside. Therefore, the incidence of prenatal deafness from these drugs is extremely low. Several reports suggest that susceptibility to aminoglycoside ototoxicity may be related to genetic factors.

Fetal ear damage due to the drugs streptomycin and dihydrostreptomycin is rare, but there have been isolated case reports of mild to severe hearing losses resulting from their use. Kidney problems in the mother for which other drugs are given, plus a prolonged course of the drugs, are responsible for the damage to the ear.

Alcohol Fetal alcohol syndrome has been documented as a cause of hearing loss in the infants of addicted mothers. One study has reported that 64 percent of children with fetal alcohol syndrome have accompanying hearing losses, either sensorineural or conductive.

Hard Drugs Hard drugs such as LSD or morphine are difficult to indict as causes of deafness, and no well-documented cases are reported. There are isolated cases of deaf children known to have been born of mothers on hard drugs, but the contribution of the drug to the loss is hard to determine.

OTHER INTRAUTERINE CONDITIONS

A number of intrauterine conditions have been implicated in hearing loss, but there are few well-documented cases that establish them as definite causations. Among these are maternal diabetes, hypothyroidism, toxemia of pregnancy, and severe malnutrition or anemia. General anesthetics and x-ray exposure have also been suggested. Although these factors have not been definitely implicated, it is well to avoid them.

Bibliography

Bergstrom, L., and W. G. Hemenway (eds.): "Symposium on Congenital Deafness," *Otolaryngology Clinics of North America*, 1971.

Bess, F. (ed.): *Childhood Deafness: Causation, Assessment and Management*, Grune and Stratton, New York, 1977.

Fraser, G. R.: *The Causes of Profound Deafness in Childhood*, Johns Hopkins University Press, Baltimore, 1976.

Gerkin, K. P.: "The High Risk Register for Deafness," *Asha*, pp. 17–23, March 1984.

Harris, S., et al.: "Clinical Note: Congenital Cytomegalovirus Infection and Sensorineural Hearing Loss," *Ear and Hearing*, pp. 352–355, 1984.

Marion P. Downs

Perinatal and Postnatal Causes

Many factors can cause hearing loss in utero, at delivery, or after birth. (The perinatal period extends from approximately one month before delivery to one month after birth. The postnatal period is from delivery to one year after delivery; it includes the neonatal period, from delivery to one month of age.) A sensorineural loss in the postnatal period often is unsuspected because the external ear looks normal, and the infant babbles normally and may even respond to some sounds. A conductive hearing loss in the postnatal period is usually due to otitis media; it is often overlooked because the ear canal is narrow and the tympanic membrane is small and difficult to see. Therefore, hearing loss in the postnatal period is difficult to detect, and yet the effect may be devastating on speech, language development, and general behavior.

PERINATAL PERIOD

In the perinatal period of fetal development, the inner ear is still maturing with increasing myelinization of the nerve structures. Either infections or ototoxic drugs may interrupt normal development and create a hearing loss. Other agents may damage the already-developed inner ear structures.

Cytomegalovirus is a significant infectious agent that can give rise to hearing loss in the ninth-month fetus. Exposure to the virus has been documented serologically in 50 percent of middle-class women in the childbearing age. Virus shedding occurs in the urine and increases from 1.2 percent in the first trimester to 5.9 percent in the third trimester; shedding in the cervix is increased from 1.3 to 13.4 percent during the same period. It appears that reactivation of latent infection does occur in pregnancy, especially in the third trimester. In addition, in congenital cytomegalovirus infection, the virus can cross the placenta, and some infants will become infected. Even an inapparent cytomegalovirus infection in pregnant women is responsible for a bilateral sensorineural hearing loss in 11 percent of their babies, an IQ below 79 in 49 percent, microcephaly in 3 percent, and neurologic defects in 10 percent.

Another infection that typically produces a congenital sensorineural hearing loss, and less commonly a conductive hearing loss due to stapes fixation, is rubella. When infection occurs in the first trimester, 68 percent of infants are deaf, and in the second trimester, 40 percent. In the third trimester, the percent of deaf newborns is considerably less but still occurs.

Two other significant infections are toxoplasmosis and syphilis. Toxoplasmosis is a protozoan infection. If it occurs during pregnancy, deafness results in 17 percent of affected newborns. Congenital syphilis is associated with stigmata at birth called Hutchinson's triade, which includes interstitial keratitis (a corneal inflammation), knotched central incisor teeth, and a sensorineural hearing loss. A progressive sensorineural loss also may occur.

Among ototoxic drugs, streptomycin has most often been the cause of perinatal hearing loss because it was used to treat tuberculosis in pregnant women. A sensorineural loss ranging from a mild high-frequency loss to a severe bilateral 60–90 decibel loss occurred when streptomycin was given in any trimester. Kanamycin rarely produced a sensorineural loss. The drugs neomycin, ethacrinic acid, and furosemide, when given to pregnant females, do not cause a sensorineural loss in newborns. Thalidomide has caused teratogenic defects in the developing ear, but only when given during the first trimester.

POSTNATAL: AT DELIVERY

Several conditions at birth may be related to hearing loss. These include low birth weight, oxygen deficiency, excessive bilirubin, and birth canal infections. Low birth weight refers to newborns of 1500 grams (3.3 pounds) or less. Approximately 30 percent of low-birth-weight newborns are full-term, and 70 percent are premature. Full-term infants with a low birth weight are described as small for gestational age. No increased hearing loss is noted in this group. Premature infants with a low birth weight have a short gestational age. In these premature infants, the risk for sensorineural hearing loss is approximately 5 percent. There may be a range from a mild high-frequency loss to a severe sensorineural loss.

Significant asphyxia at delivery may occur, especially when the pregnant woman has no antenatal care in her sixth (or more) pregnancy, or has severe preeclampsia. Asphyxia is characterized as mild (when there is increased tone and irritability requiring therapy), moderate (when hypotonia and suppressed primitive reflexes occur for several days), or severe (when the newborn is stuporous with persistent hypotonia and suppressed primitive reflexes for two weeks). Mild sensorineural hearing loss occurs in 3 percent of newborns with significant asphyxia. Severe sensorineural hearing loss occurs in another 3 percent of newborns with significant asphyxia.

It is believed that hyperbilirubinemia, that is, high levels of unconjugated bilirubin, damage the cochlear nuclei in the brainstem by deposition of pigment in the gray matter—a condition known as kernicterus. Fortunately, therapy for hyperbilirubinemia, using Rh-immune globulins for Rh-sensitized mothers, as well as phototherapy, exchange transfusions, and drug therapy, are all lessening the number of newborns with kernicterus.

Viruses and bacteria can live in the vagina and may transmit birth canal infections to the newborn. This will be discussed below in connection with neonatal otitis media.

POSTNATAL: AFTER DELIVERY

Infections of the middle ear at birth—neonatal otitis media—to six weeks of age are most often caused by *Streptococcus pneumoniae* (often associated with bacteremia) and *Haemophilus influenzae*. These infections may be diagnosed by physical examination, aspiration of the middle ear, and autopsy examination.

Maternal infections may also be responsible for neonatal otitis media. These are transmitted to the fetus via the blood, causing neonatal sepsis, pneumonia, or meningitis. Amniotic fluid could become infected from a maternal systemic infection or via an ascending infectious agent from the vagina during the latter part of pregnancy. The infected amniotic fluid, known to be swallowed by the fetus, may be pumped up the eustachian tube into the middle ear, creating an otitis media, all prior to birth.

Acute otitis media is the most common cause of hearing loss in the postnatal period. Etiologic agents are *S. pneumoniae* (33 percent), *H. influenzae* (20 percent), *Streptococcus* Group A (8 percent), *Branhamella catarrhalis* (3 percent), and other bacteria. Antibiotic therapy usually cures the infection, and hearing returns to normal within two to six weeks. Viruses, mycoplasmas, chlamydia, and other unusual organisms also have been documented as causing hearing loss.

Recurrent otitis media is defined generally as recurrence of more than three middle-ear infections in six months, or four infections in a year. Each occurrence of acute otitis media will produce a transitory hearing loss. When these episodes are frequent, the hearing loss extends over more and more time during the year. If the hearing loss occurs for more than 50 percent of the time in the first years of life, it may produce a speech and language delay, behavioral changes, and later education difficulties. This cycle of hearing loss can be interrupted either with prophylactic antibiotics or with tympanotomy tubes.

Chronic otitis media is a persistent middle-ear inflammation with an effusion that may be serous, mucoid, or purulent. Serous or mucoid otitis media most often follows an episode of acute otitis media that has been rendered sterile by use of antibiotics. The viscous nature of these fluids prevents them from being absorbed by the middle-ear mucosa, or from flowing down the eustachian tube. Drug therapy does not cure the problem. The serous or mucoid effusion is a good growth medium for microorganisms; when an upper respiratory infection occurs the middle ear quickly becomes infected. If the fluid lasts over six weeks, a tympanotomy tube is recommended to improve hearing, and in most cases it will prevent the recurrence of otitis media.

Bacterial meningitis is one of the most common causes of acquired sensorineural deafness during the postnatal period. The hearing loss ranges from mild to profound; about 50 percent of infants have a profound loss. The sensorineural loss is permanent except in some isolated cases where recovery occurred. Otitis media with a conductive hearing loss occurs in 15 percent of infants with meningitis. The infection can be cured with antibiotics, and hearing is restored. Neonatal meningitis is primarily due to gram-negative bacteria, especially *Escherichia coli*. The prognosis is poor, with 50 percent of the survivors having severe neurologic handicaps, including hearing loss, mental and motor retardation, seizures, and hydrocephalus.

Until the 1980s, testing the hearing levels in infants was difficult, although it was known that hearing loss from meningitis occurred. Brainstem auditory-evoked response testing has been done in a large series of infants and children with bacterial meningitis. Approximately 10 to 20 percent of 230 children examined in these studies had a persistent unilateral or bilateal sensorineural hearing loss. Cochlear damage, which occurs when bacteria from the meninges enter the cochlea along the cochlear nerve or cochlear ducts, was found in two-thirds of the children. Brainstem problems were found in one-third of the children. The brainstem may be damaged when the infection spreads directly into the brainstem tissue, or when the infection invades small vessels under the meninges to produce an arteritis or venous thrombophlebitis. *See* AUDIOMETRY: Auditory Evoked Potentials.

Infrequent causes of hearing loss in the postnatal period include head trauma, noise trauma, barotrauma, ototoxic drugs, sickle-cell anemia, and tumors.

Bibliography
Abroms, I.: "Non-Genetic Hearing Loss," in B. Jaffe (ed.), *Hearing Loss in Children*, pp. 367–375, University Park Press, 1977.
Bluestone C., and S. Stool: *Pediat. Otol.*, 1:402–408, 1983.
Dodge, P., et al.: "Prospective Evaluation of Hearing Impairment as a Sequela of Acute Bacterial Meningitis," *NEJM*, 311:869–874, October 4, 1984.
Klein, J., and C. Bluestone: "Management of Pediatric Infectious Diseases in Office Practice," *Pediat. Infect. Dis.*, 1:66–73, January 1982.
Ozdamor, O., N. Kraus, and L. Stein: "Auditory Brainstem Responses in Infants Recovering from Bacterial Meningitis," *Arch. Otol.*, 109:13–18, January 1983.
Panjvani, Z., and J. Hanshaw: "Cytomegalovirus in the Perinatal Period," *Amer. J. Dis. Child.*, 135:56–60, January 1981.
Robertson, C. (Edmonton, Alberta, Canada): Personal communication, 1978.

Burton Jaffe

Causes in Adults

Hearing loss is commonly classified as one of the following types: conductive, sensory, neural, sensorineural, mixed, or pseudohypacusis (nonorganic hearing loss). These terms are based on the anatomic site of the damage (lesion). Causes of conductive hearing loss are those pathologic conditions that disturb the function of the external ear canal or the middle ear. A hearing loss caused by pathology in the cochlea or in the auditory neuron is termed sensory hearing loss or neural hearing loss, respectively. However, the term sensorineural hearing loss is more commonly used because sensory and neural hearing losses often cannot be differentiated. When a conductive and sensorineural hearing loss coexist, it is called a mixed-type hearing loss.

Because the above classification of the hearing loss is based on the location of the lesion, this section will review various pathologic conditions in the external ear, middle ear, inner ear, and auditory nerve that would cause a hearing loss in adult life. There are also some genetic hearing losses that do not appear until the late teens or later.

EXTERNAL EAR CANAL
Blockages of the external ear canal may cause hearing loss. They usually result from impacted earwax, foreign bodies in the canal, or a narrowing or closure from any of several pathologic conditions.

Impacted Cerumen (Earwax)   This is not a disease, but if cerumen is hardened and occludes the external ear canal, conduction of sounds to the middle ear is blocked, causing a mild conductive hearing loss that affects high frequencies more than low frequencies. Some people produce more cerumen than other people.

Foreign Bodies Foreign bodies such as toothpicks, pins, or matches are found more often in the ears of young children than in adults. They do not, however, cause a serious hearing impairment unless the external ear canal is completely obstructed or penetration of the tympanic membrane occurs and injures the middle ear structure. Secondary infection of the middle ear also may occur. If the labyrinth is damaged, a sensory hearing loss may develop.

Acquired Narrowing (Stenosis) and Closure (Atresia) The external ear canal can become very narrow or completely closed at times as a consequence of various pathologic processes. One of the pathologic conditions that could cause such a conductive hearing loss is chronic otitis externa due to deep infection of the skin. Inflammatory disorders of the skin of the external ear canal are caused by bacterial, viral, or fungal infection, allergic reaction, and injuries. The primary symptoms are pain or itching, with redness, edema, swelling, and discharge in the canal. In the acute state, hearing is usually not affected but will be impaired if chronic infection results in extensive stenosis of the canal.

Another cause of stenosis or atresia is perichondritis, an infection of the connective tissue covering the cartilage, primarily the cartilage of the pinna. The cartilage may be destroyed, and as a consequence, a marked deformity of the pinna may develop. The stenosis also may occur after surgery and corrosive burns. Most cases require surgical excision of the stenotic lesion and reconstruction of the canal.

Tumors Malignant or benign tumors can occur in the external ear canal, but they are not common. Some originate in the middle ear, causing extensive destruction. The most common aggressive tumor in the external ear canal is cancer. Like cancer of any other part of the body, its behavior is characterized by rapid growth, destruction of the adjacent tissue, and metastasis to the regional lymph nodes and to remote areas.

MIDDLE EAR

Pathologic conditions in the middle ear, including the tympanic membrane, can cause up to 60 dB conductive hearing loss, even if there is no involvement of the inner ear. Because there is more than one vibrating system in the middle ear, each with its own mass, stiffness, and friction, the pattern of the audiogram is highly variable, depending on the pathologic condition. Alterations of just the middle-ear structure can, in some cases, cause eleva-

tion of bone conduction thresholds and can mimic a mixed-type hearing loss. Identification of the middle-ear pathologic condition, therefore, cannot depend solely on audiologic evaluation. Detailed history taking, otomicroscopic examination, radiologic evaluation, and at times, exploratory middle-ear surgery (tympanotomy) are required to identify the cause of the hearing problem. The etiology of conductive hearing impairment includes congenital malformation, injuries, inflammations, neoplasms, and disease of the otic capsule. *See* AUDITORY DISORDERS, EVALUATION AND DIAGNOSIS OF.

Injuries A variety of injuries to the head, including sudden changes in external atmospheric pressure, may produce damages to the middle ear and result in hearing loss.

Foreign Bodies: Various foreign bodies described in the previous section can penetrate the tympanic membrane and disrupt the connection of the ossicles, resulting in a conductive hearing loss. Even a sensorineural hearing loss or mixed-type hearing loss could occur if the stapes footplate is pushed into the vestibule. Many cases of ossicular disconnection can be surgically corrected.

Head Trauma: Severe head concussions or blows from auto accidents, falls, or hits with hard objects often are accompanied by fracture of the temporal bone. The middle ear can be involved if a fracture line runs along the long axis of the temporal bone, causing either fracture or dislocation of the ossicles. The joint between the incus and stapes is most often separated. Ossicular discontinuities could occur without fracture of the temporal bone.

Barotrauma: This is an injury to the middle ear caused by imbalance in air pressure between ambient air and the middle-ear cavity. When the eustachian tube cannot comply with rapid change in atmospheric air pressure during descent in an airplane or scuba diving, for example, people experience sharp earache and develop serous otitis media. The tympanic membrane may rupture. Even a slap directly over the opening of the external ear canal or an exposure to a blast sometimes results in perforation of the tympanic membrane.

Inflammations Inflammations in the middle ear are a common cause of temporary or permanent hearing loss in children, but they also can affect the hearing of adults.

Acute Suppurative Otitis Media: Suppurative is applied to those conditions where pus is formed or contained in the middle ear. Bacterial or viral infection of the nasopharynx can spread to the eustachian tube and into the entire lining of the middle-ear cleft. Bacteria may enter the middle ear through traumatic rupture of the tympanic membrane. A variety of organisms can be isolated, but those most commonly found are streptococcus pneumonia, staphylococcus aureus, and hemolytic streptococcus. In the acute stage, the patient suffers from throbbing earache and fever. If the tympanic membrane ruptures and drainage occurs, the patient experiences immediate relief of pain. When infection spreads into the mastoid and pus remains in the air cells, it is called mastoiditis, which often requires surgery. As the inflammatory process continues to spread, a variety of complications such as labyrinthitis, meningitis, paralysis of the facial nerve, or paralysis of the abducent nerve (which controls lateral movement of the eye) may occur.

Chronic Suppurative Otitis Media: Inadequately treated acute otitis media, repeated middle-ear infections, and mastoiditis unresponsive to antibiotics often develop into a chronic inflammatory condition. This is characterized by permanent perforation of the tympanic membrane, persistent or intermittent discharge, conductive hearing loss, and absence of earache. The degree of hearing loss varies from slight to moderate. The hearing loss sometimes becomes less when the middle-ear cavity is moist with discharge.

Cholesteatoma: Cholesteatoma is one of the chronic middle-ear inflammatory diseases and involves a cystlike lesion that contains proliferating, keratinizing skin debris. There are congenital and acquired cholesteatomas. The congenital form, which is rare, may occur in any part of the temporal bone. Acquired cholesteatoma can occur from the attic retraction pocket, which is caused by persistent eustachian tube stenosis. If the negative pressure persists in the middle ear, Shrapnell's membrane (the upper portion of the tympanic membrane) may be retracted and form an invaginated sac in the attic of the middle ear. The sac, which is called a retraction pocket, gradually distends. Acquired cholesteatoma also may result from migration of the skin epithelium of the external ear canal into the middle ear through a marginal perforation of the tympanic membrane. As the cholesteatoma grows, the surrounding bone is eroded and the middle-ear structure is damaged, causing a conductive hearing loss of varying degrees. The invasive nature of the cholesteatoma can cause serious complications such as secondary infection, labyrinthitis, facial nerve paralysis, meningitis, or brain abscess. If the labyrinth is involved, the hearing loss is a mixed type.

Nonsuppurative Otitis Media: This is also called serous otitis media, secretory otitis media, or glue ear. It is the most common cause of hearing loss in children, but can also occur in adults whenever the eustachian tube fails to function because of a cold or because of barotrauma during flying or diving. If nonsuppurative otitis media persists in adults, a nasopharyngeal neoplasm should be ruled out. Continuous negative air pressure in the middle ear because of eustachian tube dysfunction causes retraction of the tympanic membrane and forces nonpurulent fluid out of the lining of the middle ear. One of the serious complications of persistent negative air pressure is the development of an attic retraction pocket that can lead to the formation of a cholesteatoma.

Adhesive Otitis Media: This is a result of chronic middle-ear infection. Following a long-standing otitis media, the tympanic membrane may become scarred and collapse, resulting in adhesion to the ossicles and middle-ear promontory.

Tympanosclerosis: This is another middle-ear abnormality resulting from chronic otitis media. It is a new bone formation caused by calcification of the fibrous tissue of the middle-ear lining. A deposit of calcium often is seen as a white patch in the tympanic membrane.

Otosclerosis   Otosclerosis is a genetic disease of the otic capsule, but the clinical symptoms of hearing loss usually begin between 20 and 30 years of age. The otic capsule first becomes soft because of increased vascularity and resorption of bone. This condition is called otospongiosis. This spongy bone is gradually replaced by hard bone. Because this new bone formation often occurs around the oval window, it immobilizes the stapes, resulting in a progressive conductive hearing loss. Otospongiosis also can occur in the cochlear wall without involving the oval window. This clinically silent lesion can be found in about 8 percent of Caucasian temporal bones. The incidence is twice as common in females as in males. The clinical manifestation occurs in 10 to 12 percent of those who have the lesion, and is characterized by a very slowly progressive bilateral conductive hearing loss and constant tinnitus of various kinds. Unilateral clinical otosclerosis has been found in about 15 percent of the cases. As the pathologic process continues, the hearing loss becomes a mixed-type and can end up as a severe sensorineural hearing loss. It has been reported that pregnancy may accelerate the lesion.

Neoplasms   Neoplasms of the middle ear are relatively rare. The most commonly reported types are squamous-cell cancer and glomus tumor.

Squamous-Cell Cancer: As with any other cancer, squamous-cell cancer of the middle ear and mastoid can spread rapidly. It may occur after chronic suppurative otitis media but also may occur with no predisposing factor at any age, although it is most common in a person's fifties. Hearing loss is conductive in type until the tumor invades the labyrinth. Discharge from the ear often is blood-stained, and pain may become intense in later stages.

Glomus Tumor: This is a slow-growing tumor, which is a collection of chemoreceptor tissue in the outermost covering of the jugular bulb or which arises from the nerve on the promontory. A conductive hearing loss and pulsating tinnitus are the earliest symptoms of the tympanic glomus tumor. A sensorineural hearing loss, dizziness, and multiple cranial nerve palsies may develop later. The diagnosis can be made only by biopsy, and surgical removal is usually required. These tumors are seen more often in females than in males.

INNER EAR

The identification of the cause of an inner-ear pathology is not as easy as identifying the cause of a middle-ear disorder. The cochlea is embedded deep in the hard bone of the temporal bone and is beyond the limit of direct visual inspection through the otoscope or surgical microscope. Therefore, careful history taking and general physical examination, including various clinical laboratory studies, are most crucial for diagnosis. The sensorineural hearing loss is not an isolated ailment in many cases. The causes of many sensorineural hearing losses remain unknown or undetermined at this time. Such is the case with Ménière's syndrome and idiopathic sudden hearing loss.

Injuries Injuries not only affect the middle ear. They may also produce severe damages to the inner ear, leading to a sensorineural hearing loss.

Temporal Bone Fracture: With the progress of industrialization, accidents have increased alarmingly. Head trauma with basal skull fracture involving the temporal bone is one of the frequently seen injuries for both otolaryngologists and audiologists. The head is involved in three-quarters of all automobile accidents. It has already been noted that longitudinal temporal bone fractures usually involve the middle ear, and therefore result in a conductive hearing loss. However, if the fracture occurs at right angles to the long axis of the petrous bone, the inner ear or internal auditory meatus often is involved. This is called a transverse fracture, and may cause sensorineural hearing loss, vertigo, tinnitus, and facial nerve paralysis. A transverse fracture usually occurs when the front or back of the head receives a blow. Even without fractures of the temporal bone, severe blows to the head can damage the organ of Corti, possibly due to violent movement of the basilar membrane.

Barotrauma: Rapid or forceful air pressure changes during diving or aircraft ascent and descent may damage the membrane structure of the cochlea, producing sensorineural hearing loss or vertigo. The round-window membrane, oval-window membrane, or Reissner's membrane may rupture. The hearing loss may be fluctuant or steady, temporary or permanent.

Noise-Induced Hearing Loss: Noise exposure probably causes the greatest number of hearing losses among adults. This causal factor is discussed separately in another section of this article.

Inflammations An inflammatory condition of the inner ear is called labyrinthitis. Bacteria, viruses, or toxic agents may enter the inner ear either from the middle ear, from the meninges, or through the bloodstream. The most common route is from the middle ear. When the patient has acute or chronic otitis media, mastoiditis, or cholesteatoma, the bacteria may invade the inner ear through the eroded labyrinthine capsule. Infectious organisms can be transmitted at the time of a stapes operation or mastoidectomy, through fracture lines of the temporal bone, or via fistulas of the oval or round window. Suppurative labyrinthitis usually causes a profound sensorineural hearing loss, often total deafness, and violent vertigo.

Meningeal labyrinthitis occurs when an organism is transmitted to the cochlea via the internal auditory meatus, vestibular aqueduct, or cochlear aqueduct. This is more common in children than adults.

The organisms that cause labyrinthitis via the bloodstream are usually viruses. Certain viruses known to attack the inner ear include mumps, measles, influenza, rhinovirus, chicken pox, and varicella-zoster virus. The sensorineural hearing loss is usually severe or profound, and onset is sudden.

When a patient develops sudden flat sensorineural hearing loss with poor speech discrimination or sudden progression of fluctuation of sensorineural hearing loss with no apparent cause, syphilis may have to be ruled out. Syphilitic labyrinthitis is usually the result of congenital syphilitis, but it may occur as late as age 60. Acquired syphilitic labyrinthitis is rare and occurs in the secondary or late tertiary stage. Hearing loss is characterized by asymmetric fluctuant sensorineural hearing loss associated with dizziness. In females, the fluctuation of hearing loss may be related to menses or pregnancy. The clinical manifestation sometimes mimics Ménière's disease, toxic or viral labyrinthitis, or a tumor of the VIIIth cranial nerve.

Ototoxicity Certain antibiotics and diuretics are known to cause toxic effects on the cochlear or vestibular structures. Some are more toxic to the vestibular organ than to the cochlear organ, and vice versa, though most of them are toxic to both systems. The ototoxic antibiotics are aminoglycosides, such as those listed in Table 3.

Table 3. Ototoxic Antibiotics and Degree of Severity as Indicated by the Number of Plus (+) Signs

Drug	Cochleotoxicity	Vestibular Toxicity
Streptomycin	+	+ + +
Kanamycin	+ + +	+
Gentamicin	+ +	+
Tobramycin	+ +	+
Netilmycin	+	+
Vancomycin	+ +	+
Neomycin	+ + + +	+

The ototoxic effects depend not only on the dose but also on kidney function. Poor kidney function results in high blood levels of the drug for a longer period of time. Sensorineural hearing loss caused by aminoglycoside toxicity is either gradual or sudden and is usually associated with tinnitus. The progression of hearing loss can continue even after cessation of administration of a drug such as kanamycin. It is usually not reversible, as the toxic effects include hair cell damage and secondary degeneration of the auditory nerve endings. The mechanism of the ototoxicity still is not well understood.

Diuretics known to cause ototoxicity are ethacrynic acid and furosemide. Sensorineural hearing loss is usually transient, but may become permanent in high doses or if it is used together with an ototoxic aminoglycoside. The patient may experience vertigo.

Other ototoxic drugs include salicylates, quinine, and *cis*-platinum, which is used as a cancer chemotherapeutic agent. Hearing loss resulting from salicylate ototoxicity occurs only when the drug is used in high doses, and it is usually reversible. Quinine ototoxicity also is reversible if the dosage is kept low. *Cis*-platinum may produce gastrointestinal toxicity, nephrotoxicity, bone marrow depression, and sensorineural hearing loss in high frequencies that may be reversible or permanent.

Ménière's Disease Ménière's disease (as distinct from Ménière's syndrome) was first described by a French physician, Prosper Ménière, in 1861, as a disease characterized by sudden attacks of vertigo, fluctuating or progressive sensorineural hearing loss that often is unilateral, and tinnitus. These clinical manifestations were found later to be the results of an extraordinary distention of the membranous labyrinth. The disease is also called idiopathic endolymphatic hydrops because its etiology is unknown. Various causative factors have been suggested, including viral infections, cranial trauma, endocrine disturbances, sodium retention in the body, allergy, autonomic nervous dysfunctions, and psychosomatic disorders. The classic audiologic findings are unilateral sensorineural hearing loss with loudness recruitment and poor speech discrimination disproportionate to the pure-tone audiogram. However, a bilateral hearing loss has been found in 10 to 25 percent of the cases, and some patients demonstrate good speech discrimination. A hearing loss commonly begins in low frequencies, and then the high frequencies are gradually involved.

Aging Process (Presbycusis) As seen in other parts of the body, the aging process also takes place in the auditory system. In the inner ear, the aging process occurs as gradual degeneration of hair cells and supporting cells of the organ of Corti, beginning in the basal turn of the cochlea. Atrophy of spinal ganglion cells and stria vascularis and loss of elasticity of the basilar membrane also occur. Sensorineural hearing loss due to the aging process is called presbycusis, and will begin to occur in the high frequencies, usually between ages 55 and 60. Presbycusis is frequent, progressive, and characterized by poor speech discrimination ability, particularly when the cochlear neurons are predominantly involved (neural presbycusis). For many elderly people with neural presbycusis, speech is difficult to understand if spoken fast or in a noisy environment. This makes it difficult for them to use a hearing aid, causing a serious problem of psychosocial isolation. *See* DEAF POPULATION: Aged.

Systemic Diseases Some vascular, metabolic, and other systemic diseases are known to produce a sensorineural hearing loss. Several types of genetic syndromes with a hearing loss begin in adult life. The development of hearing loss usually is gradual but can occur suddenly. Histopathologic study of the inner ear yields no specific character or lesion. If such hearing loss occurs in the later decades of life, it is difficult to differentiate from presbycusis.

Vascular Disorders. A sudden sensorineural hearing loss occurring in patients with high blood pressure, arteriosclerosis, or other vascular disorders may be attributed to spasm of the internal auditory artery, formation of a clot in the internal auditory artery, or hemorrhage in the cochlea. The disturbance of blood supply to the cochlea results in degeneration of spiral ganglion cells and atrophy of stria vascularis and spiral ligament. Lack of oxygen because of disrupted blood supply may destroy hair cells.

Diabetis Mellitus. Diabetis mellitus is a metabolic disease characterized by a high level of blood glucose due to inadequate secretion of insulin from the pancreas, which promotes glucose utilization, storage of fat, and synthesis of protein. Because diabetes tends to cause degenerative changes in blood vessels and affects a number of peripheral nerves, blood supply to the ear and internal auditory canal may be disturbed, and cochlear and vestibular nerves may degenerate.

Thyroid Dysfunction. Diminished production of thyroid hormone (hypothyroidism) may be related to a sensorineural hearing loss, but it is not as well documented in adults as is Pendred's syndrome, which is a genetic (autosomal recessive) hearing impairment associated with a goiter. The pathophysiologic mechanism is not clear.

Renal Dysfunction. A sensorineural hearing impairment often is found in patients with renal disease who underwent hemodialysis and renal transplantation. Osmotic disturbances, electrolyte imbalance, inadequate dialysis, or ototoxicity of diuretics and aminoglycosides may affect the stria vascularis and biochemical components of inner-ear fluid, causing alteration of normal physiologic functioning of the cochlea.

Cogan's Syndrome. Also known as oculovestibuloauditory syndrome, this is a nonsyphilitic inflammation of the cornea characterized by a sudden onset of vertigo, tinnitus, and severe sensorineural hearing loss. The cause is unknown. Pathologic changes include endolymphatic hydrops, new bone formation around the round window, and degeneration of the organ of Corti and cochlear neurons.

Paget's Disease. This is one of the genetic hearing impairments and usually begins at middle age. It is a generalized bone disease characterized by thickening and softening of bones. It affects the skull as well as the long bones of the legs. The hearing loss is mainly sensorineural, but a mixed type is seen at times because of stapedial fixation. It may be associated with tinnitus and dizziness.

Alport's Disease. This is a genetic disease characterized by progressive kidney inflammation (nephritis), sensorineural hearing impairment, and ocular lens abnormalities. The kidney disease is usually noted in childhood, but hearing impairment usually occurs in the second and third decades. It is more common and severe in males than in females.

AUDITORY NERVE AND CEREBELLOPONTINE ANGLE

The two most common causes of adult hearing loss that originate in the auditory nerve and cerebellopontine angle (angle between the cerebellum and the pons) are the space-occupying lesions, eighth-nerve schwannoma and meningioma. The lesion is a slowly growing tumor. A congenital cholesteatoma, described previously, may develop in the internal auditory canal or petrous apex with similar clinical features. The hearing loss is usually unilateral and of gradual onset, but it can occur abruptly. The degree of hearing loss and the shape of the audiogram are not uniform. Auditory function is characterized by poor speech discrimination disproportionate to the audiogram. Unilateral tinnitus and vertigo or unsteadiness usually are present. Depending on the location and size of the tumor, the facial nerve and trigeminal nerve also may be involved.

VIIIth-Nerve Schwannoma   This is a histopathologically benign tumor and is often called acoustic neuroma and neurinoma. The tumor arises in the covering membrane of the VIIIth nerve, called the sheath of Schwann. The growth usually is slow and often is undetected for many years. The tumor has sometimes been found in the cochlea. It occurs unilaterally, but bilateral tumors may be found in von Recklinghausen's disease, which is a neurofibramotosis with multiple lesions.

Meningioma   This is a benign tumor that originates in the membranes covering the brain, the meninges. They account for approximately 15 percent of all intracranial tumors, but they are uncommon in the cerebellopontine angle. They usually occur in adults older than 30 years. Because of the location, the symptoms are similar to those produced by an VIIIth-nerve schwannoma.

SUDDEN HEARING LOSS

Some of the hearing losses described above develop gradually and some are characterized by sudden onset. The following are causes of hearing losses in adults that can occur suddenly or develop rapidly within hours or a few days: injuries to the ear by foreign bodies, head trauma with and without temporal bone fracture, barotrauma, acoustic trauma, otologic surgery, vascular causes, viral infection, Ménière's disease, meningitis, encephalitis, syphilis, Cogan's syndrome, suppurative labyrinthitis, ototoxicity, psychogenic causes, and idiopathic (cause unknown) sudden sensorineural hearing loss.

Bibliography

Davis, H., and S. R. Silverman: *Hearing and Deafness,* 1970.

Goodhill, V. (ed.): *Ear Diseases, Deafness and Dizziness,* 1979.

Martin, F. N. (ed.): *Medical Audiology,* 1981.

Northern, J. L. (ed.): *Hearing Disorders,* 2d ed., 1984.

Hiroshi Shimizu

Nonorganic

Nonorganic hearing loss refers to a hearing problem that has no identifiable basis in physical or physiologic function of the ear itself or of the auditory pathways of sound. The nonorganic component may be superimposed or overlaid on a hearing loss that has some physical basis, or it may be seen in conjunction with normal hearing.

Other terms for this phenomenon are functional hearing loss, hysterical or psychogenic loss, and pseudohypacusis. None of the terms identifies the degree of conscious knowledge the person has of the problem.

MOTIVES AND BEHAVIOR

There has been disagreement and controversy over the self-conscious perception of this disorder by the individual. Some have theorized that all nonorganic hearing loss represents simulation, some that all instances are psychologically or emotionally based, and still others that the condition is a gray area with both aspects of consciousness represented.

Motives for the behavior generally are considered complex, even though superficially they may seem simply and directly related to some form of compensation, whether it be financial, emotional, or social. In some instances the reward is an excuse for poor life performance, or in the case of children, poor academic performance. The motives may be conscious at some early stage of the disorder, but gradually the individual may come to believe the disorder, especially as reinforcement from the rewards increases.

Nonorganic hearing loss is not easily identifiable on the surface. Those who have the disorder appear to have trouble communicating, and some even wear hearing aids. Most investigators who have reported on the topic list characteristic communicative and general behaviors, including: (1) exceptionally good or exceptionally poor speechreading (lipreading) ability; (2) excessive straining to hear; (3) activity diametrically opposed to instructions; (4) arrival for an appointment two hours early or two hours late; (5) reporting an excessive number of symptoms that do not represent a logical set of organic symptoms.

During conventional hearing tests, the relations between pure-tone air conduction and speech audiometry are poor. Only halves of words may be repeated when equal stress has been put on each part of a two-syllable word in the delivery of the signal to the listener. The person may respond to general questions but will not respond to test materials at the same intensity levels. In the case of unilateral loss, the individual may not respond to loud signals in the nonorganic ear at a level that consistently represents a crossover level (that is, interaural attenuation of the head space), whereas the organic-loss listener will respond as if the signal were in the better ear. Many other clues of similar nature have been described.

INCIDENCE

The incidence of nonorganic hearing loss varies in social environments according to the degree with which its presence is rewarded. Immediately following World War II, the disorder increased in percentage among veterans. When the group was examined for service connection, the incidence increased from 10 percent to nearly 50 percent. Decreases in incidence occur in times of improved, sophisticated audiologic testing, as well as with early and careful counseling of the individual. In the early 1980s the estimated figures were between 1 and 5 percent of the general population. Incidences between 5 and 10 percent are estimated for the veteran and industrial-worker population.

IDENTIFICATION AND QUANTIFICATION

Several auditory tests help in the identification and quantification of nonorganic hearing loss. Conventional speech and pure-tone tests can be revised and improvised and their presentation manipulated by an experienced tester both to identify the presence of and to quantify the degree of loss.

When automatic or Békésy-type audiometry is used, both the LOT (lengthened off-time test) and BADGE (Békésy ascending-descending gap evaluation) are applicable methods. The LOT is a screening test designed to use pulsed tones with both a standard off-time and a lengthened off-time and to compare the response to these signals with those to a continuous tone. The person with nonorganic hearing loss is believed to be unable to set consistent loudness levels when the parameters of time are changed. Persons with known organically based auditory disorders do not trace better thresholds for continuous tones than for interrupted tones, but nonorganic responders may. BADGE also uses continuous and pulsed tones that are manipulated with respect to intensity from below threshold presentation, and the responses then are compared for consistency of threshold.

The speech and pure-tone SAL (sensorineural acuity level) are tests in which a noise is delivered through a bone conductor to the forehead and the conventional signal is presented through an earphone. Norms must be established in each clinical environment for this method. Initially the test was designed to determine sensorineural sensitivity. The noise through the bone conductor at the center of the forehead caused a larger shift in threshold for the signal in the normal listener or the listener with conductive hearing loss than it did for one with sensorineural hearing loss. The test also has been found somewhat useful in detecting nonorganic hearing loss in children. The noise through the bone conductor disrupts the listener's ability to maintain a consistent threshold for the signal, and the bone-conducted shift is similar to that of a normal ear or one with conductive loss. Other tests must be used to rule out conductive loss since organic hearing levels are not provided by this procedure.

Special tests for the investigation of nonorganic hearing loss using conventional signals that provide quantitative data are as follows: Lombard, pure-tone and speech Stengers, Doerfler-Stewart test, pure-tone and speech-delayed auditory feedback. The Lombard test is based on the presentation of above-threshold signals to the ears, assuming the intensity of the vocal response will reflect that the person hears the signal loudly. The pure-tone and speech Stengers are primarily applicable to unilateral losses. They are based on the interaural attenuation data available. The individual who has an organic hearing loss will continue to respond when a potentially interfering signal has been presented to the ear with the loss. One with nonorganic loss stops responding. For example, if a speech signal is presented to the better ear of a listener with organic unilateral loss at a hearing level of 30 decibels (dB), he or she will continue to indicate hearing in the better ear until the level of the poorer ear is increased to 70 dB. Then the listener will indicate that the signal is coming through the poorer ear or that there is confusion as to where the signal is. The response is a voluntary one. In the case of the listener with nonorganic loss or good hearing in both ears, there will be a response to the 30-dB hearing level signal in the better ear, but only until the level of the signal in the poorer ear is increased to the point where it will mask that in the better ear. At that point, the listener will stop responding.

The Doerfler-Stewart test is designed to indicate binaural nonorganic loss. It relies on speech stimuli delivered through earphones and a speech noise (a noise that has its greatest energy within the speech frequencies 300–3000 Hz) delivered simultaneously to a level at which noise interferes with speech. Further manipulation of the speech and noise provides five measures that are compared to a set of norms. Psychologically, the noise is highly disruptive to the nonorganic listener, and inconsistent responses to the speech signals result frequently in lower thresholds. The results lead to an interpretation concerning a binaural threshold of hearing. Pure-tone and speech-delayed auditory feedback use finger tapping to the former signal and the reading of speech material for the latter. These motor responses are then delayed in time and fed back through earphones at various levels of intensity until a disturbance of the motor response occurs. The response differences can be measured in terms of seconds so that an organic threshold of hearing is inferred. *See* AUDIOMETRY: Speech Sensitivity.

Electrophysiologic tests also are used to provide quantitative organic threshold information. These tests rely on the objective rather than the subjective responses of the individual. The tests include contralateral and ipsilateral acoustic reflexes, speech and pure-tone electrodermal audiometry, early and middle components of auditory evoked potentials, and electrocochleography. *See* AUDIOMETRY: Electrophysiologic.

Contralateral and ipsilateral acoustic reflexes are conventionally examined in conjunction with tympanograms. Elicitation of acoustic reflexes requires a loud signal. If the individual has a moderate or severe loss of hearing, reflexes will not be elicited. If there is normal hearing or a mild loss, reflexes will be present.

Speech and pure-tone electrodermal tests have fallen out of favor because of the need to condition the individual to an electric shock. Both early and middle components of auditory-evoked potentials and electrocochleography are accomplished by affixing electrodes to the individual and recording physiologic responses, usually to clicks or tones, for comparison to normative data. Intensity changes are one set of variables that can be examined with these procedures, and that aid in determination of organic thresholds.

PROFESSIONAL RESPONSIBILITY
The professional position of the audiologist is to establish whether there is an organic hearing loss, and if so, to determine the degree of the organic component. Investigation of motives and treatment of the disorder are under the aegis of other professionals.

Bibliography
Hopkinson, Norma T.: "Speech Tests for Pseudohypacusis," in J. Katz (ed.), *Handbook of Clinical Audiology*, Williams and Wilkins, Baltimore, pp. 291–302, 1978.

Martin, Fred N.: "Pseudohypacusis Perspectives and Pure Tone Tests," in J. Katz (ed.), *Handbook of Clinical Audiology*, Williams and Wilkins, Baltimore, pp. 276–290, 1978.

Rintelmann, William F.: "Pseudohypacusis," in W. F. Rintelmann (ed.), *Hearing Assessment*, University Park Press, Baltimore, pp. 379–424, 1979.

Norma T. Hopkinson

Effects of Long-Term Mild Loss
The long-term effects of mild hearing loss may be more detrimental to language development and academic achievement than is generally realized. Currently, the concept of an educationally handicapping hearing loss is undergoing dramatic changes. Traditionally, it has been thought that hearing thresholds poorer than 25 decibels (dB) might put a child at risk for educational purposes or language-learning skills. However, clinicians have found that pure-tone screening at 25 dB misses a high percentage of medically significant ear disorders, and have pointed out the role of mild or minimal hearing loss, that is, less than 25 dB, in delayed speech and language development and lower school achievement. While there is uncertainty about whether a fluctuating conductive-type hearing loss or a sensorineural-type hearing loss is more likely to cause language-learning or educational dysfunctions, the point is that even the mildest degree of hearing loss must not be ignored.

Mild hearing losses can affect language development and learning in several ways. The first occurs because of a reduction in the overall loudness of speech. Those who sustain a mild loss of hearing perceive conversational speech at a softer level. This loss of loudness has a varying effect on individual speech sounds. The acoustic energy, with its corresponding loudness of speech, is heavily concentrated in the vowel sounds, followed by the voiced consonants. The weakest sounds in terms of acoustic energy are the unvoiced consonants that are produced by creating friction in the breath stream rather than by vocalization from the larynx. Many of these unvoiced-consonant sounds fall below the threshold of the normal hearing individual, but the message content can be interpreted from the remainder of what is heard. It is important, however, for a preschool child to hear all of the speech sounds in a new word. When speech sounds are heard inconsistently or missed entirely, the usual learning strategies of the child become confused and disorganized. For the child who is still learning language, a mild hearing loss places a strain on listening abilities. One result is distortion or omission of speech sounds and words in listening and speaking, and consequently, a possible delay in overall (expressive and receptive) language development. *See* SPEECH, ACOUSTICS OF.

Different studies provide support confirming the acoustic liabilities of mild hearing loss. The following outcomes were observed from one source: there is a potential loss of transitional information, especially plural endings and related final-position fricatives; and very brief utterances or high-frequency information can conceivably be either distorted or degraded if signal-to-noise conditions are less than satisfactory. A child with a 20-dB conductive or sensorineural hearing loss might be further handicapped acoustically in the following ways: (1) morphologic markers (segments of words, phrases, or sentences critical to meaning) might be omitted or sporadically misunderstood, rendering the utterance meaningless or nonsensical; (2) very short words that are slurred in connected speech will lose considerable loudness because of the critical relation between intensity, duration, and loudness; and (3) inflections, or markers, carrying suprasegmental features such as questioning and related intonation contouring can be expected to come through inconsistently. In addition, markers for the beginnings and endings of words and ideas can be inconsistently noted. *See* SPEECH PERCEPTION.

Poor auditory development may also be related to critical periods of language and learning and to early auditory deprivations that may be caused by mild hearing loss. The theory of critical periods states that there are certain periods in development when a person is programmed to receive and use particular types of stimuli, and that subsequently the stimuli will have gradually diminishing potency in affecting the person's development. In the case of audition, it means that at a certain developmental stage auditory signals will be optimally received and used for important prelingual activities, but once this stage has passed, the effective use of these signals gradually declines. An appropriate concept for language development maintains that language input must be experienced at a certain stage, or it becomes increasingly ineffective for use in emergent language skills. The research on early experiential deprivation has been distinct from that on early auditory deprivation, yet the two are closely related. Language may be an innate function that is dependent on early experience, but the requisite experience comes largely through the sensory avenue of auditory perceiving. There seems to be little doubt that auditory processing must develop while the brain is still plastic, and that if any sensory deprivation occurs at this time, there may be permanent and irreversible deficits in the perception of the acoustic signal.

Bibliography

Dobie, R. A., and C. I. Berlin: "Influence of Otitis Media on Hearing and Development," *Ann. Otol. Rhinol. Laryngol.*, vol. 88, suppl. 60, 1979.

Holm, V. A., and L. H. Kunze: "Effect of Chronic Otitis Media on Language and Speech Development," *Pediatrics*, vol. 43, 1969.

Jordan, R. E., and E. L. Eagles: "The Relation of Air Conduction Audiometry to Otologic Abnormalities," *Ann. Otol. Rhinol. Laryngol.*, vol. 70, 1961.

Northern, J. L., and M. P. Downs: *Hearing in Children*, 2d ed., Williams and Wilkins, Baltimore, 1978.

Webster, D. B., and M. Webster: "Neonatal Sound Deprivation Affects Brainstem Auditory Nuclei," *Arch. Otolaryngol.*, vol. 103, 1977.

Allan O. Diefendorf

HEARING REHABILITATION QUARTERLY

The *Hearing Rehabilitation Quarterly (HRQ)* is published four times a year by the New York League for the Hard of Hearing. The current title and format were established in 1976. The publication grew out of a succession of the league's earlier periodicals dating back to the early 1920s. Its earliest forerunner was the *Chronicle*, which was published in 1921–1923. This was succeeded by the *Bulletin of the New York League for the Hard of Hearing*, which was published monthly beginning in February 1923. The *Bulletin* contained articles concerning events of the league, activities of members, notes of meetings of the board of trustees, and letters from readers. In 1961 the *Bulletin* was succeeded by *Highlights of the New York League for the Hard of Hearing*. This was a more comprehensive and ambitious publication; it emphasized articles of interest to hearing-rehabilitation professionals and hearing-impaired clients and consumers while continuing to keep the reader abreast of the league's activities.

At present, *HRQ* reflects the overall growth and current status of the New York League for the Hard of Hearing as an agency whose reputation and influence extends beyond the geographical limits of New York City.

AUDIENCE

HRQ is designed to bridge the gap between periodicals in hearing rehabilitation that are designed for a readership made up of rehabilitation professionals, and other periodicals designed to appeal to the hearing-handicapped individual or the interested layperson. The audience of *HRQ* is hearing-rehabilitation professionals (including audiologists, otologists, speech pathologists, hearing-aid technicians, psychologists, physicians, social workers, teachers, vocational rehabilitationists, and students) and also hearing-impaired individuals and consumers, including parents of hearing-impaired children, the concerned layperson, and political and corporate leaders who have an interest in the problems of hearing-handicapped people. In addressing this varied audience, *HRQ* seeks to balance its content. Its circulation is 1500 copies per issue. Copies are sent to professional and educational libraries as well as to individual subscribers. *See* PERIODICALS.

PURPOSE

HRQ provides information concerning recent advances in the various fields of hearing rehabilitation, information concerning therapies available to those afflicted with different degrees and types of hearing loss, consumer guidance and advocacy, employment opportunities for hearing-impaired people, advances and innovations in technology to aid deaf and hard-of-hearing people, and news of organizations serving these people. Articles present new approaches to the problems of hearing rehabilitation or summarize the state of the art in the various disciplines that concern hearing-impaired people. The articles are usually written in a style that makes them accessible to professionals across the different fields that affect the rehabilitation of deaf and hard-of-hearing people, and also to educated, concerned hearing-impaired persons and parents of hearing-impaired children. In addition to individual articles, *HRQ* carries regular information features for both professionals and laypersons.

CONTRIBUTOR INFORMATION

HRQ invites previously unpublished articles concerning any area of hearing rehabilitation. It accepts articles primarily from professionals or students (graduates or interns) in the fields of audiology, otology, prosthetics technology, communication therapy, education, psychology, and rehabilitation. *HRQ* also accepts articles and brief informational items generated by other organizations and agencies that the publisher feels would be of interest to the readership. Occasionally, first-person accounts are published.

HRQ has an honorary editorial board consisting of 27 distinguished professionals, researchers, and scholars in the areas of audiology, technology, education, communication therapies, otology, psychology, and rehabilitation. The board members are available for advice and judgment concerning any article proposed for publication.

Style and format of *HRQ* are of particular importance. Because *HRQ* seeks to addresss a broad audience, the writing style is primarily concerned with clarity. The language avoids the overly technical and the jargon of any one discipline, keeping in mind the goal of articulating to professionals across disciplinary lines and also addressing the concerned, intelligent general reader who may be hearing-impaired. The format of articles includes headings and subheadings, if possible, especially in articles of some length and complexity.

Subscription to *HRQ* is available only through membership in the New York League for the Hard of Hearing.

J. McKendry

HEINICKE, SAMUEL
(1727–1790)

Samuel Heinicke is regarded as the father of pure oralism, sometimes called the German method of deaf education. Although others before him had emphasized the importance of speech in the instruction of deaf persons, Heinicke was the first to postulate that spoken language is a necessary foundation for the development of abstract thought. None of his predecessors, moreover, had applied the principles of oralism so consistently over so many years of practice. *See* EDUCATION: Communication.

EARLY YEARS

Heinicke was born on April 4, 1727, in the town of Nautschütz in the Electorate of Saxony (now part of East Germany). As the son of a well-to-do farmer, he was expected to inherit the estate and follow in his father's footsteps. However, a quarrel arose over his refusal to marry the girl his father had chosen for him. As a result, he left home and, for lack of anything better to do, joined the Saxon army, whereupon he was stationed in Dresden.

His military duties left him with much free time, which he used to strengthen his deficient education. He also passed on his knowledge by becoming a private tutor. In 1754 or 1755 he acquired his first deaf pupil, a boy whom he taught by means of manual alphabet. In 1754 he also married Johanne Elisabeth Kracht. The following year they had a son, the first of eight children Heinicke was to have by his two marriages. *See* SIGNS: Fingerspelling.

The pleasant life which Heinicke had established was disrupted by the outbreak of the Seven Years' War in 1756, when Frederick the Great's Prussian troops surrounded Dresden and captured thousands of Saxon soldiers, including Heinicke, intending to induct them forcibly into the Prussian army. Heinicke escaped with his family and made his way to Jena, where he began to study at the university.

In 1758, however, sensing that the Prussians were on his trail, he fled again. He first went to Altona, near Hamburg and at that time under Danish rule, then finally settled in Hamburg in 1760. For some years he was employed as a private secretary and tutor in the household of the Danish Count von Schimmelhausen. In 1768 he obtained the positions of sexton, organist, and schoolteacher in nearby Eppendorf.

In 1769 Heinicke had the occasion to teach the deaf son of a local resident, and soon thereafter other deaf pupils came to Heinicke. At first Heinicke used the written language to teach them but

Samuel Heinicke, from a painting in the church of Eppendorf.

dissatisfied with the results, he gradually came to believe that he could achieve far greater success by means of the spoken language.

THEORIES AND PRACTICE OF DEAF EDUCATION

The development in Heinicke's early theories on deaf education can be seen in three newspaper articles he wrote between 1773 and 1775. In the first he maintained that the written language provided a natural transition to speech, but he criticized those who began by teaching the spoken language, claiming that they used an unnatural method. Half a year later, in a revision of this article, he omitted the criticism. In the third article, written the following year, he stated that he taught his pupils both to write and to speak, but he emphasized his method of teaching speech by substituting the pupil's sense of feeling in the speech organs for the lacking sense of hearing. Thereby he laid the basis for his later conversion to oralism.

In 1775 Heinicke also published the first textbook ever written expressly for the instruction of deaf pupils; it consisted of a number of stories taken from the Old Testament. On the basis of his demonstrated success, Heinicke's reputation as a teacher of deaf persons grew, and it became his desire to be freed from his other duties so that he might devote himself fully to this vocation.

Thus in 1777 he accepted an offer from Friedrich August III, the Elector of Saxony, to return to his homeland to establish an institute for mute persons in Leipzig. Before undertaking his new mission, however, he remarried, having been widowed since 1775. His new wife, Anna Elisabeth Kludt, was a young widow and the sister of two of his deaf pupils. He finally left for Leipzig in April 1778, taking nine of his pupils with him to continue under his tutelage. He opened his new school, the first of its kind in Germany, on April 14, 1778, under the name Electoral Saxon Institute for Mutes and Other Persons Afflicted with Speech Defects. The Samuel Heinicke School for the Deaf (now relocated) in Leipzig descends directly from the school founded by Heinicke.

During the 12 years of Heinicke's administration, the institute achieved only limited success. The enrollment remained low; and although the school was state-supported, the economy of Saxony was depressed in the aftermath of the Seven Years' War and funds were not made available for his ambitious goals for expansion.

Before his move to Leipzig, Heinicke had further revised his pedagogical theories, as can be seen in his *Observations Regarding Mutes and Human Language* (1778), and had essentially formulated the final version of his system of oralism. After becoming director of the Leipzig institute, he continued to elaborate on and defend his system.

His fundamental goal had become teaching deaf pupils to speak. In a complete reversal of his earlier position, he maintained that to teach the written language first was both dangerous and harmful; the written language should be derived from the spoken language, as it is with hearing people. He had noted the importance of the spoken language in hearing people's development of the thinking process and the comprehension of abstract ideas. But an uneducated deaf person, he wrote, can think only in terms of concrete objects which he or she has seen or perceived through the senses, and has little concept of the intellectual world. Once this person has been taught to speak, however, he or she will develop the ability to think abstractly through articulated language just as the hearing person does by hearing the spoken word.

The task of teaching speech to deaf persons, Heinicke believed, was by no means as difficult as one might expect, since they, like hearing people, have an inner drive to speak. He remarked that 10 deaf children, through their articulated sounds, make more noise than do 20 drunken peasants in a pub. He further noted that each child consistently voiced his or her own set of words, syllables, and interjections in particular kinds of situations. *See* SPEECH.

He no longer believed that the senses of sight and touch were the basis for the education of deaf pupils. Rather, it was substitution of what he referred to as the sense of taste for that of hearing through which the deaf pupil could be taught to articulate. This skill, in turn, led naturally to the development of the ability to think abstractly.

Heinicke's method consisted in part of using "speech machines," an artificial throat and tongue, to help his pupils produce sounds by visual and tactile means. Despite Heinicke's claim to the contrary, the Abbé de l'Epée was certainly right when, in a letter to Heinicke, he argued that the contact of the speech organs which produces sounds actually has nothing to do with the sense of taste. *See* L'EPÉE, ABBÉ CHARLES MICHEL DE.

In the manuscript of his much discussed *Arkanum*, of which he made a great secret during his lifetime, Heinicke reveals how, in his opinion, certain taste sensations cause the mouth to reflex to assume the proper positions for the pronounciation of the vowels (for example, the taste of vinegar for *i*, vermouth extract for *e*, plain water for *a*, sugar water for *o*, and olive oil for *u*). However, aside from the questionable validity, this techinque seemingly played only an incidental role in Heinicke's teaching methods. *See* SPEECH TRAINING.

Although Heinicke was absolutely convinced of the superiority of oralism, he did not completely eschew the use of manual signs, as some of his followers have done. As he informed l'Epée, he did occasionally find signs helpful for conveying the meaning of a concept. Once his pupils had learned to speak, however, they were expected to converse orally among themselves in his presence, as well as with other people. Heinicke maintained they would soon learn that the spoken language was the quickest and most comfortable means of expressing thoughts.

CONTROVERSY

It was inevitable that Heinicke's theories and practice of deaf education would put him at odds with his renowned French contemporary, the Abbé de l'Epée, the founder of manualism. In a spirited, protracted exchange of letters between the two men, each defended his own system and criticized that of his adversary. Heinicke realized the futility of the debate in his second letter, in which, noting the wide divergence between their views, he expressed doubt of any reconciliation.

As a result of the controversy, l'Epée submitted the question to several academies for their opinions. Although a number declined to take sides, the rector and fellows of the Academy of Zurich decided in favor of l'Epée in 1783. It was a still greater blow to Heinicke when the University of Leipzig, with which Heinicke's institute was affiliated, also sided with l'Epée the following year.

During this period, too, Heinicke found it necessary to defend himself against the accusation that he had treated his pupils harshly. With his methods and practices being called into question, it is not surprising that Elector Friedrich August, though sympathetic to Heinicke's goals, definitively rejected his request to expand and reorganize the institute. Nor is it surprising that in the following years the number of pupils enrolled in the institute decreased sharply.

Still certain that he was right, Heinicke vehemently defended his position in print and counter-attacked his critics. He complained of the difficulty of trying, all alone, to defend deaf people against the unenlightened who treated them as though they were not human beings. In spite of the setbacks during his last years, he continued to write not only on the subject of deaf education but also on general pedagogy, revealing the deplorable conditions of the educational system in Germany and urging thorough reforms.

Heinicke died suddenly of a stroke on April 30, 1790, in Leipzig. Though the institute was indeed in a state of decline, under the directorship of his wife it did survive the onslaughts which continued to batter it through the early years of the nineteenth century.

For a time it appeared, too, that oralism was virtually defunct. However, eventually Heinicke's theories and methods were revived, even though they were interpreted and applied differently over the years. The conflict between oralism and manualism, touched off by Heinicke and l'Epée, to this day has not been resolved. *See* HISTORY: Sign Language Controversy.

Bibliography

Garnett, C. B.: *The Exchange of Letters Between Samuel Heinicke and Abbé Charles Michel de l'Epée*, 1968.

Heinicke, S.: *Beobachtungen über Stumme and über die menschliche Sprache in Briefen*, Erster Theil, 1778.

————: *Biblische Geschichte alten Testaments zum Unterricht taubstummer Personen*, Erste Abtheilung, 1776.

————: *Gesammelte Schriften*, edited by G. and P. Schumann, 1912.

————: *Ueber die Denkart der Taubstummen*, 1780.

————: *Wichtige Entdeckungen*, 1784.

————: "Ueber Taubstumme," *Deutsches Museum*, vol. 2, no. 9, 1785.

Schumann, P.: *Geschichte des Taubstummenwesens vom deutschenn Standpunkt aus dargestellt*, 1940.

Stötzner, H. E.: *Samuel Heinicke, Sein Leben and Werken*, 1870.

Robert Harmon

HISTORY

Deaf people do not appear in traditional history texts. Focusing on those who wield power in politics, economics, social movements, or the arts, historians have ignored groups whose numbers are slight and influence negligible. An occasional exception occurs when historians mention as an aside or curiosity that a well-known historical figure, such as French poet Pierre de Ronsard, German composer Ludwig van Beethoven, or Russian scientist Konstantin Tsiolkovsky, had a hearing impairment. Although each of these individuals confronted some of the situations that other deaf people faced, the experience of none typifies the lives of their deaf contemporaries. By merely stating that a few outstanding individuals could not hear very well, historians have revealed little that assists in understanding the deaf experience. *See* BEETHOVEN, LUDWIG VAN; RONSARD, PIERRE DE; TSIOLKOVSKY, KONSTANTIN EDUARDOVICH.

TRADITIONAL STUDIES

The people seemingly most interested in deafness in ancient times were philosophers, law givers, and physicians. Their accounts reveal that the ancient world often recognized a connection between deafness and speechlessness, that some thought deafness indicated a curse from God, and others believed that the congenitally deaf person, invariably lacking intelligible speech, also lacked a soul and perhaps all ability to reason. The everyday life of deaf people, however, is mostly left out of these accounts.

The historical record improved very little with the Enlightenment and the awakening of learning. From the early seventeenth century until far into the twentieth century, educators and physicians dominated historical writing about deaf people. To physicians and educators, however, deafness is a pathology and deaf individuals are problems. Their accounts focused on describing and remedying the disabilities caused by lack of audition. Early texts, such as teacher Juan Pablo Bonet's *Simplification of the Method of Teaching Deaf-Mutes to Speak* (1620) or physician John Bulwer's *Philocophus, or the Deafe and Dumbe Man's Friend* (1648), exemplify this tendency. The latter, for example, is primarily an anatomy lesson with some ideas thrown in about speechreading. *See* PABLO BONET, JUAN.

The accounts of physicians do reveal that early medical treatment for deafness, such as pouring hot oil into ear canals or stuffing them with animal dung, must have been awful and seldom undertaken voluntarily. Similarly, accounts of attempts to produce speech by cutting the ligaments at the base of the tongue to "loosen" it are horrifying, but they reveal more about doctors' ignorance and brutality than about the condition of deaf people.

The histories and contemporary descriptions written by teachers almost invariably focus on deaf students' educational shortcomings. Instead of presenting a picture of what deaf people did or thought or how they lived, they describe in great detail what deaf people usually could not do, that is, talk and easily acquire facility in an oral language. Their humanity, the characteristics that hearing and deaf persons share, seldom appear in this kind of history, which, like that of the physicians, tells more about the writers than about the subjects.

PIONEERING STUDIES

By the late twentieth century, a new respect for deaf people and their experience led to a few pioneering studies of their history, rather than only studies of how medicine or education applied to them. Two monographic works were particularly significant: Jack Gannon's *Deaf Heritage: A Narrative History of Deaf America* (1981) and Harlan Lane's *When The Mind Hears: A History of the Deaf* (1984). While the latter to some extent focuses on education, though from the reconstructed viewpoint of a deaf man, the former, actually written by a deaf individual, demonstrates the rich potential inherent in a historical perspective broader than that of physicians or educators.

To the extent possible, the following seven sections of this article adopt this wider perspective.

Each section examines segments of the history of deaf people from ancient times to the late twentieth century. Because deaf people have never controlled their own country, and because they began to create identifiable cultures only in the nineteenth century, there are neither flowing continuities nor clearly defined epochs in their history. The sections, therefore, overlap in their chronology.

They begin with a discussion that relies on physicians' treatises, sacred texts, and philosophers' statements to describe speechless people, and what was known and thought about speechlessness, from the earliest recorded western history until the eighteenth century. The focus is on speechlessness, for this was seen as the major characteristic of deaf people, the one factor that truly set them apart from others.

The history of Martha's Vineyard in Massachusetts, a community with an unusually high rate of genetic deafness, provides a rare example of deaf and hearing people interacting as though each considered the other normal. This is the subject of the second section.

The third, fourth, and sixth sections each deal in a different way with the issue of education and deaf people. The first of these focuses on the relationship of deaf education to reform movements and reformers in nineteenth-century United States, while the other two examine closely the seemingly never-ending controversy about sign languages in schools and the dramatic events of the 1880 Congress of Milan.

The fifth and seventh sections, more than the others, try to look at historical issues the way deaf persons saw them. One discusses the idea of a separate community for deaf people alone—a colony somewhat isolated from the hearing world where deaf people would rule. This idea, popular among some deaf people, contrasts sharply with the Martha's Vineyard experience.

The last section presents a synthetic overview of the progress and problems of deaf people, especially deaf Americans, in the twentieth century. It identifies the major concerns of deaf people during the twentieth century, relates their attempts to deal with these concerns, and comments on the dilemmas inherent in the deaf experience.

John V. Van Cleve

Understanding Speechlessness: Pre-Enlightenment Views

Speechless people and deaf people (since deafness was usually associated with speechlessness) have been of considerable interest to physicians, philosophers, and theologians throughout recorded history. Discussion of these conditions has varied according to the beliefs and methods of the investigators; if speech is a physiological function, then speechlessness is a medical problem, but if speech is a function of a separate soul, speechlessness requires a philosophical or theological remedy.

The problem of what speech is, and how it differs from thought, language, voice, or articulation, is still much debated. A popular attitude has been that humans are the only creatures capable of communicating in the complex vocal expression of language called speech; animals certainly communicate effectively, but not with the complexity of syntax and the depth of abstraction possible to humans. Because spoken language has been thought a uniquely human attribute, disruption of that process has been a subject of great concern.

The most extreme sort of speech disorder is speechlessness—a term covering various problems of producing sounds and articulating them correctly and clearly. This is not the same as a language disorder, which stems from problems producing the thoughts that then are expressed in speech. The mental processes of the speechless may well be perfectly in order. A speechless person may have language in his or her brain, but cannot express it vocally. This important difference was not always recognized.

Before the advent of written language, speech was the only means of communicating thoughts, aside from "body language" like facial expression and gesture, and so the speechless person was cut off from society in a dramatic way, the isolation even more complete if the person was also deaf—the commonly held cause of speechlessness. Deaf mutes might be considered peculiar, imbecilic, or even cursed or inhabited by evil spirits. While ignorant, such prejudices are understandable in ages when physiological causes of deafness and speechlessness were not understood.

The English word "dumb" stems from old Teutonic language roots, from words meaning "stupid" as well as "incapable of speech." The colloquial "dummy" attests to the popular prejudice that the speechless were stupid. The attribution of "dumb" to the animal world signifies a relegation of the rest of creation to lesser orders that make noises but do not truly speak.

From classical times until the Enlightenment, speechlessness and varying degrees of speech problems were seen more as psychic than physical ailments, as theologians and physicians wrestled with the relationship of body and soul. Some physicians from ancient Egyptian times in the third millennium B.C. recognized that head injuries caused temporary or permanent speechlessness or deafness, but the faculty of speech itself remained a mysterious spiritual component of humanity.

BIBLICAL TRADITION

Ancient Hebrew tradition, which recognized each human as an entity, a unity created when God's breath entered the simple clay, taught that bodily impediments came from God. In Exodus 4:10 ff.,

Moses complains to God that he is "slow and hesitant of speech," and so should not be charged with liberating the Hebrews from Egypt. God replies, "Who is it that gives man speech? Who makes him dumb or deaf? Is it not I, the Lord? Go now; I will help your speech . . . "

Courtesy and compassion toward deaf individuals is indicated in one of the early laws, remembered in Leviticus 19:14: "You shall not treat the deaf with contempt." Even if such afflictions were sent from God, one was to pity and help the unfortunates. A sign of the Messianic Kingdom foretold by Isaiah was that deaf people would hear and dumb persons speak. Centuries later, Jesus as the personification of the Messiah was to heal those deaf and dumb.

Although "deaf ears" is an English translation of an expression used in the Bible to signify those who do not choose to hear, that is, "hear the message," deaf people were understood as being curable, in Jesus' miracles. Mark 7:32 was often cited in later centuries as showing a connection between deafness and dumbness, but the passage itself signifies a separate treatment for separate ailments:

"They brought to him a man who was deaf and had an impediment in his speech, with the request that he would lay his hand on him. He took the man aside, away from the crowd, put his fingers into his ears, spat, and touched his tongue. Then, looking up to heaven, he sighed, and said to him, 'Ephphatha,' which means, 'Be opened,' and at the same time the impediment was removed and he spoke plainly . . . [The people said] 'He even makes the deaf hear and the dumb speak.' "

Mark 9:25 ff. records a confrontation between Jesus and an "unclean," "deaf and dumb" spirit. Although this may be the only Biblical reference to "deaf and dumb" together, later commentators assumed the connection.

CLASSICAL TRADITION

In the *Iliad* and the *Odyssey* Homer describes different forms of speechlessness, using the terms *aphasia* (speechlessness caused by emotion) and *anaudos* (speechlessness caused by not being a human). *Aphonos*, meaning having no voice, or mutism, is described in Herodotus' *History* in the story about King Croesus' mute son overcoming his handicap by crying out for his father's life to be spared. This story was of continuing interest to physicians and philosophers for centuries.

In the fifth century B.C., Greek Hippocratic physicians emphasized the connection between deafness and speechlessness; their statements were to be repeated for almost 2000 years. In the voluminous writings of the Hippocratic School there are many observations and speculations about the causes and cures of speechlessness. Clinical causes range from apoplexy to head trauma. The writings differentiate between loss of voice and loss of speech, placing the origin of speech in the head. People make sounds because they have lungs with windpipes attached; sounds are then shaped by the lips, tongue, palate, and teeth. But if the tongue does not properly articulate the air coming out of the lung through the windpipe into the mouth, the person cannot speak properly. The proof, it was said, was that people born deaf never learn to articulate, and so, although they have voice—that is, can make noises—they have no speech.

THE SOUL AS THE SOURCE

Plato reported that Socrates considered thought as the conversation of the soul, and speech as audible thought. The physiological process of hearing occurred as sound came by air through the ears, and then traveled by blood to the brain and finally to the soul.

Aristotle, who believed that speech is the distinctive characteristic of humans, wrote that for any being to have voice, it must have lungs and a pharynx. Articulate voice, he wrote, is the combination of vocal and nonvocal sounds, that is, vowels and consonants. One born deaf can make sounds but cannot articulate, an acquired skill. When the soul sets into motion the breathed-in air, the air creates sound by hitting the windpipe. Animals can make noises indicative of pleasure or pain, but they cannot have true speech, which sets forth ideas and morals and is related to the rational principle which animals lack. Aristotle wondered if hearing and voice came from a single source. He made the odd observation that deaf people speak through their nostrils, and that dumb persons make noise nasally because they do not use their tongues. Drunken speech is slurred because of too much moisture, an excessive coldness which alienates the psyche.

Aristotle's beliefs influenced theories of speech for thousands of years, especially his description of speech as the result of the soul acting on bodily parts people shared with animals which had no soul. This belief was the foundation of the Stoic doctrine that the logos, the rational principle of life, was the source of speech.

ROMAN AND PATRISTIC IDEAS

Cicero considered speech the foundation of a civilized society. Some Stoics used the concept of human speech as the basis for all ethics. They wrote that speech was not a natural development from animal sounds, as Epicurus had written, but was a stream of thought from the soul. Natural reason led to natural language.

The second-century Greek physician Galen inherited these Stoic thoughts, but also wrote of the physical bases for speech. He divided human sounds into voice, articulation, and speech, and analyzed the larynx, trachea, and cerebral nerves activating these processes. He was among the first to center the origin of speech and reason in the brain; yet he also promulgated traditional ideas: speech was the messenger of the soul.

Stoic ideas permeated Roman life; the soul ruled over the tongue and any other physical components of speech. (New Testament passages attest to the belief in the spiritual origin of speech. Luke 1 describes Zacharias' temporary speechlessness because of his lack of faith that he and his wife would bear a child in their elderly years.) The soul was seen as the Creator's supreme achievement, and speech was the supreme achievement of the soul, the external logos from the internal logos of reason. In the fourth century, Nemesius wrote about the Creator's plan of an ascending ladder of communicative ability in the creation, from cows to parrots to people.

There were, of course, physicians who continued exploring the physical causes of deafness and speechlessness, like the sixth-century Byzantine physician Aetius of Amida, who investigated paralysis of voice structures he thought possibly curable by therapy. Yet even he was not interested in the brain or nervous system as sources of speech.

The Justinian Code (A.D. 529) documents attitudes toward deaf people and those without speech. In this codification of Roman law, a speechless person was considered a legal impediment, and speech was necessary for citizenship. A speechless child, one writer said, had not intellect, which was the truly human factor. Children were thought to develop true speech by around the age of seven. A deaf person could not make a promise in a court of law, though later such courts distinguished between those who had been deaf from birth and those who had become deaf through accident, after their speech faculties had been developed. The latter type of unfortunate could make a written will, since it was assumed he understood the meaning of language. (An aside is that blind persons might have a valid will if it were witnessed, but deaf people had to write the will in their own handwriting.) A mute might not serve as custodian of a minor. Nor could a mute or deaf person administer his own properties; a curator was appointed.

Thus it seems clear that under Roman law the ability to reason and the ability to speak were indissolubly connected. Persons deaf and mute were associated with minors or those incurably diseased or insane as being incapable of handling their own affairs.

AN ENGLISH EXAMPLE OF BODY AND SOUL

An interesting example of the belief that speechlessness was a theological more than a physical problem occurs in the writings of the Venerable Bede, a seventh-century English cleric. In his lively, well-regarded history, Bede wrote of a destitute mute boy healed by Bishop John of Hexham. The boy, who had never spoken, also suffered from "scabs and scales" on his bald head. John of Hexham ordered the boy to stick out his tongue, and after the bishop made the sign of the cross, he told the lad to pronounce certain sounds. The boy's tongue was "loosed," and he spoke well from that time on. Whatever one's analysis of this cure for speechlessness, it is interesting that while the bishop cured the muteness, he referred the boy to a physician to cure his skin problems.

THE MIDDLE AGES

In the writings of Eastern Christianity, the monk Meletius serves as an example of reliance on earlier scholarship; echoing previous philosophy and theology, he wrote that communication between souls was possible only through speech and hearing. Animals might communicate through voice and hearing, but speech was distinctively human. Angels, he added, communicated through intellect alone, and so did not need speech.

Medieval writers often used the classical doctrine of the four humors to explain human physiology and behavior. These ideas were based on Greek philosophy developed into systems by Islamic writers. The Persian scholar Avicenna, for instance, wrote that melancholic hearts were too hot, so in combat their brains became too humid, this imbalance resulting in an inability to speak except by repeated syllables (stuttering?).

Avicenna rejected Galen's idea of the brain as the source of speech, and echoed Aristotle that the heart was the primal organ, the agent of the soul whose intellect manifested itself in uniquely human speech.

Other medieval writers investigated the role of air in producing speech, and wrongly linked Greek *aude* (voice) and Latin *aures* (ears) etymologically, trying to prove the unbreakable link between speech and hearing.

In the twelfth century William of St. Thierry wrote that just as the use of hands separates people from animals anatomically, speech separates them spiritually, as the soul expresses its faculty of reason through the spoken word. Thus, if a mute person could not use his hands, he did not have the reasoning faculty, and was considered subhuman.

Although in the late Middle Ages there was increased study of speech defects and possible cures, including some surgery, reverence for ancient authority and interest in emphasizing speech as the special property of the soul prevented investigators from reliance on empirical evidence.

TURNING POINTS

Understanding of human anatomy was gradually increasing, as postmortem examinations were conducted more frequently. The Italian surgeon Massa described injuries to the meninges (membranes covering the brain) and, for the first time, wrote about cerebrospinal fluid. Cranial damage from falls and from traumas like being kicked in the head by a horse were described in detail; Massa removed some bone from a head wound of a young man injured by a spear, and the patient immediately regained his lost speech. Elizabeth I's physician wrote that a patient's speechlessness resulted from a fall in London's Bear Garden; the fractured cranium pressed on the dura mater (one of the brain membranes). Interest in brain dissection grew as techniques of careful dissection improved; anatomists often used heads of decapitated criminals.

A real turning point came in the work of the physician Andreas Vesalius, who made possible modern scientific study of the brain. Although he believed in the soul, Vesalius denied that it could be found anatomically, and he entirely repudiated the theory of a thousand years that brain function was centered in the cerebral ventricles.

Among those whom Vesalius so deeply influenced was the physician Mercurialis. The latter explained that brain injury was the cause of speechlessness, although other physical injuries, like tongue traumas, could cause lesser problems like those with articulation. He wove together classical sources and empirical observations. Congenital deafness was the major source of speechlessness, he wrote; if a child never heard anything, he lacked the stimuli necessary for the mind to instruct the bodily parts responsible for articulation.

The connection between mutism and deafness was of great interest to sixteenth-century physicians. Cures for mutism were possible if the person could hear, but the deaf-mute person was often considered a hopeless case without divine intervention.

The Milanese scholar Jerome Cardan, however, wrote that deaf-mute people could be taught to express themselves, and even invented a Braille-like system to prove his point. He denied that thought was impossible without speech, pointing out that deaf individuals could "hear" by reading, and mute persons could "speak" by writing. He broke down the ancient idea that the speechless person was without language, and so without reason or soul.

The German physician Salomon Alberti wrote that impairments to speech and hearing were independent. And so Aristotle and Hippocrates had been wrong in believing that mutism and deafness inevitably went together. Alberti pointed out that for centuries investigators had relied too much on classical tradition, and so had compounded their errors. He, however, relied on empirically derived knowledge. Through dissection, one could understand anatomy, and trace the nerves of the tongue and ears as they entered the brain on their separate routes. Alberti maintained that speech was an acquired skill, not a divine gift to the uniquely human. Deaf and mute persons were, then, fully rational, fully human. As a man of his era, Alberti believed in the soul, and that man was created in the image of God, but he did not believe that damaged hearing or speech came about from a damaged soul. Congenital deafness, he wrote, was an embryonic mishap in no way separating a person from the Creator or from a full humanity.

Building on the accomplishments of investigators like Vesalius and Alberti, scholars from many different disciplines attacked the problems of individuals who were deaf and dumb. Physicians, educators, mathematicians, linguists, psychologists, anatomists, epistemologists, all had their say as Renaissance minds relied more and more on empirical evidence, leading toward an intellectual milieu popularly called the Enlightenment.

No longer was there much dispute about whether or not deaf and mute persons could be taught speech. The question was not if, but how. Different suggestions abounded, as success in the burgeoning field increased.

In 1587 the French physician Laurent Joubert wrote that one must be very patient in teaching deaf-mute individuals to imitate the facial expressions and actions of those about them, but absorbing from their environment, children would learn to speak without hearing themselves.

Juan Pablo Bonet, the learned Catalan official, wrote about deaf-mute people in an influential book published in 1620. He discussed causes of the problem—deafness and tongue defects—and suggested that the best cure would use the child's sense of sight first to learn letters, and then to pronounce them by copying the teacher's use of lips, teeth, and breath. Pablo Bonet included pictures of the alphabet and of hand signals to represent each letter. He spelled out the details of instruction: the child and teacher must be in a good light so the child can see into the teacher's mouth; the teacher should start with easy vowels, then move to consonants, words, sentences, and arithmetic; the teacher should encourage the child to communicate by asking him what he has been doing all day and what he thinks of certain books the teacher should offer; each step in learning speech must be understood before proceeding to the next challenge.

In England, the Royal Society published papers on acoustical experiments, including how sound is produced, travels, and is perceived. There were numerous pamphlets and articles written, including opinions by Christopher Wren. Experiments in teaching particular deaf-mute individuals to speak were discussed, with some difference of opinion as to the comparative values of lipreading and signing with the hands. English pioneers acknowledged their debt to Continental investigators. Kenelm Digby, a man of encyclopedic knowledge, wrote accounts of European teaching of deaf and dumb persons, referring probably to Bonet's works.

In 1641 John Wilkins published a pamphlet describing the complex possibilities of sign language. Three years later, John Bulwer expanded on the subject, commenting that one sense can take over the duties of another—the eye for the ear, the hand for the tongue. He impatiently dismissed the old notions that deafness might derive from spiritual cause, and focused instead on the empirical evidence.

Experiments in teaching deaf and dumb people to speak continued enthusiastically and ever more expertly as the seventeenth century advanced. An important contributor was George Sibscota, who wrote extensively about deaf-mute persons, citing numerous classical authors, including Galen's point that a cause of deafness could be a defect in the eardrum.

In 1680 George Dalgarno published an influential book which was reprinted a century later. He stressed the connection between the senses, describing them in incredibly complex schemes. He was fortunately more simple in describing the learning process. He wrote that while the eye and the ear take in knowledge, the hand and the tongue give knowledge out. But if one sense in either pair is defective, the other will take over; ear and tongue, or hand and eye, can suffice. He stated that people blind from birth learn more quickly than deaf-mute people because through the ear they absorb language from infancy; yet deaf persons overtake blind persons in learning as they mature, since the eye is a more essential sense than the ear.

And so different and sometimes contradictory opinions about deafness and muteness proliferated, as Enlightenment empiricism supplanted more traditional beliefs. The study of speech and hearing returned to the science of medicine. Popular prejudices might persist, but observations about deafness and speechlessness proved that they were physical afflictions, and so possibly curable conditions. The creativity of the Enlightenment mind delighted in finding ways to help deaf and dumb people join in the exciting conversations of an increasingly scientific society. While the mystery of "what brings words to the tongue" remained unanswered, people without speech and deaf individuals were never again to be considered less than human or as victims of damaged souls.

Bibliography

Benton, A. L., and R. J. Joynt: "Early Descriptions of Aphasia," *Archives of Neurology*, vol. 3, pp. 205–222, 1960.

Brain, W. R. (Lord Brain): *Speech Disorders*, 1961.

Critchley, M.: *Aphasiology and Other Aspects of Language*, pp. 41–125, 1970.

Eldridge, M.: *A History of the Treatment of Speech Disorders*, 1968.

Mullett, C. F.: " 'An arte to make the dumbe to speake, the deaf to heare': a seventeenth-century goal," *Journal of the History of Medicine and Allied Sciences*, 26(2):123–149, April 1971.

O'Neill, Y. V.: *Speech and Speech Disorders in Western Thought Before 1600*, 1980.

Ynez Violé O'Neill

Martha's Vineyard

For 2½ centuries, from 1690 to 1950, a high rate of hereditary deafness appeared in the population of the island of Martha's Vineyard, Massachusetts. Hereditary deafness is one of the most common of all inherited disorders, and many cases have been reported worldwide; Martha's Vineyard is one such example. It is of interest because, in addition to existing long before and then beyond the reaches of the wider American deaf culture, the adaptation by the hearing members of this community to those who were born deaf was markedly different from that found on the mainland.

Background

Martha's Vineyard lies five miles off the southeastern shore of Massachusetts. Settled by Europeans in the 1640s, it was, until the twentieth century, a fairly isolated, highly endogamous island with a population that averaged about 3100 individuals. The type of deafness found in this population was a recessive form of profound congenital deafness. The origin for such a trait presumably begins with the occurrence of a single genetic alteration in one individual. If descendants of this individual marry other carriers for the trait, there is a one-in-four chance that each of their children will be born deaf.

It is impossible to say in whom this initial genetic change occurred; however, the individual must have been born before 1630 in an isolated region known as the Weald in the English county of Kent. All the Vineyard families in whom deafness would later occur can trace their ancestry back to a small group of adjoining Wealden parishes.

In the 1630s, about 200 inhabitants of these parishes left as a group for New England, following their local minister, Jonathan Lothrop. They sailed on the *Hercules* and *Griffin*, which arrived in Boston harbor in September 1634. They first settled in the recently founded town of Scituate, 20 miles southeast of Boston. A decade later these immigrants from Kent chose to move again, this time settling on the newly opened frontier of Cape Cod. With families that averaged six to seven children each—and often included a dozen or more—within a generation, lower Cape Cod had become crowded, at least by seventeenth-century standards. More land was needed, and Martha's Vineyard, lying just to the south, had a considerable amount of inexpensive land still available. Between 1660 and 1690 a number of families originally from Kent moved there.

DEAF INDIVIDUALS

The first known deaf man on Martha's Vineyard was born on Cape Cod in 1657 and arrived on Martha's Vineyard with his wife and family in 1692. The appearance of deaf persons in the island population rose steadily for the next 12 generations as intermarriage spread the recessive trait throughout the population. By the nineteenth century, when approximately 1 out of every 5700 Americans was born deaf, the ratio was 1 in every 155 on Martha's Vineyard. This figure does not represent the actual distribution of deafness on the island, however, for in some towns deaf individuals were even better represented. In one town 1 person in every 25 was born deaf. In one neighborhood, where about 60 people lived, 1 person in every 4 was affected.

The 12 generations of deaf people who lived on Martha's Vineyard make this an example of one of the oldest known continuous deaf populations. Yet this is of itself not the most interesting aspect of the deaf heritage on Martha's Vineyard. It was not the number of deaf individuals in the population, but the linguistic and social adaptation to their deafness that makes the Vineyard a significant part of deaf history.

ADAPTATION TO DEAFNESS

From the midseventeenth century to the early years of the twentieth, the island population was bilingual, almost all hearing members of the community being fluent in both English and sign language. Most Vineyarders began to learn signs in early childhood. Even if no immediate member of one's family was deaf, the probability that a playmate, neighbor, or friend would be made the almost daily use of sign language a necessity.

It is probable that the early Vineyard sign language was initially based on a regional British sign language. It is known that a sign language was in use during the 1630s and 1640s in some of the villages of the Weald from which individuals who later settled on the Vineyard came. It is also known that the first deaf islander was fully able to express himself in sign language. He may, of course, have invented his own sign language, but examples of independently invented systems of sign communication by deaf persons seem to have allowed their inventors only rudimentary communications with others. The language spoken by the first deaf islander seems to have been far more complex, allowing him full participation in all aspects of island life. Not only does he seem to have been heir

to a sign language generations or even centuries old, but his ability to function in the larger hearing society also indicates that hearing people were already willing and able to communicate in signs. *See* SIGNS: Home Signs.

During the seventeenth and eighteenth centuries, Vineyard sign language was probably only one of a number of local sign languages or sign systems that, as Woodward has theorized, existed before French Sign Language was introduced at Hartford, Connecticut, in 1817. It later combined to some extent with American Sign Language, as deaf Vineyard children began to attend the American School during the 1820s and 1830s. However, it never became identical to American Sign Language. *See* SIGN LANGUAGES: American.

The regular use of sign language by all members of the society had not only linguistic but also social implications for the deaf members of the community. Unlike many deaf people in the larger American society who are cut off to some extent from full participation because hearing persons are unable to communicate with them effectively, deaf members of the Vineyard society had no such barriers to overcome.

As written and oral history indicate, from earliest childhood deaf Vineyarders were full participants in all aspects of their society. Deaf men were fishermen, farmers, or boat builders; deaf women tended farms and raised families. Their incomes were identical to those of their hearing counterparts, most making a comfortable living and a few becoming wealthy by island standards. They married at the same rate and had the same number of children as their hearing neighbors. They regularly attended town meetings, voted, and held town offices. In only one aspect were deaf Vineyarders slightly different. After the American School opened, many deaf Vineyarders were sent to Hartford, Connecticut, to take advantage of what was then considered an outstanding educational opportunity. Since there was state assistance for those who attended Hartford, some were able to receive several years of education beyond that of their hearing siblings. The result was that, on the island, deaf people as a group were considered unusually well educated. An indication of this was that they were sometimes asked to interpret newspaper accounts and legal documents for their less literate hearing neighbors. *See* AMERICAN SCHOOL FOR THE DEAF.

Perhaps because there were so many deaf islanders, little attention was paid to an individual's inability to hear. Significantly, when hearing islanders in the twentieth century were asked to recall who had been deaf, many had a difficult time listing names—even of people they had known well. Deafness was considered to be only one aspect of a person's identity. Deaf individuals do not appear to have considered themselves a separate group and do not seem to have shared the supportive aspects of a deaf community so important off-island. Deaf members of the community did not gather together by themselves. To socialize only or even primarily with other deaf people, deaf Vineyarders would have had to pass over hearing spouses, family members, neighbors, and lifelong friends, all of whom would have felt slighted. Traditionally, social gatherings were always open to all members of the small island communities.

IMPACT

Martha's Vineyard was until recently an island removed from mainstream American society. Even in the eighteenth century, visitors regularly remarked on how isolated and old-fashioned life there seemed. The Vineyard deaf population was no exception, having relatively little contact with the larger deaf society on the mainland. While most nineteenth-century deaf Vineyarders attended Hartford for a time, almost all returned home to settle. Few maintained contact with off-islanders, deaf or hearing. With the exception of passing references to Martha's Vineyard in several deaf publications in the late nineteenth century, the wider world seems to have paid little attention to deaf Vineyarders.

While Martha's Vineyard was not a strong presence in nineteenth-century American deaf culture, it continues to exert an indirect influence on the larger deaf world. In the nineteenth century, proponents of the eugenics movement, the best remembered of these being Alexander Graham Bell, used the deaf Vineyarders as an example. Most of his conclusions on the "deleterious effects" of deaf intermarriage were based on data he gathered from Martha's Vineyard. While Bell never published the Vineyard data he collected over the course of four years, this research formed the basis of his book *On the Formation of a Deaf Variety of the Human Race*. The reason Bell never published directly on Martha's Vineyard was because he could not understand why not all deaf parents had deaf children and why many hearing parents had deaf offspring. The root of Bell's problem lay in the fact that he, as well as others dealing in the field of human genetics in the late nineteenth century, did not have the insight of Mendel's theory of recessive inheritance, which received attention only at the turn of the century. Without the benefit of Mendel's concept, most of the conclusions Bell drew about how deafness was inherited, including his fears that marriages of deaf individuals would produce deaf children and that the gathering of deaf children together at schools for deaf people would produce a "deaf race," are simply wrong. *See* BELL, ALEXANDER GRAHAM.

In fact, the beginning of the end of deafness in

communities such as Martha's Vineyard started as children from such isolated populations began to be sent away to schools in the 1830s and 1840s. There they met and married individuals who did not share the same genetic trait for deafness. If deaf Vineyarders had remained at home and married local people, hearing or deaf, their chances of having deaf children would have been much higher. The change in marriage patterns among deaf Vineyarders began to occur as more and more hearing Vineyarders also chose off-island mates. This was important, for with a recessively inherited trait, a person need not be deaf to have deaf offspring. In fact, 85 percent of the deaf islanders had two hearing parents. As marriage patterns changed, the number of new deaf Vineyarders born in each generation plummeted. In the 1840s, there were 15 children born deaf. In the 1880s, there was only one. She was to be the last, dying in 1952. It continues to be possible that new deaf children may be born into old island families.

CONCLUSION

Perhaps the most important insight that Martha's Vineyard provides is a window on a deaf community that developed before and then beyond the larger national deaf culture. Although a number of communities such as Martha's Vineyard existed around the world, little is known about them. What is needed, at this point, are a number of studies of such communities. The social and cultural expectations for deaf individuals may differ markedly from place to place.

Bibliography

Bell, Alexander Graham: *Memoir upon the Formation of a Deaf Variety of the Human Race*, private printing, Washington, D. C., 1883.

Groce, Nora E.: *Everyone Here Spoke Sign Language*, Harvard University Press, Cambridge, Massachusetts, 1985.

Kuschel, Rolf: "The Silent Inventor: The Creation of a Sign Language by the Only Deaf-Mute on a Polynesian Island," *Sign Language Studies*, 3:1–28, 1973.

Shuman, Malcolm: "The Sounds of Silence on Nohya," *Language Science*, 2(1):144–173, 1980.

Washabaugh, William, James Woodward, and Susan DeSantis: "Providence Island Sign: A Context Dependent Language," *Anthropological Linguistics*, vol. 20, no. 1, 1978.

Woodward, James C.: "Historical Bases of American Sign Language," in R. Siple (ed.), *Understanding Language Through Sign Language Research*, Academic Press, New York, 1978.

Nora E. Groce

Deafness and Reform: Nineteenth Century

It may be a truism to say that significant reform efforts like those on behalf of deaf persons during the nineteenth century were social movements. However, the literature which recounts the history of deafness reform too often has narrowed the relevant "social" forces to individuals and actions which affected deaf people. They rarely use the experience of deaf reform to understand broader underlying social dynamics. Moreover, historians of the deaf minority have weighted their histories toward one of several distinct approaches for training deaf children. In order to avoid both myopia and presentism, it might be well to consider how reforms for deaf people arose when they did, what were the external sources that gave them unexpected surges of energy and support, and how particular efforts altered the work of both leaders and followers in later generations. Neither the notions of movement (disparate individuals and organizations in a common cause) nor generation (a cohort of individuals whose births and lives are distinguished by contemporaneous experiences and values) should be thought neatly mechanical here; however, both notions provide a focus and interpretive order that structures historical comparisons. Such ideas invite reflections about distinctive, historical changes. If movements do not arise of their own momentum, if the established leaders of a reform were not always the controlling forces of legend, precisely how did individuals and social forces interact to shape the history of deaf reform in America?

REFORM IN PROVINCIAL AMERICA (1815–1845)

The pioneers of deaf education in America belonged to the first generation (born in the late 1780s and 1790s) raised in the new, postrevolutionary republic. They belonged to a distinctively self-conscious group who understood that the separation from Great Britain carried with it both dangers and opportunities in unequal portions. They entered upon their intellectual maturity debating the character of that new nation. Regularly their boasts of independence, ingenuity, and novelty ill concealed their fears of vulnerability in the face of older and more formidable European powers. They knew the force of British tradition could not be set aside by fiat or treaty. In economics and politics, no less than in matters such as the instruction of deaf students, the course of the British empire seemed to draw the United States back into familiar, traditional orbits. For America's first native-born generation, the preeminent problem was the novelty of the nation's provincial culture, the ambivalence of recognizing how bound they were to English habits of thought and behavior while extolling the merits of their revolution and their new nation.

This very provincialism, at once a dilemma and a dynamic force, was itself the primary cause of the extensive spate of social reforms spawned in

this generation. Between 1815 and the Panic of 1837, all commentators enthusiastically described the advances in internal improvements—canals, railroads, steamboats—as well as the creation of primitive models of industrial production. Similarly, the increasing concentrations of population in cities highlighted social problems that required new "benevolent" services geared to the dangerous and dependent classes: criminals, insane persons, vagabonds and orphans, the ignorant, and the sick. For all these groups, not the least of which were deaf persons, institutions displaced the traditional role of the family and transcended familiar, local authorities. Often organizations which claimed to be unprecedented began as little more than adaptations of older community associations and Old World institutions. Quickly they became something else entirely. In 1816, when he journeyed to England to learn the Braidwood method of deaf instruction, Thomas H. Gallaudet (1787–1851) was a man made desperate by the inadequacies of local American schools in this special sphere. His effort to fill this need would produce a special prototype service, representative of his generation as a whole. He would forge an organization which would serve not only a single local community but a network of towns.

EVANGELICAL ORIGINS OF REFORM

Gallaudet's provincial drive drew powerful sustenance from an expansive evangelical tradition whose roots went back deeply into the eighteenth century. Like the Reverend John Stanford, whose work in a New York almshouse introduced him to deaf persons and prompted his later creation of the New York Institution for the Instruction of the Deaf and Dumb (1818), Gallaudet discovered deaf persons as a vocation related to his formal religious training and missionary aspirations. In this period, one's specific religious denomination began to matter less than one's witness through action and service to any fellow Christian. Indeed, one of the conceptual efforts of these provincials to stabilize and mature their work and that of their society was to identify American Christianity with a religious nondenominationalism. In this period, the older geographical limitations upon a religious community were regularly breached by itinerant preachers, no less than by itinerant communicants. The dislocations of older traditions were particularly accentuated in population concentrations in New England and the Middle States. When doctrine began to count less than effective action, ministers and reformers opened lines of competition and merger which would parallel their counterparts in business. They began to construe the notion of congregations more broadly and fashioned quasireligious communities from communicants of many different denominations. If one were to serve deaf people in a Christian spirit, one would serve members of all denominations. *See* GALLAUDET, THOMAS HOPKINS.

The singular feature of this aggressive provincialism was its lateral rather than its vertical mobility. The influx of immigrants accentuated the regional migrations of native populations, creating an ubiquitous sense of ferment, bringing in its wake both possibility and peril. Before his efforts gave rise to a nascent school for deaf children, the Reverend John Stanford had created and served a number of Baptist parishes in New York, New Jersey, Pennsylvania, and Connecticut. Among the numerous schools and "charitable corporations" he set up in each of his congregations, the most notable was the House of Refuge, which he established in New York City in 1825. Similarly, by the time he turned to deaf people in 1816, Gallaudet had experimented with no less than five other occupations. After his graduation from Yale in 1805 he had studied law, had tutored at Yale, had worked as a merchant in Western Ohio-Kentucky, had shifted his merchant skills to New York City, and finally in 1811 had entered Andover Theological Seminary in Massachusetts from which he received the license to preach. While awaiting the call of a congregation, he discovered in the instruction of a neighbor's deaf child the possibility of a special quasi-religious mission. Similarly, Gallaudet's contemporary, Amos Kendall (1789–1869), left Massachusetts to pursue careers in law and in journalism in Kentucky. He later served as a state politician, a government official, a member of Andrew Jackson's "Kitchen Cabinet," as Postmaster General under Martin Van Buren, as journalist again with several newspapers sequentially, as business agent for Samuel F. B. Morse's telegraph company, all before devoting himself to work with deaf children and the creation of the Columbian (Washington, D.C.) Institution for the Deaf and Dumb (founded in 1857, now Gallaudet College), where he served as first president of its board of trustees. These multiple careers and dislocations could be duplicated for most of the major and minor social reformers of this generation. *See* GALLAUDET COLLEGE.

This extraordinary occupational and geographical mobility contrasted markedly with the language of order and stability which reformers used to explain their activities. At times, individuals of this provincial generation glossed their lives with conceptions of independence and ingenuity, notions which accommodated the dislocations of their careers. None, however, missed the chance to characterize their work as a reaffirmation of a larger, divine design. Perhaps their own careers made them especially sensitive to the absence of tradition and routine in their society and culture. The evangelical rhetoric in behalf of deaf instruction typifies the

effort to put some order into conceptions of behavior, if not into behavior itself. In an 1819 report on the New York Institution for the Instruction of the Deaf and Dumb, the author defined the school's purpose "to elevate a fellow being from a situation of the most ignorant, forlorn and helpless to the intelligent, noble, accountable and interesting character intended by the Creator." The first report of Gallaudet's American Asylum for the Education and Instruction of the Deaf and Dumb characterized the institution as a "gate of heaven for those poor lambs of the flock who have hitherto been wandering in the paths of ignorance like sheep without a shepherd." The metaphors of rescue, deliverance, and resurrection abounded in this period, ranking the treatment of deaf people as one more variation on a profoundly religious (though nondenominational) endeavor. The conceptions of evangelical benevolence which transcended the petty divisiveness of particular denominational dispute achieved an intellectual unity in this period that was not achieved in practice. Nevertheless, this cultural habit of thought—never a small achievement in a democracy—developed sufficient authority and cohesion in this early period to last the century and influence several successive generations.

NOVELTY OF EVANGELICAL INSTITUTIONS

If evangelism gave rise to a coherent mode of conception which often contrasted with practice, this first generation of practitioners, however erratically, revolutionized the work of reform: they created institutions to sustain and control efforts to change the work of social improvement. Among numerous examples from this earlier period (1815–1845), one might mention the American Education Society (founded 1815), the American Institute of Instruction (1830), the American Tract Society (1825), the American Home Mission Society (1826), the American Lyceum (1826), not to exclude the first general hospitals, reform schools, mental asylums, and penitentiaries in America. In a single generation these institutions experienced numerous mutations, failures, relocations, redirections. Like the work in behalf of deaf people, the focal point of the effort was a place apart: a special convention, a building, an asylum. It was a locus for the energies of many disparate individuals, of resources from many different locales. These institutions represented a network of abilities and concerns which could no longer be contained within single towns and communities.

The asylums represented the insight and achievement of nineteenth-century provincialism, which sought to widen the reach and dependence of social endeavor without repeating the worst of the Old World political and religious traditions. These institutions, which invested education itself with unprecedented social power, nevertheless did not always avoid the destructive properties of these older traditions. At their best, conceptually anyway, newer reform institutions considered themselves nonpolitical, the embodiments of a higher spirituality. They were not, as eighteenth-century workhouses and almshouses were, mere defenses or checks against the threatening instabilities in a particular locale. In an enlarged missionary tradition, nineteenth-century institutions were to make a new beginning, a society-wide revival on behalf of an expanding moral order. It was no accident that ministers and their acolytes were in the forefront of early-nineteenth-century institution building. Many of them, like the Reverend Thomas H. Gallaudet, made careers of riding circuit not only town to town but also reform to reform. In fact, Gallaudet ended his multireformist career as chaplain to an insane asylum.

Retrospective examination of these institutions often overstates their solidity and permanence. Like the experience of their leaders, reform organizations were models of pragmatic expediency and tenuousness. Virtually all originated out of voluntary associations and short-term institutes. Again, Gallaudet's experience is indicative. His medical neighbor and influential Hartford citizen, Dr. Mason Cogswell, capitalized on a chance encounter between Gallaudet and his deaf daughter to organize a voluntary group which would sponsor first the training of Gallaudet in Europe, then the establishment of a school for deaf children in Hartford, Connecticut. The success of this first association led to an irregular sequence of associations which met over two years, ultimately creating the American Asylum for the Deaf and Dumb. These initiatives produced two unexpected but precedent-setting features in the history of this reform movement. First, the group set aside its effort to imitate the British model of deaf instruction when its owners, the Braidwood family, insisted on a five-year apprenticeship to learn their "oral" method of instruction. Gallaudet turned to France, the Abbé Sicard, and the manual or sign method, whose elements, the French boasted, could be learned and taught more rapidly. The second precedent of this voluntary sponsorship was the involvement of state support. In support of Cogswell's and Gallaudet's efforts, Connecticut contributed from its public funds and thereby became the first state in America to appropriate public money for a benevolent institution. If other reforms were less fortunate, they were no less serendipitous. Their success was not permanent but—more important for this stage of American culture—an arousal of social conscience, an influence upon ever-broader yet analogous voluntary efforts for benevolent work. *See*

BRAIDWOOD, THOMAS; COGSWELL, ALICE; SICARD, ABBÉ ROCH AMBROISE CUCURRON.

SYSTEMATIZING CIVIC REFORM (1845–1875)

Within a generation, this notion of success began to narrow. Much of the language of evangelical benevolence was still prevalent, but its élan diminished. The first generation had attempted to convince people generally of the moral worth of benevolent reform. They succeeded extraordinarily in spreading conviction and a general conception about democratic behavior. They invested association with a new social import. Their preeminent power was rhetorical, and they did succeed in attracting talented individuals to their work. In contrast, the second generation (born roughly in the 1810s and 1820s) differentiated their effort in two ways: they attempted faithfully to carry out the work of reform on the exact lines of conception established by their first-generation mentors; yet they realigned the priorities and nature of reform with little grasp of how profound a change they were introducing. In part, this transformation was a function of the didactic and abstract nature of evangelical rhetoric. Its overstatement and bold spiritual conception made many distinct reform efforts appear to be far more compatible and cohesive than they ever were in practice. Once the work of practical operation began, it became abundantly clear that asylums for criminals differed from those for, say, ignorant, poor, or deaf individuals. Mere association on behalf of benevolent reform did not quickly clarify lines of authority, priorities of purpose, or strategic points of action. Success for the first generation involved the establishment of moral associations, geographically and conceptually; for the second, success became the more prosaic but no less worthy effort of methodical implementation, implicit in the original promise of association. It was not Thomas H. Gallaudet who refined and formalized the institutional plan for deaf instruction. Actually, he resigned from the American Asylum for the Deaf and Dumb in Hartford once the school was popularly considered established. It remained for succeeding generations of reformers in the education of deaf students, like Isaac L. Peet (1824–1898) and Edward M. Gallaudet (1837–1917), to realize and regularize the original promise of better education for deaf people.

The very success of associations seemed to systematize contact between practitioners and wealthy individual sponsors, whose initiatives remained the constant stimulus for additional reform organizations throughout the century. The state rarely initiated institutions for social reform of any sort; it sometimes intervened, but only in the wake of some voluntary effort. The precedent set by Mason Cogswell in Hartford continued to repeat itself through the first half of the nineteenth century in the persons of the Reverend Dexter King, founding sponsor of the Boston School (later Horace Mann School) for Deaf Mutes, or Lewis J. Dudley and Gardiner Greene Hubbard, founding sponsors of the Clarke School for the Deaf and Dumb at Northampton, Massachusetts. Like Cogswell, several of these men had deaf daughters. The force of family connection can be seen as well in the practitioners who, like Issac Peet, Edward M. Gallaudet, or Edward A. Fay, all had fathers who taught deaf students. It was also not uncommon for significant advocates, like both Edward M. Gallaudet or Alexander Graham Bell, to have had deaf mothers. This family connection established common ground between practitioners and sponsors. Unlike the philanthropists later in the nineteenth century, these early antebellum sponsors, often wealthy businessmen, actively participated in the causes and institutions they capitalized. Their presence and close contact with organizational staff illuminates the progressive shift from an evangelical to an entrepreneurial spirit in the second quarter of the nineteenth century.

Such entrepreneurs, like Gardiner Greene Hubbard (1822–1897), guaranteed a special brand of maturity both to America's reform momentum and to its provincial culture. Their special contribution was the fascination with organization which brought both private profit and civic improvement in roughly equal measures. Though trained as a lawyer and successful in that work, Hubbard had by age 35 also successfully introduced systems for gas lighting and for a fresh water supply in Cambridge, Massachusetts. In addition, he had built one of the earliest streetcar lines in America, connecting Cambridge with Boston. However, he would be best remembered for his early grasp of the profit and public service rendered by a properly run telephone system. With the profits from his ventures he helped found the Clarke School for the Deaf and Dumb, served for a dozen years on the Massachusetts Board of Education, and with his son-in-law, Alexander Graham Bell, founded the American Association To Promote Teaching of Speech to the Deaf (1890), the National Geographic Society (1888), and the publication *Science* (1883) as the official forum for the American Association for the Advancement of Science. He also headed a presidential commission for the reorganization of the U.S. Postal Service and served as trustee for many scientific associations like the Smithsonian Institution. He took the risks and designed the formats which delivered on other individuals' insights and inventions. Entrepreneurs like Hubbard contributed to the work of social improvement in a special way; they guaranteed the

ongoing mechanisms for social change. Indeed, the knowledge which maintained these mechanisms introduced a new and distinctively American education claim: mechanical and methodical knowledge—science—produced rather than hindered creative invention. *See* CLARKE SCHOOL.

The second generation then could claim its own distinctive contribution to American social change: it guaranteed the endurance of particular ingenious devices and created a means for disseminating them to any receptive party, whatever their wealth or station. By midcentury there were sufficient mechanisms to make America's technical virtuosity a part of the American promise, the very reason America appeared as both asylum and opportunity to immigrants and indigenous youth alike. These two midcentury conditions—the spread of ingenious mechanisms for improvement, plus population growth and movement—made the cultivation of proper speech a powerful democratic imperative. Virtually all public and private schools, whatever region or social class they served, featured practical instruction in elocution and modes of social discourse. No one needed to have it stated explicitly that modes of speech signaled one's social place, a preoccupation particularly keen for societies with a continuous influx of idioms and pronunciations. This preoccupation with elocution and the search for a "science" of speech was to have great impact upon many areas of social improvement, deafness included. The connection would be made explicit for Samuel Porter, a teacher of deaf students from 1832 to 1866 in both the American Institute in Hartford and the New York Institution for the Deaf and Dumb—Porter's *Guide to Pronunciation* served as a preface to *Webster's International Dictionary*.

MIDCENTURY LEADERS OF DEAF EDUCATION

The process by which these broader instruments of Americanization came to affect the instruction of deaf youth can be well illustrated by two individuals, both elocutionists, both contemporaries of the second generation of reformers. Alexander Melville Bell (1819–1905) was a Scottish immigrant to Canada via Great Britain. He had spent much of his life attempting to refine his father's method of removing speech impediments. His diction, however, recommended him more to Scottish provincials as entertainer and lecturer than scientist. He supported his family largely through popular readings and as private tutor of stammerers and ambitious clergymen until the publication of *Visible Speech: The Science of Universal Alphabetics* (1867). Bell claimed to have reduced all languages to a system of 29 symbols which were accompanied by 52 consonants, 26 vowels, and 12 diphthongs. Though successful in the hands of Bell and his sons, the method proved too intricate for his fellow elocutionists and scientists. Undaunted by the cool reception within his own country, Bell traveled to America to prosyletize on a wide circuit on behalf of his discovery. His claims attracted the attention of the ever-vigilant Gardiner Greene Hubbard, who arranged six lectures for Bell before the influential Lowell Institute. Hubbard sensed the possibilities of Melville Bell's method for deaf people and had him visit the Clarke School in Northampton, Massachusetts, the first permanent American school to experiment with "articulation" over sign as a means of deaf instruction. Hubbard's warm support of Bell and his science of recording sound began the successful challenge to the dominance of "sign" instruction, the mode which Gallaudet had made the traditional American norm a generation earlier.

The native American parallel to Melville Bell was Lewis B. Monroe (1825–1879), also best known as an elocutionist, and a contemporary of both Melville Bell and Hubbard. Like Bell, Monroe contributed to deaf instruction in ways both indirect and profound. He too staked his reputation and made his career upon an ability to convince the public of his skills in "voice culture." He too had traveled far in behalf of his emerging theory from his native Charlestown (Massachusetts) through rural New England, back toward Boston, then to New Orleans, to Europe, first for further study of voice culture in Paris, then as a tutor to sons of wealthy Central Americans. Like Bell, Monroe advanced his ideas about voice culture on a secular circuit of teachers' institutes, seasonal teaching at established schools like Williams College and the new Massachusetts Institute of Technology, as well as inspectorships and short-term superintendencies in public school systems. Wherever he went, he insisted that one might analyze a person's character by the qualities of voice, had one the proper method.

In the late 1860s Monroe began a series of school readers and, more important, published his methodology of voice culture or voice gymnastics, *A Manual of Physical and Vocal Training* (1869), which he had sent to Melville Bell in the wake of the Lowell Institute lectures. Monroe established a private and successful school for elocution, which became in 1873 the School of Oratory of Boston University. As dean of the school, he would be better known in history as the employer of Melville Bell's son, Alexander Graham Bell. Monroe energetically supported the younger Bell's applications of electricity to the study of sound and speech. That support won Monroe the invitation to verify (along with the ubiquitous Gardiner Greene Hubbard) Bell's first telephone message (March 12, 1876). For both Melville Bell and Lewis Monroe, the social and career implications of elocution introduced the power

of speech to instruction and compelled a shift toward the oral tradition of deaf instruction. Even more important, communication via speech promoted the fortunes of Alexander Graham Bell (1847–1922), one of the most important third-generation figures in the American history of deaf persons.

The cumulative achievement of these first two generations appears in Henry Barnard's 1852 survey of United States institutions for deaf children. Of the 19 schools he reported operative by 1852, virtually all had some state support. Southern states supported nine, but the greater fiscal outlay and the majority of individuals served by instruction reflected the greater commitments of the northern and midwestern state legislatures. The largest schools were the oldest—the American Asylum in Hartford, Connecticut, and the New York Institution for the Deaf and Dumb—each of which could boast over 1000 graduates. These two schools accounted for over 50 percent of the graduates of all 19 institutions in the early 1850s. These numbers are significant in arguing how aggressive and thorough the nineteenth century's benevolent tradition could be, since the entire national population of deaf persons in the early 1850s, according to Barnard's (now suspect) figures, totaled 9717 individuals. (Present-day estimates would have put the figures at about 23,000, based on a probability of one deaf person per thousand.) Nearly half that number, so Barnard's calculation implies, received some form of formal training in these nascent institutions. Furthermore, most of these schools employed deaf instructors, from one-third to one-half their staff. Most important, all of this formal instruction operated within a tradition of training by sign language, which became authoritative for provincial America at the very moment it was being rejected by France's Abbé Sicard, the instructor of Thomas H. Gallaudet. Not until the third generation of deaf leaders would America reconsider the Braidwood method in Britain or the powerful example of "articulation" in Germany. It should also be noted that after the 1860s sign itself had begun to incorporate many complex modes of manual communication: pantomimic, alphabetic, symbolic, single- and double-handed, and combinations of them. *See* EDUCATION: History.

PROFESSIONALIZATION OF DEAF INSTRUCTION

Two larger forces, well outside the aegis of the established signing institutions, account for the rapid reception of the new articulation or oral method of training for the deaf population. The first was the influx of immigrants, particularly Germans, whose own tradition of oral instruction found little support in America. The difficulty of surmounting both linguistic and ethnic barriers led to the founding of smaller private schools, in urban areas particularly. Bernard Engelsmann opened a school for Jewish children in New York within months after his arrival from Vienna in 1864. In 1867 he founded the New York Institution for Improved Instruction of Deaf Mutes and thereby offered an alternative to the second oldest school for deaf children located in New York City. In 1869 St. Joseph Institute for the Improved Instruction of Deaf Mutes opened in New York City under Catholic sponsorship and the direction of Madame Victorine Boucher. This school also espoused the articulation method.

The second historical factor to challenge the existing tradition was the expanding presence of women in work outside the home. After the Civil War, the failure of men to return to occupations like teaching made such roles women's preserve. This abrupt shift altered the staffing of public and benevolent systems at the very moment that some, like the public school, became a mass institution for the first time. The break with the traditional pattern of female employment enabled women, like Anne Sullivan, the teacher of Helen Keller, to rely more on trial and error and her own ingenuity than any formal training (though she did have some in Samuel Gridley Howe's Perkins Institute for the Blind). One might number women like Harriet Rogers (1834–1919), the first principal of the Clarke Institution for Deaf Mutes in Northampton, Massachusetts, or Sarah Fuller (1836–1919), for 41 years the principal of the Horace Mann School for the Deaf in Boston, as examples of the postwar generation who received whatever deaf training they did well after they had engaged the work of deaf instruction. Harriet Rogers traveled to Germany in 1871–1872, four years after founding her school for deaf students, to learn the oral methods firsthand. Fuller, a graduate of the West Newton (Massachusetts) Normal School and a successful public school teacher of language and elocution, turned to deaf instruction at the request of the Reverend Dexter King, state legislator and philanthropist. She studied first with Harriet Rogers at the Clarke School, then later with Alexander Graham Bell, who tutored her in "visible speech" while under her employ in the Horace Mann School. The combined force of German methodology and female teachers introduced a major countercurrent which dramatically affected the instruction of the deaf. *See* KELLER, HELEN.

This countercurrent provided a background for the central feature of the next generation's work—the professionalization of deaf instruction. The precise reason that both immigrants and women found it difficult to establish themselves in the existing institutions lay less with their espousal of the oral method of instructing deaf students and more with the challenge they represented to the Protestant and male traditions which American institutions and professions in general enshrined. The old evangelical dynamics still sent trained and ordained ministers, like the Reverend Lewellyn Pratt and the Reverend John Chickering, into the instruction of deaf people. These representatives of the third generation (born in the late 1830s and 1840s) now regularly graduated from the New England liberal arts colleges; they often received formal training in deaf instruction before spending entire careers in this work. No longer did prominent spokespersons for deaf people experience multiple occupations and frequent career shifts. The post–Civil War generation shifted infrequently, passing within institutions for deaf students. Job Williams (1842–1914) of the American School for the Deaf; Joseph C. Gordon (1842–1903) and Edward A. Fay (1843–1923), both of the National College for Deaf Mutes (founded 1864); Albert L. E. Crouter (1846–1925) of the Pennsylvania Institution for the Deaf and Dumb; or Charles W. Ely (1839–1912) of the Maryland School for the Deaf shaped entire careers at the head of single schools. These careers represented the entrenchment of institutional systems and the force of a new educational hierarchy, remarkably different experiences from their immigrant and female peers who began to criticize the teaching of sign. These differences over modes of communication soon joined broader debates at the end of the century, particularly the debates over the role and place of distinctive-individuals in American society. *See* FAY, EDWARD ALLEN.

IDEOLOGICAL DEBATE AT THE TURN OF THE CENTURY

The central contribution of the third-generation deaf reformers, particularly given the ethnic, gender, and social class divisions among practitioners, was the introduction of an ideological competition, one which sought the best method for normalizing any educational or social deviation. Both sign and oral arguments always went well beyond the literal pedagogical terms of discussion. Hence, this contentiousness was an essential part of the professionalization process in this special area. The very technicality of the debate always carried connotations that went beyond technique to deep-set notions of proper social adaptation and social power. It was the reverse, in a way, of the first generation's experience, employing the expansive, evangelical rhetoric of divine plan and a soul-saving mission among deaf persons, inflating the rhetoric to accommodate potentially any technique. The third generation sought (but did not quite achieve) a rank order of technical application and a preferential selection between different sorts of expert treatment. By the end of the nineteenth century, debates became ritualized over day schools versus residential schools for deaf children, over sign versus oral and lipreading methods, over the instructional capacities of adventitiously versus congenitally deaf persons, over the age of earliest deaf training, over the very titles of deaf institutions, that is, the connotations of "asylum" versus "school." Each side had its champion: the oral tradition defended commandingly by the immigrant inventor Alexander Graham Bell; the sign tradition by Edward Miner Gallaudet, who both merited and inherited the honor from his father, the Reverend Thomas H. Gallaudet. Each side had its professional organization and bastion school: the sign professionals organized themselves into the Convention of American Instructors for the Deaf (which once denied Bell membership) and the only institution of higher education for deaf persons, the National College for Deaf Mutes, of which Edward Miner Gallaudet served as president from its founding in 1864 until 1911; the oral professionals with Alexander Graham Bell's American Association for the Promotion of Teaching Speech to the Deaf (founded 1890) which adopted the Clarke School as its normal school. *See* ALEXANDER GRAHAM BELL ASSOCIATION FOR THE DEAF; CONVENTION OF AMERICAN INSTRUCTORS OF THE DEAF.

Before the end of the century, the oral tradition had achieved clear parity, most likely because its success promised, like the public school's Americanization of the immigrants, the appearance of less heterogeneity and overt deviance among individual citizens. Articulation became a skill employed by 50 percent of teachers of deaf students. In excess of 4200 deaf children, nearly half the deaf student population, received instruction in this method. The instruction of deaf people had shifted in states like Massachusetts from the Board of State Charities to the State Board of Education. It was no longer a matter of voluntary philanthropy or charity, but an educational right. Once roundly criticized for his emphatic endorsement of the Prussian (oral) approach to the deaf, Horace Mann became a rehabilitized hero at the end of the century for his educational prescience in this special field. Finally, the advocates of sign, including Edward M. Gallaudet himself, conceded the applicability of the oral method in certain contexts after the demonstrable record of the Clarke School and its allies in successfully teaching not only "partially deaf" (which the school initially preferred for articulation) but congenitally deaf persons. Gallaudet's institution, renamed Gallaudet College in 1894 for his father, introduced a combined method, which employed articulation ("the artificial method") for advanced or especially adept pupils. Still, Gallaudet always put primary stress on sign ("the natural method"). On his part, Alexander Graham Bell

welcomed even unreconstructed signers into his fold. Bell's extraordinary prestige as inventor of the telephone did much to override divisive problems, and his reputation helps explain the rapid acceptance of the oral method as a technique for *all* deaf people, not simply the advanced or the adept. *See* GALLAUDET, EDWARD MINER.

By the end of the century, though leaders and their organizations provided forums for continued debate, each camp turned its attention to empirical research. Bell founded and financed the Volta Bureau (1887) in Washington, D.C., and through its research and publications broadened the basis for his own self-described life achievement: a "teacher of the deaf." Gallaudet's faculty published their researches in the *American Annals of the Deaf and Dumb*, which under Edward A. Fay, a member of Gallaudet's faculty, became the established source of information on the deaf population. Their researches, definitive for their time, established, for example, that in America and the British Isles there was 1 deaf person for every 1600 citizens, with approximately 40 percent of the deafness being of congenital origin. The collaborative work on behalf of new scientific insights and authority did not eliminate the ideological divisions of the third generation; however, it did bring a momentary, outward neutrality to work for deaf people. The neutrality became for this generation a kind of professional ("scientific") standard itself, obscuring for a time the ongoing divisions within which subsequent generations, in turn, would also shape new social and educational traditions. *See* AMERICAN ANNALS OF THE DEAF.

Paul H. Mattingly

Bibliography
Bruce, Robert: *Bell: Alexander Graham Bell and the Conquest of Solitude*, 1973.
Douglas, Ann: *The Feminization of American Culture*, 1977.
Gallaudet, Edward M.: *The Life of Thomas H. Gallaudet*, 1910.
Haskell, Thomas: *The Emergence of Professional Social Science*, 1977.
History of Education Quarterly, 1960.
Lane, Harlan: *The Wild Boy of Averyon*, 1975.
Mattingly, Paul H.: *The Classless Profession: American Schoolmen in the 19th Century*, 1975.
Rothman, David: *The Discovery of the Asylum*, 1971.
Smith, Timothy: *Revivalism and Social Reform: American Protestantism on the Eve of the Civil War*, 1957.
Tyack, David, and E. Hansot: *Managers of Virtue: Public School Leadership in America, 1820–1980*, 1982.

Sign Language Controversy

For the last 200 years the most acrimonious dispute among educators of deaf persons, and occasionally among deaf persons themselves, has been over communication methods. This argument has focused on how deaf people should best communicate with each other and with hearing people, and whether sign languages should be used, particularly in educational settings.

Sign languages use body movements, especially of the hands, head, and fingers, to express ideas visually. Proponents, referred to as manualists, argue that sign languages are natural to deaf people, since they are based entirely on readily visible gestures, movements, and facial expressions, and support sign language in all contexts and for all purposes. Therefore, according to manualists, deaf people should be encouraged to use signs. Opponents of sign languages, often called oralists, reject all use of sign language. Most oralists deny that sign languages are languages, that they are natural to deaf people, or that they should be a communication method. Oralists insist that deaf people should communicate orally, expressing themselves with speech and reading speech from the lips to receive information.

The sign language controversy has involved a variety of intermediate positions between those of the oralists and the manualists. Some persons have favored the use of fingerspelling, but not sign language, in educational settings. Fingerspelling is the spelling out, letter by letter, of each word to be communicated. For example, the word "red" becomes three distinct handshapes, one for each letter. Fingerspelling may occur alone, or it may be accompanied by speech and lipreading. *See* SIGNS: Fingerspelling.

Other intermediate alternatives are various mouth-hands systems. In these a person speaks, thus permitting lipreading, while using a variety of handshapes held next to the mouth to clarify the precise meaning of words or sounds expressed on the lips. Proponents argue that mouth-hands systems assist both in lipreading and in teaching speech to deaf children. *See* MOUTH-HAND SYSTEMS.

Many schools for deaf children in the United States tried to resolve the methods controversy through another intermediate position, called the combined system. This system had numerous variations, each involving a combination of oral and manual approaches. Speech and lipreading generally were taught to all children in the school, but those who failed to make progress after a trial period were segregated into manual (sign language) classes.

Yet another position between that of the manualists and the oralists is the simultaneous method, wherein a person speaks and signs at the same time. Usually the sign vocabulary is borrowed from the national sign language, but the signs are arranged in the same word order as the spoken language. In American residential schools for deaf children today, where the simultaneous method

predominates, American Sign Language (ASL) sometimes is modified further by the addition of grammatical indicators to the signs, such as the verb endings *ed* and *ing*. *See* SOCIOLINGUISTICS: Simultaneous Communication.

Despite numerous attempts to compromise, the methods controversy prevails among educators, parents, school administrators, and deaf persons. It has involved government bodies, professional groups, and organizations of deaf people. It was not until the 1960s that studies of the effectiveness of various communication methods began to reduce the emotions and invective of two centuries.

EUROPEAN BACKGROUND

Manualism and oralism were often referred to during the nineteenth century as the French and German methods, respectively. The origin of these labels, and indeed the start of the whole controversy, lies in a public quarrel between two leading eighteenth-century educators of deaf persons—Abbé Charles Michel de l'Epée of Paris and Samuel Heinicke of Leipzig. *See* L'EPÉE, ABBÉ CHARLES MICHEL DE; HEINICKE, SAMUEL.

Abbé de l'Epée, head of the French Royal Institute for the Deaf and Dumb in Paris, was the first person to advocate the use of sign language, which he called Methodical Signs, in the instruction of deaf persons. L'Epée reasoned that, for deaf persons, signs could take the place of sounds as signifiers of ideas. Like the seventeenth-century English philosopher John Locke, l'Epée believed that all spoken and written language was artificial, that there was no logical connection between sounds and the ideas that they denoted. Therefore, l'Epée used signs to teach deaf people "to think with order, and to combine their ideas," as he explained. All of his instruction was carried out with Methodical Signs that he either invented or borrowed from those indigenous to Parisian deaf persons. The only exception was proper names. These l'Epée communicated with fingerspelling, using a one-handed manual alphabet.

Although l'Epée believed that signs, together with some fingerspelling, were adequate to instruct deaf people in all forms of language, he claimed to have success in teaching speech and lipreading. The teaching of these skills, however, was never very important to him, for he believed that they were not essential to opening the minds of deaf persons.

Samuel Heinicke took the opposite view. He initiated the methods controversy in a series of letters, first with Abbé Stork of Vienna, who had studied l'Epée's methods in Paris, and then with l'Epée himself. Heinicke argued that neither writing nor signs were adequate for instructing deaf people, because these methods could not convey abstract thought. Moreover, he believed that written or signed words could not be remembered and that signs could not convey subtleties of meaning.

The heart of the controversy between Heinicke and l'Epée emerged from their differing views of the connection between sound and thought. L'Epée believed that there was no natural connection, that sounds were arbitrary designations for thoughts or ideas, and that ideas were of primary importance. Heinicke insisted on the transcendent significance of sound, arguing in a letter to l'Epée that sounds are "the dark mainsprings which play upon our faculties of desire, bringing about random notions, and lifting our reason to what is grounded in these, namely, universal, abstract, transcendental forms of thought in which throughout our lives we must think, judge, and reason, but always in a tonelike manner." Heinicke even claimed that people dream, not in terms of objects or ideas themselves, but in terms of sound, a spoken language.

Consequently Heinicke denounced signs as useless and claimed to employ pure oral methods to instruct his deaf pupils. Although his pupils could not be influenced by spoken language in the same way as hearing people, Heinicke insisted that they grasped sounds through the means of another sense. This other sense Heinicke termed "taste," which l'Epée interpreted to mean the feelings caused by movements of the tongue, throat, and mouth in speech.

In an exchange of letters between Heinicke and l'Epée in the 1780s, neither convinced the other of the superiority of his methods. For a few decades at least, l'Epée's belief in the value of signs held sway in France. Heinicke's method predominated in Germany and to a lesser extent in England. Thus the long controversy between the German and French methods began with two radically different philosophical positions on the nature of language, sound, and thought and their interrelationships.

PREDOMINANCE OF MANUALISM IN AMERICAN INSTITUTIONS

The sign language controversy was not felt strongly in the United States until after the Civil War. From the opening of the first permanent school for deaf students in 1817—the American Asylum for the Deaf and Dumb in Hartford, Connecticut—until the late 1860s, instruction of deaf people in the United States was based on l'Epée's method. Two people were primarily responsible for this: an American, Thomas Hopkins Gallaudet, and a Frenchman, Laurent Clerc.

Gallaudet, who founded the American Asylum, learned the manual method "by accident" and brought it back from Europe. Gallaudet originally went to Europe to learn the method of educating deaf persons in England and at the exclusively oral Braidwood School in Scotland. The English school

Gallaudet visited and the Braidwood School either refused to instruct him in their methods or set conditions he found unacceptable. Thus, he left England in frustration and went to France, where he was welcomed at the Royal Institution for the Deaf and Dumb at Paris, under the direction of l'Epée's successor, Roch Ambroise Cucurron Sicard.

While in Paris, Gallaudet became more familiar with l'Epée's manual system, was impressed by it, and decided to use it as the foundation for the school he hoped to open in the United States. To help accomplish this, Gallaudet convinced Laurent Clerc, a star pupil of the Paris Institution and an instructor there, to accompany him back to the United States. Clerc and Gallaudet, then, both firm believers in the value of sign language and fingerspelling, established an early manual tradition in American schools. *See* CLERC, LAURENT.

Gallaudet believed that sign language had many advantages, including the fact that signs were natural to deaf persons. Moreover, signs, because of their concreteness, lent themselves to "the instruction and moral training of minds." Gallaudet was hardly unaware of the German oral method, but claimed that teaching lipreading was a difficult process, even if there was complete success in rare instances. Similarly, teaching deaf persons to speak was regarded by Gallaudet as a long and difficult process. He also believed that oral methods required two or three years, and sometimes more, before communication could begin between pupil and teacher.

In the 50 years after the American Asylum was established, more than 25 schools for deaf students were opened in the United States. Most were state-supported residential institutions and, as with the American Asylum, their instruction was firmly based on the French method. Some of these schools, at various times, taught speech and lipreading, but as separate classes like English or mathematics. Nowhere in the United States, until the late 1860s, was the oral method the basis of instruction. By then, however, the sign language controversy had crossed the Atlantic.

CHALLENGE OF ORALISM IN THE UNITED STATES

Education reformer Horace Mann was the first important American proponent of oralism. He and Samuel Gridley Howe, superintendent of the Perkins Institution for the Blind, toured European schools for blind children and deaf children in 1843. They returned impressed by the progress made in German and English schools that used voice and lipreading to teach deaf pupils. Mann then reported his observations and attempted to open an oral school in Boston. Supporters of the American Asylum in Hartford, which drew deaf students from Massachusetts as well as from Connecticut, defeated Mann's attempt. Nevertheless, Mann's efforts had some effect, for the American Asylum began to teach articulation (speech), but only as an addition to the curriculum rather than as a basis for instruction.

Other Americans followed the example of Mann and Howe, visiting European schools to learn more about oral methods. George E. Day, of the New York Institution, visited Europe in 1844 and 1859. Lewis Weld, from the American Asylum, accompanied Day on his 1844 trip, and in 1851 Harvey P. Peet, principal of the New York Institution for the Deaf and Dumb, also visited Europe. Day, Weld, and Peet (unlike Mann) were not overwhelmed by the educational results of the oral schools they visited. All three were thoroughly familiar with the French method, had used it during their professional careers, and would never call for its replacement by another method. This call would have to come from outsiders, people not professionally and personally involved with manual instruction; it did in the 1860s.

Parents of three deaf children in New England refused to accept sign language for their children and helped to organize a school based on German oral methods. They were fortunate in getting the assistance of John Clarke, a wealthy business person who was losing his hearing. Clarke donated over $300,000 to endow the Clarke School at Northampton, Massachusetts, which became in 1867 the first permanent school in the United States to base all its instruction on the twin pillars of oralism: speech and lipreading. At about the same time that the Clarke School opened, Isaac and Hannah Rosenfeld began a private oral school in New York City that later became the Institution for the Improved Instruction of Deaf Mutes.

These events did not go unnoticed by the manualists. In 1867 Edward Miner Gallaudet, son of T. H. Gallaudet and president of the Columbia Institution in Washington, D.C. (later renamed Gallaudet College), went to Europe to see for himself what oralism was all about and what it could accomplish. The result of his European tour was the First Conference of American Principals of Schools for the Deaf, held at the Columbia Institution in 1868. Gallaudet's action in calling this meeting was shrewd. He recognized that the established schools for deaf students would have to meet the challenge presented by oralism, for the latter method had natural attractions to the public at large and particularly to parents. If the established schools did not confront this challenge, did not find some way to meet the criticism of oralists, then these state-supported schools might lose popular and political support, and sign language would cease to be a method of instruction in American schools.

Gallaudet addressed the assembled principals in 1868 with a long paper, "The American System of Deaf-Mute Instruction; its Incidental Defects and their Remedies," in which he outlined his plan for meeting the claims of the oralists. He began with an argument that to some extent conflicted with the premises of l'Epée and his own father: instruction leading to full competence in using and understanding written language constitutes the chief work of deaf students' education. L'Epée had stressed the importance of opening closed minds; T. H. Gallaudet had emphasized the importance of teaching moral truths. For these purposes, as even most oralists admitted, sign langauge was acceptable. But the question was whether sign language, with its gestures, uncertain grammar, and word order so different from English, could be used to teach English. The younger Gallaudet said that it could.

He told the assembled principals that two major changes were needed to improve deaf students' grasp of English and hence their ability to function successfully in the society. First, he would extend the term of studies, accepting students into the institutions at earlier ages. Second, he encouraged the principals to emphasize fingerspelling, rather than signs, with more advanced students, for fingerspelling clearly was based on English words and English word order.

Gallaudet went even further in his attempt to seize the initiative from the oralists. He said that American schools for deaf children should combine the methods of l'Epée and Heinicke. The schools should teach speech to all children who could benefit from it, especially those who were either hard-of-hearing or adventitiously deaf. The speech controversy, according to Gallaudet, could be solved easily by adding facilities for speech and lipreading instruction for all pupils capable of benefiting.

The principals in attendance in Washington in 1868 were shocked by Gallaudet's apparent break from his father's staunch manualism and by his criticism of American schools. Nevertheless, they accepted the reality of oralism's challenge with two unanimously accepted resolutions, both proposed by Gallaudet. The first stated that all educational institutions for deaf and dumb persons must provide adequate instruction in articulation and lipreading to those pupils capable of deriving some benefit. The second called on the boards of directors of all institutions to provide funds to hire teachers skilled in speech and lipreading instruction.

Gallaudet was attempting in 1868, and would attempt for the remainder of his life, to find a way for signs and speech to coexist as legitimate communication methods among deaf people and in educational situations. His suggestion that l'Epée's and Heinicke's methods be combined was in fact misleading, for he did not support the idea of using speech and sign language simultaneously. Rather, he wanted students to be taught subject matter with signs, fingerspelling, and reading, while speech also would be taught—and given much greater emphasis. Despite the inaccuracy of the term, the combined method became the rallying cry for people who wished to find some legitimate place for sign language. To committed oralists, however, the combined method would never be acceptable.

Instead, oralists in the United States and abroad attacked sign language and, in some cases, fingerspelling. In the United States, where most deaf persons were taught in state-funded residential institutions with strong commitments to manualism, oralists created alternatives, either private residential or day schools that used only speech and lipreading. They were fairly successful, for by 1880, according to a survey conducted by the *American Annals of the Deaf*, there were 11 pure oral schools in the United States. At the same time, according to the *Annals*, there were 35 combined schools and 8 manual schools, plus staunchly manual Gallaudet College.

ARGUMENTS OF AMERICAN ORALISTS

Influential oralists in the United States never accepted the extreme philosophical position of Samuel Heinicke and other early European proponents of speech and lipreading. Though they often denied that gestures could constitute a language, they did not say (as Heinicke did) that deaf pupils could not learn in a signing environment. Instead, the arguments made by oralists in the United States were more practical, usually focusing on two issues: the best means of teaching English, and the most successful method of integrating deaf people with the hearing community. Underlying both of these was a third proposition that most deaf people, even those born profoundly deaf, could learn to speak and read lips well enough to profit from instruction without signs or fingerspelling.

The most important oralist in the United States for almost 50 years was Alexander Graham Bell, a one-time speech teacher, son of a hard-of-hearing woman, and spouse of a totally deaf woman. Bell argued vociferously in publications, among his many influential friends, to school boards, and to state legislators that oral methods would work, that a deaf child could be taught to read speech by observing the lips and to speak understandably. His wife, Mabel Hubbard Bell, who lost her hearing at age five from scarlet fever, was a model oral deaf person. She had no use for signs, which she never learned; she was well read and informed; she carried on normal social interaction with hearing people; and she had no interest in fraternizing with other deaf people. In the perception of Bell and

other oralists, this was exactly how all deaf people should behave.

Bell and others criticized sign language for two reasons. First, they said that it interfered with deaf people's ability to learn English. They used the parallel of a person learning a foreign language. In their opinion, this could best be accomplished only by forcing the person to use the foreign language day-in and day-out. If deaf people were allowed to use sign language, analogously to Americans allowed to use English when the goal was to learn French, then they would do so, for it was easier than mastering English. Therefore, they must be placed in an environment where signs and usually fingerspelling—though Bell had mixed feelings about this—were absolutely prohibited. All information they received must be in English, either spoken or written. With total immersion in an English environment, the American oralists argued, deaf people would learn to speak, read lips, read, and write in English. Thus, they would in effect be normal, and not be excluded from society.

Oralists made another significant argument against sign language. They said that its use, especially in residential institutions where children lived apart from their families, tended to drive a communication wedge between parents and children.

As the nineteenth century drew to a close, American oralists were attacking not only manualism but also the concept of residential institutions, deaf clubs, reunions of deaf people, and special newspapers by and for the deaf community. All of these, oralists argued, tended to isolate deaf people. They encouraged deaf adults to remain clannish, outside the mainstream, a class apart from society. Parents of deaf children, about 90 percent of whom had normal hearing, were very susceptible to these arguments.

Bell added more fuel to the oralists' arguments with his paper, delivered to the National Academy of Sciences on November 13, 1883, and called "Memoir upon the Formation of a Deaf Variety of the Human Race." Bell's bombshell was the result of his investigation of the causes of deafness in the Hartford (Connecticut), New York, Ohio, Indiana, Illinois, and Texas schools for the deaf. He found that 39 percent of the students were congenitally deaf. He assumed, incorrectly, that congenital deafness meant hereditary deafness and discovered that 29.5 percent of all pupils had deaf relatives. He was leading up to the startling conclusion that a deaf variety of the human race was being formed as more deaf people married each other and produced more deaf offspring. *See* HEARING LOSS: Genetic Causes.

Bell was interested in more than genetics, however, for he wished to discover the causes of intermarriage among deaf people and to eliminate them. His 1883 paper listed various contributing factors to intermarriage, such as special periodicals, deaf teachers in the residential schools, the formation of deaf communities, false notions among hearing people about deaf people, and deaf associations. The main causes, however, were segregation for educational purposes and the use of a unique language. Bell's conclusion was not that deaf people should be forbidden by law to marry each other, but that sign language should not be taught or used and that day schools should replace institutions.

Bell's preference for day schools began to yield results in the late nineteenth century. The first state to support special facilities for deaf students in public, nonresidential schools was Wisconsin. At the urging of the Phonological Institute of Milwaukee, and after Bell had visited Madison, the state capital, the Wisconsin legislature passed in 1885 a bill allocating $100 per deaf pupil per year to any school district that established a day school for deaf students in conjunction with its regular public school. Oralists called this the Wisconsin Plan and repeatedly urged it on the other state legislatures. *See* EDUCATIONAL PROGRAMS: Day Schools.

By the 1880s, American manualists were in retreat. Proponents of speech and lipreading blamed sign language for the myriad problems deaf people seemed to have: slow educational advancement, poor English, inability to get professional jobs, clannishness, alienation from hearing parents, and even the frequency of occurrence of deafness itself. In Europe, however, the methods controversy was even more favorable to the oralists.

EUROPEAN ADOPTION OF ORAL METHODS

By the middle of the nineteenth century, European schools, even those in France, accepted the idea that deaf persons should be taught to communicate primarily with speech and lipreading rather than with signs and fingerspelling. German schools all used oral methods, as did all 17 schools for deaf pupils in Austria-Hungary, half the schools in Denmark, 7 of the 10 schools in Belgium, and virtually all schools in Italy. The major controversy on the European continent in the second half of the nineteenth century was whether signs and fingerspelling had any value or should be forbidden altogether.

This question was raised as early as 1846 at a conference of German teachers held at Esslingen. One conference member proposed to banish sign language from all institutions. The majority of German teachers did not approve this proposal, for many still believed that teaching deaf persons to speak and read lips left them without comprehen-

sion of the substance of language. But support for the proposal grew, especially in Italy.

In 1869 and 1873 Italy led the way in pointing toward the outcome of the methods controversy in Europe. In 1869 the Royal Institute for Deaf-Mutes, at Milan, adopted speech alone as the basis of all instruction of deaf people. Four years later, at the Siena Congress of Teachers of Deaf-Mutes, the Milan precedent was accepted, with the congress declaring its belief in speech as the principal method of communication in schools for deaf persons.

In England, meanwhile, matters moved slowly, for the English were more eclectic than their continental colleagues. At the third meeting of British Educators of the Deaf in 1877, the main topic was the methods controversy. No agreement was reached, with some teachers favoring oralism, some manualism, and some the combined method. English eclecticism is reflected in statistics published by the *Annals* showing that in 1880 England had 9 manual, 5 oral, 11 combined, and 1 "writing" school. The last, in Llandaff, Wales, claimed to have dispensed with both speech and sign language, carrying on all instruction in writing.

The situation in France in the late 1870s was changing rapidly. In Paris, the 1878 International Congress for the Improvement of Deaf-Mutes went on record as favoring oral methods. The congress was not really international, for all delegates but one—from Italy—were French. Moreover, the 1878 congress was followed in 1879 by the First Convention of French Teachers of Deaf-Mutes, at Lyon. It declared that articulation was superior to sign language, especially in restoring the deaf mute to society, but it also agreed that articulation alone could not be the basis for instruction. Therefore, a majority of the convention delegates accepted a compromise resolution indicating that signs should be used for purposes of instruction but speech and lipreading also should be taught. This moderate approach was completely refuted at the Second International Congress, held at Milan in 1880.

The Milan congress marked an important turning point in the methods controversy in Europe, though there is no evidence that it affected directly the controversy in the United States. The Milan congress, unlike that in Paris in 1878, was truly international, with delegates from Italy, France, Germany, Scandinavia, Belgium, England, Switzerland, and the United States. It was carefully organized by staunchly oralist Italian teachers, most of whom were ecclesiastics or members of Catholic religious orders, as were their equally vociferous oralist colleagues from France. Together the Italians, with 87 of 164 official delegates, and the French, with 56, dominated the proceedings. The Italians and the French were determined to force the delegates to accept the argument that pure oral methods should be adopted as official policy by all teachers of deaf students. The methods controversy consumed, almost exclusively, the time of the convention.

The convention passed eight resolutions, five of which were addressed to the question of methods. The first, most important resolution set the tone for the entire conference: "The Congress, considering the incontestable superiority of speech over signs in restoring the deaf-mute to society, and in giving him a more perfect knowledge of language, declares that the oral method ought to be preferred to that of signs for the education and instruction of the deaf and dumb." The only votes against this sweeping resolution were from the American delegates and one English delegate, Richard Elliott, headmaster of the London Institution for the Deaf and Dumb. The attitude of the congress was clear, and the protests (particularly of E. M. Gallaudet) to allow sign language and fingerspelling in addition to speech instruction were ignored.

Outside of England, which retained some combined schools for a few more years, and some Scandinavian countries, which never abandoned them completely, the Milan congress of 1880 settled the methods controversy in Europe for nearly 100 years. Oralism became dominant everywhere. Signs were relegated to deaf clubs and small groups of deaf people, losing their continuity and halting their development as true languages. The few remaining deaf teachers lost their jobs, and the instruction of deaf persons in Europe became a monopoly of hearing people, for they alone could teach speech.

ORALISM'S RISE TO DOMINANCE IN THE UNITED STATES, 1880–1930

From about 1880 to 1930, speech and lipreading drastically changed the nature of American education of deaf students. Those who believed that sign language and fingerspelling had a place in deaf education constantly were thrown on the defensive by oralists and their allies in the educational establishment and state legislatures. By 1930 oralists had convinced almost everyone that speech and lipreading was the wave of the future, that the method would work with all deaf persons, and that it had economic, educational, and social advantages over other communications methods. Nevertheless, what occurred in most European countries did not happen in the United States. Sign language did not disappear but remained the basis of instruction for at least some students in most state residential institutions, and for all undergraduate students at Gallaudet College.

The public day-school movement, begun in Wisconsin through the efforts of the Phonological Institute of Milwaukee and the personal intervention of Bell, grew in strength around the turn of the century as it promised to offer a relatively inexpensive and socially beneficial method of education. State legislatures in Ohio, Illinois, Michigan, and California accepted this rationale and voted to allow public school districts to teach deaf children in purely oral day-school classes. The comparative cost figures of residential-school and day-school education provided a justification.

In 1900 in Wisconsin each student in the state residential school at Delavan cost the state $316 per year, compared with $150 per year in the day schools. Similarly, a 1910 Massachusetts study showed the per capita cost of residential schools as either $244 or $400 per year, depending upon the institution attended, while the average cost per capita in day schools was only $192 per year.

To advance the cause of oralism, a new, semi-professional organization was established in 1890, the American Association to Promote the Teaching of Speech to the Deaf (AAPTSD), or the Association as it was commonly called. It was the result of oralists' desire to have an organization of their own, separate from the older Convention of American Instructors of the Deaf (CAID), and the largesse of Bell, who gave the Association $25,000 and became its first president. The Association carried on a variety of activities designed to acquaint the public and influential individuals with the goals of oral instruction. It published a journal, the *Association Review*, which competed with the *American Annals of the Deaf*, the official organ of the CAID. *See* VOLTA REVIEW.

The AAPTSD sought to do more than just convince people that deaf persons should communicate orally. It was the Association's goal, as the board of directors declared in 1916, to encourage an "exclusive speech atmosphere" for deaf students, because this would lead to "the highest mastery of speech and lip-reading by deaf children." An exclusive speech atmosphere meant that schools either would have to be completely oral, that is, permit no signs with any students, or must segregate some students in an exclusively oral department and others in a manual department. The latter is what usually happened in state residential schools for deaf children.

The Pennsylvania School for the Deaf at Mount Airy was a pioneer in trying to resolve the methods controversy by, in effect, setting up one school for oral methods and one for manual methods. The reasoning behind this was twofold. First, A. L. E. Crouter, the school's principal, believed strongly in the advantages of oral methods in a purely oral atmosphere. He believed that whenever students were allowed to use signs they would do so, to the detriment of their speech, lipreading skills, English, and general educational progress. Second, however, even Crouter and some other principals realized that not all deaf students could make educational progress without resort to manual communication. For these students, dubbed "oral failures," a manual department was necessary. This worked as follows: when admitted, pupils were placed under oral instruction, and continued their entire education under that method, unless they were found to be mentally or physically disadvantaged, in which case they were given special attention along manual lines.

By the early twentieth century, most residential schools followed this system or a variation of it, establishing both manual and oral departments. The latter grew steadily until after World War I, when about 75 percent of the deaf pupils in American schools were taught entirely or principally by the oral method. By way of comparison, when the *Annals* began compiling methods statistics in 1893, only 25 percent of the students in American schools were instructed primarily through speech and lipreading.

Despite the popularity of oral methods in the early twentieth century, oralists were not satisfied. Indeed, some of them realized just how shrewd E. M. Gallaudet had been in 1868 when he urged the combined method on school principals. John Dutton Wright, principal and founder of the Wright Oral School in New York City, expressed this clearly in 1914, when he wrote, "I believe . . . that the growth of so-called oralism in the essentially manual atmosphere of the 'combined' schools is the greatest danger that *real* speech for the deaf has to face." Wright went on to argue that teaching speech in combined schools would eventually prove to be fatal to oralism, because oralism was not given a fair chance, and thus its results were meager, when deaf students had any familiarity with signs or signers. His solution was the total isolation of deaf children from deaf adults or other deaf children who might engage them in signing.

Sentiments such as those of Wright, though widely held, never succeeded in banishing sign language among deaf persons or in American schools. Sign language persisted in the United States in manual departments of state residential schools, in dormitories away from the watchful eyes of hearing teachers and supervisors, at Gallaudet College, and in the clubs, organizations, and religious groups that knitted together American deaf persons.

DEAF PEOPLE'S RESPONSE TO THE METHODS CONTROVERSY

Deaf people never were completely united in their stance toward the methods controversy. Most wanted to preserve sign language, while recognizing that deaf persons who had intelligible speech and could read lips possessed distinct advantages over those who could not.

Many deaf people in the United States and Europe fought to save sign language. In 1883, for example, the Second National Convention of Deaf-Mutes, with several hundred deaf persons in attendance, unanimously adopted the following resolution: "This Convention, representing the intelligence of 34,000 deaf-mutes of these United States, declare their sentiments in favor of the 'combined system' over the 'pure oral' . . ." In 1891 a moving petition, signed by more than 800 German deaf persons, was sent to William II, Emperor of Germany, begging that the method of teaching deaf people be reconsidered and that, besides articulation, sign language be introduced into their instruction. Similarly, conventions in 1896 at Geneva, 1900 at Paris, and 1902 at Berlin reaffirmed most deaf people's desire to retain sign language in schools for deaf students.

In the United States, the National Association of the Deaf (NAD), especially under the leadership of presidents Olof Hanson (served 1910–1913) and Jay Howard (1913–1917), led the fight for sign language and against pure oralism. During the crucial early years of the twentieth century, the NAD issued publications, passed resolutions, started a film collection to preserve sign language, and wrote letters to newspapers. The NAD also took an active role in state politics when legislators, under pressure from parents and the public relations efforts of the AAPTSD, considered bills to convert their state residential institutions from the combined method to pure oralism. *See* HANSON, OLOF; HOWARD, JAY COOKE; NATIONAL ASSOCIATION OF THE DEAF.

The NAD's stance reflected the reality that pure oralism, a communication method that prohibits sign language and fingerspelling, is pernicious to most deaf people. One reason is that it is an extremely difficult and frustrating method. Persons who lost their hearing after they learned speech, or those who have enough residual hearing to comprehend some speech sounds, usually can be taught intelligible speech without undue effort. For those born profoundly deaf, however, learning to speak well enough to be understood by strangers is a difficult task, requiring many hours of practice. *See* SPEECH TRAINING.

Learning lipreading is not any easier. Many English sounds look the same on the lips. Lipreading skill depends upon a person's ability to guess at the meaning of words from their context. This guesswork is, in turn, dependent on a person's knowledge of English language patterns. The problem is: how can a congenitally deaf person, who had never heard these patterns, acquire an intimate knowledge of them? *See* SPEECHREADING.

Sign language and fingerspelling, by contrast, are easy to learn. They depend upon gross body movements to convey meaning and thus are easily seen, distinguished, and understood. Deaf people argued that sign language, because it can be perceived as easily by the eyes as can sounds by the ear, is "natural," whereas speech and lipreading are "artificial."

Deaf people also struggled against oralism because it would mean the demise of deaf teachers. In 1870, for example, 42 percent of the teachers in American schools for deaf pupils were themselves deaf. By 1920, when oralism had reached the peak of its influence, only 15 percent of the teachers were deaf. Teaching was more than a job for deaf adults, providing professional status, visibility, and respectability within their communities, keeping them in touch with educational trends, and allowing them to influence the lives of deaf youngsters.

The last point is especially crucial, for sign language is not only a communication method. For many deaf people, sign language represents a cultural achievement, a source of pride and identity, not unlike French for francophones in Quebec or Spanish for Chicanos in the American Southwest. Deaf people have maintained that they can never function comfortably and easily with oral communication. Sign language gives deaf people an identity of their own, and allows free and easy communication both in and out of the academic environment. Thus, as the NAD stated in resolutions in 1910 and 1913, sign language is a beautiful language that is priceless to the deaf. The NAD encouraged schools to preserve, and improve, this sign language, and to give systematic instruction in its proper use.

Finally, deaf people challenged the educational claims of oralists. They insisted that instruction in speech and lipreading, while useful to hard-of-hearing or adventitiously deaf children, took time from more important tasks. Instead of learning chemistry or history, they said, students were spending hour after hour in speech and lipreading drill. Thus they might become like parrots, able to repeat sounds on cue, but unable to think about or to know the content needed in their life's work.

THE METHODS CONTROVERSY SINCE THE 1920s

From the late 1920s until the 1960s, the methods controversy languished. European educators remained solidly in favor of pure oral methods, while American educators generally accepted the tenets of oralism but applied them less strictly. Most public residential institutions in the United States continued the combined system that had become standard by the 1920s: elementary-school-age children were taught orally, while signs were used in at least some classes at the high school level. Various private and day schools used pure oral methods for all students, and a few residential schools experimented with the Rochester method, which combined fingerspelling and speech. In the late 1960s, however, the methods controversy, especially in the United States, came back to life.

Studies in the 1960s and 1970s began to analyze the educational achievement of deaf children, and the results called into question the effectiveness of the basically oral approach then in use. The studies showed that only a small percentage of deaf students ever reached a tenth-grade reading level. Moreover, some researchers claimed to discern a positive causal relationship between the use of signs at an early age and deaf people's subsequent maturity, educational achievement, language development, and even lipreading skills. Whatever the validity of these studies, they encouraged a renewed interest in sign language among educators. *See* PSYCHOLINGUISTICS: Language Development.

The American civil rights movement of the 1960s influenced the methods controversy, too. Many deaf persons, especially those who used signs as the primary communication method, saw themselves as a minority group that had suffered a long history of discrimination. Deaf activists, with the assistance of a stronger, reorganized NAD, pushed sign language "out of the closet." They advocated the right of deaf children to learn through their "natural" language of signs, and the right of deaf adults to have trained, certified, sign language interpreters in courtrooms and other places where effective communication was essential to protect deaf individuals' civil rights.

Studies by some linguists, especially William Stokoe and his colleagues at Gallaudet College, also affected attitudes toward communication methods. These linguists began to study ASL to see what it had in common with oral and written languages. They concluded that ASL was a legitimate language, that it had rules of grammar, and that it was capable of expressing abstract ideas and subtleties of thought. Thus, sign language, which had been on the defensive in the United States for 100 years, began to take the offensive against oral methods.

A major outcome of this reawakened interest was the growth, particularly in the 1970s, of a new philosophy called total communication (TC). This term was used as early as 1968 to describe a flexible, try-anything approach to communication in the Santa Ana, California, public schools. In 1968 it also became the basis of communication at the Maryland School for the Deaf. TC implied that schools would use gestures, sign language, voice and lipreading, fingerspelling, reading and writing, and residual hearing.

TC became almost a fad in the 1970s as more and more public residential schools adopted it as their official communication policy. It seemed to have the potential to satisfy everyone, because it was supposed to fit the method—whether oral, aural, or manual—to the needs of each individual.

In practice, however, TC schools most often rely on another compromise, called the simultaneous method and usually dubbed Simcom. *See* SOCIO-LINGUISTICS: Total Communication.

Simcom is a true combined method. It uses manual and oral methods simultaneously. Usually, a manual system with signs for each word and English syntax, such as Signing Exact English or Signed English, is signed while the person also speaks or at least uses lip movements that correspond to the word being signed. In this way, it is claimed, both persons who read lips and those who read signs—or the majority who do a combination of both—are served. *See* MANUALLY CODED ENGLISH.

Despite this latest compromise, the argument over methods, though considerably muted, continues. Oralists claim that Simcom does not produce good speech skills, while proponents of ASL argue that manual systems linked to English are mere pidgin languages. The former would like to eliminate all signs, but the latter would just as soon eliminate all speech as an instructional method.

Today, most people regard l'Epée's and Heinicke's positions as extreme and unrealistic. Knowledge can be transmitted quickly and efficiently with signs, despite what Heinicke said, and speech, for some deaf people at least, is both possible and advantageous, despite what l'Epée believed. More than ever, deaf people themselves are influencing communication decisions, usually advocating greater emphasis on manual communication with young children as well as with older persons.

Bibliography
American Annals of the Deaf (1847–1935).

Bell, Alexander Graham: *Memoir upon the Foundation of a Deaf Variety of the Human Race*, Alexander Graham Bell Association for the Deaf, Washington, D.C., 1969.

Bender, Ruth E.: *The Conquest of Deafness: A History of the Long Struggle to Make Possible Normal Living to Those Handicapped by Lack of Normal Hearing*, rev. ed., Case Western Reserve University, Cleveland, 1970.

Best, Harry: *Deafness and the Deaf in the United States*, Macmillan, New York, 1943.

Boatner, Maxine Tull: *Voice of the Deaf: A Biography of Edward Miner Gallaudet*, Public Affairs Press, Washington, D.C., 1959.

Bruce, Robert V.: *Alexander Graham Bell and the Conquest of Solitude*, Little, Brown, Boston, 1973.

Evans, Lionel: *Total Communication: Structure and Strategy*, Gallaudet College Press, Washington, D.C., 1982.

Gannon, Jack: *Deaf Heritage: A Narrative History of Deaf America*, National Association of the Deaf, Silver Spring, Maryland, 1981.

Garnett, Christopher, B., Jr.: *The Exchange of Letters Between Samuel Heinicke and Abbé Charles Michel de l'Epée*, Vantage Press, New York, 1968.

Moores, Donald F.: *Educating the Deaf: Psychology, Principles, and Practice*, Houghton Mifflin, Boston, 1978.

Volta Review (formerly *Association Review*) (1899–1930).

John V. Van Cleve

A Deaf Commonwealth
The idea of specific minorities isolating themselves in independent enclaves, or separate states, was a spasmodic refrain in the nineteenth-century United States. The American deaf community was not immune to these notions of separation. As early as the 1810s, Laurent Clerc, Thomas Hopkins Gallaudet's French protégé, made a reference to deaf people emigrating to Alabama. But Clerc's plan was not as bold as future proposals. Clerc earlier had alluded to the fact that Congress had donated a tract of land to the American School for the Deaf to aid in raising funds for the school. Clerc believed that, if necessary, part of the land could be sold as funding for the American School and the remaining piece used as a headquarters for the deaf community where some could emigrate after they received an education. Clerc's plan did not elaborate on these general conceptions.

FLOURNOY'S PLAN
Clerc, however, did not have in mind the wide-ranging and perhaps impossible scheme of John Jacobus Flournoy. Flournoy, a Georgian and rather eccentric man, who early became deaf, was born, probably in 1800, in Chatham County, Georgia. He was married three times, and two of the women ran away shortly after the marriage. Flournoy briefly attended the University of Georgia, leaving when he became an object of derision among the students. He was briefly connected with the American School for the Deaf. He committed himself to a South Carolina insane asylum, later releasing himself when he realized he was not going mad. For the latter part of his life he lived on a 600-acre plantation in Jackson County. Flournoy was a cauldron of reforms. He aided in the establishment of a school for deaf students in Georgia, but perhaps because of Flournoy's strange behavior, the legislature later passed a law, which according to Flournoy was promulgated to make "deaf and dumb persons idiots in law and to provide them guardians." Flournoy claimed that he had permitted no one "to insult me with the application of such a law." One of Flournoy's more controversial ideas was a "scheme for a commonwealth of the deaf and dumb."

In 1855 Flournoy, through a pamphlet circulated in the United States and Europe and letters to newspapers and the *American Annals of the Deaf and Dumb*, fanned the flames of controversy by proposing a separate state for deaf people to be controlled solely by them. Suggested names for the area included "Deaf-Mutia," or for euphonics sake, "Gesturia," and finally "Gallaudet." The Georgian proceeded from the premise that hearing people regarded those who were deaf as "inferior and unworthy of profit, influence or authority when well educated." It sharply assessed nineteenth-century hearing attitudes. Advocating the formation of a "Deaf State" out west, about the size of Rhode Island or Connecticut, Flournoy wanted individual control, the government to guarantee this prerogative; the deaf state would pay "pre-emptive right-money" for the land. "This Government," he emphasized, "is to be sacred to the Deaf alone." To the "mute" community would be secured the government and offices of the "small territory or State . . ." The "design" was to exhibit deaf "competency for public and other affairs," thus the "peremptory necessity of this guaranty" from the government.

Flournoy, who considered himself a "sage," did not expect the "entire" United States deaf population to migrate to his proposed commonwealth, only a portion. Believing that deaf people were quite as capable as hearing people, Flournoy stated that the "old cry about the incapacity of men's minds from physical disabilities, I think it were time, now in this intelligent age, to *explode!*" Flournoy was of the opinion that because of the "prejudice" and even "malignance" of the hearing, deaf people were deprived of legitimate offices. "We do not claim *all* offices, nor to do *every* thing," he wrote in a published letter, but to be excluded from many facets of political life was simply not fair. At Hartford, Connecticut, he saw discrimination in relation to deaf people, and although it might be better in New England in the 1850s, the South "contemned, spurned, degraded and abhorred" those who were hearing-impaired. To obviate this discrimination, Flournoy believed it was necessary to form a "powerful oligarchy" and control an area in the west, where no hearing man would be allowed to hold a "lucrative office," in short, a "Deaf-mute Republic." Flournoy desired a "political independence, a STATE SOVEREIGNTY," which solely benefited an "unfortunate *down-trodden* class, for they are down-trodden enough, when the human soul is denied its right because of our bodily imperfection."

REACTION TO THE COMMONWEALTH

Flournoy's scheme received a variety of attention in the deaf community, most of it hostile. Some viewed his sentiments as "impracticable." Edmund Booth, a graduate of the American School, for a time an instructor, and an emigrant to Iowa, claimed that Flournoy belonged to a "class of dreamers," who "while tracing out his castle in the air, gives but superficial attention to the nature of the materials with which it is to be built, or the foundation on which it is to be laid." The "best plan," in Booth's eyes, was for "deaf-mutes to follow the general current, and settle, a few in each neighborhood, and work at whatever mechanical occupation they may have learned while in school." The wisest course was to "let the mutes remain as they are—scattered and in one sense lost—among their hearing

associates." Thomas Gallaudet thought Flournoy's plans the "result of a morbid state of feeling, a dislike to the society of hearing men." To most it seemed better to remain where they were comparatively well situated than to "follow what might prove to be a '*will-o-the-wisp*' leading us onward to the swamps of speculation and vagabondism." *See* BOOTH, EDMUND.

Although several considered Flournoy and his plan impossible and impractical, much of the debate centered around the idea of owning land and keeping control of it among deaf families. Flournoy wanted to assure this fact legally, but others felt that it would never be accepted constitutionally. In addition, the suggestion that hearing children be sent away was unthinkable because it broke "endearing ties." Booth, who did not favor emigration to the west, and other important individuals in the deaf community aligned themselves against Flournoy. The Reverend William W. Turner, principal of the American School for the Deaf, made his objections known in print. The editor of the *American Annals*, Samuel Porter, referred to Flournoy's plan as "obnoxious sentiments" which he persisted in "promulgating." He asked his readers if they would be "any better received if uttered by a hearing man." Some, like P. A. Emery, a deaf instructor at the Indiana Institution for the Deaf and Dumb, favored a compromise such as buying a specific amount of land, encouraging migration by deaf people, and waiting for the results. Unquestionably, however, Flournoy's idea for a separate deaf state was the most elaborate in the nineteenth century. *See* AMERICAN ANNALS OF THE DEAF.

Later in the nineteenth century, Alexander Graham Bell, who feared the "formation of a deaf variety of the Human race," vehemently opposed Flournoy's idea. Desirous of completely integrating deaf people into the hearing world, Bell worried that large deaf families would migrate to Flournoy's community and produce more deaf offspring, who would in turn marry other children of parents with genetic deafness. It could be anticipated that in a few generations there would be established a "permanent race of deaf-mutes with a language and literature of its own." Bell simply could not tolerate this idea, suggesting that a law be enacted forbidding intermarriage among deaf people. Bell was frightened that the concept of a separate deaf community might still be favored by some individuals and could "therefore be revived in organized shape at any time." Apparently it had, for Bell was informed that a European philanthropist had begun the colonization of a tract of land in Manitoba with the arrival of 24 deaf members.

The debate over the establishment of a segregated deaf enclave brought out another issue directly related to controlling communities. Flournoy's conception seemed to imply isolation from the hearing world that would be strictly supervised. Apparently because he was rather "odd,' Flournoy had suffered numerous rebuffs by hearing persons and felt that a self-imposed boundary was necessary. Those like Booth and Turner, the leading spokespersons for the deaf community, believed that deaf people did better by being scattered throughout the nation. This integration assured interaction between the two worlds and would hopefully benefit all concerned. They detested the suggestion that deaf people should willingly remove themselves from most contact with hearing society; the mixture of deaf and hearing, although deaf persons in the nineteenth century were the subject of much derision, should not be destroyed by a fanciful scheme such as Flournoy's.

COMPARISON WITH BLACK SEPARATISTS

Spanning much of the nineteenth century, the idea of a deaf commonwealth or some kind of separate entity owned and controlled by deaf people did not differ dramatically from the calculations of others who desired something akin to this for black people. The difference was that the idea relating to a segregated deaf enclave died by the turn of the twentieth century but continued until recent times among Afro-Americans, especially the black Muslims. Some deaf people must have felt as segregated from the hearing world as blacks did from whites through legal separation. Thus, the desire to control one's own fate without outside interference led to the proposal of these schemes. Moreover, the fact that deaf people were treated through much of the nineteenth and early twentieth centuries as a distinctive minority gave further support to those who suggested a separation from hearing society. The American deaf community resisted such plans and continued to struggle for their rights and fought for concessions within the confines of the hearing world.

Bibliography

American Annals of the Deaf and Dumb, correspondence, vol. 8, 1856, vol. 10, 1858.

Bell, Alexander Graham: "Upon the Formation of a Deaf Variety of the Human Race," paper presented to the National Academy of Sciences, New Haven, Connecticut, November 13, 1883, Rare Book Collection, Gallaudet College Archives.

Booth, Edmund: "On Emigration to the West by Deaf Mutes," *American Annals of the Deaf and Dumb*, vol. 10, pp. 46–51, 1858.

Coulter, E. Merton: "John Jacobus Flournoy," in Kenneth Coleman and Charles Stephen Gurr, *Dictionary of Georgia Biography*, vol. 1, pp. 313–314, University of Georgia Press, Athens, 1983.

Barry A. Crouch

Congress of Milan

The Congress of Milan was a momentous event. In September 1880, a group of educators from several European countries and the United States met in Milan, Italy, and declared that sign language had no legitimate place in the education or the lives of deaf people. Deaf persons should speak and lipread in their national oral language, the congress stated, for oral skills would rescue them from their ignorance and brutish ways; their communication problems, isolation, and clannishness would disappear; and they would be restored to society. The old debate over the relative value of sign language and speech, the congress declared, was concluded.

The ramifications of the congress spread beyond northern Italy, touching deaf Europeans, deaf Americans, and many of those deaf persons who lived, or would live, in Asia, Latin America, and Africa. Hearing teachers and missionaries to deaf people carried the message of Milan throughout the world. Far from western Europe and the United States, oralism was victorious.

While this much is generally accepted by scholars, they disagree about the value of the congress. Those who agree with the resolutions passed at Milan see it as the turning point that liberated deaf individuals and initiated an era of educational progress and social integration. Those who advocate sign languages, however, argue that the Congress of Milan was the worst disaster to befall the deaf community in modern times, that forcing all deaf people to communicate orally imprisoned them in decades of social frustration, weakened their cultural heritage, rendered education ineffective, and blocked them from developing their full human potential by robbing them of their natural language.

FIRST CONGRESS

The immediate catalyst for the Congress of Milan was a seemingly insignificant meeting two years earlier in Paris, a gathering that demonstrated how a small group of committed individuals can exert influence far greater than their numbers warrant. During the 1878 French Universal Exhibition, a self-proclaimed International Congress for the Improvement of the Condition of Deaf-Mutes resolved that "preference should be given to the method of articulation and lip-reading" in educating deaf persons. It further declared that a future congress should be held in Italy to discuss this issue and others related to deaf welfare, and it appointed a Committee of Organization to arrange the congress.

Despite its grandiose title, however, the Paris Congress was hardly representative of experienced educators of deaf pupils. For one thing, it was international in name only. A mere 27 delegates attended, 23 of whom were from France. Second, of the 23 French representatives, only one, Abbé Lambert, chaplain of the French National Institution established by the Abbé de l'Epée, was from a school that used sign language; yet, in 1878, these schools constituted a majority in France. The unrepresentative nature of this meeting apparently was due to its sponsors, the Pereire Society of France, and the unwillingness of many French teachers and administrators to be associated with this group.

Isaac and Eugene Pereire, wealthy grandsons of Jacobo Rodriguez Pereire (1715–1780), were behind the Pereire Society. Its purpose was twofold. First, it was designed to restore the name of Jacobo Pereire to prominence as the founder of education for deaf children in France. A Portuguese who emigrated to Bordeaux, France, Pereire had used speech and lipreading, aided by finger movements to indicate positions of the speech organs, to teach a small number of deaf students in exchange for substantial fees. His work impressed mideighteenth century Frenchmen, when two of his most able pupils gave demonstrations of their speech and lipreading ability before the Academy of Sciences in Paris. Later, though, Pereire was eclipsed by l'Epée, who taught many more pupils, used sign language, and established a large institution that would accept anyone, even indigent pupils.

The second goal of the Pereire Society, then, was to discredit l'Epée and sign language by encouraging the use of speech and lipreading. To this end, the society established the oral Pereire School in Paris and funded various projects to convince the public that deaf people were best taught by oral means. One of these projects was the International Congress for the Improvement of the Condition of Deaf-Mutes, the Paris Congress, one of whose organizers was Monsieur Magnat, the principal of the Pereire School.

Magnat also was a member of the Committee of Organization selected by the 1878 meeting to plan future congresses. Its other members were mostly French supporters of oral teaching methods, though Abbé Lambert of the Paris Institution and two foreign oralists, Monsieur Borg of Stockholm and the Abbé Balestra of the school for deaf children in Como, Italy, also were chosen. Isaac and Eugene Pereire served as honorary members of the Committee of Organization.

The machinations of the Pereire Society and its Paris Congress succeeded because the climate of opinion already had begun swinging toward the idea that each nation's oral language should supplant sign language as the best communication method for deaf people. This idea, new to the United States, France, Italy, and to some extent England, was rapidly gaining proponents in the late nineteenth century. It was attractive to parents of deaf children, to neophyte teachers without sophisticated sign language skills, to certain wealthy individuals (especially Alexander Graham Bell in the United States, B. St. John Ackers in England, and the Pereires in France), to a nationalistic public, and to many of the clerics who dominated deaf education in France and Italy.

METHODS IN FRANCE

By the late 1870s French oralists and their influential supporters were pressuring the French government to change its policy for educating deaf pupils. Since l'Epée's time, French public institutions for deaf children had been overwhelmingly manual in their orientation, that is, they used sign language as the basis for instruction. In the parlance of the day, the "French method" was the term used to describe teaching in sign language, as opposed to the "German method" that followed the principles of the German oralist teacher Samuel Heinicke. But this was changing rapidly.

In the late 1870s, the French Ministry of the Interior, responding to the entreaties of oralists, ordered a report made of French methods of educating deaf people. Oscar Claveau, Inspector General of the Ministry of the Interior, and a person who knew no sign language himself, prepared the report.

Claveau argued that sign language lacked grammar and therefore was unsuitable as a vehicle for instruction. He went on to say that a switch from the use of signs to the use of oral French alone might injure the general education of deaf people. He considered this an insignificant drawback, however, for he commented that deaf persons would know French and be able to communicate with the rest of society, a point always emphasized by oralists. In the heightened nationalism of the late nineteenth century, when European nations gloried in their national language, Claveau's report met a positive response.

The Minister of the Interior acted on these illusions. He ordered that all schools under the Ministry's control use only oral French to instruct their deaf pupils, and he fired the principal of the important Paris Institution, Martin Etcheverry, a supporter of the use of both sign language and French, the so-called combined system. The Minister then named Louis Peyron, an otologist, to replace Etcheverry.

The selection of an otologist to head France's largest and most influential school for deaf people was in itself a significant step. It indicated that the pathological perspective on deafness had gained the forefront in France. To a medical person, deafness is above all a disease, a pathology, to be cured or minimized. Oralism, with its promise of restoring the deaf person to society or making him or her figuratively less "diseased" and more normal, easily fits the pathological model. Sign language, on the other hand, recognizes deaf people's unique situation and attempts to help them accommodate to it, not to deny their differentness. Peyron, thus, was a willing oralist.

The Minister of the Interior's directive banishing sign language had ramifications beyond Paris. The Ministry directly controlled the three national institutions for deaf children, enrolling some 600 pupils, and also controlled the regional and departmental schools throughout France. Moreover, private schools that received state support felt the effect of the Ministry's decree. France, however, was not alone in its rapid conversion from sign language to oralism.

METHODS IN ITALY

The Congress of Milan was a joint effort of French and Italian teachers, who were drawn together by political events. In 1858 and 1859, under Napoleon III, France assisted the Italian state of Sardinia in its quest to restore the northern province of Lombardy, which had been taken by Austria. The French also were involved in Italy's unification, and in 1870, as a result of the Franco-Prussian War, France withdrew its soldiers, who had assisted the Pope in controlling central Italy, thus removing a final obstacle to the establishment of a single Italian nation under a central, and secular, government. Ironically, although oral methods were identified throughout most of the nineteenth century with German educators, German representation and influence at the Congress of Milan was minimal. The Franco-Prussian War and France's consequent loss of Alsace-Lorraine to Germany divided the French and Germans but drove the French and Italians together.

Like their French counterparts, Italian schools at first used sign language to teach deaf pupils. Abbé Silvestri, who had studied with l'Epée, opened the first school for deaf Italians in Rome in 1784, basing its instruction on the methods Silvestri learned in Paris. Similarly, Ottavio Assorotti, a disciple of l'Epée's successor, Abbé Sicard, established the second Italian school for deaf children in Genoa. Later schools founded on the manual method were those of Father Tommasso Pendola at Siena, Abbé Balestra at Como, and Abbé Giulo Tarra at Milan. As late as 1866, when Edward Miner Gallaudet, president of the National Deaf-Mute College in Washington, D.C. (later renamed Gallaudet College), visited Italy, Tarra told him that no more than one-third of his pupils could be taught successfully with speech alone. By the 1870s, however, Tarra no longer admitted this.

Abbé Balestra was the first important Italian educator to change to oralism. He then convinced Pendola of oralism's benefits, and Pendola set out to convince other Italian teachers and administrators. By 1871 the schools at Turin, Venice, Bologna, Rome, Naples, Palermo, and the Royal Institution at Milan all were using oral Italian rather than sign language to teach their deaf pupils. Tarra had switched his Milan school for indigent deaf children in 1870. Pendola, with the zeal typical of a convert, launched a journal dedicated to oralism, *Dell' educazione dei sordo-muti en Italia*, and moved to unify support for oral language by calling the first Italian Congress of Educators of the Deaf at Siena in 1874. This occurred five years before the first French National Congress, sponsored by the Pereire Society, convened at Lyons in 1879.

The French-Italian connection was strengthened by the personal efforts of Balestra. The Abbé was one of the few non-French representatives to attend the International Congress at Paris in 1878, and he was the only non-Frenchman who played a significant role. Predictably, he argued to the congress that it should declare itself fully in support of oralism and totally opposed to the use of sign language or fingerspelling in any context. Although the congress did not completely accept Balestra's recommendation, it did name him one of the two non-French members of the Committee of Organization for the next international congress, and it did agree to hold that meeting in the staunchly oral Italy.

PARTICIPANTS

In early 1880 the Committee of Organization sent invitations "To the Teachers and Friends of the Deaf and Dumb" in Europe and the United States, urging them to attend the Milan convention "for the improvement of the condition of the deaf and dumb." The invitation said that French would be the official conference language, but oral comments in other languages were welcome. The committee stipulated no rules for convention membership; all persons, whether principals, teachers, or friends, were equally welcome and would be heard. Among the nations attending, only the United States attempted to send an official or representative group of delegates.

The Conference of Principals of American Institutions for the Deaf selected the American delegates. They constituted an impressive group with years of professional and personal contact with the deaf community. The leader was Edward Miner Gallaudet, the president of the National Deaf-Mute College and the son of a deaf woman, Sophia Fowler Gallaudet, and of the founder of the American School for the Deaf, Thomas Hopkins Gallaudet. Gallaudet's older brother, Thomas, rector of St. Ann's Church for the Deaf in New York City, was another delegate. Also from New York were the Reverend Charles A. Stoddard, a member of the board of directors of the New York School for the Deaf, and Isaac Lewis Peet, principal of the same school. The sole deaf delegate to the Milan conference was James Denison, the principal of the Kendall School in Washington, D.C., a position he held for 40 years. Together, these five Americans, representing the Conference of Principals, attended on behalf of 51 schools and some 6000 pupils.

The delegates from England each attended on his or her own, not as an elected delegate of a representative group of educators, and all but two were committed oralists before they went to Milan. Two were essentially private individuals, B. St. John Ackers and his wife, Louisa M. J. Ackers, who had a deaf child. They had established the Society for Training Teachers of the Deaf and for the Diffusion of the German System in England, a group similar to the Pereire Society in France and to Alexander Graham Bell's American Association to Promote the Teaching of Speech to the Deaf in the United States. Two others were associated with the Ackers: A. A. Kinsey, the principal of the Training College for Teachers of the Deaf, on the German system, and David Buxton, the secretary of the Society for Training Teachers of the Deaf. Susanna Hall and Thomas Arnold, two other attendees from England, both headed strictly oral private schools for deaf children, the former at Kensington and the latter at Northampton. The only English delegates who were skeptical about oralism were the Reverend W. Stainer and Richard Elliott, headmaster of the Old Kent Road Asylum for the Deaf and Dumb in London. The English-speaking delegates, in any case, were far outnumbered by those from Italy and France.

Eighty-seven delegates of the total 164 were from Italy. Of these, 46 were from Milan. Together these 46 people represented less than half of the students of one English delegate, Richard Elliott. Nearly all were ecclesiastics, either priests or, more frequently, members of Catholic religious brotherhoods, and few were experienced teachers or administrators of schools for deaf children. After the convention met, they all voted in favor of oral teaching.

The French delegates were a similar group. There were 56, the majority of whom were members of the Brotherhood of Saint-Gabriel, some of whose convention expenses were paid by the Pereire Society. The French delegates too, despite private reservations expressed to the Americans, voted in favor of eliminating sign language from the instruction and lives of deaf people.

A smattering of persons from other countries attended as well. Three of these—Madam Rosing of Norway, M. Kierkegaard-Ekbohrn, the rector of the Swedish Institute for the Deaf and Dumb at Bollnas, and Herr Treibel, the director of the Royal Institute for Deaf-Mutes in Berlin—actually took part, to some extent, in the conference's proceedings. Nevertheless, from start to finish, the Congress of Milan was planned, orchestrated, and concluded by the huge bloc of Italian and French oralists.

PROCEEDINGS

The Congress of Milan convened on September 6, 1880, in the Royal Technical Institution of Santa Marta with an opening address by Augusto Zucchi, the president of the Council of the Royal Institution for the Deaf of Milan, and proceeded according to the plans of the Committee of Organization. The reading of the rules was followed by election of officers from a list prepared in advance. The president was Abbé Guilio Tarra, an eloquent defender of oral language. The other major officer was another Italian, Pasquale Fornari, a teacher at the Royal School for the Deaf in Milan, who was chosen general secretary. Eight other delegates held positions, but they were largely honorary, giving their holders no direct influence over the convention's proceedings. Of these, only Peet, the vice president of the "English-Speaking Section," was not already committed to oralism.

The real business of the conference began on the second day. It was moved and passed that the conference should discuss first the question of methods in the teaching of deaf children. Although this issue was placed third on the agenda prepared by the Committee of Organization, it was in fact the major reason for the convention.

The opening tribute to oralism was delivered by Louisa Ackers. Reading her paper in French, she recounted how she and her husband had studied all educational methods to discover the best one for their deaf child. They concluded that the German system, with its alleged ability to teach oral language and make deaf children fit comfortably into society's mainstream, was the best. Eleven other speakers followed. The Gallaudet brothers and Richard Elliott spoke in favor of the combined system, the rest in favor of "pure oralism," that is, education by means of speech and lipreading alone.

The Abbé Tarra briefly eulogized the oral system and then proposed a resolution in its favor. Peet moved the resolution be referred to committee, since this was only the first day of a six-day convention and because the question of methods was so central to deaf education. Peet's motion was defeated, and the following resolution was offered: "The Congress considering the incontestable superiority of speech over signs in restoring the deaf-mute to society, and in giving him a more perfect knowledge of language, declares that the Oral method ought to be preferred to that of signs for the education and instruction of the deaf and dumb." Only the five Americans and Elliott voted against it.

The following days of the convention were divided between further discussions, passages of resolutions, and demonstrations of the speaking and speechreading abilities of Italian students. The longest speech was the presidential address of Tarra, which was spread over two days and consisted of a long emotional harangue against sign language. Leaving this issue aside, Edward Gallaudet spoke in favor of establishing colleges for deaf people. Here too, however, the conference's majority demonstrated their differences with the Americans and the American approach to deaf people.

Despite their professed allegiance to the elevation and education of deaf persons, the conference delegates could not agree with Gallaudet that college education was an important issue. Monsieur Hugentobler, head of a private school in Lyons, insisted that there were not enough deaf people to warrant a separate college. Padre Marchio, from the Royal Institution for the Deaf in Siena, argued that too many deaf people lacked even a common school education for the conference to endorse a college. A. A. Kinsey from England patronizingly said that deaf people were not yet ready for college, since they lacked perfect knowledge of English, which, he insisted, was more important than higher education. Only Madam Rosing from Christiana, Norway, protested Kinsey's remarks, saying that Norway had two university-educated deaf individuals who held responsible government positions. The result was not ringing support for the idea that higher education should be open to deaf people, but merely a resolution urging all national governments to educate their deaf citizens.

DEMONSTRATIONS

For many participants, the highlight of the Congress of Milan and the most convincing evidence in support of the pure oral method was the series of exhibitions or demonstrations arranged by the Italian schools. The conference organizers called these "examinations." In brief, a child's teacher would ask, in spoken Italian, a question of one of his students. The student, in turn, would then reply in spoken Italian, and all commentators agreed that the answers were given in understandable speech and were appropriate to the question, presumably showing that the student had lipread the teacher perfectly. Moreover, it was explained to the delegates that these were students who had been trained in the pure oral method, without any use of signs whatever. At least some delegates, however, were suspicious of these claims.

For one thing, Elliott, Edward Gallaudet, and Denison, who all published reports on the congress, stated their impression that on several occasions the students began their answers before the questions were completed. All three men believed this indicated that the questions and answers had been rehearsed beforehand. Additional evidence of this was that the questions all followed a written program, prepared ahead of time and distributed to the delegates. If this was true, then the impression that the students were understanding the questions through lipreading was false.

The significance of the students' clear speech also is questionable. The delegates were not given any information about the background, the degree of deafness, and the age at onset of hearing loss of the students who spoke. Children who lose their hearing after learning speech or who suffer from mild hearing impairments naturally have intelligible speech, while those who are born profoundly deaf do not. Denison reported that Italian teachers told him privately that the star pupils, those to whom most questions were addressed, were all adventitiously deaf. Moreover, the entire Italian educational effort apparently was directed disproportionately at those deaf people most likely to succeed with speech and lipreading.

The oralists' own statistics, distributed at the Congress of Milan, appear to support this conclusion. In the province of Lombardy, congenitally deaf persons outnumbered those who were adventitiously deaf nearly six to one. Yet in the Royal Institution at Milan, 63 percent of the students were reported as adventitiously deaf, as were 70 percent of those in Tarra's Milanese school for indigent deaf children. Fifty percent of all deaf children in Italian schools were adventitiously deaf, but only 18 percent of the entire Italian deaf population became deaf after birth. While there is always the possibility that these statistics do not reveal other vital information, the conclusion seems inescapable that Italian schools practiced their oral methods primarily on those deaf people who could, as even sign language proponents agreed, most easily benefit from and demonstrate the success of speech.

The unusual perspective of Denison, as the only deaf individual attending this international convention for the good of deaf people, provided one more critique of the "examinations." Denison wrote in his report that during the demonstrations of speech and lipreading he was sitting near the door where he could observe pupils before they entered the room to be examined. There, outside the gaze of their teachers and, they believed, unseen by adults, they signed among themselves. Later, Denison continued, he met some of the students outside the building and engaged them in sign language conversation. They admitted using signs when alone, thus calling into question the Italian and French teachers' claims that their methods were so successful that their students neither knew nor wanted to use sign language.

EFFECTS

There is little doubt that the Congress of Milan did have an impact on deaf education and the history of deaf people, especially in Europe. It served as a symbol and as a useful argument to those who would eliminate signs and instruct deaf children with oral language alone, and it occurred at a propitious time.

In both Europe and the United States, the late nineteenth century was a period of rapid expansion of educational programs. To a greater extent than before, mass education was touted as a tool of social engineering, one that would assist diverse groups in blending into the national culture. Faith in the application of new ideas and methods to solving humanity's problems was never higher. It seemed reasonable and proper, people believed, that deaf persons should learn English, or French, or Italian and thus free themselves from the results of a disability that formerly had set them apart from hearing society and that had caused them suffering. The Congress of Milan gave oralists, who shared these beliefs with most people, added momentum, and they pushed their advantage.

They were assisted in their efforts by popular impressions of the congress. Although its delegates were overwhelmingly from France and Italy, and even though they expressed extreme positions that were hardly representative of the whole body of persons involved in deaf education, the congress was seen by an innocent public as something different from what it actually was. A few days after the congress closed, for example, the London *Times* favorably reported on its proceedings. The *Times* claimed that "no more representative group could have been collected." Furthermore, the paper asserted that the congress demonstrated such "virtual unanimity" for teaching deaf people in oral language that it seemed "to overbear all possibility of opposition." Such strong statements were repeated elsewhere and exploited by all oralists.

The Society for Diffusing the German System in the United Kingdom prepared a report on the Milan Congress, for example, and followed this with a convention in 1881. Meeting in London, 30 delegates from English oral schools discussed the Milan Congress. They passed resolutions in favor of oral teaching and urged A. J. Mundella, the Minister of Education, to put the government solidly behind teaching in spoken English rather than in sign language.

Even Richard Elliott, the sole non-American proponent of the combined system in Milan, succumbed to pressure from the public and from parents after his return from the congress. He recommended that his school try pure oralism, though he admitted he was not optimistic about the experiment. In 1881 he visited seven schools in Belgium and France and found they all had banished sign language. Most perceptively, Elliott noted that although he found the orally trained Italian deaf students intellectually inferior to manually educated English students, the former "possessed what nine people out of ten would value more, because they understand it better, a readier means of communication." That is, they could talk.

Following the Congress of Milan, European schools for deaf children nearly unanimously converted to oralism. European deaf communities, robbed of facile communication in their schools, without deaf teachers to pass on their cultural heritage, and without linguistic continuity, declined in influence. Deaf Americans, although influenced by the Congress of Milan, never succumbed completely to its demands.

Bibliography

Arnold, Thomas: *Education of the Deaf*, revised by A. Farrar, National College of Teachers of the Deaf, London, 1923.

Bender, Ruth E.: *The Conquest of Deafness*, Case Western Reserve, Cleveland, 1970.

Denison, James: "Impressions of the Milan Convention," *Americans Annals of the Deaf*, 26:41–50, 1881.

Elliott, Richard: "The Milan Congress and the Future of the Education of the Deaf and Dumb," *American Annals of the Deaf*, 27:146–158, 1882.

Fay, Edward A.: "The International Congress," *American Annals of the Deaf*, 24:56–57, 1879.

Gallaudet, Edward M.: "The Milan Convention," *American Annals of the Deaf*, 26:1–16, 1881.

Hull, Susanna E.: "Letter to Miss Harriet B. Rogers," *Clarke School for the Deaf*, *Reports*, pp. 35–43, 1880.

Kinsey, A. A.: *Report of the Proceedings of the International Congress on the Education of the Deaf*, W. H. Allen, London, 1880.

Lane, Harlan: *When the Mind Hears: A History of the Deaf*, Random House, New York, 1984.

John V. Van Cleve

Twentieth Century

In the twentieth century deaf people have struggled to define to the hearing world exactly who they are. In the eighteenth and much of the nineteenth centuries, when social reformers first discovered deaf people, this problem was less acute: those who could not hear were assumed to be unfortunates, incomplete humans, individuals to be pitied and perhaps saved. Thus, hearing persons who felt a religious mission to uplift those less fortunate often shaped deaf people's lives. American Thomas Hopkins Gallaudet and Frenchman Abbé de l'Epée epitomized the interaction of reformers and deaf people in a simple past. Each had a burning zeal to seek moral justification for his existence, a justification each found in his missions to deaf people.

In the United States, however, this simplistic and paternalistic attitude toward deaf persons quickly gave way to more complex considerations. By the late nineteenth century deaf Americans were emerging as something very different from forlorn objects of pity. With education open to them, with concentrations of deaf people in urban areas and around residential schools, with the relatively fluid and extremely mobile nature of American society, deaf individuals joined together to take control of their own lives and form a cultural community. They married each other, established their own organizations, chose their own leaders, taught in schools for children like themselves, founded their own businesses, and began their own periodicals. By 1900 a deaf culture had begun to emerge in the United States; yet, decades later, the hearing world still did not understand or accept the identity deaf people created for themselves.

INTERNATIONAL CONGRESS OF 1900

The twentieth century began as the nineteenth had ended: deaf Americans were under pressure to assimilate, and deaf Europeans were struggling to retain minimal human rights. Americans struggled continuously and with some success, but Europeans were oppressed and demoralized by hearing educators who believed them unfit for higher education and incapable of understanding their own situation.

The International Congress for the Study of Questions of Education and Assistance to the Deaf, held in Paris in 1900, highlighted the sad state of things in Europe. Hearing organizers divided the congress into two sections, one for hearing delegates and one for deaf delegates. The hearing section, dominated by French and Germans, refused the deaf section's pleas that the congress conclude with a joint session to consider resolutions. Instead, the hearing section passed its own resolutions, designed to keep deaf Europeans weak, ignorant, and dependent. They voted to reaffirm the Congress of Milan position in favor of speech for deaf people, to support the use of textbooks prepared for deaf children, to encourage the separation of hard-of-hearing pupils from deaf pupils, to build cooperation between physicians and teachers in schools for deaf children, and to favor primary and vocational, rather than secondary or collegiate, education for all deaf people.

The deaf delegates, by contrast, showed by their resolutions that deaf Europeans in 1900 defined their needs differently than did the hearing professionals who claimed to speak for them. Specifically, the deaf section rejected the Milan resolution and favored the use of sign language and speech in education. They also pressed for secondary and higher education opportunities for deaf people, not merely primary and vocational education. They insisted that they should be considered citizens with the same employment rights as hearing people, and were particularly insistent that government employment be made available to deaf workers. They wished to see schools for deaf pupils hire qualified deaf teachers, a practice at one time common in the United States and France, but one that was being curtailed in the United States and eliminated practically everywhere else. Finally, believing that deaf people throughout the world shared a bond of common experience, and hopeful of more international exchange of assistance and encouragement, they called for the creation of a uniform sign language to be used in all nations.

The issues raised by the deaf section of the 1900 congress were not all equally relevant to Americans. Higher education was open to deaf people in the United States, for example, and schools were still hiring some deaf teachers and using sign language to instruct a portion of their students. American deaf people had achieved a level of independence and self-respect that Europeans envied. Still, at the outset of the twentieth century, deaf people in the United States were concerned about three broad issues: preservation of their nascent culture and community, elimination of the vestiges of paternalism and inequality, and employment.

CULTURAL PRESERVATION

As the twentieth century began, assimilationists, persons who wanted all deviant or different people to blend into the fabric of American life and be like everyone else, challenged the idea of a separate deaf culture. As they criticized immigrants for their languages and tendency to stick together, so too they criticized deaf people. This was most felt in the schools, because for deaf children, who usually have hearing parents, the schools were the most important socialization agents. By 1900 deaf Americans were concerned because more and more state residential schools were trying to force their students to learn without sign language, which was the bond that both united the deaf community and set it apart from hearing society. Moreover, the percentage of deaf teachers, persons who could pass on deaf culture and awareness of the deaf community to deaf children, was declining sharply: in 1870, 41 percent of all teachers of deaf pupils were themselves deaf, by 1900 less than 19 percent.

Deaf people fought against assimilation both directly and indirectly. The National Association of the Deaf (NAD), the state deaf associations, and individuals lobbied, sent letters, and wrote editorials decrying the downfall of sign language in the schools and the loss of deaf teachers. To try to preserve sign language, the NAD, under the leadership of George Veditz, began to make films of expert signers. These were to be shown to deaf gatherings and kept for future generations who might not be exposed to skilled signers. J. Schuyler Long, deaf principal of the Iowa School for the Deaf, published in 1909 and again in 1918 *The Sign Language: A Manual of Signs* to help standardize signs since they were no longer taught in schools, and to preserve the richness of sign language for the future.

Direct attempts to counter assimilation by preserving sign language may have been less significant to the long-term viability of the deaf community than the creation and strengthening of institutions. By the early twentieth century, there were deaf organizations of many kinds in the United States, and more were continuously being formed. The NAD was the oldest and most vocal. Under the strong leadership of presidents Olof Hanson, J. Cooke Howard, and Veditz, the NAD battled for deaf rights on many fronts in the first two decades after 1900. On a day-to-day basis, local social organizations like the Union League of New York were probably even more important. They fielded athletic teams, raised money for charitable causes, and provided a sense of common belonging and purpose for otherwise scattered or isolated deaf individuals.

Religious involvement also grew among deaf people during this period. Although the Episcopal Church had a long history of proselytizing among deaf persons, shortly after 1900 other denominations became involved. The Missouri Synod of the Lutheran Church, for example, established in 1903 the Ephphatha Conference of Workers Among the Deaf. John W. Michaels became the first deaf person ordained as a Southern Baptist minister in 1905; he organized the Southern Baptist Ministry to the Deaf shortly after. In 1907 Hebrew Associations of the Deaf were established in New York City and Philadelphia. *See* Religion, Jewish; Religion, Protestant.

An organization of a different kind was the National Fraternal Society of the Deaf, which was founded by a group of deaf men in 1901 and incorporated in Illinois in 1907. Its stated purpose was to provide life and disability insurance for its deaf members. All deaf people at that time had difficulty getting life insurance. The major insurers, fearing that deaf people were more liable to accidental death than hearing persons, either refused to sell them insurance, charged them higher than normal rates, or added a clause making the policy invalid in case of accidental death. In addition to providing insurance, however, the National Fraternal Society of the Deaf, like the other organizations of deaf people that proliferated in the early twentieth century, served to keep deaf people together, to provide them with opportunities to control their own lives, and to prevent their cultural assimilation into the hearing world. *See* National Fraternal Society of the Deaf.

Paternalism

Just as most deaf Americans rejected total enculturation, the majority also rejected paternalism and the discrimination it inevitably entails. The deaf community's efforts to counter this can be traced by examining their attitude toward preferential tax treatment, the administration of schools, driving rights, and deaf beggars.

The question of preferential tax treatment for deaf persons has arisen many times in the twentieth century. For example, in 1905 a Texas law exempted deaf people, along with certain other supposed unfortunates, from paying the poll tax. Deaf Texans were so irate at this that they petitioned the state legislature to remove deaf individuals from the class of those deemed incapable of paying their own taxes. When the Connecticut legislature was considering a bill in 1913 that would have classified persons who were deaf with those who were blind and thus exempt them from state taxes, deaf persons testified against the bill.

While it may seem strange that people would testify against tax privileges for themselves, deaf groups have done so repeatedly in the twentieth century. This has been necessary, they have believed, to convince the hearing world that while deaf people are different they are not inferior; and they certainly do not want to be wards of the state in matters of taxation.

Deaf people have not wished to be wards of the state in matters of education either. Together with their hearing allies in the Convention of American Instructors of the Deaf, they tried to convince states to rename their state residential institutions "schools" and to transfer authority over them to each state's education department. In 1907, for example, the NAD passed a resolution arguing that operating schools for deaf people was not an act of charity or paternal benevolence but a duty of the state. Deaf children, the NAD insisted, had the same right to free public education as hearing children. A 1919 editorial in the *Silent Worker* summarized the issue by criticizing an Illinois law that placed the state's deaf school under the jurisdiction of the Department of Public Welfare. J. H. Cloud wrote that Illinois should recognize that the state was "discharging an inherent obligation—not bestowing a charity" when it educated deaf children.

Discrimination also came under attack by deaf people in the early twentieth century, especially as it applied to driving privileges. With the spread of automobiles, increasing traffic congestion, and rising numbers of accidents, states began passing licensing laws in the 1920s, laws that sometimes classified deaf people as unfit to drive. Local groups from deaf communities in Pennsylvania and California, for instance, formed to protect the deaf individual's right to drive in those states. The NAD established a committee to compile statistics on deaf peoples' driving records and to monitor state legislation that might discriminate against deaf drivers. Accident reports seemed to show that deaf drivers were less likely than their hearing counterparts to have accidents. Although states eventually permitted deaf people to drive, the fact remains that the deaf community was forced to act to protect itself from a hearing world that could not, or would not, understand it. *See* DRIVING RESTRICTIONS.

An even more troubling problem to many deaf persons, however, was deaf beggars, who threatened to undermine all the gains deaf people had made in years of organized effort. Educated and employed deaf people were horrified by the sight of a person seeking handouts on the basis of deafness. To admit that a deaf person had reason to beg would be to admit that deaf people were appropriate objects of pity and charity, that their well-being depended upon the benevolence of the hearing community rather than on their rights as self-respecting and productive citizens. Consequently, articulate members of the deaf community railed against deaf beggars at every opportunity, and many insisted that most begging was not done by bona fide deaf persons but by hearing impostors. The NAD in 1910 went on record as favoring "stringent laws" that would make begging by deaf people or deaf impostors a "penal offense." Begging placed a deaf person in the role of supplicant to those who hear, which reenforced the paternalism against which deaf people struggled.

By the 1930s begging was no longer seen as a problem, but deaf peddling was. Peddling carried the same connotations as begging, that is, deaf people were a helpless and dependent class. Some deaf people played on the sympathy of hearing strangers by using their deafness to sell them overpriced items, especially small cards with the manual alphabet reproduced on them. The NAD, in the 1930s, called this kind of selling a "form of begging" and condemned the practice. Like outright begging, peddling implied that deaf people could not compete in the marketplace and that they should be pitied. Unlike begging, however, deaf peddling was a problem that continued beyond the 1930s and will continue as long as deaf persons are seen by the hearing world as pitiable or unemployable.

EMPLOYMENT

Deaf people have sought throughout the twentieth century to have their employment opportunities based on their skills and the requirements of the job, rather than on their deafness. As early as 1899 the NAD established a committee to study how deaf people were doing in the workplace and what could be done to improve their status. The committee, composed of Alexander Pach, Warren Robinson, and Philip Axling, surveyed hearing employers of deaf workers, deaf business persons, and deaf employees. They reported their findings, which tended to focus on industrial training in the schools, to the International Congress of the Deaf, that met in St. Louis in 1904.

In the early twentieth century, deaf people also were concerned about employment in the government, especially the federal government. At the outset of the century the federal civil service barred deaf persons from civil service jobs, classifying them with criminals and insane people. As president of the NAD from 1904 to 1910, and later as a private individual, George Veditz pressured the federal government to change this rule, and it slowly yielded. Constant pressure from deaf people, however, was necessary to keep opening employment doors. It was the 1940s, for instance, before the Civil Service Commission removed a Government Printing Office regulation that prohibited deaf printers.

Deaf people applied pressure at the state level, too, to assure employment opportunities. In the early twentieth century the Minnesota Association of the Deaf was especially strong, convincing the state government to establish in 1913 a labor bureau specifically for deaf workers within the department of labor. Similar state agencies were established in North Carolina in 1923, California in 1927, and Michigan and Pennsylvania in 1937. By the 1950s most states had one or more specialists on deaf employment within their vocational rehabilitation agencies. Still, deaf people's employment concerns have continued, for it seems that only during wartime are employers willing to treat deaf workers equally with those who hear. *See* REHABILITATION: Agencies.

WORLD WARS

The world wars did not affect deaf people exactly as they did hearing persons. Deaf men were, as a rule, barred from military service and exempt from the draft, although there were reports during World War I that some of the European combatants, especially the Germans, used deaf soldiers. The wars certainly did cause many European schools to close because they were in occupied areas, the instructors were involved in the war effort, or the building had been commandeered for war use. Even in the United States, some schools shortened their terms and lost their employees during the wars. More significantly, deaf parents, just like hearing parents, lost their children in the war. Still, most deaf people, especially in the United States, benefited from the conditions created by world war.

The wartime shortage of workers, especially draft-exempt workers, made deaf people more attractive to employers than before. World War I saw large numbers of deaf men employed in war industries in Detroit, Michigan, and Akron, Ohio. By 1919 Goodyear Tire and Rubber, for example, had almost 500 deaf employees in Akron. Goodyear's experience prompted Firestone Tire to hire deaf people, too, and Ben Schowe was hired to help build a group of deaf Firestone workers. Similarly, during World War II deaf people moved to places like Newport News, Virginia, where the demand for workers in defense industries overcame prejudice and ignorance. *See* SCHOWE, BENJAMIN MARSHALL, SR.

Desiring to demonstrate their patriotism and their independence, deaf people tried to contribute to the war effort. Many volunteered in hopes that their deafness would not be an insurmountable obstacle. In 1917, when Theodore Roosevelt was dreaming of raising his own division, a few people within the NAD wrote to him about 1000 able-bodied deaf men volunteering to fight with him. While nothing came of this offer, or of Roosevelt's personal division, deaf people contributed in other ways. During World War II, for instance, the NAD raised nearly $8000 to purchase vehicles for the Red Cross.

The situation of deaf Americans during the world wars was analogous to that of hearing women. They were not allowed to fight; their labor was in great demand; they acquitted themselves well in the workplace; and all too often they were back where they started shortly after the war ended. Following World War II, for example, employment again became a problem for deaf people, leading to a rise, or at least a perceived rise, in the old problem of deaf peddling. A deaf newspaper even commented in 1949 that deaf people were becoming a "mendicant class of human beings."

PROGRESS

Far from becoming a class of beggars, deaf people made dramatic progress after World War II. They strengthened their organizations, began cooperating with other disabled persons, made themselves heard in political circles, and, as individuals, achieved success in a variety of endeavors that once seemed closed to persons without normal hearing. Three especially important areas of progress were in higher education, recognition of deaf people's language, and reorganization of the NAD.

One major higher education advance of the postwar period was the virtual rebuilding of Gallaudet College. Although the alma mater of most of the American deaf community's leaders since the late nineteenth century, and the only collegiate program in the world for deaf people, Gallaudet College was a "sleepy" unaccredited school with less than 200 students at the end of World War II. Responding in the 1950s to pressure from alumni and the federal government, however, Gallaudet Col-

lege took steps necessary to win accreditation, and began to grow. By the 1980s it had a student population of 2000 to 2500, facilities and academic programs to rival any well-endowed small college, and an expanded role within the deaf community.

Moreover, Gallaudet College was no longer alone in providing college opportunities for deaf people. The National Technical Institute for the Deaf, affiliated with the Rochester Institute of Technology, began in 1968 providing deaf students with the technically oriented collegiate training traditionally unavailable at Gallaudet College. A few other postsecondary programs, California State University, Northridge, for example, actively recruited deaf college students. Also, many colleges, through the provision of interpreters and notetakers, became accessible to deaf people. *See* CALIFORNIA STATE UNIVERSITY, NORTHRIDGE; NATIONAL TECHNICAL INSTITUTE FOR THE DEAF.

The 1960s inaugurated the first serious study of the visual communication method used by deaf people, sign language. Hearing and deaf linguists, in the United States and elsewhere, analyzed various sign languages and discovered that they were not mere collections of gestures but were true languages with standardized grammar and syntax. Consequently, many deaf persons no longer felt embarrassed or ashamed of the language they knew best. They began to use it openly, to proclaim its value, and to emphasize its importance to their culture. *See* LANGUAGE.

Concomitant with linguistic and cultural appreciation of sign language, the state residential schools for deaf children began in the late 1960s to abandon their 60-year-old attempt to abolish sign language and to instruct most students with only speech and speechreading. The new catchword became total communication, which attempted to fit the communication method to the child. The NAD had been encouraging exactly this since the end of the nineteenth century.

The NAD itself changed drastically in the late 1950s and the 1960s. Since its founding in 1881, it had been a national organization of individuals. Difficulties of communication, as well as the natural tendency of people to identify more strongly with local organizations than with distant ones, kept the NAD politically weaker and financially less stable than it might have been. Deaf leaders recognized this, and in 1956 proposed changing the NAD into a federation of state associations. The 1957 NAD convention ratified this change, allowing the NAD eventually to establish permanent offices on the outskirts of Washington, D.C., hire a full-time executive secretary, and work in a concerted fashion to advance the interests of deaf Americans.

By the 1970s it was evident that deaf people fit differently into American society than they had 70 or 80 years before. A small but steady number of deaf individuals were receiving advanced degrees in the liberal arts, medicine, education, and law. American Sign Language was no longer hidden; it had become a source of pride to its users and a curiosity to the hearing world. The telephone, an old enemy of people who could not hear, became accessible through new technology, as did television. Some hearing people even caught glimpses of the deaf experience by attending performances of *Children of a Lesser God*, an award-winning play, or by seeing productions of the National Theatre of the Deaf. *See* NATIONAL THEATERS OF THE DEAF: United States.

PROBLEMS

Despite substantial progress, deaf people still face some seemingly intractable problems. Although they have, for the most part, eliminated vestiges of paternalism and argued successfully for full civil rights, they still have not resolved the dilemma of explaining to the hearing world exactly who they are. When pushing for civil rights or accessibility to programs, schools, and jobs, they seem to be saying that they are like everyone else except that they lack hearing. When arguing for special accommodations for their deafness, such as the installation of special telecommunications devices in government offices, they appear to be akin to other disabled persons. At other times, though, they argue that they really constitute a sort of ethnic group, a community with language, organizations, and mores different from those of the hearing majority. Thus, some deaf people argue, public policy that forces deaf children, like others with disabilities, to attend schools with their hearing peers is misguided. These deaf children will grow up without awareness of their roots, deaf adults fear, and they will be enculturated as defective hearing persons rather than as normal deaf persons.

The deaf community, then, has struggled throughout the twentieth century to avoid either an imperfect assimilation, for no deaf person can ever function in all situations exactly like a hearing individual, or a second-class, paternalistic citizenship that degrades their humanity. Not precisely hearing people, not completely an ethnic group, sharing with other disabled people only an interest in equal treatment, deaf people face a difficult and uncertain future.

Bibliography

Best, Harry: *Deafness and the Deaf in the United States*, Macmillan, New York, 1943.

Gannon, Jack R.: *Deaf Heritage: A Narrative History of Deaf America*, National Association of the Deaf, Silver Spring, Maryland, 1981.

Long, J. Schuyler: *The Sign Language: A Manual of Signs*, 2d ed., Athens Press, Iowa City, Iowa, 1918.

Schein, Jerome D., and Marcus T. Delk, Jr.: *The Deaf Population of the United States*, National Association of the Deaf, Silver Spring, Maryland, 1974.

John V. Van Cleve

HONG KONG

Hong Kong is a colony of the United Kingdom adjacent to Kwangtung Province in southeastern China. Most of Hong Kong's inhabitants live on densely populated Hong Kong island, which comprises 29 of the colony's total 399 square miles (74 of 1021 square kilometers). Chinese (Cantonese) is the major language of Hong Kong, although English also is widely used.

PREVALENCE

The exact number of hearing-impaired persons in Hong Kong is not known. In the 1982–1983 academic year, however, 1880 profoundly, severely, or moderately hearing-impaired children were enrolled in special schools for deaf students, attending special classes for partially hearing children, or receiving preschool advisory and training service and peripatetic advisory service. Audiometric screening programs in schools have shown the rate of profound deafness, defined as a hearing loss of greater than 90 decibels, to be 3.03 per 10,000, and the rate of severe deafness, defined as a hearing loss between 56 and 90 decibels, to be 5.14 per 10,000.

IDENTIFICATION AND ASSESSMENT SERVICES

In 1977, the Medical and Health Department introduced a Comprehensive Observation Scheme that provides developmental screening, including auditory assessment, for all children from birth to 5 years of age. First screening is conducted at 6 weeks, second between 8 and 10 months, third between 18 and 24 months, fourth between 36 and 42 months, and last between 48 and 54 months. Children with conditions identified during the developmental screening are referred to a child assessment center. There, a thorough evaluation is conducted to ascertain the nature of the handicap and to commence appropriate remediation or rehabilitation.

The school-age screening program, started in 1967, aims at early identification of hearing impairment among primary-2 pupils. The purpose of the screening is to provide medical and educational treatment to these pupils before the impairment develops into an educational handicap. Pupils who fail the audiometric screening test will be referred to the Special Education Services Centres of the Education Department, where audiologists conduct full-scale audiological assessments on these pupils. Remedial treatment may include medical referrals, provision of hearing aids, special seating arrangements in classrooms, provision of peripatetic advisory service, and special-education placement, if necessary.

In the 1982–1983 school year, approximately 60 percent of the primary-2 population of 53,000 pupils received audiometric screening and free follow-up audiological assessments. Results of the screening program showed that 5 to 6 percent of the screened population suffered from some degree of hearing impairment. Approximately 3 to 4 percent of the screened population required medical treatment, which is provided free by the Medical and Health Department.

Noise pollution and risks of noise-induced deafness among workers in Hong Kong have also been carefully examined since the 1970s. Legislation is being considered to protect workers' hearing. Audiological assessment service for adult patients is provided by the ear, nose, and throat unit of the Medical and Health Department at a nominal fee.

HEARING AIDS

Free provision of hearing aids to hearing-impaired children was initiated in 1971 by the Social Welfare Department. Provision of broader welfare services for hearing-impaired persons is in line with the practice in the United Kingdom, and follows the policy laid down in 1971 in interdepartmental consultations among the Social Welfare Department, Education Department, and Medical and Health Department. Since 1971, the Lotteries Fund, administered by the Social Welfare Department, has continuously subsidized hearing aids that are issued by the Education Department. Any child who is ascertained hearing-impaired by the Education Department will receive a hearing aid without a means test.

In the past, body-worn hearing aids were issued to both preschool and school-aged hearing-impaired children. Since April 1981, about three-quarters of the aids issued have been behind-the-ear hearing aids. Subject to overcoming the technical problem of making good-fitting earmolds to avoid acoustic feedback, in particular from the high-power hearing aids used by profoundly deaf children who require higher acoustic amplification, the distribution of behind-the-ear aids should result in more effective and consistent use of the aids. *See* HEARING AIDS.

The Medical and Health Department provides earmold and hearing aid repair services to hearing-impaired adults at cost. Hearing aids, however, are not issued free. They are subsidized on a means test to needy patients. On the other hand, hearing aid repair and maintenance services are provided by laboratory technicians in special schools for deaf children and in Special Education Services Centres of the Education Department.

PRESCHOOL

Since the mid-1960s, hearing-impaired children aged 6 months to 6 years have received speech and auditory training, parent guidance, and educational placement services at the Preschool Speech and Hearing Centre of the Special Education Section, Education Department. The objectives of this program are: to provide opportunities for early parental intervention; to provide a systematic approach and constructive methods in training preschool hearing-impaired children in the acquisition of speech and language and communication skills; to encourage parent and child involvement in mutual observation and learning through play; and to bridge the gap between hearing-impaired children and the family servicing centers and kindergartens in which such children are integrated.

In the 1982–1983 school year, about 200 preschool hearing-impaired children received regular individual or group training and parent guidance sessions at the Special Education Services Centres or at subsidized or private child care centers and kindergartens.

EDUCATION SYSTEM

When of age, deaf and partially hearing children are referred for educational placement according to their nature and degree of hearing impairment, extent of language acquisition, learning attitudes, and availability of resources. Education is free and compulsory from the age of 6 to 15 years. Placement may take one of the following three forms.

Special Schools There are four special schools for deaf students receiving financial assistance from the Education Department under the Codes of Aid for Special Schools and Classes. All these schools are coeducational and catering for profoundly and severely hearing-impaired children aged 4 to 20 years, as well as admitting deaf children with additional handicaps. Altogether the four schools share a capacity of 760 places, or 76 classes each accommodating 10 pupils. The classes range from preparatory through primary and secondary levels, offering 12 years of free education from preparatory to junior secondary classes. Two of the schools also provide boarding facilities. Chinese (Cantonese) is the medium of instruction, and the oral method of communication is generally adopted. Consequently, all the schools are well equipped with amplification equipment of group aids, speech and auditory training aids, overhead projectors, educational television, and video tapes. The majority of teachers in these schools are trained to teach deaf students.

As far as possible, the ordinary school curriculum is followed, with adaptations geared toward the ability and needs of hearing-impaired children. Individualized education programs are designed to adapt to the needs of individual deaf children with additional learning difficulties. Speech and language teaching, lipreading, and acquisition of communication skills are an essential element in the schools' curriculum. Other subjects taught include Chinese, mathematics, social studies, English, integrated science, religious education, physical education, music, rhythm and movement, arts and crafts, design and technology, art and design, home economics, typing, and pottery.

Special Classes In an effort to facilitate integration of hearing-impaired children, special classes are operated in ordinary government primary and secondary schools. These admit the majority of severely hearing-impaired children, some profoundly deaf children, and deaf children with additional learning difficulties. In these classes, pupils are taught by special teachers in academic subjects, while integrating with their normally hearing peers in cultural subjects like art and music, physical education, woodwork, or home economics. Class size, medium of instruction, and curriculum are similar to those in schools for deaf students. In the 1982–1983 school year, nine schools operated 35 special classes, ranging from junior secondary (middle-3) levels.

Peripatetic Advisory Service The majority of moderately hearing-impaired children and some severely and profoundly deaf children may be able to integrate successfully in ordinary classes, provided that advice and assistance of an experienced teacher of deaf students in peripatetic advisory service is made available. In 1982–1983, 715 hearing-impaired children were registered with the peripatetic advisory service. These children attended ordinary schools, special classes, special schools, technical institutes, Hong Kong Polytechnic, and the World Rehabilitation Fund Day Centre. Depending on individual needs, a hearing-impaired child may require regular visits of a peripatetic teacher at fortnightly, monthly, and tri-monthly intervals throughout his or her school life. The peripatetic teacher liaises with the heads or teachers of relevant schools and educational institutions regarding the child's educational progress and problems in learning and integration, and gives advice accordingly. The peripatetic teacher also assists the child in acquiring necessary communication skills and advises on educational placement or transfer, where necessary.

TEACHER TRAINING

Until September 1981, the Special Education Section of the Education Department operated a one-year in-service training course for teachers of handicapped children working in special schools and special classes and at Special Education Services Centres for hearing-impaired, visually handicapped, physically handicapped, slow-learning, mentally handicapped, and maladjusted children. In addition, special-education officers also lecture at colleges of education and at university extramural courses and give short talks, seminars, and courses to both government and voluntary organizations. In September 1981, Sir Robert Black College set up a special-education unit to operate two-year in-service training courses for teachers of handicapped children.

ADULT EDUCATION AND EMPLOYMENT

Adult education courses for deaf people commenced in April 1981 with a subsidy from the Education Department. Remedial courses in Chinese and basic courses in sign language, English language, typing, bookkeeping, simple accounting, and so on, have been operated by the Hong Kong Society of the Deaf. Interest groups in judo, dressmaking, Chinese painting, cookery, ribbon flower making, and other things also are run by the Hong Kong Society of the Deaf for its over 600 members.

An employment survey conducted by the Hong Kong Society of the Deaf in 1981 indicated deaf adults' dissatisfaction with their employment. Of 228 deaf employees surveyed, 154 of them indicated a change of employment for the following reasons: exceptionally low wages, excessive pressure of work, long working hours, and lack of interest in their jobs. The survey concentrated on employment of deaf clerical staff and menial staff in industries. The bulk of clerical workers had acquired a secondary standard of education, whereas the majority of menial labor and production workers were limited to the level of primary education. The majority of deaf workers, as revealed by 1981–1982 placement statistics, are finding jobs as production workers, laborers, and equipment operators. A few are service workers, and only a small minority in clerical positions. The Hong Kong government is assisting deaf as well as other handicapped persons in the newly established Selective Job Placement Service Units of the Labour Department in various Hong Kong districts.

Eva W. Kwan

HOWARD, JAY COOKE
(1872–1946)

Jay Cooke Howard became prominent in the American deaf community at a time when the compentency of users of sign language was threatened. A business person who was active as an investment

Jay Cooke Howard. (*Gallaudet College Archives*)

banker, real estate broker, and life insurance agent, he typified the attitude of diligence characterizing Gallaudet College graduates who established careers in the early twentieth century. Profit seeking, however, did not monopolize Howard's time, and he served repeatedly as a leader of local and national deaf associations. Moreover, retirement was not an allure, for Howard continued to be innovative and endeavored to find honorable labor for deaf people. Physically handicapped individuals also engaged his attention. He found time to write for deaf publications and to express his strong opinions about a variety of subjects relating to the deaf community—most important, the conflict between oralism and manualism.

Once describing himself as "100 percent deaf," Howard lost his hearing at the age of eight due to spinal meningitis. Born in Superior, Wisconsin, on May 25, 1872, he later moved with his family to Duluth, Minnesota, where he attended the state school for deaf students. Later he graduated with class honors from the Minnesota School for the Deaf at Faribault. Attending Gallaudet College between 1890 and 1895, Howard was active both athletically and academically. He was captain and quarterback of the football team, a good student, and a member of the first editorial board and, later,

editor of the college's newspaper, the *Buff and Blue*. *See* GALLAUDET COLLEGE.

After graduation, he entered business and married Minnie G. Mickle of Patterson, New Jersey, an 1897 Gallaudet graduate. Married a total of four times, Howard was the father of five children.

Howard had inherited one-half interest in a Duluth banking firm, and there began a long and rather distinguished career. Helping to organize the Howard Investment Company, he also dealt in real estate, aiding primarily deaf teachers and other deaf individuals.

Although treasurer and general manager of his own investment company, Howard found time to participate in numerous organizations and to write about a wide variety of issues affecting deaf Americans. For example, Howard was not a firm believer in trying to read lips. "I have always supposed," he wrote, "that lipreading was a substitute for hearing and, very often, a very poor substitute." Howard believed that lipreading robbed the deaf child "of a possible chance to cultivate residual hearing." Even though he seems to have had none himself, Howard "long felt that latent or residual hearing should be sought in all deaf children as soon as they enter school and, if found, cultivated." But when teachers of deaf pupils were so wedded to lipreading that they ignored the possibility of enhancing residual hearing, Howard believed they became dangerous in a school for deaf children. A graphic sign maker, Howard advocated the simultaneous communication method, in which one used voice and sign language together. He was a strong opponent of oralism and clearly delineated his thoughts on the subject. *See* SOCIOLINGUISTICS: Simultaneous Communication; SPEECHREADING.

When an attempt was made to change the New York School for the Deaf at Farnwood to a purely oral school for deaf students, Howard became enraged. "Pure (there is no such thing) oralism," he wrote, "has not a leg to stand upon." He believed it "Fad and Fancy, a Delusion and a Snare." Mentally and morally it was a "menace to the deaf" and robbed them "of the happiness and peace of mind God meant for them." *See* HISTORY: Sign Language Controversy.

Howard demonstrated his strong commitment to the broader field of deaf activities, serving four times as president of the Minnesota Association of the Deaf, as president of the Michigan Association, and as national president of the National Association of the Deaf. He maintained close ties with Gallaudet College as president of its alumni association from 1910 until 1914. Active in the National Fraternal Society of the Deaf, he also allied himself with the American Federation of the Physically Handicapped. Throughout his life Howard championed deaf causes, rights, and organizations, viewing this work as instrumental to the American deaf community. *See* NATIONAL ASSOCIATION OF THE DEAF; NATIONAL FRATERNAL SOCIETY OF THE DEAF.

Howard's financial fortunes plummeted during the depression of the 1930s, and he was essentially wiped out in his various businesses. He eventually moved to Michigan, where he became director of the Division of Deaf and Deafened for the Department of Labor and Industry. A union supporter, he worked to employ deaf people, constantly urging General Motors to do so. Writing to Ben M. Schowe in 1941, he said that while he could not claim all avenues of employment were open to deaf workers, "there are enough of these avenues open to absorb ALL of the deaf who have the least skill" and certainly all deaf persons in Michigan with a "modicum" of skills. Ignorance and discrimination often blocked his efforts, but to him the latter was more destructive as they "are two different horses." *See* SCHOWE, BENJAMIN MARSHALL, JR.

Throughout his life Howard wrote for several deaf publications, such as the *Silent Worker*, the *Michigan Mirror*, and the *Signpost*. His writings in the *American Annals of the Deaf* and the *Jewish Deaf* delineate his philosophy about communication and employment of the deaf. When he died in Detroit on January 11, 1946, a contemporary wrote that he was the "last of a long line of epochal deaf men whose services in behalf of their kind won national repute."

Bibliography

Gallaudet College Archives, Washington, D.C.: the Ben M. Schowe papers have numerous Howard letters.

Barry A. Crouch

HUGHES, REGINA OLSON
(1895–   )

Regina Olson Hughes's lifework has been aptly described by the Superior Service Award presented by the U.S. Department of Agriculture on May 18, 1962: "For outstanding performance in preparing interpretative, accurate, original, detailed illustrations of plants representing many species, and in abstracting scientific papers and translating foreign publications."

Born on February 1, 1895, in Herman, Nebraska, Regina Hughes was educated in the Herman public schools and in private schools. Gradually losing her hearing between the ages of 10 and 14, she went on to receive her bachelor's degree from Gallaudet College in 1918, her master's degree in 1920, and an honorary doctor's degree in humane letters in 1967. In 1923 she married Frederick H. Hughes, Gallaudet College dramatics professor and football coach, who died in 1956. After several years in the

Regina Olson Hughes in 1971.

U.S. State, War, and Commerce departments as a clerk and a translator of foreign languages, she joined the Department of Agriculture (USDA) in 1931 as a research clerk. Here her artistic talents were discovered and put to use. Upon retiring in 1969, she had served the United States government for 43 years as a translator and illustrator of all phases of plant life, and had earned worldwide acclaim. *See* GALLAUDET COLLEGE.

While Hughes's art education began in earliest childhood with private teachers, her botanical education grew from a passionate love of flowers, and expanded into a devotion to all the plant world. Largely self-taught in botany, she worked with taxonomists and scientists to illustrate seeds, weeds, plants, and flowers from nature and from dried specimens, making them appear lifelike. Newly discovered species, described in Latin, were given to her to make exact illustrations for publication, showing every diagnostic detail contained in the Latin description of the specimen, with precise measurements and the habit (that is, appearance) of the specimen as it is in nature. Often dependent upon foreign languages for plant descriptions, Hughes became proficient in French, Spanish, Portuguese, Italian, and German, and abstracted scientific papers in these languages.

Most of Hughes's illustrations are done in pencil or pen and ink, but others are done in watercolors. Many of her watercolors are in the permanent collections of the USDA, the Smithsonian Institution,

Hughes's illustration of *Rhus radicans*. (From *Selected Weeds of the United States*, Agricultural Handbook no. 366, Agricultural Research Service, USDA, 1970)

the Hunt Institute for Botanical Documentation, and the United States Mission to the United Nations, and in many private collections.

Upon compulsory retirement from the Agricultural Research Service, USDA, Hughes was reappointed three times without a break in service and continued two more years on contract. In 1970 she began scientific illustrating in the Botany Department of the Smithsonian Institution as artist for its National Orchid Collection. This work entailed painting orchids from life, including dissection and portrayal of all reproductive parts. She also continued scientific illustrating for the Agricultural Research Service.

In 1982 a collection of 40 beautiful and scientifically accurate watercolors of orchids by Hughes were exhibited in the Rotunda Gallery of the National Museum of Natural History of the Smithsonian Institution. Earlier, one of her bromeliad paintings graced an exhibit in the foyer of the Natural History Museum that featured the bromeliad research of Lyman B. Smith and Robert W. Reed. In 1979 this bromeliad was named *Billbergia regina* for the artist. Her extremely fine illustrations have appeared in numerous botanical papers and books by Smithsonian staff scientists.

Hughes is a versatile artist as well as illustrator, and her work in oil and watercolors is for pleasure, relaxation, and profit. Her nonscientific oils and watercolors have been exhibited in numerous one-person shows and in art exhibitions all over the United States and abroad.

Many honors came to Hughes: among them, the USDA Superior Service Award, 1962; Woman of the Year, 1970, from Gallaudet College's Phi Kappa Zeta sorority: inclusion in Marquis's *Who's Who of American Women* (6th ed.); and the Amos Kendall Award for excellence in a professional field not related to deafness, 1982. In addition to the plant species that was named for her, a plant genus and species, *Hughesia reginae*, was named in her honor in 1981.

Hughes's memberships include the Guild of Natural Science Illustrators, the National League of American Pen Women, and the Washington Watercolor Association; and she has exhibited with each of them. Her paintings also have been exhibited in the International Exhibition of Hunt Museum for Botanical Documentation at Carnegie Mellon University, at the National Arboretum, at the National Library of Agriculture, and at Gallaudet College. She illustrated the covers of numerous publications, including a cover of the *Journal of the Bromeliad Society* (vol. 33, no. 1, January–February 1983) depicting in full color the arrestingly beautiful *Billbergia rosea*.

Hughes's extensive travels took her to every continent and subcontinent, always accompanied by sketchbooks. These sketches, together with extensive notes, form the basis of many of her paintings. Her orchid paintings are permanently on public view in the National Museum of Natural History, Smithsonian Institution.

Bibliography
Partial list of publications containing Hughes's illustrations:

Correll, Donovan S., and Helen B. Correll: *Aquatic and Wetland Plants of Southwestern United States*, 1972, reprinted in 2 vols. 1980.

Gentry, Howard Scott: *The Agaves of Baja California*, California Academy of Sciences Occasional Paper no. 130, December 1978.

Gunn, C. R.: "Genus Vicia, with Notes about Tribe Viceae (Fabaceae) in Mexico and Central America," *USDA Technical Bulletin*, no. 1601, 1979.

————: "Seeds and Fruits of North American Papaveraceae," *USDA Technical Bulletin*, no. 1517, 1976.

Hermann, F. G.: "Vetches of the United States, Native, Naturalized and Cultivated," USDA Agricultural Handbook no. 168.

Hermann, F.J.: "A Revision of Genus Glycine and Its Immediate Allies," *USDA Technical Bulletin*, no. 1268, 1962.

Leppek, E. E.: *Selected Papers on Floral Evolution III, Nos. 21–40*, 1968–1976 (a rare book; only 24 copies exist in the United States and abroad).

Robinson, H. R., and R. M. King: "Revision of the Eupatorieae." *Missouri Botanical Garden*, 1983.

Smith, Lyman B.: *Flora del Uruguay IV: Bromeliaceae*, Montevideo, 1972.

Terrell, E. E.: "A Taxonomic Revision of the Genus Lolium," *USDA Technical Bulletin*, no. 1392, 1968.

USDA: *Economically Important Foreign Weeds; Potential Problems in the United States*, Agricultural Handbook no. 498, 1927 (over 6000 illustrations with seed descriptions by Hughes).

————: *Selected Weeds of the United States*. Agricultural Handbook no. 366, 1970. Issued as *Common Weeds of the United States*, Dover Press, New York, 1971; published in Canada by General Publishing Co., Toronto, 1971, and in the United Kingdom by Constable and Co., 1971.

Wurdack, John J.: *Flora of Ecuador, No. 13–138. Melastomataceae*, Smithsonian Institution, 1980.

Florence Crammatte

George E. Hyde.

HYDE, GEORGE E.
(1882–1968)

George E. Hyde was an outstanding Plains Indian historian whose many fascinating narratives became cornerstones in American Indian studies. Hyde authored some of the most important books ever written on the subject, and his works are consistently cited as references in texts of the American West. Moreover, Hyde has the distinction of having been one of the first historians to utilize Indian sources of information. His sincere interest in getting the Indian version of the past enabled him to make many Native American friends, and it also gave him the opportunity to develop both a balanced sense of history and a profound understanding of Indian identity. He is acknowledged as a significant historian because of the penetrating insights and sweeping vision he brought to American Indian scholarship. That he accomplished this while being semiblind and profoundly deaf makes his story all the more inspiring.

Born on June 10, 1882, in Omaha, Nebraska (a Great Plains state rich with Indian history), Hyde spent his entire life there. He was the only child of George W. and Lucinda Reed Hyde, and was a precocious youngster, with a passion for stories about the West. During his boyhood, Hyde became friends with the son of a local photographer who had known and recorded such legendary figures as Chief Spotted Tail and Buffalo Bill Cody. The two boys spent many halcyon days together, listening to stories and examining photographs that documented the frontier experience. Hyde's interest in Native Americans was further kindled when he befriended a group of Indians in the 1898 Trans-Mississippi Exposition in Omaha, which was attended by such celebrated characters as Geronimo.

By the time the exposition was held, Hyde had become profoundly deaf and was bothered by vision problems which resulted in semiblindness by the age of 20. Hyde was only able to complete the eighth grade, a fact that would haunt him all of his professional life. Believing that he worked in a field that overemphasized degrees, Hyde sometimes felt bitter and complained of academics "who didn't know horde from hoard, practice from practise, and led from lead." One close colleague, however, stated that Hyde's lack of academic credentials was never really an issue among peers who could recognize a good literary effort.

Early in the twentieth century Hyde turned to writing about Indians because he "was in a position to get firsthand information from several tribes." The commitment to getting the Indian viewpoint, which would become one of Hyde's trademarks, and, as one fellow historian observed, his "signal contribution" to research in the field, drew the attention of George Bird Grinnell. Grinnell was an established cultural anthropologist who had authored a book on the Pawnees, using oral accounts from Indian informants. Grinnell employed Hyde as a research assistant for a book on the Cheyennes.

The experience gave Hyde the thorough training in methodology that he might not have otherwise obtained. *The Fighting Cheyennes* was published in 1915, and Grinnell acknowledged Hyde's assistance in the preface. When he had distinguished himself as a historian, Hyde looked back at the early days and gratefully acknowledged Grinnell: "He was a fine man and gave me work when I was half blind and could not get any other employment."

By amassing an arsenal of notes through library research and correspondence with a great network of Indian friends, Hyde authored eight books during his lifetime plus a number of shorter works. Strong corrective lenses, along with a powerful magnifying glass specially ordered from Paris, enabled him to examine whatever information he could find about Indians and the West, most of which was obtained from the Omaha Public Library.

Hyde's first book was *Corn Among the Indians of the Upper Missouri* (1917), coauthored with George Will. Publication of two shorter efforts, *Rangers and Regulars* and *The Early Blackfeet and Their Neighbors*, was delayed until 1933 because of a decline in the publishing business caused by World War I and the Depression. *Life of George Bent*, which was based upon frequent letter exchanges between 1905 and 1918, was also long delayed. Unable to find a publisher, Hyde sold part of the manuscript in 1930 to the Denver Public Library for $200. It resided there for over 30 years, while Hyde kept the other half in the attic of the family home where he lived with his half-sister, a schoolteacher, who helped support him and functioned as his proofreader. Finally, in 1968, the complete book was published and met with wide critical acclaim. A gripping first person narrative of 50 years of Cheyenne life and war operations, *Life of George Bent* was hailed by the *Saturday Review* as a "treasure" that was "not just another frontier tale," while the *Los Angeles Times* said, "Its significance is immense."

Except for *Indians of the High Plains* (1959) and *Indians of the Woodlands* (1962), which were criticized by archeologists who pointed out Hyde's lack of field experience, his other books generated praise. Hyde's Sioux trilogy—*Red Cloud's Folk* (1937), *A Sioux Chronicle* (1956), and *Spotted Tail's Folk* (1961)—is considered his masterpiece. It is recognized as the most authoritative account of Oglala and Brulé Sioux history, partly evidenced by the fact that other authors have admitted in their prefaces that they perceive their efforts as being supplemental to Hyde's.

Of the three books, *Spotted Tail's Folk* is perhaps Hyde's best, having been called a literary monument to Chief Spotted Tail (1823–1881), an often misevaluated leader of the Sioux. Refuting the claim made by some biographers that Spotted Tail was unfaithful to his people, Hyde characterized the Brulé chief, who advocated peace, as a complex visionary "with more brains than any other chief." He also described the Sioux warrior and statesman as a man of "unusual ability and interesting character."

Historians of the West have used similar expressions to describe Hyde. He is considered a prolific and tough-minded writer whose straightforward style is punctuated by an intonation of objectivity. (Hyde once wrote, "I don't like skunks, whether white or Indian.") And he is remembered as a man of extraordinary character who agreed to interviews with reporters only on the condition that there would be "no sob stuff" about "fortitude triumphing over great odds," and who braved the icy streets of Omaha every December to mail Christmas parcels to Indian children at a boarding school. Upon his death on February 2, 1968, Hyde bequeathed to the Omaha Public Library the royalties from most of his books. The result was the Hyde Fund, which has been instrumental in enabling the library to increase its collection of books by and about American Indians.

Although surrounded by insightful new additions to the field of Indian research, the books written by Hyde are still recognized as foundations upon which other historians continue to build.

Bibliography

McDermott, John: "A Dedication to the Memory of George E. Hyde," *Arizona and the West*, 17:2, Summer 1975.

Panara, Robert, and John Panara: *Great Deaf Americans*, 1983.

Of Hyde's books, the following editions have forewords that provide information about his life and works: *The Pawnee Indians*, 1974; *Spotted Tail's Folk*, 1974; *Red Cloud's Folk*, 1976; *Life of George Bent*, 1968, 1983.

John Panara

I

INDIA

In the Republic of India, although great strides have been made since the late 1970s in the field of education of deaf people, there remains much to explore. Newly committed to serving handicapped students, special education is often dependent on severely limited budgets.

Provision for the education of hearing-impaired children is the responsibility of the Department of Social Welfare, or in certain states the Directorate of Education, Department of Technical Education. Because of the magnitude of the problem and lack of specific facts and figures, the needs of deaf people have to be met in partnership or with the help of voluntary agencies.

No dependable data are available regarding hearing-impaired people in India. However, if it is assumed that 1.2 people out of 1000 are hearing-impaired, then India, with a population of more than 700 million, has more than 800,000 people who are hearing-impaired, of whom 76 percent live in the rural areas. The annual birthrate is 24 million; if 1 baby in 1000 is born with a severe to profound hearing impairment, there are 24,000 more babies with hearing impairment every year, or 96,000 children in the age group from infancy to four years. Only 5.1 percent of deaf children are in schools, which are in urban or semiurban areas.

Another problem confronting the deaf child is the multilingual society. Thirty-three mother tongues are spoken in India. Of all the regional languages, Hindi is the most widespread and is spoken in more than one state. English continues to occupy a paradoxical position: in urban areas, English remains the reluctant lingua franca of the educated middle classes. By the age of eight, an Indian city child is usually trilingual, speaking the mother tongue, Hindi, and English, or the regional language, as it may be the medium of instruction at school. Thus, the language the deaf child learns varies from region to region and from school to school.

The Constitution of India (Article 46) states: "The State shall promote with special care educational and economic interests of all the weaker sections of the people and shall protect them from social injustice and all forms of exploitation." However, services for deaf people are inadequate because the emphasis within a developing country is in areas such as the uplift of the rural population, power, irrigation, and economic growth. The government has drawn up a scheme which envisages placement of handicapped children in regular schools. The support system has yet to be specified and implemented in gradual stages.

EDUCATION

India's first school for deaf children was set up by missionaries in Mazagaon, Bombay, in 1885. In 1893 the Calcutta Deaf and Dumb School was started by volunteers and is now supported entirely by the government. In South India the Florence Swainson School for the Deaf at Palayamkotai, near Madras, was started in 1897. Between 1900 and 1947, when India became an independent country, 38 schools were established; since 1947 another 162 schools have been established; and there are now slightly more than 200 schools and classes for deaf people in India. Education is not compulsory, nor is it free.

All these schools are in the urban and semiurban areas, and about 13,900 children in these areas attend schools. No figures are available for the rural areas. As screening facilities are not available, children with hearing problems in ordinary schools are sometimes termed slow learners and often not identified as hearing-impaired. There are 13 infant centers or preschool programs; most schools for deaf pupils offer elementary education; a number of schools offer prevocational training; only 14 schools are teaching up to secondary school level; 5 schools prepare students for the State Secondary School Certificate Examination, and 1 school in Calcutta prepares students for the All-India Certificate of Secondary Examination. There is no facility for postsecondary or university education (undergraduate and graduate studies) in India. However, there are a few deaf students studying at universities in the United States.

Reliable data regarding integration programs are not available. The government has set aside some funds to assist organizations in implementing programs for integration of all handicapped people. There will potentially be a great deal of variation in the support services provided for deaf children in ordinary schools.

SPEECH AND HEARING CENTERS

These centers are usually connected to hospitals. Since the establishment of the first such center, in 1964, more than 100, including private ones, have been set up. These offer services for speech problems, audiometry, development of public awareness, and early detection. The premier one is the All India Institute of Speech and Hearing at Manasagangothri, Mysore.

COMMUNICATION

India has an oralist tradition of teaching. Most schools profess to use the oral method, but in fact most children and adults in class or clubs communicate in sign language. Although an integral part of the deaf communities in India, sign language has not been used in the education of deaf children, and in most cases has been actively suppressed out of ignorance about the linguistic status of the deaf and about the sign language. Serious attempts to study sign language began in 1977, resulting in publication of a dictionary in 1980. The grammatical regularity of Indian Sign Language indicates a highly structured language. The vast majority of signs are not related to European sign languages. There is a slight regional variation in the sign language used within India. *See* SIGN LANGUAGES: Indian.

TEACHER TRAINING

Out of the 18 part-time and full-time teacher training courses held in various parts of the country, 5 are run by the government. The remaining 13 offer inservice training or a regular certificate course. Many of these courses lack information regarding new research and methodology, and fail to stress child development and language learning. Moreover, low expectations concerning achievements by deaf students are reflected in curriculum planning and teaching methods.

TECHNOLOGY

Hearing aids and their accessories are relatively expensive, so few hearing-impaired children use them. The government distributes hearing aids to children of low-income groups, but these are not always suitable for the hearing loss. There is a paucity of counseling in auditory management, resulting in inadequate knowledge of the use of hearing aids and their benefits. The making of ear molds has been carried on for some years in Bombay, Madras, and Delhi, but in Calcutta mold-making services are relatively new. The result is poorly fitting ear molds, which further add to distortion of sound. However, since 1982 more qualified audiologists have entered the field. Also body-worn hearing aids with a frequency range from 100 to 5000 hertz and output of 136 decibels SPL (sound pressure level), postaural aids to suit the partially hearing, and audiometers and auditory trainers are being manufactured. *See* HEARING AIDS: Types.

OPPORTUNITIES FOR ADULTS

Although the government reserves 3 percent of its jobs for the handicapped and a small amount of funds for assistance in placing these individuals, a large percentage of deaf people remain unemployed. Compared with hearing people in terms of opportunities for income and career advancement, deaf people are underemployed, because of the problems of general unemployment in the country. They work as fitters, turners, sheet-metal workers, weavers, printers, tailors, artists, photographers, beauticians, and as assemblers of precision instruments, electronic components, and such.

At the national level, the government has taken very positive steps. The Directorate General of Employment and Training assists in the vocational rehabilitation of physically handicapped people through the following means.

1. There are special employment exchanges (19 in the country), and vocational rehabilitation centers (11) provide psychological evaluation, vocational training, and counseling.

2. Since 1969 the government has given annual national awards for the most efficient handicapped

employee and the most outstanding employer of handicapped people.

3. The Training Centre for the Adult Deaf in Hyderabad is a government project offering two-year courses in tailoring, sheet metal work, electrical wiring, carpentry, gas welding, and photography, among other fields.

4. The All India Federation of the Deaf in Delhi actively supports a multipurpose training center for the deaf people in Delhi. It also has follow-up services for deaf adults.

5. A national institute, Ali-Yavar Jung (Indian Institute for the Hearing Handicapped), in Bombay organizes services, training, and research on deafness.

6. There are also about 50 voluntary welfare associations of deaf people offering services and assistance in vocational training, employment, marriage arrangement and counseling, athletics, and recreational activities.

General Services
Although television sets are becoming more available to the public, there is no captioning service. Telephone accessories, such as TDD, are not available. Interpreter services are practically negligible even in Delhi, Bombay, and Bangalore. There are no special services such as loop induction in public places.

Bibliography
Advani, Lal: "Rural Handicapped Child," *Mook Dhwani*, p. 4, April 1981.

Doshi, Mina B. (comp.): *Directory of Services in India for Speech and Hearing Impaired* (with special reference to the deaf).

India: A Reference Manual, comp. and ed. by Research and Reference Division, Ministry of Information and Broadcasting, Government of India, 1982.

Oza, R. K.: "Hearing Aids in India," in Prem Victor and A. Loewe (eds.), *All India Workshop for Teachers and Parents of Hearing Impaired Children*, 1981.

Statistical Outline of India 1982, Tata Services Ltd., Department of Economics and Statistics, Bombay.

Vasishta, Madan, et al.: *An Introduction to Indian Sign Language* (with focus on Delhi), Sign Language Research Inc.

Dhun D. Adenwalla

INTELLIGENCE

Intelligence is a complex psychological concept. Experts in the field disagree on its definition and how to measure it. Scores on intelligence tests are used as criteria to both accept and reject people from educational and other programs. This power has been abused and misused, and as a result intelligence testing has been plagued with controversy.

In considering intelligence, it is important to emphasize that the same definitions, measurement concepts, and classification schemes apply equally to deaf and hearing people. Yet some deaf people have been misdiagnosed on the basis of intelligence tests, although deafness itself in no way has an adverse affect on an individual's intellectual capacity.

Definition
Intelligence refers to the complex workings of the human mind. Thus, it is not a single entity, but is composed of many cognitive or thinking functions. Describing the structure and nature of these functions is the heart of the controversy in defining intelligence.

Existing definitions of intelligence range from the innate thinking capacity of an individual to the person's learning, thinking, and problem-solving abilities, or to his or her scores on intelligence tests.

Most theorists agree that existing intelligence tests are not capable of measuring most of the behaviors that can be included under the definition of intelligence. Such tests sample only a limited part of intellectual ability. Test responses given by individuals are directly related to their unique learning history.

Measurement
An intelligence quotient (IQ) refers to a specific number or score obtained on an intelligence test. It is not synonymous with intelligence, but represents a given number, earned on a given test on a given day. On standard intelligence tests, IQs are expressed as either a mental age (MA), with a corresponding ratio IQ, or as a deviation IQ.

The mental age concept assumes differences in intelligence can be identified with differences in developmental levels that are represented by the average capacities of individuals of various ages. Accordingly, the measure of an individual's intelligence is his or her mental age, or the developmental level achieved, divided by his or her chronological age (CA). The formula is $IQ = MA/CA \times 100$.

The Hiskey-Nebraska Test of Learning Aptitude, a nonverbal measure of cognitive abilities with norms for deaf and hearing children, uses the mental age concept in deriving a deaf learning age (DLA) and corresponding deaf learning quotient (DLQ) as an index of a deaf child's intelligence.

The concept of mental age has several weaknesses as a measure of intelligence. It assumes a constant relationship between mental and chronological age, which is known not to exist. The same mental age (for example, 12 years 6 months) at different chronological ages (such as 9, 12, and 24 years) indicates different intellectual abilities (su-

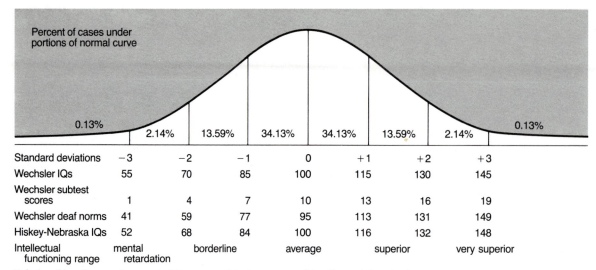

	Percent of cases under portions of normal curve						
	0.13%	2.14%	13.59%	34.13%	34.13%	13.59%	2.14%	0.13%

Standard deviations	−3	−2	−1	0	+1	+2	+3
Wechsler IQs	55	70	85	100	115	130	145
Wechsler subtest scores	1	4	7	10	13	16	19
Wechsler deaf norms	41	59	77	95	113	131	149
Hiskey-Nebraska IQs	52	68	84	100	116	132	148
Intellectual functioning range	mental retardation		borderline	average		superior		very superior

Relationship of normal curve to IQ scores, subtest scores, and intellectual functioning.

perior, average, and mentally retarded, respectively). Additional limitations are that different abilities may be measured at different age levels and individuals with the same mental age at the same chronological age may have different abilities.

The deviation IQ is an index of intellectual ability based on a comparison of an individual's performance with the mean or average performance for his or her chronological age group on the same intelligence test. Tests that yield deviation IQs are normed or given to a large number of individuals from various age groups. The resulting scores are developed into norms to which a person given an intelligence test is compared, usually on the basis of age. The Wechsler intelligence test and the hearing norms for the Hiskey-Nebraska Test of Learning Aptitude yield deviation IQs. These are standard scores with a mean of 100 and a standard deviation of 15 or 16, depending on the test.

CLASSIFICATION

IQ scores are normally distributed. That is, they can be graphed mathematically to correspond to the normal or bell-shaped curve, as shown in the illustration.

The mean or average score for most standard intelligence tests is 100. Other IQ scores are measured in terms of standard deviation units from this mean or average score. When an intelligence test is normed on a large group of persons, a normal curve of scores results. Within the mathematical model of the normal curve, it is possible to determine the percentage of scores that occur between the mean and a particular standard deviation. Accordingly, the majority of individuals (68.26 percent) earned IQ scores within the average range (IQ 85 to 115). About 13 percent earn IQs within

the superior range (IQ 115 to 130) and the borderline range (IQ 70 to 85). Some 2.27 percent earn IQs within the very superior range (IQ above 130) and the range of mental retardation (IQ below 70). An IQ score obtained on a given intelligence test can vary as a function of time, anxiety level during testing, motivation to complete tasks, and rapport with the examiner. Therefore, it is best to interpret scores on the basis of the intellectual functioning range in which they fall, rather than as a specific IQ number.

CONTENT OF INTELLIGENCE TESTS

Intelligence tests contain a variety of questions and performance tasks which generally sample the test author's conception of intelligence. Different intelligence tests sample different behaviors. For this reason, it is important to consider a given IQ on a specific test, rather than an IQ number in isolation. Most tests sample both verbal and nonverbal behaviors. Subtests are small tests within an intelligence test. They typically test a particular intelligence area (such as vocabulary) and are summed to derive a composite IQ score (such as verbal IQ). On the Wechsler Scales, subtest scores have a mean of 10 and a standard deviation of 3 (see illustration).

A verbal intelligence test measures a person's language-related reasoning abilities. These are thought to have some predictive value about a person's ability to achieve in language-related academic subjects. Verbal IQ tests usually contain items that test a person's vocabulary, fund of factual information, comprehension, memory for language stimuli, abstract reasoning abilities with language, and ability to solve language-related analogies. The verbal designation to describe such tests means that some form of language is used by the examiner to ask a question that requires a language response from the examinee. Verbal intelligence tests are generally inappropriate for use with deaf people because these tests more validly measure the language difficulties caused by the hearing impairment rather than intellectual ability. In the past, some deaf people have been erroneously diagnosed as mentally retarded on the basis of verbal IQ scores.

For this reason, nonverbal or performance-type tests are used to assess the intellectual functioning level of deaf people. Such tests do not require a language response from the examinee, but may require the examiner to use some language to explain the nature of the task. Examples of nonverbal items include discrimination tasks, detail recognition, sequencing, memory for nonverbal stimuli, pattern completion, visual-spatial abstract reasoning tasks, and motor tasks.

INTELLIGENCE TESTING WITH DEAF PERSONS

Extensive reviews of the research literature on the intelligence of deaf people indicate that their nonverbal intelligence is normally distributed. That is, as with hearing people, the mathematical graph of nonverbal IQ scores approximates the normal bell curve (see illustration). However, the distribution of verbal intelligence scores does not approximate the normal curve. This is because deafness invariably causes some language difficulty, and verbal intelligence tests measure English language thought processes. Most deaf people acquire English as a second language, and the use of existing verbal intelligence tests with them constitutes biased assessment and is therefore invalid.

Intelligence tests need to be developed to measure the language-related reasoning abilities of deaf people. The fact that most deaf people do not perform well on verbal intelligence tests in no way implies that they have deficits in thinking with language. Deficits do exist, however, in the tests that are currently available to measure the language intelligence factor within this population. *See* PSYCHOLINGUISTICS: Language Development.

Deaf people do not constitute a homogeneous group. Hearing impairment is frequently found in combination with other disabilities due to the etiological agents. Conditions that account for from one-third to one-fourth of all deafness in school age children (such as maternal rubella, meningitis, complications of Rh factor, and prematurity) are also known to be associated with school learning problems, mental illness, and mental retardation. *See* HEARING LOSS.

Research which has controlled for etiology of deafness has indicated variability in intelligence level as a function of the cause of the hearing impairment. Genetically deafened individuals are the least likely of all major causes of deafness to have ad-

ditional learning-related handicaps and, on the average, earn above-average IQs on nonverbal intelligence tests. Individuals deafened due to maternal rubella, Rh factor, and prematurity, on the average, score below the mean (IQ = 100) on nonverbal intelligence tests.

Although etiology is often a significant variable in the intellectual performance level of deaf people, it is often unknown, impossible to determine, or questionable in nature. The presence of a high-risk etiology is not necessarily associated with intellectual deficits. Conversely, the absence of a high-risk etiology is not necessarily associated with the absence of such deficits. Deaf people must be considered and evaluated individually and not as a member of a particular etiological group.

Research on the intelligence of deaf people has also indicated that they tend to obtain higher IQ scores when examiners have experience and training in the evaluation of deaf individuals. Deaf children who communicate in sign language earn higher IQ scores when the test is given in sign language than when verbal directions, pantomime, or pictures are used to explain and administer the nonverbal tasks.

Only two nonverbal intelligence tests have been normed on deaf people. These are the Performance Scale of the Wechsler Intelligence Scale for Children—Revised (WISC-R) and the Hiskey-Nebraska Test of Learning Aptitude. Both are tests for use with children and adolescents. The Performance Scale of the WISC-R was normed on some 1200 deaf children, but they were given the test in a variety of communication modes including sign language, oral speech, pantomime, pictures, gestures, and fingerspelling. This may account for the lower mean IQ of 95 found for the deaf sample compared to the mean IQ of 100 found for the hearing population. That is, some of the deaf children in the norming population might have earned higher scores if the test had been given to them in their optimal communication mode.

More existing intelligence tests need to be normed on deaf people. New and better tests also need to be developed to measure their intellectual capacity, both verbal and nonverbal. In the interim, it may be argued that existing nonverbal intelligence tests may be used with deaf people, if given in their respective communication mode, because deaf and hearing people share the same distribution of nonverbal intelligence.

CONCLUSIONS

It is important to recognize that existing intelligence tests do not measure innate intelligence and IQ scores sample only a small portion of a given deaf person's intellectual abilities. Thus, IQ scores are only estimates of ability and they can and may change over time. Perhaps most importantly, the results of an IQ test cannot tell everything that must be known in making judgments about a deaf person's competence.

Bibliography

Anderson, E., and F. Sisco: *Standardization of the WISC-R Performance Scale with the Deaf*, Series T, 0.1, Gallaudet College Press, Washington, D.C., 1978.

Moores, D. M.: *Educating the Deaf: Psychology, Principles, and Practices*, Houghton-Mifflin, Boston, 1978.

Sattler, J. M.: *Assessment of Children's Intelligence and Special Abilities*, 2d ed., Allyn and Bacon, Boston, 1982.

Sullivan, P.: "Administration Modifications on the WISC-R Performance Scale with Different Categories of Deaf Children," *American Annals of the Deaf*, 127(6):780–788, 1982.

Vernon, M.: "Fifty Years of Research on the Intelligence of the Deaf and Hard-of-Hearing," *Journal of Rehabilitation of the Deaf*, 1:1–12, 1968.

Patricia M. Sullivan

INTERNAL REVENUE CODE

The tax laws of the United States are defined in the Internal Revenue Code of 1954, which contains certain sections having special relevance to deaf individuals. Generally, these sections permit tax deductions for the special equipment and services needed by a deaf person in a hearing environment, with the most significant deductions in the category of personal medical expenses.

PERSONAL MEDICAL EXPENSES

Medical deductions are the costs necessary to diagnose, cure, treat, prevent, or ameliorate an illness or disability of the taxpayer, the taxpayer's spouse, or the taxpayer's dependents. The Internal Revenue Code considers deafness or a hearing impairment to be an illness or disability for tax purposes. Thus, taxpayers who itemize their deductions may qualify for substantial medical expense deductions.

There are several medical deductions that have particular relevance to deaf individuals. These include the cost and service of a telecommunications device for the deaf (TDD), enabling communication over the telephone lines; the cost of a telecaptioner for television sets; the cost of a hearing aid, batteries, and service; the cost of tuition at a school for the deaf, if the primary purpose for attendance is to use the resources available to relieve the disability; the cost of sign language or lipreading lessons; the cost of hiring an interpreter when necessary to facilitate communications with a deaf person; the cost of a guide dog for hearing-impaired persons as well as for the care of the dog; the cost of light signal relays as well as other special equipment to convert sound signals into visual

or tactile signals (such as a bed vibrator, a smoke detector connected to a strobe light, or a light system used by deaf parents to "hear" their baby crying or moving about); the cost of a full-view mirror in an automobile; and transportation expenses associated with any deductible medical expense, such as a visit to a hospital or a hearing aid dealer.

BUSINESS MEDICAL EXPENSES

If any medical expense is associated with a trade or business, it may be deducted, in whole or in part, as a business expense rather than an itemized medical expense. If the business is the taxpayer's, the expense is deducted from the gross income for that business. If the expense is necessary for the taxpayer to do a job satisfactorily as an employee, it may be deducted from the taxpayer's gross income. Business deductions are not limited by the five percent rule applicable to itemized medical deductions.

Business expenses fall into several categories for tax purposes. Some ordinary and necessary business expenses are deductible in the year paid, while so-called capital expenditures, such as equipment or buildings, must be depreciated over the life of the property. For example, if a person buys equipment that has a useful life of more than one year, the expense will have to be extended over a period of time appropriate to that equipment. Also, there are special tax considerations called accelerated cost recovery and investment credit with which people must be familiar if they have capital expenditures.

CONTRIBUTIONS

A taxpayer may deduct contributions made to a school or organization serving deaf people or deaf children. Services performed as a volunteer are not deductible, although a taxpayer may deduct transportation expenses associated with such voluntary work.

PERSONAL EXEMPTIONS

After taxpayers deduct their itemized deductions, they are allowed a deduction for each personal exemption to arrive at their taxable income. Taxpayers are entitled to an extra exemption if they are blind and another exemption if their spouse is blind. There is no comparable exemption for deafness or any other disability.

There is now a deduction in the Internal Revenue Code that can have some relevance to deaf individuals. A business, whether or not owned by a deaf individual, can deduct a certain amount for expenditures to eliminate architectural or transportation barriers to business facilities to make them accessible to or usable by elderly and handicapped individuals. This could mean the installation of TDDs or visual warning signals for deaf individuals.

Because the Internal Revenue Code provides additional exemptions for blindness, it appears to look more favorably on blind individuals than it does on individuals who suffer from other disabilities, including deafness. However, surveys reveal that only a fraction of blind individuals eligible for the exemption declare it. The exemption reduces taxable income; since most disabled individuals earn less than their nondisabled peers and since the United States has a progressive tax system with lower tax rates for lower incomes, the exemption is not particularly significant for most blind individuals. In addition, the exemption does stigmatize blind individuals. Deaf individuals may not declare this largely insignificant exemption, but neither do they get the added stigma associated with it.

Bibliography
Internal Revenue Service Publication 17, Part V.
IRS Publication 502.
26 C.F.R. Part 1.
26 U.S.C. 61, 63, 151, 162, 170, 190, and 213.

Michael A. Chatoff

INTERNATIONAL CONGRESS ON THE EDUCATION OF THE DEAF

International Congresses on the Education of the Deaf have been held intermittently for over 100 years. The first International Congress was held in Paris in 1878, and the most recent in Manchester, England, in the summer of 1985. These International Congresses have not traditionally had an ongoing organization with an elected board of directors and officers, but for the first 100 years a congress was held when an organization within a particular country extended invitations to representatives in other countries.

Suggestions and resolutions were made to establish a permanent international organization, but none was implemented until a procedure was adopted in a plenary session in Tokyo in 1975. At that time an International Congress Committee was established, comprising the chairpersons of the three preceding congresses. Additional members were selected by the committee itself. The committee was authorized to solicit, evaluate, and select a host country for the next congress, using seven criteria as guidelines.

MILAN CONGRESS
Certain resolutions on methodology passed at the Second International Congress held in Milan in 1880 had a great effect on the education of deaf persons throughout the world. The most influential resolutions stated: "The Convention, considering the incontestable superiority of speech over signs (1) for restoring deaf-mutes to social life, (2) for giving

them greater facility for language, declares that the method of articulation should have the preference over the signs in the education of the deaf and dumb." "Considering that the simultaneous use of signs and speech has the disadvantage of injuring speech and lipreading and precision of ideas, the Convention declares that the oral method must be preferred."

The only votes against these two resolutions were those of one English delegate and the American delegates led by Edward Miner Gallaudet. *See* GALLAUDET, EDWARD MINER.

In addition, there were other resolutions in favor of the oral method that cited long-term benefits and advocated procedures for introducing oralism into the schools.

Proponents of oral education cited these resolutions as a major justification in support of the oral method and in opposition to the use of manual communication or combined communication in the area of education of deaf pupils. Many countries changed their method of education because of these resolutions, and the resolutions were often cited as the basis for establishing exclusively oral programs in countries that did not have schools for deaf people. *See* HISTORY: Congress of Milan.

EARLY CONGRESSES
The programs of the early congresses were generally based on the discussion of questions by all those attending. In Hamburg in 1980, by contrast, there were 400 presentations, many of them going on simultaneously, so a participant could attend only a small number of the total sessions and, unless presenting a paper, did not have much opportunity to personally contribute.

French was the primary language used during the first six congresses held from 1878 to 1905, with the exception of the congress held in Chicago in 1893. English has been the primary language since 1907, although congresses have been held in the Netherlands, Sweden, Japan, and West Germany. At the 1950 congress held in Groningen, The Netherlands, the delegates received summaries of the 18 presentations in English, French, and German before the actual presentations. After each lecture the delegates were given the opportunity to ask questions and the answers were interpreted in German, French, and English.

PARTICIPATION OF DEAF INDIVIDUALS
Although the congresses were concerned with the education of deaf people, full participation by deaf individuals was minimal until recent years. There were several reasons for this. People who attended the earlier congresses, particularly those not from the host country, were predominantly heads of deaf schools, and during those years there were proba-

International Congresses on Education of the Deaf*

Place and date	Number of countries represented	Number of participants		Number from host country	Number from the United States
Paris, France, 1878	6	28		23	1
Milan, Italy, 1880	8	164		87	5
Brussels, Belgium, 1883	[Sources do not indicate number in attendance]				
Chicago, Illinois, 1893	5	211		202	202
Paris, France, 1900					
Hearing Section	16	180		?	5
Deaf Section	11	219		126	4
Liège, Belgium, 1905					
Official Congress		250	hearing		0
	19	350	deaf		0
Free Congress	8	181	hearing and deaf		0
Edinburgh, Scotland, 1907	12	220		192	9
London, England, 1925	21	500 +		420	40
West Trenton, New Jersey, 1933	8	790		778	778
Groningen, The Netherlands, 1950	23	200		?	3
Manchester, England, 1958	41	1000 +		?	?
Washington, D.C., 1963	50	1700		1393	1393
Stockholm, Sweden, 1970	50	1000		?	?
Tokyo, Japan, 1975	33	2389		1968	158
Hamburg, West Germany, 1980	64	1133		425	151

*After R. G. Brill, 1984.

bly no schools headed by deaf persons. Another factor was that there were almost no deaf teachers in European schools between 1878 and 1925, and seven of the first eight congresses were held in Europe during that time period.

The first official record of deaf participants was at the Fourth International Congress held in Chicago in 1893. There were many deaf teachers in the United States at that time and many attended the Chicago Congress.

At the Fifth International Congress in Paris in 1900, the participants were organized into two groups, a deaf section and a hearing section. Although the sections met simultaneously, there was almost no communication between the two groups. The hearing section, dominated by oral educators of the deaf, insisted on almost complete segregation of the two groups.

In 1905 there were two International Congresses held in Liège, Belgium. At the "Official Congress" there were 250 hearing participants and 350 deaf participants. The deaf and hearing members met in two separate gatherings except for the opening and closing sessions. Another meeting in Liège in the same month was called the "Free Congress." There were a total of 181 delegates from eight countries, and the majority of delegates from Belgium and France were deaf. At this Free Congress both deaf and hearing people met equally in one body.

In view of some of the resolutions adopted by the Free Congress, it is probable that the members were primarily representative of governmental public schools. The philosophy endorsed by this group directly opposed that endorsed by the Catholic schools, which were in the majority in France, Belgium, and Italy. In previous congresses it had been the Catholic group that (a) opposed the idea of having the schools under the control of the Ministry of Instruction and (b) opposed the establishment of normal schools for preparing teachers, because they would be under the control of the state. Obviously the Catholic group felt itself to be under church domination. The first of the 21 resolutions passed by the Free Congress were: (1) control of the school for the deaf by the Ministry of Public Instruction; (2) lay instruction, free and compulsory; (3) teachers of the deaf to be placed on the same plane as other teachers; (4) normal schools or classes for the preparation of teachers.

There is no record of any deaf people attending congresses held in Edinburgh in 1907 or in London in 1925, and only three deaf people attended the congress in Manchester in 1958.

The Ninth International Congress in West Trenton, New Jersey, in 1933 was jointly sponsored by four national professional organizations, including the Convention of American Instructors of the Deaf. There were many deaf teachers who were members of that organization, and as a result there were many who attended this International Congress. *See* CONVENTION OF AMERICAN INSTRUCTORS OF THE DEAF.

There were only a few deaf people attending the congress held in Stockholm in 1970. However, there was a greater participation by deaf people, primarily Americans with a Gallaudet College background, in Tokyo in 1975. *See* GALLAUDET COLLEGE.

A great change came about at the International Congress in Hamburg in 1980 when deaf people presented papers at various panels and took leading roles in presenting major addresses in plenary sessions.

The first significant manual interpreting was at the West Trenton Congress in 1933 when a substantial number of deaf teachers were present. In 1963, when Gallaudet College hosted the congress, manual interpreting was provided at all sessions throughout the congress. While there was some participation of deaf people at Stockholm in 1970, a minimum of interpreting was provided. More was provided in Tokyo in 1975, and in Hamburg in 1980 there were manual interpreters for the American Sign Language, the German Sign Language, and the Swedish Sign Language. *See* SIGN LANGUAGES.

Participation in the early congresses was almost exclusively heads of schools for deaf students along with a few other professional leaders. In most recent years teachers and other professionals working with deaf people have constituted the majority of attendees. Also, there have been included professionals from allied fields, particularly medicine, audiology, speech, linguistics, and psychology. This has greatly broadened the scope of the programs.

TOPICS

The oral-manual controversy was a prominent subject in nearly all of the congresses until recent years. In Hamburg in 1980 several participants stated that the time had come to cease the fruitless controversy and to recognize that there should be an integration of the two worlds because both oralism and manualism could be essential to deaf individuals. Because of the larger number of deaf educators participating in this congress, the oral point of view did not predominate.

At the Congress in Tokyo it was recognized that resolutions on philosophy should not be adopted by International Congresses because participants did not necessarily represent the views of their countries. Also, not all countries were represented, nor was the representation proportionate to the size of the programs in the various countries.

Subjects discussed in addition to the oral versus manual communication at various times over the more than 100-year history of International Congresses included medicine and physiology, diagnosis and assessment, educational programs at various levels including preschool and postsecondary education, speech and speechreading, auditory training, psychology, mainstreaming, vocational preparation, multihandicapped deaf children, teacher preparation, religious education, and educational programs in various countries.

It has been said that the fundamental problems of teaching deaf children are the same regardless of country, culture, language, or method of instruction. This commonality of problems may explain why educators of deaf people began to hold international meetings.

Bibliography

Brill, R. G.: *International Congresses on Education of the Deaf: An Analytical History, 1878–1980*, Gallaudet College Press, Washington, D.C., 1984.

Fay, E. A.: "The Brussels Convention," *American Annals of the Deaf*, 28:69–70, 207–208, 254–263, 1883.

———: "Resolutions of the Milan Convention," *American Annals of the Deaf*, 26:64–65, 1881.

———: "Two International Congresses," *American Annals of the Deaf*, 51:1–6, 1906.

Gallaudet, E. M.: "The Milan Convention," *American Annals of the Deaf*, 26:1–16, 1881.

Richard G. Brill

INTERPRETING

Interpreting is the act of rendering a message from one language to another language. Interpreting between hearing and deaf people also involves a change of modality. The deaf person will receive the message through visual means, while the hearing person using an interpreter will receive an auditory message. Interpreting can be thought of as a process or event. The process of interpreting engages the perception, memory, language abilities, and attention of the interpreter. The interpreter must deliver a fluent and accurate rendition of one person's meaning to the other person with little delay. The event of interpreting is the view of this process as seen by the clients or consumers. The interpreter performs a function on a particular occasion enabling people to communicate who do not share the same language or the same modalities for using language. Interpreting thus involves competence in at least two languages, an understanding of the dynamics of human interaction in two quite different modalities, an appreciation of social and cultural differences, an ability to concentrate and stay on task, and a good measure of tact and judgment. Much of the task of the interpreter goes beyond the immediate cognitive processes into the work situation, including considerations of client relations, working conditions, logistics, and advocacy for interpreting.

Sign language interpreters are becoming more aware of similarities between themselves and spoken-language interpreters. The goal of both types of interpreters is the rendering of messages between people who cannot communicate directly. Interpreters of spoken and signed languages endeavor to practice their profession without becoming intrusive or personally involved in the interaction. Where 20 years ago the interpreting with deaf people was practiced in certain circumscribed spheres of action, such as rehabilitation, medical and legal emergencies, and the occasional phone call, today changes in public laws and public attitudes have increased the integration of deaf citizens into the worlds of business and professional life, recreation and arts, education, and all aspects of social service. The increased opportunities for deaf people have expanded the interpreter's work settings as well. Spoken-language interpreters are familiar as adjuncts to international negotiations, diplomatic meetings, and technical conferences. Only since the 1980s have they been trained for work in medical settings, the courts, union negotiations, and a variety of other mundane and intimate settings that interpreters with deaf people find familiar.

The process of interpreting involves several steps that can be separated for the purpose of analysis. In actual performance, these steps are accomplished nearly instantaneously, often with no discernible break from one part of the process to another. The interpreter must perceive and understand a message in one language, and extract the meaning of the message from such diverse factors as the words or signs, intonational features or nonmanual behaviors, nonlinguistic gestural behavior, pausing, and by other cuing mechanisms. The interpreter must then reformulate that meaning into the language of the addressee. The interpreter must also monitor his or her own output to check that all the information comes out as intelligibly as was intended. For the interpreter, at least some of the time his or her attention is on this process. For the speaker or signer and the addressee, the process (when performed by a competent interpreter) is not noticeable; the audience is only aware of unintelligible communication transformed into an intelligible message.

Both hearing and deaf people function as interpreters. Hearing interpreters may come from deaf homes, or have been introduced to deaf people through community, religious, or educational institutions. Deaf people may have had an opportunity to interpret in informal settings before seeking formal training or recognition as interpreters. Several steps in preparing to take on the role of sign language interpreter may be special for deaf people:

1. Gaining awareness of one's own language use. Since signing has traditionally been part of the unacknowledged competence of many deaf people, and few have received formal instruction in signing, it is important for deaf interpreters to gain an awareness of their own language behavior. This awareness is necessary for bilingual hearing signers as well.

2. Gaining control of language varieties. The usual sociolinguistic rules dictate that a deaf person use speech with a hearing person (or perhaps a form of Signed English or other manually coded sign system) and that American Sign Language (ASL) or another natural sign language be used among deaf-only groups. A deaf sign language interpreter needs to be able to use ASL or another sign language even where hearing people are present, and even to hearing people who do not themselves have competence in this language variety. This ability to switch language varieties and to use forms that are not intelligible to all participants is an important step in being ready to interpret by using a sign language. *See* MANUALLY CODED ENGLISH; SIGN LANGUAGES: American.

3. Role rehearsal. It is helpful to rehearse staying in role for the deaf interpreter. People who have good control and awareness of their own language skills still will need practice in maintaining a neutral stance as interpreters. Since often deaf interpreters are working in teams with hearing interpreters, the rehearsal of both team members together will ensure appropriate interaction on the job. The danger for the deaf interpreter comes from potentially being seen by both deaf and hearing clients as an ally or advocate for the deaf person in the interaction. The interpreter's neutrality, both in fact and as perceived by the clientele, is crucial to the success of an interpreting assignment.

4. Ethics. Familiarity with the ethics of interpreting is equally important for deaf and hearing interpreters. Confidentiality, discretion, appropriate compensation, and appropriate professional development opportunities have a place in the conduct of any interpreter, hearing or deaf.

TERMINOLOGY

Interpreters are expected to perform in either direction—from signed to spoken language or from spoken to signed language. These are also referred to as sign-to-voice and voice-to-sign. (Sign-to-voice interpretation was previously termed reverse interpreting. This usage has declined with the recognition that one direction of interpretation does not have primary importance.) The process can be described also as taking place from a source language to a target language. The interpretation can take place immediately (simultaneous interpretation) or with a brief delay (consecutive interpretation). Consecutive interpretation may follow the source input in sentence or phrase units, or in larger units, such as a speaker's whole message. For work with spoken languages, translation refers to the act of rendering a written source text into another language in written form again. Interpretation takes place in live production, either as auditory-to-vocal or involving a visual-gestural language. Sight translation refers to the act of reading a document written in one language and expressing it aloud in another language. Sign language interpreters may also be called upon to perform sight translation from a written language into a sign language.

For sign language interpretation, separate names are increasingly used to distinguish which variety of manual communication is involved. When a true deaf sign language (for example, ASL) is either the source or target language, the process is technically called interpretation. When a manually coded form of a spoken language is one of the forms of communication (for example, Signed English), the process is narrowly called transliteration. Historically, few sign language "interpreters" have actually been competent in interpretation. Most do transliteration. The term intepretation is used generically here.

HISTORY OF INTERPRETING

Sign language interpreting has only recently become a profession, with college- and university-based educational opportunities. Until the 1960s, deaf people relied on skilled amateurs, often children of deaf adults. However, not all such children are bilingual, nor do all have the additional ability and interest to perform interpretation. In addition, such amateurs, while generally well meaning, may have no sense of appropriate ethical behavior. In the mid-1960s, United States government agencies in cooperation with professional educators and rehabilitation workers joined together to identify the appropriate training and professional role for interpreters with deaf people, and to help found a professional association of interpreters working with deaf people.

The Registry of Interpreters for the Deaf seeks to promote high-quality interpretation by providing a certification evaluation and maintaining a registry of certified and noncertified members. In recent years the evaluation process has been undergoing serious revision to assure standard administration and scoring by local teams of evaluators around the United States. It is also being revised to reflect the full repertoire of skills expected of qualified interpreters. The evaluation tests candidates on their knowledge of professional practice and ethics, as well as on interpreting skills on audio-visual materials of known difficulty. *See* REGISTRY OF INTERPRETERS FOR THE DEAF.

IMAGES OF THE INTERPRETER

The interpreter's role has been compared to a machine, a window, a bridge, and a telephone line.

All of these metaphors are in part apt, and at the same time ignore the essential fact that the interpreter is a human being.

The interpreter-as-machine is a convenient reminder that the interpreter will reproduce the message from one participant to another faithfully, accurately, and without emotional distortion or personal bias.

The interpreter-as-window metaphor emphasizes the clarity and fidelity of the interpretation. The "window" may be looked through without being looked at. The interpreter-as-bridge and interpreter-as-phone-connection likewise point to the distances or barriers between the participants who do not share the same language or communication system. The interpretation makes it possible to transmit information from one to the other.

Each metaphor can be useful in a limited way, as long as the interpreter's human qualities are not neglected. For example, a machine might be expected to give consistent performance over many hours of operation, while a human interpreter needs periodic pauses to refresh mental and physical alertness.

ETHICS

Two people who agree to use a third person to interpret between them enter into an act of trust. They must rely on the third person to be accurate and discreet. They assume that the third person is proficient. They believe that the interpreter knows how to maintain impartiality. If one or both clients feel the interpreter will not be able to remain neutral, two interpreters may be engaged, presumably to interpret into the language of each client.

By arriving in good time, dressing appropriately, and maintaining a low profile on the job, an interpreter will lay the groundwork for a process that will be remembered little. When everything is working best, the interpreter is unobtrusive and the interaction is comfortable for all. The trust involved includes a great deal of certainty about the interpreter's ability to maintain confidentiality.

During assignments, the interpreter gains access to much confidential information. The names of the people involved, the topics discussed, the decisions reached are clearly not the interpreter's to reveal. Moreover, the interpreter may hold back information about the age, sex, or other personal identifying details of the clients. Given that the deaf population is only a small and often tight-knit group in any particular region, any details of the interpreting assignment may compromise the clients' privacy. Even after the information becomes public, the interpreter still is obligated to remain mum. The only exception might be when a participant formally waives confidentiality. The careful interpreter would still want assurance of the participant's understanding of that waiver.

The time of arrival at the job site, the length of assignment, and any subsequent meeting of the parties (where an interpreter will need to be assigned) are all relevant to the payment and scheduling of interpreters. The interpreter coordinator or hiring agency may rightfully request such information. Much more problematic is a second type of request. Many schools, for example, have asked the interpreter to report if a student is absent or tardy or if problems arise (incomplete homework, inappropriate behavior). The interpreter should understand this condition and agree to it before accepting the assignment. Some interpreters find this condition a violation of confidentiality, and would argue that a deaf student has every right to be absent or tardy occasionally, just as hearing students do, and furthermore that it is the faculty's responsibility to handle student absences and monitor progress.

Accuracy in interpreting means that the interpreter will have made an assessment of the audience, will share the speaker's understanding of the intention of the message, and will be able to render a message from the speaker's language into the listener's language. When sign language is one of the languages, the interpreter will render a message from the speaker/signer's language into the listener/viewer's language, or from the source to the target language. Accuracy does not mean that there will be an equivalence between a word or sign in one language and a word or sign in the other. Messages that are fraught with idiomatic phrases or proper names (of products, of places, of official roles) often have many built-in cultural assumptions. Thus, accuracy means that the interpreter should say as much as the sender of the message, but no more. Accuracy also means giving the receiver the complete message, including the part carried by pauses, hesitation, or other silent or nonverbal signals. The interpreter transmits the full message, not merely the words.

Proficiency means that the interpreter will accept only those assignments that are within his or her capacity to perform well. Constraints of either preparation time or skill level might be considered here. In cases where interpreters do not have confidence in their ability to perform satisfactorily, they are best off declining the assignment.

Impartiality implies that the interpreter will not attempt to advise or lead either party, will resist being taken as an ally of one party, and will otherwise avoid expressing opinions about the content or procedures. There are situations in which the interpreter might not wish to be impartial. The interpreter may anticipate that one party is attempting to mislead the other. The interpreter may have strong religious, political, or other beliefs that would lead to support for one person's ideas over

another's. Acknowledging these strong feelings can be useful for the interpreter, since his or her personal feelings and attitudes ought not to come out in the interpretation. Interpreters can maintain their impartiality by staying strictly in role, functioning only to facilitate communication. They will say "no" during an assignment when the clients request that the interpreter perform some task outside the role of interpreting. By avoiding improper involvement in the interaction, the interpreter will not wrongly encourage the clients' dependency, become responsible for the outcome of the interaction, or raise an incorrect expectation about other interpreters' behavior.

While the request for compensation may seem at first to be exclusively a business concern, it is also an ethical issue. Interpreters have an obligation to the profession and to clients to state fees when the arrangements for service are made. Interpreters often find that clients, both hearing and deaf, are unaware that in many cases this service is not supported by any outside agency or organization. At the same time, provision of interpreting services may be mandated by law or regulation.

It is interesting to consider how the current conventions about ethics and etiquette have developed. Hearing children of deaf parents were the first interpreters for deaf people. Hearing children of deaf parents sometimes take on more responsibility than would be expected for their age, and sometimes feel the need to protect their parents from misunderstanding. As interpreting has become recognized as a profession by both the practitioner and the client, however, a formal distance between client and interpreter has developed. The maintenance of professional distance is now seen as an advantage in interpreting. Just as a doctor would not treat a family member, so an interpreter would avoid interpreting for close friends or relatives.

ETIQUETTE

In simultaneous interpretation in general, whether between spoken languages or between spoken and signed languages, the interpreter is expected to interpret everything that is said. Summaries, simplifications, and explanations are not the same as interpretation. Of course, in practice, it is often a matter of judgment whether a particular rendering of a text has passed beyond the acceptable limits of interpretation into one of these other forms.

Everything that is spoken in the presence of an interpreter and a deaf client must be interpreted into the client's preferred form of communication. Interpreting everything means interruptive conversations, telephone calls, public address system announcements, outside noises. The reverse is true as well: everything that is signed in the presence of an interpreter and a hearing (nonsigning) client must be interpreted into spoken language. Deaf clients will at first find it disconcerting to realize that their formerly private talk is now public, but will appreciate the reciprocal access to communication that interpreting affords. This guideline extends to coffee breaks, informal receptions, standing in line, and so on. Of course, an interpreter is permitted the time necessary to attend to personal needs and to be refreshed at agreed-upon breaks. In order to make sure that everyone knows the practice of interpreting everything, to briefly review the ethical responsibilities of the interpreter, an introduction is useful. Either the interpreter or one of the clients can take responsibility to make sure that all parties know how the interpreter will function. The introduction may also afford the interpreter an opportunity to become acquainted with clients' accents, language, or personal style.

The currently accepted practice among both spoken-language interpreters and sign language interpreters is to take the role of each person in turn by using the first-person forms of address. Rather than begin each time with "he said" or "she's asking," simply using "I" for each person avoids ambiguity and encourages the notion that the people are addressing one another directly.

Clothing, jewelry, and makeup or facial hair are all factors to be considered by sign language interpreters that are less crucial for spoken-language interpreters who are hidden in a booth. Solid-color clothing that contrasts with skin tones is recommended, as is the modest use of accessories and makeup. A male interpreter's facial hair should be well trimmed to permit clients to lipread.

SETTINGS FOR INTERPRETATION

Interpretation may occur anywhere that deaf and hearing people come together. A few of the more frequent settings are described below.

Educational Settings   In the United States, schools constitute one of the most common settings for interpreting. This situation occurs as a result of several public laws affecting access to educational opportunities. Interpreters can now be found in public schools, both elementary and secondary levels. Interpreters also accompany college students in their coursework, tutorials, and extracurricular activities, at the undergraduate and graduate levels. Most frequently the deaf person is a student in a mainstreamed setting, with many hearing classmates and hearing teachers.

Interpreters in the educational setting often are expected to serve as tutors, as classroom aides, or in other dual roles. Such multiple responsibilities can be confusing for the students and the staff if not carefully designed and executed.

Legal Settings   One of the serious challenges to interpreting in legal settings is the use of much specialized terminology in a highly formalized arena. Interpreters have a responsibility to make the technical language understandable to the client, and therefore need to undergo training to prepare for this setting.

Many jurisdictions have recognized the right of defendants to interpreters while accused of crime. Fewer provide for mandatory interpretation for deaf witnesses, jurors, or any other role in the judicial process. When interpreting in legal (as in other) settings, the interpreter considers the interaction confidential. A few jurisdictions make this ethical standard into a legal reality by granting "privileged" communication status to interpreters. Without the presence of an attorney, however, interpreters in other jurisdictions do not have the legal right to refuse to testify about interactions they have interpreted. *See* COURT INTERPRETERS ACT; STATE STATUTES: Interpreters in Judicial Proceedings.

Medical Settings   Technical language again presents a challenge in medical settings. Interpreters may also find that medical personnel do not understand the interpreter's role, and will require careful explanation that the interpreter is an aid to the medical procedures. The interpreter neither has special information about a deaf patient nor wants to limit access to the patient.

Sensitivity to matching the sex of the interpreter with the sex of the client may be necessary. Of course, this requirement is dependent on the sort of procedure anticipated. In any case, the interpreter needs to choose a physical position where the deaf client has good ability to see the interpretation, but at the same time does not feel intruded upon. The medical personnel also must be able to have easy access to the patient. As more deaf individuals find employment in medical settings (nursing, dentistry, medical technology), interpreting will not be limited to situations where the deaf person is the recipient of health care services.

Mental Health Settings   Psychological evaluations, counseling, and therapy may all involve the use of an interpreter. Interpretations that are informed by an understanding of the psychologist's or psychiatrist's purposes will achieve more useful results. Psychological evaluations, for example, require strict adherence to the principle of saying only as much as the source language has said. Introduction of "helpful" explanation by an interpreter can lead to an inappropriate evaluation. Interpreters may wish to seek orientation to procedures and to the concepts of therapeutic process. The notions of transference and countertransference should be mastered to function effectively with mental health professionals. Powerful emotions often surface during counseling or therapy; the interpreter needs to be prepared to deal with his or her own feelings resulting from the session.

Rehabilitation and Social Service Many different functions can be subsumed under this heading. Deaf individuals need communication access to vocational training and evaluation and to services provided by government or private agencies. In some cases, social service workers who are fluent in their clients' communication system may be expected to serve as interpreters as well as rehabilitation or counseling personnel. The difficulty with the dual role is the possibility that the deaf client will not be able to separate when the professional is acting as advocate and when as interpreter. Interpreters functioning in rehabilitation settings will see a variety of communication systems and enjoy a great diversity of work assignment.

Business, Industry, and Government The business world can benefit from the introduction of interpreters to assure that job responsibilities are well understood, that deaf employees have full opportunities for advancement, and that potential misunderstandings are resolved before problems develop. As deaf people take advantage of greater educational opportunities and find positions in business, the need for qualified interpreters will grow. Where existing staff of an organization have appropriate communication skills, the business can take advantage of the "in-house" interpreter's understanding of the work environment. Coworkers acting as interpreters have a special responsibility to be clear about ethical behavior in order not to violate the deaf coworker's privacy. Businesses can avoid this difficulty by hiring staff whose sole responsibility is interpreting or by using outside contractors for interpreting.

Performing Arts Deaf audiences enjoy participating in cultural events, including performance arts. While dance and mime are accessible generally without an interpreter, much theater, music, opera, and other live entertainment lose their charm without an understanding of the auditory performance. Community activities such as public dedication of a new building, celebration of holidays, or even political rallies can be categorized with performing arts, since the role of the interpreter is similar. In each of these situations, much of the performance is scripted ahead, and therefore the interpreter can be engaged beforehand and given an opportunity to rehearse alone and with the other performers. Therefore, the key to successful performance interpreting is making the arrangements sufficiently in advance. Performance interpreters can benefit from a director or adviser during the rehearsal period to serve as an informed eye. Physical placement, lighting, and costuming of the interpreters likewise can be planned ahead, in conjunction with the director or stage manager of the production. Audience development and care in seating the deaf audience to best advantage are other com-

ponents in the process. Performances by signing artists may require the interpreter's voice-over for the hearing audience's enjoyment.

Religious Settings Interpretations in religious contexts may be undertaken by the clergy who can sign for themselves or by another person acting as interpreter. In either case, the interpretation will be marked by a heightened attention to the ritualized uses and poetic senses of language. Difference in religious practices has led some to recommend that the interpreter be of the same religious background. While familiarity with the ritual and deeper meaning of the services can help the interpreter, the sensitive practitioner can offer a meaningful interpretation in the usual case. Beyond issues of language, the interpreter needs to make appropriate choices about physical position in the house of worship or meeting space.

While religious institutions accept volunteer contributions, the interpreter who expects to be paid should say so at the time the assignment is offered. The interpreter, like the organist or religious school staff, is a trained professional. As in other settings mentioned above, the issue of two roles for the interpreter, for example, religious school instructor and interpreter, has the potential to lead to misunderstanding, and thus each role must be clearly defined to the supervisory personnel as well as the congregants.

SPECIAL COMMUNICATION TECHNIQUES
Additional communication techniques may be required for some clients or situations. Clients with minimal language skills (MLS) may not share language or communication systems with the interpreter, and therefore may need special assistance to achieve understanding. Employing a trained deaf interpreter for such deaf clients can often overcome the barrier introduced by MLS. *See* LANGUAGE: Minimal Language Skills.

Deaf-blind clients will likewise have special needs that may be met on an individual basis. Some who suffer severely reduced vision may benefit from an interpreter seated closer than usual. Others may require tactile transmission of fingerspelling or signing. Still others can understand the message through tactile reception of speech. Deaf interpreters can many times fill the need for individual tactile interpreting by relaying the information from a hearing interpreter. Interpreters with deaf-blind clients may find themselves with additional tasks beyond the transmission of a message. An adequate interpretation will often include descriptions of the actions of the other people. Deaf-blind people may seek assistance in mobility and orientation as well. *See* DEAF-BLINDNESS.

Oral transmission, or oral interpreting, can be a method to help a deaf person who depends on lipreading to participate more fully. Oral transmission involves the repetition and rephrasing of the spoken message to enhance the movements of lips, mouth, and jaw. Deaf individuals who prefer this method may want to speak for themselves or may make use of the interpreter for the visual-to-spoken mode as well. Even an excellent lipreader will have difficulty interacting effectively in a group setting.

Telephones present another barrier for deaf people. When a deaf person uses an interpreter for communicating by phone, the responsibility for the call still rests with the deaf person. This implies that deaf people who wish to use the phone need orientation to the telephone and its etiquette. The interpretation usually will take place in the simultaneous mode, although on occasion an interpreter may agree to a more consecutive style. The deaf maker of the call is in charge, no matter which style is adopted, and should remain visible to the interpreter to respond. Calling a switchboard, introducing oneself over the phone, and talking to close friends and family are a few of the challenges of telephone interpreting. The professional interpreter will not assume that the deaf person is finished until both parties say goodbye.

MARKETPLACE AND WORKING CONDITIONS

The demand for interpreters continues to rise, and projections of need for the latter 1980s exceed the anticipated number of available interpreters. These projections have encouraged government organizations to support funding of training programs for interpreting. Research indicates that many interpreters need additional training in the grammar and semantics of both ASL and English as well as in the interpreting process.

Factors that affect the market for interpreting include the demographics of the deaf population; the willingness of agencies, institutions, and businesses to hire staff interpreters; and the availability of interpreters on a full-time versus part-time basis. In some large urban areas, interpreters working free-lance as independent contractors can earn as much as staff interpreters elsewhere. In less populated areas, staff interpreting is the only reasonable option for full-time employment.

Working conditions for optimum interpretation may be surprising to those who have not undertaken this demanding task. Interpreting alone cannot be a 40-hour-per-week job. Professional spoken-language interpreters will not work more than 6-8 hours per day in teams of two, so that one interpreter will not have more than 3–4 hours of interpreting in a single day. Sign language interpreters are finding similar limits appropriate for them. No single assignment should last longer than 40–50 minutes without a break of 5–10 minutes, or fatigue will begin to affect the quality of the

interpretation. Twenty hours per week, then, would be a reasonable maximum number of hours of interpreting. Full-time interpreters fill the remainder of their time with other tasks such as public education about interpreting, preparation for particular assignments, and related work.

Payment for interpreting varies depending on the assignment or position and the individual interpreter's background. An interpreter with an undergraduate degree and specialized additional training would obviously command a higher rate than a high school graduate with minimal experience. An interpreter may accept a lower rate for the security of an extended assignment. Travel compensation, for cost of travel or for traveling time, is a negotiable item. Many interpreters are now expecting all or part of the fee to be paid if the assignment is canceled with short notice. For example, the interpreter who commits to spending every weekday morning for several months at an assignment needs to be compensated if that assignment is canceled after only a few weeks. Staff interpreters, whether full- or part-time, may take a lower salary than a free-lance interpreter because of the additional benefits of health insurance, pension contributions, and paid vacation time.

Volunteer interpreting is performed at the discretion of the interpreter. Students of interpreting under the supervision of a mentor or instructor may be encouraged to volunteer as part of an internship or practicum experience. The professional interpreter, however, cannot claim any tax benefit for volunteering, whether that service is provided to a business or a nonprofit organization. Interpreting is a service that requires specialized training and demands the individual's full attention and skill. The decision to contribute this service to an individual or an organization can only be the interpreter's. People who need the services of an interpreter will be more likely to find a qualified interpreter among those who charge for the work. A qualified interpreter understands the ethical decisions inherent in any assignment, and can evaluate the communication skills and needs of the participants.

More than one interpreter may be required for a particular assignment depending on its length, physical and logistic considerations, or communication skills of the interpreters or clients. For example, a full day's business meeting will likely require two interpreters. A conference with several deaf participants taking part in different special sessions will require sufficient interpreters to cover the sessions. A panel discussion with a deaf person on the panel and other deaf people in the audience, with hearing participants as well, will require signing interpreters for both audience and panelist, and possibly voicing interpreters for the panelist and for questions from the audience. International meetings with several sign languages represented require many interpreters to meet the communication needs of all participants. As mentioned above, when clients have special communication requirements, the need for interpreters with matching skills arises. Teams of interpreters aid in working with deaf-blind, foreign, and minimal language skills clients.

PRACTICAL CONSIDERATIONS

In planning for the use of interpreters with deaf people, the important factors are visibility of the interpreters by the audience and of the deaf audience by the interpreters, and audibility of speakers by the interpreters and of the interpreters by the hearing audience. To satisfy these needs, sightlines, lighting, auditory and visual background, and the physical movement of the participants in the space all must be considered. Backlighting on the interpreter or the deaf participants is not desirable, nor is a visually busy backdrop. Specific situations should be considered well in advance so that the interpreter can alert planners to the need for a small light in a darkened room, or the need for an audio monitor if the loudspeaker system delivers a distorted signal to the podium. An interpreter coordinator can help to anticipate audience needs and plan an economical and realistic schedule for interpreting.

Clients who are not satisfied with the performance of the interpreter should communicate this to the coordinator or agency through which the interpreter was hired. If an interpreter has violated a major tenet of the Code of Ethics and is a member of the Registry of Interpreters for the Deaf, formal grievance procedures may be brought against the interpreter. Local grievance boards attempt to mediate complaints, and will refer grievances through to the national level if they cannot be resolved locally. Sanctions against an interpreter can include suspension or revocation of certification.

SUMMARY

Interpreting involves the ability to render a message from one language into another. Standards of ethical behavior monitored by a professional association have the goal of opening the way to communication for both hearing and deaf people. By keeping the interpreter solely in the role of facilitator of communication, all participants have the opportunity to deal directly and independently with one another. Anticipating one's needs for an interpreter in a particular setting can permit appropriate planning for physical needs, as well as scheduling of personnel.

Bibliography

Fink, Barbara: "Being Ignored Can Be Bliss: How to Use a Sign Language Interpreter," *Deaf American*, 34.6:5–9, 1982 (reprinted from *Disabled USA*, Fall 1981).

Frishberg, Nancy: *Interpreting: An Introduction*, RID Publications, Silver Spring, Maryland, 1985.

Seleskovitch, Danica: *Interpreting for International Conferences*, Pen and Booth, Washington, D.C., 1978.

Solow, Sharon Neumann: *Sign Language Interpreting: A Basic Resource Book*, National Association of Deaf, Silver Spring, Maryland, 1981.

Nancy Frishberg

Interpreter Training in the United States

Interpreters have been a part of life since peoples of different languages first came together and attempted to communicate. In the area of deafness, these people historically have been hearing persons who had deaf parents or deaf siblings and thus had some skill in both spoken English and American Sign Language (ASL). These early interpreters had no formal education to prepare them to mediate language and culture, but they were generally successful in facilitating communication. They worked on an informal, voluntary basis without pay or supervision. There remained, however, a need for professionalism and quality control.

DEMAND FOR INTERPRETERS

Several events in the mid-1960s expanded the social, educational, and economic involvement of deaf people in the United States and resulted in the establishment of formal interpreter training. Section 9 of the 1965 Vocational Rehabilitation Act authorized interpreting as a case service for deaf vocational rehabilitation clients for the first time. New postsecondary programs for deaf students were established, beginning with California State University, Northridge (1964), National Technical Institute for the Deaf (1968), and three regional technical-vocational programs in 1969 (Delgado College, Louisiana; St. Paul Technical Vocational Institute, Minnesota; and Seattle Central Community College, Washington). *See* CALIFORNIA STATE UNIVERSITY, NORTHRIDGE; EDUCATIONAL PROGRAMS: Higher Education; NATIONAL TECHNICAL INSTITUTE FOR THE DEAF.

These events resulted in a sudden demand for sign language interpreters that rapidly exceeded the supply. The educational institutions above began to set up interpreter training classes, hoping to increase the quantity of personnel available to meet the burgeoning educational and vocational rehabilitation interpreting needs. Initial attempts tapped a logical resource—young adults who had deaf parents or deaf siblings. These students, it was assumed, already had a command of sign language and needed only "a little polish," and thus a minimum of time, to prepare them to work as sign language interpreters. It was difficult, first, to locate these individuals, and then they were often unwilling to enter the field of deafness as a profession, or they needed more preparation than expected. It became obvious that the field of students must be broadened to include those who had an interest in learning sign language and working as interpreters, that is, people who had no background in the language or culture of the deaf community. Thus emerged a rapidly increasing number of formal, sign language classes. *See* SIGN LANGUAGE TEACHING.

Interpreting, in the formal sense, was a new phenomenon in the 1960s. William E. Stokoe had only recently shared the results of his research, declaring that ASL was, in fact, a language. The Registry of Interpreters for the Deaf had just been established in 1964 and was making the first attempts to define terminology and roles. Little was known about how to teach interpreting. No one was trained in the art of educating a sign language interpreter. No research had been conducted to determine the mental process taking place during interpreting, nor had a task analysis been completed to identify the parts of the act known as interpretation. The assumption was made that if one could sign, one could interpret.

BEGINNING PROGRAMS

Thus, early interpreter training was made up primarily of sign languge classes, two to six weeks in length, that developed conversational skills most often in a pidgin form of ASL and English. Interpreting, as such, was learned largely on the job by trial and error, where one usually worked unsupervised.

In 1973, the Rehabilitation Services Administration funded a grant that established the national Interpreter Training Consortium whose purposes were to prepare interpreter trainers, establish curriculum guidelines, train interpreters, and provide consumer education to deaf clientele. The six institutions in the consortium were the University of Arizona, California State University at Northridge, New York University, St. Paul Technical Vocational Institute, Seattle Central Community College, and the University of Tennessee. Numerous workshops were held and classes taught under the auspices of the consortium. Interpreting skills were honed; interpreters in isolated areas were brought into contact with others who were involved in the same line of work; information was exchanged and positive experiences resulted. Additional legislation was passed, resulting in an ever-increasing demand for interpreters. Training programs ranging in length from six weeks to one year began to spring up in every state. Interpreter training, however, was still in its infancy. *See* REHABILITATION: Administration.

With the depletion of consortium funds, provision was made for grant monies to be awarded to 10 regional interpreter training centers in the Rehabilitation, Comprehensive Services, and Developmental Disabilities Amendments of 1978 (Public Law 95-602, Section 304). The Conference Report for P.L. 95-602 suggested that the Office for Handicapped Individuals be redesignated as the Office of Information and Resources for the Handicapped in order to implement training for interpreters for deaf people and other information clearinghouse activities mandated elsewhere in the act. Funds were awarded and sign language interpreter training classes were provided in various regions.

MATURING PROGRAMS

Curricular materials began to appear, including a curriculum outline from New York University and a first comprehensive instructional guide, prepared by Cynthia Roy and Janice Kanda. In addition, the first interactive videotapes for the purpose of training interpreters in lifelike role-play situations was developed by deaf trainer Bob Alcorn.

Interpreter trainers, frustrated by a lack of information on how to accomplish their job, came together to discuss their common needs and interests during the 1978 Registry of Interpreters for the Deaf convention in Rochester, New York. Their concerns centered on the need for professional development, structure for exchange among trainers, and the development of educational strategies that would result in more highly skilled, rather than greater numbers of, graduates. As a result of this gathering, the first national Conference of Interpreter Trainers was held in 1979, sponsored by the Council of Directors, the National Interpreter Training Consortium, and the Registry of Interpreters for the Deaf. The conference gives innovative leadership to the task of educating interpreters. Dialogue has been established with educators of spoken-language interpreters to exchange ideas and instructional techniques. A task force was appointed to begin the initial stages of a task analysis of the processes of interpretation and transliteration.

Increased research and study led to the realization that interpreters must be bilingual and bicultural before being capable of learning the art of interpretation or transliteration. Interpreters must also have a wide range of general knowledge and life experience in order to analyze linguistic interactions and provide appropriate cultural-linguistic equivalents in the target language. The task is complex, and the education related to interpreting is beginning to reflect that complexity. Early interpreter training programs were six weeks in length, then one year, and later two years. Four-year bachelor's degree programs in sign language interpreting then emerged, and the future may see a movement toward graduate-level education similar to that found in the education of spoken-language interpreters.

A model interpreter training program will include at least the following courses: comparative English and ASL linguistic analysis; comparative cultural analysis; text analysis in various settings;

skills development in interpretation (beginning with consecutive interpreting tasks and later developing simultaneous interpreting skills—frequently integrating sign-to-voice and voice-to-sign assignments in both); an overview of the profession—code of ethics, decision-making skills, and business practices; and practicum.

Schematic models of the interpreting process have been developed by Dennis Cokely, Betty Colonomos, and others that have enabled identification of some of the components involved in the mental processing of information being interpreted as well as environmental factors that affect information transmission and interpretation. This has allowed teachers of interpretation and transliteration to teach specific skills in a sequentially appropriate manner. Rather than teaching sign skills and then jumping immediately into simultaneous interpreting practice, interpreter trainers now develop the building blocks of auditory and visual listening skills, short- and long-term memory, analytical skills specific to understanding the ASL or English text in the particular setting in which it is uttered, recomposition of the message into the target language, and self- and audience-monitoring skills.

The field of interpreter training has been in existence only since 1964. As research, program development, curriculum, and instructional techniques are improved, it is expected that sign language interpreters will increase in quantity and quality, serving to facilitate communication between deaf and hearing persons in the United States.

Bibliography

Baker, Charlotte, and Robbin Battison (eds.): *Sign Language and the Deaf Community*, National Association of the Deaf, Silver Spring, Maryland, 1980.

Caccamise, Frank, et al. (eds.): *Introduction to Interpreting for Interpreters/Transliterators, Hearing-Impaired Consumers, Hearing Consumers*, Registry of Interpreters for the Deaf, Inc., Silver Spring, Maryland, 1980.

Carlson, Rebecca H., and Anna Witter Merithew (eds.): *Proceedings of the First National Conference of Interpreter Trainers*, National Technical Institute for the Deaf, Rochester, New York, 1980.

Cokely, Dennis R: "Towards a Sociolinguistic Model of the Interpreting Process: Focus on ASL and English," unpublished dissertation, 1984.

Colonomos, Betty: "Reflections of an Interpreter Trainer," *The Reflector*, vol. 2, pp. 5–14, Winter 1982.

Roy, Cynthia B., and Janice H. Kanda: *Developing Curriculum for Interpreter Training Programs in Vocational Education*, vols. 1 and 2, Texas State Technical Institute, Waco, 1980.

Sternberg, Martin, Carol C. Tipton, and Jerome D. Schein: *Curriculum Guide for Interpreter Training*, New York University, New York, 1973.

Yoken, Carol (ed.): *Interpreter Training: The State of the Art*, National Academy of Gallaudet College, Washington, D.C., 1979.

Janice H. Kanda

IRELAND, NORTHERN

Northern Ireland comprises a total area of 5452 square miles (14,175 square kilometers) and has a population of more than 1.5 million. Administratively, Northern Ireland is divided into six counties: Antrim, Armagh, Down, Fermanagh, Londonderry, and Tyrone, together with 14 district and 12 borough councils. Belfast, the capital, and Londonderry are the principal cities. A separate parliament and executive government was established for Northern Ireland by the Government of Ireland Act 1921, but the country is ruled directly from London.

Statistics of hearing impairment are published periodically by the Departments of Education and of Health and Social Services. The numbers of hearing-impaired adults on local authority registers include more than 500 persons with speech, more than 600 deaf persons without speech, and more than 2500 hard-of-hearing. The numbers of hard-of-hearing are probably understated.

WELFARE SERVICES

Provision for the spiritual needs of adult deaf persons in Northern Ireland was pioneered by the Reverend John Kinghan, principal of the Ulster Institution from 1853 to 1884, who in 1857 commenced religious services for deaf people in Belfast. A nondenominational Mission Hall for the Adult Deaf and Dumb was established in Belfast by W. Tredennick in 1886.

Welfare services for hearing-impaired individuals are now provided on behalf of the Department of Health and Social Services by four Health and Social Services Boards under the Health and Personal Social Services (Northern Ireland) Order 1972 and the Chronically Sick and Disabled Persons (Northern Ireland) Act 1978. Voluntary organizations, however, continue to play an important role in promoting the welfare of hearing-impaired persons. Such organizations include the Kinghan Mission, the Ulster Institute for the Deaf and the St. Joseph's Centre for the Deaf in Belfast, and the Lurgan Society for the Deaf. The National Deaf Children's Society, the British Deaf Association, and the British Association of the Hard of Hearing are active in Northern Ireland. *See* UNITED KINGDOM: Organizations.

Kenneth Lysons

EDUCATION

Developments in the education of deaf people in Northern Ireland, defined as those with profound or moderate hearing loss, have from their beginnings closely paralleled those in the United Kingdom. Responsibility for securing the statutory system of public education, including that for handicapped individuals, resides with the province's five Education and Library Boards working under the oversight of the Department of Education. The boards are required to ensure that there are schools in sufficient number and variety to meet the area needs. They must also, under the Education and Libraries Order (Northern Ireland) 1972, determine those children who require special educational treatment. Deaf persons and those with partial hearing are 2 of the 10 categories defined in the regulations as requiring special educational treatment. *See* ENGLAND, EDUCATION IN.

Prior to 1960 the boards discharged their responsibilities to deaf people by obtaining their admission to the school provided by a voluntary organization named the Ulster Society for Promoting the Education of the Deaf and Dumb and the Blind, founded in 1836. The Ulster Society's school, located in Belfast since 1846, moved to its present site at Jordanstown, Whiteabbey, County of Antrim, in 1961. In 1960, however, with the formation by the Belfast Education and Library Board of the first class for partially hearing children attached to an ordinary school, a completely new dimension was added to the previous sole special educational provision available to children with hearing loss. This movement toward integration, or mainstreaming, was further intensified in 1961 with the appointment by the Antrim Education Authority (now the North-Eastern Education and Library Board) of John Darbyshire, previously a teacher of deaf persons with the Ulster Society. Darbyshire was to investigate the incidence of hearing impairment at school age within the county and to make provision recommendations. As a direct result of Darbyshire's findings and recommendations, the Antrim Authority established a peripatetic service to assist with ascertainment and to offer guidance to parents of young deaf children. The authority also was quick to establish classes for partially hearing children attached to ordinary schools at both the primary and secondary level. The remaining education authorities, or area boards as they are now termed, were soon to follow the example set by Belfast and Antrim.

There are some 27 such classes in Northern Ireland catering to approximately 240 children. In all of these an oral-aural approach to communication is used virtually exclusively with radio-link individual hearing aids increasingly replacing the more traditional hardwire group aid systems. Each of the five area boards has an established peripatetic service. *See* EDUCATION: Communication; HEARING AIDS.

Facilities for the education of deaf students in Northern Ireland were further extended in 1969 with the opening of a small school, again in the voluntary sector. This school, named St. Francis De Sales and located in Belfast, was begun by the Catholic Order of Dominican Sisters. It caters to deaf children in the nursery or primary age range and uses a purely oral approach to teaching.

As the partially hearing unit provision expanded in Northern Ireland, a corresponding decline in the numbers of children with hearing loss attending the Ulster Society's school at Jordanstown took place. Numbers declined from a peak of 164 in 1969 to a level of less than 50. The age range of the pupils has narrowed from 8 to 15 and over, and a total communication approach is used by the staff to accommodate the profound hearing losses suffered by the great majority of pupils. *See* SOCIOLINGUISTICS: Total Communication.

Again paralleling developments elsewhere in the United Kingdom, a Further Education Hostel was established by the Ulster Society on the Jordanstown site in 1979. This hostel, named the Ulster Centre, caters to deaf students in the 16 and over age bracket who are taking continuing education courses at colleges in the greater Belfast area. The hostel, under the day-to-day direction of the senior tutor, a teacher of deaf students, provides accommodation during the week for the students and back-up support to them and to the staffs of the colleges. The students, by and large, are products of either secondary school partially hearing units or the school at Jordanstown itself. The courses followed at the further education colleges include hairdressing, secretarial studies, catering, and business studies.

There are no teacher training facilities for prospective teachers of deaf people within Northern Ireland. Teachers, for the most part, undertake a one-year course either at a teacher training establishment in England or at the one that is attached to University College Dublin in the Republic of Ireland.

In April 1982 the Department of Education for Northern Ireland issued its proposals for the introduction of legislation in Northern Ireland to bring the special education services in the province broadly into line with developments in Great Britain. The main features of the proposals are: (1) replacement of the 10 categories of handicap by one based on the "special educational needs for individual children"; (2) provision for the closer involvement of parents in the decision-making process about their children's special educational needs; and (3) establishment, in law, of the principle that children with special educational needs should be integrated into ordinary schools.

The effects of the new legislation on the education of deaf children in Northern Ireland can only be minimal. Their integration into ordinary schools through the provision of partially hearing units is very firmly established. The decline of enrollment at the Ulster Society's school for deaf students at Jordanstown will no doubt continue and may very possibly lead to its demise. It is uncertain whether this will be to the long-term benefit of deaf people in Northern Ireland.

Bibliography
Education and Libraries (Northern Ireland) Order, 1972.
Handicapped Pupils and Special Schools Regulations (Northern Ireland), 1973.
Special Educational Needs: Report of the Committee of Enquiry into the Education of Handicapped Children and Young People (The Warnock Report), 1978.

J. G. McClelland

IRELAND, REPUBLIC OF

The advancement of social attitudes toward deafness in Europe was not felt in the Republic of Ireland until 1816, when the first school for deaf people was founded in Dublin by Charles Orpen, M.D. This school no longer exists. Two other nineteenth-century schools still serving deaf pupils were founded by the Catholic Institute for the Deaf at Cabra, Dublin. It was not until 1952, when a Department of Special Education was established, that the Irish government accepted financial responsibility for schools for deaf persons.

EDUCATION

Education for hearing-impaired children is free. Its aim is to prepare these children to develop their abilities, to enable them to become independent community members, and to offer them the opportunity for cultural enrichment. Since the 1940s the policy has been to provide exclusively oral education for all hearing-impaired pupils, including those who are deaf (with hearing losses in excess of 60 decibels at 125 hertz and 250 hertz and of 95 decibels in the remaining speech frequencies). Some children, however, fail to make satisfactory progress when a strictly oral approach is used. For them, two Irish schools provide supplemental manual communication in separate school and residential accommodations. Experience in these schools has shown that when speech and signs are used simultaneously, listening and lipreading skills deteriorate.

Since 1962, emphasis has been placed on early diagnosis as a prerequisite for successful educational treatment. In 1977–1980 a survey of hearing-impaired children born in 1969 in countries of the European Economic Community showed that the Republic of Ireland ranked second in having 34 percent fully diagnosed before the age of two. In that country the incidence of hearing loss sufficiently great to warrant the use of a hearing aid was 0.9 per 1000 of the school-going population. Irish medical officers and Public Health nurses administer hearing tests to all infants between six and nine months and to all school entrants. Children screened out are investigated in audiology clinics. The National Rehabilitation Board Hearing Aid Service has a statutory responsibility for supply and fitting of a wide range of hearing aids to all children irrespective of parental status, as well as to adults who are eligible for free medical treatment. This National Service is responsible for the supervision of hearing aid users. It has permanent clinics in Dublin, Cork, and Galway, as well as regular clinics in 18 other centers to cater for the needs of a comparatively small scattered rural population. Having been fitted with a hearing aid, a child is referred to a visiting teacher, who gives parent guidance during a weekly home visit. Children attending ordinary schools are seen in the schools when necessary. In 1957 a one-year full-time course in the teaching of hearing-impaired was set up at University College, Dublin, for trained primary and post primary teachers who are seconded to the course after a probationary period in a school for deaf children.

There are five schools for deaf children in the Republic of Ireland:

1. St. Mary's School for Hearing Impaired Girls, Cabra, Dublin 7, founded in 1846, is both day and residential, catering for primary and second-level (secondary) education up to entrance to third-level (postsecondary) colleges. It includes departments for hard of hearing; deaf; language disordered; and deaf with additional handicaps (including visual impairment). Attached to the school is an audiology clinic which since 1947 has been assessing children on a national basis. It also conducts courses for parents of preschool children.

2. St. Joseph's School for Deaf Boys, Cabra, Dublin 7, founded in 1857, is both day and residential and is organized on lines similar to St. Mary's. In both schools the auditory-oral approach is used except in the case of children with additional handicaps who are taught by means of total communication. Before being admitted to a particular department, each child is assessed by a team of specialists. The aim is to find the method to suit the needs of the child. In the case of children using an oral approach, classification is based on language attainment rather than on hearing loss.

3. Mary Immaculate School, Beechpark, Stillorgan, Dublin, founded in 1957, provides a full, day and residential coeducational program. The auditory-oral approach only is used.

4. Unit for Deaf, South Presentation Convent School, Douglas Street, Cork, founded in 1968, provides a day and residential coeducational program at primary level. The auditory-oral approach only is used.

5. Mid-Western Oral School, Rosbrien, Limerick, founded in 1981, provides a coeducational day program at primary level.

Special oral classes for hearing-impaired children at postprimary level were set up in 1981 in an ordinary day school—Bishopstown Community School, Bishopstown, Cork.

Four special-care units (three in Dublin and one in Cork) for mentally handicapped deaf children have been established in centers for nondeaf mentally handicapped. As of 1983, approximately 900 children were mainstreamed at primary and postprimary level. Preschool deaf children, when it is advisable and possible, attend ordinary nursery schools or play groups. At third level a small number of deaf students are integrated in colleges for the nondeaf. Mainstreaming is comparatively difficult because of bilingualism (use of Irish and English languages) in the ordinary school.

SOCIOECONOMIC STATUS

Traditionally, deaf persons have been underemployed in the Republic of Ireland, where unemployment can be said to be endemic. A report of a study carried out by the National Association for the Deaf (1974) shows that the employment rate of deaf people was much lower than that of the general population. Employment placements of deaf persons were, moreover, not in keeping with their abilities. The number in professions were small in contrast with the normal population, primarily due to the fact that until 1962 vocational rehabilitation was virtually unknown. This was changed when the National Rehabilitation Board was given responsibility for placement of deaf people in employment. Better vocational training facilities became available, a youth advisory service was established in the schools, a placement officer for deaf persons was appointed, and more emphasis was placed on state examinations as well as on prevocational training programs in the schools. These factors, together with the work of the National Association for the Deaf, have brought about a change. This association is a voluntary nonprofit charitable body founded in 1964, with the objectives of providing improved conditions and opportunities for the hearing-impaired in education, employment, and social life, and of integration into the nondeaf community. In 1980 the Government decided to employ a percentage of handicapped people in the Civil Service, and for the first time some Irish deaf people were recruited by special competition but with equal opportunity for advancement and promotion within the service.

COMMUNICATION

To understand the present situation, it is necessary to review the history of the development of methods of communication for deaf people. Ireland's first teacher used British sign language. The next two schools to be founded in Dublin selected systematic sign language developed by the Abbé Jamet at Caen, Normandy, France, and later modified by Irish teachers to reflect English. William C. Stokoe has noted similarities between it and Signed English (United States).

Pure manualism was used at St. Mary's School up to 1946, when speech and lipreading were introduced, at the request of adult deaf persons and some parents of deaf children, into an environment where the spoken word was virtually nonexistent. The introduction of the auditory-oral approach took place at a time when efficient and more powerful hearing aids were available, when emphasis was being placed on early ascertainment and parent guidance, and when a better understanding of language acquisition was made possible through international psycholinguistic research. Manual communication was retained for those who needed it. Among adult deaf people, then, one can find the following systems of communication in use today: speech and lipreading; British double-hand fingerspelling; and Irish Sign Language consisting of natural gestures, one-hand fingerspelling, and conventional sign language. For those who use only sign language or whose speech is unintelligible, written patterns are favored for communication with people unfamiliar with sign language. At lectures deaf audiences show a preference for written patterns because they are less ambiguous. A daily national television program for deaf viewers gives a shortened printed version of the news at peak viewing time.

Irislan, or basic Irish sign language, has been adapted to suit hearing mentally handicapped and autistic children who lack expressive language. Hearing persons can learn Irish systematized sign language in classes conducted in Dublin and Cork. *See* SIGN LANGUAGES: Irish.

Bibliography

"Childhood Deafness in European Community," Report of the Commission of the European Communities (EUR 6413), pp. 69–77, Belgium, 1979.

"The Doctor and the Deaf," *Medical Monthly: Journal of the Medical Union of Ireland*, pp. 5–12, April 1981.

The Education of Children Who Are Handicapped by Impaired Hearing, Report of a Committee set up by the Minister of Education, Dublin Stationery Office, The Arcade, Henry Street, Dublin 1, 1972.

Furey, J.: "New Areas of Training Being Opened Up for the Deaf," *LINK*, pp. 3–7, Summer 1982.

Good Tidings, Centenary Memorial: St. Mary's School for the Deaf, Cabra, Dublin 7, 1946.

Griffey, Nicholas: "Deaf or Language Disordered? Differential Diagnosis Through Diagnostic Teaching," *Proceedings of the International Congress on Education of the Deaf, Stockholm, 1970*, vol. 2, pp. 464–467.

————: "From a Pure Manual Method via the Combined Approach to the Oral-Auditory Technique in Educating Profoundly Deaf Children: Experience of Thirty Years of Teaching Deaf Children," *Proceedings of the International Congress on Education of the Deaf, Hamburg, 1980*, vol. 1, pp. 255–264.

————: *Irislan*, National Association for the Deaf, 25 Lower Leeson Street, Dublin, 2, 1979.

————: "Speech Methodology at St. Mary's School for the Deaf, Cabra, Dublin 7," *Proceedings of the International Conference on Oral Education of the Deaf, Northampton, USA, 1967*.

Information about the Young Adult Deaf Population of Ireland, National Association for the Deaf, 25 Lower Leeson Street, Dublin 2, 1974.

The Irish Sign Language, National Association for the Deaf, 25 Lower Leeson Street, Dublin 2, 1979.

Stokoe, W. C.: *Semiotics and Human Sign Languages*, Mouton, the Hague, 1972.

Sr. M. Nicholas, O.P.

ISRAEL

Based on a unique combination of its heritage of concern for human welfare, which goes back to the Old Testament ("Thou shalt not curse the deaf nor put a stumbling block before the blind"—Leviticus 19:14), and modern, scientifically based approaches and tools, the network of services and programs for the deaf community is well developed in Israel.

The overall incidence of deafness in Israel in the population up to 18 years of age is about 1.2 per 1000. Among Jewish children and youth of Asiatic-African origin (known as Sephardim), the incidence of deafness is about double that among those of European-American origin (known as Ashkenazim). The difference may be due to a higher rate of consanguineous marriages among the former population. From the number of deaf children in the minority population (predominantly Arab, but including Druze, Bedouin, and other communities) of Israel, it would appear that the incidence of deafness among minorities is higher than among the Jewish population, probably again on the basis of the high rate of familial marriages in the Arab villages. However, there has not been a definitive census of the deaf adult population of Israel. *See* DEAF POPULATION: Demography.

PRESCHOOL

At least 80 percent of the country's prelingually deaf children, both Jewish and minority, receive education services in one of the five Micha Preschool Centers (Jerusalem, Tel Aviv, Haifa, Beersheva, and Safed) by the age of 1–1½. The Micha organizations are voluntary, nonprofit institutions supported through fund raising and assistance from official and semiofficial sources. Referrals to the Micha Centers come from the country's well-developed network of Mothers and Baby Centers, audiology centers (every major hospital has a well-staffed and modernly equipped clinic), and Child Development Centers. All the Micha Centers are strongly auditorally and parent oriented, with two centers using total communication and three exclusively oral communication. A similar, comprehensive preschool program is offered in the French Hospital in Nazareth. *See* SOCIOLINGUISTICS: Total Communication.

The typical Micha program includes individual lessons two to four times a week, with parents generally observing through one-way windows: special nurseries for 2–4½ year olds, two to four days a week; and parent courses and discussion groups. Local variations include home training, sign language instruction for parents, and toy-lending libraries. On the mornings of the six-day Israeli week that children are not in Micha, they usually attend regular nurseries near their homes.

More than 90 percent of the Jewish deaf children 5–6 years of age attend free, compulsory integrated kindergartens—various combinations of about 3–8 deaf children and 25–30 hearing children with 2 teachers, one trained to teach deaf pupils. The others, less than 10 percent, attend special kindergartens for deaf children.

EDUCATION

At the elementary school level, there are four educational options:

1. Special schools for deaf children. These are located in Jerusalem (the only one with residential facilities), Tel Aviv, Haifa, Beersheva, and Nazareth (two schools—one for Jewish children and one for Arab children). While the Tel Aviv school has a number of Arab children scattered in various classes, the Jerusalem and Beersheva schools each have a small number of special classes in which the language and culture of the class, in keeping with Israel's culturally pluralistic approach, are Arabic.

2. Integrated classes (self-contained classes of the hearing-impaired, that is, deaf and hard-of-hearing children in regular schools). Such classes are conducted in schools in Tel Aviv, Haifa, Ashdod, Ramat Gan, and 16 Arab villages in various parts of Israel. Each school has its own formula for the amount of integrated learning and activities. Generally speaking, for most academic studies the deaf children study separately with their own special teacher, while for all of their nonacademic studies and activities the deaf children are with the hearing children.

3. Individual integration in regular classes. This approach is generally reserved for the more intellectually developed deaf child, and sometimes is an alternative to traveling to distant schools or classes. All the major cities, many smaller towns, and a

number of *kibbutzim* (cooperative villages) have deaf children in regular classes. Supportive services are usually available.

4. Individual multidisabled children in special schools and institutions.

Until about 1976 the only official method of communication in the school system was oral. After careful study, the system decided to encourage and assist teachers to learn the Israeli Sign Language in order to use a combined communication approach where appropriate. Today in most of the classes in schools for deaf children some form of total communication is used, while in all integrated classes the oral method is used, sometimes with some signing and fingerspelling as support. Some teachers use a few sign markers. As of 1984, at least one child was being taught via cued speech in an integrated kindergarten. *See* MOUTH-HAND SYSTEM: Cued Speech; SIGN LANGUAGES: Israeli; SIGNS: Fingerspelling.

At the secondary school level, there are three educational options:

1. Vocational high schools. There are two such schools, both in Tel Aviv: the four-year Vocational High School, operated by the International Jewish Service Organization (ORT), which offers three vocational choices; and the two-year High School for Working Youth, which offers training in two professions (two days a week in academic studies and four days a week in the vocation).

2. Integrated classes. There are five integrated classes in several comprehensive high schools around the country.

3. Individual integration. Throughout the country, there are individual deaf youths in regular classes, generally in vocational high schools. A limited number of deaf youths attend academic high school.

The Vocational Evaluation and Counseling Service of the National Ministry of Labour and Social Welfare has a network of centers which offer disabled individuals, including those who are hearing-impaired, a comprehensive service of vocational evaluation, training, and placement.

The National Ministry of Education, through its Inspectorate of Special Education and Education of the Hearing Impaired, offers 3–4 hours of private tutoring to hearing-impaired children in regular classes.

In addition, the network of five Shema Centers (Jerusalem, Tel Aviv, Haifa, Beersheva, and Safed) offers supervision and guidance to regular classroom teachers on management of the hearing-impaired children. (Shema, founded by parents of deaf children, is also a voluntary, nonprofit organization which receives support from various authorities and special funds.) Other Shema Center services include a range of supportive services for hearing-impaired children in regular classes in Tel Aviv

(the country's only comprehensive Media and Resource Center for hearing-impaired children), and social-recreational afterschool activities.

Amplification plays an important role in the field of education of deaf students. Classrooms are equipped mostly with Israeli-made hard-wire group hearing aids. Attempts are being made to switch over to wider use of FM wireless hearing aids in education of deaf and hard-of-hearing children in regular classes. Community assistance is available for the purchase of personal hearing aids, from such sources as the Ministries of Health and of Labour and Social Welfare, the Histadrut (National Labour Union) Health Insurance, and various special funds of the voluntary organizations. *See* HEARING AIDS: Types.

The governmental Bituach Leumi (National Insurance) Agency plays an important role in the habilitation and rehabilitation of deaf persons through its regulations on assistance to disabled people. Parents of children between the ages of 3 to 8 with more than a moderate hearing loss receive a monthly assistance grant. For those above the age of 18, there are various provisions of assistance for educational and vocational training.

ADULT ORGANIZATIONS

There are three organizations for hearing-impaired adults. The oldest and biggest is the manually oriented Aguda (Association of the Deaf in Israel), founded in 1944 by a group of deaf adults who had long been meeting informally in Tel Aviv. Today it has about 3500 members in 10 branches all over the country, with the biggest and most active in Tel Aviv, and can point to a long record of considerable achievements in many directions. The Aguda offers a range of recreational and social activities in all its branches; created, and supports, a very strong sports organization which participates actively in the International Olympics of the Deaf; provides various professional services to its members; created the world-acclaimed Kol U'Demama deaf dance group; was the driving force in the creation of the ORT Vocational High School and provides residential facilities for many of its students; and sponsors the Annual National Deaf Children's Day in Israel. The Aguda also helped found, and serves as the headquarters of, the World Congress of Jewish Deaf. *See* COMITÉ INTERNATIONAL DES SPORTS DES SOURDS; RELIGION, JEWISH.

The second organization of deaf adults is the much smaller Shema-Hod Club network, an orally oriented young adult group founded in 1970. Shema-Hod provides a range of activities and services, including social events, cultural activities, and a summer work camp in a *kibbutz*.

The third organization, founded in 1981, is Keshev (Hard of Hearing and Deafened Persons Organization). There is one club at present in Tel Aviv.

The Aguda and Shema-Hod, working together, helped bring about the decision by the Israeli Defence Forces in 1975 to accept hearing-impaired volunteers into their ranks, and also persuaded the Israeli Broadcasting Authority (IBA) to provide a brief, daily televised captioned news summary. The IBA provides sign language interpretation for a popular children's program. Also, all the voluntary and adult organizations have been working together on a computer-based telecommunication system for deaf Israelis.

SIGN LANGUAGE

Israeli Sign Language probably goes back to the start of the deaf community at the beginning of the twentieth century in Jerusalem. However, it received its major thrust in the late 1930s and 1940s with the growing immigration, including deaf children and adults, from all over the world. The immigrants brought their own sign languages and tended to perpetuate them for a while as they settled in various parts of the country. In the late 1940s and 1950s, with the growth and development of the Association of the Deaf, the Israeli Sign Language began to become a more unified national language. Only in 1977 was a signed Hebrew alphabet created, as a result of internal deaf community needs and the requests of the educational establishment when it wanted to use sign language in the school system. Today the Aguda maintains a sign language committee which is constantly creating new signs, reflecting the increasing usefulness of sign language.

SOCIOECONOMIC STATUS

Although no comprehensive study has yet been made of the socioeconomic and occupational pattern of the adult deaf community, there are certain observable patterns. Deaf males and females typically work in a wide range of occupations, including: teaching in schools for deaf children, small business ownership, architecture, drafting, graphic arts, office work, and various trades and industries (for example, metal, wood, and diamonds) at levels from semiskilled to skilled. Some have held high-level professional positions (physician, mathematician, psychologist, magazine editor) as well. One study revealed that 90 percent of a particular sample of hearing-impaired graduates of various elementary school settings pursued some kind of postelementary study before entering the work market. Of a sample of 105 graduates (average age 22.7 years) from postelementary settings, 94 percent were working, and 61 percent of these worked in only one or two positions in the several years after graduating. The study also reported that there was a higher percentage of skilled and trained workers in this sample than was reported in two earlier similar studies. It is not clear, however, how the distribution of occupations of deaf workers compares with distribution within the normally hearing population.

PERSONNEL TRAINING AND PROFESSIONAL ORGANIZATIONS

There is one program in Israel, in the School of Education of Tel Aviv University, which offers a bachelor's degree in education of hearing-impaired persons. Previously, teachers were trained in an annual special course sponsored by the Ministry of Education in conjunction first with Tel Aviv Micha, and afterward with the NIV–Tel Aviv School for the Deaf. Students may also specialize in education of hearing-impaired persons in special education programs in various universities and teachers' seminaries in Israel. The School of Communication Disorders of the Sackler Medical School of Tel Aviv University offers programs leading to bachelor's and master's degrees in speech and audiology.

There are three professional organizations related to the area of deafness: the Israeli Speech and Hearing Association, the Israeli Association of Teachers of the Hearing Impaired, and the Association of Psychologists of the Hearing Impaired.

RESEARCH

Basic and applied research in a wide range of areas—physiology, audiology, medicine, education, psychology, social activity—related to hearing-impaired persons is conducted in a variety of settings. These include Tel Aviv University, Bar Ilan University, Hadassah–Hebrew University Hospital (Jerusalem), and Rambam Government Hospital (Haifa), all working closely together with the schools and special centers for deaf children.

Because Israel is a small country which must use its resources carefully, it has been possible to achieve a relatively high degree of coordination among the organizations, various authorities, and the hearing-impaired community. They would all agree that future agendas should include: improving the range and quality of the technology available for hearing-impaired persons; strengthening the communication skills of deaf people (speech, language, and the use of hearing); advancing the Israeli Sign Language; expanding the secondary and postsecondary educational options available to hearing-impaired individuals; and broadening the range of services for the adult hearing-impaired community.

Bibliography

Borus, J., and J. Reichstein: in H. J. Oyer (ed.), *Communication for the Hearing Handicapped: An International Perspective*, chap. 13, University Park Press, Baltimore, 1976.

Proceedings of the International Congress on Education of the Deaf, Hamburg, West Germany, 1980, vol. I, pp.

335–340, 727–729; vol. II, pp. 70–84; vol. III, pp. 186–192, 232–234, 334–337, 449–452.

Zweibel, A.: *The Relationship of Cognitive Development in Deaf Children from Different Communicative Family Backgrounds to Oral Versus Manual Communication and the Degree of Their Development*, Ph.D thesis, Bar Ilan University, 1979.

Jerry Reichstein

ITALY

The condition of deaf people in Italy resembles that of other minority groups whose specific needs and identity are to a large extent disregarded by the great majority. This is clearly evidenced by the lack of sufficient, updated information. The exact number of deaf Italians is not known. A 1955 national census, and a 1980 survey by the Central Statistical Institute (ISTAT), indicate that there are at least 70,000 profoundly deaf people, including 9000 of school age. There is evidence that the incidence rate of deafness in the general population (ISTAT estimate, 0.14 percent) is higher in the southern regions compared with the central and northern regions (ISTAT estimates, 0.2 percent versus 0.15 and 0.09 percent, respectively). Besides, it appears to decrease in the youngest generations. A study of deaf children by the Commission of the European Communities (CEC), and another study including deaf adults, suggest that a significant proportion of deaf people are multihandicapped (CEC estimate, 19.5 percent).

The educational, health, and social services for deaf people, to be described in this article, show severe deficiencies. These are in part due to the general lack of adequate information on deaf people within the hearing society. Yet Italian deaf persons possess a specific sociocultural and linguistic identity. They have a national organization with 40,000 members which has played a key role in improving their conditions: the Ente Nazionale Sordomuti (ENS), officially recognized by the government since 1942. Furthermore, they have their own sign language and a growing linguistic tradition. These had been ignored, but are beginning to achieve official recognition within the hearing society.

EDUCATION

The educational system for deaf Italians is severely limited and inadequate. It provides special educational services only from preschool (children 3 to 6 years of age) through compulsory education (6 to 14 years). Higher educational services exist only as notable exceptions. As for the whole educational system (for hearing and for deaf individuals), all schools must follow national laws and regulations, whether they are run directly by the government or by private institutions. The educational system for deaf children suffers from the general failings of Italian education, which has not been able to keep pace with the profound socioeconomic transformations since the early 1940s. Countless reforms have kept the entire system in a restless state. Education for deaf people suffers from the fact that the entire educational system is undergoing a difficult restructuring.

Educational System   Several laws and regulations introduced from 1975–1977 onward have changed the educational system for deaf students. The previous system was established in 1923–1928 and was partially expanded by initiatives of the ENS and spontaneous adjustments of the deaf schools. The present situation is clearly one of transition in which the previous system still strongly influences the new one. It is thus necessary to refer to both of them.

The educational system for deaf people must be considered in connection with the one for the hearing population. The latter includes the following programs: preschool (from 3 to 6 years), optional; elementary (from 6 to 11 years), compulsory; first-grade secondary or *scuola media* (from 11 to 14 years), compulsory. Further education programs, all optional, include: vocational training of various types (from 14 to 16 or 17 years); higher secondary education (from 14 to 19 years, comprising the traditional second-grade secondary schools or *licei*, and several other types of vocational and technical schools), university and postuniversity programs. It should be noted that the system for compulsory education, formally established in 1923, was effectively extended to the general population only later, following a 1962 reform of the *scuola media*.

The old educational system for deaf students provided optional preschool (from 6 to 8 years) and compulsory elementary programs (from 8 to 16 years). These programs were offered only in special schools or classes for deaf individuals: 3 state and approximately 80 private schools, run mainly by religious organizations, and day classes in ordinary public schools. Children were taught by specialized teachers who provided both special education and speech therapy. Teachers were trained in one-year programs designed for preschool and elementary school teachers. Educational principles, methodology, and practice put great emphasis on the acquisition of spoken and written Italian. The use of manual communication and sign language was officially forbidden but in practice tolerated among deaf pupils. Beyond elementary education many schools for deaf students often provided small apprenticeship programs in trades such as tailoring, shoemaking, carpentry, and printing. Beginning in the late 1940s and 1950s, however, the ENS established several vocational training programs, and the first *scuole medie* for deaf people. In the 1960s most schools for deaf students also began to offer *scuola media* programs. At the same time, and in connection with a general increase of special education for underprivileged children at large, the number of special classes in ordinary public schools increased significantly. Finally the ENS founded three higher secondary education schools offering vocational and advanced technical instruction.

The new regulations formally extend to deaf children the same preschool, elementary, and *scuola media* programs available to hearing children, as described above. Placement regulations have also been changed and now offer the option between enrollment in the existing special schools or in ordinary classes of ordinary schools with hearing children. Special classes for deaf children in ordinary schools have been abolished. In special schools, special educational provisions remain largely the same as in the past. Such schools are mostly residential, but several of them educate day pupils. New provisions have been established for children integrated in ordinary schools, where they are taught by ordinary teachers. These include individualized programming and supportive, specialized teaching help which, however, is provided under strict time limitations. New, two-year teacher training programs have been established for preschool, elementary, and *scuola media* teachers. The new regulations emphasize the need for education directed to foster the child's whole sociocognitive, cultural, and linguistic development, albeit limited to the acquisition of spoken and written Italian. The use of manual communication methods or sign language is not considered, but it is still tolerated among deaf pupils as in the past.

The choice between ordinary and special schools is significantly influenced by the uneven distribution of special schools in the country, which does not adequately match the uneven distribution of deaf children, and by the suppression of special classes within the public school system. Although there is not sufficient information on the number of deaf children attending special and ordinary schools, the CEC report mentioned above indicated that in 1977 they were almost evenly distributed between special and ordinary schools, and that 63 percent attended day schools and 21 percent residential schools.

Beyond compulsory education there are no regulations for special educational services. There are only the three schools, all now state schools, located in Padua, Turin, and Rome. They offer: vocational programs of various types, lasting two or three years and providing qualifications as mechanics and as graphics and electrical workers; and five-year technical-vocational programs, professionally oriented, which qualify students as surveyors, bookkeepers, and dental technicians. The curricula of these schools are the same as those for hearing students, but manual communication and sign language are reportedly used, along with speech, for communication and instruction purposes. In principle, all five-year programs provide access to university education. There are no *licei* and no university programs. Although the possibility has been formally provided by the new regulations for teacher training programs, there are no deaf teachers of deaf students.

Educational Achievements The few quantifiable data currently available on educational achievements provide a general picture of the failure of deaf Italians to make significant educational progress. Over 20 percent of deaf Italians are illiterate; almost 39 percent have no formal education; and only 2.5 percent have received university educations.

Data reported by the schools of Rome and Turin provide additional information. During 1961–1981 a total of 912 students graduated: 95 percent of these achieved a vocational degree, and only 5 percent a higher secondary degree. These data, along with more general information provided by the ENS and other ongoing studies, show that the educational level of the deaf population is highly unsatisfactory. In addition, there is some evidence that the educational and cultural disadvantage of deaf individuals is even more profound: their actual achievements may be significantly lower than those formally attested by a given degree. Several studies show poor cultural achievements and poor skills in the production and comprehension of spoken and written language, despite the emphasis in the educational system on such skills.

SOCIOECONOMIC STATUS

The economic and social conditions of Italian deaf people betray the complex problems of a minority group, within a hearing society, struggling for identity. The economic and social integration of deaf persons began only recently, as shown by the following: (a) until 1961, as reported by the ENS, only approximately one-third of all deaf workers were employed, and many of these were underemployed; (b) until 1942 the Italian laws did not even recognize deaf people as autonomous individuals, but put them under guardianship.

On the economic side, significant changes have occurred. Under pressure from the ENS, legislative measures to promote the employment of deaf workers were established in 1958 and 1968. In 1979 the ENS reported that 85 percent of all qualified deaf workers were employed. In 1980 ISTAT data gave the same employment rate for the deaf and general populations. Another study of deaf workers found that all were employed. In contrast with these positive trends, however, there is evidence that a significant proportion of otherwise unimpaired deaf people (32 percent according to one study), rather than seeking employment, live on a small government subsidy assigned to low-income and unemployed deaf people since 1953. Official data indicate that 15,432 out of the estimated 70,000 received much subsidy in 1978. It is not known whether they actually live on it or receive support from their families.

It appears that despite efforts toward achieving vocational and educational qualifications, more than one-half of all deaf workers are concentrated in manual occupations. The remaining are in seemingly white-collar occupations, but due to their limited education they have little access to superior, management careers and are mainly occupied in subordinate, low-level clerical work. Unfortunately, as a consequence of significant increases in the unemployment rate in the general population, especially in the youngest generations, the deaf employment situation is expected to deteriorate. This general economic trend could thwart the successful efforts made toward higher educational and vocational qualifications.

On the social side, there are severe deficiencies in the health and social services for deaf people. As shown by the CEC report, the health services available do not provide effective screening and hearing-aid-provision programs. Language intervention programs within the health system have been established. With a few notable exceptions, these are primarily concerned with the development of spoken language skills, often to the detriment of the child's whole communicative and linguistic development. There are no national counseling and guidance programs for deaf children and their families. In social services, deficiencies are, for example, the lack of official directories or guidelines to help deaf people in the educational and occupational choices, and the lack of telecommunication services despite the efforts made along this direction by the ENS. A positive achievement is that the need for professional interpreting has been recognized, and the first interpreter training programs were established in 1981 (chiefly by the ENS and a few regional administrations).

The profound deficiencies of the health, social, and educational systems severely hamper the integration of deaf people. Direct, albeit hardly quantifiable, information on this topic can be found in the official newspaper of the ENS. The most frequently debated problems regard the lack of information and particularly telecommunication services, the fact that the hearing society shows a lack of knowledge and consideraton for the specific educational and communication needs of deaf people, the resulting alienation of deaf people as a group, and the existence of a communication barrier between the deaf and the hearing populations. These problems are reflected in the difficulty deaf people appear to encounter in starting a family, especially with hearing partners. ISTAT data show that almost twice as many deaf people are single as compared with the general population. Also, the majority of married deaf people (80 percent of the men and 100 percent of the women) have a deaf spouse.

While the current socioeconomic trends negatively influence the organization and funding of community services at large, deaf people are engaged in a strong, albeit difficult, battle for obtaining all the health and social services necessary for full participation in the hearing society.

COMMUNICATION

The entire educational system has pressed deaf people to use only spoken language as their means of communication. Sign language largely remains officially forbidden in schools, albeit tolerated in actual practice. However, visual-manual signs are the predominant means of communication among deaf people. Some deaf people seem to prefer vocal communication, and various degrees of proficiency can be found among sign users. In general, however, deaf adults use signs in their private conversation and in their public meetings. "Underground," in the schools for the deaf students, children sign among themselves and more or less with their teachers as well. There are also two theaters of the deaf with deaf signing actors, and a few deaf poets who produce their performances in signs. *See* NATIONAL THEATERS OF THE DEAF: Italy.

All professionals working with deaf people know of Italian signs, but the definition of signs as "gestures" or "mime," and the view that, unlike spoken language sounds, these signs cannot convey symbolic thought, are still prevalent. Statements on the negative effects of the use of signs on the development of spoken language are also widespread in the literature on the topic, but no relevant evidence has been provided.

Signed communication among deaf Italians is organized into a proper linguistic system. This has been called Lingua Italiana dei Segni (LIS). Researchers have provided the first linguistic description of the lexicon of LIS and of some of the main components of the signs, morphological and syntactic rules that govern the organization of the signs into sentence patterns. It must be noted that although signers of different areas appear to communicate fluently among themselves, variations among the signs used in different regions, or even within the same region, have been observed. The evidence available is limited, and further research is needed to assess the nature and the import of linguistic variations throughout the country. Psycholinguistic studies of the acquisition of LIS and Italian by deaf children have also been undertaken. *See* SIGN LANGUAGES: Italian.

Researchers are also investigating the major psychological and educational implications of signs use within educational, family, and clinical contexts. Preliminary findings provide evidence that sign use, and manual communication in general, play a significant role in the overall cognitive-emotional development of deaf children. Other studies have focused on the possibility of employing signs in therapeutic and counseling contexts designed for deaf people.

These avenues of research, although promising, are framed within a social context that has traditionally attempted to absorb all minority groups by imposing upon them its sociocultural standards, and has ignored and often overtly repressed, sociocultural and linguistic diversity. This has been applied to deaf signers as to speakers of the many different Italian dialects and to otherwise socioculturally disadvantaged groups. This social context, along with the one created by the strong Italian oralist tradition, has negatively influenced the sociolinguistic status of LIS, and in general the acceptance of manual communication. It has also interfered with the growth of a specific awareness, among deaf people as a group, of a linguistic identity through LIS.

Yet the existence of a spontaneous, underground culture, producing theater and poetry by means of signs, reveals that LIS is obviously as powerful as any other language, and that there is a growing linguistic tradition. It is likely that this tradition, along with the results of the research on LIS, will have a positive impact on both the sociolinguistic status of LIS within the hearing society and the growth of linguistic self-awareness among deaf people as a group.

Bibliography

Biscaro, B.: *L'Istruzione degli Handicappati*, 1980.

Caselli, M.C.: "Communication to Language: Deaf Children and Hearing Children Development Compared," *Sign Language Studies*, p. 39, 1983.

Cimino, E.: *Psicopedagogia del Bambino Sordo*, 1978.

Commission of European Communities: *Childhood Deafness in the European Community*, CEC Report EUR 6413—Medicine, 1979.

Francocci, G.: *Il Sordomuto*, 1960.

Istituto Centrale di Statistica (ISTAT), "Analfabetismo e Grado di Istruzione della Popolazione," *Annuario Statistico dell'Istruzione Italiana*, vols. 15 and 16, 1965.

———: "Indagine Statistica sulle Condizioni di Salute della Popolazione Italiana," *Supplemento al Bollettino Mensile di Statistica*, no. 12, 1982.

Magarotto, C. (ed.): *L'Ente Nazionale Sordomuti*, 1961.

Magarotto, C.: *L'Ente Nazionale Sordomuti nel 1979*, 1979.

Montanini Manfredi, M., and L. Fruggeri: "Linguaggio dei Segni e Indagine di Personalitá in Soggetti Privi di Udito," In G. Attili and P.E. Ricci Bitti, *I Gesti e i Segni*, 1983.

———: M. Facchini, and L. Fruggeri (eds.): *Dal Gesto al Gesto*, 1979.

Pigliacampo, R.: *Indagine Medico-Socio-Culturale su Soggetti Affetti da Sordomutismo*, 1982.

Volterra, V. (ed.): *I Segni come Parole*, 1981.

Volterra, V., et al.: "Word Order in LIS," *European Meeting on Sign Language Research*, Brussels, 1982.

Elena Pizzuto

J

JAPAN

The education and welfare of hearing-impaired persons in Japan have improved remarkably since World War II. Gains have been registered in education, welfare, voluntary services, and the socioeconomic status of deaf Japanese.

EDUCATIONAL SYSTEM

Japan's education of hearing-handicapped children is carried out according to the School Education Law, and cabinet orders and ministry regulations for the enforcement of the School Education Law. Schools for deaf people have six-year elementary, three-year lower secondary, and three-year upper secondary divisions, and kindergarten divisions. Elementary and lower secondary education is compulsory. The compulsory education period is through nine years of school, from ages 6 through 15.

The Japanese school system treats deaf and hard-of-hearing children differently. Each prefectural government must establish schools for the deaf children in its own district. Public and private primary and secondary schools may establish classes for hard-of-hearing children, but this is not obligatory. Guardians are helped with school expenses for their deaf children according to their ability to pay. Children who are educated in deaf schools are those whose loss of hearing is 90 decibels or more with both ears, and those whose loss of hearing is between 90 and 50 decibels and who find it impossible or extremely difficult to comprehend ordinary speech even with the use of a hearing aid. Children with less severe hearing difficulties are educated in special classes or in regular classes in ordinary schools. In each division of the different schools for deaf children, education is carried out according to the curriculum organized by that school, based on the Course of Study of Schools for the Deaf given by the minister of education. Textbooks in such subjects as Japanese language and music are often prepared by the Ministry of Education. The teacher qualifications in schools for deaf children are regulated by the Law for Licensing Educational Personnel. Instructors of each division of schools for deaf children must have an instructor's license for the corresponding primary, lower secondary, upper secondary schools, or kindergarten. In addition, they are supposed to hold a special license for teaching in deaf schools, but this provision of the law is flexible. There are four-year teacher-training courses for schools for the deaf children in six national teachers colleges. *See* TEACHING PROFESSION: Certification, Training.

The number of deaf pupils attending ordinary schools is increasing, and the number of pupils enrolled in special schools for deaf children is decreasing. As in other countries, mainstreaming is an important problem to be solved. Before the 1970s, deaf students usually were not admitted to colleges and universities. Now, however, an increasing number of deaf people go on to higher education in Japan's postsecondary institutions. *See* EDUCATION: Trends.

SOCIOECONOMIC STATUS

Ministry of Welfare studies indicate that there are about 300,000 adult Japanese with severe hearing impairment, defined as persons with hearing thresholds above 60 decibels in both ears or above 40 decibels in one ear and 80 decibels in the other. When those with equilibrium disturbances and speech (that is, speech intelligibility below 50 percent) and language disorders are included, the total number becomes about 320,000, representing 16 percent of Japan's physically handicapped population. Based on this total number, the socioeconomic status of these individuals will be considered below. *See* DEAF POPULATION: Demography.

Both the rate of employment and the average monthly income of hearing-handicapped Japanese are well below those of the general population. Less than 32 percent of all Japanese deaf persons over the age of 15 are employed, whereas 62 percent of the general adult population are employed outside the home. Employed deaf Japanese have an average monthly income equal to only 42 percent of the average of the general population. *See* DEAF POPULATION: Socioeconomic Status.

Deaf persons who complete their schooling through the upper secondary division and then go on to graduate from special courses beyond the secondary level have the highest employment rate. Nearly all find jobs; these, however, are in a minority. Although about 90 percent of those who graduate from the lower secondary division advance to the upper secondary division, only about 37 percent of the upper-secondary-division graduates pursue further study.

The employment situation of graduates of deaf schools has improved since the amendment of the Physically Handicapped Persons Employment Promotion Law in 1976. The law requires public agencies, public enterprises, and private businesses to employ a certain percentage (1.9, 1.8, and 1.5 percent, respectively) of physically disabled persons. Before the amendment, deaf school graduates most often worked for small and medium-sized businesses, but since its passage the number hired by large enterprises has increased. There has been a corresponding shift in the types of jobs held by deaf people. Formerly, deaf workers were concentrated in manufacturing activities, which still employ about 41 percent of the deaf work force, but now they are making inroads in service industries (21 percent) and banking and insurance (12 percent).

Studies show that most companies do not discriminate against hearing-impaired workers, and that 80 percent of the surveyed employers rate their deaf workers above average. An important problem facing modern enterprises with regard to the employment of hearing-handicapped individuals, though, is the workers' ability and willingness to change jobs as business technology develops, for this flexibility is related to their opportunities for promotion. Thus, large enterprises demand that deaf workers receive a broadly based education that emphasizes scholastic ability, communication skills, and social competence.

COMMUNICATION

Even now, most schools for deaf pupils emphasize the oral method and the use of residual hearing for instruction. Only Tochigi prefectural school has adopted the simultaneous method as a policy, and has developed an original manual system to use. Pupils of oral schools generally use natural signs as well as speech outside the schoolroom, and as they advance to lower and upper secondary divisions, their communication depends substantially on sign language. Under these conditions, the number of lower and upper secondary divisions of schools that adopt total communication as the means of teaching can be expected to increase. Most hearing-handicapped adults who have graduated from schools for deaf students commonly use sign language and written language. Deaf persons who depend principally on the oral method are in the minority. *See* EDUCATION: Communication.

Japanese Sign Language is not systematized enough to meet the requirements of the indigenous language. Research has been undertaken to extend and systematize it to meet the vocabulary and expression forms of the Japanese language. At the same time, the persons concerned have been striving to spread and promote use of sign language between hearing persons and deaf ones. *See* SIGN LANGUAGES: Japanese.

Guidance and instruction by television, as well as public and private courses for the diffusion of sign language, have been very useful. Due to recognition of the importance of social participation and integration of hearing-handicapped persons, the number of public welfare offices and other public and private facilities that provide sign language interpreting services is increasing. Sign interpreters often are provided for lectures and courses. *See* INTERPRETING.

There also has been an increase in the number of kindergarten and elementary divisions of schools for deaf children that introduce cued speech as a supplementary means of oral instruction. According to one report, 27 percent of all schools use cued speech in some form. Although many teachers in deaf schools are interested in cued speech, there is no uniform or standardized system. Adoption of this method of oral teaching probably will increase in the future. *See* MOUTH-HAND SYSTEMS: Cued Speech.

WELFARE FACILITIES AND REHABILITATION CENTERS

There are 29 residential welfare facilities for deaf children without parents or responsible guardians and 16 day-care centers for hard-of-hearing infants. Established under the terms of the Child Welfare Law, the former accommodate and protect deaf children and also provide the training and help necessary for an independent life. Residents go to school from their facilities. The day-care centers provide guidance, auditory training, and language instruction for preschool deaf children.

Three rehabilitation centers for deaf adults have been established to meet the requirements of the Law for the Welfare of the Physically Handicapped. These centers for deaf persons of 18 years or older provide the therapy and training necessary for rehabilitation. In 1979 the National Rehabilitation Center for the Physically Handicapped and the National Vocational Rehabilitation Center were conjoined in Tokorozawa City of Saitama Prefecture, and are managed together.

In the former, deaf persons receive fundamental training for rehabilitation and independent living. The latter center provides vocational guidance and training for deaf persons who have finished training in the former. Instruction is offered in vocations such as metalworking, precision industry, woodworking, chemical testing and treatment, electrical machinery, office work, information services, and the clothing industry. There are also other facilities such as the Workshop for Physically Handicapped, the Welfare Center for Physically Handicapped, vocational schools, and the Vocational Center for Mentally and Physically Handicapped. *See* REHABILITATION.

ASSOCIATIONS

The Japanese Association of the Deaf and Dumb is a national organization of deaf persons with about 20,000 members, and campaigns for the security of their rights, progress of their culture, and improvement of their welfare. It holds a national meeting every year to confer about its management, and also holds annual sports meetings for hearing-handicapped individuals. It has a branch in each prefecture to promote local activities. Another body of the hearing-handicapped persons, named Mimiyori-Kai, is mainly for those who became deaf after acquisition of language. It publishes a bulletin, *Mimiyori*.

The Japanese Society for the Study of Education for the Deaf is a national system of teachers in the deaf schools and has about 5000 members. It holds annual meetings in which practical studies of various teaching techniques are presented. The Na-

tional Conference for the Education for Children with Hard of Hearing and Speech Disorders in the Public Schools, and the Society for the Scientific Study of Education for the Deaf perform similar activities and also meet annually. The Society for Scientific Study of Education for the Deaf has about 650 members and publishes the *Japanese Journal of Research of the Deaf.*

RESEARCH INSTITUTE AND GUIDANCE CENTER

The National Institute of Special Education has an educational research department for each group of disabled persons. Its department of education for speech- and hearing-handicapped persons has four sections: Deaf, Hard of Hearing, Functional Speech Handicap, and Organic Speech Handicap. Subjects of research concerning the education of hearing-handicapped people include investigation of educational conditions, hearing compensation, speech and language acquisition, and so on; the results of the research are published in the institute's bulletin. In-service training of teachers of hearing-impaired students and educational guidance for hearing-handicapped individuals are also concerns of this institute.

The Research Institute for the Education of Exceptional Children attached to Tokyo Gakugei University has departments for hearing impairment and speech disorders. These departments are engaged in research and provide educational guidance services in much the same way as the National Institute of Special Education. It publishes an annual bulletin, *RIEEC Report.* Sixteen prefectural special education centers also carry out research and offer educational guidance services.

The Tokyo Metropolis Welfare Center for the Mentally and Physically Handicapped is a general guidance clinic. Of its 11 sections, the section of hearing and speech disorders provides services for all age groups with hearing and speech disorders. These services include a determination of the degree of the handicap, medical guidance, fitting and testing of hearing aids, training in the use of hearing aids, language teaching, communication training, and vocational and living guidance. This center publishes a bulletin, *Research Reports.*

VOLUNTARY WELFARE ORGANIZATIONS

The Society for the Education and Welfare of the Hearing Handicapped carries out such projects as an itinerant short course for mothers and children. Moving from city to city, it lends hearing aids, provides a course on marriage and baby care for hearing-impaired adults, produces and distributes educational films and publications about the welfare and education of hearing-handicapped persons, and so on.

The Informational Culture Center for the Hearing Handicapped produces and lends video tapes and movies with superimposed printed dialogue or signs.

The National Federation of PTAs of Schools for the Deaf and the Society of Parents of Hard of Hearing Children are engaged in activities promoting the welfare and education of hearing-handicapped children. The former has about 13,000 members and improves connections with other educational bodies. The latter publishes the periodical *Bell*. The National Association of the Principals of Schools for the Deaf, with about 100 members, is active in appealing to government and local authorities for support for schools for deaf children. It requests grant increases commensurate with enrollment and for the acquisition of equipment, lobbies for reform of the system of teacher education, and carries out similar activities.

Bibliography

Japan IBM Company: *Report of the 16th IBM Welfare Seminar*, 1981.

Japanese Society of Rehabilitation for the Disabled: "Physically Handicapped Persons in Japan," *Report of the Investigation into the State of the Physically Handicapped Held by Ministry of Welfare in 1980*, 1981.

Section of Rehabilitation, Ministry of Welfare: *The Welfare for Those with Disabilities*, 1980.

Section of Special Education, Ministry of Education: *The Special Education in Our Country*, 1980.

———: *Materials for Special Education*, 1981.

Isamu Arakawa

JONES, JACK
(1923–1983)

Jack Jones was a cultural historian, social critic, fiction writer, and poet. Born in Dallas, Texas, on September 28, 1923, John Timmins Jones was the younger of two children of Fisher Graham Jones and Edith Timmins Jones. He grew up in Scarsdale, New York, and lived most of his life in New York City. Both he and his sister Yvonne were hearing-impaired from early childhood, she hard-of-hearing and he profoundly deaf. A proficient lipreader and avid reader, he graduated from the prestigious Dwight School in New York City in 1942. His first literary work appeared a year later when he was 19. Between then and 1955, he attended Swarthmore College, New York University, The New School for Social Research, and the Vassar Summer Institute; worked at a number of factory jobs; and published poetry and short fiction in such journals as *Discovery*, *Accent*, *Politics*, *Village Voice*, and *i.e., The Cambridge Review* (Harvard), and in *New Directions*. These early works were praised by the critic Maxwell Geismar, who described Jones as "bringing to the forms of symbolist and surrealist fiction an unusual kind of humanity and humor."

In the early 1950s, however, having become convinced that "in the face of totalitarianism, art was living out its last decades," Jones turned to the study of history and ideology, embarking on an extraordinary program of self-education in which he proposed to read hundreds of scholarly works. During this period he also worked as a reader of published and unpublished fiction and nonfiction for the Curtis Brown Company and Twentieth Century Fox, and as an occasional reviewer for *The Nation*, *New Republic*, and other periodicals.

Ideologically a Marxist in his youth, Jones was led by events and the consideration of Stalinist practices in the Soviet Union to realize the need for a radical reevaluation of what he had then come to view as "the enigma of Marxism," namely, "of why things turned out and are still turning out so badly in the Communist countries." He completed his analysis, entitled "To the End of Thought," in 1953, and tried for two years to have it published. Finally, in late 1955, it appeared in *i.e., The Cambridge Review* under the pseudonym John Hurkan (perhaps a reference to the West Indian and Guatemalan god and giver of life, Hurakan). In this essay, which was subsequently reprinted in a mimeographed version in 1958 by the small New York publication *newspaper*, Jones presented what he believed to be the causes of the "reasonable" fanaticism of the communist movement, its loss of moral sensitivity in the interest of a world-historical morality, its capacity to do terrible things in the name of what is "good" and "necessary," and its peculiar ability to get inside of and disorganize the minds of its opponents through a kind of "undertow of the mind." According to Jones, the last-mentioned capacity of Marxism not only causes many liberals to be uncertain about it, and to respond inadequately to its threat, but explains what he perceived to be the rapidly proceeding ideological downfall of the West.

Jones maintained that at its most fundamental level the present world crisis is not a socioeconomic one involving the issue of capitalism versus communism, and has nothing to do with the problems or oppressions of "the worker" or "the people." It is rather a crisis of the world intellectual class. He based this claim on two observations concerning human psychology: (1) that it is possible for the human organism and, by extension, society to lose large areas of its functioning and, even worse, to be unaware of the loss; and (2) that all ideologies and all thinking are expressions of particular modes of human functioning. The loss of functioning is related to repression, and particular modes of human functioning are but different types of repression of natural, or "free," human functioning.

Since the Enlightenment, Jones observed, it has been assumed that freedom is something which can be attained by or added to the rational form of consciousness, and that absolute freedom consists of the absolute triumph of rationality. This is, for him, the hidden but actual driving principle of Marxism and explains why it will never stop short of this absolute. For Marxism, the maximum rational control of all aspects of economic, political, and social life will result in maximum freedom for "the worker," who is in Marx's view (according to Jones) equivalent to "natural man." But for Jones, since freedom is something that has actually been subtracted from the rational mode of consciousness, freedom cannot be obtained by it; freedom is for rationality something of the past and never of the future. Thus, unless halted, the further development of the rational power, especially under totalitarianism, will continue inexorably toward the negation of freedom.

Jones believed that the totalitarian logic can be defeated only if the destructive power and hidden ascetic negation within the rational faculty are understood. This meant that the concept of freedom must be disengaged from the rational power. Freedom must be understood to be organic or "biophysic," involving the relative absence of restrictions on the individual's organic functioning. Thus, in opposition to the totalitarian idea that freedom is fully realized in the unlimited application of the rational power, he attempted in his later works to develop "the general theory of limits" according to which the limitation of the rational power must take place at some point where the cost is seen to exceed the benefits in all of the manifestations in science, industrialization, social organization, and so on.

Jones expanded "To the End of Thought" into a book in which he set forth a more general theory of history and religious consciousness and elaborated the psychology and ideology of humanity prior to the Enlightenment. This book was never published, but the many articles that he did publish over the next 25 years may be viewed basically as chapters from it.

Although very productive, Jones suffered severe eye problems during this period. With a detached retina in one eye and cataracts in the other, he was declared legally blind in late 1974. He persisted in his research and writing, aided by magnification and a large-print typewriter.

Jones died of cancer on January 10, 1983, and was buried in King David Cemetery in Putnam Valley, New York. His papers, consisting of correspondence, notes, and manuscripts of published and unpublished articles and books, are in the Gallaudet College Archives.

Bibliography

Some of Jones's writings, not cited in the article are (in chronological order):

"Otto Rank: A Forgotten Heresy," *Commentary*, vol. 30, no. 4, 1960.

"Inhibition and Innocence," *Modern Age*, Spring 1961.

"Depth Conservationism: A Post-Marxist Ideology?", *Centennial Review*, vol. 10, no. 3, Summer 1966 (first published in *Kultura*, Paris, in Polish, 2 parts, 1964 and 1965).

"Otto Rank," *International Encyclopedia of the Social Sciences*, 1968.

"Herbert Marcuse and the Cunning of Revolution," *Michigan Quarterly Review*, vol. 9, no. 2, Spring 1970.

"The Idea of Socialism: The Ninety-Degree Turn," *Abraxas*, vol. 1, no. 3, Spring 1971.

"Que est-ce que Humanism?", *Esprit*, May 1972.

"Five Versions of Psychological Man," *Salmagundi*, no. 20, Summer 1972.

"Who Thinks Left? Who Thinks Right? Who *Thinks Radically*?", *Human Context*, vol. 4, no. 3, Autumn 1972.

"President from a Far Land?", *Columbia Forum*, vol. 3, no. 4, Fall 1974.

"Does God Exist?", *Human Context*, vol. 3, no. 3, Autumn 1975.

"Art Between Magic and Revolution," *Psychoanalytic Review*, vol. 63, no. 3, 1976.

"Freud's *Moses and Monotheism* Revisited," *Ethics*, vol. 90, no. 4, July 1980.

"Solzhenitsyn's Warning: A Secular Reinterpretation," *Chicago Review*, December 1980.

"Social Darwinism Reconsidered," *Political Psychology*, vol. 3, no. 1/2, Spring/Summer 1981–1982.

"The Deepening World Ecological Crisis," *Commentary*, 1982.

"The Reaganauts," *Bennington Review*, Winter 1982.

"How Marx Went Fatally Wrong," *This World*, Winter 1983.

Gary F. Seifert

JOURNAL OF AUDITORY RESEARCH

The C. W. Shilling Auditory Research Center, Inc., was created in 1957 as a nonprofit organization to foster scholarship, research, and publication in the field of hearing. The *Journal of Auditory Research*, together with the Amphora Press, forms the publication branch of the center. The journal was established in 1961 to serve a need for an interdisciplinary forum to be utilized by otologists, sensory and comparative psychologists, auditory neurophysiologists, musicologists, audiologists, speech scientists, psychoacousticians, engineers and bioengineers working with audioprostheses, and all workers seriously interested in the scientific study of hearing.

The editorial policy board consists of two otologists, three audiologists, and representatives of experimental and comparative psychology, psychoacoustics, and speech science.

Attempting to break down artificial barriers among those who read only journals on clinical audiology, animal hearing, otology, physiological and psychological acoustics, or deaf education, each issue of the *Journal of Auditory Research* offers a spectrum of topics to enlarge the mind of the reader. This journal also tries to indicate how information from fields similar in aim to the reader's, but different in methods and technologies, may be brought to bear on the reader's problems.

As an archive primarily for experimental papers, the *Journal of Auditory Research* is not designed to be directly helpful to those seeking assistance with their own hearing impairments, but its pages contain valuable information for those wishing to understand the basic nature of their dysfunction. Any paper based on experimental data on any phase of hearing is welcome if it will be of importance or interest to others studying the human or animal ear.

Special editorial policies include rapid and thorough editing and lowest possible cost for reprints. An editorial decision is promised within a month or less, either to publish immediately, to suggest though not necessarily to demand reworking the article, or to invite the author to submit further evidence in the form of control studies, cross-validation, further statistical analysis, and so on. The editor is particularly receptive to the beginning writer. For example, the editor will work with an author to achieve a publishable succinct version of an otherwise unwieldy thesis or dissertation that contains valuable data. The journal even welcomes the longer manuscript, which can be handled expeditiously and at far less expense than usual. Furthermore, word processing, photo reproduction, and large-scale printing and binding keep expenses low. Economic considerations alone never dictate whether a table or figure should be included; there is no charge to the author for anything. Finally, no material is copyrighted. Citation or even republication is encouraged if it will advance in any way the sciences of hearing.

When a manuscript is submitted for publication, it is given a first reading by the editor to determine whether its subject matter is appropriate for the readers of the journal. If, for example, it is a collection of unsupported opinion, however well expressed and valuable, it will not be considered appropriate for the journal. Such a paper is returned to the author without prejudice and with suggestions as to which journals might find it publishable. Any paper with improper or incomplete experimental design, causing its data to be fatally flawed, will be immediately returned with notes as to how the problems can be remedied. Once a decision is made to publish, copies of the paper are sent to two reviewers whose comments are used by the editor in subsequent informal correspondence with the author. Complete anonymity of authors to reviewers and of reviewers to authors is maintained.

The subject matter of the *Journal of Auditory Research* is so broad that no board of review editors is maintained. Appropriate reviewers are culled from the editor's knowledge of the field, from the references in the paper in question, and from subject and author indexes in abstracting journals of similar work.

It is the opinion of the editorial policy board that a mix of auditory-related topics will increase the reader's grasp of the problems faced in the reader's own workplace. It is also hoped that the reader may see that good auditory research need not always consist of full-scale studies demanding years of full-time efforts done in the few large and well-equipped laboratories devoted to human and animal hearing, laboratories for the most part not accessible to the reader.

Subscriptions to the *Journal of Auditory Research* are welcomed from any individual or from libraries, laboratories, clinics, and teaching institutions with interests in the hearing of humans or animals.

J. Donald Harris

JOURNAL OF COMMUNICATION DISORDERS

The *Journal of Communication Disorders* has broad interests and discusses the history, current status, and future of the science. Articles related to pure experimental research as well as to the clinical and theoretical contributions are welcome. American contributions and papers that are international and interdisciplinary in nature are published.

MANUSCRIPT SELECTION

The pages of the *Journal of Communication Disorders* are open to all who wish to submit manuscripts. Manuscripts are sent to the editor, who then sends them to consulting editors for review with regard to the appropriateness of the content, the quality of the work, and the adequacy of the report. Comments are made by the consulting editors; the editor then indicates the nature of the comments to the contributor by an accept-reject decison, or in the form of suggestions for changes that might make the manuscript acceptable for publication. Editors cannot conduct a review process on the basis of a letter of inquiry; the manuscript itself must be submitted. The status of the author submitting a manuscript is irrelevant; consulting editors know the author's identity, but make their decisions solely in terms of the quality of the manuscript.

No charge is made for the publication of any manuscript in the journal. Manuscripts are published in the order of their acceptance, except on the rare occasions when a particular article is published ahead of schedule. The editor selects the lead article for each issue. The *Journal of Communication Disorders* is aimed at psychologists, psychiatrists, specialists in speech and hearing sciences and communication disorders, linguisticians, neurologists, and ear, nose, and throat specialists. Circulation of the journal is approximately 1000.

The journal gives priority to articles on problems related to various disorders of communication. Subject material includes the normal communicative processes as they relate to the disorders of communication, anatomical and physiological aspects of communication disorders, psychopathological elements in communication disorders, psychodynamic aspects of communication disorders, and diagnostic and therapeutic aspects of communication disorders.

A general policy is that all articles accepted must add to knowledge in some way, whether they are experimental reports, case studies, or theoretical papers. Experimental studies should be of sufficiently high quality to make an original contribution. A paper that is based primarily on simple enumeration of the characteristics of subjects in some diagnostic category but does not present hypotheses and comparisons with other groups in order to substantiate hypotheses is not acceptable. Studies with negative results are acceptable.

Long experimental articles should present a substantial body of data, rather than report on a single short experiment in an overexpanded way. Generally this would be derived from a series of interlocking experiments. Short experimental notes must be solidly based on experiments, but need not be of the same scope as the longer articles.

Reviews and theoretical papers will be accepted provided they present new ideas, offer a revision of existing views, or organize ideals or problems in new and useful ways. Because such papers tend to be lengthy, they can be accepted only if they are on topics of particular pertinence to communication disorders. Short, critical notes in the scholarly tradition may be accepted, again provided they bring new thoughts and views to bear on an important problem. Case studies will be accepted when they are of high quality.

History

The *Journal of Communication Disorders* grew out of a book entitled *Speech Pathology: An International Study of the Science*, edited by Robert Brubaker and R. W. Rieber and published in 1966 by North Holland Publishing Company of Amsterdam. The book was well received, and the publisher soon requested a second edition. Revising the book only a year after publication did not seem appropriate to the editors. After consulting with a number of the contributors to the volume, the editors proposed the creation of an international journal on communication disorders. Most of the people consulted agreed that this would fill a great need in the profession, and the publisher quickly decided to undertake the venture.

In beginning the *Journal of Communication Disorders*, the editors received the cooperation of professionals from around the world who offered suggestions and agreed to act as referees for the new publication. The first issue was printed in May 1967 and contained a number of articles that attracted a great deal of attention in the field, such as Hobart Mowrer's paper "Stuttering as Simultaneous Admission and Denial," which was reprinted in several other periodicals. Also, a portion of the issue was devoted to a series of papers that was originally presented at a conference entitled "Psychodynamic Principles and Their Importance to the Field of Communication Disorders," which was held on March 26, 1966, in New York City. The major papers presented at this conference and reprinted in the first issue of the *Journal of Communication Disorders* were written by Oliver Bloodstein and Lewis Wolberg.

Since the first issue, the journal has continued to grow, gaining the respect of professionals throughout the field. In recent years, a number of special issues have been published. In March 1977, for example, a special double issue, entitled "The Problem of Stuttering: Theory and Therapy" (vol. 10, no. 1–2), was published. This special issue was based on papers presented at the Second Annual Emil Froeschels Conference on Communication Disorders, held at Pace University in New York City in January 1975. In addition to being an important international contributor to the clinical and experimental research in the field, Froeschels was an early supporter of the journal and a member of its editorial board. In 1978 the *Journal of Communication Disorders* published a special double number entitled "Problems in Hearing and Deafness" (vol. 11, no. 2–3). This issue reflected an interdisciplinary approach to these fields, demonstrating the work of linguists, psychiatrists, and psychologists, as well as professionals in the mainstream of hearing and deafness research.

Most issues of the journal also contain a mixture of different articles, including an international review of books and other publications dealing with various aspects of communication disorders.

R. W. Rieber

JOURNAL OF REHABILITATION OF THE DEAF

The *Journal of Rehabilitation of the Deaf* is the official publication of the American Deafness and Rehabilitation Association. Since the first issue in April 1967, the journal has been published quarterly without interruption. In addition to the regular issues, monographs, which serve as supplements, appear irregularly. Circulation is approximately 2500, and a subscription is included as a benefit of membership in the American Deafness and Rehabilitation Association. *See* AMERICAN DEAFNESS AND REHABILITATION ASSOCIATION.

The journal accepts for review material that is relevant to the area of deafness and hearing impairment. Submitted manuscripts are reviewed by professionals who represent a variety of professional backgrounds, such as medicine-psychiatry, psychology, vocational rehabilitation, and education. Reviewers recommend whether a manuscript be accepted for publication, returned for revisions, or not accepted. Specific suggestions as to the nature of revisions are required. Reasons for rejection must be stated. Authors then receive an appropriate notice, and in the case of an unacceptable manuscript a specific critique which is intended to assist the author should he or she wish to rework the manuscript.

Letters are encouraged and, if suitable, are published in the "Forum" section. Short opinion articles may also be published in the "Forum" as well as general items deemed to be of potential value or interest to the readership. Book reviews appear from time to time and are managed by a book reviews editor, who solicits books and other materials for review purposes and has them reviewed by appropriate persons.

The editor for the first two issues of the journal was Roger M. Falberg, who continues to serve as a reviewer. The editor since the third issue has been Glenn T. Lloyd.

The editorial board is appointed by the editor. Each editorial board member serves as a manuscript reviewer and is asked to review materials in a major area, as well as in other areas of qualification. All articles submitted to the journal are reviewed. When there are conflicts between reviewers, the editor usually makes the decision as to the disposition of the manuscript.

Glenn T. Lloyd

JOURNAL OF SPEECH AND HEARING DISORDERS

The *Journal of Speech and Hearing Disorders* (*JSHD*) celebrated its fiftieth anniversary in February 1985. *JSHD* was first titled the *Journal of Speech Disorders* (*JSD*) and was the official journal of the American Speech Correction Association, the predecessor to the American Speech-Language-Hearing Association. When the former association broadened its purpose to include audition in 1947, it changed its name to the American Speech and Hearing Association (ASHA) and the name of its journal to the *Journal of Speech and Hearing Disorders*. When ASHA again changed its name in 1982, adding "Language" to its title, *JSHD* retained its second designation. *See* AMERICAN SPEECH-LANGUAGE-HEARING ASSOCIATION.

CONTENT

JSHD remains one of the six official periodicals of ASHA. It is published quarterly, and has grown from an initial 500 subscribers in 1936, to a readership in excess of 50,000. *JSHD*'s principal audience comprises the practitioners within ASHA, and its main focus is on clinical practice. The journal's articles deal with the nature and treatment of disordered speech, hearing, and language, and with the clinical and supervisory processes by which this treatment is provided. Acceptance or rejection of manuscripts depends most heavily on their interest to practitioners. Since sound clinical practice is based upon heuristic as well as clinical experiences, ASHA is sensitive to the need for scientific publications with which to bolster these unjustified professional claims. Articles relating to speech, hearing, and language science based on theoretical and experimental studies are directed to *JSHD*'s sister publication, the *Journal of Speech and Hearing Research*. Members of ASHA are entitled to receive both of the journals. *See* JOURNAL OF SPEECH AND HEARING RESEARCH.

In addition, ASHA publishes proceedings of relevant conferences and materials on single subjects that are too long to publish as journal articles. The former are printed in *ASHA Reports* and the latter in *ASHA Monographs*. Originally, monographs had been printed as supplements to *JSHD*, but after the fourth monograph in 1952, the policy changed and *ASHA Monographs* was established as an independent series. Further differentiation of the material in *JSHD* is done in *Language, Speech and Hearing Services in Schools* (*LSHSS*) and *Asha*. *LSHSS* focuses on language, speech, and hearing services for children, especially in school settings, including supervision, programming, and general philosophy of management of these services. *Asha* is the association's official voice, dealing with administrative issues and other matters of broad interest to all of the association's members, including articles about the history, theory, and politics of disordered communication science and practice. The editorial posture of *JSHD* is further defined, then, by reference to the areas covered by ASHA's other five publications. *See* Asha; Language, Speech and Hearing Services in Schools.

JSHD accepts three kinds of manuscripts: articles, reports, and letters. Articles are essays on the philosophy, conceptual basis, or theoretical foundations of clinical practice in language, speech, and hearing, as well as full descriptions of clinical research projects. Reports present empirical data, either resulting from clinical practice or from experiments of limited scope but of clinical interest. Case studies can be accepted as reports. Reports tend to be less complex than articles, often presenting data about groups or individuals whose disorders have high clinical interest but who do not provide representative sampling of the population and thus do not offer a basis for generalization. Letters may present rejoinders to papers previously published by *JSHD*, summarize pilot studies, provide case studies, or support a position with respect to clinical practice. Articles are usually the longest and letters the shortest manuscripts printed by *JSHD*.

EDITORS

The first editor of *JSHD* (then *JSD*) was G. Oscar Russell (1936–1942). The second was Wendall Johnson (1943–1947), who was the editor when *JSHD*'s name was changed. He was a strong proponent of the merger of audiology and speech pathology and would probably have applauded the further broadening of the organization to its present explicit interest in languge as well as speech and audition. The other editors have been Grant Fairbanks (1949–1954), Gordon E. Peterson (1955–1957), Mary Huber (1958–1961), William R. Tiffany (1962–1965), Maryjane Rees (1964–1966), Margaret C. Byrne (1965–1968), Elizabeth Carrow (1969–1974), Ralph L. Shelton (1974–1978), William H. Perkins (1978–1981), Janis M. Costello (1982–1985), and Laurence B. Leonard (1986–   ). Editors are now appointed for three-year terms. Nominations are requested from the ASHA members, but the selection is made by the publications board of the organization.

Assisting the editor are 10 assistant editors and over 100 editorial consultants. These individuals provide the consultation that the editor needs to judge the many highly technical manuscripts. No single editor can be expected to have the essential expertise to evaluate all subject matter of interest to the speech, hearing, and language professionals. Before manuscripts are accepted for publication, they are usually considered by at least two consultants and an assistant editor, as well as by the editor. If need be, the editor can call upon guest reviewers who have special knowledge of certain topics. This review process is intended to assure high-quality published material. It is *JSHD*'s policy that reviews be made anonymously and that a de-

cision to publish a particular manuscript be concluded, to the extent possible, within six months of receipt of the manuscript.

Authors of articles accepted for publication need not be members of ASHA. A bill for page charges is presented to authors of accepted manuscripts; however, payment is voluntary, and failure to pay is not a criterion in the decision to accept or reject a manuscript. In preparing their materials, authors are requested to follow the *Publication Manual of the American Psychological Association*. *JSHD*'s editor still assumes principal responsibility for style decisions, but ASHA endeavors to maintain stylistic consistency across all of its publications through its publications board.

While *JSHD* is an official publication of ASHA, subscriptions are generally available to nonmembers.

Bibliography

Bilger, Robert C.: "JSHD Is 50 Years Old!" *Journal of Speech and Hearing Disorders*, vol. 50, no. 3, 1985.

Enid G. Wolf

JOURNAL OF SPEECH AND HEARING RESEARCH

In 1957 the American Speech and Hearing Association (ASHA) declared its intention to alter its major publication structure to provide two journals instead of one. These two journals were tentatively titled *Journal of Research in Speech and Hearing* and *Journal of Therapy in Speech and Hearing*. After final acceptance of the proposal, the foundation was laid for the *Journal of Speech and Hearing Research* (JSHR) to commence publication in 1958. Until that time, ASHA published only the *Journal of Speech Disorders* (JSD). *See* American Speech-Language-Hearing Association; Journal of Speech and Hearing Disorders.

In 1947 ASHA changed its name from the American Speech Correction Association, to accommodate the broadened interest in both expressive and receptive communication. (While retaining the same acronym, ASHA again changed its name to the American Speech–Language–Hearing Association, thus making linguists explicitly welcome among the audiologists and speech pathologists.) ASHA also changed its *Journal of Speech Disorders* to the *Journal of Speech and Hearing Disorders* (JSHD). That one journal had covered both speech and hearing research and matters of solely clinical interest. By 1957 the number of manuscripts submitted had grown so large and the interest in the scientific study of speech, hearing, and language increased to such an extent that ASHA's administration felt compelled to introduce a new publication that would more likely appeal to the scientific, as opposed to the clinical, membership.

CONTENT

Like JSHD, JSHR is published quarterly. It focuses on studies of the processes and disorders of speech, language, and hearing. Submissions may be in the form of experimental reports; theoretical, tutorial, or review papers; research notes; and letters bearing upon relevant issues. As the years have passed, the clear-cut differences the Committee on Publications saw between clinical and scientific have blurred, so that readers encounter original research and directly applicable studies in both journals, though their editors do strive to maintain the distinctions that the committee on publications, now known as the publications board, envisioned in 1957.

In the fourth issue of volume 7, 1964, JSHR announced changes in its editorial policy. The two major changes were: (1) to broaden the scope of the journal by including applied or clinical research; and (2) to add a "Reports" section to provide for formal reports of specific experiments, rather than reports of more general research projects. These manifest changes have been followed by a subtler evolution of the journal's role within ASHA, as additional journals have been added and as new editorial staffs have reinterpreted the original mandate. JSHR has largely eliminated book reviews, leaving these to *Asha*, another ASHA journal. Abstracts of publications also have not been carried since ASHA joined with Gallaudet College to publish the quarterly abstracting service *dsh Abstracts*. As a result, the journal is almost completely filled with long and short reports of empirical studies, reviews of large bodies of related research, and occasional essays on technical issues. *See* ASHA; ABSTRACTS.

EDITORS

The first editor of JSHR was Dorothy Sherman of the University of Iowa; she was succeeded by James Jerger in 1963. During his seven-year tenure as editor, Jerger moved from Gallaudet College to the Houston Speech and Hearing Center and later to the Baylor College of Medicine in Houston. Jerger began his editorship with controversy by questioning the quality of research that clinicians submitted for publication in the December issue of volume 6, 1963. His mildly disparaging, candid remarks about the state of research as represented by the papers he was given to edit provoked letters from some of ASHA's distinguished members, who saw his editorial stance as an attempt to divide the membership. Others felt that his comments were untimely, coming at a time when ASHA's professional members were attempting to build their prestige and while efforts were being made to introduce more research-oriented material into the curriculums for speech pathologists and audiologists. JSHR published a sampling of these letters in

the first issue of volume 7, 1964, and followed it with the editor's critical response. Jerger's reply constituted a thoughtful plea for high-quality research, and the controversy quickly subsided. No comparable dispute has arisen in the editorships of those who have succeeded Jerger. His standards have become the journal's standards, and those standards have been reflected in research throughout ASHA.

The sympathy of ASHA's administration and membership for Jerger's point of view may be inferred from the fact that the association selected one of his assistant editors to succeed him. In 1970 Robert C. Bilger became the third editor of JSHR. He was followed in 1974 by Thomas J. Hixon and in 1978 by Raymond D. Kent. Tanya M. Gallagher became the seventh editor in 1982, and in 1984 Theodore J. Glattke took over the editorship.

Supporting JSHR's editor is a staff consisting of an assistant to the editor, associate editors, and 90 editorial consultants. This staff referees the submissions and advises the editor as to their suitability for publication. Anyone having appropriate material may submit it to JSHR, regardless of whether he or she is a member of the association. Upon acceptance of a manuscript, the author is billed for page charges, but payments are voluntary and failure to pay is not a criterion in the decisions to publish submitted manuscripts. Authors are requested to prepare their submissions according to the style guidelines in the *Publication Manual of the American Psychological Association*. JSHR's editor assumes ultimate responsibility for decisions affecting style, but ASHA endeavors to maintain stylistic consistency across all of its publications through its publications board. Readership has grown to over 50,000, and while JSHR is one of the official publications of ASHA, subscriptions are also open to nonmembers.

Enid G. Wolf

JOURNAL OF THE ACOUSTICAL SOCIETY OF AMERICA

The *Journal of the Acoustical Society of America* is the sole periodical publication of the society. It is published montly (with two volumes per year) for the society by the American Institute of Physics, of which the society is one of the founding members. The journal has maintained its present name since the founding of the society in May 1929. The society's charter states that its purpose is "the increase and diffusion of the knowledge of acoustics and the promotion of its practical applications." At the beginning it was decided that to achieve this aim would require not only the holding of meetings for the presentation and discussion of research papers, but also the publication of a journal to contain technically acceptable articles in all branches of the subject.

History

It is a curious fact that neither in the constitution of the society as originally adopted nor in the original bylaws is there any mention of a journal. It seems to have been understood that the first secretary, Wallace Waterfall, at that time on the staff of the Celotex Company, would arrange for the publication of such and edit the first issues. The first issue came out in October 1929 and contained 163 pages with eight technical articles devoted mainly to room acoustics and speech communication. It also contained the abstracts of papers presented at the first meeting of the society on May 9–11, 1929. The journal was originally published quarterly and continued thus until January 1947, when it became a bimonthly. In January 1957, monthly publication was inaugurated and has continued since.

With the appearance of volume 3 in 1931, a regular editorial board of seven members was put in charge, with Wallace Waterfall as managing editor and Floyd R. Watson of the University of Illinois as chairperson. Other members were E. C. Wente, Paul E. Sabine, H. W. Lamson, F. A. Saunders, and Dayton C. Miller. Professor Miller served ex officio in his capacity as he was then president of the society. It was the function of the members of the editorial board to determine the acceptability of manuscripts submitted for publication. They were assisted by appropriate reviewers with expertise in the fields represented by the manuscripts.

The growth of the society naturally led to a corresponding increase in the size of the journal. This has been steady except for a slowdown during World War II. Even at that time the journal profited from the Navy's interest in underwater sound in connection with submarine signaling. After the war, growth accelerated. Volume 19 (1947), with which bimonthly publication was started, contained 1036 pages. Volume 30 (1958), which appeared just after monthly publication began, had 1222 pages. Continued acceleration has led to 4353 pages in volume 74 (1983, July through December).

Acoustics is a science covering a very wide range of phenomena connected with all forms of human activity. Though it historically grew up primarily as a branch of physics concerned with the natural properties of sound, acoustics is now deeply involved with physiology, psychology, all branches of engineering, music, medicine, and geophysics, including oceanography, aerodynamics, and seismology. It has been noted that the relatively enormous number of words in the English language relating to sound is probably greater than that as-sociated with any other physical phenomenon connected with the human body.

Content

The *Journal of the Acoustical Society of America* accepts and publishes technically qualified manuscripts in the following branches of acoustics: general linear acoustics, nonlinear acoustics (macrosonics—high-intensity sound), aeroacoustics and atmospheric sound, underwater sound, ultrasonics—high-frequency sound (including quantum acoustics and physical effects of sound), mechanical vibration and shock, vibration of plates and shells and random vibration, noise and its control, architectural acoustics, acoustic signal processing (including the statistical theory of signals), physiological and psychological acoustics (the ear and hearing), speech communication, music and musical instruments. bioacoustics (including the general effects of sound on biological systems), acoustical measurements and instrumentation, and acoustical transduction. The technical level of contributed manuscript is that expected of basic scientific and technological researchers in universities and in government and industrial research laboratories. Except for review and tutorial articles, all published papers are expected to be the result of original research.

Editorial Policy

The editor in chief of the society acts as editor of the journal. The editor has general management of all aspects of its publication, examines the proof of every article accepted for publication, and monitors the index classification assigned to it. The editor is assisted by a corps of associate editors, one of whom is assigned to each branch of acoustics as listed above (two in cases in which the publication activity is particularly great). Associate editors are expected to be recognized authorities in their fields. The associate editor has the responsibility of accepting or rejecting manuscript, acting on the recommendations of one or more competent reviewers to whom the manuscript is sent for examination. The journal thus operates on the usual peer review system. The editor enters into the reviewing process only when a controversy arises between the contributor and the associate editor.

A page charge is requested of the institution supporting the research of each contributor. However, payment is not mandatory, and even if the institution is unable to meet the charge, all technically acceptable papers are ultimately published, though occasionally with some delay.

In addition to papers in the technical areas mentioned above, each issue also contains sections on news of society activities, calendars of meetings of other relevant societies, book reviews, and reviews of acoustical patents. News of acoustical standards and of acoustical activities abroad appears on a bimonthly basis.

SUPPLEMENTS

Three separately paged supplements are published each year. Two of these are the programs of the two meetings of the society each year, containing abstracts of all presented papers. These, along with all material published in the journal, are indexed in each June and December issue at the end of the relevant volume.

The third supplement is *References to Contemporary Papers on Acoustics*, a bibliography of recent articles on acoustics from all sources throughout the world. It is usually published in midsummer.

The journal and its supplements are provided gratis to all members of the society. Nonmember subscriptions are available through the American Institute of Physics.

The journal is designed to meet the needs of teachers and research workers in colleges and universities as well as industrial and governmental laboratories. This, of course, includes acoustical consulting firms.

Except for some review and tutorial articles, articles are not solicited. The principal exceptions would be those from meeting symposiums—the papers presented are often collected by the appropriate associate editor and after the usual review are published as a group.

Bibliography

Lindsay, R. Bruce: *Journal of the Acoustical Society of America*, 68:2–9, 1980.

Waterfall, Wallace: *Journal of the Acoustical Society*, 1:5–9, 1929.

R. Bruce Lindsay

JOURNAL OF THE ASSOCIATION OF CANADIAN EDUCATORS OF THE HEARING IMPAIRED

The *Journal of the Association of Canadian Educators of the Hearing Impaired* (also known as the *A.C.E.H.I. Journal* or *La Revue ACEDA*) was founded in 1971. The first two volumes appeared as *Canadian Teacher of the Deaf*, but after the formation of the Association of Canadian Educators of the Hearing Impaired (ACEHI) in 1973, the title was changed to its present form. For the first nine years the journal was published as "a learning experience" by the students of the Technical Vocational School on the campus of the Atlantic Provinces Resource Centre for the Hearing Handicapped in Eastern Canada. In 1980 publication was moved to the University of Alberta in Western Canada, and

the journal is now published by the Publication Services Unit of the Faculty of Education. In Alberta, a fully computerized production and distribution process was adopted, using the facilities of the university's Amdahl computer.

Papers for publication in the journal are selected by an editorial board and reviewed by the editors, associate editors, and/or members of the editorial board. Other reviewers may also be used, but so far this option has not been necessary. Both solicited and unsolicited submissions are subjected to the same review process. The content and format of a particular issue is determined by the production staff at the University of Alberta. Attempts are made to balance different interests, but also to produce a series of linked papers and reviews.

OBJECTIVES

The logo of the journal describes its primary objectives. Two differently colored circles represent the French and the English heritages of Canada, intertwined to represent union. The maple leaf suggests the Canadian flag; the arrow indicates progress and purpose. In its first editorial, the journal focused on the need for a national Canadian conference to form an organization that eventually resulted in the ACEHI. The theme recurred constantly during the first volume of the journal, linked with some underlying concerns about whether teachers of deaf children should form a separate organization or join with teachers of other groups of exceptional children. The issue of French/English bilingualism was also of paramount importance, subsequently resolved by a definitive and continuing commitment to publish the journal in both official languages of Canada. It has not always been possible to achieve the objective of a completely bilingual publication; nevertheless, the objective has always been clear.

The first year of publication also raised two other concerns subsequently emphasized in the journal: the need for financial, moral, and literary support for the journal; and recurring apologies for lateness in publication. The two problems are interactive—the journal always has been produced with a mainly voluntary staff, and the lack of financial support has made it difficult to buy services that would streamline production and dissemination.

HISTORY

The journal reflects the personalities of the times and the changing fashions of the profession. Michael Marsden was closely involved in the founding of the *Teacher of the Deaf*, and used it as a forum to develop the First National Convention of Canadian Teachers of the Deaf held at the Ontario School for the Deaf, Belleville, August 22–25, 1973. Following Marsden's death, Russell Fisher took over as editor and continued until Bryan Clarke and Michael Rodda were appointed as joint editors in 1981. David Tingley, Gary Bunch, and Michael Clare have also been associated with the journal from the beginning and were instrumental in steering it through its infant years. In 1983 Christianne Morrow-Lettre was appointed as an associate editor in the French language, and in 1984 Steve Carey was appointed as French language production editor. It was hoped that the appointment of French language editors would give a continuity to French language production and thus increase the subscribership in countries where this language is widely used.

The pages of the journal are a chronology of the major events in the education of deaf children in Canada since the early 1970s. The major event in 1971–1972 was the founding of the journal itself. In 1973, 320 delegates from across Canada convened for the First National Convention of Canadian Teachers of the Deaf, and ACEHI was born. In 1975 the second national convention set the fledgling association on its feet, and a Committee on Professional Standards for Educators of the Hearing Impaired was established. In 1977 the proposals of this committee were reported in the journal for subsequent discussion and approval at the biannual meeting of ACEHI in Edmonton, Alberta, in August. Later correspondence between the National Director of ACEHI, Gary Bunch, and the Minister of Education for British Columbia, W. G. Hardwick, focused on fears about the future of the Jericho Hill residential school for deaf students in British Columbia. The "national exposure" through the journal of these fears alerted other provinces to the affection with which schools for deaf students are held in the deaf community, and made officials of provincial departments of education tread cautiously when advocating policies which are seen as a direct threat to them. *See* CANADA: Education, Teacher Training.

EDITORIAL FOCUS

The early 1980s saw a shift in focus in the journal toward deaf students in regular schools and mainstream programs. Art and creative writing contests were sponsored by ACEHI and conducted by and through the pages of the journal. The level of work submitted was extremely high, reflecting creditably on the students who took part in the contests and on their teachers. When the journal moved to the University of Alberta its technical quality improved

due to the support ACEHI received from the Publications Unit Faculty of Education.

The journal started to publish just when total communication was emerging as an educational philosophy in the education of deaf students, and some of the more insightful articles and letters are about this issue. As the content became more concerned with mainstreaming, it reflected issues concerned with language, speech, and communication. *See* SOCIOLINGUISTICS: Total Communication.

In the early 1980s the journal also moved toward a more definitely Canadian image. Like their counterparts in other Canadian activities, teachers of deaf students are reflecting on their ethnic identity and their individuality as Canadians. However, the trend also reflects the growing maturity of the journal and of ACEHI. An "Entre Amis" edition was published to coincide with the joint North America Conventions of Associations of the Hearing Impaired in Winnipeg in 1983. Unashamedly Canadian, it failed to sell to the Americans, but the Francophone motto rather than the English translation ("Between Friends") left an indelible impression. It is said that the "Entre Amis" edition was a landmark which established the journal as a viable professional publication. The publication is now capable of holding its own with other journals, and looks to achieve international recognition and financial stability.

Bibliography

Ainsworth, S.: "Report on the National Convention of Canadian Teachers of the Deaf," *Canadian Teacher of the Deaf*, 2:6–7, 1972–1973.

Bunch, G. O.: "The Journal Logo," *A.C.E.H.I. Journal*, 9:148, 1983.

Clarke, B. R.: Editorial, *A.C.E.H.I. Journal*, 8:33, 1981–1982.

———— and M. A. Winzer: "A Concise History of Education of the Deaf in Canada," *A.C.E.H.I. Journal*, 9:36–51, 1983.

Gervais, G.: "Report of National Director," *A.C.E.H.I. Journal*, 2:6–9, 1975.

"Les Normes Progessionelles des Educateurs de Deficients Auditifs," *A.C.E.H.I. Journal*, 3:127–134, 1975–1976.

Minto, H.: "Committee on Professional Standards for Educators of Hearing Impaired," *A.C.E.H.I. Journal*, 2:3, 1975.

"Professional Standards for Educators of the Hearing Impaired," *A.C.E.H.I. Journal*, 3:121–126, 1976–1977.

Tingley, D.: Editorial, *Canadian Teacher of the Deaf*, 2:2, 1972–1973.

Michael Rodda

K

KELLER, HELEN
(1880–1968)

Helen Keller, blind and deaf from early childhood, became world-famous for the strength and determination with which she conquered her handicaps and for her achievements as writer, lecturer, and social activist. She graduated from college, published books and articles, traveled and spoke on every continent, and experienced the satisfaction of useful work and loving friendships. *See* DEAF-BLINDNESS: Communication, Education.

Born June 27, 1880, on a farm in Tuscumbia, Alabama, she was the daughter of Kate (Adams) Keller and Arthur H. Keller, a former officer in the Confederate Army. When, at 19 months, an illness (never identified) deprived her of hearing and sight, the lively child became a wordless and frustrated creature whose energy boiled over into wild and capricious rebellion. Helen's parents learned that in Boston, Massachusetts, 50 years before, Samuel Gridley Howe of the Perkins Institution for the Blind had educated deaf-blind Laura Bridgman, and following the advice of Alexander Graham Bell in Washington, they asked Howe's successors to recommend a tutor for their daughter. *See* BELL, ALEXANDER GRAHAM; BRIDGMAN, LAURA DEWEY.

YEARS WITH ANNE SULLIVAN

On March 3, 1887—a date that Helen later celebrated as her true birthday—Anne Sullivan, a recent graduate of the Perkins Institution, arrived at the Keller home. Young, poor, and herself of impaired vision, Sullivan proved to be an inspired and intuitive teacher. Using the manual alphabet, she constantly spelled into the child's hand the words for objects around them, until one day Helen made a connection between the pattern traced by her teacher's fingers and the substance she felt at the pump—"water"—and in a moment of revelation, understood that "everything has a name." She rapidly acquired a sizable vocabulary and began to read Braille. Helen, Sullivan realized, was a child of remarkable powers, and told herself "something within me tells me that I shall succeed beyond my dreams." *See* SIGNS: Fingerspelling.

In Boston, reports of Helen's progress attracted wide attention and financial aid. With Anne Sullivan as interpreter, Helen continued her education at the Perkins Institution, the Wright-Humason School in New York, and the Cambridge School for Young Ladies. Enchanted by words, she read eagerly and insisted on learning to "speak with her mouth," soon acquiring a voice intelligible at least to her close companions. Her bright intelligence and loving nature won the hearts of such eminent persons as Phillips Brooks, Edward Everett Hale, and Samuel Clemens. In 1900 she entered Radcliffe College and in 1904 was graduated *cum laude*.

Keller and her teacher then purchased a country house in Wrentham, Massachusetts, where they were joined by the young writer John Macy, who married Anne Sullivan in 1905. In those happy years, the three enjoyed the stimulating company of many writers and activists of the Boston area. In 1914, however, John Macy left the household; three years

Helen Keller (left) chatting with Anne Sullivan and Alexander Graham Bell in 1894. (Library of Congress)

later Keller, Anne Sullivan Macy, and a new assistant, Polly Thomson, moved to Forest Hills, Long Island, where "Teacher" died in 1936. With Polly Thomson, Keller moved in 1939 to a house in Westport, Connecticut, her home until her death on June 1, 1968.

WRITINGS AND LECTURES

In 1903, with editorial assistance from John Macy, Helen Keller had published her first book, *The Story of My Life,* a classic account of her "soul's sudden awakening," of her love of poetry, of nature, and of friends. In *The World I Live In* (1908), she analyzed the ways in which she perceived her environment. *Out of the Dark* (1913) consisted of essays on public questions. In *Midstream* (1929), she resumed her autobiography, and in *Helen Keller in Scotland* (London, 1933) recorded her impressions of a journey on which she visited schools and physicians concerned with deaf persons and blind persons, and received an honorary degree from the University of Glasgow. *Helen Keller's Journal,*

1936–1937 (1938) traced her recovery from the sorrow of Anne's death. In 1955 she published her last book, *Teacher: Anne Sullivan Macy: A Tribute by the Foster-Child of Her Mind.* Besides these and other books, she produced countless speeches, letters, and magazine articles.

Although her voice required interpretation for most audiences, Keller nevertheless made public speaking a career. In 1924, after 12 years of lecturing and appearing on the vaudeville circuit throughout the country, she and Anne Sullivan Macy accepted a proposal to raise funds for the newly organized American Foundation for the Blind. This became Keller's enduring affiliation, and under its auspices or those of related groups she traveled and spoke all over the world.

CHARACTER AND BELIEFS

Helen Keller maintained contact with her surroundings by a variety of means. Fingerspelling was indispensable, but she also attained skill in lipreading with her fingers. Sensitive to vibrations, she shuddered at the din of the subway, thrilled to the applause of a crowd, and delighted in the rhythms of music. Braille provided "that knowledge which comes to others through their eyes and their ears"; books were her "compensation for the harms of fate." Except for signing her name, she wrote on a typewriter. Her voice, though imperfect, was of "incalculable service." A cultivated sense of smell enabled her to discriminate among different environments or to enjoy the fragrance of a garden. Through her hands, the sense of touch provided the essential bridge to other beings.

In personal relations, Keller was dependent on a small circle. Anne Sullivan Macy, though completely devoted, tended to be jealously possessive. And when, in her middle thirties, Keller planned to marry, she yielded to the anger of her mother and put aside her dream. "The brief love will remain in my life, a little island of joy surrounded by dark waters."

When she was young, doubly handicapped Americans could count on little sustenance from stable organizations or governmental bodies. For persons who were deaf or blind, public funds were inadequate, private charity whimsical or patronizing; deaf-blind people were left to vegetate. By good fortune, Helen Keller found those who would help and, with quick comprehension, retentive memory, and strength of spirit, was able to pursue her opportunities; even so, she had to lean on a few close friends.

In forming opinions she could make her own choices from a wide range of available information and ideas. Unaffected by Sullivan's skepticism, she adopted the faith of Emanuel Swedenborg, which assured her of a Divine Presence in the world and the promise of immortality to come; and, again in

Helen Keller. (American Foundation for the Blind)

contrast to her teacher, she ardently advocated woman suffrage. With pain, she rejected the racist attitudes and practices of her beloved family and her native South. In 1909 she joined the Socialist party; later, disregarding criticism, she defended the Industrial Workers of the World, called for a general strike against war, rejoiced at the Bolshevik Revolution, and frequently pointed to economic inequality as the underlying source of most physical disabilities. Although less vocal after 1920, she expressed herself sufficiently to acquire a dossier in the Federal Bureau of Investigation and, with some digression during the Second World War, retained her pacifist and socialist convictions to the end.

From the age of 10, when she persuaded the Boston elite to establish a fund for a deaf-blind boy, Helen Keller acted to represent handicapped people, to explain their needs and to set forth their claims on society. In her twenties she lobbied for blind persons in Massachusetts and boldly took up an "unmentionable" subject: blindness of the newborn caused by venereal disease. Finding that "it was not humanly possible to work for both the blind and the deaf at the same time," she devoted herself primarily to those who were blind, and yet on many of her tours she also investigated conditions of those who were deaf. Much as she enjoyed

the enthusiastic welcome she received everywhere, she could speak sharply, whether reproving Israelis for creating a separate "blind village" or, as in one Australian city, castigating the directors of a bleak charitable institution for deaf people for failing their trust. Repeatedly she pleaded for help for "the loneliest people on earth, those without sight or hearing."

SIGN LANGUAGE–VOICE TRAINING CONTROVERSY

Circumstances committed Helen Keller to one side in a bitter controversy: the question of sign language versus voice training for deaf children. Although many schools, including Gallaudet College, employed signs, certain educators insisted on teaching visual lipreading and speech. Leading the oral party was Alexander Graham Bell, who denied that sign language had any place in instruction of the young.

Helen Keller counted Bell as one of her earliest and dearest friends and loved his associate John Hitz as a "foster-father." To her needs, sign language seemed irrelevant, while voice had proved its value. As she herself had been "set free" from isolation, she demanded that blind persons and deaf persons be liberated and enabled to find companionship and employment in the larger society. Like Bell, she maintained that "every deaf child should be given an opportunity to speak and to read the lips. That is his birthright." Yet, uneasy in a position that alienated many of the deaf community, she attempted to conciliate those of a different view. In 1913, in *American Annals of the Deaf*, published by partisans of sign language, she acknowledged that "no method is perfect." She continued, "I realize that I have had exceptional advantages . . . skillful teaching and the constant, watchful care of devoted friends to keep my speech intelligible . . . Without the sign language, many hundreds of deaf people would be isolated." Whether they used signs or speech, "I want the deaf of this country, and indeed of all lands, to have every advantage that ingenuity, science, and education can give them." *See* AMERICAN ANNALS OF THE DEAF; HISTORY: Sign Language Controversy.

HER CONTRIBUTIONS AND LATE THOUGHTS

To a commonly posed question, Keller in her advancing years replied that she had concluded "after a lifetime in silence and darkness that to be deaf is a greater affliction than to be blind . . . Hearing is the soul of knowledge and information of a high order. To be cut off from hearing is to be isolated indeed." When she was young—she recalled on her seventy-fifth birthday—the opportunity to help blind persons had come up first, but "I imagine if I had been given a choice I would have taken up work for the deaf first." She answered the inquiry of a student debater: "I have imagination, the power of association, the sense of touch, smell and taste, and I never feel blind, but how can I replace the loss of hearing?"

Keller awakened public concern and awareness for all handicapped persons and inspired hope among those who were disabled. Her constant insistence that aid was a right of those in need, an obligation upon the whole society, contributed to a growing recognition of governmental responsibility. Her pleas for doubly handicapped people helped bring about new training programs and, in the early 1970s, the establishment, with federal financing, of the Helen Keller National Center for Deaf-Blind Youth and Adults, in Sands Point, New York.

Mystical religious faith lightened Helen Keller's moments of sadness and assured her that friends she had outlived still guided her from another world, where all could see and hear. Vitality infused the existence of a woman who could "sing with joy, the magnificence of living!"

Bibliography

Alexander Graham Bell Collection, Library of Congress.

Braddy, Nella: *Anne Sullivan Macy: The Story Behind Helen Keller*, Doubleday, New York, 1933.

Collections of Helen Keller's letters and papers at the American Foundation for the Blind (New York City), the Perkins Institution in Watertown, Massachusetts, and the Volta Bureau in Washington, D.C.

Helen Keller Souvenir, Volta Bureau, Washington, D.C., vol. 1, 1891, and vol. 2, 1899.

Lash, Joseph P.: *Helen and Teacher: The Story of Helen Keller and Anne Sullivan Macy*, American Foundation for the Blind, New York, 1980.

Jean Christie

KENDALL DEMONSTRATION ELEMENTARY SCHOOL

The first school for deaf pupils established in the National Capitol Region of the United States was the Kendall School. It was founded by Amos Kendall, a journalist and politician. The school was located on property owned by Kendall and was permanently endowed when he persuaded the Congress on February 16, 1857, to authorize the establishment of the school under the name of Columbia Institution for the Deaf, Dumb and Blind. Kendall himself helped guarantee the early expenses of the school and hired its first superintendent, Edward Miner Gallaudet. *See* GALLAUDET, EDWARD MINER.

EARLY YEARS

During its early years, the school served both deaf students and blind students of elementary and high school age. Early reports of Superintendent Gallaudet provided evidence of student progress to the

school's board of directors and the Congress. In 1864 Kendall and Gallaudet were successful in convincing the Congress and President Lincoln to expand the authority of the Columbia Institution to allow conferring of baccalaureate degrees, and the history of Gallaudet College commenced. Kendall School continued to serve students of elementary and high school age. In 1885 the name of the elementary and high school program on campus were changed to the Kendall School. When a normal school (a teacher training program) was established at the college in 1891, Kendall School began to serve as the laboratory school for this training program, and has continued to serve that function. *See* GALLAUDET COLLEGE.

Over the years, Kendall School has played an important role in American education of deaf children. Many of the teachers who trained at the school went on to become master teachers and, in some cases, successful administrators in other schools for deaf students. *See* TEACHING PROFESSION: Training.

DEMONSTRATION SCHOOL

In 1970 new legislation transformed the historic Kendall School into a national demonstration elementary school. This legislation, still in effect, changed the name of the school to the Kendall Demonstration Elementary School (KDES) and charged the school with a dual mission. In addition to providing an exemplary education to students in the National Capitol Region, the school was obligated to engage in research and dissemination activities which would stimulate the development of similar programs throughout the nation.

Public Law 91-587 (the Kendall Demonstration Elementary School Act) authorized the provision of yearly appropriations as necessary for the establishment and operation of the school, including allocations for construction of facilities and purchase of equipment. The legislation also specifically stated that the school must give maximum attention to excellence of architecture and design, works of art, innovative auditory and visual devices, and installations appropriate for educational functions. Similar legislation established a new high school for deaf secondary students at Gallaudet College in 1966. Following the opening of the Model Secondary School for the Deaf at Gallaudet in 1969, the Kendall School phased out its high school program. *See* MODEL SECONDARY SCHOOL FOR THE DEAF.

NEW BUILDING

In the early 1970s, Congress appropriated $15,000,000 for the construction and equipping of a new facility for KDES. Construction began in 1976 and continued until the facility was occupied in the spring of 1980. The complex contains over 180,000 square feet (16,700 square meters) of space with modern and flexible instructional areas, a television studio, a full-size gymnasium, a therapy pool, a complete library, testing areas, and 18 housing units for visiting parents and professionals. The interior walls of the building and carpeting are treated with materials with special acoustic qualities which not only absorb sound but provide an array of warm colors as well. The building is barrier-free, as required by federal law, and has become a model of excellence in architecture and design.

STUDENTS

Students enrolled in KDES range in age from early infancy to 15 years. All students seeking admission to the school must reside in the National Capitol Region and have a hearing loss severe enough to require placement in a special education program such as KDES. KDES enrolls approximately 200 students, slightly less than half of whom reside in the District of Columbia. The remaining students reside in nearby counties in Virginia and Maryland. All students commute to and from school daily as the KDES program has no residential component. KDES provides special services to multiply handicapped children and enrolls a large number of children with deaf parents due to its location and the large deaf population in the Washington area.

DEMONSTRATION RESPONSIBILITY

As part of its demonstration responsibility, KDES supports the development and dissemination of instructional materials, curriculum guides, computer software, and tests. Products developed are often pilot-tested in KDES classrooms and field-tested in other programs for deaf children prior to final revision and dissemination to educators in the field of deafness. KDES also supports basic and applied research projects designed to improve the educational achievement of deaf students and the quality of life for all deaf people. Research findings related to social and emotional aspects of deafness, parent-child interaction patterns, and the acquisition of reading and writing skills by deaf students are examples of how this research at KDES has resulted in the improvement of instructional techniques and practices.

Each year KDES is visited by over 1000 individuals from all over the world. Seminars are conducted to train professionals from all parts of the United States and occasionally from foreign countries who work with deaf people. It is also common for the school to play host to royalty and heads of state. In addition to serving as a practicum site for the many graduate training programs of Gallaudet College, KDES also accepts a limited number of practicum students and interns from other graduate programs across the country.

Since becoming a demonstration school in 1970, the KDES program has risen in stature to where it now plays a critical and prominent role in the education of elementary-aged deaf students. The school's curriculum products, instructional methods, research findings, and computer technology are being applied in a growing number of schools and programs for deaf students. It is precisely this type of role which Congress envisioned for KDES when it passed the Kendall Demonstration Elementary School Act in 1970.

Bibliography

Atwood, Albert W.: *Gallaudet College: Its First 100 Years*, Gallaudet College, Washington, D.C., 1964.

Cinelli, Pattie: "Celebrating 125 Years for Kendall School," *Gallaudet Today*, vol. 13, no. 4, Summer 1983.

Michael Denninger

KENYA

Kenya is endowed with a rich cultural heritage which has for many years bound families together, enabling them to cater for the social and economic needs of its members without any discrimination. This implies a mutual responsibility by society and its members to do their best for each other, with the full understanding that if society prospers its members will share in that prosperity.

However, over the years Kenya has experienced rapid social and economic development which has caused changes in life styles of the community. Due to these changes, provisions for handicapped persons, including those who are deaf, were initially realized by voluntary organizations in residential institutions where care, treatment, and education were available. However, soon after independence, the government began to take major responsibilities in providing services for disabled persons in health, social services, and education.

The deaf persons receiving these services in Kenya are those who are unable to hear within normal limits due to physical impairment or dysfunction of auditory mechanisms. They are impaired in processing linguistic information through hearing, with or without amplification.

EDUCATION

The government gives high priority to the development of education by providing universal free primary education for all children. To achieve this, there are national education goals for guidance. In addition, there are some specific objectives for the development of education of deaf persons, which aim at the following:

1. The overall development of the individual spiritually, mentally, socially, and physically to the highest degree.

2. The development of the potential, productive, and creative abilities of the individual so that he or she may be an asset to society.

3. The development of the individual to attain a fuller degree of independence in his or her life.

There are 26 schools and units for deaf Kenyans distributed throughout the country that enroll approximately 2000 children annually. Of these schools and units, 22 are residential and 4 are day.

Quite a large number of children with undetected minor hearing impairment are to be found in the regular school system. In order to adequately serve those children who are not in special schools, there is a small-scale but successful integration program going on in some parts of the country where facilities are available. A peripatetic program has been initiated in two major cities (Nairobi and Nakuru) to facilitate integration, detection, and counseling services. Some deaf children under five years of age who have acquired some useful speech at home receive intensive preschool training at home from peripatetic teachers in the oral-aural method, accompanied by parental guidance, until they are old enough to attend the appropriate schools or units. Others are encouraged to continue education in the normal school environment, receiving special advice and instruction from trained peripatetic and resource teachers.

A number of hearing-impaired children are admitted to nursery classes attached to special primary schools for deaf children as early as age three, where they progress to the infant classes before joining primary level—a total of eight years of education. Although it is agreed that the aim of providing primary education to deaf pupils is to develop their spiritual, physical, and communication potentials—all geared toward achieving secondary education—the great majority do not achieve this. Therefore in order to enable the deaf students to acquire essential living and communication skills, prevocational, craft-oriented skills including business techniques and agriculture are taught as part of the curriculum.

Every class teacher is entirely responsible for all specialist subjects with all the children in each class. When feasible, one or more additional specialist teachers are posted to special schools for deaf students so that extra attention can be given to individual speech and language development. The teacher-pupil ratio in these schools does not exceed 1:12, and the average annual enrollment is about 120 children.

The maintained and assisted schools for deaf students are under the management of the boards of governors appointed by the Minister for Education as stipulated in the Education Act. Special units for deaf children attached to regular primary schools are directly under the management of the respective school committees. They are considered an integral part of these schools, receiving the same attention as any other classes.

The Kenya government permits any private managers wishing to establish services for deaf persons to make an application to the ministry through its heads in the various districts.

There also exists a national adult literacy program which provides an educational service to those who need it, including deaf persons.

The Kenya Society for the Deaf has been one of the main organizations offering a wide range of services for deaf persons in this country.

SOCIOECONOMIC STATUS

Kenya, like many other developing countries, has experienced an acute problem of unemployment and a rising cost of living. This has reduced the employment opportunities for handicapped persons generally and particularly for deaf persons.

Kenya is an agricultural country, and therefore rural development based on crop and livestock industries is encouraged. Urban areas, however, provide the best opportunities for deaf workers in wage-earning employment despite the large unemployment and underemployment figures among the able-bodied. Whenever deaf persons are given the opportunities, they are able to undertake a wide range of skilled and unskilled work in industry, where the able-bodied workers have no precedence over deaf workers, nor have the latter any right to special privileges of employment. Deaf persons have ordinary rights to pursue employment, although restricted by the traditional beliefs about disabled persons.

Unfortunately, most of the rural areas, where 90 percent of the population live, do not provide salaried employment, especially in agricultural areas, where the employers equate deafness with incapacity. In such areas, deaf persons aim for self-employment. They are encouraged to grow not only subsistence crops but cash crops, which they can market through the local cooperatives and marketing boards.

Other deaf persons who live in rural areas and who have received training in such areas as tailoring, knitting, leatherwork, and local crafts are given opportunities to set up small shops in their local trading centers, where they work in groups and as individuals. Through the income from such small businesses, they are able to be self-supporting, providing their families with a reasonable standard of living.

Although there are no statistics available on the number of employed deaf persons in Kenya, the government is doing all that is possible to include legislation in the constitution on the employment of disabled persons. However, deaf persons have always received assistance in placement with various government departments and private firms in both the rural and urban sectors.

COMMUNICATION

The Ministry of Basic Education recognizes that no one type of curriculum, school, or method of communication can effectively provide for the needs of all hearing-impaired. This view has also been expressed by the deaf persons themselves. Thus the ministry is introducing other methods of communication such as the simultaneous method. *See* SOCIOLINGUISTICS: Simultaneous Communication.

In addition to the problem of method of communication, many children come from different nationalities and tribal backgrounds, posing an even greater problem of language of instruction in schools. To ease the problem, it is the government policy for all children to be educated in their mother tongue languages whenever possible during the early years and then move to national languages (Kiswahili and English) at third-grade level.

The responsibility of providing welfare services for deaf persons rests at present with various government ministries such as the Ministries of Health, Basic Education, and Culture and Social Services. These ministries play a vital role in providing information on the identification, early intervention, preventive, and curative measures of deafness.

The Ministry of Health conducts curative and preventive programs through maternal health services, nutrition programs, and early medical treatment.

The Ministry of Basic Education provides information on basic education and further training. This ministry disseminates the information to the schools and general public from the Inspectorate, the Kenya Institute of Education (which is a National Curriculum Development Centre), and administrative sections. The ministry coordinates information programs which are broadcast to the general public and schools through the schools broadcast network.

Information on vocational rehabilitation, recreational opportunities, and job placement is provided through the Ministry of Culture and Social Services.

In addition, Kamwenja Teachers' College, where specialist teachers for deaf persons are trained; Kenyatta National Hospital (ENT Clinic), where diagnostic assessment and screening of deafness is conducted; and the Kenya Society for the Deaf, which runs clinic services in major towns, are good sources of information.

Finally, it is envisaged that Kenyatta University College, which offers advanced courses on special education, and the Kenya Institute of Special Education will become information and intensive research centers in the future.

Bibliography

International Labour Organization: *Report to the Government of Kenya on the Development of a National Programme on Vocational Rehabilitation of the Disabled*, 1972.

Republic of Kenya: Development Plan, 1979–1983.

———: Education Act, 1969.

———: Ministry of Basic Education Draft Policy for Special Education, 1981.

———: *Report of a National Committee on Educational Objectives and Policies*, December 1976.

Catherine M. Abilla

KITTO, JOHN
(1804–1854)

John Kitto was an eminent Bible scholar. Despite a physical handicap, a childhood filled with privation, and little formal education, he achieved recognition for his contributions in biblical literature.

Kitto was born on December 4, 1804, in Plymouth, England, the eldest son of John Kitto, a stonemason, and Elizabeth Picken. The family suffered from intemperance and poverty, and at the age of four Kitto was sent to live with his maternal grandmother.

Grandmother Picken instilled in Kitto a love for nature and reading, and he read every book he could procure, including the family Bible. Her encouragement and a neighbor who told him stories kindled in Kitto an intense desire for learning.

On February 13, 1817, while helping his father, Kitto was climbing a ladder carrying a load of slates.

Portrait of John Kitto.

He missed his footing and fell 35 feet, losing consciousness. On awakening two weeks later, Kitto could no longer hear, and his speech was imperfect. The loss of hearing affected his balance, causing him to walk unsteadily. Thereafter he expressed himself in writing; at other times he used signs. When his voice returned, he spoke with a guttural sound.

On recovering his health, Kitto took up sign painting but without any success. Due to his parents' destitution, he was placed in a Plymouth workhouse where he learned shoemaking. Being permitted to sleep at home afforded Kitto an opportunity for mental cultivation, as he had a great thirst for knowledge. He kept a journal and recorded his daily observations and thoughts, a practice which helped to develop his mental faculties.

For two years, he was apprenticed to two shoemakers. His leisure hours were devoted to reading, and to writing essays which were published in the *Plymouth Weekly Journal*.

In 1823, certain gentlemen, recognizing Kitto's superior abilities, took up a public subscription to further his literary pursuits. Kitto was granted permission to read in the public library and, with his discharge from the workhouse, he spent many happy hours there.

Many branches of knowledge claimed Kitto's attention, but his preference was for history and morality. An interest in biblical literature was further developed when A. N. Groves, an Exeter dentist and a Christian, taught Kitto the trade of dentistry and fostered his spiritual growth.

Time strengthened Kitto's religious beliefs and, though unable to serve in the pulpit, he wrote articles on topics of a religious nature. By this time he had mastered several languages, including Hebrew.

After learning the printing trade under the auspices of the Church Missionary Society in London for two years, Kitto accompanied a group to a missionary station in Malta in 1827. There he helped to print tracts in several foreign languages to be sent to missionaries in the Near East.

Kitto's tenure with the society was terminated in 1828 as the society was displeased with his devotion during leisure time to intellectual pursuits, fearing that his health would be impaired. He returned to England.

For four years, beginning in 1829, Kitto toured the Near East with a private mission party organized by Mr. Groves. The experiences resulted in a series of biblical books which he wrote after his return to England in 1833.

In the same year, Kitto was married to Annabella Fenwick, a hearing woman. Throughout their 21 years of marriage, she collected the materials needed for his writings.

Kitto wrote for the Society for the Diffusion of Useful Knowledge, which published his articles in its periodical, *Penny Magazine*. Other contributions were printed in different magazines.

Among the 21 books he wrote were *The Pictorial Bible* (1835–1838) and the *Pictorial History of Palestine and the Holy Land* (1840). These volumes were useful to students of sacred literature. His greatest work was the *Cyclopaedia of Biblical Literature* (1845), two tomes of nearly 2000 pages, which entitled him to a foremost place among Bible commentators.

In 1845, his autobiography, *The Lost Senses*, appeared. Many other biblical works, including travel books, came out. His final book, *The Daily Bible Illustrations*, was published in Edinburgh from 1849 to 1853. Between 1848 and 1853, Kitto founded and edited the *Journal of Sacred Literature*.

In 1844, the University of Giessen in Germany honored Kitto, though a layman, with the degree of doctor of divinity. In 1845, the Royal Society of Antiquaries made him a Fellow. In 1850, he was granted a pension of 100 pounds a year from the Royal Civil List in recognition of his literary works.

The daily habit of intensive writing finally took its toll on Kitto's health. In 1851, he suffered a severe neuralgic attack in the back of his head, and doctors advised him to curtail his activities and take daily walks.

In 1853, Kitto experienced a blow when his youngest child died. He was very fond of his children, all of whom could hear, and he longed to hear their voices. Members of the household and friends communicated with Kitto by fingerspelling the letters of the manual alphabet. However, Kitto rarely used fingerspelling, preferring to write or talk. His knowledge of signs as used by deaf people was limited.

In his autobiography, Kitto wrote that sign language is the natural language of deaf people and that other modes of communication are, to them, "artificial." He believed that to be successful, deaf persons must master written language.

Early in 1854, he suffered a paralytic stroke and sank into unconsciousness. He recovered but was constantly bothered with an agonizing headache. In August, with financial assistance from friends, Kitto traveled to Germany with his family. They settled at Cannstatt, Württemberg, hoping that the effect of mineral waters would be beneficial to him.

Kitto's health continued to decline, and he died on November 25, 1854, at the age of 49. He was interred in the cemetery at Cannstatt, where a handsome monument was later erected over the site by Charles Knight, the publisher of his last work. Professor John Eadie, of Glasgow, in his biography of John Kitto, said: "The name of Dr. Kitto is now immortally associated with Biblical study and literature. The measure of his success is not more amazing in its amount than in the means by which he reached it. Neither poverty, nor deafness, nor hard usage . . . chilled the ardor of his sacred ambition."

Bibliography

Eadie, John: *Life of John Kitto*, Oliphant, Anderson and Ferrier, Edinburgh, 1882.

Kitto, John: *The Lost Senses*, Charles Knight, London, 1845.

Knight, Charles: *English Cyclopaedia Biography*, vol. 3, 1854–1872.

Ryland, J. E.: *Memoirs of John Kitto*, William Oliphant and Sons, Edinburgh, 1856.

Thayer, William M.: *From Poor-House to Pulpit; or The Triumph of the late Dr. John Kitto*. E. O. Libby, Boston, 1859.

The Western Antiquary, vol. 3, pp. 33–35, 1883.

Francis Higgins

LANGUAGE

As a salient property distinguishing human beings from other creatures, and enabling people to be reasoning, social beings, language occupies a special place in human awareness. Consequently, the definition of language is complex and problematic, and the choice of definitions has political implications. Virtually any definition is apt to be both controversial and incomplete. But it is instructive at least to try to formulate definitions.

DEFINITIONS

A definition of language can be approached by several paths. One can ask what a language consists of (what are its building blocks or concrete units), or what are the abstract properties of language (such as its hierarchical structure), or what are the functions of language (such as the transmission of thoughts and feelings).

Such definitions assume that there exist properties characteristic of all human languages (called linguistic universals) that differentiate languages from nonlinguistic communicative systems such as animal communication or the communicative strategies of computers. However, since there have been many thousands of natural human languages over the four or so millennia, it is impossible that all of these could be exhaustively studied and categorized. In fact, formal study of natural sign languages has only recently been initiated. Thus claims of universality must always be treated with some

suspicion. However, with that caveat, it is possible to attempt a definition of language based on what is known so far about spoken and signed languages.

Building Blocks Returning to the first type of definition, one could say that a language consists of symbols, words or signs, arranged by rigorous rules into sentences. These symbols are composed, by equally rigorous rules, of smaller parts: in spoken language, sounds; in signed languages, body positions and movements. Thus, different symbols, in different languages, all represent a particular object. This object is called the referent of the symbol, what the symbol means.

The English symbol, written as "tree," has three sounds—t, r, and the vowel ee. These sounds, following the rules of English, could be combined differently to form the word "reet"—a possible, but presently nonexistent, word. However, the rules of English do not permit the formation of a word like "*rtee." (An asterisk before a word or sentence means that utterance breaks the rules of the language, is ungrammatical.) Most English speakers could not give a specific rule forbidding this sound combination, but simply would say that it sounds "funny" or "foreign."

Similarly, the sounds s and t can be combined in English to form words like "stop," "nest," and "cats." But the combination ts cannot occur at the beginning of a word, as in "*tsap." However, in other spoken languages like German and Bantu, it is fine for words to begin with the sounds ts. All

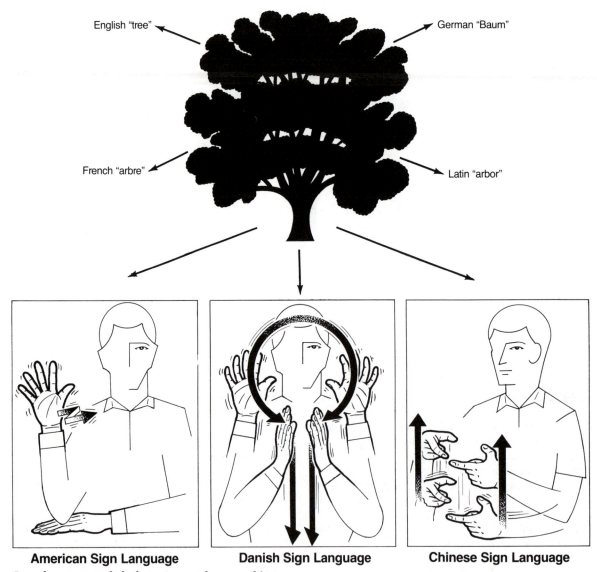

English "tree"

German "Baum"

French "arbre"

Latin "arbor"

American Sign Language   **Danish Sign Language**   **Chinese Sign Language**

Seven language symbols that represent the same object.

spoken languages have a set of rules that determine which sounds can occur in that language and how they can be combined to form words.

The same is true for signed languages, but here the rules concern body positions and movements. The extended middle finger handshape that occurs in signs in British Sign Language and Taiwan Sign Language, for example, never occurs in American Sign Language (ASL) or French Sign Language (FSL). Similarly, the T handshape in ASL does not occur in FSL. *See* SIGN LANGUAGES: America, British, French, Taiwanese.

The F handshape of ASL also occurs in Chinese Sign Language (CSL); however, the rules for how this handshape can be used are different in the two languages. In ASL, when signs with this handshape contact a part of the body (like the face or chest), the contact must be made at the point where the thumb and index finger meet, or on the side of the thumb and index finger. It would be ungrammatical to form a sign in ASL where contact is made with the ends of the three upright fingers. However, a number of signs in CSL are made by contacting those three fingers. All signed languages have rules determining which body positions and movements can occur (such as which handshapes, locations on the body, and facial expressions can be used) and how these can be combined to form signs.

For both spoken and signed languages, the study of the smallest units in a language is called phonetics. The study of how those smallest units can be combined to form words or signs is called phonology. Words or signs then are structured into sentences; the study of the rules of sentence formation is called syntax. These are some of the areas of

Handshape for "brother" in Taiwan Sign Language.

A "marked" handshape for T.

Handshape used in American Sign Language that occurs in signs like CAT and IMPORTANT.

focus within the field of linguistics, the scientific study of language.

Both linguists and lay people speak of grammatical rules. But the linguist's notion of a rule of grammar is strange to the uninitiated. As previously illustrated, the linguist's rules are implicit, or unconscious—speakers make use of them without knowing they are doing so, without being able to quote the rule they are using. Thus, the fluent speaker of English senses a relationship between sentences (1) and (2) below: they have the same meaning (neither could be true if the other was false), but each expresses the meaning in different syntactic patterns.

(1) It's Jane who came in.

(2) Jane came in.

Speakers also know that not everything needed to understand what a sentence means is to be found in its actual form. So an imperative sentence like (3) is understood as meaning (4) even though the subject "you" is not found explicitly in (3).

(3) Wash yourself!

(4) You wash yourself!

The rules of the grammar inform speakers of the relationship between (1) and (2), and enable them to infer an appropriate subject in (3).

Just as languages differ at the phonological level (for example, in how sounds can be combined to form words), so also the syntactic rules of languages differ. For instance, rules concerning word order differ from language to language. Normally the words in an English sentence are organized in the order: subject—verb—direct object.

(5) The man   read   the book.
    subject   verb   object

(6) *The book   read   the man.
    object   verb   subject

Other languages employ different orders, or require no particular order at all. In the latter case (as in a language like Latin), other means are available to distinguish subjects from objects—endings on words, for instance. Examples (7) and (8) illustrate the flexibility of Latin word order made possible by endings on the nouns (which distinguish the subject from the object).

(7) Vir   librum lēgit.   "The man read
    subject object verb   the book."

(8) Librum vir   lēgit.   "The man read
    object   subject verb   the book."

(9) *Liber   virum   lēgit.   "*The book read
    subject object verb   the man."

Linguistic research is just beginning to provide information on the syntactic structure of natural signed languages. Signed languages like ASL have rules concerning both word (sign) order and something that is functionally like word endings—changes in the movement of signs, in particular, verbs.

An understanding of how signers use space is a key to understanding the grammatical structure of signed languages. When talking about people, places, or objects not present in the immediate area, signers will assign spatial locations (for example, to the right or left) which then represent a particular person or place. Then by moving a verb like GIVE-TO from one location to another, the signer indicates who is the subject and who is the object. For example, if the right location means "Peter" and the left location means "Jane," moving the verb from right to left means "Peter gives to Jane." It would be ungrammatical to sign the verb first if the locations for Peter and Jane had not previously been assigned. Similarly, it would be ungrammatical to move the verb from the area in front of the signer's body, instead of from the right, if the meaning is "Peter gives to Jane."

In summary, all languages consist of symbols and rules determining both how the symbols are composed and how they are combined with other symbols to form sentences. Of course, sentences are then combined to form larger units: conversational turns, for instances, or paragraphs, which are studied respectively by the fields of conversa-

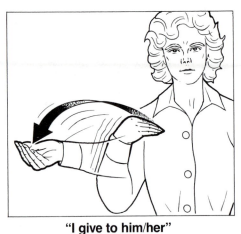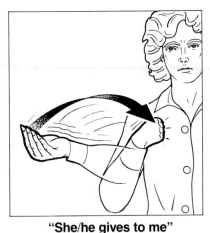

"I give to you"   "I give to him/her"   "She/he gives to me"

Changes in the movement of the verb GIVE-TO indicate different subjects and objects. (After C. Baker and D. Cokely, "What Is a Language?" in *American Sign Language: A Teacher's Resource Text on Grammar and Culture*, T. J. Publishers, Silver Spring, Maryland, 1980)

tion analysis and text analysis. And all linguistic communication attempts to achieve some effect on those who hear or see it: the study of how linguistic form relates to this social function is called pragmatics.

Features Alternatively one can define language in terms of its more abstract properties. For example, the relationship between the symbols of a language and their referents is relatively arbitrary. Symbols do not look or sound exactly like the things they represent. If they had to bear a direct resemblance, then languages would be very limited. For example, a language could not have a word for "love" or "virtue" since these meanings do not have a concrete visual or auditory form that the language could copy.

For those referents that can be seen or heard, the symbols still are relatively or completely arbitrary. For example, the word "tree" in English does not look or sound like the object depicted in a drawn tree. The sign TREE in ASL does bear some visual resemblance to the thing it represents, but it does not look exactly like a tree. If the sign is shown to people who do not know ASL, they will not know what it means. The sign TREE is iconic in that there is some visual resemblance to its referent, but it is also relatively arbitrary. Consequently, signs for "tree" vary considerably in different sign languages.

Another feature of language is that it is hierarchical—smaller elements are combined to form larger units. For example, there are about 60 sounds in English that are used to form all of the words of English (variously estimated as between 10,000 and 30,000). These words are used to form a potentially infinite number of sentences that are used to form an infinite number of paragraphs, conversational turns, soliloquies, books, and so on.

Similarly, the smaller elements of signed languages include handshapes, hand orientations, movements of the hands and arms, places where those movements are made, facial movements, head movements, eye movements, and movements of the torso. These elements combine to form signs and grammatical signals that then create sentences, and so on.

Another feature of language, illustrated above in the section "Building Blocks," is that there are rigorous rules operating at each level of the hierarchy. Languages are systematic.

Another feature of language is that it changes over time. Some changes are necessary, such as certain types of vocabulary change that enable users of a language to converse about any topic of their choosing, for example, computer "bytes," "quarks," and "quasars." Languages have this productive ability to create new vocabulary. Many languages, like ASL and English, often create new signs and words by compounding—for example, in English, "video" + "tape" becomes "videotape"; in ASL, a sign showing waves of electric current combines with a sign outlining a rectangular shape to form the compound sign that means "microwave oven."

Functions One can also work toward a definition in terms of what language is good for, what its functions are. A language is, first of all, a mode of communication: it is social, allowing human beings to inform one another of their needs, desires, and ideas. But it is cognitive as well, allowing individuals to formulate those needs, desires, and ideas in their minds.

Arising out of these properties and functions is an important aspect of human language, differentiating it (as far as is known) from animal communication: it allows its users to refer to the nonpresent. The nonpresent includes things that exist at the time of the utterance but are not physically observable by participants, like the leftover roast in the refrigerator; things that are not currently in existence, but were or will be, like a dentist's appointment tomorrow; and things that never existed except in the imagination, like trolls. Furthermore, a language allows speakers to characterize both concrete objects (a roast) and abstract concepts (virtue).

Hearing professionals sometimes have denigrated natural signed languages by claiming that these languages were unable to express abstract concepts. However, linguistic study of signed languages has disproven this myth. Indeed public lectures have been given in ASL on the molecular structure of DNA, the "crab theory" of group dynamics, and the relationship between language and culture. Similarly, at the 1980 International Symposium on Sign Language Research, a deaf user of Thai Sign Language gave a presentation on the elaborate inflectional system in her language; a deaf user of Swedish Sign Language gave a lecture on sentence structure in his language; and a deaf user of Danish Sign Language described the use of "proforms" in figurative signing. *See* SIGN LANGUAGES: Danish, Swedish.

Another key function of language is enculturation. Each language embodies and reflects the history, values, and ways of thinking of its past and present users. When children learn a language, they also learn the "world view" encapsulated in that language, which then enables them to participate freely in the culture with other language users.

PRESCRIPTIVE AND DESCRIPTIVE GRAMMAR

As seen in the preceding sections, the linguist writes rules that predict how a fluent speaker or signer might evaluate different conceivable combinations—of sounds or words, body movements, and positions or signs. But traditional grammarians have a different perspective, seeing the task of grammar as filtering out, among actually occurring forms, the chaff from the grain. They have tried to determine which forms are "good" and which are "bad." This is called prescriptive grammar, to be distinguished from the linguists' task, descriptive grammar. The prescriptive grammarian would have no position on (10): since it is never disputed, it need not be judged. But a judgment is necessary on (11), which is found in the speech of some fluent speakers of English, with the same meaning as (10).

(10) I never did anything to anybody.

(11) I never did nothing to nobody.

Prescriptive grammarians argue (on dubious grounds in terms of both historical English grammar and formal logic) that (10) is grammatical and (11) is not, and should be weeded out. But sentences like (11) are common in English. The linguist is interested in how such sentences are formed, as well as who uses them, and when; and

why (11) continues to flourish although it is discouraged by the authorities.

VARIATION

Variation among spoken and signed languages is great. But even within what people think of as the same language, there is much variation. One person may speak or sign differently from another based on membership in different social groups (ethnic, regional, or socioeconomic, for instance), or because as individuals they are psychologically different (one may be more formal, one more indirect). Similarly, people have access to several forms of speech or sign, depending for instance on whether they are conversing with a spouse, a friend, a child, or an employer.

Differences based on group membership are called dialects: people are said to sign or speak different dialects (rather than separate languages) if they can still understand each other. Sentences (10) and (11) are from two different dialects of English, with (10) being the standard form, (11) the nonstandard form. Speakers of nonstandard dialects usually must learn to use the standard dialect in certain situations; they must learn to code-switch. The study of socially determined linguistic variation is called sociolinguistics. *See* SOCIOLINGUISTICS.

Individual variation (called idiolects when the grammars of individuals are being compared, and register when speaking of variations among a single speaker's range of communicative styles) is the province of both sociolinguistics and pragmatics. As an example of the latter, a speaker who wants to get someone else to do something might say (12) or (13). Both have the same meaning, but imply a different relationship between the speakers, and might have different consequences. Example (14) is also a possible way of communicating (12).

(12) Open the window!

(13) I wonder if it would be too much trouble to get the window opened.

(14) It's hot in here.

Pragmatics attempts to describe how and when people use utterances like (13) and (14), and how such utterances differently affect the addressee.

CONCLUSION

As a science, compared with biology or physics, linguistics is very new (most of what has been discussed above has been known only since the 1960s or so), and its findings are still controversial and open to debate. But some assumptions are universally held among serious students of language: that language is systematic; that a set of rules for the production and understanding of linguistic forms is discoverable; that any language, provided it enables its users to express clearly what they need and desire to express, is equivalent in power and utility to any other such system; and that the serious scholar of language seeks to describe its properties, not to restrict or circumscribe them.

Bibliography

Baker, C., and D. Cokely: "What Is a Language?" in *American Sign Language: A Teacher's Resource Text on Grammar and Culture*, T.J. Publishers, Silver Spring, Maryland, 1980.

Bolinger, D.: *Aspects of Language*, Harcourt Brace Jovanovich, New York, 1968.

Chomsky, N.: *Language and Mind*, Harcourt Brace Jovanovich, New York, 1968.

Greenberg, J.: *Universals of Language*, MIT Press, Cambridge, Massachusetts, 1963.

Labov, W.: *Sociolinguistic Patterns*, University of Pennsylvania Press, Philadelphia, 1972.

Sapir, E.: *Language*, Harcourt Brace Jovanovich, New York, 1921.

Robin Lakoff; Charlotte Baker-Shenk

Acquisition

All normal children have the mental or cognitive capacity for learning language. This capacity, however, requires sufficient amount of linguistic input. There is some feature in the human brain that allows young humans, when they have had the opportunity to interact with language users, to develop the ability to use the rules of the language to which they are exposed. For the purposes of this article, "acquisition" will mean the normal process by which infants and young children learn the language of their primary caregivers as a first, or native, language. In normal acquisition, children in any language community learn the language of the home without any "lessons" or conscious teaching from parents or other adults. First-language acquisition is accomplished without reinforcement, teaching, or study.

Such a definition excludes the issue of deaf children with hearing parents, as well as the teaching of English to deaf children. This article assumes that American Sign Language (ASL) is the only possible native language for deaf children of American deaf adults and is potentially one of two native languages for hearing children of American deaf adults. The question of language acquisition by hearing children of deaf parents will not be addressed.

CHARACTERISTICS

Infants are virtually bathed in language input, and the input is natural, not taught. Caregivers have no real notion of what babies might need to learn and do not have a set of lesson plans in order to accomplish certain goals. Importantly, the input is concerned with concrete topics and context-related references: babies and their caregivers normally "talk" about the here and now. Language is thus treated as a means of communication, not as an abstract or isolated system. Throughout the process, caregivers provide responsive and interactive support, in which infants learn to manage social interactions. This means that language for infants and their caregivers is very much of a social tool, rather than a cognitive or intellectual one.

Much of the current thinking in the general field of language acquisition focuses on the importance of prelinguistic activities and the foundation laid for language in the interaction between infants and their caregivers. In the period prior to infants' real usage of langauge, caregivers and babies engage in a variety of "games" in which langauge and rules for language use are embedded. As infants are socialized, they are also learning about certain basic characteristics of communication, such as reciprocity, turn-taking, topic management, and eye gaze behaviors.

ISSUES

Researchers interested in language acquisition (psychologists, anthropologists, and linguists) recognize the value of all acquisition data in simply increasing understanding of the human brain and of the acquisition process. Yet, there are particular reasons for the special interest in acquisition of signed languages.

The first issue that makes this particular process of interest is that, prior to the surge of general interest in signed languages, researchers assumed that deaf children could not acquire language normally. These children were only of interest to the degree that they continued babbling, and continued to display "normal" vocal behaviors. Now that linguists generally accept the notion of signed languages as legitimate members of the family of human languages, the question of acquisition is an interesting one: do deaf children acquire signed languages normally? So, in some sense, this issue reflects the status of signed languages in comparison to spoken languages.

Second, the issue of modality is of some concern: everything researchers know about normal language acquisition is based on auditory and spoken languages. How might the shift to a visual and gestural language affect understanding of the process itself? What are the implications of the use of a different set of articulators and a different system for comprehending language? If the similarities and differences between hearing babies and deaf babies (of deaf parents) in the acquisition process can be sorted out, there will then be the opportunity to identify what is truly universal, truly human, about language. If the differences are not significant, then there is some sort of verification (a "test case") for previous language acquisition research and conclusions already suggested. An initial hypothesis, for example, was that the iconic nature of signed languages would facilitate earlier acquisition by deaf babies.

PROCESS

Anecdotal evidence indicates that, in fact, infants learning ASL acquire their first lexical items (usually MILK or MOTHER) considerably earlier than infants learning any spoken language; this has been confirmed through careful analysis of available data. It seems that this advantage can be traced to modality differences: gross motor control develops earlier than the physical abilities needed for spoken language. Later developments in the acquisition of ASL (such as syntax and complex morphology), however, seem to coincide with those in spoken languages. This suggests that these linguistic developments depend on cognitive and linguistic maturation.

General deictic points are among the first communicative gestures made by all children, both deaf and hearing, appearing well before first words and at approximately the same time as first signs. That is, all infants use pointing to communicate certain basic notions ("What is that?", "I want that," and the like). However, a strict approach can be taken to these deictic points, considering them to be truly linguistic (that is, pronouns) only if they appear in combination with a lexical or referring sign. Given this definition, they can be counted as beginning at roughly 1,8 (ages are given as "year, months"; thus 1,8 equals 20 months of age). The work of L. A. Petitto is particularly interesting, since she focuses on those points that should be "easiest" for the deaf child: I and YOU. Her evidence indicates, however, that deaf children exhibit pronoun reversals (similar to those of youngsters learning spoken languages), despite the obvious spatial relationship of these forms to their referents.

Deaf children acquiring ASL face the necessity of comprehending and producing an extraordinarily complex morphology, both derivational and inflectional. The first linguistic forms to appear in children's lexical repertoires are unaffected, however, by the morphological complexities of caretakers' language. This situation holds true until about 2,0. At this time, various parts of the morphological complex begin to appear in the child's production. For instance, noun-verb distinctions (CHAIR vs. SIT-IN-CHAIR) begin to appear between ages 2,0 and 2,11, but they do so inconsistently. It is not until sometime around 6,0 that children display control over these distinctions.

Similarly, verbs of motion and location (frequently known as classifers) remain in simplified, or frozen, form until about 2,9. These verbs are morphologically highly complex, and include morphemes that indicate the type of object that moves (such as vehicle vs. animate object), the manner (such as bounce), path (such as arc), and spatial relationships between the moving object and a secondary object (such as next-to). Even though such verbs often are fairly iconic, young deaf children do not appear to view them as such; rather, they appear to tackle the job in much the same way that hearing children cope with complex morphology. That is, only some of the morphemes appear initially, one at a time. Others are added piece by piece, until the entire subsystem is under control, in this case at about 5,6. So, for example, a young child attempting to produce a motion verb form that requires two simultaneous morphemes for direction and type of movement will instead only include one of these morphemes. At a later stage, children will produce all of the morphemes, but sequentially rather than simultaneously.

These data gathered in relationship to a variety of morphological structures suggest that deaf children acquiring ASL proceed through at least three stages before becoming competent adult users: first, they omit or ignore morphological markers altogether; second, they include some of the markers but omit others; third, they produce all of the morphology but in a sequential fashion. This indicates that simultaneity—a markedly distinctive characteristic of ASL morphology—is difficult for deaf children, and that iconicity is of little or no value to children in the process of acquisition. This latter observation is especially evident, since many of children's utterances are less iconic than the target adult model.

The actual production of signs also displays developmental progressions. Four stages of acquisition of handshapes in ASL have been suggested and confirmed. Handshapes produced by deaf babies learning ASL primarily reflect their ability to discriminate between and to control their fingers. In terms of semantic relationships, early utterances of deaf children focus on the same issues as do those of other (hearing) children: the existence or nonexistence of objects, possession of objects, and the location of objects are among the earliest notions that are expressed.

It becomes apparent that in every important respect the acquisition process is similar, regardless of the human infant's hearing status. Researchers find differences in some interesting but noncrucial areas, such as age at acquisition of first lexical items. This, as stated above, can be explained by earlier maturation of both the visual and gross motor systems. Later, deaf children display the same principled behaviors as other children so far studied: they give evidence of an initial inability to produce morphologically complex items, of forming increasingly sophisticated hypotheses about the nature of language and about the specific rules of the language they are learning, and of slowly conquering this highly complex language. Just as with other infants learning language, deaf babies gradually progress from the early use of crude communicative tools (such as deictic points) to using language (in a highly sophisticated form) in order to make their needs known.

One clearly crucial factor is the unhindered, natural interaction—both social and linguistic—between caregiver and child. This is the single factor that separates deaf children with deaf parents from their peers with hearing parents. And, indeed, it is this that makes them similar, even identical, to those children of other language communities that have been studied previously. That is, deaf children acquire signed languages "normally"—they make all the sorts of errors that other children do in the process of becoming competent language users. Equally significant is the fact that the iconicity of signed languages does not appear to assist deaf children in any way in their task. Rather, the complexity of the forms themselves seems to be a challenge that can be overcome only by the gradual maturation of cognitive abilities.

Bibliography

Bonvillian, J., M. D. Orlansky, and L. L. Novack: "Early Sign Language Acquisition and Its Relation to Cognitive and Motor Development," in J. Kyle and B. Woll (eds.), *Language in Sign: An International Perspective on Sign Language*, Croom Helm, London, 1983.

Launer, P. B.: " 'A Plane' Is Not 'To Fly': Acquiring the Distinction Between Related Nouns and Verbs in American Sign Language," unpublished doctoral dissertation, City University of New York, 1982.

Loew, R.: "Roles and Reference in American Sign Language: A Developmental Perspective," unpublished doctoral dissertation, University of Minnesota, 1984.

McIntire, M.: "The Acquisition of ASL Hand Configurations," *Sign Language Studies*, 16:247–266, 1976.

Meier, R. P.: "Icons, Analogues, and Morphemes: The Acquisition of Verb Agreement in ASL," unpublished doctoral dissertation, University of California, San Diego, 1982.

Newport, E. L.: "Constraints on Structure: Evidence from American Sign Language and Language Learning," in W. A. Collins (ed.), *Aspects of the Development of Competence, Minnesota Symposia on Child Psychology*, vol. 14, Lawrence Erlbaum Associates, Hillsdale, New Jersey, 1981.

Newport, E. L., and E. Ashbrook: "The Emergence of Semantic Relations in American Sign Language," *Papers and Reports on Child Language Development*, 13:16–21, 1977.

Newport, E. L., and R. P. Meier: "Acquisition of American Sign Language," in D. I. Slobin (ed.), *The Cross-Linguistic Study of Language Acquisition*, Lawrence Erlbaum Associates, Hillsdale, New Jersey, in press.

Petitto, L. A.: "From Gesture to Symbol: The Relation Between Form and Meaning," paper presented at Third International Symposium on Sign Language Research. Rome, Italy, 1983 (*Proceedings*, Linstok Press, in press).

Supalla, T.: "Structure and Acquisition of Verbs of Motion and Location in American Sign Language," unpublished doctoral dissertation, University of California, San Diego, 1982.

Volterra, V.: "Gestures, Signs, and Words at Two Years: When Does Communication Become Language?", *Sign Language Studies*, 33:351–362, 1981.

Marina L. McIntire

Disorders

There are two major sources of information on the human brain mechanisms used in communication. One derives from various indirect sensory and motor methods for assessing brain organization in normal people. The other source is the effect of natural disruptions of the central nervous system on communication in patients who have strokes or tumors of the brain. It is known from such studies that communication in most hearing persons depends critically on the left half, or hemisphere, of the brain. The question naturally arises whether this is true also for deaf people. To the extent that both the deaf and hearing populations employ complex self-generated movements in communicating, they appear to have similar brain mechanisms. Although hearing persons employ primarily oral movements and deaf persons employ primarily manual movements, there is much evidence that the programming of both types of movement requires similar mechanisms and is controlled primarily by the left cerebral hemisphere.

Even if the basic brain organization for communication (and indeed for noncommunicative function) is equivalent in deaf and hearing persons, however, one must keep in mind that the methods for acquiring information may be quite different in the two groups, due to their differing use of auditory and visual modalities. One would expect that skills dependent on auditory-phonemic-syllabic channels in hearing persons would be largely unavailable to deaf people, but that, where possible, alternative skills would be acquired through visual (or other) channels. This could be achieved by an experientially based variation in the use of brain pathways which emphasizes one modality over another, rather than by any fundamental brain reorganization in deaf persons. These differences between deaf and hearing persons in modes of acquisition must be recognized in examining studies on brain organization, a factor which becomes apparent when considering brain mechanisms in reading.

BRAIN ORGANIZATION: PERCEPTUAL-MOTOR ASYMMETRIES

A major approach to studying brain mechanisms in communication makes use of the presentation of visual, auditory, or tactual stimuli to the left or right side of the body, with a comparison of accuracy or speed of perception between the two sides. The general assumption, confirmed by a great deal of research, is that stimuli perceived better when presented to one half of the body or of space are dependent primarily on the opposite brain hemisphere for processing. This is due to the fact that sensory and motor anatomic systems in the brain are primarily crossed, with one hemisphere controlling the opposite side of the body.

For example, a higher score for the right visual field than for the left when reading briefly presented words is taken to reflect the fact that the left hemisphere is specialized for this kind of reading. The parallel technique on the motor side would involve a comparison of the two hands, a left-hand preference or superiority taken to indicate a right-hemisphere specialization or dominance for the particular motor acts involved, and vice versa. This type of approach is useful in that it can be applied to normal persons, but it is limited in its application because it typically permits statements only about which hemisphere is dominant for a particular process. It does not easily permit statements about which region within a hemisphere (or in both hemispheres) may be specially involved. The laterality method thus yields only a crude measure of functional specialization of the brain, concerned primarily with functional brain asymmetry, but it has the advantage that one does not have to wait for brain damage to occur in order to study a problem.

In hearing people, words tend to be perceived more accurately when presented to the right ear (left hemisphere) than when presented to the left ear (right hemisphere), reflecting the specialized function of the left hemisphere for verbal processing. Similarly, words and letters are perceived more accurately when flashed to the right visual field (left hemisphere), while certain visual-spatial tasks are performed better when presented to the left visual field (right hemisphere).

There is a question of whether the same neural organization holds for deaf people whose communication system appears to tap visuospatial systems. Several studies have reported that words and letters are not perceived better in the right field in deaf persons, though they are in hearing persons. One inference from such findings has been that the brain organization for communication is different in deaf people, perhaps because they fail to utilize those regions in the left hemisphere which are "prewired" for auditory speech processing.

There are alternative interpretations, however. Reading almost certainly does not proceed by the same means in deaf as in hearing persons, and therefore differences in cerebral hemispheric processing may not indicate any basic difference in cerebral organization but rather a different strategy in reading. For deaf individuals, reading is not syllabically based but presumably involves more of a visual match between a printed word and its referent. This would result in a different cerebral representation much like the difference between Japanese syllabic (*kana*) and idiographic (*kanji*) written languages. In hearing persons the former appears to be left-hemisphere-dependent and the latter not so. Deaf readers may thus employ brain pathways very similar to those employed by hearing persons when reading idiographic systems.

It has also been shown that manual signs, which are unequivocally language symbols for deaf people, do not show the right-visual-field superiority which would indicate left-hemisphere processing for such material. In fact, some reports indicate the reverse asymmetry. This does not necessarily mean that deaf persons use primarily their right hemispheres when processing signs, since it must be remembered that signs presented briefly to a visual field are static, whereas in reality they are moving. (The technical constraint of presenting stimuli to only one hemisphere requires a presentation time much less than a second in order to restrict access to one visual field, and essentially forces a static presentation.) Thus a briefly presented "sign" may not be seen as such, but as a static spatial array. Analysis of such spatial arrays is processed in hearing persons preferentially by the right hemisphere, not by the left. The fact that hearing persons also tend to favor the left field when identifying static "signs" suggests that, in both deaf and hearing individuals, the signs are being treated as spatial patterns, not as means of communication.

An attempt by one researcher to circumvent this difficulty, by presenting three different "stills" or phases of a sign within the short time limit, has met with some success in shifting the accuracy advantage to the right visual field and thus suggesting that the left hemisphere is involved in perception of real moving signs. However, on the whole it may be that the limitations of the brief presentation method simply make it inappropriate for studying the dynamic aspects of signing. *See* Psycholinguistics: Language Processing.

Brain Organization: Electrographic Recording

Somewhat more direct measures of brain activity may be gleaned from electrographic recordings, made by means of scalp electrodes, during the various cognitive or communicative activities of normal persons. This method also potentially allows more precise definition of the specific region involved in a process. Several studies have reported that the electrographic activity in the brains of deaf persons is different from that of hearing persons.

Specifically, deaf subjects do not show the changes in particular areas of the left hemisphere during reading of words that hearing subjects show. Therefore, it is claimed, the usual development of pathways for language-related processes has been altered in deaf people.

Unfortunately, brain-wave studies suffer from some serious interpretation problems when applied to complex functions, and for this reason have not fulfilled their initial promise as sources of information in this area. For one thing, the fact that there is a difference in brain activity appearing over the two brain hemispheres does not in itself permit the attribution of specialized processing to one hemisphere or the other. For example, reduced amplitude of electrographic activity in one hemisphere or in a particular area is often taken to indicate regional brain involvement in an ongoing process, but it is not an invariable indicator. (This is quite apart from possible artificial contributions such as asymmetrical skull thickness on the two sides or asymmetric placement of electrodes.) More important, perhaps, is the fact that electrographic activity is also very susceptible to the presence and type of motor response required, not just to the "cognitive" demands of the task.

Moreover, when a reading task is processed in the brain of a hearing person as compared with a deaf person, the same problems of interpretation arise as discussed earlier. The reading habit was acquired and is currently achieved by quite different means in the two populations, and while the cerebral mechanisms are, by that very fact, bound to be different, this does not address the more fundamental question of brain organization in deaf persons. Nevertheless, despite their limitations, both perceptual asymmetry studies and electrographic recordings are important adjunct methods to the main source of information about brain mechanisms in communication.

HEARING PERSONS WITH CENTRAL NERVOUS SYSTEM DAMAGE

The second major source of information about brain mechanisms in communication comes from the effects of central nervous system damage on communicative function. Damage to the nervous system has been a fruitful source of information for many years about how communication operates. Most of this information has come from hearing persons, but there is a growing body of data on deaf persons as well. As indicated earlier, the motor programming of both oral and manual movements employs similar mechanisms and is controlled primarily by the left cerebral hemisphere of the brain. The highly visual nature of manual signing, at least on the receiving end, has led some investigators to suggest that the brain systems employed for its transmission and reception should be quite different from the auditory-molded speech system in hearing persons. Although there certainly is scope for different brain systems to be involved in signing and speaking, it appears that the determining characteristic for brain organization in both kinds of communication is the motor control aspect, which has resulted in parallel forms of brain organization in the two cases.

Motor Systems in Arm and Hand Control   Since the basic brain mechanisms in limb control are the same for hearing and deaf persons, one can learn a great deal about manual control systems without studying deaf people directly.

There is substantial evidence that the brain pathways involved in control of the distal muscles, or those farthest from the body axis (that is, fingers and hand), are not the same as those involved in proximal arm movements, closest to the trunk. The distal movements depend on a more lateral pathway to the spinal cord, while the proximal arm movements may be controlled by the same systems or by a ventromedial pathway which also controls movements of the trunk. The system which controls fingers and hands is almost entirely a crossed system, meaning that it receives fibers almost entirely from the opposite cerebral hemisphere, whereas the proximal control system receives fibers from both cerebral hemispheres. This means, in effect, that each hemisphere controls individual arm, hand, and finger movements on the opposite side of the body, but on the same side controls only arm movements. Thus, in primates including people, the left half of the brain can control proximal movements of the left and right arms, but can control distal movements primarily of the right hand. The right hemisphere works similarly for arm movements, but controls distal movement of the left hand.

In terms of basic motor control, then, if damage is limited to the left cortical motor or corticospinal pathways, there will be inability to move the fingers of the right hand individually with accompanying weakness of wrist and elbow movements, but little impairment of shoulder movements. The lateral converse will be true after damage to the right cortical motor system. In terms of signing, movements most affected by the contralateral motor weakness, or hemiparesis, will be fingerspelling actions and signs which depend on particular handshapes. If only the basic motor systems in one hemisphere are involved, these difficulties will be restricted to one side of the body, and the other side will be relatively unaffected. Since manual signing, although typically bimanual, can be achieved fairly intelligibly with only one limb at a time, this would not in itself constitute a serious disruption of communication.

Motor Programming and the Left Hemisphere Although the basic motor pathways just described are probably fairly equivalent in the two cerebral hemispheres, a very important aspect of motor control is not so symmetrical. This is a function that might be described as a motor programming or motor selection function, and in humans it appears to depend critically on the left hemisphere. As a consequence, when a person sustains damage to the left hemisphere, the ability to carry out specified movements to command or imitation is often seriously impaired, especially if particular brain regions (parietal, midfrontal) are affected. This disability, called apraxia, is typically present in both limbs, and can occur even when there is good strength and motility of the right arm and hand, indicating that the basic motor systems are not involved. In severe cases of apraxia, the inability to carry out specified movements may extend even to well-practiced familiar movements such as demonstrating how to use a key or how to wave goodbye; but in milder cases such well-learned movements may be unaffected, while the copying of unfamiliar, less meaningful movements is affected.

The phenomenon of apraxia has been intensively studied in hearing persons and has generally been found in close association with a speech disorder (vocal aphasia), as well as with a difficulty in making a series of oral movements. These facts suggest that the system affected is involved in general motor selection functions, at least of the oral and brachial musculature. Thus a hearing person with vocal aphasia commonly has difficulty performing correctly a series of nonspeech movements of the oral musculature, as well as of hand or arm movements not related to communication.

NERVOUS SYSTEM CONSTRAINTS ON NORMAL SIGNING

Certain predictions about the motor characteristics of signing follow from the assumption that the manual and brachial movements, including signing, are controlled from one system, and that this motor programming system is based in the left hemisphere for most people. One prediction relates to the degree to which movements in the two arms can be different. The single system theory would predict that there should be a preponderance of mirror-image movements, since these movements result from identical messages going to the musculature of the two arms—for example, adduction and flexion. Another common movement should be alternation of identical commands to the two arms, since this can also easily be achieved by a single system. Relatively uncommon, because difficult to program, would be asymmetric movements in the two limbs, even when these are spatially parallel—for example, the two hands actually making different (nonalternating) movements, or both arms moving to the left (or right).

Related predictions about what should happen when the two handshapes are different are that only one hand should move, and that this hand will typically be the right hand since, although the left hemisphere programs both hands, there is an advantage for the opposite hand.

Some constraints on manual signs have been described under the labels "symmetry" and "dominance," which indicate that both the above limitations operate in actual signing behavior. Thus although both hands appear to be active in signing and appear to be making disparate movements, asymmetry is actually minimal. Asymmetry is most apparent in the distal musculature, in that handshapes are often dissimilar in the simple representative form of a sign (citation form). Much signing may be achieved by a rapid turn-taking of movements of the left and right arm, which is not detected at the speed of regular conversation.

CASES OF SIGN LANGUAGE APHASIA

Studies on hearing persons with nervous system damage have indicated that the left hemisphere is extremely important for programming or selecting the oral and manual movements to be performed. Disruptions to parts of the left hemisphere result in an apraxia, or inability to perform correctly the required movements. It would of course be expected that a limb apraxia, affecting motor selection of both sides of the body, would have a devastating effect on a communication system employing arm movements. A number of cases have now been reported of individuals who have manual signing disorders from damage to the central nervous system.

Most of the cases of so-called aphasia in deaf people are of very limited use in understanding the details of neural mechanisms in signing. They rarely have adequate information on the person's history of deafness or of the person's signing ability, either before or after the brain damage. Usually, the descriptions of the locus of central nervous system damage are also inadequate. Typically, however, it is possible to say whether the left or the right hemisphere was affected. Of the reported cases with sign aphasia, all of the right-handers have had a left-hemisphere lesion, while of the two left-handers, one had a left-hemisphere lesion and one a right-hemisphere lesion. This pattern of representation of communicative function for left- and right-handers bears a remarkable resemblance to the pattern in hearing persons. Thus, whatever the nature of the left hemisphere's predilection for communication, it appears to hold for both vocal and manual systems.

Another feature of disorders of signing is that

comprehension is affected in every case where it has been tested, though not always to the same degree. This finding is especially remarkable when one considers the high order of visual processing which is required to perceive signs, and which might therefore lead one to expect that the right hemisphere would be more involved in sign comprehension than in speech comprehension. While there is no easy way to equate a comprehension impairment in signing and in speaking disorders, there is no suggestion as yet that comprehension deficits after left-hemisphere damage are significantly less in deaf aphasics than in hearing aphasics.

A more convincing answer to the question of whether the right hemisphere contributes more to the comprehension of manual signs than to comprehension of speech might be provided by a careful study of the communicative function of right-handed deaf signers after right-hemisphere damage. Only one such case has been reported, with relatively mild damage. The apparent absence of any change in communicative ability, including sign comprehension, in this case, however, suggests that signing may be quite different from the other visuospatial functions known to depend on the right hemisphere. In general, it makes sense that the comprehension and production aspects of a communication system should overlap enormously, that is, signing and sign comprehension should both depend critically on the left hemisphere.

The precise nature of the manual signing disorders after left-hemisphere damage has only begun to be studied. Earlier reports suggested that the sign language disorder was limited to the movements employed in language and did not extend to other, nonlanguage movements. Thus the claim was made that sign language aphasics did not suffer from apraxia, the general motor programming defect described above, but rather from a language-specific defect. This claim was based largely on the fact that the particular patients reportedly had no difficulty in performing the familiar well-practiced movements by which apraxia is typically tested in the neurological examination. However, this kind of test is less sensitive to motor programming defects than are less familiar movements. When, in fact, sign language aphasics are asked to copy unfamiliar nonlanguage movements, they fail at these also, at least in the only two cases in which this has been attempted. This suggests that the sign language difficulty is a manifestation of a broader motor programming deficit, rather than a specifically linguistic problem. The same argument has been made for vocal aphasia, which is almost inevitably accompanied by difficulties in reproducing nonverbal, unvocalized movements of the oral (and often of the brachial) musculature.

One possible explanation is that both vocal and signing aphasias are manifestations of a motor programming defect of the oral and manual musculature, respectively, and that these "aphasias" are in fact not usually specifically linguistic.

The actual errors produced by signing aphasics have been reported in detail only rarely. In one case, the errors in hand posture, for example, were typically the production of another hand posture used in signing, usually a more common one. One interpretation of this phenomenon has been that, although the sign aphasic may have a manual apraxia, there is a linguistic defect as well, since the patient would otherwise not produce another sign hand posture. This point of view, however, fails to take into account the probability that a motor programming defect will result precisely in such selection of related but incorrect movements. Manual apraxia commonly results in either the repetition of a movement recently made (perseveration) or the selection of other movements made in the context, whether correct or not. In other words, the orderliness of the errors produced is not in itself an argument in favor of the idea that special linguistic processes are affected.

An interesting feature of the "aphasia" of deaf signers is that reading ability appears to be relatively spared. Admittedly, information on the prepathological reading level is not very precise, and it appears that many of the cases did not achieve a very advanced level of reading. Within these limitations, however, the relative sparing of reading function underlines the conclusion that reading is achieved by different mechanisms in deaf and hearing individuals.

SUMMARY

The left half of the brain in both hearing and deaf persons is known to control their communication systems. The fact that the deaf manual system is highly visual does not seem to have altered this basic fact of functional brain asymmetry. Studies which show a different brain representation in deaf people for reading processes are probably demonstrating a different strategy of reading, rather than a basic reorganization of brain mechanisms. The similarity in brain organization between deaf and hearing persons for communication may be based on the fact that both communication systems require precise control of complex self-generated movements. *See* PERCEPTION.

Bibliography

Battison, R.: *Lexical Borrowing in American Sign Language*, Linstock Press, Silver Spring, Maryland, 1978.

Chiarello, C., R. Knight, and M. Mandell: "Aphasia in a Prelingually Deaf Woman," *Brain*, 105:29–51, 1982.

Kimura, D.: "Neural Mechanisms in Manual Signing," *Sign Language Studies*, 33:291–312, 1981.

Poizner, H., and R. Battison: "Cerebral Asymmetry for Sign Language," in H. Lane and F. Grosjean (eds.), *Recent Perspectives on American Sign Language*, pp. 79–101, Lawrence Erlbaum Associates, Hillsdale, New Jersey, 1980.

Doreen Kimura

Minimal Language Skills

Minimal language skills (MLS) is a term used to describe the diminished or idiosyncratic communication repertoire of certain (deaf) individuals. The term was coined in the 1970s, replacing the near-synonymous "low verbal" which was deemed pejorative and imprecise. Minimal language skills is used to label individuals who probably do not exhibit a unified syndrome, but who happen to show similar lacks in their language behavior because of a variety of differing circumstances. There is currently no instrument or set of instruments that might be used reliably to identify linguistic accomplishment or communicative competence in the gestural realm, and thus, minimal language skills as a term is equally open to criticism as being imprecise or vague. It may, then, be most efficient to specify the term by defining what it is not.

CHARACTERIZATION

Minimal language skills does not mean simply the lack of spoken language skills. The confusion over the term "language" as used within deaf education and rehabilitation has contributed to some misunderstandings in identifying language skills and language deficiencies: "language" has often incorrectly been used interchangeably with the term "speech" or in place of the term "English." Minimal language skills is not intended to identify deaf persons who do not speak intelligibly, do not speechread reliably, or do not have literacy skills. These people sometimes have been characterized as having minimal English language skills, that is, they are "not literate" or "do not know English."

Minimal language skills does not describe the language skills of deaf persons who share a standard sign language with other deaf persons in their community. Thus, "monolingual" deaf signers who are competent in American Sign Language (ASL), for example, are not among the group classed as minimal language skills, despite the fact that their signing may be fraught with regionalisms, or lacking in borrowings from English (no fingerspelling, no technical terms). Sometimes a deaf person who has left the educational system at 18 or younger may appear limited in language, when in fact it is exposure to a social context larger than town, family, or workplace that is lacking. Such limitations may be termed provincial but do not qualify the

person as minimal language skills. Minimal language skills may describe a deaf person who uses a highly idiosyncratic signing system, such as home sign. *See* SIGNS: Home Signs.

Minimal language skills presumably differs from "low verbal" as a label in that it is more scientific. Low verbal has been criticized for confusing verbal in the sense of linguistic, relating to language, with verbal in the sense of spoken (that is, vocal) language. Low verbal apparently was previously used to denigrate the language skills of people who are linguistically competent but ignorant of English. For example, it was inaccurately used to label deaf persons who are competent ASL signers. Some signers have countered, half in jest, with an alternative rating scale for judging competence in signed (that is, visual) language, namely, high or low visual. So, a deaf monolingual signer might be assessed as high visual, low verbal. And an incompetent hearing signer might be evaluated as low visual!

A deaf individual who has been trained orally (for example, in spoken English) but has very limited competence in English may be characterized by minimum language skills—if the person has limited or no competence in a sign language. The signing culture would use low verbal, low visual to describe this person.

Minimal language skills has never been the term to characterize the amount of communication that an individual engages in. One person might be very gregarious, while another much more reserved, but both may show minimal language skills. Communicative competencies that may be linked with minimal language skills include appropriately initiating and sustaining conversations, responding to questions, jokes, requests, commands, promises, and so on, as well as being able to use language for these purposes.

Minimal language skills does not specify whether the individual has additional disabilities. Some persons who might be correctly called minimal language skills also show limited cognitive abilities and learning, memory, or reasoning skills.

FAMILIAR TYPES

Several composite case histories illustrate familiar types of minimal language skills individuals:

Case 1. Deaf person graduates from an oral school program, but has limited language skills (unintelligible speech, poor lipreading, able to write and read single words or simple sentences only). Finds employment in a service occupation where no literacy skills are required; communicates by teaching hearing coworkers own gestural system. At this point, might be classed minimal language skills. Later in contact with larger deaf community begins to learn more standard signs, ASL grammar, and eventually looks like a late learner of ASL.

Case 2. Deaf person never attends school. Participates in family business, as an adult. In family, communicates by gestural system which mother or siblings invented with deaf family member.

Case 3. Deaf person attends residential school for a few years, but then leaves. Lives with family member(s), with only limited contact with other deaf people or nonfamily persons.

Case 4. Deaf person misdiagnosed as mentally retarded, autistic, or mentally ill and subsequently institutionalized. Does not respond to treatment, but may become a contributing member of the community within the institution, possibly developing a consistent, albeit limited, gestural repertoire. If this deaf person is later reexamined and found to be deaf, the language abilities at the point of discovery are likely to be judged minimal language skills. If there follows a period of formal or informal rehabilitation within a deaf milieu, the gestural repertoire may approach ordinary monolingual ASL usage, although in other ways the communicative competence may still show habits of prolonged institutional confinement.

COMMUNICATION

Since each person who exhibits minimal language skills uses an individually determined symbol system, the hearing or deaf person who encounters a minimal language skills person cannot be trained reliably in advance in how to communicate with that person. However, interpreters, rehabilitation personnel, and others who need to communicate in this way should take several steps: (1) Become familiar with the usual context of the communication with family members or coworkers. Often highly communicative, minimal language skills people are accustomed to introducing others to their own private gestural systems. (2) Use props, environmental objects, or the like to aid communication; maps, clocks, calendars, pictures, and tactile stimuli may be useful. (3) Consider involving a deaf intermediary or a deaf person with certification in sign-to-voice interpreting to assist in the communication, particularly when the consequences of the communication may affect the health or welfare of the deaf person classed as minimal language skills. Such an individual can be helpful for two reasons. First, deaf persons, especially those who have attended residential schools, have much experience in interacting with other deaf individuals whose language skills are in all stages of development and whose signing behavior may range from totally nonstandard to totally conventional. Second, deaf persons who have training as interpreters are likely to understand role separation and know how

to take on only the responsibility of relaying messages between the minimal language skills person and the others who need to communicate with him or her.

Bibliography

Baker, Charlotte: "On the Terms 'Verbal' and 'Non-Verbal,'" in I. Ahlgren and B. Bergman (eds.), *Papers From the First International Symposium on Sign Language Research*, National Association of the Deaf, Stockholm, 1980.

Smith, Jess: "Interpreting for Deaf Persons with Severely Restricted Language Skills," in S. Quigley (ed.), *Interpreting for Deaf People*, U.S. Department of Health, Education and Welfare, Washington, D.C., 1965.

Nancy Frishberg

Reading and Writing

As a group, people who have lost their hearing in the first few years of life tend to have considerable difficulty with reading and writing. Two studies have reported that it is unusual for an 18-year-old deaf person to read at or above the fifth-grade level. This poor performance may be traced to several sources: (1) among deaf children of hearing parents, reduced language input in the early years; (2) inadequate methods of teaching written language to deaf children, in part due to the controversy concerning modality (sign or speech) and in part due to a failure to appreciate fully the complexities of the language acquisition process; and (3) reading instruction that narrowly focuses on one aspect of reading (sentence interpretation) to the detriment of other aspects (decoding, inferencing, paragraph and story structure).

A large part of what hearing people know about their native language comes from auditory input. Hearing children are observers of and participants in the many uses of spoken language. By the time that hearing children begin to learn to read, they have considerable mastery over their spoken language, and they can transfer some of their knowledge of the spoken language to reading print. The majority of children who have lost their hearing at an early age do not receive linguistic input to the extent that hearing children do. As a result, they do not come to the reading task with the same level of skill in sentence formation, vocabulary, and use of English as hearing children. An exception to this generalization would be the small group (approximately 10%) of deaf children whose parents are also deaf and who use sign language as a primary means of communication. These children are believed to be similar to hearing children who must learn to read in a second language, and their performance on reading and writing tasks tends to be better than deaf children who have hearing parents and who did not use signing from an early age.

The majority of deaf children, then, are faced with the task of learning a first language and learning to read at the same time.

The printed mode of English plays a central role in the general educational process. Because speech frequently cannot be used as the primary means of communication, many teachers of young deaf children attempt to use reading as a way of teaching English. Such an approach differs from that used with hearing children, who normally have fluent use of English before formal reading instruction is begun. The process by which hearing children learn to read is in many respects still a mystery. Many levels of processing are involved: decoding or word recognition ("cracking the code"); acquiring, storing, and retrieving word meanings; extracting sentence meaning from words and syntactic structures; realizing what is not stated but implied (inferencing); and using the structure of the text to organize, store, and recall information. The relative importance of each component, how and when each is acquired by hearing and deaf children, and which ones are most problematic for deaf children are matters of theoretical debate.

CODING SKILLS

Part of the process of teaching hearing children to read includes developing skills in letter and word recognition. Many approaches to teaching reading involve teaching the children to associate written letters (graphemes) with sounds, so that they may sound out the word, hear it, and recognize it. Other methods involve teaching the children to recognize an entire word on sight, rather than letter by letter. (These approaches work only if the child already knows the vocabulary word.) Once recognized, the children then pronounce the word. Either way, a major component of teaching hearing children to read is the development of an association between print and sound. Fluent readers frequently report an "inner voice" when they read silently. As the noise in the background increases, hearing readers may begin to mouth the words or even to read out loud to block out the interfering noise and increase concentration. Thus, the association of speech with print is an integral part of the reading process.

The translation from print to speech, whether silently or out loud, is referred to as phonological or sound recoding. Sound recoding also seems to be involved in memory. When attempting to remember telephone numbers, shopping lists, instructions, or other complex information, hearing people find that their memory is improved if they code the information in spoken form and rehearse it, either silently or out loud.

Despite the fact that the deaf child may not have ready access to an already developed spoken language, techniques for teaching deaf students to read routinely parallel those for hearing children. Students are taught letter-sound associations and sight word recognition, using whatever residual hearing and speech skills the child may have. Beginning deaf readers are expected to be able to read out loud, as a means of developing not only reading skills but also speech skills. For the most part, this tends to be the case regardless of whether the educational program is oral-only or uses simultaneous communication (speech with signs). In simultaneous (total) communication settings, additional practice may involve signing the sentences "out loud," but the primary emphasis is on some form of sound recoding. Because sound recoding is so prevalent in hearing readers, a question arises as to whether this skill (sometimes referred to as inner speech) is necessary for reading or merely an accompaniment to it. Studies of deaf readers show that some deaf people are able to use some type of sound recoding for reading and memory. However, several other codes are also used, including signs, fingerspelling, and an internal visual representation of the letters of the words (referred to as graphemic coding).

Studies also show that deaf individuals do not use a single code, but may use two or more codes. It is not known if this use of multiple codes is less efficient than use of a single code. Also, the relationship between the types of recoding used and reading proficiency is not clear. Some research does indicate that deaf readers who use some form of sound recoding have reading achievement scores as much as 2½ years higher than those deaf students who do not use sound recoding. There is also a strong relationship between the extent to which a deaf reader uses sound recoding (if more than one type of recoding is used) and the reading achievement score. Whether this is evidence that a single code is more effective than multiple codes or that sound recoding is more effective than other types of coding remains to be investigated. Other factors, such as the age at onset and degree of hearing loss, may also affect the type of recoding used, as well as the reading level attained. The interpretation of these findings must also take into account the use of sound recoding procedures in the teaching of reading to deaf children. That is, although deaf people may be able to develop highly efficient procedures for recoding into signs, fingerspelling, or graphemic representation, the fact that they are not taught to use these codes when learning to read may influence the findings in reading studies, as compared to memory studies. Also, the presence of sound recoding in memory tasks does not ensure that sound recoding is used during the reading process or that its use is beneficial to the reader.

Vocabulary

The advantage of speech coding for hearing children who are learning to read lies in the possibility that a word may be identified if the child can sound it out and recognize it as a word that has been heard before. It is estimated that the young hearing child has a vocabulary of 3000 to 5000 words when entering kindergarten.

Attempts to estimate the vocabulary size of deaf children on entering school are confounded by several factors. A deaf child who has deaf parents may be able to carry on a fluent conversation in American Sign Language (ASL) when entering school for the first time, but may not be able to speak or read any English words. If the school reading program attempts to build on the child's oral language, the child's vocabulary size would be essentially zero. If the school's reading program attempts to relate the printed English words to signs, the child's vocabulary size would be quite large. If only the words that a child can actually read are counted, a different estimate would be obtained. As a result, most researchers are reluctant to report a figure for vocabulary size for deaf children. Using knowledge of printed English words as the criterion, one study reported that 14-year-old deaf students fall considerably below their 10-year-old hearing counterparts, while another study reported that 18-year-old deaf students have an average vocabulary level of fourth grade. A comparison of deaf students' writing samples with hearing students' revealed that deaf students use fewer different words and hence have a great redundancy in word usage. None of these studies has compared the English vocabulary level of deaf students with the vocabulary level of hearing students who are learning a second language.

Several studies have attempted to determine which words deaf students usually know at particular age levels so that guidelines for usage can be established. One of these studies used the deaf students' abilities to provide synonyms or to understand dictionary definitions. For example, to demonstrate understanding of the word "day," the student had to choose "time between sunrise and sunset" from several response choices. This task probably underestimates the student's word knowledge, because a student who knows the word "day" may not necessarily know "sunrise" or "sunset," or understand the time relationship involved.

Another problem with attempting to determine vocabulary for deaf students is the presence of multiple meanings for individual words. Frequently, a word with multiple meanings will be known to a student in only one or two of its senses. A word such as "run" may be known to deaf students in the sense of an exercise activity, but not in the sense of to run an office, or to run for office, or a run on a popular toy or food, or a run in a stocking. Some of these senses are more difficult than others. One vocabulary book ranks words by grade level, giving each meaning a separate listing if necessary. The word "attend" is listed several times: at grade level 4 for the meaning "to be there," at grade level 6 for the meaning "to accompany," at grade level 8 for the meaning "to pay attention," and at grade level 10 for the meaning "to take care of." The degree to which deaf readers are able to make use of the context to determine the correct meaning of a word with multiple meanings is a matter for future research.

It has been estimated that as much as two-thirds of written and spoken English involves some type of figurative language. One major type of figurative language is the idiom, an expression of one or more words used in a nonliteral sense. The meanings of idioms cannot be determined from the knowledge of the individual words or from the sentence structure in which they occur. In this way, idioms contrast with metaphors, the meanings of which can usually be figured out from context and general cultural knowledge. The meanings of idioms must be learned in much the same way that one learns other vocabulary. Some researchers even consider idioms to be simply "big words," that is, an idiomatic expression of several words may be treated as though it were one word. Thus, the meanings of such expressions as "to spill the beans" or "to let the cat out of the bag" are thought to be learned in the same way as their single-word synonyms "snitch," "tattle," and "squeal."

Like other tests of vocabulary items, deaf students' performance on tests of idiom knowledge is affected by the types of tasks used. One study found that deaf students' comprehension of idioms was significantly poorer than their hearing counterparts' from third grade on. Another study found that if deaf students are given both the literal meaning and the figurative meaning for an idiomatic expression in a multiple-choice task, they prefer to choose the literal meanings. However, if their knowledge of the literal meanings is tested separately from their knowledge of the figurative meanings, they will choose the correct figurative meaning more frequently. Thus, the assessment of figurative knowledge is influenced by the choices available at one time.

Another study of 20 frequently used idioms reported a surprisingly high level of idiom knowledge for deaf students in reading levels 1 through 10. This study calls into question the general attitude of educators of deaf students that figurative language cannot or should not be extensively taught until deaf students have a better command of literal English. Studies of other types of figurative language show that deaf students do have some competence with similes and metaphors, but in all cases the deaf students' performance is considerably poorer than that of young hearing children.

IMPORTANCE OF SYNTAX

Most deaf individuals never gain complete control of English syntax (sentence structure). Extensive studies have investigated the levels of performance of deaf people on specific sentence types, looking at both comprehension and the ability to detect and correct syntactic errors. Control of these English structures in the deaf population seems to develop much later than in the hearing population. Indeed, some processes, like relative clause formation and embedding (sentence complementation), are not mastered by most deaf students by age 18. Given the differences in quality and quantity of input, this is not surprising.

This English language deficit would seem to have profound implications for deaf children learning to read. Hearing children learning to read already have oral control over most of the structures in their language. Once they have learned to decode printed words, they can easily understand most sentences in early reading materials. Deaf children, however, may not be able to understand a sentence even if they can read all of the words because they may not be able to use the syntactic information present in a sentence. For example, most seven- or eight-year-old hearing children would have no trouble deciding who was the agent in the sentence "The boy was hit by the girl," because they can use both the lexical (word meaning) and syntactic (word order) information. Most deaf children of the same age have not mastered the passive voice structure. They might interpret this sentence using active (subject-verb-object) word order, and conclude that the boy, being the first noun, was the agent, as in "The boy hit the girl."

Nonactive sentences appear very early in basal readers, the reading materials most used by teachers of deaf children. As a result, most programs for deaf children do two things: teach these structures directly, so that students will be able to use this information when reading and writing; and modify reading materials to simplify syntax. Methods of teaching these structures to deaf students largely concentrate on individual sentences. Often, the sentence structure is introduced, sometimes with a pattern or formula for making the structure. The students then practice producing these sentences, again in isolation (as opposed to using them in connected prose). It is assumed that this skill will then transfer to reading. Research, however, has thus far failed to support this assumption.

Related to this attempt to teach syntactic structures directly is the concern expressed by many teachers that reading materials are too syntactically complex for most deaf students. This has led to the development of "linguistically controlled" reading series. In these readers, sentence structure is controlled, and new and more difficult structures are introduced gradually, usually accompanied by sentence-level practice. Other materials, especially content-area texts, are often adapted by individual teachers, who try to change complex or difficult structures into simpler ones. In this way, they hope to teach social studies or science or health information without having the students become hopelessly entangled in difficult syntax.

Although these techniques can contribute to the readers' ability to extract meaning from text, they are based on a somewhat simplistic view of the reading process, namely that "meaning" is a combination of syntactic and lexical information within the sentence. Increasingly, however, psycholinguists and other researchers have shown that meaning depends not only on the information present in a sentence but on the reader's cognitive structures (past experiences, expectations, knowledge of text structure, and so on). In other words, the reader takes the information in the printed text and interprets it in light of what he or she knows or expects about that sentence. Sentences that a reader may not be able to interpret correctly in isolation may be understood if the reader uses information from context or prior knowledge.

It seems important, then, not only to take steps to simplify syntax for deaf students but to prepare them to interpret these sentences correctly. This may involve discussing the probable context of a selection based on title, pictures, subheadings, and so on; familiarizing students with the topic of the selection by relating it in some way to their personal experiences; or discussing unfamiliar terms or idioms in advance. It is also important, when altering text, to be sure that it remains coherent and well structured, as these factors also assist the reader in comprehension.

THE MOVE AWAY FROM SYNTAX

Research has reflected an increasing awareness that there is more to teaching deaf students to read than syntax and word recognition. Many models of reading stress that it is a process that involves not only text-based or "bottom-up" processing (for example, decoding words and deciphering syntax) but reader-based or "top-down" processing as well. This top-down processing refers to the readers' use of prior knowledge (of the topic, the story, the characters, similar situations, and such) to make and test hypotheses about the text.

A simplified view of one such model can be illustrated as follows: The reader decodes the title of the passage and perhaps looks at the accompanying illustrations. Using what is known about the meaning of the words in the title, the topic, the characters involved, and other prior knowledge, the reader makes predictions about the content of the text. While reading, the individual "samples" the text in order to test the hypotheses made. These hypotheses are used to interpret new information (words decoded, syntax encountered).

An example of an ambiguous sentence illustrates this point. In isolation, the sentence "The chickens were too hot to eat" could have two equally probable interpretations. Nothing in the sentence indicates whether the chickens were alive or about to be eaten. If the sentence appeared in a story entitled "A Hot Day on the Farm," the reader would tend to interpret the sentence in light of what is known about the effect of high temperature on farm animals. If the next sentence in the passage was "They just lay in the shade and refused to move," this hypothesis would be confirmed and the reader would go on. If, however, the next sentence was "We sat at the diningroom table and sipped our lemonade, waiting for them to cool," the reader would revise the hypothesis and reinterpret the first sentence in light of this new information.

Comprehension theory suggests that readers attempt to construct a coherent mental representation of a passage based on both textual information and the reader's prior knowledge. The syntactic structure of a sentence is but one clue to its correct interpretation. Understanding the syntax may not always be entirely necessary or, as in the example above, sufficient for correct interpretation in connected text.

Research has indicated that the basic mechanics of reading are the same for both hearing and deaf readers. Both seem to form working hypotheses about the meaning of a story or other connected text, to use these hypotheses to interpret subsequent sentences, and to modify them in light of contradictory information. If sentences with difficult syntactic structures are encountered in the midst of an otherwise comprehensible passage, the deaf individual is more likely to apply a correct interpretation than if these sentences were read in isolation, when the only source of information available is word meaning and sentence structure.

One possible extension of this theory concerns teaching both reading and writing. Written English is probably the clearest source of information about the structure and use of English available to the deaf person. It does not depend on a defective sensory channel for communication (as does speech), and all its components are visible (unlike speech-reading). Unlike Signed English, written English is less variable from school to school or from signer to signer. If teachers can develop in deaf students the nonsyntactic skills of reading discussed earlier, difficult sentences can be introduced in context without necessarily disrupting comprehension. This provides the deaf student with experience not only in comprehending these sentences but in their appropriate use as well. *See* Manually coded English: Signed English.

With extensive exposure to these structures in context, deaf students may begin using them in their written language. At this point the student may be more receptive to guidance in correct formation and usage.

Metacognition and Strategic Reading

Metacognition, in reading, deals with the knowledge and the control that individuals have over their own reading and studying. Specifically, it refers to the readers' knowledge of text variables (difficulty, structure, familiarity, and such), task variables (affecting storage and recall of information), strategies to enhance storage and recall, learner characteristics (ability, motivation, perceived purpose, and such), and how these variables interact to produce learning. Metacognition also involves the reader's control of self-regulation of these four variables and their interaction.

Few studies have investigated the metacognitive abilities of deaf readers. However, research on other readers, both skilled and less skilled, indicates that training in metacognitive skills may be an important means of improving reading abilities.

Metacognitive skills in reading seem to develop with proficiency in learning. Younger and poorer readers have a less adequate understanding of the four variables and their effect on reading, and therefore read and study less efficiently. Deaf readers likely fall into this category. Training studies on hearing students who have comprehension difficulties have thus far shown that instruction and practice in these skills can have positive, durable effects on the reader's ability to gain and remember information from text. Although further research is needed, this approach appears to hold promise for teaching deaf individuals to read. However, it is important to view this line of research not as a panacea, but as one more tool in teaching reading to deaf students.

Writing

The skilled writer, like the skilled reader, must be able to perform several tasks: (a) determine the structure of the text to be produced—narrative, expository, directive, (b) construct paragraphs that convey the major points, (c) construct and sequence grammatical sentences, (d) choose the appropriate vocabulary words, (e) spell the words correctly, and (f) produce legible handwriting. All of this must be done while keeping in mind what the intended readers already know and need to know in order to understand the passage.

Very little is known about the development of writing skills in deaf individuals. The available research is restricted to constructing grammatical sentences, vocabulary choice, and spelling. In many respects, deaf people's problems with writing are parallel to their problems with reading, and reflect the same general deficiency in English. Deaf writers frequently display primary concern with the structure of individual sentences. Some deaf adults even keep card files of sentences that they have had hearing people check for grammaticality.

The paragraphs that deaf people write appear stilted and do not flow easily from sentence to sentence or from topic to topic. For example, the sentence "She cannot find her shoes" is completely grammatical, but pragmatically inappropriate as the first sentence of a story (except for the most sophisticated writer who might choose to keep the reader in suspense for a while). Skilled writers tie their sentences together with words like "then," "so," "after a while," "while." These words help place the thoughts or events in reference to some other time frame, thought, event, or activity. Deaf writers tend to omit such words and tend to place events in the order in which they happen. As a result, the story structures of deaf writers lack complexity in terms of temporal sequence, highlighting main information against background information, topic flow, and topic shift. Vocabulary choice is also restricted to a smaller number of different words than those used by comparable hearing writers.

There is an obvious lack of creativity in deaf students' writing that may presumably be traced to the manner in which they are taught and the types of writing tasks they are expected to perform. Many researchers now feel that the traditional practice of using writing samples to assess deaf students' competence in English inaccurately reflects their actual capabilities. Their reading comprehension and general knowledge of English may be far greater than they are able to display in their writing samples.

Extensive investigations into more appropriate methods for teaching deaf students to write, and into the particular problems faced by deaf writers, are needed. Special efforts must be made to help deaf writers express the thoughts and creativity that they frequently express in signs or orally. One promising area is the use of telecommunication devices (TDDs) that deaf people use to make phone calls. In order to carry on a conversation with the party at the other end, one must type out the message. This provides deaf people with a motivation to master not only sentence structure but also spelling, vocabulary choice, and conversational etiquette, in order to make a better impression on the phone. Some researchers have been analyzing the

improvement in deaf students' writing ability after they have been given access to TDDs at school. Other researchers have been taking advantage of the recent increased interest in personal computers. They have written programs intended to help deaf students learn to write better. Some of these programs provide direct instruction in writing. For example, they correct spelling and syntax in sentences that students have typed into the computer. More sophisticated programs that include contexts larger than a sentence, such as a paragraph or an entire story, will help extend these efforts into areas that will greatly benefit deaf writers.

Bibliography
Shulman, J., and N. Decker (eds.): *Readable English for Hearing-Impaired Students*, Caption Center, WGBH-TV, Boston.

Volta Review, special issue on reading and the hearing-impaired, September 1982.

Ronnie Wilbur

LANGUAGE, SPEECH AND HEARING SERVICES IN SCHOOLS

Language, Speech and Hearing Services in Schools (LSHSS) is one of three scholarly journals published by the American Speech-Language-Hearing Association (ASHA). All ASHA journals are distributed free to members of the association and are available on a subscription basis to others. The editor of the journal is appointed by the executive board of the association with the advice of the publications board and serves, unpaid, for a term of four years. Published quarterly, the journal has a circulation of 45,000.

The journal appeared in 1970 in response to requests for a publication that was relevant to the needs of speech-language clinicians working in schools. The inclusion of "language" in the title was a recognition that the treatment of language disorders is an important part of the speech pathology profession. The journal is also of interest to individuals who are working with school-aged handicapped children and to speech-language clinicians working with children in nonschool settings.

The journal publishes a wide range of manuscripts dealing with normal speech, language, and hearing in children and with the speech, language, and hearing problems found in children. Papers include studies of the assessment and management of disorders of speech, hearing, and language, and descriptions of program organization, management, and supervision, as well as scholarly discussion of philosophical issues related to school programming. All manuscripts and letters submitted to the journal are reviewed by an associate editor and two or more editorial consultants. Manuscripts are judged on their scholarly contribution and on their applicability to children and to problems encountered in a school setting. Manuscripts must not have been previously published, and contributors are expected to follow the style specifications of the *Publication Manual of the American Psychological Association*.

Patricia A. Broen

LARYNGOSCOPE

The *Laryngoscope* is the oldest monthly medical journal devoted to speech and hearing still being published in the United States. It began publication in August 1896 and has continued without interruption. Its founders and first editors were Frank M. Rumbold and Max A. Goldstein, two otolaryngologists who lived in St. Louis, Missouri. The city remains the publishing home of the *Laryngoscope*, and the Washington University School of Medicine, with which Goldstein was affiliated, also continues its editorial relationship to the journal. *See* GOLDSTEIN, MAX AARON.

EDITORIAL POLICY

The first issue of the *Laryngoscope* set forth the editorial policy of being a monthly journal devoted to the diseases of the nose, throat, and ear that endeavors to occupy a middle ground between the general and strictly special journals, and to be of interest to general practitioners and specialists who treat diseases of the nose, throat, and ear. While the trend toward specialization has overwhelmed medicine since the turn of the century, the *Laryngoscope's* interest in the general practitioner is not misplaced, as ear, nose, and throat problems are among the most frequent encountered in the daily practice of medicine.

The *Laryngoscope* printed in its second issue an article by H. A. Alderton, a physician in Brooklyn, New York, entitled "The Influence of Deafness upon the Development of the Child." The article, written eight decades before the passage of Public Law 94-142 (Education of All Handicapped Children Act), has a remarkably modern conclusion: "The child with impaired faculties is as much entitled to public instruction as the healthy child; the fact that unusual methods and special teachers are required should be no rightful bar to its (sic) claim. Let these things come to pass, and the reproach of preventable deafness would pass from us with all its attendant expense to the body politic." *See* EDUCATION OF THE HANDICAPPED ACT.

The connection between the *Laryngoscope* and deafness becomes even clearer when it is realized that Max Goldstein later founded one of the most famous schools for deaf children in the United States,

the Central Institute for the Deaf, in St. Louis. Goldstein presented to the medical profession the needs of deaf people; he developed innovative procedures for auditory training, emphasizing the importance for developing residual hearing. With his driving energy and keen foresightedness, Goldstein assumed full editorship of the *Laryngoscope* in 1899. In 1900 he listed himself on the masthead as editor and proprietor, and in 1903 he dropped the proprietor from his designation. Shortly thereafter, in 1905, the Laryngoscope Company emerged as publisher. It remained in that capacity until 1982, when the publication became the official journal of the American Laryngological, Rhinological, and Otological Society, Inc., often referred to as the Triological Association. With this change, the editorial policy shifted somewhat from its original position. The *Laryngoscope* describes itself now as "a medical journal for clinical and research contributions in otolaryngology, head and neck medicine and surgery, facial plastic and reconstructive surgery, broncho-esophagology, communicative disorders, and maxillofacial surgery." The emphasis appears to have shifted more toward specialization than was evident in the initial attempt to find a middle ground between generalist and specialist. *See* CENTRAL INSTITUTE FOR THE DEAF.

The *Laryngoscope* has been editorially concerned with organizational and professional relations within the fields it addresses. In 1904 Goldstein commented on the question of separation and independent consideration of the three specialties, otology, rhinology, and laryngology. Eight decades later, the American Medical Association's members voted to split otology from rhinology and laryngology and to restructure its divisions and reorganize their journals.

EDITORS

The first editorial board for the *Laryngoscope* had four associate editors from the United States and six foreign associate editors, one each from Austria, Canada, England, Germany, Japan, and Scotland. The 6:4 ratio represented the interest in research and practice outside the United States. Such attention to other countries has slowly disappeared from the *Laryngoscope's* masthead as the world centers of research in medicine have shifted to the United States. This is not to say that the *Laryngoscope* is a parochial journal with no concerns for activities in the field outside of the United States, but rather to point out the changes that have taken place in medical and scientific research since the journal was founded just before the twentieth century.

Among the recent editors, almost all have been associated with the Washington University School of Medicine. Joseph H. Ogura was succeeded in 1984 by Stanley E. Thawley, who was then listed as acting interim editor. In 1985 Thawley was joined by coeditor Gershon J. Spector. All of the editors, beginning with Rumbold and Goldstein, have been otolaryngologists. The editorial boards have tended in recent years to be largely made up of medical teachers and practitioners from the United States.

MONOGRAPH SUPPLEMENTS

From time to time, the *Laryngoscope* has published monograph supplements to print material too copious for its regular journal. It also publishes proceedings of the Triological Association meetings and papers by its members. A section called "How I Do It" contains articles about procedures for resolving various medical problems. The *Laryngoscope* publishes the "Directory of Otolaryngologic Societies," lists new books, prints letters to the editor, but largely focuses on articles dealing with the medical aspects of ear, nose, and throat problems. While it is committed to publishing Triological Association papers and proceedings, the *Laryngoscope* does accept articles submitted from outside that organization. Subscriptions are also open to all.

It remains unresolved as to why Rumbold and Goldstein chose to name the journal the *Laryngoscope*. A laryngoscope is an apparatus used by laryngologists to visualize the larynx. A parallel instrument used by otologists is the otoscope. In view of the expressed interests of the editors, why did they elect the laryngoscope as their journalistic symbol rather than the otoscope? Selecting the one instrument in disregard of the other (and in disregard of other medical tools, such as the pharyngoscope used by otolargyngologists) suggests an initial bias. Whatever the reason for the choice, the name has succeeded for nearly a century in attracting precisely the wide readership the editors originally sought.

Enid G. Wolf

LAWYERS, DEAF

Law is a demanding and competitive profession requiring a high degree of ability in written and spoken language. Generally, lawyers spend much of their time communicating: reading and writing legal documents, talking to clients on the telephone, talking to witnesses before a court reporter, taking part in conferences and meetings, and engaging in court proceedings. Thus, of all the professions a deaf person might enter, law would seem to be one of the most difficult, with obvious conflict between the requirements of the work and the nature of the disability.

However, some deaf persons have entered law school, obtained law degrees, passed bar examinations, and become capable lawyers. Indeed, some have been outstanding in the legal field and have gained considerable reputations.

A deaf person, to succeed in law, must have certain abilities: (1) a good mind—legal problems can be complex; (2) total command of both spoken and written English, although it is not necessary to be able to speak or hear; (3) determination, diligence, and patience—law school and legal work are difficult, and people who are impatient, easily bored, or easily distracted are not likely to do well in the legal field.

Many deaf individuals who have become successful lawyers were postlingually deafened, and thus acquired a command of spoken and written language aurally; others were deaf from birth. Among the latter was an English attorney, John William Lowe, who was probably the first deaf person to become a lawyer. Born profoundly deaf in 1804, he was unable to speak clearly and was educated in a special school for deaf children. From childhood he showed tremendous intellectual prowess. Having decided to follow the same profession as his father, he studied law under some of the leading attorneys in London and was admitted to the bar in 1829. He then maintained a successful practice in real estate law for 42 years.

Lowe was interested in foreign laws and reportedly learned to read Greek, Latin, French, German, Italian, Spanish, Portuguese, Dutch, Danish, and Hebrew. He had a unique method of learning foreign languages. He would simply buy a Bible written in the language that he wanted to learn and then compare the English Bible with the foreign-language Bible. With no other help of any kind, he thus taught himself to read the foreign language. He believed that anyone could learn a foreign language by this method.

Lowe married and had three children, all of whom had normal hearing. He communicated with his children by speaking (they could understand his defective speech), and they communicated with him in the English manual alphabet. He communicated with strangers by writing notes. He died in 1876 at the age of 72.

Another nineteenth-century lawyer who was born deaf was Theodore Grady, an American. Grady attended the California School for the Deaf in Berkeley, and later became the first deaf person to receive a degree from the University of California. He was admitted to the California Bar in 1897. At that time, bar examinations were always given orally, but he received special permission to take a written examination.

Grady appeared as cocounsel in a California case at least once, in a matter involving deaf persons. However, he specialized in legal research, taught at the California School for the Deaf, worked as a tax collector, and edited the *Oakland Daily Times*.

Perhaps more typical of deaf individuals who have become lawyers was Joseph G. Parkinson, born in 1849. Parkinson became deaf due to scarlet fever when he was nine years old. He was admitted to the American School for the Deaf at Hartford, Connecticut, and graduated from Gallaudet College in 1869. *See* GALLAUDET COLLEGE.

Parkinson entered the United States Patent Office and progressed to the position of chief examiner of patents. In 1883 he was admitted to the bar of the U.S. Supreme Court. He then opened an office for the practice of patent law with his brother (who had normal hearing and apparently was also an attorney). During the following years he was frequently mentioned as being one of the leading patent attorneys in the nation. His speech was said to be fairly intelligible to those who knew him. He died prior to 1914.

Some American Examples

Many more deaf individuals have become lawyers in the twentieth century. Since a definitive listing is impossible, below are brief sketches of a sample of deaf American lawyers.

HAROLD DIAMOND

Harold Diamond was born in 1925. He lost most of his hearing at the age of 14, due to an automobile accident. He attended high school in Philadelphia and completed undergraduate work in three years at the University of Pennsylvania, where he received his bachelor's degree with a major in economics. At the University of Pennsylvania Law School he completed the three-year program in two years and received his law degree in 1947. He used no interpreters in school and was admitted to the Pennsylvania Bar in 1948.

Diamond entered the general practice of law in Philadelphia, with most of his work being in the field of criminal law, divorce, probate, and appellate cases. He has done a great deal of courtroom work without the use of an interpreter. An excellent lipreader with some residual hearing, he learned sign language at the age of 49.

Diamond was admitted to membership in the fraternal society of Masons, though it had a strict rule against the admission of any handicapped person. A noted and outstanding public speaker and a member of numerous civic groups and organizations of every kind, Diamond received many awards for his civic work, some of which was on behalf of handicapped people.

LOWELL MYERS

Lowell Myers was born in 1930; both parents were totally deaf. He became deaf gradually, starting at about 12 years of age and becoming totally deaf by

18. However, he developed good lipreading ability and learned sign language at about age 15.

Myers attended public schools that had no special facilities for deaf students. In 1951 he received a bachelor's degree with a major in accounting and later a master's degree in business administration from the University of Chicago. He received a Juris Doctor degree from the John Marshall Law School in 1956 and was admitted to the Illinois Bar that same year. He attended law school at night while working full time as a tax auditor. He did not use an interpreter in college or in law school but made arrangements with other students to copy their classroom notes.

In 1956 Myers became a tax attorney for a large corporation and also started a part-time practice as a general attorney. During the following 30 years he handled thousands of cases of all kinds, including numerous appeals, using an oral interpreter in the courtroom.

In 1964 he wrote *The Law and the Deaf*, the first book on law as it applies to deaf people. It was published by the federal government and distributed to judges and law libraries throughout the nation. In 1968 he wrote a shorter book for children, *The Law and the Deaf: Student Edition*, which was used in schools for deaf children throughout the nation. Myers also has written numerous articles and pamphlets.

In 1965 he wrote the first statute in the nation to provide for the payment of interpreters by a state (Illinois) when they are needed by deaf persons in civil (noncriminal) cases. The statute was attacked by Illinois state officials who claimed that the state could not be forced to pay for an interpreter in a private civil case. Myers took the case to the Illinois Supreme Court, which upheld the validity of the statute in the case of *Myers v. County of Cook*. Thereafter, the Illinois statute was copied and enacted in many other states of the nation.

In another case, Myers sued the Chicago Police Department arguing that deaf people were being abused by the police. The case was settled in federal court, and the police department initiated a training program to instruct police in the proper way of handling criminal cases involving deaf persons; the program was later copied by police departments in other cities.

Myers represented Donald Lang in the murder case involving a deaf person who was totally unable to communicate. The case reached the Illinois Supreme Court and later was publicized in the book *Dummy* and the subsequent motion picture.

MICHAEL A. CHATOFF

Michael A. Chatoff was born in New York in 1946. As a child he had normal hearing and attended

Top row, left to right: **Michael A. Chatoff, William H. Matarazzi, Robert J. Mather, Lowell Myers.** Bottom row: **Michael A. Schwartz, Robert M. Silber, Bonnie P. Tucker, Charles H. Winkler.**

ordinary public schools. In 1967 he received a bachelor of arts degree from Queens College, New York, and then entered Brooklyn Law School. During his first year in law school he developed a medical condition that soon left him completely deaf. Nevertheless, he completed law school without special help, received a Juris Doctor degree in 1971, and was admitted to the New York Bar later that year.

Chatoff then attended New York University School of Law and earned the master of laws degree in 1978; he worked full time and attended classes at night. In 1972 he accepted a position with a large legal publishing company, where he became a senior legal editor. He has also written numerous articles on various aspects of law.

Chatoff has handled important legal cases that affect deaf persons. For example, the case of *Chatoff v. Public Service Commission* involved the issue of the proper telephone rates to be charged to deaf persons who use special telephone equipment. Chatoff won the case and obtained a rate reduction for all deaf persons in New York State who use such equipment. This led to similar rate reductions in

other states. Chatoff also did important work in connection with the drafting and enactment of the Federal Court Interpreters Act.

Chatoff was the first deaf lawyer to argue a case before the United State Supreme Court. In *Board of Education v. Rowley* he used special equipment in court so that he could read and answer the judges' questions.

JOHN D. RANDOLPH

John D. Randolph was born in 1923. He completely lost his hearing following a series of illnesses between the ages of 3 and 12. His father and grandmother were also deaf. He attended the Texas School for the Deaf and then Gallaudet College, where he received a bachelor of science degree in chemistry in 1945. He then attended the University of Texas and received a master of arts degree in 1948, with a major in organic chemistry. He attended Georgetown University Law School at night from 1956 to 1960 and received a Juris Doctor degree. He was admitted to the Maryland Bar in 1972.

Randolph joined the United States Patent Office in 1957 and received numerous awards for outstanding performance as a patent examiner, handling difficult problems in the field of organic chemistry. He retired in 1981.

Randolph developed good speech and became adept at lipreading and sign language. In 1982 he received the Amos Kendall Award for excellence in a professional field from the Gallaudet College Alumni Association.

ROBERT J. MATHER

Unlike many deaf lawyers, Robert J. Mather was born profoundly deaf in 1950. He received his undergraduate degree from the National Technical Institute for the Deaf in 1974 and a Juris Doctor degree from DePaul University in 1977. He was admitted to the Illinois Bar in 1977 and became a member of the bar in Maryland and the District of Columbia as well.

He accepted a position as an attorney at the National Center for Law and the Deaf. Later he was deputy general counsel at the U.S. Architectural and Transportation Barriers Compliance Board. In 1982 he took a position with the U.S. Department of Justice, doing noncourtroom work on civil rights cases and administrative law.

WILLIAM H. MATARAZZI

William H. Matarazzi was born in 1953 and became severely hard-of-hearing at the age of 2½. He attended ordinary public schools where he relied on lipreading and a hearing aid. In 1975 he received a bachelor of business arts degree from the University of Notre Dame, and in 1978 he received a Juris Doctor degree from Washburn University of Topeka School of Law. He was admitted to the Kansas Bar in 1978. He learned sign language at the age of 30.

Matarazzi was employed by the Office of the Appellate Reporter for the Kansas Courts, as a staff attorney doing legal research and editorial work. He was later named president of the board of directors of Topeka Resource Center for the Handicapped.

CHARLES H. WINKLER

Charles H. Winkler was born in 1954. He became profoundly deaf due to an illness at about three years of age and thereafter used hearing aids. He attended schools which had no special facilities for deaf children and became an adept lipreader; he did not learn sign language.

Winkler received a bachelor of business administration degree from Emory University in 1976. In 1979 he received a Juris Doctor degree from Northwestern University School of Law. He was the managing editor of the *Northwestern University Journal of International Law and Business*. He was admitted to the Illinois Bar in 1979. Upon leaving law school he accepted a position with the Chicago law firm of Kanter & Eisenberg, which specializes in tax law. Winkler has also written articles on taxation.

BONNIE P. TUCKER

Bonnie P. Tucker was born in 1939; she was found to be totally deaf at age 2½. She became an excellent lipreader, never used a hearing aid, and did not learn sign language.

She attended public schools without special facilities for deaf students and went on to receive a bachelor of science degree with a major in journalism from Syracuse University in 1961. In 1980 she received a Juris Doctor degree from the University of Colorado. She graduated first in her class, was editor in chief of the school's *Law Review*, and was also a member of Order of the Coif, the honorary legal scholastic organization. Tucker did not attend classes in law school but simply read the assigned materials and took the examinations. She was admitted to the Colorado Bar in 1980, and can also practice in Arizona and California.

Upon leaving law school, Tucker worked for one year as a law clerk for the U.S. Court of Appeals. In 1981 she was employed by the law firm of Brown & Bain in Phoenix, Arizona, to handle litigation work involving corporations, antitrust actions, securities law, and so on. She has handled courtroom work, using an oral interpreter, in the Arizona state courts and federal courts and has written many legal articles.

SHEILA CONLON MENTKOWSKI

Sheila Conlon Mentkowski was born in 1951 and became profoundly deaf at an early age. She uses a hearing aid, lipreads, and learned sign language at age 21.

She received a bachelor of arts degree with a major in English literature from the College of Our Lady of the Elms in Massachusetts in 1972. She then earned a master's degree in education of the hearing-impaired. She received a Juris Doctor degree from Georgetown University in 1980, where she used an interpreter. She was admitted to the Massachusetts Bar in 1980.

She was formerly a teacher of deaf students. Since 1981 she has been employed as a staff attorney by the National Center for Law and the Deaf in Washington, D.C. Many of her cases have involved discrimination against deaf persons.

ROBERT M. SILBER

Robert M. Silber was born in 1954 and became deaf when he was four years old. He attended public schools that had no special facilities for deaf students. Silber lipreads, uses a hearing aid, and learned sign language at age 19.

Silber received a bachelor of science degree from the National Technical Institute for the Deaf in 1977 and a Juris Doctor degree from Antioch School of Law in 1980. Silber was admitted to the bar of the District of Columbia in 1980. Upon leaving law school he became a staff attorney for the National Captioning Institute, dealing with contracts, trademarks, copyrights, and communication law.

MICHAEL A. SCHWARTZ

Michael A. Schwartz was born profoundly deaf in 1953. He attended public schools that had no special facilities for deaf children. He is a good lipreader and does not use a hearing aid. He learned sign language at the age of 22.

Schwartz received a bachelor of arts degree in 1975 from Brandeis University, with honors in English, and a master of arts degree from Northwestern University in 1976, with a major in theater arts. He received a Juris Doctor degree in 1981 from New York University School of Law. Schwartz was admitted to the New York State Bar in 1982.

In 1981–1982 Schwartz was a law clerk for the U.S. District Court, Southern District of New York. At various times he was a teacher at the North Carolina School for the Deaf, a law intern with the American Civil Liberties Union, and an actor for the National Theatre of the Deaf. In 1983 he became an assistant district attorney for New York County, and has presented cases in the Appellate Division of the New York courts and also in federal district court.

Bibliography

American Annals of the Deaf (Lowe), vol. 22, no. 1, January 1877.

Chatoff v. Public Service Commission, 60 App. Div.2d 700, 400 N.Y.S.2d 390.

Gallaher, J. E.: *Representative Deaf Persons in the United States* (Grady), p. 17, 1898.

Graddock, G. C.: *Notable Deaf Persons* (Parkinson), p. 155, 1975.

Leader v. Cullerton (Myers), 53 Ill.2d 1, 289 NE2d 431, 1972.

Myers v. Briggs, 46 Ill.2d 281, 263 NE2d 109, 1970.

Myers v. County of Cook, 34 Ill.2d 541, 216 NE2d 803, 1966.

Roberts v. Cullerton (Myers), 48 Ill.2d 323, 269 NE2d 465, 1971.

Lowell J. Myers

Judicial Perspective

The experience of Richard S. Brown demonstrates that deafness need not preclude an individual from serving successfully in a judicial career. Brown is both profoundly deaf and the presiding judge of the Wisconsin Court of Appeals, District II, in Waukesha. There are four districts in Wisconsin, each consisting of three judges. Each district has one presiding judge who is responsible for the administration of that district. Brown's duties include daily telephone conferences with central staff in Madison, weekly conferences with the other judges in the district to decide cases, monthly oral arguments, and daily discussion with chambers staff concerning ongoing court business.

Brown lost the hearing in his right ear in early childhood; doctors surmise this was due to measles. During his undergraduate years, he began experiencing hearing problems in his left ear, which caused him to wear a hearing aid during law school. In 1980, at the age of 36, his left ear problem was diagnosed as an acoustic neuroma, a small tumor that envelops the acoustic nerve. Surgery in January 1983 left him deaf. *See* EAR: Pathology.

Since the tumor was slow-growing, Brown was urged by his physician to have a cochlear implant placed in his right ear before the acoustic neuroma was removed. Brown also took extensive speechreading instruction to prepare for his deafness. His lipreading proficiency was approximately 85 percent with the use of the implant, and improved with time. Brown uses a computer to assist with telephone conferences. The caller's voice is heard over a speakerphone in the judge's chamber. Brown's secretary, a shorthand reporter, records what the caller is saying on a stenographic machine attached to the computer, whose software translates the reporter's strokes instantaneously into English. The result appears on the screen seconds after the word has been spoken by the caller. Using his speechreading skills, cochlear implant, and computer, Brown is able to conduct the affairs of his office in much the same way as before the operation. *See* COCHLEAR IMPLANTS.

It is important to note that Brown is an appellate judge, not a trial judge. The difference is significant because the sense of sound is not as important in the appellate position. A trial judge has the responsibility of conducting an adversary proceeding in a clear, orderly manner. Because of a trial's adversary nature, colloquy or argument between attorneys is likely to occur. Sometimes it is highly inflammatory or prejudicial and can measurably detract from the order and dignity of the proceeding. The trial judge must have the physical ability to be aware of such colloquy and to stop it. Additionally, witnesses must be treated with fairness and consideration; they should not be ridiculed, humiliated, or shouted at. The trial judge should be physically capable of immediately understanding the questions asked, so that the examination does not get out of hand, and of hearing the witness's testimony to determine its credibility. Also, a trial judge should give strict attention to the questioning of a witness in order to be prepared to make immediate rulings on routine objections to questions without asking for repetitions. Finally, in trials without a jury, a trial judge is expected to take notes of the facts so as to aid in ruling on evidentiary matters and in making findings of fact immediately following trial. Someone dependent upon visual communication might have difficulty keeping track of the proceedings and taking notes at the same time.

An appellate judge does not hear trials where lawyers question witnesses. It is the appellate court's job to decide whether an error occurred in the trial court requiring reversal of the case, after the trial is over. An appellate judge reads the "cold" paper record already made in the trial court and legal briefs of the attorneys. In some cases, the appellate judge hears oral argument by the attorneys, but this is more of a scholarly dissertation on the law and acts as a complement to the legal briefs. The main duty of the appellate judge is to decide the case and to write opinions. While a trial judge must pay strict attention to every word that is said, the appellate judge pays strict attention to every written argument that is made. This difference in the two types of judgeships makes a substantial difference to the hearing-impaired person. A hearing-impaired person who desires to be a trial judge must make sure that the handicap is not a barrier to successful management of the courtroom.

In his appellate position, Brown is able to control the pace of oral argument. The attorneys stand in front of the three-judge panel and discuss legal aspects of the case. The judges often interrupt and ask questions of the lawyers. The proceeding is more like an ongoing dialogue in a small group discussion than a courtroom atmosphere where the pace of speech is controlled by the lawyers and witnesses. Thus, Brown is able to function quite well.

Richard S. Brown

LEGAL SERVICES

Deaf people in the past had been reluctant to see lawyers about their legal problems because of difficulties in communication. Lawyers would try to write back and forth or ask deaf people to read their lips. Confusion and frustration would often result because of language problems. Many deaf people, especially those who became deaf before they learned to talk, have difficulty with written English. Also, most deaf people miss a great deal when they must depend solely on lipreading. Deaf people were also not able to call attorneys directly because of the lack of telecommunication devices (TDDs) for deaf people in lawyer's offices. Prior to 1975 there were no legal services established to meet the special needs of deaf people. *See* TELECOMMUNICATIONS: Telephone Services.

NATIONAL CENTER FOR LAW AND THE DEAF
The National Center for Law and the Deaf (NCLD) at Gallaudet College was the first national legal center established to meet the unique legal problems of hearing-impaired people. Hearing-impaired people are often denied equal opportunities in education, employment, health care, legal services, and governmental programs because of communication barriers. Since 1975 the NCLD has worked to eliminate these barriers through legal education, technical assistance nationally, and legal services to lower-income hearing-impaired people in the metropolitan Washington, D.C., area. NCLD has been instrumental in improving state interpreter laws. It has helped to shape all federal regulations implementing the Rehabilitation Act of 1973. Also, it has effected changes in federal agency internal policies that respect the communication needs of deaf people. *See* GALLAUDET COLLEGE; REHABILITATION ACT OF 1973.

The staff of NCLD has been trained in sign language, and qualified interpreters are available for interviews. Several telecommunication devices for deaf people are in regular use. Finally, the staff has developed expertise in legal issues related to deafness.

Legal Education Conferences, Workshops, and Classes   One of the NCLD's primary objectives is to provide deaf individuals with legal information that is both understandable and useful for improving their daily lives. Due to the complexities of legal terminology and the difficulties that many deaf people have with the English language, the NCLD specially designs these presentations to be both highly visual and adapted to sign language.

The NCLD offers educational programs to employers, teachers, hospital personnel, judges, lawyers, police officers, and court clerks. The presentations promote compliance with federal and state laws designed to give disabled people an equal opportunity to lead productive lives. The programs also demonstrate cost-effective ways to overcome communication barriers.

The NCLD also provides legal information on a national basis in response to inquiries from organizations, individuals, and service providers.

Deaf Law Student Program   Prior to the establishment of the NCLD, there were few hearing-impaired attorneys. The NCLD seeks to remedy this situation by encouraging qualified hearing-impaired individuals from all over the country to consider law as a career. The NCLD has presented Law School Orientation Workshops since 1975. These two-day workshops present information to hearing-impaired college students on the Law School Aptitude Test, career possibilities in law, and the realities of law school life.

The NCLD also encourages law schools to reconsider their misconceptions about the abilities of deaf people. Information from the NCLD on the potential of hearing-impaired applicants and the importance of reasonable accommodations helps law schools create equal success for hearing-impaired law students.

Today there are many more hearing-impaired law school graduates in the nation, most of whom were assisted in their efforts by the NCLD. Despite this progress, much must be done to expand opportunities for deaf individuals in law school and law-related fields. *See* LAWYERS, DEAF.

Legal Services Clinic The NCLD has the first legal services clinic in the country providing legal assistance specifically for deaf people. The clinic provides free legal assistance to Gallaudet College students and lower-income hearing-impaired individuals in the Washington, D.C., metropolitan area.

One important aspect of the clinic is its focus on helping clients become more independent. The clinic legal staff has taught many deaf clients crucial life skills, including consumer awareness, understanding of government benefits, and knowledge of legal rights. This is particularly important to young deaf people, such as Gallaudet College students, who are just beginning to live independently.

During the school year, the clinic has the services of law students supervised by NCLD staff attorneys. The clinic gives these students an understanding of the legal and communication needs of hearing-impaired people. George Washington University and Catholic University law schools offer courses for credit with the NCLD. The presence of these former students in communities across the country creates a valuable legal resource for the entire hearing-impaired population.

State Legislation Upon request, the NCLD provides assistance to state legislators, state associations and commissions of the deaf, and other organizations in enacting state laws that provide equal access for hearing-impaired people.

Significant progress has been made on improving state interpreters laws that ensure the appointment of qualified interpreters in criminal and civil court proceedings, police interrogations, and administrative hearings.

Too often deaf people have been victims of misdiagnosis, mistreatment, or nontreatment in mental institutions. The NCLD played a key role in innovative legislation in Maryland that established a mental health facility especially adapted to meet the communication and psychological needs of deaf individuals and their families. This legislation continues to serve as a model for other states.

Federal Legislation The NCLD regularly provides hearing-impaired citizens with information on the current status of federal legislation affecting them. The center also responds to frequent requests from members of Congress for technical assistance on legislation to benefit hearing-impaired people.

An early example of this legislative assistance helped make television more accessible for the nation's 50,000 hearing-impaired students in schools for the deaf. With NCLD assistance, Congress endorsed the copying, captioning, displaying, and sharing of broadcast television programs within nonprofit schools for hearing-impaired persons as a fair use in the 1976 Federal Copyright Law. The NCLD distributes information on the 1976 copyright law to schools and professionals serving hearing-impaired students. *See* TELECOMMUNICATIONS: Captioned Television.

Many deaf people are unable to participate in court proceedings because of the government's failure to appoint and pay for qualified interpreters. At the request of certain members of Congress, the NCLD provided information and testimony that led to specific protections for hearing-impaired people in the Federal Court Interpreters Act (1979). This law provides for the appointment of qualified interpreters for any hearing-impaired person in criminal and civil federal court proceedings initiated by the United States. *See* COURT INTERPRETERS ACT.

The NCLD also assisted organizations of hearing-impaired people and congressional staffs on the passage of the Telecommunications for the Disabled Act of 1982. This act requires the Federal Communications Commission (FCC) to ensure disabled persons reasonable access to telecommunication systems. The act specifically requires the FCC to adopt rules mandating compatibility between hearing aids and essential telephones.

The NCLD continues to play an important role in responding to congressional requests on the needs of hearing-impaired citizens.

Administrative Activities The NCLD successfully supports the legal rights of hearing-impaired people before federal and state administrative agencies. This support emphasizes the critical areas of television and telephone access.

When fires ravaged wide sections of California in 1970, officials used loudspeakers, radio, and television to warn residents to evacuate threatened areas. Several hearing-impaired people were burned to death because they could not hear these warnings. The NCLD's first federal agency action was a successful petition before the FCC to require all television stations to present emergency information in visual form.

The NCLD also assisted the Public Broadcasting System in its successful petition to reserve line 21 of the television vertical blanking interval for closed captioning to hearing-impaired viewers. The closed captioning system permits captions on the television screens of viewers who have purchased and installed a special decoding device. The NCLD continues to work with organizations of deaf people to increase their access to television programming.

New technology, including TDDs, enables hearing-impaired people to have access to the vital services of the telephone. The NCLD's comments to the FCC resulted in an FCC rule ensuring that directory assistance and telephone business offices will be accessible to deaf people with TDDs. In areas in which this FCC rule does not protect the needs of deaf consumers, the NCLD is requesting that the FCC reconsider its rule.

Deaf people using TDDs in the past had to pay proportionately more than hearing people for long-distance calls, because typing a message takes 5 to 10 times longer than an oral conversation. The NCLD developed a manual, *Strategies for Obtaining Reduced Intrastate TDD Rates for TDD Users*, which has helped state associations of the deaf and other consumer groups convince 36 state regulatory commissions to lower their intrastate rates.

In 1981 AT&T responded to these state efforts by successfully petitioning the FCC for reduced interstate rates for hearing-impaired TDD users. The NCLD regularly disseminates information on these rate reductions to the deaf community. It also continues to assist states in efforts to reduce intrastate rates.

The AT&T divestiture threatened many of the advances made on behalf of hearing-impaired telephone users. One advance threatened by the divestiture was local telephone company provision of TDDs in several states. The NCLD successfully petitioned the FCC to clarify that state public utility commissions would retain the authority to consider provision of special equipment. The NCLD continues to monitor the divestiture order and FCC proceedings to ensure that the needs of the hearing-impaired community are met.

Another major administrative focus of the NCLD has been commenting on the federal regulations pursuant to the Rehabilitation Act of 1973. As a result, all final Rehabilitation Act regulations contain langauge recognizing the importance for communication access with hearing-impaired people.

The NCLD has also worked with federal agencies, including the Social Security Administration, the Immigration and Naturalization Service, and the Small Business Administration, to develop policies on providing interpreters to hearing-impaired people using their services. These written policies help the agencies communicate effectively with hearing-impaired people.

The NCLD, due to funding limitations, cannot initiate litigation.

National Association of the Deaf Legal Defense Fund

In 1976 the National Association of the Deaf (NAD) established a Legal Defense Fund for the specific purpose of bringing lawsuits in court to advance and protect the rights of deaf people throughout the country. These court actions are often filed to enforce deaf people's rights pursuant to the Rehabilitation Act of 1973. Cases have been brought where deaf people were discriminated against and denied equal access to employment, education, physical and mental health care, social services, and the administration of justice. Some of the NAD Legal Defense Fund court settlements have served as persuasive models for compliance in similar subsequent cases.

A significant example was the court settlement resulting in the state of Maryland establishing a model treatment program for mentally ill deaf patients in state mental hospitals. The model unit features a staff with training in sign language and deafness, and sign language interpreters. Deaf patients from other state hospitals are transferred into the special unit, where they can communicate with each other and with therapists. The mental health program is intended to reverse years of chronic neglect of deaf patients in state mental institutions.

The lawsuit was brought on behalf of a deaf woman who had been a patient in a Maryland mental hospital for more than 20 years. Because no one could communicate with her, she had received no services or treatment. Her mental condition had deteriorated to the point that she was considered "uncommunicable" and untreatable. Despite urgings from outside psychologists and experts in deafness, the state of Maryland had not given her a hearing aid, a treatment program, or sign language interpreters who could explain her problems to therapists or enable therapists to treat her.

The woman was transferred to the model mental health unit. Her condition, appearance, and ability to communicate greatly improved once she received appropriate treatment and services at the model unit. *See* Court decisions: Pyles v. Kamka; National Association of the Deaf.

Local Law Centers

Local law centers to serve deaf clients in their metropolitan areas were started in Philadelphia, Minneapolis, New York, and the Bay Area of Northern California. All of these legal centers use qualified interpreters and have TDDs.

The Legal Advocacy Project for Hearing Impaired Persons in Minneapolis serves hearing-impaired people in the Minneapolis metropolitan area. It provides legal representation for hearing-impaired persons on problems that are disability-related. They have helped hearing-impaired persons file numerous employment discrimination complaints with the Office for Federal Contract Compliance of the Department of Labor and the Minnesota Human Rights Department. After investigations, several of these hearing-impaired persons have been reinstated to their jobs, have received cash settlements, or have received needed interpreter services. The project also played a key role in securing legislation requiring all private employers in Minnesota with 50 or more employees to provide reasonable accommodations for handicapped workers.

The Legal Advocacy Project sued the state of Minnesota for failure to provide appropriate and accessible treatment for deaf mentally ill patients. A settlement agreement was signed to provide appropriate treatment, including hiring qualified staff and funding community-based residential services for hearing-impaired mentally ill persons.

Project personnel also assist parents on special-education issues for hearing-impaired children. Finally they provide community education regarding legal rights of deaf people.

The Bay Area Center for Law and the Deaf at the Deaf Counseling, Advocacy and Referral Agency in Northern California provides legal representation on discrimination cases based on hearing loss. It assists deaf people in obtaining interpreters for the judicial system, social service agencies, and employment situations. The center also represents parents on special-education issues for their hearing-impaired children.

CONCLUSION

The NCLD working with sections of the American Bar Association and local Bar Association committees on legal services for hearing-impaired people has made the private bar more aware of the special communication needs of deaf people. Training has also been provided to legal service programs. More and more communities have lawyers interested in taking deaf clients and providing interpreter and TDD services. But continued awareness and training is necessary to ensure equal access to legal services.

Bibliography

DuBow, S., et al.: *Legal Rights of Hearing-Impaired People*, 2d ed., 1984.

———— and S. Geer: "Communication Barriers," *Legal Advocacy for the Handicapped*, 1981.

Sy DuBow

LITERATURE, DRAMATIC CHARACTERS IN

In drama, characterizations of deaf persons, or mutes as they used to be called, have tended to reflect the status of deaf people in society. Deaf scholar and playwright Eugene Bergman has observed that deaf characters as conceived by hearing writers are rarely described as equal to hearing people. Lacking speech, they often appear less than human, or they are used merely as symbols of human alienation and despair.

In comedies, playwrights may use a character with late-onset deafness, often an elderly person, whose communication difficulties are exaggerated for comic effect. In the case of any of these stereotypes, their deafness makes them creatures of a different order for most authors unless those writers are themselves products of the deaf culture.

Stage Productions

In past centuries, there was also an obvious limit to the utility of a deaf character in a drama written to be spoken on stage. Not until sign language was systematized in eighteenth-century France was an attempt made to characterize a deaf person by means of spoken or signed lines.

THE ABBÉ DE L'EPÉE

The Abbé de l'Epée was a play supposedly based on an actual event in the career of l'Epée, who established the first school for deaf children in Paris in the mideighteenth century. Since original authorship was difficult to establish before copyright laws were written, playwrights and directors felt free to adapt, supplement, and rewrite plays to fit local tastes, available talent, and the moral message they chose to convey. *The Abbé de l'Epée* was widely performed in a variety of versions and by 1817 was being performed in America. *See* L'EPÉE, ABBÉ CHARLES MICHEL DE.

The melodrama is about a young deaf-mute of noble birth who is orphaned at age 10. In order to claim the boy's fortune, his greedy uncle takes the child to Paris, ostensibly to obtain treatment for his deafness, only to abandon him on a snowy bridge at midnight, dressed in beggar's rags to conceal his noble origins. The critical oversight is in not throwing the boy over the railing into the icy Seine. A kindly gendarme rescues the child and takes him to the Abbé de l'Epée's school where he is soon recognized as being of a background belying his humble appearance.

The boy proves a remarkably apt pupil. At age 18, the youth is taken by the Abbé on a walking tour of the south of France in the hope that he will recognize his home town. When they arrive at Toulouse, the drama of the inevitable showdown with the evil uncle is heightened by the astonishing intellect the young man displays. In answer to the question "Who is the greatest genius that France has produced?" after only a brief pause the young man writes: "Science would decide for d'Alembert, and Nature say, Buffon; Wit and Taste present Voltaire; and Sentiment pleads for Rousseau; but Genius and Humanity cry out for de l'Epée; and him I call the best and greatest of all human creatures."

It was the Abbé who was given most of the credit for the boy's remarkable achievements by Laurent Clerc, himself a deaf product of the Abbé's school. Clerc wrote, "(It is) to achieve a deed like that of the Creator" to educate a deaf person who is otherwise "condemned to grow old in a long childhood." Having first seen the play in Paris, probably around 1800, Clerc wrote in the preface to an 1818 American edition, "The piece, when first acted in Paris, caused tears to trickle from the spectators' eyes, and obtained a brilliant success." *See* CLERC, LAURENT.

The play was produced in America in, among other places, Hartford, Connecticult, the year after Clerc arrived to assist Thomas Hopkins Gallaudet with the new Connecticut Asylum (later the American School for the Deaf). Its popularity contributed in some measure to the successful efforts to raise financial support for schools for deaf children. *See* AMERICAN SCHOOL FOR THE DEAF; GALLAUDET, THOMAS HOPKINS.

WARNINGS

Warnings (1913) by Eugene O'Neill dramatizes the torment of James Knapp, who is losing his hearing. He is a ship radio operator, and his job and the safety of the ship's passengers depend on his acute hearing. Knowing his hearing is failing rapidly, he wants to quit his job, but his wife persuades him to make one last voyage to forestall the family's financial ruin. When he fails to hear radio warnings of a submerged derelict, the ship is damaged; worse, he cannot hear replies to his S.O.S. appeals and the ship sinks. Instead of joining others on the lifeboats, he kills himself in horrified realization of his failure.

This is the first work that attempts to portray a deaf person's own view of his life and disability. The character does not disprove Bergman's observation, however, since James Knapp is not a "real" deaf man. He had been functioning as a hearing person who speaks "like anyone else." Yet instead of showing encroaching deafness as a comic inconvenience, O'Neill dramatizes its isolating and terrible consequences.

THE CHAIRS

The Chairs by French dramatist Eugène Ionesco uses a deaf character symbolically to show the absurdity and impossibility of communication. In the theater of the absurd, life itself has no meaning; people do not, therefore, communicate meaningfully.

An old man is preparing to die at the end of a long, unimportant life. But he has something of great value he feels he must pass on to humanity. He and his wife invite the entire community and set up chairs for all of the (invisible) people who come to this final momentous occasion. The old man introduces each newcomer to the invisible on-stage audience (represented by empty chairs) and then to the theater audience. He knows the Orator will come to deliver the important message. Then he and his wife turn and leap out of the window into the sea—oblivion.

The Orator appears and begins to deliver the message. He gestures to show he is deaf and mute, and he tries to sign to the invisible audience. Becoming aware he is not communicating, he begins to use guttural and unintelligible speech. Finally, he writes on the blackboard some cryptic and meaningless words. He then bows ceremoniously and leaves. Only the empty chairs remain.

THE MIRACLE WORKER

The Miracle Worker was first written as a television movie in 1957. It was so successful that William Gibson adapted it for the stage, where it won the Tony Award for Best Play of 1959. Having originally been conceived as a narrative accompaniment for a dancer, there is much physical violence in the encounters between the determined young teacher and "the deaf mute, blind bundle of fierce flesh . . . [who] had lived . . . like an animal—worse, with a soul, shackled, wild with rages and despair."

The subhuman behavior of the seven-year-old Helen Keller permits the character of Annie Sullivan to glow with almost superhuman qualities, reminiscent of the saintly Abbé de l'Epée. It is the patient and sensitive young teacher, not Helen, who is the heroine of the play. Only in the context of the brilliant later accomplishments of the celebrated Helen Keller can Gibson's characterization of the child be seen as something other than grotesque sensationalism. *See* KELLER, HELEN.

MY THIRD EYE

My Third Eye (1971) was the first original production of the National Theatre of the Deaf, and the first major public presentation by deaf people based on their own stories of growing up deaf in a hearing world. *See* NATIONAL THEATERS OF THE DEAF: United States.

The confusion of the deaf child caught in the ongoing controversy of educational philosophies is expressed by actor Bernard Bragg: "It took me weeks and weeks before I was able to make my 'K' sound right. At the end of my first school year there was a demonstration for parents and visitors. I came up on a platform and made just that one letter. The audience applauded, but my mother who is deaf just stared at me as if to ask, 'Is that all you learned during all that time?'"

Joe Sarpy remembers how speech lessons felt: "The teacher put a stick to hold down my tongue and it touched my windpipe. The teacher wanted to hear my say 'Ah . . . Ah . . . Ah . . .' and I almost vomited."

Mary Beth Miller adds, "My teacher would use the same stick for all the children."

SIGN ME ALICE

Sign Me Alice (1973) by deaf actor and playwright Gilbert Eastman was an adaptation of George Bernard Shaw's *Pygmalion*, with touches from A. J. Lerner and F. Loewe's musical version, *My Fair Lady*. Eastman lampoons the new versions of Signed English and cued speech, satirizing the efforts of teachers to instruct deaf children in the varieties of new sign languages. *See* MANUALLY CODED ENGLISH: Signed English; MOUTH-HAND SYSTEMS: Cued Speech.

Heroine Alice Babel is frustrated by her inability to communicate with hearing people: "Where I go? Who I belong? Who I am? No place. People never understand me. I must force myself to understand them."

She offers to participate in an experiment with a Dr. Zeno who has invented a version of Signed English he calls U.S.E. (Using Signed English). Like many deaf people, Alice has been taught that command of the English language will be a liberating force. She believes Zeno when he calls her a "creature with . . . bad English that will keep her in the dark world," and when he compares her to "apes that gesticulate in a cage."

The romantic interest in the play is slow to be developed and resolved. Mark Newton is the deaf son of a hearing social worker and uses a version of cued speech to communicate. Since Mark has sold out to the traditional enemies, Alice can't take him seriously: "Not real Deaf. You oralist. Different world. Stay-out. You not belong to us."

Mark protests that he is "Deaf . . . talk same deaf." But not until he gives up his role as a cued speech demonstrator can he convince her of his sincerity, though he tries to explain: "I sign different to hearings because they never understand our real Sign."

This is, in fact, why Alice herself has undertaken the transformation into a "lady" who can sign proper English. But the experience teaches her, as it taught her prototype "Eliza," that being a lady does not depend on superficialities of language. "A lady can use Sign . . . U.S.E. has nothing to do with Sign. Sign is another language." And for a real deaf person, "In my heart, Sign real mine."

The play was a manifesto for the deaf community. It articulated the resentment of generations of deaf persons who felt violated by hearing teachers who suppressed the use of sign language in schools. The depth of feeling in such images as "apes that gesticulate in a cage" is hard to ignore.

A PLAY OF OUR OWN

A Play of Our Own also made its debut in 1973, marking another milestone in the coming of age of the theater of the deaf. Deaf writer and poet Dorothy Miles was interested in nurturing a drama that would not be a window on the mainstream culture but a genuine expression of values and experiences of deaf people.

Working with a community theater group of deaf actors, Miles adapted the plot of the popular film *Guess Who's Coming to Dinner*. The Hartford Thespians brought the Daniels family to life. When the deaf couple got the news that their deaf daughter, Ruth, was bringing her new hearing boyfriend home, they experienced as much consternation as if she were violating a racial norm. For the deaf family to welcome David Bone and his parents, they had to define and strengthen their own identity.

As is true with any minority, deaf people are more accustomed to adapting to the hearing world than hearing people are to the deaf world. David's efforts to learn sign language, his obvious love of Ruth, and Mr. Bone's fascination with the family's TTY finally persuade the Danielses that David might fit in.

Miles, writing from the heart of the deaf culture, was able to develop her characters as equals, without making that the central issue of the play.

TALES FROM A CLUBROOM

Tales from a Clubroom was coauthored in 1980 by deaf actor and writer Bernard Bragg and deaf playwright Eugene Bergman. While many of the 19 deaf characters are typical of any small town community, there are a number who are unique products of the deaf culture. *See* BRAGG, BERNARD.

The plot centers on the crisis confronting members of a club for deaf people when their President Green discovers that their long-admired treasurer, Jim Yakubski, has been embezzling club funds. The club's board is unforgiving, even when Yakubski confesses he has been driven to the crime to help his drug-addict son. When the board votes to expel him, he protests their decision: "To be kicked out of the club is the worst punishment you can give any deaf person. (With increasing violence) Where can I go? . . . Punish me in any other way, if you like, but why kick me out?"

But other betrayals are forgiven. Shirley Klaymans, a "thrice divorced blonde," appears to have learned her lesson. The club members understand that she has been exploited by her hearing husband: "Aw—I should've known better, marrying a hearie. And he said he didn't want me coming to the club because only low-class stupid deaf people sign. He calls deaf signers stupid. Hah! . . . I told the SOB to get out of my house!"

Even despised "oralist" Spencer Collins is welcomed, once he has seen the error of his ways. He is taken under the wing of members who try to protect him from the consequences of his ignorance when he accosts the flashy ABC card peddler, Carswell. The men try to explain to Collins why Carswell is not only accepted in the deaf community but admired: "The hearies already think so little of the deafies, what's the difference? . . . We respect him because he fools the hearies. They always take advantage of the deaf, but that peddler, a deafie, takes advantage of them for a change. Can't you see that?"

Carswell himself elaborates: "It's the deaf teachers and other high-class snobs who hate me the most . . . Average deaf people accept me and understand . . . that's good enough for me."

The most memorable character in the play is Spivey, who is described in the script as a pariah. A mute, uncommunicative young man in ill-fitted clothes, Spivey faces the world with a vacant stare and a self-effacing smile. Possibly retarded, though this is not clear, he does not sign or become involved in any club activities. Content to come each night and watch, he is the eternal observer, but it is doubtful that he understands much of what is going on. He seems to symbolize the plight of a deaf person in the hearing world, uncomprehending, always smiling, and painfully eager to oblige. Of the large cast of characters, Spivey was the one most often identified as familiar by members of the audience. It appeared that every local club had a Spivey.

CHILDREN OF A LESSER GOD

Children of a Lesser God by Mark Medoff was the second play that marked 1980 as a banner theater year for deaf people. Twenty-one years after *The Miracle Worker* had won the Tony Award for Best Play, history repeated itself with Medoff's stunning success. The play also earned deaf actress Phyllis Frelich a Tony Award for Best Actress. Medoff's friendship with Frelich and her hearing husband, Robert Steinberg, inspired him not only to write the play but to attempt to understand the mind and heart of a deaf woman. *See* FRELICH, PHYLLIS.

The heroine Sarah Norman (Frelich) had suffered a fate that befalls some children born deaf. Considered mentally retarded until she was 12, she felt unwanted at home. Her father had deserted the family after Sarah had been sent to the state residential school for the deaf. On weekend visits home as a teenager, she had been sexually exploited by her sister's boyfriends. Now 25, she works

as a maid at the school, pretending to attend classes, because she feels at home nowhere else.

When the new speech teacher, Jim Leeds, falls in love with her, it first appears that their romance will bridge the chasm between the hearing world and Sarah's silent secret world of stored-up pain. When they marry, she is thrilled with her newfound domesticity. She is "equal" at last; even beating her mother and the school principal at bridge—the ultimate female victory.

At first she rejects the efforts of her former schoolmate Orin Dennis to persuade her to assist him in a discrimination complaint against their school. He appeals to her loyalty to the deaf community: "We're deaf. Don't forget it!"

Actually, Orin is not "real deaf," only "hard of hearing." He speaks well and is a militant advocate of equal employment for deaf workers. Sarah finally joins Orin in his effort. She writes her own speech and refuses her husband's offer to interpret it for her at the commission hearing.

In an argument with Jim over her refusal to learn to speak, Sarah emphasizes that she will not do anything she cannot do well. She has proved she can do many things well—cook, play bridge, write speeches, and love. But Jim wants her to keep trying to learn to speak, and oversteps his bounds in his efforts to help her. She leaves him—perhaps forever: "Until you let me be an individual, an 'I' just as you are, you will never truly be able to come inside my silence and know me. And until you can do that, I will never let myself know you. Until that time, we cannot be joined. We cannot share a relationship."

Sarah comes a long way from the young woman who first explained to Jim why she would let no one get close enough to hurt her, afraid she "would shrivel up and blow away." But she still needs to protect her silent secret world from anyone who feels a deaf person is less a person because she does not speak. While she admits to Jim that "someone inside me loves you very much," she still is not sure enough to herself at the end of the play to risk returning to him.

THE WHITE HAWK

The White Hawk by John Basinger was first performed in 1981. Basinger worked with his star, Bernard Bragg, in a conscientious effort to portray the delicate balance of independence and sensitivity a deaf person feels when relating to the world of hearing persons.

In the play, actor and mime John Green is not satisfied to remain in the deaf community as a performer since, successful as he is, he feels that: "It has to be hearing people (in the audience). They are the door we have to open . . . The Deaf . . . that's a dead end . . . If I succeed (in the hearing world of theatre, then) the Deaf will have something to be proud of."

With a sympathetic pianist, Green develops a musical show that is so successful that a screenwriter becomes interested and creates a movie role for a deaf performer. Ironically, the role is written not for the creative and talented Green but for his hard-of-hearing friend and interpreter, Rachel, who is not even a "true deaf" person. Green is left without either the coveted film role or an interpreter for his show.

Rachel has been less trusting of the hearing world from the beginning. As a product of its unrealistic perceptions of deaf people, she has no illusions about what to expect: "The hearing people don't really like the deaf. They think we're strangers. We make them feel uncomfortable, we frighten them. And then they become cruel." Rachel's story is familiar to many marginally deaf persons. She elaborates: "When I was growing up my father wanted me to be normal . . . I had to wear those huge hearing aids to understand . . . It was as if I were in a bubble. I had to wait until I was grown to escape from all that and be what I really am, deaf."

Later in the final performance of his show, Green does a moving pantomine of the death of a white hawk, a metaphor for his career. It is an assertion of independence for which he refuses the services of his on-stage interpreter, letting his signs speak eloquently for themselves.

THAT MAKES TWO OF US

That Makes Two of Us (1982) is a one-act romantic comedy by Bernard Bragg. A pretty young deaf fashion illustrator, Cheryl, who has had an oralist education, meets her first real deaf man, Bruce. The romance winds its way through her misconceptions about deaf people who sign, and her self-consciousness about her own deafness.

By the time Cheryl learns to sign, the two realize they are in love. Bruce surprises her at the airport just as she is about to leave on a six-month job assignment to Paris. He produces tickets of his own and announces that he is going with her, which he is able to do because he is the successful owner of a car import and repair business.

Bragg portrays a deaf person who is not willing to sign as someone displaying denial of personal deafness and rejection of all deaf people.

MORNING AFTER THE MIRACLE

Morning after the Miracle by William Gibson was a sequel to *The Miracle Worker*. It concerns the tense ménage à trois that developed when Annie Sullivan fell in love with the young Harvard graduate student, John Macy, who had worked with Helen and Annie to edit Helen's autobiography.

At the time of the play, Helen is an honors student at Radcliffe; both she and Annie are national celebrities, with their lives so intertwined that they are emotionally and intellectually connected. Helen becomes jealous, and is suspicious of and threatened by Annie's romance. John thinks he can live with the unique situation and agrees not to separate the two women. He marries Annie and moves into their house.

Gibson's characterization of the adult Helen romanticizes her, giving her a degree of physical attractiveness she hardly possessed in life. This makes a near-seduction scene between Helen and John somewhat believable. Given the cloistered existence Helen had led before Macy moved into her house, the awakening of her sexuality is a natural development, albeit a complicating one.

By the time Macy realizes his mistake in marrying Annie, he has become an angry alcoholic and knows he must leave to save himself. The two women seem resigned to the fact that they are destined to live out their symbiotic relationship: "No power on earth can separate us—even the power of love," Annie announces at the end of the play. The price is high, but as Helen had earlier observed, "I have found that pain can be . . . useful."

SIGN ME ALICE II

Sign Me Alice II (1983) is Gilbert Eastman's sequel to his first play. In it, Alice Babel-Newton is happily married to Mark Newton, who is now more interested in baseball than in sign language but who supports his liberated wife in her various activities.

The misguided Dr. Zeno of *Sign Me Alice* (I) has recommended Alice to testify before a congressional hearing on education of deaf students, assuming she will support and demonstrate the wisdom of his system of U.S.E. (Using Signed English). Since it has been 10 years since he last saw Alice, he does not know that she has long since abandoned his methods and is now a strong advocate of a new method of teaching visual gestures as a base for bilingual education of deaf children.

In preparing her testimony, Alice consults her best friend, Barbara, a deaf actress who is a militant advocate of American Sign Language. Barbara describes herself as "a complaining person. Why? The hearing people do not treat me right. . . . Their ideas are false. They are hypocrites. They mold many deaf people's lives. Not mine. Not my soul. I won't let them reshape me. . . . Deep in my body there is a flame." Barbara helps Alice express some of the discontent the deaf community has with the hearing educators who still do not consult deaf consumers about educational methodologies. *See*

EDUCATION: Communication; SIGN LANGUAGES: American.

After her testimony, however, Alice is not satisfied. While everyone except Dr. Zeno appeared pleased with her presentation, she still questions herself: "They must listen to me. Now I am not speaking for myself. . . I say 'we'. . . I represent the world of deaf people. . . do I? . . . Oh, I don't know. I did not say enough. . . Maybe I said too much. . . It doesn't matter, they remain ignorant."

The impossibility of adequate communication between the two worlds seems to remain, despite deaf people's best efforts.

FISH NOR FOWL

Fish nor Fowl (1984) by Eugene Bergman is another play that joins the battle against oralism. Winona, daughter of a wealthy family, has renounced her elitist oralist private school background to marry a "real" (signing) deaf man, printer Harry Grodin. When classmate Wilbur Davenport comes to visit her after 20 years, Winona's mother conspires to pair her daughter with Wilbur as soon as she can persuade her to divorce Harry, who is, after all, "only half-human, being deaf." She pleads with her daughter: "Can't you understand the horror, the mortification, repugnance that you inspire in others when they see you gesticulating with that cripple? It's beyond my strength to be present as a constant witness to this revolting spectacle. . . That horrible deaf-mute makes me sick."

But Winona understands her mother all too well: "My tinny voice embarrasses you in public. . . You were and are ashamed of me. You conveniently got rid of me by hiding me away at a boarding school for deaf children. . . You swallowed all that muck fed (to) you about the value of an oral education."

Harry's seems the only voice of sanity. After meeting Wilbur and hearing about Winona's classmates, he asks, "Why is it that deaf children of poor parents, who attend a regular school for the deaf, are normal and lead normal lives, while children of rich parents go to oral schools and become such weirdos?"

These oralist deaf people apparently fall between the cracks, belonging to neither world, ". . . neither fish nor fowl. Hearing society won't accept them, and they don't fit into deaf society."

The resounding anger in Bergman's play can hardly be escaped. But there is another message, announced by Wilbur: "Don't believe it when they tell you that suffering enobles. . . Suffering cripples." This contrasts strikingly with Helen Keller's observation about suffering in *Morning after the Miracle*, written by a hearing playwright who may not have experienced the pain firsthand.

WOMAN TALK

Woman Talk (1984) is a one-act play by deaf actor and playwright Bruce Hlibok. It is a savage portrait of two deaf women who meet and compare notes on the physical and mental abuse they have undergone, one at the hands of a hearing husband.

Sandra, the more assertive of the two, has already left her deaf husband and her hometown. Her husband had beat her, and her family had disowned her after she aborted an unwanted pregnancy. She now lives in a different city, where nobody knows she works in a nearby town as a striptease dancer.

"It's good money," she explains to Molly. And Sandra does not want to work at jobs all other deaf people do, ". . . printers, clerks, mechanics—locked into the system of this society. I knew I could do something different."

Different she is. Sandra not only has broken the stereotype of the submissive deaf housewife, but has become so alienated from society that at first she even refuses the friendship of her new deaf neighbor, Molly. Finally she begins to listen to Molly's story, which soon moves her to outrage.

Molly's hearing husband is a professional killer, a hit man who married Molly mostly because she couldn't talk: ". . .because nobody would believe me," Molly explains to Sandra. "You know, the world in general doesn't listen to deaf people?"

Outraged at Molly's descriptions of the beatings her husband inflicts on her, Sandra persuades Molly to kill him. Together the two women butcher the drunken husband, storing his body parts in Sandra's freezer.

Molly moves in with Sandra and fulfills her ambition to be a dancer by getting a job as a stripper where Sandra works. In the final scene the two women inspect Sandra's electric knife as they await a visit from Sandra's exhusband.

Hlibok describes the play as a "cartoon." In the contemporary genre of black comedy, the women are caricatures of women's liberation and are only incidentally deaf. It has been said that when a minority group feels secure enough to laugh at itself, it has arrived. *Women Talk* may be viewed as having achieved this level of comedy.

IN THE HANDS OF ITS ENEMY

In the Hands of Its Enemy (1984), Mark Medoff's second play written for Phyllis Frelich, is also about an abused wife who kills her husband. The play is not, as was *Children of a Lesser God*, about being deaf, but about self-exploration.

In the play-within-a-play structure, Marieta (Frelich) is a deaf playwright. Encouraged by a director she had met 13 years earlier, Marieta decides to produce her first play, and with the director's insistent efforts is challenged to strengthen the characterizations by using a degree of honesty that she is not prepared to give.

Marieta's script is revealed to be based on her own childhood. It develops that Marieta herself had been abused as a child by her (hearing) father. Her deaf mother felt helpless to prevent what she knew was happening to her deaf daughter, and finally killed the husband. At her mother's trial, the young Marieta had not come forward to contradict the explanation of wife abuse that her mother offered the court for the murder. As a result, the mother was sentenced to prison where, as a lonely deaf person, she was doomed to harassment and eventual death. The now adult Marieta is still torn by guilt for not having testified at her mother's trial, and also by unresolved anger at her mother. Marieta arranges for her 15-year-old daughter Amanda to play the role based on her own life in the play she has titled "Fury's Gift." When Amanda realizes that she is acting her mother's real-life role, she is horrified.

She asks why she is being given this "Fury's Gift" of more truth than she ever wanted to know, and Marieta explains: "I tried to do it through fiction. I wanted somehow to communicate. . .me to you without having to tell you the truth." She explains to Amanda that her birth "proved to me that I didn't have to remain a victim of my father's sickness. . . I thought for so many years that anyone who looked at me could see what I was. . . I began to see my deafness as the punishment of God, who knew when I was conceived what I would grow up to be. I deserved to miss the sound of your laughter. . . I thought it would be embarrassment enough for you to go through life with a deaf mother . . . without telling you the truth about me."

In the final scene, mother and daughter are reconciled, and Amanda compliments her mother with: "If I had imagined a mother, she would be you!"

Medoff's play achieves the equality of characterization usually so lacking in plays written by hearing authors about deaf people. It is another example that characterizations of deaf persons have come of age in the theater.

Film and Television

During the twentieth century, writers have been able to project their characterizations to the general public with increasing definition and vividness due to film and television. These characterizations reach a vastly larger audience than do those of the theater and an incomparably larger one than those of the theater of the deaf.

Ironically, however, the impact of these media has usually been inversely proportionate to the authenticity of the characterizations of deaf persons.

The economics of residuals and reruns of early films has left a legacy of ill-conceived deaf characters.

The National Association of the Deaf has protested portrayals of one-dimensional or subhuman caricatures of deaf persons, especially when these roles were performed by actors who were not deaf. But for many years film producers ignored the National Association's criticisms and suggestions. By the late 1970s noticeable changes were being made by major networks and TV studios, thanks in large measure to the persistence of the National Association and to the widely acclaimed talent of deaf performers in the National Theatre of the Deaf. *See* NATIONAL ASSOCIATION OF THE DEAF.

THE STORY OF ALEXANDER GRAHAM BELL

The Story of Alexander Graham Bell (1939) starred Loretta Young in an appealing performance as Mabel, Bell's vivacious and charming deaf wife. In this film she was portrayed as an expert lipreader who spoke in a pleasing manner. The romantic and idealized story of a "mixed marriage" certainly glamorized the image of a deaf person in the eyes of American filmgoers. *See* BELL, ALEXANDER GRAHAM.

While historically accurate, Young's characterization probably had a somewhat demoralizing effect on generations of young deaf children and their parents who were struggling with the limitations of the exclusively oralist educational systems in schools for deaf children at that time.

JOHNNY BELINDA

Johnny Belinda (1955, 1983) dramatizes the life of a young deaf woman, Belinda, who is a stereotypical deaf-mute without language or education, living on a subsistence farm in Nova Scotia. She is raped by a brutish farmer who takes advantage of her inability to speak and identify him. As a result, Belinda has a son, Johnny, whom she adores. Belinda is befriended by the village doctor in the 1955 version (a government worker in the 1983 version), who helps her to learn sign language. He falls in love with her and helps to rescue Johnny from his suddenly possessive father.

The stereotype of a deaf person without language as being less than human is somewhat redeemed by Belinda's salvation through sign language, effected by the charitable intervention of a kindly hearing person. While these portrayals of the deaf-person-as-victim do little for the dignity of deaf individuals, *Johnny Belinda*'s fairy tale happy ending has made it a classic.

THE MIRACLE WORKER

The Miracle Worker was such a success as a 1957 television film that William Gibson rewrote it for the stage. The deaf and speechless Helen Keller is portrayed as scarcely human. Patty Duke's memorable portrayal of the child trapped in her silent dark world made the achievement of signed language between her and her teacher appear truly miraculous.

A fortuitous by-product of the television production was the great interest Anne Bancroft developed in the culture of deaf people while learning sign language for her role as the teacher, Annie Sullivan. She later became an influential advocate for the establishment of the National Theatre of the Deaf.

SHOES

"Shoes" (1976) was an episode in the popular television detective series *Baretta*. A young deaf shoeshine boy, Shoes is a kind of poolhall mascot who helps the police detective solve a series of rape-murders. Posing as a policeman, the killer ignores the boy he knows to be deaf and mute, and attacks the heroine. But Shoes interrupts the attack and later helps the police find the murderer, saving the heroine a second time. The heroine explains at the end of the episode that as Shoe's reward, she and he are going together to a sign language class.

The characterization of the brave young mute is intended to be a flattering one, though a deaf boy in a modern urban area being totally without language is anachronistic in the mid-1970s.

DEAF FRIEND

"Deaf Friend" (1978), an episode of the television series *James at Fifteen*, stars deaf actor Kevin van Wieringer, and describes the difficulties of a deaf teenager being mainstreamed into a suburban high school. Scott Phillips (van Wieringer) is a fine soccer player, and James believes this will be sufficient to ensure his deaf friend a warm welcome at Bunker Hill High School. Scott thinks the challenges of the hearing high school will help him learn more about the real world beyond his deaf school.

He is first rebuffed by the coach, who does not want a deaf player on the team; this is compounded by the rejection of a pretty blonde classmate. Devastated, Scott is ready to return to the deaf world that understands him, but James persuades him not to leave. James also manages to convince the coach that Scott deserves a place on the team, even a chance to play. With a spectacular last-minute goal, Scott becomes a hero on the soccer field and wins a place in the hearing world.

Sports proves to be a universal language; the episode was well received. The characterization of Scott Phillips is one that establishes the "equality" of the young deaf person by virtue of his athletic superiority.

AND YOUR NAME IS JONAH

And Your Name Is Jonah (1979) was a teaching film, which dramatized the plight of a family who had just discovered that their son was deaf rather than mentally retarded. The deaf child actor Jeffry Bravin performed the role of five-year-old Jonah with an endearing mix of mischief and innocence. The popular actress Sally Struthers helped to guarantee the film's success, along with the assistance of deaf actor and playwright Bernard Bragg as technical consultant and performer.

The story is the painfully familiar one of a deaf child diagnosed by the family doctor as retarded and institutionalized for three years. When the error is discovered and Jonah returns home, his mother (Struthers) works overtime to make up for the "big mistake," and her marriage collapses from the strain. After struggling through the maze of audiologists and speech therapists, she meets a deaf couple who invite her to a deaf club. She discovers sign language, which proves to be the magic solution; now there is a new vision of life for her son. He is enrolled in a school for deaf pupils where he happily spells the name he has finally learned as his.

And Your Name Is Jonah marks a shift in the century-long battle between the different philosophies of education of deaf children. The cast comprised a majority of deaf actors, presenting sign language as the educational modality of choice for deaf children.

BARNEY MILLER

Barney Miller, a popular television police series, presented an episode in 1980 that starred deaf actress Phyllis Frelich in the role of a prostitute. This less-than-flattering portrait was considerably enhanced by her ability to lipread and sign a sophisticated discussion of modern art with the handsome detective who booked her. Further balance was provided by the characterization of her deaf lawyer, who paid her bail and informed the captain that he was entering a charge of police entrapment for his client.

Scriptwriter Nat Mauldin apparently felt the need to glamorize his deaf characters, but at the same time it was obvious that the deaf girl was not getting special treatment because of her handicap. The message was clear: Deaf people are like anyone else, some good, some bad. The law was going to treat her as an equal, and so can the viewing public.

Film and television writers have come a long way in attempting to avoid the traditional stereotypes of deaf characters. Television and film makers appear to realize that most deaf people are just people who cannot hear.

Bibliography

Bergman, Eugene: Paper on *Fish nor Fowl* delivered at the Modern Language Association Convention, Washington, D.C., 1984.

Kalem, T. E.: "The Odd Trio" (*Monday after the Miracle* by William Gibson), *Time*, p. 79, June 14, 1982.

Nascimento, Daniel: Bibliography in Trent Batson and Eugene Bergman (eds.), *The Deaf Experience*, Merriam-Eddy, South Waterford, Maine, 1976.

Panara, Robert: "Deaf Characters in Fiction and Drama," *Deaf American*, May 1972.

Schuart, Adele: "A Play of Our Own, a Write-up," *Deaf American*, December 1973.

Willimon, William H.: "The High Cost of Miracles," *Christian Century*, pp. 864–865, August 18–25, 1982.

PLAYS

Some plays are listed with city and date of first production since they are presently available only in unpublished manuscript form. Since many productions are written and performed locally by deaf actors for deaf audiences, no complete register of plays is yet available. This listing is based on information from a number of researchers, among them Eugene Bergman, Thomas Harrington, Francis Higgins, Daniel Nascimento, and Robert Panara. It does not purport to be complete. Thomas Harrington of the Gallaudet College Media Center has compiled a list of dramatic film and television productions and would appreciate receiving information on additions to the list.

Auber, Daniel François Esprit: *The Dumb Girl of Portici*, five acts, 1828, translated from Italian, 1845.

Bates, Arlo: *Her Deaf Ear*, one act, comedy, Walter H. Baker Co., Boston, 1907.

Basinger, John: *The White Hawk*, Washington, D.C., 1981.

Bergman, Eugene: *Fish nor Fowl*, three acts, 1984.

Bragg, Bernard: *That Makes Two of Us*, video, Gallaudet College Television, Washington, D.C., 1982.

———— and Eugene Bergman: *Tales from a Clubroom*, Gallaudet College, Washington, D.C., 1980.

Bouilly, Jean Nicolas: *L'Abbé de l'Epée*, five acts, André Luitieme, Paris, 1800, translated by A. A. Matson, I. E. Chillcott, Bristol, 1870.

————: *Deaf and Dumb; or the Orphan Protected*, five acts, historical drama about l'Epée, translated from French, D. Longworth at the Dramatic Repository, Shakespeare Gallery, New York, 1817.

————: *The Lost Heir; or the Abbé de l'Epée*, three acts, translated from German, Dick and Fitzgerald, New York.

Chantel, Lucien: *Le Silence*, three acts and five tableaux, Paris, 1926.

Curtis, H. Pelham: *None so Deaf as Those Who Won't Hear*, one act, Walter H. Baker, Boston, 1880.

Desboutins, André, et Rosenberg: *Le Sourd*, one act, Paris.

Dukes, Ashley: *The Dumb Wife of Cheapside*, two acts, Samuel French, New York, 1929.

Eastman, Gilbert: *Sign Me Alice*, Washington, D.C., Gallaudet College Press, 1974.

————: *Sign Me Alice II*, Washington, D.C., 1983.

————: *Laurent Clerc: A Profile*, video, Gallaudet College Television, Washington, D.C., 1962.

France, Anatole: *The Man Who Married a Dumb Wife*, two acts, translated by Curtis Hilden Page, Dodd, Mead, New York, 1926.

Gibson, William: *The Miracle Worker*, 1959, Tamarack Productions, 1960.

————: *Monday after the Miracle*, New York, 1981.

Giradoux, Jean: *The Madwoman of Chaillot*, adapted by Maurice Valency, Random House, New York, 1949.

Harris, Elmer Blaney: *Johnny Belinda*, three acts, adapted by Sorrel Carson and John Hanau, Samuel French, London, 1956.

Hlibock, Bruce: *Woman Talk*, New York, 1984.

Holcroft, Thomas: *Deaf and Dumb*, historical drama, London, 1794.

Ionesco, Eugene: *The Chairs*, translated by Donald M. Allen, Grove Press, 1958.

Kerr, Geoffrey: *Stone Deaf;* in William Joseph Farma (ed.), *Prose, Poetry and Drama*, first series, Harper, New York, 1930.

Kotzebue, August Friedrich von: *Deaf and Dumb; or The Orphan*, five acts, translated from German by Benjamin Thompson, Vernor and Good, London, 1902.

Leavitt, A. J., and H. W. Eagan: *Deaf as a Post*, New York, 187?.

Medoff, Mark: *Children of a Lesser God*, two acts, James T. White, Clifton, New Jersey, 1980.

————: *In the Hands of the Enemy*, Los Angeles, California, 1984.

Miles, Dorothy: *A Play of Our Own*, Hartford, Connecticut, 1973.

National Theatre of the Deaf: *My Third Eye*, video, Gallaudet College, 1973.

O'Neill, Eugene: *Warnings*, one act, 1913, in *Ten Lost Plays*, Random House, New York, 1964.

Oxley, Selwyn Amor Nathaniel: *St. John of Beverly*, 2d. ed., Pearson, Shaftesbury, 1932.

————: *The Deaf of other Days*, 12 episodes, Ferrier, London, 1928.

Pilon, Frederick: *The Deaf Lover*, two acts, London, 1780, Charles Wiley, New York, 1825.

Pitrois, Yvonne: *L'Abbé de l'Epée*, six tableaux and finale, an apotheosis, Rogan, 1923.

Poole, John: *Deaf as a Post*, one act, T. H. Lacy, London. 18??.

Scott, Aimee: *The Deaf Man*, Baker International Play Bureau, Boston, 1935.

Searing, Laura Catherine: *An Autobiographical Drama*, Harr Wagner Publishing Co., San Francisco, 1921.

FILM AND TELEVISION

1939	*The Story of Alexander Graham Bell* (MGM)
1954	"My Very Good Friend Albert" (series: *Medic*)
1955	*Johnny Belinda*
	Sound Off My Love
	"There's No Need To Shout" (series: *Robert Montgomery presents the Johnson's Wax Program*)
	Big Story
1956	"No. 5 Checked Out" (series: *Screen Directors Playhouse*)

"You Gotta Have Luck" (series: *Alfred Hitchcock Presents*)

The Listening Hand

1957 *The Miracle Worker*, by William Gibson, directed by Arthur Penn

1958 "Song Out of Silence" (series: *Frontiers of Faith*)

1963 "Rage of Silence" (series: *Dick Powell Playhouse*)

1964 "A Woods Full of Question Marks" (series: *Ben Casey*)

1968 *The Heart Is a Lonely Hunter*, based on a novel by Carson McCullers (MGM)

1971 "Hands of Love" (series: *The Man and the City*)

1973 "Wall of Silence" (series: *Medical Center*)

1975 "Silent Kill" (series: *Harry O*)

"Child of Silence" (series: *Marcus Welby, M.D.*)

"The Foundling" (series: *The Waltons*)

Good Times (series)

1976 "Shoes" (series: *Baretta*)

Mary Hartman, Mary Hartman (series)

1977 "The Sound of Sunlight" (series: *Westside Medical*)

"The Hardy Boys" (series: *The Hardy Boys/Nancy Drew Mysteries*)

1978 *Dummy*, screenplay by Earnest Tidyman, based on a book by Harvey O'Higgins

"Deaf Friend" (series: *James at Fifteen*)

The American Girls (series)

"Mom and Dad Can't Hear Me" (series: *ABC Afterschool Special*)

1979 "Sounds of Silence" (series: *The Love Boat*)

The Miracle Worker (remake of 1957 feature)

Lou Grant (series)

And Your Name Is Jonah

Silent Victory: The Kitty O'Neil Story

1980 "Silent Promises" (series: *Little House on the Prairie*)

Barney Miller (series episode)

Amy (Disney Studios)

1981 *Fantasy Island* (series episode)

Nurse

1982 *Bosom Buddies* (series episode)

Little House on the Prairie (series episode)

1983 *Johnny Belinda*

Deaf characters appear also in the children's television series *Rainbow's End* and *Sesame Street*.

Catherine Elmes-Kalbacher

LITERATURE, EDITORS AND JOURNALISTS IN

A number of deaf persons in the United States have had successful careers in the field of journalism as editors and publishers. The written word provides a communication link between deaf people and hearing people. Many deaf students learned both printing and journalism working on their school "Little Papers." *See* LITTLE PAPER FAMILY.

EDMUND BOOTH

Edmund Booth (1810–1905) was owner of the *Anamosa (Iowa) Eureka*, a newspaper that is still published today. He was one of the earliest settlers in Jones County, where the newspaper was located, and in 1856 he purchased an interest in the *Eureka*. He later became its sole owner and installed the first power-driven press in the area. His eldest son took over the publication on Booth's retirement. Booth was a graduate of the American School for the Deaf, and he chaired the organizational meeting of the National Association of the Deaf in Cincinnati, Ohio, in 1880. *See* AMERICAN SCHOOL FOR THE DEAF; BOOTH, EDMUND; NATIONAL ASSOCIATION OF THE DEAF.

LAURA SEARING

Laura Redden Searing (1840–1923) was a journalist and poet who was deafened at the age of 11. She began her newspaper career in 1859 as an assistant editor with the *Presbyterian and Our Union*, a religious newspaper in St. Louis, Missouri, following her graduation from the Missouri School for the Deaf. Women reporters were not popular in those days, which may account for the fact that many of Searing's writings appeared under the pen name of Howard Glyndon. While with the *Union* she began contributing articles and poems to the *St. Louis Republican*. This led to a job with the *Republican*, and at the outbreak of the Civil War the newspaper sent her to Washington, D.C., as a correspondent. In Washington, in 1862, Searing published her first book, *Notable Men in the House of Representatives*, a collection of biographies of famous leaders that she had met and interviewed. Following the war, Searing traveled to Europe, where she continued to write for the *Republican* and for two other newspapers, the *New York Sun* and the *New York Times*. In 1868 she joined the staff of the *New York Evening Mail*. Her writings appeared in many other publications and she authored five books. *See* SEARING, LAURA.

WELLS L. HILL

Wells L. Hill (1850–1929) was the influential editor and publisher of the *Athol (Massachusetts) Transcript* and one of the most successful deaf newspaper publishers. Deafened at the age of 12, he was a graduate of the American School for the Deaf and Gallaudet College. As a college student he was the Washington, D.C., correspondent for two Massachusetts newspapers, the *Transcript* and the *Worcester West Chronicle*. Following graduation from college, he purchased a share in the *Transcript*, eventually became the owner, and turned it into an outstanding newspaper. Many of Hill's editorials were reprinted in other newspapers. The

Transcript was given credit for Athol's steady growth, and an account of Hill's life appears in the history of Athol written by L. B. Carwell. *See* GALLAUDET COLLEGE.

WILLIAM W. BEADELL

William W. Beadell (1865–1931) is recognized as the inventor of the classified ad page in newspapers. For 31 years he was editor and publisher of the *Arlington* (New Jersey) *Observer*. His newspaper career began when he and a friend learned to handset type and run the presses in his friend's father's newspaper printing plant. Beadell eventually rose to city editor of the newspaper.

At the age of 11, Beadell was deafened by meningitis. He later enrolled at Gallaudet College, and on his graduation his father presented him with the ownership of the newspaper at Yellow Creek, Illinois. One of his first moves as the new editor was to persuade the citizens of Yellow Creek to change the name of the town to Pearl City. Beadell later sold the *Pearl City News* and tried teaching at the Minnesota School for the Deaf. After a year, he returned to the newspaper field as managing editor of the *Middlebury* (Vermont) *Register*.

In 1900 Beadell acquired the *Arlington Observer* and remained with that newspaper until his death, missing only two publication days during his 31-year span. As an editor, Beadell influenced the growth of Arlington and the neighboring community of Kearney, and was held in high esteem by business associates and neighbors. As a writer, he was quoted often and many of his articles were reprinted in other publications.

It was at the *Observer* that Beadell invented the classified ad section. He also initiated the method of distributing newspapers by encouraging newsboys to become entrepreneurs by establishing their own newspaper routes.

OWEN G. CARRELL

After teaching at schools for deaf students in Texas, Oklahoma, and Kansas, Owen G. Carrell (1878–1960) entered the newspaper field in North Carolina in 1923 when he purchased an interest in the *Duplin Record*. He published the *Pender Chronicle* for 17 years, and at one time was printing three other newspapers in his plant. In 1935 he started the *Wilmington Post* and made the daily newspaper a going concern in a city that already had two other dailies.

OTHERS

The nineteenth century produced many other, lesser known deaf editors and journalists. Among them were the following.

James G. George Born in 1825, George was the editor and publisher of the *Richmond* (Kentucky) *Messenger*. He acquired the newspaper during the Civil War, and his outspoken editorials in support of the North got him in trouble with Southern sympathizers, who drove him out of business. He started the printing trade at the Kentucky School for the Deaf, where he began publishing the *Kentucky Deaf-Mute* in 1874.

Joseph Mount Mount wrote extensively for many publications under a variety of pseudonyms. In the early 1860s he started a newspaper in Kansas called the *Home Circle*. It was not successful, and in 1864 he purchased the *City Observer* in Baldwin (where the Kansas School for the Deaf originated). He abandoned the newspaper when he was appointed superintendent of the Kansas School. He was later associated with two other newspapers, the *Prairie Banner* in Missouri and the *Sunny Clime* in Texas.

William W. Chamberlain Chamberlain (1832–1895) was well known in the deaf community. He started the *Gallaudet Guide and Deaf-Mutes' Companion*, the first publication exclusively for the deaf community, and he edited the weekly *Marblehead* (Massachusetts) *Messenger* and the *Boston Owl*. He also taught at the Central New York School for the Deaf, where he started the printing trade and the school's publication, the *Register*.

Michael J. Smith and Alfred J. Lamoreaux Smith and Lamoreaux first worked together, starting the *Merry World* in Pueblo, Colorado, in 1887. It became a success in a short time. After a year, Lamoreaux sold his interest in the *World* and moved to La Junta, Colorado, where he started the *Derrick* and where he was correspondent for United Press International. He later sold the *Derrick* and was a foreman of the Denver *Daily News*, and then of the *Pueblo Evening Star*. After several years Smith left the *World* and wrote for the *Globeville News*, the *Denver Dispatch*, and the *East End Echo*.

F. H. Flint Flint was connected with four Michigan newspapers. He started a newspaper in Hickory Corners, Michigan, and also started the *Barry County Democrat*. In addition, he published the *Sunfield News* and was part owner of the *Augusta Times*.

Joe G. Bradley With his brother, Bradley founded the *Sulphur Rock Wheel* in Arkansas. They later published the *Batesville* (Arkansas) *Journal*. Bradley also taught printing at the Mississippi School for the Deaf.

John H. Howlett Howlett was city editor of the *Chicago Sunday Hero*, a newspaper for the black community. He later started the *Afro-American World* (later renamed the *Topic*), a publication for members of the black deaf community in Minnesota. He was editor of the weekly *Atchison* (Kansas)

Blade, the *Protest* in Texas, and the *Oskaloosa* (Kansas) *Gazette*.

Bibliography

Gannon, Jack R.: *Deaf Heritage: A Narrative History of Deaf America*, National Association of the Deaf, Silver Spring, Maryland, 1981.

Braddock, Guilbert C.: *Notable Deaf Persons*, edited by Florence Crammatte, Gallaudet College Alumni Association, Washington, D.C., 1975.

Panara, Robert, and John Panara: *Great Deaf Americans*, T. J. Publishers, Silver Spring, Maryland, 1983.

Jack R. Gannon

LITERATURE, FICTIONAL CHARACTERS IN

Deaf characters in literature are of two kinds: those conceived by hearing writers and those by deaf writers. The division is more than merely formal, it is illustrative of a division in attitudes toward deaf people. With rare exceptions, hearing writers combine empathy for deaf characters with a striking display of misconceptions and ignorance about them—for example, when they exaggerate the lip-reading and speech abilities of their deaf characters. Despite their misconceptions, however, great hearing writers such as Ivan Turgenev, Guy de Maupassant, and Alfred de Musset became sufficiently overwhelmed by the deaf characters they created to portray them with fairness and a measure of sympathetic understanding. Deaf writers, on the other hand, are personally more involved in aspects of the deaf experience. Their accounts are usually written in the first-person mode, because to them the struggle for dignity and assertion of the self in a hearing environment is an overriding and passionately absorbing concern.

CHARACTERS CONCEIVED BY HEARING WRITERS

The faithful mute servant (often with his tongue cut out), as in Lew Wallace's *A Prince of India* or in Jean Cocteau's *The Eagle with Two Heads*, has been a stock character in Western literature. But as early as the eighteenth century writers tried to portray somewhat more individualized deaf characters. Of these writers, the first was Daniel Defoe, best known for *Robinson Crusoe*. Defoe's interest in the subject was awakened by his father-in-law, Henry Baker, a teacher of deaf children.

Defoe's *The History of the Life and Adventures of Mr. Duncan Campbell* (1720) is a fictionalized autobiography of a well-born deaf Scotsman who gained fame and notoriety in London as a quack doctor and raffish philanderer. Written before Defoe had yet polished and refined his writing skills, this book contains vast stretches of sanctimonious prose interspersed with occasional witty narration,

as in the Susanne Johnson episode in which a hysterical girl is brought in a paralytic state to Duncan's house. Duncan has her carried upstairs to his bedroom and remains alone with her for "above half an hour," whereupon she reappears completely cured. Yet it is more than just a piquant anecdote when, on close reading, it is noticed that the quack doctor, instead of speaking, signifies to the company that the girl is in dreadful condition and writes them that they should be in good heart. In short, he uses the same means of communication, but by signing and writing, as the average deaf person does today—a circumstance that adds realism to the story.

Nineteenth Century Nearly a century was to pass before another deaf character was to appear in literature. Alfred de Musset's tale "Pierre et Camille" contains a deaf heroine, the lovely Camille des Arcis, whose deafness ruins the happiness of her parents, causing her own father to shun her and plunge into depression because "Everywhere, even in Paris, in the most advanced civilization, deaf-mutes were looked upon as a kind of beings separate from the rest of humanity, stamped with the seal of the wrath of Providence." There is hardly any attempt at character delineation: Camille is as passive as she is beautiful and the story focuses more on the trials and tribulations of the parents of a deaf child than on the deaf girl herself. Camille, looked upon as a freak by almost everyone, is left to grow up without even knowing how to read and write. Ultimately, there is a happy ending, after Camille meets and marries a young deaf man, the Marquis de Maubray, and her father finally accepts her. On coming to see Camille's child, des Arcis at first recoils, dreading that it might be "Another mute!" and becomes reconciled only after he hears the child speak. Illustrative of the self-concept that society had forced on Camille is the fact that her supreme moment of happiness comes when her child turns out to be hearing, thus removing the "curse" which God, for reasons unknown, had supposedly placed on her father, and therefore prompting him to pardon her. To a deaf reader the ending is ironic, for it is the father who should beg his daughter's pardon for having rejected and abandoned her.

Another similar deaf character is Sophy, a typical depersonalized Victorian heroine in Charles Dickens's "Doctor Marigold." Like Camille, she is a "prop," not a person in her own right but a means of making other happy. Also like Camille, Sophy's ultimate deed is in giving birth to a hearing child. But despite her one-dimensionality, Sophy is a little more actively involved in life than Camille. Before her marriage, Sophy had given meaning to the life of her adopted father, a traveling tinker, and made him feel less lonely.

In the same league belongs Ambrose Bierce's

"Chickamauga," a short story of a little boy who watches a Civil War battle and, because he is deaf, does not understand what is happening. The boy's deafness is thus used to emphasize the brutality and grotesqueness of war, of men killing each other. Bierce is not interested in the deaf character per se. As unconcerned as Bierce seems about deafness itself, he unwittingly illustrates how deaf persons are forced to be "phantoms of beings," unaware of the life going on around them. A passage from "Pierre et Camille' illustrates essentially the same idea: " 'We speak and you do not,' everyone [at the opera] seemed to be saying. 'We listen, we laugh, we sing, we love, we enjoy everything; you alone enjoy nothing, you alone hear nothing, you alone are but a statue here, the phantom of a being who looks on life from a distance.' "

In *Mumu*, a novella by Turgenev, the protagonist is the deaf serf Gerassim, who has a natural and unfailing dignity. He stoically bears the blows that his capricious and ignorant mistress deals him when she orders Tatyana, the woman he loves, to be betrothed to a hearing drunkard. Gerassim understands perfectly what is happening, but in spite of his enormous physical strength he obeys the will of his mistress. When afterward he fixes his affection on a dog, Mumu, he is forced to give the animal up as well. Ultimately, unlike Camille and Sophy, he rebels by escaping to his native village and withdrawing into a misanthropic existence.

In character development, *Mumu* is markedly superior to all other literature containing deaf fictional characters. The various touches added by Turgenev result in the composite portrait of Gerassim as a man in whom extreme delicacy of feeling is combined with self-esteem and unselfishness. This is brought out skillfully by the Russian writer in his depiction of the relationship between Gerassim and Tatyana. The girl is terrified of the gigantic mute serf and readily persuaded by the other servants to fake drunkenness so as to get rid of Gerassim, since his aversion to drunks is well known. But Gerassim is immediately aware that she is playacting and personally brings her to the drunkard to whom she is to be betrothed. A year passes and the drunkard's condition becomes so hopeless that Gerassim's mistress commands the drunkard and Tatyana to return to their native village. As the two depart, Gerassim gives Tatyana a handkerchief as a farewell present, and she—who had formerly been so frightened of the inarticulate giant—kisses him farewell. He has won her respect and affection, but it is too late. When Gerassim is later commanded to give up his pet dog, Mumu, because it makes too much noise, he thumps his breast to indicate that he himself will be the executioner. Until the last, he remains the master of his fate.

Turgenev has thus altered the image of a deaf character from that of a brutish animal or a passive, docile being to that of a person with dignity, stature, and a firm identity. As William Faulkner was to restate later in the person of Lucas Beauchamp in *Intruder in the Dust*, Turgenev showed that even an uneducated serf can rise above his circumstances solely by strength of character, that dignity and nobility of feeling are something innate.

A different deaf character is portrayed by Guy de Maupassant in his short story "The Deafmute." Gargan, a deaf shepard, is married to a girl nicknamed "Drops" for her propensity to have intercourse with anyone who offers her a glass of alcohol. This is unknown to Gargan, who is the butt of jokes by the community. When one day he discovers "Drops" in the hay with a peasant, he murders her. His violent defense of his conjugal honor earns him, finally, the respect and acceptance of the hearing community, and he is acquitted by the judge after he shows that he understands the meaning of marriage and honor, that is, he demonstrates that he is a human being and not a brute just because he is deaf.

"The Deafmute" is a curiously modern story that has a bearing on the present situation of deaf people. These "gamest of men," as Harry Best once termed them, are now becoming vocal in the defense of their rights, realizing that only thus can they win respect and recognition from the larger hearing society.

Another idea that surfaces in literature about deaf people is that of strangeness, grotesqueness. In *The Hunchback of Notre Dame*, Victor Hugo makes the protagonist not only hunchbacked but also deaf to stress his oddity and unnaturalness. Bierce's "Chickamauga," which shows the strangeness and brutality of war seen through the eyes of the little deaf boy, also belongs in this category. The boy rides horseback over wounded soldiers until he comes home and sees his home burned and his parents dead—and only then does the horror sink in and he becomes traumatized. Approximately a century later, Harry Crews was to revert to the grostesqueness motif in *The Gypsy's Curse*, whose main character is a deaf dwarf.

Twentieth Century Another addition to the list of deaf characters is in Mary Montague's "Why It Was W-on-the-Eyes," a story of a little boy, Webster, living in a school for deaf children. The plot centers on the question of why Webster's name sign is "W-on-the-Eyes." Sweet-tempered little Webster perplexes his teachers by constantly getting into fights with other boys when they tease blind boys or ridicule him for wearing ill-fitting shirts sewn by his mother. The mystery is resolved when the teachers learn that Webster's mother is blind.

"Why It Was W-on-the-Eyes" is outstanding for the artful simplicity of its style and for the profound knowledge of life in a residential school for deaf students described by Montague, who in real life was the wife of the superintendent of the West Virginia School for the Deaf. It remains a classic. The fact that this story focuses on the meaning of a single sign illustrates how often the signs of deaf people have significant and revealing roots.

On the whole however, twentieth-century deaf fictional characters are completely different from their counterparts found in the literature of the nineteenth century. In the twentieth century a curious emphasis is placed on both the mystique and the ordinary qualities of deaf characters. The contrast between two well-known novels about deaf people, *In This Sign* by Joanne Greenberg and *The Heart Is a Lonely Hunter* by Carson McCullers, could not be greater.

Abel and Janice of *In This Sign* lead lives of unrelieved despair. Outcasts in a hearing society in which they function only imperfectly, owing to their troubles with the English language, they see the happiness of their married life blighted from the outset when Abel is swindled by a car salesman into signing a contract that practically makes him a slave for life to the finance company. Their life is a chronic struggle against poverty and the prejudices of the hearing world.

The contrast between this deaf couple and John Singer of *The Heart Is a Lonely Hunter* is great. In the figure of Singer, McCullers has created a deaf mythic hero patterned on Christ. He has some lip-reading skill and sometimes resorts to a pad and pencil, but the rapport he attains with the hearing community is based on much more than this limited mode of communication. There is an extraordinary air about him that compels the attention of hearing people and makes them look up to him as if to their savior. Of course, his charisma works, not because he sits and stares with his magnetic gaze at others, but because of his many little acts of kindness and understanding that make him loved and admired: He lights the cigarette of a black man—an unthinkable act in the American South in the early 1940s; he contributes to a Christmas party for poor black children; he helps in the search for a runaway boy, and when the boy is found and has an attack of hysteria, he quiets him down simply by his commanding presence. He cannot walk down the street without people exchanging rumors about "that man of mystery." The other major characters in the story orbit about him like satellites and see in him the means of solving their personal problems. Yet this Christ-like figure ultimately shoots himself through the heart—an act that has a double meaning. His death represents a crucifixion motif, but it is also as if the author wanted to demonstrate the hero's humanity, for Singer is heartbroken because the only being to whom he is truly attached emotionally, a mentally retarded deaf man, dies in a state hospital.

It is no accident that *The Heart Is a Lonely Hunter* and *In This Sign*, probably the two most important novels about deaf people to be written in this century, offer such diametrically opposed views of the deaf experience. They mirror the split in public awareness of deaf persons. To hearing people deaf persons are different and can never be their equal. This leaves two basic alternatives as to how deaf individuals are to be viewed: either as "phantoms of being," people who are socially and intellectually inferior to those who hear and who somehow are deprived of the ability to lead complete lives, or as extraordinary individuals possessing some enigmatic "sixth sense" and who seem to know something more than most mortals.

The deaf mystique motif is recaptured in Prudence Andrew's *Ordeal by Silence*, a novel whose main character, Philip Ganter, is an illiterate deaf-mute. His story is told posthumously from the standpoint of 10 people who testify before a cardinal of the church. The setting is thirteenth-century England, shortly after the murder of Thomas à Becket, and the cardinal is to determine whether the deaf-mute is worthy of canonization following the miracles for which eyewitnesses vouch. It appears that, despite the brutish and animallike circumstances of his life, this deaf-mute had special healing powers and a uniquely calming effect on others, including King Henry II.

Similarly, in *The Kid* by John Seelye, a black deaf character living in a small western town possesses unusual strength and occult powers.

Somewhat more conventional are novels such as Margaret Kennedy's *Not in the Calendar*, which deals with the life stories of two English girls, the deaf Wyn Harper and her childhood friend the hearing Caroline Knevett. Wyn becomes a famous artist while Caroline decides to dedicate her life to educating deaf children. In the romance genre is *And Now Tomorrow* by Rachel Field, whose heroine Emily Blair is jilted by her fiancé after she becomes deafened. She meets a young doctor, Vance, who develops a special technique for restoring hearing to deaf people. He cures Emily and they fall in love. Dr. Vance's method entails the repair of the auditory nerve and is totally unrealistic. This "miracle cure" motif is sometimes encountered in works by hearing authors. Also in this category is Florence Riddell's *Silent World*, whose main character regains his hearing following a car accident and abandons his deaf wife and falls in love with a hearing woman.

The wide variety of genres in which deaf characters figure is illustrated by Susan Yankowitz's stream-of-consciousness novel *Silent Witness*, whose deaf protagonist, Anna, leads a life of quiet desperation in a world that is circumscribed mainly by the walls of her own room.

A play that had been popular in the 1940s and was subsequently filmed is *Johnny Belinda* by Elmer Harris. it deals with the plight of an innocent deaf girl who is raped by a ruffian and then befriended by a physician who learns the manual alphabet in order to communicate with her. In the late 1970s and early 1980s two other highly popular plays, *And Your Name Is Jonah* by Michael Bortman (televised) and *Children of a Lesser God* by Mark Medoff, deal more realistically with their deaf protagonists. *See* LITERATURE, DRAMATIC CHARACTERS IN.

A separate category is formed by novels whose authors, while hearing, have a deep and special understanding of the problems of the deaf community. Prominent in this category are Carolyn Norris (*Islands of Silence; Signs Unseen, Sounds Unheard*) and Jack Livingston (*Die Again, Macready*), who specialize in the genres of romance and the murder mystery, respectively. Norris' Neo-Gothic novel *Island of Silence* focuses on a deaf protagonist who is rescued from his isolation and restored to the world by the love of his hearing tutor, while Livingston's hard-bitten deaf detective, Joe Binney, performs creditably and succeeds in winning the respect of all with whom he comes in contact.

CHARACTERS CONCEIVED BY DEAF WRITERS

The richness and variety of deaf characters in the works of hearing writers is not paralleled in the works of their deaf counterparts. Deaf writers such as John Kitto and Albert Ballin have created powerful and searing works, but their autobiographical nature precludes them from the scope of this article. Deaf novelists and short-story writers are rare, as opposed to deaf autobiographers, and with the exception of Pauline Leader, published writers such as Rachel Philbrick, Howard Terry, Eugene Relgis, and Bud Long deal mostly with peripheral aspects of the deaf experience. *See* KITTO, JOHN.

Rachel Philbrick was the first known deaf novelist, her first book, *Warp and Woof*, having been published before 1880 and her second, *Desire Wentworth, a Romance of Provincial Times*, in 1881. Unfortunately, her prose is so turgid as to be almost totally undistinguished.

She was followed by Howard Terry, a prolific novelist who wrote in the fashion of his day adventure stories and romances that are similar to pulp fiction. Although deaf himself, he does not display in his works understanding of deaf psychology and mentality. Typically, in Terry's *A Voice from the Silence* the deaf protagonist Jack Harlow, owing to his ability to lipread, discovers the murderer of his girl friend's father. *See* TERRY, HOWARD L.

Pauline Leader, on the other hand, is a writer who was born ahead of her time. The protagonist of her *And No Birds Sing* is a sensitive and intelligent Jewish deaf girl, a voracious reader, who rebels against her environment. At home her deafness makes others consider her uneducable and to be let out only under supervision. Escaping her constricting family environment, she goes to New York dreaming of a bright new future, but there too she meets with loneliness, isolation, and lack of understanding. At the novel's end, beaten by life, she is reduced to the status of a bagwoman.

Also writing in the 1930s, the Frenchman Eugene Relgis, a disciple of Romain Rolland, depicts in *Muted Voices* the blows that life deals to his deaf hero, Myron, at home where no one understands or can help him and at school where he is derided by the teachers and mocked and persecuted by the hearing boys. Relgis writes in a poetic tenor and ends his novel on an upbeat note when Myron meets the woman of his dreams and finds happiness. What is chiefly remarkable about this novel is its poetic imagery and mood of introspection.

A more recent deaf short-story writer is Bud Long, whose novelettes featuring "Comrade Dolgov of the KGB" ("The Case of the Missing Cincinnatian," "The Case of the Lombard Street Murder," "The Case of the Los Angeles Chameleon"), all written in the 1970s, include as a subprotagonist a deaf man, Karl Trevinko, Dolgov's American assistant. Although written in a humorous style, they reflect the author's bitterness about the supposedly low status of deaf persons in the United States.

Four deaf playwrights who focus on deaf characters are Eugene Bergman, Bernard Bragg, Gilbert Eastman, and Dorothy Miles. Bergman and Bragg collaborated on a play about the deaf world, *Tales from a Clubroom*, with a cast of 20 characters and the setting of a deaf club. In addition, Bergman independently wrote a play on the oralist theme, *Fish Nor Fowl*, and Bragg, a comedy, *That Makes Two of Us*, about the burgeoning of love between a deaf signer and an oralist. Eastman's *Sign Me Alice* is an adaptation of G. B. Shaw's *Pygmalion*, with the heroine learning proper sign language. Miles's *A Play of Our Own* is a romantic comedy in a deaf setting. *See* BRAGG, BERNARD.

Bibliography

Andrew, Prudence: *Ordeal by Silence: A Story of Medieval Times*, Putnam, New York, 1961.

Batson, Trent, and Eugene Bergman: *The Deaf Experience: An Anthology of Literature by and about the Deaf*, Merriam-Eddy Co., South Waterford, Maine, 1976.

Bergman, Eugene, and Bernard Bragg: *Tales from a Clubroom*, Gallaudet College Press, Washington, D.C., 1982.

Field, Rachel: *And Now Tomorrow*, Macmillan, New York, 1955.

Greenberg, Joanne: *In This Sign*, Holt, Rinehart and Winston, New York, 1970.

Harris, Elmer: *Johnny Belinda*, Samuel French Publishers, London and New York, 1939.

Kennedy, Margaret: *Not in the Calendar*, Macmillan, New York, 1964.

Leader, Pauline: *And No Birds Sing*, Vanguard Press, New York, 1931.

Livingston, Jack: *A Piece of Silence: A Murder Mystery*, St. Martin's Press, New York, 1982.

McCullers, Carson: *The Heart Is a Lonely Hunter*, Bantam, New York, 1970.

Maupassant, Guy de: "The Deaf Mute," in *Short Stories of the Tragedy and Comedy of Life*, M. Walter Dunne, New York and London, 1903.

Norris, Carolyn: *Island of Silence*, Alinda Press, Eureka, California, 1978.

Relgis, Eugene: *Muted Voices*, Oriole Press, Berkley Heights, New Jersey, 1938.

Riddell, Florence: *Silent World*, Lippincott, Philadelphia, Pennsylvania, 1914.

Seelye, John: *The Kid*, Viking Press, New York, 1972.

Terry, Howard Leslie: *A Voice from the Silence: A Story of the Ozarks*, Palisades Press, Santa Monica, California, 1914.

Turgenev, Ivan: "Mumu," in *The Novels and Stories of Ivan Turgenieff*, vol. 9, Chas. Scribner's Sons, New York, 1904.

Wallace, Lew: *The Prince of India; or, Why Constantinople Fell*, Harper and Brothers, New York, 1893.

Eugene Bergman

LITERATURE, WRITERS IN

Deaf individuals have used all the various literary forms to express themselves, most often writing about the experience of deafness. This entry discusses these individuals and their work. It is arranged by genre: poetry, history and social criticism, scholarly studies, biography, personal essays, autobiography, fiction, anthologies, and drama. Each of these sections is subdivided according to the work of particular individuals or periods.

Poetry

It is generally agreed that poetry is the oldest literary genre and the first to be given written expression. Almost the same can be said of the literary achievement of deaf people, as the first writers who produced works of genuine merit were the French poets Pierre de Ronsard and Joachim du Bellay.

RENAISSANCE

If Italy was the cradle of the sonnet form during the Renaissance, it was France that gave birth to the first deaf poet to carry on this tradition and influence future sonneteers. This was Pierre de Ronsard (1524–1585), who was aptly named "The Prince of Poets" by his literary peers and admirers, among them the three kings of France whom he served and their enemy royalties, Mary Queen of Scots and Queen Elizabeth I of England. *See* RONSARD, PIERRE DE.

It first appeared that Ronsard was destined for a life of political action because of his birth and breeding, his good looks, and his personality. A serious illness at the age of 16, however, caused severe deafness for several years and then left him hard-of-hearing for the rest of his life. It forced him to discontinue a diplomatic career at court and made him turn to the study of classical literature. In 1544, at age 20, he went to Paris where he established a literary circle (later called the Pléiade) whose purpose was to improve French poetry by imitating Greek, Latin, and Italian verse forms and by introducing new words and poetic structures, such as the Petrarchan sonnet.

As the leader of this movement, Ronsard became a lyric poet whose first collection of *Odes* (totaling 94; 1550) were modeled after Pindar and Horace of classical Greece and Rome. In 1522 he published his second major work, a collection of 181 sonnets. Entitled *Amours (Loves)* these were "flesh and blood" declarations of passion addressed to his various mistresses, both real and fancied.

Other important works by Ronsard were his *Hymns* (1555) in praise of his patrons, and numerous odes for special church and state occasions. In 1554 Henry II made him official court poet, an office that he kept under two succeeding kings, Frances II and Charles IX. During these years, Ronsard reached the peak of his fame. His poetic style and spirit not only influenced his own countrymen but also the great lyric poets of Elizabethan England and the later Cavalier Poets. His collected works (1578) included the *Sonnets to Helene*, which reveal a more serene and contemplative attitude to life and nature as well as a tone of melancholy. This influence extended to such nineteenth-century poets as William Butler Yeats.

Such was Ronsard's genius and influence. He was an imitator of the classics, and innovator who brought a new spirit and vocabulary to French poetry, and a model for future poets.

He was so absorbed with life and nature, with the real and fancied characters of his creative interests, that his own deafness never found expression in his poetry. In all his published works, there is no known record of any note of bitterness or regret about his handicap, even any mention of it. This fact is noted by many biographers as well as by Ruth E. Bender in *The Conquest of Deafness*

(1960), who also states that the opposite was true of Ronsard's contemporary Joachim du Bellay. Fortunately, du Bellay met Ronsard and derived both comfort and inspiration from him.

Joachim du Bellay (1522–1560) was born to a noble family, one of his uncles being the powerful Cardinal du Bellay. In his late teens he developed an ear infection which tormented him throughout life and caused a progressive hearing impairment. He began the study of law, but after meeting Ronsard, changed his career interest. He accompanied Ronsard to Paris, where he began the serious study of the classics and soon started writing poetry. *See* DU BELLAY, JOACHIM.

Du Bellay wrote many sonnets following the Italian models of Petrarch in which the experience of love is expressed in alternating moods of ardor and melancholy. Titled *L'Olive* (1549), this collection of 115 poems was the first sonnet sequence in French and expressed (as Petrarch did for "Laura") du Bellay's love for "Olive," who was his muse and ideal woman.

When the avant garde literary group known as the Pléiade was formed, du Bellay wrote the famous manifesto or declaration of literary independence, *La Defence et Illustration de la Langue Française* (1549). This *Defense and Illustration of the French Language* was analogous to Dante's *De Vulgari Eloquentia* (1310), which championed the use of the native Italian vernacular over the formal and medieval Latin still in use in Italian letters. Similarly, du Bellay defended the natural beauty and nobility of the French language, believing it potentially equal to the classic tongues. His work served to inject a new spirit of pride and freshness into French poetry and also inspired similar essays by later Romantic poets, such as William Wordsworth's "Preface" to *The Lyrical Ballads* (1798) and Percy Bysshe Shelley's *Defense of Poetry* (1821). In 1533 du Bellay went to Rome, where he spent four miserable years in the service of his uncle Cardinal du Bellay. During this period, he not only lost his hearing but also experienced profound loneliness and homesickness for his native France. These themes and du Bellay's dislike of Rome are expressed in two of his works, *Antiquités de Rome* and *Les Regrets* (both 1558), which contained some of his finest poetry. They also reveal how he had broken away from the influence of Petrarch so as to practice the "new poetry" of France, as described in his *Defense and Illustration of the French Language*.

So great was the achievement of these two luminaries of the Renaissance, no representative deaf poet thereafter could be said to equal the stature of Ronsard and du Bellay with respect to a classical training in belles lettres and to universal recognition of talent. Obviously, there were some sociohistorical influences responsible for this cultural disparity. One explanation could be the disappearance of patrons in later times, which made it difficult for the aspiring poet to study, practice, and create art for art's sake.

NINETEENTH CENTURY

It was not until the nineteenth century that "the silent lyre" was reawakened to the touch of a deaf poet. This happened in the United States in 1827 with the publication of *The Legend of the Rock, and Other Poems* by James Nack. It proved to be more than just the first book written by a deaf American: it was a literary first. One of the leading reviews was most lavish in praise of Nack, calling him "an intellectual wonder" and someone who showed more promise as a teenage poet than the similar efforts of Chatterton and Byron.

James Nack   James Nack (1809–1879) became totally deaf at age eight and was plagued with ill health most of his life. In spite of such handicaps, however, Nack published three other volumes of poetry: *Earl Ruppert, and Other Poems* (1839); *The Immortal, a Dramatic Romance* (1850); and *The Romance of the Ring, and Other Poems* (1859). The aging and harassed poet apparently had lost the fire and lyrical sublimity of his youth, for only passing mention is given to his later work in the literary reviews of that time. Nack could not support himself with his writings, so he also did creditable work at various times as a legal clerk, teacher of deaf people, and translator of French, German, and Dutch writings. *See* NACK, JAMES.

Not long after Nack's first published work, two other deaf poets had their work published. John R. Burnet and John Carlin, like Nack, were practically self-educated, having both been born before the first schools for deaf pupils were established in the United States.

John Burnet   John Burnet (1808–1864) lost his hearing at age eight from brain fever. Growing up on a farm in New Jersey, he was educated by an older sister and then continued learning on his own. In 1833, Burnet helped his uncle edit *The People's Friend*, a Philadelphia newspaper. Two years later, he published a book, *Tales of the Deaf and Dumb, with Miscellaneous Poems*. This work earned Burnet a significant sum of money, in addition to a budding reputation. Thereafter, he was quite productive as a writer, contributing articles and poems to various publications, including the *North American Review*, the *Biblical Repository*, and the *Newark Daily Advertiser*.

His interest in daily life and social conditions often served as thematic material for his poems. One poem reflects on the National Census of 1830, which reported that 6000 deaf people were living in America but less than 500 were in the six schools for deaf people.

> "Six thousand souls—unknowing of a God,
> Even in Christianity's most blest abode!
> Six thousand hearts—by undeserved doom,
> Lock'd up to brood in solitary gloom!"

Another poem, "The Battle of Trenton," commemorates the surprise attack of the American revolutionaries against the British on Christmas Eve in 1776, and literally paints the scene in words of Washington crossing the Delaware River.

John Carlin   John Carlin (1813–1891) was a child prodigy who graduated from the Pennsylvania Institution for the Deaf at age 12. He gained fame as a portrait painter, but also wrote a considerable number of poems. Although never published in book form, these were often widely printed in the newspapers during the years 1850–1884, and at one time drew praise from William Cullen Bryant, the famed poet and editor of the *New York Evening Post*. Readers marveled that Carlin had been born deaf, and, as such, was the first and only deaf-mute poet the world had ever known. *See* CARLIN, JOHN.

Among other deaf poets were two British writers, John Kitto and William Henry Simpson, both of whom gained some measure of distinction as poets even though they remained dubious of their accomplishment.

John Kitto   John Kitto (1804–1854) became totally deaf at age 12 and went on to become one of the highest-ranking deaf authors and a Biblical scholar of international reputation. One of his many books, *Lost Senses* (1848), is an interesting autobiography which contains 300 lines of poetry and an "apology" in which he downgrades the quality of his work in comparison with that of hearing poets. Edward Miner Gallaudet maintained, however, that Kitto's poems actually "indicate that he might have gained distinction as a writer of verse had he devoted himself to poetry with half the interest he showed in his prose works." *See* GALLAUDET, EDWARD MINER; KITTO, JOHN.

William H. Simpson   Gallaudet pointed out the same tone of doubt and self-effacement in the "Introduction" to a volume of poems, *Day-Dreams of the Deaf*, by William Henry Simpson. Simpson, who was postlingually deaf, became an instructor in the London Institution for the Deaf from where he had also graduated. In his introduction, Simpson is in full agreement with John Kitto's sentiments and refers to the difficulties that stand in the way of deaf poets. He goes on to disclaim any pretense of success. This was far from the truth, as readers of his poems discovered. One of his poems, "Lines on Reading the Narrative of Frederick Douglas, an Escaped American Slave," was both popular and widely quoted in the newspapers of that time, concluding with the stirring stanza:

> "Lift up, lift up thy voice and win
>   Many to freedom's cause;
> Rest not till all thy kith and kin
>   Live under equal laws;
> Blot from thy land one cursed sin,
>   And win the world's applause!"

Laura Redden Searing   Simpson's interest in the social issues of the time was shared by an American writer during and after the Civil War. Writing under the name of "Howard Glyndon," Laura Redden Searing was a war correspondent who sent the latest dispatches from Washington, D.C., to the *St. Louis Republican* newspaper. Readers did not know, however, that "Howard Glyndon" was actually a deaf woman—the first to succeed in journalism and poetry. *See* SEARING, LAURA.

Laura Redden Searing (1840–1923) became totally deaf at age 10 and later graduated from the Missouri School for the Deaf. During the Civil War she wrote many poems expressing her reaction to war. Many of her poems were widely quoted in newspapers and magazines. Her "Belle Missouri" became the first song for the Union soldiers from Missouri. Later her poems were published under the title *Idylls of Battle and Poems of the Rebellion* (1865). After the war, Searing continued contributing poems to newspapers and magazines in New York, such as *Galaxy, Harpers, Atlantic Monthly, Putnam's,* and the *New York Evening Mail,* for which she worked as a feature columnist. In 1874 she published a second volume of poems, *Sounds from Secret Chambers,* and in 1921 all her poems were reprinted in a complete edition. Her achievement as a poet and journalist was recognized by her peers in the literary world. She was included in the *Dictionary of American Biography* (1928), and some of her poems were featured in several anthologies of American poetry edited by such popular poets as John Greenleaf Whittier and William Cullen Bryant.

Other Women   Other deaf women who were productive as poets during the nineteenth century were Angeline Fuller Fischer, Mary Toles Peet, and Alice C. Jennings. Angeline Fuller Fischer, who was also partially paralyzed and plagued with poor eyesight since age 13, went on to become the leading feminist of the deaf world. As a columnist for various publications of the deaf community, she provided encouragement and advice to deaf women on literary, cultural, and religious matters of interest. She also campaigned for the equal rights of deaf women. Fischer wanted women to be able to participate in the social activities of the newly established (1880) National Association of the Deaf. She also wanted a separate college for deaf women, since Gallaudet College admitted only males until it became coeducational in 1887. In 1883 Fischer published a book, *The Venture*, containing over 230 pages of verse, which was highly acclaimed by readers and established poets such as Ella Wheeler Wilcox, Oliver Wendell Holmes, and Whittier. Some well-known anthologies included her work, among them *Women in Sacred Song*, which contained 21 of her poems, and *Poets of America*. *See* GALLAUDET COLLEGE; NATIONAL ASSOCIATION OF THE DEAF.

Although not as prolific as Fischer, Mary Toles Peet was regarded as an accomplished poet by both deaf and hearing admirers. Deaf since age 13, she became the wife of Isaac Lewis Peet, headmaster of the New York School for the Deaf, from which she had graduated. She raised a family and was a hostess and teacher at the school. She might be likened to Emily Dickinson, being both modest about her work and neglecting to preserve many of her poems. Her friends and daughter managed to salvage some 45 poems which were posthumously published in a volume, *Verses* (1903). *See* PEET, MARY TOLES.

Little is known about the life of Alice C. Jennings. Her poetry was of such high quality as to be widely quoted in deaf publications and published in future anthologies such as *The Silent Muse* (1960). Many poems dealing with the deaf experience are evident in two of her published collections, *Heart Echoes* (1880) and *The Fruit of the Spirit* (1903).

TWENTIETH CENTURY

The end of the nineteenth and beginning of the twentieth century brought forth several deaf poets. **Joseph Schuyler Long** Joseph Schuyler Long was both an educator and poet. While he served as principal of the Iowa School for the Deaf, he published a book of poems, *Out of the Silence* (1908), which contained many pieces that had seen wide circulation in deaf newspapers and journals. Another poet was George Moredock Teegarden. After teaching for many years at the Western Pennsylvania School for the Deaf, Teegarden began writing poems at age 50. A collected edition of his poems, *Vagrant Verses*, was published in 1929 by the Fanwood Press through the efforts of his hearing daughter. Years later, when she was teaching at Gallaudet College, Alice M. Teegarden established the George M. Teegarden Award for Excellence in Creative Poetry in memory of her father, who was both an outstanding poet and writer-adapter for the *Raindrop*, a monthly magazine featuring stories and adaptations of literary classics for deaf schoolchildren. **Howard L. Terry** Probably the most productive and best-known writer among deaf persons in the United

States was Howard L. Terry, the author of numerous works of poetry and prose. Versatile in his craft, he tried practically every form of literary expression—newspaper and magazine feature writing, poetry, drama, the short story, the novel, and greeting card verses. Most of the time he succeeded in selling his work, which was featured in a wide variety of magazines, such as the *Mentor*, *Social Science*, the *Hesperian*, *Out West*, *Poetry World*, and *Wee Wisdom*. Deafened at age 11, Terry also developed vision problems in later years that sometimes rendered him half blind. This did not stop him from buying a farm and, together with his deaf wife, raising crops for a living. Quite a few of Terry's poems deal with farm life in the Midwest, and with the beauty of nature's scenic grandeur in California, where he eventually moved. *See* TERRY, HOWARD L.

Like Carl Sandburg and Robert Frost, Terry was a close observer of humans and nature, especially as these related to contemporary events. His poetic forms and meters, however, were more attuned to those of the Romantic poets of the early and middle nineteenth century. A good example of this mix is in his poem "The Titanic," which is composed in the nine-line Spenserian stanza form of Lord Byron's *Childe Harold's Pilgrimage*; it has the same sense of excitement and dramatic irony:

> "Two thousand souls aboard, no sign of fear!
>   Oh, happy happy hearts that westward sail,
> Ye dream of loved ones till the happy tear
>   Of greetings springs too soon. Along the rail
> Ye promenade in glad expectancy,
>   Low sinks the sun, and o'er the sea the veil,
> Star-decked, of night draws on. In mighty glee
>   On plows the ship, defiant of the gale,
> Through fog and wave and ice she leaves a
>   titan trail! . . ."

Terry was affectionately known to deaf people as their "Venerable Dean of Letters." His collected poems were published in five volumes: *A Tale of Normandy* (1898); *Waters from an Ozark Spring* (1909); *The Dream: A Dramatic Romance* (1912); *California and Other Verses* (1917); and *Sung in Silence* (1929).

Annie Charlotte Dalton Another prolific poetry writer was Annie Charlotte Dalton, who became seriously deafened at age seven. She grew up in Vancouver, British Columbia, and her poetry attracted a wide following in Canada, where it was highly praised by such contemporary reviewers as Laura Davies Holt and the noted deaf author Earnest Elmo Calkins of the *Volta Review*. Calkins recognized Dalton as the poet laureate of the deaf people, as she often protested "against the constant employment of deafness as the motive for low comedy, as in Dame Edith Sitwell's 'Solo for Ear Trumpet' and the movie, *Deaf, Dumb, and Daffy*." Dalton published four books of poetry: *The Marriage of Music* (1910); *Flame and Adventure* (1924); *The Silent Zone* (1926); and *The Amber Riders and Other Poems* (1929).

Gustinus Ambrosi At about the same time, Gustinus Ambrosi was drawing rave notices in Vienna, Austria, for his creative genius as sculptor and poet. Born in Italy, Ambrosi became totally deaf at age seven and proved to be a prodigy in sculpturing from clay, wood, and stone. Because of his father's opposition to the Fascist regime, the family was exiled and moved to Austria. Here Ambrosi developed into a sculptor of worldwide renown: the Emperor of Austria gave him an entire museum for a studio. Ambrosi's sculptures were larger-than-life dynamic representations, and his bust portrayals were equally impressive (three popes asked him to make their bust replicas at the Vatican). Ambrosi also wrote poetry, especially sonnet sequences. Two of his published collections were entitled *Die Sonette an Gott* (*Sonnets to God*, 1923); and *Einer Toten* (*To A Dead Love*, 1937). *See* AMBROSI, GUSTINUS.

Silent Muse Poets The years following World War I saw an unprecedented number of deaf poets get their work published. Although many never published a collected edition of their work, their names are worthy of mention, since most of them were included in *The Silent Muse* (1960), the first anthology of poetry by deaf persons. The poets included J. S. Bowen, J. H. MacFarlane, Edith Peel Chandler, Sara Tredwell Ragna, whose short poignant verses on deafness appeared in *Contemporary Magazine*, and Guie C. Cooke, whose sonnet "In Memory of Thomas Scott Marr" (the deaf architect) has become a classic. *See* MARR, THOMAS SCOTT.

A good number of these deaf poets had attended Gallaudet College, where they had contributed poems to the student newspaper, the *Buff and Blue*, and its companion *Literary Quarterly*. These models inspired future student poets, who ushered in what is called the golden age in poetry at Gallaudet, the decade from 1930 to 1940. One influence on this poetic renaissance was the establishment in 1933 of a poetry contest by the American Association of University Women of the District of Columbia, which was open to all colleges and universities in the district, at that time numbering 10.

In 1933 Stephen Koziar won first prize with the poem "Remember Me"; and Loy E. Golladay placed second with his poem "Spirit of Chichen-Itza." In 1934 Golladay took first prize with the sonnet sequence "The Eternal Triangle," and Earl Sollenberger placed third with his poem "The Grave near Pope." In 1939 Rex Lowman took first prize with his dramatic monologue "Ulysses Remembers," and

the following year repeated his triumph with "Arachne." Another student poet, Felix Kowalewski, won second honorable mention in the 1935 contest with his poem "Epitaph for an Arctic Explorer," which also received honorable mention in the D.C. Women's Clubs Poetry Contest in 1937 and was published in *This Week*, the Sunday magazine section of the *New York Herald Tribune*.

Prizewinners who went on to publish collected poems included Sollenberger, Rex Lowman, and Kowalewski. Writing under the pen name of "Earl Crombie," Sollenberger published his first volume, *Along with Me* (1934), which enjoyed wide distribution in the midst of the Great Depression. He repeated his initial success with a second collection, *A Handful of Quietness* (1941). Sollenberger later committed suicide, abruptly ending a promising career.

Lowman won the James Patrick McGovern Poetry Contest Award while doing graduate studies at American University. In 1964 he published a volume of collected poems, *Bitterweed*. His work is a blend of rich symbolism and subtle allusions to classical literature, myth, and religion, as in the sonnet titled "Beethoven":

"This tree is music; and this rose
Is laughter rippling on a stream
Free-flowing into hills of dream
Grown phantasmal in evening's close.
The counterpoint of wind that blows
In faint, elusive gusts is theme
For all the undertones that teem
In glimmering light which fades and glows.
This woodland that is yet a world,
Peopled with all that Eden held,
Has one cold angel, forthwith hurled
From sound to silence,—he who felled
The ululation of this wound
With all the instruments of sound."

Felix Kowalewski, in addition to being a poet, was an accomplished artist and sculptor whose work has been widely displayed at exhibitions in various museums in the United States. He mastered the French language and translated many of the poems of Charles Baudelaire. These, together with his own impressive output of poems, were published in 1983 under the title *You and I: Fifty Years of Poems, Translations and Art Works*. The poems reveal Kowalewski to be not only a gifted lyricist but also a master of many poetic forms—the sonnet, the rondeau, the triolet, the aubade, the haiku, among others. He even invented his own rhyme schemes, as in "Bette":

"My lady of the dulcimer . . .
I've never heard the song of her.

My eyes can only picture her . . .
And words the sound of the dulcimer.
My lady of the dulcimer."

Another Gallaudet poet, who was actually one of the precursors of the poetic renaissance, was Alice McVan. Her talents as a translator of Spanish lyrics were greatly esteemed by her circle of co-workers and admirers, as were her reviews of numerous prose works written in Spanish, all of which appeared in the publications of the Hispanic Society in New York City, where she worked as a curator-specialist. Her most representative work as a poet appeared in a small but impressive volume entitled *Tryst* (1953). This work not only reflects an intimate knowledge of Spanish culture and folkways, as in her tour de force poem "Ballet of the Bullfight," but also highlights the deft turn of phrase and whimsical imagination, such as is evident in "Morning":

"Voices run
Like flashing sun
Up and down the scales.

Laughter spills
Like golden rills
In quiet, leafy dales.

Silence has been caught and drowned
In a swift cascade of sound."

McVan's verse is as modern in her range of subject matter, vocabulary, and imagery as many of her hearing contemporaries.

Also refreshing and unique is the poetic accomplishment of Dorothy Squire Miles. Born and educated in England, she went to Gallaudet for her higher education, where she also was active in dramatics. This led to an invitation to join the National Theatre of the Deaf and the opportunity to develop her talents as an actress and a playwright. One of her works, *A Play of Our Own*, proved to be both popular and one of the first expressions of the deaf experience on the stage. Although Miles had been writing poems before this, her association with the National Theatre of the Deaf led to "a love affair" with the language of signs and gestures. The result, as she herself expressed it in the introduction to her published poems, *Gestures* (1976), led her "to blend words with sign language as closely as lyrics and tunes are blended in song," the total effect being that "the poem should be seen as well as read". This technique is illustrated in the following Haiku poems taken from the quartet entitled "The Seasons":

Spring

"Sunshine, born on breeze

among singing trees, to dance
on rippled water."

Autumn

"Scattered leaves, a-whirl
in playful winds, turn to watch
people hurry by."

See NATIONAL THEATERS OF THE DEAF: United States.

Paul S. Pyers, Jr., takes a somewhat similar approach, while also incorporating some of the typographical metaphors used by the pioneering modernist e.e. cummings. Pyers, who became deaf at four months, published two small volumes of verse, *Man Is Marching* and *The Talking Rock and Other Poems* (1980). In one of the poems, "The Illusion of Our Mind," he observes:

" . . . And our mind speaks inwardly
So differently under the illus(trat)ion:
We see a castle of sand
Standing still under the mir(ror)-age
—The aged eyes of the sun—
But washes away under the wave
Of our thoughts."

Linwood Smith, coauthor of *Black and Deaf in America* (1983), also began writing poetry while a student at Gallaudet. In 1973 his collected poems appeared in *Silence, Love, and Kids I Know*, which brings to life the lives and feelings of the deaf children he knew and taught, as well as "the Black experience."

Three other poets of recent times have caught the public eye with book publications of their work. C. Allan Dunham, who graduated from the Rochester School for the Deaf, often appeared in print in the *Buffalo News* and the *Buffalo Courier Express*. In 1969 Dunham published a collection of 45 poems, *My Heart Can Hear*. Sharper wit and phrasing characterize the verse of another deaf alumnus of Gallaudet College, Kathleen Bedard Schreiber. Most of Schreiber's poems were written to her daughter Beth who was a student at college. Published under the title *Dear Beth—Love Mom*, Schreiber's collection of 78 poems are grouped into four categories, or states of mind.

Robert Smithdas was a deaf-blind poet and Director of Services for the Deaf-Blind at the Industrial Home for the Blind in New York. One of his best-known poems, "Shared Beauty," deals with the deaf-blind experience and the theme of compensation, as in the following excerpt:

"I only know that when I touch a flower,
or feel the sun and wind upon my face,
or hold your hand in mine, there is a
   brightness

within my soul that words can never trace.
I call it Life, and laugh with its delight,
though life itself be out of sound and sight."

Smithdas published several collections of poems, among them *Christmas Bells and Other Poems* (1954), *My Heart Sings* (1959), and *City of the Heart* (1966). *See* DEAF-BLINDNESS.

Other noteworthy deaf Americans whose poems have frequently been printed in newspapers and magazines, and who have earned a reputation despite the fact that they had yet to publish in book form before 1985, are Loy Golladay, Thomas Ulmer, Stephen Koziar, Taras Denis, Mervin Garretson, Lawrence Newman, Willard Madsen, and Robert Panara. The last two, in particular, had each written a poem on the deaf experience which became popular. Madsen's poem, "You Have To Be Deaf To Understand," received international attention and has been translated into seven languages. Panara's sonnet, "On His Deafness," has often been dramatized in sign-mime by both the National Theatre of the Deaf and the Gallaudet Dancers when on national and world tours. Panara, who graduated from Gallaudet in the war-time class of 1945, has also written more lines on the theme of *arma virumque*, or arms and the man, than any other deaf poet. His "Aftermath" expresses both the destructiveness and stupidity of warfare.

David Wright Every generation has had its flock of deaf poets, and often one whose name led the rest. In the mid-1950s such a poet was David Wright, who became totally deaf at age seven from scarlet fever in Johannesburg, South Africa. He received his early education at the Northampton School for the Deaf in England and later entered Oriel College, Oxford, where he obtained his bachelor's degree. At Oxford, Wright came in contact with other budding poets, some of whom also went on to achieve literary fame. *See* WRIGHT, DAVID.

Wright's accomplishments were many. Some of his poems were published in the leading literary magazines in both Great Britain and the United States; he translated *Beowulf* and *The Canterbury Tales* into modern English; he was widely active as an editor of anthologies and of literary magazines; he published eight books of poetry; and he wrote an autobiography, *Deafness* (1969). His urbane wit and controlled emotion lead to effective use of understatement and irony in much of his poetry. This, coupled with a cynical perception of life's paradoxes and injustices, such as his view of apartheid, or racial discrimination, in South Africa, lends his poetry a special impression. Much of this is evident in these lines from his poem "A Funeral Oration":

"Composed at thirty, my funeral oration: Here lies

David John Murray Wright, 6'2", myopic blue eyes . . .
Preferring cats, hated dogs; drank (when he could) too much;
Was deaf as a tombstone; and extremely hard to touch.
Academic achievements: B.A. Oxon (2nd class);
Poetic: the publication of one volume of verse . . . .
He could roll himself cigarettes from discarded stubs,
Assume the first position of Yoga; sail, row, swim;
And though deaf, in church appear to be joining a hymn.
Often arrested for being without a permit,
Starved on his talents as much as he dined on his wit,
Born in a dominion to which he hoped not to go back
Since predisposed to imagine white possibly black;
His life like his times, was appalling; his conduct odd;
He hoped to write one good line; died believing in God."

The Modern Poet Today, the poet's influence has greatly diminished in scope and popularity due to changing tastes in art and literature. Gone are the halcyon days of royal patronage, such as that enjoyed by Ronsard and du Bellay when poetry and belles lettres were produced for art's sake only. Accordingly, the deaf poet of the nineteenth and twentieth centuries should be praised for overcoming not only the handicap of deafness but also that of an indifferent reading public and of literary critics who maintained that the poet is not in touch with the times.

History and Social Criticism

Deaf writers have been most prolific and successful in writing nonfiction. Whether it be journalism, history, biography, autobiography, or special studies in religion, education, and linguistics, it is in such genres of nonfiction that the deaf writer has made the most impact and achieved some measure of success.

HARRIET MARTINEAU

One of the most famous and successful deaf writers was Harriet Martineau (1802–1876). This English woman, a product of the Victorian period, was a prolific translator, journalist, historian, and social commentator who wrote on many controversial issues of the times, including equality for women, religious beliefs, mesmerism or hypnotism, abolition and the slavery issue, and the education and welfare of deaf people. She often fictionalized these themes or popular social issues in order to make them easier for readers to understand. Thus she was more of an editorial writer and novelist. She also wrote books for children. *See* MARTINEAU, HARRIET.

Martineau developed a hearing loss at age 12 which became more progressive and caused her much frustration and inconvenience. Despite this, she became an independent woman who could be called today a militant and a free-spirited intellectual. She was regarded as a radical Victorian by her peers, and succeeded in making a living entirely on earnings from her writings. Among the many books she wrote were *Poor Law and Paupers Illustrated* (1833), *Illustrations of Political Economy* (1834), *Society in America* (1837), *Deerbrook* (1839), *Letters on Mesmerism* (1845), *Eastern Life, Present and Past* (1848), and her *Autobiography* (1877). The autobiography reveals her to be a strong advocate for the betterment of the lives of all women, of the poor and oppressed, and of the disadvantaged and uneducated. It also contains the classic essay "Letter to the Deaf" in which Martineau expresses her sympathy and understanding of deafness and deaf people. She also writes how she deplores the tendency of deaf persons to evade their problems, and encourages them to forget their handicap and think of other things more important and constructive. She portrays a positive attitude toward deafness, keeping with her own assertive, independent, and creative personality.

GEORGE HYDE

Another productive writer was George Hyde (1882–1968). Born in the frontier region of Nebraska, Hyde grew up hearing tales and legends of the American Indians and became an authentic historian of the Plains Indian. A mysterious physical disorder caused him to become completely deaf at age 18 and also caused the progressive blindness that was to hinder his mobility in later life. These adversities seemed to have challenged him to greater achievements. He was instilled with a dogged determination to research the facts and tell the real truth about the Indians and their mistreatment by the white historian. *See* HYDE, GEORGE.

Practically self-educated, Hyde studied and wrote about the Plains Indians so knowingly that his works are cited as references in standard texts of Western Americana. His books include *Red Cloud's Folk: A History of the Oglala Sioux Indians* (1937), which brought deserving recognition to Chief Red Cloud, one of the greatest Sioux leaders in battle and diplomacy; *The Pawnee Indians* (1951); *Indians of the High Plains* (1959); *Spotted Tail's Folk: A History of the Brule Sioux* (1961); and *Life of George Bent: Written from His Letters.*

JACK R. GANNON

Of equal importance as a historian and social commentator of deaf people in the United States is Jack R. Gannon (born 1938). Totally deafened from spinal meningitis at age eight, Gannon graduated from the Missouri School for the Deaf and then from Gallaudet College, where he later became Director of Alumni Affairs and editor of *Gallaudet Today*. It was at Gallaudet that Gannon wrote his pioneering work *Deaf Heritage: A Narrative History of Deaf America* (1981). In this book, he reveals a complete grasp of the life and times of deaf America, and he describes the deaf experience with deep insight and feeling.

Gannon also describes in his book the upward mobility and sociocultural achievement of the deaf American. Starting with the year 1880, when the National Association of the Deaf was officially organized, each of the chapters covers a 10-year period. Within each time frame, people and personalities come to life against the backdrop of historical movements and events. These are effectively interwoven and are vividly illustrated by hundreds of photographs and drawings, including many "Ripley's Believe It or Not" reproductions.

Along with the historical information, the author showcases deaf artists and architects (with vivid illustrations of their works); the National Theatre of the Deaf; sports and the Deaf Hall of Fame; national organizations for deaf people; publications for deaf people; and deaf folklore or humorous glimpses of deaf culture via cartoons and anecdotes. The result is a history of deaf Americana that is well documented, easy to read, and highly entertaining with its wealth of visual interest.

Scholarly Studies

Few deaf individuals have been professional scholars. Seldom wealthy and only infrequently found in academic positions that provide the facilities conducive to scholarly work, deaf people usually have not had the opportunity for research, reflection, and writing that such work demands. Their communication requirements also have reduced their accessibility to groups with similar intellectual concerns. Nevertheless, a handful of deaf individuals have overcome these difficulties to produce work of genuine scholarship.

JOHN KITTO

Born in poverty and afflicted with total deafness at age 12, John Kitto (1804–1854) progressed from poverty to become one of the world's most respected Biblical scholars. A voracious reader, he mastered several languages, including Hebrew, and developed an iron will and discipline which, together with his natural genius, drove him to produce 21 books from the time he began his eccle-siastical studies with the Missionary Society in London. His fieldwork as a missionary allowed him to tour Europe and Asia, particularly the Near East, which gave him firsthand knowledge of religious shrines and places of historical significance, as well as the opportunity to meet other scholars and to have access to special library collections.

Among his most important writings are *The Pictorial Bible* (1835–1838), *The Pictorial History of Palestine and the Holy Land* (1840), and the two-volume *Cyclopedia of Biblical Literature* (1845), considered to be his greatest work. Of special interest also is his autobiography, *The Lost Senses* (1845), which includes many poems and reflections on the deaf experience.

HORACE HOWARD FURNESS

As equally renowned as a scholar was Horace Howard Furness (1833–1912). Called "the greatest of Shakespeare's editors" by the *Dictionary of American Biography* (1915), his *New Variorum* edition of Shakespeare's works was one of the monuments of American scholarship of the nineteenth and early twentieth centuries. Furness did not labor under the handicap of total deafness but was victimized by progressive deafness starting at about age 25.

Furness was born in Philadelphia in fairly prosperous circumstances, the son of William Henry Furness, a Unitarian clergyman and a New Testament scholar.

Furness went to Harvard College to study law, graduated in 1859, and was admitted to the bar four years later. However, because of increasing deafness, he abandoned a legal career in favor of Shakespearean studies. After the Civil War, Furness joined the Shakespearean Society of Philadelphia and began his life's work of preparing a more definitive edition of Shakespeare's plays. Although using the First Folio edition (1623) as his primary source, he reprinted variant readings from the best authorities. He began with a collection of *Romeo and Juliet* (1871), the first of 15 volumes that he labored over for the next 50 years, the last being *Cymbeline*, published in 1913, one year after his death. His son, Horace Howard Furness, Jr. (1865–1930), joined him as coeditor in 1901 and prepared several collations of the other plays. It was evidently a family of Shakespearean devotees since Furness's wife, Helen Kate Furness (1837–1883), also collaborated with him on another important work and compiled *A Concordance to the Poems of Shakespeare* (1874).

Furness's image as a witty, genial, and scholarly gentleman is projected in his letters and correspondence, collected in two volumes (1922). Furness was not ashamed of his deafness and always carried an ear trumpet. He was awarded honorary degrees by Columbia, Yale, and Harvard universities for his accomplishments.

DEAF STUDIES

Other deaf persons have contributed greatly to a developing discipline or subject content known as deaf studies. These are not professional scholars per se, since they are engaged in other professions or occupational careers. However, with the limited time and research sources available, they take their work seriously and each has added significant findings to deaf studies.

One of the first was the Reverend Guilbert C. Braddock, whose biographical profiles, entitled "Notable Deaf Persons," ran through many issues of the *Frat*, the official organ of the National Fraternal Society of the Deaf. These proved informative to the research worker, as well as enlightening and inspirational to deaf and hearing readers alike. After his death, these profiles were published in book form by the Gallaudet Alumni Association. Over 100 were collected and edited by Florence B. Crammatte and published under the title *Notable Deaf Persons* (1975). *See* GALLAUDET COLLEGE ALUMNI ASSOCIATION; NATIONAL FRATERNAL SOCIETY OF THE DEAF.

Pursuing the same goal was Ernest Elmo Calkins, whose monthly column, "Lives of the Deafened," appeared regularly in the *Volta Review* during the 1920s and 1930s. Calkins, who was hard-of-hearing, often focused on persons with a similar hearing impairment, highlighting their success stories through the development of their speech and lipreading skills, as well as through their special talent and courage. *See* VOLTA REVIEW.

Others who have frequently contributed feature articles dealing with the successful accomplishments of deaf people in various walks of life were Winfield S. Runde for the *Silent Worker Magazine*; Frank Bowe, who interviewed notable deaf persons for the *Deaf American Magazine*; and Robert L. Swain, Jr., who featured the exploits of past and present adult deaf persons and spotlighted up-and-coming young deaf adults in his writings for the *Deaf American Magazine* and other journals for the deaf. *See* DEAF AMERICAN.

Further research and writing in an attempt to promote interest in deaf studies was done by Robert Panara and published in various professional and popular periodicals for and by deaf people. Some of his topics were "The Deaf Writer in America: From Colonial Times to the Present," "Deaf Characters in Fiction and Drama," "Poetry and the Deaf," and "Cultural Arts Among Deaf People."

Of special importance to scholars, educators, and laypersons are the comprehensive bibliographies on deaf studies and related subjects by Francis G. Higgins. These appeared in two parts in the March

1947 and the May 1950 issues of the *American Annals of the Deaf* under the broad title "The Education of the Deaf—The Book Mart, Being a List of Books on the Deaf, Speech and Speech-Reading, the Language of Signs, etc., Now in Print." Numbering over 50 pages, these bibliographical references included the works of deaf authors and extended to deaf writers in foreign countries. *See* AMERICAN ANNALS OF THE DEAF.

The outstanding contribution of Martin L. A. Sternberg as a scholar deserves special mention. Sternberg, who became totally deaf at age seven and progressed through high schools and colleges for hearing students in New York City, began his scholarly project of compiling a definitive dictionary of American Sign Language in 1962. After almost 20 years of arduous research and writing, he accomplished his objective with the publication of *American Sign Language: A Comprehensive Dictionary* (1981). The book, as well as its author, was accorded many honors. In 1982 Sternberg was awarded the Townsend Harris Medal, which signifies the highest honor the City College of New York bestows on its outstanding graduates. *See* SIGN LANGUAGES: American.

Biography

Most biographers of deaf individuals, except for those of deaf persons who have made a major impact on the hearing society, have been deaf themselves. Biographies of prominent or successful deaf people from the past serve to develop a sense of historical continuity for the adult deaf community. Stories of the lives of living and deceased deaf persons who achieved unusual goals and overcame circumstances provide important role models and heroes for deaf children.

FERDINAND BERTHIER

The first deaf person to gain recognition as a biographer was French writer Ferdinand Berthier (1803–1886). Totally deaf since early childhood, he became a master teacher at the Institute for the Deaf in Paris and the founder of the first known social organization of deaf people, the Société Universelle des Sourds-Muets, in 1838. His early works consisted of historical narratives, such as *The Deaf Before and After the Abbé de l'Epée* (1840), and a series of essays on deafness and sign language. He followed these with a short biography of Roch-Ambroise Bebian, an early educator of deaf persons. *See* BERTHIER, JEAN-FERDINAND.

A brilliant scholar who excelled in French, Latin, and Greek, Berthier developed a reputation as a linguist and exponent of the sign language that had been systemized by the Abbé de l'Epée. These studies and writings prepared him for his great work published in 1852, *The Abbé de l'Epée: His Life and His Work.* He followed this with a second biography in 1873, *An Historical Summary of the Life, Labors, and Triumphs of the Abbé Sicard,* about the educator who had succeeded l'Epée as director of the institution at Paris. Berthier also wrote a book entitled *Code Napolean* (1870), which was a handbook on French law for deaf readers. *See* L'EPÉE, ABBÉ CHARLES MICHEL DE; SICARD, ABBÉ ROCH AMBROISE CUCURRON.

Berthier was honored many times for his achievements. In 1849 the Emperor Napoleon III presented Berthier with the Cross of the Legion of Honor which also entitled him to the rank of chevalier and an annual pension by royalty. It was the first time a deaf person was so honored, and it greatly impressed some of France's most distinguished men of letters.

CORINNE ROCHELEAU

Another deaf biographer of French lineage and language to be similarly honored by her hearing peers was Corinne Rocheleau. Born in Massachusetts of French ancestors who had emigrated to Canada and then to New England, Rocheleau became deaf at age nine and went to the Catholic parochial school for deaf girls in Montreal, Canada. Since her parents spoke French and English fluently, they desired that their daughter be educated bilingually. At the Montreal school, she learned to speak and lipread so well that after graduation she enrolled in a school for hearing students and successfully completed a program in fine arts. She worked for several years at the Office of Geographical Research in Washington, D.C., and then accepted a position as manager of her brother's textile plant in Worcester, Massachusetts.

Rocheleau continued her studies in French and developed a special interest in the lives of French-Canadian women who had made pioneering contributions in various careers. This led Rocheleau to write many biographical sketches, which she later collected in book form and published under the title *Françaises d'Amerique, Heroic French Women of Canada* (1922). Her next biography, *Hors de sa Prison, Out of Her Prison* (1928), became a classic on the education of deaf-blind people. It went through several editions and was honored by the French Academy. Hundreds of case studies dealing with deaf-blind people were written by Rocheleau and published in various newspapers and periodicals. A bilingual author, she also wrote many articles and stories in English for American magazines and in French for Canadian publications.

YVONNE PITROIS

A close friend and correspondent of Rocheleau was another French deaf woman, Yvonne Pitrois (1880–1937), who provided many of the facts about

Rocheleau's life in her biographical sketch published in *Volta Review*. A severe sunstroke at age seven left Pitrois totally deaf and temporarily blind for several years. Her mother, a schoolteacher in Paris, educated her daughter and succeeded in teaching her both French and English. In 1912 she started a Correspondence Club which led to an exchange of letters with notable deaf and hearing persons in France and America and other English-speaking nations. *See* PITROIS, YVONNE.

Pitrois first published translations of English books and articles in magazines of a religious nature. In 1912 she published a short biography on the life of the Abbé de l'Epée on the bicentenary of his birth. The biography was later reprinted serially in English in the *Silent Worker Magazine*. Thereafter, she contributed regularly to the *Silent Worker* as well as to the *Volta Review* and the *American Annals of the Deaf*. In 1912 she edited and published at her own expense a bimonthly magazine, *La Petite Silencieuse (The Little Deaf Girl)*, which circulated through France, Switzerland, and Canada, and provided an open forum for advice to deaf women on personal, domestic, and educational affairs.

Her lifelong interest in deaf-blind people prompted her to edit and publish, also at her own expense, a quarterly magazine in Braille, *Le Rayon de Soleil (The Sunbeam)*. She followed this with the publication of a book, *Trois Lumières dans la Nuit (Three Lights in the Darkness)*, which glorified the achievement of three notable blind Frenchmen: Valentin Hany, Louis Braille, and Maurice de la Sizeranne. One of her last works was the publication of biographical profiles titled *Les Femmes de la Grande Guerre (Women of the World War)*.

OTHER WORKS AND WRITERS

In addition to his scholarly contributions to deaf studies, Guilbert C. Braddock has made contributions as a biographer. Born in Colorado, he became totally deaf at age four. After graduating from the Colorado School for the Deaf, he enrolled in Gallaudet College, where he obtained both the bachelor of arts and his master's degrees. He studied theology essentially on his own and succeeded so well that, after passing the canonical examinations at the General Theological Seminary in New York City, he was ordained a priest in the Episcopal Church. He served successively as vicar at St. Ann's Church in New York City; as missionary to deaf people in Washington D.C., Virginia, and Maryland; and as vicar of All Souls' Church in Philadelphia.

A brilliant scholar and writer, Braddock was a pioneer in researching and keeping records of the achievements of deaf people in the United States and in foreign lands. These he recorded in the form of biographical profiles, first published serially over

several decades in the *Frat* magazine. They not only bore the mark of an erudite scholar but were also flavored with a dry wit and penchant for humorous anecdotes that characterized the author's personality.

Braddock's explorations in the field of deaf studies ended with the first quarter of the twentieth century; other deaf writers continued the quest. Some biographies were in the form of interviews with selected men and women of different ages and career backgrounds, as in *I'm Deaf, Too: 12 Deaf Americans*, by Frank Bowe and Martin Sternberg (1973). Another book was of personal experiences by 16 "role models," most of whom were on the academic staff of Gallaudet College. The book was titled *A Handful of Stories* (1981) and was edited by Leonard Lane and Ivey Pittle. Two other books were designed to function as reader workbooks for deaf school-age children: *Successful Deaf Americans* (1978) and *Courageous Deaf Adults* (1980), both by Darlene K. Toole.

Four other works of this genre were more comprehensive and detailed in scope. One was co-authored by two Czechoslovakians, Karel Lipa and Pavel Les, and entitled *We Have Overcome* (1971). Karel Lipa, who was hard-of-hearing, covered the life stories of 27 distinguished hearing-impaired persons. Although some of these are of questionable status (the individuals developed a hearing loss late in life), quite a few are legitimately deaf or very hard-of-hearing, such as the poet Pierre de Ronsard, the composer-musician Beethoven, and the Russian scientist Konstantin Tsiolkovsky, who did pioneering work in space research and was honored as the "Father of Rockets" powered by liquid fuel. Coauthor Pavel Les was blind and covered the life stories of persons with a similar handicap; two major omissions were Helen Keller and Olga Skorochodova, the Russian deaf-blind educator and author. *See* BEETHOVEN, LUDWIG VAN; TSIOLKOVSKY, KONSTANTIN EDUARDOVICH.

The Forgotten People (1973) by Willard H. Woods, Sr., contains 10 in-depth biographies and has an impressive number of specific case histories proving that deaf people can succeed in a wide variety of occupations and professions if given the training and opportunity. It is a landmark work in stressing the need for affirmative action to eliminate the barriers and discriminatory practices of personnel managers in denying qualified deaf persons equal employment opportunities and on-the-job advancement.

With similar objectives, Ernest Hairston and Linwood Smith published the book *Black and Deaf in America* (1983). The authors, who are black and deaf, present an in-depth study of long-standing neglect and discrimination that has been the black and deaf experience in America, including under-education and underemployment. Also in the book are biographical profiles in interview form of prominent black and deaf persons who have made major breakthroughs and accomplishments in various careers.

Another book pattened after Braddock's work is *Great Deaf Americans* (1983). Coauthored by Robert Panara, who is deaf, and his son John, this book consists of 33 biographies that illustrate how deaf people have contributed not only to the deaf community but to the quality of life for all Americans. Arranged in chronological order beginning with Laurent Clerc (1785–1869), the first deaf teacher of deaf people, and concluding with Lou Ferrigno (born 1951), the body-builder and actor, the biographies describe the careers of journalists, poets, lawyers, scientists, artists, professional athletes, and entertainers, among others. A number of women and black individuals are also included.

Personal Essay

The personal essay not only deals with factual experiences of an autobiographical nature but also comes to grips with the problem of identity, with the resistance against stereotyping, and with the struggle to gain equality.

ALBERT BALLIN

One of the first of the personal essay writers was Albert Ballin, a portrait painter and calendar lithographer. In his book, *A Deaf Mute Howls* (1933), he exposed some of the absurdities and injustices practiced by dogmatic teachers in educational institutions for deaf children. He had attended such an institution and also attacked in his books its inhibiting and insular effects on the deaf child. He was years ahead of the modern trend toward mainstreaming, the placing of deaf children with hearing students in public schools, thus providing opportunities for them to have a normal home life and to interact with hearing peers. In his book, Ballin also advocates the use of sign language by teachers in these public schools, pointing out his own difficulties in learning English (which he calls his second language)—a viewpoint vigorously championed by the deaf community today.

Ballin later moved to Hollywood, where he interacted with movie stars and contributed to trade journals such as the *Hollywood Filmgraph*. One of his articles, "Motion Picture Making as Seen from a Deaf Man's View," proposed that sign language be used by film directors to overcome noise disruptions, speed up picture making, and give deaf actors opportunities to act in silent films. He also argued that sign language be used more universally—by fire fighters, by construction workers, and by others working in places affected by noise and occupational hazards.

LEO JACOBS

In his book *A Deaf Adult Speaks Out* (1974), Leo Jacobs describes the grass roots experience of growing up deaf and gives readers an awareness of what it means to be deaf. Jacobs also advocates sign language or total communication over pure oralism in the education of deaf children. However, he differs from Ballin by defending residential schools for deaf students, where he maintains they will benefit from more specialized services, become more active in athletics and extracurricular activities, and develop leadership skills. He also speaks out for deaf adults, believing that they should have more control over the influences on their lives—their education, mode of communication, consumer services, employment practices, and political issues. *See* EDUCATION: Communication; EDUCATIONAL PROGRAMS: Residential Schools.

BEN M. SCHOWE

Ben M. Schowe, Sr., takes a more objective and cosmopolitan approach to the sociological study of deafness and deaf people in his book *Identity Crisis in Deafness* (1979). Subtitled "A Humanistic Perspective," it attempts to show that self-knowledge and self-worth equate with how successfully deaf people adapt to their chosen career and social circle or cultural group. This applies alike to those prelingually and postlingually deaf, to those favoring the oral method of communication, and to those who feel at home with the manual or combined mode. He considers these groups as both disparate and similar, each having its own cultural interests and values, yet all sharing identical needs and problems because of their common handicap. This even includes the rapidly expanding population of persons developing a hearing loss after age 65. To illustrate his thesis, Schowe singles out representative individuals such as John Kitto, E. E. Calkins, and Albert Ballin, each of whom experienced an identity crisis but resolved it through a satisfying adjustment in career interests or sociocultural pursuit of happiness. *See* SCHOWE, BENJAMIN MARSHALL, SR.

Autobiography

Autobiographies, perhaps even more than biographies or personal essays, can provide access to and understanding of the ways in which individuals struggle with the vicissitudes of life. Unfortunately, the number of deaf persons who have published autobiographies is relatively small. Still, these few provide rare insight into the many facets of the deaf experience.

JOHN KITTO

Biblical scholar John Kitto wrote an autobiography, which is one of the earliest written by a well-educated deaf person. In *The Lost Senses* (1845), Kitto devotes much thought and feeling to describing in vivid detail how he became deaf, the ensuing struggle for survival against poverty, the educational deprivation, and the entire deaf experience.

ERNEST ELMO CALKINS

The experience of deafness and the identity crisis of learning to cope with this handicap is the common thread that runs through most autobiographies. In *Louder Please!* (1924), Ernest Elmo Calkins illustrates the disadvantages and advantages of being deaf by way of personal experiences and anecdotes, concluding that the assets far outweigh the liabilities. A man of many interests (a rare book collector; devotee of art and sculpture, natural science, and model boat building; and contributor to deaf studies), Calkins was a prime example of a hard-of-hearing person who adapted to the lifestyle and social circles of the hearing world but who maintained a link with deafness and deaf people. Further autobiographical sketches, enlivened by many interesting personal essays on people, places, and things, are recounted in his other book, *And Hearing Not: Annals of an Ad Man* (1946). He was the first person to receive the Edward Bok Gold Medal for distinguished service to advertising, and became senior partner of the advertising firm of Calkins and Holden.

DAVID WRIGHT

David Wright, the noted British poet, also illustrates the truth of Ben Schowe's thesis on the identity crisis in his autobiography, *Deafness* (1969). The book actually consists of two distinct writings: the first half is his autobiography, from early childhood to early adulthood; the second part is a sort of condensed history of deaf education as viewed and experienced by Wright. The first part is of special interest and is much more revealing than the second part. It describes how Wright as a deaf teenager felt lost and alienated among his peers at the Northampton School for the Deaf, mainly because of his disenchantment with sign language. After leaving that school, he finds himself a stranger in the hearing world. The realization comes that he must choose either to hide behind his deafness or participate in life; he had to overcome his shyness and start meeting and talking with people. When he attends Oxford University, he comes to realize that the less attention he pays to his own deafness, the more his hearing peers become comfortable with him and tend to forget the handicap.

JACK ASHLEY

Yet another account of identity crisis in deafness is the autobiography of Jack Ashley, *Journey into Silence* (1973). It is the life story of a British politician who rose from a poor Catholic section of Widnes, England, to a position of prominence and respect, but who suddenly lost his hearing six months after he was elected to Parliament.

Several months after his election, Jack Ashley went to have a hearing problem corrected. He was 46 years old, but the resulting operation left him totally deaf. *Journey into Silence* is about his struggle to accept his handicap and readjust to life. At first, he felt he could not function as a member of Parliament, believing his attempt would prove more hurtful to others than to himself. He considered himself a disabled person and lost his self-confidence. His party, however, gave him full support and encouraged him to remain in office. His colleagues helped him follow debates and kept him on top of discussions by writing notes and typing out abstracts of speeches. In time, Ashley learned to accept his handicap. By remaining in office, and also being reelected later, he redoubled his efforts to serve the welfare of his fellow Britons. He introduced and championed many bills to provide better services to deaf and disabled people in England. He also proved to himself, and to others, that he could function successfully as a deaf member of Parliament.

HELEN KELLER

The world's best-known autobiography of a deaf person is that of Helen Keller (1880–1968), who became blind and deaf at 19 months of age from scarlet fever, but learned to read Braille, to write, and even to speak. Her first autobiography, *The Story of My Life* (1903), described her childhood, how she was educated, and how she learned to accept her handicap and find her niche in life. It is dedicated to Anne Sullivan, her lifelong teacher, friend, and business associate. Keller went on to write several other books of an autobiographical nature—*The World I Live In* (1908), *In the Midst of Life's Stream* (1929), and *Let Us Have Faith* (1940)—which, together with her life's work in the service of Foundations for the Blind in the United States and throughout the world, made her a symbol of human determination in overcoming physical handicaps and an inspiration for all similarly handicapped people.

OTHER WORKS

One person to benefit by the example of Helen Keller was Russian-born Olga Skorochodova, who became blind and deaf at age five. She too learned to read, write, and speak with the help of a devoted teacher, a Professor Sokoljanskij, who prepared her for a college education. Skorochodova went to the University of Moscow, where she studied Russian literature and special education, and after graduating, she became an educational specialist at the Moscow Institute of Defectology, where she studied the problems of deaf-blind people. In 1947 she published the first volume of her trilogy covering her life, *How I Perceive and Conceive the World Surrounding Me.*

A number of other works not only illustrate the many facets of deafness and the deaf experience, but also reveal the unique style and personality of the writer.

Grace McGreevy has a clever and witty manner of writing about her experiences as a hard-of-hearing person in *I'm Thirsty, Too!* (1968). Scattered throughout the book are drawings of a woman, complete with assorted hearing aids, sketched in clever situations. McGreevy states that no one realized that she had a hearing problem until she entered school, nor did she comprehend this herself. She explains the dilemma by observing that many of her older relatives were extremely hard-of-hearing so that all of their conversation was carried on by loud shouting. Her parents, too, thought that she was just being stubborn when she refused to answer their calls, or that she would rather go on reading the book she had in her hands. The author's survival tactics in dealing with lipreading, speech therapy, and hearing aids is told with a sharp sense of humor, imagination, and spirit.

Julius Wiggins's autobiography, *No Sound* (1970), is the story of a totally deaf man who went from Canada to New York City, where he not only became prosperous as a furrier but also founded and published the best newspaper of deaf people in the United States, the *Silent News. No Sound* contradicts the stereotyped view of deaf people as the silent minority whose subculture runs contrary to social norms and the pursuit of true happiness. Instead, with Wiggins as the representative figure, most deaf Americans are portrayed as well-adjusted, happy-go-lucky achievers and go-getters who join clubs, gossip, and react with the spirit of the crowd at conventions, sporting events, and cultural affairs, much like their hearing counterparts. The book is refreshing in its lively and unabstract picture of the typical deaf American. *See* SILENT NEWS.

An interesting example of this representative deaf American is Frances "Peggy" Parsons, who has been called the "Total Communication Ambassador of the World" for her voluntary efforts to develop deaf awareness and acceptance of sign language in foreign lands. Starting with the Philippines in 1974, Parsons was the first deaf person to work in the Peace Corps and has since actively recruited young deaf adults to follow her example. Evidently, her cross-cultural experiences while living in Tahiti as a teenager greatly influenced her life and her outlook. Some of this is captured in her book *Sound of the Stars* (1971), which she recorded in diary form between 1939 and 1941. It is unique because it is the literary expression of a midteens deaf girl

and exhibits some of the peculiarities of "deaf English" which Parsons kept intact for publication. The total effect is a colloquial and engrossing chronicle of people, places, and customs as experienced by a lively, curious, and outgoing deaf teenager growing up in the prewar South Pacific.

Fiction

The novel developed somewhat late in literary history, first appearing in the seventeenth century when it established itself as a standard literary form. It has since emerged as perhaps the most popular literary genre today. Yet, rare is the deaf writer who attempts to compose a novel, or even novelette or short story.

HOWARD L. TERRY

One of the earliest fictional works by a deaf writer was the novel *A Voice from the Silence* (1912) by Howard L. Terry. The hero of the story is "Jack Harlow," who is humorously described "as deaf as a post" by the townspeople. The antagonist is "Gibbs," a Scrooge-like land baron in the midwestern town, who threatens to reveal the long-hidden secret that "Tom Duncan," a local farmer, had once killed a man in a fit of reckless passion. Harlow, who is looked upon as "harmlessly dumb," learns about this by lipreading the conversation between Gibbs and Duncan. He thus uncovers both the murder mystery and the blackmailing villain, and thereby wins the respect of the townspeople.

A Voice from the Silence typified the popular melodramatic novel of the second half of the nineteenth century, plodding along in episodic fashion. The dialogue is ridden with the contrived dialect, idioms, and cliches of midwestern farmers. But the deaf writer's reliance on bookish speech could be excused, providing the story line was well knit and absorbing. In fact, Terry's melodrama was suited to the silent screen, and he was paid $150 for the film rights. However, the novel was never filmed.

MARGARET PRESCOTT MONTAGUE

Margaret Prescott Montague, a hearing-impaired author who wrote regularly for the *Volta Review,* published *Closed Doors: Studies of Deaf and Blind Children* in 1915. It was a fictional portrayal of institution life at the Lomax School for the Deaf and the Blind. Featuring a series of stories, the book presents the controversy of oralism versus manualism, using characters and situations that illustrate the relative usefulness of each. It also stresses the necessity for sending deaf children to school at the earliest possible age, the need for specialized instruction by skilled and dedicated teachers, and the importance of expert medical care and diagnosis of all hearing-impaired children. The book was adapted by Walt Disney Studios in 1981 and made into a motion picture, *Amy-on-the-Lips* (later retitled *Amy*), which featured several hearing-impaired performers.

EUGENE RELGIS

In 1938 the Hungarian-born Eugene Relgis published a fictional autobiography of how he became totally deaf in childhood and of the subsequent experience of growing up in a silent world. Entitled *Muted Voices (Glasuri in Surdina)*, it was highly praised by the distinguished Austrian author Stefan Zweig. Relgis describes the deaf experience through the fictional character "Miron." The problem is that Miron becomes so obsessed with his daydreams that he rarely interacts or communicates in reality. Despite the fact that *Muted Voices* is seemingly devoid of characters that interact in social situations, real or imagined, Eugene Relgis emerges as a composite of Franz Kafka (*Metamorphosis*), James Joyce (*Ulysses*), and Thomas Wolfe (*Of Time and the River*).

HELEN MUSE

Deaf novelists have tried to keep pace with their contemporaries in content and style changes. Readers of the historical novel, for example, should appreciate the "literary firsts" produced by Helen E. Muse and James A. Sullivan. These two deaf novelists have much pride and passion for the American heritage, and unfold their stories with much local color and narrative interest.

Green Pavilions (1961) by Muse is the saga of the lives and loves of two sturdy Colonists, imbued with the American spirit, who journey to the wilds of northern Michigan to seek their fortunes. Against the background of the French and Indian Wars, these two men persevere through violence and brutality, famine and pestilence, family suffering and tragedy, until they emerge as Old Testament heroes and bring out the best qualities of humanity in the warring factions of the French, Indian, and British. Muse unfolds a tapestry of rare poetic beauty and symbolism.

JAMES SULLIVAN

James Sullivan takes a more direct and historically oriented course in his novel *Valley Forge* (1964). The story portrays the determination and bravery of the 11,000 soldiers under General Washington who withstood the terrible winter at Valley Forge during the Revolutionary War. There is no definite plot. Instead, the author vividly describes the setting, the atmosphere, and the general spirit by using vignettes and anecdotes. These reveal the generosity of the neighboring farmers toward the starved troops, the understanding sympathy and passive loyalty accorded Washington by the landed gentry who still believed that they were obligated to the king for their property rights and tenure, and the conflicts of misunderstanding experienced by these opposing factions. The charm of *Valley Forge*, however, lies in the anecdotes about General Washington told by the various characters. These interior anecdotes reveal a rich collection of Colonial folklore, and they reflect the full depth of interest and research of the author in this period of American history.

BARRY MILLER

Among science fiction writers, Barry Miller showed flashes of genius and promise as a freelance author during his twenties and thirties. This deaf writer first was successful with a short story, "The Dimensional Wasp," which appeared in *Other Worlds*; he later followed with a novelette, "Condition for Survival," published in *Amazing Stories*. He never found a popular publisher for several full-length science fiction novels he had also written, one of which was completed while he was a student at Gallaudet College.

There have been many novels and short stories produced by persons who have a slight hearing impairment or who became hard-of-hearing quite late in their careers. Many such writers are listed in the two-part bibliography compiled by Francis C. Higgins, entitled "The Book Mart" and published in the March 1947 and May 1950 issues of the *American Annals of the Deaf*. Among these are such noted novelists as Carolyn Wells, Ellen Glasgow, Rupert Hughes, Frank Swinnerton, and H. M. Tomlinson. Also listed are a number of novels by lesser known authors, reputed to be "deaf" but with sparse, if any, biographical evidence. These include Christine Whiting Parmentier, Raymond Leslie Goldman, and the German author Ruth Schaumann, whose works are not translated into English.

Anthologies

Many deaf writers have come from Gallaudet College. With a rich heritage and source of materials to draw from, it was natural for its alumni to promote the publication of a representative anthology of poetry and prose by deaf writers. This project was undertaken by a trio of deaf editors—Robert Panara, Taras B. Denis, and J. H. MacFarlane. Entitled *The Silent Muse Anthology*, the work was published in 1960 by the Gallaudet College Alumni Association and attracted widespread recognition in America and abroad. *The Silent Muse* enhanced the image of deaf people as poets, essayists, and storytellers, and also offered testimony of the motivation and cultural enrichment that can be obtained by providing higher education for deaf people in America. Many of the poems were also translated into German in 1971 under the title *Taubheit—Du Schicksal! (Deafness—My Fate, My Destiny!)*.

Another unique anthology is *The Deaf Experience* (1976), edited by Trenton W. Batson and Eugene Bergman, the latter being totally deaf. The book offers a sampling of various kinds of prose writings by deaf and hearing authors dealing with the deaf experience and with the image and function of the deaf character in fiction.

The stories taken from the nineteenth century are all by hearing authors. Among these are "Pierre and Camille" by Alfred Musset, which vividly illustrates the needless suffering and shame experienced by hearing parents who are unable to accept the reality of deafness in their child. Other stories are by Ivan Turgenev ("Mumu") and Guy de Maupassant ("The Deaf Mute"), presenting stereotyped images of the deaf serf and the deaf peasant in nineteenth-century Europe whose ignorance and naivete are preyed upon by their unfeeling peers, resulting in needless tragedies. However, there is a striking shift of tone and attitude in twentieth-century fiction. Because they seem to mirror the condition of modern people, deaf characters function as symbols and thus appear with greater frequency. Examples are "The Key," by Eudora Welty; "Talking Horse," by Bernard Malamud; and "At the Dances of the Deaf Mutes," by Walter Toman—all hearing authors. *See* LITERATURE, FICTIONAL CHARACTERS IN.

There are seven deaf authors represented in the anthology: David Wright, Howard L. Terry, Margaret P. Montague, John Kitto, Albert Ballin, Eugene Relgis, and Julius Wiggins. An added feature of *The Deaf Experience* is an annotated bibliography by Daniel Nascimento.

Drama

As with fiction writers, the deaf dramatist or playwright also faces the difficult task of reproducing the idiomatic speech and rhythms of hearing people. Until 1980, when closed captioned television programming was initiated nationally in the United States, the prospective deaf dramatist had no ready-made means of hearing and imitating the kind of talk and dialogue popularized on radio and television in situation comedies and serious drama. The result was that almost all of the published works by deaf playwrights deal with the theater of the deaf.

GILBERT EASTMAN

In 1973 two important contributions to the stage were made by Gilbert Eastman and Dorothy Miles. Both plays involved deaf people in situations common to the deaf experience and both were expressly intended for an audience of deaf theatergoers, conveyed through American Sign Language, with simultaneous, voice-over for hearing people.

Eastman's play, *Sign Me Alice*, is a humorous spoof of the various sign language systems that have been foisted on deaf people. It is a clever adaptation of G. B. Shaw's *Pygmalion*, which was later made into the musical *My Fair Lady*. In both these plays, a speech and English professor, Henry Higgins, takes on a bet and attempts to transform a Cockney flower girl of the streets, Eliza Doolittle, into a regal English lady by teaching her to speak and behave in the cultivated English manner. *Sign Me Alice* uses a similar story line.

Eastman followed *Sign Me Alice* with another play, *Laurent Clerc: A Profile*, which he completed in 1976 after spending a sabbatical leave in France. During his stay, he researched material on the life of Clerc, the first deaf teacher of deaf people in the United States, who was born and educated in France. The play dramatizes the turning points in Clerc's career and his impact on deaf education, as well as his legacy of teaching and disseminating sign language.

DOROTHY S. MILES

Dorothy S. Miles adapted her play *A Play of Our Own* (1973) from the motion picture *Guess Who's Coming to Dinner?* (1967), which deals with mixed marriage. In *A Play of Our Own*, the mixed marriage is between a deaf woman and a hearing man.

Miles was a member of the National Theatre of the Deaf when she wrote an outline of the play, and worked in collaboration with the Hartford Thespians, a deaf semiprofessional theater group in Connecticut, to develop the complete script. The play was developed naturally, via sign language and improvisation, and intended primarily for deaf playgoers.

A Play of Our Own became a perennial stage classic in deaf community theaters. It was published in book form for general circulation in 1984. Several people wrote sequels to the drama. A hearing actor with the National Theatre of the Deaf, Rico Peterson, wrote *A Play of Our Own, Part 2* (1978). Deaf playwright Steve Baldwin both wrote the script and directed *A Play of Our Own, Part 3* (1979) in Dallas, Texas, and followed it with yet another sequel, *A Play of Our Own, Part 4: Her Hands Will Dance, Her Heart Will Sing*, which premiered at Bridgewater State College, Massachusetts (1981).

EUGENE BERGMAN

In 1980 the National Association of the Deaf held its Centennial Convention in Cincinnati, Ohio. One of the main attractions was the premiere performance of the new play *Tales from a Clubroom* by Bernard Bragg and Eugene Bergman. The play focuses on a club for the deaf and on the lives of some of the deaf characters, who frequent it.

Tales from a Clubroom was published in book form in 1981.

BERNARD BRAGG

Bernard Bragg also wrote and directed a one-act romantic comedy, *That Makes Two of Us* (1979), which was taken on tour by the Gallaudet College Touring Company in 1980–1981. The play went beyond the usual comic misunderstandings that ensue when a deaf manualist romances a deaf oralist. Adding to the dilemma was the sexist issue of equal opportunity for women. In an attempt to resolve the problem of who yields to whom, as well as to what method of communication should be used, Bragg neatly manipulates the ending of the play so as to satisfy both the male lead character and the female lead character.

The play also introduced an innovative feature, taken directly from deaf culture and real life situations. These were the "interpreters," who took turns and alternated roles when translating signs to speech and speech to signs for the deaf and hearing audience, even participating in the action while doing both simultaneously.

A number of other deaf dramatists have written scripts for theater productions, though many have not been published in book form. Some of these were highly successful plays performed by professional theaters of the deaf such as the National Theatre of the Deaf and the Fairmount Theatre group. The playwrights were mostly graduates of the Deaf Playwrights Conference, sponsored annually by the National Theatre of the Deaf for the encouragement and development of deaf dramatists.

SHANNY MOW

Shanny Mow, a former actor and the resident director of the National Theatre of the Deaf's Deaf Playwrights Conference, has earned a reputation as a model for budding playwrights. In 1980 Mow created a novel adaptation of Homer's epic poem *The Iliad*. Entitled *The Iliad: Play by Play*, it was an athletic spoof of the Trojan War, using the metaphor of a football game. Costumed with fancy helmets and sparkling nylon jerseys bulging over shoulder pads, these epic heroes take on a contemporary look and become rugged participants of a "Super Bowl" war fought on a stadium battleground. However, despite Mow's satire, the story line remains faithful to Homer's epic and its tragic ending.

For the 1981–1982 season the National Theatre of the Deaf toured the United States and Japan with a revival of its adaptation of the Sumerian epic *Gilgamesh*. On the same billing was an original one-act play by Mow, *Incident at Shoshomi Junction, or The Ghost of Chastity Past*. It was a melo-

dramatic western performed in the style of popular Kabuki acting, the trademark of Japanese theater. It featured a typical cowboy setting except that the characters were dressed in Japanese costumes and performed in the slow-motion movement and mime of Kabuki actors. The result was most ingenious and hilarious, and the play proved to be a big hit, especially with deaf audiences.

In 1982–1983 Mow collaborated with a hearing person, David Hays (the founder and artistic director of the National Theatre of the Deaf), in developing another spoof, this one dealing with a version of the quest of the Holy Grail. The script's title was *Parzival: From the Horse's Mouth*, and featured various knights and ladies of King Arthur's Court in many comic excursions from the original legend. A unique feature of the play was the creation of "Nevefere," the faithful talking horse of the hero.

ADRIAN BLUE

In 1982, Adrian Blue, a veteran star of the National Theatre of the Deaf and an outstanding mime, took a one-year leave to perform and write for the Fairmount Theatre of the Deaf. While there, he wrote and directed an original full-length play, *Circus of Sign*, which enjoyed a successful run at the Brooks Theatre in Cleveland, Ohio. Blue's variety show, which showcased the deaf performer's talent for circus mimicry through mime and sign language, was named Outstanding Original Script of 1982 by the Cleveland Critics Circle.

DON BANGS

Also in 1982, fellow director and playwright Don Bangs developed a clever adaptation of Molière's classic *The Miser* for the Fairmount Theatre group. Bangs, who has several television shows for the deaf to his credit, spoofed the play with a "spaghetti western" version. The play was performed on television and earned an Emmy Award for outstanding achievement in special programming. It was also featured on national television (Public Broadcasting Service).

STEVE BALDWIN

Another product of the Deaf Playwrights Conference is Steve Baldwin, director of the drama department at the Southwest Collegiate Institute for the Deaf in Big Spring, Texas. He has been prolific as a playwright, director, and producer of many plays for college and community theater production. His *Deaf Smith* (1985) is a historical drama of the legendary hero of the Texan Revolution who was General Houston's chief scout and war spy. In 1985 Baldwin was honored as the recipient of the Cultural Achievement Award by the West Texas Chamber of Commerce in San Angelo for his sustained contributions to the theater. *See* LITERATURE, DRAMATIC CHARACTERS IN; SMITH, ERASTUS.

Bibliography

Batson, Trenton W., and Eugene Bergman: *The Deaf Experience*, Merriam-Eddy Co., 1976.

Braddock, Guilbert C: *Notable Deaf Persons*, Gallaudet College Alumni Association, 1975.

Campbell, Oscar James, and Edward G. Quinn (eds.): *The Reader's Cyclopedia of Shakespeare*, Thomas Crowell, 1966.

Encyclopedia Americana, vol. 12, p. 185, 1983.

Gannon, Jack R.: *Deaf Heritage: A Narrative History of Deaf America*, National Association of the Deaf, 1981.

Hornstein, Lillian, G. D. Percy, and Sterling A. Brown (eds.): *The Reader's Companion to World Literature*, New American Library, 1956.

Jones, Barry, and M. V. Dixon: *The Rutledge Dictionary of People*, Rutledge Press, 1981.

Kunitz, Stanley, and Vineta Colby (eds.): *European Authors, 1000–1900: A Biographical Dictionary of European Literature*, H. W. Wilson Co., 1967.

Lipa, Karel, and Pavel Les: *We Have Overcome*, TISK Brno, Czechoslovakia, 1971.

Magill, Frank (ed.): *Masterplots from the World's Fine Literature*, third series, Salem Press, 1960.

National Theatre of the Deaf: *News* (newsletter), Summer 1981, Winter 1982, Summer 1982.

Panara, Robert: "The Deaf Writer: From Colonial Times to the Present", *American Annals of the Deaf*, part 1, September 1970, part 2, November 1970.

——— and John Panara: *Great Deaf Americans*, T.J. Publishers, 1983.

Price, Max: "Iliad Given a Modern Touch," *Denver Post*, October 3, 1980.

Souvenir Program Book, National Theatre of the Deaf, 1983–1984.

Taylor, Gladys M.: "Deaf Characters in Short Stories: A Selective Bibliography," *Deaf American*, part 1, July/August 1976, part 2, October 1976.

Robert Panara

LITTLE PAPER FAMILY

The Little Paper Family began inconspicuously in 1849, when the North Carolina Institution for the Deaf and Blind began producing a small periodical titled *The Deaf Mute*. Before the end of the century, state residential schools for deaf students throughout the United States had followed the North Carolina school's example, each composing, editing, and printing its own monthly, biweekly, weekly, or even daily newspaper. Together, these school journals were called the Little Paper Family.

PURPOSE

The residential schools usually stated that their periodicals served more than one purpose. The Colorado *Index*, for example, announced that its function was to aid students in their literary work, to inform the school's patrons of important events, and to teach students the art of printing. Similarly, the Florida *Institute Herald* began in 1891 with the stated objectives of teaching printing, interesting students in reading, and keeping the public informed about the school.

The most important of the objectives was to teach printing. Beginning in the late nineteenth century and continuing far into the twentieth, printing was the single most common form of skilled employment for deaf persons, usually males, who completed secondary education. Discriminated against in many occupations, deaf people could gain employment as machine operators, particularly as operators of printing presses, and the state residential schools provided the necessary training. *See* DEAF COMMUNITY: Socioeconomic Status; DEAF POPULATION.

In addition to their academic department, or "intellectual department" as some named it, the residential schools typically had a printing department. This was presided over by an experienced, often deaf, printer, called the foreman. The foreman trained students in printing while producing the school's Little Paper. The foreman sometimes owned the paper and might have earned income from advertisements and subscription fees.

The Little Paper Family periodicals served another vital function. They helped forge a network among the widely scattered members of the deaf community. Together with other periodicals written, printed, and read by deaf people and a growing number of local, state, and national organizations, such as the National Association of the Deaf and the National Fraternal Society of the Deaf, the Little Paper Family provided a way for deaf individuals to keep in touch with their community and their culture. *See* NATIONAL ASSOCIATION OF THE DEAF: NATIONAL FRATERNAL SOCIETY OF THE DEAF.

The residential schools often were the foci of deaf culture in the nineteenth and early twentieth centuries. It was there that most deaf children, especially the large majority with hearing parents, first learned sign language, made contact with others who shared a similar set of experiences, and began to define themselves as deaf people. By means of the schools' periodicals, graduates kept in touch with the events and individuals at their alma mater and with deaf persons in other states. News about other schools, about national events important to deaf persons, and polite gossip about deaf individuals filled the pages of the Little Paper Family.

FORMAT

The format of the Little Paper Family publications during their heyday was relatively uniform. Many began their first page with a poem in the upper left corner. This might have been followed by one long article or several shorter ones that tended to be either morally uplifting or bizarre and sensational. The Arkansas *Optic* of October 17, 1891, for example, had on its first page a lengthy piece about the evils of the lottery, followed by short, didactic tidbits such as "What Mothers Are Made For," "Advice to Young Men," and "How To Keep Your Friends." The California *Weekly News* led off an 1889 issue with sensational, and suspect, stories about an elk that was trained to the harness, a 1700-pound grizzly bear that nine riflemen shot 109 times before it died, and a list of the world's 12 greatest women. When the reader's interest was captured with these oddities, borrowed from publications for hearing readers, and after the obligation to provide morally solid advice was fulfilled, the papers sharpened their focus.

Succeeding pages typically contained news of specific interest to the deaf community. A common feature was a column or page called "The Exchange" or "Exchanges" that excerpted pieces from other periodicals in the Little Paper Family. These might tell about the changes in school curriculum or, more often, personnel: who was hired, who left, who was promoted, who married, who died. In this informal but effective way, deaf people kept in touch with each other and became aware of events that affected their friends and the institutions that solidified their dispersed community.

Local news stories provided the material reprinted in other periodicals' exchange sections. Each paper provided succinct summaries of events, particularly those involving people, that might be of interest to readers familiar with the school. These news items were similar to those that might be found in any small-town newspaper, including such trivia as who was visiting whom, as well as notices of deaths and marriages.

Editorials appeared, too, but most often they were very mild. Little Paper Family editors, as one at the *Nebraska Journal* commented in a private letter during a particularly tumultuous period in the Nebraska school's history, depended on the goodwill of the school's administration for their livelihood and relatively prestigious positions. They could not afford to alienate or offend either the school's superintendent or his superiors, who usually were hearing persons.

A regular feature of many papers was a page specifically for younger children at the school. The Alabama *Messenger* typically designated this section "Our Little People" and filled it with short, simple stories and lessons. These were written in a direct style, calculated to be comprehensible to children with poorly developed English language skills, and often were intended to be inspirational.

Less inspirational, but more useful, was information about the school's structure, policies, per-

sonnel, and sometimes its curriculum. This material often appeared on the last page. The name and duties of each member of the school's staff, beginning with the superintendent and including the members of the governing board, were listed, followed by a review of the school's mandate, policies for admission, instruction units, and sometimes the school calendar.

SIGNIFICANCE

The Little Paper Family was one of the means used by the American deaf community to establish and then to retain its identity. Confronted in the late nineteenth and early twentieth centuries with demands to be assimilated into the hearing world, to abjure their language of signs, to stop teaching deaf children, to marry hearing people, to give up their clubs and associations and periodicals, deaf Americans persevered. They maintained social and professional ties and reinforced standards of acceptable behavior through periodicals, including the school papers, they exchanged.

Work on the Little Paper Family also trained a corps of deaf printers, providing steady and remunerative employment. Printers had a useful skill, one that did not depend on auditory ability. Coming together to work on large metropolitan newspapers, deaf printers provided a nucleus around which other deaf people could gather to sustain community and ties.

Many leaders of the deaf community were printers at some point in their lives. Today, printing is often seen as a vocational skill fit only for students who show little academic ability. But for deaf people it was not always so. Many of the deaf people who ultimately became professors at Gallaudet College, for instance, began their working careers as printers, using to advantage the skills developed in their residential schools (and at Gallaudet) until they could secure the education necessary to pursue a more intellectual career. Perhaps the first of these was Amos Draper, who learned printing at the American School for the Deaf while working on the *Gallaudet Guide*, and who then became a professional printer in Illinois before going to Gallaudet College. In 1872 he became a professor of Latin and mathematics at Gallaudet. George Veditz, one of the intellectual giants of the deaf community, was at one time the foreman of the printing office at the Maryland School for the Deaf. Fred Schreiber, who made the National Association of the Deaf into a dynamic and effective organization, was also a former printer. *See* GALLAUDET COLLEGE; SCHREIBER, FREDERICK CARL; VEDITZ, GEORGE WILLIAM.

The Little Paper Family periodicals also provide a valuable record of the deaf community's history and the individuals who shaped it. Examination of local news items, the exchanges, and the information about school personnel allows the reconstruction of the histories of schools and persons. Even the changes in the names of these journals are illustrative.

Most Little Papers began with the word "deaf-mute" in their titles, reflecting the common mid-nineteenth century assumption that deafness created muteness. By the 1880s or 1890s, when there was more emphasis on speech teaching in American schools for deaf people and when it was widely recognized that some deaf persons (especially those with late-onset deafness and those with some hearing in the speech frequencies) could speak intelligibly, "deaf-mute" became an anachronism. To try to eliminate from the popular mind the connection between deafness and loss of speech, many Little Papers changed their mastheads: the Arkansas *Deaf-Mute Optic* became the *Optic*; the *Mute Journal of Nebraska*, the Nebraska *Journal*; the *Mute's Chronicle*, the Ohio *Chronicle*; and so on. Little papers founded later, such as the Arizona *Cactus* in 1926, never had the derogatory "deaf-mute" in their titles. *See* SPEECH.

Another term that was considered appropriate when deaf education commenced, but which became derogatory, was "institution." Its demise, too, can be traced through the Little Paper Family. Editorials in the late nineteenth century protested the use of "institution," or the more odious "asylum," in the name of schools for deaf children, because they imputed an eleemosynary rather than an educational function to the schools. This issue was connected as well with the schools' attempts to be placed administratively under state boards of education, rather than under the board or agency that controlled prisons and mental hospitals. Hence, it is not surprising that the Florida *Institute Herald*, for example, changed its name in 1900 to the *School Herald*.

The Little Paper Family, then, is more than an artifact of the deaf community. It was an institution that helped deaf Americans forge and maintain their identity; it provided a training ground for leaders; and it led to employment for deaf people. Today, it provides an important source of historical information that is readily accessible and enjoyable to use.

Bibliography

Gannon, Jack R.: *Deaf Heritage: A Narrative History of Deaf America*, National Association of the Deaf, Silver Spring, Maryland, 1981.

Most Little Papers are available in the Gallaudet College Library.

John V. Van Cleve

M

MANUALLY CODED ENGLISH

The phrase "manually coded English" or "manual codes for English" (MCE) is used generically to refer to all artificially developed codes that aim to represent the English language in manual (sign) form. The best known of these codes—Seeing Essential English (SEE 1), Signing Exact English (SEE 2), and Signed English—were developed in the late 1960s and early 1970s in an attempt to remedy deaf students' unsatisfactory scores on English tests after decades of education under the strictly oral system. It was assumed that continuous visual exposure to a form of signing structured like English, in addition to spoken English, would aid students' acquisition of English. Other terms that have been used to refer generically to these codes are manual English and signed English, although both are also used as names for specific codes.

STRUCTURE

Like Morse code and braille, the manual codes are not languages themselves, but are codes that attempt to reflect the structure and vocabulary of a language—in this case, English. However, unlike Morse code and braille, the manual codes for English have taken some of their vocabulary from a second language, American Sign Language (ASL). When these signs were "borrowed" from ASL, they were altered in dramatic ways. In many cases, one or more significant parts of the sign were changed. The handshape of many signs was changed and replaced with a handshape from the manual alphabet that corresponds to the initial letter of a particular English word. For example, the flat open handshape that occurs in the ASL sign meaning "happy" or "glad" was replaced with a G handshape to represent the English word "glad." This change in handshape creates a new sign, just like replacement of the *c* in "cat" with a *d* creates a new word, "dat." Similarly, the movements of signs in MCE are significantly altered from their appearance in ASL. *See* SIGN LANGUAGES: American.

MCE also changes the grammatical functions of many signs from their usage in ASL. For example, signs that are verbs in ASL, like LOVE and BITE, are used as both nouns and verbs in MCE. Other signs in ASL that are verbs are used as prepositions. For example, the ASL signs that mean "to join to" and "to be above (something)" are used as prepositions in SEE 2, meaning "of" and "over," respectively. So when the SEE 2 user speaks and signs "I live over there," the ASL signer sees "I live be above something there."

This example also illustrates the area in which MCE most dramatically changes ASL signs—meaning. Since MCE frequently assigns one sign to represent one word (for example, the same sign is used whenever the word "over" appears in a sentence), signs are used to mean very different things from their usage in ASL. To the ASL signer, the SEE 2 version of "over and over again" appears as "be above something and be above something again." Similarly, SEE 2 "overweight" appears as "be above something weigh + t."

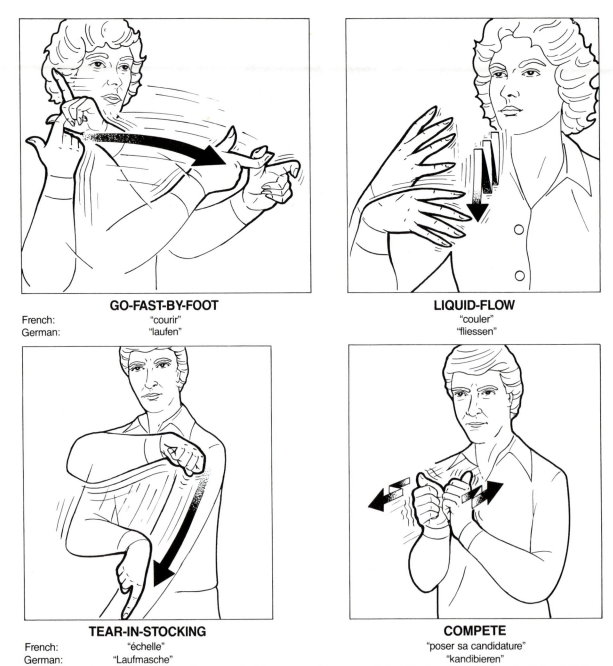

GO-FAST-BY-FOOT

| French: | "courir" |
| German: | "laufen" |

LIQUID-FLOW

"couler"
"fliessen"

TEAR-IN-STOCKING

| French: | "échelle" |
| German: | "Laufmasche" |

COMPETE

"poser sa candidature"
"kandibieren"

Meanings of the English word "run" expressed with separate signs or words in ASL, French, and German. (After C. Baker and D. Cokely, *American Sign Language: A Teacher's Resource Text on Grammar and Culture*, T. J. Publishers, Silver Spring, Maryland, 1980)

English has many multiple-meaning words, for example, "play" (which can mean a recreational activity or a dramatic production), "right" (which can mean a direction, or correct, or a legal privilege), and "pool" (which can mean a game, or an area for swimming, or a collection of things). In ASL, there are separate signs for each meaning. For example, to express the different meanings of "run" in the following sentences, ASL would use separate signs that mean, respectively, "go fast by foot," "liquid flow," "tear in stocking," and "compete": (1) She is running home. (2) She left the water running. (3) She has a run in her stocking. (4) She will run for president.

In the same way, German and French use different vocabulary items to express these different meanings. However, since English uses the same word "run," MCE uses the same sign—in this case, a variant of the ASL sign meaning "go fast by foot."

In addition to the borrowed and significantly altered vocabulary of ASL, the manual codes also include newly invented signs for English affixes like "-ing," "-ly," "-ment," and "-ness." The number of these affixes varies among the different codes. For example, SEE 2 has over 50; Signed English uses only 14.

EFFECTIVENESS

When the manual codes were introduced, developers expected that teachers and parents would learn the rules and vocabulary of a code and then use it accurately and continuously with their deaf students or children. However, research in the mid to late 1970s began to show that neither teachers nor parents were accurately using the codes. In fact, without being aware of it, they were deleting many of the required signs—deleting not only conjunctions and prepositions, but also verbs and nouns in a manner that often made the sign representation unintelligible.

Although teachers with more experience in signing were found to make fewer errors (and deaf teachers made the least errors), the deletions of even the best signers were significant. Eventually, researchers began to examine the effect of differences in signing rate and speaking rate on deletions in MCE signing. They found that it takes about twice as much time to produce a sign as it takes to say a word. So when hearing people sign each word that they say, they have to slow down their speaking rate by 100 percent. In addition, since many words like "talks" (talk + s), "went" (go + past tense), and "slowly" (slow + ly) are represented with more than one sign, the rate is made even slower. The resultant, tediously slow communication rate apparently is intolerable for MCE users, so they delete many of the required signs. Researchers also have stated that the cognitive burden of trying to think and transmit information in two modalities (speech and sign) simultaneously is too heavy and is a factor leading to the deletions and other errors found in MCE signing. *See* SOCIO-LINGUISTICS: Simultaneous Communication.

In light of these difficulties, the primary author of Signed English, Harry Bornstein, wrote in 1982 that teachers working with adolescents and adults could expect to make deletions in their signing, and suggested ways in which they might make these deletions, resulting in a "leaner version" of Signed English. However, he maintains that teachers and parents with young children should still sacrifice "comfortable transmission" for the sake of providing an accurate model of English and simply should sign slowly in order to sign "accurately."

As a result of the deletions and other errors described in research studies, deaf students clearly are not being exposed to a consistent model of MCE. However, the question remains whether even this faulty use of MCE still can help improve deaf students' acquisition of English. Research has shown that students can learn to use structures of MCE accurately in certain contexts, but it has not yet been demonstrated credibly how this skill in MCE relates to the learning of English (written or spoken).

MODEL OF ENGLISH

The assumption of the creators and users of MCE is that such codes do model accurately and completely the English language, enabling deaf students to "see" English manually. However, linguists who have studied MCE have concluded that the codes do not presently model English accurately and completely, and that they never could accurately and completely model English.

There are several reasons for this conclusion. Concerning the codes now in use, linguists note their failure to distinguish between free and bound morphemes (which is crucial in English). For example, spoken English distinguishes between "black board" (meaning a board that is black) and "blackboard" (meaning a board, that could be green, that one writes on with chalk) by changing the way the words are pronounced (in the compound, by stressing the first part of the word and reducing the second part). Written English distinguishes the two meanings by writing one as two words and the other as one word. MCE does not distinguish between the two.

Another flaw with the codes is their resistance to the kind of assimilation and reduction naturally occurring in English (for example, saying "gonna" instead of the full form "going to"), and the fact that many of their morphemes are semantically tied to another language. For example, when English speakers hear the sentence "The water is running," they do not imagine water on two legs "running." However, the MCE sign borrowed from ASL is rooted in the meaning "go fast by foot" and continues to be used with that sole meaning in ASL today. These semantic ties to ASL make MCE very different from English.

Furthermore, linguists have shown that the modality of a language (vocal-auditory versus visual-gestural) significantly shapes its structure. One cannot expect a manual code to model the structure of a vocal-auditory language like English. For example, crucial semantic, syntactic, pragmatic, and discourse types of information are carried by intonation and vocal stress in English. One simply cannot move the hands up and down to model the way that English expresses this information. Attempting to include this information in gestural form means making MCE change to look more like ASL and less like English.

RESPONSE OF THE DEAF COMMUNITY

With notable exceptions, it appears that the majority of deaf people are alienated, and some offended, by the manual codes. In fact, a deaf person's intentional signing in one of the codes is one way to elicit laughter among deaf people and make jokes at the expense of teachers and hearing people. Deaf adults frequently comment that the signs are "ugly," "odd-looking," "confusing," or "boring."

This response is not surprising for several reasons. A language is an extremely important means of unifying a group of people and expressing who they are. When someone tries to change a community's language in an unnatural way, the community naturally becomes defensive. Both explicitly and implicitly, efforts to develop and spread the use of MCE have been seen as an effort to get rid of and replace ASL. *See* SOCIOLINGUISTICS: Language Attitudes.

Another reason for the resistance to MCE is the way it changes unnaturally the structure of ASL signs, often violating the rules found to characterize many other indigenous signed languages of the world in addition to ASL. That is, the effort to make signs fit the structure of a vocal-auditory language (English) brings MCE in conflict with the structure naturally occurring in visual-gestural languages, languages that are built to fit the needs and capabilities of the eyes and body.

USAGE

In most primary and elementary schools and programs serving deaf children, some form of MCE is used by teachers (and often by interpreters in mainstream programs). In the upper grades, teachers have tended to lessen their focus on signing "exact English" and have used the forms of signing frequently referred to as Pidgin Sign English. *See* SOCIOLINGUISTICS: Sign Language Continuum.

Bibliography

Baker, C.: "How Does 'Sim-Com' Fit into a Bilingual Approach to Education?", in F. Caccamise and D. Hicks (eds.), *Proceedings of the Second National Symposium on Sign Language Research and Teaching*, pp. 13–261, National Association of the Deaf, Silver Spring, Maryland, 1980.

Baker, C., and D. Cokely: "English in the Deaf Community," *American Sign Language: A Teacher's Resource Text on Grammar and Culture*, T. J. Publishers, Silver Spring, Maryland, 1980.

Bornstein, H.: "Towards a Theory of Use of Signed English: From Birth Through Adulthood," *American Annals of the Deaf*, 127:26–31, 1982.

Charrow, V.: "A Linguist's View of Manual English," in Crammatte and Crammatte (eds.), *Proceedings of the Seventh World Congress of the World Federation of the Deaf*, pp. 78–82, National Association of the Deaf, Silver Spring, Maryland, 1976.

Cokely, D., and R. Gawlik: "A Position Paper on the Relationship Between Manual English and Sign," *Deaf American*, May 7–11, 1973.

Kannapell, B.: "Language Choice Reflects Identity Choice: A Sociolinguistic Study of Deaf College Students," unpublished doctoral dissertation, Georgetown University, 1985.

Kluwin, T.: "A Rationale for Modifying Classroom Signing Systems," *Sign Language Studies*, 31:179–187, 1981.

Marmor, G., and L. Petitto: "Simultaneous Communication in the Classroom: How Well Is English Grammar Represented?", *Sign Language Studies*, 23:99–136, 1979.

Woodward, J.: "Manual English: A Problem in Language Planning and Standardization," in G. Gustason and J. Woodward (eds.), *Recent Developments in Manual English*, pp. 1–12, Gallaudet College Press, Washington, D.C., 1973.

Charlotte Baker-Shenk

SEE

The acronym SEE is used for both Seeing Essential English (sometimes called SEE 1) and Signing Exact English (SEE 2). These are both manual codes for the representation of English on the hands, and both originated from the desire to provide deaf students with a visually clear English model. The individuals who originally worked together on Seeing Essential English in the late 1960s and early 1970s encountered some philosophical differences, and the resulting division led to the establishment of Signing Exact English.

Both systems were developed in an attempt to improve the English mastery and educational achievement of deaf students, particularly their poor showing in reading and English language scores on academic achievement tests. For over 50 years, scores reported in these two areas for high-school-aged deaf students had hovered around the level attained by fourth- and fifth-grade hearing children. A 1965 national study noted the poor educational showing, and emphasized that the chief problem was in the area of learning English. A study in the 1940s reported that only 24 words made up nearly one-third of the English words in print in popular American magazines, and these are words commonly ignored in speechreading or dropped in signing: articles, conjunctions, prepositions, pronouns, and auxiliaries. Accordingly, the SEE systems developed clear signs for such words when no sign, or a sign with various English translations, existed in American Sign Language (such as THE, IS, ARE), and signs for inflections (such as -S, -ING, -ED, -NESS). Words that previously had been combination signs in ASL (such as MOTHER-FATHER for "parents") were modified, often by the addition of the first letter of the word (such as using the P handshape in the MOTHER-FATHER movement for PARENT). *See* EDUCATION: Problems.

EXAMPLES OF SEE SIGNS

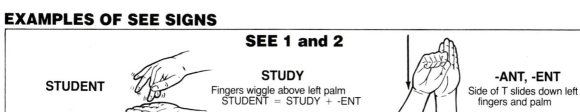

SEE 1 and 2

STUDENT

STUDY
Fingers wiggle above left palm
STUDENT = STUDY + -ENT

-ANT, -ENT
Side of T slides down left
fingers and palm

BASIC WORDS

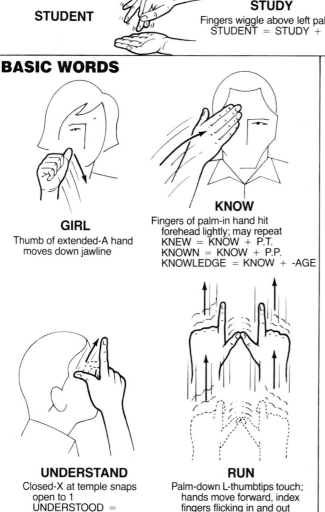

GIRL
Thumb of extended-A hand
moves down jawline

KNOW
Fingers of palm-in hand hit
forehead lightly; may repeat
KNEW = KNOW + P.T.
KNOWN = KNOW + P.P.
KNOWLEDGE = KNOW + -AGE

UNDERSTAND
Closed-X at temple snaps
open to 1
UNDERSTOOD =
UNDERSTAND + P.T.

RUN
Palm-down L-thumbtips touch;
hands move forward, index
fingers flicking in and out
rapidly
RAN = RUN + P.T.

COMPLEX WORDS

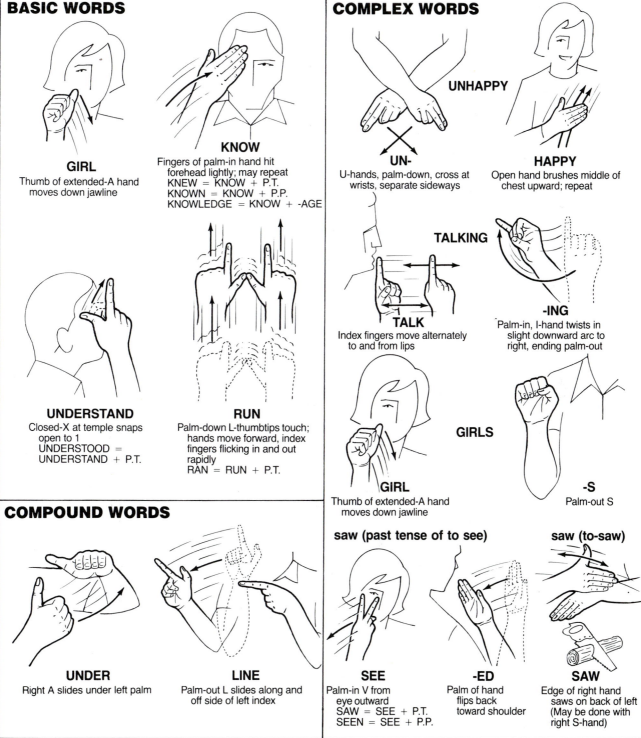

UNHAPPY

UN-
U-hands, palm-down, cross at
wrists, separate sideways

HAPPY
Open hand brushes middle of
chest upward; repeat

TALKING

TALK
Index fingers move alternately
to and from lips

-ING
Palm-in, I-hand twists in
slight downward arc to
right, ending palm-out

GIRLS

GIRL
Thumb of extended-A hand
moves down jawline

-S
Palm-out S

COMPOUND WORDS

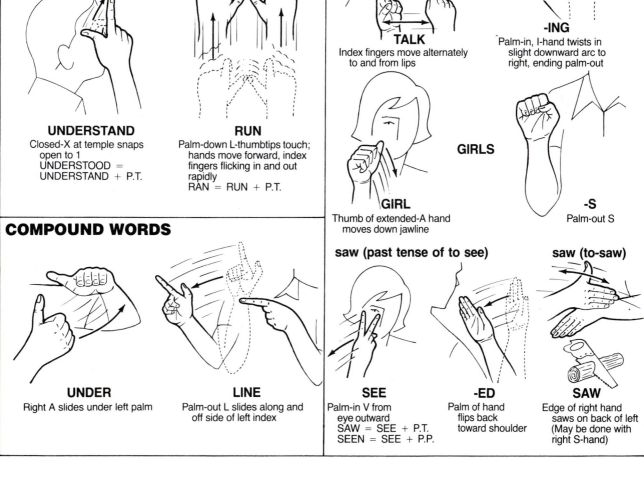

UNDER
Right A slides under left palm

LINE
Palm-out L slides along and
off side of left index

saw (past tense of to see)

SEE
Palm-in V from
eye outward
SAW = SEE + P.T.
SEEN = SEE + P.P.

-ED
Palm of hand
flips back
toward shoulder

saw (to-saw)

SAW
Edge of right hand
saws on back of left
(May be done with
right S-hand)

The split between SEE 1 and SEE 2 was caused by a difference in the degree to which English words were signed in parts or as whole words. SEE 1 followed an approach involving the signing of roots plus affixes or inflections more than did SEE 2. SEE 1, for instance, used PORT as a root sign for IM-PORT-ANT, while SEE 2 retained the ASL sign for the entire word IMPORTANT. Both systems would sign "student" as STUDY-ENT. A national survey in 1979 indicated that SEE 2 was the most widely used text in programs for hearing-impaired persons in the United States using a signed English system.

Signing Exact English, in its attempt to represent English, uses many of the same signs that are found in American Sign Language. For instance, the signs for GIRL, HOME, KNOW are the same. However, because the language being modeled is English, signs are not always used as they are in ASL. Signing Exact English divides words into three groups: basic, complex, and compound.

Basic words are considered those which cannot be subdivided and retain a complete meaning. Such words, for instance, would include GIRL, KNOW, RUN. Such words are treated according to a "two out of three" rule: if any two of the three factors of spelling, sound, and meaning are the same, the same sign is utilized. This means, for example, that RIGHT would be signed with one sign for the meanings of "right and left" and "right and wrong" since spelling and sound are the same. However, RIGHT and WRITE would be signed differently since although sound is the same, spelling and meaning differ. Similarly, PRESENT as in "the present time" would be signed differently from PRESENT in "he will present the award" since only spelling is the same, and sound and meaning differ.

Complex words are those which consist of a basic word plus an affix: GIRL-S, UN-HAPPY, TALK-ING. Once an affix is added to a basic word, the resulting combination is no longer treated as a basic word. This means, for example, that when the past tense is added to SEE to form "saw" (SEE-ED), the sign is not the same as that used for the basic word SAW in "I will saw some wood."

Compound words consist of two basic words put together. This is done only when the meaning of the basic words remains consistent. For instance, "underline" is signed UNDER-LINE, because the meanings of "under" and "line" are retained, but "understand" is signed as one word, UNDER-STAND, because there is no relation to the meanings of "under" or "stand."

If an unambiguous sign exists in ASL, that sign is retained even though it could be signed differently according to the complex- or compound-word principles. For example, "misunderstand" could, according to the complex-word principle, be signed MIS-UNDERSTAND, but since an unambiguous sign with only one English translation exists in ASL, the sign is retained for MISUNDERSTAND. Similarly, "helpless, speechless" are signed HELP-LESS, SPEECH-LESS, but because there is an unambiguous ASL sign, "careless" is signed CARELESS.

The most basic principle of Signing Exact English is to sign what is said in English. This means that idioms or multiple meanings are signed according to the English words used: "knock it off" would be signed KNOCK IT OFF rather than as FINISH or STOP.

The rapid spread of this system among parents and teachers in the 1970s led to questions as to both the possibility of signing this way without dropping signs and whether there was improvement in deaf children's English skills. Research in the late 1970s and early 1980s indicated that many individuals were not consistent about signing each word or inflection, but that when teachers were consistent the students had improved test scores in English. Teacher consistency, rather than age of student, number of years in a SEE program, sex, or degree of hearing loss, seemed to be the deciding factor. With preschool children, a study of mothers indicated that children at this age developed and used what the mother used at home rather than what was used in school.

Bibliography

Anthony, D.: *Seeing Essential English*, 1971.

Babbidge, H.: *A Report to the Secretary of Health, Education and Welfare by His Advisory Committee on Education of the Deaf*, 1965.

Crandall, K.: "A Comparison of Signs Used by Mothers and Deaf Children During Early Childhood," *Proceedings of the Convention of American Instructors of the Deaf*, 1975.

Gilman, L. A., J. M. Davis, and M. J. M. Raffin: "Use of Common Morphemes by Hearing-Impaired Children Exposed to a System of Manual English," *Journal of Auditory Research*, 20:57–69, 1980.

Gustason, G. (ed.): *Using Signing Exact English in Total Communication*, 1981.

———, D. Pfetzing, and E. Zawolkow: *Signing Exact English*, 1980.

Lorge, E., and H. Thorndike: *A Teacher's Word Book of 30,000 Words*, 1944.

Gerilee Gustason

Signed English

To some degree, deaf persons must depend upon what they see to learn the spoken language of their community. Accordingly, a number of sign systems, based upon signs drawn from the American Sign Language, have been devised to supplement and parallel speech to help deaf children and adults learn English. Signed English is a manual English system developed by a team led by Harry Bornstein,

Little Red Riding Hood kissed her mother goodbye and walked happily through the woods to Grandmother's house.

5

Sample page from *Little Red Riding Hood*, the first book to appear in Signed English.

Karen L. Saulnier, Lillian B. Hamilton, and Ralph R. Miller, Sr., at Gallaudet College in the early 1970s. It is the most rapidly growing system in use to help deaf students and adults learn English throughout the United States today. Structurally speaking, it is the least complicated of the manual English systems and can be easily modified to meet various linguistic needs and levels. *See* GALLAUDET COLLEGE.

NATURE OF THE PROBLEM

Any attempt to produce an exact manual representation of spoken English will prove to be cumbersome. This is due to the fact that a detailed signing process is much slower than the speaking process. A balance must be struck between providing a signer with adequate English vocabulary and grammar and allowing ease of signing.

PROPOSED SOLUTION

Consequently, Signed English's logic and design has been kept simple and straightforward. It is made up of two kinds of signs: sign words and sign markers. Each sign word represents a separate entry in

a standard English dictionary, with all of its various meanings. Sign words do not represent spelling or sound. The more than 3100 sign words currently in the system are essentially the most frequently used words in English and are signed in the same order as in English. In addition, there are 14 sign markers which, when added to the sign word, add to its meaning much as do affixes in English, for example, the plurals, the past. As with the sign words, sign markers were selected because of frequency of use. In Signed English one uses either a sign word alone or a sign word and one sign marker to represent a word. More complicated vocabulary is fingerspelled. *See* SIGNS: Fingerspelling.

Clearly, 3100 words and 14 affixes do not represent the whole of English. This manual model of English is limited for the following reasons: (1) Research indicates that Signed English in its present form poses a formidable learning task to parents, students, and teachers. A more complete model would necessarily be more complex and hence even more difficult to learn and use. (2) The vocabulary and structure of Signed English is complete enough to meet the communication needs of most individuals. The manual alphabet is available to represent those words and word form changes outside the bounds of the system. (3) Aspects of the English language can be gleaned through the combined input of speechreading, aided listening, and the printed text. There is no need to place the entire burden of providing linguistic information on the manual component. *See* HEARING AIDS; SPEECHREADING.

CURRENT STATUS

The Signed English system's most unusual feature is its large and attractive set of teaching aids, that is, illustrated books and posters. Although these teaching aids were initially designed with the young deaf child in mind, they are being adapted more and more frequently to the classrooms and homes of mentally, socially, or linguistically retarded individuals of all ages. The Signed English series is composed of three special-purpose books, fifty children's books, three posters, and the main reference book, *The Comprehensive Signed English Dictionary.*

FUTURE STATUS

According to a survey conducted in 1978, programs for deaf students since 1968 had made a dramatic leap in espousing the philosophy of total communication, coupled with the trend toward the use of manual English systems in the classroom. Roughly two-thirds of the programs surveyed were moving in this direction. It was suggested that this trend was greatly facilitated by the availability of manual English texts. *See* SOCIOLINGUISTICS: Total Communication.

Initial evaluations of the effectiveness of Signed English have revealed that it does have a positive effect on the language learning of hearing-impaired children. A more comprehensive evaluation awaits the completion of the Signed English materials and their systematic use from preschool through the elementary and secondary school years. It does seem clear, however, that how a manual English system is used by teachers and parents is as important as the actual design of the system. It is most likely that the future will generate efforts to monitor the language and speech development of children exposed to a variety of manual sign systems. This ongoing evaluation will almost surely lead to improvements in manual English systems.

Bibliography

Bornstein, H.: "A Description of Some Current Systems Designed to Represent English," *American Annals of the Deaf*, vol. 118, 1973.

———: "Signed English: A Manual Approach to English Language Development," *Journal of Speech and Hearing Disorders*, vol. 39, 1974.

———: "Systems of Sign," in L. Bradford and W. Hardy (eds.), *Hearing and Hearing Impairment*, Academic Press, New York, 1979.

———: "Towards a Theory of Use for Signed English: From Birth Through Adulthood," *American Annals of the Deaf*, vol. 127, 1982.

——— and K. Saulnier: "Signed English: A Brief Follow-up to the First Evaluation," *American Annals of the Deaf*, vol. 126, 1981.

———, ———, and L. B. Hamilton: "Signed English: A First Evaluation," *American Annals of the Deaf*, vol. 125, 1980.

Jordan, I. K., G. Gustason, and R. Rosen: "An Update on Communication Trends at Programs for the Deaf," *American Annals of the Deaf*, June 1979.

Harry Bornstein

MARR, THOMAS SCOTT
(1866–1936)

Thomas Scott Marr, born in Nashville on October 20, 1866, was a well-known architect in Tennessee. He was the founding partner of the firm of Marr and Holman, whose Art Deco buildings of the 1930s are of particular note. Among Marr's best-known commissions were the Methodist Publishing House (Nashville, 1906); the Tennessee School for the Deaf (Knoxville, 1924); the Noel Hotel (Nashville, 1930;

Thomas Scott Marr. (Gallaudet College Archives)

Marr and Holman's Sudekum Building (Nashville, 1930–1932; now the Tennessee Building).

renovated as the Union Planters Bank in 1973); the Sudekum Building (Nashville, 1930–1932; now the Tennessee Building), and the United States Post Office (Nashville, 1934).

Marr lost his hearing as an infant because of scarlet fever. He began his education in the Nashville public schools, and at the age of 11 transferred to the Tennessee School for the Deaf in Knoxville. After he graduated in 1889 from Gallaudet College, where he roomed with Cadwallader Washburn, Marr began his training as a drafter with the Nashville architectural firm of Thompson and Giebel. In 1892 he entered the Massachusetts Institute of Technology as a special student in architecture. *See* GALLAUDET COLLEGE; WASHBURN, CADWALLADER LINCOLN.

The economic depression of 1893 forced Marr to abandon his academic training and to return to Nashville, where he worked for various firms before establishing his own practice in 1896. Marr hired Joseph W. Holman, Sr., as an office assistant, and they formed a partnership in 1910.

The Broadway National Bank (Nashville, 1910), the Cotton States Building (Nashville, 1920; demol-

ished 1982), and the Sam Davis Hotel (Nashville, 1928) are examples of the firm's early commercial designs. Marr and Holman's use of arches, columns, pilasters, and other classical details reflects the taste of the period for the academic style. Marr's Colonial Revival design for the Tennessee School for the Deaf was appropriate for an educational complex. Brentwood Hall (Nashville, 1920), an adaptation of Andrew Jackson's Greek Revival–style Hermitage (Nashville, 1834–1836), was one of their better-known domestic commissions.

The absence of ornate neoclassical details in the lobby of the Commerce Union Bank (Nashville, 1920; demolished 1977) and the virtually unadorned limestone and brick exterior of the Noel Hotel foreshadowed the firm's best works in the 1930s. The Sudekum Building and the United States Post Office are examples of Marr and Holman's competence with the new, streamlined esthetic of the Art Deco style. Although only 13 stories tall, the Sudekum Building clearly embraced the insistent verticality and stepped-back pyramidal massing of the great Art Deco skyscrapers of Manhattan's skyline. The $1,000,000 Post Office was the first federal building approved and constructed after Franklin D. Roosevelt entered the White House. Its sleek white marble exterior, stylized carvings, and vibrantly polychrome lobby made it and the Sudekum Building the two most modern buildings of their day in Nashville.

After Marr's death in Nashville on March 2, 1936, the firm was continued by Joseph Holman, Sr.; but it moved away from the energetic Art Deco style that distinguished Marr and Holman design in the 1930s.

Bibliography

Boatner, Edmund B.: "Thomas Scott Marr," *Nebraska Journal*, vol. 65, no. 7, June 1936.

Chandler, J. B.: "Thomas Scott Marr, Architect," *The Silent Worker*, vol. 41, no. 5, June 1929.

————: "Nashville's New Post Office, Designed by a Deaf Artist," *Ohio Chronicle*, January 19, 1935.

Judy P. Mannes

MARTINEAU, HARRIET
(1802–1876)

Born on June 12, 1802, in Norwich, England, Harriet Martineau became one of the most famous of the mid-Victorians. She is an astonishing instance of a highly educated, liberated, and influential woman in a time when women had little schooling, independence, and power. What makes her fame and importance even more remarkable is that she suffered from a severe, painful hearing impairment.

Harriet Martineau received a superior schooling, largely because of her radical, Unitarian background. Her brother James became famous as a Unitarian clergyman, theologian, and philosopher. Although she could not follow in his footsteps, she became even more well known than he was. Popularizing economic, educational, sociological, and philosophical ideas and trends, she was undoubtedly the most famous woman journalist of her time. Harriet Martineau contributed to the leading periodicals, which played a major role in shaping national opinions and policy. She later collected much of her journalistic work and published it in book form.

Martineau was strong and independent enough to write as she wanted; she did not seek to become popular by writing what she thought the readers wanted. Indeed, she had many enemies because of her unorthodox beliefs. One of her controversial beliefs for a while was in the power of mesmerism (or hypnotism, as it was soon to be called), which she claimed had cured her of a grave illness. The fact that she became socially intimate with the mesmerist who supposedly cured her did not make her belief in mesmerism any easier for her readers to accept.

She was a self-confident woman, however, and went her own way regardless of consequence. For example, when she visited the United States in 1834, she was warmly received ("lafayetted" was her

Harriet Martineau in 1833.

term—Lafayette had visited the United States 10 years earlier and had received a hero's welcome). Yet the two books she wrote about her American travels (*Society in America*, 1837, and *Retrospect of Western Travel*, 1838) were critical of what she found. She was bothered by the apparent hypocrisy of American Christians in their treatment of women, Indians and blacks. Her visit to a Charleston slave market was a shocking experience, and her advocacy of antislavery made her very controversial in much of the United States. Her most notorious book, however, was *Eastern Life, Present and Past*, which was published in 1848 after touring the Near East.

During this tour she systematically studied each region and religion and arrived at an evolutionary theory of the development of religions. It seemed to her that different religions could be ranked on an evolutionary scale, from the most primitive and concrete to the most advanced and abstract. Such an objective analysis of religions, including her own Christianity, was not well received by many of her readers. A reviewer in the journal *The Rambler* called her "the enemy of Christianity and of all existing religions." And when she subsequently carried her analytic theory to its logical conclusion and espoused a form of philosophical atheism in *Letters on the Laws of Man's Nature and Development* (1851), the outcry was even greater.

Nevertheless, Harriet Martineau retained the esteem of the notables of her day, and was visited by such people as William Wordsworth, Matthew Arnold, Charlotte Brontë, and, from the United States, Ralph Waldo Emerson, Nathaniel Hawthorne, and Margaret Fuller. Her home in the beautiful Lake District of northern England (which she had built with the money earned from her writing) became a mecca for her admirers. She became something of a fairy godmother to the people of her village, doing what she could to improve their lot in life. Keeping her independence to the end, she twice turned down offers of a pension from the government.

Harriet Martineau's deafness was of central concern to her. She disliked being deaf and made no attempts to minimize its effects. She first began to notice a hearing loss at the age of 12, when she had to request a seat in the front row of her classroom. By the age of 16, her disability had become "very noticeable, very inconvenient, and excessively painful." In another 2 years her deafness became severe, but "false shame" prevented the 18-year-old young lady from using an ear trumpet; 10 years passed before she had the courage to make her deafness so obvious. From then on, she relied on a trumpet for socializing.

Hawthorne described a visit with her as follows: "All the while she talks, she moves the bowl of her ear-trumpet from one auditor to another, so that it becomes quite an organ of intelligence and sympathy between her and yourself. The ear-trumpet seems a sensible part of her, like the feelers of some insects. If you have any little remark to make, you drop it in; and she helps you to make remarks by this delicate little appeal of the trumpet, as she slightly directs it towards you; and if you have nothing to say, the appeal is not strong enough to embarrass you."

Martineau castigated the general ignorance regarding deaf people and their problems, and resented the blundering meddling by those who can hear into the affairs of those who cannot. She wrote that "those who hear should not insist on managing the case of the deaf for them." She blamed many of the ills arising from inadequate education for deaf children on parents and teachers, and wondered if adults would ever realize "how much more is learned by oral intercourse than in any other way."

Feeling solidarity with others who were deaf, she felt justified in speaking out about their shared concerns and frustrations. In her posthumously published *Autobiography* (1877), she referred to her "Letter to the Deaf" (1834), which she described as her best effort to express her thoughts about what it was like to be deaf. This article first appeared in *Tait's Magazine*, and has since been reprinted in pamphlet form. While asserting her qualifications for writing such a "letter," she frankly admitted that she had "nothing to offer to those of you who have been deaf from early childhood. Your case is very different from mine."

She addressed those who became deaf in childhood or later in life, and exhorted them to remain active in society and to use ear-trumpets to hear whatever they could. She told an anecdote about her visit to a shop to try a new trumpet model. The shopkeeper told her, "I assure you, Ma'am, I dread to see a deaf person come into my shop. They all expect me to find them some little thing that they may put into their ears, that will make them hear every thing, without any body finding out what is the matter with them." She found his complaint (still echoed today) both funny and sad.

Martineau emphasized the need to be independent and not to ask others to repeat everything. She believed that "to give the least possible pain to others is the right principle," and felt that those with disabilities "must struggle for whatever may be had, without encroaching on the comfort of others." It was better, in her opinion, to sit through an entire dinner occasionally and miss all of the conversation than to spoil the affair for everyone by continually asking people to repeat their little jokes and comments.

Life was a fatiguing struggle for Harriet Marti-

neau. She wrote: "Life is a long, hard, unrelieved working-day to us, who hear, or see, only by express effort, or have to make other senses serve the turn of that which is lost." Being deaf was neither a blessing nor necessarily a curse. Near the end of her life she argued that her deafness had forced her to become an independent woman and compelled her to try to do what she could to assuage the lot of others who shared her "misfortune" but not her education or independence. The best that she could make of her lot, as she concluded in her "Letter to the Deaf," was "to be as wise as is possible under a great disability, and as happy as is possible under a great privation."

Harriet Martineau died on June 27, 1876, in Ambleside, England.

Bibliography
Martineau, Harriet: *Autobiography*, 1877.
———: *Household Education*, 1849.
Pichanick, Valerie Kossen: *Harriet Martineau, The Woman and Her Work, 1802–76*, University of Michigan Press, Ann Arbor, 1980.

Bruce White

MASSIEU, JEAN
(1772–1846)

Jean Massieu was born in 1772 near Cadillac, department of Gironde, France, and died at Lille, department of Nord, on July 22, 1846. He had two brothers and three sisters, and all six children were deaf. What distinguished Jean from the others was exceptional intelligence, vivacity, a gift for miming, and the determination to acquire literacy and an education.

A fragmentary *Notice on the Childhood of Massieu, Deaf-Mute*, recorded by a Madame V. Celliez and published in 1851, provides insight into his thoughts and feelings as a child: He loved animals, but had no playmates among local children. Imagining that he might gain hearing and speech by imitation, he knelt for morning and evening prayers, moving his lips, imitating others. Used as a shepherd, he counted the animals on his fingers and, reaching 10, made a notch on his staff. He yearned to go to school, but his father and the schoolmaster refused. He later reminisced: "The signs I used, to transmit my thought to my parents, and to my siblings, were very different from those of educated deaf-mutes. Strangers never understood when we expressed our thought through signs; but the neighbors understood."

A local gentleman, Monsieur de Puymorin, arranged for Massieu's admittance to the school for deaf people in Bordeaux. Meeting the headmaster, the Abbé Sicard, was the turning point in Massieu's life. Sicard taught him how to read and write.

"Within three years," Massieu recalled later, "I had become like those who hear and speak." When the Abbé de l'Epée died in 1789, Sicard competed for the job of headmaster at the Paris school. A public demonstration of Sicard's method was called for: with Massieu's assistance, he won. Both Sicard and Massieu moved to Paris in early 1790. *See* L'EPÉE, ABBÉ CHARLES MICHEL DE; SICARD, ABBÉ ROCH AMBROISE CUCURRON.

During the next five years, while the political and social fabric of France was being rewoven, Sicard maneuvered adroitly to establish a secure place for the education of deaf people. Massieu was at his side when Sicard pleaded their cause before the National Assembly in 1791, before the Convention in 1795. Later, Massieu met all the Bonapartes, their uncle Cardinal Fesch, and Pope Pius VII who came to Paris to crown Napolean emperor.

During those public demonstrations of Sicard's method, visitors invariably asked Massieu tricky questions, such as: What is hearing? eternity? gratitude? a difficulty? Massieu's written answers demonstrated his intelligence and imagination: "Hearing is auricular sight;" "eternity, a day without yesterday or tomorrow;" "gratitude, the memory of the heart;" "a difficulty, a possibility with an obstacle."

Massieu served as instructor at the National Institution for the Deaf from 1790 till shortly after Sicard's death in 1822. With Sicard gone, the lid blew off Massieu's repressed emotional life. Caught in the act of corrupting two 11-year-old girls, he had to leave the institution. He moved to Rodez, department of Aveyron, married a hearing woman, fathered two hearing girls, and rose to be headmaster of the local school for deaf children. In 1831, he moved to Lille to head a school that grew from 10 to 40 pupils by the time he retired in 1839. After his death, his friends in Lille requested a pension for his widow and children; it was refused.

By far the most revealing source of information about Massieu is Sicard's *Course of Instruction of a Congenital Deaf-Mute* (1801). Teaching Massieu the alphabet meant little to the boy, but when Sicard drew pictures of simple objects with their names superimposed, "I read in his eyes, and in his whole physiognomy, surprise and curiosity." When Sicard then erased the picture and a spectator, upon request, read the word and brought the object, "Massieu was astounded." It was now his turn to ask for the names of things: "he wanted to know everything, he wanted all those words written down."

Beyond Massieu's extraordinary eagerness, Sicard documents the young man's role as teacher: "Every day he learned more than fifty words, and not a day passed when he did not in turn teach me the signs for the objects I taught him to write." A unique collaboration thus evolved: "I taught him the written signs of our language, Massieu taught me the *mimed* signs of his. This is how we prepared to converse, eventually, in that pantomime I was perfecting, while my student, through his gestures, unveiled its elements for me."

Sicard concluded: "Neither I nor my famous teacher [l'Epée] are the inventors of the language of the deaf (this must be admitted). And just as a foreigner cannot teach a Frenchman his national language, so it is not the business of a speaking man to invent signs and give them abstract meaning."

Thus Massieu was the cooriginator of Sicard's famous method.

Bibliography

Berthier, F.: *L'abbé Sicard ... son ami et son confrère a l'Institut*, Douniol, Paris, 1873.

Celliez, Mme V.: *Album d'un sourd-muet: Notice sur l'enfance de Massieu, sourd-muet, suivie de poésies*, Courbet, Lons-le-Sauliner, 1851.

Sicard, Abbé: *Course of Instruction of a Congenital Deaf-Mute*, Paris, 1801.

Dora B. Weiner

MERCER, WILLIAM
(1765–1839)

William Mercer was one of the earliest American deaf painters of which there is any record. He was born in Fredericksburg, Virginia, in 1765—the first of five children of Hugh and Isabella (Gordon) Mercer. He was born deaf. This infirmity caused the parents much anxiety. In time, they accepted their son's handicap and spared no effort to help him overcome it.

Nothing is known of Mercer's early childhood. In November 1783, two months after the end of the Revolutionary War, Mercer, then 18 years old, was apprenticed to Charles Willson Peale, a prominent American artist whose studio was located in Philadelphia, Pennslyvania. It is assumed that the profession was chosen for Mercer, but the reason for selecting Peale to teach the deaf youth is not known. Mercer was Peale's second pupil.

From November 1783 to April 1786, Mercer remained under Peale's tutelage and boarded with the Peale family, with the cost of room, board, and tuition being paid by his uncle and guardian, General George Weedon. In a letter that Peale wrote of Mercer, he said, "William was a nervous, rather timid lad, naturally cheerful in spite of the immense handicap of being deaf and dumb, and on the whole eager to learn the profession which had been chosen for him."

Mercer executed a color painting of the battle of Princeton a few years after the contest was fought (on January 3, 1777). In this action, his father,

William Mercer posed for the figure on the ground, representing his father, in Charles Willson Peale's painting (1783) of George Washington on the battlefield at Princeton.

American Brigadier General Hugh Mercer, lost his life. At the time of the battle, Mercer was living with his mother in Fredericksburg. He was too young to have been an eyewitness of the fighting to know all the details depicted in his painting. Pictures of the primitive painting have appeared in many books on American history, sometimes without due credit to the artist. The original painting, 25¼ in. × 40½ in., is owned by the Historical Society of Pennsylvania.

Another painting, also titled *The Battle of Princeton*, which hangs in the Firestone Library at Princeton University, is believed to have been done by James Peale, a brother of Charles Willson Peale. The latter fought at Princeton and may have furnished some sketches of the battlefield to James. James completed his color painting sometime between 1783 and 1786 in Peale's studio, the same years that Mercer was studying there. The painting of the battle attributed to James Peale and that by

Mercer are almost identical in every detail, so it is presumed that Mercer made a copy of James's painting in 1786.

One of Charles Willson Peale's paintings, done in 1783, shows Washington brandishing his sword on the battlefield at Princeton. To the right and behind Washington lies General Hugh Mercer. Peale used William Mercer to pose for the figure of his dying father. This is the only known likeness of the deaf artist.

Two other works of art have been attributed to William Mercer. One, a half portrait of Mercer's grandmother, Mrs. John Gordon, is supposed to have been painted about 1786–1790. It is now owned by the Historical Society of Pennslyvania. The other is an oval miniature of a prominent Virginian public official, Edmund Pendleton (1721–1803), and is signed "W.M." This miniature, 1½ in. × 1¼ in., on ivory is the property of the Virginia Historical Society of Richmond.

After Mercer's return to Fredericksburg in 1786, he began to practice his profession. Besides the paintings mentioned above, other pictures were completed by Mercer but their whereabouts remain a mystery. Two years before his death, he laid aside his brush due to age and infirmity.

Mercer's portrait of his grandmother, Mrs. John Gordon, painted about 1786–1790. (Historical Society of Pennsylvania)

At age 74, Mercer passed away on August 20, 1839, in Fredericksburg, following "a protracted sickness and great general debility."

It is believed that Mercer was interred in the Patton family plot (his sister, Anna, married Robert Patton, a great-great-grandfather of General George S. Patton of World War II fame) in the Masonic Cemetery in Fredericksburg. No tombstone marks the site.

With a dearth of information on deaf people and their accomplishments prior to the Revolutionary War period and shortly afterward, it is a rare occasion to find a deaf person who became successful. Despite his handicap, William Mercer carved a niche for himself in the chronicle of deaf lore.

Bibliography

Egbert, Donald Drew: "General Mercer at the Battle of Princeton as Painted by James Peale, Charles Willson Peale, and William Mercer," *Princeton University Library Chronicle*, vol. 13, no. 4, pp. 171–194, Summer 1952.

Flexner, James T: *The Light of Distant Skies*, 1954.

Goolrich, John T.: *The Life of General Hugh Mercer*, Neale, New York, 1906.

Sellers, Charles Coleman: *Charles Willson Peale*, 1969.

Ward, Harry M.: *Duty, Honor or Country*, Memoirs Volume 133, American Philosophical Society, Philadelphia, 1979.

Francis C. Higgins

MEXICO

The education of deaf persons in Mexico has a long history; nevertheless, the provision of educational and rehabilitation services to deaf Mexicans is still inadequate for the presumed size of the deaf population. There is little organization among the Mexican deaf persons themselves and even though there are two deaf sports associations in Mexico City, no true national organizations or regional groups exist.

EDUCATION

On April 15, 1861, President Benito Juárez issued a Public Education Law requiring, along with other provisions, that a school for deaf people should be established in Mexico City. It was not until 1866, however, that San Juan Letrán School opened, founded by Enrique Huet, a deaf person who previously had been director of a school for deaf children in Brazil. The mayor of Mexico City and the city council assisted Huet.

A second school for deaf Mexicans, La Escuela par la Enseñanza de los Sordo-Mudos (School for Teaching Deaf-Mutes), was established a few years later. Unlike the San Juan Letrán School, this school emphasized the development of manual labor and practical job-related skills in the hope that its deaf graduates would become self-supporting. The

school's emphasis on the development of manual labor skills was required by a new national regulation of January 31, 1880.

Professor Huet died in January 1882, leaving behind a legacy of both manual and oral teaching methods. Huet had encouraged lipreading and articulation for students, probably those who were hard of hearing. Most likely influenced by Abbé de l'Epée, he also employed sign language. After Huet's death, the school had 12 more directors, the last of whom was Guadalupe Garcia, appointed in 1927. *See* EDUCATION: Communication; L'EPÉE, ABBÉ CHARLES MICHEL DE.

In the middle of the twentieth century, several new institutions were established to assist deaf Mexicans, and educational methodology shifted from manualism to oralism. In 1948 Mexico's Secretary of Health and Welfare created a nursery school for young deaf children in Mexico City. Under the direction of Fidel López Larrosa until 1955, this school sought to encourage the growth of oral skills and to eliminate sign language use.

On June 1, 1951, the Centro Audiólogico y Foniatrico (Center of Audiology and Speech Production) of Mexico was founded. Renamed the Instituto Mexicano de la Audición y el Lenguaje (IMAL; Mexican Institute of Speech and Hearing) in 1952, it became a civil association under the direction of a board of trustees, composed of representatives from various sectors of Mexican society, such as industry, banking, commerce, medicine, and law. The IMAL was the first genuine "institute" relating to deafness in Latin America, and offers courses for deaf people, teachers of deaf students, audiologists, speech pathologists, and technicians in audiometry. In addition, IMAL conducts research and offers social services to deaf clients.

The emphasis in all IMAL activities is on the promotion of speech and lipreading, and the use of residual hearing. The IMAL's methods and philosophy have been influenced strongly by the Borel-Maissony Foundation of Paris, the Central Institute for the Deaf in St. Louis, the John Tracy Clinic in Los Angeles, and the multisensory method pioneered by Max A. Goldstein. To teach reading, the institute uses the Fitzgerald Key, adapted to the grammatical structure of Spanish. People from all Spanish-speaking countries except Puerto Rico and the Philippines have studied at the IMAL, as have students from Brazil, the United States, France, Angola, and South Korea. *See* CENTRAL INSTITUTE FOR THE DEAF; GOLDSTEIN, MAX AARON.

Depending on their degree of oral skills and in keeping with their abilities and interests, many IMAL students proceed to the baccalaureate. Some deaf students reach the licenciatura level in dentistry, commerce, administration, accounting, engineering, and other professional fields. A few have gone on to even more intensive academic work at the Universidad Nacional Autónoma de México in Mexico City. The evolution of deaf education over the past century has permitted deaf Mexicans to participate in professional activities that formerly were unattainable.

SERVICES

There are a variety of government-sponsored and -supported services for deaf people in Mexico. The Secretary of Health and Welfare maintains the Instituto Nacional de la Comunicación Humana (National Institute of Human Communication), established in 1953 with staff from the IMAL. This institute uses both oral and manual methods and trains specialized personnel to work with deaf people. The Hospital Central 20 de Noviembre (Central Hospital of the 20th of November) and the Hospital General (General Hospital) provide services. The former has a speech pathology unit for children, while the latter trains doctors to work with deaf patients. The Desarollo Integral de la Familia (Integral Development of the Family) is an agency in the capital with branch offices in various states that provides oral education for deaf children. Personnel who work with deaf children receive training at the Secretary of Public Education's Escuela Normal de Especialización (Normal School of Specialization), which also maintains a clinic for children with hearing problems. The Instituto Mexicano del Seguro Social (Mexican Institute of Social Security) in the National Medical Center also provides services to hearing-impaired children and to persons who use hearing aids.

Three major private organizations provide services for deaf people as well: the Instituto José David (José David Institute) in Chihuahua, Chihuahua; the Instituto Sertoma (Sertoma Institute) in Monterrey, Nuevo Leon; and the Orientación Infantil para la Rehabilitación Auditiva (Infant Orientation for Auditory Rehabilitation) in Mexico City. The last uses electroacoustic amplification to try to train the residual hearing of very young children, and it rejects lipreading.

Despite rapid growth in the training of teachers and the provision of services for deaf people in Mexico, much remains to be accomplished. The IMAL, Mexico's major training institution, has graduated only about 500 students, of whom over half have been foreigners who returned to their home countries after completing their courses. The IMAL estimates, based on normal demographic patterns, that Mexico needs about 1500 trained teachers and therapists to serve its deaf population adequately.

Bibliography

Berruecos Tellez, P.: *Investigación de la población sorda del distrito Federal, México*, IV Congreso Panamericano de Otorrino—Laringología y Broncoesofagología, Memoria, México, 1954.

Instituto Mexicano de la Audicion y el Lenguaje: "Muestreo Estratificado, con probabilidad proporcional al tamaño de los estratos—en la población escolar urbana, diurna, del Distrito Federal, México, sobre los defectos del lenguaje, de la comprensión de la lectura y la coincidencia de ambos," *Acta Audiológica y Foniátrica Hispanoamericana*, 1(2):107–120, México, 1959.

————: *Programa de los Cursos Interamericanos*, México, 1982–1987.

Juarez, R. D.: *Estudio General Archivológico de los Cursos Interamericanos (1953–1981), del IMAL*, Mexico, 1982.

Pedro Berruecos Tellez

MODEL SECONDARY SCHOOL FOR THE DEAF

The Model Secondary School for the Deaf (MSSD) was established by an act of Congress (Public Law 89-694) on October 15, 1966. The purpose of this federally supported program was twofold: to provide an exemplary secondary school program for hearing-impaired students, and to stimulate development of similarly excellent programs throughout the United States. MSSD was to serve as a regional high school to prepare deaf students for postsecondary academic matriculation or a vocational career, and as a laboratory school for all secondary programs for deaf students in the United States. This was intended to result in upgrading education for deaf youth through testing and experimentation with materials, methodology, curriculum, and management systems, all of which would emphasize confluent education, a merging of the cognitive and affective experiences of the learner.

MSSD was the result of the educational climate of the times, with the publication of James B. Conant's *The American High School Today*, and a report on the status of deaf education in the United States from a national committee chaired by Homer Babbidge, *Education of the Deaf: A Report to the Secretary of the Department of Health, Education and Welfare, by his Advisory Committee on Education of the Deaf*. As a result of Conant's study, public secondary school education was undergoing significant changes, including consolidation of existing smaller high schools. His studies recommended a high school enrollment of at least 500 in order to permit individualization of programs, to carry a comprehensive curriculum, to meet the needs of differing levels of interest and achievement among the school population, to maintain a diverse pool of trained subject-matter specialists, to provide adequate guidance and counseling, to justify capital outlay for a relevant high school program, to provide the necessary variety and scope for peer interaction, and to cover all other support services requisite to an effective and meaningful secondary program.

The Babbidge Report identified a broad array of needs caused by gaps and lacks in educational programming for hearing-impaired students in the United States. Among the findings of the study committee were that the average deaf school graduate had less than an eighth-grade education; less than 1 percent of educational costs in deafness was expended in research and development; the United States lacked a focal point of responsibility for developing new and modified programs for deaf children; and due to the low population density of deafness, there were no comprehensive high schools for deaf students.

Criteria for admission into the new school were a minimum age of 14 years, a reading level with at least a third-grade equivalent, a hearing loss of 70 decibels or more in the better ear, and no other major handicaps. With the passage of the Education for All Handicapped Children Act (P.L. 94-142), these original criteria were modified and made more flexible. *See* EDUCATION OF THE HANDICAPPED ACT.

The primary service area for MSSD students is the District of Columbia, Maryland, Delaware, Pennsylvania, Virginia, and West Virginia, with students admitted from other states across the nation if space is available. Preference is to be given to students without access to a full-service high school program. MSSD is both a residential and a publicly supported but privately operated day school.

On May 16, 1969, Gallaudet College entered into an agreement with the Department of Health, Education and Welfare to operate MSSD on its campus. That fall the first group of 12 teachers was recruited along with an acting principal to receive training and orientation to deafness and to begin the planning process. In January 1970 a small pilot class of nine students enrolled. *See* GALLAUDET COLLEGE.

By the fall of 1970 Doin Hicks had been recruited from the Dallas (Texas) Pilot Institute for the Deaf in the Callier Hearing and Speech Center to become director of the fledgling school. Hicks had previously been principal of the Arkansas School for the Deaf at Little Rock and was knowledgeable about both oral and manual communication. Mervin D. Garretson came on board as principal and director of instructional services. Profoundly deaf from the age of five, he had served 12 years as principal of the Montana School for the Deaf, five years as associate professor of education at Gallaudet, and three years as executive director of the Council of Organizations Serving the Deaf. *See* COUNCIL OF ORGANIZATIONS SERVING THE DEAF.

Guy Watson of New Mexico State University be-

came director of curriculum development and media, but resigned a year later to be replaced by Paul Watson of the University of Illinois, Chicago campus. Joseph Rosenstein was named director of research and development. The son of deaf parents, Rosenstein had served at the Lexington School for the Deaf and the Bureau of Education for the Handicapped in the U.S. Department of Education. Victor H. Galloway, deaf from infancy, was recruited from the National Technical Institute for the Deaf to become director of pupil personnel services and residence programs. *See* NATIONAL TECHNICAL INSTITUTE FOR THE DEAF.

With 70 new students from the surrounding five-state area, and a new faculty and staff, the school opened for business in a temporarily leased structure on the southeast corner of the Gallaudet College campus. In 1976 the functional multilevel facilities on the 17-acre northwestern corner were ready for occupancy. Today the academic complex, residence halls, health facilities, dining and infirmary levels, and playing fields serve about 400 deaf high school students annually. Also, MSSD has great outreach as a national demonstration school serving all secondary programs for hearing-impaired children. In addition to curriculum and media development and dissemination, the school arranges for workshops, seminars, internships, and visitations, and publishes a professional journal for teachers, *Perspectives*, and a national high school student publication, *The World Around You*.

A Parent Advisory Council meets regularly to advise and react to school programs, both academic and extracurricular. The school also has a National Advisory Council to assist MSSD to maintain its sense of direction and emphasis. The constantly revised and updated curriculum offers 180 courses, both required and elective, such as Spanish, art, and theater arts. Approximately three-quarters of the student body reside on campus, with the remainder commuting from the metropolitan Washington area. Over 70 percent of the graduates go on to postsecondary schools in various parts of the nation.

Mervin D. Garretson

MORGAN, DALE L.
(1914–1971)

Dale Morgan was a scholar and historian of the American West, and an authority particularly on the frontier fur trade. His outstanding publications, books, and articles have earned him wide respect.

Born on December 18, 1914, in Salt Lake City, Utah, Morgan was one of four children in the Mormon family of James Lowell and Emily Holmes

Morgan. At age 14 he suffered an illness that left him totally deaf and with impaired physical co-ordination that changed his gait. Nonetheless, he completed high school and entered the University of Utah, where he majored in commercial art, graduating in 1937.

Morgan's deafness placed severe limitations on his opportunities for employment, and the economic chaos of the Great Depression further reduced his chances to find work. Undaunted, he persisted until he was hired as a clerk for the Utah Writers Project by the Works Progress Administration. His emergent talents as a writer and editor helped him advance quickly to the position of state supervisor. Under his authorship, the WPA published the Guide Series book *Utah: A Guide to the State* (1941). This success prompted Morgan to turn his attention to the pursuit of history.

In 1942 Morgan moved to Washington, D.C., where he worked in the Office of Price Administration. In his spare time he began compiling a bibliography of Mormonism. For 30 years he continued work on this project, which at one time was supported by a Guggenheim grant.

From 1948 to 1953 Morgan struggled to support himself through work at the Utah State Historical Society and as a free-lance editor. In 1954 the Bancroft Library at the University of California hired him as an editor and author. Finally secure in a sound professional position, and surrounded by a wealth of research materials on the American frontier, Morgan entered his most prolific scholarly era. He authored three frontier works and edited five more. His death left unfinished his plans for a major study of the fur trade in North America, and his Mormon bibliography.

All of Morgan's historical writing is notable for its precision and attention to detail. Two works in particular, *Jedediah Smith and the Opening of the West* (1953) and *The West of William H. Ashley* (1963), are models of meticulous research and skilled craftsmanship, and earned him his reputation for excellence.

Morgan received numerous awards from members of his profession. His honors included the Utah State Historical Society Fellow Award (1960) and two awards from the California Historical Society—the Henry R. Wagner Memorial Award (1961) and the Fellowship Award (1962). Morgan died of cancer on March 30, 1971, in Baltimore, Maryland.

Bibliography

Cooley, Everett L.: "A Dedication to the Memory of Dale L. Morgan: 1914–1971," *Arizona and the West*, vol. 19, Summer 1977.

Correspondence of Dale L. Morgan, Bancroft Library, University of California, Berkeley: and Marriott Library, University of Utah, Salt Lake City.

Anne M. Butler

MOUTH-HAND SYSTEMS

Mouth-hand systems are aids to speechreading, and they are sometimes used in speech training. They consist of a small number of arbitrary handshapes made close to the speaker's mouth to distinguish phonemes that appear the same when spoken. Thus, mouth-hand systems are not languages or self-sufficient communication methods. They are adjuncts to the visual transmission of spoken languages.

Mouth-hand systems often appeal to parents and educators who desire prelingually deaf children to acquire first-language competence in a spoken, rather than a signed, language. The effectiveness of mouth-hand systems in achieving this objective has not been proven, but many programs for deaf children, in the United States and elsewhere, are experimenting with mouth-hand systems. There are two major mouth-hand systems: Danish and Cued Speech.

DANISH

The Mouth-Hand System (MHS) has been widely used in Denmark since 1900, when it was invented by Georg Forchhammer. He was headmaster at the oral school for deaf children in Fredericia and, although he did not accept sign language, he considered visual means of communication to be necessary for deaf and severely hard-of-hearing people. Also, his marriage to a hearing-impaired woman inspired him to construct this visual system "in order to make lipreading as clear for the eye as hearing is for the ear." The system depends only on the pronunciation of a word, not on its meaning or its spelling. *See* DENMARK.

The MHS consists of 14 different hand positions, each supplementing a specific sound that is otherwise difficult or impossible to lipread. The hand positions are constructed so that they symbolize the sound. For example, "n" is grouped with the other nasal sounds [m] and [n] by a downward twist of the hand, with other alveolar sounds ([d] and [t]) by the extension of the index finger, and with other voiced sounds (such as [b] and [g]) by the fact that the wrist is not bent outward.

The most frequently used sounds have the most easily made hand positions. In using the MHS, it is important to have simultaneity between the movements of the hand and the mouth.

In Denmark the MHS is the main visual aid used by deafened and hard-of-hearing people with no knowledge of sign language. It is rather easy to learn and use and has, through many years of experience, proved to be of vital importance in daily conversation and during interpreting for the above groups. As a consequence, courses for relatives, friends, and professionals working with hearing-impaired people are readily available.

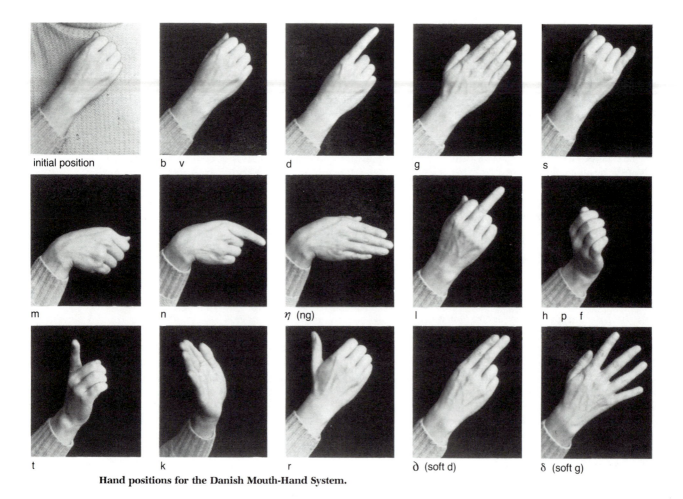

Hand positions for the Danish Mouth-Hand System.

When MHS is used as the only visual aid of communication, however, it has disadvantages. The simultaneous production of hand movements and spoken words slows down speech. It is quite tiring to produce and to read over extended time periods, because it demands heavy concentration and also restricts the use of spontaneous gesturing. Finally, the necessity of simultaneous lipreading makes it hard to understand MHS communication over longer distances, for example, while attending large meetings or following an MHS interpreter. Some of these disadvantages can be lessened by combining MHS with gestures and conventionalized signs for commonly used expressions.

MHS also has a firm position within the deaf population, but it is used in a different way than within the above-mentioned groups of hearing-impaired people. It has traditionally been used as a method to improve speech training. By exercising various hand positions and movements of the wrist, the students are made aware of the comparable sounds and positions of the speech organs. When hand positions have become routine, they can be used to correct faults in pronunciation and to support the production and the comprehension of speech.

Due to the long tradition of MHS in Denmark, it has also become an integrated part of sign language comparable to the role of fingerspelling in other sign languages. It is used to specify names of places and people, and to clarify the perception of words which have no equivalence in sign language.

Several signs actually have their root in MHS. For these lexical borrowings, the hand positions and movements have changed to follow the rules of sign constructions.

MHS can be used along with any spoken language, but it is usually necessary to adjust or add hand positions to symbolize sounds which do not exist in Danish. Hand positions have been constructed for English, French, German, Norwegian, and Swedish.

Bibliography

Birch-Rasmussen, S.: *Mundhåndsystemet* (in Danish, English, French, and German), Døves Center for Total Kommunikation, 1982.

Forchhammer, G.: *Om Nødvendigheden af Sikre Med-*

delsesmidler i Døvstummeundervisningen, J. Frimodts Forlag, 1903.

Skamris, N. P.: *Mund-håndsystem efter naturmetoden,* Audio Aid, 1982.

Britta Hansen

CUED SPEECH

Cued Speech (developed in 1966) is a system for visual representation of spoken language. It provides visual information about phonemes, syllables, primary stress, duration and, when desired, intonation. In English it utilizes eight handshapes and four hand locations near the face to supplement the oral manifestations (lips-teeth-tongue) of speech so as to eliminate the ambiguities of speechreading.

Cued Speech is distinct from all other mouth-hand systems in that it is characterized by the following basic principles: (1) Each phoneme must be read from the mouth, since the hand cues identify only groups of phonemes. (2) All phonemes appear visually different from each other, either on the mouth or on the hand—that is, Cued Speech clarifies visually all the discriminations needed for accurate perception of spoken language. (3) Cued Speech is based on phonemic distinctions, not phonetic distinctions. Early in the development of Cued Speech, the writer attempted to incorporate phonetic distinctions along with phonemic distinctions, to the extent feasible. The attempt to do this reduced the levels of visual contrast (on the mouth) between phonemes. Thus, the decision was made to maximize phoneme contrasts within groups identified by each hand cue, regardless of phonetic characteristics.

Cued Speech has thus far been adapted to many languages and dialects, and audiocassette lessons designed for self-instruction by hearing persons are available in a wide variety of languages. The system is essentially consistent across languages and dialects in that, with a few exceptions, a given phoneme will tend to be cued the same way in all languages and dialects. The only exceptions are cases in which deviations are necessary in order to maximize visual contrasts or ease of cueing for the language in question.

Organizations National Cued Speech organizations exist in the United States (founded 1983), France (1978), and Switzerland (1982). There is a National Center for Cued Speech in London. Regional Cued Speech representatives identified by the Office of Cued Speech in the Department of Audiology at Gallaudet College are located in most states and several countries. There are state Cued Speech associations in Massachusetts, Connecticut, West Virginia, and several other local associations, in addition to the Washington Metropolitan Area Cued Speech Association. One regional association

has been formed: the Gulf Coast Cued Speech Association (six-state area). There are several other staffed centers for Cued Speech in the United States in addition to the one at Gallaudet College. The earliest of these was the Cued Speech Center, Raleigh, North Carolina, which has been operating since 1979. *See* GALLAUDET COLLEGE.

Use. Estimates of the extent of use of Cued Speech in the United States are of uncertain accuracy, because in most locations where it is used, only one to five hearing-impaired children are involved, usually in a home-clinic-preschool situation, or a public school with a few hearing-impaired children, and thus not on official lists of special programs serving hearing-impaired children. In some locations there are substantially larger numbers: these include the Washington, D.C., area; Milwaukee, Wisconsin; Raleigh, North Carolina; Louisville, Kentucky; Dayton, Ohio; Fresno, California; Richardson, Texas; Conroe, Texas; Sedalia, Missouri; and Fredericksburg, Virginia.

Relation to Spoken Language The development of Cued Speech was prompted by the fact that most congenitally deaf persons do not become competent readers. Four months of study led to the conclusion that the underlying problem was the lack of a reasonable (easy, natural, enjoyable) way to learn spoken language as a young deaf child. A child can use her or his speech skills for expressive communication with others, become a good speechreader, or learn to read easily and effectively, only if the child knows a spoken language. *See* LANGUAGE: Reading and Writing.

Cued Speech fits very easily into aural-oral programs for hearing-impaired children, where it attempts to clarify and speed up the process of learning spoken language. It should be used in concert with good auditory and auditory-oral training. Its greatest advantage lies in the fact that it facilitates the learning of the language of hearing parents and siblings in the natural setting of the home during both preschool and school years.

In a total communication program using some form of signed English, Cued Speech can be used to help accomplish the one thing most total communication programs fail to achieve, the learning of spoken language along with written and signed forms. In this context it is simply another tool to be used for a special purpose, not to replace anything except the frustration of the unclear auditory-oral input that is otherwise available for presenting the spoken form. *See* SOCIOLINGUISTICS: Total Communication; SPEECH TRAINING.

Advantages Among the claims made for Cued Speech are that it makes spoken language visually clear; that it solves the communication problem in the home; that it causes the young deaf child to learn spoken language receptively at apparently the same rate as a similar hearing child for the same amount of exposure; that the visual analog of spoken language acquired by the child is fully applicable to the child's needs for use of expressive speech, development of speechreading skills, and development of reading skill; that it can be used effectively in a class containing children of widely different hearing losses; that it can be used effectively in concert with any good system for development of auditory-oral-speech skills; that the basics of the system can be learned by the average hearing person in 12 to 20 hours; that, for the skilled user, normal speech speed in the classroom is relatively easy.

Research There is some research evidence that Cued Speech achieves its objective of making the spoken language clear through vision alone. Apart from formal research, however, it is easy to demonstrate the effectiveness of Cued Speech in improving the perception of spoken language by asking a profoundly deaf child (hearing aids off) who knows Cued Speech to repeat words in a language which the child does not know but which contains only sounds the child is capable of producing, when they are presented in Cued Speech.

Research is needed, with appropriate controls, to compare the long-term effectiveness of Cued Speech with that of other systems, as regards language development, reading, speechreading, general knowledge, and so on. The difficulties of establishing and maintaining appropriate controls for such studies is obvious. A good many such studies have been planned and abandoned because of these difficulties. Other needed research includes: evaluation of variations in the readability of Cued Speech with distance, rate of presentation, illumination, and so on; expressive error patterns in experienced and inexperienced users; and time required for mastery.

Bibliography

Cornett, R. Orin, et al.: "A Theoretical Model for Development of Reading in Hearing-Impaired Children," *Directions*, 1(1):43–68, 1979.

Nicholls, Gaye H.: *Cued Speech and the Reception of Spoken Language*, McGill University, Montreal, 1979.

Sbaiti, Mary Elsie: *Annotated Bibliography on Cued Speech*, Cued Speech Center, Inc., Raleigh, North Carolina, 1982.

Shafbuch, Linda: *Final Program Review of the NCRC Cued Speech Project*, Kendall Demonstration Elementary School, Gallaudet College, 1979.

R. Orin Cornett

MUSICIANS

The loss of hearing is one of the greatest blows a musician can suffer. Ironically, though, nineteenth-century Europe produced not only some of history's finest music but five supremely talented yet hearing-impaired musicians. The most famous was Ludwig van Beethoven (1770–1827), the German-born composer and pianist, who suffered from a severe and progressive hearing loss during his most productive years. Beethoven's deafness is well known; the hearing impairment of other nineteenth-century musicians is less so. *See* BEETHOVEN, LUDWIG VAN.

ROBERT SCHUMANN

Robert Schumann (1810–1856) wrote and composed much, in particular piano works. Among his teachers was Friedrich Wieck (famous piano pedagogue and also expert on deafness and hearing aids) whose daughter, Clara, Schumann married in 1840 after earlier determined legal opposition from Wieck had become futile. Schumann's compositions were as numerous as his articles for the *Neue Zeitschrift für Musik*, of which he was the editor.

Schumann was haunted in his teens by fears of losing his mind. His only sister died a physical and mental invalid in 1826. His father was suffering from a nervous disorder and died in the same year. Mental instability and syphilis (contracted perhaps as early as 1832) led by 1839 to his first manifestations of "choral trumpets." Until his death in an insane asylum, where he was for the last two years of his life, Schumann endured aural hallucinations.

BEDŘICH SMETANA

Bedřich Smetana (1824–1884) hoped to emulate Franz Liszt in technique and Wolfgang Amadeus Mozart in composition. His greatest achievements are the creation of Czech national opera and six symphonic poems, *My Fatherland*.

Smetana had suffered sporadic incidences of hearing impairment as early as 1860. On the night of October 20, 1874, he became completely deaf. His deafness was the symptom of complete disintegration of his nervous system; the cause was syphilis. He continued to compose without hearing the last four of his six symphonic poems; he continued to play. He also enjoyed watching others play his music or music he knew well. (Beethoven had enjoyed watching singers without hearing a sound himself. He had also "improvised for more than an hour, with his hearing aid on the sounding board," as Friedrich Wieck recollected of a visit he and seven-year-old Clara had made in 1826.)

ROBERT FRANZ

Robert Franz (1815–1892), a prodigious composer of songs and especially of choral music, experienced his first hearing loss at age 28. He, too, suffering from a nervous malady. At age 52, he became totally deaf and had to relinquish all of his official positions. He continued to compose until 1886, though he lamented his inability to hear his own music whose effect was so vividly expressed upon the faces of the members of the audience. "Such a sight," he wrote, "I would not wish my worst enemy."

GABRIEL FAURÉ

In the 1860s, Gabriel Fauré (1845–1924), a French musician trained for the organ, became acquainted, under the guidance of Camille Saint-Saëns, with the music of Schumann, Liszt, and Richard Wagner. Fauré was especially fond of Schumann's music. In later years, he prepared a revised edition of all of Schumann's piano compositions. Fauré was a composer, pianist, and teacher. His contribution to the French song matched those of Schumann and Franz for German *Lieder.*

When in 1903 Fauré was certain that he would become deaf—his brother Amand had been deaf for several years—he wrote to his wife that it would be disrespectful to recall Beethoven. Yet had not the second part of Beethoven's life been one of long despair? This was not the melancholy, the depressions he had gone through some 20 years earlier. Arteriosclerosis not only caused the deterioration of his hearing; it distorted his hearing; the tones he heard were not those he read or thought of. Yet he continued to compose, including his great lyric drama *Pénélope* (which he never heard). He was music critic of *Le Figaro* (1903–1921) and director of the Paris Conservatory from 1905 until 1920. By the time he was completely deaf, according to his son and biographer Philippe Fauré-Fremiet, he suffered the torments of Schumann and the long despair of Beethoven.

Fauré achieved in his later compositions, during his third period, a sublimity and serenity that transcended the passions of his hearing years.

Bibliography

Brockway, Wallace, and Herbert Weinstock: *Men of Music*, 1939.

Cooper, Martin: *Beethoven, The Last Decade (1817–1827)*, 1970.

The New Grove Dictionary of Music and Musicians, vols. 6 and 16, 1980.

The Oxford Companion to Music, 10th ed., 1970.

Kurt Beermann

N

NACK, JAMES
(1809–1879)

Though recognized as one of America's first published deaf authors, James Nack seems to have suffered the consequences of being before his time. The era in which he lived was one of practical growth rather than of cultural pursuit, a fact that he realized once his teen-age literary triumphs wore off. Throughout the life of this self-made but much-too-sensitive scholar, poverty, ill health, and social withdrawal took turns usurping whatever imaginative creations he dared undertake. And the works were many—whether unpublished, anonymous, or even destroyed by his own hand. By impulse or perfectionism, James Nack was a poet first, a deaf person last.

Born on January 4, 1809, in the competitive climate of New York City at a time when the financial misfortunes of his merchant father bore heavily on the family, young Nack was fortunate to receive some home-grown instruction from an older sister, and learned to read at the age of four. When he was eight, his talent for verse and rhyme became evident. However, at that age a serious accident occurred, causing lifelong complications. Tripping on a stairway, he reached out and dragged a heavy object down upon his head. It was several weeks before he recovered, but had lost his hearing completely.

According to the official register at the New York School for the Deaf (then the New York Institution for the Instruction of the Deaf and Dumb) under the heading "Information in Regard to Early Pupils, 1818–1852," Nack was admitted on August 5, 1818, at the age of nine. Although he excelled in grammar and arithmetic, it was poetry that preoccupied him until he left school in December 1823.

When he was 14, he wrote the poem "The Blue-Eyed Maid," which caught the fancy of the Clerk of the City and County of New York, Abraham Asten, who subsequently introduced Nack into the city's literary circle. On the advice of some of its members, the prodigy collected 68 of his poems composed before he was 18 and published his first book, *The Legend of the Rocks and Other Poems* (1827). James Nack became something of a celebrity.

Hailed as another "teen-age Lord Byron," Nack was befriended by a wealthy lawyer, in whose employ he was afforded extensive use of the gentleman's fine library. The happy deaf youth lost no time in catching up on numerous volumes dealing with all kinds of subjects, including languages, which he picked up easily. Soon after, Asten hired Nack as an assistant in the County Clerk's Office, where for more than 30 years he performed admirably, albeit mulling over the dull details of legal copy. In 1838, Nack married a hearing woman named Martha W. Simon and went on to publish his second collection of poetry, *Earl Ruppert and Other Tales and Poems* (1839). A family man, generous, sincere, and fond of children, he and Martha raised three daughters, all of whom had normal hearing.

In 1850, Nack wrote *The Immortal, a Dramatic Romance, and Other Poems*, reprinted in 1852 under the title *Poems*, and several years later completed his final volume, *The Romance of the Ring and Other Poems* (1859). During this period Nack also rendered translations from the French, Dutch, and German which critics found remarkable, considering the fact that he had neither ear for nor actual experience in foreign communication.

James Nack died on September 23, 1879, in New York City.

The poetry of James Nack reflects the sentimentality of the period. Despite his loss of hearing at an early age, he had a gift for transcending silence, even adding rhythm and music. Euphony remained at least latent in his aesthetic makeup. However, nurturing and developing such talent, especially amid the hail of problems and pressures which pummeled him repeatedly, required an extraordinary combination of persistence and pertinacity. In sum, the perspective on Nack's life is perhaps not gained from his poetry or his deafness, but rather from his determination to do what he wanted most, and to do it as best he could.

Bibliography

Nack, James: "Bell Song," translated from the original German text by Schiller, *American Annals for the Deaf*, (2):82–83, January 1848.

———: *Earl Ruppert and Other Tales and Poems*, with a memoir of the author by P. M. Wetmore, Adlard, New York, 1839.

———: *The Immortal, a Dramatic Romance, and Other Poems*, with a memoir of the author by G. P. Morris, Stringer and Townsend, New York, 1850.

———: "In Memory of the Late John R. Burnet," *American Annals for the Deaf*, 23(3):180–181, July 1878.

———: *The Legend of the Rocks and Other Poems*, E. Conrad, New York, 1827.

———: *The Romance of the Ring and Other Poems*, with a memoir of the author by G. P. Morris, Delisser and Procter, New York, 1859.

Panara, Robert F.: "The Deaf Writer in America from Colonial Times to 1970," Part 1, *American Annals for the Deaf*, p. 510, September 1970.

Taras B. Denis

NATIONAL ASSOCIATION OF THE DEAF

The National Association of the Deaf (NAD) is a voluntary, self-help organization founded in 1880 in Cincinnati, Ohio, with the declared objectives "to bring the deaf of the different sections of the United States in close contact and to deliberate on the needs of the deaf as a class." That initial meeting was called the First National Convention of Deaf-Mutes, and characterized NAD members with the statement, "We have interests peculiar to ourselves which can be taken care of by ourselves."

FOUNDING

The association was preceded by other organizations of deaf people. The New England Association of the Deaf brought leaders of the deaf community together in 1853 for the first time in the United States. Shortly after the Civil War, New York and Ohio established state associations. The growing opposition to sign language in the late nineteenth century, expressed by educators at the Berlin and Milan Congresses and by influential individuals such as Alexander Graham Bell, was a factor in encouraging deaf people to unite to protect their interests. The perceived threat against sign language and the encouragement from the earlier, successful organizational experiences of deaf people at state and regional levels prompted the call for the initial nationwide gathering in 1880. *See* BELL, ALEXANDER GRAHAM; HISTORY: Congress of Milan.

The association was the first organization in the United States founded by disabled persons. Until 1964 only deaf persons were accepted as members, so it was truly an association of deaf people. After 1964 membership opened to persons willing to support the association's objectives, regardless of their hearing ability. However, fewer than 100 of the 15,000 members are nondeaf persons, and most of them are professionals serving deaf clients.

Following its sixth convention in 1900, the association was incorporated in the District of Columbia. Its meetings have been held biennially except in 1942 and 1946 when the conventions were postponed due to World War II travel restrictions. In 1893 the association hosted the Second World Congress on Deafness, held in conjunction with the Columbian Exposition, in St. Louis, Missouri. In 1975 the association hosted another international meeting, the World Congress of the Deaf, in Washington, D.C. In 1980 the NAD Centennial Convention, held in Cincinnati, registered over 3000 persons in its week-long activities, which included selection of Miss Deaf America, luncheons, banquets, theatricals, exhibits, the passage of 112 resolutions on all phases of deaf life and adoption of NAD's biennial budget, which had increased dramatically from $25,000 in 1964 to $2 million in 1980. The National Association of the Deaf is a member of the World Federation of the Deaf. *See* WORLD FEDERATION OF THE DEAF

ACTIVITIES

One of the association's major efforts through the years has been to provide equal employment opportunity for deaf Americans. In 1908 it succeeded in opening the federal civil service to deaf workers, and fought similar battles on behalf of deaf participation in the Civilian Conservation Corps during the 1930s and the Job Corps during the 1960s. During the economic depression of the 1930s, the association sought legislation to eliminate "deaf" peddlers, many of whom were not deaf. It has aided its state associations on behalf of more positions for deaf teachers and against attempts to limit deaf persons' driving privileges. It continues to promote the use and preservation of American Sign Language, most recently through its Communication Skills Program, which sponsors classes throughout the United States, and the National Consortium of Programs for Training Sign Language Instructors. *See* DRIVING RESTRICTIONS; SIGN LANGUAGES: American.

To honor Thomas Hopkins Gallaudet, who helped establish the first permanent school for deaf persons in the United States, the association commissioned the statue of him and Alice Cogswell, sculpted by Daniel Chester French, which now stands at the front of the Gallaudet College campus. The association's efforts have not been confined to issues relating to the deaf population, however, for it engaged in fund raising to buy ambulances and other equipment for the Red Cross in both world wars. *See* COGSWELL, ALICE; GALLAUDET, THOMAS HOPKINS; GALLAUDET COLLEGE.

Originally an association of individuals, in 1960 the National Association of the Deaf altered its structure to become a federation of state associations, represented in the national body by the 13 elected members of the governing board. Since 1960 the daily affairs have been managed by a full-time, paid executive secretary and staff. In 1964 the association moved its home office to Washington, D.C., and since 1971 the headquarters has been located in Silver Spring, Maryland. The association usually leases excess space in the three-story building to organizations with an interest in deafness.

NATIONAL SCOPE

After its move to the Capitol area in 1964, the association became increasingly active in education and rehabilitation at the federal level. In 1969 it obtained funds for the National Census of the Deaf Population, the first nationwide attempt to enumerate deaf persons in 40 years, and the resulting report, *The Deaf Population of the United States*, has become an authoritative source of data. The association's two major publications are *The Deaf American* (called *The Silent Worker* until 1960), a monthly magazine, and *The Broadcaster*, a monthly newspaper which began publication in 1979. Typically, the association responds to 1000 mail and telephone requests a month for information about deafness and deaf people. *See* DEAF AMERICAN.

The association also publishes and distributes books on deafness and sells special equipment used by deaf people. It jointly owns and operates with the Massachusetts State Association of the Deaf a rehabilitation facility near Boston called DEAF Inc., which serves adolescents and adults throughout New England. The association also has a subsidiary, Deaf Community Analysts, Inc., which conducts survey research and provides consultation on scientific matters. Additionally, the NAD supports a legal defense fund, subsidizes the International Association of Parents of the Deaf, holds an annual Youth Leadership Camp for deaf adolescents, and maintains the Junior National Association of the Deaf for its school-age members. *See* LEGAL SERVICES.

Among those who have addressed the National Association of the Deaf conventions over the last 100 years, one of the most memorable was Mayor Fiorello H. LaGuardia, who introduced the 1934 convention in New York City: "I speak today to people who can understand although they cannot hear, while all day long I speak to people who can hear but cannot understand."

Bibliography
Gallaudet College Alumni Association: *The Gallaudet Almanac*, Washington, D.C., 1974.

The NAD Story, National Association of the Deaf, Silver Spring, Maryland.

J. D. Schein: "The Deaf Community," in H. Davis and S. R. Silverman (eds.), *Hearing and Deafness*, pp. 511–523, Holt, Rinehart and Winston, New York, 1978.

F. C. Schreiber: "National Association of the Deaf," in L. J. Bradford and W. G. Hardy (eds.), *Hearing and Hearing Impairment*, pp. 563–568, Grune and Stratton, New York, 1979.

Jerome Schein

NATIONAL CAPTIONING INSTITUTE

The National Captioning Institute (NCI) is a private, nonprofit, tax-exempt corporation that was established in 1979 for one specific purpose: to open new educational horizons for all hearing-impaired Americans through access to television.

A private company operating in the public interest, NCI is the only organization in the United States established solely to provide closed captions, which are hidden subtitles that, when "opened," look much like those in foreign-language movies. The captions are triggered by a special decoding device called a TeleCaption adapter that is hooked up to any television set, thereby enabling hearing-impaired viewers to read information on the television screen, rather than hear it. *See* TELECOMMUNICATIONS: Captioned Television.

NCI was established by a unique coalition of private and federal investments, coupled with the determination of deaf people, to make use of miniaturized technology to facilitate access to the exciting medium of television. At its suburban

Washington, D.C., office and its operations facility in Hollywood, California, NCI captions prerecorded television programs, home video movies, commercial messages, and public service announcements as well as live events such as network news programs, Presidential press conferences, and speeches and other significant live television programs as they are broadcast.

NCI is also charged with a variety of other activities. These include marketing the closed captioned service so that it is available through all television delivery systems including broadcast and cable television, home video, and satellite; identifying new applications for closed captioned television; informing the public; developing expanded distribution channels for the TeleCaption adapter; keeping abreast of technological developments; and attracting new funding sources.

EARLY DEVELOPMENT

The first closed captioned television demonstration took place in Knoxville, Tennessee, in November 1971. Three months later, a second demonstration was conducted at Gallaudet College in Washington, D.C. The concept might have ended there had it not been for the foresight of the United States Office of Education (later called the Department of Education). In those initial experiments and investments, the Office of Education supplied seed money for development and perfection of the captioning technology and decoder. In 1979 it advanced seed money in the form of a four-year $6.9 million decreasing grant which helped establish NCI. Today, the Department of Education continues to be deeply involved with the development and expansion of closed captioned television. *See* GALLAUDET COLLEGE; ORGANIZATIONS: Governmental.

Others have been involved, too. In December 1976 the Federal Communications Commission formally reserved line 21 of the vertical blanking interval of the television signal for the transmission of the closed captioned signal, thus clearing the way for extending the benefits of television to hearing-impaired Americans. In March 1983 the commission reaffirmed this special use of line 21 for at least another five years.

In early 1977 negotiations began on other fronts to secure commercial network support for closed captioning and to ensure mass production of the TeleCaption adapters. Federal financial support was augmented by a $3.5 million loan from four insurance companies. In the fall of 1978 the national television networks agreed to participate voluntarily in the service on the condition that a responsive, free-standing nonprofit organization be established to provide the captioning service. It was for this reason that NCI was established.

By March 1979, all the pieces needed to launch the national closed captioned television service were in place. ABC and NBC agreed to join PBS in providing five hours a week of prime-time programming. At the time, CBS, having decided to pursue development of other technology, declined participation; however, CBS agreed in 1984 to offer closed captioned programs using line 21 along with its teletext service. Sears, Roebuck & Co. agreed to manufacture and market the TeleCaption adapter.

THE SERVICE IS LAUNCHED

The nationwide service began on March 16, 1980, when PBS aired *Masterpiece Theatre* and *Once upon a Classic*; NBC broadcast *The Wonderful World of Disney*; and ABC telecast *The ABC Sunday Night Movie*—all with closed captions. Fifteen hours of programming per week constituted the closed captioned television schedule in those days.

Since then, as government grants terminated in 1982, private-sector support of the service has steadily increased. Today, ABC-TV and public television annually invest hundreds of thousands of dollars to closed-caption many of their prime-time programs. Program producers and other television delivery systems also have begun to share financially in the effort to expand the availability of the service.

In 1983 a Corporate Advisory Council to NCI was formed with the objectives of extending the service to at least a half million TV households and increasing the volume of programming to at least 100 hours weekly by 1988. Council members include representatives of many of America's most prestigious corporations, including the Kellogg Company, Prudential Insurance Company, Equitable Life Assurance Society of America, Nabisco Brands, Mobil Corporation, Xerox, and AT&T.

Also in 1983, the NCI Caption Club was formed for the purpose of accepting annual contributions from individuals, families, and organizations, in whatever amount they feel appropriate, toward expanding the volume of closed captioned programming. These funds are to be matched by contributions from corporations, foundations, and various groups in the television industry, and will be allocated under the supervision of NCI's Consumer Advisory Board which includes deaf and hard-of-hearing people from various regions of the country.

More than 40 hours of television programs are closed-captioned every week; major Hollywood movie releases and other programs are also closed-captioned on home video as well as other programs that are available only on pay cable systems around the country.

NEW TELEVISION USES

As electronic technology moves from the laboratory into the homes of America, a profound change is taking place in the home and family. No longer just a place to return to after a day of activity elsewhere, the home is once again becoming the focus of people's lives. Parents and children are able to work together, to be entertained and to learn as family units. A significant development along these lines was the agreement in 1983 between the Council of the Annenberg/CPB Project and NCI which made possible the closed captioning of eight educational telecourses in 1984 which can be taken for college credit or personal interest.

Recent demographic studies indicate that the closed captioned television audience averages 3.5 viewers per decoder, primarily in the 20–44 age group. Family income of decoder owners averages $23,000. Closed captioned program preferences ranked in descending order are: movies, prime-time series, news and public affairs programs, talk shows, game shows, sports programs, and soap operas.

Among awards bestowed upon NCI was the 1983 "Caring Bear Award" from Action for Children's Television, which recognized NCI for its efforts to expand the benefits of closed captioned television to programs that appeal mostly to young people; and the 1984 ViRA Award, for technical achievement from *Video Review* magazine, which recognized NCI for its efforts to expand closed captioning throughout the home entertainment industry.

POTENTIAL BENEFICIARIES

The potential for closed captioned television is far greater than what has been experienced thus far. Not only are there many more millions of severely hearing-impaired people who could benefit significantly from closed captioning, but there are also millions among the aging population, the learning-disabled, speakers of English as a second language, and those adults who need continued help in developing functional reading skills.

Closed captioned television is a vital service, greatly needed by deaf people and an increasing number of other Americans with language and reading difficulties. It is the only viable means available to ensure that vast segments of the population are not isolated from the long-term benfits of America's ever-changing electronic communications technology.

PUBLICATIONS

Each September, NCI publishes its *CAPTION* newsletter. The *CAPTION* newsletter is available free of charge to all interested parties. In addition, the company publishes a monthly *Marketing Memo* that is sent primarily to commercial advertisers and corporations, and periodic consumer research reports.

John E. D. Ball

NATIONAL CONGRESS OF JEWISH DEAF

A call for the first United States–Jewish deaf gathering in 1956 was prompted by a concern for the future of deaf Judaism. Although local groups of deaf Jews existed in New York, Philadelphia, Baltimore, Cleveland, Chicago, and Los Angeles, the need to form a common bond among the deaf Jews and to upgrade the religious, educational, and cultural services on a national basis was declared a vital goal.

ORGANIZATION

The initial meeting, titled the National Convention of Jewish Deaf, was held in New York City in the summer of 1956. Philip Hanover, Harold Steinman, and Anna Plapinger headed this venture. Attended by hundreds from around the nation, the assembly saw fit to support this new concept and founded the National Congress of Jewish Deaf (NCJD). Conventions have been held biennially since 1962.

The Congress is largely financed by dues from the members and 18 affiliates, donations, and a 25 percent contribution from the net profits of each convention. Its officers serve on a voluntary basis, and the executive director performs assignments from home.

MEETINGS AND PROGRAMS

Conventions usually register over 1500 persons, with program, in addition to regular business sessions, including panel discussions, receptions, religious and rabbi workshops, the Miss NCJD beauty contest, teenage programs, entertainment, Sabbath Dinner, Sabbath Services, awards, and the grand ball. At the Sabbath Dinners a Christian clergyman often is invited to "break bread" with the members in an effort to foster brotherhood between Jews and non-Jews. The Sabbath Services are officiated by a rabbi trained in sign language and include audience participation. The Congress is open to both deaf and hearing individuals of all denominations.

The primary focus of the Congress has been on the welfare of Jewish deaf individuals. It represents them on the President's Committee for the Handicapped and in projects involving homes for aged persons, interpreters, consumer services, legal rights, census, employment, mental health, education, sports, and other activities. It also serves as a referral center and is a clearing house for information about religion, education, and cultural programs.

In the early 1960s, since there were no ordained deaf rabbis to serve deaf needs, the Congress urged the Hebrew Union College to accept deaf candidates for the rabbinate and/or to train its students to intern among deaf communities, and the NCJD

Endowment Fund was established to assist with this program. Such awareness produced many student rabbis to work with deaf Jews. The Congress was also instrumental in setting up a Religious Section during the existence of the National Council of Organizations Serving the Deaf in the late 1960s and laid the groundwork to include Judaism in the Spiritual Care Commission of the World Federation of the Deaf. *See* WORLD FEDERATION OF THE DEAF.

In order to keep Congress members, affiliates, and rabbis informed of developments, the *N.C.J.D. Quarterly* has been published since 1958. A newsletter for rabbis is issued at intervals, and local affiliates also produce their own newsletters.

The Congress has assisted several other denominations with proper signs concerning Judaism and has campaigned against offending signs for "Jews" or "Jewish." It also published *Signs in Judaism*, a book helpful for rabbis, religious tutors, interpreters, advisers, parents of deaf children, and deaf persons themselves.

In 1970 the congress hosted a workshop on "Orientation of Jewish Religious Leaders and Lay People to Deafness and Vocational Rehabilitation," supported by a grant from the Department of Health, Education, and Welfare. Two national surveys on the education of Jewish youths in American schools have been conducted. It maintains an NCJD Hall of Fame which enshrines Jewish deaf personalities for their accomplishments; an archivist preserves historical materials.

In 1965 when the World Games for the Deaf took place in Washington, D.C., the Congress and its Baltimore affiliate hosted a reception for Jewish athletes and visitors from around the world. This occasion was repeated in 1985 with affiliate Temple Beth Solomon in Los Angeles as cohost, and a drive for funds to help defray the lodging and meals costs of the Israeli team was conducted.

The Congress encourages its affiliates and members to support Israel's existence by purchasing Israeli bonds and to participate in and support national and local campaigns to raise funds for Jewish welfare; deaf volunteers contact their deaf friends via TTDs to solicit donations.

The Congress played an influential role in the founding of the World Organization of Jewish Deaf in 1977, which serves deaf Jews in Europe and Israel, and though based in Tel Aviv, Israel, has been headed by an American official of the Congress since its founding. When the 1977, 1981, and 1986 Congresses were held in the Holy Land, the Congress chartered tours to Israel, and future projects call for youth exchange programs and the hosting of the World Congress in America.

Bibliography

Fleischman, Alexander, Rosalind Rosen, and Bess Hyman (eds.): *N.C.J.D. Quarterly*, Gallaudet College Library.

The NCJD Story, National Congress of Jewish Deaf, Greenbelt, Maryland.

Shuart, Adele K. and National Congress of Jewish Deaf: *Signs in Judaism*, publication pending.

Strassfeld, Sharon and Michael (eds.): *Second Jewish Catalog*: "The Jewish Deaf Community," Jewish Publications Society of America, 1976.

Tillem, Ivan L. (ed.): *Jewish Directory and Almanac*, Pacific Press, 1984.

Alexander Fleischman

NATIONAL FRATERNAL SOCIETY OF THE DEAF

The National Fraternal Society of the Deaf (NFSD) is a fraternal benefit order, operating under the same rules and regulations that state insurance departments impose on other nonprofit organizations such as the Knights of Columbus and Woodmen of the World. The society has divisions in all parts of the United States and Canada.

HEADQUARTERS

Erected in 1975, the society's headquarters building in Mt. Prospect, Illinois, a suburb of Chicago, accommodates the eight officers and employees who carry out the daily operations. Modern equipment facilitates direct contact with the society's 13,000 members and 106 divisions. The library, named after A. L. Roberts, one of the society's Grand Presidents, contains hundreds of books on deafness as well as insurance-related reference books. It also serves as the meeting room for the society's board of directors. The nine board members sit at a round table which was selected to maximize the visual aspect of communication since all board members are deaf. The divisions donated the chairs and table to the library in 1975.

HISTORY

The society had its beginning in 1901, the idea of some boys in the Michigan School for the Deaf. At that time there was a national society known as the Coming Men of America, composed primarily of boys in their teens and fostering lofty principles of patriotism, honor, and manhood. The older boys at the Michigan School proceeded to organize their own lodge of the Coming Men of America, known as McKinley Lodge No. 922.

The Coming Men of America had a brief life, but it strongly influenced the lives of many youths, particularly those at the Michigan School. A number of the graduates held a meeting in Chicagto to discuss the concept of a fraternal society solely for deaf people. This meeting was followed by a meeting of former members of the Coming Men of America at a reunion at the Michigan School in Flint, on June 12, 1901. Plans for the formation of the Fraternal Society of the Deaf (FSD) were presented and adopted. Present at this meeting were Alexander McCuaig, William Minaker, Fred Wheeler, John Polk, Eugene McCall, Frank Drake, Carl Anderson, John Miller, Hugh Babcock, Harold Preston, Howard Blodgett, Charles Pettit, and John Berry.

The Fraternal Society was incorporated as a mutual benefit organization by the state of Illinois on August 12, 1901. It was brought out that deaf persons were unable to obtain adequate life insurance except by paying exorbitant premiums, and that almost no insurer would provide deaf persons with disability coverage. The theory at that time was that deaf persons did not live long and were prone to have accidents. Thus, a very legitimate reason to form the Fraternal Society of the Deaf was given. However, the Fraternal Society did not offer insurance as it is now known. It was largely a good fellowship organization with meager benefits in case of illness, accident, or death. The benefits were based on a haphazard plan, which depended on the collection of assessments from its members. At the first convention of the Fraternal Society in Chicago in 1903, there was a membership of 90 and $279.94 in the treasury.

On December 2, 1907, a charter was granted by the state of Illinois to operate as a fraternal insurance body, and the society's name was changed to its present form. However, the inequities of the voluntary assessment system then in operation led to much indifference and distrust. It was evident that the society had to be placed on a more secure financial basis. At the 1909 convention, Charles A. Piper, who was then president of the National Fraternal Congress and who had become interested in the work that the society was trying to do for the deaf, advocated the adoption of a legal reserve basis with an adequate rate table. The delegates lost no time in following Piper's suggestion. Thus, the society met all the requirements of the state of Illinois to operate as a bona fide fraternal benefit society with sound actuarial principles.

Confidence in the society grew and members began to enroll at an increasing pace. By 1912 there were 1319 members, and the number of divisions throughout the United States had grown from 25 to 35. By 1984 there were 106 divisions and assets had grown to $9,000,000.

Canada gave the society an international flavor when Toronto petitioned for the granting of a charter as a division in 1924. Efforts to change the name of the society due to its operating across the United States border were futile.

OBJECTIVES

The objectives of the society are substantially the same as those given when it applied for its charter: "To unite fraternally all deaf men and women, relatives of members and others involved in the field of deafness, all of whom are not more than sixty years of age at the time of becoming members and are possessed of good bodily and mental health, and are of good moral character and industrious habits; to give moral aid and support to its members in time of need; to establish and disburse endowments, annuities, cash surrender, loan values, paid-up insurance and income options; and, on demise of members, to pay death benefits to those who have been named as beneficiaries in accordance with the laws of the Society. The Society shall also aim to uphold honor, fraternity and good citizenship, to encourage industry, ambition, honesty and perseverance; to prevent, if possible, members from being wronged, swindled or imposed upon, or ill-treated in any manner deemed unfair or disgraceful."

MEMBERSHIP AND SERVICES

While the original concept of the society was to unite men between the ages of 18 and 55, it was inevitable that women would enter the picture. As early as 1915, efforts to admit deaf women were made, but the men argued that a woman's place was in the home. However, the persistence of women prevailed, and in 1937 they were permitted to form social auxiliaries to promote the best interests of the divisions with which they were affiliated. They had no voice in the management of the affairs of the society until 1951 when, with the social auxiliaries numbering 39 and membership around 1500, the Chicago convention acceded to their demand for regular insurance membership. Women now play a very important role in the affairs of the society—not only do they serve as officers in their own divisions, composed entirely of females, but they also serve as officers in divisions composed of men and women.

The admission of women as insured members was a breakthrough which resulted in unanimous approval to insure deaf children in 1964. But the membership age to receive division privileges remained at 18. Restrictions regarding race were removed by convention action in 1967. Also in 1967, at the New York City convention, hearing children of deaf parents who are members of the society were approved for insurance coverage, and in 1971 grandchildren of members were added to the eligibles. In 1979 the society decided to admit hearing persons involved in the field of deafness. That is the status of membership eligibility and juvenile insurance coverage at the present time.

ORGANIZATION

Since 1901 the society has had 11 chief administrative officers. Peter Hellers of Detroit was the first Grand President (1901–1903), followed by Francis

P. Gibson (1903–1905), J. J. Kleinhans (1905–1909), E. M. Bristol (1909–1912), H. C. Anderson (1912–1927), F. J. Neesam (1929–1931), A. L. Roberts (1931–1957), L. S. Cherry (1957–1967), F. B. Sullivan (1964–1984), and Robert R. Anderson (1984 to present). The most prominent officers were F. P. Gibson and A. L. Roberts. Although Grand President only briefly, Gibson had been a mainstay of the society since its office opened in Chicago in 1901, serving as secretary and as editor of the society's publication. Roberts led the society through its turbulent depression years and was also a gifted writer and speaker. He was honored by Gallaudet College in 1942 with an honorary degree of doctor of humane letters.

It was to Roberts that F. P. Gibson uttered the words "Carry On," which have appeared by convention decree since 1931 on the masthead of the society's publication, *The Frat*. In 1929 Roberts was Grand Secretary-Treasurer of the society while Gibson was Grand President. Gibson died rather suddenly from complications following surgery. Prior to surgery, Roberts visited Gibson in the hospital and as he was leaving, Gibson said, "Bobs, if anything happens to me, carry on." So popular was Gibson among the society's members that "Carry On" became their rallying cry, and influenced Roberts's decision to assume the office of Grand President in 1931.

The society holds conventions quadrennially; in 1983 the convention was held in Denver, and New Jersey was selected as the 1987 site. At the Denver convention, reorganization took effect, with the executive officers being chosen by a nine-member board of directors instead of by delegates, as was previously done.

The official organ of the society, *The Frat*, is published bimonthly. Members receive the publication free; others pay a minimal subscription price. *The Frat* contains important business and social announcements pertaining to the society, and editorials relating to the deaf community frequently appear.

The society undertakes a wide range of community activities. On a national level, All-America awards have been presented to athletes in schools for the deaf since 1950. These awards recognize outstanding performances in football and basketball. The United States and Canadian participants in the World Games for the Deaf have been recipients of flight bags from the society since the United States played host to the Games in 1965. An "Athlete of the Year" award has been given annually since 1968. An award of a U.S. saving bond to an outstanding graduate of each school for the deaf in the United States has been in effect since 1970, and Canada awards cash to its winners. Ten schol-

arships have been granted since 1970 to members of the society pursuing postsecondary studies.

ACTIVITIES

Local divisions of the society have their own pet projects in their communities. Donations of clothing, money, and incidentals to residents of homes for aged deaf people are common, as are annual contributions of toys and clothing to needy children. Divisions are also frequent contributors to sporting events of deaf people and often take part in activities with other organizations of deaf people.

The National Fraternal Society of the Deaf is quite active regarding legislation that discriminates against deaf people or that helps them. With the widespread chain of divisions, the society headquarters can immediately contact divisions within a state and request the support of members to oppose or support legislation concerning deaf persons.

Obtaining automobile insurance for deaf drivers at standard rates was a critical issue in the early 1940s. Because insurance was involved, the society was able to prevail upon one insurer to accept deaf drivers at standard rates and keep a record on claims paid out. Not all deaf drivers were enrolled in this program, but the fact that the insurer continues to accept qualified applicants testifies to the good record established by deaf drivers over the years. When legislation detrimental to the interest of deaf drivers was introduced in some states, letters from the agency handling the placement of insurance were helpful in defeating the legislation.

The problems of deaf drivers received the attention of Federal Judge Sherman Finesilver of Denver. Beginning with a symposium on deaf drivers in 1962, Judge Finesilver continuously presented the deaf driver favorably, and the society cooperated with him in setting up driver improvement classes in various parts of the country. Later public statements by Judge Finesilver convinced insurers that deaf drivers could be insured at standard rates. Today the deaf driver with a good driving record experiences no problem obtaining auto insurance. *See* DRIVING RESTRICTIONS.

Ironically, the society now finds itself in competition with other life insurers which had previously avoided insuring deaf persons, except at increased rates. However, having come a long and successful way, the society is meeting this competition and continuing its service to the deaf community.

Bibliography

Mudgett, D.: "The NFSD Story: Diamond Jubilee 1901–1976," *The Deaf American*, June 1976.

Roberts, A. L.: "Lean Years and Lush," *The Frat*,

June–October, December 1944; August–September 1945.

Sullivan, F. B.: "From Acorns to the Mighty Oak," *The Frat*, March–April, May–June 1971.

Frank B. Sullivan

NATIONAL TECHNICAL INSTITUTE FOR THE DEAF

The National Technical Institute for the Deaf (NTID), was established in 1965 as the first technological college for deaf students in the world. It is a federally funded institution located on the campus of the Rochester Institute of Technology (RIT), an independent college in Rochester, New York. Approximately 1250 deaf students share the same campus with more than 8500 hearing students.

NATIONAL TECHNICAL INSTITUTE FOR THE DEAF ACT

Peter N. Peterson, a deaf teacher at the Minnesota School for the Deaf, wrote in 1930: "A national technical institute for the deaf . . . located in a large manufacturing city, is what deaf young America needs more than anything else . . . such an institute should include 'several buildings filled with modern machines, appliances, tools, materials, school buildings, dormitories . . . a gymnasium, library, tennis courts, trees, shrubs, flowers, a director . . . a staff of competent instructors, and 500 students. A national technical institute for the deaf. A dream, yes, and a possibility.' "

It became a reality in 1965 when the National Technical Institute for the Deaf Act (Public Law 89-36) created the institute, and a final bill drafted by Congressman Hugh Carey of New York was signed into law by President Lyndon B. Johnson on June 8. Among the provisions of the act were that the institute be established within the context of an already existing institution of higher learning, that it be an institute that provides for at least the baccalaureate degree, and that there be established immediately a National Advisory Board to advise the Secretary of Health, Education and Welfare about procedures and guidelines with respect to the establishment of the institute.

Public Law 89-36 further defined NTID as a postsecondary educational and residential institution with eight basic responsibilities: to provide semi-professional and professional technical programs for postsecondary deaf students; to provide special support services to encourage personal, social, and cultural development among deaf students; to encourage qualified deaf students to pursue graduate studies; to conduct research into the occupational and employment-related aspects of deafness; to develop and evaluate new, imaginative instructional

technology; to conduct training programs, seminars, and short courses related to deafness for staff and graduate students preparing to work professionally with deaf people; to disseminate information regarding NTID curricula, courses of study, special services, and research findings to various publics; and to develop and modify the educational specifications, to design and construct the facilities, to procure the equipment, and to develop and maintain the staff necessary to meet the objectives of NTID.

HOST INSTITUTE

The National Advisory Board unanimously selected the Rochester Institute of Technology from 20 applicants to be the host institution for the National Technical Institute for the Deaf. The Rochester Institute of Technology's qualifications for hosting NTID were impressive: in its 137-year history, the institute had developed a specialization in professional and technological education, with a majority of its graduates moving directly into careers in science, technology, the arts, and business. Additionally, the Rochester Institute of Technology had a long history of providing technical education of the caliber now provided to deaf students. Since 1912 the Rochester Institute has provided cooperative work experiences for students, the third postsecondary school in the United States to do so. Also, the National Advisory Board members found the local business and industry of Rochester highly receptive to having an institute for deaf persons in their community.

DESIGN OF THE INSTITUTE

The U. S. Department of Health, Education and Welfare formally entered into an agreement in 1966 with the Rochester Institute to design a facility. The planning and construction team for NTID needed to design a program for it, including exact requirements and the number of students to be served; to design a facility to respond to these requirements; and to protect the public interest by ensuring adherence to the legislation that initiated the project.

The architects had three major concerns in planning the NTID complex: to provide close integration with the Rochester Institute campus in buildings that would express the identity of NTID; to incorporate the sophisticated technology required for the education of deaf students; and to use light, color, texture, and space to heighten the educational use and enjoyment of those perceptions in which deaf students have no handicap.

While these construction plans were being finalized, NTID admitted its first class of 70 students in September 1968. These students attended classes with their hearing peers on the institute's new suburban campus in Henrietta, New York.

Groundbreaking for NTID's three-building facility took place in June 1971, and the complex was completed in 3 years. The Lyndon Baines Johnson Academic Building, the Mark Ellingson–Peter N. Peterson–Alexander Graham Bell residence hall complex, and the Hettie L. Shumway Dining Commons all conformed to the special needs of the Rochester Institute's hearing-impaired students.

The residence halls, built to accommodate 750 students, are designed in living-group arrangements, using movable modular furniture, and are equipped with special visual alarm systems to signal evacuation, message, and visitor. Windowless classrooms in the academic building encourage close attention to instructors during classes. This building also houses faculty offices, a theater, learning laboratories, shops, and studios. Between classes students can relax in a bright, airy hallway known as "the street," filled with plants and colorful murals.

The first director of NTID was D. Robert Frisina, an internationally recognized educator and consultant in the field of deafness. He previously had served as dean of the Graduate School of Gallaudet College and as adviser to the U.S. Social and Rehabilitative Service, National Institutes of Health, and State Education Departments. Frisina served as director of NTID from 1967 until 1977. He was succeeded by William E. Castle, who previously had served as dean of NTID. Before joining NTID, Castle was associate secretary for research and scientific affairs for the American Speech and Hearing Association. He became president of the Alexander Graham Bell Association for the Deaf in 1982. Castle has a long history in the fields of speech, hearing, and postsecondary education for deaf persons.

PREPARATION OF STUDENTS

An applicant to NTID must be a United States citizen or permanent resident; have an overall eighth-grade achievement level or above with good grades, and have a hearing loss of 70 decibels (ISO) or greater (without a hearing aid) in the better ear that seriously limits the student's chances of success in a regular college program.

NTID's students have come from every state, Washington, D.C., and Puerto Rico. Many come from mainstreamed public schools, others from residential secondary-school programs for deaf students. Their communication preferences range from oral to manual to simultaneous communication. All are supported by NTID's eclectic approach to communication. *See* EDUCATION: Communication.

As one of nine colleges at the Rochester Institute of Technology, NTID prepares its students for careers in such fields as accounting, data processing, architectural drafting, medical laboratory technology, photography, optical finishing technology, and applied art. Students may pursue NTID certificate, diploma, and associate degree programs in business, science and engineering, and visual communication careers. In addition, those who have the interest and capability may pursue baccalaureate and master's degree programs in other colleges at the Rochester Institute, including the Colleges of Applied Science and Technology, Business, Engineering, Fine and Applied Arts, Graphic Arts and Photography, and Liberal Arts.

SUPPORT SERVICES

Interpreters In NTID classes, students, teachers, and interpreters communicate with sign language, speech, fingerspelling, facial expression, body language, and all types of media. Qualified students who enroll in the other colleges of the Rochester Institute of Technology may request support services in the form of interpreters, tutors, and notetakers. Interpreters also are available for religious services, student activities, theater, sports, and cultural events; in counseling; and for personal needs.

Communications NTID recognizes the need for good communication skills and has established services covering all types of communication. Instruction and related services are provided for students in reading, writing, use of residual hearing, speechreading, speaking, and manual–simultaneous communication. A Communication Assessment and Advising Department offers a course to help students understand their own communication strengths and weaknesses. This department also offers a course to introduce students to hearing-aid use. Communication-skill assessment, hearing-aid selection, a hearing-aid shop, and individual communication advising are other services of this department.

Learning centers offer students self-paced instruction, small-group classes, and individual attention. These centers are set up for instruction in English, mathematics, physics, reading, science, telecommunications, and writing. Self-instruction labs encourage students to practice their communication skills.

Computer-Assisted Instruction Computer-assisted instruction is used at the Rochester Institute of Technology for teaching and research. Students can use computers to receive information and to study subjects such as mathematics and science. Students may take tests by computer. Computer-assisted instruction also is used to counsel students about their career goals.

RESEARCH

NTID has worked with other institutions carrying out research related to the general problems of deaf people. Through cooperation with institutions like the Salk Institute and Western Ontario University,

NTID actively works to solve the educational and economic problems of deaf people.

Within the institute, research is conducted in three major areas: communication assessment and training, education and cognition, and graduate accommodation. Benefits derived through communication research have been improved communication skills of students; procedures for identifying reading and writing skill levels, speech and voice disorders, and sign-language skills; and development of materials for improving reading and writing skills, manual-simultaneous communication abilities, functional skills in audition and speechreading, and speech and voice production.

Educational research has focused on making the deaf student an independent, active learner and on ways to improve the teaching-learning process for deaf individuals. Research on the deaf Rochester Institute of Technology's graduates evaluates how successful NTID has been in preparing graduates for employment. The institute also evaluates changing demographic characteristics of deaf people nationwide and monitors the changing job market.

ADVANCING PROFESSIONALS

One of NTID's goals is to influence professionals who serve the deaf population. Since 1969 the institute has been helping to fulfill that goal through its internship program. Graduate internships offer master's and doctor's degree students the opportunity to practice their professional skills with a population of deaf college students. Professional internships offer a unique opportunity for people from business, industry, and education to develop their skills in a supervised experience with deaf college students and NTID staff members. The Rochester Institute of Technology and the University of Rochester cosponsor a graduate program designed to improve the quality of education and services for deaf people. The program qualifies educators to work with deaf people at the secondary-school level in teaching, providing support services and serving as resources on deafness to schools that mainstream deaf students in regular school systems. The Rochester Institute offers an Interpreting for the Hearing Impaired program which prepares graduates to provide interpreting and other educational support services to hearing-impaired people.

PLACEMENT

Historically, more than 95 percent of NTID's graduates who enter the labor force find jobs. A majority are employed in the Middle Atlantic, New England, and east North Central regions of the United States. They are upwardly and occupationally mobile, and are choosing employment op-

portunities away from their hometowns. The majority of those who do not seek jobs continue their education. NTID has an individualized placement program to teach students job-search skills. Employment advisers help students develop ways to find jobs, and also help employers understand the programs of NTID and how well prepared its graduates are in technical and communication skills.

The National Center on Employment of the Deaf (NCED) offers services to employers, professionals serving deaf individuals, and qualified deaf persons. Center staff members assist employers in recruiting, hiring, and accommodating deaf people. A continuing career development service helps graduates continue to move upward in their jobs and gives employers strategies to promote their deaf employees' career growth. A career-matching system matches qualifications of deaf persons seeking jobs with the needs of employers nationally. It is designed to facilitate career and geographic mobility.

CONTINUING RESPONSIBILITY

NTID must keep in mind its mission and basic responsibilities as defined by the National Advisory Board when it was created. It needs to constantly evaluate and improve existing programs, design curricula to meet the needs of the twentieth century, and increase options for deaf students while endeavoring to increase the number and percentage of deaf students who cross-register into the major programs of other colleges at the Rochester Institute of Technology.

Bibliography

National Technical Institute for the Deaf, Public Information Office: *Focus* (magazine).

———: "RIT Official Bulletin."

William E. Castle

NATIONAL THEATERS OF THE DEAF

Theater performed by deaf individuals for mixed deaf and hearing audiences is a relatively new phenomenon. It is an idea, however, with international appeal, and more and more countries are witnessing the establishment of national theater groups composed mostly of deaf people. Some of these groups have been successful in developing talent, attracting audiences, and gaining financial stability. Others have collapsed after their initial enthusiasm waned. One event that has encouraged the growth of deaf theater is the international Pantomime Festival of the Deaf.

INTERNATIONAL PANTOMIME FESTIVAL
OF THE DEAF

Held during the third week in November every other year, the International Pantomime Festival of the

Deaf brings together the best professional and amateur deaf mimes in Brno, Czechoslovakia. First organized in 1970, it is on the International Theatre Institute calendar as one of the important cultural events. The seventh festival coincided with the First World Theatre Festival of the Deaf in 1981. Chosen as the best in the festival were the Union of Invalids of Czechoslovakia for *Ideal Society*, the Central Cultural Group of the Federation of the Deaf and Hard of Hearing from the German Democratic Republic for *A Different One*, and Stanco Jordan of Bulgaria for his *The Sunflower Seed*. The eighth festival drew 200 mimes from 12 nations. Debbie Anne Rennie of the United States captured the grand prize for the best individual performance, and her ensemble from the Fairmount Theatre of the Deaf took the Most Appreciated Show award for their entry of *SMIRCUS: A Sign Mime Circus*. See FAIRMOUNT THEATRE OF THE DEAF.

FIRST WORLD THEATRE FESTIVAL OF THE DEAF
An indication of the growth of interest in deaf theater was the establishment of the First World Theatre Festival of the Deaf, in Brno, Czechoslovakia, November 14–22, 1981. It attracted 218 artists from nine countries. Ten more countries were represented by observers. Sixteen full-length performances were given and every one was sold out. The purpose of the gathering was to show the artistic work of the best professional and amateur deaf theater groups, to present an overview of the current situation and level of the field, and to encourage further creative activities among the world's deaf performers. The event was commissioned by the World Federation of the Deaf and sponsored by the Union of Invalids in the Czechoslovak Socialist Republic. See WORLD FEDERATION OF THE DEAF.

Despite the diversity of styles of presentation, an international jury agreed to use intelligibility as one major judging criterion. Were deaf people the only ones who could comprehend the performance? Top honors went to the Olsztyn Pantomime of Poland for its production of *Apocalypse*. Also honored were the Moscow Theatre of Mime and Gesture for *The Pulse of My Parallel* and the Theatre of the Deaf from Barcelona for *The Great Theatre of the World*.

The biennial International Pantomime Festival and the First World Theatre Festival of the Deaf underscore the fact that the time has arrived for deaf theater groups to gain acceptance. In addition to the National Theatre of the Deaf in the United States, the deaf theater groups that have had some success include Australia's New South Wales Theatre of the Deaf, Canada's A Show of Hands Theatre Company and Théâtre Visuel des Sourds, Czechoslovakia's Pantomima of the Union of Invalids, Denmark's Døves Teater, England's Interim Theatre Company, France's International Visual Theatre, Israel's Kol Demama Dance Company, Italy's Compagnia Teatrale di Mimo and Senza Parole, Japan's Theatre of the Deaf, Poland's Olsztyn Pantomime, the Soviet Union's Moscow Theatre of Mimicry and Gesture, and Sweden's Tyst Teater.

AUSTRALIA
In 1974, following a tour and workshops by the National Theatre of the Deaf of the United States, the New South Wales Theatre of the Deaf was formed under the auspices of the Elizabethan Theatre Trust and the Adult Deaf Society of New South Wales. It started as an amateur group and became in 1979 a professional theater-in-education company that uses sign language, mime, gesture, and dance with hearing narrators. Made up of three deaf actors, one hearing actor, and a hearing actor–production manager, the company tours schools with a repertoire of plays that promotes deaf awareness—for example, *Theodora*, about a deaf girl caught in the French Revolution, *Signposts in History*, about communication through the ages, and *Actions Speak Louder than Words*, a humorous piece about auditioning for a film using body language rather than voice. The group also gives workshops.

Within its organizational structure, there is a part-time, semiprofessional company of 15 deaf actors who perform exclusively at the Adult Deaf Society with productions such as *The Threepenny Opera*. The New South Wales Theatre of the Deaf also has sponsored Talent Quest and the Annual Deaf Community Revue. In a 1979 joint effort with Griffith Theatre Company, it presented *Alex . . . or the Automatic Trial*. See AUSTRALIA.

CANADA
Reflecting its bilingual population, Canada has two deaf theater groups, A Show of Hands Theatre Company and Théâtre Visuel des Sourds. A Show of Hands originated in 1980, when a grant to study a theater of and for deaf people was set up with a professional director, Frank Canino, and the deaf community. The result was the small production *If Only You Weren't So Wishy Washy, Charlie Brown!* It was performed at a cultural festival in 1982. A name for the performing group was requested for the program brochure, and A Show of Hands Theatre Company was thus created. The company consists of four deaf actors in addition to a deaf associate director among a staff of three. It also draws talent from the deaf community. The company's other offering was *The Shooting of Dan McGrew*, a poem dramatized by Jim McDermott, who had signed the World Theatre Day speech while it was delivered by Tony-winner Len Cariou at the St. Lawrence Centre. A sign language theater, the company seeks to provide a theatrical learning experience for deaf Canadians and has performed

almost exclusively to them. The company is based in Toronto.

Founded by a group of young deaf performers in 1968, Théâtre Visuel des Sourds is an independent, semiprofessional company based in Montreal. The company makes video productions as well as performs plays. It has five deaf members, including founders Serge Briere, Jean Goulet, and Gerard Courchesne, and one hearing member. Among its numerous video productions, the company has made a 30-minute tape on how to teach the Quebec French Sign Language to hearing people. In 1983 the company toured with a special play for children. Pantomime is almost extensively used, with some sign language mixed in. The company is very involved with the affairs of the Montreal deaf community. See CANADA.

CZECHOSLOVAKIA

Pantomima of the Union of Invalids is the central representative ensemble of a nationwide pantomime program sponsored by the Union of Invalids in the Czechoslovak Socialist Republic. It tours extensively around the country and abroad, performing in East Germany, West Germany, Bulgaria, Poland, and the Soviet Union. Started in the 1960s, the program grew in scope and quality during the 1970s. There are at present six regional ensembles and five groups of special interest for deaf people. The best mimes are selected for the two central representative ensembles. Pantomima of the Union of Invalids contains 23 members, 2 art leaders, engineers, and illuminators. They are amateurs, but the Union of Invalids covers all their expenses for Pantomima activities.

An all-evening program usually opens with short scenes of humor and educational subjects, followed by the feature play presenting historical themes involving the struggle against individual and collective violence. The regional and special-interest ensembles specialize in short similar works.

The Union of Invalids sponsors the biennial International Pantomime Festival of the Deaf in Brno. Its own entry, *Ideal Society*, took the top honors at the seventh festival in 1981.

DENMARK

Based in Copenhagen, Døves Teater is an association with 90 paying members, almost everyone being deaf. Its main audience is deaf, and it performs to hearing groups for a fee. Members of its Children Theatre Group work professionally. Financial supports comes from various sources, including the Danish Ministry of Culture.

Døves Teater offers various types of productions. It has presented drama (such as *Mother's Two Daughters*), mime performances (*Woman Clown with a Doll*), a dance performance (*Between Integration and Segregation*), a debate performance (*What is Culture of the Deaf?*), children's theater (*Deaf in a Hearing World*), and cabaret in sign language. Experimentation is important in its work. While the Døves Teater encourages its members to develop deaf plays, it also employs a ballet dancer from the Royal Theatre in Copenhagen.

The company was founded in 1960 following the Nordic Conference held in Denmark that year. A hearing director, Alfred Hansen, and a deaf actor, Gudmund Kjaer Soerensen, had encouraged deaf Danes to stage a Ludvig Holberg play. From the applause of the conference audience, Døves Teater (Theatre of the Deaf) was born.

One Døves member, Alida Rasmussen, has appeared in the Danish version of *Children of a Lesser God*. Several members studied at the National Theatre of the Deaf's Professional School in the United States. Døves Teater was the host of the Second World Theatre Festival of the Deaf, held in Copenhagen on May 4–10, 1986. See DENMARK.

ENGLAND

The Interim Theatre Company was founded in 1978 by Terry Ruane and Chris Harrowell to continue the work of the defunct British Theatre of the Deaf formed in 1968. In its initial season, it produced *The Fisherman and His Soul* and *The Streets of London* and followed with *Medieval Tales* the next year. It performed in national venues, including the Traverse in Edinburgh, the Cockpit in London, Theatre Clwyd in Mold, Wales, and various small arts centers around the country. One of its members, Jean St. Clair, played the lead of a deaf girl in the Birmingham Repertory Theatre production of *Hearing* (1979), which featured a memorable relationship between a deaf girl and her overprotective and guilt-ridden mother. It brought several American actors in for its production of *Equus*.

On the belief that contemporary theater relied too much on the spoken word for impact, Interim sought to offer the alternative of a visual experience. The company conducted drama workshops in special schools, deaf clubs, and community centers. It also continued the week-long summer school program initiated by the British Theatre of the Deaf.

FRANCE

In January 1976 the American and French Centers of the International Institute launched a project to promote the growth of international deaf culture and to establish an international deaf theater and cultural center based in Paris. The center was to be called the International Visual Theatre. Three deaf Americans, Jane Wilk, Alfred Corrado, and Julianna Fjeld, were asked to help establish it. Wilk was appointed the administrative director. Scenic artist Corrado flew immediately to Paris and teamed up with hearing French director Jean Gremion to conduct experimental workshops with deaf children from French schools for deaf pupils. They were soon joined by Fjeld. International Visual Theatre's five year plan called for, among other things, an exploration of the natural expression of deaf people in the theater and the development and spread of an international sign language. *See* FRANCE.

ISRAEL

With 7 deaf dancers and 10 hearing dancers moving together, Kol Demama (Voice of Silence) Dance Company seeks to create a language beyond words that expresses a full range of emotions. Dancers take their cues from the flow of the sequence and from each other's movements, by sight, touch, and vibrations. The audience cannot tell which dancers are deaf, which are not. Kol Demama's production of *Psalms to Jerusalem* is a blend of religious motifs representing the major faiths. Symbols of Judaism, Christianity, and Islam are created through dramatic hand movements to a musical mix of Gregorian themes, Jewish prayers, ancient Samaritan chants, and oriental melodies. In *Alter Ego*, one dancer symbolizes the ego, another the alter ego. One dances in a soft romantic style, the other in a determined and energetic style. For a moment they clash, the next they merge, thus portraying humans' inner dualism.

The company is based in Tel Aviv and is directed by Moshe Efrati, a dancer and choreographer formerly with the Batsheva Dance Company. He was invited to work with deaf people at the Helen Keller Center. Later, he formed the Efrati Dance Company and a second one, Demama Dance Company, for deaf individuals. In 1979 he merged the two groups into Kol Demama. The company has danced on three continents, and it toured the United States in the fall of 1984. *See* ISRAEL.

ITALY

Senza Parole is a mime company of the Italian Theatre of the Deaf established in 1979. Semiprofessional and based in Milan, it is sponsored by the National Deaf Organization. Members attended a school of mime at the Civic School of Dramatic Art of the Piccolo Teatro. The company survived through difficult times and produced *Prometeo* by Roberto Rossetti and Clara Delpero. It was developed through improvisation by a 15-member cast. In 1983 the company drew inspiration from the work of Samuel Beckett to produce their most important work to date, *Rendezvous*. A second official theater, for amateur deaf actors, is Gruppo Teatrale "Ciclope" in Palermo, Sicily. *See* ITALY.

JAPAN

Tremendous crowds and press coverage of the winter tour in Japan by the United States' National Theatre of the Deaf, and the patronage of popular television personality Tetsuko Kuroyanagi, created the perfect climate for the formation of Japan's Theatre of the Deaf in April 1980. It held its first theater seminar in Tokyo the following summer. The semiprofessional company consists of 11 deaf persons and 4 hearing persons and is headed by Akihiro Yonaiyama, a deaf actor who toured with the National Theatre of the Deaf in Japan and in America in 1979. Another member, Tetsuya Izaki, spent 1½ years with the American company.

The Japanese Theatre of the Deaf performs four types of productions: sign-mime (such as *All One's Life*, *Dracula*, *All the Year Round*), silent theater (*The Sea*, *Baseball*), kyogen of sign language (*The Six Jizos*, *Black Paint*), and drama (*Snow White*). It entered its kyogen of sign language production in the Arts Competition by the Ministry of Culture at the National Noh Theatre in the fall of 1984. Japan's Theatre of the Deaf is based in Tokyo, and receives financial support from the Totto Foundation, of whom Tetsuko Kuroyanagi is the chairperson.

In Hitomi, a group of four deaf and six hearing persons have performed Deaf Puppet Theatre since 1981. The group won the jury prize at the 1983 International Pantomime Festival of the Deaf in Brno. One of the group's members is Yutaka Ohsugi, who also edits the *Deaf Theatre News*. This publication reports news, trends, and performance schedules of theaters of deaf people around the world. It published its first issue in October 1983, and its enterprises include summer theater sessions, festivals, and an employment agency. It has headquarters in the VAIS (Visual Arts Information System) office in Tokyo. *See* JAPAN.

POLAND

The work of Olsztyn Pantomime, Poland's deaf theater group, is characterized by powerful visual impact and reflects the philosophy of its managing director, Bohdan Gluszczak, who has been with the group since its formation. In 1959 it was set up under the auspices of the Polish Union of the Deaf and attached to the Voivodship House of Culture. The ensemble features 35 deaf members recruited from among the workers in cooperatives for disabled persons. As amateurs, they devote about 200 evenings a year to rehearsals and work in the theater.

The group's first performance was Aleksander Fredro's comedy *Jestem zabójca* (*I Am a Killer*). For other subject matter, they draw from Francisco Goya's pictures (*Caprichos*), Albrecht Dürer's woodcuts (*Apocalypse*), St. John (*The Revelation of St. John the Evangelist*), Federico García Lorca, and folk art. Work on a play takes about three years, prepared in various stages, from sketches to scenario. In developing complex interrelationships and intricate visual stories, a great deal of attention is given to making the right choice of gesture, posture, or pantomime. Music plays an important role in their work and is carefully composed for each production. A 1984 production, *The Banquet*, is based on several plays by Witold Gombrowicz, an outstanding playwright of the Polish avant-garde theater. Olsztyn Pantomime is frequently invited to perform outside Poland and has won many prizes from international festivals.

SWEDEN

An independent group with the Swedish National Theater Center in Solna, Tyst Teater (Silent Theatre) tours the country each fall and spring. A small ensemble consisting of only deaf actors, it performs a repertoire of classical plays and plays that focus on the situation of deaf people in society. Actors use sign language and perform to associations for deaf people, schools, and institutions. The plays are discussed with the audience following each performance. The company also teaches creative drama.

Tyst Teater started as an amateur group in 1970 and presented *To Be Deaf in Sweden* at the 1975 World Congress of the World Federation of the Deaf in Washington, D.C. Joining the National Theater Center in the summer of 1977, Tyst Teater turned professional and has since produced *My Ear Itches*; *Waiting for Godot*; *Marianne*; *That for You*; *Not All Thieves Come to Steal*; *Miss Julie*; *Always Second*; *At Sea*; *The Shot*; *Animal, Nature and Smart Guy*; and *The Proposal and the Bear*. *See* SWEDEN.

UNION OF SOVIET SOCIALIST REPUBLICS

The Soviet Union's deaf theater group is a professionally licensed company, the Moscow Theater of Mimicry and Gesture, that employs over 100 people, of which 40 percent are actors. All actors except four are deaf. Others serve as directors, designers, stagehands, and administrative personnel. The company performs in a modern 750-seat sloping amphitheater in Moscow, complete with a revolving stage and a 10-instrument orchestra. The theater houses, in addition to rehearsal and storage space and dressing rooms, two lecture halls, a film projection room, a library, a studio for amateur painters and sculptors, and a well-equipped sports complex. Primarily a resident theater, the company makes an occasional tour in major cities in the Soviet Union and eastern Europe.

The repertoire includes contemporary and classic Russian plays such as Leo Tolstoy's *War and Peace*, Shakespeare's *Twelfth Night*, Alexandre Dumas's *The Three Musketeers*, and musical comedies, as well as the company's own special productions. Four major productions are presented each year, and plays are constantly rotated. Its 1973 production of *Prometheus Bound* featured American guest artist Bernard Bragg, appearing as part of an exchange program with the United States' National Theatre of the Deaf. The Moscow Theatre's Michael Sliptchenko, in turn, appeared in the National Theatre of the Deaf's production of *Dybbuk* the following year. *See* BRAGG, BERNARD.

The company uses sign language in its productions but does not stress signs as a dramatic medium. With microphones, speakers are situated in the front, offstage. They synchronize the deaf actor's lip movements, word by word, with voice. When songs and dances are presented, actors keep in time with music but otherwise perform in a conventional manner.

The Moscow Theatre of Mimicry and Gesture was founded in St. Petersburg (Leningrad) in 1917 and moved to Moscow the next year, when Lenin reestablished the government in Moscow following the revolution. It was disbanded during World War II but was revived shortly after the war. In 1962 it became professional upon the state's decision to subsidize it.

In Kiev there is also a professional troupe called the Rainbow, consisting of deaf acrobats, dancers, and jugglers.

UNITED STATES

Since its 1967 debut, the National Theatre of the Deaf (NTD) has given over 3000 performances across four continents. Based in Chester, Connecticut, the company of 12 to 14 professional actors opens with a new production each fall and spends 27 weeks a year touring. It has appeared on Broadway, at the Kennedy Center in Washington, D.C., at Lincoln Center in New York City, and in major theaters of the world. When it performed at Las Vegas, Nevada, in November 1980, it became the only theatrical company to have performed in all 50 states. NTD presented *The Hero with a Thousand Faces* at the 1984 Olympic Arts Festival in Los Angeles as one of the four American representatives.

Language The members of the almost entirely deaf cast use sign language in an enlarged and elaborated theatrical form. The choice of sign may be made so its handshape or location will differ from the sign preceding it, thus offering esthetic variety. New signs may be created to meet the demands of dramatic expression. Actors work with scripts in English and translate them into sign themselves with assistance from a sign master. Prominent deaf dramatists Eric Malzkuhn, Robert

Panara, and Bernard Bragg have served as translators. Two hearing actors provide voice translation in addition to speaking for themselves, since 90 percent of NTD's audience is composed of hearing people.

With the company interpreter at their side, directors of Broadway and international acclaim guide the company in the process of scene development. Experimentation, improvisation, and collaboration constitute vital elements of the five-week rehearsal period. Dance, mime, acrobatics, and music have been incorporated into many productions. The repertoire includes both classics and original works. When it is necessary, portions of a script are adapted to accommodate the deafness of the actors. For example, in *All the Way Home* (1984) directed by Colleen Dewhurst, who had appeared in the original award-winning production, all members of the two families become deaf characters except for a child who remains hearing so he can receive the phone calls essential to the plot of the play.

Deafness and sign language were the subjects of the company's first original piece, *My Third Eye* (1971). Actors related their fears, frustrations, and joys while growing up as deaf parents. A side show in the vein of *Gulliver's Travels* commented on the strangeness of creatures who talked instead of signed. In *Parade* (1975), the actors staged a march to Washington, D.C., to press their demand for the "New Deaf Dominion." Each actor gave a monologue on being a deaf individual in search of a personal version of the Holy Grail in *Parzival, from the Horse's Mouth* (1982). Edmund Waterstreet and Shanny Mow formed the first deaf director and deaf writer team to produce *The Iliad, Play by Play* (1980). On June 5, 1977, at the Shubert Theatre in New York City, NTD received Broadway's highest tribute for theatrical excellence when it was presented with the Antoinette Perry (Tony) Award.

Little Theatre of the Deaf Little Theatre of the Deaf (LTD), an offshoot of NTD, performs to children in schools, libraries, museums, and parks throughout the United States. It has appeared in India, the Far East, Scandinavia, and Trinidad. Founded in 1968, it soon expanded to two companies of five actors each to meet the growing demands for appearances. Each company offers a one-hour program of short stories, fables, fairy tales, poems, and often an introduction to sign language. At the end of each performance, the cast improvises on suggestions from the young audience. As an example of one of America's best in children's theater, LTD performed in 1972 at the Fourth International Congress of the International Association of Theatres for Children and Youth. For its 1977 Children's Arts Festival, the Kennedy Center commissioned NTD to produce a new work, *Sir Gawain and the Green Knight* by Dennis Scott. Dur-

ing the holiday seasons, at home in Chester, LTD has presented *A Christmas Carol* and *A Child's Christmas in Wales*. In summers, it presents storytelling hours at the Village Green and other places.

Theatre in Sign Theatre in Sign, another NTD project, performed *Gin Game* (1979) featuring Patrick Graybill and Phyllis Frelich. The play was directed by Linda Bove, and the dialogue was communicated entirely in American Sign Language. A trio of one-act plays, *Here We Are*, *The Bear*, and *Bedtime Story*, was performed the following year. *See* BOVE, LINDA; FRELICH, PHYLLIS; SIGN LANGUAGES: American.

Professional School Each summer NTD conducts the Professional School for Deaf Theatre Personnel in Chester. Starting at 7:30 with morning calisthenics, students attend classes in acting, dancing, movement, and theater literature and arts. Participation, experimentation, and leadership are stressed by a faculty of noted artists and the NTD Company. The Professional School is accredited by Connecticut College. A federal scholarship of tuition and room and board is awarded to each deaf American citizen who qualifies on the basis of dramatic aspirations or involvement in community or educational theater. Since 1967 the Professional School has been a source of new talent for NTD as well as other theaters across the country. Foreign students who attend take their training back home to establish or strengthen drama programs in Europe and Asia. An NTD team of Andrew Vasnick, Michael Posnick, and Edmund Waterstreet taught at Japan's Theatre of the Deaf's First Annual Summer Theatre Seminar in Tokyo in 1981.

The Deaf Playwrights Conference is held at the same time as the Professional School. New plays by aspiring deaf writers are developed under the guidance of a dramaturge, rehearsed by the NTD actors, and critiqued by professionals in staged readings open to the public. Five writers attended the first conference in 1977.

The NTD Company conducts workshops on visual/sign language theater. It participates in workshops as well. In 1972 the company spent three weeks with Peter Brook at his famed International Centre for Theatre Research in Paris. Deaf actors from the Soviet Union, Sweden, and Japan have performed with NTD as a part of the artist exchange program. From NTD, Bragg went to the Russian Theatre of Mimicry and Gesture, and Carol Aquiline and Benjamin Strout lent their expertise to Australia's N.S.W. Theatre of the Deaf. In an advocacy endeavor to create roles and place deaf artists in television, film, and stage, NTD first published *Deaf Players' Guild*, a listing of skilled deaf performers, in 1979.

Television NTD's pilot project at the time of its inception was a one-hour television special taped in March 1967 for NBC's *Experiment in Television.* It featured Bragg, Audree Norton, Gilbert Eastman, June Russi, Ralph White, Howard Palmer, and Lou Fant in various sketches and a scene from *All the Way Home.* It was directed by Joe Layton and hosted by Nanette Fabray. It was aired nationally after objections from oral organizations were offset by support from the deaf community. NTD has since made frequent appearances on television. *A Child's Christmas in Wales* with Sir Michael Redgrave was taped in England in 1973 and carried by CBS. With WGBH of Boston, the company produced *Who Knows One* (1977) and the three-part *Festival of Hands* series: "The Silken Tent" (1980) with Jason Robards, "The Road to Cordoba" (1981) with Chita Rivera, and "Issa's Treasure" (1981) with Tetsuko Kuroyanagi.

History The success of the 1958 Broadway production of *The Miracle Worker* prompted Edna Simon Levine, a psychologist in the area of deafness, to share her idea of a professional theater of deaf actors with the director and star of the play, Arthur Penn and Anne Bancroft. They expressed enthusiasm and were soon joined by David Hays, a set designer, and Gene Lasko, a New York director. An initial request for federal funding was turned down. Hays, who had been deeply impressed by the Gallaudet College production of *Our Town*, persisted with the idea and was met with a recurring question from his theater colleagues and philanthropists: "A theater of the *what?*" In 1964 he became involved with George C. White in setting up the Eugene O'Neill Theater Center in Waterford, Connecticut. Located on an estate overlooking Long Island Sound, the center would provide an ideal environment for exploration and experimentation with new and bold concepts such as Levine's dream. Once more Hays sought government assistance. He argued that there was no better way to address social ills and correct the prevailing misconceptions of deaf people than to present deaf persons at their best, as articulate, highly skillful actors on the legitimate stage. It was a bold, even radical, idea in the late 1960s. Though his concerns were artistic, Hays received support from Mary Switzer, head of the Vocational Rehabilitation Administration, and from Boyce Williams, Edwin Martin, and Mac Norwood. *See* GALLAUDET COLLEGE; WILLIAMS, BOYCE ROBERT.

A planning grant was awarded in 1965. In the following summer, the Gallaudet Theatre production of *Iphigenia in Aulis* was brought to the National Playwrights Conference in Waterford. The favorable response of professionals in the audience convinced the planners to go ahead with a theater of the deaf. Hays was chosen as the managing director. It was decided that NTD would be a language theater. Mime would only emphasize mute-

ness. Hays then turned to the deaf community for help in locating deaf talent. Along with the 7 who appeared in *Experiment in Television*, the founding company of 16 was completed with the addition of Joe Valez, Andrew Vasnick, Charles Corey, Violet Armstrong, Phyllis Frelich, Mary Beth Miller, and Timothy Scanlon, and hearing actors William Rhys and Joyce Flynn. The first tour took place in the fall of 1967. Two years later, NTD made its first international tour.

Early in 1981 NTD separated from the Eugene O'Neill Theater Center and became incorporated as a nonprofit organization. It moved to Chester in 1982. The new home, the Hazel E. Stark Center, is a converted mill and residence housing offices, rehearsal space, classrooms, and theater shops, and was made possible by a $257,000 gift from Connecticut businessman Irving Stark in memory of his wife.

Basic funding for NTD comes from the Media Services and Captioned Films section of the Office of Education and from performance fees. Through the years, NTD has also received generous support from foundations, corporations, art commissions, and individuals.

NTD STAGE PRODUCTIONS

1967	William Saroyan, *The Man with His Heart in the Highlands*
	Tsuruya Namboku, *The Tale of Kasane*
	Tyger! Tyger! and Other Burnings (selected poems)
	Giacomo Puccini, *Gianni Schicchi*
1968	Richard Brinsley Sheridan, *The Critic*
	Federico García Lorca, *The Love of Don Perlimplin and Belisa in the Garden*
	Blueprints (selected poems)
1969	Dylan Thomas, *Songs from Milkwood*
	Molière, *Sganarelle*
1970	Georg Büchner, *Woyzeck*
	Journeys, from the collection of Richard Lewis
1971	*My Third Eye*, first original piece
1972	*Gilgamesh*, adapted by Larry Arrick after the Sumerian legend
1973	*Optimism*, from Voltaire's *Candide*
1974	S. Ansk, *The Dybbuk*
	Priscilla, Princess of Power, second original piece
1975	*Parade*, third original piece
1976	Virgil Thomson and Gertrude Stein, *Four Saints in Three Acts*
	Anton Chekhov, *On the Harmfulness of Tobacco*
	Eric Marshall and Stuart Hample, *Children's Letters to God*
1977	Alexandre Dumas, *The Three Musketeers*
1978	Stefan Zweig (after Ben Jonson), *Volpone*
	Dylan Thomas, *Quite Early One Morning*
1979	Thornton Wilder, *Our Town*
	David Hays, *The Wooden Boy* (after Carlo Collodi's *Pinocchio*)
1980	Shanny Mow, *The Iliad, Play by Play*

1981	Shanny Mow, *Gilgamesh* (after Larry Arrick after the Sumerian legend)
	Shanny Mow, *The Ghost of Chastity Past or the Incident at Sashimi Junction*
1982	Shanny Mow and David Hays, *Parzival, from the Horse's Mouth*
1983	Larry Arrick, *The Hero with a Thousand Faces* (adapted from the book by Joseph E. Campbell)
1984	Tad Mosel, *All the Way Home*

Shanny Mow

NAVARRETE, JUAN FERNANDEZ DE
(1526–1579)

Juan Fernandez de Navarrete, known as El Mudo (The Mute), was born in Logroño, Spain, in 1526. He was a painter of the Madrid School who belonged to the transitional period of Spanish art between the mannerist movement of the sixteenth century and naturalism in the seventeenth century. As court painter to Philip II of Spain, he was the most important of the group of Spanish and Italian painters commissioned to work in the Escorial. Almost all his works portrayed religious subjects. In them, he endeavored to portray the feeling of enjoyment in the images without sacrificing their devotional qualities. Learned in the fine arts, an independent thinker and innovator, El Mudo was the first in Spain to abandon mannerism and the first to use the dynamic lights and darks of Tintoretto, which he modified and adapted to Spanish realism. He was the bridge to naturalism exemplified by the work of Caravaggio.

El Mudo became deaf at 3½ years of age from an unknown cause and began to express his wants by sketching with a piece of charcoal or other material. He received his first art lessons at the Hospice of the Star of the Hieronyomite order in Logroño, and remained there until his teacher, Fray Vicente de Santo Domingo, recommended that his parents send him to study in Italy. There he examined the great artworks of Naples, Rome, Florence, Milan, and Venice and probably studied in the studio of Titian. Shortly after 1560 he was summoned to Madrid by the king. By 1566 he was working at the Escorial, employed first as a restorer of paintings and a copiest. In 1568, he was named painter to the king. His early commissions comprised religious personages done in grisaille for cabinet doors and such—all are lost. Next he executed a series of pictures for the convent of the Escorial; those that remain hang in the gallery of the upper cloister. In 1576, he was given a commission to paint the pictures for 30 altars in the Basilica of the Escorial. He completed only some of these large pictures, depicting well-postured figures of two apostles or two saints, in the chapels on each side of the main altar. However, he suffered so much pain from physical ailments that he left his work at the Escorial, sought medical help in Segovia, and later moved to Toledo. He died there in the home of his friend, the sculptor and silversmith Nicolás de Vergara, on March 28, 1579.

Throughout his career, Juan Fernandez de Navarrete showed enthusiasm for the coloring and masterful composition of the Venetians. However, as a consequence of his precise drawing and dynamic chiaroscuro, he added more vigor and relief. The chiaroscuro was not arbitrarily managed as in the case of the tenebrists—those artists who emphasized violent contrasts of light and dark—but was used to enhance his pungent realism by means of a more profound modeling. Also, he never adhered to the intellectual conceits of the mannerists in vogue at that time. Instead he worked independently toward concrete statements of greater simplicity and naturalism. Perhaps he was influ-

Juan Fernandez de Navarrete's *The Beheading of the Apostle Saint James Mayor*, in the Escorial, Spain.

enced by the forthrightness of the sculpture groups by the Leoni brothers that featured the Emperor Charles V and Philip II, arranged in cenotaphs on each side of the high altar of the basilica. His evolution as an artist, though not radical, was constant due to his continued search for new means to enrich his style. He showed the influence of Titian and Correggio in his earliest works, such as the *Baptism of Christ* in the Prado, Madrid, conceived with great feeling, fluidity, and gentleness, whereas later his enthusiasm stemmed from the terminal works of Raphael and the dynamic movement and luminous lighting of Tintoretto. At this period, El Mudo became more intent on substance than form, but he never neglected or became careless with his technique. He not only insisted on making his style suit the needs of his themes, but also felt that his pictures should be painted so as to engender the desire to share their devotional message. Those pictures that are in the Escorial reveal this aim: In the *Holy Family* and *Jesus of the Column* he imbued his composition with a sense of monumentality; in his unfinished work *The Interment of Saint Lawrence*, he returned to the problems of chiaroscuro; and in the pairs of apostles and saints for the basilica he made each figure fill the picture plane, thus creating a composition that responds to the grandeur of the architectural complex.

The picture *The Beheading of the Apostle Saint James Mayor* still speaks for El Mudo. Originally part of a retable in the sacristy in the chapter room of the Escorial, this picture now hangs in the upper gallery of the main cloister. The artist has interpreted the horrible and tragic moment of death of the patron saint of Spain with both expression and intensity. He arrested the emotional impact of the foreground by placing, in a dispassionate setting, the background scene, which shows the battle between Christians and Moors with the saint on horseback ravaging the enemy. The artist painted this dramatic theme from a high point of view with an elevated horizon, acute foreshortening, and intense chiaroscuro to engender empathy, to make spectators feel as if they were there when it happened.

Although the works of Juan Fernandez de Navarrete did not enjoy immediate success, they did impress one of Spain's outstanding poets and dramatists, Lope de Vega. His epitaph for the artist put into words the effect of the expressive quality of El Mudo's works:

"Heaven did not intend that I should speak because with my understanding it gave greater feeling to things that I painted and such life that I gave to them

with only a brushstroke since I could not speak I made them so that they should speak for me."

Bibliography
Aznar, José Camón: *Summa Artis—Historia General del Arte*, vol. 25, Espasa-Calpe S.A., pp. 27–30, 1977.

El Escorial—Eighth Marvel of the World, Patrimonial National, Madrid, pp. 38, 181, 240, 458, 1967.

Enciclopedia Universal Ilustrada, vol. 23, Espasa-Calpe S.A., pp. 798–800.

"Pintura del Siglo XVI," *Ars Hispaniae—Historia Universal del Arte Hispanico*, vol. 12, Plus-Ultra S.A., pp. 251–252, 257.

Siguenza, Fray José de: *La Foundacíon del Monasterio de el Escorial*, Aguilar Ediciones, pp. 220–221, 241–245, 269, 318, 335–336, 1963.

Elva Fromuth Loe

NETHERLANDS

The Netherlands has 14,400,000 inhabitants. About 400,000 (3.4% of the population) are hearing-impaired to the extent that understanding speech in a quiet environment is difficult. About 28,000 people are deaf, that is, have no functional hearing at all. Each year about 175 children of pre-preschool age (up to three years) are diagnosed as deaf by sociomedical services (mostly audiologic centers) and are enrolled in home training programs. There are five schools for deaf pupils, with a total enrollment of about 1500 pupils. *See* DEAF POPULATION: Demography.

EDUCATION
The Netherlands' five educational centers for deaf students are designed for preschool, grade school, and vocational and limited academic possibilities, as well as having special facilities for students with multiple handicaps. They are located in Amsterdam, Groningen, The Hague (in the suburb Voorburg), Rotterdam, and St. Michielsgestel. All are state schools in the sense that they are fully supported and controlled by the Ministry of Education. The background of the institute in the Hague is Protestant and that of the school in St. Michielsgestel, Catholic. These two and the school in Groningen have residential facilities, whereas the schools in Amsterdam and Rotterdam have day-student facilities only. Methodologically, there are no great differences between the schools. As far as the preferred mode of communication is concerned, St. Michielsgestel is the one most evidently orally oriented; Groningen uses total communication; the others are best characterized as moderately oral, but open to new developments and other means. All five schools use nonoral means of communication for multiply handicapped pupils. In St. Mi-

chielsgestel these pupils are housed on different campuses, and the country's only full-fledged department for deaf and blind persons is included. The Netherlands, furthermore, has realized since the early 1950s the need for schools intermediate between those for deaf children on the one hand and regular facilities for hearing children on the other (that is, schools for hard-of-hearing pupils, located within easy reach for day students). There is little mainstreaming, and the instances of deaf persons pursuing higher education are rare. *See* EDUCATION: Communication.

SOCIOECONOMIC CONDITIONS

Most deaf people holding jobs function between the levels of skilled and unskilled labor, with very few in higher income brackets. As a group, moreover, deaf individuals seem to be harder hit by unemployment than the general adult population. The integration within the population at large ranges from fairly to very high, if integration is taken as the display of sufficient skills in speech and speech-reading for basic interchange at the work and public level. Complete integration, with little or no contact with other deaf persons, is not unusual but seems to be reserved for a minority, although orally oriented educators like to disagree. Yet, it is fairly obvious that most deaf people participate one way or another in mutual contacts, usually through alumni associations and via the different activities of the local deaf clubs; this participation appears to be on the increase. One of the reasons is probably the changing attitude toward the use of signing—in the schools, among the specialists, and in society at large. Compared with other countries, such as the United States, there seems to be less intermarriage among deaf persons, and a smaller proportion of children of deaf parents.

In a socialized country such as the Netherlands, there are numerous special provisions for handicapped persons in general and for deaf persons in particular. One is a social service system of aftercare (that is, after the school years are completed) in which some of the institutes mentioned above are active. Some deaf persons consider these services patronizing. Other desirable provisions are lacking, such as interpreting services and psychiatric care.

COMMUNICATION

For decades oralism has prevailed from pre-preschool home training programs all the way through school methods, and even in the social aftercare programs for deaf adults. There are, however, some evident changes in attitudes and practices. Early detection of deafness and guidance for deaf children and their parents have been well organized for decades through the audiologic centers. Nowaways, more and more programs run by

these centers are beginning to acknowledge the manual-visual nature of the first interaction, and to organize this communication in a more structured way. One center, the Dutch Foundation for the Deaf and the Hard of Hearing Child, in Amsterdam, is developing a total communication–like parent-child program. Deaf adults vary quite a bit in their modes of communication (depending on their skills, preferences, and fluency, as well as on the sociolinguistic situation), ranging from speech-only to signing-only under all circumstances. *See* SOCIOLINGUISTICS: Sign Language Continuum.

Obviously, the extremes of this range occur rarely. The communication among deaf persons is mostly characterized by the regular use of signs as well as by the incorporation of lip movements, usually voiceless. For deaf persons there is no clear-cut dominance of Dutch Sign Language, and speech often plays a part in their own interchange. Although a theoretical distinction between Signed Dutch and Dutch Sign Language exists, and pure forms of each do sometimes occur, blends of the two seem most commonly used. *See* SIGN LANGUAGES: Dutch.

RESEARCH

A large part of the ongoing research in the Netherlands focuses on signing. Reports on it have been given at the International Congresses on Sign Language Research in Bristol (1981) and Rome (1983), at the European Congress in Brussels (1982), and at the Second European Congress on Sign Language Research in Amsterdam (1985). At the Institute for General Linguistics of the University of Amsterdam, preparation of a dictionary of signs with some 3000 entries was undertaken, for use by parents, teachers, interpreters, and the deaf people themselves. The preparatory work involved the analysis of videotaped spontaneous and prompted interchange in signing between native informants from five regions, related to the five schools and using different varieties of signs. The dictionary project started as the realization of a child dictionary of signs with about 2000 entries, and is part of a larger project aimed at advancing the communicative opportunities of deaf persons. The other part has been carried out at the Dutch Foundation for the Deaf and Hard of Hearing Child, in close cooperation with the University of Amsterdam institute and with the preschool of the Amsterdam School for the Deaf. This part of the project relates to the improvements of the early interaction and communication between hearing parents and their deaf child. In cooperation with the University of Groningen, the Groningen School for the Deaf started a research project to evaluate and guide its total communication programs.

At the Institute for Linguistics of the University of Amsterdam, a project on the status of sign language in the communication of deaf adults and in the schools in all European countries was completed. Moreover, projects have been undertaken on the psycholinguistic characteristics of the communication of deaf adults among themselves, and on interpreting from speech into sign language and vice versa. Apart from research related to signing, research has been carried out over the years at the St. Michielsgestel school; it focuses mainly on differential diagnosis of multiply handicapped deaf children, and on the special educational implications of so-called dysphasic, deaf-blind, and other multiply handicapped deaf children.

NATIONAL ORGANIZATION

The national organization of deaf people has been realized relatively recently, mostly by the foundation of the Dutch National Deaf Council (NCD; Stichting Nederlandse Doverrenraad), initiated and run mostly by deaf people and comprising all local chapters of the deaf clubs, the deaf sports organizations, and the like. The NCD holds office in Utrecht, and presented itself to the nation publicly for the first time in 1981 through its First National Congress. A second national congress was organized in 1983.

The development of the NCD points to the growing self-esteem of the Dutch deaf community. The organization promotes the use of Dutch Sign Language and Signed Dutch, supporting linguistic, psycholinguistic, and sociolinguistic research related to communication. The NCD also advocates the use of deaf teachers or assistant teachers, and publicizes its opinions among parents of deaf children, the public, and officials. The NCD's activities frequently encounter criticism from orally oriented parents, the influential school at St. Michielsgestel, and some education officials.

PERIODICALS

The joint schools for deaf and hard-of-hearing students publish a monthly periodical on broad educational issues, mainly directed at the teachers. The periodical name, *Van horen zeggen* (From Hearsay), has come under some criticism for being hearing-biased. Under the auspices of the NCD, a monthly is published, *Woord en Gebaar* (Word and Sign). It carries a broad spectrum of information, from popularized summaries of theoretical issues—such as the requirements for a dictionary of signs, or the implications of cued speech—to information on sports, local events, and personal notes. Deaf editors present this information in a nontechnical format that deaf readers can readily understand.

Bibliography

Ligtenberg, C. L. van, and H. Hoolboom: *Over horen en slechtoren*, Alphen van de Rijn, Stafleu, 1982.

Stritchting Nederlandse Doverrenraad: *Wie niet horen Kan moet maar zien: Een visie op het communiceren met doven*, Muiderberg, Coutinho, 1981.

Tervoort, Bernard T. (ed.): *Hand over Hand: Nieuwe inzichten in de communicatie van doven*, Muiderberg, Coutinho, 1983.

Bernard T. Tervoort

NEW ZEALAND

New Zealand, well over 100,000 square miles (260,000 square kilometers) in area, has only 3 million people. Except for Auckland (population about 1 million) and other main centers, the population is thinly distributed. The challenge, then, is to ensure that deaf children throughout the country receive equitable education benefits.

EDUCATION

In 1874 the government began considering educational provisions for deaf children, and in 1878 Gerrit Van Asch was chosen to begin the first school. Earlier Van Asch had left Rotterdam for London, where he had established his own school for deaf students, reportedly very successful. Writing in 1865 in the *Quarterly Journal of Science*, he argued for reform in deaf education. In advocating the development of oral methods of communication, he anticipated the marked changes that were to occur in education of deaf students in England. The school that Van Asch established in New Zealand in 1880 was the first oral school for deaf pupils in the British Commonwealth, and probably was the first oral school in the world to be established and completely maintained by a government.

Education of deaf children became compulsory in New Zealand. When Van Asch retired in 1906, he was recognized by educational authorities for developing a very high standard of work. Later principals of the school continued using basic approaches developed by Van Asch. Moreover, they succeeded in establishing clinics for hard-of-hearing people and for speech problems in several cities. Their work was endorsed by Alexander Graham Bell, who visited the school in 1911. *See* BELL, ALEXANDER GRAHAM.

In 1940 a new principal who had received training at the University of Manchester under Sir Alexander Ewing began prompting some important changes: More formal teacher training began in 1943, and free hearing aids were instituted in 1949. A nursery school was established in 1940, and in 1957 guidance programs for parents of preschool children were offered.

During World War II a second school was established in the North Island. Then each school for the deaf became responsible for the educational management of all deaf children in its own area representing half the population of New Zealand.

In 1955 a class for deaf children in a Wellington school was the forerunner of a system of such classes in ordinary schools. This development, coupled with a service providing itinerant resource teachers for deaf students, enabled the schools for deaf pupils to promote a range of community-based educational programs from kindergarten through high school. Repeated epidemics of rubella (there was a very serious one in 1964–1965), sometimes resulting in deafness in the newborn, have led to the development of extensive facilities for deaf pupils within ordinary schools. See HEARING LOSS: Prenatal Causes.

Since 1960 the trend has been toward developing new and existing services: classes for deaf children in ordinary schools, resource teachers of deaf pupils, two state schools and one Roman Catholic school for deaf students, and an advisory service for deaf children. The advisers help to locate and audiologically assess deaf children, and provide guidance programs for parents of preschool deaf children and for general teachers who have some deaf students. The advisers also play a major role in hearing aid fitting and monitoring.

The Education Department Directory of Special Education and Guidance Services reports that over 140 children attend classes for deaf children in ordinary primary schools with specially trained teachers. More than 120 others are in similar classes in secondary schools, and a few children attend classes attached to kindergartens. The itinerant resource teachers instruct about 230 deaf children in ordinary schools, and advisers are responsible for over 1000 deaf children attending ordinary classes from kindergarten through secondary school. The two state schools have about 200 children on campus.

To facilitate advanced education, the schools for deaf pupils have developed liaisons with polytechnic colleges and community colleges, so that tutors and other supportive teaching are available. The entry of a New Zealand deaf student into Gallaudet College is paralleled by the acceptance of deaf students in New Zealand universities, with the support of university committees on disabled students. See GALLAUDET COLLEGE.

Originally using only the oral approach, education for deaf New Zealanders was modified by the advent of total communication. The 1979 statement on total communication by the New Zealand Department of Education specifies that a standardized sign system (the Australian or Victorian sign system) and two-handed fingerspelling will be used.

Parents of a deaf child must be consulted in selecting either total communication or the oral approach. Because of the small population, the establishment of schools based on only one communication methodology is avoided and respect for both approaches is encouraged.

Moreover, the school system endeavors to provide options in school placement, more academic opportunity, and choice in career preparation. See EDUCATION: Communication; SOCIOLINGUISTICS: Total communication.

SOCIOECONOMIC STATUS

Generally, deaf workers have positions that are not commensurate with their overall ability. Increased opportunities for higher education have led to a greater degree of training for some deaf people, and thus better jobs. However, this improvement has been limited by the rise in unemployment for all New Zealand adults since 1970 due to worldwide economic decline. Notably, overall employment rates for deaf adults compare favorably with those of the rest of the population.

There is a lack of detailed research into national employment patterns for deaf adults. Data suggest that deaf people hold a wide spectrum of jobs, and this favorable situation might be explained as follows. Because New Zealand has a small, thinly distributed population, occupations that elsewhere were traditionally reserved for deaf adults, such as printing, were not viable. Deaf people in country areas often had to find relationships within groups of hearing people, such as sport and employment groups. Deaf people in cities and large towns were able to make wider employment choices because supportive deaf clubs were available. A range of other support services, including vocational guidance, are provided.

COMMUNICATION

Because of an oral tradition in the schools, a formal sign system was not established. A New Zealand sign language developed among deaf persons themselves, but no fingerspelling was used. New Zealand signs have some features in common with English signs, and more recently with those of other countries. The introduction of total communication brought a wider range of signs and two-handed fingerspelling.

Bibliography

Allen, A. B.: *They Hear with the Eye*, School Publications Branch, Department of Education, Wellington, 1980.

Havill, S. J., and D. R. Mitchell: *Issues in New Zealand Special Education*, Hodder and Stoughton, Auckland, 1972.

Parsons, Michael B.: "The Education of Children with Hearing Disabilities in New Zealand," *Australian Journal of Special Education*, vol. 5, no. 2, November 1981.

Michael B. Parsons

NEWSAM, ALBERT
(1809–1864)

Albert Newsam was born deaf on May 20, 1809, in Steubenville, Ohio. He became an outstanding engraver and lithographer.

His father, a boatman, drowned shortly after Newsam's birth. Nothing is known of his mother, and the orphan was raised by a guardian, Thomas Hamilton, who kept a hotel in Steubenville. Since he could neither hear nor speak, young Newsam made his wants known by sketching the desired objects on paper, board, and even on the ground. Throughout his childhood, his artistic talent was developed by this self-training.

In 1819, when Newsam was 10 years old, William P. Davis, a beggar who passed himself off as a deaf and mute person and who lodged with Hamilton, noted the boy's artistic talent. Davis feigned an interest in the young artist and persuaded Hamilton to let him take the lad to the newly established school for deaf students in Philadelphia. Davis's actual intention was to exploit the boy to gain people's sympathies and contributions. On the journey east, Davis had Newsam demonstrate his skill in drawing to the public. He also referred to him as his brother.

In May 1820, Davis and Newsam reached Philadelphia. One day, a sketch that the boy was making on a city watch-box attracted the attention of Bishop William White, the first president of the board of directors of the Institution for the Deaf and Dumb there. This chance meeting resulted in Newsam being rescued from Davis and admitted to the institution on May 15, 1820.

In school, Newsam was a model pupil with a strong memory. He displayed a great talent for drawing, and it was encouraged by his teachers. He graduated in 1826 but remained in school for another year as a monitor while instructing the pupils in the art of drawing.

In 1827, at the age of 17, Newsam was apprenticed to Cephas G. Childs of Philadelphia, first in the trade of engraving on copper and later in lithography. His teacher was Peter S. Duval, a Frenchman. Newsam worked for Childs for four years and attended evening classes at the Pennsylvania Academy of Fine Arts. His love for sketching was so great that he used to say, "Other artists paint to live, but I live to draw or paint." By great personal industry, he was able to excel in his chosen profession. As a delineator, or copyist, of portraits for lithographic reproduction, Newsam was unsurpassed. His remarkable portrait copies made his name and his money.

At different times, Newsam was a student of Hugh Bridport, George Catlin, and James R. Lambdin. In 1855, Newsam received lessons from Lamb-

Portrait of Albert Newsam. (Gallaudet College Archives)

din in portrait painting, but this was a field which he never was able to master.

In 1858, at Hartford, Connecticut, deaf Americans honored Thomas H. Gallaudet, the pioneer educator, by unveiling a monument which Newsam had designed. *See* GALLAUDET, THOMAS HOPKINS.

Newsam's works were numerous, as was his collection of books in his profession. Part of his valuable lithographs were later taken and sold by a treacherous friend, and another part, along with his collection of books, were destroyed in a fire in 1856 in Duval's lithographic establishment in Philadelphia. The Historical Society of Pennsylvania owns some of the artist's remaining works.

Newsam's marriage to a hearing woman, Rosanna Edgar, in 1834, lasted only a week.

Newsam was always in robust health, but in the fall of 1857 his right eye failed and he became partially blind. In October 1859, he became partially paralyzed, losing the use of his right hand, and could no longer draw. Through the help of friends, Newsam was placed in the Pennsylvania Hospital for a year and later in the Living Home for the Sick and Well near Wilmington, Delaware, where he died November 20, 1864, at the age of 56. His remains lie in Laurel Hill Cemetery in Philadelphia.

Newsam's work drew much praise from some of the artists of his day. In the words of one admirer, "The name of Albert Newsam is indelibly associated with the rise and progress of the lithographic art in America."

The only known portrait of Newsam is the frontispiece of Pyatt's *Memoir of Albert Newsam*, published in 1868.

Bibliography

Pennsylvania Magazine of History and Biography, October 1900, January 1901, April 1901.

Peters, Harry T.: *America on Stone: Other Printmakers to the American People*, Garden City, New York, 1931.

Pyatt, Joseph O.: *Memoir of Albert Newsam*, printed for the author, Philadelphia, 1868.

Stauffer, David McNeely: *American Engravers upon Copper and Steel*, vol. 1, Grolier Club, New York, 1907.

Francis C. Higgins

NIGERIA

Of Nigeria's population estimated at over 80 million, more than 70,000 are believed to be deaf. Nearly 7000 deaf persons are of school age, although less than half are actually in school. Specific information about the main causes of deafness and other related factors is difficult to obtain because there have been no censuses of deaf people and pertinent medical records are scanty. Even where there are medical data on birth and early childhood development, information cannot be used as a basis for generalization as to prevalence, causes, and onset of deafness. The reason is that often deafness in children is not detected early enough, especially if the parents are illiterate. Even when deafness is noticed, nothing may be done until the child has reached school age. In areas where hospitals are few, the majority of births take place outside the hospitals and medical authorities rarely have contact with the newborn child. Thus, any hearing disability may go unnoticed until much later when it becomes difficult to specify the original cause of the problem. Finally, the general negative attitude toward disabled children and their parents compels some parents to hide their handicapped children at home, until it is too late for medical authorities to determine why the children have lost their hearing.

Despite this lack of consistent information, it is believed that most cases of deafness are adventitious (occurring after birth). In the past, occasional outbreaks of diseases that affect expectant mothers have given rise to a prevalence of congenital deafness in an area. However, some studies have confirmed that a large number of deaf persons lost their hearing in adult life, or at least, after they had acquired speech and established language; hence, many deaf persons in Nigeria have very good speech. Specific causes of deafness frequently mentioned in medical records include measles, meningitis, premature birth, and heredity. Notably, there was once a serious outbreak of meningitis in parts of northern Nigeria, and many children in that area were left deaf or blind.

EDUCATION

The beginning of formal education for deaf children lagged behind establishment of regular education by more than a century, because few had any idea that a deaf child without speech and language could be taught to read and write. Moreover, superstitious beliefs, by which physical disabilities were regarded as a punishment by vengeful gods for wrongs done by the afflicted or the parents, were against any attempts to educate deaf persons. It was also the general reasoning in colonial days that scarce public funds expended on education of handicapped people was a waste, in view of the high level of illiteracy among the able-bodied population and the unlikelihood that an educated handicapped person could find suitable employment. Thus, the earliest efforts to educate deaf children were made by voluntary organizations and Christian missionaries.

The first school for deaf persons, the Wesley School in Lagos, was started in 1957 as a goodwill venture by the Society for the Welfare of the Deaf, organized a year earlier through the efforts of retired government officers and religious leaders. In 1960 the Ibadan Mission School for the Deaf (which merged with the Ibadan School for the Deaf in 1974) was founded at Oke Ado, Ibadan, by Andrew Foster, a deaf American missionary (who had also established the first school for deaf children in Ghana two years earlier). These two schools, with their oral (Wesley) and manual (Ibadan Mission) methods of communication, provided the pattern for the other schools that followed. *See* FOSTER, ANDREW JACKSON.

Schools There are 20 schools for the deaf and 11 deaf units (offering day classes in regular schools). They are distributed as follows among the 19 states that make up the federation: Oyo State, 14 schools and units; Ogun State, 4; Anambra, 2; Kaduna, 2; Benue, 2; Imo, Plateau, Kwara, Bendel, Lagos, Ondo, and Sokoto states, 1 school or unit each. Approximately 2100 deaf children attend these primary schools. Seven of the schools cater also to other types of handicapped children such as the mentally retarded, the physically handicapped, and the blind. Nearly all special schools in the country are owned and managed by the respective state governments directly, or through a management board. A 1977 National Policy on Education includes a section on special education, which states that education of handicapped children shall be free up to the university level. This has given much encouragement not only to handicapped children and their parents but also to state educational planners.

Since 1979, secondary school programs for deaf children have been established in three existing residential schools for the deaf (Ibadan School for the Deaf, Kwara State School, and Plateau School) and in a day secondary school for hearing students (Methodist Grammar School, Bodija, Ibadan). Total enrollment of deaf students in these secondary programs averages well over 300. The Ijokodo High School (the secondary section of the Ibadan School for the Deaf) has adopted "reverse" integration, hearing students are integrated into all the classes, led by teachers using total communication. All schools for deaf Nigerians follow the academic curriculum used in schools for hearing children. They also prepare their pupils for the same school-leaving certificate examinations. Subject such as speech training, speechreading, auditory training, and vocational courses are somehow squeezed into the regular curriculum, and are overseen by specialist teachers.

Range of Educational Programs Most schools begin at the Primary Class I level, and enroll children six or seven years of age. Some of the older schools like Wesley, Ibadan, and Kwara have preprimary classes which admit children aged five years. Apart from the four secondary programs described earlier, deaf primary school-leavers may be accepted by any secondary school for hearing children, but most of them go to vocational schools for the hearing. For three or more years they learn trades such as welding, signwriting, auto panel beating, electrical wiring, and cabinetmaking. Although most obtain their trade certificates, many find it difficult to cope with the theoretical part of the course, owing to language and communication problems.

A qualified deaf student who has passed two or more prescribed subjects at the advanced level of the General Certificate of Education may apply, through the national Joint Admissions and Matriculation Board, to any of the more than 20 universities in the country. A few deaf students have struggled through the difficult programs of some of these universities, without supportive services, and graduated with credit. Since the 1970s, however, many vocational school graduates have been encouraged to advance their education overseas by the examples of three Nigerian deaf graduates of Gallaudet College, who returned to Nigeria to open two flourishing schools for deaf pupils or to accept a university teaching job. Over 50 deaf students from Nigeria study in the United States annually, pursuing academic and vocational courses at institutions such as Gallaudet College, Western Maryland College, California State University at North-

ridge, Delgado Community College, Columbus Technical Institute and Seattle Community College. Fortunately, since 1974 Nigeria's state and federal governments have been disposed to award scholarships for overseas training to qualified handicapped persons, including those who are deaf. *See* EDUCATIONAL PROGRAMS: Higher Education.

TEACHER TRAINING
Prior to 1974, most teachers were trained in Britain, sponsored by the British Commonwealth Society for the Deaf. The University of Ibadan offered admission to its own first group of deaf-education teacher trainees in September 1974. Since then, an average of about 10 persons each year have been trained as teachers of deaf children. The University of Jos and the Federal Advanced Teachers' College for Special Education, Oyo, also provide training for teachers. Sponsored by Nigeria's government, a considerable number have been trained in the United States at the University of Northern Colorado and at Lenoir Rhyne College, in North Carolina; and at institutions in the United Kingdom.

COMMUNICATION METHODS
All Nigerian schools use the English language in all classes. Some use the vernacular (local dialect) in the preprimary classes, and also teach it as a subject in the primary classes, while others use only the English language throughout. The advantage of the early adoption of English is that deaf children are helped to develop some proficiency in it to improve their performance in the school-leaving certificate examination, where they must compete with hearing peers who have had a longer experience in the use of English. The disadvantage is that many deaf children "brought up" on English at school are unable to communicate with their parents who do not understand it.

Presently, nearly all schools use the American manual alphabet and sign language. At one time, Wesley School in Lagos stood out as Nigeria's only purely oral school. It achieved much more success than others in teaching speech and speechreading. *See* SIGN LANGUAGES.

SOCIOECONOMIC STATUS
Little is known about the socioeconomic status of most illiterate deaf adults, except that many of them are fully integrated into their extended family units. Deaf primary school-leavers with no vocational training usually find low-paying jobs as cleaners, farm workers, and manual workers in factories, shops, and government establishments. Their wages, though low, compare favorably with those of hearing peers, although they have fewer opportunities for advancement than hearing persons. However, a large number of this class of deaf people, who

live in large cities like Lagos and Ibadan, beg alms in the streets rather than find jobs. Deaf vocational school graduates are employed by some government agencies to do the kind of work for which they are trained. They are usually paid established wages for the jobs. Studies, however, have shown that once deaf workers are employed, they receive neither promotion nor encouragement; and they rarely advance to managerial positions. As the many deaf people undergoing advanced technical and vocational training overseas return to Nigeria, they will encounter difficulties in obtaining employment commensurate with their skills, for there remains the low expectation of what a deaf person can do or be.

ORGANIZATIONS

The Nigerian Association of the Deaf, comprising deaf people, was formed in the early 1970s, but became defunct after about five years due to poor leadership. A more successful organization, the Nigerian Advisory Council for the Deaf (NACD) is an offshoot of a Society for the Care of the Deaf (formed in Lagos in 1956). The NACD, whose membership is made up of hearing-education officers, retired government workers, and heads of schools for deaf students, receives substantial annual subventions from the federal government. Since its beginning in the early 1970s, it has been concerned mainly with the welfare of deaf children in primary schools. Consequently, many deaf adults feel alienated.

Bibliography

Afolabi, B.: "The Deaf at Work," unpublished thesis, Department of Special Education, University of Ibadan, 1980.

Dike, C.: "Employment Opportunities for Deaf Primary School-Leavers," unpublished thesis, Department of Special Education, University of Ibadan, 1980.

Mba, P. O.: "Attitudes Toward the Handicapped in Developing Countries and Steps Toward Attitudinal Change," *ERIC Reports*, Reston, Virginia, 1978.

————: "Trends in the Education of the Hearing-Impaired in Developing Countries," *Proceeding of the International Congress on Education of the Deaf, Hamburg, Germany, 1980.*

————: "Special Schools and Programmes in Nigeria (1979–80)", unpublished table, Department of Special Education, University of Ibadan, 1980.

P. O. Mba

O

ORGANIZATIONS

The lives of deaf people are powerfully influenced by numerous organizations. The organizations of greatest importance to deaf adults are those that involve other deaf people, that is, organizations of, rather than for, deaf people. The deaf community has duplicated to a large extent the institutions that characterize the vastly larger general community. As children, deaf people are typically under the authority of adults who can hear. Once matured, deaf people tend to create and manage their own organizations.

The independence of typical deaf adults challenges popular conceptions of disabled people as weak and demanding of sympathy and aid. That picture does not represent the majority of those who are deafened in childhood. Such individuals tend to join the deaf community, that is, to associate largely with other persons who have been deafened in childhood. Conversely, those who become deaf in adulthood seldom become members of the deaf community; they strive to retain their lifelong relations with friends and relatives whose hearing remains intact. It is these tendencies of early-deafened persons to seek each other's company and of late-deafened persons to remain aloof from those who are early deafened that give the deaf community its unique character. *See* DEAF POPULATION: Deaf Community.

Cogent evidence of the deaf community's existence are the organizations that provide its structure. Deaf people in the United States have built a comprehensive organizational network that fills the gaps in meeting their psychological and social needs.

Historical Perspective

The seedbeds for organizations of deaf people have been the schools for deaf children. Lacking easy communication and common interests with members of their nuclear families, deaf children have tended to establish strong bonds with each other. These relationships typically have grown out of meetings with other deaf children in the schools. By 1836, only 19 years after the first school for deaf children was established, some deaf adults in New England formed one of the first organizations of deaf people in the United States. Shortly thereafter, such organizations—largely alumni groups—sprang up throughout the United States. The relationship between schools and organizations continued throughout the nineteenth century, as other states opened schools for deaf students and the graduates of those schools set up structured means of continuing to meet socially. At a national level, the organizational tendencies culminated in the formation of the National Association of the Deaf in 1880, less than 20 years after the establishment of the first college for deaf people in the world. *See* EDUCATION: History; NATIONAL ASSOCIATION OF THE DEAF.

Before assuming that the schools alone account for the organizational growth of the deaf community, scholars are confronted with the parallel case of blind people. A similar community and a similar organizational structure do not exist among blind people. There are ample organizations for blind people, many established decades ago, but no organizations of blind people were established until the 1950s. Even then, the organizations of blind people did not compare in number or strength to those of deaf people. While the reasons for this difference are certainly complex, a salient factor is communication: deafness interrupts communication with the general public, blindness does not. Blindness evokes sympathy; deafness tends to evoke frustration and hostility. Thus, blind people have long had supporters who have been willing to do for them what they would have difficulty doing for themselves. Deaf people, on the other hand, have tended to be ignored by the general public, which seems to prefer to avoid them because social interchanges are so difficult. "The blind leading the blind" seems ludicrous, while the deaf communicating with the deaf does not. Blindness interferes with mobility, something that sighted people can assist blind people to overcome. Deafness only inhibits communication with those who cannot communicate manually, something with which deaf people can assist each other. The fact that blindness has brought support from the general public and deafness has caused its members to seek each other for support may be the critical one in accounting for the differences between these two sensory disabilities.

Governmental Organizations

Among the earliest intrusions of governments into the affairs of deaf people are those found in the Talmud—the writings gleaned from the Bible and the commentaries of religious authorities which make up the Jewish civil and religious law. According to Halakha, the interpretations of the Talmud, a deaf-mute person cannot enter into contracts and cannot attain full citizenship within the religious community. The laws group deaf-mute persons with minor and mentally retarded persons as individuals who must be protected by the community against exploitation by those who would take advantage of their lack of understanding. *See* RELIGION, JEWISH.

The ancient Romans took a similar view of deafness, though one considerably less benign. Children could be murdered at three years of age, if they were judged to be a liability to the state. Since Roman law as late as A.D. 170 decreed that deaf-mute persons lacked intelligence and hence had no legal rights, they were at risk of being legally executed. By 530 the Emperor Justinian modified the laws to appoint guardians for deaf-mute persons, thus affording them the protection intended by the Talmud.

In all of the historical research on deafness, no evidence appears of more than tolerance for the deaf-mute person until the emergence of Christianity. The Venerable Bede (ca. 685) was said to have instructed a deaf-mute youth. Isolated instances of enlightened views of early deafness convinced Rudolph Agricola, a Dutch scholar, and Girolamo Cardano, an Italian physician, that persons born deaf could (and should) be educated. They set forth their opinions in books published in the sixteenth century. While they expressed their views eloquently and probably did much to convince others, neither is known to have ever treated a deaf person. Nor did their reasoned arguments have any immediate impact on their governments. Similarly, the actual successes by the two Spanish priests Pedro Ponce de Leon and Juan Pablo Bonet in teaching children born deaf to aristocratic parents had no influence on their governments' policies toward early-deafened people. *See* PABLO BONET, JUAN; PONCE DE LEON, PEDRO.

FOREIGN GOVERNMENTS

The seminal work of Charles Michel de l'Epée in the eighteenth century led to the establishment of the first public school for deaf students. Initially funded by a grant from King Louis XVI, the school continued through the French Revolution and survives to this day. The Institut National des Sourds-Muets (National Institute for Deaf-Mutes) in Paris is the oldest permanent school for deaf students in the world, and therefore is the oldest governmental organization devoted to deafness. Its establishment was followed within a few years by schools, mostly government-supported, in other European countries. Today, almost all countries provide educational services for deaf children, either by directly funding schools or indirectly supplying subsidies that enable parents to obtain educational services. Thus, the most common governmental organizations for deaf persons are educational. *See* L'EPÉE, ABBÉ CHARLES MICHEL DE.

Rehabilitation facilities are most often government-sponsored, as is true in the United States. The models for such efforts consist of the government's establishing an agency which is charged with providing services to disabled persons and which, in turn, either directly provides those services or reimburses voluntary agencies for the costs of the services they render on behalf of disabled persons. the Soviet Union, Yugoslavia, Argentina, and the Republic of China (Taiwan), among many others, follow the former model. *See* CHINA, REPUBLIC OF.

The second model for dealing with deaf citizens in the population makes use of existing voluntary agencies' efforts to serve disabled persons. The government may not be firmly committed to supporting the voluntary organizations, but in practice they are heavily subsidized. For example, the British government provides a substantial portion of the funds needed to carry out the work of the Royal National Institute for the Deaf (RNID) in London. Nonetheless, RNID was founded privately and remains, in principle, independent of the government. Similar groups exist in West Germany, the Scandinavian countries, India, and many other countries. While it is possible for governments to do so, few appear to leave the matter of rehabilitation solely to voluntary agencies. Those countries that do, such as Sudan, are poor and industrially underdeveloped. *See* DENMARK; GERMANY, FEDERAL REPUBLIC OF; INDIA; SWEDEN; UNITED KINGDOM.

The involvement of government in the social sphere of deaf persons' activities occurs in many foreign countries. It is not unusual for the leader of the national organization of deaf people to be a hearing person. The rationale is that the hearing person is needed to provide the liaison with the government and the general public. Even when deaf persons head these organizations, they are often mere figureheads. An examination of the organizational structure reveals that nondeaf persons actually control its affairs. That situation, most common through the middle of the twentieth century in foreign countries, is now changing. Taking their cue from their colleagues in the United States, deaf persons in foreign countries are becoming increasingly militant about managing their own destinies.

The same holds true of voluntary agencies. For example, the RNID's chief executive officer serving in 1985 had no hearing difficulty, yet he was well accepted by the majority of deaf persons in the United Kingdon. The same would not be true in the United States, where only deaf people lead organizations of deaf people. Such choices reflect institutionalized attitudes toward deaf people and deafness. Whether deaf people in these countries are better or worse off because of self-leadership or leadership by hearing people depends upon definitions of good and poor accommodations. Independence has its price as well as its benefits. While RNID has a powerful influence on the lives of deaf people in Great Britain, there are other organizations to which deaf people can lend, or from which they can withhold, support. The British Deaf Association (BDA), for instance, is the counterpart to the United States' National Association of the Deaf. It is an organization of deaf people. It does not have the governmental connections of the RNID, neither does it attempt to provide the range of services nor to conduct the research that RNID does. BDA offers an additional option to deaf people seeking organizational involvement with their government; unlike RNID which is professionally staffed, BDA is a consumer group. *See* UNITED KINGDOM: Organizations.

UNITED STATES GOVERNMENT

In viewing the organizational structure that impinges upon the lives of deaf people in the United States, three distinct levels of government must be considered: the federal, the state, and the local. Deaf people can expect, and indeed do receive, different treatment at the hands of the various levels of government. However, those differences were a long time in coming; the concept of a federal responsibility for the welfare of individual citizens emerged slowly in the United States.

Deaf leaders tend more often to look to the federal government, not the state or local governments, for assistance. The problems of greatest concern to the deaf community are best resolved on a national basis, and the deaf community's strength maximizes at the national level, being progressively weaker at state and local levels due to the low incidence of deafness in the general population. The various groups within the deaf community can be brought together more effectively on a nationwide basis as their collective strength is sufficient to be felt at the national level.

Federal Agencies The federal government has two offices specifically charged with responsibility for the welfare of deaf people; the Office of Deafness and Communicative Disorders, and Media Services and Captioned Films for the Deaf. Both were part of the Department of Education and Welfare before it was subdivided into the Department of Health and Human Services and the Department of Education. Begun in 1966, the Office of Deafness and Communicative Disorders (ODCD) in the Rehabilitation Services Administration has been a major contact point for all agencies of the federal government, as well as for citizens and agencies outside the federal government with an interest in deafness and deaf people. Boyce R. Williams was ODCD's head from its inception until his retirement in 1983. Williams was a late-deafened man who came to Washington from his position as a rehabilitation counselor in Indiana to take the newly created post of Consultant for the Deaf, the Hard of Hearing, and the Speech Impaired, in 1945. The permanent staff of ODCD has usually consisted of only a single assistant and one or two clerical positions. Despite its tiny size, ODCD answers all inquiries received from the public and government alike, provides technical assistance, and represents deaf people when it is appropriate to have government personnel do so. *See* REHABILITATION: Agencies; WILLIAMS, BOYCE ROBERT.

Media Services and Captioned Films for the Deaf is in the Office of Special Education, Department of Education. When established in 1958, it was called only Captioned Films for the Deaf in recognition of its functions, which were to bring to deaf persons understanding and appreciation of those films which play an important part in the general and cultural advance of hearing persons; to provide through these films enriched educational and cultural experiences by which deaf persons can be brought into better touch with their environment; and to provide a wholesome and rewarding experience which deaf persons may share together.

Captioned Films for the Deaf grew out of a private nonprofit corporation established with a grant from the Junior League of Hartford (Connecticut) and the encouragement of the Convention of American Instructors of the Deaf. During the years of silent films, deaf people as well as hearing audiences could enjoy movies. However, once sound films came into vogue, silent (captioned) movies largely disappeared from the screen, leaving deaf people without a principal means of entertainment and information. The task of running such a substantial enterprise on a nationwide basis soon outstripped the resources of the small company. Educators lobbied Congress, and in 1958 Public Law 85-905 set up Captioned Films for the Deaf as a government enterprise to put titles on sound films, thus making them intelligible to deaf audiences. The private corporation was disbanded, and its films were transferred to the new federal program. A measure of Captioned Films for the Deaf's success is the move to broaden its operation to include other disabled people. In 1965 Congress changed the name to Media Services and Captioned Films for the Deaf. The expanded purview, however, did not materialize, as subsequent Congresses did not appropriate the funds that would permit it to provide media services to all disabled groups. However, the change in legislation did enable Captioned Films for the Deaf to extend its activities to cover other media for deaf people. *See* TELEVISION AND MOTION PICTURES: Silent Films.

Legislation   Legislatively, the concerns of deaf people are usually brought before the Subcommittee on the Handicapped of the House of Representative's Committee on Education and Labor, and the Subcommittee on the Education and Rehabilitation of the Handicapped of the Senate's Committee on Labor and Human Resources (formerly the Committee on Labor and Public Welfare). These are the subcommittees that oversee the budgets of Gallaudet College and the National Technical Institute for the Deaf and that originate the legislation that provides the appropriations for Captioned Television for the Deaf. Thus, these two legislative bodies have a direct impact on the lives of many deaf people, and they are appropriate targets of lobbying by those organizations and individuals seeking legislation on behalf of the deaf community. *See* GALLAUDET COLLEGE; NATIONAL TECHNICAL INSTITUTE FOR THE DEAF.

State Governments   The state governments in the United States were first to respond to the problems of deaf people. The Connecticut legislature provided funds to support the first permanent public school for deaf students in the United States in 1817. New York in 1818, Pennsylvania in 1820, and Kentucky in 1823 followed. By the end of the Civil War, most states had opened schools for deaf children. The federal government did not become directly involved in the education of deaf children until 1857, when the Columbia Institution for the Instruction of the Deaf and Dumb (later called the Kendall School for the Deaf and then the Kendall Demonstration Elementary School) opened in the District of Columbia on the grounds of what has become Gallaudet College. *See* EDUCATION: History.

In rehabilitation, the earliest efforts were directed by the state agencies that regulated labor. Minnesota, for example, established a Bureau of the Deaf in 1915 within its department of labor. Its first head and sole employee was a deaf woman, Petra Howard. Three other states had offices in their labor departments that concentrated solely on the problems of deaf people: North Carolina, Michigan, and Wisconsin.

As the federal-state partnership in rehabilitation came into being, efforts to establish similar programs in state departments of labor ceased. The states varied somewhat in their initial acceptance of deaf clients in vocational rehabilitation programs. Their reluctance was based on the requirement, existing at one time in the early rehabilitation legislation, that clients must have a possibility of obtaining employment upon completion of their individual programs. In time, however, all states have opened their rehabilitation programs to those who are deaf. The Model State Plan for Rehabilitation of Deaf Clients, which was distributed initially in 1973, had been endorsed by all states, according to a survey completed in 1977. This show of interest in deaf people marks the current attitudes of state vocational rehabilitation agencies toward their deaf constituency.

State Commissions on Deafness   In 1971 the Texas legislature established the first permanent commission on deafness in the United States. Within the decade, 16 states had followed Texas's lead. Despite these agencies' importance, they have had comparatively little attention from the deaf community. The National Association of the Deaf sponsored the first National Conference for State Commissions on Deafness in 1977, when only 10 states had them, but the National Association of the Deaf has not sponsored a similar conference since that time. Subsequent meetings between commission representatives have been informal and largely unpublicized. The average deaf citizen does not seem to have realized the potential these commissions have for improving economic, social, and vocational conditions in their states, nor have most of the professionals who devote all or a major part of their practices to deaf people fully grasped the state commissions' potential influence on the service delivery systems of those states that have them.

In addition to the states that have commissions, there are states that have active programs providing a broad range of services that do not meet the definition of a commission. That fact should not reflect on the worth of such agencies. Rather, such states have made a choice, explicitly or implicitly, of how they wish to serve their deaf citizens. The important issue is not whether the state has a commission but whether its deaf people are well or poorly served.

The scopes of the commissions differ greatly from state to state. Some commissions have fairly narrow purviews, others very broad. No single function has been assigned by all of the legislatures to all of the commissions. Advocacy comes closest to being a "universal" mandate. Only Arizona's legislation does not indicate that its commission is to undertake that function. Most states want their commissions on deafness to coordinate services, to eliminate duplication, and to assure that essential services are not being overlooked. Four commissions, however, do not have such a role to play in their states: Nebraska, North Carolina, Texas, and Virginia. They may, nevertheless, be providing this important service, even though it is not specified in their legislation.

The legislation setting up the commissions typically allows them considerable latitude in determining their operations, and state commissions do go beyond the particulars of their charters. Iowa, for instance, does not have statewide planning specified in its charter, yet the commission has recently developed a statewide plan for mental health services for deaf people. All commissions have some involvement in the provision of interpreting services, though only a few have that function spelled out in their enabling acts. All of the commissions provide some advocacy and engage in information gathering and dissemination as part of their actual functions. Only Texas has legislation for telecommunications, but seven other state commissions are active in this area. Some services are as yet untouched by most of the commissions. Only New Jersey and Texas have been involved with transportation problems. Only Texas has been specifically engaged in serving elderly deaf people, a growing segment of the deaf population and one badly in need of assistance. Oklahoma, however, is developing programs tailored for deaf senior citizens. Texas also has received pioneering authority to serve deaf-blind adults, who are traditionally assigned to commissions for the blind in most states. *See* DEAF-BLINDNESS.

The state commissions are under the direction of boards that range in size from 7 to 19 members, with the median number of members between 11 and 12. The state governors are generally responsible for selecting board members. The laws require particular groups in the states to be represented. All state commissions, except Wisconsin, are required to have deaf people on their boards. The proportions of the memberships that must be deaf vary widely, from none (Wisconsin) to 75 percent (Massachusetts). Of course, the actual number of deaf people may greatly exceed the legally set minimum, and governors may follow unwritten laws (precedents) to appoint a specified number of deaf members.

While ten states do require that state governments be represented on their boards, five do not. Six states specify professional members; seven require parent representatives, and five make interpreter representatives mandatory. Eight state commissions must have board members who represent the general public. Kansas and Kentucky require that one at-large member be from an agency serving deaf people. Wisconsin's entire board is left to the governor's discretion. Careful study of the composition of each of the boards provides one clue to the state legislators' ambitions for the commissions.

The commissions have adopted a number of different operating modes. Some, like Texas, work largely through contracts to existing agencies within their states. Others, like Connecticut, provide much of the services by acquiring staff. Most commissions have some combination of these modes, contracting certain services and attempting to provide others by inhouse staff. The particular operational style must depend upon many factors, including funding, geography, and legislative and administrative standards. However, it should be clear that a well-functioning commission can perform its duties effectively by a variety of means.

Local Governments At the city and county levels of government, no provisions are made exclusively for the welfare of deaf people. The numbers of deaf persons are too few at the local level to be a sufficiently large problem to attract the sustained attention of local government officials. Many cities now have "ombuds" persons who negotiate for citizens seeking aid or redress from the government. For disabled people, there are often mayors' offices for the disabled—agencies that have a specific assignment to provide advocacy for disabled people. Such offices are frequently inaccessible to deaf people because the agency officials are unable to communicate manually and are sometimes reluctant to use, or unable to locate, interpreters. Often such offices expect to be contacted mostly by telephone, hence they provide limited office space for private meetings with individuals who may wish to consult with them about their problems. While satisfactory for most disabled people, this arrangement actually denies proper access to deaf people, since they have such grave difficulties using the telephone. Only occasionally do such agencies have telephonic adapters (TDDs) for communication with deaf persons. Even when a local agency does purchase a TDD, it is often no more than a token. No one has the task of monitoring the line dedicated to the TDD, and often no one on the staff has been trained to operate the device, so transmissions are garbled and unsatisfactory.

Rehabilitation and Education at the Local Level
State rehabilitation agencies generally have local offices, but the policies and procedures governing the activities of such offices come from the state level. However, much authority is granted to the local education authority (LEA) concerning education. Parents of deaf children must now negotiate with the LEA to determine the children's educational placement according to the federal regulations. LEAs are required to establish Committees on the Handicapped which meet with the parents to plan jointly the disabled child's educational program for the forthcoming school period. What emerges from such meetings is the Individualized Educational Program (IEP) which sets forth the educational progress that the child is expected to make during the specified period of time, the educational strategies that will be used, and the persons responsible for them. The parent must concur in these decisions. If parents do not agree with the Committee on the Handicapped's decisions, and if negotiations fail between the interested parties, then various rights of appeal may be exercised by the parent on behalf of the child. The legal process is open to parents to defend their disabled children's rights, but deaf people encounter difficulties when they deal with politically sensitive local authorities. The public is seldom sympathetic because the issues are not easily made clear to persons who are otherwise uninformed about deafness, regardless of whether those individuals are laypersons, administrators of government agencies, or court judges. Furthermore, the numbers of deaf people at the local level are rarely large enough to give deaf people much political weight in any struggles with local government officials.

International Organizations
Two organizational movements operate internationally. One, over a century old, is the gathering of educators to discuss the education of deaf students; the other, relatively new, is the World Federation of the Deaf, an organization of, for, and by deaf people. A third organization, the Comité International des Sports des Sourds has a specialized international function.

INTERNATIONAL CONGRESSES ON THE EDUCATION OF THE DEAF

In 1878 in Paris, a group of educators representing Austria, Belgium, France, Italy, and Sweden met to discuss the problems of educating deaf students. In addition to the 26 individuals from these five countries, J.D. Philbrick from the United States attended as an observer, since he was not a teacher of deaf students. The invitation that had been sent to Edward Miner Gallaudet, president of the college for deaf students in Washington, D.C., did not reach him until weeks after the meeting. The participants modestly billed their conference as the International Congress for the Improvement of the Conditions of Deaf-Mutes. Subsequent meetings that grew from this historic conference adopted the name International Congress on the Education of the Deaf (ICED). The attendees of the first conference were largely from schools that preferred the oral method of instruction in the classrooms, as opposed to the use of manual communication. Despite this background, the Congress elected as its president the retired director of the French national school, and the only one who had had experience with the manual methods of instruction pioneered by the Abbé de l'Epée. Not surprisingly, the congress adopted a resolution supporting the use of oral instruction, though it recognized the value of manual communication and did not directly oppose it. *See* GALLAUDET, EDWARD MINER.

The second meeting had the most long-lasting influence on the education of deaf children. For almost a century after the International Congress on the Education of the Deaf held its meeting in Milan in 1880, the oral method of instruction supplanted the use of manual communication in the classrooms of the world. The meeting was from the first a dramatic encounter between those who supported oralism and those who chose the simultaneous method, which combined manual communication with speech and lipreading. The agenda was lengthy, but the methods controversy actually absorbed most of the delegates' time and passions. At the conclusion of the deliberations, the delegates adopted a series of eight resolutions, the first two (and most famous) becoming known as the Milan Manifesto. The Milan Manifesto declared that the oral method was the preferred method of communication for deaf people. *See* HISTORY: Congress of Milan.

The third ICED met in Brussels in 1883. Astonishingly, the oral-manual controversy did not appear on the agenda. The Committee on Arrangements has been appointed at Milan, and it concluded that the issue had been resolved and was not deserving of further deliberation. How valuable were the actual discussions and how important was the adoption of the particular resolutions (for example, the question of teacher training was tabled as too disputatious) remain unresolved questions. Some commentators feel the International Congress on the Education of the Deaf was useless and others that its work was important. Nonetheless, the long-term impact of the Brussels meeting has proved to be negligible.

As a means of bringing together educators of deaf children from different countries, the International Congress on the Education of the Deaf appears to be a success; its most recent congresses have been attended by over 1000 delegates. The program listings have grown from a handful of issues narrowly focused on a few problems to an array of issues that cover virtually every aspect of deaf people's lives. However, congresses also have pretended to a representativeness they did not have; some have been manifestly unfair, rude, and even contemptuous of the very group they are dedicated to serve. This contemptuous attitude is now disappearing from the International Congress and the institutions that it represents. The future of ICED as an information vehicle that will serve deafness seems assured. *See* INTERNATIONAL CONGRESS ON THE EDUCATION OF THE DEAF.

WORLD FEDERATION OF THE DEAF

In 1951 in Rome, representatives of 25 countries attended the first World Congress of the Deaf. The delegates, almost all of whom were deaf, voted to form the World Federation of the Deaf (WFD), headquarters of which are in Rome. The WFD president for most of the years since WFD was founded was Dragoljub Vukotic of Yugoslavia, a deaf man who had spent sufficient time in the United States to develop an excellent command of American Sign Language. He was elected at the second international congress in Zagreb, Yugoslavia, in 1955. He was succeeded by another deaf man, Swedish-born Yerker Andersson, a member of the Gallaudet College faculty in sociology. Andersson moved from vice-presidency to the presidency in the elections at the international congress in Palermo, Italy, in 1983. The secretary general of WFD, Cesare Magarotto, is the hearing son of deaf parents.

Serving under the president are nine vice-presidents, who together with the secretary general and the president make up WFD's bureau, which acts as an executive committee for the organization. WFD meets every four years. The title of the quadrennial meetings is sometimes rendered in English as "International" and sometimes as "World" Congress of the Deaf. The correct title, acording to the secretary general, is neither; it is Congress of the World Federation of the Deaf, with the number of the congress placed first. Thus, in 1975 the United States for the first time played host to the VII Congress of the World Federation of the Deaf, held in Washington, D.C. Sofia, Bulgaria, was the site for the 1979 congress; Palermo, Italy, for the 1987 congress; and Helsinki, Finland, for the 1987 congress. The distribution of meetings sites leaves little doubt

of the intentions of the WFD to prevent its activities from being dominated by any one bloc of nations or interests.

When the congress is in session, the assembly, made up of delegates from the member nations, acts as the legislative body for WFD. For purposes of organizing the congress activities, WFD has established nine commissions which can also function as vehicles for action and information between congresses. Each has an international president and, in congress years, a national president who makes the local arrangements. The commissions are: art and culture, communication, medicine and audiology, pedagogy, psychology, social aspects of deafness, spiritual care, technical assistance to developing countries, and vocational rehabilitation. Nondeaf persons may be delegates to the congresses, the choice being left to the individual nations. For example, the head of the Commission on the Social Aspects of Deafness, Josif Gueljman from Leningrad, has normal hearing, but his parents were deaf.

A most fascinating aspect of WFD is communication. With 57 member nations, WFD constantly faces the language problem, made even more complicated by the fact that most of the delegates depend upon sign language for communication. WFD has adopted French and English as its official languages. All material is printed in these two languages. Attempts to expand the number of official spoken languages have been sternly rebuked on the grounds that to do so would strain unbearably the financial resources of WFD. Recognizing the diversity of sign language dialects even in the same country, WFD sponsored a committee of sign language experts from among its members to develop an international sign language. Beginning in 1959, the committee produced *The First Contribution to International Dictionary of the Language of Signs, Conference Terminology.* It was followed by a second edition in 1965. The current edition was delivered to the 1975 congress, and bore the name coined by Magarotto, *Gestuno–International Sign Language of the Deaf.* Gestuno, like Esperanto, appropriates signs from existing sign languages. The final selection of 1470 signs was made by a small committee chaired by Allan B. Hayhurst of Carlisle, England, and had representatives from Denmark, Italy, the Soviet Union, and the United States. Gestuno solves the question of syntax by ignoring it; the committee recognized the problem, but left it open to future generations to solve. The committee attempted to select signs that had the most natural referents, were most iconic, and were easily produced. By emphasizing economy of gesture, they hoped to smooth the path to the adoption of Gestuno in settings other than WFD meetings. At plenary sessions of the congresses, three sign language interpreters are now required, one each for English, French, and Gestuno. *See* GESTURES; SIGN LANGUAGES: International.

WFD provides international visibility for deaf people, and has been successful as a means of exchanging information and opinions between deaf people from different countries. Dedicated to full citizenship for all deaf people, WFD has represented them before such international bodies as UNESCO. WFD's meetings are well attended and bring together deaf people from a large array of countries. The work on signed communication has been impressive and effective. *See* WORLD FEDERATION OF THE DEAF.

COMITÉ INTERNATIONAL DES SPORTS DES SOURDS
In 1924 the first World Games for the Deaf (originally called International Games for the Deaf) were held in Paris. An organization grew out of that immediately popular event, the Comité International des Sports Silencieux, subsequently called the Comité International des Sports des Sourds (CISS). The United States did not enter the games until 1935, when a coach from the Illinois School for the Deaf, Robey S. Burns, took two of his athletes to London to participate. The United States' deaf community did not join the CISS until 1957, when the American Athletic Association for the Deaf (AAAD) helped send 40 participants to the games. In 1965 the AAAD hosted the games in Washington, D.C., attracting a record turnout of athletes and viewers. The 1965 games also set a record because deaf people alone organized and managed all aspects of the affair, from starting gun to closing banquet, without any government support. The United States handled the games so successfully that they won the bid for the 1985 event, held in Los Angeles. CISS also sponsors winter games for the deaf, held in various countries since 1949. The United States held the winter games in Lake Placid, New York, in 1975. While patterned after the Olympics, the games for deaf persons are not intended to replace them, and occasionally deaf athletes have participated in the Olympics. The World Games for the Deaf provide deaf athletes with the same opportunities to compete internationally and to meet their peers in other countries that the Olympics provide for hearing persons. *See* AMERICAN ATHLETIC ASSOCIATION OF THE DEAF; COMITÉ INTERNATIONAL DES SPORTS DES SOURDS.

Advocacy

There are advocacy groups that deaf people have organized for themselves and others that purport to speak on their behalf. The foremost organization representing deaf people in the United States is the National Association of the Deaf (NAD). Since 1964, when it moved its home offices to the Washington,

D.C., area, the NAD has increasingly appeared before the U.S. Congress to testify on legislation of interest to the deaf community, before administrators of federal programs to promote the addition of services deaf people desire and to urge improvements in the quality of those already being provided, and before the judiciary through its Legal Defense Fund which was established in 1976. Through its state affiliates, NAD extends its influence to the state and local levels of government. It also has a crucial role in presenting deaf views to the general public, as well as mobilizing the support of individual deaf persons for various causes. These issues are debated at the biennial national conventions and presented in various NAD publications, such as the *Deaf American*, the *Broadcaster*, and *Interstate*. NAD is also a social and service organization, but its role as advocate for deaf people provided the rationale for its founding, and so both the deaf community and the general community look to it for leadership in those matters of greatest interest to deaf people. *See* DEAF AMERICAN; NATIONAL ASSOCIATION OF THE DEAF.

The NAD and its state affiliates are not alone among deaf groups in their lobbying efforts. In 1901 the National Fraternal Society of the Deaf (NFSD) was founded, 21 years after NAD came into being, by 13 deaf men who were concerned about the problems deaf people were having in purchasing life insurance. Originally known as the Fraternal Society of the Deaf and providing only burial benefits, it became national in 1907, when it also changed its programs to include life insurance. NFSD, while basically an insurance company today, also devotes energy to forwarding the general welfare of deaf people. Through its membership distributed across the country in numerous chapters (divisions), NFSD can quickly and effectively make direct contacts with legislators and government administrators. Its officers, especially its grand president, serve on many boards and advisory committees of influential organizations. In these ways, the ability of NFSD to contribute to policy development is greatly multiplied. *See* NATIONAL FRATERNAL SOCIETY OF THE DEAF.

Other organizations of deaf people play less frequent but often significant roles in providing advocacy. Telecommunications for the Deaf, Inc., has been principally directed to problems associated with developing telephone services for those who use the Weitbrecht modification that makes such services available to deaf users. Telecommunications for the Deaf, however, does lend its support to numerous other causes, and it has taken strong positions with respect to captioned television. The American Athletic Association of the Deaf, while not politically inclined, does join with other organizations occasionally. It contributes to public awareness of the physical achievements of deaf youths and adults. Among the most active state associations are the Pennsylvania Society for the Advancement of the Deaf and the Wisconsin Association of the Deaf. The Pennsylvania Society has a long history of effective dealings with its state government. The Wisconsin Association has likewise done very well, having had a contract with the state for almost half a century to provide services to deaf people. Other state associations have had good, though perhaps less spectacular, records of working with their governments to achieve particular objectives desired by their members. *See* TELECOMMUNICATIONS FOR THE DEAF, INC.

In 1964 the Alexander Graham Bell Association established an Oral Deaf Adult Section to bring greater participation of deaf people into its affairs. The Bell Association's policies, however, are established by a board whose membership is completely dominated by people who hear. The title of the organization inspires the confidence of legislators who call upon it for testimony and of administrators who encounter its policy statements, but the Bell Association's policies with respect to communication often directly conflict with those of organizations in the deaf community. For instance, in 1967 when the National Broadcasting Company announced that it would telecast a sign language production by the National Theatre of the Deaf, the Bell Association's director wrote a strong letter of protest for "any programming which indicates that the use of the language of signs is inevitable for deaf children or it is more than an artificial language, and a foreign one at that, for the deaf of this country." The opposition caught NBC by surprise, but the counterreaction in support of the program mustered by the deaf community restored the balance, and the program was aired on schedule. The incident served to remind deaf people of the Milan Manifesto and the precariousness of their minority position on communication. *See* ALEXANDER GRAHAM BELL ASSOCIATION FOR THE DEAF.

Other advocacy groups that may or may not act in concert with the views of the deaf community include the Conference of Educational Administrators Serving the Deaf (formerly the Conference of Executives of American Schools for the Deaf) and the Convention of American Instructors of the Deaf. These two organizations are closely affiliated with each other, sharing an executive director and jointly publishing the *American Annals of the Deaf.* As professional educators, they have had considerable influence with the Congress. A much newer group, the American Deafness and Rehabilitation Association, has also had a role to play in shaping legislation bearing upon the lives of deaf people. Neither group is affiliated with its larger counterpart, the National Education Association or the National Rehabilitation Association. Their sole emphasis on

deafness makes these organizations particularly forceful as spokepersons on the affairs of deaf people. While these three professional groups have deaf members, none has a deaf majority within its membership. While that fact shapes the representativeness of their views, it does not seem to reduce the impact of their testimonies on issues predominantly affecting deaf people. The Congress is as apt to accept their judgments of the reactions of the deaf community as the judgments of the National Association of the Deaf or the National Fraternal Society of the Deaf. *See* AMERICAN DEAFNESS AND REHABILITATION ASSOCIATION; CONFERENCE OF EDUCATIONAL ADMINISTRATORS SERVING THE DEAF; CONVENTION OF AMERICAN INSTRUCTORS OF THE DEAF.

Federal officials and deaf leaders recognized the governmental dilemma when faced with competing voices, all claiming to speak for deaf people. The problem arose at the historic Workshop on Community Development Through Organizations of and for the Deaf, held at Fort Monroe, Virginia, in 1961, and best known as the Fort Monroe Workshop. To reduce the cacophony that has sometimes obscured major issues affecting the deaf community, the participants in the Fort Monroe Workshop recommended that an umbrella organization be established that would provide a forum for debates within the deaf community. Organizations could debate important issues among themselves, reach compromises, and then present a unified position to the government. The idea had great appeal, not only among members of the deaf community but also among sympathetic federal officials.

In 1967 the Council of Organizations Serving the Deaf was formed with the aid of a grant from the federal Social and Rehabilitation Service. The council brought together the National Association of the Deaf and the National Fraternal Society of the Deaf with the Bell Association, the Council of Educational Administrators Serving the Deaf, the Convention of American Instructors of the Deaf, and the American Deafness and Rehabilitation Association. For a brief time it appeared that harmony would be achieved; however, the council collapsed soon after the withdrawal of federal funds. The executive secretary of the National Association of the Deaf, Frederick C. Schreiber, had seen the embodiment of an ideal, and he proposed that a new organization be created without any government involvement. He named it the Mutual Alliance Plan and campaigned assiduously among his organizational colleagues for its adoption. He died before it could be established. *See* COUNCIL OF ORGANIZATIONS SERVING THE DEAF; SCHREIBER, FREDERICK CARL.

The Council on Education of the Deaf is composed of representatives of the Bell Association, the Council of Executives, and the Convention of American Instructors of the Deaf. It provides the kind of forum on educational matters that Schreiber had hoped could be had on all issues involving deaf people.

Parent Groups

Parents have a major stake in areas involving their children, but parents of deaf children have not been well organized. The Bell Association has attracted many parents to membership, and it provides them with information and support. However, its monolithic interest in speech does not appeal to all parents. Those seeking a broader reaction to deafness are inclined to join the International Association of Parents of the Deaf, an organization of parents that is closely related to the National Association of the Deaf. Smaller groups of parents in local and state communities spring up, often in the wake of epidemics, such as the 1964–1965 rubella outbreak, or particular crises, such as the threats of school closings. These local groups occasionally join the national organizations, but often remain unaffiliated and hence less potent politically.

Parent organizations exist for more than advocacy purposes; their major function is to provide emotional support to their members. Meeting people who share the same problems can, in itself, give strength to those who are struck by what they regard as a tragic blow. Since most parents of deaf children can hear and have had no direct experience with deafness, finding other parents of deaf children ameliorates somewhat the emotional distress. Furthermore, parents need advice about rearing children whose condition appears to deviate markedly from their own experience. When they seek expert advice, parents are often confronted with contradictory opinions and unrealistic programming. They find themselves in continuous befuddlement as to how to proceed, and they are little helped by intimations that, if they fail to "do the right thing," they will irreparably impair their deaf children's futures. When they join with other parents of deaf children, they often find swift relief by learning that they are not alone in being confused.

Professional

Professional organizations serve a number of functions, including advocacy, self-promotion, self-regulation, and service provision. Organizations serving the deaf community may be subdivided into three broad categories: education, rehabilitation, and related services.

EDUCATION

Educators of deaf students and the administrators of their programs typically join the Convention of American Instructors of the Deaf or the Council of Executives of American Schools for the Deaf. Some prefer the Council for Exceptional Children, though its purview is all disabilities, not deafness alone. Others might prefer the American Speech-Language-Hearing Association, whose members are largely speech pathologists and audiologists. The majority of teachers of deaf students, if they join a professional organization, join the Convention of American Instructors. *See* AMERICAN SPEECH-LANGUAGE-HEARING ASSOCIATION.

The Council on Education of the Deaf was founded in 1960 because the representatives of the constituent groups—the Bell Association, the Convention of American Instructors, and the Conference of Executives—felt that they had more in common than in opposition with respect to educating deaf children. The council accredits teacher-training programs. This function entails developing requirements for various teaching certificates, communicating with the universities that prepare teachers of deaf children, and inspecting the programs prior to accreditation. The cooperative spirit that prevails in deafness education is made apparent by the fact that university programs welcome the council's accreditation and willingly pay the expenses of visiting teams of educators who make onsite examinations of the institutions' faculties and facilities. Nonetheless, the council is a weak organization because its constitution provides that all its activities must have unanimous consent of the members. While this provision is an understandable compromise essential to the Bell Association, it inhibits the organization from taking a position on controversial issues. Thus, when conditions call for a strong voice to override two or more warring factions, the council is likely to be powerless to speak. At the very least, though, the council provides a forum for the discussion of whatever concerns the education of deaf children. *See* EDUCATIONAL PROGRAMS: Accreditation.

REHABILITATION

The Professional Rehabilitation Workers with the Adult Deaf (PRWAD) was formed in 1964 in response to a feeling among providers of rehabilitation services to deaf clients that they needed an organization separate from the National Rehabilitation Association, which dealt with all disabilities, and separate from the educational organizations that paid little heed to the problems of deaf adults. PRWAD has developed over the years into an organization that, though small numerically, assumes large tasks. It conducts annual meetings to inform its membership about recent research and other developments of interest and to promote improved practices. It publishes a quarterly, the *Journal of Rehabilitation of the Deaf*, and a periodic newsletter. In 1980 PRWAD changed its name to

American Deafness and Research Association (ADARA). ADARA has discussed the possibilities of accreditation of rehabilitation workers, but has not yet established a certificate program. *See* JOURNAL OF REHABILITATION OF THE DEAF.

Another rehabilitation organization that emerged in the 1960s is the Registry of Interpreters for the Deaf. The organization radically changed interpreting in the United States from a haphazard, unregulated favor to a paid activity, with a code of ethics and a certificate program. At a 1964 conference at Ball State University, the National Registry of Professional Interpreters and Translators for the Deaf (later shortened to the Registry of Interpreters for the Deaf) was established with 42 regular and 22 sustaining members. The Registry quickly grew to over 1000 members, most of whom were working interpreters. Originally, it accepted as members deaf persons who supported its principles and hearing persons who, though they were not available to interpret, could do so. The latter were often administrators of schools and programs for deaf people who signed as part of their daily work but who were not free to accept assignments outside their regular duties. Early in its history, the Registry saw the necessity for adopting and maintaining performance standards. The certification program has been notably successful in raising the standards of interpreting in the United States. Though even older, well-established organizations find the certification process a difficult one to maintain, the Registry has persevered with little outside support to maintain its certification process. As a professional group, it has studiously avoided appearing as an advocate for deaf people. *See* INTERPRETING; REGISTRY OF INTERPRETERS FOR THE DEAF.

OTHER PROFESSIONAL ORGANIZATIONS

Audiologists and speech pathologists, otologists, and psychologists all perform critical functions at one or another time in the lives of deaf people. Audiologists and speech-language pathologists are generally represented by the American Speech-Language-Hearing Association, best known by its earlier acronym ASHA. Until recent years, deaf people have tended to be hostile toward audiologists and speech pathologists, and the latter have often ignored deaf people. Deaf people resent audiologists because they deliver bad news. Audiologists typically have little to do with the early-deafened population because they feel they can often do nothing for them beyond making the diagnosis. With the advent of more powerful, better-constructed hearing aids, the audiologists' attitudes have begun to change. In addition, many early-deafened adults look back at their experiences with speech-language pathologists as having been largely negative, a struggle to meet incomprehensible (to the child) demands for performance that mean next to nothing to them—that is, to speak, which the child cannot hear, and to lipread, which the child does with great difficulty. ASHA moved to redress this situation, and among the ways in which it did this was to form a corporation with Gallaudet College to publish *dsh Abstracts*, a quarterly journal that summarized the recent literature on deafness, speech, and hearing. The research conducted by ASHA's members has become increasingly relevant to deaf people, and ASHA's acceptance of American Sign Language as a true language, not just a coding strategy, has done much to improve its relations with the deaf community. *See* DSH ABSTRACTS.

Deaf people also do not have much interaction with physicians concerning their deafness. The organization that represents otologists, the medical specialists in aural pathology, is the American Academy of Otology in the American Medical Association. Traditionally, physicians favor the oral approach to educating deaf children, an attitude that does not win favor in the deaf community. Furthermore, many early-deafened adults recall that as children they had painful experiences with physicians. However, the otologists have little influence either favorably or unfavorably on the deaf community.

In recent years, psychologists have come to recognize the fallacies present in the testing of deaf people. The principal organization of psychologists, the American Psychological Association (APA), has held a number of meetings, some in conjunction with the National Academy of Sciences, to discuss and reformulate guidelines for the testing of deviant groups such as deaf people. Because psychology covers so much of human behavior, the relations between the American Psychology Association and the deaf community can be important. With psychologists beginning to recognize their inadequacies, the American Psychological Association has moved into a position more congenial to deaf people.

Service

Organizations providing direct services to deaf people play important parts in the deaf community. Early-deafened people require specialized education and rehabilitation services, as well as accommodations in the workplace and at home.

EDUCATION

The apex of education for deaf students is Gallaudet College, the only institution of higher education in the world solely devoted to deaf persons. Founded during the American Civil War, the college continues to exert a strong influence not only on the education of deaf students but also on other aspects of their lives. In addition to its educational facilities, it maintains an extensive research program that looks broadly at the problems engendered by deafness. A substantial portion of deaf leadership comes from Gallaudet College's graduates. During their college days, they expand their horizons, polish their leadership skills through student organizations, develop relations that often flourish a lifetime, and catch the spirit of accomplishment that surrounds them.

For a hundred years, Gallaudet College was virtually the only possibility for those deaf students seeking higher education. In 1967 Congress passed the legislation establishing the National Technical Institute for the Deaf (NTID). The following year the Rochester Institute of Technology (RIT), having won the competition held to select a site for NTID, opened its doors to deaf students and their own faculty. NTID's own portion of the RIT campus was completed in 1974. NTID is already experiencing some success in spreading its influence.

Also in the 1960s there emerged several other programs that greatly expanded the choices of deaf students seeking postsecondary training. California State University at Northridge (CSUN) opened its Leadership Training Program (LTP). This program prepared educational administrators at the master's level. After its first seven years, the program began to accept deaf students, and has had considerable success in attracting those who have quickly moved into top positions in the deaf community. See CALIFORNIA STATE UNIVERSITY, NORTHRIDGE.

Three schools, Delgado Community College in New Orleans, St. Paul Technical-Vocational Institute, and Seattle Community College, won grants from the federal government to develop postsecondary programs for deaf students. Because of their geographical placement, the three institutions came to be known as the Triangle Schools. They have established the models for incorporating deaf students into postsecondary schools with minimum expense to the institution and maximum benefit to the students. The postsecondary and higher-education programs encourage the elementary and secondary programs to improve their offerings so that more deaf students can have the opportunity to continue their education.

None of the postsecondary programs was initiated by a deaf person. These programs are largely under the direction of governing bodies that do not include more than token deaf participation. The programs all make special arrangements for communication with the deaf students, and they usually provide for their social lives outside the classrooms. Educational policies and planning for deaf students, however, are in the hands of representatives of the general community, with varying but small amounts of advice solicited from the deaf community, which has no authority to alter whatever paths these institutions elect to follow. *See* EDUCATIONAL PROGRAMS: Higher Education.

REHABILITATION

The voluntary agencies adopt one of three models for the delivery of rehabilitation services. They may attempt to be comprehensive service centers (CSC), providing deaf clients with the majority of social and rehabilitation services. They may choose to provide a single service or a very limited number of related rehabilitation services, becoming limited service centers (LSC). They may become information and referral centers (IRC) that brokers use for their deaf clients; that is, instead of attempting to provide the broad range of services deaf people need, the centers determine the deaf clients' needs and then contact the appropriate community agency. To be successful, the information and referral center must be able to provide interpreting and, if necessary, technical assistance to the agencies to which the deaf clients are referred.

The oldest voluntary agency in the United States still exclusively devoted to serving deaf clients is the New York Society for the Deaf (NYSD) in New York City. Chartered in 1913 by the state to provide social and vocational services to deaf clients, NYSD was originally called the Jewish Society for the Deaf, in recognition of its religious origin; it was founded by Rabbi Felix Nash. After his death, his widow Tanya Nash took charge of the agency. In 1968 the agency changed its name to its present nonsectarian title, reflecting the fact that its services are available to all deaf persons, regardless of their religious preferences, although the agency continues to receive major support from the Federation of Jewish Philanthropies. NYSD is basically a comprehensive service center, though in recent years it has considered brokering more of its services. Because over the years sophisticated services for deaf clients have greatly increased, the agency finds that hiring all of the needed expertise is uneconomical when compared to locating qualified experts and agencies in the community, making the arrangements for the deaf client and, if warranted, providing interpreting and technical assistance to the other service providers. NYSD offers personal adjustment training, communication skills development, vocational placement and guidance, and social casework services; directs a regional interpreter service; manages Tanya Towers, a housing facility in Manhattan for elderly deaf persons; makes referrals for legal services; and conducts religious, social, and recreational programs. NYSD also has special programming for deaf-blind clients. In addition, NYSD acts as an advocate for deaf people, working with the deaf community to coordinate efforts at the state level of government. *See* SOCIAL WORK AND SOCIAL WELFARE.

Deafness Evaluation and Adjustment Facilities (DEAF, Inc.), in Boston, is another example of a comprehensive service center. However, it differs from NYSD in that it is wholly owned by the deaf community, which employs the administrative personnel to run the agency and establishes its policies through a board made up of deaf people. Originally, DEAF, Inc., was a joint venture of the National Association of the Deaf and the Massachusetts State Association of the Deaf. Since 1983 the latter has managed DEAF, Inc., by itself, with the financial support of the Massachusetts Rehabilitation Commission. DEAF, Inc., offers vocational evaluation, training, and placement, job development, personal counseling, and independent-living services. It also makes available to other rehabilitation agencies its expertise in managing the problems of deaf clients.

GLAD, an acronym for Greater Los Angeles Council on Deafness, is a similar comprehensive service center in Los Angeles owned and managed by deaf people. Like DEAF, Inc., GLAD was started by deaf people. Both organizations began operations in the latter 1970s, a period in which Congress passed such landmark legislation as the Rehabilitation Act of 1973. For DEAF, Inc., and GLAD, providing communication in the client's native language or preferred mode of communication—as required by the Rehabilitation Act—causes no difficulties. Assuring the cooperation of the deaf community in case management is also no problem. Since these are agencies of the deaf community, they encounter no delay in establishing their credentials with deaf people, and they have the advantages that come from being a part of the group they are established to serve. These two organizations demonstrate the ability of deaf people to provide for deaf people. *See* GREATER LOS ANGELES COUNCIL ON DEAFNESS INC.; REHABILITATION ACT OF 1973.

An example of a limited service center is the South Dakota Communications Services for the Deaf (SDCSD). Founded in 1975 by a contract with the state, SDCSD basically coordinates the interpreting activities in the state. It has advocacy, information dissemination, and some referral activities, but its energies are largely directed toward meeting the communication needs of deaf South Dakotans. The South Dakota Association of the Deaf holds the contract, making SDCSD another agency that has been developed and is owned by deaf people to serve deaf people. Other limited service centers in rehabilitation typically focus on the closely related areas of job development and job placement—a feature growing out of the original vocational orientation of the federal-state rehabilitation pro-

gram in the United States. *See* REHABILITATION: History.

The information and referral center model developed at the New York University Deafness Research and Training Center, under a grant from the Social and Rehabilitation Services, was designed to bring minority deaf persons who were not being reached through the established agencies into the rehabilitation process. Recognizing that these clients when located would require all of the services that other deaf clients need plus specialized communication, New York University chose to concentrate on identifying the clients, introducing them to the service-delivery system, and providing the specialized communication they would need to make use of the established system. A key figure in the information and referral center was the neighborhood liaison, a deaf person who lived in the target area but who had good communication skills in both American Sign Language and the local sign dialect. This approach was dictated by the fact that, for instance, a severe difficulty in New York City's Spanish Harlem was that the language used was a mixture of Puerto Rican, Cuban, and American sign languages. The target group for the center was made up of clients from the Caribbean, most of whom had little or no formal education. The neighborhood worker could communicate easily with the target groups, was not a disruptive element in the community, and could communicate well with the New York University staff. Having made the contacts, the neighborhood worker brought the clients to the center for preliminary evaluations. Based on those assessments of the clients, the appropriate agencies were contacted and arrangements made for the clients to receive the services they needed. The model proved to be both effective and economical, avoiding duplication of services while bringing into the service-delivery system many individuals who would otherwise not have been able to access it.

Social Organizations

Multipurpose associations like the National Association of the Deaf could be classified as social organizations, but this section considers only the athletic and religious organizations.

ATHLETIC

Athletics have a prominent place in the social life of the deaf community. Many deaf adults attend sporting events primarily to meet their deaf friends, rather than to watch the athletes perform.

The premier sports organization in the deaf community is the American Athletic Association of the Deaf (AAAD), first called the American Athletic Union of the Deaf. Founded in 1945 following the first annual National Basketball Tournament, AAAD promotes competition among the deaf clubs, establishes rules for the competitions, supervises regional tournaments and since 1957 assists deaf athletes to attend the International Games for the Deaf. AAAD's charter also states that it will provide social outlets for its members—a provision in keeping with the finding that much support for athletics comes from those actually seeking companionship rather than from those wishing to observe a competition between opposing athletes. AAAD divides its purview into seven regions, containing over 150 affiliated clubs. It sponsors annual basketball and softball tournaments. It also has an AAAD Hall of Fame in which the outstanding deaf athletes, coaches, and sports figures are honored.

Bowling has brought into being a large number of organizations, dating back to the 1930s when the Chicago Club established a bowling league. Several states have bowling organizations; regionally, there are 10 bowling organizations. The Great Lakes Deaf Bowling Association refers to itself as the American Bowling Congress of the Deaf. Its annual tournaments enroll as many as 130 teams and 650 bowlers. The American Deaf Women's Bowling Association is its female counterpart, holding its tournaments concurrently with the Great Lakes Association and attracting like numbers of participants. Since 1963 a nationwide organization, the National Deaf Bowling Association, has held a World's Deaf Bowling Championship and publishes a quarterly newsletter, the *Deaf Bowler*.

RELIGIOUS

No religion is without deaf members. The scant evidence available suggests that the religious preferences of the deaf population are very close to those for the general population. The proportions of Catholics, Jews, and Protestants in the deaf community are probably much the same as in the population at large. Similar findings might be expected for church membership and religious participation, though these matters have had little systematic study.

The Episcopal Church was the first in the United States to have a congregation exclusively made up of deaf people. St. Ann's Church for the Deaf in New York City was established by the oldest son of Thomas Hopkins Gallaudet. The son, Thomas, became an Episcopal priest in 1851 and shortly thereafter founded St. Ann's. The second church for deaf people was All Soul's Church in Philadelphia, in association with St. Stephen's Church, which originally held special services for its deaf members. All Soul's first religious leader was a deaf man, the Reverend Henry W. Syle, who was the first deaf person in the United States to be ordained as an

Episcopal priest. Episcopal deaf congregations have been established throughout the United States.

The second religion in the United States to establish a church for deaf worshipers was the Lutheran Church, which organized one in Chicago in 1896. Our Saviour Lutheran Church for the Deaf was followed two years later by Emanuel Lutheran Church for the Deaf in Milwaukee. Many Lutheran congregations have been served by pastors who are assigned to more than one city. Most geographical areas were at least in contact with one of the 14 or more missions to deaf people that supervised the programs and provided for their maintenance.

The first Methodist church for deaf people was formerly established in Chicago in 1894, when Philip J. Habenstab, a teacher at the Illinois School for the Deaf, became the first deaf person ordained by the Methodist Church. The Chicago Mission for the Deaf was succeeded by the Christ Methodist Church in Baltimore in 1896, and the Cameron Methodist Church in Cincinnati in 1910.

Catholic deaf people usually have not had separate congregations, though they have had signed masses, that is, worship services in which an interpreter or the priest signs the spoken portions of the mass. However, St. Mary Magdalene Church for the Deaf in Denver, Mother of Perpetual Help Church of the Deaf in Omaha, St. Francis of Assisi Catholic Church and Center for the Deaf in Landover Hills, Maryland, St. John's Deaf Center in Warren, Michigan, and Catholic Deaf Center in New Orleans are exceptions.

The Southern Baptist Ministry to the Deaf (SBMD) took a somewhat different approach to its deaf people. Founded in 1906 by John W. Michaels, SBMD sought separate space in existing churches or the use of their space at different times in order to hold services for deaf people. Michaels was not concerned with whether the church was of the Baptist denomination, and set up deaf Sunday schools and congregations in Methodist and Presbyterian churches. SBMD also encouraged the publication of sign dictionaries, in recognition of the need for interpreters and manually proficient ministers.

Other religions have provided for deaf congregants with more modest facilities. The Church of Latter Day Saints (the Mormons) authorized a separate congregation for its deaf members in 1917. Judaism, however, has paid little attention to its early deafened coreligionists, and Jewish deaf people have tended to fend for themselves. In New York City, for instance, deaf Jews maintain three separate congregations without noteworthy assistance from the Jewish community. Another example of deaf adults striking out on their own is the Christian Deaf Fellowship. Begun in 1944 as a nondenominational group, it affiliated with the Central Bible Institute and Seminary in Springfield,

Missouri, for purposes of preparing deaf ministers. While the idea came from a hearing minister whose parents were deaf, the fellowship is entirely managed by its deaf leadership.

In keeping with their tendencies to organize, deaf people have also formed organizations on the basis of their religious preferences. One of the oldest such groups is the Episcopal Church's Conference of Church Workers among the Deaf, which was founded in 1881. Another long-established organization is the Ephphatha Conference of Workers among the Deaf, which started in 1903. The International Catholic Deaf Association, which has headquarters in Toronto, Ontario, Canada, has both hearing and deaf members, although its principal membership is deaf. In 1956 the National Congress of Jewish Deaf was formed. *See* NATIONAL CONGRESS OF JEWISH DEAF; RELIGION, CATHOLIC; RELIGION, PROTESTANT.

RELIGIOUS SCHOOLS

Since schools for deaf pupils have generally instigated the growth of organizations in the deaf community, religious schools need to be considered. The Catholic church maintains nine parochial schools for deaf students: St. Mary in Buffalo, Holy Trinity in Chicago, St. Rita in Cincinnati, St. John in Milwaukee, St. Francis de Sales and St. Joseph in New York City, Archbishop Ryan in Philadelphia, DePaul Institute in Pittsburgh, and St. Joseph in St. Louis. The Lutheran church sponsors two schools for deaf children, one in Detroit and the other on Long Island. The only Jewish religious school for deaf children in the United States is the Hebrew Academy for the Deaf, which accommodates about 60 students in New York City. Founded in the 1970s, the school is expanding its enrollment to include students with a variety of other educationally handicapping conditions.

Commercial

Deaf people have not tended to dominate any particular industry as entrepreneurs. Nor has any industry been dominated by its interest in serving deaf people, unless one considers education a commercial enterprise. In the eighteenth and nineteenth centuries, before public education became ubiquitous, proprietary schools for deaf students did appear occasionally, but today most private schools for deaf children are heavily subsidized by the state governments and are, for all intents and purposes, public schools. Similarly, proprietary interests have not had any important role in rehabilitation, which has grown in the United States as a state-federal responsibility. Nonetheless, some commercial interests—particularly communications, travel, and entertainment—have held greater attraction for the deaf community than others.

PRINT MEDIA

With oral communication difficult and manual communication relatively little known in the general population, deaf people have a substantial stake in print media. Earlier in the twentieth century, deaf people were stereotyped as printers, and a few were publishers. Generally, deaf publishers direct their efforts toward deaf audiences, as did Julius Wiggins, publisher of the *Silent News*, most of whose 3000 readers are deaf. Most publishers of materials for deaf people have engaged in the specialty as the outcome of another activity, such as school bulletins and alumni publications, or as a sideline, as in the case of Wiggins. The major publishing associations do not have divisions or special interest groups for deaf publications. An organization that does bring together the publications aimed at deaf readerships is the Little Paper Family. However, it is not a commercial organization in the sense that it supports businesses. *See* LITTLE PAPER FAMILY; SILENT NEWS.

Two large exceptions are the National Association of the Deaf and TJ Publishers. The National Association of the Deaf publishes books for and about deafness as well as selling such books by other publishers. TJ Publishers is owned and managed by Terry J. O'Rourke, an early-deafened Gallaudet College graduate. Beginning with a book he authored, *A Basic Course in American Sign Language*, O'Rourke now publishes a large list of books about deafness and also sells books on deafness published by other companies.

HEARING AIDS

The manufacturers of hearing aids have not found deaf people to be enthusiastic consumers of their products. Various studies have shown that, of hearing-impaired persons, only a small proportion (about one in five) purchase hearing aids, despite the fact that most deaf children are introduced to hearing aids no later than the time they enter school. Now that more powerful, better-constructed aids are being manufactured, increasing efforts are being made to increase the market. Manufacturers' organizations, however, take indirect approaches like sponsoring Better Hearing Month and similar campaigns. Hearing aid dealers usually see manual communication as frustrating their sales, rather than supplementing them. Direct involvement of early-deafened people and their organizations in the management of these campaigns are infrequent, most likely because of the manufacturers' attitudes toward manual communication. The National Association of the Deaf and the National Fraternal Society of the Deaf usually join in support of Better Hearing Month, for instance, but they do not participate in its planning or execution. Cochlear prostheses may alter the hearing aids situation. *See* Cochlear implant; Hearing aids.

TELEPHONE

Robert Weitbrecht's invention of a modem to facilitate the use of the telephone by deaf people has led to a number of commercial attempts to profit from what he freely gave to the deaf community. From 1964 to the present, there have been at least a dozen manufacturers of electronic equipment who have attempted to capture the market for the telephonic attachments (essentially, a teletypewriter connected via a modem to telephone lines and sending signals that activate similar devices at the other end). No single manufacturer has cornered the market. The principal organization involved in the distribution of the devices is Telecommunications for the Deaf, Inc. Founded in 1968 by three deaf leaders, Latham and Nancy Breunig and Jess Smith, to distribute obsolete teletypewriters donated by American Telephone and Telegraph for use by deaf people, Telecommunications for the Deaf, Inc., now has 24 chapters in the United States and authorizes over 100 service agencies in the United States and 1 in Canada. In addition to its efforts to work with manufacturers for the improvement of the attachments, it publishes the *International Telephone Directory of the Deaf*, which lists owners of telephone attachments, both hearing and deaf. It also holds a biennial convention for organizational purposes and to promote the use of the equipment.

TELEVISION

The principal organization involved with television is the National Captioning Institute. It is a private, nonprofit organization whose owners list no members of the deaf community. It has received multimillion-dollar support from the federal government, as well as fees from the networks and from advertisers, who pay to have their programs captioned. The National Captioning Institute does have an advisory board of members of the deaf community, and it employs a number of deaf people in such roles as public relations and research; however, its control rests outside the deaf community. *See* National Captioning Institute; Telecommunications.

TRAVEL

Denied most telecommunications and being aware that there is much to be seen outside their hometowns, deaf people tend to travel a great deal. Such travel can be greatly aided by having a travel agent, but deaf people on tour need special arrangements not easily made. Finding English-speaking local guides to foreign facilities is difficult enough, but locating one who knows American Sign Language is often impossible. The answer is to bring one along from the United States. Such arrangements have been made through Herbtours, managed by a deaf Gallaudet College graduate, Herb Schreiber. The Gallaudet College Alumni Association also sponsors tours. The travel arrangements made by specialists who handle only deaf clients assure not only qualified interpreters but also congenial companionship, since most of the other members of the tour will be deaf. There are general travel agencies that will efficiently handle deaf tourists, and some have agents who can communicate manually. The specialist in serving deaf travelers, however, is aware of additional problems that they may encounter, and makes provisions to avoid such difficulties as failing to hear announcements over airport public address systems, negotiating with hotels over inadequate accommodations, and responding to custom agents inquiries. *See* Gallaudet College Alumni Association.

ENTERTAINMENT

The National Theatre of the Deaf (NTD) was established by a grant from the Social and Rehabilitation Service in 1966. It has toured the world in productions that feature deaf actors, whose signs are interpreted over loudspeakers that enable hearing persons in the audience who do not know sign to follow the play. Its director, David Hays, firmly believes that NTD should demonstrate the capabilities of deaf actors and should open places for them in the theatrical world. NTD has been successful, with many of its alumni having had impressive careers on television and Broadway. *See* National Theaters of the Deaf: United States.

Summary

Increasingly over the years deaf people in the United States have gained control of significant organizations in their lives. They have little direct involvement in the federal government, having only two groups especially directed to deafness. However, at least 16 states have commissions on deafness. Locally, the numbers of deaf people are usually too few to have much impact on the government. Internationally, deaf people have developed organizations that are within their control and enable them to fulfill their immediate, though limited objectives. Advocacy by deaf people has been at least as successful in attaining its objectives as advocacy for deaf people, and the former affords the deaf community considerably more satisfaction. Deaf people have also made some advances in establishing their own economic influence among commercial organizations. They appear to be making headway in developing commercial enterprises that are adequately responsive to deaf consumers.

Regardless of the type of organization, deaf people have made great progress in improving their communicative access. Deaf people who prefer manual communication have far more opportunities to exercise that preference in contact with all kinds of organizations. Where manual communication is not feasible, many organizations that work with or cater to deaf persons have provided other communication options to ensure that there is adequate two-way interchange of ideas. It is likely that organizations of deaf people will continue to flourish within the deaf community.

Bibliography

Bender, Ruth E.: *The Conquest of Deafness*, 3d ed., Interstate Printers and Publishers, Danville, Illinois, 1981.

Brill, Richard G.: *International Congresses on Education of the Deaf*, Gallaudet College Press, Washington, D.C., 1984.

Gannon, Jack R.: *Deaf Heritage*, National Association of the Deaf, Silver Spring, Maryland, 1981.

Lane, Harlan: *The Wild Boy of Aveyron*, Harvard University Press, Cambridge, Massachusetts, 1976.

Schein, Jerome D.: *Speaking the Language of Sign*, Doubleday, New York, 1984.

Jerome D. Schein

OTOLARYNGOLOGY— HEAD AND NECK SURGERY

Otolaryngology—Head and Neck Surgery is directed to serve the clinical and continuing education needs of specialists in otolaryngology and head and neck surgery. Each issue contains approximately 120 pages of original scientific contributions submitted exclusively to the journal. Articles cover a wide range of subjects, including general otolaryngology, general head and neck surgery, laryngology-bronchoesophagology, rhinology and allergy, otology and neuro-otology, esthetic surgery, and audiology and speech. The journal is published eight times a year.

This is the official journal of the American Academy of Otolaryngology—Head and Neck Surgery, the largest association in this specialty. It is the second most widely read specialty journal among United States otolaryngologists, received by each of the 5600 academy members.

The American Academy of Otolaryngology—Head and Neck Surgery represents United States physicians specializing in the treatment and surgery of the ear, nose, and throat and related structures of the head and neck. It serves the specialty's scientific and educational needs and represents otolaryngology in governmental and socioeconomic matters.

The academy holds an annual meeting, the largest clinical meeting of its kind. It includes an intensive continuing education program for the otolaryngologist, offering over 300 hours of instruction to acquaint specialists with the latest breakthroughs and advanced techniques occurring in the field. Topics include cosmetic facial reconstruction, cancer and tumor surgery, management of patients with loss of hearing and balance, endoscopic examination of air and food passages, and treatment of allergic, sinus, laryngeal, thyroid, and esophageal disorders.

The academy was first called the Western Ophthalmic and Oto-laryngologic Association, from 1896 to 1903. At the eighth annual meeting in 1903, the name was changed to the American Academy of Ophthalmology and Otolaryngology, and this title was used from 1904 through 1977. Upon separation of the two specialties—ophthalmology and otolaryngology—the name American Academy of Otolaryngology was adopted in 1978. In 1981 the name was changed to the American Academy of Otolaryngology—Head and Neck Surgery to reflect the full range of specialties represented by the organization.

The academy's official journal has also undergone name changes. It was called *Transactions* from 1896 through 1977. This was changed to *Otolaryngology* in 1978 and to *Otolaryngology—Head and Neck Surgery* in 1979.

The journal has always been edited by a doctor of medicine. The first editor, Clarence Loeb, was appointed in 1920. He served until 1930, when he was succeeded by Arthur Proetz. W. P. Wherry assumed the editorship in 1932, followed by William L. Benedict in 1940, W. Howard Morrison in 1969, and D. Thane R. Cody in 1976. In 1977 Mansfield F. W. Smith was appointed editor.

The journal brings to the academy members papers of scientific merit that are carefully reviewed by their peers. The primary source for manuscripts is the presentations at the annual meeting of the American Academy of Otolaryngology—Head and Neck Surgery. Unsolicited manuscripts are also submitted, from workshops and from other meetings within the specialty. The journal receives approximately 350 submissions a year. These are reviewed by the distinguished authorities of the Editorial Review Board. The journal will publish illustrations in four colors.

The journal has features as well: A case-report section, a drug and device capsule review section, occasional letters to the editor, and several book reviews in each issue. The news and announcements page informs readers of upcoming events.

Two special issues are published each year: the academy's Section on Instruction issue (May), which contains abstracts for approximately 275 courses offered at the annual meeting, and the Annual Meeting Scientific Program issue (September), which summarizes programs, meeting times, and room assignments.

Mansfield F. W. Smith

PABLO BONET, JUAN
(1579–1623)

Juan Pablo Bonet was the author of the first published book dedicated to the instruction of deaf people at a time when such teaching was universally unknown. Juan Pablo was born July 1, 1579, in a little Spanish village, Torres de Berrellén, near Zarogoza. He was the son of Juan Pablo (whose parents were Martin Pablo and Isabela de Cerreta) and María Bonet (daughter of Francisco Bonet and Gracia Guerguete). Thus, his family name was Pablo, not Bonet as frequently stated. His family were old Christians, that is to say, they were neither Arabs nor Jews, both of whom were numerous in his village. There was no deafness in his family.

At an early age he went to Madrid where he lived with an uncle who was in the military. Pablo enlisted in the army and took part in expeditions against the Berbers and pirates in the Mediterranean and in the struggles in North Italy between the Spaniards and the Savoyards. These continuous travels gave him an opportunity to learn Italian and French.

In 1607 the constable of Castile, Don Juan Fernández de Velasco, Duke of Frias, took Pablo into his service. While serving Fernández de Velasco, Pablo married Mencia de Ruicerezo, and the couple had one son, Diego Pablo (who died without children in 1652). The second son of the constable, named Luis, was deaf, supposedly because of a disease suffered when he was two years old. The constable had two deaf uncles and two deaf aunts,

however, indicating that the deafness of Luis may have been hereditary.

Fernández de Velasco died in 1613 and his widow, Doña Juana de Córdoba, Duchess of Frias, asked Manuel Ramírez de Carrión to be Luis's teacher. Ramírez, who also had educated other deaf members of the Velasco family, followed the methodology of Pedro Ponce de León, but he never published anything about his work. Juan Pablo, as secretary to the duchess of Frias, was able to observe Ramírez teaching young Luis. *See* CARRIÓN, MANUEL RAMÍREZ DE; PONCE DE LEÓN, PEDRO.

When Ramírez returned to his village in 1619, Pablo offered to continue as Luis's teacher. He did not introduce any original methods in his teaching but followed the techniques of Pedro Ponce and Ramírez as he had seen them applied. Pablo's role as teacher may have lasted about three years and certainly alternated with his other obligations in the ducal house. In 1620 he published his renowned book, *Reduction de las letras, y arte para ensenar a hablar los mudos* (Simplification of the Alphabet, and the Art of Teaching Mutes to Speak).

The pedagogic description in this book is not original, for Pablo limited himself to an exposition of the method employed by Ramírez, which he, in turn, borrowed from Pedro Ponce. This has led many investigators to believe that Pablo's book is only an edited manuscript originally written by Ponce and then lost. What is certain, however, is that 74 authors are quoted in the book, but neither Pedro Ponce nor Manuel Ramírez, from whom Pablo learned everything, is quoted. The book's censor, Fray Antonio Perez, abbot of the Benedictine monastery of St. Martin in Madrid, who authorized and recommended publication of the book, wrote in the preface that it was "Ponce de León who gave birth to this marvel of making mutes speak."

Thus it is clear from the preface that Pablo was not the originator of the pedagogic method discussed in the text. The method consists of teaching the deaf pupil the correct position of the organs of articulation and the correct method of expelling air to form the sound of each letter of the alphabet. To obtain the positioning, the teacher put his fingers into the child's mouth, using a leather tongue to show the exact tongue position that the pupil must imitate. To demonstrate expiration, the teacher pressed the pupil's lips with his fingers, put the palm of his hand at various distances from the mouth to measure the intensity of the vocal emission, and made a paper strip vibrate to teach the trilled "r." Pablo does not mention the use of a mirror to allow the student to verify the exact position of his or her tongue, perhaps because the poor quality of mirrors in those days rendered them useless. His descriptions of the articulatory positions are excellent, and they have helped modern phoneticians understand the articulation of seventeenth-century Spanish. Pablo was the first writer to make a clear distinction between voiced and unvoiced phonemes.

He also defended the teaching of reading and spelling. He argued that if children knew how to articulate each letter and how to join them in the expiration of voice, they could read in a loud voice in a very short time. This did not mean, though, that the children understood everything they read. Concurrently with speech instruction, which he believed should begin when the child was between six and eight years old, Pablo recommended the teaching of dactylology or fingerspelling. He placed importance on the value of simultaneously reading, showing the pupil pictures, and fingerspelling. His book has nice pictures of the finger positions for each letter, copied from a book by Melchior de Yerba that appeared in 1593. This finger alphabet is the same as the one handed alphabet in use in many countries today. With it, one can express anything correctly. Interestingly, he did not teach lipreading, which he believed had negative effects.

Pablo's grammatical descriptions are remarkable. He distinguished among verbs, nouns, and conjunctions, the last including words that lack gender, number, and tense. He understood past, present, and future tenses and wrote that there are concrete and abstract nouns. The former he called "real nouns" and the latter "non-real nouns." Pablo insisted that adjectives had to be thought of in contrasting binary pairs.

Juan Pablo Bonet died on February 2, 1623, in Madrid. Although he did not originate a method for teaching deaf pupils, his book was important in spreading the idea that a deaf child could be educated orally. He aroused in other European teachers curiosity and interest in this kind of education. We can consider Juan Pablo Bonet not the creator but the disseminator of the oral method for the education of deaf children. *See* SPAIN.

Bibliography

Bejarano, Eloi: *L'Espagne et les sourdmuets*, Madrid, 1905.

Best, Harry: *Deafness and the Deaf in the United States*, 1943.

Giangreco, C. and M.: *The Education of the Hearing Impaired*, 1970.

Navarro, Tomás: "Doctrina fonética de Juan Pablo-Bonet," *Revista filológica española*, vol. 7, p. 150, 1920.

————: "Juan Pablo-Bonet," *La paraula*, vol. 3, p. 23, 1920.

Perelló, Jorge: *Lexicón de comunicología*, Barcelona, 1977.

————: *Sordomudez*, Barcelona, 1978.

Read, Malcolm K.: "Linguistic Theory and the Problem of Mutism," *Historiografía lingüistica*, vol. 4, p. 303, 1977.

Rodriguez González, Angles: *Aspectos lingüísticos del lenguaje gestual del sordo*, doctoral thesis, Valladolid, 1983.

Jorge Perelló

PARENT EDUCATION

The diagnosis of deafness in an infant or young child creates a tremendous crisis for hearing parents and other family members. During the ensuing days, months, and years, most parents experience a wide range of feelings including anger, guilt, confusion, helplessness, and sorrow. While such feelings are both common and normal, the ability to express and cope with these emotional states is varied and greatly affects the family environment as well as the deaf child.

The personality and cognitive development of deaf children are greatly influenced by their early and continued interactions and relationships with their parents. Further, due to the ubiquity of their communication delay and the limited number of individuals who can communicate with most young deaf children, the family's adaptation to and understanding of deafness is especially critical for their deaf child's growth.

Given this situation, it should not be surprising that parental or family education and counseling is believed to be a critical component of educational intervention for deaf children, especially in the early stages. This article discusses the history of parent education efforts, the role of parent educators, models of parent education, the processes of family adaptation to deafness and deaf culture, and critical issues relating to these endeavors.

HISTORICAL ISSUES

Historically, parents have received little or no assistance or counseling following diagnosis of a child's hearing impairment. This is still common in rural and impoverished areas that do not have adequate early intervention services. Prior to the 1960s, the few early intervention programs that existed were not affiliated with either public school programs or state-supported residential schools for deaf pupils. They were supported primarily through private means, and they did not reach the general population of deaf children. Typically, services were provided by audiologists and speech therapists, and teachers of deaf people were usually not involved. In such programs, educational considerations received low priority, and the problems of deafness were usually perceived within a medical framework or as involving an inability to speak, rather than as an inability to hear, which could be remediated simply by proper fitting of hearing aids and training in articulation and oral fluency. This naivete was compounded by the fact that those affiliated with such programs usually had no knowledge of the programs for deaf people in which most children eventually were enrolled; nor did they have social or professional contacts with deaf adults. Further, these programs rarely employed parent counselors; thus, parent education was characterized by its inadequacy and ideological confusion. As manual communication was strongly discouraged, parent-child communication was often minimal, and behavior problems were common. The child's failure to speak clearly was usually attributed to either poor parenting or developmental problems. Many parents wavered between guilt and resentment as their child failed to speak.

During the early 1970s, three major changes occurred. First, the recognition of the needs of disadvantaged and disabled children led to the emergence of many early intervention and preschool programs for deaf children. Second, these programs were usually linked to public or residential school programs and directed by educators of deaf people. Third, the philosophy of total communication emerged as a viable and rapidly growing educational alternative. However, parent education services were often less than optimal as teachers of deaf children assumed the responsibilities of parent counselors, infant development specialists, educational audiologists, and psychologists—roles for which they were professionally unqualified. *See* EDUCATIONAL PROGRAMS.

COMMUNICATION CONTROVERSY

If parents are able to secure early intervention for their child, it is only the beginning step in deciding between the two major approaches to teaching deaf children: oral or total communication. The "pure oral" school asserts that with amplification of residual hearing, auditory training, speechreading, and speech training, most deaf children can develop sufficient oral skills to function successfully in the hearing world. This philosophy is based on the notion that full integration of deaf persons in the hearing world is both possible and desirable. The John Tracy Clinic, established in 1943, is probably the most famous oral early intervention program. It was one of the earliest systematic attempts to assist parents, and it developed a free correspondence course for parents of preschool deaf children. For many parents this service was critical and provided their only source of professional support in assisting their young child. For many severely and profoundly deaf children, however, this method often resulted in limited progress: children who were functionally illiterate with no means of communication and parents who were disappointed and disillusioned.

The second approach, total communication, incorporates all possible means of communication (sign language, pantomime, gesture, speech), and has revolutionized the early education of many deaf children. The total communication philosophy has frequently been utilized as the educational method of simultaneous communication, in which a manual signing system based on English syntax is used simultaneously with speech. *See* SOCIOLINGUISTICS: Total Communication.

This shift to total communication came about as the acquisition and use of language became better understood and more precise differentiation was made between the terms communication, language, and speech. Total communication also grew in prominence as the deaf community became more involved in its own education, sign language was recognized as a legitimate language and one natural to the deaf population, and research documented the positive effects of early manual communication. This new understanding and knowledge of language and deafness helped parents to recognize the unalterable differences that are caused by early childhood deafness and the critical importance of encouraging early language use (not to be confused with speech) and communication.

Both of these philosophies have their ardent proponents regarding which approach should be used with deaf children. Due to the lack of available services or inadequate early counseling, parents may be forced to adopt one approach without sufficient evaluation or information.

DIAGNOSIS AND FAMILY ADAPTATION

Deafness is difficult to diagnose in a very young child, and its infrequency, invisibility, and its sharing of symptomatology with other childhood ailments have often led to misdiagnoses such as retardation, autism, language delay, or brain damage. Further, the long delay of usually 6 to 18 months between suspicion and confirmation of a hearing loss is traumatic and often leads to justifiable anger at professionals. *See* AUDIOMETRY.

The diagnosis of deafness leads inevitably to a series of emotional reactions in hearing parents that follow a four-stage process. Acute reactions include shock, denial, disbelief, and an overwhelming feeling of helplessness. Such feelings are often followed by self-blame, blaming of one's spouse or even the deaf child for this "misfortune," anger directed toward professionals, and depression. Through the process of self-reflection and the assistance of supportive others, including parent educators, parents begin to adapt to this new reality and the family reaches a new equilibrium. Finally, if the parents have good ego strength, a supportive network, and adequate educational and counseling resources, they will come to accept the reality of their child's deafness. Each family copes with the initial diagnosis in different ways, and it is believed that these initial reactions are not necessarily predictive of later family or child functioning.

A child's deafness confronts hearing parents with a new reality which is often unexplainable. It calls for the development of new skills, increased time commitments to parenting, and numerous financial burdens. Successfully meeting these new demands requires that the family correctly recognize and explore their emotional reactions to their child's disability and share these thoughts with empathic listeners. This process is best accomplished in the context of counseling combined with exposure to other hearing parents of deaf children and to deaf adults.

The most difficult hurdle for many parents is their desire for normality. It is natural for parents to deny the reality of the differences that result from deafness. This is evidenced early by "shopping around" for alternative diagnoses or searching for a curative operation or religious experience. While these forms of denial are quite obvious and usually short-lived, more subtle forms may continue. As long as parents hold onto the belief that deafness is primarily an inability to speak, they strive to create a speaking child who can "overcome" his or her deafness and be normalized. Since this goal is unattainable for many deaf children, this denial may lead to placing a child with little speech potential in an oral program and depriving the child and family of critical early communication. This process eventually leads to grave disappointment, poor family functioning, and poor self-concept and behavioral disturbance in the child. The understanding that deafness is irreversible and the acceptance of its unalterable differences is crucial to a healthy parent-child relationship and is an important sign of the family's acceptance.

Further, many deaf and hearing professionals believe that much of the parents' fear of deafness and its implications can be dispelled by encouraging early and continued contact between hearing parents and deaf adults. Through such experiences, in concert with counseling, parents can begin to realize that deafness is not primarily an audiological deficit, but instead that it constitutes a rich and varied minority cultural group with a proud history, normative values, and language. By establishing links to the deaf community, the parents can also expose the child to deaf adult role models and prevent later conflicts in the child between loyalty to their hearing family and their assimilation into the deaf community. Such experiences facilitate further acceptance of the differences that deafness involves. *See* DEAF POPULATION: Deaf Community.

PARENT EDUCATORS

Most educational programs in the elementary and secondary years focus almost solely on the child and often ignore many of the needs of parents or families of the deaf child. This has led to feelings of alienation, inadequate understanding and support systems for parents, and poor family communication. In order to prevent such difficulties the role of parent educator has recently been recognized as a necessary and integral part of the intervention services offered to families with deaf children. However, this recognition has not led to the rapid introduction of such services.

Until recently the role of "parent educator" was usually provided by untrained teachers of deaf pupils. This role has now changed considerably, and demands that parent educators have special training and knowledge.

As parent educators can provide services from a variety of settings (for example, residential or public schools, speech and hearing centers, and community mental health centers), their roles, goals, and functions can vary considerably. Parent educators frequently assume the role of liaison between schools or education programs and health and social service agencies and usually provide direct services such as instruction and counseling. Instruction may include providing materials and resources for families as well as classes in areas such as parenting skills or sign language. Their role as counselors may include providing individual counseling following the diagnosis, parent discussion groups, and being "on-call" for crisis situations. The parent educator can also act as an advocate for parents' needs and rights within the school or education system.

Family education programs presently utilize a variety of service delivery models. Education programs are offered in single night or weekend workshops, or on a weekly, biweekly, or monthly basis to discuss topics such as child development, parenting skills, the Individual Educational Placement (IEP) Process, parents' rights, sign language instruction, and so on. Innovative learning vacations or camps also have been developed by the Deaf Children's Society of British Columbia, International Association of Parents of the Deaf, and Gallaudet College, for example, where the whole family attends and receives an in-depth, time-limited experience. Such learning vacations are one of the first examples of attempts to assist siblings and other relatives. The development of local, national, and international parent associations (American Society for Deaf Children, International Parents Organization of the Alexander Graham Bell Association) has been especially noteworthy in providing material resources as well as social support to many parents of deaf children. *See* ALEXANDER GRAHAM BELL ASSOCIATION FOR THE DEAF; AMERICAN SOCIETY FOR DEAF CHILDREN; GALLAUDET COLLEGE.

DEVELOPMENTAL ISSUES
Many parent educators provide services in parent-infant programs. Their work with parents usually ends when the deaf child reaches the age of four or five years and enters preschool. This early parent education is crucial, yet it is vitally important that parent education continues with parents of older deaf children as well.

Because of the transactional nature of a child's development at any given time, characteristics of the family, child, and environment are affecting, as well as being affected by, the intervention process. Despite the value of early intervention, it is extremely important to give credence to continued changes and difficulties that families may encounter in raising their deaf children. Donald Moores, using a family life cycle model, posited four major points of stress and transition in families with deaf children: the diagnostic crisis, school entry, beginning adolescence, and early adulthood. The family and the deaf child confront very different concerns, frustrations, and stresses at different stages of the child's development, and therefore require different interventions to learn new ways to cope and grow.

The initial concerns and goals of parent programs and education may include the development of relaxed, mutually satisfying communication between parent and child, understanding and allowing expression of grief and other negative emotional states, and restoring the parents' confidence in their parenting skills. However, the fact that a family has shown a healthy adaptation to one stage does not ensure that the painful feelings first felt during the diagnostic crisis will not reemerge as new developmental demands (such as independence, responsibility, or school problems) are faced by the family and deaf child. Thus, "acceptance"

of deafness by the family is a relative, not absolute, state and does not imply that all is fine. Further, it is important for parents and parent educators to realize that chronic or periodic sorrow may occur simultaneously with healthy coping and acceptance.

CURRENT AND FUTURE CHALLENGES
Three changes in deaf education have resulted from the Education for All Handicapped Children Act: (1) More services are now provided for preschool deaf children. (2) There has been strong encouragement for mainstreaming deaf children in local public schools, which has resulted in a reduction in the proportion of children who attend residential schools. (3) The IEP Process has led to demands for greater parent involvement in their child's educational programming. Thus, there has been increased pressure on families to assume a more important role concerning their deaf child. It is not accidental that there has been a parallel rise in interest in parent services. However, while some new services are being provided, parent education at the elementary and secondary levels is still a very low priority in deaf education. There is a need for school administrators to realize that it is not possible to educate successfully a deaf child without providing continuing services (counseling, information, sign language training) to their families. Clear linkages have been established between family adaptation and provision of services and the child's emotional maturity and educational attainment.

Two additional changes face the field of parent education. First, services to families usually involve only services to mothers. There is a great need for the demonstration of service delivery models that can significantly affect fathers as well as other important persons in the child's life (siblings, grandparents, neighbors, and so on). Second, there has been a historical lack of communication, and at times even hostility, between public school programs for deaf children and the deaf adult community. Deaf adults are clearly an invaluable resource for deaf children and their hearing parents. It is the challenge of parent educators to begin to build healthy relationships between deaf persons, hearing parents, and local school programs.

Bibliography
Buscaglia, L.: *The Disabled and Their Parents*, Charles B. Slack, Thorofare, New Jersey, 1975.

Freeman, R. D., C. F. Carbin, and R. C. Boese: *Can't Your Deaf Child Hear? A Guide for Those Who Care about Deaf Children*, University Park Press, Baltimore, 1981.

Greenberg, M. T., and R. Calderon: Early intervention for deaf children: Outcomes and issues, *Topics in Early Childhood Special Education*, 4:1–9, 1984.

Luterman, D.: *Counselling Parents of Hearing Impaired Children*, Little, Brown, Boston, 1979.

Meadow, K. P.: *Deafness and Child Development*, University of California Press, Berkeley, 1980.

Mindel, E., and M. Vernon: *They Grow in Silence*, National Association of the Deaf, Silver Spring, Maryland, 1971.

Moores, D. F.: *Educating the Deaf: Psychology, Principles, and Practices*, Houghton Mifflin, Boston, 1982.

Naiman, D. W., and J. D. Schein: *For Parents of Deaf Children*, National Association of the Deaf, Silver Spring, Maryland, 1978.

Parent Education Resource Manual, Gallaudet College Division of Public Services, Washington, D.C., 1982.

Schlesinger, H. S., and K. Meadow: *Sound and Sign*, University of California Press, Berkeley, 1972.

Spradley, T., and J. Spradley: *Deaf Like Me*, Random House, New York, 1978.

Mark T. Greenberg; Rosemary Calderon

Parent Resources

More than 90 percent of parents with children who are deaf or hard-of-hearing are themselves hearing. They may know nothing about deafness, may never have met a deaf person or another parent with a deaf child. They often feel lonely, confused, and isolated. Raising a child who has a disability that interferes with the communication process of a family is difficult and often painful if the parents do not have informative and supportive resources.

At different periods of the chld's (and the parents') growth, there will be a need for different types of information. Early in the child's life there will be the need for information about deafness in general, hearing aids, communication systems, and infant and preschool programs. The parents of a school-age child want information about schools, legal rights, language development, reading levels, and social development. The parents of an adolescent or young adult will want information about college, career, vocational rehabilitation, legal rights, independent living, and the deaf community. Throughout the search for information is the search for resources on a local and national level.

Until the 1970s, the primary resource for parents was the school the child attended. The school provided much or limited information depending on the program's interest in parents. Since 1975 when the Education for All Handicapped Children Act came into effect, parents have played a more important role in school programs and educational planning for their children. Awareness has increased as to the needs and skills, both psychological and intellectual, of parents. As parents have become more sophisticated, they look for increased, in-depth information so they can raise their child with knowledge and confidence.

Sixty-eight percent of hearing-impaired children are now in regular schools in mainstreamed programs, and schools no longer play the centralized role they did before 1975. Mandated busing of handicapped children has eliminated the daily contact which parents had with schools as they drove their children to and from school. Public schools with no more than one to five deaf children may not have the resources to answer parents' specific questions about deafness and raising a deaf child.

Informational and supportive resources can provide parents with knowledge which leads them to make informed decisions for their child. With a broad range of resources, parents have more options from which to make choices that will have a life-long impact on their child.

Resources may be parent-to-parent organizations or professional organizations; may be specifically concerned with deafness or may deal with general disabilities; or may be accessible through telephone books, directories of local services, schools, and colleges for the deaf, and other parents.

As of the mid-1980s, the prime source of information about resources for parents continued to be schools and parents. Word-of-mouth at parent meetings, school meetings, and community meetings were another source of information, as were newsletters and journals. Associations for and of deaf people, for and of educators and other professionals, and for and of parents provided individualized information valuable to parents searching for appropriate resources to support their decisions about their child.

Bibliography

Mendelsohn, Jacqueline Z.: "*A Family Begins*," International Association of Parents of the Deaf, 1982.

National Center for Law and the Deaf, *Legal Rights of Hearing-Impaired People*, 1982.

1980 Summer Writing Team/Hearing Impaired, Anoka-Hennepin District No. 11, Minnesota: *Very Important People: A Resource Guide About Deafness for Parents and Children*, 1980.

Ogden, Paul W., and Suzanne Lipsett: *The Silent Garden*, 1982.

Jacqueline Z. Mendelsohn

PEET, MARY TOLES
(1836–1901)

Mary Toles Peet wrote verses for her family and friends, taught deaf pupils, and officially conducted the social affairs of her hearing husband who was the administrator of a school for deaf students. Her beauty, intelligence, and charming manners attracted all in her presence, including noted educators, artists, political figures, and businessmen—an unusual accomplishment for a deaf woman whose early life was spent in a rural environment.

Shortly after Mary was born on a farm in Green

Township, Pennsylvania, in 1836, the Toles family moved to Arkwright, Chautauqua County, New York, where she spent her childhood. At the age of 13, an attack of brain fever caused a permanent loss of hearing. Two years later, in 1851, she was admitted into the New York Institution for the Instruction of the Deaf and Dumb (now New York School for the Deaf).

The gifted young girl had no trouble mastering all subjects, especially English. An avid reader, she took naturally to the study of the classics and exhibited a fondness for poetry. In 1853, she graduated with the highest honors of her class. Her teacher Isaac Lewis Peet fell in love with her and married his bright student on June 27, 1854.

Almost immediately, the new Mrs. Peet shouldered the responsibilities of both wife and hostess for her husband, who was also the school's vice-principal. Substituting in his place whenever administrative duties interfered with his classroom schedule, she eventually served as a regular teacher until 1867, when her husband succeeded his father, Harvey P. Peet, as principal. In the following years, her wit, elegance, and good taste permanently established her as the school's first lady, off campus as well as on. At the same time she was raising a family of four children. In 1891, Mrs. Peet contracted a serious illness that forced her to forego her societal role at the school, although occasionally she continued to entertain close friends at home.

Following the death of her husband in December 1898, she went to live with her only daughter, Elizabeth, in Providence, Rhode Island. Two years later, she moved to Washington, D.C., where Elizabeth had secured a position at Gallaudet College, then the only institution of higher learning for deaf students in the world. Though Mrs. Peet was there only a short time, some of the happiest moments of her life were spent in and around its campus on Kendall Green. *See* GALLAUDET COLLEGE.

Mary Toles Peet died on March 5, 1901, in Washington. It is unfortunate that only 45 poems written by Mary Toles Peet exist. They were published in 1903 in a little volume titled *Verses*, with an introduction by Edward Allen Fay. Also included in the private publication is a note by Elizabeth Peet which best tells why so few were printed: "It is only due to my mother to say that this little collection of verses falls far short of being complete. She herself valued her own writings so lightly that but few of her verses were preserved, and it is only through the kindness of her friends that I have been able to secure the comparatively small number contained in this book." *See* FAY, EDWARD ALLEN.

Bibliography

Braddock, Gilbert C.: *Notable Deaf Persons*, edited by F. B. Crammette, pp. 12–13, Gallaudet College Alumni Association, Washington, D.C., 1975.

Fox, Thomas F.: "Chronology of the New York School for the Deaf," *Fanwood Journal*, 1935.

Gallaudet, E. M.: "The Poetry of the Deaf," *American Annals of the Deaf*, 29:209–210, 1884.

Jenkins, I.: "The Peet Family," *N.Y.S.D. Annual Reports*, 46:308–309, 1901.

Peet, Mary Toles: *Verses*, printed privately, 1903.

Taras B. Denis

PERCEPTION

Perception is the process by which environmental stimulus information, conveyed by light, sound, and other forms of energy, is detected by the various senses (vision, hearing, touch, and so on) and processed by the brain to provide an awareness and knowledge of objects and events in the surrounding world. This definition specifies a dynamic process involving coordinated activity of all the senses in picking up, extracting, and responding to information in the energy that is stimulating them. For example, when people pick up a crying infant, they actively seek information through vision, hearing, touch, and smell. This information is integrated and combined with existing knowledge to provide a perceptual experience of a familiar infant with a certain size, weight, and other physical attributes, who is emitting a cry with distinctive characteristics associated with discomfort, and who is moist in a certain location.

Since perception involves the coordinated activity of all the senses, it is of theoretical as well as practical importance to understand the perceptual effects of sensory impairment. The most common sensory impairments are blindness and deafness, and the most obvious perceptual effect is to reduce or eliminate information that would otherwise be provided by the impaired sensory system. Thus, a blind person can have no perceptual experience of color, for example, and a deaf person cannot perceive speech sounds. In addition, since there is coordination and interaction between sensory systems, it is possible that impairment in one sense modality might affect performance in the other senses. There are two major hypotheses about this effect: (1) the generalized perceptual deficiency hypothesis, which states that impairment in one sensory system tends to be accompanied by deficits in the other sensory systems as well; and (2) the perceptual compensation hypothesis, which proposes that impairment in one sensory channel will lead to development of superior capabilities in one or more of the other sensory systems. The proposition that a sensory impairment, such as deafness, produces an experiential deficiency resulting from lack of exposure to certain kinds of environmental information or experience (for example, information communicated through spoken language) is related to the deficiency hypothesis. This experiential deficiency may contribute to a delay in the development of certain cognitive and perceptual abilities. These hypotheses can serve as a theoretical framework for research on perception and deafness.

DEAFNESS AND VISION PROBLEMS

Ophthalmological studies with deaf subjects generally indicate that there is a higher incidence of vision problems among hearing-impaired students than among normal-hearing children. Specifically, hyperopia (farsightedness), astigmatism, and ocular pathology (physical or physiological abnormalities of the eye) occur more frequently among deaf than hearing children. The most notable exceptions to this pattern are myopia (nearsightedness), which occurs in deaf children at about the same rate as with hearing children, and color vision defects, which seem to occur somewhat less frequently among hearing-impaired children (males).

In some cases the factors causing deafness also produce visual defects. For example, maternal rubella infection during pregnancy is known to increase the frequency of ocular pathology and vision problems in addition to deafness. Certain hereditary disorders also affect both the auditory and visual systems. Usher's syndrome, for example, produces congenital deafness combined with retinitis pigmentosa, a progressive deterioration of the retina of the eye. However, in other cases there is no clear relationship between the etiology of deafness and the occurrence of visual disorders. *See* HEARING LOSS: Genetic Causes.

Since deaf individuals must rely heavily on vision to provide sensory information, there is a clear need for early visual screening and ophthalmological examination. Early identification of vision problems, and correction of these problems where possible, can significantly benefit the educational and social development of any child, but particularly in cases where there is a hearing impairment.

TESTS OF VISUAL PERCEPTUAL ABILITIES

Research conducted in the 1950s seemed to support a generalized deficiency hypothesis by revealing inferior performance of deaf subjects as compared with hearing subjects on certain perceptual tests. For example, deaf subjects performed more poorly on tests requiring them to reproduce a specific pattern of lines, dots, or marbles, or to identify a certain figure embedded in a concealing background. This deficiency was originally interpreted as a difficulty in perceiving abstract stimuli (arrangements of lines or dots) that are not readily associated with familiar objects or experiences. Some of the subsequent studies conducted with many of the same or similar tests, however, found that deaf subjects performed at an equivalent or superior level by comparison with hearing subjects.

Fortunately, research comparing visual memory for stimuli presented either simultaneously or sequentially provides some clarification. Several studies have shown that when stimulus elements (for example, cubes, lines, or letters) forming a pattern are presented simultaneously, deaf children are able to reproduce the pattern from memory as well as, or better than, hearing children. However, when stimulus items are presented consecutively, hearing children tend to show better recall of the sequential pattern. The performance decrement for deaf children with certain kinds of sequentially presented stimuli may represent a developmental lag, by comparison with hearing children, that is overcome with increasing age. There is also research indicating that training in visual sequential memory can improve general performance of deaf children in this area.

Deaf children's poor performance on tests involving embedded figures, or differentiation of figure and background, is related to a perceptual characteristic known as field dependence/field independence. This terminology refers to the ability to distinguish a certain figure (object, shape, pattern, and so on) embedded in a background structure. Field independence means the ability to perceive a figure as separate from a surrounding background (or field). Field dependence refers to a tendency to perceive the figure and background as a whole structure, with perceptual difficulty in differentiating the figure embedded in the structured field. There are large individual differences in this perceptual trait or style, with a general developmental trend toward greater field independence with increasing age. Deaf subjects are generally more field-dependent than hearing subjects of the same age. The distinction between field dependence and field independence is usually interpreted as a difference in perceptual processing strategy, rather than perceptual capacity, and the generally greater field dependence of deaf individuals probably reflects, in part, the sensory and social deprivation experienced by many deaf children.

In summary, the evidence from research with various tests of visual perceptual abilities indicates that deaf children are equivalent or superior to hearing children in the ability to recall and reproduce visually perceived patterns when the pattern elements are presented simultaneously. However, when pattern elements are presented sequentially, deaf children show poorer performance than hearing children. On tests of field dependence/independence, deaf subjects generally reveal a more field-dependent, holistic perceptual strategy in comparison with hearing subjects of the same age.

COLOR DISCRIMINATION

Deaf and hearing children have been compared in studies of preference for color or form in tests involving matching or sorting (categorizing). For example, the subject may be presented with sets of three figures that vary in both color and shape. The subject's task is to identify two figures from each set that appear most similar. Hearing children generally prefer to match stimuli on the basis of form after about four years of age, with a tendency to prefer color prior to that age. Deaf children, however, continue to show a color preference in this task until at least the age of 10 or 12 years. Corresponding to these preferences, deaf children tend to show better color discrimination ability than hearing children, while hearing children discriminate form variations better than deaf children. Thus, for both deaf and hearing subjects, the stimulus dimension that is preferred and attended to for purposes of categorization or matching is also differentiated more accurately.

Another phenomenon related to color perception is known as the Stroop effect. This effect refers to the conflict that occurs when a subject attempts to name the color of ink when the print forms a conflicting color-word association, for example, if "GREEN" is printed in red ink. In this situation, color naming or identification is slower than if the ink or paint color is simply presented as a colored patch or disk. This effect has been demonstrated with normally hearing and deaf subjects.

In research with deaf people, static pictures of signs for colors and color-word associations were printed in ink of a conflicting color or in ink of a consistent color. Both deaf students whose first language was American Sign Language and English-speaking hearing subjects with some knowledge of sign language showed interference from Stroop (color-conflict) stimuli, as measured by time required to identify the color. However, deaf subjects showed more interference from the stimuli in sign language than did the hearing subjects. This probably reflects the greater familiarity with or assimilation of sign meanings by deaf subjects, which increases the conflict between the color represented by the sign and the color of the ink in which it is printed. This research also points out the interaction between perception and the cognitive effects of linguistic stimuli. *See* SIGN LANGUAGES: American.

LINGUISTIC PROFICIENCY AND PERCEPTUAL/COGNITIVE DEVELOPMENT

Some studies concerned with the relationship between language and cognitive or perceptual development have employed deaf subjects. The reason is that children who are congenitally deaf or who became deaf at an early age (that is, prior to about three years of age) are usually deficient in their comprehension of spoken language and in their reading and writing abilities. Therefore, it is reasoned that if the development of cognitive and perceptual abilities is affected by linguistic competence, deaf subjects should show deficiencies or differences in comparison with hearing subjects. Actually, the research in this area has revealed all possible outcomes, with inferior performance or a developmental lag by deaf subjects in some abilities, but evidence for equivalent and superior performance in other areas. Some of these findings have been noted above. Some investigators have argued that the research showing equivalent performance by deaf and hearing subjects indicates that cognitive/perceptual development (at least in certain areas) does not require linguistic support. However, these studies generally do not document sufficiently the linguistic competence of deaf subjects, and it is entirely possible that they possess a level of proficiency in sign communication (or even English) sufficient to mediate performance in the cognitive/perceptual tasks being studied.

PERIPHERAL VISION

Human vision consists of two anatomically and functionally distinct (but interrelated) parts. The fovea, located in the center of the retina of each eye, is a small area that provides clear, sharp vision (visual acuity) for detecting detail (such as print on a page) and discriminating colors under conditions of adequate illumination. When people position their eyes to look at an object, that object is in their central field of view and forms an image on the fovea in each eye. The retinal area surrounding the fovea is called the peripheral retina and does not provide good resolution of detail or good color discrimination. However, the peripheral retina can respond to stimuli under conditions of very dim illumination, and serves an alerting or orienting function for the visual system by detecting stimuli outside the central field of view. For example, the sudden appearance of a moving car at the edge of the visual field attracts the observer's attention and may produce an orienting response of the head and eyes to examine the object in more detail with foveal vision.

Deaf people may depend on this alerting/orienting function of the peripheral retina even more than hearing people do. A deaf person, attending to information in central vision, must rely almost exclusively on peripheral vision to monitor stimuli and events taking place in the peripheral environment. However, a hearing person can use the auditory system, in addition to peripheral vision, to detect peripheral stimuli. The information provided by peripheral vision has obvious adaptive significance for the deaf individual, and the greater dependence of deaf people on peripheral vision may lead to the development of differences in the functioning of the peripheral visual system. Research indicates that while deaf and hearing subjects are similar in general ability to detect and respond to peripheral stimuli, deaf subjects appear to be better able to change the focus of attention from one part of the peripheral visual field to another, while simultaneously monitoring a foveal stimulus. That is, if the observer is presented with foveal information and simultaneously a stimulus appears in some area of peripheral vision, deaf subjects seem to be better able to redirect their attention to the unexpected location of the peripheral stimulus. This greater flexibility in redirecting peripheral visual attention, in the presence of competing foveal information, may be one of the developmental consequences of increased reliance on peripheral vision for maintaining contact with peripheral environmental stimuli.

TACTUAL PERCEPTION

The tactual system can provide a deaf person with vibratory information that a hearing person would detect auditorily, as well as other information such as the surface quality (texture, hardness), shape, and weight of environmental objects. As with vision, the tactual system in deaf persons might reveal either areas of deficiency or the development of superior abilities, in partial compensation for deafness. Unfortunately, there is very little research with deaf subjects on tactual sensitivity and perception. There is research to indicate that deaf subjects are more sensitive to vibration (vibrotactile sensitivity) and better able to detect tactually the separation between two points (two-point threshold) than hearing subjects. However, other measures of tactual sensitivity, including discrimination of roughness or surface texture, shape discrimination, and tactual-vision comparisons for object identification, have revealed equivalent performance by deaf and hearing subjects. The greater vibrotactile sensitivity of deaf subjects may represent the compensatory development of a higher level of attunement or attention to vibration, since many sound-emitting objects in the environment (such as moving objects or objects emitting high-intensity or low-frequency sounds) can be detected in the form of tactile vibrations.

Research has also been conducted on tactile displays that aid in speech perception by deaf people. These electromechanical devices analyze the acoustic features of the speech signal, and display these features to the deaf user as coded patterns of vibrotactile stimulation. (Similarly, visual displays have been developed to represent speech in the form of luminous patterns of lines or dots presented, for example, through eyeglasses.) Currently, there are some potentially useful tactile and visual systems being developed, such as display systems for cued speech. Research on tactile (and visual) aids indicate that they have not been successful in significantly improving speech perception by deaf people in everyday communication. A basic reason for this lack of success is that the tactile and visual systems are limited in discriminating a rapid, sequential flow of stimulation in comparison with the auditory system. However, it may be possible to overcome this limitation, to some extent, by devices that represent higher-order units of articulation through patterns of tactile (or visual) stimulation. *See* MOUTH-HAND SYSTEMS: Cued Speech; SENSORY AIDS.

CONCLUSIONS

There is no consistent trend in the results from research on perception with deaf subjects. Deficiency, or a developmental lag, has been found for certain vision problems (ophthalmological), visual memory for sequentially presented stimuli, field independence, persistence of preference for color over form in figure-matching tasks, and shape discrimination. Equivalence of deaf and hearing subjects has been reported for visual memory for simultaneously presented stimuli, Stroop effect interference in color naming, detection of peripheral stimuli, and tactual discrimination of surface texture and object shape. Deaf subjects have been found to perform at a superior level in comparison with normally hearing subjects in color discrimination, redirecting attention to peripheral visual stimuli, vibrotactile sensitivity, and two-point tactual discrimination ability. This pattern of research results indicates that generalizations about the perceptual abilities of deaf individuals are not justified. Perceptual deficiency, equivalence, and compensatory superiority are a function of individual differences and the nature of the perceptual/cognitive task or situation.

Bibliography

Furth, H. G.: "Linguistic Deficiency and Thinking: Research with Deaf Subjects, 1964–1969," *Psychological Bulletin*, 76:58–72, 1971.

Hoemann, H.: "Perception by the Deaf," in E. Carterette and M. Friedman (eds.), *Handbook of Perception*. vol. 10: *Perceptual Ecology*, Academic Press, New York, 1978.

Parasnis, I.: "Visual Perceptual Skills and Deafness: A Research Review," *Journal of the Academy of Rehabilitative Audiology*, 16:148–160, 1983.

Reynolds, H. N.: "Perceptual Effects of Deafness," in R. D. Walk and H. L. Pick (eds.), *Perception and Experience*, Plenum Press, New York, 1978.

H. N. Reynolds

PERFORMING ARTS

The developing interest and pride of the deaf community in their own culture and language, or modality of expression, is highly significant. When deaf persons can identify with their deaf counterparts on stage, television, and the movies, it serves to remove the "stigma" and "stereotype" of deafness. They discover a new self-image and develop greater confidence and a more positive attitude toward life and society. It also encourages them to seek other role models in the performing arts.

PERFORMING ARTISTS

In many ways, deaf persons as individuals have blazed new pathways in the performing arts for others to follow. One of these individuals is Bernard Bragg. He studied mime with Marcel Marceau in Paris and then toured the United States with his one-man show in many of the best night clubs and theaters. His numerous television appearances include his own weekly show *The Quiet Man* in San Francisco (1960–62), frequent appearances on BBC programs in England, and guest spots on television talk shows in the United States. Bragg also helped to establish the National Theatre of the Deaf (NTD) and was one of its brightest stars for over 10 years. The publication of his biography, *Signs of Silence* (1974), by Helen Powers, is an inspiration for all deaf youth. *See* BRAGG, BERNARD.

Another performer who often appeared on television was Linda Bove. A member of NTD since 1968, she played a leading role in productions of the Little Theatre of the Deaf. Moreover, she was the first deaf person to be seen in the daytime television serial *Search For Tomorrow* (1973); she later became a permanent member of the popular children's program *Sesame Street*. She had the lead role in *Children of a Lesser God* during the years when the national touring company performed in the United States and Canada, and she also had a role in a full-length Sesame Street movie, *Follow That Bird* (1984). By communicating with "hands that talk," Linda Bove has helped develop deaf awareness and shown how deaf individuals can contribute to the world of entertainment. *See* BOVE, LINDA.

For deaf people, the biggest breakthrough in the theater world occurred in June 1980, when deaf Phyllis Frelich, a former member of NTD, won the Antoinette Perry ("Tony") Award for best actress in the play *Children of a Lesser God*. The original production also featured two other deaf persons in supporting roles, Lewis Merkin and Julianna Gold. Frelich's achievement not only proved that a talented deaf person could succeed on Broadway if given the opportunity, but also opened the door to other deaf performing artists. The long-running Broadway play was so successful that several other professional companies were formed to take it to theaters outside New York City. In each of these, a deaf actress played the leading role of "Sarah Norman." The national touring company, playing in major cities throughout the United States and Canada, featured Linda Bove; the second national touring group had Freda Norman in the lead role; and the London (England) company starred Liz Quinn. Other groups have since played in Australia and South Africa, and repeat performances continued to captivate audiences in regional theaters throughout the United States. Altogether, scores of deaf persons have been employed in leading or supporting roles or as understudies and substitutes. The film rights to the play were purchased by a Hollywood production company in 1984. *See* FRELICH, PHYLLIS.

A few people who had acquired hearing impairments had already made an impact in Hollywood before Frelich and Bove. Among them were Nanette Fabray and Johnnie Ray, both of whom had the unusual distinction of being singers. *See* FABRAY, NANETTE; RAY, JOHNNIE.

TELEVISION

One of the first profoundly deaf persons to appear on prime-time television was Audree (Bennett) Norton, who had toured nationally with the NTD. Norton had a featured role in *Mannix* (1968), a detective series starring Mike Connors. It was a drama in which Norton not only was the heroine but also exposed audiences to deaf awareness and deaf culture (it was probably the first time in a television show that a flashing light bulb was used to draw attention to a ringing doorbell). She also portrayed a deaf character on the police show *Streets of San Francisco* (1971).

On November 15, 1971, Jane (Norman) Wilk and Peter Wechsberg, both former members of the NTD, started the first television program with profoundly deaf newscasters. This was *NewSign Four*, a daily news program integrated with the *Today Show* in the early morning for deaf persons in the San Francisco Bay area. Wilk and Wechsberg used sign language and fingerspelling to communicate the news of the world, as well as "what was happening and where" in the local deaf community. *NewSign Four* proved so successful that it was honored with an Emmy Award.

A second Emmy Award went to Wechsberg in 1973 for his documentary television film *My Eyes Are My Ears*, which featured success stories of deaf people who contributed to the cultural, educational, and economic growth of California. In 1975 Wechsberg established *Sign-Scope*, a motion picture production company in Portland, Oregon. This led to the production of a full-length movie in Technicolor, *Deafula*—a deaf-culture parody of the classic horror film *Dracula*. It proved that deaf performing artists could be inventive and versatile, for Wechsberg not only wrote the script but also directed the movie and played the leading role. He later followed this with another comedy, *Think Me Nothing*, which also featured deaf performers spoofing trendsetters and deaf culture.

Deaf culture was the focus of another West Coast venture into television programming for deaf and hearing viewers in 1975 when D.E.A.F. Media, Inc., produced *Silent Perspectives*, which acquainted the public with deaf people and their culture; it won an Emmy Award.

This led to the creation of an original and imaginative program for deaf children, *Rainbow's End* (1980), featuring a magical television studio where a group of people, most of them deaf, produce television shows. The star attraction of *Rainbow's End* was Freda (Norman) Peterson, another NTD leading lady. The series, which was funded by the Bureau of Education of the Handicapped, U.S. Office of Education, and developed in cooperation with television stations in San Mateo and San Francisco, also stressed creative approaches to teaching English visually to deaf children. It was the first program of its kind, winning an Emmy Award in 1980 and the hope of deaf people everywhere that it would have continued production as a deaf version of *Sesame Street*.

Los Angeles took pride in displaying its own television celebrity in the person of Herb Larsen, called "the deaf Johnny Carson." As host of *Off-Hand*, celebrity talk show, Larsen captivated deaf and hearing viewers as a master of ceremonies and as a stand-up comic for the half-hour show seen weekly in Los Angeles and on the Silent Network Satellite Service. His co-host and interpreter was Lou Fant, the hearing son of deaf parents, who helped establish the National Theatre of the Deaf and later had a long list of television and film credits as an actor. By the end of 1984, *Off-Hand* had a string of 200 performances, produced by Silent Network. Created by Sheldon Altfeld, the Los Angeles-based company is dedicated to producing nationwide television programming that showcases deaf talent and deaf culture.

COMEDIANS

Two people who put deaf culture to use in original and creative ways were George Johnston and Mary Beth Miller. Johnston, a gifted impressionist, could mimic almost any well-known personage, deaf or hearing, and could sing and dance with perfect timing to suit the comedy situation. Also, he could depict "the deaf Archie Bunker" using the mannerisms, hang-ups, and folklore peculiar to deaf people and their culture. Featuring his one-man *Gee Jay Show* (named for his initials), Johnston's repertory of deaf jokes and skits, his improvisations in pantomime and slapstick comedy, and his catchy song and dance numbers were a great success.

Mary Beth Miller had distinguished herself as a popular comedian and dramatic actress with the NTD Company before going freelance and then helping to found the New York Deaf Theatre. For the latter, she wrote and directed performances of *Travelling Road Show* and *A Play of 1,000 Words*, also performing in both as the major character. Her talents for mimicry and dramatic monologue, comedy sketches, and slapstick earned her nationwide acclaim whenever she went on tours of the United States and Canada.

CHILD STARS

It was inevitable that by the 1970s an increasing number of stage, screen, and television productions should feature deaf child and teenage performers. The first of these to have a featured role on the Broadway stage was the 17-year-old Bruce Hlibok, who portrayed "Hubbell," the deaf teenage rebel in the musical *Runaways* (1978). He "sang" in fluent and eloquent sign language; always on stage with Hlibok was his interpreter, who provided voice-over as well as signs for those scenes when he was off stage. It marked the first time in New York theater history that deaf audiences could follow and fully understand an interpreted musical, thereby serving as a model or prototype for the New York Theatre Access Project of sign-interpreted performances for deaf people, which began in 1980. *Runaways* captured five Tony Award nominations.

In 1979 10-year-old Jeffrey Bravin, the deaf son of deaf parents, had the featured role in the movie *And Your Name Is Jonah*. As "Jonah," Bravin enacted the all-too-common story of a boy who is diagnosed as mentally retarded but later discovered to be deaf. Bravin's co-star was Sally Struthers, the movie and television celebrity; the film also featured other deaf persons, including its consultant, Bernard Bragg, all of whom provided realistic situations and environments to convey "the deaf experience" in what was probably the best-made and most honest movie on the subject up to that time.

Other teenagers appearing in television dramas were Kevin Van Wieringen as "Scott Phillips" in an episode of the series *James At 15* (1978). Another was 13-year-old Johnny Kovacs, who appeared in six episodes of the series *Second Family Tree* (1983). Kovacs, who is the son of deaf parents, also played "the Wild Boy," who is mute (not deaf) and needs to communicate in sign language in an episode of the television adventure drama series *Little House On the Prairie* (1982).

In 1982 15-year-old Otto Rechenberg appeared

in movie theaters throughout the United States in *Amy*. Originally titled *Amy-on-the-Lips*, the movie was an adaptation of a short story, "Why It Was W-on-the-Eyes," by Margaret Montague, a teacher of deaf children. The film also featured Nanette Fabray.

If anyone ever loomed larger than life on both the movie and television screen, it was "the Incredible Hulk" of Lou Ferrigno. Born and raised in Brooklyn, New York, he developed an ear infection at age three that caused a severe hearing loss and made learning to speak quite difficult. Ferrigno was called "dumb Louie" by his peers and grew up shy and withdrawn, and a skinny weakling. However, he took up body-building and developed into a tall, muscular man. His first movie appearance was in the classic film on body-building, *Pumping Iron*, in which he co-starred with Arnold Schwarzenegger. Like Schwarzenegger, Ferrigno was a champion body-builder, having won both the "Mr. America" and "Mr. Universe" titles. He then went on to win international fame as "the Incredible Hulk" in the weekly television adventure drama. He also had the lead role in the Italian remake of the epic film *Hercules* (1983), and made frequent appearances in various serials.

Equally exciting and daring was the career of Kitty O'Neil, deaf from infancy, who has been called "Hollywood's most amazing stunt woman." For many years, O'Neil was a "stand-in" for Hollywood and television actresses whenever the scene proved dangerous. Her roles included substituting for Linda Carter in *Wonder Woman* and for Lindsay Wagner in *The Bionic Woman*. O'Neil, who was a platform diving champion as well as the holder of many speed racing records for women (she set the world land speed record for a woman in 1976), also was featured in the television movie *Silent Victory: The Kitty O'Neil Story* (1979). Although Hollywood actress Stockard Channing played the title role, O'Neil performed all the stunts herself.

DANCE

Some deaf persons have excelled in dance. Two individuals bear special mention—Helen Heckman and Frances Woods. During the mid-1920s, Heckman impressed audiences in small night clubs of various European cities with her interpretive dances. Despite total deafness from infancy, she spoke with natural speech qualities—accent, modulation, inflection, rhythm. Her talents, her dedication to hard work and practice, and her intuitive sense of timing and artistry of body movement she transformed into dance. All this she recounts in her autobiography, *My Life Transformed* (1928).

Probably the greatest individual achievement by a deaf person in the field of dance was made by Frances Woods, named Esther Thomas at birth. A premature baby, she weighed only two pounds and was born without ear drums; the doctors did not expect her to live. However, she survived, grew up to be very athletic, and developed a fine sense of rhythm for dancing. It was on the dance floor that she met her future husband, Anthony Caliguire, who began teaching her to dance by playing the piano, getting her to feel the rhythm of the music, and then having her perform the dance steps to follow the particular rhythm. *See* WOODS, FRANCES.

One of the first deaf dance groups was the American Deaf Dance Company (ADDC). With Yacov Sharir, a normal-hearing dancer, as their artistic director, the ADDC developed a unique set of dance numbers without the use of music which impressed audiences by their visual and intuitively conceived rhythms. A talented group of deaf professionals, the ADDC made several successful tours of the United States, and also conducted workshops and training programs in cooperation with the Summer School of the NTD.

Another major dance theater group is Musign (an acronym of "music" and "sign"), featuring a talented quartet of deaf professional performers—Rita Corey, Bob Hiltermann, Ed Chevy, and Marjorie Tanzar. Musign went on national tours in the fall of 1982, after debuting at the World's Fair in Knoxville, Tennessee. They have performed in New York City's Lincoln Center, gone on two tours of the Far East, make numerous appearances on television, and won the Theatre Critics Circle Award, San Francisco, in 1983. Based in Berkeley, California, Musign has created an original form of visual music using sign language, mime, and dance to interpret an ever-changing variety of popular songs. The result is a fast-stepping musical revue, punctuated with unusual lighting effects and costumes, which is captivating and appealing to hearing and deaf audiences.

THEATERS OF DEAF PEOPLE

The National Theatre of the Deaf (NTD) has helped awaken the public to deaf awareness. Since its establishment in 1967, NTD has influenced millions of hearing people throughout the world, in the theater and on television. In their hands, the sign language of deaf people is transformed into a form of visual expression that paints pictures in the air. Similarly, NTD has presented deafness in positive ways to people unfamiliar with it; they have dramatized the deaf experience with honest realism. The same is true of the Little Theatre of the Deaf, which dramatizes fables, folklore, and poetry. *See* NATIONAL THEATERS OF THE DEAF: United States.

Although most deaf people in the United States live in metropolitan areas, their handicap excludes them from many of the cultural arts programs enjoyed by hearing people in their localities. This includes many residential schools for deaf students as well as public schools and colleges in which deaf students are mainstreamed or integrated with hearing students. To meet this cultural lag, an unusual touring company was initiated in 1980 at the National Technical Institute for the Deaf (NTID), called Sunshine Too.

A complement to the established NTID Educational Theatre program which involves both deaf and hearing students on campus, Sunshine Too enjoys the status of a professional traveling show that gives performances and workshops in public schools for deaf children, and colleges, as well as offering evening programs for deaf and hearing adults and their families. Sunshine Too productions include one-act plays, mime, personal stories and monologues, poetry, song, and even an introduction to sign language and deafness. Every production is done in sign language and voice by deaf and hearing performers who have traveled around the United States and Canada over the years, and performances have been enthusiastically received by audiences of all ages. See NATIONAL TECHNICAL INSTITUTE FOR THE DEAF; THEATER, COLLEGE.

Community theaters of the deaf are doing activities similar to those of Sunshine Too in metropolitan centers. Among the more active groups in years past were the New York Theatre Guild of the 1930s; the New York Hebrew Association of the Deaf's Drama Guild of the 1940s; the Chicago Silent Dramatic Club of the 1940s; the Bay Area Players of San Francisco-Oakland in the 1950s, and Spectrum Deaf Theatre of Austin Texas in the 1970s.

Beginning with the 1960s there was an increasing number of deaf community theaters, some of which became so successful in point of longevity as to become models for other newcomers. Probably the best organized and most famous of these was the Hughes Memorial Theatre based in Washington, D.C., which evolved from the Dramatics Guild of the District of Columbia Club of the Deaf, starting in 1959. The Hughes Memorial Theatre offers stage productions of vintage and popular plays, from serious drama to comedies and musicals. Another community theater, begun in 1979, was the New York Deaf Theatre, Ltd. Equally active was the Fairmount Theatre of the Deaf of Cleveland, Ohio, which began as a community theater in 1980 but later matured to become the only other professional deaf theater in the country other than NTD; it was widely acclaimed by deaf and hearing audiences wherever they performed. See FAIRMOUNT THEATRE OF THE DEAF.

SIGNED PERFORMANCES

Yet another attempt to eliminate cultural barriers and create equal opportunities for deaf people to derive the same kind of "theater experience" as hearing patrons do is the dedicated work of organizations providing special sign-interpreted performances.

One of the first to offer this service was Project D.A.T.E. (Deaf Audience Theatre Encounter) which began in December 1978 at the Mark Taper Forum, Los Angeles, with 35 deaf persons attending a performance of A Christmas Carol. Although the performance was not interpreted in sign, a post-play discussion was, and as a result of the dialogue and feedback with the deaf community, D.A.T.E. developed a viable program. Thereafter, two performances of each of the five events in the annual season of plays were sign-interpreted. Also included were advance summary workshops and post-play discussions. Project D.A.T.E. could also be considered as the springboard for the production of Children of a Lesser God which premiered at the Mark Taper Forum on October 29, 1979. Coordinator for the project was Joe Castronovo, a deaf actor and performing arts administrator who was also a former member of the NTD.

As the result of a survey made in 1979 by the Theatre Development Fund (TDF) of New York City, a program known as the Theatre Access Project (TAP), supported by TDF general operating funds, was set up to serve deaf people who strongly expressed the need for interpreted performances. For the December 2, 1980, signed performance of Elephant Man, 82 deaf persons bought tickets and attended. Since then, over 22 popular shows have been interpreted at various Broadway and off-Broadway theaters, among them: A Chorus Line, Annie, Amadeus, Pirates of Penzance, On Your Toes, and Dreamgirls—an average of six such performances per year.

With the encouragement and assistance of Ann Silver, a deaf person who has long been active in promoting theater and cultural programs for deaf people in New York City, even the New York City Opera featured an interpreted performance of The Merry Widow in the fall of 1983; this operatta was sung in English and signed in American Sign Language. Later, they presented a sign-interpreted production of the tragic opera Susannah, which drew a large audience of deaf people. Deaf theatergoers now have the option of play selection and the opportunity to become regular theater patrons.

Bibliography

Brown, Ruth S.: "TAP Sign Interpreted Performances Start Fifth Year," Silent News, January, 1985.

"Deaf Theatre Goers in Los Angeles Enjoy Varied Program" (news item), NAD Broadcaster, November/December 1979.

Heckman, Helen: My Life Transformed, Macmillan, New York, 1928.

"Introducing Herb Larsen," *Silent Network* (publicity brochure), Beverly Hills, California, Winter 1984–85.

"Johnny Kovacs: New Deaf TV Star," *World Around You*, vol. 4 no. 8, December 16, 1982.

Panara, Robert: "Cultural Arts Among Deaf People," *Gallaudet Today*, Washington, D.C., Spring 1983.

————, and John Panara: *Great Deaf Americans*, T.J. Publishers, Inc., Silver Spring, Maryland, 1983.

"Rainbows End" (publicity brochure), D.E.A.F. Media, Inc., Oakland, California, 1981.

Swain, Robert: "Deaf Teenage: A Runaway Success," *Deaf American*, January 1979.

Robert Panara

GALLAUDET DANCERS

The Gallaudet Dancers is a performing dance company composed of hearing-impaired students at Gallaudet College. The company has given live performances throughout the United States and abroad, and has appeared on television in the United States. Data from the national television networks indicate that over 100 million television viewers have witnessed the Gallaudet Dancers in performance. They continue to be important emissaries for Gallaudet College and the deaf community. *See* GALLAUDET COLLEGE.

Early Years The Gallaudet Dancers were established in 1955 by Peter Wisher, a Gallaudet College basketball coach and physical education teacher. Wisher had studied dance under the leading dancers of that era, such as Martha Graham, Doris Humphrey, Hanya Halen, and José Limon. When he arrived at Gallaudet College, there were no dance classes or dance organizations on campus. The prevailing philosophy seemed to be that since deaf people could not hear they could not dance. After witnessing a group signing the Lord's Prayer at a religious service, Wisher concluded that since deaf people are used to communicating with movement, dance could prove to be a prime activity for them. Moreover, the enthusiastic response of the students upon being introduced to dance inspired further exploration of dance and its effects upon hearing-impaired young people.

When the performing dance group was established in the fall of 1955, membership was on a voluntary basis and was limited to hearing-impaired students. Since the dancers at that time were novices, techniques and choreography were kept on an elementary level. However, a new art form was introduced: dances based on signs. Inasmuch as hearing dancers abstract human gestures in composing dances, it follows that deaf persons could abstract signs in their choreographic efforts. This form of expression made an impact on hearing audiences. Invitations to perform poured in from schools, churches, national organizations, television networks, and foreign countries.

Due to the many invitations to appear at pres-tigious events, it became necessary to terminate the voluntary aspect of the group. To be a member, students had to forego all extracurricular activities that might interfere with rehearsals, travel, and appearances. The media kept referring to the group as the Gallaudet Dancers. Members of the company felt that it was an appropriate name and adopted it.

Performances Over the years the dancers have appeared with countless national celebrities—individuals as diverse as entertainers Nanette Fabray and Ray Charles, athletes Hank Aaron and Nancy Lopez, and politicians Lyndon Johnson and Andrew Young. They have appeared on television programs such as the *Mike Douglas Show*, *60 Minutes*, *P.M. Magazine*, *Panorama*, and *Evening Magazine*, and performed at the National Democratic Convention in 1968 and at the Presidential inaugural ceremonies in 1980 at the Kennedy Center. The Gallaudet Dancers have traveled abroad, giving performances in France, Israel, England, Denmark, Peru, Canada, and Costa Rica.

The experience gained in the Gallaudet Dance troupe has benefited its alumni. Several former dancers, for instance, have appeared in the television programs *Fame*, *Sesame Street*, and *Happy Days*, and in the award-winning play *Children of a Lesser God*. The group's success also has prompted others to support deaf dancers. Subsequently, several performers and organizations have sponsored deaf dance groups, such as Jacques D'Amboise, Edward Vilella, and the Joffrey Ballet.

Instruction One of the most essential considerations in dance for deaf people is the method of accompaniment, both in learning new rhythmic patterns and in performing. One instrument seems to satisfy all levels of hearing loss—the drum. Everyone can either feel or hear its beat, and once patterns are mastered music can replace the drum. Many of the group's most successful dances, however, have been performed without musical accompaniment; feelings and moods set the quality and duration of appropriate movements.

Advantage is taken of those dancers with some residual hearing. Because they can follow the rhythm of various kinds of accompaniment, they are sometimes given leadership roles. The profoundly deaf members, in turn, respond to visual cues, and hand signals are used to help them establish the required rhythm. Once the basic rhythm is perceived by the dancers, they do not seem to have a problem maintaining it throughout the number being performed.

Contrary to popular opinion, deaf dancers do not follow rhythm by feeling vibrations in the floor. Standing still and with a proper floor, dancers can sense vibrations; however, when they move through space this contact is lost. The Gallaudet Dancers, therefore, are not limited to particular dancing surfaces. They have performed on bare ground, brick, concrete, and wooden stages.

Significance The success of the Gallaudet Dancers has important implications. For one thing, it indicates that deaf students are intensely interested in dance. The Gallaudet Dancers have been willing to sacrifice much during their college years to participate in the troupe. Dancing provides a means to express feelings and emotions; it takes advantage of deaf people's interest in body movements; it is intensely visual; and it provides an opportunity to interrelate with others.

The ability of the Gallaudet Dancers to project abstract conceptions is significant, too. Some studies of deaf people have questioned their competence to conceptualize and think abstractly, but—while the dancers may not be typical of the general deaf population—their performances certainly indicate that, through body movement, they can express abstract notions. Dance provides a communication medium that does not depend upon oral language skills, and hence is equally accessible to those who hear and those who are deaf. *See* INTELLIGENCE.

For the participants themselves, the experience of performing with the Gallaudet Dancers has had several benefits. Among the rewards listed by members have been the value of physical and mental exercise, the opportunity to learn rhythmic body movement, the acquisition of new communication skills, the chance to show that deaf people can succeed in a field dominated by hearing people, assistance in overcoming self-consciousness, and the rewards of performance and travel. As a former member said in a letter to the troupe's director: "My four years with the dance group were the best years of my life. I miss it."

Peter A. Wisher

PERIODICALS

When Johann Gutenberg invented movable type in the 1400s, he did not realize what a favor he was doing deaf people. Printing became a leading trade and an excellent occupation for deaf people in the United States. This development led naturally to the publication of periodicals by and for deaf people, and moreover to specialized print media including information about various aspects of deafness.

History

Residential schools for deaf people in the United States were probably the first to offer vocational training programs. Soon after many of these schools were founded, they acquired some type and manually powered presses and began teaching their students the printing trade. These schools were very proud of their printing capabilities, and many documents began appearing with the school's "Printing Office" by-line. These print shops produced most of the school's printing, including annual reports, stationery, and complicated forms.

DEAF PRINTERS

The experience and excellent training that deaf students acquired in these school print shops led many of them into well-paying positions on large metropolitan newspapers, on smaller dailies, and in commercial shops.

For years deaf printers labored over California job cases, handsetting stick after stick, galley after galley of type. Deaf printers were fast and accurate, and had a high level of concentration. Then came Merganthaler's Linotype, a machine with some 3000 moving parts, on which an operator could quickly cast a slug, or line, of type by typing on a keyboard. This new invention threatened to put many deaf printers out of business (and indeed, did so) because the owners were reluctant to entrust such a complicated and expensive machine to a person who could not hear it. But some deaf printers rose to the challenge, learned how to operate the Linotype, and became fast and skilled. Schools began acquiring the new typesetting machine, and soon the Linotype was also providing an excellent livelihood for deaf printers. There are no known statistics on the number of deaf printers in the United States, but when Linotype was at its peak probably every large metropolitan newspaper in the United States had at least one deaf printer.

LITTLE PAPER FAMILY

With access to a print shop and a need to keep their students occupied in a hands-on, meaningful way, many schools began publishing their own periodicals. Most periodicals began appearing in newspaper formats and later changed to magazine formats. Many originally were printed monthly, but as the typesetting skills of the students improved, a number began appearing more frequently. By the 1890s at least 3 schools were publishing daily newspapers and more than 30 were printing weeklies.

These school publications were used to teach and encourage good writing skills, to provide the students with an opportunity to write for publication, and to reward them with the thrill of seeing their names in print. Some of these students later became writers, editors, and journalists. *See* LITTLE PAPER FAMILY.

COMMUNITY PUBLICATIONS

Levi Backus, a graduate of the American School for the Deaf where he was taught by Laurent Clerc, is credited with starting the first commercially produced newspaper for the deaf community. He was editor and proprietor of the weekly *Canajoharie* (New York) *Radii.* He began printing a news column of interest to local deaf citizens. (*Canajoharie* was initially the location of the Central New York School for the Deaf.) Backus later received an appropriation from the New York legislature to mail the newspaper to deaf people in the state. *See* CLERC, LAURENT.

In 1860 the *Gallaudet Guide and Deaf-Mutes' Companion* began appearing monthly. It was the first publication devoted exclusively to deaf readers and was edited by William M. Chamberlain and printed in Boston. It served as the official organ of the New England Gallaudet Association of the Deaf.

About 1870, Henry C. Rider began publishing the *Deaf-Mutes' Journal.* This became the first weekly newspaper of the deaf community, and the New York School for the Deaf later assumed its publication.

The first attempt at a literary magazine for the deaf community was started in Washington, D.C., in 1871 by Melville Ballard, John B. Hotchkiss, Joseph P. Parkinson, and James Denison, and was named the *Silent World.* It did not catch on and ceased publication after five years.

The *National Exponent* appeared in 1894. Published by O. H. Regensburg in Chicago, it had some well-known deaf writers on its staff, among them Robert P. McGregor, James H. Cloud, J. Schuyler Long, George W. Veditz, and James E. Gallaher. It reached a circulation of 1200, but folded after two years. *See* VEDITZ, GEORGE WILLIAM.

In 1887 the *Silent Worker* made its debut at the New Jersey School for the Deaf. The *Silent Worker* ceased publication in 1929, but was revived in 1948 as the official organ of the National Association of the Deaf. The magazine had a succession of editors, including Bill R. White, Loel F. Schreiber, and Byron B. Burnes. In 1949 Jess M. Smith, vice-president of the National Association of the Deaf and a teacher at the Tennessee School for the Deaf, assumed the editorship of the magazine. It was printed for a while at the Tennessee School for the Deaf and at Pettingill's Printcraft, a commercial print shop in Idaho owned by Don G. Pettingill. In 1964 the *Silent Worker* was renamed the *Deaf American,* and in 1980 the editorship was transferred to the National Association of the Deaf's home office in Maryland. The National Association had also begun publishing the *NAD Broadcaster,* a tabloid newspaper, in 1979. *See* DEAF AMERICAN.

The *American Deaf Citizen* made its debut in 1929 (the same year the *Silent Worker* ceased publication), and was edited by Roy B. Conkling and printed in Ohio. It ceased publication in 1942.

In 1937 Leo Lewis, a printer and the president of the Texas Association of the Deaf, began publishing the *Modern Silents.* It was a high-quality magazine with modern design and was comparable in quality to the old *Silent Worker.* Unfortunately, it too ceased publication after only two years.

In 1938 Willard H. Woods began publishing the *Digest of the Deaf.* It had a format similar to the *Reader's Digest* and focused on the accomplishments of deaf people in the arts, sciences, and industry. It was edited by Woods and Eleanor E. Sherman. Charles Moscovitz was the managing editor and Florence B. Crammatte associate editor. Guilbert C. Braddock, Petra F. Howard, Wesley Lauritsen, Margaret E. Jackson, and Howard L. Terry, most of them well-known writers during their time, were among the contributing editors. It folded in 1940. *See* TERRY, HOWARD L.

In the 1940s the *Silent Cavalier* appeared. It was started as an organ of the Virginia Association of the Deaf by Reuben Alitzer. When the newspaper was moved to Washington, D.C., Allan B. Crammatte became editor and turned it into one of the most vocal newspapers of its day, and "Silent" was dropped from its flag. The *Cavalier* acquired the *Silent Broadcaster* and the mailing list of the old *Deaf-Mutes' Journal* and grew into a national newspaper. At its peak it had over 4000 paid subscribers.

The *Cavalier* was later sold to Edgar M. Winecoff and Luther Bunn and moved to North Carolina, where it was merged with the *Southerner* and Troy Hill's *American Deaf News* to become the *National Observer.* The *Observer* ceased publication in 1956.

In 1969 the *Silent News,* a tabloid, appeared. It was published by Julius Wiggins and his wife, printed in their shop in New Jersey, and edited by Walter M. Schulman. It quickly grew in circulation, and now it appears monthly and has news about the deaf community from across the United States. *See* SILENT NEWS.

In the early 1970s Clarence Suppala of Beaverton, Oregon, began publishing a small, typewritten, collated, and stapled newsletter named the *Deaf Spectrum.* The *Spectrum* was probably the closest thing to muckraking the deaf community has seen. The state of education of deaf children, especially in Oregon, and the heavy emphasis on oral education in the United States was a favorite *Spectrum* topic, and the editor attacked the subject with relish. It was a pro–total communication supporter and a very strong advocate of the rights of deaf people. This little newsletter attracted quite a national audience, mostly readers who agreed with Supalla and admired his spunk. It folded in 1979. *See* SOCIOLINGUISTICS: Total Communication.

Ye Silent Crier, the *Empire State News,* and the *WAD Pilot* are among the oldest state publications. The *Deaf Episcopalian* and the *Deaf Lutheran* are among the oldest religious publications appearing today.

The *Dee Cee Eyes*, published by the Metropolitan Washington (D.C.) Association of the Deaf, is perhaps the oldest club periodical in continuous publication. It was started by Frederick C. Schreiber in 1961.

There are over 500 publications related to deafness in existence today. In recent years the deaf community has seen the appearance of such special-interest publications as *Black Deaf News*, the *Deaf Angler*, and the *Deaf Skier*. Over 60 have used the word "silent" in their flag. Publications have appeared with such names as *Helping Hands*, *Listen*, *Listener*, *Listening*, *Light for the Deaf*, *Out of the Chatterbox*, *Sights and Sounds*, *Sign Language*, *Sign Waves*, *Silent Success*, *Silent Optimist*, and *Vibrations*.

The *Ranch Hand*, a colorful religious newspaper published at the Bill Rice Ranch in Murfreesboro, Tennessee, is probably the most widely disseminated publication in the deaf community, with a circulation of around 100,000. Other leading national publications today are the *Deaf American*, the *Silent News*, the *NAD Broadcaster*, the *American Annals of the Deaf*, the *Volta Review*, the *Gallaudet Alumni Newsletter*, the *Frat*, the *NTID Focus*, and *Gallaudet Today*.

Jack R. Gannon

Specialized Print Media

Deaf people in the United States have tended to develop specialized print media. This section deals with publications that are largely about deafness and that view it from the perspective of particular diciplines, which are numerous and varied because deafness affects every aspect of life.

Historically, the oldest, continuously published educational journal in the United States dedicated to deafness is the *American Annals of the Deaf*, which first appeared in 1847, and except for the period of the Civil War, has been distributed every year since. *See* AMERICAN ANNALS OF THE DEAF.

Social scientists in the United States have been interested in deafness almost from the inception of their field. Psychologists published articles about the testing of deaf children before Binet's pioneering assessment of the intelligence of Parisian schoolchildren was translated into English. Linguists directed their attention to the sign language of deaf people in the sixteenth century before they had invented the term linguistics. Similarly, very early concern with deafness can be found among rehabilitation and social workers, though not sociologists. Much of this attention is reflected in the periodicals erected to mirror the professional interest in deafness.

Interest in multiply handicapped deaf persons

was present a century ago. E. A. Fay wrote articles on mental retardation and deafness in issues of the *American Annals of the Deaf*, with the first appearing in 1879. In the same year, A. A. Fuller presented an article on deaf-blindness. Similar early evidence can be found for other areas of concern, such as psychometrics and the intercultural aspects of sign language. This means to professionals in the field that the periodical literature projects a picture of a continuity of interests that extends over a century and a half. *See* FAY, EDWARD ALLEN.

The periodical literature has helped deaf people to define their culture. That there is such an entity as the deaf community is evidenced by its printed record. The major associations of deaf people have depended upon periodicals to maintain contact with their constituents. As a result, these journals have assumed substantial influence in deaf people's social and political affairs. They not only record the events of interest to the community but also provide the forum for structuring future events. For example, the debate that led to reshaping the National Association of the Deaf's administration appeared in its periodical in the late 1950s, laying the groundwork for its reorganization in 1962 and 1964. Periodicals like the *Frat* and the *Deaf American* are edited and largely written by deaf people. Their content reflects the breadth of the deaf community, ranging from philosophical essays and scientific reports to news of beauty contests, social gatherings, and sporting events. Like periodicals of general circulation, periodicals in the deaf community vary from gossipy to profound, from bare announcements to thoughtful articles. *See* NATIONAL ASSOCIATION OF THE DEAF.

CLASSIFICATION

The major periodicals related to deafness and deaf people can be grouped under four headings: deaf affairs, communicology, education, and rehabilitation. Deaf affairs covers the social, political, and recreational lives of deaf people. Probably the most influential journals in this category are the *Frat* and the *Deaf American*. However, these two publications, which represent respectively the National Fraternal Society of the Deaf and the National Association of the Deaf, must share the sphere of influence with many state and local publications and the Little Paper Family. Without known exception, every organization that is concerned with the social lives of deaf people has a periodical, be it a monthly newsletter or a fairly elaborate journal. *See* LITTLE PAPER FAMILY.

Communicology is a term suggested by Wendell Johnson, a giant in the development of the speech and hearing professions in the United States. He wanted a term that would encompass the diverse points of view taken by acoustics, audiology, linguistics, otology, special education, speech pathology, speech science, and other disciplines that are concerned with human communication and the factors that disrupt it. The term did not catch on among the professionals, but it will serve for the limited purpose of bringing together journals dealing with the disruption of communication by deafness. The appropriate periodicals are: *American Speech; Annals of Otology, Rhinology, and Laryngology; Archives of Otolaryngology; Asha; Audecibel; Audiology and Hearing Education; Communication Outlook; Ear and Hearing; Ear, Nose and Throat Journal; Hearing Aid Journal; Human Communication Research; Journal of the Acoustical Society of America; Journal of Auditory Research; Journal of Communication Disorders; Journal of Speech and Hearing Disorders; Journal of Speech and Hearing Research; Laryngoscope; Otolaryngology and Head and Neck Surgery; Sign Language Studies;* and *Sound and Vibration.* The disciplines represented—acoustics, audiology, cybernetics, linguistics, otology, psycholinguistics, speech pathology, and so on—support the choice of the term communicology to cover their diversity, while indicating their link with deafness and related specialties.

While education could easily fit under communicology, it deserves separate consideration here because of the critical role it plays in the lives of early-deafened people. Education, or the lack of it, makes the difference between whether deafness is considered a disability or a handicap. Its pervasive influence on deaf people's lives is reflected in the numerous journals devoted to it. Important journals dealing with education of deaf persons are: *American Annals of the Deaf; Journal of the Canadian Association of Educators of the Hearing Impaired; Language, Speech and Hearing Services in the Schools; Teaching English to the Deaf;* and *Volta Review.* Both the *Annals* and the *Review* serve as forums for their respective sponsoring organizations, and they often contain material that moves beyond a strict construction of the term education, especially bringing to the fore the concerns of parents of deaf children. The other three journals are more specifically addressed to educators of deaf students.

Rehabilitation actually should be considered along with education and be placed with it into the category communicology, since both involve many of the same procedures under different names (training instead of instructing, and vocational evaluation rather than educational asessment) and hence attract persons with similar interests. However, in the United States, the social-welfare structure has a distinct place for services given to disabled adults, including those who are deaf. Journals devoted to rehabilitation include: *ACCD Action, American Rehabilitation, Journal of Rehabilitation of the Deaf,*

Rehabilitation Literature, and *Rehabilitation Psychology.* The only publication that deals exclusively with the rehabilitation of deaf persons is the *Journal of Rehabilitation of the Deaf,* which was founded in 1966 as the voice for professional rehabilitation workers with deaf adults (whose organization is now called the American Deafness and Rehabilitation Association). The other four journals have occasional articles about deafness, as well as articles dealing more broadly with the rehabilitation process as it influences and is influenced by various disability groups. *See* AMERICAN DEAFNESS AND REHABILITATION ASSOCIATION.

ABSTRACTING SERVICES
The information explosion has encouraged the parallel eruption of services to assist readers in locating relevant material. The problem confronting most literary searchers is how to eliminate masses of print that impede finding the specific items desired. Glut, not paucity, is the difficulty, and so abstracting services have emerged.

In 1960 Gallaudet College and the American Speech and Hearing Association established Deafness Speech and Hearing Publications, Inc., with a four-year grant from the Federal Office of Vocational Rehabilitation (the predecessor to the Rehabilitation Services Administration). The corporation used the grant funds to subsidize publication of *dsh Abstracts,* a quarterly journal of abstracts of the literature on deafness, speech, and hearing. The editors for the first volume, which was completed in October 1961, were Stephen P. Quigley and Jerome D. Schein.

The *dsh Abstracts* published nonevaluative summaries of the contents of relevant journal articles, books, monographs, and conference proceedings. No editorial comments about the materials abstracted were permitted, as the function of the journal was to inform, not criticize. The journal addressed students and professionals in disciplines that found its materials pertinent, such as audiologists, educators of hearing-impaired students, otolaryngologists, physiatrists, sensory and clinical psychologists, rehabilitators, speech pathologists, and sociologists. *See* DSH ABSTRACTS.

There are, of course, many other journals of abstracts and computerized data bases. These include *Abstracts for Social Workers, Child Development Abstracts and Bibliography, Exceptional Child Education Abstracts, Mental Retardation Abstracts,* and *Psychological Abstracts.* Among the computer-accessed services are *Educational Research Information Center (ERIC)* and *Psych Info.* Some are broad, encompassing whole disciplines, such as social work (*Abstracts for Social Workers*), psychology (*Psychological Abstracts*), and special education (*Exceptional Child Education Ab-*

stracts). Others follow a more specialized coverage, such as child development and mental retardation.

Jerome D. Schein

PERU

Peru is a South American country of about 496,000 square miles (1,290,000 square kilometers). The total population is slightly more than 17 million. The deaf people have their own organizations, are recognized by the national government as an important responsibility, and generally are educated according to models imported from Europe and from other nations of Latin America.

EDUCATIONAL HISTORY

Organized education of deaf Peruvians began in 1936. Paquita de Benavides, wife of the president, brought a group of Franciscan nuns from Spain to take charge of the first school for deaf pupils. The school was established on June 18, 1936, in Barranco, in accordance with the government's Supreme Resolution Number 283.

The Barranco school began as a boarding school and used sign language as the primary means of communication until the 1970s, when it converted to the oral method. In 1980 the boarding facilities were closed, and the buildings that had been used to house students were converted into workshops to provide vocational training. The Barranco school, which has graduated an average of 10 persons per year, is called the Immaculate Conception Center for Special Education (Centro de Educación Especial "La Immaculada") and accepts deaf and hard-of-hearing students between the ages of 3 and 18. *See* EDUCATION: Communication.

Neuhaus and Grimensa Wiese opened a second school for deaf students in 1959, the Peruvian Center of Hearing and Speech (Centro Peruano de Audición y Lenguaje); this school follows the oral methods of Pedro Berruecos Téllez of the Mexican Institute. Berruecos Téllez is an adviser to the foundation that operates the Peruvian Center of Hearing and Speech, and the Mexican Institute trains the Peruvian professionals who work at the school. *See* MEXICO.

Law 19326 marked a significant turning point in the education of deaf Peruvians. Enacted on March 21, 1972, and known as the Law of Educational Reform, it mandated education for all special students, including those who are deaf. Recognizing that education of exceptional students was lamentably negligent, the law provided for the incorporation of special education into the public school system, with the state assuming responsibility to serve the needs of handicapped young people.

To accomplish this, the government created the Office of Special Education, a technical and pedagogical organization in charge of regulating, orienting, coordinating, supervising, and evaluating actions that respond to special-education demands. The office attempts to integrate various services, such as education, vocational training, and programs, provided for each student.

EDUCATION TODAY

There are more than 70 schools or educational centers that serve deaf and hard-of-hearing children in Peru. Five of these schools are private, but they receive some support from the government through subsidies and the payment of teachers' salaries. The remaining schools are free, with all costs borne by the Ministry of Education.

None of the schools offer boarding arrangements. Students attend classes five hours daily in two shifts. Some schools provide food, and free exercise books on articulation, lipreading, and grammar. The state has developed standardized materials for teachers and staff of these schools. Materials include guides to the use of special-education materials, rhythmic movement guides, the basic curriculum for beginning students, an evaluation guide, and instruction in orientation and implementation techniques.

Educational policy in Peru aims to integrate or mainstream deaf students into regular classes, either at the late primary or beginning secondary level. For those students who cannot successfully be mainstreamed, due to late commencement of their education or the presence of handicapping conditions in addition to hearing loss, there are vocational programs. Training in these programs is offered in tailoring, shoemaking, jewelry making and repair, dental-machine repair, bookbinding, photography, weaving, and similar skilled occupations. *See* EDUCATIONAL LEGISLATION: Mainstreaming.

COMMUNICATION

The oral method predominates in Peruvian schools for deaf children. All but three schools—those beginning to employ total communication—use it exclusively. However, it is evident that the great majority of deaf students use sign language outside the classroom. In recognition of this fact, preparation of a sign language manual was undertaken to try to unify and codify the signs that deaf Peruvians use. *See* SOCIOLINGUISTICS: Total Communication.

The interest of deaf Peruvians in sign language as manifested in other ways as well. The government television channel has a daily program entitled "Family at Noon" (*Mediodía Familiar*), which is interpreted into sign language and is watched by many hearing-impaired people. There are also three-minute microprograms, called "Help Me" (*Ayúdame*), interpreted in sign language and broadcast to the community at various times.

TEACHER TRAINING

The training of teachers was begun in 1966 in accordance with an agreement of the Peruvian Center of Hearing and Speech with the Catholic University of Peru (Pontificia Universidad Católica del Perú) with the professional advice of Julio Bernaldo de Quiros, director of the Medical Center of Phonetic and Audiological Research of Buenos Aires (Centro Médico de Investigaciones Foniátricas y Audiológicas de Buenos Aires). This training, which lasts two years, demands as a prerequisite that the teacher have a teaching degree, which requires four years of study. This requirement considerably limits the number of candidates because of the expense and time required. The frequent result is that the majority of graduates do not work in the schools, but rather as private consultants. Thus a high percentage of the staff of the educational centers is not specialized. This constitutes a serious problem and has motivated the presentation of an emergency plan to the Ministry of Education to train teachers in special education. As part of the plan, an agreement was signed with the Women's University of the Sacred Heart (Universidad Feminina del Sagrado Corazón) to train schoolteachers in four summer sessions, with financing from the Department of Education. This program began in January 1982.

DEAF ADULTS

Most deaf Peruvians are employed and able to support families. While some work in factories, family businesses, or their own companies, the most successful financially are specialists in commercial drawing or in accounting and bookkeeping. A few have achieved engineering positions, and some deaf Peruvians are in universities and preparing for professional careers.

Three organizations of deaf Peruvians, all in Lima, are officially recognized: the Peruvian Association of the Advancement and Integration of Deaf People (Asociación Peruana de Promoción e Integración del Sordo), the Peruvian Association of the Deaf (Asociación de Sordos del Perú), and the Silent Sports Union of Peru (Unión Deportiva Silenciosa del Perú).

Shirley Mukarker

PETERSON, ROBERT BAARD
(1943–   )

Robert Peterson is an American painter who developed a reputation as an important artist in the Southwest. Although he studied art at Gallaudet College (1960–1962) and then at the University of New Mexico (1962–1965), he is essentially self-taught. Born in Elmhurst, Illinois, in 1943, he developed an interest in art begun during childhood, when he was hospitalized in Chicago at the age of four for one year as result of rheumatic fever. It was at this time that his deafness was diagnosed. In 1951 his family moved to New Mexico, where he attended public schools in Albuquerque and then the state school for deaf people in Santa Fe.

Peterson began to paint full-time in 1968. He is a figurative painter who shares with contemporary artists such as Andy Warhol and Richard Estes a concern for depicting common objects and realistic scenes. However, he cannot be classified as a pop artist or photorealist. His subjects, whether they are abandoned railroad signals, empty oil drums, concrete sewer pipes, or a crate of eggs, are always recognizable, but his primary interest is in presenting the abstract qualities of these objects.

His earliest paintings, such as *Red Tractor* (1970), were straightforward depictions of idle, isolated objects. As his style developed, his works became increasingly simplified in both shape and color. By distilling an object to its basic form, removing it from—or exaggerating its relationship to—its natural environment, and dramatizing the effects of light and shadow, Peterson concentrates on capturing the essence of the object itself. In most of his works since the early 1970s (for example, *Eggs*

Robert Peterson. (William Waldron)

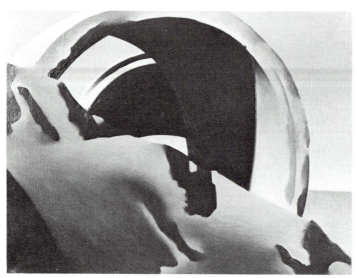

Two Pipes **(1981) by Peterson. (Gallaudet College Collection)**

in a Crate, 1971), color is minimized. His more recent subjects (plain red bricks, cardboard boxes, and shop towels) have reached a new degree of simplicity. In *Shop Towel over Box* (1982), for example, Peterson's exploration of opposites, such as darks and lights and voids and solids, was extended to color and texture.

His works are the epitome of a rationally ordered world, but the brilliance of his light and the clarity of his air give his subjects an other-worldly aura. His paintings are not only about things but about the element of time as well. In the tradition of many American painters (such as the nineteenth-century luminists John Kensett and Frederick Church, or Edward Hopper of this century), space and light have a content of their own. The intensity of Peterson's light gives his objects a universality and permanence. He has stated that painting is "especially adapted to deal with the ambiguity and flux of life. Such is existence that even to be rational can be absurd."

Peterson has works in more than 15 private, corporate, and museum collections, including the Anschutz Collection, Denver; First City Bank of Chicago, Brussels, Belgium; Museum of Albuquerque; Museum of New Mexico, Santa Fe; Northern Trust Company, Chicago; and the University of New Mexico Art Museum, Albuquerque. He has received the following awards: Purchase Prize and Honorable Mention, Southwest Fine Arts Biennial, Santa Fe, 1970; Purchase Prize, Fuller Lodge Competition, Los Alamos, New Mexico, 1970; Jurors Award, Southwest Fine Arts Biennial, Santa Fe, 1972; Purchase Award, the October Show, Albuquerque, 1981; and Albuquerque Arts Board 1% for Art Project, 1982.

Bibliography
 Shirley, David L.: Review, *New York Times*, January 8, 1972.
 Strohl, Earl: "Robert Peterson," *Artspace*, July 1983.

Judy P. Mannes

PHILATELY

Philately, or stamp collecting, is the study of imprinted stamps, envelopes, postmarks, and other materials that are issued by a governing authority. These philatelic materials feature a range of topics, such as persons and events. Miniature designs adorn the philatelic items to convey a message to the general public about the specific subject matter. Postage stamps, stamped envelopes, postal cards, and airletter sheets are purchased at a post office as means of prepayment for an intended postal use.

STAMP ISSUES

Recognition has been given by various postal authorities to a number of famed personalities, including Ludwig van Beethoven, Alexander Graham Bell, Thomas A. Edison, Francisco de Goya, Helen Keller, Juliette Gordon Low, and Samuel F. B. Morse, who were either deaf or connected with the deaf community. Postal recognition was given to them, however, because of their achievements outside the deaf community. *See* BEETHOVEN, LUDWIG VAN; BELL, ALEXANDER GRAHAM; KELLER, HELEN.

Stamps have also been issued throughout the world to recognize the deaf community and its related areas. In 1959 France issued a postage stamp honoring Charles Michel de l'Epée, the founder of the first free school for deaf students in the world, the National Royal Institution for the Deaf in Paris. Thomas Hopkins Gallaudet visited this school and befriended a deaf student, Laurent Clerc. As a result of this friendship, Gallaudet brought Clerc to America and established the Connecticut Asylum for the Education and Instruction of Deaf and Dumb Persons in Hartford, the first permanent school for deaf persons in the United States. The United States recognized Gallaudet with a postage stamp in 1983. Hungary honored Andras Cházár, the founder of deaf education in Hungary, with a stamp in 1962, and also honored Dr. Gustav Barczi, an ear doctor and a promoter of deaf education methods in Hungary, with a postal card in 1975. Samuel Heinicke, the founder of the National Institute for the Education of the Deaf in Leipzig, Germany, was honored with a pair of stamps from East Germany in 1978. Philatelic recognition was also given to Henri Daniel Guyot by the Netherlands in 1935; Johann Fredrich Oberline by West Germany in 1954; Canon Petrus Jozef Triest by Belgium in 1962; Saint Francis de Sales by France in 1967; and Frans Van Cauwelaert and Ovide Decroly by Belgium in 1980 and 1981, respectively. *See* AMERICAN SCHOOL FOR THE DEAF; CLERC, LAURENT; GALLAUDET, THOMAS HOPKINS; HEINICKE, SAMUEL; L'EPÉE, ABBÉ CHARLES MICHEL DE.

World Federation of the Deaf Congress meetings were commemorated on stamps by Yugoslavia in 1955, by Poland in 1967, and by Bulgaria in 1979. World Games for the Deaf were recognized with a postage stamp from Yugoslavia in 1969 and with a six-envelope set from Romania in 1977. Poland issued a pair of stamps to honor the First World Chess for the Deaf Championship in 1956. The Eleventh International Audiology Congress was recognized with a 1972 stamp from Hungary. The Soviet Union had a stamped envelope for the fiftieth anniversary of the Russian Society for the Deaf in 1976. Iran issued a stamp in 1977 to recognize the First Regional Seminar on the Education and Welfare of the Deaf. Austria commemorated 200 years of deaf education in Austria with a stamp in 1979. West Germany issued an embossed ear stamp to commemorate the Sixteenth International Congress for the Training and Education of the Hard of Hearing in 1980. In 1981 South Africa issued a pair of stamps to honor the hundredth anniversary of the Institute for the Deaf and Blind in Worcester, South Africa. *See* COMITÉ INTERNATIONAL DES SPORTS DES SOURDS; WORLD FEDERATION OF THE DEAF.

The 1981 International Year of Disabled Persons theme year saw a number of deafness-connected stamps from various countries. Also, at other times, some countries have issued stamps showing sign language, speech training, ear portrayal, or earphones to focus on the disability of deafness or to commemorate a deafness-related event.

POSTMARKS

Postmarks are used to cancel stamps, preventing them from being reused. Besides the regular postmarks seen on daily mail, there are slogan postmarks, first-day-of-issue postmarks, postal history postmarks, and special pictorial cancellation postmarks. Slogan postmarks publicize an event or carry a message. "Help us build the Helen Keller Home—Organisation of the Deaf-Mutes in Israel" was used as a slogan postmark on mails originating from Tel Aviv-Yafo in 1956. Italy in 1957 had a slogan postmark "Ente Nazionale Sordomuti—Manifestazioni Internazionali Sportive e Culturali—25–30 Agosto-Milano—1–30 Septembre-Roma" (literally, "The National Deaf-Mute Institute has an International Sports and Cultural Show during the period of August 25 to 30 in Milan and September 1 to 30 in Rome"). Also, "Make friends with a deaf child," "The British Deaf Association cares," "The British Deaf Association cares about lifelong deafness," and "National Deaf Childrens' Society—A deaf child needs your friendship" were used as slogan postmarks in England during the 1970s.

First-day-of-issue postmarks are special one-day postmarks that note the city where the stamp is first issued. They have the words "First day of issue" along with the city designation which, in most cases, has a relationship with the stamp's subject. For example, the T. H. Gallaudet stamp was first issued in West Hartford, Connecticut, on June 10, 1983. West Hartford was honored as the first day city because it is the locale of the American School for the Deaf. Other post offices in the United States could not sell the Gallaudet stamp until the next business day.

Postal history postmarks depict various types of postmarking devices used years ago. The postmark from the town of Gallaudet, Indiana, shows the history of a post office that was established in honor of T. H. Gallaudet on January 30, 1854, and that lasted until November 30, 1903.

Special pictorial cancellation postmarks are made and used for special events. The United States Postal Service used such special pictorial cancellation postmarks between June 29 and July 5, 1980, for the National Association of the Deaf Centennial Convention in Cincinnati, Ohio; on June 25 and 26, 1982, for the Alumni House ("Ole Jim" restoration project) opening at Gallaudet College, Washington, D.C.; and on May 27, 1984, for the International Committee of Silent Chess Eighth World Individual Chess Championship of the Deaf at Gallaudet College, Washington, D.C. Internationally, special pictorial cancellation postmarks were provided for several World Federation of the Deaf Congress meetings, several World Games for the Deaf, the inauguration of the Helen Keller Home (with the Tel Aviv-Yafo, Israel, August 1, 1958, postmark date), the Second World Chess for the Deaf Championship (with the Portoroz, Yugoslavia, September 4, 1960, postmark date), and the First World Congress of Jewish Deaf (held in Tel Aviv-Yafo Israel, from July 31 to August 4, 1977). Other special pictorial postmark cancellations were used for certain deafness-related events by several other countries. *See* GALLAUDET COLLEGE.

METERED SLOGANS

Postage-metered slogans are another form of philately which are usually used for high-volume mail. At the discretion of the meter user, the user can add a meter slogan to the metered mail printout. Some deafness-related meter slogans that were used by various United States companies and organizations are "Deaf workers are good workers—have you tried one?", "Full citizenship rights for all deaf people," "Deaf people can phone now," "A hearing aid is a mark of intelligence. . .It shows consideration for others," "Help little deaf children—Contribute to John Tracy Clinic," "That the deaf may speak," and "Give that the deaf may speak—Clarke School—Northampton, Mass." The Helen Keller Home for the Deaf in Israel used a "Help rehabilitate the deaf mute in Israel" meter slogan. *See* CLARKE SCHOOL.

INDICIA

Postage indicia are privately made imprints done on mailing pieces. Payment is made when the volume mailing is brought to the post office. The Australia Association for Better Hearing used a printed postage indicia, and Sign Post (of Australia) used a rubber-stamp-and-ink applied postage indicia on their mailings.

POST CARDS AND CACHETS

Post cards and cachets (envelopes with imprinted designs) are an integral part of philately. They are usually privately made and appropriately designed to give a nice appearance when used with any philatelic-oriented cancellations. First-day-of-issue postmarks, along with cachet designs, are called first-day covers and are available for purchase at most first-day ceremony sites. Post cards were made for the 1975 Eighth World Winter Games for the Deaf at Lake Placid, New York, and for the 1980 National Association of the Deaf Centennial Convention. *See* NATIONAL ASSOCIATION OF THE DEAF.

SEALS

There have been several privately made stamps, known as seals, for fund-raising purposes or for publicizing a cause. Some World Games for the Deaf as well as some deaf sporting events issued decorative seals. Two notable examples are France's National Educational and Social Assistance Organization for Deaf Persons (the seal has an Abbé de l'Epée portrait) to help raise funds for the Deaf Social Center in France, and the United States Gallaudet Home Fund—Empire State Association of the Deaf (the seal has a picture of Thomas Gallaudet, the oldest son of T. H. Gallaudet) to raise funds for the Gallaudet Home for Aged and Infirm Deaf in New York State.

ARTWORK

There are three hearing-impaired persons whose artworks were used on stamps. Louis Frisino of Maryland had four of his wildlife designs portrayed on State of Maryland wildlife revenue stamps. Like many other states' wildlife revenue stamps, these are issued as permits for the stamp holder to hunt or fish for the permitted wildlife game and are means of income for the state government to maintain its wildlife program. Afework Mengsha, a hearing-impaired person, has etched some designs onto several stamps from Ethiopia. Also, Norway,

in honoring the 1979 International Year of the Child theme year, chose a Mathias Stoltenberg painting as one of the stamps in a two-stamp set. Stoltenberg was a hearing-impaired artist who lived from July 21, 1799, to November 2, 1871.

Bibliography

Andersson, Yerker: "Stamp Collecting—With a Special Interest," *Gallaudet Today*, vol. 9, no. 2, Winter 1979.

Gannon, Jack R.: *Deaf Heritage: A Narrative History of Deaf America*, National Association of the Deaf, Silver Spring, Maryland, 1981.

Henricks, Sylvia, C.: "Gallaudet: Famous Name and Forgotten Indiana Town," *American Philatelist*, vol. 98, no. 5, May 1984.

Kenneth S. Rothschild

PHILIPPINES

There are about 300,000 hearing-impaired individuals in the Republic of the Philippines representing approximately 3 percent of the estimated 10,000,000 persons with handicaps.

EDUCATION

Special education for deaf and other handicapped people is controlled by the Minister of Education, Culture and Sports through the regional directors (13 of them throughout the country). To date the National Capital Region (NCR), Metro Manila area, has a concentration of special education programs which necessitates the organization of the Special Education Unit to assist the regional director in supervision the public and private special schools and special programs in regular schools.

The Philippine School for the Deaf (PSD) is a national day-residential school located in Pasay City that, in 1982, served nearly 600 deaf children, two-thirds in the elementary level and one-third in the high school. For half a century it was the only school that admitted deaf children, until the opening of special classes for deaf children in regular schools. These special classes increased as teachers were trained at the Philippine School for the Deaf, the University of the Philippines, and the Philippine Normal College by virtue of Republic Act 5250. By 1982 over 2000 deaf children were enrolled in government-supported educational programs.

There also are private educational programs for deaf pupils. The Philippine Association of the Deaf (PAD) School at Makati, Metro Manila; the Deaf Evangelistic Alliance Foundation (D.E.A.F.) at Cavinti, Laguna; the Kinder U at Malate, Manila; the Southeast Asian Institute for the Deaf (SAID) at Maryknoll College Compound, Quezon City; and the Bible Institute for the Deaf (BID) at Malinta, Valenzuela, Bulacan, established their schools in the order mentioned. Except for the Kinder U, all four were still in existence in 1982 and served a total of less than 400 elementary and high school students.

For years segregated programs for deaf students prevailed. The advent of integrating handicapped with normal children as an educational trend has had an impact on deaf education in the country. The special classes for deaf children in regular schools started what may be considered partial integration, because deaf students gradually find themselves with the hearing peers in some school subjects and activities, with some special help from the regular teacher and the special education teacher.

Full integration has been tried in a pilot-school setting with a group of deaf children at the elementary level and at least some groups at the high school level in public schools. Available are interpretive services of special education teachers assigned to help the deaf students understand the regular teachers' explanations and to assist them in their assignments while in the resource room. The few who pursue higher education usually find themselves with hearing students who try to help them in the lectures and assignments. A vocational placement coordinator makes instructors aware that a deaf student is in the class, so that assistance is more readily given. Some parents employ a special education teacher to interpret lectures in college to their deaf children.

At the elementary level the focus is on the development of communication skills to help deaf students in their school subjects. Likewise, the school develops the deaf children's work skills very early in the grades to prepare them for vocational exploratory courses in the upper levels. Alongside of academic subjects in the high school, deaf students continue to take up vocational courses. They specialize in a course of their choice by the third and fourth years. For many deaf people, high school becomes a terminal school. Efforts, however, have been directed to offer short-term vocational courses to graduates or school leavers who have slight chance to continue in other schools. The vocational placement coordinator conducts annual career guidance sessions before deaf students graduate from high school.

The PSD has shifted from one communication method to another depending upon the training of the incumbent administrator of the school. From the combined method, it shifted to the oral method, then to total communication with emphasis on the oral components in the lower grades. The PAD School, the SAID, the D.E.A.F., and the BID all use total communication. The Kinder U during its three years' existence used the oral method. Special classes in the field use varied methods depending upon the orientation of the special education teacher. Because of the integrated setting of these classes, there is a logical emphasis on the oral method. *See* EDUCATION: Communication.

Most special schools for deaf pupils have preparatory levels (preschool) through grade 6. Only SAID offers grade 7. Two of the private special schools are preparing (as of 1983) to offer high school. The PSD and the D.E.A.F. offer both elementary and high school levels.

Some of the deaf high school graduates pursue postsecondary courses in vocational schools through the assistance of the vocational placement coordinator. A few go to universities and colleges to pursue fine arts, commercial arts, home economics, culinary arts, teaching, architecture, commercial science, and other subjects. Some adult deaf persons who are not able to enroll in schools for the deaf go to the National Vocational Rehabilitation Center for some vocational training and literacy courses.

SOCIOECONOMIC STATUS

In a study conducted by S. G. Esguerra, *Correlation of Hearing Loss, Speech Intelligibility, Lipreading Ability, Intelligence, and Educational Attainment to Occupational Success*, 81 percent of the 120 deaf subjects were found employed in private firms, while 19 percent were in public offices. Sixteen percent were in professional, technical, and managerial occupations; 12.5 percent in clerical and sales jobs; 10.0 percent in machine-trades occupations; 8.3 percent in bench-work jobs; 1.7 percent in structural occupations; and 6.7 percent in miscellaneous occupations. The greatest number, 45.0 percent, were in service occupations. The study did not include those who were self-employed in tailoring, cosmetology, fishing, agriculture, and other areas. Those who were employed were observed to be earning as much as their hearing peers who were doing the same jobs at the time. Likewise, many kept their jobs until retirement age.

COMMUNICATION

Many deaf persons who graduate from special schools communicate manually with other deaf persons and with hearing people who understand sign language. Occasionally, those who develop good speech while in school manage to speak intelligibly with hearing persons when properly motivated and as the need arises. Those who have not gone to school at all use natural signs, and those who learned to write on their own communicate by writing. A majority of the deaf people who graduate from the field programs manage to carry on orally with some gestures.

Bibliography

Datuin, Gregoria M., et al. (eds.): *People of the Silent World*. Philippine Association of the Deaf, Makati, Metro Manila, 1976.

Esguerra, Sergia G.: *Correlation of Hearing Loss, Speech Intelligibility, Lipreading Ability, Intelligence, and Educational Attainment to Occupational Success*, unpublished doctoral dissertation, Arellano University, 1972.

1982 Annual Report of the Special Education Division, Bureau of Elementary Education, Ministry of Education, Culture and Sports, Manila.

1982 Annual Reports from the Philippine School for the Deaf and the Four School Divisions in Metro Manila (Manila, Quezon City, Pasay City, and Caloocan City).

Sergia G. Esguerra

PHONETICS

Phonetics is the science and art of describing speech sounds. Historically, phonetics has centered upon the study of how sounds are articulated, but it has expanded in the mid-twentieth century to include the study of how sounds are constituted physically and how they are perceived. Phonetics is often divided into several overlapping areas: acoustic vs. articulatory phonetics and experimental vs. descriptive phonetics. Speech sounds can be studied in terms of how they are produced (an articulatory description); their physical nature (an acoustic description); or their function in language (a linguistic description). The linguistic description of speech sounds is a more abstract description; it makes use of both articulatory and acoustic facts to describe either (1) how the sounds of a language change over time or (2) how the sounds function in a language at a given point in time.

BRANCHES

Acoustic phonetics is the study of the physical characteristics of speech sounds. It has provided much useful information about determining which particular acoustic attributes of each phoneme (the smallest unit of a speech sound) are the most important for the accurate perception of that phoneme. Acoustic phonetics rests upon the scientific groundwork of physics and psychophysics. Once a word has left a speaker's mouth, it consists physically of nothing more than vibrations of air molecules. Acoustic phonetics studies speech in this domain with a variety of physical measuring devices which analyze the vibrations in different ways. The actual waveform can be displayed and studied on an oscilloscope. The sound spectrograph can display a physical graph of speech along three dimensions: the frequency of sound is displayed in the vertical dimension; the course of time is in the horizontal direction; and the physical intensity of sound is shown as the relative darkness.

Articulatory phonetics is the study and description of how sounds are produced by the musculature of the human thorax, neck, and head. A great variety of different techniques can be used to study articulation. A speaker can be recorded on videotape or film, which can be slowed down or even examined frame by frame. Electromyographic techniques involve the insertion of small electrodes into specific muscles to study which particular ones are most responsible for individual speech sounds. X-ray technology can be used to document the movement of articulators that are not outwardly visible.

Experimental phonetics is the study of how speech is produced or perceived using physical measurements, psychophysical tests, or other laboratory techniques. In contrast to experimental phonetics, descriptive phonetics is a more general area of study of speech sounds with particular emphasis upon the practical techniques of phonetic transcription. The task of descriptive phonetics is to arrive at a written description of particular speech acts. The skills that are acquired by the study of descriptive phonetics can be of great use to language instructors, teachers of deaf people, and speech pathologists.

HISTORY

Phonetics is a modern science, but it has old roots. The conceptual distinction between consonants and vowels is as old as Latin. The phonetic fact that the tongue is the primary articulator of speech is implicit in many languages by use of the word "tongue" to mean language. Among many early phoneticians, a substantial motivation to study speech sounds was in part the desire to teach deaf persons.

One such early work, *Elements of Speech*, was written by William Holder in 1669. His work is subtitled "An Essay of Inquiry into the Natural Production of Letters with an Appendix Concerning Persons Deaf and Dumb." Holder divided the articulation of speech into a material cause and a formal cause, by which he referred to the modern distinction between the voice source and articulation or resonance. Holder also arrived at a classification of the English nasal and oral occlusives which is not substantially different from that used today. He classified them by place of articulation (labial, gingival, and palatick) and by manner (mute, murmur-mute, and nasovocal). Holder, and other early phoneticians, did not arrive at a good schema for vowel articulation. Holder summarized vowel articulation in this way: "The vowels are made by a free passage of Breath Vocalized through the Cavity of the Mouth, without any appulse of the Organs; the said Cavity's being differently shaped by the postures of the Throat, Tongue, and Lips, some or more of them, but chiefly the Tongue."

UNITS OF SPEECH

For the purpose of phonetic description, modern phonetics views speech as composed of discrete sounds, or segmental units, and prosody (rhythm) or suprasegmentals. The segmental sounds are the result of analyzing an utterance into a finite set of sounds that follow each other in sequence. The prosody of the utterance (that is, its suprasegmental structure), on the other hand, is continuous and cannot be easily segmented into discrete parts. Prosody consists of the aggregate changes of fundamental frequency, intensity, duration, and in some cases, phonetic quality, and is thus often viewed as superimposed upon the string of discrete sounds that compose an utterance.

The basic or smallest unit of sound production recognized by phoneticians is the syllable. However, the syllable is a hard unit to define strictly. It does not correspond to any single articulatory event, and even in acoustic terms there is no unique physical parameter that defines it well. In most instances, a syllable appears to consist of a vocalic nucleus and one or more consonants that are articulated as a unit. In this definition, "oh" [oᵘ] and "sixths" [sIksθs] both consist of one syllable. While it is usually not difficult to enumerate the number of syllables in a word, deciding exactly where the boundaries are between them can be difficult. For example, it is not difficult to determine that the word "constitute" contains three syllable peaks, but it is difficult to decide their boundaries: Does the /s/ sound belong in the first or the second syllable?

The dichotomy between vowels and consonants is closely related to the definition of the syllable. While it is true that there are many objective differences between vowels and consonants, the crucial distinction between the two rests upon a difference in their function in the syllable. Consonants are those sounds that do not function as the nucleus of a syllable, whereas vowels do. The distinction between vowels and consonants thus depends upon function. Some sounds may function as both vowels and consonants in different syllables. For example, in the word "bird" the /r/ phoneme functions as a vowel; in the word "red" it functions as a consonant. As a group, vowels tend to be voiced, more intense, and longer than consonants. Sounds which are intermediate in their function are called semivowels (for example, [ᵘ] as in the English "coo" [kʰuᵘ]), or glides (for example, [j], as in "abuse" [abjuᵘz]).

INTERNATIONAL PHONETIC ASSOCIATION ALPHABET

All areas of phonetics rely upon some form of phonetic alphabet to describe the segmental sounds of speech. The most widely used phonetic alphabet is that of the International Phonetic Association (IPA). The first table shows the main consonant and vowel symbols used in the IPA alphabet. Most of the symbols are variants of Roman letters, and are supposed to be usable to describe speech in any dialect. The ultimate goal of a transcription into a phonetic alphabet is to allow someone to read the transcription and arrive at the spoken version of the written transcription.

The IPA alphabet makes use of basic symbols and secondary symbols, called diacritics. Diacritics are placed above or below, before or after the primary symbols to indicate smaller differences in sound. In the use of diacritics, the IPA adheres to two principles: (1) Diacritical markings should be used to indicate small differences of sound, such as between allophones of a phoneme, for nasalization of vowels, and for length, stress, and intonation. (2) If a difference of sound is phonemic (that is, one that can be used to carry a difference of meaning, such as in the sound contrast of "sty" /staⁱ/ and "spy" /spaⁱ/), then two different letters should be used.

In using the IPA, or any other phonetic alphabet, the phonetician listens carefully to the target word or phrase and transcribes the sounds into letters. The phonetic symbol that the phonetician chooses is shorthand for a more complete articulatory description of how the sound is produced. For example, the IPA symbol [f] means "continuant voiceless labiodental fricative consonant." Small differences can then be noted by diacritics, perhaps on rehearing the target sound. A distinction is made between a broad and a narrow transcription. The broad transcription is a skeletal description of the speech act, and it might not include diacritics. The narrow transcription makes ample use of many supplementary diacritics to describe the speech act in the fullest detail possible.

A trained phonetician can describe a given utterance in enormous detail, primarily by listening repeatedly to the utterance, by watching the speaker, and sometimes by attempting to reproduce the utterance himself or herself. Nevertheless, all phonetic transcriptions are imperfect or inaccurate to some degree. First, phonetic transcription uses a finite (and extremely small) number of symbols with which to describe the quasi-infinite universe of human sound production. Theoretically, the physical utterance will be different each time the same word is said, even when repeated by a single individual. Second, the number of physical acoustic differences that utterances can exhibit is far greater than the number of such differences that the human auditory system can register as different. Third, a phonetic transcription uses the human auditory system and brain as a sound-measuring device. Each

Symbols of the International Phonetic Association for the Transcription of Vowels and Consonants

Consonant: PLACE OF ARTICULATION

Consonant: MANNER OF ARTICULATION	Bilabial	Labiodental	Alveolar/dental	Retroflex	Palato-alveolar	Palatal	Velar	Uvular	Pharyngeal	Glottal
Plosive	p b	·	t d	ʈ ɖ	·	c ɟ	k g	q G	·	ʔ
Nasal	m	ɱ	n	ɳ	·	ɲ	ŋ	N	·	·
Lateral	·	·	l	ɭ	·	ʎ	·	·	·	·
Lateral-fricative	·	·	ɬ ɮ	·	·	·	·	·	·	·
Rolled	·	·	r	·	·	·	·	R	·	·
Flapped	·	·	ɾ	ɽ	·	·	·	R	·	·
Rolled-fricative	·	·	ɼ	·	·	·	·	·	·	·
Fricative	ɸ β	f v	s z θ ð	ʂ ʐ	ʃ ʒ	ç j	x ɣ	Χ ʁ	ħ ʕ	h ɦ
Continuant/semivowel	w ɥ	ʊ	ɹ	·	·	j	·	ʁ	·	·

Vowel: PLACE OF ARTICULATION

Vowel: DEGREE OF OPENING	(Unrounded)			(With lip-rounding)		
	Front	Central	Back	Front	Central	Back
High	i	ɨ	ɯ	y	ʉ	u
	e		ɤ	ø		o
		ə				
	ɛ		ʌ	œ		ɔ
		ɐ				
Low	æ			Æ		
					ɒ	
	a	ɑ				

OTHER PHONETIC TRANSCRIPTIONS

human, however, speaks a particular dialect of a particular language, and the phonological rules of that language can exert a powerful influence upon perception. Finally, most systems of phonetic transcription rely heavily upon a description of the segmental phonemes, while the prosody of the utterance is often not described in great detail.

OTHER PHONETIC TRANSCRIPTIONS

Most dictionaries indicate pronunciation by use of their own phonetic symbols. The symbols are usually defined to the readers by means of key words, such as "root (rōot)," where the long mark over the double "o" is said to indicate a "long o" as in "boot." Other alphabets have been proposed, but not many have found widespread use. A system of an alphabetic notation for extremely precise phonetic transcription was proposed by K. L. Pike in 1966, but it has never been widely used, even by its originator. The Northhampton System uses alphabetic symbols to describe English pronunciation which were selected because they represent common spellings and are thus useful in teaching deaf children. An earlier phonetic alphabet, called Visible Speech, was proposed by Alexander Graham Bell in *The Mechanism of Speech* (1906). Bell's Visible Speech alphabet was designed to facilitate the teaching of speech to deaf people. Each letter of the alphabet was actually a tiny visual code that specified such phonetic features as the place of articulation and the presence of occlusion, voicing, or nasality. However, this alphabet was also never widely used. In a different direction, an attempt was made by R. Potter, G. Kopp, and H. Kopp to devise symbols for speech sounds based upon an abstraction of their acoustic appearance on spectrograms. Vowels were to be symbolized by horizontal bars representative of their formant structure, whereas stop-consonants were drawn as a long vertical line (representing their burst) and a short vertical line (representing the frequency of the burst). *See* BELL, ALEXANDER GRAHAM; VISIBLE SPEECH.

Consonant sounds are traditionally described by specifying the place and manner of articulation; vowel sounds are described by reference to extreme articulatory targets, called cardinal vowels. For this purpose, phoneticians make use of a cross section of the vocal tract, which is divided into regions that correspond to the most common places of articulation; these divisions do not correspond in all cases to specific anatomical divisions or structures. English /p, b, m/ are called labial or bilabial, since they are produced with the closure of both lips. English /f, v/ are called labiodental, since their articulation makes use of the upper teeth and lower lip. English /θ, ð/ are called dental when made with the tongue tip against the teeth, or interdental when made with the tongue between the teeth. English /t, d, n, s, l, z/ are made by articulation of the tongue tip against the alveolar ridge, and are called alveolar consonants. Sounds such as /s, z/ are made with the tongue blade against the palate and are called palatal consonants. English /k, g, ŋ/ are called velars, since they are made with the dorsum of the tongue at the velum. In some languages, the tongue dorsum and the uvula can produce uvular consonants. The tongue root can be used to make a constriction against the pharynx wall, and these sounds are called pharyngeals. Finally, the glottis itself can be used as a place of articulation. A glottal stop is produced in "uh-uh" [aʔa] meaning "no."

In addition to the place of articulation of consonant sounds, a traditional phonetic classification specifies the manner of articulation, which refers to any description of articulation other than the primary place of articulation. Some of the most important and common manners of articulation follow.

Voiced sounds are those during which the vocal folds are in vibration; during voiceless sounds there is no vocal fold vibration. Vowels can be voiceless, as in whispered speech. The sounds /θ, p, s/ are examples of voiceless consonants in English, whereas /d, v, g, l, ʤ/ are examples of voiced consonants. When the velopharyngeal port is open, then air is allowed to resonate in both the oral and nasal cavities. English /a, o, p, k, v/ are all oral sounds, whereas /m, n, ñ/ are called nasal consonants. Vowels also may be nasalized, as in the informal English exclamation "hunh?" [hə̃], meaning "what?" Glottalized consonants (which are often represented by a consonant symbol followed by a glottal stop) are sounds released with a tightly closed glottis. Sounds produced with heightened tension of the articulatory muscles are called tense; those without such tension are called lax. The vowels /I, ɛ, U, ə/ are called lax vowels, whereas /i/ or /u/ are called tense. Some phoneticians view English /p, t, k/ as tense consonants, and their voiced counterparts as lax.

Among consonants, it is useful to distinguish continuants and noncontinuants as well as obstruents and nonobstruents. Continuant sounds involve the relatively unobstructed passage of air, for example, /s/ or /l/. Continuants may vary in length, and may be prolonged so long as the speaker's air supply is not exhausted. Stops, affricates, and some kinds of r-sounds are noncontinuants; their production involves a sequence of discrete events. The term "obstruent" refers to those sounds in which the airflow is blocked or impeded, as in stop consonants. Nonobstruents are called resonants.

Cross-sectional diagram of the vocal tract, indicating major places of articulation of speech sounds.

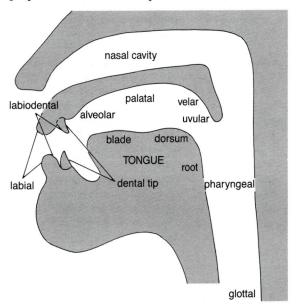

Occlusives are speech sounds that involve some closure of the vocal tract at some point of articulation, and include stop-consonants and affricates. Stop-consonants are produced by momentary complete closure of the vocal tract and sudden release. Such sounds are said to consist of closure (the period of time during which the vocal tract is completely closed), burst (the sudden release of energy at opening), and release (a brief period of frication noise). Affricates are essentially stop-consonants coarticulated with a homorganic fricative release, such as /tʃap/ "chop" or /dʒʌdʒ/ "judge."

Fricatives are consonants produced by partial occlusion of the vocal tract so that turbulence or noise is created by the passage of air between the closely approximated articulators. All fricatives involve acoustic noise; this noise may also be combined with vocal fold vibration. Acoustically, fricative noise may be relatively evenly spread throughout the spectrum, as in the case of /o/, or it may be relatively concentrated in a particular frequency range, such as /s/ or /ʃ/.

Nasal consonants are produced by oral occlusion and free resonance of air in the nasal cavity. Because nasals all share the same manner of production, they also share a marked perceptual similarity. There can be as many different places of articulation for nasals as for stop-consonants, and like all other consonants, nasals may be either voiced or voiceless, although voiceless nasals are much less common than voiced ones.

The class of liquids (informally referred to as r-like or l-like sounds) occupy an unusual status within phonetics. Liquids are a class of sounds that appear to be identified and grouped together based upon a vaguely specified perceptual commonality—they are said to share a "liquid" perceptual element. Articulatorily, the class of l-like sounds is defined as those continuant sounds produced with incomplete closure of the vocal tract by contact of the tongue tip and the anterior mouth roof. In this way, the air is free to pass on either side of the tongue for l-like sounds. The class of sounds said to have r-quality is extremely diverse and is much harder to define, either articulatorily or acoustically. The r-like sounds may be produced at many different places of articulation in the vocal tract, and in many different manners. For example, the American English /r/ is produced as a vocalic continuant, /ɹ/; the /r/ in Italian is produced as a tip trill in "Roma" [roma]; and the /r/ in Parisian French is produced as a uvular fricative in "rire" [RiR].

Clicks are an unusual class of speech sounds that occur primarily in the indigenous languages of South Africa, although they occur as marginal sounds in languages elsewhere. The sound of disapproval, symbolized orthographically in English as "tsk, tsk, tsk," is in reality a series of clicks, as is the clucking sound made to urge on horses. However, in some languages of South Africa, these sounds combine with vowels and function in the language as consonants; specialized phonetic symbols are used for them. Clicks appear to involve a degree of suction created by occlusion of the tongue in two places; the tongue is pulled from the closure, creating an audible suction burst and a brief ingression of air.

Vowels are also describable phonetically with reference to place and manner of articulation. However, the specification of place of articulation for vowels is complicated by the fact that vowels do not involve a contact of articulators; it is more the shape and position of the tongue that is important, which is often difficult to describe. In the phonetic system of the IPA, vowels are described with reference to cardinal vowels, whose symbols are shown in the first table. The cardinal vowels involve extremes of articulation, and act as reference points for the description of all vowels. For instance, cardinal /i/ is the most front, most high, and most unrounded vowel that it is possible to make. Phoneticians learn to produce and to recognize these cardinal vowels by imitation and practice. Diacritics are used in combination with cardinal vowel symbols to describe a particular vowel as more front, more back, more high, more low than a given cardinal vowel. For example [e$^{\wedge >}$] indicates a vowel more high and more back than cardinal /e/.

Diacritics are also used to show different manners of vowel articulation. A voiceless vowel, as in a whispered word, can be specified [ḁ]. Also, vowels are susceptible to nasalization, and this can be indicated phonetically as [ã]. Another important secondary characteristic of vowels is the length of articulation. Very noticeable differences of vowel length may occur in different utterances, as in the words "bit" and "bees." The diacritic for vowel length is a colon, partial colon, or double colon. For example, five different productions of the vowel /a/, from shortest to longest, could be shown as [a], [aˑ], [aː], [aːˑ], [aːː].

The position of the tongue and the shape of the vocal tract are crucial determinants of vowel quality. Since articulation in speech is dynamic, differences of vowel quality over the course of a single syllable are common. Vowels that are constant in sound quality are called monophthongs. Vowels that have some noticeable change of quality are described as a vowel nucleus plus and an offglide or onglide. For example, the vowel of the English word "goon" is said to have a labial offglide, and may be transcribed [guⁿn]. Vowels that appear to have two noticeably different target values are called diphthongs, and are commonly transcribed by writing the most prominent vowel target as the nearest cardinal vowel equivalent, and the less prominent one as a superscript vowel. For example, the diphthong in the English words "lied" and "coin" could be written as [a^{i}] and [ɔ^{i}]. The difference between a diphthong and a sequence of two separate vowels is directly related to the number of syllable peaks, whether one or two.

Suprasegmental Transcription

The transcription of prosody or supersegmentals is a weaker area of descriptive phonetics than the description of segmental sounds, and it is an area where experimental phonetics holds the promise of creating new knowledge. Prosody refers to the dynamic rhythm of speech and includes the pitch of the voice (fundamental frequency), duration (length of phonemes or words), and loudness (the physical amplitude of sounds). The description of prosody poses a number of difficulties within the confines of descriptive phonetics. First, the production fundamental frequency, intensity, and length involves gestures within the larynx that the phonetician cannot directly observe. Second, the production of prosody is continuous. It extends over an entire utterance and does not consist of discrete events that can be easily named and described. Finally, the perception of prosodic quantities also is continuous rather than discrete or categorical, and the perception of each prosodic dimension is mutually dependent upon the others.

The most immediate need for suprasegmental description in phonetics arises in situations where the suprasegmental causes a change in the meaning of a word or phrase. This is the case in many tonal languages, such as Chinese, where the "tone" [that is, some combination of F_0 (fundamental frequency), duration, length, and phonetic quality] of the word determines its lexical meaning. However, even in English, clear differences of accent or stress can be found among the syllables of individual words or among the words of a phrase or sentence. These stress or accent differences are closely related to syntax in English and convey important information. For example, compare the intonation of "It's home" and "Is he home?" In the first, fundamental frequency falls precipitously over the course of the word "home"; in the second, fundamental frequency rises and the word is often also slightly elongated.

Phoneticians have devised a number of different procedures to describe these suprasegmentals. The IPA notation uses certain diacritics to indicate stress, as in English "combination" [ˌk^{h}ambI'ne^{i}ʃn], and other diacritics to indicate differences of word tone, as in Chinese. Some phoneticians have attempted to categorize stress levels in English into four grades, and place the numbers 1, 2, 3, or 4 above each syllable to describe its stress level. In this way, a word like "telegraphic" could be transcribed as [$\overset{2}{\text{t}^{\text{h}}\text{ɛ}}\overset{4}{\text{lə}}\overset{1}{\text{græ}}\overset{3}{\text{fIk}}$]. Other phoneticians advocate a more continuous and impressionistic description of prosody, such as the use of a line drawn above and below the transcription to indicate the pitch contour—thus, [t^{h}ɛləgræfIk]. In these and other methods describing prosody, the actual fundamental frequency, intensity, and duration is not described; it is not revealed whether the fundamental frequency in a particular syllable was 100 Hz or 200 Hz, whether it lasted 50 milliseconds or 250 milliseconds. However, the precise physical quantities

Diacritical Marks Used To Modify the Phonetic Value of Other Phonetic Symbols

Symbol	Meaning	Example of use
~	Nasalization	ã
˚	Voicelessness	a
•	Voicing, to some degree	ṣ
⌐	Dentalization	t̪
ω	Labialization	k ω
ʔ or '	Glottalization	pʔ or p'
:	Length	a:
‿	Coarticulated sounds	t‿ʃ
< or +	Forward articulation	o< or o+
> or −	Back articulation	e> or e−
^ or •	Higher articulation	e^ or ẹ
ˇ or ˛	Lower articulation	eˇ or e˛
⌢ or ˘	Diphthong offglide	a^{u} or a^{ŭ}
ˌ	Syllabicity	b^tn̩ "button"
ˈ	Strong stress on the following syllable	ˈb^tn̩ "button"
ˌ	Medium stress on the following syllable	ˌk^{h}ambI'ne^{i}ʃn "combination"
h	Aspiration	k^{h}

of F_0, intensity, and duration can be accurately studied and described within acoustic phonetics.

USE OF PHONETIC TRANSCRIPTIONS

The phonetic transcription of speech can be a valuable tool in many different fields: anthropology, speech pathology, deaf education, primary education, linguistics. A trained phonetician can listen to speech (and perhaps examine it in other ways) and describe it in great detail. Nonetheless, there are some limitations upon phonetic description. The phonetician relies on the auditory system for a great deal of analysis, a practice that is potentially subject to bias from his or her native dialect or language. In addition, the human auditory system automatically normalizes speech differences due to size differences of the vocal tract or vocal folds. There are large acoustic differences between the speech of men, women, and children which do not appear in the phonetician's transcription. Furthermore, phonetic transcription involves categorizing or quantizing the flow of speech; many more utterances can be heard as different than can be quantified or precisely described. Articulatory phonetics describes units, which appear in the transcription as a linear sequence much like ordinary writing. In reality, however, speech is a heavily coarticulated code, where the cues for individual phonemes overlap and are spread out in time.

Bibliography

Abercrombie, David: *Elements of General Phonetics*, Aldine Publishing, Chicago, 1967.

Bell, Alexander Graham: *The Mechanism of Speech*, New York, 1906.

Catford, J. C.: *Fundamental Problems in Phonetics*, University of Indiana Press, Bloomington, 1966.

Heffner, R. M. S.: *General Phonetics*, University of Wisconsin Press, Madison, 1960.

Holder, William: *Elements of Speech*, London, 1669.

International Phonetic Association: *The Principles of the International Phonetic Association*, Department of Phonetics, University College, London, 1965.

Malmberg, Bertil (ed.): *Manual of Phonetics*, American Elsevier, New York, 1974.

Pickett, J. M.: *The Sounds of Speech Communication*, University Park Press, Baltimore, 1980.

Pike, Kenneth L.: *Phonetics*, University of Michigan Press, Ann Arbor, 1966.

Potter, R., G. Kopp, and H. Kopp: *Visible Speech*, Van Nostrand, New York, 1947.

Randall B. Monsen

PITROIS, YVONNE
(1880–1937)

Yvonne Pitrois became internationally known for her untiring correspondence, writing, and translating for English and American papers of the deaf community, and for her efforts as publisher-editor of small papers for deaf or blind people.

Pitrois was born on December 14, 1880, in Paris and lived in Tours, France, until 1912. Later she lived with her mother at Le Mans and Bordeaux, and at a seashore cottage in Brittany. Her widowed mother supported Yvonne and an older sister by conducting classes in French and English, and by translating books and articles.

Pitrois had normal hearing and sight until age 7, when she suffered a severe sunstroke. This rendered her deaf, and she was also blind until age 12. Her physician advised that she remain in a darkened room.

Pitrois's mother undertook to educate her daughter at home, and fortunately Pitrois had already learned to read. This ability was a great asset toward acquiring an education, as for many others who lose their hearing at about the age of 7. To communicate with Pitrois in the dark, her mother wrote in her hand. By this ingenious method, Pitrois absorbed information and enjoyed many hours of bilingual storytelling.

By the age of 12, Pitrois's eyesight had improved so much that she was permitted to emerge into daylight. She then advanced her knowledge of written French and English with her mother's help. She is credited with having translated several books and articles, many of a religious nature, from English to French.

Pitrois originated an international correspondence club. Among the correspondents were such notable deaf or blind persons as Helen Keller, Douglas Tilden, Thomas F. Fox, Mrs. James Muir (a deaf Australian), and Bertha Galeron de Calonne (a deaf-blind poet of France). Pitrois began contributing to the various publications of and about deaf people of France and England. She soon became recognized as a sort of unofficial "hands across the Channel" ambassador of good will among deaf persons. *See* KELLER, HELEN; TILDEN, DOUGLAS.

The year 1912 saw a World Congress of the Deaf in Paris celebrating the two-hundredth anniversary of the birth of the Abbé de l'Epée; Pitrois wrote a biography for the occasion. Her English translation appeared serially in the *Silent Worker* (now the *Deaf American*), the official publication of the National Association of the Deaf (United States). Thereafter she wrote many accounts of the founding of schools for deaf people in Europe and elsewhere. Her frequent letters and articles to the *Silent Worker* were headed "From the Old World." *See* DEAF AMERICAN; L'EPÉE, ABBÉ CHARLES MICHEL DE; NATIONAL ASSOCIATION OF THE DEAF.

Her articles gave "in intimate and feminine style, a charming panoramic impression of the continental institutions established for those bereft of hearing. Occasional notices of remarkable deaf individuals found ready place in her surveys." She said her general purpose was "to contribute towards extending the bounds of comprehension, sympathy, and affection uniting, all the world over, our great silent universal family."

During World War I, Pitrois described the suffering and wartime perils of deaf people in France and Belgium. The *Deaf-Mutes' Journal*, then a national deaf paper published at the New York School, raised and sent her $500 for relief purposes.

Pitrois strongly believed that deaf children should learn their own special heritage. Just as French children learn the history of their country and American children learn theirs, Pitrois argued, so the deaf children of all nations should learn the history of deaf people and their friends.

In 1912 Pitrois established a little magazine, in French, called *La Petite Silencieuse* (*The Little Silent Girl*). This was circulated at a nominal cost, mostly to France, Switzerland, and Canada. Full of items from her correspondents and with good advice for her "little sisters," it was said to have had a domestic character of its own that profoundly influenced many who received it. She included a page in the paper in Braille, for blind persons.

In 1928 Pitrois published at her own expense a separate magazine in Braille called *Le Rayon de Soleil* (*The Ray of Sunshine*). This was sent free to over 100 persons in France, Canada, and the United States.

These magazines were kept alive through the generosity of Pitrois and her friends. Part of the sadness that followed her death on April 23, 1937, was that these little magazines ceased to appear.

Bibliography

Braddock, Guilbert C.: "Yvonne Pitrois," in Florence B. Crammatte (ed.), *Notable Deaf Persons*, Gallaudet College Alumni Association, Washington D.C., 1975.

Loy E. Golladay

PONCE DE LEÓN, PEDRO
(?–1584)

Pedro Ponce de León has been widely acknowledged as the first teacher of deaf students. A monk of the ancient order of St. Benedict, he was born in the town of Sahagún, province of León, in northern Spain, and took his vows in the Benedictine monastery of his hometown on November 3, 1526. It is not known when Fray Pedro Ponce was transferred by his superiors from the monastery of Sahugún to the monastery of San Salvador de Oña, located in the mountains of north-central Spain, province of Burgos, where he spent the rest of his life.

EARLY TEACHING

In this monastery (chartered in 1010), Pedro Ponce met the two deaf sons of the Marquis of Berlanga, Juan Fernández de Velasco. The Velasco family had been one of the wealthiest and most powerful families in Spain since the thirteenth century. The Marquis of Berlanga was the brother of Don Pedro de Velasco, Condestable of Castile (honorary commander in chief of the armed forces) and Duke of Frías. The marquis had eight children, five of whom were born deaf. The two deaf boys, Francisco and Pedro, were sent to the monastery of Oña. Of the five daughters, Juliana, Bernardina, and Catalina were also deaf and were sent to different monasteries. This action served the double purpose of keeping the deaf children from public view and preventing them from having offspring. Deafness was very common among the Velascos, probably because many of them received a special dispensation from the Holy See to marry first cousins. The reason for these consanguineous marriages was solely financial, to prevent the breakup of the family estates.

Don Francisco and Don Pedro had been sent to Oña before the death of their father in 1546. At this time they were 9 and 12 years old, respectively. A contemporary, Don Baltasar de Zúñiga, said that shortly after their arrival in the monastery the boys became very close to Pedro Ponce, leading the abbot to entrust the boys to Fray Pedro's care. Zúñiga said that "because [Ponce] grew very fond of the boys and was very saddened by their handicap, he took to thinking of ways in which he could teach them how to speak."

Don Francisco died quite young but was able to speak somewhat. Don Pedro died in his thirties. He was taught how to write, speak, and read and understand books in Italian and Latin. Zúñiga added that on some occasions Don Pedro went to the city of Salamanca to visit his sister Inés, who married the Count of Monterrey. Her children, by express order of Pedro Ponce, would speak to Don Pedro, their uncle, using movements of their hands with which they formed the letters of the alphabet.

TEACHING SUCCESS

Zúñiga's testimony was corroborated by a letter that Don Pedro de Velasco wrote to a contemporary humanist, Ambrosio de Morales, in which he explained how Pedro Ponce taught him. Don Pedro began by writing Spanish words and then progressed to fingerspelling and speech. With these skills, he began reading history and eventually learned Latin as well.

Justo Pérez de Urbel has corroborated the veracity of this. In the course of investigations on Fray

Pedro Ponce, he discovered a manuscript of the *Third Decade* of the Roman historian Titus Livius translated into Spanish, which bears the signature of Fray Pedro Ponce on the last page under an inscription that reads: "Don Pedro de Velasco, brother of the Condestable of Castile, and his teacher Fray Pedro Ponce borrowed this book from the house of the Count of Castro."

Pedro Ponce also taught 10 or 12 other deaf people how to speak, among them Don Pedro's sisters Doña Bernardina and Doña Catalina, as well as the son of a high official, and a monk named Fray Gaspar de Burgos who was born deaf.

Don Pedro de Velasco died in 1572. In his last will, dated September 15, 1571, he referred to Fray Pedro Ponce as "my teacher and my father" and named him among his executors. He bequeathed to him some personal effects: ". . . and I order that my teacher be given my bed with its mattresses and woodwork, blue trappings, and all bed linen and coverlets and everything else, except my white shirts and other clothes which should go to the poor . . ."

On August 24, 1578, Fray Pedro Ponce signed a document notarized by Juan de Palacios, actuary of the town of Oña, in which he made an endowment with the monies that he had received from his students. The document reads: ". . . these monies I, Fray Pedro Ponce, monk of this House of Oña, have acquired by my sayings and by bequeaths of gentlemen of whose wills I have been executor, and by gifts from pupils that I have had. The latter were deaf and mute and were taught by me by means of the art that God bestowed on me in this holy monastery. . . They were the sons and daughters of great noblemen and important people and they were deaf and mute from birth. I taught them how to read and write, count, pray, serve at Mass, understand the Christian doctrine, confess orally, and some I taught Latin and others Latin and Greek and to one even Italian."

There has been speculation for centuries concerning a book written by Pedro Ponce, according to Fray Juan de Castaniza, monk at Oña and a friend of Ponce, who mentioned it in his *History of St. Benedict*. This book was entitled *Doctrina para los mudos sordos* (*Instruction for the Mute Deaf*). While it is highly probable that such a book was written by Pedro Ponce, the manuscript was probably lost or destroyed during the great social upheavals that Spain underwent during the nineteenth century. Many monasteries like San Salvador de Oña were expropriated by the government, and the monks were forced to leave. The monasteries were then ransacked, and some of the treasures were either destroyed or stolen or sent to municipal libraries or museums. The papers and documents from the monastery of Oña were sent to the National Archives of Spain. The manuscript of Fray Pedro Ponce has not been found among Oña's bundles.

Fray Pedro Ponce de León was a monk for 58 years. His death was recorded in the monastery's registry: "Fray Pedro Ponce, benefactor of this monastery, was laid to rest in the Lord. Among the good qualities which he possessed in a high degree, he excelled in one which made him very famous in the world, namely, teaching the mute to speak. He died in the year 1584, in the month of August."

TEACHING METHOD

Although Pedro Ponce's book was lost, it is possible to speculate on the method he used in the instruction of his deaf students. The most important document is the account given by Francisco Vallés, physician to the King of Spain, who mentioned Ponce in his book *De Iis Quae Scripta Sunt Physice in Libris Sacris, sive de Sacra Philosophia* (loosely translated, *Philosophical Speculations on Natural Phenomena Described in the Bible*). Vallés met Ponce and was present at some of Ponce's lessons. He related how Ponce instructed the deaf children "first to write, pointing with his finger at those things that were symbolized by those characters [that he had written]; after by prompting (*provocando*) the movements of the tongue that correspond to the letters (*characteribus*). And thus, while with those that hear one begins by the spoken language, with those whose ears are closed one begins more properly (*rectius*) by writing." This corroborated the account that Don Pedro de Velasco gave to Ambrosio de Morales concerning the method used by his teacher.

The manual alphabet used by Pedro Ponce was probably the same that appeared in the *Book Called Solace for the Sick*, written by Melchor Yebra, a Franciscan monk, and printed in Madrid in 1593. This book contained pictures of a hand alphabet in which each configuration of the hand preceded the alphabet of Saint Bonaventure, which is a set of maxims of Christian behavior. Yebra's manual alphabet is almost identical to that used by Manuel Ramírez de Carrión at the beginning of the sixteenth century to teach another deaf member of the Velasco family. Carrión's alphabet was the same one that Juan Pablo Bonet published in 1620 in his book *Simplification of the Letters and Art to Teach the Mutes to Speak*. See CARRIÓN, MANUEL RAMÍREZ DE; PABLO BONET, JUAN; SIGNS: Fingerspelling.

Besides the use of the manual alphabet, Ponce de León must have communicated with signs with his deaf students, since the Benedictine monks were under strict vows of silence. This was a rule observed by many monastic orders. In order to communicate without breaking their silence, the Benedictines developed signs. A detailed description of the signs used by the Benedictine monks of Cluny, France, and presumably by those on Oña, is included in the Constitutions and Rules of this monastic order, the *Vetus Disciplina Monastica*, published in Paris in 1726, which contains more than 400 signs.

Since other deaf members of the Velasco family were taught by Manuel Ramírez de Carrión and Juan Pablo Bonet two generations later, it is quite possible that these pioneers in the education of deaf people incorporated the method and intuition of Pedro Ponce in their work.

Bibliography

Chaves, Teresa L., and Jorge L. Soler: "Pedro Ponce de Leon, First Teacher of the Deaf," *Sign Language Studies*, vol. 5, pp. 48–59, 1974.

Navarro Tomas, Tomas: "Manuel Ramírez de Carrión y el arte de enseñar a los mudos," *Revista de Filologia Española*, vol. 11, pp. 225–266, 1924.

Pérez de Urbel, Fray Justo: *Fray Pedro Ponce de León y el origen del arte de enseñar a hablar a los mudos*, Madrid, 1973.

Jorge Soler

PRESBYCUSIS

Presbycusis (presbyacusis) is a general term indicating a reduction in auditory function in the later stages of life. It is usually insidious in onset and progress, beginning in midlife in some persons, but is more often noticeable by the late sixties and early seventies. It may appear at first as an inability to hear sounds as subtle as the ticking of a watch or, in digital watches, the high-pitched repetitious tone that serves as an alarm. Later there is inconsistent hearing of such sounds as a telephone ring in an adjoining room or the soft scrape of footsteps. Gradually it involves problems in the understanding of speech. It is often reported that presbycusis is the most common cause of hearing loss.

Signs

The process of presbycusis involves age-related changes in various parts of the auditory system, including the ear, the brainstem, and the brain. The sequence of the prominent signs of functional change usually are: loss of hearing for weak sounds; reduced ability to understand speech correctly even when it is heard; and increased difficulties in understanding speech correctly under unfavorable listening conditions.

A common sign of presbycusis in patients seen clinically is a greater loss of hearing for sounds whose frequencies are higher than 1000 Hz than for sounds of lower frequency. Histologic studies of the ears of older persons who had experienced such hearing show a loss of groups of hair cells in the region of the cochlea which normally is most responsive to these sounds. In a smaller proportion of cases, the hearing loss for low and high audiometric frequencies is about equal. Such frequency-related changes in hearing are depicted clinically on an audiogram. *See* AUDIOMETRY: Pure-Tone Audiogram; EAR: Anatomy.

The audiogram reveals only part of the problem of presbycusis. Gradual alterations in the ear's function are accompanied by disturbances in the listener's ability to discriminate one sound from other sounds that are similar in their acoustic properties. Thus, the most disturbing manifestation of presbycusis is the listener's confusion of some of the sounds of speech, such as /p/, /t/, and /k/, so that, for example, the hearing of "sack" may be mistaken for "sap" or "sat." As the loss of hearing progresses, such confusions in understanding what is said occur increasingly, and the sufferer and his or her close associates gradually become aware of the hearing problem.

The confusions of speech sounds apparently result in part from a breakdown in the tuning of the ear to sounds of different frequencies. In the normally functioning ear this tuning means that tiny areas (about 1 millimeter) of the ear's delicate inner mechanism will respond primarily to a sound of a specific frequency, such as 4000 Hz, and decreasingly to sounds just lower and just higher than that. Sounds still further away in frequency will not bring a response from that part of the ear unless they are made very strongly. In the aging ear this specificity of response, or tuning, becomes less precise so that sounds of such remote frequencies will interfere even when they are relatively weak. *See* EAR: Physiology; HEARING.

Another indication of decreasing processing in the ear is the requirement by older listeners of a greater-than-normal frequency separation between two tones before they are recognized as different. In the aging ear the breakdown of such tuning leads to a blurring of speech sounds that the brain must identify, such as a /t/ or a /k/. This problem is exacerbated in the presence of noise, because poorer tuning leads to greater vulnerability of such speech sounds to masking, or obliteration, by the noise.

Another problem in the presbycusic ear is the occurrence of distortions when the received sound is strong. Speaking loudly to a presbycusic listener, therefore, may cause the speech to be even less distinct than when it is quieter, in somewhat the same way that shouting into a microphone results in distortion out of the loudspeaker.

INDUSTRIAL NOISE AND SOCIOACUSIS EFFECTS

The age-associated changes in the ear's ability to hear and discriminate speech are complicated further by the cacophony of noises which differentiate modern industrial societies from more primitive environments. Studies of peoples in remote, essentially agrarian areas have revealed far less deterioration with age than has been documented in American and European surveys. Persons most at risk for large losses of hearing are those who have been engaged in noisy industrial surroundings where high-level sounds throughout the working day can cause noise-induced hearing loss. Others, who do not work under such conditions, may nevertheless suffer from socioacusis, a loss of hearing from the onslaught of the many noises in today's complex living environment. The loss of hearing that occurs in later life, therefore, apparently results from normal physiologic aging, which may reflect familial patterns, in combination with the effects of a mechanized society.

THE HIGHER "EAR"

The understanding of speech occurs most definitively as a result of the function of the brain. It is possible, therefore, to hear only parts of what is said, along with considerable distortion, and yet know the speaker's intended message. Such processing of incomplete information requires complex linguistic and cognitive activity involving a knowledge of the language's vocabulary, grammar, and expressions; of the general subject matter and of the relationship of the message to the circumstances; of psychological factors such as attention, and attitude toward the speaker and his message; and of memory, both short- and long-term. *See* PSYCHOACOUSTICS.

Research into presbycusis has, therefore, moved from an earlier concentration on the ear's loss of hearing for certain frequencies to concern for the entire process involved in the reception and understanding of speech and other meaningful sounds. Investigators now ask why an older listener, having hearing sensitivity similar to that of a young adult, has more difficulty hearing when noise is present, or when speech is rapid or distorted through the telephone (or from which parts are deleted either by bursts of noise or by electronic processing, as in transatlantic telephone calls), or when poor acoustic conditions exist, as in a house of worship or in assembly halls.

Effect of Speed A consistent finding in studies of aging indicates the slowing of many physiologic and psychologic functions. It is not surprising, therefore, that the ability to follow rapid speech is reduced in older listeners. It is clear that this problem involves changes in brain activity, since rapid speech, in which the normal rate of 8–10 speech sounds per second may be increased to as many as 25–30 per second, depends heavily on such functions for understanding.

Selection and Rejection An example of complex auditory processing that declines in presbycusis is selective listening, in which one speaker's message must be attended to against a competitive background of other talkers or when poor acoustics require that the listener reject reverberated repetitions of speech sounds in order to attend to the flow of the message.

Telephone Listening A frequent manifestation of an older person's changes in auditory efficiency is in the increasing problem in understanding over the telephone, particularly when noise is present in the listening environment.

Effect of Incomplete Information The most dramatic experimental evidence of age-related decline in the understanding of speech emerges from studies in which parts of a message are deleted, forcing the listener to synthesize the meaning from reduced information. For example, if 50 percent of a speech recording is removed by electronic interruptions, young adult listeners will understand almost all of the sentence material so treated, but 55-year-old listeners will score about 30 percent less, 65-year-old persons about 45 percent less, and 75-year-old listeners almost 60 percent less.

Effect of Talker Characteristics A common experience of persons with hearing loss is that they have more difficulty understanding some speakers than others. Research reports suggest that this is related to the acoustic characteristics that normally determine the relative intelligibility of different talkers. Presbycusic listeners who have a typical loss of hearing for sounds of higher frequency are at increasing disadvantage for speakers with hoarse voices, and some older persons find whispered speech highly unintelligible.

OTHER CONTRIBUTING FACTORS

The auditory reception and processing difficulties exhibited by older persons are affected additionally by certain age-associated psychological tendencies. Thus, besides being less alert to sounds about them, some older listeners show increasing perseverance of concentration on a particular subject, failing to note shifts in topic. Another finding is the greater tendency of older subjects to resist guessing when they are unsure of what was heard. Therefore, they tend to withhold responses in experiments rather than expose themselves to the possibility of error.

Short-term memory changes are widely reported for older persons. This has been demonstrated in studies involving spoken messages in which sentences having more than one clause are heard over strongly competing noise. Apparently in the struggle to understand and repeat one part of the sentence, the other part tends to slip out of the immediate memory.

Confusions between words heard under unfavorable conditions often are resolved with the help of a sentence's contextual clues. Experimental reports suggest that with aging the skill for accomplishing such synthetic inference is blunted.

The effects of aging on the perception of speech are even more pronounced when the language or dialect is not that to which the listener was exposed during the earliest period of language development (until about age six or seven). When such persons are tested in adulthood, their performance on tasks involving degraded speech in their current but nonnative language tends to be significantly below that of native speakers of that language. The disparity seems to be greater in older than in younger adults. Similar differences between young and older listeners have been noted for the perception of unfamiliar dialects of one's native language.

HEARING AIDS

Since there is still little that medical practice can apply to ameliorate presbycusis, the use of a hearing aid is the most recommended corrective measure. Its ability to provide a satisfactory substitute for normal hearing, however, is still quite limited, because in the signal it delivers to the ear are the very acoustic factors that cause difficulty even for a normal listener—limited frequency range, uneven amplification of sounds of different frequency, distortion of strong sounds, assorted internal noises and artifacts known as transients, and so on. It has been reported that if both young and older subjects having normal hearing sensitivity listen to speech through a hearing aid, the older listeners have considerably greater difficulty understanding the speech. The limited help that older hearing-impaired persons obtain from a hearing aid, therefore, appears to be due to both the inherent shortcomings of hearing aids and the increasing processing problems of older persons when exposed to various degradations in the quality of received speech. *See* HEARING AIDS.

SUMMARY AND CONCLUSIONS

Certain generalizations have been made about presbycusis as a condition in which there are age-related changes in auditory function, the most notable effect being in the reception and processing of speech. The most commonly documented change is loss of hearing sensitivity, usually for sounds with frequencies above 1000 Hz. The reduced understanding of speech results in part from this loss and, probably more importantly, from decreasing precision in the ear's management of incoming signals. The reduced and distorted information sent by the presbycusic ears to the brain apparently suffers poorer linguistic and cognitive processing in the older listener than in young adults with similar hearing.

A central observation of research, however, is that hearing as well as other bodily functions show increasingly larger individual variations in older people than in healthy young adults. While generalizations are informative, investigators of presbycusis are often more concerned with the proportion of older persons who show significantly worse auditory behavior than almost all of the normal young listeners. Thus, while individual older persons may hear as well as the average young adult, it is clear that each age decade, at least from the fifth (ages 40–49) upward, contains increasingly larger percentages of persons with presbycusis, with the decline in hearing most apparent after the early sixties, and with estimates of 60 to 80 percent of persons in their seventies and older. Difficulties in reconciling reported incidence figures lie in the definition of presbycusis and in the population studied. For example, people in nonindustrial areas were found to contain fewer cases of presbycusis than those of the same age in industrial societies. *See* HEARING LOSS: Incidence and prevalence.

As the population continues to show an increasingly higher median age, presbycusis, which is already the leading hearing impairment, is becoming an urgent problem which calls for research and planning in a communicating society.

Bibliography
Bergman, M.: *Aging and the Perception of Speech*, 1980.
Hinchcliffe, R.: "The Anatomical Locus of Presbycusis," *Journal of Speech and Hearing Disorders*, vol. 27, no. 4, November 1962.
Marshall, L.: "Auditory Processing in Aging Listeners," *Journal of Speech and Hearing Disorders*, vol. 46, no. 3, August 1981.
Schuknecht, H. F.: *Pathology of the Ear*, 1974.

Moe Bergman

PRINCETEAU, RENÉ PIERRE CHARLES (1843–1914)

René Princeteau, a popular nineteenth-century painter of equestrian and military scenes, made his most enduring mark on French art as Henri de Toulouse-Lautrec's first teacher. The son of a well-to-do Bordeaux wine merchant, Princeteau was born deaf at Libourne, France, in 1843. At the age of 14 he went to Bordeaux to continue his education, and there became interested in sculpture and began formal instruction in the studio of Maggesi.

Intending to pursue a career in sculpture, Princeteau went to Paris in 1865 and entered the Ecole des Beaux-Arts. Although he won two sculpture competitions during these early years, he soon turned to painting as his principal medium. He left the Ecole and set up his own studio in Saint-Honoré, a suburb of Paris.

An accomplished rider, Princeteau was fascinated with depicting horses, and he studied their anatomy and movements in detail. His interest, though, was not in the traditional approach to equestrian painting, which presented the horse and its rider in a rigid, stationary pose, but instead in conveying with fidelity the vibrancy of moving forms. Similarly, his riders were not merely passive figures, but active participants in the steeplechase or hunt scene depicted.

Although he did not associate himself with any particular contemporary artistic movement, his realistic interpretation of nature does show a subtle affinity to Jean Baptiste Camille Corot (1796–1875). While in Paris, he often painted in the forests of Fontainebleau, and his landscapes have the characteristic gentleness and softness of the Barbizon school of painters. His use of *plein air* technique (that is, painting outdoors) and his interest in capturing the immediacy of the moment allied him as well with his contemporaries among the Impressionists.

It was Princeteau's sketchlike technique which had a lasting influence on Toulouse-Lautrec. Toulouse-Lautrec's father was a friend of Princeteau and a frequent subject in his steeplechase scenes. Toulouse-Lautrec began to paint with Princeteau in 1878 or 1879 in Paris. Princeteau was a capable teacher, and he and Toulouse-Lautrec, who was 21

years his junior, would often sketch together. Sketchbooks found in the studio of Toulouse-Lautrec contain drawings by both teacher and student. Some entries are so similar in style that they are difficult to attribute correctly. Toulouse-Lautrec not only shared with Princeteau his interest in horses and racing events, but learned from Princeteau the use of small scattered brushstrokes to suggest the effects of light playing on the riders and horses. This technique left a permanent imprint on Toulouse-Lautrec's style, and it was already evident in an oil sketch he did of Princeteau in 1881.

In 1883 Princeteau left Paris and returned to the Bordeaux region to live on the estate of Château Pontus-Fronsac near Libourne. Princeteau, who had earned his reputation as a first-rank painter of horses, now turned his attention to a new subject, the cattle he observed from his quarters. He found their simple but noble beauty alluring and sought to capture all the nuances of their movements and postures. Unlike his equestrian paintings, in which he depicted his subjects in shimmering light and warm fields, these new works were set in landscapes with bare trees and ominous skies. They reflect a period of personal sadness and disenchantment which, despite his professional success, spurred his move from Paris. Ultimately, in 1885, he totally abandoned his studio in Paris to remain in Libourne.

He exhibited annually in the Salon de Paris from 1868 to 1904. *Le Relais* (The Posthouse) won an honorable mention in 1881, *Intérieur d'etable* (Inside the Stable) earned a third-class medal in 1883, and *Attelage de boeufs charroyant des engrais* (Oxen Hauling Fodder) took a second-class honor in 1885. *Chevaux effrayes par le train* (Horses Frightened by the Train) was exhibited in the Centennial Exhibition held in Philadelphia in 1876. Today, the Museum of Libourne has an extensive collection of his works. Other works are in museums in Bordeaux and Montauben, and *Le Relais* is part of the collection of the Petit Palais in Paris. Princeteau died in Fronsec, France, in 1914.

Ox Labourant by René Princeteau. (From *The Silent Worker*, vol. 10, no. 9, June 1887)

Bibliography

Lassaigne, Jacques: *Lautrec*, Edition d'Art, Skira, Paris, 1953.

Martinchard, Robert: *Princeteau 1843–1914*, Presses de l'Union, Bordeaux, 1956.

Judy P. Mannes

PSYCHOACOUSTICS

In attempting to understand human sensory inputs, such as in vision and audition, it must be remembered that what is actually experienced as sensory information is a pattern of neural impulses that are only some analog, or coding, of the external events that the senses need to register. In the general area of sensory responses, the study of this parallel between external events (the stimulus, or signal) and the eventual subjective response is known as psychophysics, and in audition specifically as psychoacoustics.

Modern technology has made it easy to measure and control the physical parameters of the signal to a desired degree. Techniques for quantifying and systematizing the responses are not so simple.

Psychoacoustics may begin with operations as simple as finding the smallest physical difference that can be reliably responded to subjectively as a change. This area of auditory discrimination or differentiation involves finding the smallest change in frequency, intensity, spectrum, duration, and so on, that makes a subjective difference to the listener. The form of these discriminable changes over the range encompassed by the system contains cues as to how the system processes sensory data. So also does the systematic portrayal of the form of the subjective response over the whole range of useful values of these same physical parameters. These latter are the psychoacoustic scales of pitch, loudness, sound quality, and so forth that the system is believed to use in recognizing and categorizing such signals as the sounds of the environment and of conversational speech.

Most of the evidence gathered indicates that when a person responds to changes in the magnitude of some physical parameter, such as a change in intensity of a sound which leads to a different loudness, the response is in ratio terms. One sound seems twice, or 1½ times, as loud as another. This is true not only in psychoacoustics but in psychophysics in general. Thus most psychophysical scales that involve a change of magnitude, take the form $R = ks^\alpha$, where R is the magnitude of the subjective response, k is a constant adjusting for the particular units employed, s is the measure of the physical parameter involved, and α is the factor that denotes how rapidly the subjective response changes with a change in the physical parameter. By taking the logarithm of the above values and transforming the expression to the form $\log R = \log s + \log k$ (a constant), it is more evident that the relation is a straight line on a log-log plot, and, thus, that making the same ratio of change anywhere along the useful range of the physical parameter evokes the same ratio of change in the subjective response.

This is the most basic illustration not only that psychoacoustics attempts to be the piecemeal eliciting and tabulating of subjective responses to acoustic stimuli, but that it attempts to build a structured model of how the auditory system reacts to and processes acoustic signals to create subjectively a useful world of sound.

Earl D. Schubert

Pitch

Pitch is the subjective property of sound that varies primarily with frequency, and it is described most often on a high-low dimension. For example, a flute has a high pitch and a tuba has a low pitch. Pitch and frequency usually vary together. Pitch refers to perception, whereas frequency is a physical property of sound, that is, the number of cycles per second in the waveform of the sound. Pitch can vary also with the physical dimensions of intensity, duration, and complexity of the sound as described below.

RELATION WITH FREQUENCY

Pitch changes with frequency in a complex manner. The relation between pitch and frequency has been measured by using the method of fractionation in which a person adjusts the frequency of a tone to divide a pitch range into subjectively equal intervals; this method was used to obtain the pitch scale for pure tones on the mel scale. The mel is the unit of pitch. Pitch in mels is plotted as a function of frequency in hertz (Hz). A sound with a pitch of 500 mels is perceived to be half as high in pitch as a sound with a pitch of 1000 mels. Likewise, 1000 mels is half as high as 2000 mels. The pitch of a 1000-Hz tone of moderate loudness is defined as 1000 mels. As shown on the mel scale, pitch is nearly proportional to frequency below approximately 1000 Hz, but increases slower than frequency above 1000 Hz. For example, a 500-Hz tone has a pitch near 500 mels, but a 3000-Hz tone has a pitch of only 2000 mels.

The mel-pitch scale is different from the musical-pitch scale. The former is defined in terms of perception, while the latter is defined in terms of physical units (such as frequency). The western musical scale is divided into octaves. The ratio between octaves is 2-to-1, so that a 2000-Hz tone is one octave above a 1000-Hz tone and a 500-Hz tone

The mel scale for pitch. (After S. S. Stevens and J. Volkman, "The Relation of Pitch to Frequency," *American Journal of Psychology*, 53:329–353, 1940)

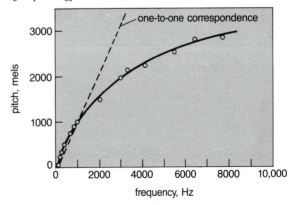

is one octave below. Each octave is divided into 12 semitones, which are equally spaced on a logarithmic scale. A semitone can be divided into cents; 1 semitone equals 100 cents. Cents are often used to describe very small musical intervals, such as in the mistuning of an instrument. Many common musical scales, such as the A major and A minor scales consist of seven tones (A through G, or la through so) one or two semitones apart. The musical scale is circular. Right above G follows an A that is one octave higher than the starting A. Although their frequencies are an octave apart, the two A's are perceptually very similar, a phenomenon called octave generalization. Due to octave generalization, a C from a cello is perceived as very similar to a C from a flute, although the frequency of the C note produced by the flute may be four or eight times (two or three octaves) higher than that produced by the cello. Because tones separated by one or more octaves are perceptually similar, musical pitch is often described by two attributes: pitch chroma, which refers to the position of the tone within the octave and is given by the name of the note (A through G), and pitch height, which refers to the pitch on a continuously increasing scale such as the mel scale. In music, the pitch height is given by the octave number of the note. In the example above, the cello and the flute were both playing the pitch chroma C, but were playing different pitch heights.

Absolute pitch or perfect pitch refers to an individual's ability to identify the pitch chroma of tonal sounds without the aid of a known reference pitch. Perfect relative pitch refers to an individual's ability to recognize musical intervals, that is, the ability to identify the pitch chroma of one tone relative to that of a reference tone. While relatively few persons have absolute pitch, it is common to find persons with perfect relative pitch, which can be learned by most people. However, some people have difficulty recognizing musical intervals and are called tone deaf.

The pitch of a tone at a fixed frequency may change with intensity. Pitch decreases with increasing intensity for tones below 1000 Hz and increases with intensity for tones above 3000 Hz. Between 1000 and 3000 Hz, pitch is relatively independent of intensity. There are large differences from person to person in the effect of intensity on pitch.

A tone loses its pitch at short durations. As a tone is made very brief, it becomes more like a click. The critical duration beyond which pitch remains stable with increasing duration is a fixed number of cycles (3 to 9) below 1000 Hz and 1/100 of a second above 1000 Hz.

The pitch of a tone may shift due to the presence of other sounds. If a band of noise and a tone are close in frequency and intensity, the pitch of the tone will shift away from the noise. While pure-tone pitch increases when the tone has a higher frequency than the noise, it does not consistently decrease when it is lower.

MULTIPLE TONES

If two or more tones are presented simultaneously at moderate or high intensities, combination tones may be heard. The frequencies of combination tones correspond to differences between multiples of the frequencies being presented. The most audible combination tone is usually the cubic difference tone, f_C, which is as many hertz below the lower of two tones as the higher is above. Mathematically, $f_C = f_1 - (f_2 - f_1) = 2f_1 - f_2$, where f_1 is the frequency of the lower tone and f_2 is the frequency of the higher tone.

The ear can analyze a sound into its constituent frequencies, at least to some degree. By analytic listening, a trained listener can hear several pitches when presented with two or more simultaneous pure tones. For example, two sufficiently different frequencies presented simultaneously may give rise to several different pitches corresponding to each of the two frequencies and their combination tones. In addition, one or more pitches may be derived from the composite of the two tones and their combination tones. The pitch of the total sound or composite is heard by synthetic listening, which is the most common manner of listening to complex sounds such as those created by musical instruments.

The composite pitch of a musical instrument or a person's voice is determined by the fundamental frequency, which is the highest frequency that can be divided into the component frequencies of the sound and is the inverse of the period of the sound. Harmonics are exact multiples of the fundamental frequency. For example, for a 100-Hz fundamental, the first harmonic is 100 Hz, the second harmonic is two times the fundamental or 200 Hz, the third harmonic is three times the fundamental or 300 Hz, and so on. Even if the fundamental frequency is absent in a harmonic complex sound, a clear pitch corresponding to the absent fundamental can be heard by synthetic listening. This pitch is called the missing fundamental, low pitch, periodicity pitch, or residue. For example, the pitch of a complex sound consisting of tones at 700, 800, 900, and 1000 Hz has the same pitch as a 100-Hz tone, which is the fundamental frequency of the complex sound. Although aural distortion can produce a tone at the fundamental frequency of a complex sound, the perception of the pitch corresponding to the fundamental frequency does not result from aural distortion. Similarly, it has been shown that the missing fundamental cannot be eliminated by a low-frequency noise, even if the noise is intense enough to make inaudible any possible aural distortion product at the fundamental frequency.

Pitch may also be associated with sounds that are not periodic (that is, noises). Noises that have their energy concentrated in bands of frequencies will also have a pitchlike quality corresponding to those bands.

DIPLACUSIS

A tone may have different pitches when presented to the left and right ears, which is a common phenomenon called binaural diplacusis. It is measured by having a person adjust the frequency in one ear so the pitch is equal to that of a reference tone in the other ear. Many persons with normal hearing have small differences between the ears. In persons with hearing loss of cochlear and retrocochlear origin, pitch may differ between ears by as much as an octave. In monaural diplacusis, a single tone may be heard as a group of tones or a noise. Diplacusis is a common symptom of persons with hearing loss of cochlear or retrocochlear origin. *See* EAR: Pathology.

Although profoundly deaf persons cannot hear pitch as other persons do, they can feel vibrations of low-frequency sounds. These vibrations can give much information.

CODING

How pitch is coded in the auditory system is not clear. Since A. Seebeck proposed the time-coding theory and G. S. Ohm and H. von Helmholtz proposed the place-coding theory, researchers have been trying to decide between them. The time-coding theories are based on the fact that the neural firings in the auditory system are in approximate synchrony with the waveform of the sound. For example, the time between neural firings to a 1000-Hz tone is near-multiples of 1/1000 of a second. Although a single neuron cannot fire faster than once every 3/1000 of a second, the composite activity of a group of neurons may maintain synchrony up to at least 4000 Hz. On this basis, time-coding theories postulate that pitch is derived from the time between firings of nerve fibers.

The place-coding theories are based on the fact that the auditory system, including the auditory areas of the brain, is ordered according to frequency. Specific neurons are tuned to specific frequencies, and which neurons respond to a tone depends on its frequency. For example, G. von Békésy discovered that the place of maximum displacement on the basilar membrane in the inner ear changes from near the oval window (and the stapes) at high frequencies to near the apex (furthest from the stapes) at low frequencies. This ordering according to frequency is called the tono-

topic organization of the auditory system. The place theories postulate that pitch is derived from the pattern of neural excitation, that is, which neurons are firing. For example, the pitch of pure tones is often thought to be determined by the location of the neurons that respond most vigorously to the tone. Place theories for perception of the missing fundamental postulate that pitch is derived through intricate transformations of the component frequencies in a complex sound. It is possible that both place- and time-coding are important for the perception of pitch and that low frequencies are processed via a temporal code and high frequencies via a spectral code.

Bibliography

Békésy, G. von: "Zur Theorie des Hörens: Die Schwingungsform der Basilarmembran," *Physikalische Zeitschrift*, 29:793–810, 1928; translation: G. von Békésy, *Experiments in Hearing*, McGraw-Hill, New York, 1960.

de Boer, E.: "On the 'Residue' and Auditory Pitch Perception," in W. D. Keidel and W. D. Neff (eds.), *Handbook of Sensory Physiology*, vol. 5, Springer-Verlag, Berlin, 1976.

de Mare, G.: "Investigations into the Functions of the Auditory Apparatus in Perceptual Deafness," *Acta Oto-Laryngologica*, S74:107, 1948.

Deutsch, D.: *The Psychology of Music*, Academic Press, New York, 1982.

Egan, J. P., and D. R. Myer: "Change in the Pitch of Tones of Low Frequency as a Function of the Pattern of Excitation Produced by a Band of Noise," *Journal of the Acoustical Society of America*, 22:827–833, 1950.

Fletcher, H.: "The Physical Criterion for Determining the Pitch of Tones," *Physical Review*, 23:427–437, 1924.

Gelfand, S.: "Pitch," in *Hearing: An Introduction to Psychological and Physiological Acoustics*, pp. 275–290, Marcel Dekker, New York, 1981.

Helmholtz, H. von: *On the Sensation of Tone*, Dover Publications, New York, 1954: original German edition, 1863; fourth (and last) German edition, 1877.

Licklider, J. C. R.: "Periodicity Pitch and Place Pitch," *Journal of the Acoustical Society of America*, 26:945, 1954.

Moore, B. C. J.: *An Introduction to the Psychology of Hearing*, 2d ed., Academic Press, New York, 1982.

Ohm, G. S.: "Über die Definition des Tones, nebst daran geknupfter Theorie der Sirene und ähnlicher Tonbildender Vorrichtingen," *Annalen für Physik und Chemie*, 59:513–565, 1843.

Plomp, R.: *Aspects of Tone Sensation*, Academic Press, London and New York, 1976.

Roederer, J. G.: *Introduction to the Physics and Psychophysics of Music*, Springer, New York, 1973.

Scharf, B., and A. J. M. Houtsma: "Audition II," in K. Boff (ed.), *Handbook of Human Perception and Performance*, John Wiley and Sons, in press.

Schouten, J. F.: "The Residue and the Mechanism of Hearing," *Proceedings of the Koninklijke Nederlandse Akademie van Wetenschappen*, 43:991:999, 1940.

Seebeck, A.: "Beobachtungen über einige Bedingungen der Entstehung von Tönen," *Annalen für Physik und Chemie*, 53:417–436, 1841.

Shambaugh, G. C.: "Diplacusis: A Localizing Symptom of Disease of the Organ of Corti," *Archives of Otolaryngology*, 31:160, 1940.

Stevens, S. S.: "The Relation of Pitch to Intensity," *Journal of the Acoustical Society of America*, 6:150–154, 1935.

———— and J. Volkman: "The Relation of Pitch to Frequency: A Revised Scale," *American Journal of Psychology*, 53:329–353, 1940.

Terhardt, E.: "Pitch of Pure Tones: Its Relation to Intensity," in E. Zwicker and E. Terhardt (eds.), *Facts and Models of Hearing*, Springer-Verlag, Berlin, 1974.

————: "Pitch, Consonance and Harmony," *Journal of the Acoustical Society of America*, 55:1061–1069, 1974.

Ward, W. D.: "Musical Perception," in J. V. Tobias (ed.), *Foundations of Modern Auditory Theory*, vol. 1, Academic Press, New York, 1970.

Wightman, F. L.: "The Pattern-Transformation Model of Pitch," *Journal of the Acoustical Society of America*, 54:407–416, 1973.

———— and D. M. Green: "The Perception of Pitch," *American Scientist*, 62:208–215, 1974.

Mary Florentine

Loudness

Loudness is the psychologic attribute of sound that is most closely related to the physical dimension of sound intensity, although other physical characteristics also influence the loudness of sounds.

As with all perceptual phenomena, the attribute of loudness cannot really be described. Psychophysicists have relied on comparative judgments to gain some understanding of the relations between physical characteristics and loudness perception. Listeners may be asked to compare the loudness of stimuli to a number scale (direct measurement), or to compare the loudness of one sound to the loudness of another (indirect measurement).

MEASUREMENT

The measurement of loudness has many scientific and practical applications. The theoretic importance of loudness comes from the information gained from loudness measurements with regard to the neural code used by the brain in auditory processing. By comparing the loudnesses of various sounds, researchers have gained some understanding of the manner in which the auditory system encodes and discriminates sound stimuli. Loudness has practical importance for diagnosing various hearing impairments and for environmental noise control. The use of loudness measures in diagnosis is based on the fact that various auditory impairments affect loudness differently. Loudness measures sometimes are helpful for distinguishing between primarily cochlear and primarily neural impairments of hearing. In environmental noise control, loudness measures are useful because the disruptive effect of noise is related more to its loudness than to its physical intensity. Noise regulations are sometimes based on calculations of the loudness of un-

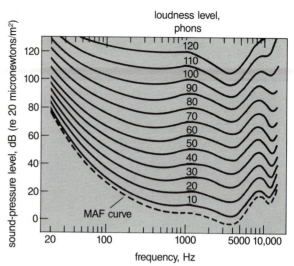

Equal loudness contours. (After A. Peterson and E. Gross, *Handbook of Noise Measurement*, General Radio Co., 1972)

wanted sounds such as aircraft and automobile noise.

Loudness measurement procedures are critical to the understanding of this perceptual dimension. Direct measurements have been employed to construct loudness scales that are analogous to scales of physical dimensions. The several scales to represent loudness on a continuum differ in their starting points (zero) and in the size of the measurement unit.

Sone Scale   The most common loudness scale is the sone scale. On the sone scale, the loudness of a binaural 1000-Hz tone at 40 decibels (dB) above threshold is defined as 1 sone. Any sound that is twice as loud is 2 sones, any sound half as loud is 0.5 sone, and so on. By asking subjects to assign numbers to sounds in this manner, a normal loudness function has been constructed and can be expressed mathematically.

Phon Scale   Another useful loudness scale is the phon scale, which is derived by matching the loudness of sound stimuli to a comparison tone. The comparison tone has a frequency of 1000 Hz, and it is adjusted in level to match the loudness of the comparison stimulus. If a stimulus has a loudness level of 60 phons, it is equal in loudness to a 1000-Hz tone, 60 dB above threshold. Thus, all sounds with a loudness level of 60 phons are equally loud. It is possible, then, to construct a family of equal loudness contours for tones. An equal loudness contour is a set of frequency-intensity combinations that result in equal loudness.

CHARACTERISTICS

These direct and indirect methods of loudness measurement have been employed to study many characteristics of loudness perception. Some examples of loudness characteristics that have been useful in understanding normal and abnormal hearing are loudness recruitment, temporal summation of loudness, and loudness adaptation.

Loudness Recruitment This refers to an abnormally rapid increase in loudness as intensity is increased. It occurs in most people with sensorineural hearing loss. Although these people require more sound intensity just to hear a sound compared to normal-hearing people, once the sound intensity is raised above threshold, the impaired person may experience normal or nearly normal loudness for that suprathreshold sound. Because the dynamic range for loudness is decreased (that is, the range from barely detectable to unbearably loud), persons with loudness recruitment have an abnormally narrow range over which the auditory system can encode intensities.

Temporal Summation of Loudness This is the increase in loudness that occurs as the duration of a sound is increased. For normal-hearing listeners, as a sound is made longer, from one-tenth to two-tenths of a second, for example, it sounds louder. Beyond about a half second, however, increasing the duration no longer influences loudness. In listeners with sensorineural hearing loss, there is a reduced effect of duration on loudness. This has been interpreted as a reduced ability of the auditory system to integrate sound over time.

Loudness Adaptation This is the reduction of loudness that occurs during continuous sounds. Just as the brightness of a light or the sensation of pressure on the skin diminishes over time if the stimulus is unchanging, the loudness of a steady sound decreases. This loudness decrement is very small in normal-hearing listeners but may be large in people with sensorineural hearing loss. Loudness adaptation is particularly marked in people with disease of the auditory nerve, and the phenomenon is used in a diagnostic test to detect pathologic conditions of the auditory nerve. *See* AUDIOMETRY: Loudness Adaptation.

Robert H. Margolis

Binaural Hearing

Binaural hearing, or hearing with two ears, has three basic advantages: (1) it enables the individual to know where sounds are coming from (that is, localization ability); (2) it helps in understanding speech in a noisy environment (that is, selective listening); and (3) it helps in detecting weak sounds (that is, binaural summation; a sound slightly too weak to be heard with one ear becomes audible when listening with two ears and an already audible sound in one ear becomes louder when listening with two ears).

Although people hear with two ears, one sound image is perceived from a single sound source. Bin-

aural fusion is the process by which sounds to the left and right ears fuse to form a single sound image. If the sounds to the two ears are similar in frequency and time, they will fuse.

LOCALIZATION ABILITY

Localization can occur in the horizontal plane and in the vertical plane. As shown in the illustration, the horizontal plane can be conceived as a circle around the head, which is parallel with the floor and at the same height as the ears. The vertical plane is perpendicular to a line connecting the two ears and intersects the midpoint of that line.

Persons with normal hearing can locate a sound in their horizontal plane (to either their left or right side), as well as in the vertical plane (either high or low). Infants with normal hearing turn their heads toward a loud click when they are only a few minutes old; thus, the ability to localize sounds is present at birth and is not necessarily learned.

The information used to locate a sound in the horizontal plane includes the difference in intensity of the sound at the two ears, called interaural in-

Schematic diagram of the horizontal plane and a sound source positioned 30 degrees to the right. The distance from the sound to the right ear, D_r, and the left ear, D_l, is shown. The inset shows the waveform of a 1000-Hz tone as the sound travels to the left and right ears.

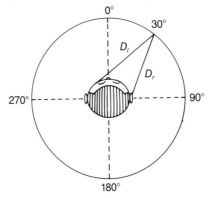

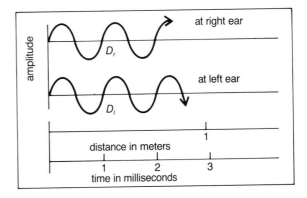

tensity difference, and the difference in time of arrival of the sound at the two ears, called interaural time difference. For example, a sound from 30 degrees to the right is more intense (2 to 12 dB depending on its frequency) in the right ear than in the left ear. The sound is weaker in the farther ear because the head reflects high-frequency sounds away from it. This head-shadow effect is much stronger at high than at low frequencies because high-frequency sounds with their short wavelengths cannot bend around the head as readily as low-frequency sounds with their longer wavelengths. For example, a tone coming directly from the right (90 degrees) is 20 dB weaker in the left ear than in the right at 3000 Hz, but only 5 dB weaker at 500 Hz. Accordingly, at frequencies above 2000 Hz, interaural intensity differences are powerful indicators of the location of a sound source.

At frequencies below about 2000 Hz, the interaural time difference indicates the location of a sound source. For example, a sound 30 degrees to the right arrives about 0.27 millisecond earlier at the right ear than at the left ear because it must travel further to reach the left ear. These time differences also can be thought of as phase differences between the ears. When the sound is a tone, the time difference is usually described as a phase difference, which is determined by the distance of the sound source to each ear and by the frequency. For a sound 30 degrees to the right, the distance to the right ear, D_r, is shorter than that to the left ear, D_l. Traveling at about 340 meters (1122 feet) per second, sound arrives earlier at the right ear than at the left ear. As shown in the inset of the illustration, the result is that the phase is different at the two ears. The figure shows a 1000-Hz tone; other frequencies from the same location would have different phase relations at the two ears.

The smallest difference in location that a person can discriminate is known as the minimum audible angle. It is measured as the smallest angle in degrees between two locations in the horizontal plane that can be discriminated and it ranges from 1–2 degrees directly in front of the head to about 10 degrees at the side of the head. The minimum audible angle is smallest for frequencies below about 1000 Hz and above about 3000 Hz. Between these frequencies, the minimum audible angle increases; between 1500–2000 Hz, sounds positioned to the side of the head in an area called the cone of confusion, are especially difficult to locate (see illustration). Fortunately, the cone of confusion rarely affects the ability to locate sounds in everyday situations for two reasons. First, most environmental sounds are composed of many different frequencies. Second, when locating sounds, people usually move their head toward the sound and listen with their head at different angles. Moving the head

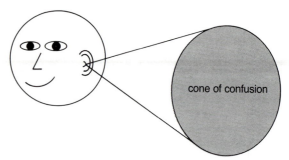

Schematic diagram of the cone of confusion for a spherical head. (After A. W. Mills, "Auditory Localization," in J. V. Tobias (ed.), *Foundations of Modern Auditory Theory*, vol. 2, Academic Press, New York, 1972)

changes the interaural time and intensity differences, helping to locate the sound.

When a sound is in the vertical plane, interaural intensity or time differences provide no information about locus because they are zero for any position in that plane. However, reflections from the pinna (the convoluted flap of cartilage around the ear canal) help to locate such sounds. Because the reflections are frequency-dependent, the pinna acts as a filter, amplifying some frequencies and attenuating others.

The preceding discussion assumes that the sound is coming directly from its source. Indoors, however, reflections of the sound from the walls, floor, and ceiling are heard. Although the reflections come from many directions, a single sound source is perceived which is localized on the basis of the first wavefront reaching the ears. This phenomenon is called the precedence effect or Haas effect. The reflections that arrive later add to the loudness and quality of the sound but do not influence its perceived location.

LATERALIZATION

Sounds presented via earphones usually are heard inside the head. Localizing sound images inside the head is called lateralization. Lateralization experiments have provided much information about the roles of interaural time and intensity differences because the two can be controlled separately for sounds preserved via earphones. Humans can hear interaural time differences as small as 10 microseconds and interaural intensity differences less than 1 dB. Lateralization experiments also have shown that interaural intensity differences can be offset by opposing interaural time differences, or vice versa. For example, if a click arrives 100 microseconds earlier to the left ear than to the right, its image normally is lateralized to the left side of the head. However, if the intensity to the right ear is increased a few decibels, its image may be lateralized at the middle of the head. A lead time to the left ear can be compensated for, at least to some degree, by an intensity increase to the right ear. This phenomenon is called time-intensity trading.

Earphones also permit presenting a different frequency to each ear. If the frequencies at the two ears are low and differ by less than about 10 Hz, the location of the fused image fluctuates. These fluctuations are known as binaural beats and reflect an interaction between the neural pathways of the two ears.

SELECTIVE LISTENING

The ability to hear a signal, such as speech, in the presence of noise is called selective listening. Relative phase relationships at both ears between the signal and the noise help people to listen selectively. If the interaural phase of a signal differs from that of a noise, the signal can be detected more easily. For example, an out-of-phase 250-Hz tone presented together with an in-phase noise background has a detection threshold that is 14 dB lower than if the tone and the noise were both in phase at the two ears. This phenomenon is called the binaural masking level difference.

BINAURAL SUMMATION AND OTHER EFFECTS

Threshold is about 3 dB lower when listening with two ears than when listening with one ear. This effect reflects binaural summation at threshold. Likewise, binaural summation of loudness makes a sound nearly twice as loud when listening with two ears than when listening with one ear.

Presenting different sounds to both ears also gives insight into hemispheric specialization. Such experiments reveal a right-ear advantage for speech and a left-ear advantage for music.

LOCALIZATION OF SOUNDS BY HEARING-IMPAIRED LISTENERS

The ability to localize sounds can be modified. For example, a person with an earplug in one ear (a type of simulated hearing loss that modifies the interaural intensity difference) can relearn to locate sounds. At first, sounds are heard toward the unplugged ear because they are louder in that ear. However, within about a week, the person can localize sounds normally.

Despite this ability to adapt to distorted interaural information, many hearing-impaired listeners have difficulty locating sounds. The amount of difficulty appears to be related to the type of hearing loss and to the amount of difference in loss between the ears. If the hearing loss is different in the two ears, localization is usually degraded more than if the loss is about the same. However, even

persons with only one intact ear can usually locate some sound sources on the side of the good ear, but they frequently make large errors when the sources are on the opposite side.

Along with difficulty in locating sounds, many hearing-impaired persons report difficulty in understanding speech in the presence of noise (that is, problems with selective listening.) Unfortunately, hearing aids rarely rehabilitate a hearing loss totally. Although hearing aids amplify speech, they also amplify noise, and they do not compensate for deficits in selective listening. However, some research shows that hearing aids in both ears help many hearing-impaired persons to improve their ability to locate sounds. *See* HEARING AIDS.

Bibliography

Durlach, N. I., and H. S. Colburn: "Binaural Phenomena," in E. C. Carterette and M. P. Friedman (eds.), *Handbook of Perception*, vol. 4, Academic Press, New York, 1978.

———, C. L. Thompson, and H. S. Colburn: "Binaural Interaction in Impaired Listeners," *Audiology*, 20:181–211, 1981.

Gelfand, S.: "Binaural Hearing," in *Hearing: An Introduction to Psychological and Physiological Acoustics*, pp. 291–322, Marcel Dekker, New York, 1981.

Green, D. M., and W. A. Yost: "Binaural Analysis," in W. D. Neff, and W. D. Keidel (eds.), *Handbook of Sensory Physiology*, vol. V(2), Springer, New York, 1975.

Mills, A. W.: "Auditory Localization," in J. V. Tobias (ed.), *Foundations of Modern Auditory Theory*, vol. 2, Academic Press, New York, 1972.

Moore, B. C. J.: "Spatial Hearing," in *An Introduction to the Psychology of Hearing*, 2d ed., pp. 150–154, Academic Press, New York, 1982.

Yost, W. A., and D. W. Nielson: "Binaural Hearing," in *Fundamentals of Hearing, An Introduction*, pp. 155–165, Holt, Rinehart, and Winston, New York, 1977.

Mary Florentine

Dichotic Listening

The integrity and function of the central auditory system can be investigated by several psychoacoustic procedures. One such technique, dichotic listening, has become increasingly popular since around 1960. In a dichotic listening test, two different signals (usually two different tokens of speech such as common words, digits, or consonant-vowel nonsense syllables) are presented simultaneously, one to each ear. For example, the syllable /pa/ might be presented to the left ear and, simultaneously, the syllable /ga/ might be presented to the right ear. Dichotic testing, where the signal in one ear provides competition for the signal in the other ear, may be contrasted with monotic testing, where one syllable, for example, /pa/, is presented to only one ear and no competing syllable is presented to the other ear.

CONVENTIONAL DICHOTIC TEST INTERPRETATION

Dichotic nonsense-syllable tests usually impose a more difficult listening task than word or digit tests. If nonsense syllables are presented monotically, listeners should recognize the syllables with nearly 100 percent accuracy. However, if nonsense syllables are presented dichotically, syllable recognition scores may be reduced to around 60 to 70 percent, even for normal listeners who have no peripheral or central hearing disorder. However, syllable-recognition scores for dichotic digits (for example, one, three, six) probably will exceed 95 percent for normal listeners. When dichotic tests are used for listeners with normal hearing, the lower scores provided by nonsense-syllable tests are advantageous because what is generally wanted is to compare the score for one ear with the score for the other ear to determine which ear has the "advantage," that comparison is meaningless if both scores approach 100 percent. When dichotic tests are used for listeners with abnormal auditory function, recognition scores for digits may be low enough to provide a meaningful assessment of the ear advantage and, in fact, a nonsense-syllable test may prove to be too difficult in most circumstances.

Normal Listeners For a group of listeners with normal central auditory function, higher scores, on the average, usually occur for syllables presented to the right ear. For example, the mean score for the left ear might be expected to be approximately 65 percent and the mean score for the right ear approximately 75 percent, which would correspond to a right-ear advantage (REA) of 10 percent. When normal listeners are tested dichotically, the mean REA typically ranges between 5 and 15 percent, but the size of the REA varies markedly among individual listeners.

Most explanations of the REA are based on three assumptions: (1) The language-dominant left hemisphere is largely, but probably not exclusively, responsible for processing both syllables. (2) The syllable presented to the right ear travels directly to the language-dominant left hemisphere, whereas the syllable presented to the left ear travels a more indirect path from the left ear to the right hemisphere and then crosses from the right hemisphere to the left hemisphere via the corpus callosum. (3) The lower score for the left ear occurs because important phonetic information for recognition of the left-ear syllable is distorted or lost during inter-hemispheric transmission from the right hemisphere to the language-dominant left hemisphere.

These three assumptions compose what might be called a strict ear-brain hypothesis, which often leads investigators to conclude that persons with an REA are left-brain-dominant and that those with a left-ear advantage (LEA) are right-brain-dominant. Thus, the ear-brain hypothesis reflects a language-dominance principle. Some believe that listeners who evidence no ear advantage have poorly established hemispheric dominance, but there is little or no experimental evidence to support that contention.

Listeners with Central Auditory Disorders Dichotic speech tests also are used clinically to help determine if a listener has a central auditory disorder. Clinical application of dichotic speech tests, however, is not based on the same language-dominance principle that is applied to normal listeners. When the person has a unilateral (that is, one side only) central auditory disorder, it is generally expected that the score for speech presented to the ear contralateral (on the opposite side) to a temporal lobe lesion will be much lower than the score for speech presented to the ear ipsilateral (on the same side) to the lesion. Thus, in the most simple case, a lesion affecting the central auditory pathways of the right temporal lobe will produce a lower score for the left ear than for the right ear, whereas a lesion affecting the auditory pathways of the left temporal lobe will produce a lower score for the right ear. That difference in scores for the two ears is often called a contralateral-ear effect because the score is lower for the ear contralateral to the lesion. It may also be called a lesion effect to contrast the clinical outcome with the language-dominance effect for normal listeners.

OTHER FACTORS IN TESTING NORMAL LISTENERS

Three factors that should be considered before invoking the conventional language-dominance interpretation for normal listeners in response to a consonant-vowel nonsense-syllable test will be discussed below.

Reversals in Direction of Ear Advantage The direction of ear advantage for an individual listener often is reversed from test to retest. Thus, an REA observed on an initial dichotic test of 30 pairs of syllables may be reversed to an LEA when the test is repeated. The different outcomes for test and retest probably reflect some form of measurement error and not that the listener demonstrates left-hemispheric dominance on one occasion and right-hemispheric dominance on the other.

The origin of the reversals may become clearer if a few statistical properties of the ear advantage are considered. Suppose that the same test of 30 pairs of syllables is administered 20 times to each listener rather than only once or twice. The following outcomes almost certainly will occur: (1) The 20 measurements of the ear advantage for any individual listener will be distributed approximately as a normal (bell-shaped) curve. (2) The mean ear advantage for an individual listener will be listener-specific and relatively unpredictable. Most listeners will probably have an REA, but the direction and size of the advantage will vary greatly among listeners. (3) The standard deviation of the 20 measurements of the ear advantage for any individual listener will be approximately 10 percent, and there will be no more than small differences in the size of the intratest standard deviation among listeners.

A typical listener with a mean REA of 8 percent and a standard deviation of 10 percent for 20 repetitions of the test may be considered. Because the multiple estimates of the ear advantage are distributed normally, a certain number of outcomes will fall one standard deviation or more away from the mean of 8 percent. Three (16 percent) of the 20 tests should produce REAs of 18 percent (8 percent + 10 percent) or larger and, more importantly, another 3 (16 percent) of the 20 tests should produce LEAs of 2 percent (8 percent − 10 percent) or larger. The likelihood of reversals in direction of ear advantage increases as the size of the mean ear advantage (either REA or LEA) approaches 0 percent. If a listener has a mean REA of only 4 percent (which is certainly not uncommon), 3 of the 20 tests should produce an LEA of 6 percent or larger; but if a listener has a mean REA of 15 percent (which is less common), an LEA on even 1 of the 20 tests would be unlikely. Thus, one or two administrations of a short dichotic test are usually not sufficient to assess either the size or direction of the ear advantage because of the relatively large standard deviation and the relatively small mean.

Reliability of Ear Advantage Test-retest or split-half reliability for assessments of the ear advantage from one or two test administrations usually lies in the unsatisfactory range of +.60 to +.70. However, the reliability problem can be largely overcome by increasing the number of test administrations. For example, if the 30-pair test is presented six times, split-half reliability should approach +.90, and the number of additional test administrations that would be required to increase reliability beyond +.90 is probably not worth the investment of time. It must be emphasized, however, that even if sufficient tests are administered to achieve a satisfactory reliability of +.90 or higher, the problem of reversals in direction of ear advantage may not be solved. If an individual listener has a mean ear advantage of 8 percent that is calculated from 100 administrations of the test, it is still expected that 16 percent of the test outcomes will produce an LEA of 2 percent or higher even if reliability approaches +1.00.

Validity of Ear Advantage With one common dichotic-listening paradigm, the listener receives a pair of syllables (for example, /ta/ in the left ear and /ka/ in the right ear), is instructed to attend equally to both ears, and is asked to select two responses from a known set of alternatives (commonly six). That conventional paradigm, however, does not allow the tester to know the extent to which the observed ear advantage reflects a true difference in sensory capacity between the auditory channels from the left and right ears in contrast to certain tendencies on the part of listeners that may bias their responses. Does the listener, for example, pay relatively more attention to one ear or the other, and is the direction of that divided attention switched from test to test? That problem had received relatively little attention; more rigorous psychoacoustic techniques are now being reported, however, that enable the tester to distinguish with greater confidence between true sensory capacity and listener proclivities.

OTHER FACTORS IN TESTING LISTENERS WITH CENTRAL AUDITORY DISORDERS

The same three factors described above for normal listeners also may contribute to the outcome of clinical dichotic tests, but their importance is probably lessened. Multiple measurements of the ear advantage are probably not distributed normally, test-retest reversals in the direction of ear advantage are less likely to occur, and researchers do not suspect that listener bias will affect the outcome appreciably. However, there are other factors that must be considered when dichotic tests are administered to persons who are suspected of having central auditory disorders.

Lesion Effect vs. Dominance Effect It was noted above that lower scores are expected for the ear that is contralateral to a temporal lobe lesion, and the common explanation for that outcome calls on principles associated with the contralateral-ear effect or lesion effect. That interpretation, however, remains controversial. Aphasics, for example, almost always have damage to the left hemisphere, and they generally evidence lower scores for the right ear on a dichotic listening test. According to the lesion-effect interpretation, the lower score for the right ear occurs because the right ear is contralateral to the damaged left hemisphere.

An alternative explanation for the same outcome focuses on the higher score for the left ear (an LEA) and describes the person as having a left-ear advantage rather than a right-ear deficit. Proponents of this viewpoint believe that the LEA occurs because the right hemisphere has taken over primary language function following damage to the left hemisphere. Although the controversy has not been resolved completely, a longitudinal study was reported in which 27 aphasics were tested with a dichotic digit test at monthly intervals from one month to six months postdamage. For most of the individuals, scores for both ears improved over the six-month interval, but the ear advantage did not change appreciably. That outcome did not support a language-dominance hypothesis, which would predict that an early REA (reflecting left-hemispheric dominance) would shift toward an LEA (reflecting a switch to right-hemispheric dominance), or that at least a small LEA shortly after cerebral insult might become a larger LEA over time.

Ipsilateral-Ear Effect According to most interpretations of the lesion-effect principle, the score will be lower for the ear contralateral to the temporal lobe lesion. However, when a deep lesion in the left hemisphere involves callosal fibers, the left ear may have the lower score. In that case, the score is lower for the ear ipsilateral to the lesion and the outcome is called the ipsilateral-ear effect. Thus, when the examiner is presented with a low left-ear score, convincing corroborating evidence should be obtained before concluding that the outcome is consistent with a lesion on one side of the brain or the other.

Choice of Dichotic Speech Test A nonsense-syllable test may be too difficult to use in a clinical environment. Furthermore, although consonant-vowel nonsense syllables appear to be quite sensitive to the presence of a central nervous system lesion, investigations have suggested that the right-ear score for a dichotic digit test shows promise as being quite sensitive to the location of a central auditory lesion. In one study, aphasics were divided into two groups on the basis of independent computerized tomography scan results: those with and those without evidence of significant involvement of Heschl's gyrus, the primary auditory reception area in the temporal lobe of the cerebral cortex. Low right-ear scores for digits occurred more frequently in association with significant primary auditory cortex damage, whereas high right-ear scores for digits occurred with individuals for whom the auditory cortex and geniculotemporal pathway appeared to be spared. Correct classification occurred for 85 percent of the 41 individuals tested.

Coexisting Peripheral Hearing Impairment Clinical dichotic speech tests should be relatively insensitive to the presence of peripheral hearing impairment as well as relatively sensitive to the presence of a central auditory deficit. In one study, four different dichotic speech tests were administered to 27 individuals with sensorineural hearing loss. The digit test appeared to be the most promising of the four tests for assessing central auditory integrity because scores on that test were only slightly affected by the peripheral hearing loss. Results of that experiment and others have provided three guidelines that should be followed when the person for whom a central auditory test is contemplated also has a peripheral hearing loss: (1) The examiner must choose the dichotic test carefully because the influence of the peripheral loss on the dichotic outcome will vary considerably among tests. (2) Monotic testing on each ear should be conducted before the dichotic test is administered. (3) At least for consonant-vowel nonsense syllables, the dichotic test should be administered at an intensity that produces asymptotic monotic scores for both ears.

Bibliography

Damasio, H., and A. Damasio: "Paradoxic Ear Extinction in Dichotic Listening: Possible Anatomic Significance," *Neurology*, 29:644–653, 1979.

Katsuki, J., et al.: "Application of Theory of Signal Detection to Dichotic Listening," *Journal of Speech and Hearing Research*, 27:444–448, 1984.

Niccum, N.: "Longitudinal Dichotic Listening Patterns for Aphasic Patients: I. Description of Recovery Curves," *Brain and Language*, 1985.

———, A. B. Rubens, and C. Speaks: "Effects of Stimulus Material on the Dichotic Listening Performance of Aphasic Patients," *Journal of Speech and Hearing Research*, 24:526–534, 1981.

Schulhoff, C., and H. Goodglass: "Dichotic Listening, Side of Brain Injury and Cerebral Dominance," *Neuropsychologia*, 7:149–160, 1969.

Sparks, R., H. Goodglass, and B. Nickel: "Ipsilateral Versus Contralateral Extinction in Dichotic Listening Resulting from Hemisphere Lesions," *Cortex*, 6:249–260, 1970.

Speaks, C., N. Niccum, and E. Carney: "Statistical Properties of Responses to Dichotic Listening with CV Nonsense Syllables," *Journal of the Acoustical Society of America*, 72:1185–1194, 1982.

———, ———, and D. Van Tasell: "Effects of Stimulus Material on the Dichotic Listening Performance of Patients with Sensorineural Hearing Loss," *Journal of Speech and Hearing Research*, 28:16–25, 1985.

Charles E. Speaks

Masking

Auditory masking means in general the interference of one sound with another, usually the interference of an unwanted sound with a desired sound, the signal. The formal definition, as approved by the American Standards Association, is more restricted. It states that masking is (1) the process by which the threshold of audibility for one sound is raised by the presence of another (masking) sound; and (2) the amount, usually in decibels, by which the threshold of audibility of a sound is raised by the presence of another (masking) sound. The definition properly emphasizes the quantifiable aspect of masking but, to conform to general use, should be extended to include the partial masking of one sound by another. Partial masking may consist of two components: the reduction of the masked sound in loudness, and whatever change a masking sound may make in a masked complex sound that may render it less recognizable, even though still audible. The partial masking of the sounds of speech or music are familiar examples of the latter phenomenon.

PATTERN OF MASKING

Most of the formal experimentation on the nature of auditory masking has made use of the comparative spectral simplicity of pure tones and noise or noise bands. The classic picture of how sound energy at one frequency raises the threshold of tones at other frequencies is illustrated. A narrow band of noise, which is designated as the masking signal, is used because pure-tone maskers interact with the masked tone to produce beats and other audible distortion products that interfere with the measurement of masking itself. A number of characteristics of masking are apparent in this portrayal. First, the closer the two sounds, the greater the interference, which is predictable because the ear does a frequency analysis. Second, for low levels of the masker, the interference occurs essentially symmetrically in either direction along the frequency scale. Finally, at higher levels the rise in threshold occasioned by the masker is much greater at frequencies above the masker than below—a parallel to a common everyday observation that low sounds mask high sounds to a greater degree than the reverse.

Each of these characteristics could be predicted from the shape of a tuning curve of the first-order neuron (auditory nerve), where the parallels are the greatest sensitivity of a neuron for a single frequency, the essentially symmetric shape of the peak, and the low-frequency skew of the tail of the tuning curve when frequency is plotted on a logarithmic scale. Even closer correspondence between neural and psychophysical behavior is evidenced if, rather than presenting a fixed masker and asking the subject to listen for other tones (which is the method used to generate the illustration), the listener is instructed to attend to the single center-frequency tone as the other tones are suitably varied to make that tone inaudible. The resulting curve looks almost like the neural tuning curve. The importance of these similarities is that they furnish compelling evidence that this form of masking begins at the periphery, that is, it is not primarily a centrally mediated process. To at least a first approximation, the interference among complex sounds, such as speech or music, can be understood from these interactions between simpler sounds.

IMPORTANCE OF MASKING

Knowledge of the process of masking is important in daily listening because people listen increasingly in the presence of other interfering signals, and defective auditory systems need special assistance in coping with such environments. In addition, upon

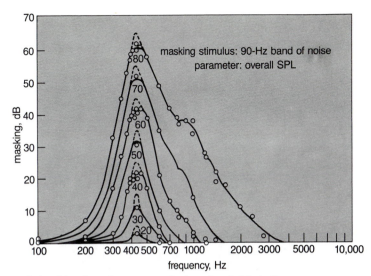

Relationship of one frequency to the tone threshold at other frequencies.

closer scrutiny, masking is seen as the failure of signal separation and, by implication, of complete signal analysis. Thus, the details of masking take on considerable importance for either the theoretical or practical study of hearing. *See* HEARING.

Most of the study of signal analysis in the auditory system has centered on frequency, or spectral, analysis. Why is it that two incoming signals are incompletely separated and therefore one is completely or partially masked? It might appear that if separation of components of different frequencies is the most useful analysis of the complex sounds of the environment, then the finest frequency analysis is the optimum kind of processing. The simplest view of auditory frequency analysis could start with the fact that the cochlea possesses about 3000 rows of hair cells, each cell (or, at least, each row) showing a narrow frequency response. From these rows come a total of about 30,000 nerve fibers. In actual operation, a single fiber performs like a filter, having a (half-power) width of about one-sixth octave and very steep sides, so that it can respond to only a very narrow range of frequencies. If the filters in each of the 3000 rows were tuned to a slightly different center frequency, there would be provision for extremely fine frequency resolution. On pursuing this further, it becomes apparent that the finer the tuning the more sluggish the temporal response, so that for rapidly changing sounds like speech or other environmental sounds some compromise must be made. Even from this superficial logic, a choice must be made between some optimum degree of interference between simultaneous sounds and a complete inability to process meaningful sounds; the ideal could not be complete or extremely fine frequency resolution. According to such an analysis, then, a certain amount of masking is inevitable, and the details of its operation figure prominently in attempts to generate a complete understanding of auditory processing. *See* EAR: Anatomy.

The specialist in the testing of defective hearing has a somewhat different view of masking because it is useful purposely to cover one sound with another.

TYPES OF MASKING

The description of masking thus far has presumed that there are two (or more) sounds present at the same time. Because interference can also occur between successive sounds, that original condition has been designated as simultaneous masking.

Forward Masking Because the auditory system is an elaborate processor rather than a simple transducer, it is to be expected that processing requires some time. After almost any kind of stimulation the system is not immediately back to its prestimulated state. For that reason a similar pattern of interference between sounds of different frequencies takes place if one sound follows another closely in time. This interference of a sound with a subsequent sound has come to be known as forward masking. Its spectral pattern, that is, how much a sound of one frequency influences subsequent sounds at other frequencies, is highly similar to the pattern for simultaneous masking. Because the system does recover quite rapidly, the pattern depends strongly on how quickly the second sound follows the end of the first, or masking, sound.

This picture of the temporal pattern of forward masking was well established as early as 1947 and takes the form shown in the graph. The numbers to the left of each curve indicate the intensity of a 400-millisecond tone that was used as the masker. The open circles show how much that previous tone changed the threshold for a brief (20-millisecond) probe tone that occurred after a silent interval as shown on the horizontal scale. This is one way of showing to what extent excitation from the previous tone still persists, or by what degree the system has still not returned to normal.

Forward masking also has both theoretic and practical implications. Some of the effects seen in simultaneous masking are attributable to such factors as suppression of one tone by another, or intermodulation distortion. Thus, by a comparison of simultaneous and forward masking some of these hidden behaviors of the auditory system can be at least partially sorted out.

Forward masking also occurs in everyday listening when sounds follow in rapid succession. Although both simultaneous and forward masking can operate in listening to speech, the effect of forward masking must be comparatively greater. It can be assumed that single sounds, where energy in one band may partially or wholly mask energy in another, have been learned originally with the same degree of masking present. Sequences of sounds, however, are sufficiently varied that perhaps some speech sounds do really interfere with the recognition of the succeeding sound.

Backward Masking More difficult to understand in logical terms is the fact that a sound can also interfere with another sound that occurred previously. This phenomenon has been labeled backward masking. It seems paradoxical, especially because, when the silent time between sounds is only a few milliseconds, an earlier sound is interfered with (backward masking) more than is true for a following sound (forward masking). Here it is important to remember that this is not a simple transmission line, and that many things may happen between a physical input and the perceptual output that is measured. It is conceivable, however, that a strong sound might mask an earlier weaker sound.

CLINICAL MASKING

In the measurement of hearing loss, the phenomenon of masking is used to make certain that the test tone is not heard by the ear not under test. In testing by air conduction, unless elaborate precautions are taken, the ear not being tested receives some small portion of the signal intended for the test ear. Usually the signal that leaks to the nontest ear is no more than 30 to 40 dB weaker than the test-ear signal. Therefore, if the difference in sensitivity of the two ears is as great as 30 dB, it becomes necessary to introduce a masking noise into the nontest ear to avoid a false cue. When the test is by bone conduction, the problem is much greater since the signal spreads almost unattenuated through the bone and tissue of the head to the ear not under

Temporal pattern of forward masking.

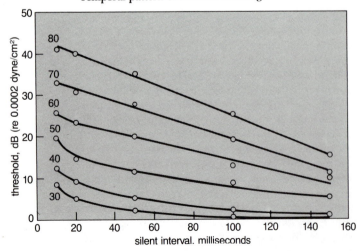

test. Thus the signal-obliterating type of masking must be used for bone conduction testing whenever the bone-conducted signal might be above threshold in the nontest ear. *See* AUDIOMETRY.

RELEASE FROM MASKING

Whenever the auditory system receives a different mixture of the desired signal and an interfering noise at the right ear than it receives at the left ear, it can detect the wanted signal more readily, that is, with a less favorable energy ratio, than when the two mixtures are identical. In the laboratory this can be made to occur by placing the signal in phase at the two ears, but the noise in some other interaural phase relation. Under the most favorable condition (signal in phase, noise in opposite phase) the audibility of low-frequency tonal signals may increase by as much as 15 dB.

Less dramatic advantages accrue to such interaural differences during everyday listening to speech when the wanted signal comes from a different direction than the interfering noise, and therefore the signal-and-noise mixture is different at the two ears. Here the measured advantage seems to be limited to 2 to 3 dB, but ease of listening is reported to be greatly enhanced. This is one aspect of the "cocktail party effect," where the desired voice can be quite readily followed in a babble of equally strong interfering voices.

CRITICAL BANDS

If the auditory system has achieved a reasonable compromise between fine frequency resolution and optimum temporal flexibility, it can be expressed as the width of the appropriate frequency-analyzing filter. The filter widths that appear to govern frequency analysis in the auditory system are labeled critical bandwidths.

The reason for using the filter analogy is that a number of auditory experiments indicate that the amount of interaction or interference between two sounds of different frequency changes with a certain frequency spacing of the sounds. Specifically, for sounds above 500 Hz, when the frequency ratio between two sounds increases above about 6/5 the interaction between the sounds decreases. This has been shown for the detection of sounds in various levels of noise, for loudness combination of sounds, for the beating of two or more sounds, and even for musical consonance.

The simpler filter model is an oversimplification of the actual auditory processing taking place. But a useful rule of thumb is that the system behaves as though some basic auditory process resembles a filter that is roughly 100 Hz wide for signals below 500 Hz and is about 20 percent of center frequency for frequencies 500 Hz and above.

Earl D. Schubert

Threshold Sensitivity

Threshold sensitivity of the auditory system refers to the softest sounds that can be detected by a listener. Usually, it is expressed as the minimum sound pressure level (SPL) that causes a defined behavioral response in a specified proportion of test trials. The experimental determination of threshold sensitivity is performed in an environment sufficiently quiet to eliminate interference from nontest sounds. The terms absolute sensitivity and absolute threshold are used interchangeably with threshold sensitivity. These terms are distinctly different from differential sensitivity, which relates to the detection of stimulus differences regardless of their intensities. Hearing loss, a major aspect of hearing impairment, is a reduction of threshold sensitivity brought about by damage to the auditory system.

Because the ear is not equally sensitive at all frequencies, threshold sensitivity is presented as a graph that describes its frequency dependence. Two types of data are compiled: minimum audible pressures (MAP) and minimum audible fields (MAF). Both are intended to estimate the best possible hearing sensitivity because the data are obtained under the quietest of conditions and the subjects are chosen to minimize the effects of age, ear disease, and exposure to noise. There are no systematic gender differences, and thresholds are generally 3 to 6 dB better when listening with two ears (binaural) rather than one ear (monaural).

There is no single low- or high-frequency limit to sensitivity. The ears' best sensitivity, however, is in the region around 1 to 3 kilohertz (kHz) with a gradual worsening above and below these frequencies. The short-term variability of human auditory sensitivity is about plus or minus 1 dB. Over the long term, however, auditory sensitivity can decline typically from the effects of aging and of exposure to noise. *See* PRESBYCUSIS.

Average minimum detectable sound pressure levels for humans, obtained from many subjects. The shape of the sensitivity curve is a direct result of the sound transmission characteristics of the outer and middle ear, and also the mechanics of the cochlear fluids and basilar membrane.

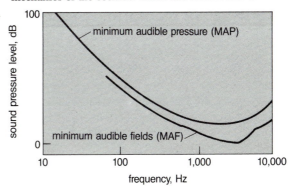

MEASUREMENT

Auditory experience is a construct of the brain and thus is different from sound or electricity, which are physical forms of energy. During perception, the detection of an event exists only in the brain of the listener. Therefore, the ability of the auditory system to detect soft sounds cannot be measured directly. Quantification of sensory experience requires special psychophysical methods. There are several different methods, but they all share a common basis: the physical stimulus is measured, a change in behavior is noted, and the effect of the stimulus is inferred.

The required equipment consists of several interconnected elements. An electric signal (that is, a sine wave) is generated and passed through an attenuator that controls the intensity of the sound generated by the earphone or loudspeaker to which the electric signal is delivered. A switch, either manual or automated, determines when and for how long the acoustic stimulus is presented.

The stimulus is measured with a sound-level meter to ensure that the magnitude or strength of the stimulus is known for all attenuator settings. The calibration is most important because it is the stimulus that is measured, while the ability to detect sounds is inferred from the subjects' responses.

When the stimulus is delivered by a loudspeaker with the subject in its sound field, the result of the threshold measure is an MAF; when it is delivered by using an earphone, the result is an MAP. There are systematic differences between the two results. Several different processes active in different frequency regions can account for the MAP thresholds being about 6 to 10 dB poorer than MAF thresholds. At a time when the discrepancy had not yet been resolved, the difference was referred to as the "missing 6 dB." If masking by physiologic noises, effects of ear canal resonances, and differences between artificial ear calibration and eardrum sound pressures all are taken into account, the discrepancy is resolved.

The subject is enclosed in an acoustically treated room to minimize the background sound that could interfere with performance of the task. There must also be a provision for the subject to inform the operator when a stimulus is detected. The response may be as simple as raising the subject's hand or as complex as pressing a button that connects to a computer.

The determination of threshold sensitivity will always take place in similar environments, but there are a number of distinctly different schemes of stimulus and response control, called psychophysical methods. There are classical methods based upon the classical theories of sensory threshold, and modern methods based upon the contemporary theory of signal detection.

Classical Methods Generally speaking, there are three classical methods: the method of limits, the method of constant stimuli, and the method of adjustment. Each uses a prescribed pattern of stimulus presentations and a specified format of subject responses. While the three differ in detail, each is an attempt to arrive at the smallest or weakest stimulus detectable in a given proportion of trials.

The earliest view of sensory threshold held that a critical amount of stimulus energy was necessary to elicit a sensory experience. Below that amount, the stimulus is never detected; above that amount the stimulus is always detected. To test this, a subject must listen to many stimulus presentations at a number of stimulus levels. The experimenter determines the proportion of correct detections of the stimulus at each stimulus level. Theoretically, the stimulus energy t would be considered the threshold because a lower stimulus would never be detected and a higher stimulus would always be detected. However, in actual experiments, as stimulus energy increases, the subject detects an increasing proportion of stimulus presentations. Because of this result, the simple theory was modified to allow for the threshold to vary from moment to moment in a random way, thus accommodating the S form of a data curve. The definition of threshold was then altered to specify a proportion of correct responses that corresponded to a single stimulus level. The value of this proportion, often 50 percent, is not entirely arbitrary because it is often governed by the method being used.

The method of limits employs a series of stimulus trials that either successively increase in in-

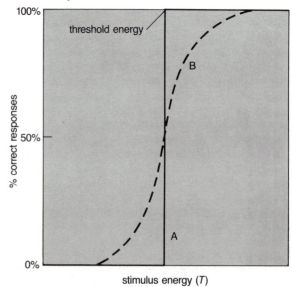

Expected (A) and actual (B) outcome of an experiment to determine the proportion of correct detections of a stimulus at many stimulus levels.

tensity until a response is obtained or successively decrease in intensity until responses cease. Many of these ascending and descending series are obtained, and the data are analyzed to determine the level that satisfies the threshold criterion. Modifications of this method are the basis of current clinical audiometry.

The method of constant stimuli requires that intensities in the region of threshold are each presented many times in a random order; the intensity corresponding to the predetermined criterion proportion is taken as threshold.

The method of adjustment gives control of intensity to the subject, who varies the stimulus until it just appears or disappears. As in the other methods, threshold corresponds to the level that produces a particular predetermined proportion of correct detections.

These methods were employed extensively during the classical era of psychophysics and are responsible for much of the data concerning auditory threshold sensitivity. However, there are some aspects of detection performance that are not accounted for by the classical theory.

Modern Methods An alternate and more contemporary view is that of signal detection theory. A major contribution based on this theory is its recognition of listener criteria as important in the assessment of stimulus detection capability. Some listeners are very conservative and must be certain that they heard the stimulus, while others will respond even if they are not at all sure. Differences in listener criteria can have substantial effects on threshold measures. A person using strict conservative criteria will yield higher (poorer) threshold sensitivities, while measures on someone with lax criteria will give lower estimates of threshold sensitivity.

Signal detection theory leads to its own psychophysical methods that provide for assessment of responses when no stimulus is presented (false positives) and the absence of a response when a stimulus is presented (false negative). These two factors allow for quantification based on listener criteria.

FACTORS THAT AFFECT THRESHOLD SENSITIVITY

The various psychophysical methods described above are not perfectly equivalent. Each has particular biases that result in different threshold curves, and there is no one curve of minimal audibility. When sufficient experimental control is exercised, however, the various methods yield remarkably similar results.

Instructions to Subject If the subject is told to respond only when a tone is distinctly heard, one result will be obtained; if instructed to respond to anything different from silence, a different result

will be obtained. Responses to tonality are at stronger stimulus levels. The difference between the two results is dependent upon frequency, but at 4000 Hz it is about 7 dB and is referred to as the atonal gap.

Masking As mentioned above, threshold sensitivity measurements are conducted in "silent" rooms because nontest sounds can interfere with the detection of the the test-stimulus presentations. The interference of one sound with the detection of another is called masking, and has the effect of elevating the measured threshold of a test stimulus. Because background noise cannot be totally eliminated, the absolute threshold sensitivity represents a practical lowest detectable intensity with the background sound held to a minimum. The threshold shift produced by a masker of moderate intensity is temporary. A lower threshold returns almost instantaneously upon withdrawal of the competing sound.

Duration Chemical measures of threshold sensitivity use a pure tone (single-frequency sinusoid) approximately 1 to 2 seconds in duration. Investigators have shown that test tones under 1-second duration have higher or poorer thresholds. For presentations under 0.25 second, the relation between stimulus duration and threshold is essentially linear regardless of frequency. For a tenfold decrease in duration the threshold increases about 10 dB. This effect sometimes is referred to as the time-intensity trading relation, and the underlying physiologic process often is referred to as temporal integration or temporal summation.

There is another reason that brief tones (that is, shorter than 250 milliseconds) are not used to estimate threshold sensitivity. As duration is reduced, the stimulus bandwidth is widened. For example, a 10-millisecond tone burst turned on abruptly could have a bandwidth wider than 2000 Hz. This cannot be considered a frequency-specific stimulus. When the frequency dependence of threshold sensitivity is being tested, a frequency-specific stimulus must be used.

Stimulus Bandwidth It is possible to measure absolute threshold with a stimulus of broader spectrum than a sine wave. Stimuli consisting of many spectral components on both sides of a test sine wave (for example, 1000 Hz) produce threshold intensities equal to those of a sine wave alone. However, the bandwidth of these stimuli cannot be increased indiscriminately. A limit is reached beyond which the intensity of a stimulus at threshold is larger than the intensity of the sine wave alone. Adding energy outside this band has no effect on the response. The spectral limit just described is called a critical band. This term, first used in an explanation of masking, has been found to apply to a wide variety of psychoacoustic phenomena, including the threshold of complex sounds. Critical bands also are frequency-dependent. For example, at 1000 Hz the critical bandwidth is about 160 Hz.

Exposure to Noise   Prolonged exposure to excessive noise can temporarily raise auditory thresholds, and is called temporary threshold shift (TTS). While recovery can occur if the ear is returned to quiet, permanent damage can result if exposures are long with no recovery period and are repeated many times over the course of years. An implication of this may be found in the area of industrial hearing testing, where workers are required to be in a noise-free environment for eight hours prior to examination. This minimizes the effects of temporary noise-induced hearing loss. *See* HEARING LOSS: Noise-Induced.

Bibliography

Gelfand, Stanley A.: *Hearing: An Introduction to Psychological and Physiological Acoustics*, Marcel Dekker, New York, 1981.

Yost, William A., and Donald W. Nielsen: *Fundamentals of Hearing: An Introduction*, Holt, Rinehart and Winston, New York, 1972.

William M. Aldrich

Temporal Factors in Audition

Each phrase and each word in a verbal string takes a specific amount of time for the speaker to produce, and in turn, each word takes a specific time for the listener to process auditorially. Between words and phrases there exist spatial intervals which are necessary for the adequate perception of speech and language. Because of the continuous nature of everyday speech, the discrete temporal requirements of words and phrases as well as the existence of these spatial elements normally are not discernible. The importance of the temporal nature of these elements, however, becomes apparent in difficult listening conditions, as exemplified by experimental manipulation and by observations of certain auditorially handicapping conditions. This section will focus on the effects that temporal factors have upon the perception of speech. Speech sounds are made up of tones and noises of brief duration, and information about the temporal nature of nonspeech sounds is important in understanding better the basis for the perception of speech sound.

CHARACTERISTICS OF TEMPORAL FACTORS

The minimum temporal interval necessary for short-duration sounds such as clicks to be perceived as separate occurrences is about 2 milliseconds. On the other hand, accurate judgment of the order of appearance of nonspeech sounds requires a temporal interval in the neighborhood of 20 milliseconds. More complex acoustic stimuli, such as speech sounds, have been found to require temporal intervals of 25 to 70 milliseconds to be perceived as separate and successive. Successive sounds tend to

fuse when separated by less than 2 milliseconds for clicks and less than 30 milliseconds for more complex stimuli. As a related phenomenon, the more intense a sound of brief duration, the longer a preceding silent interval of fixed duration will be judged by a listener.

When two sounds are judged equal in loudness, the duration of the interval between the sounds must be longer for accurate judgment of temporal order than if one on the pair of sounds is louder than the other. In fact, the threshold of the identification of temporal order changes as a function of the duration of the steady-state portion of the preceding sound. Instead, the manipulation of variables such as loudness, listener characteristics (for example, trained vs. untrained), and nature of the stimuli can result in the need for separation intervals between speech sounds of as much as 75 milliseconds in order to achieve accurate reports of order of appearance of these sounds. Individuals with sensorineural hearing losses often require even longer temporal intervals to obtain accurate perceptions of temporal order.

How long a signal must persist before a listener can realize its characteristics or even its existence is related to several factors, including the intensity of the signal. A short-duration sound of 50 milliseconds may be identifiable as a tone or even a speech sound. Further, the longer the duration of a tone of given intensity, for example, 200 to 300 milliseconds, the louder it may be judged by a listener. In turn, the duration of the tone can be reduced to below 200 milliseconds and equal loudness can still be obtained by adjusting other factors such as stimulus onset or rise time, the duration of temporal intervals between the stimuli, and the frequency characteristics of the stimulus. For example, it takes about 200 milliseconds for a tone to reach maximum loudness level for the listener. Additionally, as the duration of the signal is shortened below 200 milliseconds, the greater its intensity must be for the signal to be perceived. The improvement in threshold with increase of signal duration (up to about 200 milliseconds) is a manifestation of temporal integration or temporal summation. The phenomenon also is referred to as the time-intensity trading relation.

Temporal integration and temporal order phenomena which exist at these discrete acoustic levels also exist for speech. For example, the intensity necessary to reach thresholds for vowel identification appears to vary inversely with the duration of the acoustic steady-state portion of the vowel, as well as the durations of signal characteristics preceding and succeeding the vowel.

TEMPORAL FACTORS IN SPEECH PERCEPTION

The temporal characteristics of perception of speech sounds, known as phonemes, have a major significance for theories of speech perception. The phoneme comprises various acoustic and physiologic features which tend to characterize its nature. Generally, phonemes are classed as consonants (such as /k/ and /t/) or vowels (such as /a/), as in the word "cat." Consonants tend to be acoustically noisier than vowels, and the acoustic structure (if any) of consonants normally is less clear compared to vowels. Consonants typically are much shorter in duration and tend to be abrupt in onset and offset compared to the longer and more continuous vowel sounds. Accurate identification of vowels requires longer acoustic durations than consonants. Moreover, naturally produced vowel phonemes require less acoustic time (25 to 30 milliseconds) to be accurately identified when produced in isolation than when these same phonemes are produced in a context (50 to 70 milliseconds) bounded by consonants. Consonants, which require less duration than vowels for accurate identification, also require longer duration for identification in context (approximately 20 to 40 milliseconds) than in isolation (approximately 16 to 30 milliseconds). The error limits for phoneme identification accuracy is about 5 to 10 milliseconds, suggesting that the listener can make phonemic decisions based upon extremely small differences in phoneme duration.

Speech sounds combine to make up syllables and words, and duration again plays a role in perceptual accuracy. For example, if the duration of a silent interval between the first and second syllable of the word "rapid" is less than about 70 (± 10) milliseconds, the word will be perceived as "rabid."

Another important aspect of phoneme perception is the transition area between the consonants preceding and following the vowels. A vowel artificially produced in isolation sounds like a continuous buzz, although isolated vowels can be discriminated with some degree of accuracy. The "vowelness" of the vowel, however, becomes obvious when placed in a context with other phonemes, particularly consonants. Very brief acoustic transition areas of 3 to 10 milliseconds between the vowel and consonants serve as cues to consonant phoneme identification and discrimination. Acoustic concentration areas of the vowels vary in frequency, but flow into transition areas that point to the appropriate frequency areas for the peception of a specific consonant. If the brief durations of these transition areas is tampered with, the resulting phoneme perception can change dramatically.

Another example of the importance of temporal integrity of the speech signal relates to the perceptual cuing of the voiced-voiceless contrast which appears to depend in large part on voice onset time (VOT). For voiced sounds (such as /b/) the VOT is short, of the order of 20 to 30 milliseconds, but for voiceless sounds the VOT can run considerably longer. These effects, however, can be offset by modification of other factors, such as the intensity of the consonant burst and the overall duration and rise-decay times of various pre- and postconsonant acoustic characteristics.

Consonant perception tends to be categoric in nature, and vowel perception tends to be continuous in nature. The motor movements for consonant production tend to have abrupt articulatory boundaries, compared to the more continuous and flowing articulatory movements associated with vowel production. These phonemena, coupled with the tendency of the articulators to overshoot and undershoot their respective targets during consonant production (coarticulation), have given rise to the idea that speech perception mirrors production. The motor theory of speech perception suggests that speech production is so rapid that the listener would find it impossible to perceive speech on an acoustically oriented phoneme-by-phoneme basis. As suggested by the motor theory, the listener uses acoustic patterns in the signal in order to cue stored patterns of learned articulatory gestures during perception. Thus, the bases for speech perception, according to the motor theory, are these stored motor patterns of speech perception, which are characterized by a variety of temporal factors.

Syllable duration also plays a vital role in speech perception, at least for adults. For example, syllables of less than 200 milliseconds tend to cue the perception of a voiceless final-stop consonant (such as /t/); if greater than 400 milliseconds, consonant cuing tends to be ambiguous. Although normal speaking rates can have a significant effect on the duration of phonemes, the relative duration of syllables in a word or phrase tends to remain constant. Thus, one can argue that normal speech perception is based upon speech timing and rhythm, and that judgments of timing occur at the speech syllable level. More specifically, speech perception in normal running speech may be enhanced by reference to phonemic clauses (syntagmas), which are bound phrases that can include several words simultaneously. The boundaries between these words may be lost, in a sense, due to the coarticulation effects, yielding to the use of syntagmas as basic units of speech perception. It becomes important, therefore, to maintain not only the integrity of the relative duration of speech sounds but also the relative durations of these perceptual phrase units.

TIME-ALTERED SPEECH SOUNDS AND WORDS

Contemporary views of hearing indicate that there is at least a short- and a long-term-based storage mechanism for incoming sounds that permits the listener to integrate and interpret continuous speech signals. These views implicitly assume that the memory store has certain temporal biases. In the phrase "Pondie the dog and Sam the cat like to play together," the speech signals—whether they are independent phonemes, such as the "p" in "Pondie," or words in a statement as in "Pondie" followed by the words "the" and "dog"—enter the listener's auditory system in a specified temporal order or sequence. If each item is to be understood by the listener and then integrated into a percept that makes sense, each word and each sound in each word must have a relatively high degree of intelligibility.

It is easy to demonstrate that the intelligibility of a speech signal can be decreased by its being presented too softly or too loudly or by burying it in a high level of noise. Intelligibility of a speech sound also can be decreased if its temporal characteristics are distorted.

The temporal characteristics of speech perception can be distorted by manipulating the temporal intervals between phonemes in words (interphonemic intervals, or IPI). In the word "cat" silent intervals of varying lengths can be placed between the phonemes of the word (for example, /k/silence /a/silence/t/). When older children are presented with single-syllable nonsense words with variable IPIs, there are significant decreases in percent correct identification scores when the IPI reaches 200 milliseconds in duration. The same result is found with meaningful words, except that scores tend to rebound (improve) when the IPI reaches 400 milliseconds. The children apparently process whole words, and as the IPI increases to 200 milliseconds, the ability to do this decreases. When the IPI reaches 400 milliseconds, however, the children process individually, sequentially presented phonemes, and then are able to resynthesize these phonemes into meaningful whole-word units. This phonemenon shows the importance that temporal intervals play in the storage systems for speech perception.

One way to distort the temporal characteristics of speech is to shorten the consonants or the vowels. Because consonants are much shorter in duration than vowels, the effects of such manipulations are more apparent for consonants than for vowels. Because vowels are longer, they are considered to have more temporal redundancy and are thus less susceptible to temporal distortion than consonants. Because of this temporal redundancy and because of the more fluid nature of vowels relative to consonants, it has been shown that up to 50 percent of a vowel in a word such as "dog" can be removed without significantly decreasing intelligibility of the word to the listener. On the other hand, if 50 percent of the shorter consonants /d/ and /g/ in the word were removed, the average listener would have difficulty identifying the word accurately.

Intelligibility also can be affected by temporarily distorting whole words. Such distortions can be accomplished in a variety of ways, including simply talking faster, using a simple but tedious cut-and-splice procedure, or using sophisticated recording devices and computers. Regardless of the method employed, the general purpose is the same—to shorten or time-compress the stimulus under study. When using time-compression procedures, it is necessary to optimize the size of the intervals that are discarded from the word. For example, intelligibility decreases as the size of the discarded intervals increases and approaches the size of phonemes, syllables, and words. Another factor to consider is linguistic complexity, as exemplified by the better maintenance of intelligibility of digits as time compression increases compared to that of monosyllabic words and phrases. Generally, the intelligibility of words decreases as amount of time compression increases, with the most significant drop in intelligibility occurring at 60 percent time compression. The effects of temporal degradation upon intelligibility can be offset to a limited extent by increasing the intensity or the sensation level of presentation. The intelligibility of time-compressed words also increases as a function of increasing age in children, although it seems to decrease as a function of increasing age in geriatric populations.

TIME-ALTERED INTERSTIMULUS INTERVALS AND LINGUISTIC COMPLEXITY

Another means of studying the temporal factors in speech perception is to alter the temporal nature of the interstimulus intervals. This can be demonstrated by manipulating an entire sentence. For example, in the phrase "Pondie the dog and Sam the cat like to play together," spaces (intervals) can be observed between (inter) the words (stimuli) of the statement. Thus, if one were to verbalize this statement, the verbalization would include the stimuli and the intervals between the stimuli in a continuous verbal stream. If the statement were to be unselectively time-compressed, there would be a reduction in the length of both the stimulus items (the words) and the interstimulus intervals by a like amount. However, these intervals serve linguistic and perceptual purposes by allowing the listener time to order the incoming words into some interpretable sequence. Acceptable intelligibility of the verbal statement can be maintained when it has been time-compressed if the interstimulus interval is not destroyed. If the interstimulus interval increases too much relative to the duration of the words, the ability to synthesize the incoming signal may be reached and intelligibility again will decrease.

The optimal interstimulus interval appears to lie between 50 and 200 milliseconds. If the interstimulus interval is too short or nonexistent, the listener's auditory processing system cannot adequately store the information in proper order; if it is too long, the listener's system loses items occurring earlier in the sequence. Thus, degraded temporal factors in the speech signal can result in order errors as well as item errors. If the item is compressed, the effect of the time compression can be partially offset by lengthening the interstimulus interval, up to a point. Conversely, the interstimulus interval can be reduced significantly as long as the normal integrity of the stimulus is maintained, up to a point.

As noted above, levels of linguistic complexity can interact with the temporal factors in affecting the perception of speech. For children, the accuracy of recalling time-compressed sentences increases as a function of increasing age and decreasing sentence length and time compression. On a more complex level, one might consider the nature of recalling sentences of varying length and meaningfulness where the interstimulus intervals and the word durations have been independently altered through time compression. As might be expected, the recall accuracy decreases with increasing temporal compression of the stimulus words in word sequences. To an extent, however, this degradation in recall accuracy can be offset by increasing the interstimulus intervals within the word sequences and by increasing the meaningfulness of the word sequences. However, as words in a sequence more closely approximate natural sentences, the effect of temporal distortion of the words plays a greater role in recall accuracy compared to that of the interstimulus interval. Apparently the redundant nature of a naturally produced normal sentence allows for adequate accuracy and auditory processing of the speech up to a time-compression level of about 50 percent. When the naturalness of the sentence is reduced, as in a simple string of contextually unrelated words, the interstimulus interval needs to be increased in order to maintain accuracy of recall. Generally, both children and adults show similar effects as a result of covarying sentence length with word duration, interstimulus interval, and contextual meaningfulness.

COMPREHENSION OF TIME-ALTERED SPEECH

Generally, the recognition of the speech signal and accurate reproduction by the listener of that signal is referred to as intelligibility. Beyond intelligibility, concept of comprehension of the speech signal by the listener must be considered. Persons with high mental aptitude seem to comprehend temporally distorted passages and readings better than persons with low mental abilities. Further, it seems that recall comprehension, like intelligibility, tends to decrease significantly when the temporal characteristics and the message have been reduced to about 50 percent of their original duration. The detrimental effects of time compression upon com-

prehension, however, can be offset by reducing the linguistic complexity of the signal and by a variety of listener-training techniques. Normal listeners can be trained to tolerate time-compressed passages up to about the 50 percent level and, when asked to return to a normal listening rate, will indicate a preference for the faster signal.

A variety of complex theories and ideas have been derived to explain why temporal distortion adversely affects intelligibility and comprehension of speech. Generally, a portion of the listener's brain is devoted to processing auditory signals. If the incoming signals are too rapid, a neurophysiologic bottleneck effect can occur, resulting in item and order errors in recall accuracy. This effect is increased when the interstimulus interval is reduced, resulting in a reduction in time allotted for the listener to process a given stimulus item in the continuous stream of speech. The exact neurologic and cognitive nature of this bottleneck phenomenon, however, has yet to be explained.

APPLICATION

Temporal distortion of speech has been found to have some important applications in education and in other clinical circumstances. Central auditory neurologic mechanisms are so constituted that when some damage is done to them they often seem to be able to operate with unnoticeable deficit when confronted with normal speech under easy listening conditions. The use of time compression to reduce the temporal redundancy of the speech signal, and thereby increase the difficulty level of the signal, has been found useful in detecting subtle lesions in the auditory nervous system. The results of such tests in conjunction with other measures and medical data may be used to determine if damage to the central auditory system exists, and to determine the effect that such damage may have upon the person's ability to understand normal language. For example, time-altered speech signals may be used to enhance the diagnosis of children whose speech and language problems are primarily developmental in nature from those whose speech and language problems have a neuropathologic basis.

An understanding of the nature and limitations of the temporal factors in speech signals combined with behavioral training techniques can lead to useful applications to the general population as well as to various special populations. For example, students can be trained to use time compression to enhance self-paced learning of tape-recorded educational materials. The student can differentially increase the preferred speech of easier material and decrease that of more difficult material. Severely visually impaired persons, who rely heavily on aural communication, have made use of recorded time-altered speech for educational and recreational purposes through, for example, programs of tape-recorded books and other materials. On the other hand, severely hearing-impaired persons, who depend heavily on visual communication and who tend to perform poorly on temporally based psychoacoustic measures, have demonstrated particular talent in processing time-compressed American Sign Language video presentations.

SUMMARY

Temporal factors associated with speech signals play a major role in the perceptual integration and interpretation of the physical parameters of sound. If speech sounds or words or even sentences and passages are temporally reduced, they can be adequately perceived and understood by a normal listener up to a reduction of 50 percent. Beyond this level, however, significant reductions in intelligibility and comprehension are observed. Also, the effects of the reductions in the temporal redundancy of speech are context-dependent, and interact with interstimulus intervals inherent in the signal, with the linguistic complexity of the signal such as sentence length and meaningfulness, as well as with listener training and predisposition to tolerate such distortion.

Another means of determining the influence of temporal factors in psychoacoustics is the study of periodicity in perception. When segments of noise are presented dichotically, for example, listeners can detect a sense of periodicity or flutter in the signal presentation when the durations of the segmented noises are less than 140 milliseconds. When the noise duration increases to 200 milliseconds or more, periodicity can still be heard, but the listener senses that the periodic nature of the stimuli moves from the peripheral hearing mechanism to a more central location within the head, thereby suggesting that the temporal properties inherent in acoustic signals have both peripheral and central processing neuromechanisms. The perceived periodic nature of the stimuli, of course, can be adjusted by manipulating the interaural temporal separation in the listening task. In addition, the auditory system apparently can distinguish a series of pulses with interruption rates of 1 to 1½ milliseconds before perceiving the sound series as a continuous, uninterrupted stream of sound. Moreover, the phenomenon of jitter can be detected with temporal intervals as low as 0.1 millisecond.

The temporal resolving power of the peripheral and central auditory system is extremely sensitive to the temporal characteristics of acoustic stimuli. Such sophistication in the temporal resolution of acoustic information is necessary in order for listeners to process accurately the extremely complex acoustic signals of speech and messages of language, particularly in view of the acoustically difficult listening conditions of everyday speech.

Bibliography

Babkoff, H., and S. Sutton: "Perception of Temporal Order and Loudness Judgments for Dichotic Clicks," *Journal of the Acoustical Society of America*, 35:574–577, 1963.

Beasley, D., and D. Beasley: "Auditory Reassembly Abilities of Black and White First- and Third-Grade Children," *Journal of Speech and Hearing Research*, 16(2):213–221, 1973.

———— and J. Maki: "Time- and Frequency-Altered Speech," in N. Lass (ed.), *Contemporary Issues in Experimental Phonetics*, chap. 12, pp. 419–458, Academic Press, New York, 1976.

———— and A. Rintelmann: "Central Auditory Processing," in W. Rintelmann (ed.), *Hearing Assessment*, chap. 10, pp. 321–349, University Park Press, Baltimore, 1979.

Campbell, R. A., and S. A. Counter: "Temporal Integration and Periodicity Pitch," *Journal of the Acoustical Society of America*, 45(3):691–693, 1969.

Cole, R. A., and J. Jakimik: "Segmenting Speech into Words," *Journal of the Acoustical Society of America*, 67(4):1323–1332, 1980.

Creelman, C. D.: "Human Discrimination of Auditory Duration," *Journal of the Acoustical Society of America*, 34:582–593, 1962.

Daniloff, R. G., G. Schuckers, and L. Feth: *The Physiology of Speech and Hearing: An Introduction*, Prentice-Hall, Englewood Cliffs, New Jersey, 1980.

Duker, S.: *Time-Compressed Speech*, vols. 1-3, Scarecrow Press, Metuchen, New Jersey, 1974.

Fant, G.: *Speech Sounds and Features*, MIT Press, Cambridge, Massachusetts, 1973.

Fay, W. G.: *Temporal Sequence in the Perception of Speech*, Mouton and Co., The Hague, 1966.

Gerber, S. E. (ed.): *Introductory Hearing Science*, W. B. Saunders, Philadelphia, 1974.

Heiman, G., and R. Tweney: "Intelligibility and Comprehension of Time-Compressed Sign Language Narratives," *Journal of Psycholinguistic Research*, 10(1):3–15, 1981.

Hirsh, I. J., and C. E. Sherrick: "Perceived Order in Different Sense Modalities," *Journal of Experimental Psychology*, 62(5):423–432, 1961.

Hafter, E. R.: "Lateralization Model and the Role of Time-Intensity Tradings in Binaural Masking: Can the Data be Explained by a Time-Only Hypothesis?", *Journal of the Acoustical Society of America*, 62(3):633–635, 1977.

Huggins, A. W. F.: "On the Perception of Temporal Phenomena in Speech," *Journal of the Acoustical Society of America*, 51(4):1279–1290, 1972.

————: "Is Periodicity Detection Central?", *Journal of the Acoustical Society of America*, 71(4):963–966, 1982.

Irwin, R. J., and S. C. Purdy: "The Minimum Detectable Duration of Auditory Signals for Normal and Hearing-Impaired Listeners," *Journal of the Acoustical Society of America*, 71(4):967–974, 1982.

Kuhl, P.: "Speech Perception: An Overview of Current Issues, in N. Lass et al. (eds.), *Speech, Language, and*

Hearing: Normal Processes, vol. 1, chap. 10, pp. 286–322, W. B. Saunders, Philadelphia, 1982.

Licklider, J. C. R.: "Basic Correlates of the Auditory Stimulus," in S. S. Stevens (ed.), *Handbook of Experimental Psychology*, John Wiley and Sons, New York, 1951.

Liberman, A. M., et al.: "A Motor Theory of Speech Perception," paper presented to the Speech Communication Seminar, Speech Transmission Laboratory, Royal Institute of Technology, Stockholm, Sweden, 1962.

————— et al.: "Perception of the Speech Code," *Psychological Review*, 74(6):431–461, 1967.

Miller, J.: "Phonetic Perception: Evidence for Context-Dependent and Context-Independent Processing," *Journal of the Acoustical Society of America*, 69(3):822–831, 1981.

Nooteboom, S. G., and G. J. Doodeman: "Production and Perception of Vowel Length in Spoken Sentences," *Journal of the Acoustical Society of America*, 67(1):276–287, 1980.

Osberger, M., and H. Levitt: "The Effect of Timing Errors on the Intelligibility of Deaf Children's Speech," *Journal of the Acoustical Society of America*, 65(5):1316–1324, 1979.

Pastore, R. E., L. B. Harris, and J. K. Kaplan: "Temporal Order Identification: Some Parameter Dependencies," *Journal of the Acoustical Society of America*, 71(2):430–436, 1982.

Port, R. F.: "Linguistic Timing Factors in Combination," *Journal of the Acoustical Society of America*, 69(1):262–274, 1981.

Pantalos, J., G. H. Schuckers, and N. Hipskind: "Sentence Length-Duration Relationships in an Auditory Assembly Task," *Journal of Communication Disorders*, 8:61–75, 1975.

Pribram, K.: *Languages of the Brain*, Prentice-Hall, Englewood Cliffs, New Jersey, 1971.

Sanders, D.: *Aural Rehabilitation*, pp. 98–99, Prentice-Hall, Englewood Cliffs, New Jersey, 1971.

Scharf, B.: "Loudness and Frequency Sensitivity at Short Duration," in R. Plomp and G. F. Smoorenberg (eds.), *Frequency Analysis and Periodicity Detection in Hearing*, A. W. Sijthoff, Leiden, 1970.

Schwartz, M. F.: "A Study of Thresholds of Identification for Vowels as a Function of Their Duration," *Journal of Auditory Research*, 3:47–52, 1963.

Scott, D. R.: "Duration as a Cue to the Perception of Phrase Boundary," *Journal of the Acoustical Society of America*, 71(4):996–1007, 1982.

Shriner, T. H., and R. G. Daniloff: "Reassembly of Segmented CVC Syllables by Children," *Journal of Speech and Hearing Research*, 13(3):537–547, 1970.

Sonn, M.: *Psychoacoustical Terminology*, Raytheon Corporation, Portsmouth, Rhode Island, 1969.

Tekeli, M. E., and W. L. Cullinan: "The Perception of Temporally Segmented Spoken Vowel and Vowel-Consonant Syllables," Annual Convention of American Speech and Hearing Association, Washington, D.C., 1975.

Tobias, J. V. (ed.): *Foundations of Modern Auditory Theory*, vol. 1, Academic Press, New York, 1970.

Tyler, R., et al.: "Psychoacoustic and Phonetic Temporal Processing in Normal and Hearing-Impaired Listeners, *Journal of Acoustical Society of America*, 72(3):740–752, 1982.

Wardrip-Fruin, C.: "On the Status of Temporal Cues to Phonetic Categories: Preceding Vowel Duration as a Cue to Voicing in Final Stop Consonants," *Journal of the Acoustical Society of America*, 71(1):187–195, 1982.

Wright, H. N.: "Clinical Measurement of Temporal Auditory Summation," *Journal of Speech and Hearing Research*, 11(1):109–127, 1968.

Daniel S. Beasley

PSYCHOLINGUISTICS

Psycholinguistics is a branch of psychology primarily concerned with language behavior, that is, with the way in which people learn, use, and understand language. The field is relatively new, having begun about 1957. Research with deaf people and sign language is an even newer and burgeoning area within psycholinguistics. Psycholinguists have been primarily interested in two major areas: how children learn language and how people process language.

The section below on language development traces the learning of both sign language and English in children who are either born deaf or who have lost their hearing before acquiring language. Although the development of English language skills is typically delayed, deaf children of deaf parents learn sign language in a way that closely parallels hearing children's learning of spoken languages.

Because sign language is visual rather than auditory, it presents many interesting questions. It is especially useful for researchers interested in separating the properties of language per se from the properties of the human auditory system. The section below on sign language processing discusses how deaf people use and understand sign language. The role of the brain in sign language production and perception is compared and contrasted with hearing people's use of speech.

Robert Lee Williams

Language Development

The acquisition of language and language-related skills is of paramount importance in the development, education, and adjustment of deaf children. Normally hearing parents of deaf children are likely to aspire for their children to master spoken language. Although many hearing-impaired children do acquire proficiency in speech and speechreading, many others, depending in part on age at onset and degree of hearing loss, find that learning to communicate orally is an immensely arduous and ultimately unsuccessful task. On the other hand, when deaf children are born into families with deaf parents or other close deaf relatives, the children are much more likely to experience an early introduction to manual communication. Such children typically acquire facility rapidly with language in the manual mode; receptive and expressive communication regularly occurs, often with other signing members of the family and community. Regardless of family hearing background, however, the education of deaf students generally gives a high priority to skills tied to the dominant spoken language in the society, such as reading and writing, and the children's educational success will depend on how well they master these language-related tasks. Moreover, deaf children's facility in spoken and signed languages often has a profound impact on their social, cultural, and emotional development.

SPOKEN LANGUAGE

In most families, normally hearing children are surrounded by spoken language and, from an early age, become active participants in the vocal communication process. Even before these children are able to produce recognizable spoken words, they frequently are engaged in vocal play, and often demonstrate nonverbally their understanding of many words. By the time these children have reached their fifth birthday, they probably have mastered, with little apparent effort, most of the grammatical rules of their native language.

This seeming ease of mastery contrasts markedly with the language-learning experience of most deaf children. About 90 percent of deaf children in the United States are born to parents with normal hearing. Because most of these parents have neither a background in deaf education nor any previous experience with deafness in their families, the determination of hearing loss in their children often constitutes their introduction to deafness and precipitates a series of important decisions they will need to make about their children's language and education. In the past, hearing parents of deaf children were usually discouraged by their physicians and by speech and hearing specialists from interacting with their children through manual communication (sign language and fingerspelling); this situation continues to exist to some degree. Many have been urged to interact with their deaf children through speech alone, and have been led to believe that their children will acquire sufficient oral-aural skills through such interaction and through formal education.

Unfortunately, most hearing parents do not learn to communicate effectively with their deaf children through speech, sign language, or fingerspelling, either singly or in combination. This lack of communication often adversely affects the personal relationships between hearing parents and their deaf children. Children with impaired hearing also frequently miss out on the extensive playful language

interaction bouts that characterize caregiver-child interaction in families with a fully shared language. Instead, hearing parents' verbal interactions with their deaf children often result in strain and frustration for both parents and children. Not surprisingly, then, the onset of spoken language in hearing-impaired children typically is delayed in comparison with that of children with normal hearing. The content and structure in the early stages of spoken language use, however, appear to be quite similar, as the same syntactic and semantic forms are common to both deaf and hearing children. *See* SOCIALIZATION: Families.

Most deaf students receive years of training in spoken language, often beginning in home-based or preschool programs and continuing into high school, college, and beyond. Even after these many years of training, the speech of many prelingually profoundly deaf individuals remains very difficult to understand. The speech often is at an abnormal pitch, with distinctly different intonation patterns. For those aspects of speech production that are visible on the lips, the intelligibility is often quite good; in contrast, vowels and lingual consonants usually prove particularly difficult. Still, only a small percentage of deaf students acquire clearly recognizable speech and effective speechreading skills. The success of some of these students probably can be attributed to less severe levels of hearing loss, differential hearing loss across the speech spectrum, or postlingual onset that make such youngsters "good bets" for the production or retention of speech. Yet other deaf students' remarkable achievements in this domain cannot be so readily explained. Although it is not clear what characteristics are responsible for their achievement, deaf students who attain success in oral communication are more likely to be of above-average intelligence, to be very persistent, and to have parents and teachers who are highly dedicated to their training and progress in spoken language skills. *See* SPEECH; SPEECH TRAINING.

Despite many years of speech training, most deaf students do not acquire facility in an auditory-vocal language. Not only is their speech in most cases largely unintelligible, but their command of reading and writing often is well below that of their hearing contemporaries. Descriptions of deaf students' English usage, moreover, frequently characterize it as adhering rigidly to simple sentence patterns, with the students experiencing particular difficulty in mastering inflectional or derivational endings, deletion rules, correct word order, verb forms, and function words. Some of these difficulties probably can be attributed to the students' preferred learning and language modes; for many deaf students the mode is a visual one. That is, it is quite likely that signed and spoken languages adapt themselves to different kinds of grammatical structures because of differences between the language modalities. This interpretation is given additional credence by the findings that as students' hearing levels decrease the incidence of their syntactic errors typically increases, that particular errors in usage are common to many deaf students, and that these errors often are highly resistant to change. Some of the English usage problems of deaf students probably also should be attributed to inadequate assessment of specific individual needs and abilities in early childhood. Consequently, years of potentially valuable training and development may have been eclipsed as these individuals may not have progressed adequately in their initial educational programs.

LANGUAGE AND DEAF EDUCATION

A long-standing controversy among educators of deaf students has been the relative efficacy of manual and oral techniques in fostering the language skills and educational progress of deaf students. Although some of the first educational institutions for deaf persons founded in the United States embraced manual communication, oral communication has predominated in the education of deaf students for most of the past century. In this latter approach, all effort is made to teach the language prevalent in the society by oral means, along with auditory amplification and speechreading. Strong advocates of oral education have even argued that signing to deaf children should be strictly prohibited. Despite this oral emphasis, many deaf students who acquired the unfortunate label of "oral failure" eventually received their training through sign language and fingerspelling. *See* EDUCATION: Communication; HISTORY: Sign Language Controversy.

One reason often advanced by supporters of the oral-only approach for recommending to parents that they not communicate manually with their deaf children is that such gestures, being more easily acquired by the children, would supplant or greatly retard the children's spoken language development. Although it may seem reasonable to suppose that if one prevents children from following one avenue of communication, they will pursue another, this recommendation does not appear to be well grounded in systematic research. On the contrary, some evidence suggests that if deaf children receive training in both language modalities, their improvement in ability to communicate manually prompts improvement in their spoken language skills.

A review of the literature on the educational achievement of deaf students, moreover, suggests that a prohibition on signing probably is not justified in most cases. Indeed, in studies that compared the relative effectiveness of oral and manual methods, the students in the manual group frequently scored higher in overall educational achievement, in social adjustment, in speechreading, in mathematics, and in reading; and there were often no significant differences between oral and manual groups in speech skills. It should be noted, however, that a number of these evaluations had design limitations in that they compared the achievement of deaf students with deaf parents against the performance of deaf students with hearing parents; thus, other factors, such as parental acceptance of deafness, may also have influenced the results. Regardless, such research findings cast doubt upon the appropriateness of strictly oral programs for all deaf students.

In light of these findings, it is not surprising that the 1970s witnessed a dramatic swing in the reported dominant educational philosophies of schools for deaf children, with most programs announcing a change from an oral approach to a program of total communication. In such an approach, the emphasis is placed on teaching language and language-related skills without being limited to any specific modality, and teachers often use signs, fingerspelling, oral skills (speech and speechreading), amplified residual hearing, reading, and writing to foster these skills. *See* SOCIOLINGUISTICS: Total Communication.

In addition to the principal oral and manual programs, there have been several interesting innovations designed to facilitate language acquisition and usage in deaf students since the 1970s. Unfortunately, longitudinal evaluations of their effectiveness generally have not yet been reported in detail. One such approach is cued speech, which consists of a small number of specially designed hand movements (not signs) made by the speaker near his or her face. These gestures are designed to help deaf persons distinguish between those phonemes that cannot be read from the lips alone. A second approach, cochlear implants, consists of surgically placing a small electronic device into the ear of a deaf person. These devices send an electronic signal or impulse to the wearer that provides the sensation of sound, but current models are limited in their ability to transmit speech. A third approach consists of the use of various gestural language systems (for example, Signed English, Signing Exact English) specifically designed to render English in the manual mode. The rationale behind the development of these systems is that, because they duplicate English syntax and morphology manually, they would assist deaf students in their mastery of English reading and writing skills. Yet the very complexity of the systems themselves often results in teachers and students using incomplete or inconsistent variations of the systems. *See* COCHLEAR IMPLANTS; MANUALLY CODED ENGLISH; MOUTH-HAND SYSTEMS: Cued Speech.

SIGN LANGUAGE ACQUISITION

In most cases, the hearing parents of deaf children have had no previous experience interacting with deaf persons, except perhaps with older friends or relatives whose hearing has deteriorated. Such parents often are inadequately prepared to handle their children's deafness. They frequently receive contradictory advice on how best to rear their deaf children, and may fail to learn to communicate effectively with them. In contrast, deaf children brought up in families where one or both parents are deaf are likely to be more readily accepted, and to participate in a rich linguistic environment from early childhood. As with hearing infants learning to speak, deaf infants acquiring American Sign Language babble manually prior to producing their first lexical items. As they grow up, these deaf children learn to sign not only from communicating with their parents, but from contacts with other signers in the deaf community as well. Also, as with hearing children, deaf children will play with their language and use it in every conceivable setting. Not only will these children sign to members of their family and their friends, but they also will frequently sign to themselves, sign in a mirror, sign to their favorite animals, and perhaps even use signs in their dreams. *See* SIGN LANGUAGES: American.

The results of several recent long-term or longitudinal studies of sign language acquisition in young deaf children support the conclusion that, in most respects, the stages of sign language acquisition closely parallel those of spoken language acquisition in hearing children. Such a conclusion suggests that similar cognitive abilities probably underlie the acquisition processes in both modalities. Still, it should be noted that confirmation of this conclusion awaits the completion of larger and more detailed longitudinal investigations, and that there are certain areas of difference between the acquisition processes of sign and speech. *See* LANGUAGE: Acquisition.

One area where the two acquisition processes often differ is in the onset of the first steps of language use. Whereas most hearing children do not utter their first recognizable words until their first birthday (or later), children of deaf parents typically produce their first recognizable signs several months before the end of their first year. Many of these initial signs, however, are not used in a fully symbolic manner, as they are often tied to objects or events in the immediate environment. This relative acceleration in early vocabulary development

often continues through much of the second year, as children learning to sign tend to acquire the 10- and 50-item lexicons two or three months before children learning to speak achieve these same language milestones in speech. This initial sign advantage also is attested to by the observations that children during this period, in families with normal hearing, typically use communicative gestures (not signs) in advance of speech.

A wide range of reasons have been advanced to account for the finding that the first steps of language in the manual mode frequently occur prior to the onset of word use in children learning to speak. One frequently cited concept is that the cells in the motor areas in the brain mature more rapidly than those in the speech centers; as a result, neuromuscular control of the hands often antedates that of the vocal apparatus. A second plausible explanation is that deaf parents can readily mold their children's fingers into the correct hand configuration and then guide their children's hands through the proper sign movement. Such direct manipulation is, of course, impossible in teaching children to speak. Another developmental advantage for sign-learning children is that they can receive direct visual feedback for their sign productions, and thus they can see and compare their signs with their parents'. And because some signs clearly resemble the objects, actions, or properties they stand for, this iconic aspect may facilitate children's early sign learning. Of course, it is also possible that early signs simply may be more easily interpreted by parents than are infants' comparable initial attempts at spoken words.

Although young children learning to sign frequently show accelerated initial vocabulary acquisition in comparison with children learning to speak, the content of their early vocabularies generally is very similar, regardless of language modality. This conclusion is based on analyses of the grammatical and semantic categories of initial 50-item sign and speech vocabularies. In sign, as in speech, nominals or nouns (for example, *car*, *cookie*) typically constitute young children's largest grammatical category at this stage. This category, in turn, is generally followed by action, modifier, and personal-social words or signs, respectively. An examination of the specific lexical entries in the vocabularies of both signing and speaking children further underlines this pattern of similarity. That is, both groups of children frequently learn and use the names of the various objects, people, and activities in their environments, and these environments apparently are largely overlapping. Indeed, many of the most frequently occurring entries in young children's initial sign vocabularies also are those that appear most often on initial word lists for children learning to speak (for example, *Mommy*, *milk, dog, baby, no, shoes, ball, bye*). Another parallel in early sign and spoken language vocabulary development can be seen in the children's misnamings of items in their environment, using their available lexicons. There is some evidence that both signing and speaking children over- and underextend the use of a sign or word in comparison with adult usage. For example, a child might overextend the sign or word *dog* by applying it to all four-legged animals, or underextend the sign or word *man* by using it only to refer to his or her father. The presence of such similar error patterns in early language usage implies that similar cognitive processes underlie both language modes. There is one area, however, where the early vocabularies of signing and speaking children typically diverge, namely the grammatical category of function words (for example, *the, of*). Whereas such words play an important structural role in English, there do not appear to be equivalent American Sign Language signs for this purpose, and thus they do not constitute an important component in young signers' vocabularies.

Unfortunately, present understanding of the acquisition of correct American Sign Language grammatical usage in young children is incomplete. The few systematic longitudinal accounts that have been reported tend to support the position that the acquisition of sign language in deaf children largely parallels the development of spoken language skills in hearing children. For example, between 18 and 36 months of age, both signing and speaking children show rapid expansion of their initial vocabularies, in some cases doubling the size of their lexicons within a period of several months. Analyses of early sign and word combinations also indicate clear similarity, as the sign constructions of young deaf children closely resemble the structures and meanings in hearing children's early speech. Another index of similar parallel development is evident in the development of negation. Both speaking and signing children progress from simple negative indicators to increasing differentiation of new words for negation and use of more complex ways of integrating negative markers or constructions into their signed or spoken utterances. At the same time that the overall pattern of the development of grammatical usage in signed and spoken languages appears to be similar, the various constraints of the two language modes can result in noteworthy differences between the languages. Whereas words or morphemes necessarily are presented sequentially in spoken languages, the characteristics of the visual and gestural systems frequently enable signers to convey multiple units of information simultaneously.

The sign language input of deaf parents to their children also has been a research interest. With the exception of deaf parents' frequently greater physical involvement in shaping their children's initial sign formation, the interactions of deaf parents with their children learning to sign and of hearing parents with their children learning to speak otherwise appear to largely parallel each other. Young children growing up in a deaf family show evidence of steady improvement in their sign usage, which does not seem to come from specific training (parents often do not correct their children's sequences of signs, overregularizations of syntactic patterns, or inappropriate repetitions). Deaf parents appear to be more concerned with how their children form individual signs, the accuracy of their children's sign utterances, and the overall language interaction; these concerns are similar to those of hearing parents. Deaf children also frequently imitate their parents' signing in a manner similar to hearing children's imitation of adult usage. Correspondingly, deaf parents often recognize their youngsters' early sign combinations, and then complete their children's "telegraphic" productions with the missing elements. Adult expansions of children's early spoken utterances also are quite common.

Most deaf children do not have deaf parents, but learn to sign in schools or programs for deaf children. These children typically acquire considerable proficiency in signing, although some evidence suggests that native signers differ in their usage from nonnative learners of American Sign Language. In these schools, deaf children of deaf parents often have played an important role in teaching or transmitting sign language skills to deaf children of hearing parents. This pattern of language transmission now appears to be changing somewhat, together with many educational and societal attitudes toward manual communication. As noted before, many educational programs for deaf students adopted a total communication philosophy in the 1970s, with the result being that many hearing teachers now employ one of the varieties of English signing in their instruction and interaction with deaf students. Correspondingly, more hearing parents today are being encouraged to learn to communicate manually with their preschool hearing-impaired children. As a result, the linguistic environment of students in schools for deaf pupils has been altered—entering students with hearing parents may have an established manual means of communication, and deaf students now acquire substantial supplemental exposure to signing through teacher models. It is not yet clear how this interaction of two language systems (American Sign Language and English Signing) will affect each of them. Preliminary observations of the sign communication in such situations have indicated that the students' signing probably is influenced by both manual systems. Over time, the deaf students of hearing parents tend to incorporate such typical American Sign Language processes as conveying certain aspects of meaning simultaneously rather than sequentially, and setting the communication stage visually to transmit information. At the same time, many of the basic grammatical relations in the students' signing are expressed in correct English word order, with many of the grammatical morphemes following English structure. It would be of interest to study the long-term outcome of interactions between different manual language systems on students' signing.

Even when deaf children attend a strictly oral school and receive little or no gestural communication from their parents, they may still acquire elements of a manual language system. Observers have long reported that deaf students in oral schools that discourage or prohibit sign language frequently develop and use idiosyncratic sign and gestural systems in surreptitious communication among themselves. An unfortunate consequence of this situation is that some of these students fail to acquire proficiency in either spoken or signed languages, and thus find it difficult to communicate with both deaf and hearing persons. Relatedly, young deaf children living at home with their nonsigning, hearing parents often spontaneously begin to use a gestural system that has some of the characteristics of a language. Unlike the children of deaf parents, these youngsters do not have their hands molded or shaped into the proper sign configuration, nor do the parents model appropriate sign usage. To the contrary, many of these parents have been advised to use only oral techniques and not to respond to their children's gestures. Yet despite these formidable barriers to input and interaction, some deaf children successfully invent a variety of gestures (often with a pantomimic or iconic base) and are able to combine these gestures into short phrases. *See* SIGNS: Home Signs.

SPOKEN LANGUAGE DEVELOPMENT OF HEARING CHILDREN OF DEAF PARENTS

Many deaf parents express concern about the spoken language development of their hearing children. Although most deaf parents use manual communication in interaction within their families, many parents supplement their signing with spoken language input when communicating with their children. There is, however, a wide range in the voice quality of these parents and in the frequency with which they speak to their children. These differences, in turn, might be expected to influence their children's speech development.

At least in early infancy, maturational factors seem to play a more dominant role than speech intelligibility in determining vocal production. Systematic comparisons of the vocalizations of hearing infants born to deaf parents with those born to hearing parents have failed to show differences in cooing or crying behaviors, or in the frequency and duration of vocalizations during the first year. Although the notion of a maturational schedule often has been used to explain this absence of differences, it is quite possible that these infants depend to a large extent on the feedback they receive from their own voices. Or, it may be that the language input that hearing infants receive from their deaf parents, albeit different on a number of dimensions from that of hearing parents, is sufficient for their very early vocal development.

Differences in spoken language production between the hearing children of deaf parents and those of hearing parents become much more evident in the second year. Whereas most hearing children's speech skills grow rapidly at this time, the children of deaf parents typically are more limited in their progress in this area. Many deaf parents comment that they plan to compensate for what they perceive as inadequacies in their spoken language by having their hearing children exposed to spoken language input from hearing children, adult neighbors, relatives, and babysitters, as well as through television and other media. Exposure to television alone does not appear to foster young children's language development sufficiently, but those children with more interactive spoken language experiences seem to make satisfactory progress. Still, various studies have indicated that about half the hearing children of deaf parents have not developed fully normal speech skills by the time they are of school age. However, the actual learning of a sign language does not appear to interfere with the acquisition of a spoken language; hearing children who receive sufficient signed and spoken input readily achieve fluency in both language modes.

SUMMARY

Most deaf children grow up in families in which they are the only hearing-impaired individuals. The parents typically place a singular emphasis on their deaf children's development of speech skills. Despite years of formal training, the majority of these children never acquire proficiency in the spoken societal language, and their parents often fail to learn to communicate effectively in sign language or fingerspelling. Consequently, many deaf children are deprived in their early years not only of speech but of adequate language input and interaction altogether. The historically adverse reaction of many hearing parents and educators to manual communication appears to have changed considerably since the late 1960s. Now, most schools and classes for deaf children in the United States have incorporated some form of sign communication into their educational programs. In contrast to the development of most deaf children in otherwise hearing families, deaf children with deaf parents are introduced to a full language system early on, and readily acquire fluency in the manual mode. Although a complete understanding of American Sign Language acquisition has not yet been attained, much has been learned recently about the acquisition process. In general, the stages of sign language acquisition appear to mirror those of spoken language development. As with hearing children learning to speak, the language of sign-learning children progresses over time, from early nonadult rule systems, through many revisions, to a rule system that matches adult usage. Finally, whereas children of deaf parents typically acquire good sign language skills, the spoken language development of hearing children of deaf parents often tends to progress more slowly than that of children of normally hearing parents.

Bibliography

Kretschmer, R. R., and L. W. Kretschmer: *Language Development and Intervention with the Hearing Impaired*, University Park Press, Baltimore, 1978.

Meadow, K. P.: *Deafness and Child Development*, University of California Press, Berkeley, 1980.

Newport, E. L., and R. R. Meier: "Acquisition of American Sign Language," in D. I. Slobin (ed.), *The Cross-Linguistic Study of Language Acquisition*, Lawrence Erlbaum Associates, Hillsdale, New Jersey, in press.

Wilbur, R. B.: *American Sign Language and Sign Systems*, University Park Press, Baltimore, 1979.

John D. Bonvillian

Sign Language Processing

The processing of language is a broad domain. It includes the study of the various stages of coding and knowledge access in the perception, production, storage, and recall of language, as well as how these processes are carried out by the brain. This article is limited to aspects of the perception of American Sign Language and to brain organization for American Sign Language (ASL). The study of sign language processing provides a promising vehicle for understanding language processing in general, since ASL displays the complex organizational properties found in spoken languages but does so in ways highly conditioned by the visual-gestural modality (communication method). In order to understand the processing of ASL, it is first necessary to consider briefly some of its structural aspects.

LINGUISTIC STRUCTURE OF ASL

American Sign Language, like spoken languages, exhibits formal structuring at two levels: lexical signs are formed from a limited set of combining elements that are themselves essentially without meaning, and meaningful units are combined into signed sentences by grammatical rules. However, in the means by which these linguistic structures are conveyed, ASL deeply shows its roots in the visual modality. At the first level, ASL signs are composed of at least three major aspects: configuration of the hands, location of the hands relative to the body, and movement of the hands and arms. A fourth component, orientation of the palm, has also been discussed by researchers in the field, but it does not seem to have the same degree of status as the other three. Each of these in turn includes a number of discrete representatives. For example, there are a number of different handshapes, different patterns of movement, and different places where the sign can take place. In a sense, these can be considered analogous to the discrete sounds made in speech. In isolation they are essentially meaningless, but in combination they form signs. With respect to the second level, ASL shows a wide range of inflectional and derivational processes. Inflections are changes in a word to reflect a change in grammatical function. For example, in English the word *catch* can be inflected to *catches*. The -es indicates third person, singular, present tense. In ASL, the form of these processes is based on changing the movement and spatial contouring of signs. Through these processes, different signs have families of associated forms, all related by formal patterning. Importantly, inflections occur simultaneously as a modulation of the sign, so that the surface structure of these complex forms is highly multilayered.

The grammar of ASL not only relies on modifications of movement, but also on manipulations of space. Nouns introduced into the discourse are assigned specific points in space. Pronoun signs are directed toward these points, and verbs can move among these points to specify subject and object. For example, in the sentence "Ryan hit Jim," Ryan might be assigned a point to the left, Jim assigned a point to the right, and the verb *hit* is directed from Ryan to Jim.

PERCEPTION

Understanding a sentence in ASL involves not only comprehension of the meaning of the signs, their inflections, and the associated grammatical processes, but also the complex perceptual task of observing the information under the conditions of everyday conversations. The relationship between the structure of ASL and the sensory capacities of the human body is an interesting area for study. Researchers have focused on several major aspects: sign recognition, feature perception, movement perception, the effect of linguistic experience on perception, and information content of ASL.

Sign Recognition In order to understand how signers perceive sign language, many investigators have studied perception of the forms of signs themselves. In one procedure, called the gating paradigm, a timing circuit electronically terminates signs, so that signs can be repeatedly presented to a viewer with increasing exposure times at each successive repetition. The subject's task is to try to identify the sign at each presentation and to rate how confident the identification is. The recognition of signs, as more and more information about the signs unfolds over time, does not seem to be an all-or-none operation. Rather, deaf signers narrow in on the sign, part by part. The configuration, orientation, and location of the hands are all correctly perceived much sooner than the movement of signs. Correct perception of the sign's movement triggers the correct identification of the sign. Furthermore, in sign language as in spoken language, the recognition of signs or words is a complex process in which the observer uses partial information about the sign (or word) as it unfolds to identify it.

Feature Perception Just as signers perceive signs as consisting of subcomponents, they perceive the representatives within each of the major formational parameters (hand configuration, location, and movement) not as whole units, but rather in terms of shared features. Studies of how deaf signers perceive the hand configuration, location, and movement of signs have in general tried to construct models of how these parameters are mentally represented. They reveal that the deaf signers' representation of the various formation parameters is based on a limited set of underlying dimensions. For example, processing the hand configuration of a sign involves looking to see whether the hand is closed or whether fingers are extended from the palm, and if so, how many and which ones. Similarly, locations of the hands are processed not as an infinite set of random sign locations, but in general regions such as the face, central body, and hand and arm. Likewise for movement, features such as repetition, path shape, and plane of movement figure significantly in the perception of ASL movement forms. An organizing principle for perceiving these individual features of signs seems to be that the building blocks of signs are perceived in terms of classes whose members are psychologically similar.

The features that underlie perception of ASL hand configurations, locations, and movements are based on the capabilities of human perception and on the particular roles that components can play in ASL phonology. However, perception of movement may differ from perception of the static ASL parameters of hand configuration and location. Studies of the perception of ASL movement help to explain this difference.

Movement Perception Since the visual system is organized in large part for analyzing changing rather than static events, the study of motion perception of ASL allows the joint study of the perception of movement and the perception of language. Investigators have adapted techniques from the study of biological motion to isolate movements from sign forms so that they could study perception of movement directly. Small incandescent bulbs are placed at the major joints of the arms and hands, and signing is recorded in a darkened room so that only the pattern of moving lights appears against a black background. These point-light displays have a strong perceptual coherence. Deaf signers immediately recognize these displays as that of someone making signs, and even with such greatly reduced information are highly accurate in recognizing movement patterns and in identifying linguistic information. This accurate identification of language processes presented as only a few moving points of light demonstrates that patterns of movement form a distinct layer of structure in ASL.

Movements that are part of signs and movements that convey inflectional and derivational processes in ASL are perceived in terms of a limited set of underlying dimensions, as has been mentioned. However, the dimensions underlying perception of inflectional movement (sign modulations) are not in general the same as those underlying lexical (individual signs) movement. For example, dimensions capturing specific patterns of cyclical movement, displacement from the body's vertical axis, and length of movement repetitions figure significantly in the perception of inflectional, but not lexical, movements. Thus, significant aspects of the representation of movement differ at the two linguistic levels. These perceptual data support the claim from linguistic analysis that the formational fabric of the two levels differs. This difference might reflect the large number of dimensions available for a visual-gestural system from which a visual language can build its forms.

Effects of Linguistic Experience Studies of how hearing nonsigners perceive the formational parameters of ASL signs reveal that they, too, perceive hand configurations, locations, and movements in terms of a limited set of underlying dimensions. These dimensions provide clues to the natural perceptual categories into which representatives of the major formational parameters fall. If deaf signers and hearing nonsigners perceive the elements of ASL differently, it must be due to the linguistic experience of the deaf signers. Related experiments on the perception of speech make it clear that a speaker's perception of phonemes is determined in part by the speaker's phonological knowledge. In Japanese, for example, speakers do not distinguish between /r/ and /l/; therefore, Japanese adults, unlike infants and English-speaking adults, fail to discriminate the acoustic difference between these speech sounds. Their linguistic experience has in this case modified their innate auditory sensitivities.

No similar modifications of natural perceptual categories due to linguistic experience have been found for the two static sign parameters of hand configuration and location. Perception of the third parameter, movement, however, seems to differ in nature from perception of these static ASL parameters. For movement perception, both lexical (signs) and inflectional (modulation of signs), deaf signers differ from hearing nonsigners. Perception of movement forms are tied to linguistically relevant dimensions (for example, movement repetition), for deaf but not for hearing subjects. Thus, acquisition of a visual-gestural language can modify the natural perceptual categories into which movement forms fall.

Low-Bandwidth Transmission Researchers have also studied the perception of sign language under several methods of low information transmission. Video transmission requires a bandwidth, or information rate, of over 1000 times that of a telephone line. Methods are being developed for selectively reducing the information in the presentation of sign language while maintaining accurate comprehension, which would allow the visual transmission of sign language over existing telephone lines. Once developed, these procedures would allow signers, with appropriately modified video terminals, to use existing telecommunication facilities for ASL communication. One method that has been successfully used for reducing the information in the presentation of ASL has been to simulate a low-bandwidth transmission channel using television. In this procedure, signing is presented in a small rectangular portion of the full screen, and thus uses a fraction of the full channel capacity. Perception of ASL sentences, triplets of ASL nouns, and perception of fingerspelled words have been tested at decreasing portions of the screen (that is, at decreasing channel sizes). High intelligibility was obtained at a bandwidth only seven times that of a single telephone line. Current research on applying computer image processing to the signal may further reduce the necessary channel size to that for transmission over a telephone line.

A second method for reducing the information requirements for the presentation of ASL comes from presenting ASL as dynamic point-light displays. Gloves with 13 strategically placed light spots, plus a reference spot on the face, have been used to transmit ASL. These point-light displays effectively convey many of the subtle distinctions important to the comprehension of ASL. Furthermore, ASL signers seem to be able to communicate easily with each other when all they see are these 27 moving points of light, although controlled tests at the conversational level remain to be done. These point-light displays considerably reduce the information rate for presenting sign language, possibly to the level necessary for coding to the capacity of a single telephone line.

HEMISPHERIC SPECIALIZATION

One of the most striking findings in the study of the relation between the structure of the brain and behavioral functioning is that of cerebral dominance in humans. Although the two cerebral hemispheres are relatively close neuroanatomical mirror images, they function differently. In hearing individuals, the left cerebral hemisphere is specialized for language processing, and the right cerebral hemisphere is specialized for processing visual-spatial relations. ASL, like spoken languages, displays internal patterning, yet unlike spoken languages it relies on the processing of visual-spatial information.

ASL incorporates both complex language structure and complex spatial relations, thereby exhibiting properties for which each of the hemispheres of hearing people shows a differing specialization. Because of these dual attributes, ASL offers a valuable opportunity for refining understanding of the different functions of the two hemispheres. Investigating hemispheric specialization for sign language has taken two parallel approaches. In one, specialization for sign language is studied in normal deaf signers, and in the other, the breakdown of sign language is analyzed following localized brain damage.

Specialization in Normal Deaf Signers The visual modality provides a means of experimentally investigating hemispheric specialization in non-brain-damaged individuals. If people look at points directly in front of them, their visual world is divided into halves. Visual stimuli in the right side of the visual field are transmitted directly to the left cerebral hemisphere, and stimuli in the left visual field are transmitted directly to the right hemisphere. By measuring how accurately or how rapidly subjects respond to stimuli presented in the right visual field, as compared to when they are presented in the left field, one can infer which hemisphere predominantly mediates the task. Thus, better performance to stimuli presented in the right visual field implicates superior processing by the left cerebral hemisphere, and conversely, better performance to stimuli presented in the left visual field implicates right hemisphere specialization. For example, spatial material is processed more quickly when presented to the left visual field where the information can be sent directly to the right hemisphere. If the material were presented to the right hemisphere, it would have to go first to the left hemisphere, then to the right hemisphere.

This chain of events holds only so long as subjects are indeed looking straight ahead. If subjects move their eyes, they change their visual field and the experimenter no longer knows which hemisphere is primarily receiving the information. Thus, investigators have typically presented visual stimuli rapidly, more rapidly than it takes to move the eye, a time on the order of two-tenths of a second. Under these rapid presentations, hearing subjects are more accurate in response to printed English words presented to the right-visual field (left hemisphere), and are more accurate to spatial material, such as faces, presented to the left visual field (right hemisphere). The investigation of hemispheric specialization for sign language, however, is complicated due to the difficulty of capturing the movement of signs in the brief durations necessary to stimulate differentially one or the other hemisphere. Thus, investigators have generally presented static line drawings or photographs of signs rapidly to the left or right visual field. In general, the findings suggest that, unlike the left hemisphere advantage of hearing subjects in response to English words, deaf signers show a right hemisphere advantage to signs presented statically.

The pattern changes, however, when movement is introduced. Moving signs have been presented very rapidly to the visual fields in two ways. In one, movement was portrayed through the sequential presentation of still photographs taken at strategic points of a sign. The signs were presented too quickly for the people to move their eyes. Deaf signers tried to identify these moving signs as well as signs portrayed statically. Although the signers showed a right hemisphere advantage in response to signs presented statically, they showed no differences to the signs presented with movement. Thus, with the change from static to moving signs, there was a shift from right hemisphere dominance to a more balanced hemispheric involvement.

The severe difficulty in controlling moving signs presented rapidly to the visual fields was solved in yet another way. New procedures for computer-synthesizing signs have been used to present moving signs rapidly to the visual fields. These synthesized signs were stick figure representations that captured the different movement qualities of signs and were perfectly identifiable when presented to the subjects' central vision. When the synthesized signs were presented to the visual fields, deaf signers showed left hemisphere specialization. Thus it seems that it is the left cerebral hemisphere in normal deaf signers that is specialized for the processing of moving ASL signs.

The fact that congenitally deaf signers do show hemispheric specialization means that auditory experience is not a necessary condition for the development of hemispheric specialization. The fact that they show more right hemisphere than left hemisphere involvement in the perception of ASL signs presented statically suggests that processing the complex spatial properties of these signs primarily involves the right hemisphere. There is other evidence that requirements for spatial processing can produce right hemisphere advantages for linguistic material. For example, in hearing individuals, printlike lettering yields the typical left hemisphere advantage; whereas spatially elaborate scriptlike lettering yields a right hemisphere advantage, even with subjects vocally identifying the letters. Spatial processing of linguistic as well as of nonlinguistic stimuli can determine cerebral asymmetries, and apparently this is the case for signs presented without their characteristic movement. However, the pattern of hemispheric specialization changes for moving signs, with the left hemisphere now involved. In order to understand brain organization for sign language more fully, investigators have studied how sign language deteriorates after particular brain damage.

Aphasia Damage to the left, but not to the right, hemisphere produces language disorders (aphasias) in hearing individuals. These disorders vary depending upon the site of the brain damage. Until recently, little has been known about how unilateral brain damage affects sign language. Understanding how sign language is represented in the brain should yield clearer understanding of the basic principles underlying hemispheric specialization. It is clear that the left cerebral hemisphere is closely connected with speech. There is a neuroanatomical difference between the hemispheres in a portion of the auditory association cortex known to mediate spoken language. This area, even at birth, is larger in the left hemisphere than in the right. Researchers have suggested that this area may perform finer auditory analyses and represent a possible underlying basis for the left hemisphere's specialization for language. A related theory links the fact that the left hemisphere is specialized not only for language but also for rapid temporal analysis, a requirement for understanding speech. In this view, the specialization of the left hemisphere for language is a secondary consequence of its more primary specialization for rapid temporal analysis. However, sign language makes use of space as well as time. Furthermore, the temporal contrasts in sign language are typically stretched over longer intervals than those of speech. Thus, one would not expect left hemisphere specialization for sign language because sign language displays complex linguistic structures (governed by the left hemisphere) as well as complex visuospatial relations (governed by the right hemisphere). In sum, a more balanced hemispheric involvement is likely. *See* LANGUAGE: Disorders.

ASL thus pits the linguistic function against the form of the signal (visual) in a very pronounced manner. Studies of the breakdown of ASL following brain damage are informative. Damage to the left, but not to the right, hemisphere in congenitally deaf signers produces aphasias for ASL. Furthermore, the breakdown of sign language is not uniform but can be selective. For example, one congenitally deaf lifelong ASL signer experienced a left hemisphere stroke in the region of the frontal lobe. The traditional Broca's area, a major spoken language–mediating area, and much of the surrounding territory was damaged. The signing of this patient following her stroke was grossly impaired. Her signing became nonfluent, effortful, awkwardly articulated, and (importantly) without any of the grammatical devices of ASL. Her utterances typically consisted of only one or two signs: nouns and uninflected verbs. Her left hemisphere damage left her unable to use the grammatical devices of ASL. Her comprehension of sign language, however, was relatively intact. This pattern of impairment for sign language closely resembles that of Broca's aphasia for spoken language, and, indeed, the brain damage in this deaf signer is typical of those that produce this type of aphasia for spoken language.

Another case of sign language aphasia also had a grammatical impairment, but of a very different sort. This man easily produced long strings of signs, but with incorrect grammar. He made selection errors and additions within grammatical morphology and erred in the spatial syntax and discourse processes of ASL. Other left hemisphere damages produce yet different patterns of sign language impairments. For example, damage primarily to the left parietal lobe in a deaf signer resulted in a sign aphasia in which there was a marked sign comprehension loss. Furthermore, although the signing of this patient was smooth and fully grammatical, there were selection errors in the formational elements of signs, producing nonsense signs. The phonological level of the language was also disrupted. Thus, left hemisphere damage in deaf signers can lead to marked impairments in sign language, and these sign language aphasias take different forms depending upon the site of the brain damage. Selective impairments of sign language occur along lines of linguistically relevant components.

Visual-Spatial Capacities Although damage to the right hemisphere does not produce aphasia for sign language, it does result in severe spatial loss. Right hemisphere–damaged signers, like similarly injured hearing people, have performed poorly across a range of tests that discriminate right as opposed to left hemisphere damage. Thus, like hearing patients with damage to the right hemisphere, right hemisphere–damaged signers often show severe difficulties in spatial manipulation and perception. These appear as deficiencies in assembling three-dimensional blocks to match a picture, in drawing from memory or copying a model, in the perception of the angular orientation of lines, and so forth. These right hemisphere–damaged signers, like their hearing counterparts, also often show neglect of the left hemispace, an inattention to the left side of space.

The pattern of performance of brain-damaged signers on nonlanguage visual-spatial tests suggests that deaf signers do show hemispheric specialization for such processing, and do so in a manner similar to hearing-speaking individuals. Right hemisphere–damaged signers often show severe spatial impairments, while left hemisphere–damaged signers tend to process visual-spatial relationships appropriately. As mentioned earlier, however, the language behavior of these brain-damaged signers is much the opposite. Indeed, quite striking separations between language and nonlanguage visual-spatial functions have occurred. Signers with left hemisphere damage who have severe sign language aphasias with grossly impaired signing can do quite well on tests. Similarly, right hemisphere–damaged signers may show the opposite pattern. Thus, these data suggest that the two cerebral hemispheres of congenitally deaf signers can develop separate functional specialization even though sign language is conveyed in large part via visual-spatial manipulation.

SUMMARY

Sign language, like spoken language, has complex internal structure but conveys its structure in ways strongly affected by the visual modality. Processing sign language, however, is in many respects similar to the processing of spoken language. The perception of signs is not an all-or-none phenomenon, but rather the signer uses partial information about the sign as it unfolds in time to understand it. Furthermore, the representatives within each of the major formational classes of signs are perceived in terms of shared features, rather than as randomly related. The perception of the movement of signs, however, may differ in important respects from perception of the static parameters, hand configuration and location. Whereas hearing nonsigners and deaf signers both perceive the internal patterning within the set of hand configurations and locations similarly, deaf and hearing subjects differ in their perception of ASL movement. This difference in perception may reflect modification of natural perceptual categories as a result of acquisition of a visual-gestural language.

Sign language, as a visual language, differs from speech in its requirements for electronic transmission. In the search for methods for the visual transmission of sign language over existing telephone lines, researchers have been able to reduce the information in the presentation of sign language while maintaining accurate comprehension.

Finally, as a visual language, ASL presents an interesting area for investigating hemispheric specialization. Converging data from the study of normal deaf signers and brain-damaged signers show that the cerebral hemispheres of congenitally deaf signers are functionally specialized. Once again, the movement of signs is crucially important for normal deaf signers. These signers show left hemisphere specialization for moving ASL signs, although not for signs that are presented statically. Furthermore, signers with damage to the left, but not to the right, hemisphere show obvious sign language aphasias. These aphasias can be selective with respect to the structural components of sign language. Damage to the right hemisphere in deaf signers produces impairments in spatial abilities, and thus separate functional specialization of the two hemispheres emerge in deaf signers for processing a spatial language as opposed to processing nonlanguage spatial relations. Clearly, hearing and speech are not necessary for the development of hemispheric specialization as was once believed. Furthermore, since it is the left cerebral hemisphere that is dominant for sign language, the underlying basis for the specialization of the left hemisphere must rest, not on the visual nature of ASL *per se*, but rather on the linguistic processing operations required.

Bibliography

Bellugi, U., H. Poizner, and E. S. Klima: "Brain Organization for Language: Clues from Sign Aphasia," *Human Neurobiology*, 2:155–170, 1983.

Grosjean, F.: "Psycholinguistics of Sign Language," in H. Lane and F. Grosjean (eds.), *Recent Perspectives on American Sign Language*, Earlbaum Associates, Hillsdale, New Jersey, 1980.

Lane, H., P. Boyes-Braem, and U. Bellugi: "Preliminaries to a Distinctive Feature Analysis of Handshapes in American Sign Language," *Cognitive Psychology*, 8:263–289, 1976.

Poizner, H.: "Visual and 'Phonetic' Coding of Movement: Evidence from American Sign Language," *Science*, 212:691–693, 1981.

Sperling, G.: "Bandwidth Requirements for Video Transmission of American Sign Language and Finger Spelling," *Science*, 210:797–799, 1980.

Howard Poizner

PSYCHOLOGICAL EVALUATION

The psychological evaluation of deaf children and adults is both a science and an art. It is a science because it entails the assessment of a person's behavior in a standardized situation with specialized tests and testing procedures. It is an art because the psychological examiner must use these scientific procedures in a skillful manner and interpret the results creatively to generate clinical hypotheses. Science and art are combined to diagnose the client and make appropriate recommendations to assist the particular psychological problems of the deaf person.

The evaluation process does not focus exclusively on a test score or number. Rather, the focus is on a range of competencies that are assessed both quantitatively and qualitatively. Accordingly, tests are samples of behavior within a particular time and situation. The individual's behavior in other settings and times may differ. Test results are dependent upon the individual's cooperation and motivation. Scores may be affected by rapport and ability to communicate with the examiner, fatigue, anxiety, or stress. Test results are always interpreted in relation to other behaviors. These include, but are not limited to, cultural background, primary language, mode of communication, etiology of hearing loss, additional handicapping conditions, educational placement, type and degree of hearing impairment, age at onset, and case history information.

Tests used to assess a deaf individual must be valid and reliable. That is, they must measure what they purport to measure and do so consistently over time. Ideally, tests should have norms for deaf people. In reality, few tests are available with deaf norms. In their absence, the psychological examiner must employ tests normed on hearing individuals and apply the results to deaf clients. Tests without deaf norms must be interpreted with caution when applied to deaf individuals; that is, psychological reports should be evaluated to determine the validity, reliability, and appropriateness of psychological tests with deaf people. Some tests without deaf norms are, however, appropriate for use with deaf individuals. Examples include projective personality tests (such as the Rorschach, Thematic Apperception Test, and House-Tree-Person drawing tests), adaptive behavior scales and behavior problem cheklists (such as the American Association of Mental Deficiency Adaptive Behavior Scale), and the performance on nonverbal portions of intelligence tests (such as the Wechsler Adult Intelligence Scale—Revised). This appropriateness has been demonstrated in the clinical practice of psychologists with competence in the assessment of deaf people.

A psychological evaluation consists of evaluating the referral question, administering and scoring tests to answer the referral question, observing behavior, making recommendations, and writing a report of the evaluation. Information is gathered directly or inferred from samples of behavior. Human behavior is complex, and error is present within all attempts to measure it. The science and art of psychological evaluation are both inexact.

CONSIDERATIONS WITH DEAF CLIENTS

A major assumption underlying the psychological evaluation of any individual is that the examiner possesses the clinical competence to administer, score, and interpret the tests used in the assessment. With deaf clients, the clinical competence of the examiner ideally includes graduate-level course work and a supervised internship in the psychology of deafness as well as fluent expressive and receptive sign language skills in American Sign Language (ASL), Signed English, or Signing Exact English. The number of psychologists in the United States with this level of competence is steadily increasing, but the demand for them far exceeds their supply. *See* MANUALLY CODED ENGLISH; SIGNED LANGUAGES: American; SIGNED ENGLISH.

A less preferred level of clinical competence is an examiner who has no specific course work or training in the psychology of deafness but has acquired sign language skills and on-the-job training in deafness. After an initial learning period, these individuals are generally able to provide an adequate psychological evaluation of a deaf person.

The least preferred level of clinical competence is an examiner with no specific course work or training in the psychology of deafness and no sign language skills. These examiners either rely on an interpreter to communicate with the deaf person or use pantomime, gestures, or speech to administer tests. Psychological evaluations completed by examiners with this level of competence are generally less reliable than those obtained by examiners with deafness-specific training and sign language skills. Users of psychological evaluations of deaf people, who believe the results are unreliable because of the skill level of the examiner, should feel free to obtain a second opinion.

Verbal Tests In general, psychological tests that require reading or verbal or written language to evaluate a deaf person's intelligence or personality dynamics are inappropriate. This is because such tests measure more validly the impact of hearing loss on verbal language development than mental ability or personality structure. The language proficiency of a deaf individual is usually unrelated to the person's intelligence or personality dynamics. The use of primarily verbal assessment instruments often results in erroneous labels of mental retardation or emotional disturbance. A valid measure of intelligence, personality, or other attributes may be obtained from a nonverbal, performance-type assessment instrument.

However, most generalizations have exceptions. Sometimes it is necessary to use a verbal test to measure a psychological attribute in a deaf individual. This situation can occur when the deaf person has the sufficient English language proficiency and reading skills to complete a verbal-type test. The intent here is to measure actual achievement and not potential. Examples include the use of educational and linguistic tests to measure reading and language skills. Verbal intelligence tests can be useful in making placement decisions regarding the deaf individual's ability to handle language-based academic subjects in mainstreamed or college settings. However, results of verbal intelligence tests should never be interpreted as an intelligence quotient or used as the sole measure of intelligence with a deaf individual. Projective personality tests such as the Rorschach and Thematic Apperception Test (TAT) require a language response from the client, and are additional examples of verbal-type tests which may be used with deaf individuals, given fluent communication between the examiner and examinee. *See* INTELLIGENCE.

Mode of Communication Tests and testing procedures used in the psychological evaluation of deaf individuals should be administered in the person's native language. Native language is the normal mode of communication used by the individual, namely, oral communication, sign language, or total communication. This is mandated by Public Law 94-142 (the Education for All Handicapped Children Act of 1975) for deaf individuals between the ages of 0 and 21. Accordingly, deaf individuals who communicate in an oral/auditory mode should be tested in a communication mode that emphasizes speech, speechreading, natural gestures, and mime. Deaf people who communicate in sign language should be evaluated in American Sign Language (ASL), Signed English, Signing Exact English, or the particular sign language system used for communication. Psychological tests that require language facility between tester and testee should be avoided if the examiner is not skilled in communicating either orally or in some sign language system with deaf people.

Additional Disabilities Demographic estimates suggest that from one-fourth to one-third of the deaf population possesses additional disabilities, including visual impairment, mental retardation, cerebral palsy, additional language difficulties, learning disabilities, and behavioral or emotional problems. These additional conditions can result from some etiologies or causes of deafness, such as maternal rubella, complications of Rh factor, premature birth, perinatal anoxia, meningitis, cytomegalovirus, and some genetic disorders such as Usher's syndrome (that is, congenital deafness with progressive blindness). *See* HEARING LOSS.

Deaf individuals with additional disabilities present a challenge to psychological examiners. A deaf individual with cerebral palsy presents a particular testing challenge because most nonverbal tests contain timed subtests that require fine motor dexterity. Care must be taken to ensure that nonverbal tests that do not penalize additional handicaps are used in the psychological evaluation.

COMPONENTS OF A PSYCHOLOGICAL EVALUATION

The specific components of a psychological evaluation of a deaf person depend upon the nature and scope of the referral question. Typical referral questions include ascertainment of intellectual functioning level, determination of eligibility for or progress within a program, evaluation of behavioral or emotional status, and periodic evaluations to comply with special education laws. Each of these reasons for referral requires different psychological procedures to answer the specific referral question.

A psychological evaluation culminates in a written report which outlines the specific psychological tests administered and their respective scores, discusses the results of these tests, renders a diagnosis on the basis of these test results, and makes recommendations to benefit the client.

A consideration of the component parts of a state-of-the-art psychological evaluation is a useful means of illustrating what is involved therein. These components are as follows:

Identifying Information The initial information provided in a psychological report includes the name of the person evaluated, the date of birth, the date of the evaluation, and the person's chronological age at the time of the evaluation. Other information which may be given includes the address of the client, parent's name and address, case number of the client, school and grade placement, and the name of the examiner. Consumers of psychological evaluations should note the date of the evaluation to determine if the report contains current results. Behavior and performance on tests can change and vary over time. Diagnosis at one point is not necessarily prognosis at a later date. Some deaf people, particularly children and adolescents, have psychological evaluations within their cumulative records which contain information and diagnoses that are no longer relevant.

Reason for Referral This section explains the reasons that prompted referral and the specific referral questions to be answered in the psychological report. It also informs consumers whether or not the report addresses aspects of the deaf person's psychological status that will be of assistance to them.

Tests Administered In this section, all the tests administered and the respective results that were employed to answer the referral questions are given. These should be reviewed by the report consumer to determine their appropriateness for use with deaf clients.

Behavioral Observations The deaf person's behavioral manifestations during the psychological evaluation provide diagnostic information. Examples include the rapport established with the examiner, attention to the task, and cooperation during testing. This section describes such test-taking behaviors exhibited by the deaf person throughout the course of the psychological evaluation. It should also contain statements about the mode of communication used in the evaluation and the examiner's opinion of the reliability of test results. This reliability is generally judged to be a minimal, fair, or good estimate of the client's functioning levels. The deaf person's behavior during testing and rapport with the examiner have a significant effect on the reliability of test results.

Case History and Background Information The results of a psychological evaluation are interpreted, in part, within the context of the deaf person's specific background and case history. This section briefly summarizes the client's developmental status which includes the audiological, cognitive, motor, education, communication, family, and social histories. This section of the report may also provide information about etiology of the deafness, results of previous psychological evaluations, and current medical and medication status. These variables, in essence, describe the client's individualized psychology of deafness.

Diagnostic Impressions This section is the heart of the psychological report as it discusses the results of each test given in the psychological evaluation. It usually includes the following:

1. Measures of intelligence. This section contains the results and interpretation of the deaf person's performance on a nonverbal intelligence test. If often includes the results of more than one intelligence test. This is because most standard intelligence tests are composed of verbal and nonverbal scales. The use of the nonverbal scale constitutes only half of the test. Therefore, to obtain a large sample of nonverbal abilities, more than one nonverbal or performance-type intelligence test is administered. Examples of nonverbal intelligence tests include the Performance Scales of the Wechsler Adult Intelligence Scale—Revised (WAIS-R), the Wechsler Intelligence Scale for Children—Revised (WISC-R), the Wechsler Preschool and Primary Scale of Intelli-

gence (WPPSI), Raven's Progressive Matrices, the Hiskey-Nebraska Test of Learning Aptitude, and the Leiter International Performance Scale (LIPS).

2. Evaluation of personality structure and behavioral status. This part of the report gives the results of the personality and behavioral assessments. Projective techniques are most often used to assess the deaf person's personality dynamics, reality contact, and coping patterns. The client is shown inkblots (Rorschach Technique) or pictures (Thematic Apperception Test or Children's Apperception Test), or is asked to draw pictures (Kinetic Drawings or House-Tree-Person Test). It is assumed that the person's responses to these rather ambiguous stimuli contain projections of their inner personality structure. Results are interpreted subjectively by the psychological examiner within the context of the client's case history, clinical interview, and behavioral checklist data. A deaf person may exhibit differential behavioral manifestations, depending on the situation or environment. The examiner is limited in both interaction time and type of situation with the deaf person. Behavior checklist data provide a means of gathering information about the deaf person in areas of his or her environment outside of the examination setting. Checklists may be distributed to parents, other family members, teachers, dormitory counselors, and significant others to determine behavioral assets, excesses, and deficits in all aspects of the deaf person's environment.

3. Educational achievement. This section provides information on the deaf person's skills in the academic areas of reading, mathematics, spelling, and other school subjects. Such data are invaluable in determining a deaf child's progress in a given educational setting or communication modality, a deaf adolescent's potential to complete college work, or a deaf adult's ability to benefit from a vocational-technical program or to handle the reading requirements of a specific job-training course. It is also beneficial in ascertaining if the deaf person possesses the basic survival skills in reading and math to function in society. Specific objectives to enhance the deaf person's academic achievement may be garnered from assessment in these areas.

4. Neuropsychological screening or assessment. A neuropsychological assessment, in a broadly defined sense, evaluates brain-behavior relationships. Such evaluation is not conducted routinely and is typically given because of referral by a neurologist who suspects some type of brain dysfunction. However, selected subtests from a neuropsychological battery may also be given to a deaf client in the absence of suspicions of brain dysfunction. Such testing data provide information about a deaf person's preferred cognitive style, modality learning

strengths and weaknesses, memory, and sensory processing skills. This is useful in determining if the deaf person will require instructional modifications within a given educational program to ensure optimal learning.

5. Clinical interview and mental status examination. Clinical interviews provide valuable information about the nature of the referral questions, the deaf person's self-perceptions, the problem that prompted the psychological evaluation, and perceptions of the deaf person by significant others in the environment. A clinical interview provides an opportunity for the examiner to ask pertinent questions of the deaf person and other persons within the environment. These individuals are also provided the opportunity to communicate their questions or concerns to the psychological examiner. The mental status examination is a highly structured interviewing technique, not routinely given, which assesses a broad spectrum of the deaf person's mental functioning. Components include motor behavior, expressive mannerisms, attitude, level of consciousness, orientation, attention, concentration, memory, thought processes, reality contact, insight, judgment, mood, and affect. It is most useful with deaf adolescents and adults in the differential diagnosis of mental illness. This section of the psychological report synthesizes the information gathered from either or both of these interviewing techniques.

Summary and Recommendations These final sections of a psychological report provide a succinct summary of the deaf person's cognitive, affective, behavioral, academic, and neuropsychological functioning. Test results are integrated within the person's specific case history and interview data across these domains, and a diagnosis is rendered. Recommendations and suggestions for remediation and treatment are given and based upon these findings. Specific services, remediation procedures, viable resources, and programming options are recommended. This ensures that the psychological evaluation had a proactive effect on the deaf person's life.

Consent and Dissemination Two final points to be considered in the psychological evaluation of deaf people are informed consent of the client and who should be privy to the information about the person contained in the report. A visit to a psychologist is both a personal and a private matter. In the case of a minor child, the written permission of the parent or legal guardian is obtained before the evaluation occurs. Deaf adults referred for evaluation by vocational rehabilitation, the courts, or other agencies have the right to be informed of the purpose of the evaluation and how its results may affect their lives. The psychologist does not have the right to release the psychological evaluation to anyone, unless under court order, without the written permission of the deaf person or parent or guardian. Psychological evaluations contain sensitive material and should be released only to those individuals or agencies who will use the information prudently, respect its confidentiality, and follow the recommendations to enhance the psychological well-being of the deaf person.

Bibliography

Mitchell, J. V. (ed.): *The Ninth Mental Measurements Yearbook*, University of Nebraska Press, Lincoln, 1985.

Moores, D. M.: *Educating the Deaf: Psychology, Principles, and Practices*, Houghton-Mifflin, Boston, 1978.

Sattler, J. M.: *Assessment of Children's Intelligence and Special Abilities*, (2d ed.), Allyn and Bacon, Boston, 1982.

Sullivan, P., and M. Vernon: "Psychological Assessment of Hearing-Impaired Children," *School Psychology Review*, 8(3):271–290, 1979.

Zieziula, F. (ed.): *Assessment of Hearing Impaired People: A Guide for Selecting Psychological, Educational and Vocational Tests*, Gallaudet College Press, Washington, D.C., 1982.

Patricia M. Sullivan

PSYCHOLOGY

The phrase "psychology of deafness" is misleading. It implies that the laws and principles of psychology governing the behavior of deaf people are different from those applying to normally hearing people. Psychology is indeed a varied field, but its laws and principles are universal, applying to all people.

The field of psychology has, since the late 1960s, become extraordinarily diverse. While the layperson may be familiar with the traditional areas such as clinical, counseling, and experimental psychology, the American Psychological Association lists more than 40 subdivisions within the field. Many of these subdivisions are more closely allied with fields outside psychology than with mainstream psychology. Physiological psychology, for example, may have more in common with biology than with, say, clinical psychology. The single focus that defines the entire field, however, remains the same: the study of how organisms behave. This section examines the impact of deafness on a person's behavior.

Deafness produces changes that are at times quite predictable, such as the difficulty a child born deaf will have learning spoken languages. Other changes, personality adjustments for instance, are unique to the particular individual and may be difficult to forecast with any certainty. Much of what follows applies to deaf people as a group and may not necessarily be true for every deaf person.

An examination of how psychologists have studied the phenomenon of deafness reveals several trends. Initially psychologists studied deaf people more as an exotic curiosity, but over the years the viewpoint gradually became somewhat paternalistic and rehabilitative. Every effort was made to integrate deaf individuals into the hearing world and make them behave as much like hearing people as possible. While this was going on (with limited success) in the clinical wing of psychology, experimental psychologists occasionally used deaf people as control groups in research where speech or language was thought to play some important role. For example, at one time psychologists believed that thought was nothing more than subvocal speech (that is, small movements of the vocal apparatus). Deaf people were enlisted to see if, instead of thinking with subvocal speech, they thought with "submovement sign." Sensors were attached to their fingers to see if they made tiny movements during thoughts. (The fingers did not move.) More recently, many research ideas developed for hearing people have been relentlessly replicated on deaf people in an effort to see if any of the findings might be dependent on an aural-oral communication channel.

The sections below represent to some extent the beginnings of a new direction in psychology's approach with deaf people. The discussion of mental health clearly shows that deaf people face the same trials and tribulations in day-to-day living that hearing people face and that they overcome them in much the same manner and at the same rate of success. Because the clients are deaf, the mental health facilities and procedures must of course be modified to suit their needs, but the basic principles remain the same. This is also true when a deaf person in need of help goes to a psychotherapist.

As can be seen in the discussion of psychotherapy, the basic psychotherapeutic procedures are the same for deaf and hearing people, but the therapist must be able to communicate easily with the deaf person as well as to separate the person's deafness from his or her psychological disorders. When the client is a teen-ager, the therapist has the even more difficult task of unraveling the complex weave of deafness, normal adolescent adjustment problems, and the particular psychological difficulties which brought the person to the therapist in search of help.

The problems in adjusting to being hard-of-hearing are not the same as those faced by deaf people. Being lost between the hearing and deaf cultures and without a support group to fall back on is just one of the unique difficulties faced by a hard-of-hearing individual. This topic is explored in the section on hard-of-hearing.

In addition to being deaf, a segment of the population must cope with additional handicaps such as blindness, cerebral palsy, mental retardation, and behavioral disorders. The problems and needs of these multiply handicapped people are discussed in a separate section.

Finally, the discussion of psychosocial behavior touches on the development of thought as well as the development of social behavior in deaf children.

Robert Lee Williams

Mental Health

For centuries, deaf persons were perceived by society as dependent, defective, difficult, and limited emotionally and intellectually. Educational opportunities for deaf persons gradually opened the door to vocational and scholastic progress over the past 150 years, and the wall of silence was breached by oral and manual communication and by specialized teaching in day and residential schools. However, there were no accurate criteria for assessing affective states or personality development, and misconceptions about deaf persons' mental health persisted, while data regarding mental illness did not exist. Only since about 1960 has attention been directed by qualified professionals—psychiatrists and psychologists—to family and mental health problems in the deaf population; to development of personality and feeling in the context of family, school, and society; to the causes, prevalence, nature, and treatment of mental illness among deaf persons; to legal problems arising therefrom; and to the establishment of mental health services for the deaf community at least comparable to those available to the population at large. These endeavors have destroyed the old notion that deafness inevitably led to psychopathology, and have pointed to specific areas where preventive measures can forestall behavioral difficulties due to severe communicative deprivation.

DEFINITIONS

Mental health is a much-used term, but good definitions are rare. It can be said that mental health is simply the absence of mental illness, but it is usually thought to be something more. Freud summed it up as the ability to love and work. Developmental psychology defines mental health in terms of life stages, with specific tasks to be mastered and specific rewards to be achieved successfully at each stage. Another workable concept of mental health, and one that can be used in this discussion of mental health and deafness, is taken from a dictionary of behavioral science: a state of relatively good adjustment, feelings of well-being, and fulfillment of one's potentialities and capacities. One author emphasizes the freedom to change. Perfection is not required.

Mental illness is defined as a disorder of behavior of organic or nonorganic origin that is severe enough to require professional help. Between the definitions of mental illness and mental health lies a large area of life problems and situational difficulties for which counseling may be of great assistance.

In considering deafness along with mental health, various criteria based on decibel hearing loss, age at onset, and social affiliations have been proposed. Specialized attention to mental health problems seems warranted for a relatively homogeneous group of individuals with profound hearing loss (unable to use audition even with amplification), dating from birth or early childhood (congenital or preverbal), and socially identified with deaf persons by virtue of school, friendships, and affiliations. There are overlaps—for example, individuals identified as deaf with a lesser hearing loss or a loss acquired in their teens (prevocational), or persons with early profound deafness who have never identified themselves—but the definition omits the hard-of-hearing or deafened individual whose problems, while sometimes even more severe, are different from those of deaf persons.

Attention to the psychological and mental health needs of deaf persons requires communication ability and familiarity with the social aspects of deafness. It also requires long training, professional status, and experience in the clinical and behavioral sciences. Whether deaf or hearing (and more and more deaf professionals are entering the field), workers need a mixture of knowledge, empathy, and objectivity to advise and treat those deaf persons who seek help.

INFANCY AND PARENT-CHILD INTERACTION

Mental health results from the growth of basic human potentials, which develops through the stages of life with the aid of the environment. Various researchers have noted that infants seem to be born with certain temperaments related to such characteristics as activity, movement, social behavior, and attentiveness, and that these congenital qualities interact with the surrounding environment as the child's personality develops from infancy in the home, school, and larger social setting. The infant who is born deaf, whether because of heredity or pregnancy complications, or who becomes deaf early in life, faces a different reality than the child who can hear. The deaf child therefore has a different basic experience in the earliest years of infancy. Such children have less total sensory input since they hear little or no sound, and the ability to be in touch with persons at a distance or in another room is absent. If such infants also cannot hear their own voices, they may have a delay in defining their sense of self as separate from others. While these are problems that may result from the absence of sound, there are other problems that stem from the delayed communication that often occurs between many hearing parents and their deaf children.

Feelings or affects develop in the earliest weeks of life as the expression of biological needs and are expressed by sucking, moving, and sleeping; feelings also develop in response to sight and sound. Soon these affects are seen in communication, using facial expression, movement and, in the hearing child, voice. Later, with the development of language, feelings are increasingly defined and controlled as they appear in the interaction with significant people in the home and environment. The ability to give names to objects and to feelings provides the child with a feeling of mastery over them. A child who acts upon feelings instead of mastering them through language may be in conflict with the environment, and may develop excessive fears or feelings of guilt too early.

Persons who have been deaf since birth or early infancy have some deficit in these areas of development. Early stimulation by sound is indeed lacking; deaf infants lack the soothing quality of the mother's voice; they lack the ability to hear the mother talking, singing, or announcing her presence when out of sight. Psychologists are still trying to find out how much this experience can be replaced by vision, touch, or vibration. In addition, sound as communication is absent, which points out how important it is for parents to find other ways of communicating with their deaf infants from the cradle on. Langauge is usually delayed, though the observation of children using sign from infancy indicates that this need not be the case. It has been shown that abstract thought is present in deaf persons and that manual communication can serve as a perfectly adequate mode for the basic personality-developing functions of language.

The important arena to which these considerations point is technically known as object relations, that is, the direction of interest, need satisfaction, and feelings (such as love, hate, expectation, and disappointment) toward important persons who help or thwart the child. If lack of communication leads to impoverishment of affects, a shallow or undependable personality may develop.

Deaf children's perception of their mother is influenced not only by the mechanisms of mother-child communication, but by their mother's attitude and feelings as well. Indeed, the dedication of the parent to early communication may depend to a large extent upon the strength of her fear, guilt, and rage at discovering her child is deaf, and the consequent hopelessness with which she may approach making contact with a child who does not respond to her voice. Battles over means of communication—oral or manual—often lead to prohibitions which further affect the quantity and the quality of communication between parent and child.

As a result, deficits are often seen in empathy and impulse control in deaf persons whose parents, usually hearing, have not taken the trouble to communicate with them or to understand them. The slow process of learning how to relate to parents by trial and error, reward and admonition, is blocked by lack of attention to the pathways of communication in the earliest years. The young deaf child may have no outlet for impulsive needs and restlessness, may behave destructively, and in a vicious circle, further alienate the parents. The social sense, that is, the capacity for empathy and feeling for others gained through learning how to relate to parents, with the rewards as well as the trials, tribulations, and deprivations involved, may be shut out by isolation at home.

There are only a few observational reports of young deaf children and their families. In one study, preliminary findings indicated severe separation anxiety, a clinging to the mother, which could be explained by the need of the deaf child to keep the mother in view in order to maintain contact with her. Emotional attachment of both deaf and hearing parents to their deaf children was relatively shallow. Hearing parents reacted more intensely to a diagnosis of deafness than deaf parents—denial gave way to guilt, rage, and disappointment. During the months of such parental reactions, the child's development suffered considerably. Since only 10 percent of deaf children have deaf parents, these findings can be interpreted as the result of poor communication between hearing parent and deaf child, in either the parental or grandparental generation. *See* Deaf population: Demography.

One study of impulse control indicated that deaf children of deaf parents obtained significantly greater impulse control scores than deaf children of hearing parents, and that the earlier the deaf children were exposed to manual communication, the better their impulse control.

There are other factors involved in some of the characteristic personality difficulties of many deaf children. It is said by some investigators that, at least among the group who became deaf as a result of maternal rubella, traits such as impulsivity, motor restlessness, and hyperactivity may characterize only those children who are multihandicapped. Such a finding casts doubts upon the validity of deafness as an independent variable in psychiatric disorders of children, especially when neurologic disturbances coexist. *See* Socialization: Families.

School Environment

With entrance into school between the ages of three and six, deaf children move into the world outside their family. The earliest schools for deaf students in the United States, founded in the early nineteenth century, were residential institutions, boarding schools where students lived year-round, returning home only for vacations and year-end holidays. During the nineteenth century, there arose an increasing number of day schools, particularly in large cities; since the 1970s there have been movements toward establishing day classes in hearing schools as well as to mainstream, or teach deaf students in classes together with hearing students. Even in residential schools, most students return home on weekends, and many do so every afternoon. *See* EDUCATIONAL PROGRAMS.

A number of choices confront the parents of a deaf child. The usual reason for placement of students in a residential school is tradition, particularly for deaf children of deaf parents who had attended such a school in their childhood. A second reason is the concept of segregation, which is still fostered by some counselors, pediatricians, or otologists who indicate to bewildered parents of deaf infants that they and their child would be better off with an institutional setting. A third reason used to be geography, but with more adequate means of transportation and some decentralization of cities, geography becomes less of a determining factor.

For those students in residential schools, the school, together with the afterschool program, may be thought of as a total environment designed to foster not only the educational but the emotional and social needs of the deaf student. A time set aside for homework, consultation with houseparents and counselors regarding academic work, and weekly reports to parents may constitute an environment well suited to sustain academic achievement. On the social and emotional level, there is opportunity for contact with counselors, teachers, cottage parents, athletic coaches, and peers. Cottage parents represent a very important aspect of residential afterschool activity. While in the past cottage parents may often have been chosen because of their willingness to work in return for room and board, today more attention is given to their qualifications. Cottage parents need to function as friends, as confidants, as referees, and if properly qualified, as counselors. Regular contact between cottage parents and academic staff is important, and often requires some overlapping in work schedules between the two groups. Cottage parents can help teach deaf youngsters the principles of social interaction, of getting along with others, and can often do this in a less threatening way than teachers.

There are many programmed and unprogrammed activities after school that may broaden the students' experience in living and doing things together with other children; among these are field trips, scouting, and clubs. Athletic instruction and team sports present a special avenue for the social

as well as the physical development of the youngster and adolescent. Many deaf children who go home at the end of the school day have no opportunity for organized athletic activities, since they will often be excluded from activities with the hearing children on their block. By staying after school or by taking advantage of residential placement, a good deal may be learned about the principles of fair play, competition, and the healthy expenditure of energy. As with cottage parents and counselors, a free and easy communication between athletic instructors and teachers is essential if full advantage is to be gained from the experience.

Residential students today do not stay in school throughout the year, but go home on Friday, returning Sunday night or Monday morning. With some of the younger children, separation problems become evident; behavior on Monday and Tuesday is often indicative of the events of the weekend before. Weekend events may consist of neglect or actual abuse at home, a free license to roam the streets, or a warm and welcoming family. In the case of the abused or neglected child, anger or depression may be evidenced in school or the child may continue to act in a delinquent or defiant manner. Conversely, with an overprotected child, especially in the younger age groups, there is often a sadness and a weepiness due to problems of separation. Weekends are important, however, because they are the children's contact with their family. The nature of this contact needs to be considered by the counselors at school, and attention paid to any contrast between the home environment on weekends and the school environment during the week. Parents may bring problems to the attention of the school counselors that they have noticed on weekends but which are never noticed during the school week. Full discussion with cottage parents and afterschool personnel may indicate the child to be better adjusted in school than at home. The school must decide whether to be responsible for pointing out this difference and for making suggestions regarding the home environment. Ideally, if the child is to be seen in the total setting, the school personnel—social worker, psychologist, and others—would have to get involved in the parents' complaints about home weekends.

Similar problems arise for day students, and there are times when it is desirable to convert a day student to a residential student in spite of the geographic closeness in order to provide the child with a better environment than exists at home. Conversely, there are times when some residential students are having so much difficulty in the dormitory that they need to be converted to day students and live at home or in a foster home in spite of a rather lengthy commute each day.

Other problems of deaf students during their

school years may stem from the dependent status of special children, their expectation that things will be done for them. Deaf youngsters may tend to blame others for their misdeeds and may lack a mutual interest in each other. Sincerely motivated dating, family behavior, and responsibility may give way to rote learning.

Parents often go through a repeat of early depression as children grow into preadolescence but are unable to keep up with hearing peers in social development. Parents can no longer deny or minimize this difference, and sometimes either give up or conversely push the children beyond their capabilities. *See* SOCIALIZATION: Schools and Peer Groups.

ADOLESCENCE

In addition to the psychiatric considerations relating to deaf children, deaf adolescents have some special mental health problems. A major problem for adolescents is their identity acquisition; their worries include sex, morality, religion, popularity, vocation, and the future. A large question for deaf adolescents is whether they belong in the hearing world or not. Role models are infrequent, and as need for increased verbal skills develops, hearing peer groups separate from deaf peer groups. Alienation from the family, as a continued result of poor communication at home, is often more acute than among hearing adolescents. Dating and development of sexual identity are limited by misinformation or restriction and lack of social freedom. Drug abuse, formerly rare, has become as prevalent among some deaf youth as among hearing youth. Deaf adolescents need much guidance in the proper settings as they move into adulthood. *See* SEXUALITY.

ADULTHOOD

The adult deaf person who has weathered the vicissitudes of early family life, school days, and adolescence enters into the social world of work, marriage, and family. Mental health at this point entails absence of symptoms of maladjustment, ranging from feelings of guilt and inferiority through more defined psychiatric disorders, and also entails a satisfactory adaptation to life's requirements, freedom to achieve success commensurate with abilities, and a sense of well-being and self-esteem. Writers, sociologists, and psychiatric investigators, both deaf and hearing, have surveyed adult deaf society, and many, if not most, deaf adults approach these norms. Some deaf persons seem to have adapted by having little to do with other deaf people and groups. Some shun the deaf community because they cannot accept their condition of deafness; others maintain an identity as "oral" deaf individuals, shunning sign language. Most deaf adults have to some extent identified themselves with and joined the deaf community, rather than feeling like outsiders in a hearing world. They usually enter the labor market, though often not in the higher-paid occupations. They live active, outgoing lives and usually marry deaf persons. Hard-of-hearing persons often have the most difficult problem, not finding a place in either world; some identify with the deaf community and some become leaders. It is evident that adult mental health has to be assessed in a psychosocial context. *See* DEAF POPULATION: Deaf Community.

EARLY ASCERTAINMENT AND PARENTAL INVOLVEMENT

Since the early role of the parent—involving parental acceptance and a healthy parent-child relationship—is so important in establishing human relatedness and emotional development, it is of the utmost importance that deafness be identified early in infancy. Infants with a known risk for hearing impairment are usually watched closely for the possibility of congenital hearing loss. These include those born prematurely, those with a history of maternal rubella, and those with a family history of deafness. Deaf parents, of course, have an early interest in whether their babies are deaf or hearing (only 10 percent of such children are deaf). In most other cases it may take three or four years before deafness is definitively diagnosed. Better awareness among pediatricians and the availability of electrophysiological hearing tests that do not require the cooperation of the infant now make it possible to screen newborns, especially those with risk factors, and young infants in whom deafness is suspected. *See* AUDITORY DISORDERS, PREVENTION OF: Screening.

Once it is established that the child is deaf, parents need first to be helped in dealing with their reaction to the diagnosis. Some deaf parents have actually indicated they preferred deaf children; this is understandable and speaks to their sense of worth and equality. Others are more concerned, because of their experience with the minority status of deaf persons in society at large. Hearing parents, mostly unfamiliar with deaf persons and deafness, and harboring the worst possible prognosis, may react typically with anger, denial, and depression. Counseling in the early stages is difficult, but it is important that contact be made with professionals, with other parents of deaf children, and eventually with deaf adults. What must be avoided is projection of parental anger or denial to the child, often resulting in frequent ostracism, affective neglect, and family disruption. Early intervention may be of the greatest preventive value, and programs have been set up in some states for counselors to travel immediately to the home of parents as soon as the diagnosis of deafness in an infant is made.

Two interacting types of group programs are useful in helping parents. The first consists of counseling groups with parents of deaf children of the same or various ages to impart factual knowledge, share experiences and emotional reactions, and diminish guilt and despair. Such programs have been most helpful when conducted during the child's preschool years; if delayed until the child is an adolescent, the parents will have often given up and sought relief rather than insight.

The other important area is the parent-infant nursery, where the interactions between parents and young children can be observed and modified by trained psychologists who can spot subtle cues of rejection or noncommunication and can suggest to parents improved ways of relating to and playing with their infants.

INTERVENTION IN SCHOOL
A prerequisite for an effective mental health program in school is that the school have a mental health team that can provide formal evaluation, recommendations, and some form of counseling for each student in trouble. This team, usually consisting of a school psychologist and social worker and a consulting psychiatrist, needs to have files on each child and has to be able to consult with teachers, cottage parents, and other afterschool personnel when problems arise in school, after school, or even at home. In a residential placement, it is possible for the mental health team to observe and gain a total picture of the child's functioning in various settings. Conferences including the mental health team with cottage parents, the dean of students, teachers, psychologists, and counselors, as well as with parents or outside social workers connected with agencies responsible for the child's welfare, may result in a total corrective program to help the more disturbed children.

The school for deaf children, with its afterschool activities, may fit into a three-part mental health scheme that is slowly being put together in various locales throughout the United States. The first level involves children with emotional disturbances who are able to remain in their regular classrooms. These youngsters do not interfere appreciably with the rest of the class or, during afterschool life, with their dormitory mates. It is possible to consult with and advise their teachers and cottage parents regarding their particular problems and the ways in which the personnel may deal with these problems in the school setting. The second level consists of those children whose levels of withdrawal or disruption is such that they are uncontainable within the regular classroom or afterschool setting. For such youngsters it would be best for the schools to provide special classes and perhaps special afterschool activities designed for their particular form

of emotional difficulty and staffed by personnel specially trained. Finally, on the third level, there are those children and adolescents who are so disturbed, either because of psychotic behavior, extreme organic mental symptoms, or drug and substance abuse that they require a more medically oriented, more restrictive, more total round-the-clock care environment than the school can provide. For such youngsters, a hospital setting may have to be recommended for short-term management, and only slowly are hospitals for deaf children and adolescents being established. There are also a few special homes for treatment of deaf adolescents with severe alcohol or drug abuse problems. These forms of residential placement, while not in the usual school setting, may be thought of as special extensions of the school program for the exceptional student who needs such treatment for a limited period of time. *See* ALCOHOLISM AND DRUG ABUSE.

COMMUNITY RESOURCES FOR MENTAL HYGIENE
When deaf adolescents leave school and enter the community, they become part of the group of consumers of psychiatric counselors and treatment centers and share in the availability or lack of availability of such facilities to the general population. However, deaf people have special needs—not that they necessarily have more serious mental health problems than others, but that facilities equal to those available to hearing persons are not always at hand.

There have nevertheless been significant advances in recent years, and there is a growing network of helpful programs in the United States. A prototype of such a program is the Mental Health Services for the Deaf established by New York State in 1955. An outpatient clinic for diagnosis and treatment of adolescents and adults was followed by an inpatient hospital service with 30 beds, by consultation services to schools, and by outreach community programs, including a group home for persons unable to live alone or with family for emotional reasons. Psychiatrists, psychologists, social workers, nurses, and rehabilitation counselors work together to offer knowledgeable help. The team includes some deaf professionals. All staff are versed in sign language, and a telephone device for the deaf (TDD) is available.

A number of such programs were subsequently established in major centers in the United States and abroad. Their success depends both on the quality and dedication of the staff and upon the support and cooperation of the local deaf community. The latter is important to remove the stigma of emotional illness in the minds of deaf persons, to monitor the programs' usefulness and suggest improvements, to provide a group of lay volunteers and visitors, and to press legislative bodies for the continued funds needed to maintain the programs.

Once such a facility is established, it may offer its services to medical staff at hospitals, organize day hospital and group programs, and offer marital and family therapy sessions for hearing parents of deaf children as well as hearing sons and daughters of deaf parents. One such center in St. Paul, Minnesota, sponsors health fairs for the deaf community, offers classes in childbirth and parenting, and has produced sign language videotapes on health topics such as contraception and human sexuality. It has expanded its program to include the unique problems of hard-of-hearing persons. That program also serves as a statewide resource for hearing-impaired persons who have been sexually victimized.

MENTAL ILLNESS: DIAGNOSIS AND DISTRIBUTION

If mental health has been defined as a state of relatively good adjustment, feelings of well-being, and actualization of one's potentials and capacities, mental illness is defined as a behavior disorder of organic or nonorganic origin, which is severe enough to require professional help. There is no evidence that mental illness in adults is more prevalent among deaf persons than among hearing persons; in fact, surveys and investigations have shown that deafness as such does not increase the risk for serious adult behavior disorder. However, since diagnosis may be more difficult and depend upon communication and understanding, it will be useful to survey the types and symptoms of mental illness as seen in deaf populations.

Children and Adolescents Annual surveys of schools for deaf students have shown as many as 3 out of every 10 deaf students presented significant emotional or behavioral problems, in day as well as residential settings. While the symptoms of childhood psychosis—schizophrenia, autism, depression—are quite rare, they may be characteristic of some organically impaired deaf children and form one class of children deaf from maternal rubella.

The large cohort of youngsters deaf as a result of maternal rubella during the epidemics of 1964–1965 represented a multihandicapped group of older children. About 50 percent of these were behaviorally disturbed, with symptoms of either cerebral dysfunction, reactive behavior disorder, autism, or mental retardation. Cerebral dysfunction is diagnosed on the basis of neurological disease coexisting with behavior disorder. Among the symptoms are hypo- or hyperactivity, attention abnormalities, and impulse disorders, existing together with neurological signs. Reactive behavior disorder is characterized by the development of stress under certain environmental circumstances. The implication is that improvement of the home or

school situation may relieve the disorder. Autism, representing a childhood psychosis, includes the classic symptoms of inability to relate to people and situations from earliest days, repetitious utterance without meaning, inability to use language, limited spontaneous activity, avoiding outside stimuli, and relating best to inanimate objects. In addition to these classic symptoms, the rubella children with or without autism may show mental retardation, usually of the moderate to profound variety. In many cases, multiple psychiatric diagnoses are found, such as a combination of mental retardation and behavior disorder, autism, or cerebral dysfunction. Impulsivity in children with rubella syndrome has been found about three times as often in those with such multiple handicaps as in those who are deaf alone. Accurate diagnosis entails careful history and comprehensive physical, neurological, and psychiatric evaluation.

Childhood depression is an entity only recently recognized, and is particularly difficult to diagnose without careful observation and empathic communication. In this context, it is often necessary to distinguish between real suicide threats and the complaints of deaf youngsters who are frustrated enough to make vague statements about harming themselves or not wanting to live.

Psychological tests are helpful adjuncts in examining the disturbed deaf child. Scales of intelligence, of learning aptitudes, and of social maturity, as well as projective tests using pictures or play material, are useful; and so are visual motor tests for organicity. Achievement and vocational interest tests are also available. *See* PSYCHOLOGICAL EVALUATION.

Careful assessment of the deaf child should lead to diagnostic formulation in multidimensional terms and a corresponding program of treatment or environmental fashioning useful to parents, teachers, and clinical personnel. It should be clear that such evaluation is a specialized task, requiring on the part of the evaluator a knowledge of the many organic and developmental factors associated with deafness, a familiarity with deaf persons as a social group and with their educational and community organization, and above all a facility in total communication, including American Sign Language and other manual modes (Signed English, fingerspelling). The task of evaluation (as well as treatment) can probably best be achieved in a specialized mental health unit, staffed by psychiatrists, psychologists, social workers, rehabilitation counselors, and speech and hearing personnel. In practice, such groups can often make good use of the services of an interpreter. *See* MANUALLY CODED ENGLISH; SIGN LANGUAGES: American.

Adults Schizophrenic disorders are defined according to the *American Psychiatric Association Diagnostic Manual* in terms of delusions, hallucinations, or markedly illogical thinking accompanied by flat affect, with deterioration from a previous level of functioning, which lasts at least six months. Prodromal or residual symptoms include social isolation, peculiar behavior, impairment in work and personal hygiene, vague speech, odd or bizarre thinking, and unusual perceptual experiences.

The diagnosis of schizophrenia in a deaf person requires the ability to distinguish between certain affective and linguistic features of communication by sign language, and actual inappropriateness and concreteness of schizophrenic speech and affect. Many deaf persons in hospitals had been misdiagnosed as schizophrenic because of the examiner's lack of familiarity with deafness. Actually, when properly diagnosed, schizophrenic disorders are no more common among deaf persons than among the general population.

Depression and mania are characterized primarily by mood disorder without schizophrenic features. While depression is equally common among deaf and hearing persons, deaf patients often show a good deal of anxious agitation and bodily preoccupation, rather than slowing of movement and delusions of guilt and self-recrimination.

Organic psychoses—that is, substance abuse including alcoholism, and forms of senile dementia—are found equally among deaf and hearing persons and require knowledgeable professionals to work with the special social and family problems involved.

In the past, many deaf patients in psychiatric hospitals were diagnosed as having psychosis with mental retardation; in most cases this was a misdiagnosis resulting from unskilled testing and lack of knowledge about deafness.

Anxiety, obsessional disorder, and other neurotic conditions similar to those in hearing patients are seen by therapists for deaf patients in outpatient clinics.

TREATMENT OF MENTAL ILLNESS

In planning for psychiatric treatment of deaf persons, attention needs to be paid as much to the organization and staffing of services as to the therapeutic measures to be used. In a number of states there are comprehensive mental health centers, which include outpatient, inpatient, aftercare, and community programs. It is essential that effective communication be established with deaf patients; thus, skill in manual communication on the part of the staff is important. For some time, persons with proper professional background in the mental health field who also had communication skills were few in number. The use of interpreters in a mental health setting has many disadvantages, and they often inhibit frank discussion. Fortunately, more professionals are acquiring the necessary skill, and a group of deaf professionals has arisen to add an important dimension to the programs in question. In addition to communication skills, a thorough knowledge of educational and social aspects of deafness and the deaf community is important. Special hospital wards for deaf patients needing protective or intensive care with specially trained medical, nursing, and attendant staff have functioned well where established, and in a populated state or region can serve the needs of the deaf population. After being discharged, day hospitals, halfway centers, and residential homes provide for those unable to return immediately to family or independent living.

Other components of the center should include outpatient clinics for diagnosis and treatment of nonhospitalized patients and aftercare for previously hospitalized patients, preventive measures such as psychiatric consultation to schools for the deaf, and education of the deaf community to remove the stigma of emotional disorder. All of these require the trust and cooperation of deaf persons in the community. It has been found that an advisory committee of deaf leaders and grass-roots citizens is essential, both to secure this understanding and cooperation and to prevail on legislatures and governing bodies to provide and support the specialized services.

Modes of treatment in all these settings are similar to those used in general psychiatric practice, namely pharmacological therapy combined with various forms of psychosocial treatment, such as behavior therapy, supportive psychotherapy, and insight psychotherapy. Psychotherapy in particular, including insight and psychoanalytic methods and use of dreams, certainly requires excellent communication skills on the part of both patient and therapist, but excellent results have been reported in selected instances.

LEGAL ASPECTS

Persons have a right not to be confined against their will without adequate reason; it is becoming clearer from recent court decisions that patients, voluntary or not, have a right when hospitalized to receive more than just custodial treatment, that is, a right not to be neglected. Unnecessary hospitalization, perfunctory or merely custodial care, or indiscriminate discharge without proper follow-up facilities in the community for treatment and readjustment to daily life, may be discriminatory for the deaf population.

Similar considerations apply to legal and social problems related to delinquency and crime and to competency to stand trial. Interpreters in court and knowledgeable police and probation officers are needed. Deaf people need the protection of the law but must not get this protection at the expense of their rights. Special legislation may make the deaf person a second-class citizen. In a certain county, for example, deaf persons were once given special rights regarding punishment for crime, but at the same time they were not allowed to drive. This form of paternalism is tied to antiquated notions of deaf persons' mental and social incapability; the modern mental health concept and experience avoids any such taint. *See* DRIVING RESTRICTIONS.

PROGRAMS

In addition to the pioneer New York State program, other facilities have developed in many parts of the United States and abroad, though the total requirements of the United States and the world are by no means met. Each program has its own emphasis, and has tried to do a better job of filling the gaps and to meet the need for comprehensive psychiatric care. Programs have been established in San Francisco and Los Angeles, California; Washington D.C.; St. Paul, Minnesota; Virginia; North Carolina; Brooklyn, New York; Chicago, Illinois; Indianapolis, Indiana; Madison, Wisconsin; Columbus, Ohio; Austin, Texas; Denver, Colorado; and in England, Denmark, Norway, and Finland. With further research into psychological development, psychiatric diagnosis, and treatment modalities, and with increased accessibility to skilled and understanding professionals who are adequately supported by government and private resources, the community of deaf persons continues to move toward the ideal of receiving mental health care at least equal to that available to the population at large. *See* DENMARK; UNITED KINGDOM: Mental Health.

Bibliography

Chess, S., and P. B. Fernandez: "Impulsivity in Rubella Deaf Children: A Longitudinal Study," *American Annals of the Deaf*, vol. 125, no. 40, 1980.

Galenson, E., et al., "Assessment of Development in the Deaf Child," *Journal of the Academy of Child Psychiatry*, vol. 15, no. 1, 1979.

Harris, R. I.: "The Relationship of Impulse Control to Parent Hearing Status, Manual Communication and Academic Achievement in Deaf Children," *American Annals of the Deaf*, vol. 123, no. 1, 1978.

Rainer, J. D.: "Some Observations on Affect Induction and Ego Development in the Deaf," *International Review of Psycho-Analysis*, vol. 3, pt. 1, 1976.

Stein, L. K., E. D. Mindel, and T. Jabaley (eds.): *Deafness and Mental Health*, 1981.

John D. Rainer

Psychotherapy

This entry discusses individual psychotherapy, which involves only two participants, the client and the psychotherapist. Group psychotherapy, family therapy, marital therapy, psychodrama, and numerous other forms of psychological intervention are not covered. The general discussion serves as a backdrop to psychotherapy with deaf individuals.

CHARACTERIZATION

Psychotherapy can best be understood in terms of its basic technique and goal. The psychological technique of psychotherapy is aimed at alleviating the emotional distresses and mental suffering of clients and helping them develop effective ways of coping with conflict or stress. The ultimate goal of psychotherapy is to develop greater personal integration, self-fulfillment, and broadened responsibility.

Psychotherapy is essentially a psychological rather than a physical method, relying primarily on verbal means of intervention, that is, the "talking cure." The importance of verbal communication implies a close interpersonal relationship between client and therapist.

The therapist-client relationship is different from other forms of relationships in important and basic ways. People who make themselves available as psychotherapists are in effect socially sanctioned healers, professionals who commit themselves to helping others. Psychotherapy is a highly specialized profession in psychology and mental health that is practiced by members of many different professions, including psychiatrists, clinical psychologists, counseling psychologists, psychiatric social workers, mental health counselors, and others who have had specialized and intensive postgraduate training in psychotherapy.

The person who seeks out a therapist usually does so because of an overwhelming need. It may be to reduce psychological distress, to learn how to cope more effectively with life's demands, or to discover how to live more creatively and fulfillingly. Many clients do not know exactly what is wrong, but they are experiencing a general sense of dissatisfaction and malaise. However hidden the problems, the essential point is that the clients decide that they are in need of help and choose someone who has been socially sanctioned as qualified to provide that help.

Psychotherapy is not limited to persons who are "sick," neurotic or mentally ill. Since the 1960s a growing number of relatively well-adjusted people have entered psychotherapy because they wanted to understand themselves better, function at their potential, improve their relationships with others, face the world without fear, and live more satisfying, productive, and meaningful lives.

Common to all forms of psychotherapy is the intense, emotionally charged, confiding relationship with a helping person. Unlike an ordinary social interaction, it has an intense quality with client and therapist meeting on serious business. Confidentiality is of paramount importance. For psychotherapy to work, the client must disclose his or her problems, inner thoughts, deep feelings, and fantasies—disclosures that are typically painful, threatening, or embarrassing—and the client must feel secure that everything revealed is completely confidential.

Moreover, psychotherapy is a collaborative endeavor; a partnership, or a therapeutic alliance, in which the client is expected almost from the very beginning to play an active part. This means that clients must gradually become more autonomous, more self-directing, and more responsible for their feelings, beliefs, and actions. In order to feel better about themselves, their relationships with others, and their behavior, they must learn to make changes within themselves in their environments that permit them to feel and act differently. The process of psychotherapy is designed not to change clients but to help clients change themselves.

Psychotherapy is a generic term that applies to many different forms of treatment. They represent a wide array of theoretical orientations, schools of thought, and aims of treatment. One such orientation is classical Freudian psychoanalytic psychotherapy and its many variants devised by Freud's disciples. Other orientations include the client-centered therapy of Carl Rogers, existential psychotherapy, gestalt therapy, behavior therapy, cognitive psychotherapy, transactional analysis, rational-emotive therapy, and reality therapy. A compendium of psychotherapy lists over 250 brand-name therapies, including forms of family, marital, sex, and group therapy.

Despite this melange of psychotherapies, studies show that many practitioners are mostly in agreement regarding certain goals and approaches in psychotherapy. This is especially true of psychotherapy involving both a human relationship and psychological techniques, and largely concerned with personality and behavior change. The client who seeks help for a psychological concern or problem desires change. The client wants to feel or act differently or to live more effectively or happily, and the psychotherapist agrees to help the client in achieving the goal. A consensual view of psychotherapy sees the individual as a troubled human being often plagued with torment, suffering, and anguish that require compassion, understanding, and ultimately healing.

CURRENT STATUS

Deaf individuals do not have a wide choice of psychotherapies. "Improved, yet primitive" describes the current status of the practice of psychotherapy for deaf persons.

Mental health and the behavioral sciences, represented particularly by the disciplines of psychiatry and psychology, are still relative newcomers in the field of deafness, which was long dominated by educators. For example, while the professions of guidance counselor and school psychologist were

for many years firmly entrenched within the general public education system, such positions were virtually nonexistent in residential schools and other educational programs for deaf children. School counselors and, later, school psychologists began to penetrate deafness education when Gallaudet College established in the 1970s graduate training programs in these helping professions. The late entry of mental health in the field of deafness is a major reason for the deplorable state of psychotherapy practice with deaf people. *See* GALLAUDET COLLEGE.

Although the years since the 1970s have seen an increasing interest in new mental health programs in both hospital and community settings, mental health service delivery for deaf individuals remains inadequate and variable in quality. There are in the United States fewer than 60 mental health programs in schools, hospitals, and clinics, serving a total of more than 1000 deaf persons with psychological problems. Most of these programs, however, are of the state hospital variety, catering to the very disturbed and mentally ill, many of whom are in custodial care. Thus, there is a general neglect of deaf individuals who are not disturbed enough to be hospitalized but who nonetheless are in need of psychotherapy and likely to benefit from it. These deaf people need psychotherapy to keep themselves out of the hospital, and they represent the vast majority of deaf people in need of outpatient preventive and rehabilitative mental health services.

There is a persistently acute shortage of psychotherapists trained and qualified to work and communicate with deaf clients. Since the majority of deaf people communicate via sign language, it is essential that the psychotherapist be fluent and expert in sign language as used by clients from varied educational, social, cultural, and communication backgrounds and preferences.

This communication barrier precludes deaf individuals from gaining access to the abundant pool of psychotherapists. Contributing to this psychotherapist shortage is the scarcity of graduate and postgraduate training programs to prepare mental health specialists to work with deaf children, adults, and their families—particularly in psychological evaluation, diagnosis, counseling, and psychotherapy. Attempts by the few mental health professionals in the field of deafness to establish such training programs, through government mental health agencies or institutions of higher education, have not been successful. This shortage is reflected in the fact that although there is a rapid acceleration of psychotherapy research in general, there remains a paucity of process and outcome studies with deaf clients. This can be attributed to the chronic scarcity of psychotherapists and behavioral researchers with an in-depth familiarity with deafness and its psychosocial ramifications, with the ability to communicate with deaf people in sign language, and with the ability to operate from within the deaf individual's frame of reference, that is, the ability to see the world as a deaf person sees and experiences it.

The general theme of literature on the psychological and mental health aspects of deafness is one of deviance and maladjustment, rather than of prevention and treatment. There is a good deal of information about the psychological and social problems of deaf individuals, but it gives very little advice about treatment. This is also true of graduate training programs in the field of deafness, which place an unbalanced emphasis on the liabilities rather than on the assets, strengths, and potentials of deaf people. These courses also give little attention to intervention and treatment. It is much easier to say what is wrong with a person than to discuss corrective treatment. While literature and courses are quick to point out and enumerate the deaf person's deficiencies, they are slow to define or at least portray a relatively psychologically healthy or well-functioning deaf person. Such an entity personifies the majority of deaf people, who have normal problems of everyday living similar to those of their nondeaf counterparts. Psychologically healthy deaf people continue to be relatively elusive in publications about deafness; yet they are badly needed as role models for psychological health and integrity, and are sorely needed as guides in psychotherapy with deaf people.

Another reason for the slow progress in the practice of psychotherapy with deaf people is the problem associated with inaccurate diagnosis. Accurate diagnosis is essential and crucial in treatment planning, but it is rare for even the competent psychologist or psychiatrist who has little or no knowledge of deafness and its complex implications. Consequently, misdiagnoses often occur, thus blunting or misguiding treatment efforts, as evidenced by frequent references to deaf individuals who have been misdiagnosed and inappropriately placed in state mental institutions.

APPROACHES

Several forms of psychotherapy work well with deaf people when conditions for effective psychotherapy are present. Current approaches have been skillfully applied in work with deaf clients by qualified psychotherapists with special competencies. The major problem is not the approach per se; rather, it is the limited number of qualified psychotherapists competent to work and communicate with deaf clients. This in turn spawns misinformation, misconceptions, and myths about deaf individuals' capacity and potential for psychotherapy.

Historically, professionals involved in the lives of deaf people were teachers, athletic coaches, the clergy, social workers, and in later years vocational rehabilitation counselors. Deaf adults sought assistance from their former teachers, deaf leaders, or educated deaf people. For years these people filled in the mental health void for deaf people, providing whatever assistance and "words of wisdom" that are the proper province of highly trained mental health professionals. The type of assistance given was usually straightforward: advising, directing, instructing, lecturing, preaching, admonishing, and other means hardly conducive to the development of independent thought and behavior.

The situation improved with the arrival and growth of professional counselors and caseworkers in the field of deafness during the 1960s. However, the brand of counseling used was largely directive, presumably fitting the attributed personality, language, and cognitive limitations of deaf clients, hence leaving little room for their growth and development. In directive counseling, the counselor assumes the role of an authority offering the client an evaluation of the particular problem and defining courses of action. The counselor in this case is judgmental, telling the client what is wrong and what is right, and advising the client on how to correct the problem. This is in contrast to the therapist, who encourages the client's expression of feelings, reflecting these and helping the client to assume responsibility for them. In this way clients independently think things out for themselves, developing their own goals and planning their own course of action. Counselors may make suggestions, but the clients consider the options and make their own decisions after exploring them with the counselor.

While psychotherapy and counseling were undergoing exciting developments, growth, and experimentation with new approaches, and while psychotherapy research was coming into its own in the 1960s, the field of deafness was hampered by the outdated and anachronistic directive approach. Professional journals continued to feature articles with arguments against the use of feeling-oriented, insight-developing, and in-depth counseling approaches due to the deaf clients' supposed limitations. Arguments were also advanced against the newer cognitive or rational approaches on the grounds that they required high intellectual, logical, and abstract functioning, which, according to the authors, deaf people in general do not possess. Thus, more directive and manipulative approaches persisted.

Even with the arrival and upsurge of psychology and psychiatry in deafness mental health, the situation remains relatively bleak. The literature pertaining to psychotherapy with deaf clients is sparse.

When the subject is mentioned, it is usually in reference to the difficulty or failure in psychotherapy endeavors with deaf clients. Deaf individuals are depicted as a population who, due to their characteristics, shortcomings, language limitations, and communication disabilities, are not responsive to psychotherapy. Additionally, some assert that deaf clients are not good candidates for the insight-developing, feeling-oriented, and in-depth type of psychotherapy, especially where reflection, introspection, and internalization are required. Moreover, in preference studies, deaf persons are usually found at the bottom of the list of disability groups with which the helping professionals prefer to work.

As late as 1967, prominent psychoanalysts who had worked with deaf patients maintained that psychoanalytic therapy with deaf people was not possible because of the need of the deaf patient to face the therapist, which cannot be accomplished while lying on the couch. It was not mentioned that there are other approaches within the psychoanalytic camp that do not require the couch, and that there are psychoanalysts who do not use the couch at all.

Deaf people were thought to be best suited for a form of assistance in which the therapist plays an active role, giving advice, direction, information, reassurance, and leading the client. This propensity to stereotype deaf people as difficult and high-risk candidates for psychotherapy, as is done with poor, disadvantaged, disabled, old, and nonverbal populations, serves only to thwart the opportunity for emotional growth and psychological enhancement that can be made possible by more appropriate forms of psychotherapy.

The reported and observed difficulties and failures in psychotherapy with deaf individuals apparently reflect the therapists' skills and attitudes rather than the imputed or stereotyped limitations of the deaf client. The therapists themselves are often limited in that they are not able to communicate effectively with their deaf clients.

The nature and basic principles of psychotherapy with deaf individuals are not different from those that characterize psychotherapy with non-deaf individuals. Nor is a new approach based on a new theoretical orientation needed in psychotherapy with deaf people. Current approaches have been demonstrated to be equally applicable to deaf clients. It is their implementation that differs. For deaf clients, for example, psychotherapy is implemented by sign language or whatever communication mode is preferred by the client.

THE PSYCHOTHERAPIST

The most important variable in psychotherapy is the psychotherapist. Research has shown that two factors influence the success in psychotherapy: the training, competencies, skills, and experience of the therapist; and the personality of the therapist. The personal qualities and style of the therapist seem to have a more significant effect on therapeutic outcome than the particular approach used. The therapist's personality is crucial to the social chemistry of the relationship between therapist and client. Interpersonal factors not only are important, but in many cases can be decisive in influencing outcome.

The therapist characteristics that may influence the process of personality and behavior changes, and thus the therapeutic outcome, are warmth, friendliness, genuineness, interpersonal style, beliefs, values, attitudes, and prejudices. Others include unconditional positive regard for the client; a nonjudgmental attitude; empathy, or ability to understand clients from their frame of reference; the capacity to understand, accept, and respect the values of the client; and congruence, or the ability of therapists to say exactly what they think and feel.

These personal qualities have special meaning in the practice of psychotherapy with deaf people. They would encompass, for example, a willingness to learn about deafness and deaf people and about what it means to exist as a deaf person; an unconditional positive regard for the deaf client no matter what the client's limitations are, including the client's minimial English skills or inability to use speech; an acceptance of the client's sign language or mode of communication as part of the client's being; a freedom from traditional, stereotypic, negative and derogatory attitudes toward deaf individuals; an ability to see the deaf client as a person, and as one of worth and value; and an understanding and respect for the deaf client's values, even though they may be at variance with the therapist's. Above all, therapists should be aware of their own feelings, biases, blind spots, and limitations which may impede progress in therapy.

Technical Competencies Psychotherapists are considered qualified if they have had an extensive educational background in the behavioral sciences and mental health, advanced degrees (preferably a doctoral degree), a minimum of one year of internship and additional postdoctoral or postgraduate supervised training in psychotherapy with actual clients, and a license or certification in their respective mental health disciplines. In the case of the psychiatrist, for example, training in psychotherapy occurs only as part of a three-year residency. Because of this, a number of psychiatrists who are primarily interested in psychotherapy go on to take training after medical school and residency requirements in a psychoanalytic or other type of psychotherapy training institute.

For the clinical or counseling psychologist, the

length of graduate training is four or five years, with many requiring a longer period for completion. An internship and a doctoral dissertation are usually required. The Ph.D. degree and one or two years experience is required prior to state licensure as a psychologist. Although psychotherapy is emphasized in these programs, several psychologists enter post-Ph.D. training programs in psychoanalytic or other types of psychotherapy.

However, competency in psychotherapy with deaf persons is not achieved simply through academic psychological training, medical training, postgraduate training in psychotherapy, or in terms of degrees, certification, and licensure. A psychotherapist treating deaf clients must also possess unique competencies in order to function effectively with them. These include thorough pedagogical grounding in all aspects of deafness; successful completion of studies in the psychological, developmental, and mental health aspects of deafness, including treatment techniques; understanding of the principles, practices, and approaches in psychological evaluation and diagnosis with deaf children, adults, and families, including psychological testing and diagnostic interviewing skills; skills in crisis intervention; the experience of supervision by or in consultation with a veteran psychotherapist experienced in psychotherapy with deaf clients; possession of a working knowledge and familiarity with relatively psychologically healthy or well-adjusted deaf individuals from a variety of backgrounds; and finally, a working knowledge of the history, philosophy, and development of communication modes used by deaf individuals from all walks of life.

Communication Skill A cardinal tenet in psychotherapy is for the therapist to use the mode of communication the client prefers. Difficulty in communicating drastically reduces the effectiveness of psychotherapy. Therefore, the key competency for psychotherapy with a deaf clientele lies in the ability of the therapist to establish effective communicative relations with every type of deaf client of whatever communicative persuasion. In order for psychotherapy to work for a majority of deaf people, it must be done in sign language, for the overwhelming majority use it in its various forms. Additionally, it is the therapist's responsibility to follow the deaf client's communicative lead, whether expressed in signs, pantomime, gestures, body language, facial expression, or any combination of these. Further, communication with the client needs to take place not only in the client's own mode of communication but also in the client's own language patterns, idioms, and concepts.

Therapists also must use speech and lipreading with deaf clients unfamiliar with sign language, or with those deaf clients who subscribe to an oral communication philosophy that eschews sign language. Accommodations must also be made for clients preferring the simultaneous method, that is, the simultaneous use of sign language, speech, and lipreading. *See* SOCIOLINGUISTICS: Simultaneous Communication.

The reported difficulties, failures, and pessimism in psychotherapy with deaf clients is often related to the therapist's inability to use sign language sufficiently and appropriately, giving rise to high levels of stress and fatigue for both client and therapist. Without appropriate sign language skill, it is difficult, moreover, to gain the client's confidence, arouse expectation of help, clarify misconceptions of psychotherapy and the role of the therapist, and motivate the client to accept the condition of therapy. Some clients, for example, are able to express their deepest feeling only through American Sign Language (ASL); their feelings would be left unexpressed with the therapist who is not able to comprehend this language.

Consumerism in mental health advises that if the match between client and therapist seems to be a bad one, the client should terminate the relationship and continue to seek a better one. A client-therapist relationship with communication difficulties is a bad match, and should accordingly be terminated. Unfortunately, with the shortage of qualified therapists competent to treat and communicate with deaf people, the deaf client often endures a difficult, frustrating, unproductive, or even harmful psychotherapy experience.

INTERPRETERS

A fairly recent dimension to psychotherapy with deaf people is the use of a sign language interpreter. The results are mixed. The use of an interpreter facilitates communication where the therapist lacks the requisite sign language skills. It also may convey to the client the therapist's acceptance of the reality of their mutual communication difficulties as well as the therapist's sincere desire to understand and to be understood. There are, however, problems that noticeably alter or hinder therapy.

The involvement of an interpreter creates a triangular arrangement, precluding a direct one-to-one, dyadic relationship that, by itself, is a powerful healing and corrective experience for the client. Therapists who have used interpreters have written that this method may result in diluting and distorting the usual one-to-one relationship. The loss of visual and emotional contact between therapists and clients has negative effects. There is a shift of attention from both sides to the interpreter, thus preventing the therapist's personal characteristics and technical skills from having a direct bearing on the relationship. Nonverbal behavior, with all the nuances of body language, facial expressions, and gestures, essential in psychotherapy in general and with deaf clients in particular, may not be readily observable by the therapist.

Additionally, in the private office setting, interpreter fees are usually not covered by health insurance for psychotherapy. Further, depending on location, deaf clients and therapists are often hard-pressed to recruit a highly skilled interpreter for the psychotherapy situation, their certification notwithstanding. Another concern is that the therapist may come to habitually rely on interpreters, thus precluding or retarding their own mastery of the sign language.

There are a host of other professional, technical, and practical problems associated with the use of interpreters in psychotherapy. Still, it is better for a deaf person in locations where fully communicating therapists are in short supply or are nonexistent to have access to psychotherapy via an interpreter than to have no psychotherapy at all. It is then essential for client, therapist, and interpreter to understand the merits and limitations of the use of the interpreter in psychotherapy. *See* INTERPRETING.

TREATMENT ISSUES

Efforts to work with, communicate with, study, and provide services for deaf people may be influenced by a dangerous tendency to stereotype deaf people. A guiding principle for the therapist is not to automatically attribute the deaf client's problem to, or associate it with, deafness, as is common with many therapists inexperienced with deafness and deaf people. What must be kept in mind is that many deaf people seek psychotherapy for problems unrelated or only remotely related to deafness. Others may have problems similar to nondeaf clients, for example, communication difficulties, which may be aggravated by deafness. Thus, the psychotherapist must be extremely cautious not to view the deaf client through the stereotypic prism of deafness.

Although there is no evidence that deafness per se makes for a biological predisposition to mental health problems, and there are no forms of emotional disorders and mental illness that are not shared by both deaf and nondeaf individuals, the incidence of mental health problems is considerably greater among the deaf population than the nondeaf population. Studies have indicated that emotional problems in residential schools for deaf children are found to be five times the expected rate. Adjustment problems of deaf children mainstreamed in public schools were first mentioned in the late 1960s, and there is growing concern about the increasing number of deaf children who have difficulty in effecting satisfactory emotional and social adjustments in mainstreamed programs, especially where they do not receive professional counseling support. The incidence of schizophrenia, a major form of mental illness, is no higher among the deaf than the hearing population, but the incidence of increased emotional immaturity and of impulsive disorders appears inordinately higher.

Psychotherapy does involve work with clients who are unable or find it difficult to adjust satisfactorily to deafness. Many deaf individuals, regardless of age, age at onset of hearing loss, degree of hearing loss, and educational, social, cultural, and communication background, suffer from problems associated with poor adjustment to deafness. Some clients seek therapy specifically to help them adjust to their loss of hearing even after several years since onset of hearing loss. Others need to deal with their denial of deafness, while still others need the opportunity to mourn their hearing loss. There are also clients who need assistance in dealing with guilt feelings while learning sign language. For these clients, psychotherapy provides an opportunity to talk freely about their hearing loss and attendant problems, to help them come to grips with the reality of deafness within a very supportive climate, and finally to help them understand that although deafness for them is irreversible, it is not necessarily a stultifying or a paralyzing influence and that there are ways of compensating for or overcoming it.

An important consideration is the role of stress in deafness. Stress is a common denominator for many mental health problems, and being deaf can be a very stressful experience. How well a deaf individual copes with daily stress is a good index of the individual's mental health.

Deafness itself is a medical condition; it denotes a physical disability and becomes a handicap due to the limitations and restrictions society places on a person with it. Deafness seen as a handicap is akin to racism, sexism, and other "isms" associated with minority groups. Deaf people are placed in positions where they are forced to experience, and attempt to endure, daily insults to their persons. They continue to endure prejudice, discrimination, ridicule, and negative and devaluative attitudes of society, as many of them have since early childhood. The psychosocial effects of deafness can have a telling effect on a deaf individual's psychological makeup and integrity.

Deaf clients also bring special assets and strengths to therapy. Because of the handicapping aspects of deafness, many deaf people have had to develop special strengths against adversity. In addition, many deaf individuals have developed effective coping, compensatory, and survival skills.

RESEARCH

Since the mid-1950s, psychotherapy research has become more subtle and sophisticated in design and conception. There is increasing concern with the more complex interactions of therapist, client, therapist-client relationships, and situations under which therapy takes place as determinants of the therapeutic outcome. At the same time, there has been a shifting of interest from an almost exclusive concern with outcome (what is accomplished?) to the study of the therapy process (what goes on between therapist and client?). Newer studies are also joining process and outcome questions (which aspects of the process make a therapeutic difference?).

Research in investigating psychotherapy as used with deaf populations still has been limited. While interest and growth has been apparent in providing mental health services for deaf people, it is not as evident in research. Reviews of psychotherapy outcome studies show that psychotherapy in general has modestly positive effects on patients. There is growing support, based on psychotherapy research data, for the conclusion that psychotherapy is worthwhile for many people. However, psychotherapy outcome studies have not been performed with deaf individuals, and from the research standpoint, no conclusions can yet be made as to the effectiveness of psychotherapy on deaf clients.

An encouraging note is the direction that has been taken by Gallaudet College's Research Institute's Mental Health and Deafness Research Program. The training of Ph.D. clinical psychologists in the short-term Interpersonal Psychotherapy of Depression (IPT) was initiated in early 1985. This psychotherapeutic approach was developed by the New Haven–Boston Collaborative Depression Project at Yale University. Before conducting a clinical trials process and outcome study with deaf clients, the aim of this training is for these therapists to become certified in the IPT approach. All have extensive experience in psychotherapy with deaf clients, and all are fluent in sign language.

This is the first instance in the deafness field in which attention has been paid to a specific definition of the treatment (IPT) in order to make it possible to draw conclusions about its effects on deaf individuals under certain conditions. Apart from being a pioneering endeavor, it is the first research dealing with a specific psychotherapy approach for a specific disorder, in this case, depression, a disorder that seems to be as prevalent among the deaf population as it is with the nondeaf population.

There are complex questions in psychotherapy research dealing with deaf people. Nonetheless, findings from process and outcome studies would provide extremely valuable new information and insights, thus increasing the effectiveness of psychotherapy with deaf individuals. Most significantly, there is a great need for such controlled and measurable process and outcome research data in order to supplement and support the observations and reports by various practitioners that psychotherapy, under proper conditions, is effective with deaf people.

PROBLEMS

Deaf clients need protection against inadequately and inappropriately trained practitioners as well as from incompetent ones. They need protection also from quacks and pseudo mental health professionals in the field of deafness, where the mental health profession is largely unmonitored and where quality control is virtually nonexistent. Of special concern is the susceptibility of some deaf individuals and their families to increasingly aggressive advertising and blandishment by a confusing amalgam of licensed and unlicensed individuals representing themselves as psychotherapist, marriage and family counselor, personal counselor, social therapist, psychodramatist, personal growth leader, and so on, but who may lack the qualifications, credentials, educational background, training, competency, and experience to offer such psychological services. A very tempting lure is the use of sign language, a skill which these people possess to varying degrees. The deaf individual may not be aware that proficiency in sign language is not to be equated with proficiency in psychotherapy.

An undesirable corollary to this is the inappropriate use of medication. Many deaf clients are given prescriptions for medication because of the physician's or psychiatrist's unfamiliarity with deaf people. Thus, there is the problem of prescription of medication without psychotherapy or without referral to an appropriate psychotherapist competent to treat deaf people. While medication can facilitate treatment where it is clearly indicated, it should not be used as a substitute for psychotherapy when medication is not necessary. While medication offers symptom relief, psychotherapy deals with the causes of psychological distress. Ideally, when medication is recommended, it is employed as adjunct therapy along with regular psychotherapy sessions.

Another worrisome area concerns mental health professionals such as counselors and caseworkers who treat clients for disorders that are beyond their level of competence. It is crucial for these professionals to know their own boundaries and to refer such clients to an appropriate practitioner.

The counselor, caseworker, and other mental health professionals should know when, how, and where to refer clients for psychotherapy when their conditions require more than counseling and the practitioner is not equipped to function in a psychotherapeutic role. The counselor or caseworker, for example, does not handle resistance and mechanisms of defense by developing goals of personality and behavior change, or focusing on the early conditioning and the unconscious forces that play on the person, as is done in psychotherapy; nor does a counselor use intensive, emotionally laden psychotherapeutic techniques to penetrate the client's many-layered defenses. Similarly, the counselor does not deal with and work through the client's feelings and attitudes about other people that have been transferred onto the therapist, as is done in certain forms of psychotherapy. In sum, while casework and counseling approaches are useful for certain clients and their needs, they are no substitute for those in need of psychotherapy.

The damage that can be done by an incompetent or inappropriate practitioner may have lifelong consequences for a client, particularly for deaf clients. The immediate effects of incompetent mental health professionals or others may not be readily apparent. The damage often manifests itself in many subtle ways and may worsen over a period of time. Research has indicated that even competently administered psychotherapy, despite its overall positive results, may make some clients worse.

GUIDELINES

A deaf individual wanting a professional psychotherapist must accept the fact that finding one who can help may be difficult. There are no sure guidelines, although some "rules-of-thumb" can be followed.

A logical starting point would be a special mental health facility for deaf people, if there is one in the client's vicinity. The potential deaf client also could look in the TDD directories (directories for users of special telephone devices for deaf people). A third possibility is to inquire after therapists who have good reputations as psychotherapists within the deaf community.

Consumer-oriented literature on psychotherapy strongly advocates interviewing several therapists before making a commitment. While potential deaf clients generally do not have this luxury due to the acute shortage of competent psychotherapists, they should ask the potential therapist simple but crucial questions about education, training, clinical experience, licensure or certification, therapeutic approach, length of time in practice with deaf clients, and other skills-related questions. Also important are questions pertaining to fees and whether there are arrangements for third-party reimbursement by the client's health insurance carrier.

In general, people in need of psychotherapy typically do not know how to choose the practitioner, how to judge the therapist's level of competence, or how to ascertain the therapist's approach in therapy. This is especially true for prospective deaf clients. For these reasons, preventive mental health education should begin in the schools and continue throughout the postsecondary years.

CONCLUSION

Deaf individuals have demonstrated their capacity and potential for emotional growth and psychological enhancement through psychotherapy. Under conditions for effective psychotherapy, deaf clients have responded to and benefited from the various forms of psychotherapy. Yet, psychotherapy remains inaccessible to many deaf people in need of it.

Bibliography

Brauer, B. A.: "Perspectives on Psychotherapy with Deaf Persons," *Mental Health in Deafness*, experimental issue, no. 4, Fall 1980.

——— and A. E. Sussman: "Experiences of Deaf Therapists with Deaf Clients," *Mental Health In Deafness*, experimental issue, no. 4, Fall 1980.

Garfield, S. L., and A. E. Bergin: *Handbook of Psychotherapy and Behavior Change*, 2d ed., 1978.

Gurman, A. S., and A. M. Razin: *Effective Psychotherapy: A Handbook of Research*, 1977.

Heinik, R. (ed.): *The Psychotherapy Handbook: The A to Z Guide to More than 250 Different Therapies in Use Today*, 1980.

Levine, E. S., A. E. Sussman, and B. B. (Brauer) Sachs (eds.): *The Preparation of Psychological Service Providers to the Deaf*, PRWAD Monograph, no. 4, May 1977.

Sachs, B. B. (Brauer): "The Mental Health Needs of Deaf Americans," *Task Panel Reports Submitted to the President's Commission on Mental Health*, vol. 3, Appendix, U.S. Government Printing Office, Washington, D.C., 1978.

Sobel, D.: "Freud's Fragmelacy," *New York Times Magazine*, October 26, 1980.

Wolberg, L. R.: *The Practice of Psychotherapy*, 1982.

———: *The Techniques of Psychotherapy*, 3d ed., part 1, 1977.

Allen E. Sussman

Hard-of-Hearing

The psychology of people who are hard-of-hearing differs significantly from that of deaf people. Hard-of-hearing is used here to describe persons who have postlingually acquired hearing losses ranging from mild to profound but who can still benefit from amplification. Their speech is adequate for communication, and they use, however imperfectly, the auditory mode to receive communications. This invisible condition of diminished hearing, without external evidence such as signing, places such people in limbo. They do not belong to deaf communities, and they are usually estranged from the hearing community of which they had been a part. Uncertainty, anxiety, and the development of chronic stress produce adverse perceptions that perpetuate a vicious cycle. Fatigue, caused by the strain of concentrated listening and lipreading, reduces the hard-of-hearing person's physical and mental capability to function and to cope.

As people lose their hearing, things seem to change for them, and for those around them. Misperceptions of each other, fueled by interactions often caused by ignorance, evolve. Communication breaks down. Isolation—a feeling of being alone, even in the middle of a crowd—develops the trend toward withdrawal. Perceived rejection sets in, accompanied by poor self-esteem. The process of socialization gradually shuts down.

STRESS FACTOR

Illness and disease often occur in individuals who have experienced a series of psychologically stressful events. Regardless of age, stress and one's reaction to it appears to be the critical factor. The loss, even partial, of the sense of hearing—upon which most interpersonal communications depend—may be described as a chronic stressor. It is a major life loss. The effort for a hard-of-hearing person to stay in effective communication requires tremendous physical and emotional energy beyond that required normally by a hearing person. The breakdown of communications causes intense stress. Hard-of-hearing people live with this stress constantly. Such unrelenting pressure, involving biological and psychological reaction to threatening situations in which people find themselves at a disadvantage, causes changes in behavior. The complexity of the task of adjustment by persons who lose hearing, and the effects on the people with whom they live, has never been fully appreciated.

Chronic stress is not an inevitable cause of psychological problems. Much depends upon how the stressor (hearing loss) is perceived and what the response to it is. When a major life crisis is seen as a challenge, coping is within reach. When the same life event is perceived as a crushing blow, helplessness and depression negate effective coping. A positive attitude minimizes the scope of the problem and enhances motivation to do something about it. Once the mind grasps the need for change or a readjustment and is open to information on how best to effect such change, there is a good chance for successful handling of the problem. Not that hearing can be restored or corrected (most hearing losses cannot), but tolerance, gained through acquiring skills which help one adapt to new circumstances, is a constructive response to stress.

COMPLICATIONS

Most people handle life crises adequately, but when they come in rapid sequence things get more complicated. Aging and the onset of impaired hearing put a person in double jeopardy. Some researchers think that this poses a far greater problem for a person in those circumstances than for a person who has lost hearing as a young adult.

It is known that some 55 percent of all persons with severe bilateral hearing loss are over 64 years old and 80 percent are over 44 years old, but there is little information on their adjustment to hearing loss. Does it vary with the age at which it is encountered? What is the effect of the person's income, occupation, and education? How is adjustment affected by the degree of loss, a person's character, stability of personality prior to hearing loss, whether the person is married?

While little is known about their adjustment, it is known that persons with acquired hearing loss have adjustment problems that are sometimes severe. Everywhere such people turn, they have a communication problem—on the street, in school, at the dinner table, in bed, on the job, in the doctor's office, in the market, on the phone, watching television, at the theater. It has been estimated that seven or more years elapse between the time of onset of hearing loss and actual diagnosis. Virtually all of the research on acquired hearing loss deals with the period after diagnosis, but the process of adjustment certainly begins during that earlier period. These two distinct phases of adjustment, prior to diagnosis and after diagnosis, pose significantly different problems for each individual. However, those who actually reach the stage of seeking help with their hearing loss are far fewer in number than those who do not. And yet the effect of impaired communication on the mental health of a hearing-impaired person can be devastating. Every day, every endeavor is a fresh reason for anxiety. Failure is always imminent. Frustration is endless. Anger and resentment may be repressed or expressed in antisocial behavior. Tension and anxiety contribute to fatigue that further impedes communication. The inability of some people to project their voices, the unwillingness of many hearing people to make a special effort, to spend the extra time, lead hearing-impaired people to feel tentative, left out, suspicious, lonely, isolated, uninteresting, devalued, and depressed.

This is true of children, teen-agers, and young adults. It is especially true of middle-aged and elderly people who grew up with normal hearing and have no experience coping with an acquired hearing disability. They try the patience of family and friends. They do not want to ask people to repeat or to shout so they stay home more often, and become more withdrawn. The unaccustomed isolation leads to depression.

PERCEPTION

Perhaps most important is the degree of impairment that is felt—not the degree of hearing loss measured. The person who has a 60-decibel loss in both ears and who, for whatever reason, cannot function in those circumstances has a greater adjustment problem than a person with a 90-decibel bilateral loss who can function. Perceived problems and negative reaction to stressful events by the person add to the handicapping conditions created by society. A feeling of loss, grief over no longer fully possessing an important life sense, combine with the circumstances of each individual to define a tailor-made challenge or threat. Thus, mild and moderate hearing impairments can and do cause personal problems of serious psychological nature that require significant adjustment. Since one cannot control the environment, even a positive response to stress is no guarantee of success. For example, hearing people's views and the nature of adjustment to hearing loss and coping are often very simple. Coping means acceptance of hearing loss, reduced access to social situations, and the wearing of a hearing aid. The hearing aid is expected to correct the situation to a significant degree. Family members will then strike a balance between support and dominance so that the hearing-impaired person can be effective, independent, and a participant in family life.

It almost never works that way. Studies of persons with acquired hearing loss, particularly in the United Kingdom, point to a lack of coping and to inappropriate adjustment, which lead to dissatisfaction on the part of the individual.

British researchers have developed a model for adjustment by the person with postlingual hearing loss. Using basic assumptions about the communications process and defining three phases of adjustment, these researchers have attempted to reduce a complicated subject to manageable proportion. Within the variations of circumstances for each individual, and the complexity of hearing loss affecting a person, there are some general considerations regarding communication structure which help explain the psychological reaction of a person who is hearing-impaired. They are as follows.

1. Exchange of information is governed by various social and personal norms.

2. People, through personal and social adjustment, attempt to control the speed, intensity, and density of information they receive.

3. In normal circumstances, most people have adjusted to a specific level of control of these factors. In social circumstances, the level has been "negotiated" and agreed to.

4. The onset of hearing loss disturbs the control that a person can exert.

5. The response is to increase intensity, or increase repetition, or increase the concentration level to maximize information being received.

6. This overt added control may be unacceptable to communication partners. The situation produces a realization of hearing loss.

7. The person may take one of four courses of action: increase the level of control at any cost; accept a reduced level of control and flow of information; reject or avoid those situations where the level of control is threatened; or use a combination of the three.

The degree to which a person can tolerate the reduced and varying extent of access to information will determine the degree of adjustment. If the person is to achieve a satisfactory level of communication, every encounter between hearing and hard-of-hearing persons requires that communications contracts be negotiated with patience and sensitivity. In the choice between changing one's life style to increase control or withdrawing from those areas of previous life style that now threaten independence and control, the latter seems more likely.

ADJUSTMENT PHASES

To facilitate understanding of the forces at play when hearing loss occurs, the three phases through which a person might travel in the process of adjustment should be examined. These are described below.

Phase I The first phase is the period before the person acknowledges hearing loss and seeks help. The extent of phase I varies from days to years. Although conscious realization of hearing impairment may take a long time, adjustment is in progress. Estimates indicate that three-fourths of those with acquired hearing loss are in this phase at any given time. These are people who have not sought professional help with their problem. A common response in this phase is to increase control of loudness (turn up the television, radio, and stereo) and to increase use of social and physical means to enhance intensity of information sought (sit closer to the speaker at meetings, increase concentration, make frequent requests for repetition). The hearing person's reaction to such action includes complaints about loudness, nonverbal acts such as hands over ears, and refusal to repeat—"It isn't important." The resulting alternatives are either a reduced level of loudness or an alienation of others. In either case, the hearing-impaired person is on the defensive and has to adjust to the lesser of two evils.

As these situations occur more frequently, the hearing-impaired person moves closer to seeking help, often at the insistence of family members; accelerates the process of aggressive and antisocial behavior; or withdraws from normal social activities. The individual exists in a twilight zone, unable to hear in the sunlit world of sound, yet not enveloped in a night of silence; ambiguity becomes the problem. Phase I, combined with aging, poses an increasingly difficult problem for the hearing-impaired person which all too often has resulted in institutionalization.

Phase II The diagnosis and referral phase is normally of short duration, but it is one of great anxiety. The diagnosis of hearing loss (often progressive) opens many possibilities for the future: total deafness, loss of job, embarrassment, stigma, loss of independence, rejection by family and friends. The person is usually less focused on the physical aspects of hearing loss than on the social, economic, and personal costs of the new circumstances. How the doctor, audiologist, hearing aid specialist, family, and friends perform in this phase can be crucial to the hearing-impaired person's ultimate adjustment. The degree and direction of adjustment in phase I also has bearing on where the hearing-impaired person will go from here. Information can help. A clear understanding of what is and what is not happening to the person can contribute to a positive reaction. Awareness that there are many others in similar circumstances and actually meeting some of the problems is very useful.

Phase III Most of the literature of acquired hearing loss falls into this category—adjustment to diagnosed hearing loss. Whatever support came from family and friends in the previous two phases must now be replaced by long-term commitment. This becomes as difficult for them as for the hearing-impaired person because misunderstandings develop easily. The hearing-impaired person feels the family does not understand the problem, and the family feels the person is not accepting the hearing loss, and is not adjusting properly. For the small percentage who use hearing aids successfully, the struggle to maintain some degree of control in interpersonal relationships is enhanced, but tension is usually present and adjustment comes to mean dealing with diminished control.

The loss of independence, particularly in the older male hearing-impaired person, becomes a major problem. In the case of a married couple, the husband may make various excuses for not socializing with friends, and the wife may offer support and try to intermediate as interpreter. Opposed to such dependence, he may see the situation as relinquishing self-determination or control. He must either accept a lower level of information flow involving interpreting, or repeatedly breach social behavior norms. Progressively he increases his resistance to social involvement. There is evidence of marital breakdowns and suicidal behavior at the extreme limits of such circumstances. Key variables are the previous or expected level of control and the characteristics of life style which relate to a person's normal form of interrelationships.

Of course, in marital situations where the wife heads the household, the reverse could occur. Her loss of hearing could trigger her anxieties about dependence on her spouse in communication, and her deteriorated social life.

SUPPORT STRUCTURE FOR ADJUSTMENT

One need not become psychologically debilitated or even chronically unhappy as a result of hearing loss. But the requirements for successful adjustment are not within the sole control of the individual. The response to hearing loss is conditioned by significant others and members of the hearing health delivery system. Acquisition of information about hearing loss, learning new skills in communication, associating with others who are in similar circumstances all contribute to potential for successful handling of the problems that hearing loss poses.

Simple technical improvements in the listening environment and enhanced use of auditory reception by assistive listening devices greatly facilitate coping and reduce stress. Many hard-of-hearing people whose perception of themselves had diminished due to coping inadequately now find that there are ways of remaining in the mainstream of life. Group therapy, in the context of a self-help movement, has aided thousands in their ability to adjust more effectively to their new circumstances of hearing loss.

A survey of 6000 hard-of-hearing people, most of whom use some form of amplification, indicated strong feelings of being misunderstood, but being sustained by faith, spouse support, hearing aids, and association with other hearing-impaired people. In addition to group therapy, rehabilitative counseling of hard-of-hearing people, as well as psychological counseling, can add much to successful adjustment. By urging the hearing-impaired person to face the threat head on, to examine it, to determine what really is the source of fear, and to suggest ways to relieve the pressure and facilitate adaptation, the counselor can lead the way to successful coping. Most hearing-impaired people report that there is virtually no advice on personal adjustment from those in the hearing health field.

CONCLUSION

There are significant differences in the psychology of those people who are born deaf and those who lose their hearing later (postlingually). The latter group have lost a precious possession. They are confronted by many concerns: the ambiguity of a progressive hearing loss; the fear of worse things happening if hearing diminishes; the prejudices of being part of a hearing culture that associates deafness with stigma; the complexities of hearing loss with its many apparent contradictions; the need to adjust to amplification if usable; inadequate alternatives for action; misunderstandings caused by thinking a communication was received accurately when it was not; the humiliation of being no longer able to function adequately on the telephone; the constant fatigue from straining to hear and to lip-read; the embarrassment of being unable to maintain a communicative relationship with peers; a feeling of dependence; a gradual withdrawal resulting in poor self-esteem and low level of life satisfaction.

The effects of these variables depend on many other factors related to the person who has the problem. Generally, however, hearing loss acquired postlingually is a negative experience causing severe stress. Some individuals can handle such problems alone, but most people need help. Support structures, ranging from family and hearing health professionals to community and self-help groups, need urgent attention.

It is difficult for a person to understand what is happening as hearing diminishes. Without clear guidelines, the individual must rely on her or his basic characteristics and personality to achieve adjustment. Such inner resources are seldom enough. Hearing loss is America's most pervasive handicapping condition; hard-of-hearing people are the nation's most numerous victims. To remove them from a limbo fraught with psychological complexity will take much research, education, and attention to a problem not yet considered sufficiently serious to warrant priority action.

Bibliography

Brickman, P., et al.: "Models of Helping and Coping," *American Psychology*, no. 37, 1982.

Kyle, J. G., L. Jones, and P. L. Wood: *Adjustment to Acquired Hearing Loss: A Working Model*, School of Education Research Unit, University of Bristol, U.K., 1984.

Stone, H. E.: "Hearing Loss and Mental Health," *Shhh—A Journal About Hearing Loss*, vol. 3, no. 6, November/December 1982.

Vernon, McKay: "Psychological Stress and Hearing Loss," *Shhh—A Journal About Hearing Loss*, vol. 5, no. 4, July/August 1984.

H. E. Stone

Multiply Handicapped

Multiply handicapped deaf people have one or more significant disabilities in addition to their impaired hearing. A virtually unlimited variety of impairments co-occur with deafness; these range from mild to severe, may be present from birth or acquired later in life, and may be caused by physical factors, environmental influences, or both.

The description of a hearing-impaired person as multiply handicapped is somewhat subjective, particularly as there is no universally accepted definition of this term. There does appear to be a general agreement, however, that a sizable percentage of deaf children and adults have additional disabilities, and that these often present formidable barriers to education, communication, social development, employment, and other areas. Additional physical, intellectual, emotional, or behavioral disabilities can significantly increase the complexity of providing appropriate education and other services to hearing-impaired persons.

PREVALENCE

Estimates of the extent of multiple impairments among the hearing-impaired population vary considerably. Surveys of school-aged children and youths typically indicate that from 20 to 33 percent of students enrolled in educational programs for deaf and hearing-impaired students are classified as multiply handicapped. Almost certainly, the actual percentage of hearing-impaired persons with multiple handicaps is even higher, since the above surveys do not include hearing-impaired individuals who are served by programs designed primarily for people with disabilities other than deafness. It has been estimated, for example, that some 10 to 15 percent of the population in schools and institutions for persons classified as mentally retarded or developmentally disabled have significant hearing loss. Similarly, audiologic screenings conducted among groups of persons who are visually, physically, or neurologically impaired have found a higher occurrence of hearing impairments than would be expected for the general population. Little reliable information is available on the prevalence of multiple handicaps in hearing-impaired adults.

AVAILABILITY OF SERVICE

Prior to the 1970s, few educational or other special services were available to multiply handicapped hearing-impaired persons. This situation has changed considerably, however, particularly in response to Public Law 94-142, the Education for All Handicapped Children Act of 1975. Many schools and agencies for deaf persons now offer some degree of specialized training and assistance to those with multiple handicaps, and to their parents and families. Despite these advances, however, the probability exists that some multiply handicapped hearing-impaired children and adults have not yet been identified, nor have services been made available to meet their specialized needs. *See* EDUCATION OF THE HANDICAPPED ACT.

CLASSIFICATION

While the incidence of multiple handicaps among deaf people is generally considered to be high, some observers maintain that disability-related terms and labels are often applied to deaf people hastily or inaccurately, serving no constructive purpose. For example, some deaf children have been mistakenly classified as mentally retarded because of examiners' strict reliance on verbally based intelligence tests, while others have unfairly been characterized as autistic or emotionally disturbed because of apparent deficits in communicative and social development brought about by their deafness. Caution should always be exercised in evaluating and interpreting the behavior of deaf persons who are suspected of having multiple handicaps; such diagnoses should only be made following comprehensive and diversified assessments and observations.

Multiply handicapped hearing-impaired persons are most frequently classified according to the type of disability present in addition to deafness. Terms such as hearing-impaired/mentally retarded, deaf-blind, and deaf/emotionally disturbed are often used. These disability labels should not be rigidly applied as a basis for providing services or for grouping individuals. Some children with both visual and hearing impairments, for example, may benefit most from placement in a class for hearing-impaired children; others are most appropriately served in programs for visually impaired children; still others need highly specialized services for deaf-blind severely handicapped children. Nevertheless, the categorical labels may prove useful in considering some of the special concerns of individuals who have additional disabilities frequently identified in deaf populations.

Mental Retardation Several of the leading causes of deafness, notably prematurity, maternal rubella, Rh factor incompatibility, and meningitis, can also cause damage to the brain and central nervous system, bringing about deficits in intellectual performance and adaptive behavior. Conversely, a number of the major physical causes of mental retardation may also result in abnormalities in the auditory structures. Persons with Down's syndrome, for example, often have irregularities in the middle ear and inner ear, and are particularly susceptible to otitis media, which may result in conductive hearing loss. *See* HEARING LOSS.

The cumulative effects of deafness and mental retardation, especially when both are present from birth or early childhood, greatly inhibit the development of language and basic concepts. Most educators of hearing-impaired mentally retarded students use some form of manual communication, usually adapted or simplified, in conjunction with speech. Signs are presented through carefully structured imitation and shaping programs. Other approaches to communication emphasize natural gestures, graphic or pictorial symbols (frequently in the form of communication boards and picture books), speech, or a combination of methods. Regardless of the method used, educational and rehabilitation programs seek to enable hearing-impaired mentally retarded individuals to acquire basic expressive and receptive abilities, self-care skills,

and vocational competence. The use of functional, realistic activities and materials is emphasized, and students are encouraged to interact with nonhandicapped persons in the community.

Visual Impairment The co-occurrence of blindness (or severe visual impairment) along with deafness imposes pervasive limitations on learning, development, and communication. When the two principal channels of sensory input—vision and hearing—are absent or greatly restricted, it is very difficult for a person to gain knowledge and concepts through continual interactions with the environment. A deaf-blind person is usually defined as one who has a combination of visual and auditory impairments sufficiently severe to preclude being adequately served in programs solely for visually impaired persons (where most education and communication methods require the individual to have good hearing), or solely for hearing-impaired persons (where most education and communication methods rely heavily on adequate vision). Relatively few persons are both totally blind and profoundly deaf. The deaf-blind person must depend largely on secondary sources of information and experience and on the sense of touch. Many causes of deaf-blindness have been identified; some are associated with a wide range of physical and intellectual impairments, while others affect only a person's vision and hearing. Two causes of deaf-blindness of particular current concern are maternal rubella (German measles) and Usher's syndrome. *See* DEAF-BLINDNESS.

Several thousand children were born with severe visual, hearing, and other impairments after epidemics of maternal rubella affected many pregnant women in the United States and Canada in the mid-1960s. Usher's syndrome affects congenitally deaf persons with the visual handicap of retinitis pigmentosa. This results in a gradual loss of peripheral vision, usually in adulthood.

Motor Impairment The occurrence of motor and neurological disabilities is not uncommon in deaf persons. Rh factor incompatibility, prematurity, and perinatal anoxia (lack of oxygen around the time of birth) are among the conditions that can impair both hearing and motor functioning. Cerebral palsy is a general term applied to malfunctions of the brain that cause disorders in the voluntary motor functions. Persons with cerebral palsy may have paralysis, lack of coordination, impaired balance, muscle weakness, involuntary convulsions, and other motor disturbances. There are several fairly well-defined patterns of cerebral palsy, usually classified by the types of motor disability [for example, spasticity, rigidity, athetosis (characterized by large irregular involuntary twisting movements)], areas of the body involved [hemiplegia (one side), diplegia (major involvement of the legs, minor involvement of the arms)], and degree of severity [mild, moderate, severe]. Cerebral palsy is not considered a progressive disorder; that is, it does not ordinarily become more severe as a person ages. Intellectual impairment may accompany cerebral palsy; however, no clear relationship exists between the degree of a person's motor impairment and the degree (if any) of intellectual impairment. Some 25 to 30 percent of persons with cerebral palsy also have impaired hearing, and about 70 percent have speech disorders, usually caused by difficulties in controlling the muscles used in spoken communication. Such combinations of disabilities can impose complex barriers to communication and development. While the hearing impairment interferes with a deaf person's ability to acquire language, the motor impairment may make it difficult or impossible for the person to speak, sign, or fingerspell clearly. Regular physical therapy, careful positioning, and, in some cases, medication, surgery, and the use of specially adapted equipment and technology can help deaf persons with cerebral palsy or other motor disorders move and communicate as effectively as possible.

Emotional Disturbance Although any instance of multiple disabilities requires careful assessment and professional judgment, the characterization of a hearing-impaired person as having emotional disturbance or behavior disorders is particularly problematic. Psychologists and others who specialize in the evaluation and treatment of emotional disturbance generally maintain that a person's behavior must deviate markedly and chronically from established societal or cultural norms in order for that person to be considered to have an emotional or behavioral disorder requiring treatment.

Many deaf individuals, it is reasonable to assume, may be viewed as exhibiting behavior patterns that are "deviant" or "socially unacceptable" because of a clinician's lack of understanding of deafness or inability to communicate with the hearing-impaired client. A substantial number of deaf persons have been subjected to inappropriate diagnoses and placements and to having their hearing impairment identified late in life or not at all. Any of these externally caused factors may result in behavior that is considered disturbed or disordered. The "disturbance," however, rests more in the environment than in the hearing-impaired person.

These cautions, however, should not obscure a concern for those deaf children and adults whose behavioral or emotional problems pose serious obstacles to their education, social adjustment, or personal fulfillment. Surveys of the prevalence of emotional disturbance among deaf populations vary widely according to the definitions used; yet it is generally acknowledged that a substantial number of hearing-impaired persons exhibit symptoms of emotional disturbance at some point in their development. Estimates of the prevalence of serious behavioral problems in deaf children range from about 8 to over 22 percent; mild, moderate, and transitory behavior problems are reported to be much more frequent. Among the problems or symptoms often described in studies of hearing-impaired persons are immaturity, anxiety, rigidity, aggression, lack of social relationships, egocentricity, impulsiveness, delinquency, and bizarre or socially inappropriate behavior. Deaf children of hearing parents, it has been reported, are more likely to be considered to have psychological adjustment problems than are deaf children of deaf parents.

Clearly, communication and language acquisition are closely interrelated with social adjustment, family and peer relationships, and an understanding of acceptable and unacceptable behavior. These interrelationships, unfortunately, have often worked to the disadvantage of deaf persons. Relatively few specialists in the identification and treatment of emotional disorders have the ability to communicate readily and directly with deaf persons; it is thus difficult for such specialists to understand and address their special needs. Conversely, professionals who specialize in the education and habilitation of deaf persons frequently have been unwilling or unable to meet the needs of their students or clients who exhibit severely disturbed behavior. This situation is improving gradually, with the development of new behavior rating instruments specifically designed for use with deaf persons, and with the establishment of specialized counseling and therapy services for this population.

Bibliography

Campbell, B., and V. Baldwin (eds.): *Severely Handicapped/Hearing Impaired Students: Strengthening Service Delivery*, 1982.

Cherow, E., N. D. Matkin, and R. J. Trybus (eds.): *Hearing-Impaired Children and Youth with Developmental Disabilities: An Interdisciplinary Foundation for Service*, 1985.

Mencher, G. T., and S. E. Gerber (eds.): *The Multiply Handicapped Hearing Impaired Child*, 1983.

Tweedie, D., and E. H. Shroyer (eds.): *The Multihandicapped Hearing Impaired: Identification and Instruction*, 1982.

Michael D. Orlansky

Psychosocial Behavior

A congenital profound hearing loss presents unique psychological constellations and challenges in the child's psychosocial development. Deafness is not a single entity that uniformly affects those who are diagnosed as deaf. The physiological causes and conditions of hearing loss are varied, and different aspects of the hearing process may be differentially involved. Apart from variability in type and in extent of hearing loss, there is the added factor of time of onset. A hearing loss sustained after acquisition of language, around age two to three, has quite different effects than hearing loss earlier or at birth. In addition, there are as yet many intangibles to which no definite answers are available. One is the possibility of a neurological involvement that extends beyond hearing and complicates the psychological picture. Another is the individual variability in the use of residual hearing (whether unaided or aided) and what, for lack of a better word, can be called a special "talent" for acquisition of language in spite of severely restricted input. Finally, there is a big difference in psychosocial impact between deafness occurring in a welcoming deaf family and in an unsuspecting and unprepared hearing family.

INFANCY

To appreciate the psychological situation, it is useful to compare early deafness with the other major sensory deficiency, early blindness; but the development of healthy infants during their first 1½ years must first be considered. In this period, vision is by far the most crucial, if not the only effective, distance receptor. It is the necessary basis for the infants' knowledge of, and interest in, the world. This interest and knowledge is spontaneously shown in their actions, beginning with the coordinated reaching and exploration of persons and things by means of eyes, mouth, and hands. This is followed a few months later by active moving, first by crawling, then by walking, into the ever expanding world of objects. Moreover, vision is by far the most congenial sense modality through which the objects of actions take on substantiality. As infants come to understand that they live in a world of permanent objects (people and things), there is also beginning awareness that they are stable selves in relation to stable others. Around two years of age this psychological world of action and vision gradually becomes internalized in the young children's personal memory and fantasy. What in general is referred to as an internal mental image has usually a quite prominent visual component, and therefore the equation of mental images with internal visual pictures is for most people unproblematic.

On all these counts, profoundly blind children are at a severe disadvantage, even though in favorable circumstances and with exceptional personal care all these psychological problems and challenges can be met and overcome. Large developmental delays are invariably expected. This is in marked contrast to congenitally deaf children: they show no retardation in their early mastery of the action world, and moreover they often present to

their caretakers no definite clues through which hearing loss could be suspected, much less diagnosed. The reason for this relatively favorable psychological situation is also the reason why blindness is such a severe developmental deficiency: not hearing but vision is the developmentally first sensory channel of interpersonal communication. Vision enables face-to-face contact and with it the recognition and imitation of facial social expressions, in the form of a smile of approval and encouragement, in gestures of mutual delight, in signs of surprise, anger, sorrow, or disappointment. This is by far the most difficult problem for the parents of blind children: the difficulty of establishing mutually satisfying interpersonal communication and the long delay before hearing and speech can take over the main communicative function that in sighted children is preceded by nonverbal visual contact.

The points stressed are, first, the absolute necessity of actions as the developmental basis for meaningful contact with the world of persons and things and, second, the fact that in the beginning vision plays an infinitely more crucial role in establishing this contact than hearing. This statement must not be misconstrued to mean that hearing serves no useful function during the first year. Depending on individual differences, some infants quite early are sensitive to the sounds in their environment. However, the comparison of congenital blindness and deafness indirectly confirms the evidence that the early development of meaningful hearing leans heavily on the development of meaningful vision, and not vice versa. For this reason, blind children's psychosocial development is severely affected by lack of vision for which hearing can in no way substitute. In striking contrast, the early psychosocial development of hearing-deprived children is not necessarily negatively affected by their sensory defect.

EARLY AND MIDDLE CHILDHOOD

However, two remarkable transformations occur in the psychology of the growing child beginning around 1½ years, that is, subsequent to the developed capacity to move and act as a self in mutual relation with other people and things. One transformation is expansion of the logic of action into the logic of action-separated (abstract) thinking. The other is the formation of representative symbols extending the scope of reality beyond the perceptive here and now. Three major forms of symbols can be enumerated: gestures and symbolic (or pretend) play; internal fantasy, including the mental images mentioned above; and shared symbolic communication in the form of societal language. Thinking can then be parsimoniously described as the logical, or rather at first the prelogical, coordination of the various symbols. It must be emphasized that these new achievements develop quite gradually; in particular, the logic of thinking requires about five years of continuous further development before children between ages six and seven acquire the first general mental operations and an understanding of logical necessity. Then it takes another six or seven years to attain the more mature logical capacity of reflective theoretical thinking. Around age two, at the point when this new development in thinking and symbols has its beginning, deaf children fail to acquire competence in the language of society. Within a relatively short span, between the ages of two to four, hearing children assimilate the surrounding speech through the mutual effort of the parents and the children themselves, backed by the natural motivation to communicate. While hearing children thus quickly come to use speech as their major mode of social communication, deaf children's hearing loss effectively bars this type of easy acquisition.

Parental Role At this time the hearing loss is bound to have some profound effects on deaf children's psychosocial development. In fact, if deafness can be called a physical disability, from the psychological viewpoint it has always been recognized primarily as a potential communicative disability. For that reason, to an even greater extent than with hearing children, deaf children's development is very much dependent on the kind of social interactions they experience in their home. By now, deafness has been diagnosed. How do the parents respond to it? Have they worked through the shock, the grief, the uncertainty of the future and reached a measure of constructive acceptance? The variability of these parental responses, together with the wide range of the children's individual psychological dispositions (including the nature of hearing loss), makes it unreasonable to expect to find uniform patterns of psychological development in deaf children. Nevertheless, the first unique challenge of early deafness falls squarely, not on the child, but on the parents. Since the quality of acceptance of the deafness of their child is bound to influence the quality of child-parent interaction, this acceptance is a decisive determinant on the deaf child's ensuing psychosocial development.

Constructive acceptance implies a number of different things. First, personal resentment or guilt feelings concerning the child's sensory defect have been overcome. Second, the parents have developed the flexibility and ingenuity to use with the deaf child all available channels of personal communication and to continue the dialogue that has already started during the first two years. Finally, common sense and good judgment are required to make use of available educational programs and technical devices and to respond to the often conflicting claims and promises on the part of experts (including their veiled threats) without unrealistic expectations on the one hand or an insufficiently challenging routine on the other. Fortunately for parents of deaf children, the controversy surrounding the methods of educating deaf children, which formerly was severe and dogmatic, has generally abated; there is also more exposure of people in general to deaf people in society and to the use of sign language (for example, on television). These changes and increased tolerance for diversity has made it easier for parents to reach the desirable degree of acceptance and a reasonable commitment to help their deaf child to become a constructive part of that society. *See* HISTORY: Sign Language Controversy.

Socialization and Knowledge The children affected with deafness do not themselves experience any particular disadvantage. In fact, all the scientific and clinical evidence concurs that in spite of not having the ease of verbal exchanges (which in hearing children almost continuously occupy whatever they are doing), young deaf children develop their social and knowledge capacities well within the range of expectation for hearing children. The massive differences in amount, ease, and scope of sound and finally verbal experience are not at all matched by equal differences in psychosocial development. On the contrary, similar to hearing children, deaf children after age two engage in symbolic play, socialize with other children, and use gestures to communicate and express their feelings. Equally surprising is the overwhelming similarity of young deaf children's intellectual and logical development. If intelligence is measured in terms of verbal knowledge, then indeed deaf children are far below hearing children of comparable age. But when nonverbal tasks are devised to observe their logical thinking, no genuine and consistent differences have been demonstrated. This is in spite of many years of intensive psychological research to find precisely specific areas of knowledge capacities or strategies in which deaf children would be different or deficient as a direct function of their lack of verbal competence.

Deaf children's continued healthy psychological development after age two is, at the least, powerful evidence that verbal language by itself cannot be considered the primary source of either social or intellectual development. Rather, the evidence suggests that social relating and intellectual understanding are actively constructed by the growing children in constant interactions with other people, things, and events. Verbal language interactions, where they are present, can become precious and mutually satisfying occasions to engage in this developmental construction, but they are in no way the primary, much less the only, means to bring it about. The overall psychological normalcy of young deaf children is comprehensible only if the role of verbal speech in development is not exaggerated. More precisely, if verbal language is perhaps considered a vital component in the social relating and thinking of hearing children, then obviously deaf children must use some substitute symbolic system to compensate for their lack of verbal language. To communicate and to form symbols for communication is, however, an integral part of the developing human child, and all healthy deaf children, regardless of their achieved language competence, construct symbols and use them for social communication and, if necessary, for thinking. In fact, deaf children growing up in a home where sign language is not known, almost "invent" their own symbolic language spontaneously—in apparent contrast to hearing children to whom society freely presents its own language.

Comparison with Hearing Children An appraisal of past psychological research shows the similarities between age-comparable hearing and deaf groups on a great variety of age-sensitive tasks. In spite of some reported differences, primarily induced by experimental settings and thus only marginally related to real life, the overriding fact is that deaf children do develop mature logical thinking and understanding. This is true even though they may be very poor in the acquisition of society's language or unexposed to the model of the American Sign Language or some other visual language of signs. This language difference has the most serious consequences for their scholastic and social conduct where, with some notable exceptions, they lag conspicuously behind the hearing population. The most intense educational efforts are focused on helping deaf children acquire the knowledge and the practical use of society's language. Nevertheless, what should be of great comfort to all concerned with deaf people's well-being is the psychological robustness and autonomy of these young people. To an outsider the deaf children's speech and language discrepancy would appear an almost insurmountable psychological obstacle. Yet from their own viewpoint, they seem to accept the challenge of their peculiar situation with a routine self-assurance and positive expectation, as do all healthy children.

Provided they have had an accepting early parental home which assured them the basis of feelings of self-worth and self-esteem, deaf children are not necessarily psychologically damaged by the gradual realization that they are different and cannot as easily communicate with others as do hearing people. This statement is not contradicted by occasional observations that deaf school children seem to show a higher degree of immaturity or maladjustment than hearing children. In general, these differences are small deviations from norms

that can be easily accounted for by the strange situational context. As deaf people grow up and take their place in the world of work and adult society, there is no reliable evidence that they suffer serious mental or social maladjustments to a greater extent than the rest of the population. Repeated attempts to discover a characteristic deaf "personality" have been quite futile. As in the intellectual area, so also in the personality area deaf people fall comfortably within the expected variability of the hearing population, and any stereotypic notions are not factual.

Special Challenges The point is not to deny that there are situations and problems that are special to deaf youngsters in their psychosocial development; rather, it is to stress that their psychological responses to these challenges as a rule are quite adequate to lead to the development of an autonomous, intellectually and socially mature adult. This suggests a research strategy that in fact is now more and more employed: instead of asking how do deaf people globally differ from hearing people (as a rule, they do not), it is more profitable to search for an understanding of the way that deaf youngsters respond to their special challenges, keeping in mind that all youngsters face challenges. These special challenges include, first and foremost, the problem of communication, social identification, and possible social isolation. There are also possible problems of overprotection or dependency and the problems surrounding their formal education.

ADOLESCENCE

When a deaf boy or girl is around 13 years old, he or she must face the transition from childhood to adolescence. The age of puberty has been reached and with it the beginning of the breaking away from the state of dependent childhood to independent adulthood. Emotionally and intellectually the deaf youngsters are ready to "test reality;" now, for the first time, they have the task of accepting themselves as being deaf. The full impact of this condition has not yet been felt or reflected on during the middle childhood years; then all children in the full bloom of intellectual development are intensely but unreflectively open to ever expanding encounters with people, especially peers, social institutions (including formal education), and a vast scope of different things and ideas. But around age 13, adolescents begin to view themselves as thinking persons in their own right, and self-reflection and self-planning are part of normal development. Now, deaf adolescents experience and can reflect upon deafness as being different from the normal state of hearing. In the majority of cases this awareness and the transition into deaf adulthood proceeds without major psychosocial disruptions. The principal pitfalls to avoid are social immaturity and dependency on the one extreme, and social isolation on the other extreme. There are two major components for deaf adolescents in facing these problems: one having to do with their communication, the other with the deaf group.

A certain proportion of deaf youngsters do acquire a comfortable use of societal language; but the majority of them do not really feel at home in that language—rather the language of signs is or is fast becoming their primary language. Deaf youngsters realize this and accept it, and they do so all the more readily as they look forward to growing up into the group of deaf adults. Acceptance of deafness means, therefore, identification with the deaf social group. It is this group within which they look forward to having easy communication and the recognition of their peers, to having their friends, their recreation, their associations, eventually their families. Only with this prospect before them can they be satisfied with their rather moderate progress in education, compared to hearing standards. However, in general they can now stop comparing themselves to hearing norms, which would severely test their psychological well-being, and can focus on their psychological strengths. This strength includes an experience unique to deaf people: a sure sense of being the originators of their own language of signs and of belonging to the community of those who use this language.

Whatever can be said about the language of signs of a deaf group—and each separate society has its typical sign language for deaf people—unquestionably it is a true human language, with all the major characteristics of other languages. Its gesturelike quality in no way detracts from its cognitive equality with spoken languages. However, from a psychosocial viewpoint it has special characteristics that affect its users: it requires meaningful face-to-face contact, and it is more public and self-revealing than spoken language. An interesting neurological parallel to this connectedness is the finding that for those for whom it is their first language, sign language is believed to be bilaterally represented—in contrast to spoken language where almost invariably one cerebral side (usually the left) is dominant. *See* PSYCHOLINGUISTICS: Language Processing.

DEAF COMMUNITY

The language of signs is the chief instrument holding together what is rightly called the deaf community, and this community plays a pivotal role in the psychosocial adjustment of most deaf people. It is a unique social constellation, not easily comparable to any other social subgroup. Within it, deaf adolescents can find role models that are both challenging and realistic. Not a homogeneous whole, it mirrors the variety of people in the larger hearing society. Deaf youngsters have indeed a wide choice of options in terms of interpersonal relations and of career possibilities. While some deaf people can make a personally and socially adequate adjustment to the adult hearing society, the great majority find the solution to their psychosocial task within the deaf community. It is therefore gratifying to note that the larger society has become better informed about the life of ordinary deaf people and their way of communication, not least on account of sign language seen on television screens. At the same time there is a greater tolerance for social diversity in general, and deaf people can benefit from this positive social attitude, especially since it makes the task of accepting the state of deafness easier, both for the parents and for the young deaf persons themselves.

Psychosocial development reaches a relatively stable plateau in young adulthood and, beyond that, in adulthood proper. The results of several surveys clearly indicate that deaf people show a level of psychological adjustment comparable to hearing people. There is no greater incidence of serious mental illness or antisocial behavior among deaf people than among the population in general. As a rule, deaf people, particularly in North America but increasingly in other parts of the world, show a surprising degree of autonomy in the shaping of their own lives and in adjusting to the difference of ease of societal communication. Even though their average level of employment is below what hearing persons with comparable length of education may achieve, deaf persons show stability in their work history and have proven their capacity to adjust to the changing demands of the workplace. On a personal level, deaf people with few exceptions find their marriage partners among themselves, just as friendships, recreation, and day-to-day social contacts are generally found within the deaf community. To an outsider this attachment to the deaf group may seem restrictive so that a word or two of caution may be in order. First, when deaf persons are discovered with clear evidence of some form of psychosocial maladjustment, deafness should not automatically be identified as the major cause; often deafness may be a contributing factor but the decisive reason is found in psychological and social processes, common to deaf and hearing people alike. This comment merely exemplifies what was implied above, namely that there may be problems specific to deafness but there is no specific psychology.

With regard to the deaf community itself, it is here proposed that the deaf group is the major method through which deaf people accept and overcome the tremendous challenge that profound deafness imposes on them, a challenge that has to be worked through by all deaf persons once they reach a certain age level. Far from being the restrictive environment that superficially it may appear, it is the constructive solution for the psychosocial well-being of deaf people. The deaf community incorporates a noncomparative attitude and a realistic independence, and is the surest antidote to social isolation and immature overprotection. In fact, it is within the hearing community that deaf people surely must experience a certain measure of restriction. The deaf community is precisely the suitable context which can make up for this lack. In this sense this community is perhaps the single most important factor making possible a healthy psychosocial development of deaf children and eventually an adequate psychosocial adjustment of deaf adults.

Bibliography

Furth, H. G.: *Deafness and Learning: A Psychosocial Approach*, Wadsworth, Belmont, California, 1973.

Gregory, S.: *The Deaf Child and His Family*, George Allen and Unwin, London, 1976.

Hoeman, H. W., and J. I. Briga: "Hearing Impairment," *Handbook of Special Education*, Prentice-Hall, Englewood Cliffs, New Jersey, 1981.

Jacobs, L. M.: *A Deaf Adult Speaks Out*, Gallaudet College Press, Washington, D. C., 1974.

Meadow, K. P.: *Deafness and Child Development*, University of California Press, Berkeley, 1980.

Mindel, E. D., and M. Vernon: *They Grow in Silence: The Deaf Child and His Family*, National Association of the Deaf, Silver Spring, Maryland, 1971.

Hans G. Furth

R

RAY, JOHNNIE
(1927–   )

Johnnie Ray was once called "one of the most exciting singers in the world." At the peak of his career in the 1950s, he was known as the Prince of Wails and the Cry Guy because of his emotional and expressive style. Two of his hit songs, "Little White Cloud That Cried" and "Cry," made him an overnight sensation in 1952.

Born on January 10, 1927, in Dallas, Oregon, Ray was raised on the family farm in Salem. When he was 11 years old, he began to withdraw from schoolmates and other people. Four years later, he was diagnosed as having a hearing impairment, which was soon corrected with a hearing aid.

During the next two years, Ray joined church and choir groups, played the piano in high school bands, and sang wherever he was given the opportunity. He first breakthrough occurred at the age of 16 when he sang on an amateur radio show in Portland, Oregon. He continued to appear regularly. At 17, he composed "Little White Cloud," the song that catapulted him to fame years later. It was in Portland, too, that he landed his first professional singing job as a production singer in a burlesque show.

In 1949 Ray moved to Hollywood. He tried to support himself by singing and playing the piano in hideaway night clubs and burlesque theaters around Los Angeles. When this did not work out to his satisfaction, he decided to head for New York. Ray made his way eastward by singing and playing the piano at small supper clubs. The pay was meager, but the experience gave him the time and opportunity to write new songs for his act.

Ray's success came while he was performing in Detroit. Two of his songs, "Whiskey and Gin" and "Tell the Lady I Said Goodbye," were recorded. The local disc jockeys were so impressed that they often played his songs over the radio, and soon Ray was discovered by a recording executive. He was given a contract, flown to New York City, and scheduled for a recording session. There, he recorded "Little White Cloud That Cried" and "Cry," which together sold over 4 million copies and made Ray internationally famous.

He went on world tours and built up a tremendous fan club. He continued to write his own songs, many of which sold by the millions. Three of these topped the best record lists in Great Britain: "Such a Night" (1954), "Just Walkin' in the Rain" (1956), and "Yes, Tonight Josephine" (1957). Others that scored high in the Hit Parade lists were "Please, Mr. Sun," "Walkin' My Baby Back Home," "Broken Hearted," "Glad Rag Doll," "Look Homeward, Angel," "If You Believe," and "I'll Never Fall in Love Again." With Frankie Laine in 1957, he recorded "Good Evening, Friends," and also in the early 1950s, collaborated with Doris Day in recording three hit songs: "Ma Says, Pa Says," "Full Time Job," and "Let's Walk That-a-Way."

Ray's name was also featured on the marquees of Hollywood and Broadway musical productions. With Ethel Merman, Donald O'Connor, and Marilyn Monroe, he had a featured role in the motion picture *There's No Business like Show Business* (1954), and he acted with touring companies in such popular stage productions as *Guys and Dolls* and *Bus Stop*.

Ray's brilliance as a recording artist flickered out in the early 1960s. However, he was still very much in demand as a singer in Las Vegas night clubs, on television shows, and on concert tours. He toured Europe with Judy Garland in 1969, and sang with her in concert at the Falconer Center at Copenhagen, Denmark, in March—which turned out to be Judy Garland's final performance.

During his years of success, Ray continued his longtime interest and involvement in the education and welfare of deaf persons. He never lost sight of the many children and adults who, like himself, had a hearing impairment. Many of these were underprivileged or too poor to afford hearing aids. In 1952 Ray established the Johnnie Ray Foundation for the Deaf through personal donations and the generous contributions of other people. In addition to providing hearing aids for children in schools for deaf pupils, scholarships were granted for the training of teachers of deaf people.

Ray also became a benefactor of the Pasadena (California) HEAR Foundation in 1969, when he first learned of their work in helping deaf children through specially trained teachers and advanced hearing aids. To encourage this cause and help raise the needed funds, he donated much of his time and talent by giving benefit performances, appearing on television talk shows, and doing many promotional activities. He was elected to HEAR's board of trustees and affectionately called "our singing disciple" by fellow board members.

Although Ray was still singing in concert tours that took him across America and Europe in the 1970s, he never stopped contributing to the cause of deaf people and deafness. He also enjoyed unobtrusively visiting schools, programs, or colleges for deaf persons during his tours.

Bibliography

Elson, Howard, and John Brunton: *Whatever Happened To...? The Great Rock and Pop Nostalgia Book*, Proteus Publishing Co. (Scribner Book Co.), New York and London, 1981.

Robert Panara

REDMOND, GRANVILLE
(1871–1935)

Granville Redmond's "merry laughing way" endeared him to his classmates and teachers at the California School for the Deaf, Berkeley (CSDB). He often amused and astounded his fellow students with his hastily drawn oversize cartoons, especially those depicting historical battles. These drawings,

along with pantomime gestures and American Sign Language, were Redmond's natural outlets for his innermost feelings. He was totally deaf from age 2½ years following a bout of scarlet fever. *See* SIGN LANGUAGES: American.

Granville Redmond was born March 9, 1871, in Philadelphia, Pennsylvania. His parents, Charles Clawson Redmond and Elizabeth (Buck) Redmond, enrolled him in CSDB in 1879. His parents and classmates called him Seymour, and it was not until he opened his first painting studio in Los Angeles, California, in 1898 that he used the name Granville Redmond, which became his official signature thereafter.

Redmond's talent for drawing was soon recognized and encouraged by his first art teacher, Theophilus Hope d'Estrella. Other school subjects, however, were often neglected. Following his graduation in 1890, the board of trustees granted him money to attend the San Francisco Art Association's California School of Design. In his second year, Redmond won the W. E. Brown Award for best drawing from life in Arthur F. Mathews's competitive drawing class. Mathews, director of the art school, was one of the west coast's most influential artists. *See* D'ESTRELLA, THEOPHILUS HOPE.

Proud of Redmond's progress, the board of trustees again voted funds for Redmond to continue his studies in Paris. When Redmond arrived in Paris in 1893, he roomed with his former teacher and friend Douglas Tilden. He immediately enrolled in the Académie Julian under Benjamin Constant and Jean Paul Laurens. At first he painted religious and mythological subjects in the usual classical manner, winning several class honors. However, his painting *Matin d'hiver*, which was accepted in the official Paris Salon of 1895, suggests he was famil-

Granville Redmond, about 1925.

iar with the brushstrokes and compositions of the Impressionist painter Camille Pissarro. Redmond was also impressed with the tonal qualities of James NcNeill Whistler's atmospheric moonlight paintings. *See* TILDEN, DOUGLAS.

Gottardo Piazzoni, who had attended art school with Redmond in San Francisco, joined him in Paris. When time permitted, they sketched and painted in the nearby Fontainebleau forest. Both men admired Théodore Rousseau's Barbizon paintings.

Financial difficulties caused Redmond to leave Paris in 1898 and set up his first studio in Los Angeles. He soon fell in love, not only with the California landscape but also with a charming young deaf woman, Carrie Ann Jean. They married in 1899 and had three hearing children: Jean, Helen, and Hiram.

Since Los Angeles had few facilities for exhibition, Redmond showed his paintings at the Mark Hopkins Institute of Art in San Francisco, which was considered the art capital of the west. Between 1900 and 1906, Los Angeles newspaper references made much of Redmond's use of color as one of his strong points. He specialized in the themes of early-morning, hazy, quiet atmospheric effects and of the solitude of muted moonlight evenings in the manner of the Tonalists—few colors and thin paint. The beauty inherent in silence and solitude seemed to be at the core of his creativity—the essence of his life.

Success was assured when his *California Landscape* was accepted in the main exhibition of the Palace of Fine Arts Gallery at the Universal Exposition in St. Louis, Missouri, in 1904. The *Los Angeles Examiner* acknowledged Redmond as "the finest and boldest worker of color known to the west . . . Granville Redmond is essentially the color artist of Southern California."

The economic depression of 1907 hastened Redmond's decision to move out of the city. He moved his family northward to the rural community of Parkfield in the southeast corner of Monterey County. His productivity soared in what he called "God's country." Redmond's patrons, William Nichols and his wife, soon owned 60 of Redmond's paintings in their extensive collection of California landscapes. Urged on by the Nicholses, Redmond again moved northward to paint the famed oak trees of Menlo Park. He was now painting in a more Impressionist manner with thicker paint and lighter colors. He was also exhibiting in both Los Angeles and San Francisco.

Art critic and curator Everett C. Maxwell marveled at Redmond's new canvases, which he exhibited at the opening of the Museum of History, Science, and Art in Los Angeles in 1913. The inaugural exhibit displayed works by American artists such as George Bellows, Childe Hassam, Thomas Moran,

Matin d'hiver, an oil painting by Redmond, exhibited in the Paris Salon, 1895. (Historical Library and Museum, California; School for the Deaf, Fremont, California)

and E. W. Redfield. Following the opening, Redmond was chosen to be the first distinguished artist for a series of one-artist exhibits at the new museum.

Redmond also participated in the most significant exhibition of the era at the Pan Pacific International Exposition in 1915 in San Francisco. American Impressionist paintings dominated the scene.

With the outbreak of World War I, painting sales diminished, and Redmond, who was also a master pantomimist, decided to try his luck in the movies. His old friend Gottardo Piazzoni, acting as sign language interpreter, accompanied him to Hollywood. Redmond soon caught the eye of Charlie Chaplin, who not only provided him with bit parts in some Chaplin movies such as *A Dog's Life* and *The Kid*, but also gave Redmond space for a large sunny painting studio on the movie lot. These two "silent men" had much in common and soon became close friends. Tradition has it among deaf people that Chaplin learned much pantomime and natural-gesture language from Redmond. Redmond painted in this studio for the rest of his life. Moviemaking took up little of his time. He often painted at nearby Long Beach, Laguna Beach, and Catalina Island. *See* TELEVISION AND MOTION PICTURES.

The demand for his work, especially of California poppy-field scenes, precluded his participation in local exhibitions for several years. Illness also slowed his production, but by 1930 he was painting again. He held his last major exhibition in 1933. Arthur Millier, art critic of the *Los Angeles Times*, wrote, "Redmond is unrivalled in realistic depiction of California landscape." The artist died in Los Angeles on May 24, 1935.

In the 1980s, with the revival of inteest in California landscape painting, Redmond was again recognized as one of the foremost California landscape painters in the early twentieth century from both northern and southern California. His paintings are in several California repositories—Bancroft Library of the University of California, Berkeley; California School for the Deaf, Fremont; Laguna Beach Museum of Art; Los Angeles County Museum of Art; Mills College Art Gallery; National Center on Deafness of California State University, Northridge; Oakland Museum; and Stanford University Museum of Art—and in the New York City Museum of Art and the Springville Museum of Art, Springville, Utah.

Bibliography

Albronda, Mildred: "Granville Redmond: California Landscape Painter," *Art & Antiques*, December 1982.

————: *Granville Redmond, 1871–1935*, unpublished manuscript.

Burnes, Caroline H., and Catherine M. Ramger: *A History of the California School for the Deaf, 1860–1960*, 1960.

Impressionism—The California View, Oakland Museum, California, 1981.

Terry, Alice T.: "Moving Pictures and the Deaf," *The Silent Worker*, June 1918 (two photos with Charlie Chaplin).

Wall Moure, Nancy Dustin: *Painting and Sculpture in Los Angeles, 1900–1945*, Museum Associates of the Los Angeles County Museum of Art, 1980.

Westphal, Ruth: *Plein Air Painters of California: The Southland*, Westphal Publishing, Irvine, California, 1982.

Mildred Albronda

REGISTRY OF INTERPRETERS FOR THE DEAF

The Registry of Interpreters for the Deaf (RID) is the largest national association of interpreters or translators in the United States, with almost 3000 members, most of whom are certified interpreters, representing the 50 states. The association is working to increase the number of certified interpreters available to the deaf and hearing communities. RID was founded in Muncie, Indiana, in 1964, with the initial objective simply to maintain a registry of people who worked or who would work as interpreters in their communities. Forty-two interpreters from across the United States registered, with deaf and hearing supporters as associates. This historic meeting launched what has become one of the most active national professional associations working directly with both deaf and hearing people.

The association was first known as the National Registry of Professional Interpreters and Translators for the Deaf. Soon after the 1964 organizational meeting, the present name was adopted. The 1970s saw an increase both in membership and in interpretation: more deaf and hearing people were using interpreters to communicate effectively in conducting their daily affairs. The need for regulation of the profession became apparent.

In 1972 RID established the first national performance evaluation and certification system for interpreters in the world (it has remained the only national system of its kind for interpreters of any languages). Also in the 1970s came the establishment of local and state associations of interpreters. RID's local and state associations, in cooperation with local and state associations of and for deaf people, have been instrumental in creating a body of legislative coalitions that work for state laws on interpretation.

Since 1970, the national association has held biennial conventions. These conventions have provided workshops and seminars on issues related to interpretation and have given direct training or continuing education to students as well as practitioners of interpreting. These conventions also give opportunities for deaf and hearing consumers to learn more about the profession of interpreting and how to obtain interpreting services in their communities.

A significant change came with the 1983–1985 biennium. Prior to this, RID was a small national organization with one or two operating committees involving 7 to 14 members. During this biennium, 22 ad hoc and permanent standing committees were established. This action involved over 150 members from all over the United States.

The RID has grown from 164 members to over 2700. During the RID's first two decades, the national office budget increased from just thousands of dollars to over $280,000. Significant increases in the national evaluation and certification system necessitated annual reviews and revisions of the system to keep pace with the demand for certified interpreters. As states establish legislatively mandated interpreting services through their commissions for deaf people, an increasing number of deaf and hearing people will be using certified interpreters to conduct their daily affairs.

As stated in the new RID bylaws, its purpose is to "initiate, sponsor, promote and execute policies and activities that will further the profession of interpretation of American Sign Language and English and the transliteration of English." RID thus cooperates with other interpreters of other languages. With over 50 state and local associations of interpreters affiliated with RID, the impact of RID on interpretation of all languages in the United States could expand. For example, working with the National Association of the Deaf and other associations of interpreters, RID played a major role in the regulation passed in 1979 that requires federal courts to provide certified legal interpreters. In cooperation with the Conference of Interpreter Trainers, Translators and Interpreters Educational Society, California Court Interpreters Association, American Deafness and Rehabilitation Association, and other associations of and for deaf people and interpreter associations, RID should continue to influence public policies that will increase the number and availability of certified interpreters. *See* COURT INTERPRETER'S ACT; NATIONAL ASSOCIATION OF THE DEAF.

The RID maintains a national office with a staff of six. The office acts as a daily information and resource center for (1) interpretation (producing the national bimonthly newsletter *VIEWS* and answering questions about interpretation); (2) planning and conducting biennial national conventions (training); (3) cooperating in the development of state conventions (training); (4) advising government agencies on interpretation; and (5) working with state associations of interpreters on state and local legislation on interpretation, and marketing original texts on interpretation. *See* INTERPRETING.

W. F. Roy, III

REHABILITATION

In the United States, rehabilitation is a twentieth-century concept. Until World War I (1914–1918), the federal and state governments made no provisions for disabled citizens. Even the National Defense Act of 1916, the first recognition of a public responsibility for those disabled in its service, provided only for wounded veterans and only for their vocational training. A 1920 act moved to include disabled people more generally, but only for vocational rehabilitation. Later acts, culminating in the Rehabilitation Act Amendments of 1973 and 1978, extended the federal and state governments' coverage to all disabled citizens and to rehabilitation without regard for a vocational objective. *See* REHABILITATION ACT OF 1973.

These decisions have been critical for deaf people, a third of whom are multiply disabled and some of whom have limited or no vocational objectives. For all deaf people, the principal goal of rehabilitation—to provide the assistance that will enable disabled persons to attain their maximum feasible potential for independent living—is particularly appealing. Faced by a communication disability that alienates them from the larger society, deaf people have tended to seek the company of the similarly afflicted, and have formed the "deaf community." Given the benefits of rehabilitation services, deaf people may achieve an adjustment that enables them to succeed in the general society while continuing to enjoy the deaf community. The prevailing rehabilitation philosophy in the United States recognizes the rights of disabled individuals to their uniqueness, and does not ask that it be given up in return for the benefits offered by rehabilitation programs. *See* DEAF POPULATION: Deaf Community.

TERMINOLOGY

In discussions of rehabilitation, semantic distinctions shape more than academic thinking—they contribute to the operation of programs. Three terms basic to rehabilitation have distinctive meanings. An impairment is the total loss of a body part. A disability is the reduction in the ability to perform particular functions. A handicap is the negative social and personal consequences that arise from a disability. Thus, impaired individuals may have a disability but not a handicap. For instance, a person may have lost the nerve cells that permit the auditory discrimination of high tones. The impairment is the loss of the nerve cells, and the disability is the lost capacity to hear treble notes in music. This causes a handicap if one's occupation is a musician, but not if one has no particular interest in music. These distinctions make the rehabilitator aware that impairments need not be handicapping. Indeed, the primary purpose of rehabilitation is to eliminate handicaps by reducing disabilities due to impairments.

Degree of Hearing Impairment An essential distinction in deafness rehabilitation is between degrees of hearing impairment. Those who have any degree of imperfect hearing are referred to as being hearing-impaired. The hearing-impaired group is divided into those who are deaf (that is, unable to hear and understand speech through the ear alone, with best available amplification) and those who are hard-of-hearing (that is, have some degree of hearing impairment short of being deaf).

Age at Onset It is also critical for rehabilitators to attend to the age at onset, that is the age of the individual at the time the hearing impairment occurs. Early deafness usually severely affects language and speech development, while adult deafness does not. Early-deafened individuals tend to join the deaf community; those deafened as adults most often do not. On the other hand, emotional disruption due to hearing loss is common in adults and much less so in children.

To distinguish the ages at onset, rehabilitators modify the terms describing the degree of impairment, marking somewhat arbitrary points in human development. Prelingual refers to hearing impairment that occurs before three years of age, even though linguistic development begins at earlier ages. Congenital designates a hearing impairment that is present at birth. Prevocational refers to hearing impairment that occurs before 19 years of age, while recognizing that students become interested in vocational pursuits at earlier ages and that some have work experience prior to age 19. Adult is used to indicate that the hearing impairment develops between 19 and 65 years of age, and senile, that the hearing impairment occurs at or after 65 years of age. Prelingual deafness, then, is the inability to hear and understand speech, even with best amplification, that develops before the individual is three years old.

Utility of Language For purposes of working with a particular individual, fuller details are required, that is, the exact degree of impairment, the shape of the auditory responses at various frequencies, and the precise age at onset or, if the onset has been gradual, a description of its course to the present degree of impairment. The summary terms are needed, however, for statistical purposes and for easy communication among professionals who work with deaf persons.

Coding the Major Disabling Condition An important activity in every state rehabilitation agency is the coding of disabilities. For reporting to the federal agency as well as for internal purposes, assigning clients to predetermined categories of disabilities is necessary. The coding framework is known as the R300 codes. They provide categories that agree with the federal agency's requirements. The codes often attempt to incorporate three aspects of the disability: (1) its physical locus, (2) its severity, and (3) its probable etiology. Thus, Code 231 is "prelingual deafness due to a congenital condition." Code 630 indicates only "epilepsy." A single three-digit code, then, may incorporate a great deal of information, much of it useful to rehabilitation, or may simply indicate the medical condition. The R300 codes lean heavily on the medical model of disability as a disease, but also have some unique features, principally the coding of the sensory disabilities.

Critique of R300 Codes. The rehabilitation counselor may be clear about clients' problems until decisions must be made about their major disabling condition. For example, the counselor must decide that a person who is deaf and mentally retarded needs rehabilitation primarily because of the deafness or because of the mental retardation. The example becomes more complicated if a mentally retarded and deaf client returns for rehabilitation because of cataracts that have caused blindness, and the counselor must determine if the client is to be considered as primarily deaf, mentally retarded, or blind. These situations, faced frequently by rehabilitation agencies, are important, because most of the statistical reporting is by major disabling condition, and the coding used by the Rehabilitation Services Administration does not pro-

vide for multiple disabilities as the primary basis for rehabilitation. Statistical reporting is an important part of the state agency's evaluation. Ambiguous situations enter into the administration of the program, from the individual counselor to the federal commissioner.

The congressional mandate to rehabilitation is that priority be given to serving the most seriously handicapped individuals. Amputation of a finger is not considered a serious disability. Thus, if a deaf client is accepted for rehabilitation because a finger was lost while operating a lathe, the major disabling condition would almost certainly be noted as deafness and the secondary disability as amputation of a minor body part.

Rehabilitation administrators are often asked how many persons with particular disabilities have been served by their agencies. If the questioners are advocates for mental retardation, they will likely consider mental retardation ahead of other conditions as the major disability. Similarly, if the questioners are advocates for some other disability group—deaf people, for instance—they will view deafness as the most disabling condition. But if advocates for deaf-blind persons, they will be disappointed because the codes do not specifically recognize deaf-blindness as a major disabling condition.

How clients are coded, then, has administrative and political implications for the rehabilitation agencies. Thus, coding should be of interest to disabled people, their families, friends, and advocates. When the state agency allocates funds for particular services, knowing the expected number of persons apt to request those services is very important. Overestimations and underestimations are disruptive of rehabilitation.

Coding Deafness. The R300 codes for hearing impairment are shown in the table. The first decision that must be made regarding hearing impairment is its degree: deaf or hard-of-hearing. Deafness is not defined in the coding manual, but hard-of-hearing is specified as meeting one of the following conditions in the better-hearing, unaided ear: at least a 55-decibel (dB) loss at the speech reception threshold (SRT); a 55-dB loss at the pure-tone threshold (PTA); or a 30- to 54-dB loss at the SRT or PTA, with either speech discrimination of less than 50 percent or a statement from a physician skilled in diseases of the ear indicating a progressive loss. This definition is somewhat ambiguous. The use of the term "loss" instead of threshold leaves in doubt whether the "at least" is an upper or lower limit. While most rehabilitation counselors who have many hearing-impaired clients quickly learn to use these codes, the ambiguity is undesirable for the codes are used by those who only occasionally must consult them. *See* AUDIOLOGIC CLASSIFICATION.

R300 Codes for Hearing Impairment

Code	Condition
	Prelingual Deafness
231	Congenital condition
233	Degenerative or infectious disease
234	Accident, injury, or poisoning
239	Ill-defined, unspecified, or unknown cause
	Prevocational Deafness
243	Degenerative or infectious disease
244	Accident, injury, or poisoning
249	Ill-defined, unspecified, or unknown cause
	Postvocational Deafness
253	Degenerative or infectious disease
254	Accident, injury, or poisoning
259	Ill-defined, unspecified, or unknown cause
	Prelingual Hard-of-Hearing
261	Congenital condition
263	Degenerative or infectious disease
264	Accident, injury, or poisoning
269	Ill-defined, unspecified, or unknown cause
	Prevocational Hard-of-Hearing
271	Congenital condition
273	Degenerative or infectious disease
274	Accident, injury, or poisoning
279	Ill-defined, unspecified, or unknown cause
	Postvocational Hard-of-Hearing
281	Congenital condition
283	Degenerative or infectious disease
284	Accident, injury or poisoning
289	Ill-defined, unspecified, or unknown cause

Specification of a precise age at onset would be preferable to the terms prelingual, prevocational, and postvocational. Many experts in the field of hearing impairment accept 35 months as the upper limit of the prelingual category. However, that age is merely a convenience and is not adequate for clinical purposes or for serious research use. The same is true for the other broad categories. A far better coding would result from inserting the actual age at onset of the hearing condition.

The etiological categories are also too broad to be of much value. Congenital is redundant, since it adds nothing to the prelingual designation that precedes it. One cannot indicate, for example, that the client was deafened due to maternal rubella, an infectious disease that occurs prenatally and hence may have congenital consequences. If the mother ingested thalidomide during pregnancy, causing the baby to become deaf, it is not clear if the correct code would be 231 (congenital condition) or 234 (accident, injury, or poisoning).

An additional difficulty arises from the lack of specific directions as to the selection of major disabling conditions. The decision of whether deafness is the major disability or whether it is the secondary disability often has to be made. Such decisions have consequences on rehabilitation services.

Finally, consideration should be given to coordinating the R300 codes with other codes being used to classify disabilities. The continuous need for information about disabling conditions would be best served by optimizing data obtained from other sources. Congress has recognized this and has mandated intragovernmental cooperation by establishing in the National Center for Health Statistics, a committee to coordinate terminology and data retrieval practices.

FEDERAL-STATE PARTNERSHIP

Rehabilitation in the United States is not conceived as wholly the responsibility of the central government. Almost from its inception, rehabilitation has been organized as a partnership between the federal government and the state governments. In practice, this has meant that the federal government pays a substantial proportion of the costs of the rehabilitation programs in return for which the states agree to conform to regulations promulgated by the federal government. This arrangement has proved to be politically sensible and generally satisfactory to the parties involved. It allows for adjustments being made to rehabilitation programs in accordance with local conditions, for joint control of costs by the two governments involved since both contribute a share, and for the placement of the supervision of services close to the points of their delivery. In addition, the federal-state partnership provides a broad political base for legislation, involving two levels of government. These features probably account for much of the success of rehabilitation efforts in the United States.

REHABILITATION PROCESS

As rehabilitation has evolved over the years, it has developed a defining methodology. The rehabilitation process is a series of steps through which clients progress, from their first contacts with the rehabilitation agency, to their ultimate rehabilitation, and even on to the follow-up of their performances beyond their successful conclusion of the basic rehabilitation process. The steps in the rehabilitation process are described below.

Casefinding and Referral Rehabilitation clients are seldom knowledgeable about the availability of benefits. Disabled people sometimes languish outside the system because they are unaware that they are eligible to receive valuable services from it. For this reason, the rehabilitation process includes casefinding (actively seeking qualified candidates for rehabilitation) and referral (gaining the cooperation of individuals and agencies in sending clients to the proper points of service delivery, both within and outside rehabilitation).

Intake The point at which the client contacts the rehabilitation agency, or is contacted by it, is referred to as intake. It is the initial enrollment of the individual into the rehabilitation program.

Diagnosis In order to evaluate or diagnose the client's condition, a physical examination by a physician is required. The requisite medical personnel determine whether the individual's condition qualifies the person for rehabilitation.

Evaluation The next step in the rehabilitation process is determining the individual's prospects for vocational adjustment and independent living. Evaluation usually includes examinations by various professionals within the agency—psychologists, work-evaluation specialists, and so forth—or may necessitate sending the client to other facilities that specialize in providing these services. Once the data are assembled, the rehabilitation counselor and the client join in the preparation of the individual written rehabilitation program (IWRP), the goals and the strategies for the individual's rehabilitation.

Determination of Eligibility The client may require services that the state does not authorize, may have insufficient rehabilitation potential to be eligible for services in a particular state, or may have greater financial resources than a given state allows for those seeking its services without charge. Certain services are available regardless of the individual's ability to pay for them: diagnosis, evaluation, counseling, referral to other appropriate agencies, and vocational placement services. Others are granted under provisions specific to each state.

Physical Restoration If it is deemed medically appropriate, and if the individual meets qualifications for the service in the state in which he or she resides, surgery or other medical procedures to restore function may be undertaken within the structure of the rehabilitation process. Other therapies and means of physically compensating for the client's disability also may be undertaken.

Adjustment Training The client may require various procedures intended to make the individual employable: job-readiness training, development of communication skills, specialized therapies to overcome specific physical or emotional disabilities, and so forth. Such adjustment training may

also include independent-living services, that is, services that enable the individual to function independently despite impairments and disabilities.

Vocational Training Specific instruction to make an individual job-ready is a part of the rehabilitation process. Vocational training may include instruction in a technical institute, on-the-job training, or higher education for those whose individual written rehabilitation program calls for that level of instruction to achieve the vocational objectives set for them. In addition to paying the costs of the education and training, rehabilitation agencies may also provide for maintenance and transportation expenses that are essential to vocational training.

Counseling Throughout the rehabilitation process, the client's progress is coordinated by a counselor. The rehabilitation counselor meets with the client and with the personnel providing services to the client.

Placement The counselor assists the client in finding employment consistent with the individual's abilities and disabilities. Placement may immediately follow training or may be phased, beginning with various kinds of trial placements and progressing until the client has achieved a satisfactory position in industry.

Follow-Up Counselors should continue to maintain contact with their clients for at least two months after placement to be assured that the client needs no further services to retain the vocational adjustment. While federal regulations require a 60-day follow-up period, the states may authorize a longer period.

Postemployment Services Once the client's follow-up interviews ensure the rehabilitation counselor that the client is satisfactorily placed, it is still possible to authorize additional benefits under the provisions of postemployment services. These services are defined as those that are essential for the employee to retain the placement. They might include having interpreting services at particular times, or assistance in locating different living quarters if transportation arrangements necessitate such a move. Since necessary job skills can vary widely, the regulations do not specifically limit what services the counselor can justify. The final decision about what services may be authorized for the client are left to the agency's administration, and subject to state review.

Rights of Appeal The rehabilitation clients' rights to due process are protected by the federal-state regulations. A specific appeal process is in place, stretching from the rehabilitation counselor's supervisor to the head of the federal rehabilitation agency.

Priorities Because rehabilitation funds are limited, a state may be faced with a greater demand for services than it can finance, thus necessitating priorities as to which clients should be served ahead of others. Rehabilitation agencies had been accused of concentrating on serving the milder disabilities in an effort to build up the numbers rehabilitated per budgeted dollar. Congress reacted in the 1973 and subsequent rehabilitation legislation by requiring that the most severely disabled clients be served first. This reversal of priorities has been beneficial to deaf clients, who are among the most severely disabled groups in rehabilitation.

MODEL STATE PLAN

First published in 1974, the *Model State Plan for Rehabilitation of Deaf Clients* grew out of a need to provide state rehabilitation agencies with guidelines that would enable them to tailor programs for deaf clients in accordance with the provisions of the Rehabilitation Act Amendments of 1973. The unanimous acceptance of the plan by state directors of vocational rehabilitation was determined in 1976 by a survey of all state agencies. The model plan was revised in 1977 and 1980 to keep pace with further legislative and regulatory refinements in rehabilitation. The plan has two features that most distinguish it from other service-delivery models: an emphasis on communication, and on the necessity for specially trained rehabilitation counselors.

Communication The initial contact with the agency provides a critical moment in the rehabilitation of deaf people who are sometimes lost to appropriate agencies. If personnel capable of communicating with deaf people are not available at the initial contact, misunderstanding and discouragement can result. Once a deaf individual is within the rehabilitation process, communication determines the effectiveness of the program. The regulations governing the rehabilitation process now mandate that communication with clients be in their native language or preferred mode of communication. That stipulation from the Rehabilitation Act greatly assists deaf clients, but the model plan emphasizes that communication must be construed in broader terms than language-based messages passed between clients and agency personnel. What the agency conveys to deaf people by the visible behavior of its staff (their body language) as well as their overt linguistic expressions must also be considered.

Counselors The model plan offers several organizations of personnel that provide rehabilitation counselors who have special training to work with deaf clients. RCDs (rehabilitation counselors for deaf clients) are specialists who prepare first by becoming fully qualified rehabilitation counselors and then by adding a knowledge of the deaf community, its structure and mores, and a proficiency in manual communication. Thus the RCD can direct deaf clients to attain the maximum benefits available from the rehabilitation process.

Impact The model plan has codified those steps, of which modified communication and specialized counselors are two, that must be taken to assure that deaf people have equal access to rehabilitation facilities and can, therefore, enjoy the same benefits that have been so important to the disabled population of the United States.

Jerome D. Schein

History

Anthropological evidence shows that physical disabilities have existed since the cave dwellers. Prehistory through the early Greek and Roman times gives examples of the total rejection of disabled persons by society. For instance, the Spartans encouraged the killing of defective infants as a crude eugenics practice. Soldiers injured in battle were "mercifully" slain by their comrades to save them from falling into the hands of the enemy. Roman law contained formal approval for the destruction of deformed infants. Societal attitudes toward disabled people improved somewhat when banishment became an accepted practice. Instead of destroying physically disabled people, they were placed in asylums, institutions, and colonies, often not for therapy but to keep them out of the community's sight. Later, charitable attitudes toward disabled people became prevalent, as much to assuage the guilt of able-bodied people as to assist disabled people.

NINETEENTH CENTURY

In the nineteenth century, another marked shift occurred in attitudes toward disabled people when rehabilitation practices began. The rehabilitation philosophy shuns the destruction or abandonment of disabled people and counsels that restoration of function and vocational training are better than charity. It focuses on providing prostheses and other technical aids, instruction that restores function when feasible, and counseling on how to live and work when function cannot be restored. Rehabilitation is an optimistic, humanistic approach to physical disability that celebrates life as far more valuable than an unflawed physique.

Rehabilitation as a response to physical disability in the United States is often dated by experts from 1863, when the Hospital for the Ruptured and Crippled opened in New York City, followed by the Cleveland Rehabilitation Center (1889) and the Boston Industrial School for the Crippled and Deformed (1893). These facilities, which were crude by today's standards, differed from earlier approaches by offering physical therapy and some vocational training—the bare beginnings of rehabilitation.

Deafness Rehabilitation   The rehabilitation movement for deaf people in the United States might be said to have begun much earlier, with the establishment of the Hartford (Connecticut) Asylum for the Deaf and Dumb in 1817. Though it is undisputed as the first sustained educational program for deaf persons in the United States, the Hartford Asylum (now renamed the American School for the Deaf) also represents a rehabilitation approach by offering instruction to overcome the disability. The separation of special education from rehabilitation is somewhat arbitrary. Early educational intervention with disabled children intends to prevent the necessity for many rehabilitation services when they become adults. Thus rehabilitation can be viewed in part as an educational approach to physical disability. However, in the nineteenth century no efforts for the rehabilitation of deaf adults were made at the federal level and almost none at the state levels. *See* AMERICAN SCHOOL FOR THE DEAF.

EARLY TWENTIETH CENTURY
In the United States the majority of what is accepted today as rehabilitation has developed in the twentieth century, with much growth having taken place during and after World War II. Federal legislation for rehabilitation dates from the National Defense Act of 1916. It was the first recognition of America's obligation to disabled veterans. That law provided vocational training, but only for wounded veterans. Early-deafened persons did not come under its provisions. The emphasis of the act was upon vocational training, preparing the disabled soldiers for return to gainful employment. Provisions for physical restoration, counseling, adjustment training, and other aspects of rehabilitation as it is now known were largely absent. So closely was rehabilitation tied to the idea of occupational placement that, when the Soldier Rehabilitation Act of 1917 was passed, Congress selected the Federal Board for Vocational Education to administer the new law's rehabilitation provisions. This board had been established by the Smith-Hughes Act of 1916.

SMITH-FESS ACT OF 1920
In 1920, under the Smith-Fess Act, Congress extended the vocational rehabilitation programs to include nonmilitary persons. The Smith-Fess Act also changed somewhat the manner in which the program was administered. Through the Federal Board for Vocational Education, it provided matching grants to the states to enable them to offer counseling, job training, orthotic and prosthetic appliances, and job placement. It was necessary to involve some form of education or training to be eligible for vocational rehabilitation. The states were required to pay half the cost of the program, matching the federal share dollar for dollar. Within

18 months after the passage of the 1920 law, 34 state legislatures had enacted the legislation that was needed to meet the Smith-Fess requirements for federal-state partnership in rehabilitation.

Eligibility for Rehabilitation Services   Those to be served under the new law were disabled veterans and persons injured while employed in industry (originally, war-related industries). The inclusion of all physically disabled adults did not emerge until later legislative acts were passed. Another limitation on client eligibility was the stress on employment potential. During the early years of vocational rehabilitation, the authorized services were limited to those that would train or educate the disabled individual to obtain employment. This approach meant that individuals whose disabilities seemed to preclude their gainful employment were usually not accepted into the rehabilitation process. Furthermore, if a disabled person only needed counseling and job placement, these services could not be provided under the act. Thus, disabled applicants could be rejected because they needed too much or too little rehabilitation. In addition, the Federal Board decreed that the minimum age for eligibility would be the minimum age for legal employability in each state.

Federal Attitude Toward Rehabilitation   Despite the radical change in policy that the Smith-Fess Act represented, the federal agency assigned to administer it was reluctant to establish a new federal program. In its first announcement the Federal Board stated, "Under this act the Federal Government does not propose to undertake the organization and immediate direction of vocational rehabilitation in the states, but does agree to make substantial financial contributions to its support." Congress reinforced this hesitant attitude by passing temporary legislation, which it annually renewed for the next 15 years, in the hope that the states would develop programs that, aside from funding, would not require federal interaction.

SOCIAL SECURITY ACT OF 1935
In 1935 the Social Security Act was passed, initiating a new era for older Americans. Within that legislation were provisions that made vocational rehabilitation a permanent federal-state program. To administer the program, the Vocational Rehabilitation Division was established in the Office of Education, which moved into the newly created Federal Security Agency that emerged in 1939. In 1933 President Franklin D. Roosevelt had severed the direct link between vocational education and vocational rehabilitation by removing control of the latter from the Federal Board to the Department of the Interior. The Federal Security Agency merged the national health, education, and welfare activities.

Federal Attitude Toward Rehabilitation Changes
The Social Security Act also greatly increased the
funding for vocational rehabilitation services and,
most importantly at that time, increased the federal involvement in the administration of vocational rehabilitation: Congress authorized a 75 percent increase in grants to states and a 25 percent
increase in the budget for the federal administration of the program. One year later Congress passed
the Randolph-Sheppard Act authorizing states to
license blind persons to manage vending stands in
federal buildings. The philosophy underlying these
shifts in the congressional view of vocational rehabilitation was spelled out by the House Ways and
Means Committee in its report accompanying the
Social Security Act of 1935. It declared that the
provision of increased aid for vocational rehabilitation was made in recognition of its role "in a
permanent program for economic security"—an
evocative phrase during those years of the Great
Depression. The Social Security Act also provided
for crippled children and for elderly persons; programs for both groups joined vocational rehabilitation in the new agency. *See* SOCIAL SECURITY ACT.

BARDEN-LAFOLLETTE ACT OF 1943
The next great shifts in rehabilitation policies occurred as the nation fought World War II. In 1943
the Vocational Rehabilitation articles of the Social
Security Act were amended to authorize physical
restoration and related medical services to enable
physically disabled persons to return to work. The
amendments, embodied in the Barden-Lafollette Act
of 1943, also introduced provisions for preventive
services to eliminate or reduce disabilities, extended services to include those who were mentally
ill or mentally retarded, and brought into the authority of the act those agencies for the blind that
were separately established in some states.

Office of Vocational Rehabilitation Administratively, the Federal Security Agency established the
Office of Vocational Rehabilitation, its status parallel to the Office of Education, which was in the
same agency. Other federal agencies sought out the
Office of Vocational Rehabilitation during the war
crisis. Referrals came from the Selective Service
agency, which sent draftees who were rejected because of physical disabilities. The Employment Security Commission and the War Manpower Office
also referred people whose efforts were welcomed
in the defense industries.

Inservice Training The importance of formal
training for counselors surfaced for the first time
in bulletins issued by the Federal Security Agency
in the 1940s. Leaders in the development of vocational rehabilitation had emphasized the key role
of counseling, but had not acknowledged that there
existed a transportable body of theory, skills, and

knowledge that would justify formal preparation
for counselors of disabled people. The first responses to counselor training were in the form of
inservice training. Not until 1954 did the federal
government offer support to preservice education
for rehabilitation personnel.

**President's Committee on Employment of the
Handicapped** The value of improving public information about disabilities and attitudes toward
disabled people, especially those of potential employers, gained formal recognition when Congress
passed a joint resolution establishing the President's Committee on Employment of the Handicapped. Passed in August 1945, the resolution also
designated the first week in October as National
Employ the Handicapped Week. The activities of
the week highlight the abilities and downplay the
disabilities of handicapped people.

LATTER TWENTIETH CENTURY
In 1951 a new director, Mary E. Switzer, took charge
of the Office of Vocational Rehabilitation and served
for almost two decades. Switzer guided the agency
through a variety of administrative changes of name
and location within the federal hierarchy. Her influence has pervaded subsequent rehabilitation focus. She is justifiably identified with the strong,
positive image that the field, as reflected in the
federal-state partnership, has enjoyed during the
second half of the twentieth century.

VOCATIONAL REHABILITATION ACT AMENDMENTS OF 1954
In 1953 President Dwight D. Eisenhower transformed the Federal Security Agency into the Department of Health, Education and Welfare, moving the Office of Vocational Rehabilitation into a
greatly enhanced status in the federal administration. Switzer seized the opportunity to propose an
enlarged program that suited the President's "dynamic conservatism" by aiming to remove individuals from the welfare rolls and into productive employment. The Vocational Rehabilitation Act
Amendments of 1954 proposed as its principal objective to rehabilitate "physically (and mentally)
handicapped individuals so that they may prepare
for and engage in remunerative employment, thereby
increasing not only their social and economic well-
being but also the productive capacity of the nation."

Preservice Training Among the 1954 act's provisions was the establishment of training grants to
develop rehabilitation personnel, including physicians, occupational and physical therapists, psychologists, and rehabilitation counselors. (While it
would be more appropriate to refer to the funding
of degree programs in higher education as "education grants," federal protocol reserves that term
for programs supported by federal education agen-

cies, and "training grants" for similar programs of higher-education support by the other federal agencies.) Provisions that contribute to the development of professional rehabilitation personnel have been a part of subsequent rehabilitation legislation. This step confirmed the characterization of rehabilitation as a professional activity, not a charitable enterprise.

Changes in the Federal-State Partnership The 1954 act carried two sections that altered the federal-state partnership. One freed the states from the federally imposed necessity of housing their programs in conjunction with vocational education boards. Under the new law, they could, if they chose, establish independent vocational rehabilitation agencies or place them within other administrative units. The second permitted the states, for the first time, to use the joint funds to expand or remodel buildings to make them suitable for rehabilitation. Not only did this provide further evidence of the new status of the federal-state program, but it also enabled the states to develop further rehabilitation centers and sheltered workshops in support of their overall efforts.

1965 VOCATIONAL REHABILITATION ACT AMENDMENTS

The 1960s can be characterized by the fact that the 1965 Vocational Rehabilitation Act Amendments were passed unanimously by both houses of Congress. Vocational Rehabilitation, under Mary E. Switzer, was enjoying a heyday in Congress.

Significant Changes The contents of the 1965 act were impressive. Funding received a manifold increase, enabling substantial expansion of vocational rehabilitation services. In keeping with the additional funding, eligibility requirements were broadened to include "socially handicapped persons" (for example, physically normal juvenile delinquents and adult offenders). The act also authorized extended evaluation, thereby effectively waiving the requirement that clients, following rehabilitation services, must have a reasonable expectation of gainful employment.

Rehabilitation Facilities Special grants to state agencies and some private, nonprofit agencies were authorized for construction and operation of rehabilitation facilities, including sheltered workshops. These grants proved harbingers of further liberalization of the congressional attitude toward the creation of rehabilitation facilities.

SOCIAL AND REHABILITATION SERVICE

In addition to her positive relations with Congress, Switzer enjoyed excellent relations with her administrative superiors. In 1967 Secretary of Health, Education and Welfare John W. Gardner organized the Social and Rehabilitation Service, an umbrella agency that merged under one administrator five agencies: the Children's Bureau, Administration on Aging, Medical Services Administration, Public Welfare Assistance Payments Administration, and the newly named Rehabilitation Services Administration. Gardner chose Switzer to head this conglomerate, signaling that the rehabilitation concept would prevail in the administration of these massive programs.

1967 VOCATIONAL REHABILITATION ACT AMENDMENTS

Funding levels continued to be high in 1967 congressional activities, but basic changes in vocational rehabilitation did not appear in the legislation. However, the Vocational Rehabilitation Act Amendments of 1967 took an action important to those interested in deafness. They established the National Center for Deaf-Blind Youth and Adults, the first federal recognition of this severe disability, previously considered unfeasible for vocational rehabilitation. *See* DEAF-BLINDNESS.

1968 VOCATIONAL REHABILITATION ACT AMENDMENTS

Another significant year for rehabilitation legislation was 1968. A new funding formula of 80 percent federal and 20 percent state matching funds was established. The prohibitions on the use of these funds for new construction were removed. States were permitted to share their funding and administrative responsibilities with other state agencies, which cleared the way for joint projects in the states.

Eligibility Eligibility for vocational rehabilitation was extended to "individuals disadvantaged by reason of age, youth, low educational attainments, ethnic, or other factors such as prison and delinquency records." By this definition, Congress intended to extend the rehabilitation concept to include a very broad range of social ills—poverty, delinquency, age discrimination, racial and ethnic prejudices, as well as physical and mental disabilities. Under Switzer, vocational rehabilitation had won the confidence of the legislative branch.

Redefinition of Rehabilitation The 1968 legislation also rewrote the definition of rehabilitation to cover (1) services to families of handicapped individuals, when the services can significantly assist in the rehabilitation of a group of individuals, and (2) services needed to maintain a rehabilitated client in employment. Like the 1965 amendments, the 1968 alterations in rehabilitation legislation significantly extended its range of activities.

REHABILITATION ACT AMENDMENTS OF 1973

The dramatic improvements of the 1960s, instead of establishing the apex of rehabilitation development in the United States, merely foreshadowed even greater developments in the federal-state posture toward disabled people. Congress changed the name of the rehabilitation legislation in 1973 by dropping "Vocational" from its title. Changing the title to the Rehabilitation Act signaled Congress's shift from economic to social motivation for rehabilitation. The requirement that rehabilitation clients must have, at least in principle, a vocational objective had been weakened in the preceding legislation. Now Congress signaled that it had radically altered the meaning of rehabilitation. The law added provisions for independent living services, removed age restrictions for services by federally funded rehabilitation agencies, and broadened the range of services to cover telecommunications and recreation.

The greatest innovation in the law was to affirm social services as rights of disabled people, regardless of economic return to society. Title V, with its now-famous Section 504, is sometimes called the Bill of Rights for Disabled People. Its power derives, in part, from its brevity. Four sections spell out the rights of disabled people.

Title V: Sections 501, 502, and 503 Section 501 forbids employment discrimination by federal agencies on the basis of physical or mental disability. Section 502 establishes the Architectural and Transportation Barriers Compliance Board (later renamed the Architectural, Transportation and Communication Barriers Compliance Board to include activities that discriminate against hearing- and speech-impaired individuals). This board oversees the laws passed to eliminate environmental impediments to the use of facilities by disabled people. Section 503 requires that contractors seeking to do business with the federal government must have affirmative action plans to employ disabled people. The Department of Labor, which has the enforcement authority, has the power under this act to withhold federal funds from those who fail to comply with the law's provisions.

Title V: Section 504 The full text of Section 504 consists of one sentence: "No otherwise qualified handicapped individual in the United States . . . shall, solely by reason of his handicap, be excluded from participation in, be denied the benefits of, or be subjected to discrimination under any program or activity receiving federal financial assistance." The lack of ambiguity in the wording of the section provides much of its power. Congress left no doubt as to its intention to defend the equal rights of disabled individuals to enjoy federal benefits without discrimination. Because of the ubiquity of federal funds and their importance to many businesses and institutions, their threatened loss can be a powerful means of enforcing Section 504's provisions. The general nature of Section 504's phrases further strengthen it: it forbids discrimination in

any program or activity receiving federal financial assistance, not just employment or education. For example, a conference that uses federal monies cannot be held in a meeting place that is inaccessible to physically disabled persons. Advocates for disabled people regard Section 504 as the most powerful legal tool for preventing and correcting abuses.

EDUCATION FOR ALL HANDICAPPED CHILDREN ACT

Shortly after passing the Rehabilitation Act, Congress enacted further landmark legislation by adopting Public Law 94-142, known as the Education for All Handicapped Children Act. This act establishes that education for disabled children is not a privilege, a charity, a sympathetic gesture, or a measure for the economic good of the community, but that it is a civil right. Emerging from a series of lawsuits by parents in various states, the act codified what the courts had been saying: if any part of the government provides free education for some of its citizens, the government must provide it for all. The passage of this legislation immediately following the Rehabilitation Act Amendments of 1973 reflects the then-reigning attitude of Congress toward disabled people. It offers evidence of how far the people of the United States have come in accepting the rehabilitation concept for dealing with disabled people.

PLACEMENT OF REHABILITATION IN THE FEDERAL STRUCTURE

Under the Soldier Rehabilitation Act of 1917 and the Smith-Fess Act of 1920, the administrative authority for rehabilitation rested in the Federal Board for Vocational Education. The Social Security Act of 1935 set up the Vocational Rehabilitation Division within the Office of Education. The next move occurred under the Barden-Lafollette Act of 1943; the Federal Security Agency established the Office of Vocational Rehabilitation. When the Department of Health, Education and Welfare (DHEW) was created, rehabilitation changed its name (and its status) to Vocational Rehabilitation Administration. Under the Social and Rehabilitation Service which was created within the Department of Health, Education and Welfare, it became Rehabilitation Services Administration. With the splitting of the Department of Health, Education and Welfare into the Department of Health and Human Services and the Department of Education, rehabilitation moved to the latter and retained its name and status as an administration. While all of these moves and name changes may seem trivial, they actually reflect the federal attitude toward rehabilitation. Originally, it was merely an appendage to vocational education. It gained in stature as it advanced within the federal government from an office, to a division, to an administration—each representing a step up in the hierarchy of federal agencies. The name change from Vocational Rehabilitation Administration to Rehabilitation Services Administration further reflects a change in the agency's philosophy, as authorized by Congress. The dropping of "Vocational" from the title signified a sharp turn in the agency's mission.

WAR AND REHABILITATION

World War I sparked the first federal recognition of a public obligation to serve those who were injured in its service. For the next three decades rehabilitation changed slowly, evolving toward a more liberal image. World War II greatly accelerated changes in rehabilitation concepts. The clear demonstration of the contributions that disabled people could make to the national defense supported substantial changes in federal legislation. The Vietnam conflict provided an impetus to liberalization of rehabilitation, especially with the inclusion of those for whom the usual vocational objectives are infeasible. Though not yet fully realized, the independent living movement marks yet another step forward in the treatment of the disabled population. It stands out among the many innovations in the 1973 Rehabilitation Act Amendments. Throughout the twentieth century, the course of federal legislation has been toward affirmation of the rights of disabled persons to full citizenship—rights that physical and mental disabilities cannot prevent, rights that deserve the vigorous support of the nation to assure that its most afflicted citizens enjoy them.

Jerome D. Schein

Administration

The vocational rehabilitation program is a cooperative partnership administered by the federal and state governments. It is the primary public program for helping handicapped youths and adults obtain or maintain employment.

STRUCTURE

Vocational rehabilitation began as a grant-in-aid program for providing services to handicapped individuals under the Smith-Fess Act of 1920. The Federal Board of Vocational Education was the administering agency. In 1935 the vocational rehabilitation program was transformed into permanent legislation, and was administered by the Federal Security Agency under the authority of the Social Security Act. During the 1940s and 1950s, the legislation was broadened and administered by the Vocational Rehabilitation Administration (VRA).

During the 1960s the Vocational Rehabilitation Administration was brought into the formation of the Department of Health, Education and Welfare as a program unit. In 1966 it became the Rehabilitation Services Administration and in 1967 was placed into the Social and Rehabilitation Services of the department.

In 1973 Congress, responding to the concern for the program's integrity voiced by state administrators, handicapped individuals, and other concerned citizens, established in law the Rehabilitation Services Administration and made the commissioner's position one appointed by the President and confirmed by the U.S. Senate. When the Department of Health, Education and Welfare was divided into the Department of Health and Human Services and the Department of Education, the Rehabilitation Services Administration was placed in the Department of Education's Office of Special Education and Rehabilitative Services (OSERS). This office also includes the National Institute of Handicapped Research and Special Education Programs. The Rehabilitation Services Administration is responsible for the administration and leadership of the program, and has central office staff in Washington, D.C., and other staff located within 10 administrative regions throughout the nation. The regional offices act as the primary liaison between the federal and state agencies.

FUNCTION

The Rehabilitation Services Administration establishes overall national policy concerning vocational rehabilitation and independent living programs. Its functions include formulating rules, regulations, and policies applicable to vocational rehabilitation services; providing leadership to states in planning, developing, and coordinating overall programs; reviewing state plans to ensure that they conform with all legal requirements; and monitoring and evaluating the states' program performance and accomplishments. State vocational rehabilitation agencies provide the rehabilitation services to handicapped individuals.

The Rehabilitation Services Administration also administers grants, some of which are for workerpower development and training programs, others of which are discretionary because the administration requests proposals annually for funding these special areas of emphasis. Included in the discretionary grants program are special demonstration projects for severely disabled individuals, handicapped migrant workers, projects with industry, recreation for handicapped persons, and independent living projects. The project proposals submitted are judged competitively against published criteria in the *Federal Register*, and each applicant's proposal is reviewed by panels of peers and ranked according to merit. The commissioner uses this information in making the awards.

The worker-power development and training grant program provides support to institutions of higher education and state vocational rehabilitation agencies to assure training of rehabilitation personnel in a variety of professions. Grants for in-service training are made to state vocational rehabilitation agencies to assure that state staff have the skills needed to serve handicapped clients, including training to improve communication skills for staff serving deaf people.

The Rehabilitation Services Administration also coordinates services among federal agencies that relate to the well-being and concerns of handicapped individuals, especially those seeking employment. These agencies include the Department of Health and Human Services, the Department of Transportation, and the Department of Labor.

Similarly, the administration works with associations of handicapped persons, such as the National Association of the Deaf, and maintains liaisons with the Council of State Administrators of Vocational Rehabilitation. The latter is an association of vocational rehabilitation directors whose purpose is to provide a forum for exchange of information and issues concerning handicapped people and to strengthen the vocational rehabilitation program. *See* NATIONAL ASSOCIATION OF THE DEAF.

The commissioner is required to report annually to the President and Congress on the status of the program's efforts in assisting handicapped citizens. This reporting includes that over which the commissioner exerts direct control, such as project grants and program demonstrations, as well as that part of the federal-state program of vocational rehabilitation administered by the state under a plan approved by the commissioner.

STATE PLAN

States are not required to have a vocational rehabilitation program. However, each state has established a legislative authority that enables it to develop a state plan that reflects the Federal Rehabilitation Act, along with the implementing regulations, that governs the vocational rehabilitation program. A state under its plan for vocational rehabilitation approved by the Rehabilitation Services Administration commissioner both administers and directs the vocational rehabilitation program within that state. The director and the staff are to spend full time on the activities of the program. Decisions on eligibility of applicants for service, provision of services, and the nature and scope of services provided to handicapped individuals are under the authority of the state agency, not the federal government.

The state plan is the key instrument by which

the vocational rehabilitation program operates. It is a formula grant-in-aid program that allows each state to establish and maintain a program of vocational rehabilitation for its handicapped citizens. The state is required to pay a minimum of 20 percent of the costs of the program.

The state plan can be viewed as a contract agreement that is periodically affirmed by the state and amended as needed to reflect changes in the legislative base. The form of the plan is a pre-print document that is used to assure that all state vocational rehabilitation programs conform to the mandated and basic requirements of the Rehabilitation Act. It also allows states, through options and attachments, to individualize their plans as to the priorities, resources, conditions, and scope of services that will be provided. The state plan essentially is an assurance that the respective state vocational rehabilitation programs will comply with federal statutes. Should a state wish to amend its plan, the amendments must be sent to the state's governor for review and comment, and then to the commissioner for review and approval or disapproval.

The Rehabilitation Services Administration has responsibility for monitoring the implementation of, and assuring compliance with, the approved state plan. This role is further supported by state and federal audit agencies that periodically study both expenditures of federal and state funds and program effectiveness.

A change in the state plan is required when there is a substantial change in state laws, organization, policy, or administration affecting the state plan. In addition, each state is required to submit annually: (1) the estimated number of handicapped people to be served and rehabilitated, (2) the methods used to expand and improve services to the most severely handicapped individuals, (3) changes in the order of selection and outcome and service goals, and (4) changes in policies resulting from statewide studies and annual program evaluations.

FUNDING

The states receive funds appropriated annually by Congress for implementing the vocational rehabilitation program on a formula basis. This formula is based primarily on the state population and per capita income. The federal funding of the vocational rehabilitation program is different from many other federal programs in that the funding appropriated must be obligated (expended) within the relevant fiscal year and cannot be used by the state in the following year's program. Consequently, in the latter part of the fiscal year, some states, unable to utilize all of their federal funds, will release them for reallocation to another state's vocational rehabilitation program. Federal funds not used by states are returned to the U.S. Treasury.

State legislatures do not always appropriate the full amount needed to match appropriated federal funds. State vocational agencies may use cash equivalents, such as the salaries of state personnel of other public agencies contributing to a cooperative program of vocational rehabilitation, to acquire the state matching needed to secure the federal appropriation available. Donations of funds to be used to match available federal dollars may be accepted from private individuals or organizations. These funds may be used to initiate or support a vocational rehabilitation program for a particular group of disabled individuals—a vocational rehabilitation program to initiate services to low-achieving deaf individuals, for example.

The formula grant-in-aid program provides grants to assist states in meeting the needs of their handicapped citizens preparing to secure employment commensurate with their capabilities. Acceptable employment can be through business or industry, self-employment, homemaking, or sheltered employment.

FACILITIES

Rehabilitation facility is a broad term used to describe a place where various services may be offered handicapped persons. They may be state-operated agencies or private nonprofit operations. State vocational rehabilitation agencies may support either type of program or a combination of both. The facility may be an entire building or a part of a building.

An important part of the rehabilitation program is that up to about 25 percent of those persons served by an agency receive services from a rehabilitation center or workshop. Approximately 30 percent of the case-service dollars that a state agency expends is through facility services. Services by such centers vary widely, but most include: (1) evaluation: a study of the handicapped person's ability to function at home, in the community, and in society, as well as the individual's potential to benefit from rehabilitation services in terms of becoming employed; (2) adjustment: assisting handicapped people to develop attitudes, behaviors, personal habits, and relationships, and responses to a work setting that will enable them to satisfactorily perform a work activity; (3) skill training: organized instruction designed to prepare a handicapped person to successfully accomplish a specific work activity, trade, or profession; (4) extended employment: a work activity accomplished as an employee in a sheltered workshop for an indefinite period of time; and (5) job placement: assisting a handicapped individual through a variety of services, in-

cluding counseling and guidance, to obtain employment suitable to the person's skills and abilities.

Some state agencies have established centers or workshops to meet the special needs of deaf individuals, either through the state itself, or with the cooperation of a private nonprofit organization. These facilities have staff skilled in communication and knowledgeable about hearing impairments. The federal government has recognized that many deaf individuals want postsecondary training, and it has stimulated and supported a number of specialized institutions to respond to this need. Gallaudet College, in Washington, D.C., and the National Technical Institute for the Deaf, in Rochester, New York, are two examples of such institutions offering programs in higher education. A number of federally supported postsecondary programs, such as the Technical-Vocational Institute, in St. Paul, Minnesota, provide opportunities for skill training to deaf youths. *See* GALLAUDET COLLEGE; NATIONAL TECHNICAL INSTITUTE FOR THE DEAF.

INDEPENDENT LIVING PROGRAMS

The Rehabilitation Act, as amended, authorized a formula grant-in-aid program similar to that of the vocational rehabilitation program. Its goal is to enhance or improve handicapped people's ability to live independently within their communities. Unfortunately, appropriations have not been made to initiate this part of the act. However, Congress has funded independent living projects, with the purpose of demonstrating the potential this program may have for handicapped persons who may not have an employment goal.

Most states do have independent living projects, which may be state-operated or administered by private nonprofit organizations. The projects are community-based and do not typically provide services statewide. The main services offered by many of these projects are to have knowledge of handicapped persons and to coordinate services they need. These most often center on self-care, housing, transportation, and employment.

It is intended that such projects have staff available who are skilled in serving hearing-impaired persons. Such programs contribute much to the adjustment of handicapped persons, and the results of such services may raise their potential for employment. Such projects are also open to serve handicapped persons who are not of employment age.

IMPLICATIONS FOR DEAF PERSONS

There are a number of areas within the administration of the Rehabilitation Services Administration and state vocational rehabilitation agencies that may be of interest and concern to deaf persons. The quality and commitment of services to hearing-impaired clients may be reflected in a number of factors.

Points of leadership, training of staff, staff assignments, allocation of funds, and facilities available reflect the manner and priority that the agency has established in rehabilitating hearing-impaired people.

The number, experience, and qualifications of persons assigned to work with hearing-impaired clients, and the agency's hiring practices, career development policies, and practices reflect upon its affirmative action.

The manner in which the views of other organizations, professionals, deaf persons, or those interested in deaf persons are considered in formulating the organization's policy is significant. It determines the formation of advisory committees, the reviews and frequency of complaints, the undertaking of special studies, and other topics.

The means that the organization uses to determine the effectiveness of its program of services to hearing-impaired people is important. Measures used to determine how successful the agency effort has been may include the numbers served and rehabilitated, percentage of those served who successfully achieve an employment goal, occupations and wages at time of case closure, time needed to close each case, average cost of case services expended, and rehabilitation agency trends comparing agency experience with other groups over a number of years.

Henry Warner

Agencies

Rehabilitation agencies divide into three types: governmental—those that are established and managed in accordance with legislative or administrative authority; voluntary—those that are established to provide services on a nonprofit basis; and proprietary—those that sell their services. These types may operate in four jurisdictions, that is, on a national, regional, statewide, or local basis. Taken together, these categories yield 12 groups of agencies.

1. National governmental agencies. The Rehabilitation Services Administration (RSA) in the Department of Education is the government agency charged with responsibility for civilian rehabilitation. The Veterans Administration also devotes a sizable portion of its resources to rehabilitation. Programs for the vocational training of deaf youths, such as the program at the St. Paul Technical-Vocational Institute, accept clients from across the United States, but are essentially local agencies even though partial funding comes from the federal government (for example, control of the program at the St. Paul Technical-Vocational Institute is manifested by the St. Paul Board of Education).

2. Regional governmental agencies. The Rehabilitation Services Administration maintains 10 regional offices, each of which has responsibility for monitoring the rehabilitation programs of the states in its geographical area, and each of which provides technical assistance and informational services to rehabilitation agencies in its area.

3. State governmental agencies. Every state maintains at least one rehabilitation authority that has responsibility for planning, budgeting, and supervising rehabilitation agencies in its jurisdiction. Some states have two rehabilitation agencies: a general agency and a separate agency for blind rehabilitation clients. The activities of the two agencies may be coordinated within the state government.

4. Local governmental agencies. Local governments in the United States do not maintain rehabilitation facilities completely independent of the state authority. While the extent of their freedom to act independently varies from city to city and county to county, local government rehabilitation facilities are, in fact, branches of the state's program.

5. National voluntary agencies. Voluntary rehabilitation organizations at the federal level are usually fund-raising bodies that provide support for state and local rehabilitation programs. Other organizations bring together individuals who have professional interests in common, such as the National Rehabilitation Association, or who share an interest in a particular disability group, such as the Epilepsy Foundation of America. These organizations may serve advocacy functions and may direct efforts to improve the quality of services by those who work with disabled people, but they do not deliver direct services to clients.

6. Regional voluntary agencies. Unlike the federal-regional structure, regional voluntary agencies are not necessarily subunits of national bodies but are usually formed to work across state lines. An example is the Regional Programs for Educational Services to Deaf-Blind Children, most of whose members have served several states. For example, the Mountain Plains Regional Center has served in Colorado, Kansas, Nebraska, New Mexico, North Dakota, South Dakota, Utah, and Wyoming.

7. Statewide voluntary agencies. Voluntary rehabilitation agencies that serve an entire state are uncommon. The New York Psychiatric Institute manages a program for the rehabilitation of mentally ill deaf persons in New York State. Housed at Rockland State Hospital in Rockland County, the agency accepts patients from anywhere in the state. Other examples may be found in states, such as Rhode Island, where the distinction between state and local tends to blur because of their small size.

8. Local voluntary agencies. The majority of voluntary rehabilitation agencies operate locally. Al-

most every large city and county has one or more agencies serving deaf people.

9. National proprietary agencies. Recently a few proprietary agencies have emerged at the national level to vend an array of rehabilitation services, though most are presently involved in activities such as replacing body organs with manufactured replacements (for example, the artificial heart). The House Ear Institute has developed a national network of otologists to provide cochlear implants to profoundly hearing-impaired individuals. *See* COCHLEAR IMPLANTS.

10. Regional proprietary agencies. Like the regional voluntary agencies, those proprietary agencies that fall into this category do not represent subdivisions of national organizations. They are formed to sell their services over an area that crosses state borders.

11. Statewide proprietary agencies. Private rehabilitation agencies are not often developed at the state level. An exception that may become more prevalent is the interpreter service for deaf people. While most such services are being provided by voluntary and governmental agencies, a few proprietary agencies are offering interpreter services on a statewide basis. *See* INTERPRETING.

12. Local proprietary agencies. Proprietary rehabilitation agencies most often function at the local level. Among the services they vend are psychological evaluation and counseling, physical and occupational therapy, restorative surgery, and interpreter services. The following sections deal in depth with this categorization of agencies, expanding upon the differences that are found among them.

Jerome D. Schein

FEDERAL AGENCIES

The Executive Branch of the United States government consists of the Executive Office of the President, 13 departments, and many independent agencies. Almost everybody has contact with a federal agency during a year—for example, with the Internal Revenue Service and the Social Security Administration. Frequently, however, federal assistance is more indirectly offered to states and local agencies through aid used to provide a program of services, such as special education for disabled children, food stamps, Head Start (children's educational development), and Medicaid. Knowing the kinds of assistance available and where to find it is a difficult task for many people unfamiliar with government. This discussion addresses some overall and general aspects of government programs and provides specific information on those programs most frequently sought by the public.

Federal assistance programs are authorized by the U.S. Congress through legislation and are then provided an appropriation for the fiscal year Oc-

tober 1 through September 30. The Executive Branch is responsible for the implementation of the laws passed by Congress and the management of the respective programs. The Judicial System resolves questions of interpretation of laws and responsibilities associated with them when challenges are made through the federal court system. While there are many authorities establishing both federal and federal-state assistance programs, the following is a sampling of those most often of concern to disabled persons.

Department of Education The catalog of Federal Domestic Assistance lists approximately 90 different Department of Education programs of assistance to states, organizations, or individuals. Most often identified by the public are student loans and grants, assistance to handicapped children, vocational education, regional education programs for deaf and other disabled persons, and Handicapped Media Services and Captioned Films.

Department of Energy The most significant programs of the Department of Energy include authorization assistance for low-income persons and Office of Minority Economic Impact loans.

Department of Treasury The Department of Treasury provides three major programs for disabled individuals: taxpayer service, tax counseling for elderly citizens, and General Revenue Sharing (state and local government assistance).

Small Business Administration The Small Business Administration has three programs of particular interest to disabled people: loans to small businesses, management assistance to small businesses, and handicapped assistance loans.

Department of Transportation The Department of Transportation has approximately 40 programs. Two of these are of special interest: urban mass transportation capital and operating assistance formula grants, and boating safety.

Department of Labor Of the approximately 30 programs of the Department of Labor, 6 are of major significance to individuals with disabilities: unemployment insurance, job training partnership, nondiscrimination and affirmative action by federal contractors, occupational safety and health, and apprenticeship training.

Department of Justice The Department of Justice operates five programs with particular relevance to disabled people: desegregation of public education, equal employment opportunity, civil rights of institutionalized persons, civil rights compliance activities, and fair housing and equal credit opportunity.

Department of Housing Urban Development Three of the Department of Housing and Urban Development's approximately 70 different programs are significant to disabled individuals. These include housing for elderly or disabled people, public housing, and low-income housing (home ownership opportunities).

Department of Health and Human Services The Department of Health and Human Services has the greatest number of programs directly relevant to disabled persons. These 10 programs are family planning services, community health centers, Head Start, work incentive program, child welfare services (state grants), programs for aged persons, Social Security Disability Insurance, Supplemental Security Income, primary care (block grants to states), and maternal and child health services (block grants).

Department of Commerce The three programs of the Department of Commerce that especially concern disabled citizens are Census Bureau data products; Business Assistance, Services, and Information; and public telecommunication facilities.

Department of Defense The Department of Defense has two programs that may be applicable to disabled persons: industrial equipment loans to educational institutions, and donations or loans of obsolete property.

Department of Agriculture The Department of Agriculture has six significant programs for disabled individuals: human nutrition information service, food stamps, school breakfast program, commodity supplemental food program, rural rental assistance payments, and business and industrial loans.

Information Resources There are many agencies of the United States government operating programs of domestic assistance. The person seeking knowledge or assistance from federal programs faces a bewildering task. Questions of what is the responsible federal agency, law, or authority; eligibility factors; a description of the operating program; and what funding has been appropriated all seem difficult information to secure. However, there are a number of information sources that can begin to answer these questions.

The *Catalog of Federal Domestic Assistance*, available from the Government Printing Office, is published annually and provides information and guidance on applying and preparing proposals for grant assistance. Each program of assistance is identified by the responsible department or administering agency, the authorization (law) upon which the program is based, objective of the program, eligibility requirements, and other important information.

Another useful publication is *Programs for the Handicapped*. This bimonthly periodical is published by the Department of Education's Office of Special Education and Rehabilitation Services, and can be obtained free.

A third reference publication is the *Federal Staff Directory*. It annually provides organizational listings of departments and independent agencies of the federal government, and includes telephone numbers and biographical descriptions of key federal executives.

State vocational rehabilitation agencies also are good sources of information. Part of the responsibility of each state's Vocational Rehabilitation Program administration is to establish and maintain information and referral programs that provide disabled individuals with accurate vocational rehabilitation information and appropriate referrals to other federal and state programs and activities. The staff of these agencies should include, to the maximum extent feasible, interpreters for deaf clients.

Federal Information Centers provide information about and assistance for problems related to the federal government. They are located throughout the United States in 70 major metropolitan areas. Individuals may write or telephone the centers with questions concerning Social Security, patents, copyrights, tax assistance, wage and hour laws, Medicare, and federal employment. These centers work closely with information and referral agencies of state and local government. Business owners or managers can use them when buying from or selling to the federal government. They are also a source of other business-related information.

The United States Commission on Civil Rights puts out *Clearinghouse Publication 81*, which addresses the issue of reasonable accommodation, a central consideration in handicap discrimination law. This publication provides information about disabled people, the barriers they face, and their legal rights. Part of it also makes suggestions on ways to resolve legal issues concerning disabled people's rights. Furthermore, it "identifies major social and legal mechanisms, practices, and settings," in which discrimination of disabled people arises, and it lists major federal statutes concerning disabled people, with a brief summary of their purposes and contents.

Affirmative Action Most federal agencies are required to have affirmative action programs for assuring equal employment and career opportunities for minorities, including disabled people. Departments of the federal government have been required to implement regulations for Section 504 of the Rehabilitation Act of 1973, as amended, to assure that grantees or receiving organizations contracting with the government do not have discrimination in their hiring or employment practices.

Federal agencies may allow, through the Office of Personnel Management, disabled individuals to be appointed to a position temporarily to demonstrate their ability to fulfill that position competently, rather than have them compete in the normal personnel recruitment process. Adjustments may be allowed on written examinations, when appropriate, to assure that disabled persons receive an opportunity to compete fairly with the general public.

Disabled persons should expect reasonable accommodations to assure their accessibility to programs that are supported in part or wholly through federal funding. For deaf persons this may require the services of an interpreter in job training, in education programs, or when seeking assistance from public agencies. Frequently, personnel of federal programs have little understanding of hearing-impaired persons and their problems in accessing federal assistance programs. It will be necessary for those interested in hearing-impaired and deaf people to assure that their rights are understood and respected. Frequently, advocacy offices can be of assistance in these matters. The civil rights offices of the respective departments can often be helpful.

Bibliography

Brownson, Charles B., and Anna L. Brownson: *1984 Federal Staff Directory*, Congressional Staff Directory, Ltd., Mount Vernon, Virginia.

Office of Information and Resources for the Handicapped: *Programs for the Handicapped Clearinghouse on the Handicapped*, Washington, D.C.

Office of Management and Budget: *1983 Catalog of Federal Domestic Assistance*.

Office of Technology Assessment: *Technology and Handicapped People*, Washington, D.C., May 1982.

Henry C. Warner

STATE AGENCIES

This section addresses the manner in which state plans are implemented. Although each participating state agrees to meet the basic requirements of the Rehabilitation Act under its approved state plan, the choices and philosophy of leadership, state legislative support, and organization of state government can cause profound differences in the vocational rehabilitation program offered.

The term state agency means the sole agency in a state designated to administer the state plan for vocational rehabilitation services. It includes the state agency for blind persons, if designated as the sole state agency with respect to that part of the plan relating to vocational rehabilitation of blind individuals.

Designated state unit, or state unit, can mean one of two things. It can mean the state agency, vocational bureau, division, or other organizational unit which is primarily concerned with vocational rehabilitation or vocational and other rehabilitation of handicapped individuals, and which is responsible for the administration of the vocational rehabilitation program of the state agency. Or, it can mean the Independent State Commissioner Board or other agency that has vocational rehabilitation or vocational and other rehabilitation as its primary function.

The state agency is the administering and supervisory organization for the unit providing vocational rehabilitation services. The state unit implements the state plan, and is therefore a subdivision of the state agency, or is the same as the state agency in those states that have an independent rehabilitation agency.

Location The Rehabilitation Act, as amended, allows for placement of the state unit within several different state government settings. It may be in (1) a state agency primarily concerned with vocational rehabilitation or vocational and other rehabilitation of handicapped individuals; (2) an independent organization, such as a commission, that functions both as sole agency and as the designate state unit (this allows the vocational rehabilitation program to establish its own priorities, develop and present budgets to legislative bodies, manage its resources, and operate within the general parameters of state government); or (3) a state education or vocational education agency or another state agency that includes at least two other major organizational units, each of which administers one or more of the state's major programs of public education, public health, public welfare, or labor.

The second or third category above places the vocational rehabilitation unit in a supervisory structure of a sole agency. The sole agency may exert strong influence on the vocational rehabilitation unit's priorities for program direction, control of its budget development and presentations, management of its resources, and personnel. It may properly charge indirect costs to the agency for various support services available to the vocational rehabilitation unit. Examples of these services might be legal services, administrative work associated with personnel actions, statistical and financial reporting, and other shared costs of state administration.

Some states have placed a heavier burden of supervising structures on vocational rehabilitation than on other program units utilizing mostly federal funding. The range of direct and indirect administrative costs to the vocational rehabilitation agency is generally within the range of 6 to 15 percent of the vocational rehabilitation unit's total funding.

The location of the vocational rehabilitation unit in a human resource agency is likely to result in the coordination of the vocational rehabilitation program with its companion programs and in support of the overall department objectives. If the designated vocational rehabilitation unit is within a department of human resources, it may place greater emphasis on the vocational rehabilitation of disabled public assistance recipients than if it is located elsewhere. Similarly, if it is in a department of education, its greatest emphasis may be on the vocational rehabilitation of disabled youth.

Staffing Changes have occurred in the manner in which state directors of the vocational rehabilitation program are selected. Since the 1960s, these positions were changed from being protected by state merit systems to that of appointment. This has often strengthened the political influence and direction of the program. Administrators of sole agencies have the power of appointment for positions not covered by state merit systems. There also has been a tendency to exempt from state merit systems the administrative positions at the second and third level of responsibility of state vocational rehabilitation units.

State directors of the vocational rehabilitation units are required by the approved state plan to have a full-time vocational rehabilitation staff with clear lines of supervisory authority. The vocational rehabilitation units are expected to maintain control of all vocational rehabilitation program functions.

The commissioner of the Rehabilitation Services Administration is prohibited by law from exerting influence on the selection of any state official employed by the program. However, the commissioner's approval of the state plan does commit the state vocational rehabilitation program to having adequate staff available to fulfill the unit's needs for program planning and evaluation, staff development, rehabilitation facility development and utilization, medical consultation, and rehabilitation counseling services. The state plan also requires that personnel be available to communicate with applicants for services in their native languages or preferred modes of communication, including nonverbal methods or devices.

Program One of the greatest assets of vocational rehabilitation programs is the degree of flexibility that the Rehabilitation Act provides in meeting the rehabilitation service needs of its clients. The vocational rehabilitation program can be individualized to meet each client's needs in achieving employment. This is formally accomplished through the development of the individual written rehabilitation program which is developed jointly by the rehabilitation counselor and the client.

Section 103 of the Rehabilitation Act, as amended, mandates that the state plan make available certain services to meet the needs of handicapped individuals. The mandated services are intended to be available to meet individual needs; not every individual receives every service listed.

For each of these mandated services, the state vocational rehabilitation program is required to have a written policy describing the kind and extent of the service and the conditions upon which the service

will be provided. For example, most vocational rehabilitation agencies apply a financial needs test for services, dependent upon the client's resources available to support the jointly developed individual written rehabilitation program. The mandated services are: (1) evaluation of vocational rehabilitation potential; (2) counseling and guidance; (3) physical and mental restoration; (4) vocational and other training; (5) maintenance; (6) transportation; (7) services to family members when in support of the individual written rehabilitation program; (8) interpreter and notetakers; (9) reader service, rehabilitation teacher services, and orientation and mobility services for blind persons; (10) telecommunication, sensory, and other technological aids and devices; (11) recruitment and training services in public service employment; (12) placement in suitable employment; (13) postemployment services necessary to maintain suitable employment; (14) occupational licenses, permits, or other written authority required by a state, city, or other governmental unit for an occupation or business, tools, equipment, initial stocks, and supplies; and (15) other goods and services that can reasonably be expected to benefit a handicapped individual in terms of employability. No financial requirements, however, may be placed upon evaluation of rehabilitation potential (except those provided under an extended evaluation plan), counseling, or guidance referral and placement services.

Vocational rehabilitation agencies are both encouraged and required to develop cooperative relationships and programming with other organizations serving handicapped individuals. The intent is for vocational rehabilitation programs to use the resources of the community and other public agencies when there is a population of mutual interest to both the vocational rehabilitation agency and the cooperating agency. Such resources might be the state medicaid program, student financial assistance, food stamps, public housing, mental health services, or other education and training resources.

In addition, the Vocational Rehabilitation Act provides the authority for the vocational rehabilitation agency under its approved state plan to establish and construct rehabilitation facilities for the primary purpose of providing vocational rehabilitation services to handicapped individuals. This authority may be utilized to develop facilities operated by the state agency or in cooperation with other public or private nonprofit agencies.

A state vocational rehabilitation agency may decide to develop rehabilitation service providers outside of the state government for a variety of purposes. These include the desire to increase financial and public support of a local community, the attempt to expand the base of rehabilitation resources beyond the state vocational rehabilitation organizational unit, the need to bypass administrative and bureaucratic obstacles that can restrict the development of a state-operated program, and the effort to establish a system of rehabilitation service providers that could not be achieved through state government.

State vocational rehabilitation policies vary in a number of ways. One is in the provision of a telecommunication device for deaf or severely hearing-impaired individuals. Criteria to determine this policy include such factors as how closely related and supportive is the device to the hearing-impaired person's effort to secure or maintain employment, how developed the individual's language ability is, and whether there are other units in sufficient quantity within the community to make it useful.

The state written policy can be reviewed by the public. It should assist the handicapped individual in reaching the chosen employment goal, and can be changed if it is shown not to be effective in managing the program.

Bibliography

Rehabilitation Act of 1973, as amended, Sec. 101(a) and 103(a).

Transmittal of Report on State Vocational Rehabilitation Agency Expenditures Under the Basic State Grants Program for FY 1982, Rehabilitation Services Administration Information Memorandum 83–43.

Henry C. Warner

LOCAL AGENCIES

State vocational rehabilitation agencies have great flexibility in the manner in which they choose to allocate, establish, and develop rehabilitation resources under the Rehabilitation Act of 1973, as amended. This is easily evidenced when reviewing the manner in which different states have approached the establishment and use of statewide materials of rehabilitation facilities.

While the goal of vocational rehabilitation facilities is to prepare or provide opportunities for handicapped individuals to become employed, some vocational rehabilitation agencies have developed supportive objectives for rehabilitation facilities to assist in meeting the overall agency goal. It should be understood that participating nonprofit organizations, such as Goodwill Industries or Jewish Vocational Services, may have other programs and goals outside the setting of vocational rehabilitation, and only part of these organizations' activities may be directly related on a contractual or cooperative arrangement with vocational rehabilitation programming of the state agency.

An example of an activity not directly related to vocational rehabilitation programs are work activities programs offered by sheltered workshops, which have the primary purpose of providing a therapeutic environment rather than productive gainful employment. Another program emerging in the rehabilitation field is that of independent living, which has the goal of assisting handicapped people in living more independently.

Definition The term local agency usually means an agency of a unit of general local government or of an Indian tribal organization (or a combination of such units or organizations) that has the sole responsibility under an agreement with the state agency to conduct a vocational rehabilitation program. This is done in the locality under the supervision of the state agency in accordance with the state plan. Presently there are no local vocational rehabilitation agencies operating under the supervision of a state agency's approved state plan. However, the Rehabilitation Act does provide the possibility of geopolitical subdivisions of a state conducting a vocational rehabilitation program. The state agency, working through the designated state unit, would develop a written agreement with assurances for the local administration of the state plan. The designated state unit would supervise the administration of the local agency.

The term local agency can also refer to facilities at the community level. These rehabilitation facilities and workshops are a major resource to state agencies in developing appropriate programs of vocational rehabilitation services. The states use a number of different mechanisms to initiate and support such programs: grants, contracts, fees for services, and so forth. The services most frequently obtained from local resources are: (1) evaluation of rehabilitation potential; (2) personal, social, and work adjustment training; (3) skill training; (4) treatment services; (5) extended employment; and (6) guidance and placement services.

State Facilities Plan The state facilities plan is a document prepared by the agency indicating facilities being utilized by the vocational rehabilitation program. The facilities plan should be updated each year, and should include (1) a list of local facilities used, (2) the utilization rate of these facilities, and (3) the priorities for new or expanded facility programs. Some state agencies have developed and implemented systematic means of evaluating the effectiveness of the facilities they use. Goals are established and costs projected. Performance of the facility is then measured against the established goals. Negotiation periodically takes place between the local facility and state agency on the cost-performance record, and is often adjusted based upon experience. Goals for facilities and workshops vary significantly. Some examples of annual goals might be: to place a certain percentage of clients into competitive employment; to provide vocational evaluation services to a specific number of agency applicants or clients; and to provide personal and work adjustment training to a specific number of clients.

The state vocational rehabilitation agency generally establishes standards of operation that facilities are required to meet as contractors or providers. The standards may be based on the National Council for Accreditation of Rehabilitation Facilities (CARF) standards or on criteria judged to be equal to or stronger than these. Depending upon the local facility's mission and the services it provides, certification or accrediting by the National Council for Accreditation of Rehabilitation Facilities or other bodies, such as the American Hospital Association or state Medicaid certification, may be required by the state agency.

The state facility plan must be developed cooperatively with the service provider and must be available for public review. Some states have interpreted the facility plan in a more limited way and include only rehabilitation workshops in their facility planning, while others include comprehensive rehabilitation centers and medically oriented rehabilitation facilities.

Initiating or Expansion of Local Facilities The Rehabilitation Act of 1973, as amended, provides a number of provisions that allows the state agency to establish or construct rehabilitation facilities. The state agency may choose to utilize these provisions to develop state-operated or nonprofit programs. In cooperative arrangements to develop a new or expanded program of vocational rehabilitation services, the state agency may accept funds from a nonprofit agency or another appropriate donor to meet the state share to secure federal matching funds. The local share can be no less than 20 percent of the total cost of the establishment project. The establishment provision allows the funds to be obligated for space, equipment, and initial or expanded staffing of the rehabilitation facility. Funds made available under the establishment authority provision are not to be used for continued operating costs of the facility.

For example, if the state agency chooses, it may establish a sheltered workshop program in a rehabilitation facility to provide for productive employment for handicapped individuals. It may supply the needed space through the expansion or remodeling of a building, purchase the necessary equipment to meet work contract requirements, and engage the necessary staff to supervise and manage the program. It cannot use establishment funds to purchase such things as consumable materials or to pay utility bills. These costs of operation must come from other sources, such as the sale of products or services produced by the handicapped workers.

Construction authority is used in a similar manner; however, there are additional assurances to be met. This authority requires that the state matching share be 50 percent of the total cost of the project.

The use of these authorities (Establishment or Construction) is made frequently at the end of the federal fiscal year when some state agencies release funds that they are unable to obligate. The Rehabilitation Services Administration then distributes the funds to states having the available matching state funds and desiring to initiate or expand their vocational rehabilitation programs.

Utilization of Facilities Most state agencies coordinate the use of local rehabilitation facilities through their rehabilitation counselors. The rehabilitation counselor directs or authorizes services to be provided to a client by the facility for a specific period of time. Payments to private nonprofit or private for-profit facilities are usually made on a contract or fee-for-service basis.

Deaf Service Centers There are a growing number of deaf service centers developing in the United States. Many of the services they provide are not directly related to vocational rehabilitation programs. The basic services offered are telephone-relay and interpreter services. However, a number of the larger centers offer a variety of services, such as counseling, recreation, job assistance, and information and referral to other assistance agencies.

In the southeastern United States in 1985, approximately one-third of those centers surveyed had annual budgets of over $150,000. All were private nonprofit organizations and received support from a variety of sources, such as community donations, state grants, and fees for services. The majority of the centers reported having cooperative working relationships with police, court systems, hospitals, mental health centers, vocational rehabilitation agencies, schools, employment services, and local businesses and employers.

In some states deaf service centers have formed a statewide network in coordinating efforts to assist deaf people. In other states the deaf service centers operate essentially independently.

Henry C. Warner

VOLUNTARY AGENCIES

Voluntary agencies constitute another system that serves the deaf population. Deaf people have traditionally been served by federal, state, and local government agencies, but there are also nongovernmental agencies that are designed to provide services and programs for deaf citizens.

The major difference between federal, state, and local agencies and voluntary agencies is their financial base. Government funds are the major source of financial support for federal, state, and local agencies. Voluntary agencies receive most of their funding from contributions or donations offered by individuals, foundations, and organizations that raise money for specific disability groups, such as the American Cancer Society and the United Way. When the government supports an agency, it can place special qualifications or requirements on who will be served, what services will be provided, and what the cost, if any, will be. Government agencies provide a wide variety of services, but they may not be available to the total population.

Voluntary agencies, on the other hand, usually are nonprofit organizations, and the fees they charge for services are usually based on the client's ability to pay. Voluntary agencies usually are open to all individuals.

Voluntary agencies often provide awareness programs and information about the activities, programs, and services being offered by different programs. For example, the agencies are often aware of the special needs of hearing-impaired people, and can generally provide counseling and educational programs on hearing loss and productive ways to better understand and cope with hearing problems.

Many voluntary agencies are based in the community or the state. However, some have national headquarters with branch offices or local programs established in the communities. A list of national organizations serving hearing-impaired persons is available from the National Information Center on Deafness at Gallaudet College.

Bibliography

Services for Hearing Impaired People, Gallaudet College, Washington, D.C., 1982.

James D. Dixon

Process

The focus of the rehabilitation process is upon the sequential delivery of services designed to assist the handicapped person in obtaining and successfully engaging in employment or other gainful activity. Services are provided by a broad spectrum of rehabilitation professionals and from a diverse pool of service agencies and rehabilitation facilities. Critical to the integrity and success of this process is the concept of the individualized rehabilitation plan, which provides both the professional and the handicapped person with the framework around which goals can be developed and services can be offered.

The rehabilitation process is based on an established set of principles that have been developed over the past 60 years. These principles can be summarized as follows: clients must be provided with all information necessary to understand the role of rehabilitation and to maximize their own involvement in the process and outcome; rapport must be established and continued throughout the entire time that the clients are being rehabilitated; and each service must be planned and monitored to develop an accurate assessment of the clients' potentials and goals. Designed to maximize client participation in rehabilitation, these principles encourage independence and are unique to the field of rehabilitation. The responsibility for these activities lies primarily with rehabilitation counselors. They coordinate all phases of the rehabilitation process and work closely with the clients to ensure their participation. At an appropriate time early in the process, an individual written rehabilitation program (IWRP) is jointly developed by the client and the counselor. This plan assures client participation and serves as a guide and a commitment to the client.

The process begins with either the client's self-referral or the referral from another source, and ends with the client's successful adjustment or vocational placement. The process can be best understood by dividing it into four phases: evaluation, planning, treatment, and termination. The state-federal rehabilitation program further divides the process into sixteen phases signified by two-digit status codes.

The evaluation phase takes place in four steps: (1) an intake interview conducted by the counselor; (2) a general medical examination to establish the existence of a physical or mental disability, functional limitations, and the need for possible future medical intervention; (3) specialist examinations, such as audiological, otological, ophthalmological, or psychological evaluations, depending on the handicapping conditions that exist; and (4) evaluations of ability to work, ranging from simple observations of the client at work to sophisticated vocational evaluation systems in specialized rehabilitation facilities. A client may be found to be ineligible for services at this point. The criteria for eligibility of services are generally that the person have a medical or physical disability, that the disability engender a substantial functional limitation to employment, and that it be feasible for the individual to be rehabilitated.

The second phase of the process is the planning of rehabilitation services needed and their sequencing to maximize the success of future preparation. This phase begins after the counselor has collected all of the information sought during the evaluation phase. The planning phase calls for active client participation and a thorough knowledge of vocational information on the part of the counselor. The process of rehabilitation planning is an integration of the client's abilities, limitations, interests, and goals. Possible vocations, based on existing job opportunities, are selected by and suited to the individual client. Vocational training ranges from learning very basic activities of daily living to university graduate-level education. Planning also includes an analysis of the types of services needed, and where they can be obtained.

The third phase of the rehabilitation process includes the offering and completion of all of the services found necessary during the preservice phase.

The rehabilitation process is flexible. In cases where the disability becomes more severe or is unstable, services may be interrupted or other services introduced. After successful employment has been obtained, postemployment services to maintain the client's goal of vocational success can be authorized.

Bibliography

Bitter, James A.: *Introduction to Rehabilitation*, C.V. Mosby, St. Louis, Missouri, 1979.

Rubin, Stanford E., and Richard T. Roessler: *Foundation of the Vocational Rehabilitation Process*, University Park Press, Baltimore, Maryland, 1978.

Wright, George N.: *Total Rehabilitation*, Little, Brown, Boston, Massachusetts, 1980.

Gary F. Austin

CASEFINDING

The Rehabilitation Act of 1973, as amended, provides the basis for casefinding and indicates the ways that agencies are to direct their casefinding effort. For many agencies, the disabled population potentially eligible for vocational rehabilitation services is far greater than the agency resources, so administrative decisions are made consciously to emphasize services to certain groups.

Legal Basis The Rehabilitation Act specifies that the state will address in its own plan the various plans, policies, and methods to be followed in its administration and under its supervision, including a description of the method it will use to expand and improve services to individuals with the most severe handicaps. Second, the state plan must provide satisfactory assurances to the commissioner that the state has studied and considered a broad variety of means for providing services to individuals with the most severe handicaps.

In addition, the state plan includes provisions for the state agency to enter into cooperative arrangements with other public agencies and into agreements with private or nonprivate organizations and other programs for handicapped individuals. The act requires specific arrangements for the coordination of services to eligible individuals and those served by the Education of the Handicapped Act and the Vocational Education Act. *See* EDUCATION OF THE HANDICAPPED ACT.

While the state vocational rehabilitation agency establishes the basis for casefinding, implementation is typically the responsibility of the vocational rehabilitation counselor. Almost without exception, the counselor is delegated the responsibility of establishing eligibility for vocational rehabilitation services under the state plan. The counselor develops and manages a caseload and promotes services to applicants and potential clients of the agency within a geographic region of the state.

Essentially, casefinding has two major levels of responsibility: administrative and supervisory level, and that of vocational rehabilitation counselor practicing in the community. How the state agency allocates its resources affects casefinding. If the counselor has a large caseload and small case-service funds, casefinding is likely to be at a minimum. The policies of vocational rehabilitation agencies that support and emphasize services to severely handicapped individuals are most often reflected in their staffing patterns.

Casefinding and the Rehabilitation Counselor State agencies vary substantially in staff size and in the manner in which assignments are made. Typically, counselors are assigned to general caseloads (serving all handicapped individuals). Less often, they may be assigned to work in a cooperative program or to function as a specialist for certain handicapped populations. Development of an adequate number of referrals for the counselor serving a general caseload is usually not a problem. More often than not, referrals of disabled individuals exceed the counselor's time and resources. The cultivation of community referrals is often developed through membership in civic organizations, committees, businesses, and through contacts with employers, physicians, other professionals, and public and private agencies. In cultivating and encouraging referrals on a selective basis, counselors can significantly manage the types and kinds of referrals received from a particular geographic area.

For the counselor assigned to a cooperative program, such as in an institutional or school setting, identifying and cultivating referrals is a more focused procedure. Securing the awareness and understanding of the cooperating agency and its staff is a primary objective. Developing the cooperating staff's confidence in the counselor's ability to provide appropriate and needed services is essential. Acceptance is earned by providing an appropriate program of services to clients.

Rehabilitation Counselors and Services for Deaf People Casefinding for rehabilitation counselors serving deaf persons is more complex. Frequently, states have assigned staff to serve hearing-impaired individuals and those with other communicative disorders. This prevents the counselor from giving complete attention to seeking and providing rehabilitation services to deaf clients. Outside of a residential or large day school, which may have a built-in caseload, the counselor's efforts may be much more perplexing. Acting as a field counselor, the counselor must become known to deaf people and those organizations that serve them. Periodic visits to clubs, hearing societies, schools, places of worship, Social Security field offices, traveler's aid societies, and employers known to hire deaf individuals help establish an awareness of the counselor's mission.

The easily identified deaf persons are those who have been in residential or day school programs. Unfortunately, deaf people are still frequently misdiagnosed and placed inappropriately into facilities such as nursing homes or institutions for mentally ill or mentally retarded persons. Some parents of deaf children have sheltered them from society so they may not be known in the community until they have become young adults. In other instances, deaf youth have been misplaced in school and are not correctly identified as potential clients for vocational rehabilitation services.

Those deaf individuals outside the normal counselor contact points require a more vigorous outreach effort. Frequently these deaf individuals have minimal language skills and little sophistication in dealing with public agencies. Their referral to a vocational rehabilitation agency is most likely dependent on some informed third party, who may not identify the individual as being deaf, but rather as having communication or mental problems.

Another group of deaf individuals who have not been part of the deaf culture are those who lost their hearing later in life. Most often they are faced with social, communication, and emotional anguish over their hearing loss, and are treated as hard-of-hearing individuals.

Many counselors serve a combined caseload of various communicative disorders. For those counselors who are not highly skilled and comfortable with manual communication skills, working with hearing individuals may appear more productive and less frustrating than working with deaf individuals. Lack of regular contact with deaf individuals will lessen the counselors' effectiveness, and their communication skills and knowledge of deafness and the deaf community will not grow.

Statistical Information and Analysis The collection and analysis of the state's handicapped population and studies to determine the manner in which each group of disabled persons is served is a part of the state agency's responsibility. These studies can lead to decisions about underserved populations of disabled people. Frequently, the largest percentage of referrals to state vocational rehabilitation agencies are from public-education and other public institutions. Self-referral continues to be a major referral source for state agencies.

Public Information The state vocational rehabilitation agency often has a public information program to publicize the programs it offers to handicapped individuals. Brochures, films, television and radio announcements, and publications are generally available explaining the vocational rehabilitation program and where to seek additional information and services. State staff are generally available to make presentations to civic organizations and other interested groups. These mechanisms have generally been effective in reaching many handicapped persons. However, deaf persons frequently are not reached by these programs.

Henry C. Warner

COUNSELING

There are no accurate figures available that would indicate how many counselors in the United States have been trained specifically to assist deaf children, adolescents, and adults. Yet the deaf world has progressed from the survey of the 1960s that showed rehabilitation counselors assigned to deaf people had very little if any formal training in deafness. Other research showed that through the early 1970s less than half of all schools for deaf children in the United States had guidance counselors on staff to assist students, and only a small percentage of these counselors had satisfactory training in counseling and deafness. Today, a general sense of optimism prevails among rehabilitation and education experts that more qualified counselors are in contact with deaf people than in any time in the past.

There is reason to be concerned about counseling services, especially in the process of providing appropriate rehabilitation service to deaf people. Counseling is a tool of the rehabilitation trade that has been important since rehabilitation counselors began differentiating themselves from other helping roles. Rehabilitation counselors agree that they are experts in "counseling" rehabilitation clients, yet most disagree about what counseling is.

Theories For all the disagreements, there are similarities to be found among all proponents of differing counseling theories. First, all theorists agree that counseling is a process involving a unique interpersonal relationship between an expert in human relations (counselor) and a client or clients. Second, the process of counseling is highly dependent upon clear, open, and concise communication between the expert and client. Third, the ultimate goal of the process is to alter in some way the client's present pattern of behavior. Beyond these three assumptions, volumes have been written arguing the merits of different theoretical approaches, exploring detailed steps that should occur in the process, and substantiating success or failures in counseling outcomes.

Counseling as a unique process of rehabilitating deaf clients was not given serious attention until the 1970s, when increased federal support of training, research, and demonstration programs, as well as improved social acceptance of culturally deviant groups, provided a social environment where quality rehabilitation services were given greater attention. This resulted in a thorough examination of rehabilitation practices used with deaf people, specifically the role of counseling in the rehabilitation process. During that decade questions arose about professional skills necessary to counsel deaf clients and about the applicability of certain theoretical approaches when counseling deaf people.

Issues There have been a number of spokespersons who have helped improve counseling services for deaf people. For example, Larry Stewart and Allen Sussman, both deaf psychologists, gave importance and credibility to this specialty. Psychologists, rehabilitation workers, and psychiatrists, represented by people such as McCay Vernon, Norman Tully, Jerome Schein, Douglas Watson, Robert Sanderson, John Rainer, and Kenneth Altshuler, investigated critical questions that clarified the uniqueness of the field.

Differing opinions about the nature of counseling deaf people include the beliefs that: (1) counseling consists primarily of attempting to effect a better functioning relationship between deaf clients and their environment; (2) one of the goals of counseling should be deaf clients' better understanding of their attitudes towards hearing persons; (3) the goal is to help deaf clients better understand themselves; (4) counselors should help deaf clients learn to control impulsiveness as well as to improve social relationships and raise low self-images; (5) the counselor should aim at developing what types of employment are best suited for the deaf client; (6) the unique aspect in counseling deaf people is in helping them make appropriate decisions independently; and (7) counselors should take a more aggressive, active role with deaf clients, give greater attention to changing their social and physical environments, and devote a greater proportion of time to preventive rather than remedial programming.

Counseling with Deaf People, the first major publication devoted entirely to this specialty, appeared in 1971. It considers the counseling of deaf people to be a multidimensional process involving a unique relationship between the client's background resulting from his or her disability and the counselor's attitudes and feelings toward someone who is culturally and physically different.

The primary barrier to providing effective counseling services to deaf people is communication. Effective communication is contingent upon the client's verbal and nonverbal expressive ability, as well as the counselor's ability to communicate with the client in the client's native and natural language. Most of the burden of communication falls on the counselor, who must become proficient in American Sign Langauge or its variations in order to interact effectively with a large number of deaf clients. *See* Sign languages: American.

A second major issue in counseling deaf people is one of attitude—the attitude of the counselor toward disabled people in general and deaf people in particular, and the attitude of the deaf client toward hearing people and deaf people. Genuine concern for and acceptance of clients are, in part, built upon a counselor's attitudes toward people in society. Likewise, openness to change on the part of the client via interaction between client and counselor is highly dependent upon a client's past and present attitudes toward significant others who may be symbolically represented by the counselor.

The third issue that a counselor for deaf people faces is the need to have a thorough understanding of the culture of deaf people, of the special circumstances experienced by deaf people living in the hearing world, as well as in a deaf world. These dual cultural experiences affect the counseling relationship, the presenting problem, and the plan for the resolution of the problem.

The fourth issue of importance to the counseling of deaf clients is an awareness and understanding on the part of the counselor of the conceptual limitations and experiential deprivation resulting from the disability of deafness. This issue is deeper than a mere difference in communication systems. The counselor must have a true sense of the possible difference in the thought processes of the deaf person, which result from a lack of auditory stimulation. This should be remembered especially as a counselor attempts to understand clients' analyses of their current problems and the logistical solutions to these problems.

The fifth issue that a counselor must be aware of is the situational barriers that deaf people encounter in a hearing world. Frequently, deaf clients bring to counseling very real situational problems that unknowledgeable counselors may view as delusions. Solutions to problems must take into account the reality of discriminatory practices that exist in society and that may be encountered by deaf persons as they attempt to change their lives.

The sixth issue that counselors must be concerned about is the deaf individual's privacy and confidentiality. The subculture of deaf people is so closed and small that professional and social roles are often intertwined. Deaf people worry about rumor and innuendo that can often cross state boundaries in a matter of hours. They have realistic fears of opening themselves up to ridicule and misunderstanding if information is loosely shared or unintentionally made public.

Lastly, counselors with deaf people must often be information givers and referral agents. The absence of contact with other helping professionals means that deaf persons often seek advice or information from rehabilitation counselors on subjects not necessarily related to counseling issues. A counselor must know when to provide direct information, when to assist clients in seeking answers to questions independently, and when to make referrals to other help providers.

The applicability of various theoretical counseling approaches used with deaf people has received a great deal of attention, yet very little scientific research. Most counseling approaches have been used with deaf clients and in a wide variety of educational and rehabilitation settings. These approaches include behavior modification, behavioral counseling, transactional analysis, reality therapy, psychodrama, play therapy, rational-emotive psychotherapy, Adlerian therapy, client-centered therapy, biofeedback therapy, gestalt therapy, and psychoanalysis, as well as eclectic approaches. Some experts argue that no specific counseling approach should be discarded for use with a deaf person on the basis of an individual's deafness alone. Some counselors believe that deaf people are unable to benefit from insight-oriented counseling approaches because of the conceptual limitations imposed by deafness; others believe insight can be achieved with deaf persons when they are assisted by a competent counselor knowledgeable in deafness, fluent in American Sign Language, and experienced with deaf people. See PSYCHOLOGY: Psychotherapy.

Training Training of counselors who will work with deaf people requires time, special university faculty, and access to deaf people as clients. A number of universities began in the 1970s to offer graduate training programs in deafness counseling that could meet these requirements—for example, the University of Arizona, University of Arkansas, Gallaudet College, California State University at Northridge, New York University, and Western Oregon State College. Students attending these training programs receive formal courses in manual communication, psychological and social aspects of deafness, audiology, legislation related to deafness, and practicum with deaf people, in addition to traditional counselor education courses.

In 1972 Gallaudet College, through its graduate school, initiated a master's-level training program in school counseling with deaf children. Previous to this, the sole focus of training in counseling services for deaf people was on the deaf adult in traditional rehabilitation or mental health agencies. Schools for deaf children were sorely deficient in providing appropriate counseling services to children of school-age range. Individuals who occupied positions as guidance counselors felt unprepared to handle the problems they faced and requested more specific counselor training. The master's program is the only training program in the world that focuses on the preservice preparation of counselors who will work in elementary, secondary, and postsecondary educational institutions that serve deaf children and adolescents.

In the future, counseling with deaf people will deal with such issues as the use and influence of interpreters in counseling sessions, the appropriateness of group counseling techniques for specific problems, the counseling of deaf people with multiple disabilities, and the need for the specialty areas of parental, marriage, and gerontological counseling for deaf people. The future appears bright as more counselors are better trained to work with the special needs of deaf people, and as more knowledge is uncovered to assure that the best possible counseling approaches are used when working with a wide variety of deaf clientele.

Bibliography
Curtis, M. A.: "Counseling in Schools for the Deaf," *American Annals of the Deaf*, 121(4):386–388, 1976.
Scott, W. D.: "Counseling with Deaf Persons: An Overview of Literature Dealing with Definitions, Situations, and Types of Approaches Used," *Journal of Rehabilitation of the Deaf*, 11(4):16–22, 1978.
Sussman, A. E., and L. G. Stewart (eds.): *Counseling with Deaf People*, Deafness Research and Training Center, New York University, New York, 1971.
Tully, N. L.: "Role Concepts and Functions of Rehabilitation Counselors with the Deaf," unpublished doctoral dissertation, University of Arizona, 1970.
Zieziula, F. R.: "An Alternative Approach in Service to Deaf Individuals: Community Counseling," *Journal of Rehabilitation of the Deaf*, 14(1):1–5, 1980.

Frank R. Zieziula

DIAGNOSIS

Confirmation of a client's hearing impairment and a detailed report of its nature is required by federal regulations. In addition, a thorough medical examination is necessary to determine if the client has other physical limitations that may impede rehabilitation and should therefore be included in the individual written rehabilitation program (IWRP). This step in the rehabilitation process sometimes annoys prelingually deaf individuals, who have had their ears probed again and again over the years. Since they regard their condition as incurable, the otological and audiological examinations may seem a waste of time. However, it is more than a bureaucratic interruption of the deaf individual's efforts to obtain assistance. The possibilities remain that the person's hearing may change, and the condition might be alterable by recently developed techniques. Records from school hearing tests are often out of date and sometimes too vague to be accepted in place of the current information obtained by audiologists and otologists selected by the rehabilitation agency.

Examination Applicants for vocational rehabilitation must have a physical examination to determine if they are eligible, by virtue of the nature and extent of their disability, to receive services from the federal-state program. For those whose presenting complaint is one of hearing impairment, a careful audiological-otological examination is essential.

Audiometry. The diagnosis of the hearing impairment must establish its extent and, if possible, its etiology. The extent of hearing impairment is typically expressed as the average thresholds for pure tones at 500, 1000, and 2000 Hz in the client's better ear, that is, the better-ear average (BEA). For rehabilitation purposes, however, this summary term is inadequate. The BEA does not direct the fitting of a hearing aid; it does not contribute to an understanding of etiology; and, most critically, it does not show how the client uses any remnant hearing. Whether a client can hear and understand speech cannot be determined solely from the BEA. Some individuals with BEAs of 90 dB are able to conduct conversations with little or no visual support, provided they have well-fitted hearing aids. Others with the same hearing levels for speech derive little or no assistance from hearing aids. The reasons are complex: the BEA does not differentiate the slope of the loss, nor does it reflect other aspects of pathology such as the amount of middle-ear involvement or the possibility of retrocochlear damage. *See* AUDIOMETRY: Pure-Tone Audiogram.

Speech Audiometry. At least two measures of ability to understand speech are valuable in rehabilitation planning, speech-reception threshold (SRT) and speech-discrimination scores (SD score or discrimination score). The SRT is the threshold at which the hearing-impaired individual can repeat half of the series of spondees (equally stressed two-syllable words) that are presented at progressively louder intervals through earphones. The discrimination score is the percent of words that the patient can repeat when presented at levels 30 or 40 dB above the SRT. *See* AUDIOMETRY: Speech Discrimination, Speech Sensitivity.

Site of Lesion. Determining the locus of the impairment is also essential. Audiologists classify hearing impairments according to the site of the lesion. If the cause of the hearing impairment is located anywhere from the pinna through the middle ear up to, but not including, the inner ear, it disrupts the transmission of sound to the hearing end organ, the cochlea. Such impairments are called conductive impairments, and most can be treated surgically or medically, leading to partial or total restoration of hearing. Damage to the cochlea or elsewhere along the auditory nerve is referred to as sensorineural impairment. Damage to the auditory cortex is classified as central impairment. Combinations of conductive and sensorineural impairments are referred to as mixed. The designations conductive, sensorineural, central, or mixed have implications for rehabilitation, and audiologists now have a sophisticated set of diagnostic tests that enable them to determine the likely site of the hearing impairment. *See* EAR: Anatomy.

Unilateral vs. Bilateral Hearing Impairments. The use of the BEA betrays a widely held conviction that unilateral hearing impairments are of little consequence. The notion is prevalent that if one ear functions normally, the loss of hearing in the other will only be disabling for purposes of sound localization. It will otherwise be an inconvenience, since difficulty can occur when a noisy source imposes on the unaffected ear, and a threat, since the loss of the one ear makes the individual's overall hearing more vulnerable. However, evidence now suggests that the individual with a unilateral hearing impairment does suffer an overall loss of auditory functioning that is not indicated by the normal BEA. The rehabilitation counselor needs to be alert to the hearing problems that unilaterally hearing-impaired clients face in their daily activities.

Etiology. The hearing specialist's determination of the etiology of the client's hearing impairment can be helpful in rehabilitation planning. Many hearing impairments are associated with other disabilities, which can help indicate the likely course of the disability, as well as point to additional problems that must be considered in rehabilitation. For example, a client with Ménière's syndrome (intermittent hearing impairment and vertigo) may be far more disabled than a client with a larger chronic hearing loss, because Ménière's syndrome, when active, prevents the individual from performing almost any sustained work. Or, a youth whose prelingual deafness is diagnosed as part of Usher's syndrome suffers from a progressive loss of vision that will conclude in blindness in early adulthood. Determining the etiology of the hearing impairment can also provide clues to the age at onset if it has not been determined by other information. It is important to decide whether any language delay has resulted from an early hearing loss or might be evidence of mental retardation.

Other Hearing Data. The audiologist will also determine the ability of the individual to tolerate loud sounds. This information will be helpful in fitting a hearing aid, if one is necessary. Also, if there is some question about whether the prospective client has the claimed hearing impairment, the audiologist has tests that can detect deception. In addition to the battery of electrophysiological tests, the hearing specialist must also take a careful history of the client. A preliminary case history may be difficult or impossible to obtain directly from the client, in which case reliance must be placed on examining earlier records and on informants, such as the client's parents, spouse, or other relatives. Combining the results of audiometry, tympanometry, and other hearing tests with the historical information, and often with other information about the individual's physical condition, makes diagnosis somewhat subjective. Counseling will be enhanced if the rehabilitation counselor conveys the value of these procedures to a client who regards them as mere delays in getting services from the agency. Clarifying that this step is not only mandated but also useful can replace hostility toward the agency with goodwill. *See* AUDIOMETRY.

Visual Examination. Deaf rehabilitation clients are also required to undergo a thorough visual assessment. Prelingually deaf children have a higher rate of visual difficulties than children in the general population. The notion that deaf people can see better and that blind people can hear better has no empirical foundation.

For deaf people, vision is the principal means by which to obtain information. Defects in the visual system that would be minor for hearing persons may be serious for deaf people. A regulation of the Rehabilitation Service Administration specifies that deaf clients must have a visual evaluation from a physician skilled in eye diseases or from an optometrist. Obtaining this evaluation need not delay the client's progress through the rehabilitation process, since eligibility depends upon establishing the hearing impairment, not the visual impairment. The client's eligibility determination can go forward, with the information on vision only becoming critical during the evaluation stage and when the individual written rehabilitation program is being prepared.

Examiners Finding personnel to provide accurate diagnostic information is a problem that many state rehabilitation agencies face. Most agencies contract for the highly specialized services that deaf clients need. Aside from needing experienced, well-educated personnel to conduct the examinations and interpret the results, a thorough hearing evaluation requires a sizeable investment in equipment, with costs that cannot be justified by the typical general rehabilitation agency that serves only an occasional deaf client. Identifying qualified personnel is made especially difficult by the problems faced when examining a deaf individual. Few diagnosticians are fluent in manual communication; while they can make use of an interpreter, some find this time-consuming and awkward. Locating diagnosticians who have had experience dealing with the kinds of pathology that many deaf clients present is an even greater problem. Some conditions that are obvious to those who have had extensive experience with

deaf persons might be missed by less experienced diagnosticians. Obtaining the cooperation of specialists is not easy in states with outdated fee schedules that put practitioners in the position of subsidizing the state when examining their rehabilitation clients.

Jerome D. Schein

EDUCATION AND TRAINING

Education and training for rehabilitation of deaf individuals has undergone dramatic change since the mid-1960s. Beginning in the late 1950s, there was unprecedented activity in the rehabilitation of deaf individuals. A landmark study in the 1960s was the "Occupational Status of the Young Deaf Adults of New England and the Need and Demand for a Regional Technical Vocational Training Center." This study was conducted to determine the occupational status of young deaf adults in New England and to determine their need and demand for a regional vocational training center. The study was replicated several years later in the southwestern states. Organizers at a national workshop in 1964 concluded that a combination of one national vocational-technical school along with perhaps four regional vocational schools attracted the support of the greatest number of workshop participants. Organizations such as the Conference of Executives of American Schools for the Deaf, the Alexander Graham Bell Association, and the Council for Exceptional Children were among the early leaders to support improved vocational and occupational opportunities for deaf people. *See* ALEXANDER GRAHAM BELL ASSOCIATION FOR THE DEAF; CONFERENCE OF EDUCATIONAL ADMINISTRATORS SERVING THE DEAF.

The legislative history developed rapidly, and on June 8, 1965, President Lyndon B. Johnson signed into law the National Technical Institute for the Deaf Act (Public Law 89–36). The creation of the National Technical Institute satisfied one part of the concerns expressed by leadership in the field of deafness. The second main concern expressed in the 1960s was for the establishment of regional programs. This resulted in the establishment of three regional, federally funded model postsecondary programs that were located in two-year postsecondary institutions for students with normal hearing, and that were under joint sponsorship of the Bureau of Education for the Handicapped and the Rehabilitation Services Administration. Requests for proposals for five-year research and demonstration programs were issued in the late 1960s, with program awards going to Delgado College (New Orleans), Seattle Community College, and the St. Paul Technical-Vocational Institute. The research component was initially housed at the University of

Pittsburgh, and later at the University of Minnesota. *See* EDUCATIONAL PROGRAMS: Community Colleges.

Legislation In 1973–1974 a program of legislative action was pursued that moved the regional postsecondary education programs from a grant basis to a legislated basis with the passage of Section 625 of the Education of the Handicapped Act. During 1975 California State University at Northridge replaced Delgado College as a federally funded program, with Delgado College regaining federally funded status in 1976. The University of Tennessee replaced Delgado College in 1983 as one of the postsecondary education programs for deaf students. *See* CALIFORNIA STATE UNIVERSITY, NORTHRIDGE; EDUCATION OF THE HANDICAPPED ACT.

In the span from 1965 until 1969, postsecondary education opportunities for deaf people changed dramatically, moving from the historical position of Gallaudet College standing alone for 100 years as the only postsecondary program for deaf people, to the point where deaf people had two national and three regional federally funded postsecondary programs.

Other kinds of legislative actions occurred in the late 1960s and in the 1970s which in combination with the federally funded programs profoundly affected the lives of deaf people. The first was the passage of the Vocational Education Amendments of 1968, which mandated that 10 percent of vocational education funds be set aside for handicapped persons. In 1973 the Vocational Rehabilitation Act provided meaningful affirmative action plans through Sections 501, 503, and 504 of its Title V. The Education for All Handicapped Children Act of 1975 was further landmark legislation. These three pieces of federal legislation each have their state counterparts and have been amended regularly.

Major effects of the legislation of the 1960s and the early 1970s was to alter the rehabilitation service delivery patterns for deaf persons, in education, job training, and job placement. Services historically performed in rehabilitation facilities in the 1960s and early 1970s are now often performed in education environments.

A hallmark of the 1960s was rehabilitation center programs developed and maintained on federal grant funds and oriented toward work evaluation and work adjustment training with minimum emphasis on vocational or technical training. Successful programs were established in Hot Springs, Arkansas, St. Louis, Missouri, and Boston, Massachusetts, but all were terminated with the expiration of federal funding.

In the late 1960s, the National Technical Institute for the Deaf (NTID) and the regional programs at Delgado College, Seattle Community College, and the St. Paul Technical-Vocational Institute began to enroll students and demonstrated that deaf students could succeed in institutions that historically had served only hearing students. Additional postsecondary institutions started to establish their own programs for deaf students, leaning heavily on the expertise of the federally funded programs. Primary sources of their funding were vocational education funds and vocational rehabilitation funds.

The total number of postsecondary education programs grew from 1 program at Gallaudet College in 1965 to over 100 programs in the 1980s. Basic information about 108 programs can be found in the fifth edition of *College and Career Programs for Deaf Students.* This publication reports that there were 4838 deaf students enrolled in postsecondary education programs in the fall of 1982, with 2361 in federally funded programs and 2477 in locally supported programs. Eight of the programs serve over 100 students each, 8 serve between 50 and 100 each, 12 serve between 25 and 50 each, and 80 serve less than 25 each.

Program Models These 108 programs can be cast into four basic models: (1) Gallaudet College, a self-contained model; (2) the National Technical Institute for the Deaf, a combined model featuring components of the self-contained model and the support-service model (in the host institute of the Rochester Institute of Technology); (3) a support service model comprising preparatory programs, counseling, interpreting, notetaking, tutoring, speech and hearing services, supervised housing, and inservice training programs (the federally funded postsecondary education programs maintain this model); (4) selective support-service models which provide some, but not all, of the basic support services outlined in (3).

Approximately half of all deaf individuals pursuing postsecondary education will choose option 1 or 2, and half will choose option 3 or 4. Attendance at Gallaudet College and the National Technical Institute for the Deaf is dependent upon successful completion of preadmissions testing. The majority of the programs that comprise options 3 and 4 have some form of open-admission policy. Open admission almost always applies to general courses of study, while admission to specific courses of study usually requires minimum performance standards.

A continuing concern for rehabilitation personnel is the question of referral to in-state versus out-of-state training programs, which has also been addressed by the Council of State Administrators of Vocational Rehabilitation. Its position, endorsed by the Commissioner of Rehabilitation Services in 1983, is that vocational rehabilitation counselors are uniquely qualified to orient clients to available postsecondary programs and to assist them in making the best possible choice. As with hearing students, great care should be taken in the selection of the proper and most appropriate postsecondary education facility. A survey conducted several years ago among graduates of the St. Paul Technical-Vocational Institute program for deaf students revealed that deaf students selected a postsecondary program for three major reasons: (1) availability of high-quality special support services, (2) ability to get short-term, specific training which leads to skilled jobs, and (3) recommendations.

The appropriate matching of the student with the institution is fundamental to the rehabilitation process. The selection of the institution should include reasonable assurances that major areas of study offering the student opportunity for success are available. Once these assurances have been received, careful attention should be given to the needs of the student in terms of support services. Each component of the available support services should be carefully examined to determine which services a student will need. Not all students will need all services all of the time, but the majority will need all of the services some of the time.

A minimum support-service model comprises preparatory programs, counseling, interpreting, notetaking, tutoring, speech and hearing services, supervised housing, and in-service training programs. Additional components of a support-service program will vary depending upon a variety of factors, including the make-up of the host institution, funding availability, and other local geographical factors. At some schools additional programs are available for deaf students, such as consortiums with other postsecondary institutions, continuing education for deaf adults, outreach and dissemination programs, and recreation and leisure activities. Some postsecondary programs for deaf students maintain interpreter training programs which can enrich the educational program for deaf students.

Success Factors There are several concepts that determine the success of deaf students in postsecondary institutions that historically have served only hearing people. One of these concepts is known as critical mass and has evolved from experiences at the St. Paul Technical-Vocational Institute. Critical mass is defined as a minimum number of students to form a cohesive peer group that permits individual differences to prevail in developing adequate interpersonal relationships within the peer group. The development and confidence of self in the peer group yields confidence for individual members of the peer group to compete adequately in the larger academic and social environment (the hearing environment). The precise minimum number of like students to form a critical mass will vary from program to program, but the number should be large enough to form a meaningful social group.

Another concept often necessary for successful integration of deaf students is the hearing norm. Postsecondary institutions present a community image that comprises a minimum set of performance expectations for all graduates. For example, carpenters are expected to know carpentry, engineers to know engineering, and history majors to know areas of history. The community at large views these minimum performance expectations first, and deafness second; the same is true in training institutions. Regular instructors have minimum performance standards that must be met, which are based on hearing norms. In other words, the majority rules, and in essentially all integrated classes there will be more hearing students than deaf students. The acceptable norm of performance in the classroom, therefore, is based on the hearing-norm majority.

The severity of the impact of early profound deafness has not changed appreciably over time; such deafness continues to affect language development, the communication process, and the total development of the person. What is changing is the educational background of students. Until the early 1970s, approximately 80 percent of deaf youths were educated in residential schools, with the remaining students receiving their education in a variety of other specialized facilities. A total reversal of the educational process has taken place, with the majority of youths now receiving their education in mainstreamed environments. Several implications for rehabilitation and postsecondary education personnel are that the deaf culture is changing: there will be an emerging bimodal population with more high-achieving students, more low-achieving students, and fewer midrange students; communication styles will vary widely; and the range of support services required will be extended beyond services presently available.

Because deafness continues to influence the educational process, adjustments and modifications need to be continually made by the support-service staff. These accommodations can be described through the "Four C's": (1) Correction—The deaf student in the hearing educational environment is constantly correcting behaviors and acquiring new skills. The host institution is simultaneously adjusting to the deaf student. (2) Circumvention—The deaf student learns to survive in the new environment, avoiding painful situations where possible. The institution may modify or substitute course requirements to better permit success for the deaf student. (3) Compensation—The deaf student builds strengths and assets in social and educational coping skills. The host institution compensates or accommodates by the provision of support services to assist the deaf student in competing. (4) Crisis— At least one crisis will probably occur almost daily. The deaf student matriculates in a hearing environment, gains independence, manages budgets, pays rent and is involved in all aspects of independent living skills. Crises that occur should be faced and made an integral part of the overall learning process.

Widespread postsecondary educational opportunities for deaf individuals have enhanced the relationship between vocational rehabilitation and postsecondary education. The relationship is unique, with many shared and common goals. One of the primary goals is training, with employment the ultimate goal. Both vocational rehabilitation and postsecondary education provide counseling as a core service, and both are concerned that individuals function at their best physical and mental capacity. Vocational rehabilitation is a primary supplier of services for clients and postsecondary education is a direct provider.

JOB PLACEMENT

Follow-up is often an integral part of the job placement process, which can be complex because of the large numbers of variables involved, such as ability to work, physical capacity, educational levels, and employment opportunities. Essentially all deaf persons are eligible for vocational rehabilitation services. Becoming a client of vocational rehabilitation is a necessary first step for all persons with hearing loss. The provision of vocational rehabilitation services has become more complex, but employment remains the goal.

Today's job market is changing and competitive. Persons involved in the job placement process need to be knowledgeable about local employment conditions. In numerous communities the local employment news includes large numbers of job seekers, plant closings, displaced workers, retraining programs, and rapidly changing needs of employers. Networking has emerged as a key technique for all persons seeking employment, including deaf people. Networking can be broadly defined as multiple components banding together to reach a common goal. A typical networking effort might include the client as the central figure, together with representatives from vocational rehabilitation, postsecondary education, state employment services, parents, and projects with industry. Networking for jobs specifically contains elements of cooperation with a variety of agencies that are employment-oriented, counseling and guidance services, postsecondary institutions, job clubs for support and guidance during actual job seeking, assistance from interpreters as necessary, and job follow-up practices.

The federal government has consistently provided leadership in the rehabilitation process through a variety of initiatives, including emphasis on transition programs, which the Office for Special Education and Rehabilitative Services defines as building bridges from school to work and independent living. Within the transition framework there are different areas of emphasis: (1) making secondary school curricula more relevant to employment needs, (2) improvement of employment opportunities, including the provision of incentives to employers to hire handicapped individuals, (3) improvement of postsecondary opportunities, (4) improvement of existing services, such as vocational rehabilitation and programs available through the Job Training Partnership Act, and (5) supported employment. Supported employment, vestibule training, on-the-job training, and other forms of direct employer intervention, usually with monetary subsidies, are all creative ways of providing meaningful employment opportunities for deaf individuals.

History indicates that job placement, while viewed as the goal and a major component of the rehabilitation process, has rarely been given the full attention, in terms of time and effort, that is required for it to be effective. The rationale for this lack of effort tends to be the press of other rehabilitation duties, which force job placement to a less important position. In light of economic conditions, it does appear that more emphasis is being placed on highly systematized job placement approaches such as networking and individualized rehabilitation placement plans.

Marketing also has a place in the job placement process for deaf people. The National Center on Employment of the Deaf at the National Technical Institute for the Deaf is an exemplary model for marketing jobs for deaf and hearing-impaired individuals. In general field of disability, there are numerous other marketing plans that affect industry acceptance and employment of handicapped individuals, including deaf people. Among such efforts are the Job Accommodation Network (JAN), which is coordinated by the President's Committee on the Handicapped; Hireability, a Minnesota consortium program; and McJobs, a national cooperative effort jointly sponsored by Goodwill, Easter Seals, and McDonald's.

Vocational Evaluation Vocational evaluation has evolved as a professional discipline within the field of deafness. The findings from a qualified vocational evaluation assessment can often be a key factor in the overall success of a rehabilitation plan, and can provide important indicators of directions needed in the job training and job placement process. Select postsecondary institutions offer vocational evaluation services as an integral part of their support services.

Bibliography

Gallaudet College and National Technical Institute for the Deaf, *College and Career Programs for Deaf Students,* 5th ed. 1983.

Karchmer, Michael A.: "Demographics and Deaf Adolescents," Gallaudet Research Institute, Center for Assessment and Demographic Studies, Gallaudet College, 1983.

Lauritsen, Robert R.: "Five Factors for Post-Secondary Education for Deaf and Hard of Hearing Students," St. Paul Technical-Vocational Institute.

"The National Directory of Rehabilitation Facilities Offering Vocational Evaluation and Adjustment Training to Hearing Impaired Persons," Rehabilitation Research and Training Center, Deafness-Hearing Impairment, University of Arkansas, Little Rock, 1984.

Robert R. Lauritsen

EVALUATION

Deafness places few limitations on the vocations in which deaf people can succeed, as has been demonstrated over the years by the accomplishments of deaf people in almost every vocational field. Yet the vocational accomplishments of deaf people have not led the rehabilitation field to invest the efforts necessary to create or adapt evaluation procedures that would not penalize deaf clients and would more precisely indicate those areas in which they are most likely to perform well. Confronted by the gaps in evaluation procedures revealed over the years, rehabilitation specialists in deafness have begun to refine existing approaches to vocational evaluation and to develop global assessment procedures that correctly reveal the individual potentials of deaf clients. The model for vocational evaluation seems not to differ for deaf individuals or other clients; in practice, however, numerous accommodations to the deaf client are indicated by logic and experience.

Definition Vocational (work) evaluation uses actual or simulated industrial tasks as part of a procedure that incorporates cultural, economic, educational, medical, psychological, social, and vocational information to arrive at an individual client's optimal occupational placement. Also implied are some aspects of other definitions, such as prediction of the client's vocational behavior as one of the objectives of work evaluation. All extant definitions agree that the process includes the use of work samples (whether on the job or invented for assessment purposes) to provide some of the information, and that such information is only part of what enters into the evaluation. The additional information that the work-evaluation specialist utilizes ranges widely across the client's interests and abilities and takes into account the work settings in which the client can be expected to seek employment. All of the definitions agree on the objective of the process, which is to contribute to the client's vocational adjustment.

Client-Evaluator Relationship The professional who guides the client's evaluation should take the time to explain the process and to relate it to the client's individual written rehabilitation program (IWRP). The goals of vocational evaluation are to assess individuals' assets and limitations in order to optimize their ultimate vocational achievements. Clients should know that they will not "pass or fail" the evaluation and that they have a stake in determining as closely as possible their true abilities and liabilities. They should not be overanxious, but should be motivated to perform the various assessments as well as possible with reasonable effort. Providing initial counsel to the client on these points is an important precursor to effective evaluation.

In the course of evaluation, in which they may be interviewed and tested by several experts, clients will ideally be directed by a single evaluator, who should develop good rapport and excellent communication. The various examinations will be conducted by experts in areas such as psychology, occupational assessment, and education, but the one evaluator will be given the responsibility for combining all of the information and conveying it to the client's rehabilitation counselor in the most useful manner. For some agencies, the rehabilitation counselor directs the client's evaluation, purchasing the necessary services from vendors approved by the agency. The counseler, then, assumes the responsibility for combining the evaluation data and arriving at the recommendations used to develop the individual written rehabilitation program. Some agencies, however, assign evaluation to another facility as a package; that is, the outside facility does the complete vocational evaluation, after which the results are returned to the referring counselor. If the counselor at the rehabilitation agency is a specialist in deafness, he or she will be in the best position to reassure the client about any points in the evaluation that provoke anxiety and to explain those aspects which the client questions. In this way, the evaluation itself can be a positive growth experience for the deaf client.

Extended Evaluation Legislation now permits the agency to broaden the client base by offering extended evaluation to clients whose latent talents cannot be determined in the usually short evaluation time. The concept of extended evaluation takes into account the fact that some clients, particularly multiply impaired deaf clients, may require a much longer, more intensive evaluation to establish their vocational potential. Once the U.S. Congress had directed vocational rehabilitation agencies to give priority to the most severely disabled clients, this evaluation strategy became essential to bring into the rehabilitation process cases that earlier would have been declared infeasible, and unable to make a vocational adjustment. Granting rehabilitation agencies the flexibility to increase the length of evaluation time greatly facilitated the implementation of the congressional intent concerning priorities in selecting clients.

Initial Evaluation   The first phase in the evaluation will establish the client's level of communication, determine educational background, and consider all prior work experience. These analyses indicate the directions to be followed in the subsequent phases of the evaluation.

Communication Skills. Deaf clients vary widely in the modes of communication they can use and in their degree of fluency in each. A thorough communication assessment should include testing of English language skills in reading, writing, speaking, and listening. Testing of both receptive and expressive fluency in American Sign Language should also be made, although no standardized tests are available, so the examiner must make a subjective assessment. Other manual communication skills may also be tested, such as fingerspelling, any of the versions of Manual English, or cued speech. Whatever methods the client uses should be assessed, and the client's preferred method for daily communication should be used in further evaluations in accordance with federal regulations. If the evaluators are not familiar with the communication mode the client prefers, interpreters should be sought. The evaluators should bear in mind that the purpose of the communication assessment is to assist in determining the type of training which clients can best profit from and which will lead to eventual job placements. *See* Manually coded English; Mouth-hand systems: Cued Speech; Signs: Fingerspelling.

Educational Background. During the educational history interview, more than just a listing of educational settings that the client has attended should be explored. Because most states do not have a unified curriculum for deaf students, and because the achievement levels associated with grades in schools for deaf children are so different (usually much lower) than for those of children in ordinary schools, the grade levels and other measures of achievement cannot be interpreted without considerable information about the school. If the evaluator is not familiar with schools for deaf students, then knowledgeable authorities in the state education department should be consulted. Neither should home instruction be ignored, underestimated, or overestimated. Some deaf clients have spent so little time in school and derived so little benefit from it that their organized learning comes

essentially from instruction in their home, by parents, siblings, neighbors, or relatives. Deaf immigrants from the Caribbean, for example, sometimes arrive with little or no formal education, yet they may have good self-care skills and a well-developed work orientation that they have acquired in their homes. The lack of formal education will mean distinct limitations on the training programs in which they can participate, largely because of their lack of linguistic skills, but their attitudes toward employment and their basically good physical condition may make them job-ready with only a small amount of training directed at the specific workplace. The interview may uncover vocational instruction that the client has already had, which may provide excellent insight into what the client is likely to do in similar training situations.

Work History. In taking the work history, the interviewer should be alert to evidence of good or poor work habits that may be exhibited to nonindustrial employment, such as family employment. When the client has held a number of jobs before entering the evaluation, the interviewer should be prepared to contact former employers. At a minimum, the interview should establish the basic details of the prior employment (date hired, types of work performed and positions held, earnings, date terminated, reason for termination), the client's attitudes, and any information about any skills that may not be evident from the job titles.

Follow-up on Initial Information. Obtaining information from other sources is an important initial step in the evaluation, although replies to inquiries about the client's background may not be received until the evaluation is nearly completed. More is desired than simple verification of the client's statements. It must be determined how other significant people regard the client, whether valuable information about the client has not been provided, and if some of the client's factual statements are in dispute. Discrepancies between client's statements and those from other sources can be used in later interviews to assist the client in preparing for the work world. The evaluation should be seen as a learning experience for the client as well as a means of gathering data. Discovering that information they are giving to others may be challenged and can be independently verified can teach clients a valuable lesson before facing employment interviews, in which misinformation can result in loss of a potential job.

Psychological Evaluation   The psychometric evaluation provides data about the client's interests, attitudes, intelligence, educational achievements, and personality. Tests of specific functions, such as short-term memory, perceptuomotor skills, and manual dexterity, will also be included in the psychometric battery. All data may not be directly relevant to job placement for a particular client, but the data provide supplementary information that aids in the shaping of the individual written rehabilitation program, particularly when judging the extent to which the client may benefit from available vocational and personal-adjustment training possibilities. In addition to the psychometric interpretation, the psychologist may contribute clinical impressions that, in the case of deaf clients, may be as valid as the interpretations of test scores. Few psychometrics have been developed or norms established specifically for the deaf population, which is why experience with deaf clients is an asset to psychologists in rehabilitation. The experienced clinician makes use of observations of the client, which are essential for deriving meaning from the psychometrics and for formulating judgments that will be used to interpret the psychological evaluation.

Work Samples Structured tasks that are designed for their high face validity form a key part of the work evaluation. Work samples are selections of activities presented in a manner simulating the environment in which the actual work would be conducted. The instructions for the work, the effort required to complete the task, the criterion for evaluating the products, and the client-evaluator interaction are all intended to reproduce the situation that the client would face in an actual employment situation.

The wide variety of commercial work samples (Valpar, Singer, TOWER, and so forth) seldom have norms for deaf clients. The modification of the standardized instructions and tasks for use with deaf persons may affect the way the results should be interpreted. Work evaluators need to be especially attentive to research that will determine the extent to which modifications in the procedures affect the validity of the work samples. Where the size of the deaf caseload justifies it, the agency should consider developing its own work samples. The tasks would be those most relevant to placement of deaf individuals residing in the agency's geographical area. The instructions would be developed for administration to deaf persons and might involve a variety of approaches replicating the kinds of communication to be expected in the industrial settings to which deaf clients are typically sent by the agency. The interpretations would be based on the agency's own normative data and in accordance with the evidence it gathers for checking the reliabilities and validities of the procedures.

Trial Placements Another means for determining the client's work potential is on-the-job placement. Cooperative employers may accept clients with the understanding that they may be accepted for full-time employment if they prove ready, but that if they are found unacceptable, they can be replaced

without jeopardizing the company's unemployment insurance or harming the company in other ways. The rehabilitation counselor must remain in close contact with the employer. If the employee does not succeed in the placement, information should be gathered as to which of the client's characteristics need modification. Even if modification is successful, the client may not find the work satisfactory. This does not prove the placement was a failure; to the contrary, it will have given valuable data about the client's interests.

The federal government, one of the largest employers in the United States, makes specific provisions for the employment of disabled workers. Under a 700-hour appointment, disabled workers can demonstrate their ability to handle a particular workload, without the necessity for taking civil service examinations. This waiver is helpful to the placement of deaf clients who may be unable to pass the qualifying tests because their linguistic skills are inadequate, but who may be able to manage adequately the demands of the position.

Concluding the Evaluation No matter how technically adequate each element of the evaluation may have been, the final interpretation of the findings is more subjective than scientific. The culmination of the procedures is not the specification of a job, but rather the specification of job families that will satisfy the client's interests and aptitudes and that will provide enough opportunities for employment in the area in which the client will reside. The client must be maximally involved throughout the evaluation process to assure that he or she understands and is satisfied with the final recommendations.

Jerome D. Schein

INDIVIDUAL WRITTEN REHABILITATION PROGRAM

Following the determination of eligibility, the counselor and the client jointly develop a program of services to meet a vocational goal. The concept of a vocational rehabilitation plan was expressed in the literature and training of rehabilitation professionals many years before it became formalized as a legal requirement of the state plan within the Rehabilitation Act of 1973. This formal requirement of professional practice of rehabilitation counselors is known as the individual written rehabilitation program (IWRP).

Purpose The IWRP is a record of the case planning and management needed to establish an employment goal. It also assures that the views, needs, and desires of the client are considered. The initial IWRP is viewed as a starting point, and it is expected that changes may be made in the course of a client's rehabilitation. The IWRP also establishes the objectives, time frame for services to be provided, and the conditions to be met by both the client and the agency. When agreement between the client and counselor has been reached, one copy of the IWRP is given to the client and the other retained in the client's case record. In some states, the client and the vocational rehabilitation counselor sign the IWRP. The client, when appropriate, may be represented by a parent, guardian, or other representative to assure that the client's best interests are met. Deaf people have the right to clearly understand this process. They can insist that a manual or oral interpreter be present during discussions of the IWRP, and that the plan be written in language they can understand.

Extended Evaluation Although the primary purpose of the IWRP is to outline and implement a plan leading to an occupational goal, it is occasionally used to establish rehabilitation potential. When the counselor does not have sufficient information to determine whether there is a reasonable expectation of employability or that providing rehabilitation services will result in improving the handicapped person's chance of employment, a period of extended evaluation can be authorized. The extended-evaluation IWRP is formed in the same manner as a usual one except that its goal is to establish rehabilitation potential and its duration is limited to the time necessary to make that decision, which cannot exceed 18 months. Only those services necessary to complete a decision of eligibility for vocational rehabilitation are provided under an extended-evaluation IWRP.

Form State vocational rehabilitation agencies have developed their own preprint forms that conform to the legal requirements of federal and state laws and policies. The forms may be available in large print or braille for those individuals with visual problems.

Typically, the first pages of the IWRP explain the responsibilities of the counselor, the state agency, and the client. If the state agency applies an economic-needs test, it will likely be stated in the IWRP. While the IWRP and conditions are to be explained orally (and manually, if appropriate), a copy of the agreement is an important reference for later review if misunderstandings between client and agency occur.

It would be appropriate to note in the IWRP for some hearing-impaired persons an available telecommunications device for the deaf (TDD) number and under what conditions interpreter services will be provided. The IWRP developed jointly by the counselor and client also contains the results of the necessary diagnostic and evaluative studies that were needed to establish eligibility and rehabilitation potential.

Content The individual written rehabilitation program will contain:

1. The basis upon which eligibility for vocational rehabilitation was determined, or in the event that rehabilitation potential has not been decided, the need for extended evaluation to determine eligibility.

2. Statements describing the rights and responsibilities of the client and agency, ways of resolving disputes between the two, and conditions upon which the program will be provided. Examples of such conditions include: (a) use of client's resources (savings, transportation, insurance benefits), (b) application for assistance from other public agencies needed to fulfill the program (student financial aid, health care), (c) satisfactory progress in the program, and (d) availability of agency funds to support the program.

3. The establishment of long-range goals and supporting objectives needed to accomplish the program, including the time period proposed to achieve each objective and vocational goal. For example, the objective may be to complete satisfactorily a course of training in welding at a technical institute within 12 months, while the goal may be to achieve employment as a welder within 18 months.

4. Specific services to be provided to meet the objectives and vocational goal. These are to be listed along with the beginning and completion dates of each service. Included within the statement of services are those services to be arranged or provided by the client and those sought from other sources, such as education scholarships from private or public sources.

5. A statement of the handicapped individual's views on the program. The client's agreement to the jointly developed program and interest in achieving the vocational goal should also be in the IWRP. If appropriate, the views of the parent or guardian may also be included. The IWRP also offers the client an opportunity to express opinions about any portion of the program that is not completely satisfactory, such as location of training, costs of participation by the client, or any inadequacy of the services.

6. A description of the measures, timing, and manner in which the progress of the program is to be gauged. Some measures used include training progress reports, medical reports, and achievement of objectives or vocational goal.

7. A statement saying that services from the state's client-assistance program have been explained to the client and that notification has been given to the client as to contacts that may be used should unresolvable misunderstandings occur regarding any part of the IWRP.

8. While not a part of the initial IWRP, the closing of the client's case record. This requires that the client receive written notification of the action and the reasons behind the decision. If the individ-

ual's case is being closed because the potential for achieving the vocational goal no longer exists, the client is entitled to an annual review to determine if potential for vocational rehabilitation has improved.

Joint Review There is a requirement that the IWRP be reviewed jointly by the counselor and client at least annually. The time for the review needs to be in the IWRP. The results of the evaluation must be shared with the client. A review of the program is appropriate whenever major changes are being considered.

Closure When a case is closed as unsuccessful for any reason except ineligibility, the reasons must be documented in the case folder. Examples of this action would be if the agency has lost contact with the client or if the client has died or has moved and left no forwarding address.

Postemployment services are those necessary to maintain or secure other suitable employment after case closure. Postemployment services may be part of the planning of the initial IWRP or may become part of the amended IWRP at any time during the rehabilitation process. They may be provided even after the case record has been closed, so long as the case record remains known to the agency (case files are frequently destroyed after three years) and the client's disability has not substantially changed or become more complex. Postemployment services most frequently take the form of additional counseling, guidance, and job-placement services, and less frequently, as additional skill training or refresher courses.

Relation of IWRP to IEP When a handicapped individual is receiving services under the authority of the Education for All Handicapped Children's Act, the IWRP is to be coordinated with the individual education program (IEP). Under these circumstances, joint staffing of representatives of vocational rehabilitation and special-education and perhaps other agencies to coordinate the goal, objectives, scheduling, and provision of services is appropriate. Parents, guardians, and the deaf individual should also be involved, and legislation strongly encourages their participation.

Bibliography

Federal Register, Part XIX, U.S. Department of Education, 34 CFR Part 361, State Vocational Rehabilitation and Independent Living Rehabilitation Programs.

Program Regulation Guide, RSA-PRG-75-5, April 21, 1975, *Rehabilitation Services Manual*, Individual Written Rehabilitation Program, Chapter 1507.

Henry C. Warner

INTAKE

In rehabilitation terminology, intake means the management of referrals and applications for vocational rehabilitation services. State vocational rehabilitation agencies are required to establish and maintain written intake standards and procedures. These begin with a referral, which the *Rehabilitation Service Manual* defines as a person for whom the following information has been supplied: name and address, reported disability, age, sex, date of referral, and source of referral. Next, the individual seeking services becomes an applicant by signing an application and being assigned to a counselor. The counselor's role is to collect information necessary to determine the applicant's eligibility for services. Counselors may decide to develop extended evaluation programs if they cannot decide whether vocational rehabilitation services will benefit a particular applicant's employment opportunities.

State vocational rehabilitation agencies may vary in their intake procedures, depending on such factors as size and assignment of caseloads, geographic area to be covered, and special populations to be emphasized or served.

The person seeking vocational rehabilitation services generally will first contact a receptionist, secretary, or case assistant, who most often will set up an appointment to meet with a rehabilitation counselor if one is not then available. Some counselors are assigned to geographic areas rather than to one specific office and often travel to see clients. Counselors who serve a number of small communities may meet clients or persons interested in vocational rehabilitation at county health offices, state employment service offices, or almost anywhere of mutual convenience.

Intake has several specific purposes. One is to secure the information necessary to identify the person as a referral or to assist the individual in seeking a more appropriate resource for assistance. Another is to decide on the assignment of the referral to a particular rehabilitation counselor. Finally, data are collected and analyzed over a period of time to determine how clients are being referred to the agency. This information assists the agency in knowing how well it is extending services to the disabled population.

Initial Interview The first meeting of client and rehabilitation counselor is referred to as the initial interview. An application for vocational rehabilitation services is generally completed at that time. While each state vocational rehabilitation agency develops its own form, most seek similar information: a description of the client's disability, hospitalization, visits to physicians, medical insurance, residence, previous rehabilitation service, family members, family income, training and education, work history, vocational possibilities, prospects for employment, primary source of financial support, public assistance received, work status, Social Security Disability Insurance benefits, references, and an evaluation of the applicant's mobility.

This information will provide an overview of the

applicant's background, experience, and interests, and will establish a basis for deciding what other information will be needed to make a decision on eligibility for services. An initial step toward that decision is securing an appraisal of general health and, when indicated, specialty examinations, such as hearing and vision. These examinations are done to determine the loss or limitation of function caused by the disabling condition, to determine if other conditions are present that would prevent or reduce employment possibilities, and to provide recommendations for treatment when possible. Through these initial procedures a preliminary study is completed that leads to a decision on eligibility for vocational rehabilitation services.

The meeting with the rehabilitation counselor enables the applicant to learn how the program may assist him or her in becoming more employable, what services are available, what his or her rights are, and where additional assistance may be found. The sharing of information, interests, goals, problems, and desires is an important part of the development of a working relationship between the counselor and the applicant. From this developing relationship, the planning for the client's rehabilitation program is started. Good communication and understanding during the initial interview is basic to the program's success.

Implications for Vocational Rehabilitation Agencies   Contacting public agencies has often been a disappointing experience for many deaf individuals. The communication barriers are so severe for some deaf individuals that public agencies are not seen as helpful. Vocational rehabilitation agencies should assure that staff who have first contact with the public be prepared and oriented to greet and assist deaf individuals. If staff are not skilled both in communication with deaf and hearing-impaired persons and in the use of telecommunications devices, interpreters should be employed. Agencies also should provide periodic, systematic training to staff having responsibilities for greeting the public, to assure that a positive and helpful atmosphere is established. Staff assigned to work with deaf people should also be encouraged to be involved with organizations associated with persons having hearing impairments.

Implications for Deaf Clients   Deaf individuals who wish to apply for vocational rehabilitation services should call or write the vocational rehabilitation office for an appointment, notifying the agency if a qualified oral or manual interpreter is needed. There is no charge for interpreter services, and advance warning allows the agency time to make proper arrangements. If the deaf individual cannot understand the interpreter or counselor at the initial meeting, another meeting should be requested.

Individuals with minimum language skills may also wish to consider having someone act as a representative or guardian. Client assistance or advocates are often available from state-supported organizations to act in the applicant's interest.

Implications for Rehabilitation Counselors   The basic barrier faced by hearing-impaired and deaf individuals is communication and understanding. Determining the most effective means of communication is an important initial step in establishing a helpful relationship. Communicating in the manner or language that is most comfortable for the applicant should be one of the first considerations of the rehabilitation counselor. If an interpreter is needed for understanding, the counselor must assure that one is available. Environmental conditions should also be of concern, such as lighting to assure that facial expression and lips can be clearly seen, and an area that is comfortable and affords privacy for the free exchange of information.

Counselors may wish to observe or assist applicants in completing their applications. The completion of the application can often give an initial assessment of language skills and comprehension. It may also give insight into the kinds of services the individual will need to become employable.

Important aspects of the interview can be reinforced by handouts or a follow-up letter of explanation. These actions will vary, depending on the severity of the disability and on functional limitations. For example, printed or written material may not be readily understood by some deaf individuals, and one-to-one assistance may be needed by the counselor, interpreter, or case aide to assure that an examination or other supportive service by another agency is properly arranged. Giving the applicant a business card with the counselor's name, address, and telephone number or telecommunications device (TDD) number should be a routine procedure.

An individual or organization referring a client to a vocational rehabilitation agency should receive follow-up information describing the action planned by the agency. This procedure helps keep the communication channels open and reflects upon the counselor's and agency's desire to act in a businesslike manner. It also is an opportunity to reinforce appropriate referrals of handicapped persons to the agency.

Henry C. Warner

PHYSICAL RESTORATION

The state rehabilitation agencies are empowered to finance necessary restorative measures to improve a client's possibilities for employment. Such measures can include underwriting surgery, medical treatment, prosthetics, and therapeutic programs to assist the individual in recovering the lost function. The two approaches most relevant to deaf clients are surgery and hearing aids. Medical treatment for infectious problems of the auditory system may also be indicated for some clients.

Surgery Rarely, individuals are born without an opening into the middle ear, a condition known as congenital atresia. Such individuals usually suffer from other defects, such as an agenesis of the middle-ear bones (the ossicles), so reconstructive surgery involves more than creating an opening to the auditory canal. For example, building a substitute for the ossicular chain or restoring its function if it is not in proper working order may also be required. Other defects of the external auditory meatus may be due to tumors, which block the entrance to the middle ear and can easily be removed.

Middle Ear. Far more common than absent auricular openings, though still relatively infrequent, are conductive hearing impairments due to injury or to middle-ear disease that may be caused by chronic otitis media or otosclerosis. For example, the tympanum, the membrane that separates the outer ear from the middle ear, may be punctured, reducing its conductive efficiency. Surgery can close the opening. In addition, damage to the ossicles— the incus, malleus, and stapes—can be repaired in a number of ways. The stapes mobilization operation consists of freeing the stapes by jiggling it with a surgical probe when it has ankylosed and become immobile. However, that operation has almost entirely been replaced by the stapedectomy, in which the stapes is replaced with an artificial part made of one of several different materials, such as Teflon. The invention of the surgical microscope and the development of antiseptic conditions have made middle-ear surgery a relatively simple, successful procedure for restoring hearing that has been lost due to disruptions in sound conduction. *See* AUDITORY DISORDERS, REMEDIATION OF: Surgical Treatment.

Cochlear Implant. Formerly, damage to the inner ear, causing sensorineural hearing impairment, was untreatable. The profoundly hearing-impaired individual for whom hearing aids provide no benefit has been beyond assistance from modern technology or medical-surgical treatment. In November 1984 the United States Food and Drug Administration accepted the cochlear implant as safe for use with profoundly hearing-impaired adults and approved its continued experimental use with children for whom hearing aids have been unhelpful. The cochlear implant consists of one or more electrodes that are surgically implanted in the temporal bone so that contact is made with the cochlea. The implanted wires are then connected to an internal coil that makes contact through the skin with an external coil held in place magnetically behind the ear. The external coil connects to a transducer that converts auditory impulses from a microphone placed in the auditory meatus.

This system transmits mild electrical impulses to the auditory nerve which initially perceives the stimuli as a buzzing or other nonspecific sound. In time, some implanted individuals are able to make some discriminations with the device. Its principal early successes have been in improving lipreading scores and in putting the implanted individuals in auditory contact with their surroundings. Reliable speech discrimination has not as yet been achieved.

In the rehabilitation of deaf adults, the provision of cochlear implants by the government is questionable. The rehabilitation counselor must be able to demonstrate that the prosthesis will enhance the client's vocational potential. Such justification may be easier if evidence of the effectiveness of the implants grows. As technology improves, pressure can be expected to mount for a wider use of the cochlear implant in rehabilitation. Since the cost of the device and its operation is substantial, the agencies will be faced with serious budgetary problems if they have a sizable number of profoundly hearing-impaired clients.

Medical Treatment The most common medical problem involving the outer ear is impacted cerumen (earwax) which, if the tympanic membrane is completely obstructed by it, can result in raising the auditory threshold by 40 decibels (dB). Removal of the wax should be done by qualified medical personnel, as a careless procedure could result in a rupture of the tympanum. If the tympanum is breeched, serious infection could result from using water under pressure to remove the obstruction.

Infections that lead to the buildup of fluid in the middle ear (serous otitis media) are among the most prevalent causes of hearing impairment in children. If untreated or improperly treated, this condition can lead to cholesteatomas (squamous cysts) that may become life-threatening. Other serious consequences could also result. Treatment with antibiotics is indicated, and their early use is usually sufficient to eliminate or control the problem. A client found to be suffering from any of these conditions, whether identified as the primary or the secondary cause of application for rehabilitation, should be given treatment according to the regulations governing rehabilitation. The costs of such treatment are relatively low compared with the costs of unemployment.

Hearing Aids The rehabilitation counselor should authorize purchase of hearing aids whenever there is evidence that they will contribute to clients' occupational adjustment and to their capacity to meet the demands of daily living. In auditory rehabilitation, the hearing aid is a key prosthesis; anyone with an irreversible hearing impairment should be considered a candidate for one.

Definition and Operation. Technically, a hearing

aid is any device that amplifies sound or brings it more effectively to the ear. Hence, ear trumpets, acoustic fans, a hand cupped behind the ear are all aids to hearing. Today, however, hearing aids refer to electroacoustic devices for the selective amplification of sound. They consist of a microphone that converts sound into an electrical signal, an amplifier that increases the strength of the signal, and an earphone that converts the electrical energy back to acoustic energy. These battery-powered instruments are capable of greatly increasing the energy of any sound, but they are selective because uniform amplification of every sound in the environment would be counterproductive for most hearing-aid wearers.

The frequency response of the hearing aid refers to the range of frequencies that it does amplify. Frequencies that carry linguistic information—from approximately 250 to 2000 Hz—are usually amplified more than lower frequencies, since hearing impairments occur more often at the higher frequencies. The ability to amplify selectively makes the modern hearing aid a more potent instrument in correcting hearing impairments than any device that amplifies without regard to frequency. In addition, the electroacoustic hearing aid cuts off amplification when sounds reach amplitudes beyond the wearer's tolerance. The problem of overamplification would make it impossible to use the aid in noisy situations.

The electroacoustic aids also introduce some distortion in the sound delivered to the ear, giving a reproduction that deviates somewhat from the original signal. For persons with sensorineural hearing impairments, any degree of distortion can seriously lower the hearing aid's value.

Types. Hearing aids take a number of configurations: body-worn, postauricular, all-in-the-ear, and eyeglass types. Body-worn hearing aids have a microphone and power unit that is worn on the body and is connected by wire to the earpiece. Body-worn hearing aids were the most common design before miniaturization led to the other forms, and they have fallen out of fashion for several reasons: they are bulky, they cannot provide true binaural hearing, and they are subject to a great deal of noise due to clothing rubbing on the wire connecting receiver and earphone. Postauricular (behind-the-ear) aids overcome these disadvantages, though they introduce problems of auditory feedback and lower power. Newer designs have overcome these disadvantages, and the development of printed electrical circuits has led to the all-in-the-ear hearing aids. Aids can also be built into eyeglass frames. For some types of hearing impairment, an aid in each ear is advisable, which is possible with the latter three types of aids.

Fitting. To ensure that individuals receive maximum benefit from their hearing aids, they should be examined and fitted by specialists, such as otologists and audiologists. Hearing-aid dealers may not be wholly objective in determining the type of aid that is best for the client. Hearing aid fitting is not an exact science. The type of distortion that the aid introduces is not specified in the measurements, so it must be determined by trying the aid at several different settings in a variety of situations. Clients should be encouraged to try different aids and to select the one they prefer. Federal regulations now give them the right to return the aid and exchange it for one that provides better results. An aid that works well in a dealer's soundproofed environment may be unsatisfactory in the client's usual noisy work environment. The trial-and-error aspects of fitting can be best managed by a specialist.

Auditory Training. Weeks may be necessary to adapt to the new way in which the world sounds with a hearing aid. Optimal use of a hearing aid results from auditory training—learning to discriminate sounds and to combine the information given by the hearing aid with other information that enhances interpretation of sounds in the acoustic environment. The hearing aid is a highly complex electronic instrument, and clients should be given instruction in its use. They need to learn such things as how to make simple tests to determine if the aid is functioning properly, how to adjust the aid to give best reception, and how to replace worn-out batteries. Obtaining good auditory training for the deaf client who has been fitted with a hearing aid is a wise move for the rehabilitation counselor who wants to assure that restorative measures indicated for the client have been made. *See* HEARING AIDS.

Other Measures A hearing-ear dog may be purchased for the client if the rehabilitation counselor considers it important for vocational adjustment. These dogs are trained to alert their deaf owners to important environmental sounds, such as doorbell, telephone, and smoke-detector or alarm-bell sounding.

Another device that might warrant purchase by the rehabilitation agency for its deaf clients are alarm clocks that activate lights in the bedroom or a vibrator placed under the client's pillow. Clients may need the device to assure that they will awaken in time for work. The key criterion for such purchases is whether they will enhance the client's employability.

Client Consent The client has the right to refuse treatment such as surgery, medical treatment, or the wearing of a prosthesis without losing the eligibility for rehabilitation. All surgery has some risk, and the client may not believe the benefits outweigh the risks. To assure that the client is making a reasonable, informed decision to refuse a proposed treatment, the counselor should take sufficient time to explain in detail the procedures and to respond to the client's questions. If the counselor does not feel qualified to respond to technical questions, the aid of experts should be enlisted.

Jerome D. Schein

Personnel

Rehabilitation service for deaf persons has featured some important gains over the years due to the emergence of professionals specializing in the area of deafness. The presence of counselors and other rehabilitation staff skilled in communicating with deaf people has elevated the quality of service available in public and private agencies, and improved the effectiveness of rehabilitation programs. Moreover, deaf people have been encouraged to actively seek appropriate services for themselves.

The field of rehabilitation itself has gained from specialization in deafness. Specialization is usually a sign of growth within a profession, and in this case has been addressing the needs of a definitive group within the community of persons with disabilities. Progress in overcoming communication barriers for deaf persons, for example, has yielded benefits for other groups of disabled persons, who frequently also have communication difficulties.

REHABILITATION COUNSELOR FOR DEAF CLIENTS

Principal among these specialized rehabilitation professionals is the rehabilitation counselor for deaf clients (RCD). It is an occupational role with deep roots in the profession of rehabilitation counseling and in the legislative history of vocational rehabilitation. Most state vocational rehabilitation agencies and many private rehabilitation facilities now employ professional counselors with specialized skills and knowledge in deafness.

Overall progress in establishing RCD positions within private and public rehabilitation agencies is indeed not complete. In fact, the bureaucratic process which has responded to the demand for such counseling specialists has been a long and problematic one. Many deaf persons are still not able to obtain services from professional counselors capable of responding to their preferred mode of communicating. The National Census of the Deaf Population (published 1974) found that only half of the adult deaf persons involved in the study's sample of cases had sought assistance from vocational rehabilitation programs. One possible explanation for this response is that accessible programs and quality counseling were not as readily available to deaf persons as they were to persons with other disabilities.

Fortunately, the number of qualified RCDs finding employment in public and private agencies has been increasing steadily. A qualified RCD meets the minimum conditions for employment as a rehabilitation counselor, which generally include a graduate degree in rehabilitation counseling, or another type of advanced degree, plus relevant work experience. In addition, the qualified RCD possesses manual and oral communication skills to enable communication with most deaf clients, knowledge of deafness, and the ability to establish rapport with the deaf community. The talented RCD is one who can consistently apply these skills and knowledge to coordinate timely services, to develop appropriate vocational plans with deaf clients, and to assist deaf persons in achieving the kinds of employment and job satisfaction that they deserve.

The conditions of employment for RCDs vary from agency to agency, or from community to community. Sometimes, for instance, the RCD must engage in developing community services, which requires thoughtful planning, public relations, and service coordination with individuals who usually have had no experience with deafness. RCDs must be prepared to spend extra hours in accomplishing some basic service provisions. They are typically characterized by the ability to acquire and use a second language (since most are not native signers), by knowledge acquired frequently through personal experience, and by a special dedication to the field of deafness.

The presence of many qualified RCDs within the rehabilitation system is an outcome of several converging factors. Above all, however, it was the concerted effort of a select and dedicated group of individuals that produced results. Against the background of social changes affecting minorities in the United States in the 1960s and 1970s, deaf and hearing leaders within the deaf community applied the concepts of self-advocacy, consumer rights, and affirmative action toward the development of the RCD role.

Laws and regulations provided a basis for the emergence of RCD positions. The Rehabilitation Act of 1973 (Public Law 93-112) placed emphasis on services to persons with severe disabilities, and required federally supported programs and services to eliminate communication barriers and to make reasonable accommodations for persons with disabilities. The Rehabilitation Act Amendments of 1978 (Public Law 95-602) required the development of provisions relating to the establishment and maintenance of minimum standards to assure the availability of personnel trained to communicate in the client's native language or preferred mode.

The *Model State Plan*, a published set of guidelines for implementing the concepts of accessibility in terms of deafness rehabilitation, defined the role of RCD in the context of the vocational rehabilitation system. Conceived in the early 1970s and refined through several revised publications, the *Model State Plan* has been adopted in some form by all state rehabilitation agencies. The recommended function and qualifications for RCDs, as well as for the state coordinator for deafness (SCD) and other related positions, are presented as reference material for state officials planning personnel selection, assignments, and training. Perhaps no other document in this field has equaled the effect that the *Model State Plan* has had on the development of specialized positions in deafness rehabilitation and on the acceptance of these positions by public and private agencies.

The formation of a professional organization on deafness rehabilitation also has promoted the development of the RCD position. The American Deafness and Rehabilitation Association (ADARA), formerly known as the Professional Rehabilitation Workers with the Adult Deaf, has fostered professional identity and conduct within the ranks of RCDs. ADARA has conducted quality training conferences for RCDs and has provided a forum for research and innovation. *See* AMERICAN DEAFNESS AND REHABILITATION ASSOCIATION.

Finally, the gradual acceptance of manual forms of communication as legitimate modes of learning, teaching, and communicating, together with the growing recognition of American Sign Language as a separate language, has reinforced the need to staff agencies with professionals who possess manual communication skills and are able to communicate with most deaf people.

OTHER SPECIALISTS

Subspecialties within the position of RCD have arisen as a result of varying job demands and the complexity of serving deaf persons through social and rehabilitation programs. Two specialties have developed around counseling functions; three other specialties are outgrowths of the function of service coordinator and do not necessarily require professional counselor training.

Vocational Evaluator The RCD vocational evaluator combines expertise in the area of evaluation and assessment techniques with expertise in deafness rehabilitation. Like general vocational evaluators, the purpose of the RCD vocational evaluator is to match the evaluated skills, aptitudes, interests, and behavior of a client with an appropriate vocational goal. Utilizing standardized tests, simulated or real work situations, and counseling techniques, the evaluator observes, records, and analyzes the work readiness of a client. Recommendations on the client's future course of rehabilitation are made for the benefit of the client and for the rehabilitation counselor overseeing the client's case. The recommendations properly incorporate perti-

nent medical, educational, psychological, and social information known to and analyzed by the evaluator. At the essence of the evaluation process is communication between evaluator and client. The evaluator who can communicate fluently with the deaf client optimizes evaluation. Without the meaningful and timely exchange of information, the proper rapport, and the counseling sessions which make the results understandable, the vocational evaluation may amount to a mere exercise in test taking. Evaluators generally work within rehabilitation facilities offering specialized services for deaf persons. Through experience and training, these evaluators have acquired a unique understanding of how methods of vocational evaluation can be applied to deaf persons over a full range of linguistic skills and life experiences.

Placement Specialists RCD placement specialists concentrate on providing vocational counseling and placement services to deaf persons who are ready to begin employment. This particular subspecialty merges expertise in job placement with knowledge and skills in deafness rehabilitation. Knowledge of current labor market conditions, access to information on job vacancies, skill in developing relationships with employers, and expertise in matching client potential with job demands all characterize the placement specialist.

The RCD placement specialist possesses communication skills and an understanding of employment implications for deaf persons, and is able to convey some knowledge, information, and any necessary follow-up service to the employer to ensure a client's successful adjustment to the employment setting. Placement specialists work either in rehabilitation facilities ordinarily offering placement services to significant numbers of deaf clients or in state vocational rehabilitation agencies serving large populations of deaf persons.

Other notable subspecialties that are based on counseling functions include mental health specialists and deaf-blind specialists. These two specialties are not based on counseling roles within the rehabilitation process, but focus on the nature of the clients (particularly those with certain dual disabilities) and upon the separate systems in which these clients are served. Specialists working with these clients must acquire additional knowledge in the areas of psychiatric treatment or deaf-blindness.

State Coordinator in Deafness Among the subspecialties that are derived to some degree from the RCD role but that are based on the function of service coordination, the role of state coordinator in deafness (SCD) is most closely linked to the RCD. The state coordinator's primary purpose is to coordinate the planning and delivery of deafness rehabilitation services. The position is an administrative one within the hierarchy of a state vocational rehabilitation agency, and is typically in an advisory rather than a supervisory capacity. The coordinator works closely with the agency's RCDs to form a network of services within the state agency.

Assistant The assistant supports the RCD in coordinating the delivery of services to clients. The RCD assistant generally performs all of the duties and activities to facilitate the progress of a client through the rehabilitation system, with the exception of providing professional counseling services. Quite often it is the frequent contact and special help provided by the assistant that ensures a successful experience for the client. Assistants usually work under the direction of an RCD within state agencies or in rehabilitation facilities offering specialized services for deaf persons.

Independent Living Specialists Independent living specialists work either with deaf clients who are receiving vocational rehabilitation services or with those who are not pursuing vocational training or employment. Such specialists concentrate on helping deaf persons achieve higher levels of independence in the overall control of their lives and in the performance of daily activities. They assist deaf people in gaining access to community programs and services, and may provide direct services, such as mobility training, personal care training, peer counseling, and a variety of social and survival skill training. Most often, they are employed by independent living centers in local communities or by rehabilitation facilities providing specialized services to deaf persons.

TRAINING

For many years most RCDs acquired their professional training on the job. There were few graduate training programs in the nation providing preemployment training in deafness rehabilitation. Although there are still a limited number of graduate programs, the number of graduates searching for and entering RCD positions has increased significantly. At the same time, the availability of pretrained applicants for RCD vacancies has encouraged state agencies to create separate position titles and testing procedures. Such changes enable state agencies to attract and hire qualified applicants for RCD positions.

Preemployment training in deafness rehabilitation has had a definite impact upon the quality of practicing RCDs. Yet on-the-job training continues to be a necessary source of counselors who are able to work effectively with deaf clients.

TRENDS

It seems inevitable that specialization in this field will continue and that national standards will be developed for the RCD position. Acceptance of these standards will enhance the quality of programs and services for deaf persons. Also, the presence of RCDs will continue to be extended into less-populated geographical areas and into more generically oriented agencies. RCDs working under such conditions will need knowledge of other disability groups. Finally, much greater use of technological devices will improve the ease and effectiveness of communication between counselor and client.

Bibliography

Schein, J. D. (ed.): *Model State Plan for Rehabilitation of Deaf Clients: Second Revision*, National Association of the Deaf, 1980.

Eugene F. Joyce

Psychology

Rehabilitation psychology is concerned with the provision of psychological services to individuals who have chronic illness and disability. Rehabilitation psychologists working with deaf or hearing-impaired individuals must be cognizant of the profound impact that deafness has on an individual's life and of the additional impediments to rehabilitation presented by this condition. These psychologists must be familiar with and understand the unusual life circumstances that surround a hearing-impaired or deaf individual.

The successful prevention of handicapping conditions that result from disability is the real goal of rehabilitation. Therefore, the psychologist must help deaf people address those environmental as well as individual problems that are likely to create a handicapping condition. Not every disability will produce handicapping conditions, and individuals with the same disability will face different handicaps.

ASSESSMENT OF HEARING-IMPAIRED PERSONS

A major problem faced by the psychologist attempting an assessment of a deaf person is the lack of testing instruments that have been standardized on or adapted for this population. The psychologist must be alert to the necessity for individualized interpretation and recognize that clinical judgment becomes of paramount importance. In addition, tests administered by psychologists inexperienced in working with hearing-impaired clients are subject to greater error variance than tests administered by psychologists experienced with deaf persons. This is especially true of work with deaf children because of their irregular attentiveness. Evaluations of hearing-impaired persons should always begin with a performance measure; this score will likely be higher and more valid than scores obtained on language-dependent instruments. *See* PSYCHOLOGICAL EVALUATION.

The life experiences of deaf individuals are often so vastly different that psychologists must be especially sensitive to the implications of these experiences for psychological assessment. Deafness alters the individual's environment so dramatically that personality development and organization are drastically affected. Whether the norms established for personality instruments may be appropriately applied to deaf persons is therefore open to question. The factor that determines the extent to which assessment procedures must be redefined is the extent to which the deaf person's communication skills have been affected.

Generally speaking, persons who suffered severe and profound hearing loss before they were able to develop a knowledge of language and communication should be tested with nonverbal performance measures to evaluate intelligence, and with fingerspelling and sign language during interviewing and personality assessment. Preferably, the psychologist should use case history data and interviewing techniques to establish rapport and to determine personality functioning from the clinical interview. In general, standardized personality tests have questionable validity for deaf persons because these tests do not have normative data for deaf populations.

The hearing-impaired individual must be considered within his or her world rather than within the normally hearing world with which the psychologist is familiar. The psychologist may wish to gather as much information as possible from real-life observation of the individual. The information gathered in the case history can provide valuable insight into the problem-solving capabilities that the hearing-impaired individual typically brings to situations. This portion of the assessment sequence also allows for a broader understanding of the family history of the client and may shed some light on those factors that have contributed to the development of the individual.

The psychologist's attitudes and nonverbal communications are also critical to the relationship established with the hearing-impaired person. Psychologists especially need to be aware of their own attitudes, anxieties, and stereotyped notions, which will affect their interaction with the hearing-impaired person and their interpretation of the person's data. These preconceived attitudes will also be perceived by the hearing-impaired person and will affect the way he or she interacts with the psychologist.

PSYCHOTHERAPY

Psychologists engaged in psychotherapy with hearing-impaired individuals must be extremely sensitive to the subtle interpretive differences in various forms of manual communication. Meanings can be easily distorted unless the psychologist is quick to note unexpected reactions or attitude changes in the client. For this reason the development of rapport and a sense of trust is critical to the therapeutic relationship with deaf clients.

Because the emotional development of deaf persons may be dramatically delayed and certain developmental stages may have remained unresolved, it may be necessary for the psychologist to work diligently with a deaf client on such issues as integration, separation, and individuality, development of trust and autonomy, and other factors affecting an individual's sound emotional adjustment to life. Despite what may appear to be severe regression which would be labeled as serious pathology in a normally hearing person, deaf clients may simply be delayed in their emotional development.

Bibliography

Stewart, L. G.: "Counseling the Deaf Client," in L. K. Stein, E. D. Mindel, and T. Jabaley (eds.), *Deafness and Mental Health*, Grune and Stratton, New York, 1981.

Vernon, M., and P. Ottinger: "Psychological Evaluation of the Deaf and Hard of Hearing," in L. K. Stein, E. D. Mindel, and T. Jabaley (eds.), *Deafness and Mental Health*, Grune and Stratton, New York, 1981.

Zieziula, F. R. (ed.): *Assessment of Hearing-Impaired People*, Gallaudet College Press, Washington, D.C., 1982.

Mary A. Jansen

REHABILITATION ACT OF 1973

The Rehabilitation Act of 1973 is a comprehensive federal statute providing diverse training programs and services for handicapped people. The act also includes a civil rights chapter (Title V) that has been called the handicapped person's "Bill of Rights." Title V (especially Section 504) has received the most public awareness and media attention; significant lawsuits have enforced the rights to services and accommodations granted by Title V.

BACKGROUND AND PURPOSE

The Rehabilitation Act of 1973 was passed in an era of advocacy for the civil rights of minority and disadvantaged groups. Since the 1920s, the federal government has provided some funds for assisting and training handicapped people and disabled veterans. The 1973 act promotes much more than job training. It includes recognition that handicapped people have a legal right to equal treatment and fairness in a variety of contexts, such as jobs, removal of architectural barriers in public places, education, and public services. Title V of the act is similar to other federal statutes prohibiting race, sex, and religious discrimination.

The act became law on September 26, 1973, but detailed regulations implementing it were not promulgated until 1977, after angry public demonstrations and protests about the delay. Important regulations carrying out the purposes of the act have since been adopted by almost every department and agency of the federal government.

The act has also been amended several times. For example, the definition of handicapped person was greatly expanded in 1974. As a result, the act now protects people with virtually any physical or mental disability, as well as people who are misdiagnosed as having a handicap or who have a history of a handicapping condition that subjects them to discrimination.

In 1978 Title V was expanded to cover programs operated by the federal government. The enforcement provisions of Section 504 were strengthened, and courts were authorized to award fees to attorneys who could prove that a defendant discriminated against a handicapped person. Special service programs such as interpreter training centers were authorized for deaf individuals. In 1984 the Client Assistance Program was enhanced, and more clients were made eligible for vocational services.

Congress stated explicitly the purpose of the act: "To develop and implement, through research, training, services, and the guarantee of equal opportunity, comprehensive and coordinated programs of vocational rehabilitation and independent living." To accomplish this, the Rehabilitation Services Administration, now within the Department of Education, implements the programs and projects of the act. *See* REHABILITATION: Administration.

TITLE I: VOCATIONAL REHABILITATION

Title I authorizes grants to the states to provide vocational rehabilitation services for handicapped persons. Vocational rehabilitation services are intended to help the clients become employable through counseling, training, and placement.

In exchange for federal funding, state vocational rehabilitation agencies must meet minimum federal criteria. Any disabled individual who may become employable after receiving vocational rehabilitation is eligible for certain services.

The state vocational rehabilitation agency must prepare an individual written rehabilitation program for each client. Each program must specify long-range rehabilitation goals, the services that will be provided, how long the services will continue, and evaluation procedures and schedules to ensure that the client is making progress. The client must help to develop his or her own rehabilitation program.

The act lists services that a state agency must provide: diagnostic testing and evaluation; counseling, referral, and placement services; job and academic training; medical services (including audiology and hearing aids); maintenance costs (living expenses) during rehabilitation; interpreter and reader services; occupational licenses, tools, and equipment; transportation; and telecommunications devices. *See* TELECOMMUNICATIONS.

Special funds are provided for state Client Assistance Programs. Client Assistance Program counselors advise clients about vocational rehabilitation benefits and make sure they receive services to which they are entitled. Client Assistance Program projects attempt to resolve problems that clients experience with vocational rehabilitation agencies; they help dissatisfied clients pursue legal remedies to enforce their rights under the act. Deaf clients have used Client Assistance Program projects to confront vocational rehabilitation counselors with whom they cannot communicate or who refuse to fund requested training and support services.

TITLE II: RESEARCH AND TRAINING

The goal of Title II is to provide a comprehensive, coordinated approach to research and demonstration projects for rehabilitation services. The National Institute of Handicapped Research provides grants for research and special vocational rehabilitation service projects. It coordinates all federal programs and policies related to research in rehabilitation, and it disseminates educational materials and training programs on research and engineering advances in rehabilitation pertinent to the problems of handicapped individuals.

The grants are intended to develop innovative methods of applying advanced medical technology and scientific achievement to rehabilitation problems. Priority research topics include spinal cord injuries, end-stage renal disease, international research programs, the use of telecommunication systems, rehabilitation of children and of individuals aged 60 or older, captioning services for deaf individuals, and employment services.

TITLE III: TRAINING, SUPPLEMENTARY SERVICES, AND FACILITIES

Title III authorizes federal funds to pay up to 90 percent of the cost of providing vocational training services to handicapped individuals by public or nonprofit private rehabilitation facilities. Services include training in occupational skills, work evaluation and testing, occupational tools and equipment, job tryouts, and weekly living allowances. Special attention is to be given to individuals with the most severe handicaps, including deafness.

Title III also authorizes grants and loan guarantees for the construction and staffing of rehabilitation facilities. Comprehensive rehabilitation centers provide a broad range of services to handicapped individuals, including information and referral, counseling, job placement, and health, educational, social, and recreational services.

Training rehabilitation personnel is an important component of a successful program, and a special section of Title III authorizes training a sufficient number of interpreters to meet the communication needs of deaf individuals. The act authorizes up to 12 interpreter training programs throughout the United States. Other grants are available for interpreter services within each state. Interpreter service programs must be conveniently located to serve the maximum number of deaf individuals. They are coordinated with the information and referral programs established in another section of the act, and they must assure that participating interpreters meet minimum competency standards. *See* INTERPRETING.

Other special programs include demonstration programs using model techniques of comprehensive vocational services, services for migratory workers, and the Helen Keller National Center for Deaf-Blind Youths and Adults (funded separately from the act after 1984 legislation), which demonstrates methods of specialized intensive services for the rehabilitation and training of persons who are both deaf and blind. *See* DEAF-BLINDNESS.

TITLE IV: NATIONAL COUNCIL ON THE HANDICAPPED

The National Council on the Handicapped sets general policies for the research and service programs conducted under the act, and advises federal officials on the development of rehabilitation programs. The National Council consists of 15 members, including representatives of handicapped individuals, national organizations, service providers, researchers, business concerns, and labor organizations. At least five members of the National Council must be handicapped individuals or parents or guardians of handicapped individuals.

TITLE V: "BILL OF RIGHTS"

The civil rights protections in Title V have been widely celebrated as a "Bill of Rights" for handicapped people. Title V and its regulations require equal access to jobs, education, and services. Legal mechanisms for enforcing those rights are available through complaints filed with federal agencies or through lawsuits in federal courts. Although Title V does not guarantee universal equal access for disabled Americans, it does create important substantive rights and remedies to challenge discrimination.

Section 501: Federal Employment   The U.S. Congress committed the federal government to equal employment opportunity for disabled federal employees in Section 501 of the act. Section 501 requires all federal agencies and departments (including the Postal Service) to submit annual affirmative action program plans for the hiring, placement, and advancement of handicapped individuals in federal employment. The plans also describe how the special needs of handicapped employees are being met.

The regulations implementing this section protect any handicapped applicant or employee who can perform the essential functions of the job without endangering his or her health and safety or that of others. The regulations do not define precisely what is meant by essential functions of a job. Employers must examine job descriptions for the most significant tasks and, if necessary, eliminate nonessential tasks that are barriers for handicapped workers. Employers must also provide reasonable accommodations such as sign language interpreters, telephone devices for the deaf (TDDs), special training, special supervision methods, and modified equipment or machinery to enable handicapped workers to perform essential job tasks successfully. Employers do not have to provide accommodations that would cause undue hardship on the agency or its operations.

Regulations for processing complaints of discrimination based on physical and mental handicap were not adopted until 1978. Responsibility for handling complaints of handicap discrimination in federal employment has been transferred from the Civil Service Commission to the Equal Employment Opportunity Commission.

Complaints that a federal agency has discriminated on the basis of handicap must be submitted to each agency's Office of Equal Employment Opportunity (EEO) within 30 days of the discriminatory incident. Deaf individuals have successfully complained about an agency's refusal to hire them or to promote them to a position for which they were qualified, refusal to provide qualified interpreter services for job training and meetings, and other discriminatory conduct. If the grievance cannot be resolved through EEO investigation, mediation, and hearings, the individual has a right to file suit in a federal district court.

Section 502: Architectural Accessibility   Section 502 created the Architectural and Transportation Barriers Compliance Board which enforces the 1968 Architectural Barriers Act. This law requires most buildings and facilities designed, constructed, altered, or leased with federal money after 1968 to be accessible to disabled people. The potential impact of this law is great, since there are many federally owned or leased facilities in the United States. *See* ARCHITECTURAL BARRIERS ACT.

Minimum standards for accessibility under the Architectural Barriers Act are established by the American National Standards Institute. The standards are primarily concerned with physical accessibility for persons with mobility impairments.

In 1978 the Compliance Board was given explicit authority to investigate communication barriers (such as the absence of telecommunication devices in public facilities) and to adopt its own accessibility standards to replace those of the American National Standards Institute. This is significant for the deaf community, since the institute's standards are ambiguous about communication needs of deaf individuals. They do not include solutions to communication barriers such as telephone amplifiers, TDDs, or visual warning signals for fires and other emergencies.

Complaints about architectural barriers can be filed with the Architectural and Transportation Barriers Compliance Board, which will investigate and attempt to achieve voluntary compliance with the law. If this is not successful, the Compliance Board can hold a hearing before an administrative law judge, who can order modifications to public facilities for violations of the architectural barriers law and can withhold federal funds for noncompliance.

Deaf individuals have filed complaints leading to the installation of TDDs in post office buildings, doorbells with flashing-light relays in federally funded housing, visual warning systems on fire alarms, and security systems that are not wholly dependent on operation of an auditory intercom. Section 502 and the Architectural Barriers Act might also be used to require the spotlighting of interpreters and the installation of appropriate supplementary acoustic devices such as audio loops in meeting rooms and auditoriums.

Section 503: Federal Contractors Section 503 requires affirmative action in the hiring, placement, and promotion of qualified handicapped individuals by employers who have contracts or subcontracts of $2500 or more with the federal government. Contractors with 50 or more employees or a contract exceeding $50,000 are required to have written affirmative action plans to explain what steps they will take to actively recruit, hire, and promote qualified handicapped people. More than 300,000 businesses, including most major corporations, are federal contractors.

Federal contractors must comply with requirements that are similar to those for federal employment. The law protects any handicapped individual who is "capable of performing a particular job, with reasonable accommodation to his or her handicap." Federal contractors must consider the same commonsense modifications that would permit deaf and other handicapped people to perform their jobs successfully and safely, including modifying equipment and workplaces, restructuring jobs to eliminate nonessential tasks, and using interpreters for deaf employees. If a handicapped individual can perform a job with these reasonable changes, failure to hire or promote because of the handicap is discriminatory.

Complaints of handicap discrimination by federal contractors must be filed with the U.S. Department of Labor Office of Federal Contract Compliance (OFCCP) within 180 days of the discriminatory incident. Regional offices of the office of Federal Contract Compliance investigate each complaint and enforce violations of the law. Formal enforcement mechanisms include bringing suit in federal court, withholding payments due on existing federal contracts, terminating existing federal contracts, and barring the contractor from receiving future federal contracts. If a formal enforcement hearing is held, the handicapped individual who brought the complaint is not a participant because the dispute is primarily between the Office of Federal Contract Compliance and the contractor. Individual complainants are not always satisfied with the Compliance Office's resolution of their complaints. Although the Compliance Office's own figures indicate that it closes most cases of handicap discrimination, the complaint process is long and time-consuming.

Section 504: Federal Recipients Section 504 is considered by many handicapped people to be the broadest protection of their rights, since it prohibits discrimination against qualified handicapped individuals in any federally assisted program or activity.

Almost all public institutions, such as school systems, police departments, libraries, courts, jails, transit systems, and public assistance programs, are recipients of federal financial assistance. Many private schools, hospitals, colleges, nursing homes, airports, museums, and other facilities also receive federal financial assistance for some of their activities.

Every federal agency that provides federal financial assistance has detailed written rules that spell out the nondiscrimination obligations of its recipients. The first agency to publish Section 504 regulations was the U.S. Department of Health, Education and Welfare (HEW) [divided in 1980 into the Department of Education and the Department of Health and Human Resources]. The Department of Health, Education and Welfare also issued guidelines for other agencies to follow in developing their own Section 504 regulations. Therefore, each agency's rules are generally consistent with each other and with the model regulation of the Department of Health, Education and Welfare. Authority to supervise compliance with Section 504 was given to the U.S. Department of Justice in 1980.

If an institution receives federal financial assistance for one part of its activities, then the Section

504 regulations require it to obey Section 504 in any of its activities that receive or benefit from the financial assistance. This concept may greatly widen the ability of Section 504 to reach discriminatory activities not directly funded by federal agencies. However, the Supreme Court created confusion in 1984 when it decided in *Grove City College v. Bell* that a similar nondiscrimination law applied only to the specific program or activity that actually received federal aid. Congress is attempting to clarify whether Section 504 and other nondiscrimination laws apply to all activities of a federal recipient.

Section 504 requires recipients to give handicapped people an equal opportunity to participate in its programs and activities. A recipient cannot refuse to allow a deaf person to benefit from its programs merely because of a handicapping condition. For example, a college cannot refuse to admit a deaf person just because he or she is deaf. However, a deaf person can be rejected for failure to meet certain reasonable eligibility criteria.

A deaf person must be given an equally effective opportunity to benefit from a recipient's programs. If a mental health counseling center cannot communicate with a deaf patient in sign language, the deaf patient will not have the same opportunity to get help as a hearing patient.

Sometimes handicapped people will need different or special treatment in order to get true equal opportunity. Title V is different from the civil rights laws based on race or sex, which usually require treating people in exactly the same way. Title V often requires recipients to give handicapped people some special assistance or accommodation, such as sign language interpreters or ramps for wheelchairs. However, the Section 504 regulation prohibits unnecessary special or different treatment if it would tend to stigmatize handicapped people. Special or separate services for handicapped people are prohibited unless they are necessary to provide services that are as effective as those provided to others.

The Section 504 rules against discrimination prohibit communication barriers as well as physical barriers. In many contexts, recipients of federal financial assistance must take appropriate steps to make sure that hearing-impaired people can communicate effectively. The appropriate steps depend on the particular situation and the needs of the particular hearing-impaired person, but the usual accommodations are qualified sign language interpreters, TDD-equipped telephones, and telephone amplifiers.

The Section 504 rules contain the same kind of employment discrimination rules discussed above for federal agencies and federal contractors. They also contain explicit rules for certain types of facilities as follows.

Health and Social Services. Health care facilities and social service agencies must meet the communication needs of deaf persons. Deaf people frequently receive inadequate health care and social services because no one on the staff can communicate with them. Agencies with 15 or more employees must provide, when necessary, appropriate auxiliary aids to hearing-impaired people and to people with impaired sensory, manual, or speaking skills to give them an equal opportunity to benefit from the services. This means that if a deaf patient cannot understand the doctors and nurses, a hospital must provide free sign language interpreter service to make sure that the patient's illness is properly diagnosed and that the medical staff and patient understand each other. Agencies are also expected to have TDDs or to use effective TDD relay systems to make sure that deaf people have the same telephone access to their programs that hearing people have.

Smaller agencies may also be required to provide auxiliary aids when doing so would not be unduly burdensome; interpreters can be hired for a reasonable hourly fee and TDDs can be purchased for a few hundred dollars. Although an agency is not expected to have an interpreter on staff at all times, it should have a system for scheduling appointments when interpreters are available and for contacting interpreters in emergencies.

Elementary Education. Most school systems and educational agencies receive some form of federal financial assistance. The Department of Education's 504 regulation requires school systems to provide handicapped children with a free, appropriate public education, regardless of the nature of their handicaps. If the local school system does not have the facilities or staff to educate a handicapped child, it must send the child to another school that does, even if this means paying the child's tuition at a private school.

Section 504 also requires schools to provide equal opportunity to deaf parents. A school system should provide a qualified interpreter when a deaf parent meets with a child's teacher to discuss the child's school program.

Specific policies for the education of handicapped children are codified in Public Law 94-142, the Education for All Handicapped Children Act. *See* EDUCATION OF THE HANDICAPPED ACT.

Postsecondary Education. Colleges and universities that receive federal financial assistance must be accessible to handicapped students and teachers in recruitment, admissions, and programs. However, the college is not required to make substantial changes in the requirements of its academic program, and may require "reasonable physical qualifications" for admission to its programs.

Qualified handicapped students must be given an equal opportunity to benefit from the program without being unnecessarily segregated or limited in their participation. The Section 504 regulations require colleges to provide auxiliary aids that a deaf or blind student needs to participate fully in the educational program. Interpreters, transcripts, notetakers, copies of notes, taped texts, and readers have been used as auxiliary aids.

A college can refer a handicapped student to another source for the provision of auxiliary aids. Many deaf students receive their school interpreter services from state vocational rehabilitation agencies, but the college remains ultimately responsible for ensuring that students do receive the necessary services.

Enforcement. Strong enforcement provisions are essential to assure that the nondiscrimination rules are obeyed. All recipients of federal financial assistance are required to evaluate their own programs to identify and eliminate barriers for disabled people. If barriers remain, complaints can be brought against the agency either by filing an administrative complaint with the agency that provides the federal funds or by filing a lawsuit in federal court. The Department of Justice has oversight supervision, but each federal agency enforces its own Section 504 rules, using the same procedures that are used to enforce Title VI of the Civil Rights Act of 1964.

Administrative complaints must be filed with the agency's Office for Civil Rights within 180 days of the discriminatory event. The agency will investigate the complaint, interview witnesses, and collect evidence of discriminatory policies. If it finds discrimination has occurred, the agency will try to get appropriate relief from the recipient. If the recipient refuses to reach a satisfactory resolution, the agency can institute formal enforcement proceedings to terminate federal financial assistance to the recipient.

Since investigations of administrative complaints can take a long time, a handicapped person can choose to bring a lawsuit to federal court. Although litigation is expensive, attorney's fees and other costs can be awarded if the person wins the case.

TITLE VI: EMPLOYMENT OPPORTUNITIES

Title VI authorizes innovative pilot programs to encourage employment of handicapped individuals. For example, funding was provided for community service employment and the Community Employment Training Act (CETA) programs under this chapter. Title VI also encourages handicapped individuals to get jobs in private industry by providing joint financing of training and employment projects in realistic work settings, including provision of supportive services and special equipment.

TITLE VII: INDEPENDENT LIVING

Centers for Independent Living were established by Title VII of the act. Through the centers, severely handicapped people develop skills that will enable them to live and function independently. The centers offer counseling and referral services, housing and transportation, group living arrangements, education and training, physical rehabilitation, therapeutic and health maintenance programs, peer counseling, and advocacy services.

Title VII also authorizes grants to states for advocacy systems to protect the rights of handicapped individuals. Protection and advocacy offices must have the legal authority to pursue legal, administrative, and other appropriate remedies to ensure the protection of the rights of handicapped individuals, and must be independent of state rehabilitation agencies.

Bibliography

Grove City College v. Bell, 465 U.S. 555, 104 S. Ct. 1211 (1984).
  34 CFR § 104.1 et seq.
  29 U.S.C. § 701 et seq.

Sara Geer; Mary-Jean Sweeney

Southeastern Community College v. Davis

In a decision titled *Southeastern Community College v. Davis*, the U.S. Supreme Court first interpreted Section 504 of the Rehabilitation Act of 1973, which prohibits agencies that receive federal funds (including colleges) from discriminating against handicapped persons. The case involved a hearing-impaired woman, Frances Davis, who was denied admission to the nursing program of Southeastern Community College in North Carolina.

BACKGROUND

Davis, a licensed practical nurse, sought to advance in her nursing profession by seeking admission to Southeastern Community College's nursing school program to become a registered nurse. Her hearing loss was apparent in the admission interviews, and the college requested that she be evaluated by an audiologist. The hearing evaluation showed that she had a moderately severe bilateral sensorineural hearing loss, and, even with a hearing aid would need to use her vision to supplement her hearing. The audiologist found that Davis could be expected to respond only when spoken to directly, but that she was an excellent lipreader. *See* EAR: Pathology.

The college then consulted with the director of the North Carolina Board of Nursing, who believed Davis's hearing loss made her unsafe to practice as a nurse, arguing that there would be several situations where Davis's hearing disability would make her inadequate to respond to the patient's needs. Consequently, the director recommended that the college not admit Davis to its nursing program.

The college also asked the director of nursing services of a nearby hospital whether she would employ Davis as a registered nurse. The director indicated that she would employ Davis as a registered nurse if she had a vacancy, and thought Davis could do well in areas of long-term care, in a doctor's office, or in an industrial setting. Nevertheless, the college rejected Davis's application for the registered nurse program on the basis of her hearing disability, and Davis took the issue to court.

DISTRICT COURT OPINION

Davis filed suit in federal district court alleging both a violation of Section 504 of the Rehabilitation Act and a denial of equal protection and due process under the Fourteenth Amendment to the U.S. Constitution. The district court ruled in the college's favor, believing Davis's handicap would prevent her from becoming a competent nurse. The district court declared that in many situations, such as an operating room, intensive care unit, or postnatal care unit, the wearing of surgical masks would make lipreading impossible. Moreover, a registered nurse often would be required to follow instantly a physician's voiced instructions for getting different instruments and drugs.

Thus, the district court held that Davis was not an "otherwise qualified handicapped individual," meaning an individual protected from discrimination by Section 504. The federal judge defined "otherwise qualified individual" as meaning a person "otherwise able to function sufficiently in the position sought in spite of the handicap, if proper training and facilities are suitable and available." The district court also held that there was no violation of Davis's constitutional rights.

COURT OF APPEALS DECISION

Davis appealed the district court's decision to the Court of Appeals for the Fourth Circuit. The court of appeals considered Section 504 of the Department of Health, Education, and Welfare (HEW) administrative regulations that had been issued while the appeal was pending, and unanimously reversed the earlier court's decision. The case returned to the district court for reconsideration of Davis's application in light of these intervening regulations.

The appeals court ruled that the district court erred in considering only the nature of Davis's handicap in determining whether she was "otherwise qualified" for the nursing program. Under the 504 regulations, the court of appeals decided, applications to postsecondary education programs should be considered on the basis of the disabled applicant's "academic and technical qualifications." Instead, the district court had focused only on Davis's handicap. The appeals court acknowl-

edged that the college could consider other relevant subjective and objective factors used when picking other candidates for enrollment in the nursing program. However, it was decided that admission should not be denied to an applicant who meets all the other admission criteria solely because she may not successfully perform every task a registered nurse may confront.

The appeals court also requested the district court to consider modifications of the college's nursing program to allow Davis's participation, for HEW regulations required modifications to accommodate disabled persons. Some of the relevant modifications in Davis's case included provision of auxiliary aids, substitution of specific courses required for the completion of degree requirements, and adaptation of the manner in which specific courses were conducted. The college's position was that it was not prepared to modify its nursing program, especially the clinical training, to meet the needs created by Davis's deafness.

The court of appeals did not find Davis qualified or order that the college admit her. It only stated that, as required by HEW regulations, she should be considered for admission on the basis of her academic and technical qualifications.

SUPREME COURT DECISION

The U.S. Supreme Court granted review because of the importance of the issue to the many colleges and universities that receive federal funding and therefore are subject to the requirements of Section 504. The Supreme Court decided unanimously that Southeastern Community College had not violated Section 504 when it refused to admit Davis. The Court defined the issue narrowly, saying that it was deciding whether Section 504 "forbids professional schools from imposing physical qualifications for admission to their clinical training programs."

Justice Lewis Powell, writing for the Court, found that Section 504 does not compel schools to disregard the applicant's disabilities "or to make substantial modifications in their programs to allow disabled persons to participate." Instead, the Court interpreted Section 504 to mean "that mere possession of a handicap is not a permissible ground for assuming an inability to function in a particular context."

The Supreme Court concluded that in Section 504 "otherwise qualified individual" means "one who is able to meet all of a program's requirements in spite of his handicap," and said that this definition was consistent with HEW's interpretation. For example, HEW's analysis to its regulation states that legitimate physical qualifications may be essential to program participation. Moreover, HEW noted that Congress intended Section 504 to apply to those persons who were qualified in spite of their handicap rather than to those who were qualified except for their handicap.

The Supreme Court then looked at whether the physical qualifications the college required of Davis, that is, greater ability to hear, were necessary for the nursing program. The Court concluded that "the ability to understand speech without reliance on lipreading is necessary for patient safety during the clinical phase of the program." The Court then considered whether Davis could meet these necessary requirements with modifications of the program and decided that it was unlikely she could successfully participate in the clinical program with any of the accommodations the HEW regulations require. The Court concluded that either the college would have to provide Davis with close individual faculty supervision when she was working with patients or it would have to change the nursing program curriculum to limit her participation to academic classes. These requirements, the Court said, were greater modifications than Section 504 regulations require. The Court rejected the court of appeals view that it was not necessary that she be trained to do all tasks a registered nurse may perform since there were some positions she could perform satisfactorily as a registered nurse. The Court held that a qualified handicapped person must do all the functions of a registered nurse.

The Supreme Court's decision in this case recognized that the 504 HEW regulations do require educational institutions that receive federal funding to modify their programs to accommodate disabled persons. However, the Court held that the 504 statute did not compel substantial modifications. Furthermore, the Court noted that Section 504 does not impose an affirmative action requirement on recipients. Since Congress included affirmative action requirements for Sections 501 and 503 in the statute, the Court reasoned that Congress's failure to do so for Section 504 indicated it did not intend it. The Court acknowledged, however, that it is difficult to draw the line "between a lawful refusal to extend affirmative action and illegal discrimination against handicapped persons." The Court realized there would be situations where qualified handicapped persons could be arbitrarily deprived of the chance to participate in a federal recipient's program.

In this case, the Court found that Davis could not participate in the college's nursing program unless the college substantially lowered its admission standards. The Court concluded that Section 504 does not require colleges and universities to make substantial modifications of standards for handicapped people.

Bibliography
DuBow, S., et al.: *Legal Rights of Hearing-Impaired People*, 1982, 2d ed., 1984.

Hull, K.: *The Rights of Physically Handicapped People*, 1979.

Southeastern Community College v. Davis, 424 F.Supp. 1341 (D.N.C. 1976); *rev'd and remanded*, 574 F.2d 1158 (4th Cir. 1978); *rev'd* 442 U.S. 397 (1979).

Sy DuBow

Camenisch v. University of Texas

University of Texas v. Camenisch was the second case, after *Southeastern Community College v. Davis*, to be decided by the U.S. Supreme Court on the rights of deaf college students under Section 504 of the Rehabilitation Act of 1973. In *Camenisch*, the Supreme Court refused to decide whether the University of Texas was financially responsible for paying for a sign language interpreter for a deaf graduate student. A federal district court had granted the student a preliminary injunction ordering the university to provide the interpreter. An appeals court affirmed the preliminary injunction even though the student had graduated by the time the case reached the appellate level. The Supreme Court found that the issue of whether the district court should have granted preliminary relief was moot because the terms of the preliminary injunction ordering interpreter services had been fulfilled. The Court returned the case to the lower court for a final decision on the university's claim that it was entitled to recover from the student the money it had paid for interpreter costs.

BACKGROUND

Walter Camenisch was a deaf man employed at the Texas School for the Deaf as acting dean of students. He was also a graduate student at the University of Texas at Austin. His employment was contingent upon his supplementing his education and getting a master's degree. He planned to obtain his degree and become permanent dean of students at one of the campuses of the Texas School for the Deaf. Without the services of an interpreter, Camenisch could not successfully participate in the master's program, and therefore would lose his job as acting dean of students.

In the fall of 1977 Camenisch asked the university to provide funds to pay for an interpreter so he could attend classes, but he was turned down. Because he was earning $11,000 per year, he did not meet the university's criteria for financial assistance to graduate students, even when the expenses of the interpreter were added to his other expenses for determining his eligibility.

Camenisch made a similar request for interpreter services to the Texas State Rehabilitation Commission, which also informed him that it would not provide funds for interpreter services.

In the winter of 1977 his attorneys, the National Association of the Deaf Legal Defense Fund, asked the university to provide funds for interpreter services, but again the university refused the request. *See* LEGAL SERVICES; NATIONAL ASSOCIATION OF THE DEAF.

Until the filing of the law suit, the university had not provided interpreter services for Camenisch while he had been a student in the university's master's degree program. As a result, Camenisch himself paid $1245 for interpreter services for nine graduate courses at the university.

DISTRICT COURT DECISION

In 1978 Camenisch filed a complaint in U.S. District Court for the Western District of Texas, Austin Division, requesting that the University of Texas provide sign language interpreter services for one class. In the complaint, he claimed that the failure of the university to provide interpreter services violated Section 504 of the Rehabilitation Act of 1973. Camenisch also relied on regulations of the Department of Health, Education, and Welfare implementing Section 504. These regulations provide that: "(1) A recipient to which this [Auxiliary Aids] subpart applies shall take such steps as are necessary to ensure that no handicapped student is denied the benefits of, excluded from participation in, or otherwise subjected to discrimination under the education program or activity operated by the recipient because of the absence of educational auxiliary aids for students with impaired sensory, manual, or speaking skills. (2) Auxiliary Aids may include taped texts, interpreters or other effective methods of making orally delivered materials available to students with hearing impairments, readers in libraries for students with visual impairments, classroom equipment adapted for use by students with manual impairments, and other similar services and actions. Recipients need not provide attendants, individually prescribed devices, readers for personal use or study, or other devices or services of a personal nature."

The parties to the case were in agreement on most of the pertinent facts, so there was no need for a trial or a jury. The parties also agreed on some important legal points: (1) The University of Texas was a state-supported institution of higher education which received federal financial assistance from the United States. (2) The plaintiff was a handicapped individual, defined in federal law as "any person who (a) has a physical or mental impairment which substantially limits one or more of such person's major life activities, (b) has a record of such an impairment, or (c) is regarded as having such an impairment." (3) The plaintiff was a qualified handicapped individual as defined by the Department of Health, Education, and Welfare regulation to Section 504 of the Rehabilitation Act of 1973 in that he was a "handicapped person who

meets the academic and technical standards requisite to admission or participation in the recipient's education program or activity." (4) The University of Texas at Austin received federal financial assistance in the fiscal year 1978 in excess of $31,400,000, and the budget for the year ending August 31, 1978, was in excess of $200,000,000.

On May 17, 1978, based on that Stipulation of Facts, the federal district court ordered a preliminary injunction requiring the university "to procure an interpreter or other effective method of making orally delivered course materials available to plaintiff during his completion of his master's work at defendant University." The court conditioned the preliminary injunction by ordering Camenisch to post a security bond in the amount of $3000 "pending the outcome of this litigation." Finally, the court ordered Camenisch to file an administrative complaint with the U.S. Department of Health, Education, and Welfare and halted further court action.

HEW COMPLAINT

While the case was on appeal to the U.S. Court of Appeals for the Fifth Circuit, the Department of Health, Education, and Welfare issued a letter of finding in the administrative complaint. The department concluded that the university was "in violation of Section 504 of the Rehabilitation Act of 1973 by failing to provide educational auxiliary aids to students with impaired sensory skills, thus denying handicapped students equal educational opportunities." The Department stated that the "requested interpreter services were necessary for Camenisch to fully participate in the educational program in which he was enrolled" and that the financial status of a qualified handicapped student was not an acceptable criterion for determining whether necessary auxiliary aids would be provided.

COURT OF APPEALS DECISION

The U.S. Court of Appeals for the Fifth Circuit agreed with the federal district court's order granting preliminary injunctive relief. Although Camenisch had already received the relief he sought, the case was not moot, according to the appeals court, because the injunction bond preserved the issue of who was responsible for the cost of interpreter services. The appeals court decision was divided into three parts.

First, the court of appeals held that Camenisch could sue in federal district court under Section 504. Such relief was not limited to judicial review of a federal agency administrative decision.

Second, the appeals court held that the federal district court erred in conditioning the grant of preliminary injunctive relief on Camenisch's filing of an administrative complaint with the U.S. Department of Health, Education, and Welfare. A suit to enforce the rights of qualified handicapped individuals under Section 504 could be brought without resort to administrative remedies.

Third, the appeals court held that the Department of Health, Education, and Welfare regulations required educational institutions to provide support services in their academic programs to handicapped persons, including the provision of sign language interpreter services to deaf students. The appeals court distinguished *Southeastern Community College v. Davis* by noting that the "Supreme Court's decision in *Southeastern Community College* says only that Section 504 does not require a school to provide services to a handicapped individual for a program for which the individual handicap precludes him from ever realizing the principal benefits of the training." The appeals court pointed out that the hearing-impaired plaintiff in *Southeastern Community College* sought admission to a nursing program and was not otherwise qualified because of her disability, while in the present case the hearing-impaired person was otherwise qualified and could "obviously perform well in his profession" as a teacher and administrator at a school for deaf students.

SUPREME COURT DECISION

In his legal brief before the U.S. Supreme Court, Camenisch argued that the University of Texas conceded that the federal regulation required it to provide a sign language interpreter for him. The regulation struck a balance between the nondiscrimination mandate of Section 504 and the list of compliance actions by education institutions receiving federal financial assistance. The plaintiff also argued that *Southeastern Community College v. Davis* did not mean that Section 504 was not intended to impose any financial obligation on a college or university. The Supreme Court noted that the elimination of discrimination under Section 504 might involve some costs. In addition, the Supreme Court recognized the role of the Deparment of Health, Education, and Welfare in identifying "those instances where the refusal to accommodate the needs of a disabled person amounts to discrimination against the handicapped." Finally, the plaintiff argued that he could sue for injunctive relief against the university without first filing an administrative complaint with the federal agency providing the university with financial assistance.

The Supreme Court did not reach a decision on the substantive issues raised in the case. Instead, it declared the decision of the appeals court null and void, and sent the case back to the lower courts for a final decision on whether the university was obligated to pay the cost of interpreter services. The issue before the Supreme Court on whether the fed-

eral district court should have awarded preliminary relief was moot because the plaintiff had been provided an interpreter and had successfully completed his educational program.

In a concurring opinion remanding the case for trial, Chief Justice Burger noted that the university was willing to permit Camenisch to have a sign language interpreter present in the classroom at his own expense. The Chief Justice also noted that the university's refusal to provide for an interpreter was based on the fact that Camenisch did not meet the university's financial needs tests for assistance to graduate students. The Chief Justice suggested that the trial court should "among other things, decide whether the federal regulations at issue, which go beyond the carefully worded nondiscrimination provision, of Section 504, exceed the powers" of the federal agency under Section 504.

On remand, the federal district court never had to decide the merits of the dispute. The case was settled out of court with each side being responsible for its own costs. Camenisch was not required to reimburse the university for the costs of the interpreter.

Bibliography

Camenisch v. University of Texas, 616 F.2d 127 (5th Cir. 1980), *vacated and remanded as moot*, 451 U.S. 390 (1982).

Section 504 of the Rehabiliation Act of 1973, 29 U.S.C.§794.

Southeastern Community College v. Davis, 442 U.S. 397 (1979).

U.S. Department of Education implementing regulations to §504, 34 C.F.R. Part 104.

Marc P. Charmatz

Gottfried v. Community Television of Southern California

In a series of legal actions taken on behalf of the deaf community of Los Angeles, it has been held that the Rehabilitation Act of 1973 does not in itself require the United States government to issue regulations compelling broadcasters to caption television programs. In *Community Television of Southern California v. Gottfried* (1983), the U.S. Supreme Court decided that the Federal Communications Commission (FCC) did not have to impose additional requirements on "public" (educational) television stations beyond those that the commission imposes on conventional, commercial television stations, even though as recipients of federal financial assistance, public stations are subject to the Rehabilitation Act. The Court did recognize, nevertheless, that no broadcaster "may simply ignore the needs of the hearing impaired in discharging its responsibilities to the community which it serves."

In a separate action in 1984, the U.S. Court of Appeals for the Ninth Circuit held that the government did not have to issue specific regulations to interpret the Rehabilitation Act with respect to access by deaf individuals to programs aired by television station recipients of federal financial assistance. The act, said the court, could be enforced by ad hoc adjudication rather than rulemaking.

BACKGROUND

In 1975 the ABC Television network began making available to noncommercial educational (public) television stations a version of its nightly network newscast with open captions (visibile to all viewers) on the TV screen. Although the program aired on more than 100 stations nationwide at no cost to the stations, Los Angeles public television station KCET, licensed to Community Television of Southern California, declined to air the program.

Sue Gottfried was a hearing-impaired resident of Los Angeles, active in the Greater Los Angeles Council on Deafness (GLAD), a local umbrella organization for deaf and hearing-impaired persons. Her husband, attorney Abraham Gottfried, asked KCET management why it did not carry the free program for deaf individuals. After several exchanges, GLAD picketed the station in May 1977. KCET began airing the program shortly thereafter. This incident triggered a closer inspection by GLAD and the Gottfrieds of a broadcaster's legal obligation to serve deaf persons. *See* GREATER LOS ANGELES COUNCIL ON DEAFNESS.

PETITIONS TO FEDERAL COMMUNICATIONS COMMISSION

In October 1977 Sue Gottfried, individually and on behalf of other deaf individuals, filed petitions with the FCC to deny the licenses of eight Los Angeles television stations—seven commercial VHF stations and public station KCET. GLAD was also a petitioner. The grounds Gottfried alleged for denial were (1) that the stations had not met their responsibilities under the Communications Act to ascertain and program to meet the needs and problems of their community, and (2) that the stations were subject to the Rehabilitation Act of 1973 because they held valuable governmental licenses, and that they violated this act, as well as the First Amendment, by not making their programs accessible to hearing-impaired viewers. The latter charge was enhanced in the case of KCET by recitation of the station's failure to air the ABC News program during most of the relevant license term covering the previous three years.

FCC DECISIONS

The seven-member Federal Communications Commission unanimously denied all of the petitions in 1978, refusing to hold a hearing on the license renewal applications of the subject stations. Gottfried

had not met the commission's strict standard of showing specific facts raising substantial and material questions of fact to ascertain whether renewal of the licenses would serve the "public interest, convenience and necessity."

The ascertainment requirement is general, and the stations met the FCC's minimum requirements. There was no specific FCC requirement to develop demographic data on the deaf population or specifically to ascertain the needs of deaf people. Nor were there any FCC regulations or guidelines requiring captioning or other techniques to make television programming accessible to deaf viewers, although since 1970 the FCC had encouraged broadcasters to help deaf audiences with visual aids. The commission found that it would be "unfair" to broadcasters to jeopardize their licenses for failure to do something not theretofore formally required.

The commission also held that the commercial licensees were not subject to the Rehabilitation Act solely by reason of their government licenses. And even if KCET, which received over 30 percent of its funding from the federal government, was subject to the act as a recipient of federal financial assistance, the FCC was not the funding agency and therefore declined to enforce the act before the appropriate agency actually found a violation.

The FCC denied Gottfried's and GLAD's petition for reconsideration in 1979, and the deaf groups sought judicial review.

COURT OF APPEALS REVERSAL

In an extensive decision issued in April 1981, a three-judge panel of the U.S. Court of Appeals for the District of Columbia Circuit affirmed, by a two-to-one vote, the FCC decision with respect to the seven commercial stations, but reversed the renewal grant to KCET. Judge J. Skelly Wright, writing for the majority, held that the commercial stations' licenses to broadcast on the public airwaves were commodities of great value. In passing the Rehabilitation Act, however, Congress had not intended government grants of licenses to be "federal financial assistance" which triggered Section 504 of the act.

Still, the court stated, commercial broadcasters had a general obligation under the Communications Act to serve the pubic interest, and this included "some accommodation for the hard of hearing." But the court relied on a series of FCC actions since 1970 designed to encourage broadcaster service to the deaf community, and on FCC assurances that this course would continue, to defer to the commission's expertise and judgment in the matter for the time being. "However," the court cautioned, "should the Commission fail to fulfill its obligations to the nation's hearing impaired minority . . .

judicial action might become appropriate at a later date."

The court found that as a recipient of federal funds for equipment and programming, station KCET was subject to Section 504. This law requires that no otherwise qualified handicapped individuals may, solely by reason of their handicap, be discriminated against or denied participation in or the benefits of the programs and activities by recipients of federal financial assistance.

The court then reasoned that the FCC, in interpreting the "public interest" standard of the Communications Act in connection with the station's renewal application, had to take into account the legal obligations of licensees subject to the Rehabilitation Act.

"It is unreasonable to believe that a public station could give service cognizable as being 'in the public interest' without at least making efforts to satisfy its statutory obligations [under the Rehabilitation Act]." On remand, the court provided the commission with flexibility to decide what procedures and accommodations would be appropriate.

In a separate opinion, Chief Judge Carl McGowan objected to the different treatment accorded to commercial and public broadcasters. Like the majority, he preferred a rulemaking proceeding by the FCC to determine "how the broadcast industry is required to provide the enjoyment and educational benefits of television to persons with impaired hearing." But McGowan dissented to the remand of KCET's license, preferring to treat all the broadcasters alike, at least until they had advance notice of what was, and could reasonably be, expected of them.

Both Community Television of Southern California and the FCC sought review from the Supreme Court. Gottfried sought review of the decision as it related to the commercial stations. The Supreme Court, which has discretion in these matters, accepted the petitions of KCET and the FCC, but declined Gottfried's petition to review the lower court's decision.

SUPREME COURT REVIEW: COMMUNITY TELEVISION OF SOUTHERN CALIFORNIA V. GOTTFRIED; FCC V. GOTTFRIED

On February 22, 1983, the Supreme Court reversed the court of appeals by a seven-to-two vote and affirmed the FCC's original renewal grant to KCET. Justice Stevens, writing for the majority, agreed that "the public interest would be served by making television broadcasting more available and more understandable to the substantial portion of our population that is handicapped by impaired hearing." And Stevens reiterated that no broadcaster "may simply ignore the needs of the hearing impaired."

But the Court found no congressional intent to have the FCC enforce the Rehabilitation Act. To the contrary, enforcement comes from the funding agencies, and the FCC is not a funding agency. More technically, the FCC does not have "original jurisdiction" of claims of violation of the Rehabilitation Act, although it can and should take other agency's findings of violations into account in considering the "public interest" merits of license renewal applicants.

The Court then set forth its narrow holding of the case, and left open the possibility of differential treatment in the future. "But unless and until such a differential standard has been promulgated, the Federal Communications Commission does not abuse its discretion in interpreting the public interest standard . . . when it declines to impose a greater obligation to provide special programming for the hearing impaired on a public licensee than on a commercial licensee."

Dissenting Justice Marshall, joined by Justice Brennan, agreed with Gottfried's argument that agency deliberation under the public interest standard cannot ignore a relevant act of Congress. The commission abused its discretion, they contended, by giving no consideration to the Rehabilitation Act. Furthermore, the dissenters noted, under the court of appeals holding, the commission did not have to treat public broadcasters more strictly than their commercial counterparts. Under its broad authority, the FCC could impose equal or greater obligations on the commerical licensees if rationally based. The ability to afford specialized programming might be one such basis.

While some of the language in the *Gottfried* decision was quite favorable to deaf people, the FCC's reaction was not. The commission continued to deny individual adjudications on the same basis as in the 1978 *Gottfried* decision—that there is no rule or requirement of captioning, or any other specific aid to deaf audiences, and therefore, short of a finding of violation of a relevant law, there is no reason for a hearing.

Meanwhile, Gottfried and GLAD had been seeking in a separate federal action a court order mandating government regulations from the FCC and other responsible agencies with respect to captioning programs on television.

GREATER LOS ANGELES COUNCIL ON DEAFNESS V. COMMUNITY TELEVISION OF SOUTHERN CALIFORNIA: THE DISTRICT COURT DECISION

Pursuing what they claimed was a "Catch-22" situation, Gottfried and GLAD sued KCET, the public broadcasting network (PBS), and the Corporation for Public Broadcasting, as well as the relevant governmental funding agencies, in federal district court for violation of Section 504 of the Rehabilitation Act. There could not be violations of the act if there were no standards or guidelines applicable to public broadcasters. And no agency was proceeding with rulemakings to address the question.

The Catch-22 arose from an administrative complaint which Gottfried filed in March 1978 with the Department of Health, Education and Welfare (HEW) against KCET. The department had the coordinating responsibility for governmental implementation of the Rehabilitation Act, and also was one source of federal financial assistance to public broadcasters.

Two weeks later the department stated that it was unable to act on the complaint without a policy clarification as to how the Rehabilitation Act related to public broadcasters.

After the FCC denied the license challenges to KCET in September 1978, in part because there was no violation of the act found by a funding agency (such as HEW), Gottfried, GLAD, and GLAD's executive director, Marcella Meyer, filed a class action suit in December 1978 representing the hearing-impaired population of greater Los Angeles against KCET, PBS, the Corporation for Public Broadcasting, the FCC, and HEW. The suit sought the issuance of governmental regulations to require public broadcasters to comply with Section 504 of the Rehabilitation Act, or the termination of federal funding to grantees not complying with the act. GLAD was later dismissed from the case on procedural grounds.

In an affidavit submitted to the court in October 1979, HEW agreed that public broadcasters were subject to Section 504, but requested remand of the case in order to develop an appropriate standard for compliance with the act. In March 1980 the district court, per Judge Manual Real, ordered the department to promulgate such a compliance standard "with all speed possible."

When HEW was restructured into two separate departments in 1980, this project fell within the jurisdiction of the Department of Education, which supplied funding to public broadcasters. To further complicate the matter, however, later in the same year President Carter transferred overall coordination responsibilities for implementation of the Rehabilitation Act to the Department of Justice. In January 1981 the Department of Education issued a notice of intent to issue regulations for public broadcasters.

Although the Department of Education had received extensions of time from the court to promulgate a rule, it abandoned the rulemaking in August 1981, and chose instead to rule specifically on whether KCET had complied with the act. It held that KCET satisfied the requirements of Section 504 by airing the "closed captioned" versions of programs supplied by the Department of Education, but that the station did not need to add its own captioning to other programs in view of the substantial financial burden such a requirement would impose.

The district court then resumed its trial of the matter, and held on November 17, 1981, that the government was discriminating against hearing-impaired viewers by failing to promulgate regulations making programming aired over public broadcast stations accessible to deaf people, implying that only open captioning would suffice for compliance with the Rehabilitation Act.

Judge Real enjoined the Department of Education from disbursing federal funds for public broadcasting until it adopted nondiscriminatory regulations, exempting from the order funds to aid in captioning. The judge also ordered the FCC and Attorney General to issue compliance regulation for public broadcasters.

GLAD v. COMMUNITY TELEVISION OF SOUTHERN CALIFORNIA: NINTH CIRCUIT DECISION

On appeal, a three-judge panel of the U.S. Court of Appeals for the Ninth Circuit reversed the district court order on November 3, 1983, several months after the Supreme Court's decision in the first *Gottfried* case. Judge Hug, writing for a unanimous panel, found error in the court's termination of funding without a particular finding that the recipients of such funding had failed to comply with a specific governmental funding requirement.

The Attorney General had coordination responsibilities, but was not a funder of public broadcasting. Since responsibility for enforcement of Section 504 was with the funding agency, the court found error in the district court's mandating the Department of Justice to issue regulations.

Similarly, relying on the Supreme Court decision in the first *Gottfried* decision, the court held that the FCC had "no responsibility for enforcement and no duty to promulgate regulations."

Finally, the court decided that the Department of Education had discretion as to whether to proceed by rulemaking or adjudication. Although it began with rulemaking, the court would not find an abuse of discretion in the department's switch to individual adjudication. "From a practical standpoint," the court opined, "the decision not to proceed by rulemaking will permit the Government to remain responsive to the developing technology in this area." It thus reversed the district court's decision to require rulemaking.

The court of appeals also affirmed the district court's dismissal of the class action against the "private defendants" KCET, PBS, and the Corporation for Public Broadcasting.

PETITION FOR SUPREME COURT REVIEW

Gottfried and Meyer sought Supreme Court review, arguing that the government had created a Catch-22 for deaf viewers. Individual adjudications were favorable to broadcasters because it would be unfair to hold them to a standard of compliance without first issuing a rule or guideline. Yet no government agency would issue a general standard for compliance by public broadcasters.

The petitioners also raised other constitutional and statutory grounds. But in June 1984, the Supreme Court denied review, thus leaving the Ninth Circuit decision intact.

IMPACT OF GOTTFRIED CASES

The initial decisions of the court of appeals in the first *Gottfried* case and the district court in the second *Gottfried* case created an atmosphere of pressure on the public broadcasting community to turn to closed captioning as a rational alternative to the more serious sanctions which could arise in litigation. This, along with governmental funding of captioning and a sincere desire to meet the needs of deaf viewers, led to a significant increase in closed captioning during the early 1980s. Ironically, that increase in captioning, which was disclosed to the courts at each level of appeal, may well have contributed to the ultimate success of the broadcasters in winning the litigation.

Although captioning increased and television became much more accessible to the deaf population, the essential legal paradox posed by the Gottfried litigation remained: until there is a specific governmental standard as to what constitutes compliance with the nondiscrimination dictates of the Rehabilitation Act, the act will not be enforced against public or other broadcasters. Yet no agency has taken the responsibility to issue comprehensive compliance standards. Furthermore, is it unfair or unreasonable to require public broadcasters to meet requirements in this area that more affluent commercial broadcasters may avoid? How does the government factor the cost of captioning into the need for reasonable accommodation for hearing-impaired persons? These questions, essentially unanswered by the *Gottfried* litigation, are not likely to disappear. Nor is the question of how America's significant hearing-impaired population will obtain access to the programming presented over the nation's airwaves. *See* TELECOMMUNICATIONS: Captioned Television.

Bibliography

Gottfried I: License Renewals—Los Angeles, 69 F.C.C.2d 451 (1978), *reconsid'n denied*, 72 F.C.C.2d 273 (1979), *aff'd in part and rev'd in part sub nom.* Gottfried v. FCC, 655 F.2d 297 (D.C.Cir. 1981), *aff'd in part and rev'd in part sub nom.* Community Television of Southern California v. Gottfried, 459 U.S. 498 (1983).

Gottfried II: Greater Los Angeles Council on Deafness v. Community Television of Southern California, Civil No. CV-78-4715R (unreported) (C.D.Cal. 1981), rev'd 719 F.2d 1017 (9th Cir. 1983), *cert. denied sub nom.* Gottfried v. United States, 104 S.Ct.3535, *reh'g denied*, 105 S.Ct.21 (1984).

Heldman, Television and the Hearing Impaired, 34 Fed.Comm. L.J. 93 (1982), plus the following notes on the case: 69 ABA J. 666 (1983); 5 Whittier L. Rev. 435 (1983); 31 Catholic L. Rev. 699 (1982); 9 J. Coll. & U.L. 1 (82–83); 130 U.Pa. L. Rev. 957 (1982); 7 Mental Disability L. Rep. 84 (1983); 4 B.C.L. Rev. 893 (1985).

Charles M. Firestone

Schornstein v. New Jersey Division of Vocational Rehabilitation Services

The Rehabilitation Act of 1973 established two means by which deaf college students can be provided interpreters. As part of its mandate of non-discrimination, Section 504 requires federal financial recipients, such as colleges, to provide interpreters to deaf persons who need them to use the program's services. In addition, Title I of the Rehabilitation Act of 1973 provides federal funds to states for vocational rehabilitation programs for disabled persons; it specifies that certain services, including interpreters and training, must be provided when necessary to achieve an individual's vocational goal. Both Section 504 and Title I are interpreted by regulations developed by the U.S. Department of Education.

Many deaf persons in their state's vocational rehabilitation programs attend training institutions or colleges which are federal financial recipients. A controversy has arisen, therefore, as to which facility is responsible for funding of the deaf student's interpreter—the federally funded college or training institution, or the state vocational rehabilitation agency which otherwise funds the student's training.

Two federal courts of appeals have reviewed this issue. In both cases the courts found that the primary obligation for provision of interpreters to vocational rehabilitation clients rests with the vocational rehabilitation agency, but the decisions rested on two different legal theories. In 1980 deaf vocational rehabilitation clients in New Jersey whose vocational rehabilitation plan included college or other training faced a dilemma. The New Jersey Division of Vocational Rehabilitation Services (NJDVRS) had a written policy to refuse to provide sign language interpreter services for training or college attendance. It based this policy on the argument that Section 504 required colleges to provide interpreters. However, many of the colleges in New Jersey also refused to provide interpreter services. The colleges based their refusal on a letter from the state which maintained that colleges had no such Section 504 obligation. One of the vocational rehabilitation clients affected, Ruth Ann Schornstein, brought suit against both her college, Kean College, and the state vocational rehabilitation agency. She asked the U.S. District Court for the District of New Jersey to decide which, if either, of these state institutions should provide her with the interpreter services she needed to attend college, and to thereby achieve vocational skills.

There was no dispute as to the facts. Schornstein had been accepted by vocational rehabilitation as an eligible client, and as required, an individual rehabilitation plan had been developed for her. The plan set forth the agreed-upon vocational goal, which required college training, and noted that interpreter services would be necessary in order for Schornstein to receive this training. The vocational rehabilitation agency provided her with funds for tuition, books, and transportation, but refused to provide funds for interpreter services. Similarly, Kean College acknowledged that it was a federal financial recipient, that Schornstein was eligible to attend Kean, and that she needed interpreter services. However, Kean College also refused to provide a fund for interpreter services.

The U.S. district court found that the state vocational rehabilitation agency's blanket policy denying interpreter services to every deaf client receiving training violated Title I of the Rehabilitation Act. Title I authorizes grants to assist states in their vocational rehabilitation of handicapped persons, but the states that elect to participate in this program must comply with the terms and conditions that Title I sets forth. One of the terms of Title I is that the state vocational rehabilitation agency must prepare an individualized rehabilitation plan tailored especially for each individual client. Additionally, Title I defines the scope of vocational rehabilitation services that must be provided to an individual to render the individual employable. Title I lists examples of goods and services to be provided by vocational rehabilitation, and specifically includes "interpreter services for deaf individuals." The court found the New Jersey vocational rehabilitation policy particularly objectionable in that it was based on colleges' obligations to provide interpreters, although New Jersey itself denied that colleges had any obligation to provide interpreter services.

The court also found that the vocational rehabilitation agency has no authority to deny an individual deaf client interpreter services if they are needed to achieve the client's vocational goals. Title I requires that vocational rehabilitation agencies must give priority in delivering services to "severely handicapped individuals," which includes deaf persons. Therefore, deaf persons who meet vocational rehabilitation eligibility standards must be accepted as clients. Once a client has been accepted to receive services, the vocational rehabilitation agency has little discretion as to what services must be provided. The services listed in Title I, including interpreter services, must be provided to the client when necessary to achieve his or her vocational goal. The vocational rehabilitation agency may adopt an "economic needs" test for provision of these services, and must seek "similar benefit" programs to provide alternative sources of funding for the required services. However, the court found that New Jersey's vocational rehabilitation agency had adopted no "economic needs" test for interpreter services to deaf persons, and could point to no "similar benefits" programs to provide interpreter services.

Therefore, because the vocational rehabilitation agency had accepted Schornstein as a client and had conceded that she needed interpreter services to meet her vocational goals, the court found that Title I required the agency to provide those services. Since the court found the agency responsible under Title I, it held that it did not have to decide whether Kean College or the state agency had a Section 504 responsibility to provide interpreter services as federal financial recipients. The decision of the district court was affirmed by the U.S. Court of Appeals for the Third Circuit.

Jones v. IDRS

The same issue arose in Illinois that same year. The courts there arrived at a conclusion similar to that of the courts in *Schornstein*, but based their conclusion on different legal grounds.

In the Illinois case, Charles Jones was a client of Illinois Department of Rehabilitation Services (IDRS). His vocational plan called for attendance at the Illinois Institute of Technology (ITT). In Jones's case, however, vocational rehabilitation and the college were actively pointing to each other as being responsible for providing the necessary interpreter services, and based their refusals on the premise that the other was responsible. Therefore, Jones sued both the college and the vocational rehabilitation agency, asking the court to decide which was responsible.

The agency defended itself on the section of Title I which requires a vocational rehabilitation agency to look for a "similar benefits" program to provide necessary services to a client. The agency claimed that this section prohibits vocational rehabilitation from providing interpreter services to a college student because the college's Section 504 obligation to provide interpreter services constitutes a "similar benefit." The college based its defense on a section of the Department of Education Section 504 Regulation's Analysis, which states that auxiliary aids for students, such as interpreters, will usually be paid for, not by colleges, but by agencies such as vocational rehabilitation.

The U.S. district court declined to base its decision on Jones's rights as a vocational rehabilitation client on Title I. It found that an individual cannot bring suit under Title I because Title I creates an express administrative remedy for vocational rehabilitation clients who are dissatisfied with an action by the state vocational rehabilitation agency.

However, the court found that, under Section 504, both the agency and the college had an obligation to provide interpreter services to Jones because both were federal financial recipients, and Jones required an interpreter to benefit from either program. The court found that the agency had the primary obligation to provide interpreter services. It held that a college's obligations under Section 504 do not render it a "similar benefit," and that it was the intention of the Department of Education that vocational rehabilitation agencies rather than colleges provide interpreters for vocational rehabilitation clients at college. However, the court noted that the college was responsible for providing an interpreter for Jones if he should ever cease to be eligible for vocational rehabilitation assistance. A U.S. court of appeals affirmed this court's decision.

Therefore, on two different legal theories, courts have determined that vocational rehabilitation agencies have the primary obligation to provide interpreter services to deaf college students who are clients.

Elaine Gardner

REHABILITATION LITERATURE

Rehabilitation Literature is published by the National Easter Seal Society, the United States' oldest and largest voluntary health agency concerned with the total rehabilitation of persons with disabling conditions. As an interdisciplinary journal, *Rehabilitation Literature* is intended for use by professional personnel and students in all areas pertaining to the physical and mental rehabilitation of disabled individuals. It is dedicated to the advancement of knowledge and skills and to the encouragement of cooperative efforts by professional members of the rehabilitation team. *Rehabilitation Literature* serves to promote communication among medical and health practitioners and to alert them to the literature on development and progress both in their own areas of responsibility and in related areas. It informs readers through original articles, abstracts of current literature, book reviews, information on new products, film reviews, and notices of new programs and research projects. As a reviewing and abstracting journal, it identifies and describes current books, monographs, and periodical articles pertaining to the care, welfare, education, and employment of children and adults with disabilities.

AUDIENCE
Rehabilitation Literature is the primary service publication of the National Easter Seal Society (formerly, the Society for Crippled Children and Adults), headquartered in Chicago, Illinois, and its 47 affiliated state societies in the United States and Canada. The journal is circulated to hospitals, libraries, universities, health organizations, independent living centers, rehabilitation centers and agencies, as well as rehabilitation practitioners throughout the United States, Canada, Mexico, and over 45 other countries. The readers of *Rehabilitation Literature* represent virtually every rehabilitation-related discipline, including physicians, nurses, psychologists, counselors, social workers, medical librarians, therapists (speech, occupational, physical), administrators, and teachers. *See* REHABILITATION: Personnel.

Rehabilitation Literature has a paid subscription list of over 4500. Because approximately 40 percent of the journal's subscription list is made up of institutions—hospitals, universities, colleges, libraries, rehabilitation centers, welfare and social agencies—the number and types of readers reached by a single subscription are difficult to estimate. Readership surveys indicate that a single copy of the journal is routinely read by more than eight people.

HISTORY
The current *Rehabilitation Literature* evolved out of the *Bulletin on Current Literature* and its successor, *Rehabilitation Literature* (1940–1958), both compilations of book reviews and abstracts in mimeographed form. In January 1959, the new journal was introduced with added contents, including original review articles written by authorities in particular phases of rehabilitation activities, book reviews, digests of selected articles of significance published in current issues of other journals, a critical book review by an expert in the area covered, and a section of comments and events of interest to the readers.

When the new publication was about to be introduced, editor Earl Graham dedicated the journal to the rehabilitation professions and to their members who worked with disabled persons. He stated that *Rehabilitation Literature* would report on the advancement of knowledge and skills in the various areas of rehabilitation and encourage cooperative efforts among professional members of the rehabilitation team. He also established the journal as an independent undertaking, in no sense the house organ of the National Society for Crippled Children and Adults, whose contributors would give free expression to their own ideas and opinions. Thus, the journal has always covered the broad area of rehabilitation and has not confined itself to the specific interests of the National Easter Seal Society.

Rehabilitation Literature's features have chronicled the emergence of rehabilitation both as a movement and as a profession. Its articles have addressed basic principles and views of rehabilitation as process and philosophy. The writings of eminent rehabilitation authorities have appeared over the years and have helped to shape not only approaches toward rehabilitation treatment but also society's attitudes toward disabled persons.

The evolution of *Rehabilitation Literature* since 1959 shows a variety of changes, especially since the mid-1970s. Issues from 1959 to 1975 were published monthly and consisted of 32 pages. In 1976 a decision was made to publish ten issues per year, with two issues (June/July, November/December) having 56 pages. Since the 1980 volume, *Rehabilitation Literature* has been published bimonthly, with issues running 64 to 80 pages.

An editorial advisory board was formally established in January 1981. Although the journal's staff had formerly used the services of selected authorities for manuscript evaluation, the board's structured peer review strengthened the journal's credibility and prestige, and facilitated the publication of general scholarly articles characteristic of the journal's interdisciplinary focus. The current 16-member board provides the basis for a network of reviewers and advisers, and assists the staff with the development of special features which regularly appear in the journal.

Paid advertising was initially accepted beginning in February 1981, and now comprises approximately 6% of the journal's pages.

FORMAT

Contents of the journal consist of a feature article, special articles or special reports, commentary, new products section, events and comments, rehab calendar, film forum, feature book review, general book reviews, abstracts of current literature, and author index. Publishers and addresses of periodicals abstracted in each issue are listed alphabetically. An annual index, of articles and authors only, is printed in the November/December issue.

The feature article is usually a review article in which the author summarizes current knowledge and recent developments in a specific field. The present status of the subject is often documented by a review of the literature as well as by a presentation of the author's own experience and personal observations. In the course of the review, the author reports, evaluates, and criticizes what is being

done and what is known. It is essential that current and recent research activities be discussed in terms of their implications for general rehabilitation efforts. Six thousand words are allotted to the feature article.

The special articles or special reports run 1500 to 3000 words. These may be an expression of opinion by the author; a report of a clinical experience, program, or project; or pragmatic observations and information in an area of concern to a particular segment of the readership.

In October 1981, *Rehabilitation Literature* published a special issue commemorating the International Year of Disabled Persons. Since then a series of special issues have been published on a variety of timely subjects, such as women and disability, attitudes, technology, aging, vocational rehabilitation, and childhood disabilities. These issues are usually 72 pages and afford a comprehensive summary of the most up-to-date materials on the featured subject.

Contributed articles in *Rehabilitation Literature* are selectively indexed by most of the major abstracting and indexing services.

Bibliography

Graham, E. C., and M. M. Mullen (comp. and eds.): *Rehabilitation Literature 1950–1955: A Bibliographic Review of the Medical Care, Education, Employment, Welfare, and Psychology of Handicapped Children and Adults,* McGraw-Hill, New York, 1956.

Regnier, S. J., and M. Petkovsek (eds.): *Rehabilitation: 25 Years of Concepts, Principles, Perspectives,* National Easter Seal Society, Chicago, 1984.

Stephen J. Regnier

REHABILITATION PSYCHOLOGY

Rehabilitation Psychology is the journal of the Division of Rehabilitation Psychology of the American Psychological Association (APA). This division began as a special interest group in 1949 and was entitled the National Council on Psychological Aspects of Disability. In 1954 the forerunner of the journal was first published as the *Newsletter*. In 1957 its name was changed to the *Bulletin*, and it began to publish more scholarly material in addition to news items about the National Council. In 1958 the National Council on Psychological Aspects of Disability became an official division of the American Psychological Association, and in 1960 the division's name became Psychological Aspects of Disability. In 1969 the name of the *Bulletin* was changed to *Psychological Aspects of Disability* to reflect its new status as a scholarly journal in response to growing recognition of the importance of psychological factors in disability, and to the need to disseminate scholarly information on the topic to those working in the field. In 1972 the names of the journal and the division were changed to Rehabilitation Psychology.

Rehabilitation Psychology is an interdisciplinary journal of relevance to all concerned with psychological perspectives in rehabilitation. The journal publishes articles that address the psychological and behavioral aspects of rehabilitation in a wide range of settings and from a number of perspectives. A variety of issues and populations within rehabilitation and psychology are considered appropriate for study by professionals working with the psychological and psychosocial aspects of rehabilitation. The journal publishes manuscripts that deal with issues of chronic illness, and physical, mental, or emotional disability throughout the entire life span, and include such populations as persons with developmental disabilities and elderly people. Manuscripts that detail sound empirical research, theory, clinical practices, and policy issues in rehabilitation psychology are published, as are reviews of pertinent topics. Additionally, the journal incorporates Brief Research Reports and Brief Clinical Reports sections for studies whose sample size is small. A Book Review section presents reviews of newly published, relevant books. From time to time an entire issue of the journal is devoted to a topic of particular importance or interest to the readership. Suggestions for special issues are welcomed by the editor.

In order to change prevalent psychological attitudes about disability, the journal has established a policy of avoiding language that contributes to the continuation of myths about persons with disabling conditions. Therefore, the journal encourages authors to maintain the integrity of persons with disabling conditions in the conduct of research, interpretation of data, and use of terms. Authors should avoid language that equates persons with the conditions they have, such as "epileptics" or "postpolios," or language that implies that the person as a whole is disabled, as in the expression "disabled person."

Mary A. Jansen

RELIGION, CATHOLIC

Without church programs for deaf people in the past, the present status of deaf education might have been delayed for another hundred years. The pioneers of these early programs were motivated by religious ideals and believed in the worth of all individuals. Eventually, the pioneer programs of church groups were outnumbered by tax-supported public programs, and the influence of religious groups waned in an increasingly secular society. Yet although the church seemed to lose a

leadership role, it remained a constant influence on the lives of deaf persons. However, a new era has dawned with the growing awareness of the importance of church programs for hearing-impaired individuals. More and more persons, both hearing and deaf, are being drawn into this ministry.

There are approximately 50,000,000 Catholics in the United States, of whom at least 100,000 are deaf. To meet their needs, 92 dioceses—more than half of the church's 167 dioceses—have appointed salaried personnel to minister with deaf Catholics. The number of persons working in this special ministry varies from diocese to diocese. It is difficult to number those who do pastoral work with deaf Catholics because the situation is in constant flux, but approximately 400 persons contribute varying amounts of expertise—full-time, part-time, and volunteer.

BEGINNING OF CATHOLIC MINISTRY WITH DEAF PERSONS

Historically, it might be said that the Catholic church began its service to deaf Americans on April 15, 1817, in Connecticut. On that date the American Asylum for the Deaf and Dumb, at Hartford, opened its doors as the first permanent school for deaf students in the United States. The school's founder, Thomas Hopkins Gallaudet, had obtained the teaching services of a Catholic deaf man from France, Laurent Clerc. Bishop John Cheverus, the first bishop of Boston (whose See included the state of Connecticut) had been a contributor to the Hartford school. However, these early roots were terminated when Clerc converted to Protestantism and led the Catholic children in his path. All students were required to attend regular Protestant chapel exercises, and no Catholic priest was allowed to enter the school and minister to its deaf pupils until 1896. *See* AMERICAN SCHOOL FOR THE DEAF; CLERC, LAURENT; GALLAUDET, THOMAS HOPKINS.

The establishment of private Catholic schools for deaf children was the major factor that kept the faith alive among American deaf persons. This influence began with the opening of St. Joseph's Institute for the Deaf in St. Louis, Missouri, by the Sisters of St. Joseph of Carondelet in 1837, and grew with the opening of St. Mary's School in Buffalo, New York, in 1859. Several other Catholic schools for deaf children were established in the nineteenth century, including St. Joseph's in the Bronx, New York (1869), St. John's in Milwaukee, Wisconsin (1876), Ephpheta in Chicago, Illinois (1890), Chinchuba Institute in New Orleans, Louisiana (1895), St. Joseph's in Oakland, California (1895), and the Boston School at Randolph, Massachusetts (1899). Six more Catholic schools were established in the twentieth century: St. Gabriel in Puerto Rico (1902),

DePaul Institute in Pittsburgh, Pennsylvania (1908), Archbishop Ryan Memorial Institute (1912), St. Rita School (1915), and St. Francis deSales, all three in Brooklyn, New York (1960), and Cleary School on Long Island, New York (1963). After the Ephpheta School in Chicago closed in the early 1950s, Catholic Charities opened special classrooms for deaf students in existing Catholic day schools beginning with St. Mel–Holy Ghost. This concept of providing separate rooms in day schools allowed deaf students to live at home and grow up with hearing children while receiving specialized education. The Holy Trinity program began in 1957 with one room for deaf students and then acquired its own building. For over 150 years graduates of these schools have been leaders and Christian role models for their peers and descendants. *See* EDUCATION: History; EDUCATIONAL PROGRAMS: Day Schools.

PIONEER MINISTERS

Several notable persons can be credited with nurturing the faith of American Catholic deaf persons: Mother Mary Anne Burke, who for more than 60 years served every interest of the students at St. Mary's; Mother Borgia of St. Joseph's in St. Louis, much admired by older deaf people who, because of her, exhibit generosity of faith, nondependence in their personal lives, and enthusiasm of spirit; Father Gehl, a dynamic speaker around the country for the benefit of St. John's; and Monsignor Waldhaus at St. Rita's.

Father Daniel D. Higgins, a Redemptorist priest, is among these pioneers. From 1906 to 1959, he gave missions to deaf people from coast to coast and was unsurpassed in visual catechetics. His special gift was the understanding of movement and pantomime. His sermon outlines resembled a set of stage directions as he moved characters around for visual effect. He spent much of his time with deaf children in state schools. Years later, deaf adults across the country remembered the priest with magic in his hands.

Father Higgins missed no opportunity to promote this apostolate and to draw laborers into the Catholic church. Wherever he traveled, he gave talks at seminaries and convents, urged priests whose parishes were near schools for the deaf to "hear" the word of God. Due to his promptings, many seminaries initiated classes in the language of signs. His legacy to his own religious community, the Redemptorists (C.Ss.R.), was the establishment of a tradition of priests to work with deaf people.

MINISTRY WITH DEAF ADULTS

Early in the twentieth century, many Catholic deaf societies were established. Many of the pioneers who established Catholic schools for deaf students were responsible for beginning these Catholic deaf associations for adults at approximately the same time. Several of these early deaf societies published magazines or newsletters for disseminating information, most on a monthly basis. Two were published at DePaul Institute: the *DePaul Alumni News* and the *Catholic Deaf Bulletin*. The *Catholic Auditor* carried announcements and news of interest to deaf Catholics of the Trenton, New Jersey, diocese, and *The Spokesman* was published for deaf persons in Philadelphia, Pennsylvania. An early national publication for deaf Catholics was the *Catholic Deaf Mute*, begun in 1899. This publication continued until 1936, when its name was changed to *Ephpheta*. *Ephpheta*, the offical organ of the National Catholic Education Association, included articles of general interest, pertinent problems of the day, special feature articles, use of color, and many pictures and photographs. Publication ceased in 1969. The Catholic Knights and Ladies of de l'Epée, a national society with headquarters in Chicago and councils in Cincinnati, Boston, Philadelphia, Scranton, Baltimore, Providence, Milwaukee, Altoona, and Toledo, also published a national newsletter, the *De l'Epéean*.

Perhaps the golden age of work with deaf adults in the United States was the period between 1945 and 1960, when over 30 priests were assigned to this apostolate in various dioceses, most of them on a full-time basis. It was during this time that the International Catholic Deaf Association (ICDA) was born. Through the initiative of a group of Catholic deaf laypersons from various cities in Canada and the United States, particularly Marcel Warnier of Toronto, and a group of priest-chaplains, the association was founded in 1949. This lay organization is led by persons who are themselves deaf. The main objective of the association is to give the deaf person a sense of identification with the church. Specifically, it promotes unity among deaf Catholics throughout the world, promotes the teaching and principles of the Catholic church, and is actively engaged in good works pertaining to the educational, social, and ethical advancement of deaf persons. The purpose of the association is spiritual.

Father John Gallagher, C.Ss.R., served as chaplain of the International Catholic Deaf Association from 1952 until his death in 1960. His enthusiasm for the association motivated deaf Catholics around the country to establish local chapters. Always desiring to strengthen the status of the association among church authorities and Catholic organizations, Father Gallagher even wrote to Pope Pius XII about the progress of the association and obtained his apostolic blessing. Father Thomas Cribbin followed Father Gallagher as chaplain, and for 12 years inspired united Catholic action within the organization. He promoted prayers and sacrifices one day a week as a special appeal to God to lead the many strayed deaf Catholics back to Catholicism. He also encouraged use of the association's Mission Fund for many worthwhile projects.

The International Catholic Deaf Association has an annual convention and publishes the *Deaf Catholic* bimonthly. The Mission Fund, maintained by voluntary contributions from association members and other interested persons, has helped to provide retreats in schools for deaf students, missions for deaf adults in areas where there is no pastor, and a salary for the priest who serves as missionary to deaf Catholics in the United States.

FATHER DAVID WALSH

Greatly responsible for building up association membership and establishing new chapters was Father David Walsh, another Redemptorist, who labored from the 1950s as a missionary to deaf persons and officially as a missionary for the association from 1962 until 1976. He traveled around the country and gave retreats and missions, counseled people, visited schools and catechized the students, celebrated special liturgies, and administered the sacraments. Because his extensive travel convinced him that the work of the church with deaf people needed more of everything (Catholic deaf leaders, chaplains, sisters, brothers, pastoral workers), he lost no opportunity to encourage anyone who expressed an interest in this ministry to pursue it. In fact, a second "golden age" of deaf ministry can be identified between 1965 and 1975, when a large number of sisters joined the ranks of pastoral workers. A third period is evident, too, after 1975, when lay persons entered the field on a full-time, professional basis.

Because special education is necessary for those involved in catechizing deaf Catholics, Father Walsh began organizing national religious education workshops. The first one was held in 1960 at DePaul University in Chicago and ran for 10 days; 16 more workshops were to follow in various cities. These workshops provided professional training in sign language and teaching techniques and produced sets of religious lesson plans for nationwide circulation. Video-taped presentations for distribution were produced at the 1982 and 1984 workshops.

Father Walsh envisioned and developed another type of national annual workshop, the Pastoral Week; the first one was held in 1971 in Jacksonville, Florida. At these workshops, pastoral workers who often work alone in widespread geographical areas come together for mutual support and sharing. They spend a week listening to professionals on such topics as scripture, spirituality, counseling, sign language, liturgy, and sacraments. The religious education workshops and the Pastoral Weeks have united

pastoral workers and have served to greatly advance work with deaf Catholics.

A program exclusively for deaf persons is the Cursillo. Cursillos are retreat experiences which bring together up to 70 persons for prayers, religious instruction, and leadership training. Cursillos are conducted by a team of deaf lay persons aided by several priest-spiritual directors. Father Walsh organized the first national Cursillo for deaf Catholics in 1970 and held it in Chicago. Since then, over 1000 deaf persons have participated in 1 of 23 Cursillos and the movement has grown in popularity.

A follow-up to this experience is the Ultreya, a gathering of Cursillistas in a given area on a regular basis. Its purpose is twofold: for the group to give visible evidence of their life in Christ, and for members to share with each other their life in Christ. They come together to inspire each other. Ultreyas continue regularly in local areas, while some have been organized nationally.

NATIONAL CATHOLIC OFFICE FOR THE DEAF

During the years that Father Walsh was traveling and organizing national workshops, he envisioned the establishment of a national office which would coordinate religious service with deaf Catholics. In July 1971, at the convention of the International Catholic Deaf Association, the priests in attendance voted to establish a national pastoral office for the deaf under the direction of Father Walsh. These priests, who had been working a number of years with deaf people, recognized the need to coordinate and develop the church's work at a national level. They knew that often there was no chaplain for deaf Catholics in a diocese or, if there was, his work was part-time, and he was seldom available; that very few priests had learned to communicate well with deaf people; and that there was a continuous turnover of chaplains and teaching personnel in the religious education programs. Father Walsh accepted the mandate and began to operate this national office from Liguori, Missouri. By 1973, pastoral workers had elected a steering committee of 19 members, who drew up goals and objectives for this organization and elected a five-member board of directors for a term of 3 years.

All steering committee members agreed that pastoral service to bishops, pastors, pastoral workers, catechists, parents of deaf children, and to deaf individuals themselves was the central concept of the National Catholic Office for the Deaf (NCOD). They set down the following objectives for the National Catholic Office: (1) to influence bishops and pastors through information concerning hearing-impaired persons; (2) to coordinate the efforts of all persons and organizations involved in the church's work with hearing-impaired persons; (3) to provide information concerning the religious needs of hearing-impaired Catholics and conduct catechist training workshops; (4) to prepare and distribute specially adapted liturgies, catechetical lessons, Marriage Encounter, Teens Encounter Christ, and Cursillo manuals; and (5) to serve as a resource center for religious education materials for hearing-impaired Catholics.

Father Walsh opened an office in 1976 at Trinity College in Washington, D.C. He continued organizing and developing the above-mentioned programs and initiated two more significant advances in deaf ministry. One was the publishing of a bimonthly journal called *Listening*, an international magazine for pastoral workers, parents of deaf children, and the deaf community that features articles on pastoral ministry and religious education. Special issues have focused on subgroups such as deaf Hispanics and aged deaf persons.

The other important advancement was the establishment of a training program for those wishing to enter ministry with deaf persons. The program invites college graduates, deaf as well as hearing persons, and persons of all religious faiths to use the resources of Catholic University and Gallaudet College. Persons can study theology and pastoral ministry at Catholic University and sign language and deaf psychology at Gallaudet College. The program was designed to be flexible and tailored to the specific needs and interests of each trainee. Upon the completion of 24 academic credit-hours, a seminar, a practicum, a research paper, and an evaluation by a board of experienced pastoral workers, candidates are awarded a certificate issued by the National Catholic Office. *See* GALLAUDET COLLEGE.

Father Walsh continued as executive director until 1980, when the board of directors selected Sister M. Alverna Hollis, O.P., as his successor. One of her significant contributions to the ministry was the writing and illustrating of *Signs for Catholic Liturgy and Education*, a manual of religious signs with suggestions for interpreting various prayers.

The National Catholic Office for the Deaf is a membership organization of five geographical regions: the West, the South, the Midwest, the Great Lakes, and the Atlantic Seaboard. Board members represent each region at board meetings and assist the region by discovering the needs of deaf Catholics in the region and encouraging programs in undeveloped areas; acting as liaison persons between bishops and deaf Catholics; initiating an annual regional workshop; maintaining contact with pastoral workers and taking their suggestions to board meetings.

The National Catholic Office could never have been opened without generous financial assistance. The Loyal Christian Benefit Association (LCBA), first under the presidency of Bertha Leavy and later under Catherine Kelly, funded the major programs of the National Catholic Office (Cursillos, Pastoral Weeks, *Listening* magazine) since its founding. An incorporated, benevolent, fraternal, insurance association, the Loyal Christian Benefit Association is dedicated to providing fraternal activities and fraternal life insurance plans for Christian women, children, and men.

DEAF PRIESTS AND DEACONS

The Catholic church in the United States can boast of several deaf priests, including Father Thomas Coughlin, O.S.S.T., Joseph Bruce, S.J., and Raymond Fleming. All of them have led retreats, missions, and prayer days throughout the country. From the time of his ordination in 1977, Father Coughlin wanted to establish an organization dedicated to Christian development of deaf youth. He named the organization Mark Seven, from the scripture passage about Jesus curing the deaf man. The goals of Mark Seven are to establish a national deaf youth camp, to promote religious vocations, and to establish a permanent retreat house.

A significant event in the history of deaf Catholics was the private audience of Pope John Paul II with Father Coughlin on June 14, 1979. An appeal was made to the Holy Father to recognize the spiritual needs of deaf Catholics. Father Coughlin told him of the hope to establish a permanent youth camp and retreat center. The Holy Father endorsed the constitution of Mark Seven. Within 3 years, Father Coughlin purchased land and a hotel at Old Forge, New York.

Camp Mark Seven began its first season in the summer of 1982. Attending the two youth leadership and religious development programs were students from St. Joseph's School in the Bronx and teens from Kentucky, Illinois, and Ohio. Their experience at the camp included sessions on moral and spiritual development, group discussions, games, outdoor recreational activities, and prayers. Later, the camp hosted a private directed retreat and a community week for New Yorkers. The calendar for a second season filled up immediately upon the close of the first summer's activities.

Another advance in ministry with Catholic deaf persons was the ordination of deaf men to the diaconate. Upon completion of seminary studies, Jerome Kiel and Paul Pernecky were ordained in 1975, William Koch in 1981, and Thomas Ryan and Patrick Graybill in 1982.

DEAF SISTERS

Precisely how many deaf women have been admitted into religious communities is not clear. The earliest known record of a deaf girl entering a convent appears to be that of Sister Patricia, who graduated from the Pennsylvania School for the Deaf and was received into the Community of the Sisters of St. Joseph in 1880. Honora Benedict Wholihan, known as Sister Xavier Mary of St. Hubert, entered the Mission Helpers of the Sacred Heart in Towson, Maryland, in 1901. Most of her life was spent as housemother to the deaf children who attended St. Gabriel School for the Deaf in Puerto Rico. Suffering from poor eyesight and later from spasmodic muscles, she returned in 1926 to the motherhouse infirmary and remained there until her death in 1943.

In 1929 a semireligious organization of deaf women, known as the Sisters of the Pious Union of Our Lady of Good Counsel, was accepted into the order of the Sisters of Charity of Cincinnati. Many of these sisters became teachers at St. Rita's School. The Sisters of Charity discontinued accepting hearing-impaired persons in 1935. The Sisters of St. Francis of Assisi of St. Francis, Wisconsin, accepted four deaf sisters.

Sister Mary Immaculate Grassi, a deaf woman of the Sisters of St. Joseph of Chestnut Hill, works pastorally with the deaf of Philadelphia. Sister Maureen Langton of the Sisters of St. Joseph of Carondelet ministers in New York City.

Special retreats for the hearing-impaired priests, sisters, brothers, and deacons of the United States have been organized nationally. Some participants use sign language, some lipread, others (who have recently become deaf) depend upon the written word. Special effort is made to communicate with all those gathered for the prayer experience.

MINISTRY TODAY

The backbone of religious service with deaf Catholics is the routine of activities carried out on the local level: the regularly scheduled worship services and religious education programs; weddings, baptisms, and funerals; visits to the sick and shut-ins; counseling; interpreting; meetings of local deaf associations and the chapters of the International Catholic Deaf Association; and Marriage Encounter and Engaged Encounter weekends. Catholic action varies according to the creativity and interests of each group. Usually, each diocese or Center for the Deaf publishes a monthly newsletter which announces a schedule of religious events and prints news concerning the community.

Pastoral workers face two great challenges concerning ministry with deaf Catholics. Although Pope Paul VI's encyclical of 1975 on Evangelization in the Modern World and the United States Catholic Bishops' Statement of 1978 on Handicapped People both establish priority of ministry with disabled persons, all dioceses have not implemented these exhortations. Many dioceses lack programs and trained personnel to minister with deaf individuals.

The other challenge is to develop religious-education materials and programs that will reach deaf people in depth. There has been little research into deaf people's understanding of religion. However, in 1974 the first major research on the religious thinking of deaf persons appeared in Father Anthony Russo's *The God of the Deaf Adolescent*. His monumental work, based on 4 years of research including interviews with 150 deaf students, has verified that the texts and programs available have not been able to reach deaf persons in depth. This is not because the deaf persons are restricted by any intellectual limitation, but because catechists have not as yet developed religious-education materials specifically designed for deaf Catholics. The great challenge facing catechists is to develop the content that Father Russo describes in his book.

Bibliography

Bergin, Rev. Robert: "The Catholic Church's Ministry with the Deaf in the Archdiocese of Hartford," *Listening*, vol. 4, no. 4, September–October 1981.

Higgins, Father Daniel D.: *Catechism with Pictured Signs*, 1943.

————: *How to Talk to the Deaf*, 1923.

Hourihan, Rev. John P.: "Church Programs for the Hearing Impaired," in Bradford and Hardy (eds.), *Hearing and Hearing Impairment*, Grune and Stratton, New York, 1979.

Jacquet, C. H.: *Yearbook of American and Canadian Churches—1976*, Abington Press, Nashville.

Russo, Rev. A.: *The God of the Deaf Adolescent*, Paulist Press, Paramus, New Jersey, 1975.

Stone, M. E., and J. P. Youngs, Jr.: "Catholic Education of the Deaf in the United States, 1837–1948," *American Annals of the Deaf*, pp. 409–510, 1948.

Walsh, Rev. D.: "Let Us Now Praise Great Men: Unusual Man—Daniel D. Higgins," 1975.

————: "The Role of the Clergy Serving the Deaf," in Stein, Mindel, and Jabaley (eds.), *Deafness and Mental Health*, Grune and Stratton, New York, 1981.

————: "Statement on the Work of the Catholic Church for the Deaf in the United States," 1975.

Sister M. Alverna Hollis, O.P.

RELIGION, JEWISH

Judaism is probably the oldest monotheistic religion in the world, and the oldest book in Judaism, the Bible, is full of references to deaf people. To understand the present situation of deaf Jews, a brief review of the Jewish law concerning deafness from the talmudic period (200–500 of the Christian Era) up to the present is necessary.

EARLY HISTORY

In Talmud, the deaf person (*heresh*) is negatively defined as follows: A person who can speak at all, even poorly, is not considered a *heresh*. A person who can hear the loud slamming of a door is not considered a *heresh*.

In Talmudic times, both religious authorities and the laity were of the opinion that deaf Jews should be excluded from religious rituals. They based their decision on the notion that the inability to hear deprived deaf persons of the opportunity to listen and be educated, to gain knowledge of the Torah, and to respond in prayer. The rabbinic exclusion of deaf people from Jewish ritual life needs to be properly understood. It was not motivated by malice but by the desire to relieve deaf Jews of religious burdens and protect them from inadvertently breaking any laws. The rabbis, who functioned more like modern lawyers than clergy, developed laws to exempt deaf persons from various civil and religious duties. Over time, however, these exemptions were interpreted as prohibitions, and so they became restrictions.

It is interesting to note that in the Mishnah (a Jewish legal code compiled about 200 C.E.) the rabbis explicitly allowed marriages by means of "gestures" (*remizot*), possibly the first reference to signing in Jewish literature. In some rabbinic legends, Mordecai, the hero of the book of Esther, is portrayed as so adept a linguist that he could understand the language of deaf people. This tradition not only confirms the existence of an early system of manual communication among deaf people, it also suggests that Mordecai was the first interpreter.

The development of Jewish law reveals a liberalizing trend. Jewish law, regarded by many as revealed by God, cannot be changed by fiat. Instead, when the law makers are confronted with a law that has become odious, like capital punishment, they simply define it out of existence by establishing such strict rules of evidence that convicting someone of a capital offense is virtually impossible. In the case of laws concerning deaf persons, the rabbis repeatedly narrowed the legal definition of deafness until there were very few people who qualified as being deaf (*hereshim*). Azriel Hildesheimer (1820–1899), a leading orthodox rabbi in Berlin, argued with his slightly older Hungarian contemporary Maharam Schick over this point. Hildesheimer believed that deaf people's advances when taught by modern methods had demonstrated their mental competence beyond any question. As a consequence, Hildesheimer felt that very few deaf persons should be considered *heresh* (mentally incompetent, nonspeaking, and totally deaf).

IMMIGRATION ERA

Renewed hopes and faith in religious freedom attracted over 2,000,000 eastern European Jews to American soil in the late nineteenth and early twentieth centuries. These Jews settled mainly in northeastern cities, where employment could be found. Community life became established around the synagogue and other institutions. Families then were adamant in carrying out religious practices, and deaf people were given a somewhat homemade educational course in Torah and Talmud by their peers. In order to satisfy the old, established restrictions against deaf persons performing religious rituals, while granting them their right to live as members of the Jewish community, hearing male family members often stood up for deaf individuals in religious ceremonies such as circumcisions, weddings, and funerals.

When deaf Jews observed the decades of successful education of non-Jewish deaf children, they felt that their own education had been neglected. They desired to keep to the traditions of their parents and to observe the religion into which they were born, so they united to organize Hebrew associations patterned after the benevolent societies in the Old World. Their chief goal was to provide places for their members to convene for social and welfare activities and religious observations such as services for the High Holy Days, Passover seders, and Sabbath services. New York City, the port of entry for most eastern European immigrants, received the largest number of deaf Jews, and hence became the oldest site for such associations. One such association, the Hebrew Congregation of the Deaf (later known as the Hebrew Association of the Deaf), was founded in 1907 under the leadership of Marcus L. Kenner, who served as its first president. By 1911 the congregation felt the need for some assistance from the hearing community and formed the Society for the Welfare of the Jewish Deaf (later known as the New York Society of the Deaf). It served the deaf community in job placements and counseling, and it coordinated educational and athletic activities, hobby clubs, and aid to the newly arrived immigrants. The congregation's first religious leader was Rabbi Albert J. Amateau, who had formerly led a congregation of Turkish Jews; he was followed by A. Felix Nash, fresh out of rabbinical college and the University of Chicago School of Social Work. Both learned sign language and adjusted themselves to the demands of this unfamiliar work. The Hebrew Association of the Deaf (HAD) enjoyed its association with Nash for only two years, until his death in 1932. A year earlier, Tanya, his wife, also had begun to serve deaf people; she accepted the post of executive director of HAD after her husband's death. Her impressive dedication to this work for some 40 years was recognized when a low-income senior citizen apartment house near the New York School for the Deaf was named Tanya Towers.

For 10 years, beginning in 1915, the Society for the Welfare of the Jewish Deaf (SWJD) supported a lively magazine, the *Jewish Deaf.* It was edited at various times by Rabbi Amateau and Marcus Kenner, among others. The list of contributors to this monthly periodical included many distinguished deaf persons of that period: J. H. Cloud, I. Goldberg, T. F. Fox, Alice Terry, and G. W. Veditz. Original papers by hearing Jewish and Christian clergy, educators, and professionals and business people were also published in the *Jewish Deaf.* Its editorial policy was most liberal and vigorous, so that the *Jewish Deaf* became a worthy organ of the National Association of the Deaf. *See* NATIONAL ASSOCIATION OF THE DEAF; PERIODICALS: History; VEDITZ, GEORGE WILLIAM.

The Society for the Welfare of the Jewish Deaf later became an agency of the Federation of Jewish Philanthropies and took the Hebrew Association of the Deaf under its wing. It expanded its base of service to include the needs of the non-Jewish deaf population and offered a variety of programs, including vocational training, rehabilitation, family counseling, summer camping for the elderly, communication skills training, and psychological testing.

Jewish communities organized on behalf of their deaf in other cities as well. In Philadelphia, a branch of Friends of the Deaf was formed. The Baltimore Society of Jewish Deaf was organized under the sponsorship of the Baltimore branch of the National Council of Jewish Women. In addition, the Brooklyn Hebrew Society of the Deaf, the Cleveland Hebrew Association of the Deaf, and the Los Angeles Hebrew Association of the Deaf were created.

EUROPE DURING WORLD WAR II

Nazi policy was to declare disabled people, including deaf people, "genetically diseased." In order to "purify the race," the Nazis tried to eliminate the "defect" of deafness. Deaf people were denied marriage licenses, over 15,000 were sterilized, some were experimented upon, and many were murdered. Many deaf people were betrayed by those they trusted most. Some teachers of deaf students, several principals of deaf schools, even a few of the deaf community leaders themselves collaborated with the Nazis to victimize deaf people.

Among the millions of victims of Nazi terror were thousands of deaf Jews. One case of Nazi persecution occurred at the Israelite Institute for the Deaf, a private Jewish residential school for deaf children founded in 1873 in Berlin-Weissensee. In May 1942, Nazis dragged 146 Jewish deaf citizens from the school and murdered them. In Vienna there was a school, founded in 1864, that trained deaf children to speak Hebrew and read Jewish texts; this, too, was demolished. In the Netherlands of this time

most organizations and programs for deaf persons were administered by Jewish leaders, and as a result of the Nazi invasion, were destroyed.

RECENT HISTORY

After World War II, many Jewish leaders of deaf people in the United States realized there was a need to join together to foster Judaism among deaf people on the national level. They were encouraged by respected persons in the fields of education, finance, social work, and law, including Judge Montefiore Levy, Simon Osserman, Tanya Nash of New York's HAD, Rose Olanoff of Philadelphia, Helen Coblenzer of Baltimore, and Irving Fusfield of Gallaudet College. Deaf leaders who joined in the drive for national acceptance were Leonard Warshawsky of Chicago, Alexander Fleischman of Washington, D.C., and Bernard Teitelbaum of Pittsburgh. Anna Plapinger of New York generously financed the first convention. The turnout was large, the enthusiasm was overwhelming, and the National Congress of Jewish Deaf was established in New York City in July 1956. *See* NATIONAL CONGRESS OF THE JEWISH DEAF.

By this time, the American Jewish population was over the 5,000,000 mark, and there were an estimated 170,000 deaf and hearing-impaired Jews in the United States. The aims of the National Congress of Jewish Deaf were to aid in the growth and preservation of the religious spirit among deaf Jews; to foster fellowship among Jewish deaf people; to maintain among deaf persons the warmth and the traditions of the Jewish home; to promote cultural growth in keeping with Jewish ideals; to instill in Jewish deaf youth a sense of oneness in the faith of their parents; to develop closer relationships between Jews and non-Jews; and to establish an endowment fund to promote the attainment of these aims.

A variety of activities began with the founding of the National Congress. These included representing Jewish deaf people in all matters concerning their welfare and rights as citizens of the United States; serving as a clearinghouse for information about religion, education, and culture; promoting religious services at schools for deaf children and for community organizations serving deaf persons; training rabbinical candidates in sign language; serving as an information and referral center for and about deaf Jews; supporting camps and leadership programs for Jewish students; promoting conventions; cooperating with all branches of Judaism to upgrade educational and religious services to deaf persons outside Jewish population centers; representing Jewish deaf people on the U.S. President's Committee for the Employment of the Handicapped; and establishing such assistance as homes for the aged, interpreters, consumer services, surveys of the legal rights of deaf people, a census of the deaf Jewish population, and employment and mental health counseling.

Philip Hanover chaired the first convention and was elected president for one term. Alexander Fleischman carried the banner for the next 16 years, and edited the newly founded *NCJD Quarterly*. As a public relations medium designed to stimulate interest in the Judaic movement among the scattered Jewish deaf community, the quarterly helped to bring in new members and donations to the Congress. New affiliates joined the Congress: the Hillel Club of Gallaudet College (sponsored by B'nai B'rith International), the Boston Hebrew Association of the Deaf, Congregation Bene Shalom of the Hebrew Association of the Deaf (Chicago), Temple Beth Or of the Deaf (New York City), and Temple Beth Solomon of the Deaf (Arleta, California); the last three groups are the only congregations for Jewish deaf people in the United States.

The Congress expanded with the affiliation of the New York Society for the Deaf, the Washington Society of Jewish Deaf, Beth Torah of the Deaf (Brooklyn, New York), the Jewish Community Center Association of the Deaf (Fort Lauderdale, Florida), the Hearing Impaired Chavura (Fellowship) (Rochester, New York), the Chabad House (Los Angeles, California), and the Toronto Jewish Society for Hearing Impaired (Canada). Each affiliate is represented by a delegate the NCJD biennial conventions. The gatherings are an opportunity for Jewish deaf people to get together amid educational and spiritual uplift. Highlights are panel discussions about Judaism and workshops on religious signing and other topics. An Award of Merit ceremony honors outstanding workers, who are recommended by the affiliates themselves. Added later was the Anna and Henry Plapinger Leadership Award to those who have performed meritorious services.

One of the main concerns of the Congress is to encourage rabbis to work with deaf people, learn sign language, and become familiar with the needs of deaf people. A scholarship is provided to student rabbis serving Jewish deaf persons. The Congress also supplements the salaries of rabbis after they are ordained and start serving a deaf congregation, and assists affiliates in arranging religious service for their members. In addition, the Congress provides orientations on deafness to encourage student rabbis to work with deaf individuals, sends instructors to teach sign language to student rabbis, and publishes and markets books on religious signing. Finally, it seeks to foster their Jewish heritage among deaf people by providing funds for lay religious education and by establishing and maintaining the archives of the Congress. Solomon Dietch of Chicago spearheaded the endowment-fund drive in the

beginning, and Betsy Blumenthal of Baltimore chaired the fund for 10 years.

When it began to encourage the major rabbinical seminaries to admit deaf candidates, the Congress faced another problem. The subject of deafness had no status in the pastoral psychology or special-education courses. Most rabbinic and education students completed their studies without once discussing deafness or becoming aware of the existence of deaf Jews and their religious needs. Furthermore, no course in sign language was offered. Given this situation, many people believed deaf rabbis would serve and understand their deaf congregations more effectively. Unfortunately, for a long time the seminaries were not approached by any qualified deaf candidates.

It took extra efforts to convince the institutions of this neglect of a minority group of Jews. The first accepted hearing-impaired applicant at Hebrew Union College (Reform) at Cincinnati, Ohio, was Alton Silver of Los Angeles, California. Many remember how admirably he officiated at the Chicago and New York NCJD conventions. After that, there was no question that the long wait for a Jewish deaf clergy was over. Unfortunately, Silver's rabbinnic dreams were short-lived; he died in his senior year of college, only 27 years old.

While Jewish deaf people were waiting for a deaf rabbi, a few hearing rabbis dedicated themselves to the various deaf communities. Douglas Goldhamer (Reform) of Toronto, Canada, rapidly mastered sign language and spoke to many hearing congregations, declaring that "sign language brought life to my hands." After ordination, he established himself as the rabbi for Congregation Bene Shalom in Chicago. Doubling as a TV newscaster, he also interpreted the news to Chicago-area deaf persons. Rabbi Moshe Ebstein (Orthodox), the father of two deaf sons, established the Hebrew Institute for the Deaf in Brooklyn, New York, an Orthodox oralist day school (the only Jewish day school program for deaf students in the country). Rabbi Eliezer Lederfeind (Orthodox) of New York City, the hearing son of deaf parents, spearheaded a deaf youth movement called Our Way and conducted retreats and religious-educational tours to Israel. A handful of other Reform student rabbis served their internship with deaf congregations and were taught sign language via grants from the NCJD Endowment Fund.

With more women rabbinical candidates studying at seminaries, women also took up internships with Jewish deaf people. First was Lynn Gottlieb, who officiated at Temple Beth Or for 2 years. She was a member of New York Havurah, a puppeteer at the Jewish Museum, and director of Bat Kol Players—Portraits of Women. She also had a short stint with the New York Hebrew Association, tutoring young people. Elyse Goldstein, who served her internship at Temple Beth Or while still a student at Hebrew Union College (New York), was the next intern. After her ordination in 1983, Rabbi Goldstein accepted a position with Holy Blossom Temple in Toronto, Canada, where she assisted the Toronto affiliate. She became the first rabbi to be certified as an interpreter.

Many other events affecting deaf Jews have occurred in recent years. Affiliated associations have developed new programs, and a variety of festive ceremonies assisted by selected rabbis have taken place. In addition, cultural, religious, sign language, and interpreting classes have been offered. In support of the State of Israel, deaf individuals and organizations for deaf persons have purchased Israel bonds. The Sisterhood of Temple Beth Or sponsored luncheon and fashion shows whose proceeds went to support Beth Or's rabbi, and they also honored their Woman of the Year. Congregation Bene Shalom trained a choir to perform songs in music and sign language and printed their own prayer book. The National Congress of Jewish Deaf and the Baltimore Society of Jewish Deaf jointly hosted a reception for Jewish deaf athletes from Israel and other nations participating in the 1965 World Games for the Deaf in Washington, D.C., and Temple Beth Solomon hosted the same during the 1985 Games in Los Angeles. B'nai B'rith International endorsed and supported the organization of a unit of hearing-impaired Jews in Washington, D.C. The World Federation of the Deaf advocated a Spiritual Care Commission at its Congress in Paris (1971) and appointed an American Jewish deaf leader on the committee. The Drama Department at Gallaudet College presented a moving performance of *The Diary of Anne Frank*. Washington and California deaf persons assisted in the Super Sunday Telethon, collecting donations from deaf individuals. In this drive, communication was through portable teletypewriters. Temple Beth Solomon sponsored a youth retreat that attracted some 40 young people. Jewish Family Social Service in Maryland included deaf people in its programs. The New York Society of the Deaf sponsored a seminar at the New York City Brookdale Center (Hebrew Union College–Jewish Institute of Religion) on "The Deaf Jew in the Modern World." National Congress affiliates pledged to assist in financing Israel's athletes participation in the 1985 World Games for the Deaf in Los Angeles. Under the editorship of Adele K. Shuart, the Congress published a Hebrew sign language book. *See* WORLD FEDERATION OF THE DEAF.

The local Hebrew Associations have provided leadership training and other opportunities so that many Jewish deaf men and women could assume important positions in a variety of other organizations. Frederick Schreiber, Art Kruger, Leonard Warshawsky, Alexander Fleischman, Gerald Burstein, Allan T. Hurwitz, Bernard Bragg, and Rosalind Rosen, among many others, have played major roles in the National Association of the Deaf, the National Fraternal Society of the Deaf, Gallaudet College, the National Technical Institute for the Deaf, the National Theatre of the Deaf, and the American Athletic Association of the Deaf. *See* AMERICAN ATHLETIC ASSOCIATION OF THE DEAF; BRAGG, BERNARD; GALLAUDET COLLEGE; NATIONAL ASSOCIATION OF THE DEAF; NATIONAL FRATERNAL SOCIETY OF THE DEAF; NATIONAL TECHNICAL INSTITUTE FOR THE DEAF; NATIONAL THEATERS OF THE DEAF: United States; SCHREIBER, FREDERICK CARL.

WORLD ORGANIZATION OF JEWISH DEAF

Israeli deaf persons, recognizing the growth of the NCJD and its programs and affiliates, in 1975 decided to found a World Organization of Jewish Deaf, with its headquarters located on the premises of the Israel Association of the Deaf. Subsequently, Alexander Fleischman of the United States and Chaim Apter, Moshe Shem Tov, and Issachar Goldrath of Israeli (all deaf except Goldrath) met with Israel's Chief Rabbi, the Honorable Shlomo Goren, to seek his assistance by recognizing the new organization and to request that he give the keynote address at the first convention. In 1977, in Tel Aviv, well over 400 people attended the new organization's first convention and participated in interesting sessions and a free exchange of thoughts and goals. In his address, Chief Rabbi Goren declared his confidence in the educational status of deaf Jews, their respectable citizenship in their communities, and their acceptance of responsibility in employment and family life; therefore, he called for a removal of all barriers against Jewish people who were deaf. A nine-member bureau of the new organization elected Fleischman president, Apter secretary general, and Moshe Bamberger (Israel) treasurer. Israel, Great Britain, France, and the United States, all countries having national Jewish bodies, became charter members of the World Organization of Jewish Deaf.

Deaf Jews have come a long way, amid trials and hardships. Yet, the Jewish hearing world is not fully aware of the existence of hearing-impaired Jewish people. The latter's religious needs are equal to those of their hearing peers. Because there are not enough rabbis available to work with deaf persons, perhaps the best solution would be to train interested deaf people to become teachers and leaders in their own Jewish communities. Future generations of deaf Jews will need these teachers' help to arrive at a clear understanding of their culture, heritage, and religion, and to carry on the work of the pioneers.

Bibliography

Bleich, J. D.: "The Status of the Deaf-Mute in Jewish Law," *Tradition*, 16(5):79–84, Fall 1977.

Eilani, T., and B. Meir: *The Status of the Deaf Person in Jewish Law*, Tel Aviv and Ramat Gan, Association of the Deaf in Israel and Bar-Ilan University, 1981 (a digest of a computer-based study of Jewish legal decisions concerning deaf people in Hebrew).

Fleischman, A., R. Rosen, and B. Hyman (eds.): *NCJD Quarterly*, Gallaudet College Library, Washington, D.C., 1956–1983.

Ginsberg, L.: *Legends of the Jews*, Jewish Publication Society, Philadelphia, 1954.

Goldhamer, D.: *The Heresh in the Talmud*, rabbinic thesis, Hebrew Union College, 1970.

Greenstone, J.: "Deaf and Dumb in Jewish Law," *Jewish Encyclopedia*, 1907.

Grosness, L.: *The Matter of Reading the Torah by a Deaf Person*, responsum of the bet din of London (BM 663 G75), Jewish Theological Seminary, New York, 1963.

Hafeta, E.: *The Task of the Deaf*, 2 vols., New York, 1874–1885 (in Hebrew).

Kenner, M. L. (ed.): *The Jewish Deaf*, National Association for the Deaf and Gallaudet Library, Washington, D.C., 1915–1925.

National Congress of Jewish Deaf Papers, *Minutes and History*, files of NCJD Archives and Executive Director, 1956–1983.

Perlstein, D. (ed.): *Genesis 2*, vol. 13, no. 2, Boston, November 1981.

Proceedings of the Fred Milfred Memorial Conference on the Deaf Jew in the Modern World, New York Society of the Deaf, 1981.

Proceedings of the Workshop on Orientation of Jewish Religious Leaders and Lay People to Deafness and Vocational Rehabilitation, U.S. Department of Health, Education and Welfare, Rehabilitation Service Administration, Washington, D.C., 1970.

Proceedings of the World Federation of the Deaf, Rome, W.F.D. Spiritual Care Commission, 1971–1983.

Proceedings of the World Organization of Jewish Deaf Congress, Association of the Deaf, Tel Aviv, 1977–1983.

Rabinowitz, L.: "Deaf Mute," *Encyclopedia Judiaca*, 1974, and *EJ Yearbooks*, p. 405, 1974, and pp. 200–201, 1977–1978.

Schwartz, H.: "To Open the Ears of the Deaf," *Conservative Judaism*, vol. 27, no. 2, Winter 1974.

Strassfeld, S. and M. (eds.): *Second Jewish Catalog*, Jewish Publication Society of America, Philadelphia, 1970.

Alexander Fleischman

RELIGION, PROTESTANT

The major Protestant denominations in the United States have made organized efforts to serve and sometimes to proselytize deaf people. These activities are described below in three sections. The first describes the activities of various nonliturgical Protestant churches: the Methodist, American Baptist, Southern Baptist, Mennonite, Christian, Church of Christ, Presbyterian, Assemblies of God, and the Church of Jesus Christ of Latter-Day Saints. The second section discusses the deaf ministry of the Episcopal Church, and the third section that of the Lutheran Church.

Nonliturgical

Most nonliturgical Protestant churches believe that hearing persons should be coordinators or directors of their deaf ministries to facilitate communication with the hearing church. Since a church is an autonomous unit in most of the nonliturgical Protestant denominations, any hearing person, even one with minimal or mediocre sign language skill, may start a deaf ministry. This may help explain the rapid growth of deaf church units and hearing workers in several denominations, notably the Baptists, the Assemblies of God, and the Churches of Christ.

An interpreted worship type of ministry with a separated Sunday school class or a separated department of Sunday school classes for deaf parishioners accounts for nearly 90 percent of all nonliturgical Protestant deaf units in the United States. The majority of teachers and leaders of Bible classes for deaf persons are deaf themselves, while the hearing workers serve as interpreters of worship services and other church functions. Some denominations, which in the past had focused on beginning new deaf missions, are now seeking to provide interpreted services for deaf people in other local churches. Other denominations with a heavy emphasis on local interpreted services are encouraging strategic deaf units to become self-supporting deaf missions and churches. Most of the missions and churches of and for deaf persons have hearing pastors who are assisted by capable deaf leaders, deacons, or committees. Some of these missions and churches are housed within hearing churches, and others have their own facilities that are given to the deaf congregation or owned by the hearing mother churches. Few deaf congregations have bought their own church buildings, with or without the help of their hearing families and friends. There are, moreover, few religious instruction classes, missions, and churches under the total leadership of deaf persons without any guidance and financial assistance from any hearing church, mission agency, or hearing public. See INTERPRETING.

METHODIST CHURCH
The Methodist work with deaf people owes its beginning to Dr. Philip G. Gillet, superintendent of the Illinois School for the Deaf, who is regarded as its pioneer. The First Methodist Church in Chicago established monthly service for deaf persons in 1890. Dr. Philip Hasentab became the first deaf person

to be ordained into the Methodist ministry, and was followed by the Reverend Henry Rutherford, an Illinois School for the Deaf graduate who was ordained in 1908 and preached to deaf people in Illinois, Iowa, Kansas, Nebraska, and Missouri.

In the United Methodist Church there are over 15 organized ministries and conference-wide programs of deaf ministry and a growing interest in promoting special programs and interpreted services for deaf people in the hearing churches. Two agencies within the General Board of Global Ministries of the United Methodist Church, the National Division and the Division of Health and Welfare Ministries, cooperate to provide project support through the General Advance Special Program and leadership and mission development through the Offices of Urban Ministries and Ministries with Persons with Handicapping Conditions.

The United Methodist Congress of the Deaf was organized officially in Washington, D.C., in 1977, though annual, informal workshops began in 1972. Its purpose is to build support systems among deaf and hearing-impaired Methodists, to advance deaf awareness in hearing churches, to encourage the development of curriculum materials, and to cultivate growth and understanding of missions.

AMERICAN BAPTIST CHURCHES

Although the Baptist Churches belong to different fellowships, as a group they exhibit the largest growth and greatest strength of any churches in their work with deaf parishioners. The American Baptist Churches have been involved in the deaf ministry since the early twentieth century—the Temple Baptist Church in Los Angeles has had a deaf congregation since 1933. John Clark, a deaf pastor, established the annual Baptist Deaf Fellowship of America at Forest Hills Baptist Church in Decatur, Georgia. This fellowship is held in a different town each year. The American Baptist Convention's work with deaf persons has not been as intense and widely promoted as the Southern Baptist Convention's ministry.

The independent Baptist churches owe much of their work with deaf people to Dr. and Mrs. Bill Rice, who founded the Bill Rice Ranch Camp for the Deaf in Murfreesboro, Tennessee, on July 24, 1950. Dr. and Mrs. Rice felt the need for spiritual training for deaf persons after they learned that one of their daughters had become deaf at the age of two due to spinal meningitis. In 1953 the Bill Rice Ranch, an independent Baptist camp, has 12 young deaf people, and the number has grown each year, with over 1000 deaf persons attending annually. It is responsible for camps in Apache Creek, New Mexico, the Caribbean Islands, Brazil, and Mexico. The camps conduct an intensive sign language school for two weeks in May and November

of each year. These two-week schools have provided the impetus for the establishment of more than 800 Sunday school classes for deaf children in the independent, fundamentalist Baptist churches across America and in foreign countries. The Bill Rice Ranch also publishes printed materials for deaf people such as a songbook, Bible lessons, tracts, and the *Ranch Hand*, a newspaper. They produce sign language sermon films and have two deaf and two hearing evangelists who travel, preach, and teach in the churches.

The independent Baptist churches have a good number of deaf ministers as well as hearing ministers for deaf persons, a corps of lay ministers, and approximately 1000 interpreters. They have a high school, a Bible diploma program, and a college degree program for deaf students at Tennessee Temple University in Chattanooga, Tennessee, and a school for deaf children at Providence Baptist Church in Riverview, Florida.

SOUTHERN BAPTIST CONVENTION

The Southern Baptist Convention began its ministry to deaf persons in 1902. Myrtle Morris, a Georgia School for the Deaf graduate who learned that there was no school for deaf Cubans, was appointed as a missionary to deaf people in Cuba under the Home Mission Board in late 1904. The Reverend John Michaels, a Virginia School for the Deaf graduate and principal of the Arkansas School for the Deaf, became a state worker under the Arkansas Baptist Convention in 1905 and a missionary to deaf people in the United States under the Home Mission Board in December 1906.

The Southern Baptist Convention has about 800 churches with deaf work, 38 missions and churches for congregations, more than 1000 interpreters, several hearing home and state mission leaders, several deaf and hearing pastors, a large corps of lay ministers, two college programs for deaf students (Dallas Baptist College in Dallas, Texas, and Gardner-Webb College in Boiling Springs, North Carolina), a high school program for deaf students (Harrison-Chilhowee Baptist Academy in Seymour, Tennessee), and a Bible program for deaf young people (Boyce Bible School in Louisville, Kentucky).

The Southern Baptist Convention churches are the backbone of the denomination's ministry to deaf people and are largely responsible for their work. The Convention, through its two conference centers, the Baptist Sunday School Board, the Home Mission Board, and the state Baptist conventions, provides curriculum materials for deaf people, facilities for training deaf teachers, leaders, and interpreters, audio-visual materials for both deaf and hearing workers, pastoral assistance, financial assistance to national and state organizations of deaf persons, state and area mission leadership in the field of deafness, seminary extension training, state and national Baptist newsletters for deaf people, interpreters, and printed materials such as *A Manual of Religious Signs*, *A Handbook for Religious Interpreters for the Deaf*, and *Manual for Work with the Deaf*.

The Southern Baptist Conference of the Deaf, Junior Southern Baptist Conference of the Deaf, Junior Southern Baptist Conference of the Deaf Association of Southern Baptist Interpreters for the Deaf, Pastor's and Missionary's Conference, and 19 Baptist state conferences of the deaf are held annually. The purpose of these conferences is to promote fellowship, to provide training, to support volunteer missions, to channel funds for support of world missions, to foster spiritual growth, to promote better understanding of church roles, and to provide choir and athletic competitions.

MENNONITE CHURCH

The earliest recorded work with deaf persons in the Mennonite Church was at the Harrisburg (Oregon) Mennonite Church in 1911, which has services interpreted for deaf people. During the 1950s the Scottdale (Pennsylvania) Mennonite Church provided a meeting place for deaf people, with Paul and Ferne Savanick, deaf lay leaders, imparting continuity and enthusiasm to the work for many years. In 1956 the First Deaf Mennonite Church was established in Lancaster, Pennsylvania, pastored by Raymond Rohrer, the only deaf pastor in the denomination. In the 1970s other Mennonite churches began having interpreted worship services and Bible classes for deaf persons in several northern states. In 1976 a Deaf Ministries central office was established at the Mennonite Board of Missions in Elkhart, Indiana. The Deaf Ministries office serves as a consultant and advocate for deaf individuals, families, and churches. The *SIGNING* newsletter, begun in 1979, is a bimonthly forum for people interested in deaf ministry. Deaf Ministries sponsors Christian education events for deaf persons, helps people find resources, and assists in developing and strengthening deaf ministries.

CHRISTIAN CHURCHES

The independent Christian Churches and (instrumental) Churches of Christ began their deaf ministry with interpreted services at the First Christian Church in Gooding, Idaho, in 1957, and at the First Christian Church in Miami, Oklahoma, in 1958. A third was established at Boulevard Church of Christ in Charleston, West Virginia, in February 1960, and the fourth was the ministry at First Christian Church in Norfolk, Nebraska, in 1968. Today the Christian Churches and (instrumental) Churches of Christ have many interpreted services and churches of deaf congregations, ministries at some state schools for

deaf children, and Bible camps. There are a few deaf and ordained ministers, many lay ministers, and more than 100 interpreters. Thirteen Bible colleges supported by them offer some courses in the field of deafness.

Deaf Missions in Council Bluffs, Iowa, staffed by ministers and workers of the Christian Churches and (instrumental) Churches of Christ, prepares and distributes Bible visuals for deaf people. They train Christian workers and do personal work among deaf persons. Deaf Missions has a catalog of visual and printed materials for use in deaf ministries. It publishes *Deaf Missions Report* and *Daily Devotions for the Deaf*. One of its important activities is the Omega Project, which is an effort to translate the Bible visually into American Sign Language (ASL). One deaf and one hearing person are the ASL translators of several one-hour segments on the Scriptures. Deaf Missions videotapes the *Daily Devotions for the Deaf* in sign language for cable television stations that agree to broadcast them. *See* SIGN LANGUAGES: American.

CHURCH OF CHRIST

The (noninstrumental) Church of Christ began its deaf ministry in Austin, Texas, in 1935 when Gladys (Mears) Holland, who had deaf members in the family, established the first service for deaf persons near the Texas School for the Deaf. In 1945 the Church of Christ deaf congregations sprang up in Nashville and Knoxville, Tennessee. A noninstrumental Church of Christ is a church congregation that is opposed to "human innovation" in the use of instrumental music and missionary societies. As a result of controversy about this issue, the Churches of Christ and the Christian Churches were officially separated in 1901. The Churches of Christ do not accept musical instruments, including pianos or organs, whereas the Christian Churches use them in their worship.

The (noninstrumental) Church of Christ has approximately 140 churches with deaf ministries, over 200 interpreters, several deaf ministers, deaf missionaries, and two training centers for deaf people (Deaf Department of the Sunset School of Preaching, Sunset Church of Christ, in Lubbock, Texas, and the Birmingham Bible School for the Deaf, Roebuck Parkway Church of Christ, in Birmingham, Alabama).

The local Churches of Christ finance their own deaf work. Since each church is independent, there is no central agency to sponsor the deaf ministry. A Church of Christ, however, may request sister congregations to support the deaf work if they agree to do so. Deaf persons having genuine skills are welcomed into leadership positions, but so far there are no deaf elders in the Churches of Christ. The Church of Christ has an annual national Christian

Workshop for Workers with the Deaf. Local congregations take turns hosting this workshop. A Rome, Georgia, Church of Christ has a student center near the Georgia School for the Deaf. A Memphis, Tennessee, Church of Christ prints *LIGHT for the Deaf*, a newsletter for deaf people. The World Bible Translation Center in Arlington, Texas, has translated Old and New Testaments for deaf persons and also for hearing persons whose second language is English. The Bible translation is the *New Testament, English Version for the Deaf.*

PRESBYTERIAN CHURCH

Presbyterian ministries to persons who are deaf and hard-of-hearing have existed in several local churches since the early 1930s, but they only reached a semiorganized status in 1981. The local Presbyterian churches finance local deaf ministries, often in conjunction with area governing bodies, while general assembly agencies support program development through synod and churchwide conferences. The first nationally sponsored Presbyterian workshop on ministry with hearing-impaired persons was held in Washington, D.C., in November 1982 under the auspices of the General Assembly Program Agency and the Presbyterian Disabilities Concerns Caucus. A by-product of this meeting was a Deaf Awareness/Consciousness Workshop in Maysville, Kentucky, in April 1984 for the Synod of the Covenant (Ohio, Michigan, and Kentucky). The consensus of the November 1982 workshop was to involve people with hearing impairments in all leadership and decision-making levels of the church. This consensus is supported by the plan for reunion of the Presbyterian Church (USA), which guarantees full participation by persons with disabilities in the life of the church.

Two hearing persons in the Social Welfare Program Agency and the General Assembly Mission Board and several church pastors, including the Reverend Larry Correu, a hearing-impaired pastor, have been responsible for the growing interest of the Presbyterian Health, Education and Welfare Association, and work closely in advocacy and program development with both the Program Agency in New York and the General Assembly Mission Board in Atlanta, Georgia.

CHURCH OF JESUS CHRIST OF LATTER-DAY SAINTS

In 1896 in Salt Lake City, Utah, the Church of Jesus Christ of Latter-Day Saints began a class for deaf children under Thomas Cott Griggs, who had a deaf daughter. Later the class moved to Ogden, the home of the Utah School for the Deaf, and was taken over by a hearing teacher at the school for the deaf who later became principal. In 1917 the class was organized into a branch with the principal as its first president and with several deaf members serving as officers and teachers.

The Church of Jesus Christ of Latter-Day Saints has 3 wards for deaf people with deaf bishops, 9 branches for deaf persons with deaf presidents, 22 groups with deaf leaders and interpreters, 6 seminaries for deaf students in the United States, and 16 interpreter services and 5 deaf groups in foreign countries. There are 58 Mormon missionaries to deaf people, and half of them are deaf. They serve in 19 different states.

The Law and Fast Offering of the Church of Jesus Christ of Latter-Day Saints finances the church's expense and the welfare for needy members. The church holds area conferences for deaf people. These conferences include workshops, lectures, and other activities, all of which help deaf people understand the Bible and Mormon church doctrines. The church provides facilities, services for hearing-impaired persons, curriculum for deaf people, purchase of telecommunication devices for deaf persons, videotape hardware, and special member services. It has training programs and uses many videotapes with interpreter inserts and captioning. It uses deaf persons in the role of leadership to bring better understanding to deaf members and to encourage members to take part in their various positions. *See* TELECOMMUNICATIONS.

ASSEMBLIES OF GOD

The Assemblies of God started its work among deaf people with Elsie Peters visiting the home of a deaf family, Mr. and Mrs. Sullivan Chainey, in Springfield, Missouri, in 1919. Mrs. Peters moved with her husband to Los Angeles and established the First Full Gospel Church to the Deaf on October 29, 1929, becoming the only female minister to deaf persons in the United States on May 9, 1930. Sullivan Chainey, as a result of Mrs. Peter's ministry, became the first deaf home missionary under the Assemblies of God.

The Assemblies of God promote and produce many indigenous churches as the best way of evangelizing and discipling deaf people. They have conducted annual workshops and conferences for deaf persons and hearing workers and published special materials for use in deaf work. Two of their excellent publications are Edgar Lawrence's *Ministering to the Silent Minority* and Croft Pentz's *Ministry to the Deaf*, both of which are practical helps for beginning a deaf ministry and for working with deaf persons. The Assemblies of God have 20 churches for deaf parishioners, 20 churches for deaf people affiliated with hearing churches, 340 deaf church groups with interpreters, 80 credentialed ministers, a large corps of interpreters, and 2 college programs for deaf students (Central Bible College in Springfield, Missouri, and North Central Bible College in Minneapolis, Minnesota).

CHRISTIAN DEAF FELLOWSHIP

The Christian Deaf Fellowship was created by three deaf and two hearing people who met in Springfield, Missouri, in the fall of 1945. The first convention of the Christian Deaf Fellowship was held in Tulsa, Oklahoma, in the summer of 1946, with approximately 125 people in attendance. The Reverend John Stallings, son of deaf parents and pastor to a deaf congregation in Virginia, served as its first superintendent and then president from 1946 to April 1963.

The Christian Deaf Fellowship is a fellowship and spiritual support group of Christian deaf and hearing people from different denominations working together in their evangelistic program. For the first 20 years of its existence its main ministry was in the United States; recently it has gone on an international scale, having established two mission centers for deaf people in Jamaica and Bolivia. It has sponsored 23 missionaries to deaf people in Mexico, Bolivia, Colombia, and Jamaica. The Christian Deaf Fellowship also has cooperating fellowship with mission works in Africa, Argentina, the Bahamas, Brazil, Canada, Germany, Greece, Korea, Lebanon, and Peru. The organizations affiliated with the Christian Deaf Fellowship are the Deaf Christian Fellowship of Ireland, England, and Sweden; the Christian Deaf Fellowship of Germany and Japan; the Deaf Ministries International in Concord, California; the Deaf Evangelistic Alliance Foundation, Inc., in Laguna, Philippines; and the Bible School for the Deaf in Downey, California. Like the Southern Baptist churches, the independent, fundamental churches carry on their own deaf ministries.

The long-range plans and trends indicate that there will be many more new Bible classes and churches for deaf people. Sign language courses and training programs will continue to be offered to the hearing churches that are interested in beginning deaf ministries so that new workers and teachers, both hearing and deaf, can be trained to serve deaf persons. Curriculum materials for special groups of hearing-impaired persons, such as those who are also blind or mentally retarded, deaf preschoolers, and primary-school-age deaf children, will be developed and printed. Denominational colleges and seminaries will be encouraged to provide training programs for hearing students who want to work with hearing-impaired persons and also degree programs for deaf students.

Carter E. Bearden

Episcopal

For the deaf people of the United States, the nineteenth century was a time of exceptional advance and enlightenment. In 1817 at Hartford, Connecticut, the Reverend Thomas Hopkins Gallaudet, an Episcopal clergyman, established the first permanent school for deaf students in America. It was destined to serve as a model for deaf education in almost every state, so that by the end of the century some 45 state residential schools for deaf students had been established. *See* GALLAUDET, THOMAS HOPKINS.

The two sons of Thomas Hopkins Gallaudet also were destined to play important roles in the advancement of deaf Americans by providing ministry for their spiritual needs and higher educational opportunities. The older son, the Reverend Thomas Gallaudet, became a missionary-priest in the Episcopal church and for nearly 50 years gave his time and talents to raise the status of deaf persons and provide for their spiritual edification. The younger son, Edward Miner Gallaudet, became the founder and first president of Gallaudet College in Washington, D.C. This college made an important contribution to deaf individuals invested in the ministry, particularly in the Episcopal church, by providing the college education that ordinarily is required of those who wish to enter the ordained ministry. *See* GALLAUDET, EDWARD MINER; GALLAUDET COLLEGE.

BEGINNINGS

In 1850 Thomas Gallaudet started a Bible class for deaf people at St. Stephen's Church in New York City. This class soon outgrew its meeting room. Several adults were baptized and some were presented to the bishop for confirmation. Gallaudet's pastoral relationship with a New York School for the Deaf student who had become consumptive and died convinced him that deaf people had a great need for the spiritual ministrations of the church and that he should devote his life to that ministry. Furthermore, Gallaudet began to feel that the deaf people of New York City should have their own church. With the approval of his Episcopal bishop and other leaders, he set about to establish such a church. On the first Sunday of October 1852 he held a service in the small chapel of New York University on Washington Square. This is considered the beginning of St. Ann's Church for the Deaf. In 1859 the new congregation acquired a church and rectory located at 18th Street near 5th Avenue—the first church for deaf people in the world.

Thomas Gallaudet was not content to limit his ministry to this New York congregation. He wanted deaf persons everywhere to come to the knowledge and faith in God that was central to his own life.

Thomas Gallaudet. (Gallaudet College Archives)

Henry Winter Syle.

Soon he was making trips to other cities to have services for deaf people. In 1859 he started work in Baltimore, Washington, D.C., and Philadelphia. But he could not carry on this work unaided; to his assistance came men of unusual talent and integrity. One, the Reverend John Chamberlain, became Gallaudet's assistant at St. Ann's and served the Episcopal church and the deaf community from 1872 until his death in January 1921. Other Episcopal priests of note were Francis Joseph Clerc, the son of Laurent Clerc, the deaf Frenchman who accompanied Thomas Hopkins Gallaudet to America to help him establish the school at Hartford; Thomas B. Berry, who, in addition to his missionary work among deaf people, was the founder of the school for deaf children at Sioux Falls, South Dakota; and J. Stanley Searing, who served deaf individuals in the Boston and general New England area. *See* CLERC, LAURENT.

Despite the contributions to the ministry of these hearing priests, Gallaudet saw that there was a need for many more workers, both clergy and lay, if there was to be expansion in the mission field.

DEAF PRIESTS
Thomas Gallaudet met a deaf man of unusual intellectual gifts and of high moral character—Henry Winter Syle, the son of a missionary to China. Although there was no record of a deaf man being given holy orders by a Christian church anywhere

in the world, Gallaudet decided to present Syle to the Right Reverend William Bacon Stevens, fifth bishop of Pennsylvania, and request that he be admitted as a candidate for holy orders. Despite some objections from the clergy of the Episcopal church, Bishop Stevens was pleased to take steps to provide for Syle's training and eventual ordination to the order of deacons. On October 8, 1876, at the Church of St. Stephen in Philadelphia, Syle was ordained a deacon by Bishop Stevens. Less than four months later, on January 25, 1877, another deaf man, Austin Ward Mann, who had been a teacher in the school for deaf people at Flint, Michigan, was made a deacon by the Bishop of Ohio at Grace Church, Cleveland. Both Syle and Mann together were advanced to the priesthood at a ceremony held on October 14, 1883, in the Church of the Covenant in Philadelphia. Both of the above-named bishops officiated, and Thomas Gallaudet preached the sermon.

Syle established the All Souls' Church for the Deaf in Philadelphia, and he was largely responsible for the formation of the Pennslyvania Society for the Advancement of the Deaf. In 1901 the Pennsylvania Society established a home for aged and infirm deaf people at Doylestown. Furthermore, it was probably at the urging of Syle that an organization known as the Conference of Church Workers Among the Deaf (CCWAD) came into being at a meeting held on October 6, 1881, at St. Ann's Church for the Deaf in New York City. Its purpose was to give unity and support to those engaged in Episcopal church work with deaf people.

Mann became an untiring missionary in the north-central states of Ohio, Indiana, Michigan, and Illinois. He also established the deaf mission at the Christ Church in St. Louis, Missouri. Only twice in his ministry did Mann take a vacation, and he refused to retire from his arduous labors even when nearing the age of 70. He dropped dead at the Union Railroad Station, in Columbis Ohio, in 1911. The funeral requiem eucharist was held in Grace Church in Cleveland, the church where he had been ordained a deacon 34 years earlier.

After Mann's death, a succession of deaf men endeavored to carry on his work. They were highly respected in the deaf community and had served the Episcopal church as layreaders for a number of years before being made priests. Many were already past middle age when ordained, however, so their priesthood was in most cases of short duration. One such man was the Reverend Horace B. Waters, who continued his secular employment with the Ford Motor Company in Detroit while ministering to deaf people at several cities in Michigan. Similarly, Swedish-born Bengt Olaf George Almo was ordained a priest in Cincinnati in 1939. He held services for deaf parishioners in all the major cities in Ohio, and for a time in West Virginia as well, until he retired in 1965.

One particularly influential person in attracting deaf persons to the Episcopal priesthood was the Reverend James Henry Cloud. At a convention of Episcopal church workers held in Philadelphia in 1926, there were 16 deaf missionary-priests assembled. The Reverend Cloud had arranged the convention but was ill at his home in St. Louis. Cloud had served the church and the deaf community with exceptional industry. For three consecutive terms he was the elected president of the National Association of the Deaf; yet he found time to visit and hold services in the Los Angeles and Denver areas. In the summer of 1915 he led a mission at St. Paul's Church in Los Angeles and influenced the British-born hearing-impaired priest Clarence E. Webb to learn sign language and serve deaf people in the Los Angeles area as missioner (Webb retired in 1934). *See* NATIONAL ASSOCIATION OF THE DEAF.

At the invitation of Bishop Fred Ingley of Colorado, Cloud left St. Louis in those months having five Sundays so that he could conduct services for deaf people in Denver churches. In 1922 he spent the entire month of August in Denver. Several deaf persons were baptized, and he presented a class of 15 to Bishop Ingley for confirmation, including Homer E. Grace. Two years later Cloud presented Grace to the bishop for ordination to the diaconate. After he was ordained a priest in 1925, the Reverend

Grace became missioner to deaf people throughout the Episcopal church's Sixth Province (Colorado, Nebraska, South Dakota, Iowa, and Minnesota) and continued this ministry until his retirement in 1959.

Another man who was influenced by Cloud, and probably also by Grace, was the Reverend Olof Hanson, who was ordained a priest in 1927 at the age of 66. His field was the Pacific Northwest (Washington and Oregon, and Vancouver in British Columbia). Hanson had made a name for himself nationally in the deaf community in 1908 by writing a letter to President Theodore Roosevelt that resulted in the rescinding of a ruling of the Civil Service Commission in Washington that prohibited deaf persons from taking the examinations for government employment. *See* HANSON, OLOF.

In the South, a long and laudatory ministry was done by the Reverend Robert C. Fletcher between the years 1929 and 1972. He established two churches for deaf people in Alabama, one in Birmingham and the other in Mobile. In 1952 he was awarded an honorary degree by Gallaudet College, and in 1972 he was named an honorary canon of the Cathedral Church of the Advent in Birmingham.

Following the death of the Reverend S. Stanley Searing in 1910, the ministry in New England was carried on by a layreader of note, Edwin W. Frisbee, and the Reverend George H. Hefflon, who was ordained that year. In 1925 Hefflon was struck by a trolley car in Providence, Rhode Island, and died shortly afterward. Hefflon was succeeded the following year by the Reverend J. Stanley Light, who had first served the Boston mission as layreader before ordination. A monument to his ministry is St. Andrew's Center and Chapel at Boston. It was consecrated shortly before his death in 1963. Gallaudet College conferred upon him in 1954 the honorary degree of doctor of humane letters.

Another deaf priest who made noteworthy contributions to the growth and strengthening of the Episcopal ministry was the Reverend Oliver J. Whildin, who was ordained in 1901 and appointed to work as a general missionary in the South, with Baltimore, Maryland, as his home base. Whildin had a gift for drawing other young men into the ministry. One, the Reverend George F. Flick, went to Chicago, where he established the All Angels' Church for the Deaf. The Reverend Herbert C. Merrill became missioner to deaf people in the upstate New York area. The Reverend Hobart L. Tracy in later years came up from Mississippi to work in the Washington, D.C., field which included Virginia and West Virginia.

Whildin initiated work at Durham, North Carolina, which at first was merely a Bible class meeting at St. Philip's Church but grew into a congregation of considerable size under the leadership of layreader Roma C. Fortune, a deaf man who was ordained a priest in 1929. Two years later a new church, named Ephphatha Church for the Deaf, was consecrated at Durham. Upon the death of Fortune, a hearing son, James R. Fortune, took steps to enter the ministry and was ordained a priest in 1945. The ministry of the son continued in North Carolina until his retirement in 1977.

Whildin was concerned about the need for more financial support for the ministry to deaf people. For the purpose of soliciting money, he founded the Society for the Promotion of Church Work Among the Deaf in the province of Washington, D.C., and he widely circulated his own monthly newsletter. As a result, the Conference of Church Workers Among the Deaf (CCWAD) received a bequest of $8000 and, through the beneficence of a wealthy Pittsburgh churchwoman named Margaret Fleming, a second capital fund was started.

ORGANIZATION

At the 1926 meeting of the Conference of Church Workers Among the Deaf in Philadelphia, Whildin was elected president. From that time until 1956 the organization met every three years in various cities about the country; since 1956 annual meetings have been held. The newsletter that Whildin started in 1924 became the official organ of CCWAD, although it has gone through several name changes and now is published quarterly as the *Deaf Episcopalian*. At the 1970 convention the name of the organization was changed to Episcopal Conference of the Deaf.

In the 1950s CCWAD took steps to obtain a greater measure of recognition and financial support from national Episcopal church headquarters in New York. At the request of the Conference, Presiding Bishop Henry Knox Sherrill appointed an advisory committee of four bishops to meet with the workers at their 1957 convention. This led to greater involvement of the national church in the deaf ministry. An advisory committee composed of bishops, priests, and outstanding lay people became a permanent feature of the organization of the Conference. Several hearing men, in some cases seminarians, were recruited and became either full-time or part-time missioners to deaf people. In 1960 a full-time chaplain to the Episcopal students at Gallaudet College was appointed, with financial support coming from the national church.

Another innovation was the appointment of a full-time executive secretary of the Episcopal Conference of the Deaf in 1974. Receiving the appointment was a deaf layman of Birmingham, Alabama, Robert W. Cunningham. Upon Cunningham's death in 1979, a retired hearing priest, the Reverend Arthur R. Steidemann, was appointed to succeed him. The new executive secretary is the son of the Reverend Arthur O. Steidemann, a deaf man who served the congregation of St. Thomas' Mission in St. Louis for many years, first as a layreader, then as an ordained priest, until his death in 1950.

In 1977, for the first time a woman priest was appointed to serve a congregation of deaf people. The Reverend Columba Gillis, a hearing woman who was a member of the Order of St. Helena, was given pastoral oversight of St. Ann's Church for the Deaf in New York.

Of course, there have also been some setbacks. For example, in 1949 St. Ann's Church for the Deaf in New York City was sold to the National Bible Institute. The congregation then used facilities in various parish churches. In 1968 the All Souls' Church for the Deaf in Philadelphia was put up for sale. The congregation moved its services of worship and other activities to St. Stephen's Church in downtown Philadelphia.

Bibliography

Berg, Otto B.: *A Missionary Chronicle: Being a History of the Ministry to the Deaf in the Episcopal Church (1850–1980)*, St. Mary's Press, Hollywood, Maryland, 1984.

Gallaudet, Thomas: *A Sketch of My Life*, Gallaudet College Archives, Washington, D.C.

Sampson, Robert C.: *The Reverend Henry Winter Syle, M. A., Friend, Scholar and Teacher*, Gallaudet College, Washington, D.C.

Otto B. Berg

Lutheran

United States Lutheran congregations are organized into national synods. The three largest of these synods (the American Lutheran Church [ALC], the Lutheran Church in America [LCA], and the Lutheran Church–Missouri Synod [LC-MS]), both at the congregational level and at the synodical level, have ministered to deaf people, most often as the result of some specific need expressed by a parent of a deaf child or a deaf person.

EARLY EFFORTS

The earliest work of Lutherans among deaf people in the United States may have been the establishment in 1874 of the Evangelical Lutheran Institute for the Deaf in Detroit, Michigan. There Pastor Georg Speckard began by instructing deaf children using methods he had practiced before he came to the United States at the Deaf Institute of the Grand Duchy of Hesse in Germany. Pastor Speckard was actually hired to be director of an orphanage, but when he came to his post he had two young deaf girls with him. Since he was teaching these girls Luther's *Small Catechism*, Lutheran parents of other deaf children begged that he take their children in for instruction as well. Soon the orphanage became a de facto school for deaf children. This work led eventually to the national ministry of the Lutheran Church–Missouri Synod among deaf people.

A geographic coincidence led the Pennsylvania Synod of the Lutheran Church of America to begin a ministry at the Pennsylvania Institute for the Deaf, which was to be located across the road from the Lutheran Seminary in Mount Airy, Pennsylvania. Beginning in 1889, the work led to a confirmation of nine deaf persons in 1895.

Three years later another coincidence was responsible for the establishment of ministry among deaf persons under the sponsorship of the United Norwegian Lutheran Synod (later to merge into the American Lutheran church). Professor Olav Lee on the faculty of Saint Olaf's College was the father of three deaf boys who attended the Minnesota State School for the Deaf in Faribault. He and a Pastor Larson began religious instruction for pupils of the school. In 1898 because of his urging, the Ephphatha Mission to the Deaf and the Blind was established, with the responsibility for specialized ministries.

MINISTRY TO ADULTS

These early efforts involved teaching deaf pupils in a school setting. These pupils eventually graduated and entered adult life wishing to have meaningful liturgical worship experiences in a language they could understand (sign language). In 1884 Edward Pahl, a deaf man who had graduated from the Lutheran Institute for the Deaf in Detroit, wrote to his school complaining that there was no qualified pastor working among Lutheran deaf adults. In response, the director, Herman Uhlig, wrote to Pastor August Reinke in Chicago about the letter. Pastor Reinke learned sign language and on March 4, 1895 (usually considered the birthday of the Missouri Synod mission work among deaf people), he preached to a group of 16 deaf persons on the text "God is Love."

After a short time, word of Reinke's work spread, and he traveled to several cities in the Midwest to conduct services for deaf people. At its Forth Wayne, Indiana, convention of 1896, the Missouri Synod officially established the Deaf Mission Commission. No funding was granted from the synod, and members of the commission were forced to solicit contributions. Toward the end of the nineteenth century two more pastors, Traugott Wangerin and Herman Bentrup, took up the work, and the first deaf congregation was organized in Chicago, with the name First Evangelical Lutheran Deaf-Mute Congregation of Our Savior.

AMERICAN LUTHERAN CHURCH

Similarly, the American Lutheran Church work begun in Faribault, Minnesota, was expanding. Services were being conducted in Sioux Falls, South Dakota, by 1911, and a Pastor Bjorlee was riding a circuit covering the upper-Midwest-area cities in which there were pockets of deaf people. In the 1930s work began in Minneapolis–Saint Paul, that led to the establishment in 1950 of the Bread of Life Lutheran Church for the Deaf. In 1959 the synod established a home office for work among deaf people (blind persons were also included) with Pastor Sterling Simonson as the director. This office was moved to Minneapolis in 1981, and in 1983 it was reorganized into a synodical umbrella unit responsible for the church's work among several other groups of disabled persons as well as deaf people. In 1984 the American Lutheran Church listed three pastors working full time in the deaf ministry and 116 congregations with some form of ministry among hearing-impaired people.

LUTHERAN CHURCH OF AMERICA

While the American Lutheran Church thus concentrated its efforts in the upper Midwest, the work among deaf people under the auspices of the Lutheran Church of America was centered mainly in Pennsylvania. The inner Mission Society of the Ministerium of Pennsylvania supported pastors Francis Shearer, Gustave Bechtold, and Frederick Goos who worked among deaf people in the Philadelphia area for many years, building on the early work done at the Mount Airy school. There was also expansion across Pennsylvania, most notably with the beginning of a ministry among the Harrisburg deaf population by Pastor George Harkins in 1947. This ministry was taken up shortly thereafter by Pastor Kendig Bergstresser, whose interest grew in part because he had several hearing-impaired children. The Central Pennsylvania Synod of the Lutheran Church of America in the early 1970s established a part-time office to coordinate deaf ministry in its area, but no comparable national office has been established.

MISSOURI SYNOD

The Missouri Synod developed the largest full-time deaf ministry in the United States, more so than its two national counterparts. As previously noted, by 1903 seven pastors were involved in deaf ministry and had organized themselves into a conference of pastors.

In 1909 Pastor Martin Wangerin began publication in Milwaukee of the *Deaf Lutheran* magazine. It provided articles for the spiritual and moral betterment of deaf Lutherans and cited various events among the churches serving deaf people.

By the 1930s the Missouri Synod was ministering to deaf people in most of the large urban centers in the United States as well as in some smaller cities with large populations of Lutheran people. The basic strategy for this work was to have a full-time itinerant missionary who conducted worship services in sign language in several cities in a rather large geographic area, and who also visited state schools for deaf students to give religious instruction. All of this work was supported by funding from the national synodical budget. As the work grew and the need for more workers became apparent, the national conventions in 1932 and 1935 resolved that sign language instruction should be made available to students at the synod's large seminary in Saint Louis. It was hoped that these students would then go into the expanding deaf mission of the synod.

By 1943 it was clear to the members of the Deaf Mute Mission Board (the successor to the Deaf Missions Commission) that the work had grown to a point where an administrator was needed to coordinate the effort. Pastor John Salvner of Minneapolis was appointed executive secretary to the board and set up an office in that city. He served in the post until he was succeeded by Pastor William Reinking in 1958. At that time the office for deaf ministry was moved to the headquarters of the Missouri Synod in Saint Louis.

In 1967 the synod was restructured, and the special board for deaf ministries was dissolved, leaving the deaf ministry work in the hands of the larger Board for Missions. However, the Missouri Synod continued to expand and fund its deaf ministry as a national mission until 1973, when the national convention in New Orleans passed a resolution placing financial responsibility for the work in the smaller synodical unit, the geographic District. This action considerably changed the role of the executive secretary more into that of an adviser or consultant. Another reorganization occurred in 1981, placing the deaf ministry work in the hands of a nine-member Board for Mission Services, but establishing a specific advisory Standing Committee on Deaf Ministry.

Simultaneous with the changes in administrative structure were changes in the activities of the deaf members of the churches. In 1951 the Lutheran Deaf Mission Society was founded. This organization gave deaf people an opportunity to support work among deaf persons outside of the United States. Lutheran work was begun in Hong Kong and in Nigeria and other foreign countries.

The International Lutheran Deaf Association (ILDA) was organized and held its first convention in Chicago in 1971. This organization's purpose was to "promote the Christian faith and life of Lutheran deaf persons . . . throughout the world." As an association of lay persons, it offered assistance to the deaf ministry of the synod and financially supported mission efforts to other deaf people in the world. The original Lutheran Deaf Mission Society was absorbed into the International Association in 1975.

In the late 1940s another lay organization, Lutheran Friends of the Deaf, was established in New York City. Its purpose was to explore the possibility of starting a second Lutheran school for deaf children in the New York City area. The members gathered funds, bought property on Long Island, and in 1951 opened Mill Neck Manor Lutheran School for the Deaf. This group has expanded its work to include the publication of religious education materials for deaf children, the awarding of a medal, and the support of various projects to help deaf people around the world. In 1979 the organization's Mill Neck Foundation established and funded the John of Beverley Chair of Deaf Ministry at Concordia Seminary, Saint Louis. This was the first full-time professorship in the United States designed to promote and train students to work among deaf people.

In 1984 there were 40 full-time pastors working among deaf people in the various districts of the Missouri Synod. Of these, 5 were deaf themselves. William Ludwig was the first deaf person to be ordained into the ministry of the Missouri Synod, having graduated in 1959 from Concordia Theological Seminary in Springfield, Illinois. Concordia Seminary in Saint Louis did not graduate a deaf person until 1977 when a Norwegian deaf student, K. Omahr Mork, completed his work. He was followed by Robert Case and Edwin Lot Bergstresser, the son of Kendig Bergstresser who had worked among the deaf people of the Harrisburg, Pennsylvania, area.

Changes in the area of education of deaf people in the United States have brought about modifications of the mission work done among deaf people under the auspices of the three largest Lutheran bodies. The American Lutheran Church has over 116 pastors working part time among deaf people in mostly interpreted ministries. While the Missouri Synod has the largest full-time deaf ministry, within this synod as well as within the Lutheran Church of America there is a growing number of congregations with partial ministries to deaf people.

Bibliography

Berg, Otto: *A Missionary Chronicle*, St. Mary's Press, Hollywood, Maryland, 1984.

Fangmeier, Ruth (ed.): *"Moses, My Servant, Is Dead," and That Leaves You and Me*, Proceedings of the Convocation on Deaf Ministry, Board for Mission Services of the Lutheran Church–Missouri Synod, Saint Louis, 1983.

Pokorny, Daniel, and Raymond Hohenstein (eds.): *The Word in Signs and Wonder*, Arno Press/MSS Information Corporation, New York, 1977.

Schlund, Steven: *Deaf Ministry in the LC-MS*, research paper, Concordia Seminary, Saint Louis, 1982.

———: *The Lutheran Annual 1985*, Concordia Publishing House, Saint Louis.

Daniel H. Pokorny

RONSARD, PIERRE DE
(1524–1585)

Pierre de Ronsard, premier poet of the French Renaissance, suffered a significant hearing loss at age 15 which blocked a promising diplomatic career and led him to dedicate himself to literary pursuits.

During his lifetime, he was widely acknowledged as the "Prince of Poets" in France, and accomplished a profound renewal and enrichment of poetic language and form. After his death his poetic reputation suffered at the hands of the next generation of classicist critics and poets, particularly Boileau and Malherbe, and for two centuries his work was held in relatively low esteem. In the early 1800s, however, the advent of Romanticism brought reappraisal by critics such as Saint-Beuve, and Ronsard continues to be regarded as one of the most significant poets in the history of French literature.

EARLY LIFE

Pierre de Ronsard was born on September 11, 1524, in the castle of Possonière in the Vendôme region of France. His father, Louys de Ronsard, had been appointed to the royal household of Louis XII in 1498, and had married Jeanne Chaudriers, a widow, in 1515. Of five children born to the couple, only three survived to adulthood; Pierre was the youngest.

The Renaissance culture that Louys de Ronsard acquired through his travels in Italy is reflected in the elaborate ornamentation of the Possonière castle, which he rebuilt in 1515. He was a man of letters, and is reputed to have passed time in Spain with the children of Louis XII (hostages of Charles V) composing poetry.

Little is known of Pierre de Ronsard's earliest education; he may have received some of it from his uncle Jean de Ronsard, priest of Bessé-sur-Braye, who at his death willed his personal library to his literary nephew. At age 9 to 10, Pierre was enrolled for six months in the college of Navarre in Paris (benefiting, by his own account, not at all), after which he entered the service of the Dauphin (Crown Prince) Francis as a page. When Francis died only three days later, Ronsard was passed along to Charles, Duke of Orleans, Francis's youngest brother. In 1537 he accompanied Charles's sister, the princess Madeleine of France, to Scotland following her marriage to King James V. After the death of Madeleine and remarriage of James V to Marie of Lorraine, Ronsard returned to the service of the Duke of Orleans and was "graduated" from page to squire in the royal stables. He met the future Henry II of France, who would become his generous patron.

In May 1540 Ronsard accompanied the humanist Lazare de Baïf to Hagenua, in Alsace, to the Diet at which the Emperor of Germany and the King of France hoped to mitigate Protestant-Catholic hostilities. Lazare de Baïf was to have a critical influence on Ronsard's literary development. He was the quintessential humanist, corresponding easily in Greek, maintaining ties with Erasmus and Guillaume Budé, and acquainted with many of the Italian poets and humanists whose work Ronsard would later study and imitate.

Returning from Hagenau in August 1540, Ronsard was stricken with a high fever and what was perhaps a type of otitis, from which he emerged "half-deaf." Ronsard offers relatively little insight in his writings into the emotional impact of his deafness, but one immediate practical consequence was the need to redirect his aspirations. The dual careers of soldier and diplomat, so promisingly begun in his service to the royal household, were now closed to him. His social and economic position dictated only two choices: the clergy and *belles lettres*.

CAREER

Although continually reproached by his father for his impracticality, Ronsard determined to dedicate himself to literature. His first efforts were in Latin, but as early as 1541 he began to write poetry in his native French. Acceding to his father's desire to make him eligible for ecclesiastical stipends and pensions, he was tonsured in 1543. This very preliminary step toward ordination obligated him to celibacy, but as one biographer notes, Ronsard "never was constrained by it, either in his conduct or in his writing."

The death of his father in 1544 allowed him to pursue his literary interests more freely. He accepted Lazare de Baïf's invitation to come to Paris as the tutor and companion of Baïf's son, Jean-Antoine. The two young men studied together under the tutelage of Jean Dorat, a poet and Hellenist of profound erudition who introduced them to the then little-known glories of Greek literature.

In 1547 when, on the death of Lazare de Baïf, Ronsard and Jean-Antoine followed Dorat to the College of Conqueret to continue their studies, one of the most intense and revolutionary movements in the history of French literature began to unfold. Joined by Joachim du Bellay (who had a hearing loss that was ultimately greater than Ronsard's), Ronsard became the head of the Brigade, a group of aspiring poets intent on infusing new life and vigor into the French poetic tradition by drawing on classic and Italian models. *See* DU BELLAY, JOACHIM.

POETRY

The Defense and Illustration of the French Language was published in 1549, written by du Bellay but reflective of many of Ronsard's own ideas as well as those of the Italians Sperone Speroni and Pietro Bembo. This theoretical exposition of the ideas of the Brigade was followed first by du Bellay's *Olive*, which introduced the sonnet into French vernacular poetry, and then in 1550 by Ronsard's *Quatre Premiers Livres d'Odes* (*First Four Books of Odes*), which imitated the form and themes of Horace, Pindar, and other poets of classical antiquity.

Although Ronsard at first deprecated the Petrarchan sonnet as a verse form less noble than the ode, he capitulated to popular sentiment and published his next volume, *Les Amours de Cassandre* (*The Loves of Cassandra*), thus establishing his own mastery of the form introduced by du Bellay. The woman named in the title was Cassandre Salviati, whom Ronsard met briefly at the royal court during its residence at Blois. She was 14 at the time; the poet was 21.

By 1556 the Brigade of the College of Coqueret had been winnowed down to the most significant and dedicated of its many adherents, and included Ronsard, du Bellay, Pontus de Tyard, Antoine de Baïf, Jacques Pelletier, Rémy Belleau, and Etienne Jodelle, with their mentor Dorat. The group came to be known (probably at Ronsard's instigation) as the Pléiade, after a group of seven Greek tragic poets of Alexandria in 280 B.C.

Continuing to publish poetry at a steady rhythm, Ronsard also began to occupy a series of ecclesiastical charges—Mareuil-les-Eaux in 1553, Challes in 1554—awarded to him by Henry II. During the reign of his childhood friend, Ronsard played an increasingly important role at court. After the death in 1558 of the official court poet, Saint-Gellais, he became the *aumonier ordinaire* to the king, charged with handing him his kneeling cushion and holy water.

When Charles IX acceded to the throne in 1560, Ronsard, then Canon of the Cathedral of Mans, received a generous pension; in the same year he published the first collective edition of his poetry.

As an important spokesman of the court, Ronsard involved himself in the religious and political controversies of the times through a series of *Discourses*, including a "Response to Preachers and Ministers of Geneva." Less controversial and more entertaining were his collected *Elegies*, *Mascarades*, *and Bergeries*, which appeared in 1565.

The ability of Ronsard to assume the role of defender of the Catholic faith in print (for which he was rewarded with the Priory of Saint-Cosme-en-l'Isle and the Priory of Croixval) while at the same time falling in love with, and immortalizing in verse, a series of ladies of the court was characteristic both of the times in which he lived and of his own pragmatic view of his semiclerical state. Income from church properties was, of course, a means of rewarding service to king and church at that time and in no way reflected the degree of personal piety exhibited by the recipient.

The biographical reality behind Ronsard's love poetry (that for which he is most famous) has been a subject of considerable critical discussion. In an era when fidelity to classical stereotypes of feminine beauty was considered desirable, the absence of individualism in descriptions of the beloved may or may not point to a purely imaginary relationship. In most cases the women about whom Ronsard wrote—Cassandre Salviati, Marie du Pin(?), Hélène de Surgères—have been identified. What is not known is the extent to which his courtship of them was purely literary or genuinely personal. In considering Ronsard not only as a significant poet but also as a deaf poet, this question is particularly tantalizing.

It is known that Ronsard was not prevented by deafness from engaging in face-to-face communication (unlike du Bellay in later life); but whether his hearing loss had a significant impact on his personal relationships is very difficult to determine. In one poem, Ronsard uses his deafness as an excuse for asking his beloved to come closer. Du Bellay, in his poetic homage to Ronsard, notes that "You complain, Ronsard, of being deaf," but this statement serves as a device for introducing elaborate praise of Ronsard's interior poetic "ear." There is really very little to suggest that, once Ronsard reoriented his career toward poetry, he ever let his hearing loss impede him personally or professionally.

The publication in 1572 of Ronsard's four-volume epic poem, *The Franciade*, was the greatest artistic disappointment of his career. The project of writing a French national epic along the lines of the *Iliad* or the *Aeneid* had been conceived by the Pléiade poets around 1550, in their early zeal to provide for France an equivalent for all the important literary works of classical antiquity. It was to Ronsard, their acknowledged master poet, that the charge was given, and he worked on it sporadically for the next 20 years.

The four volumes cover French "history" from the Trojans, from whom (following medieval tradition) he has the French royal house of Valois descend, to Pepin. He himself gives the death of Charles IX as the reason for abandoning the project, but as one biographer points out, Ronsard was "too much of an artist not to know when he was making a mistake." *The Franciade* was certainly a contributing factor in the long eclipse of critical esteem that his work suffered.

While the death of Charles IX may not have been the real reason for cutting short his epic poem, it nevertheless put an effective end to Ronsard's role as court poet. Finding the mores of the court of Henry III and his *mignons* distasteful in the extreme, Ronsard chose to retire to his favorite priories, spending several months at each, while he was supplanted at court by the new favorite, Desportes. It was during this period that he wrote the noted "Sonnets pour la Mort de Marie" ("Sonnets for the Death of Mary") and "Sonnets pour Hélène," both of which appear for the first time in the edition of his complete works published in 1578. He worked continuously until his death, despite the torments of gout and persistent insomnia, at reediting his poetic legacy, striving to secure the "glory"—the artistic immortality and undying fame—that was his lifelong aspiration. He died on December 27, 1585, at his favorite priory of Saint-Cosme. Two months later, in Paris, the poets whom he had inspired celebrated his literary achievements in several languages at a spectacular public funeral.

SIGNIFICANCE

Since the critical reevaluation of Ronsard's poetic works by Sainte-Beuve and other Romantic critics and poets, Ronsard's position of signal importance in the history of French poetry seems assured. It has been noted that Ronsard is a poet known to the general French-speaking population, primarily through a small number of poems that everyone recognizes at once: several of his sonnets are memorized by French schoolchildren as a matter of course. His greater importance, though, lies in his pivotal role in moving the French language into the realm of great literature and in greatly expanding its poetic possibilities. In the words of the French poet and critic Pierre de Nolhac, "Ronsard renewed from top to bottom the matter and the form, the inspiration and the vocabulary of our poetry."

Bibliography

Armstrong, Elizabeth: *Ronsard and the Age of Gold*, Cambridge University Press, Cambridge, 1968.

Bishop, Morris: *Ronsard, Prince of Poets*, University Press, London, 1950.

Boyer, Frederic: *Pierre de Ronsard*, Editions Pierre Séghers, series Poètes d'hier et d'aujourd'hui, Paris, 1958.

Braun, Sidney David (ed.): *Dictionary of French Literature*, Philosophical Library, New York, 1976.

Cave, Terrence (ed.): *Ronsard the Poet*, Methuen, London, 1973.

Cohen, Gustave: *Ronsard, sa vie et son oeuvre*, Gallimard, Paris, 1956.

Dassonville, Michel: *Ronsard: Etude historique et literaire*, vols. II and III, Droz, Geneva, 1976.

Lagarde, A., and L. Michard, (ed.): *XVIe Siecle: Les grands auteurs français du programme textes et litterature*.

Lewis, D. B. Wyndham: *Ronsard*, Sheed and Ward, London, 1944.

Malignon, Jean: *Dictionnaire des Ecrivains Français*, Editions du Seuil, Tours, 1971.

Reid, Joyce M. H. (ed.): *The Concise Oxford Dictionary of French Literature*, Clarendon Press, Oxford, 1976.

Ronsard, Pierre de: *Oeuvres Completes*, ed. by G. Cohen, Gallimard, Paris, 1950.

Catherine Ingold